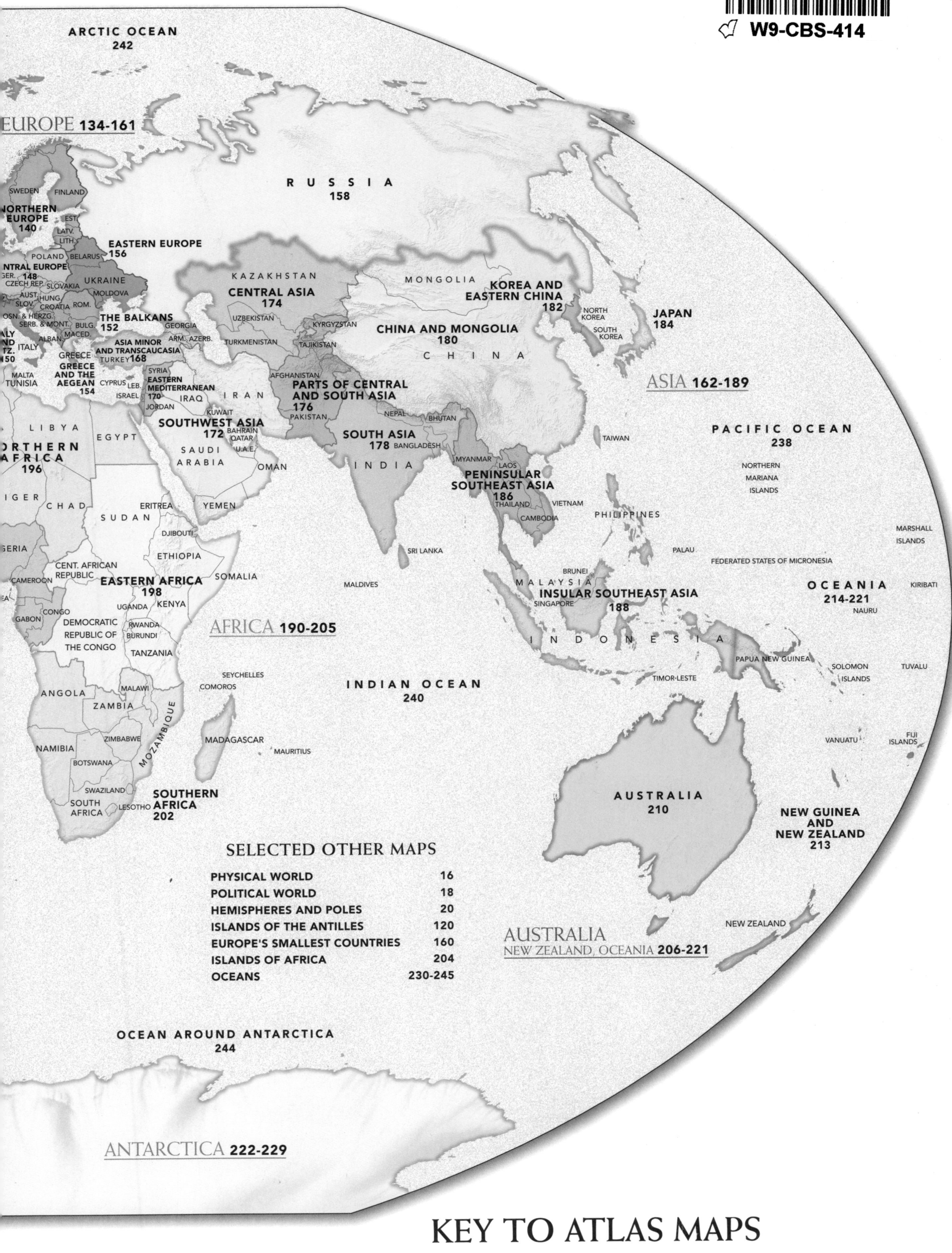

ARCTIC OCEAN
242
EUROPE 134-161
RUSSIA
158
SWEDEN
FINLAND
EST.
LATV.
LITH.
POLAND
BELARUS
EASTERN EUROPE
156
UKRAINE
MOLDOVA
CZECH REP.
SLOVAKIA
AUST.
HUNG.
SLOV.
CROATIA
ROM.
SERB. & MONT.
BULG.
MACED.
ALBAN.
ITALY
GREECE
THE BALKANS
152
GEORGIA
ARM.
AZERB.
ASIA MINOR AND TRANSCAUCASIA
TURKEY 168
GREECE AND THE AEGEAN
154
MALTA
TUNISIA
CYPRUS
LEB.
ISRAEL
SYRIA
EASTERN MEDITERRANEAN
170
JORDAN
IRAQ
IRAN
KUWAIT
SOUTHWEST ASIA
172
BAHRAIN
QATAR
U.A.E.
SAUDI ARABIA
OMAN
YEMEN
KAZAKHSTAN
CENTRAL ASIA
174
UZBEKISTAN
TURKMENISTAN
KYRGYZSTAN
TAJIKISTAN
AFGHANISTAN
PAKISTAN
PARTS OF CENTRAL AND SOUTH ASIA
176
NEPAL
BHUTAN
SOUTH ASIA
178
BANGLADESH
INDIA
SRI LANKA
MALDIVES
MONGOLIA
CHINA AND MONGOLIA
180
CHINA
KOREA AND EASTERN CHINA
182
NORTH KOREA
SOUTH KOREA
JAPAN
184
ASIA 162-189
TAIWAN
MYANMAR
LAOS
PENINSULAR SOUTHEAST ASIA
186
THAILAND
VIETNAM
CAMBODIA
PHILIPPINES
BRUNEI
MALAYSIA
SINGAPORE
INSULAR SOUTHEAST ASIA
188
INDONESIA
TIMOR-LESTE
PAPUA NEW GUINEA
PACIFIC OCEAN
238
NORTHERN MARIANA ISLANDS
PALAU
FEDERATED STATES OF MICRONESIA
MARSHALL ISLANDS
OCEANIA
214-221
KIRIBATI
NAURU
SOLOMON ISLANDS
TUVALU
VANUATU
FIJI ISLANDS
LIBYA
EGYPT
196
CHAD
SUDAN
ERITREA
DJIBOUTI
ETHIOPIA
SOMALIA
CENT. AFRICAN REPUBLIC
CAMEROON
EASTERN AFRICA
198
UGANDA
KENYA
GABON
CONGO
DEMOCRATIC REPUBLIC OF THE CONGO
RWANDA
BURUNDI
TANZANIA
AFRICA 190-205
SEYCHELLES
COMOROS
MALAWI
ANGOLA
ZAMBIA
ZIMBABWE
MOZAMBIQUE
NAMIBIA
BOTSWANA
SWAZILAND
SOUTH AFRICA
LESOTHO
SOUTHERN AFRICA
202
MADAGASCAR
MAURITIUS
INDIAN OCEAN
240
AUSTRALIA
210
NEW GUINEA AND NEW ZEALAND
213
NEW ZEALAND
AUSTRALIA
NEW ZEALAND, OCEANIA 206-221
OCEAN AROUND ANTARCTICA
244
ANTARCTICA 222-229

SELECTED OTHER MAPS

KEY TO ATLAS MAPS

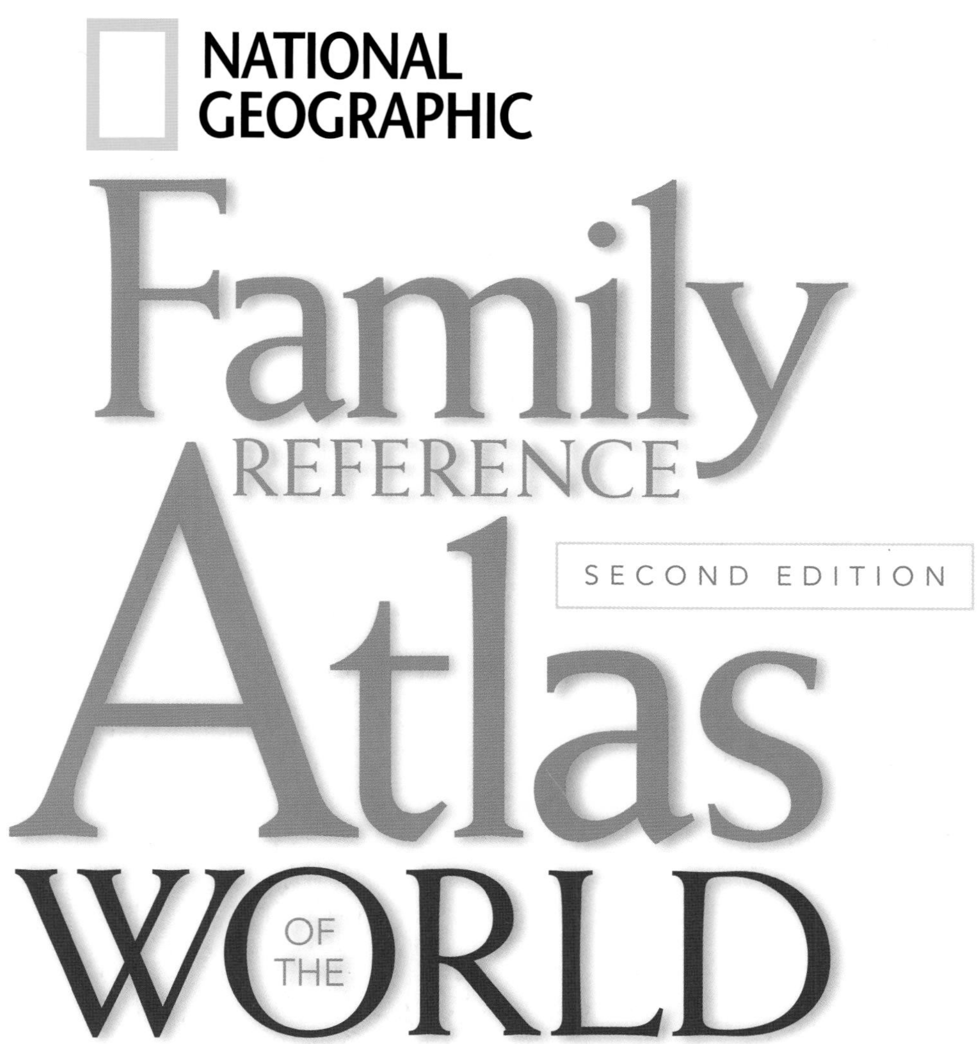
NATIONAL GEOGRAPHIC
Family
REFERENCE
SECOND EDITION
Atlas
OF THE
WORLD

NATIONAL GEOGRAPHIC
Family
REFERENCE
Atlas
SECOND EDITION
OF THE
WORLD

NATIONAL GEOGRAPHIC
WASHINGTON, D.C.

Founded in 1888, the National Geographic Society is one of the largest nonprofit scientific and educational organizations in the world. It reaches more than 285 million people worldwide each month through its official journal, NATIONAL GEOGRAPHIC, and its four other magazines; the National Geographic Channel; television documentaries; radio programs; films; books; videos and DVDs; maps; and interactive media. National Geographic has funded more than 8,000 scientific research projects and supports an education program combating geographic illiteracy.

For more information, please call
1-800-NGS LINE (647-5463)
or write to the following address:

National Geographic Society
1145 17th Street N.W.
Washington, D.C. 20036-4688 U.S.A.

Log on to nationalgeographic.com;
AOL Keyword: NatGeo.

For information about special discounts
for bulk purchases, please contact
National Geographic Books Special Sales:
ngspecsales@ngs.org

Library of Congress Cataloging in Publication data is available upon request.

ISBN-10: 0-7922-5567-4
ISBN-13: 978-0-7922-5567-3

This atlas was made possible by the contributions of numerous experts and organizations around the world, including the following:

Center for International Earth Science Information Network (CIESIN), Columbia University

Central Intelligence Agency (CIA)

Conservation International (CI)

Cooperative Association for Internet Data Analysis (CAIDA)

Earth Science System Education Program, Michigan State University

Global Land Cover Group, University of Maryland

International Monetary Fund (IMF)

International Union for the Conservation of Nature and Natural Resources (IUCN)

Lunar and Planetary Institute (LPI)

National Aeronautics and Space Administration (NASA)
NASA Ames Research Center, NASA Goddard Space Flight Center, NASA Jet Propulsion Laboratory (JPL), NASA Marshall Space Flight Center

National Geospatial-Intelligence Agency (NGA)

National Oceanic and Atmospheric Administration (NOAA)
National Climatic Data Center (NCDC), National Environmental Satellite, Data, and Information Service (NESDIS), National Geophysical Data Center (NGDC), National Ocean Service (NOS)

National Science Foundation (NSF)

Population Reference Bureau (PRB)

Scripps Institution of Oceanography

Smithsonian Institution

United Nations (UN)
UN Conference on Trade and Development (UNCTAD), UN Development Programme (UNDP), UN Educational, Scientific, and Cultural Organization (UNESCO), UN Environment Programme (UNEP), UN Millennium Project, UN Population Division, UN Refugee Agency (UNHCR), UN Statistics Division (UNSD), Food and Agriculture Organization of the United Nations (FAO), International Telecommunication Union (ITU), World Conservation Monitoring Centre (WCMC)

U.S. Board on Geographic Names (BGN)

U.S. Bureau of the Census

U.S. Department of Agriculture (USDA)

U.S. Department of Energy (DOE)

U.S. Department of the Interior
Bureau of Land Management (BLM), National Park Service (NPS), U.S. Geological Survey (USGS)

U.S. Department of State: Office of the Geographer

World Bank

World Health Organization (WHO)
Pan American Health Organization (PAHO)

World Resources Institute (WRI)

World Trade Organization (WTO)

Worldwatch Institute

World Wildlife Fund (WWF)

For a complete listing of contributors, see page 380.

Introduction

WHY GEOGRAPHY? Today as never before, geographic information provides a powerful key to understanding an increasingly complicated world. While maps still record political boundaries and landforms, they now do far more than record country borders and mountains and seas: They track the more elusive boundaries that result in cultural divides, religious divides, and the borderless, global community created by communication and technological advances. In this second edition of the *Family Reference Atlas,* maps become pictures that tell stories of natural phenomena and of human hopes, desires, disasters, and successes.

National Geographic has been at the forefront of cartographic innovation for nearly a century, but the mapmaking technologies we now use surpass the wildest imaginings of our predecessors. Those master craftsmen made maps by the time-honored pen-and-ink method; today, satellites and computer systems allow us to acquire, combine, and overlay data in moments. By marrying the artistry of mapmaking with science and technology, we can track how a change in ocean temperatures in one region can give rise to superstorms in another; how the growing trend toward urbanization in many countries is depleting resources, affecting weather patterns, and encouraging poverty and diseases; and how shrinking populations in other countries are impacting economic growth and future opportunity. In this single volume you can quickly gain an understanding of these and other changes and their implications for regions, continents, the planet, and humankind.

In order to bring you a more detailed picture of certain parts of the globe, we've expanded the European and Caribbean sections. And we've added or enhanced world thematic maps on globalization, technology and communication, hot spots of conflict and terror, even the Internet and Internet-spread viruses. We've also included maps of our planetary neighbor Mars, based on data sent back by rovers Spirit and Opportunity and more recently, by the Mars Reconnaissance Orbiter (MRO).

Ours has never been a static planet, but the pace of change on Earth has accelerated with the explosion of the human population and the proliferation of human technologies. Large questions loom for the future—what will the continued growth of India and China mean for the planet; how will melting glaciers, rising sea levels, and an ever more volatile climate impact us all? Can we, in our daily lives, help improve life on Earth? When people "discover that they must be part of the solutions," Wangari Maathai, the Kenyan activist and environmentalist said in accepting her Nobel Peace Prize, "they realize their hidden potential and are empowered to overcome inertia and take action." We hope this atlas will serve to empower you, giving you and your family the knowledge you need to be engaged global citizens.

JOHN M. FAHEY, JR.

PRESIDENT AND
CHIEF EXECUTIVE OFFICER

Table of Contents

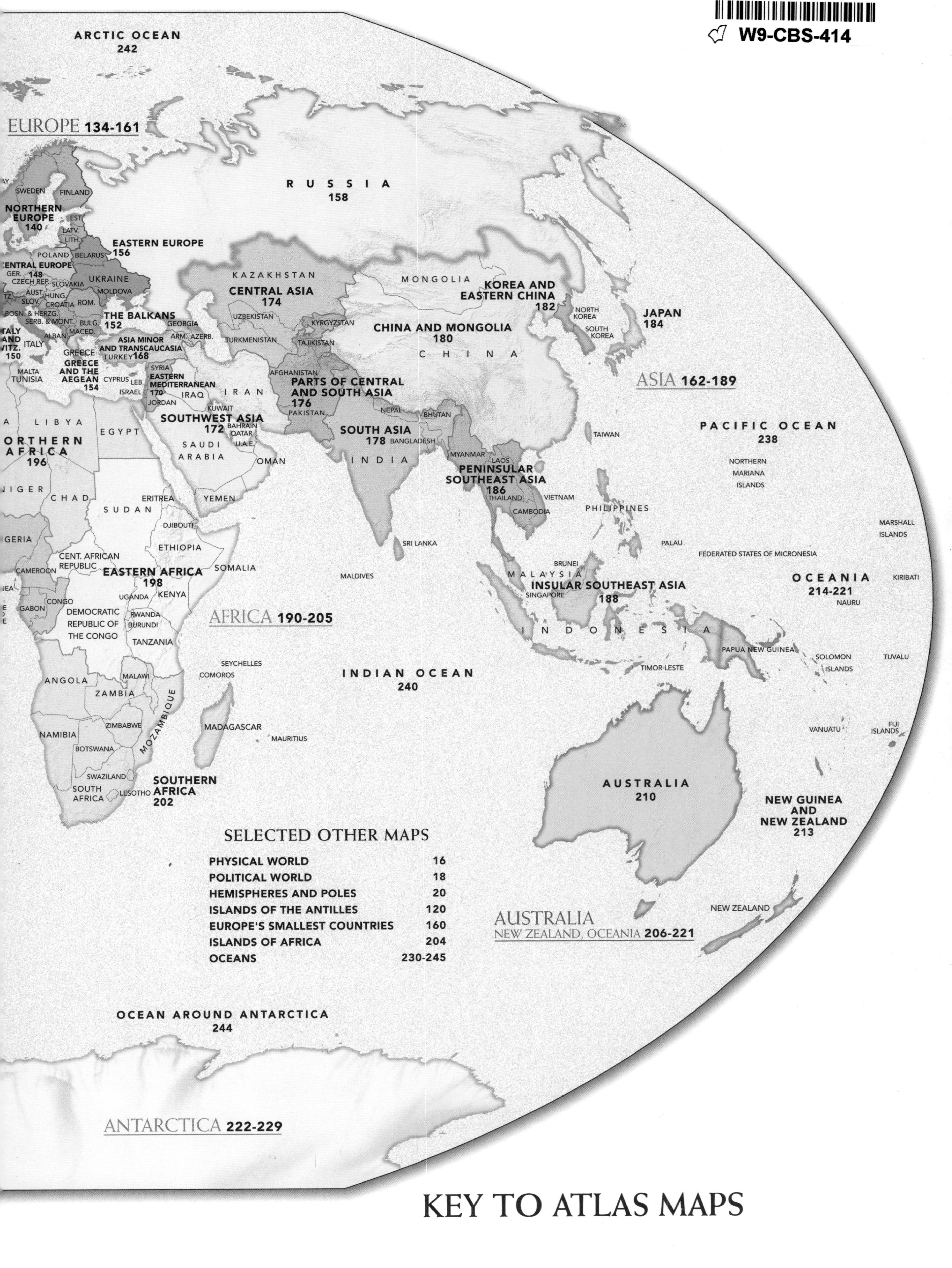

ARCTIC OCEAN
242
EUROPE 134-161
RUSSIA
158
SWEDEN
FINLAND
NORTHERN EUROPE
140
EST.
LATV.
LITH.
EASTERN EUROPE
156
POLAND
BELARUS
CENTRAL EUROPE
GER.
148
CZECH REP.
SLOVAKIA
UKRAINE
MOLDOVA
AUST.
HUNG.
SLOV.
CROATIA
ROM.
BOSN. & HERZG.
SERB. & MONT.
BULG.
MACED.
ALBAN.
THE BALKANS
152
ITALY
GREECE
GREECE AND THE AEGEAN
154
MALTA
TUNISIA
CYPRUS
LEB.
ISRAEL
SYRIA
EASTERN MEDITERRANEAN
170
JORDAN
IRAQ
KUWAIT
ASIA MINOR AND TRANSCAUCASIA
TURKEY
168
GEORGIA
ARM.
AZERB.
KAZAKHSTAN
CENTRAL ASIA
174
UZBEKISTAN
TURKMENISTAN
KYRGYZSTAN
TAJIKISTAN
AFGHANISTAN
PARTS OF CENTRAL AND SOUTH ASIA
176
PAKISTAN
IRAN
SOUTHWEST ASIA
172
BAHRAIN
QATAR
U.A.E.
SAUDI ARABIA
OMAN
YEMEN
MONGOLIA
KOREA AND EASTERN CHINA
182
NORTH KOREA
SOUTH KOREA
JAPAN
184
CHINA AND MONGOLIA
180
CHINA
NEPAL
BHUTAN
SOUTH ASIA
178
BANGLADESH
INDIA
SRI LANKA
MALDIVES
ASIA 162-189
TAIWAN
PACIFIC OCEAN
238
NORTHERN MARIANA ISLANDS
MYANMAR
LAOS
PENINSULAR SOUTHEAST ASIA
186
THAILAND
VIETNAM
CAMBODIA
PHILIPPINES
PALAU
MARSHALL ISLANDS
FEDERATED STATES OF MICRONESIA
BRUNEI
MALAYSIA
INSULAR SOUTHEAST ASIA
188
SINGAPORE
OCEANIA
214-221
KIRIBATI
NAURU
INDONESIA
PAPUA NEW GUINEA
SOLOMON ISLANDS
TUVALU
TIMOR-LESTE
LIBYA
EGYPT
NORTHERN AFRICA
196
NIGER
CHAD
SUDAN
ERITREA
DJIBOUTI
ETHIOPIA
NIGERIA
CENT. AFRICAN REPUBLIC
CAMEROON
EASTERN AFRICA
198
SOMALIA
UGANDA
KENYA
CONGO
GABON
DEMOCRATIC REPUBLIC OF THE CONGO
RWANDA
BURUNDI
TANZANIA
AFRICA 190-205
SEYCHELLES
COMOROS
INDIAN OCEAN
240
ANGOLA
MALAWI
ZAMBIA
MOZAMBIQUE
ZIMBABWE
MADAGASCAR
MAURITIUS
NAMIBIA
BOTSWANA
SWAZILAND
SOUTH AFRICA
LESOTHO
SOUTHERN AFRICA
202
VANUATU
FIJI ISLANDS
AUSTRALIA
210
NEW GUINEA AND NEW ZEALAND
213
NEW ZEALAND
AUSTRALIA
NEW ZEALAND, OCEANIA 206-221
SELECTED OTHER MAPS
PHYSICAL WORLD 16
POLITICAL WORLD 18
HEMISPHERES AND POLES 20
ISLANDS OF THE ANTILLES 120
EUROPE'S SMALLEST COUNTRIES 160
ISLANDS OF AFRICA 204
OCEANS 230-245
OCEAN AROUND ANTARCTICA
244
ANTARCTICA 222-229
KEY TO ATLAS MAPS

Winkel Tripel Projection, Central Meridian 0°
SCALE 1:80,470,600
1 CENTIMETER = 805 KILOMETERS; 1 INCH = 1270 MILES AT THE EQUATOR
0 500 1000 1500 2000 2500
KILOMETERS
0 500 1000 1500 2000 2500
STATUTE MILES
Longitude East of Greenwich
20° 40° 60° 80° 100° 120° 140° 160° 180°
90° 80° 70° 60° 50° 40° 30° 20° 10° 0° 10° 20° 30° 40° 50° 60° 70° 80° 90°
POLE PLAIN
NANSEN RIDGE
NANSEN BASIN
MAKAROV BASIN
North East Land
George Land
Graham Bell Island
Franz Josef Land
Vize I.
Komsomolets Island
October Revolution Island
Bol'shevik Island
Cape Chelyuskin
North Land
CONTINENTAL SLOPE
CONTINENTAL SHELF
New Siberian Islands
EAST SIBERIAN SEA
Wrangel I.
LAPTEV SEA
Taymyr Peninsula
Lake Taymyr
North Siberian Lowland
KARA SEA
Novaya Zemlya
BARENTS SEA
Edge Island
CONTINENTAL SHELF
North Cape
Gyda Peninsula
Yamal Pen.
Kolguyev I.
Kola Pen.
White Sea
Timan Ridge
Ural Mountains
Chukchi Range
ARCTIC CIRCLE
Chersky Range
Verkhoyansk Range
Kolyma Range
Central Siberian Plateau
West Siberian Plain
S I B E R I A
Lake Onega
Lake Ladoga
Gulf of Finland
Baltic Sea
Source of the Volga
Northern European Plain
Pinsk Marshes
Central Russian Upland
E U R O P E
Carpathian Mts.
Danube
Balkan Peninsula
Apennines
Sicily
Crete
Cyprus
Black Sea
Sea of Azov
Crimea
Caucasus Mts.
El'brus 5642
Caspian Depression -28
Caspian Sea
Aral Sea -56
Ustyurt Plateau
Turan Lowland
Qizilqum
Garagum
Amu Darya
Syr Darya
The Steppes
Kazakh Uplands
Lake Balkhash
Dzungarian Basin
Altay Mountains
Mongolian Plateau
GOBI
Tian Shan
Turpan Depression -154
Victory Peak 7439
TARIM BASIN
Taklimakan Desert
Altun Shan
Kunlun Mountains
Muztag 6987
Hindu Kush
K2 8611
Source of the Yangtze
Plateau of Tibet
HIMALAYA
Mt. Everest 8850 (29035 ft)
Brahmaputra
Ganges
Indus
Great Indian Desert
ANATOLIA (ASIA MINOR)
Mt. Ararat 5137
Elburz Mts. 5671
Zagros Mountains
Mesopotamia
Syrian Desert
Dead Sea -416 (-1365 ft)
Nile Fan
Qattara Depression -133
Western Desert
Libyan Desert
Sinai
An Nafūd
Eastern Desert
ARABIAN PENINSULA
Rub al Khali (Empty Quarter)
Persian Gulf
Gulf of Oman
Red Sea
Nubian Desert
Tibesti Mts. 3415
Marra Mts. 3088
Lake Chad
Blue Nile
White Nile
Ethiopian Highlands
Gulf of Aden
Socotra
Somali Peninsula
Lake Turkana (L. Rudolf)
Cameroon Mt 4100
Congo
Congo Basin
Ruwenzori 5109
Lake Albert
Lake Victoria
Sources of the Nile
Kilimanjaro 5895
Lake Tanganyika
Mitumba Mts.
Congo Canyon
Lower Guinea
Zanzibar I.
Katanga Plateau
Lake Malawi
Victoria Falls
Lake Kariba
Zambezi
Kalahari Desert
Namib Desert
Thabana Ntlenyana 3482
Drakensberg
Great Karroo
Cape of Good Hope
Cape Agulhas
AGULHAS PLATEAU
AGULHAS BASIN
Meteor Seamount
Madagascar
Comoro Is.
Aldabra Is.
Amirante Isles
Seychelles
MASCARENE PLATEAU
MASCARENE BASIN
Mascarene Islands
Mauritius
Réunion
Rodrigues
MADAGASCAR BASIN
NATAL BASIN
MADAGASCAR PLATEAU
MOZAMBIQUE PLATEAU
PRINCE EDWARD FRACTURE ZONE
Prince Edward Islands
Crozet Islands
CROZET BASIN
SOUTHWEST INDIAN RIDGE
Ob Tablemount
Lena Tablemount
ENDERBY PLAIN
Cosmonaut Sea
Riiser-Larsen Peninsula
Cape Ann
Enderby Land
Prydz Bay
Queen Maud Land
Cape Poinsett
ANTARCTIC CIRCLE
South Magnetic Pole
Balleny Is.
Ice thickness 4776
Victoria Land
Transantarctic Mountains
Ross Sea
Ross Ice Shelf
A N T A R C T I C A
OWEN FRACTURE ZONE
CARLSBERG RIDGE
SOMALI BASIN
Coco-de-Mer Seamounts
ARABIAN SEA
ARABIAN BASIN
Indus Fan
Deccan Plateau
Western Ghats
Eastern Ghats
INDIA
CHAGOS-LACCADIVE PLATEAU
Maldive Islands
Chagos Archipelago
Diego Garcia
CHAGOS TRENCH
MID-INDIAN RIDGE
MID-INDIAN BASIN
Sri Lanka (Ceylon)
CEYLON PLAIN
Nikitin Seamount
BAY OF BENGAL
Ganges Fan
Andaman Islands
Nicobar Islands
Andaman Sea
NINETYEAST RIDGE
COCOS BASIN
Cocos Islands
OSBORN PLATEAU
INVESTIGATOR RIDGE
Christmas I.
WHARTON BASIN
Wallaby Plateau
EXMOUTH PLATEAU
North West Cape
Cape Inscription
PERTH BASIN
BROKEN RIDGE
DIAMANTINA FRACTURE ZONE
Cape Naturaliste
Amsterdam
St. Paul
Kerguelen Islands
KERGUELEN
Heard Island
PLATEAU
SOUTHEAST INDIAN RIDGE
SOUTH INDIAN BASIN
INDIAN OCEAN
Indochina Peninsula
Gulf of Thailand
Gulf of Tonkin
Hainan
Malay Pen.
Strait of Malacca
Sumatra
Kerinci 3800
Java
Java Sea
JAVA TRENCH
JAVA RIDGE
Greater Sunda Islands
Lesser Sunda Islands
Borneo
Kinabalu 4101
CONTINENTAL SHELF
INDONESIA
Celebes
CELEBES SEA
CELEBES BASIN
SULU BASIN
Mindanao
Flores
Timor
Timor Sea
Arafura Sea
Banda Sea
Buru
Jaya Peak 4884
New Guinea
SOUTH CHINA SEA
Mt. Pinatubo
Luzon
Luzon Strait
Taiwan
Philippine Islands
PHILIPPINE TRENCH
PHILIPPINE BASIN
PALAWAN TROUGH
PHILIPPINE SEA
RYUKYU TRENCH
Ryukyu Islands
EAST CHINA SEA
Yellow Sea
North China Plain
Qin Ling
Yangtze
Qinghai Hu
Korea
SEA OF JAPAN (EAST SEA)
JAPAN TRENCH
Honshu
Fuji 3776
Shikoku
Kyushu
Hokkaido
Manchurian Plain
Greater Khingan Range
Amur
Sikhote Alin Range
Sakhalin
SEA OF OKHOTSK
Kuril Islands
KURIL TRENCH
Stanovoy Range
Yablonovyy Range
Lake Baikal
Eastern Sayan Mts.
Kamchatka Peninsula
Koryak Range
BERING SEA
ALEUTIAN BASIN
ALEUTIAN TRENCH
Aleutian Is.
Attu
Detroit Tablemount
EMPEROR SEAMOUNTS
EMPEROR TROUGH
HESS RISE
NORTHWEST PACIFIC BASIN
SHATSKY RISE
Isakov Seamount
Makarov Seamount
Grosvenor Seamount
MAPMAKER SEAMOUNTS
NORTH PACIFIC OCEAN
TROPIC OF CANCER
MID-PACIFIC MOUNTAINS
Wake I.
BONIN TRENCH
MARIANA TROUGH
Mariana Islands
MARIANA TRENCH
Challenger Deep 10920
Guam
WEST MARIANA BASIN
EAST MARIANA BASIN
MAGELLAN SEAMOUNTS
Marshall Islands
Bikini Atoll
Enewetak Atoll
Kwajalein Atoll
Taongi Atoll
MICRONESIA
Caroline Islands
YAP TRENCH
PALAU TRENCH
WEST CAROLINE BASIN
EAST CAROLINE BASIN
Chuuk
Pohnpei (Ponape)
CENTRAL PACIFIC BASIN
EQUATOR
Nauru
Banaba
Beru
Gilbert Islands
Admiralty Is.
Bismarck Archipelago
New Ireland
New Britain
Bougainville
Solomon Islands
Solomon Sea
Guadalcanal
Nanumea
Tuvalu
VITYAZ TRENCH
CONTINENTAL SHELF
Cape York Pen.
Gulf of Carpentaria
Great Barrier Reef
CORAL SEA BASIN
CORAL SEA
NORTH NEW HEBRIDES TRENCH
Vanuatu
NEW HEBRIDES TRENCH
NORTH FIJI BASIN
Fiji Islands
New Caledonia
TROPIC OF CAPRICORN
SOUTH FIJI BASIN
NEW CALEDONIA BASIN
LORD HOWE RISE
Lord Howe I.
Kimberley Plateau
NORTH AUSTRALIAN BASIN
Great Sandy Desert
Western Plateau
Macdonnell Ranges
AUSTRALIA
Great Victoria Desert
Nullarbor Plain
Lake Eyre -16
Central Lowlands
Great Artesian Basin
Great Dividing Range
Great Australian Bight
Darling
Murray
Mt. Kosciuszko 2228
CONTINENTAL SLOPE
SOUTH AUSTRALIAN BASIN
Bass Strait
Tasmania
TASMAN PLAIN
TASMAN SEA
Gascoyne Tablemount
SOUTH TASMAN RISE
EAST TASMAN PLATEAU
NEW ZEALAND
North Island
South Island
Mt. Cook 3754
Stewart Island
CAMPBELL PLATEAU
Auckland Is.
Macquarie I.
MACQUARIE RIDGE
SOUTH PACIFIC OCEAN

Longitude West of Greenwich
ARCTIC
North Magnetic Pole 2006
QUEEN ELIZABETH ISLANDS
ELLESMERE ISLAND
PARRY ISLANDS
Knud Rasmussen Land
GREENLAND
(KALAALLIT NUNAAT)
Denmark
BEAUFORT SEA
BAFFIN BAY
BAFFIN ISLAND
DAVIS STRAIT
VICTORIA ISLAND
Wrangel I.
Monday
Sunday
Date Line
RUSSIA
Brooks Range
ARCTIC CIRCLE
ALASKA
U.S.
Barrow
Nome
Fairbanks
Mt. McKinley (Denali) 6194 (20320 ft)
Anchorage
Bethel
Valdez
Kodiak
BERING SEA
Aleutian Islands
Alaska Peninsula
Cold Bay
Alexander Archipelago
Prince Rupert
Queen Charlotte Islands
Juneau
Skagway
Whitehorse
Inuvik
Great Bear Lake
Great Slave Lake
Yellowknife
Hay River
Fort Smith
Fort St. John
Peace River
Fort McMurray
Edmonton
Prince George
Calgary
Saskatoon
Regina
Winnipeg
Lake Winnipeg
CANADA
HUDSON BAY
Cambridge Bay
Taloyoak
Resolute
Pond Inlet
Igloolik
Bathurst Inlet
Chesterfield Inlet
Arviat
Whale Cove
Iqaluit
Kuujjuaq
Nain
Sanikiluaq
Chisasibi
Fort Severn
Fort Albany
Thompson
LABRADOR
Labrador City
Sept-Îles
Chibougamau
Timmins
Thunder Bay
Québec
Montréal
Ottawa
Toronto
ISLAND OF NEWFOUNDLAND
St. John's
Charlottetown
Halifax
St.-Pierre & Miquelon France
LABRADOR SEA
Qaanaaq (Thule)
Upernavik
Nuuk (Godthåb)
Narsarsuaq
Reykjavík
ICELAND
Denmark Strait
Vancouver I.
Victoria
Vancouver
Seattle
Portland
Eugene
Boise
Helena
Billings
Fargo
ROCKY MOUNTAINS
Minneapolis
Milwaukee
Chicago
Detroit
Buffalo
Boston
New York
Philadelphia
Washington
Salt Lake City
Reno
Sacramento
San Francisco
Las Vegas
Los Angeles
San Diego
Tijuana
Mexicali
Phoenix
Santa Fe
Albuquerque
Denver
Kansas City
Omaha
Indianapolis
Columbus
UNITED STATES
Oklahoma City
Tulsa
Nashville
Memphis
Charlotte
Atlanta
Birmingham
Dallas
El Paso
Ciudad Juárez
Chihuahua
San Antonio
Austin
Houston
New Orleans
Jacksonville
Tampa
Orlando
Miami
Mississippi
Baja California
Isla Guadalupe Mexico
Nuevo Laredo
Laredo
Monterrey
MEXICO
GULF OF MEXICO
Tampico
Mazatlán
Guadalajara
Mexico
Puebla
Veracruz
Mérida
Cancún
Acapulco
Islas Revillagigedo Mexico
Isla Clarión
Bermuda Islands U.K.
Nassau
BAHAMAS
Turks and Caicos Is. U.K.
Havana
CUBA
Cayman Is. U.K.
JAMAICA
Kingston
HAITI
Port-au-Prince
DOMINICAN REP.
Santo Domingo
PUERTO RICO U.S.
Virgin Is. U.S. & U.K.
ST. KITTS AND NEVIS
ANTIGUA AND BARBUDA
Guadeloupe France
DOMINICA
Martinique France
ST. LUCIA
BARBADOS
ST. VINCENT AND THE GRENADINES
GRENADA
Port-of-Spain
TRINIDAD AND TOBAGO
GREATER ANTILLES
LESSER ANTILLES
CARIBBEAN SEA
Belmopan
BELIZE
Yucatán
Tuxtla Gutiérrez
GUATEMALA
Guatemala
HONDURAS
Tegucigalpa
San Salvador
EL SALVADOR
NICARAGUA
Managua
San José
COSTA RICA
PANAMA
Panama
Clipperton France
Isla del Coco Costa Rica
Isla de Malpelo Colombia
Barranquilla
Cartagena
Maracaibo
Curaçao Neth.
Aruba Neth.
Caracas
Mérida
VENEZUELA
Puerto Ayacucho
Georgetown
GUYANA
Paramaribo
SURINAME
Cayenne
FRENCH GUIANA France
Medellín
Bogotá
Cali
COLOMBIA
Boa Vista
Mitú
Quito
ECUADOR
Guayaquil
Cuenca
GALÁPAGOS ISLANDS (ARCHIPIÉLAGO DE COLÓN) Ecuador
Macapá
Belém
São Luís
Fortaleza
Arquipélago de Fernando de Noronha Brazil
Barcelos
Óbidos
Santarém
Manaus
Amazon
Itaituba
Caxias
Natal
Juazeiro do Norte
Leticia
Iquitos
Manicoré
Marabá
Carolina
Recife
Piura
Trujillo
Eirunepé
Cruzeiro do Sul
Rio Branco
Porto Velho
BRAZIL
PERU
ANDES
Lima
Ayacucho
Cusco
Ica
Ji-Paraná (Rondônia)
Guajará-Mirim
Vilhena
Trinidad
Porangatu
Peixe
Feira de Santana
Aracaju
Salvador (Bahia)
Ilhéus
BOLIVIA
La Paz
Cochabamba
Tacna
Arica
Santa Cruz
Sucre
Cuiabá
Cáceres
Corumbá
Brasília
Goiânia
Montes Claros
Belo Horizonte
Vitória
Rio de Janeiro
São Paulo
Campo Grande
Bauru
Iquique
Antofagasta
San Salvador de Jujuy
Salta
Asunción
PARAGUAY
Curitiba
Florianópolis
Posadas
Porto Alegre
Pelotas
San Miguel de Tucumán
La Rioja
Córdoba
Salto
URUGUAY
Montevideo
Buenos Aires
Mar del Plata
Cerro Aconcagua 6960 (22834 ft)
Santiago
Mendoza
Río Cuarto
Concepción
Santa Rosa
PAMPAS
Paraná
Bahía Blanca
Neuquén
Viedma
Península Valdés
Puerto Madryn
Valdivia
Puerto Montt
CHILE
ARGENTINA
PATAGONIA
Comodoro Rivadavia
Puerto Deseado
Balmaceda
Península de Taitao
Río Gallegos
Punta Arenas
TIERRA DEL FUEGO
Ushuaia
Stanley
FALKLAND ISLANDS (ISLAS MALVINAS) U.K.
Shag Rocks U.K.
South Georgia U.K.
South Sandwich Islands U.K.
Islas Diego Ramírez Chile
SCOTIA SEA
Drake Passage
S. Shetland Is.
S. Orkney Is.
ANTARCTIC PENINSULA
WEDDELL SEA
Riiser-Larsen Ice Shelf
Ronne Ice Shelf
Filchner Ice Shelf
Berkner Island
ANTARCTICA
ELLSWORTH LAND
Vinson Massif 4897 (16067 ft)
MARIE BYRD LAND
ROSS SEA
Ross Ice Shelf
TRANSANTARCTIC MOUNTAINS
Scott I.
ANTARCTIC CIRCLE
NORTH ATLANTIC OCEAN
SOUTH ATLANTIC OCEAN
NORTH PACIFIC OCEAN
SOUTH PACIFIC OCEAN
Midway Is. U.S.
HAWAII United States
Kaua'i
Honolulu
Maui
Hilo
Hawai'i
TROPIC OF CANCER
Johnston Atoll U.S.
Palmyra Atoll U.S.
Kiritimati (Christmas I.)
LINE ISLANDS
Howland Island
Baker Island U.S.
EQUATOR
Jarvis I. U.S.
PHOENIX ISLANDS
KIRIBATI
TOKELAU N.Z.
MARQUESAS ISLANDS France
Îles SAMOA
Apia
AMERICAN SAMOA U.S.
Pago Pago
Wallis France
SAMOA IS.
COOK ISLANDS New Zealand
TUAMOTU ARCHIPELAGO
Rangiroa
Papeete
Tahiti
SOCIETY IS.
FRENCH POLYNESIA France
Lau Group
Fiji Islands
TONGA IS.
TONGA
Nuku'alofa
Niue N.Z.
Rarotonga
Tubuai
Îles Gambier
AUSTRAL ISLANDS (TUBUAI ISLANDS)
Rapa
United Kingdom
Ducie Island
Pitcairn Island
TROPIC OF CAPRICORN
Isla Sala y Gómez Chile
Easter Island (Isla de Pascua) Chile
Isla San Félix Chile
Isla San Ambrosio
Archipiélago Juan Fernández Chile
Kermadec Islands N.Z.
Chatham Is. N.Z.
Sunday
Monday
Date Line
Ilha de Trindade
Ilhas Martin Vaz Brazil
St. Peter and St. Paul Rocks Brazil
Ascension U.K.
Tristan da Cunha Group U.K.
PORTUGAL
Lisbon
Azores (Açores) Portugal
Madeira Islands Portugal
Canary Islands (Islas Canarias) Spain
Santa Cruz
Laayoune
Casablanca
Marrakech
WESTERN SAHARA Morocco
Cap Barbas
Atar
Nouakchott
CAPE VERDE
Praia
SENEGAL
Dakar
GAMBIA
Banjul
Bamako
GUINEA-BISSAU
Bissau
GUINEA
Conakry
Freetown
SIERRA LEONE
Monrovia
LIBERIA
180° 160° 140° 120° 100° 80° 60° 40°
90° 80° 70° 60° 50° 40° 30° 20° 10° 0° 10° 20° 30° 40° 50° 60° 70° 80° 90°

Longitude East of Greenwich
20° 40° 60° 80° 100° 120° 140° 160° 180°
ARCTIC OCEAN
FRANZ JOSEF LAND
Russia
SVALBARD
Norway
Spitsbergen
Nordaustlandet
SEVERNAYA ZEMLYA (NORTH LAND)
Ostrov Komsomolets
Ostrov Oktyabr'skoy Revolyutsii
Ostrov Bol'shevik
NEW SIBERIAN IS.
EAST SIBERIAN SEA
Wrangel Island
LAPTEV SEA
KARA SEA
BARENTS SEA
NOVAYA ZEMLYA
ARCTIC CIRCLE
R U S S I A
URAL MOUNTAINS
Verkhoyanskiy Khrebet
Khrebet Cherskogo
Stanovoy Khrebet
Murmansk
Arkhangel'sk
Vorkuta
Noril'sk
Dudinka
Igarka
Dikson
Khatanga
Tiksi
Yakutsk
Magadan
Oymyakon
Anadyr'
Petropavlovsk-Kamchatskiy
KAMCHATKA PENINSULA
SEA OF OKHOTSK
SAKHALIN
BERING SEA
Aleutian Islands U.S.
Sunday
Monday
Date Line
Kuril Islands
FINLAND
Helsinki
Oulu
Turku
SWEDEN
NORWAY
Stockholm
Oslo
Tallinn
ESTONIA
LATVIA
Riga
LITHUANIA
Vilnius
BELARUS
Minsk
St. Petersburg
Moscow
Nizhniy Novgorod
Kirov
Perm'
Yekaterinburg
Chelyabinsk
Kazan'
Ufa
Samara
Omsk
Novosibirsk
Barnaul
Krasnoyarsk
Irkutsk
Ulan Ude
Chita
Blagoveshchensk
Khabarovsk
Vladivostok
Komsomol'sk na Amure
Lake Baikal
POLAND
Warsaw
Berlin
Prague
Vienna
Budapest
UKRAINE
Kiev
MOLDOVA
Chişinău
ROMANIA
Bucharest
Belgrade
Sofia
Skopje
GREECE
Athens
ITALY
Rome
Naples
Palermo
MALTA
Tunis
TUNISIA
Tripoli
Benghazi
LIBYA
EGYPT
Cairo
Alexandria
Aswân
Luxor
TURKEY
Istanbul
Ankara
İzmir
Adana
BLACK SEA
CASPIAN SEA
GEORGIA
T'bilisi
ARMENIA
Yerevan
AZERBAIJAN
Baku
Rostov
Volgograd
Krasnodar
KAZAKHSTAN
Astana
Almaty
Aral Sea
Lake Balkhash
UZBEKISTAN
Tashkent
TURKMENISTAN
Ashgabat
KYRGYZSTAN
Bishkek
TAJIKISTAN
Dushanbe
AFGHANISTAN
Kabul
Herat
Kandahar
PAKISTAN
Islamabad
Lahore
Faisalabad
Quetta
Karachi
IRAN
Tehran
Tabriz
Mashhad
Esfahan
Shiraz
Bandar-e Abbas
IRAQ
Baghdad
Mosul
Basra
SYRIA
Damascus
LEBANON
Beirut
ISRAEL
Jerusalem
JORDAN
Amman
CYPRUS
Nicosia
KUWAIT
Kuwait
SAUDI ARABIA
Riyadh
Mecca
Jeddah
Medina
BAHRAIN
Manama
QATAR
Doha
UNITED ARAB EMIRATES
Abu Dhabi
Dubai
OMAN
Muscat
Rub al Khali
YEMEN
Sanaa
Aden
Socotra
Yemen
Gulf of Aden
DJIBOUTI
Djibouti
SOMALILAND
Hargeysa
ETHIOPIA
Addis Ababa
ERITREA
Asmara
SUDAN
Khartoum
Omdurman
Port Sudan
SOUTH SUDAN
Juba
CHAD
N'Djamena
NIGER
Agadez
NIGERIA
Kano
Abuja
Zaria
CAMEROON
Yaoundé
CENTRAL AFRICAN REPUBLIC
Bangui
GABON
Libreville
CONGO
Brazzaville
DEMOCRATIC REPUBLIC OF THE CONGO
Kinshasa
Kisangani
Lubumbashi
UGANDA
Kampala
KENYA
Nairobi
Mombasa
RWANDA
Kigali
BURUNDI
Bujumbura
TANZANIA
Dodoma
Dar es Salaam
Zanzibar
Kilimanjaro 5895 (19340 ft)
SOMALIA
Mogadishu
Chisimayu
ANGOLA
Luanda
Huambo
Benguela
Lubango
Namibe
ZAMBIA
Lusaka
MALAWI
Lilongwe
Blantyre
ZIMBABWE
Harare
Bulawayo
MOZAMBIQUE
Maputo
Beira
Nampula
NAMIBIA
Windhoek
BOTSWANA
Gaborone
Francistown
KALAHARI DESERT
SOUTH AFRICA
Pretoria
Johannesburg
Bloemfontein
Kimberley
Durban
East London
Port Elizabeth
Cape Town
LESOTHO
Maseru
SWAZILAND
Mbabane
MADAGASCAR
Antananarivo
Toamasina
Mozambique Chan.
COMOROS
Moroni
Mayotte France
SEYCHELLES
Victoria
MAURITIUS
Port Louis
Réunion France
St.-Denis
Mascarene Is.
Rodrigues Mauritius
Agalega Is. Mauritius
Cargados Carajos Bank Mauritius
Tromelin I. France
Chagos Archipelago (Oil Islands)
Diego Garcia
British Indian Ocean Territory
MALDIVES
Male
Maldive Islands
LAKSHADWEEP India
INDIAN OCEAN
ARABIAN SEA
BAY OF BENGAL
INDIA
Delhi
New Delhi
Jaipur
Kanpur
Ahmadabad
Vadodara
Surat
Bhopal
Indore
Nagpur
Mumbai (Bombay)
Pune
Hyderabad
Bangalore
Mysore
Chennai (Madras)
Madurai
Kochi
Trivandrum
Kolkata (Calcutta)
Vishakhapatnam
SRI LANKA
Colombo
Kandy
Jaffna
NEPAL
Kathmandu
Mt. Everest 8850 (29035 ft)
BHUTAN
Thimphu
BANGLADESH
Dhaka
Chittagong
MYANMAR (BURMA)
Yangon (Rangoon)
Mandalay
ANDAMAN ISLANDS India
NICOBAR ISLANDS India
THAILAND
Bangkok
Chiang Mai
LAOS
Vientiane
VIETNAM
Hanoi
Haiphong
Hue
Ho Chi Minh City
CAMBODIA
Phnom Penh
MALAYSIA
Kuala Lumpur
SINGAPORE
Medan
Padang
Kepulauan Mentawai
Jambi
Palembang
INDONESIA
Jakarta
Bandung
Semarang
Surabaya
Yogyakarta
Denpasar
Bali
GREATER SUNDA ISLANDS
LESSER SUNDA ISLANDS
Java Sea
BORNEO
Pontianak
Balikpapan
CELEBES
Ujungpandang
Manado
Ambon
Jayapura
Flores
Timor
TIMOR-LESTE
Dili
Kupang
Christmas I. Australia
Cocos (Keeling) Islands Australia
CHINA
Beijing
Tianjin
Shanghai
Nanjing
Hangzhou
Wuhan
Chongqing
Chengdu
Xi'an
Lanzhou
Xining
Taiyuan
Zhengzhou
Jinan
Qingdao
Shenyang
Anshan
Fushun
Changchun
Jilin
Harbin
Qiqihar
Baotou
Datong
Yinchuan
Ürümqi
Kashi
Hami
Lhasa
Guiyang
Kunming
Nanning
Guangzhou
Changsha
Nanchang
Fuzhou
Xiamen
Hong Kong
Macau
Haikou
HAINAN
TIBET
Taklimakan Desert
TIAN SHAN
KUNLUN MOUNTAINS
ALTAY MOUNTAINS
GOBI
INNER MONGOLIA
DONGBEI
SINKIANG
MONGOLIA
Ulaanbaatar
NORTH KOREA
Pyongyang
SOUTH KOREA
Seoul
Busan
JAPAN
Tokyo
Yokohama
Osaka
Kyoto
Hiroshima
Fukuoka
Sendai
Sapporo
HOKKAIDO
HONSHU
SHIKOKU
KYUSHU
SEA OF JAPAN (EAST SEA)
YELLOW SEA
EAST CHINA SEA
TAIWAN
Taipei
Kaohsiung
SOUTH CHINA SEA
PHILIPPINES
Manila
Quezon City
Baguio
Cebu
Davao
Zamboanga
LUZON
MINDANAO
PHILIPPINE SEA
Spratly Islands
Paracel Is. China
BRUNEI
Bandar Seri Begawan
SABAH
SARAWAK
PACIFIC OCEAN
NORTH PACIFIC OCEAN
TROPIC OF CANCER
Bonin Islands
Volcano Islands
Iwo Jima
Daitō Shotō Japan
Minami Tori Shima (Marcus I.) Japan
Wake Island U.S.
NORTHERN MARIANA ISLANDS U.S.
Saipan
Guam U.S.
PALAU
Koror
Yap Islands
FEDERATED STATES OF MICRONESIA
Palikir
CAROLINE ISLANDS
MARSHALL ISLANDS
Majuro
Ralik Chain
Ratak Chain
Bikini Atoll
KIRIBATI
Tarawa
Gilbert Islands
EQUATOR
NAURU
TUVALU
Funafuti
PAPUA NEW GUINEA
Port Moresby
NEW GUINEA
BISMARCK ARCH.
New Britain
New Ireland
Admiralty Islands
SOLOMON ISLANDS
Honiara
Guadalcanal
Bougainville
Santa Cruz Islands
Louisiade Archipelago
VANUATU
Port-Vila
Espiritu Santo
FIJI ISLANDS
Suva
Viti Levu
New Caledonia France
Nouméa
Loyalty Is.
Coral Sea
Arafura Sea
Timor Sea
Gulf of Carpentaria
AUSTRALIA
Darwin
Nhulunbuy
Weipa
Cape York Pen.
Cairns
Townsville
Mackay
Gladstone
Gympie
Brisbane
Newcastle
Sydney
Canberra
Melbourne
Adelaide
Port Augusta
Perth
Albany
Esperance
Kalgoorlie
Rockingham
Carnarvon
Denham
Port Hedland
Derby
Alice Springs
Tennant Creek
Great Sandy Desert
Great Victoria Desert
Simpson Desert
Great Australian Bight
Great Dividing Range
Bass Strait
TASMANIA
Hobart
TROPIC OF CAPRICORN
SOUTH PACIFIC OCEAN
Lord Howe I. Ball's Pyramid Australia
Norfolk Island Australia
TASMAN SEA
NEW ZEALAND
NORTH ISLAND
SOUTH ISLAND
Auckland
Hamilton
Wellington
Christchurch
Dunedin
Auckland Is. N.Z.
Macquarie I. Australia
Île Amsterdam France
Prince Edward Islands South Africa
Crozet Islands France
Kerguélen Islands France
McDonald Is.
Heard Island
Shag I.
Australia
ANTARCTIC CIRCLE
ANTARCTICA
QUEEN MAUD LAND
ENDERBY LAND
WILKES LAND
Riiser-Larsen Peninsula
Amery Ice Shelf
West Ice Shelf
Shackleton Ice Shelf
South Magnetic Pole 2006
Balleny Islands
Transantarctic Mountains
ROSS SEA
Ross Ice Shelf
Winkel Tripel Projection, Central Meridian 0°
SCALE 1:80,470,600
1 CENTIMETER = 805 KILOMETERS; 1 INCH = 1270 MILES AT THE EQUATOR
0 500 1000 1500 2000 2500
KILOMETERS
0 500 1000 1500 2000 2500
STATUTE MILES
International boundaries and disputed territories, where scale permits, reflect de facto status at the time of publication.

Hemispheres and Poles

Western Hemisphere

Eastern Hemisphere

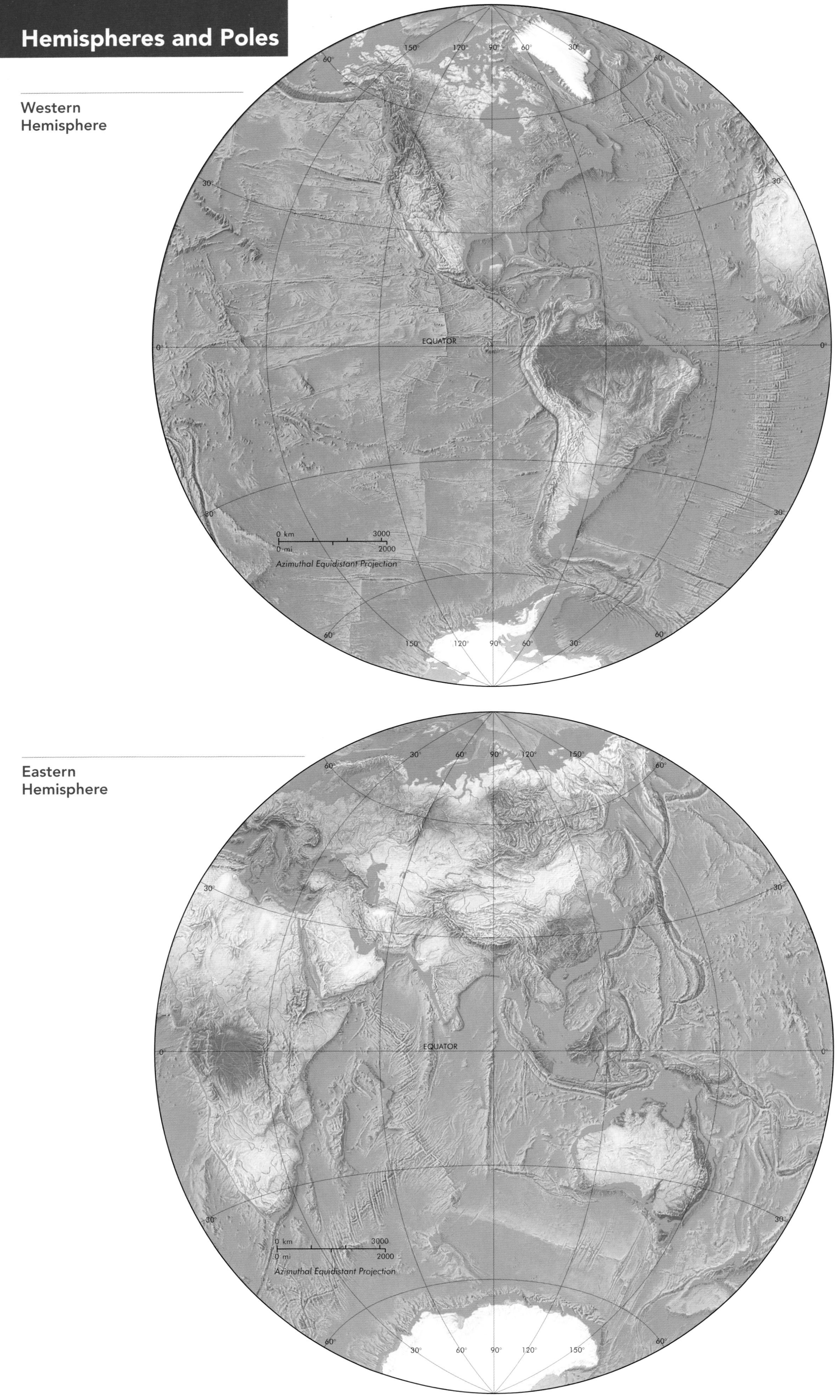
150°
120°
90°
60°
30°
60°
30°
EQUATOR
0°
0 km 3000
0 mi 2000
Azimuthal Equidistant Projection
30°
60°
120°
150°
EQUATOR
0 km 3000
0 mi 2000
Azimuthal Equidistant Projection

North Pole

South Pole

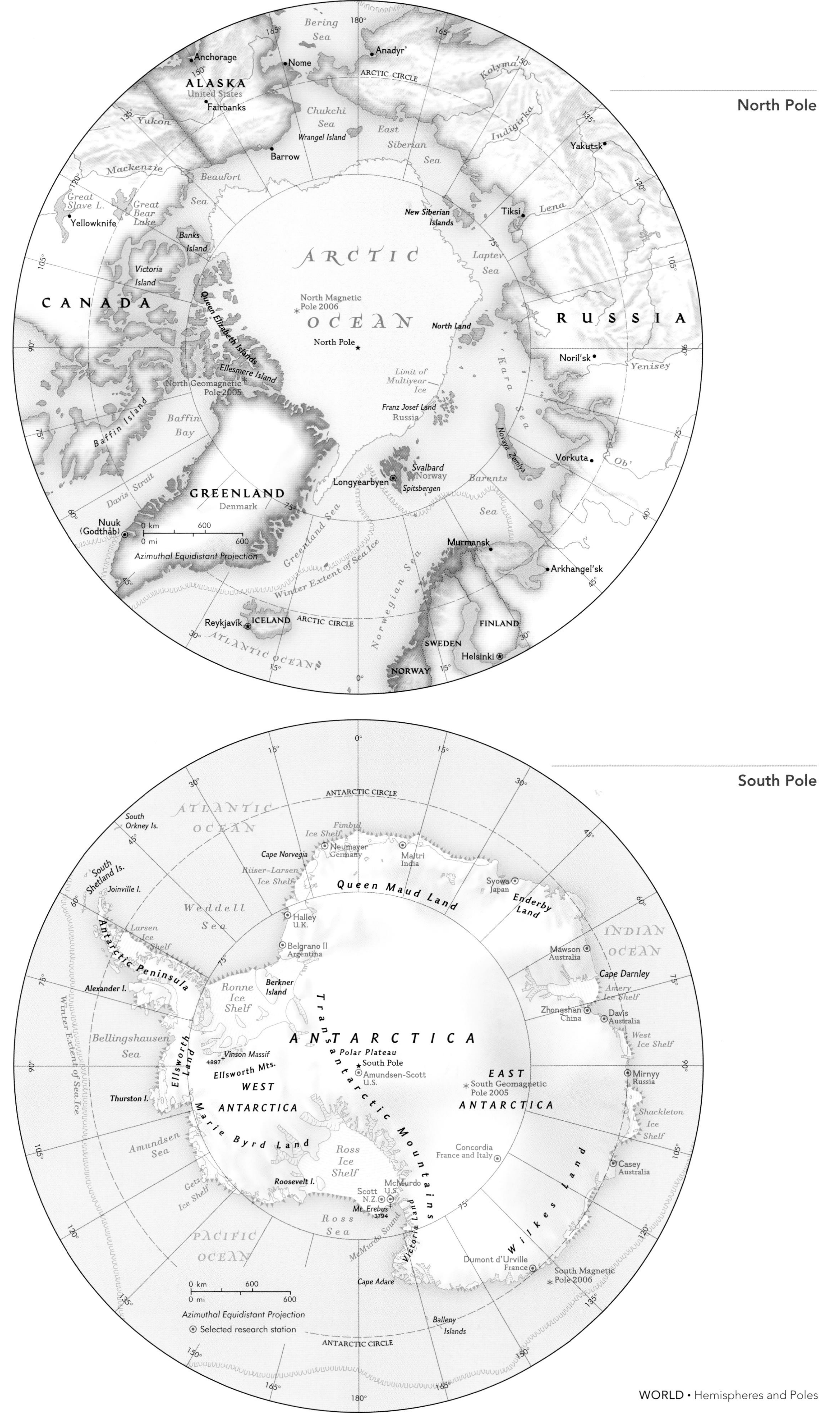

Bering Sea
Anchorage
Nome
Anadyr'
ARCTIC CIRCLE
ALASKA
United States
Fairbanks
Chukchi Sea
Wrangel Island
East Siberian Sea
Kolyma
Indigirka
Yakutsk
Yukon
Barrow
Mackenzie
Beaufort Sea
Great Slave L.
Great Bear Lake
Yellowknife
New Siberian Islands
Tiksi
Lena
Banks Island
ARCTIC OCEAN
Laptev Sea
Victoria Island
North Magnetic Pole 2006
CANADA
Queen Elizabeth Islands
North Land
RUSSIA
North Pole
Noril'sk
Yenisey
Ellesmere Island
North Geomagnetic Pole 2005
Limit of Multiyear Ice
Kara Sea
Franz Josef Land
Russia
Baffin Island
Baffin Bay
Novaya Zemlya
Vorkuta
Ob'
Davis Strait
GREENLAND
Denmark
Svalbard
Norway
Longyearbyen
Spitsbergen
Barents Sea
Nuuk (Godthåb)
0 km 600
0 mi 600
Azimuthal Equidistant Projection
Greenland Sea
Winter Extent of Sea Ice
Norwegian Sea
Murmansk
Arkhangel'sk
Reykjavík
ICELAND
ARCTIC CIRCLE
FINLAND
ATLANTIC OCEAN
SWEDEN
Helsinki
NORWAY
ANTARCTIC CIRCLE
ATLANTIC OCEAN
South Orkney Is.
Fimbul Ice Shelf
Cape Norvegia
Neumayer Germany
Maitri India
South Shetland Is.
Joinville I.
Riiser-Larsen Ice Shelf
Queen Maud Land
Syowa Japan
Enderby Land
Weddell Sea
Halley U.K.
Larsen Ice Shelf
INDIAN OCEAN
Belgrano II Argentina
Mawson Australia
Antarctic Peninsula
Cape Darnley
Alexander I.
Ronne Ice Shelf
Berkner Island
Amery Ice Shelf
Zhongshan China
Davis Australia
Bellingshausen Sea
Ellsworth Land
ANTARCTICA
West Ice Shelf
Vinson Massif 4897
Polar Plateau
Ellsworth Mts.
South Pole
Amundsen-Scott U.S.
EAST ANTARCTICA
Mirnyy Russia
Winter Extent of Sea Ice
WEST ANTARCTICA
South Geomagnetic Pole 2005
Thurston I.
Transantarctic Mountains
Shackleton Ice Shelf
Marie Byrd Land
Amundsen Sea
Ross Ice Shelf
Concordia France and Italy
Casey Australia
Getz Ice Shelf
Roosevelt I.
Scott N.Z.
McMurdo U.S.
Mt. Erebus 3794
Victoria Land
Wilkes Land
Ross Sea
McMurdo Sound
PACIFIC OCEAN
Dumont d'Urville France
South Magnetic Pole 2006
0 km 600
0 mi 600
Cape Adare
Azimuthal Equidistant Projection
Selected research station
Balleny Islands
ANTARCTIC CIRCLE

Structure of the Earth

LIKE ICE ON A GREAT LAKE, the Earth's crust, or the lithosphere, floats over the planet's molten innards, is cracked in many places, and is in slow but constant movement. Earth's surface is broken into 16 enormous slabs of rock, called plates, averaging thousands of miles wide and having a thickness of several miles. As they move and grind against each other, they push up mountains, spawn volcanoes, and generate earthquakes.

Although these often cataclysmic events capture our attention, the movements that cause them are imperceptible, a slow waltz of rafted rock that continues over eons. How slow? The Mid-Atlantic Ridge (see "spreading" diagram, opposite) is being built by magma oozing between two plates, separating North America and Africa at the speed of a growing human fingernail.

The dividing lines between plates often mark areas of high volcanic and earthquake activity as plates strain against each other or one dives beneath another. In the Ring of Fire around the Pacific Basin, disastrous earthquakes have occurred in Kobe, Japan, and in Los Angeles and San Francisco, California. Volcanic eruptions have taken place at Pinatubo in the Philippines and Mount St. Helens in Washington State.

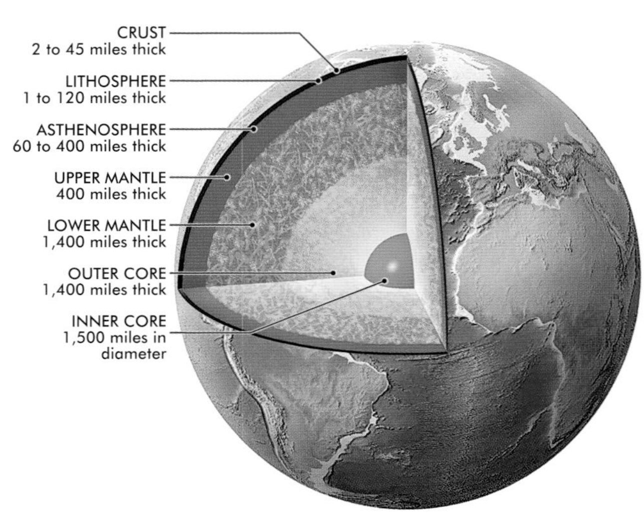

CRUST
2 to 45 miles thick
LITHOSPHERE
1 to 120 miles thick
ASTHENOSPHERE
60 to 400 miles thick
UPPER MANTLE
400 miles thick
LOWER MANTLE
1,400 miles thick
OUTER CORE
1,400 miles thick
INNER CORE
1,500 miles in diameter

Continents Adrift in Time

With unceasing movement of Earth's tectonic plates, continents "drift" over geologic time—breaking apart, reassembling, and again fragmenting to repeat the process. Three times during the past billion years, Earth's drifting landmasses have merged to form so-called supercontinents. Rodinia, a supercontinent in the late Precambrian, began breaking apart about 750 million years ago. In time, its pieces reassembled to form another supercontinent, which in turn later split into smaller landmasses during the Paleozoic. The largest of these were called Euramerica (ancestral Europe and North America) and Gondwana (ancestral Africa, Antarctica, Arabia, India, and Australia). More than 250 million years ago, these two landmasses recombined, forming Pangaea. In the Mesozoic era, Pangaea split and the Atlantic and Indian Oceans began forming. Though the Atlantic is still widening today, scientists predict it will close as the seafloor recycles back into Earth's mantle. A new supercontinent, Pangaea Ultima, will eventually form.

KEY TO PALEO-GEOGRAPHIC MAPS

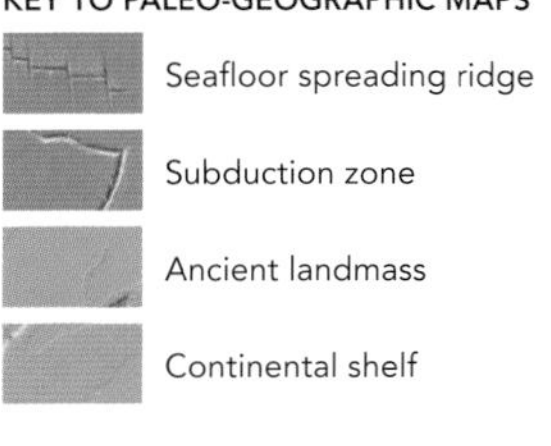

Seafloor spreading ridge
Subduction zone
Ancient landmass
Continental shelf

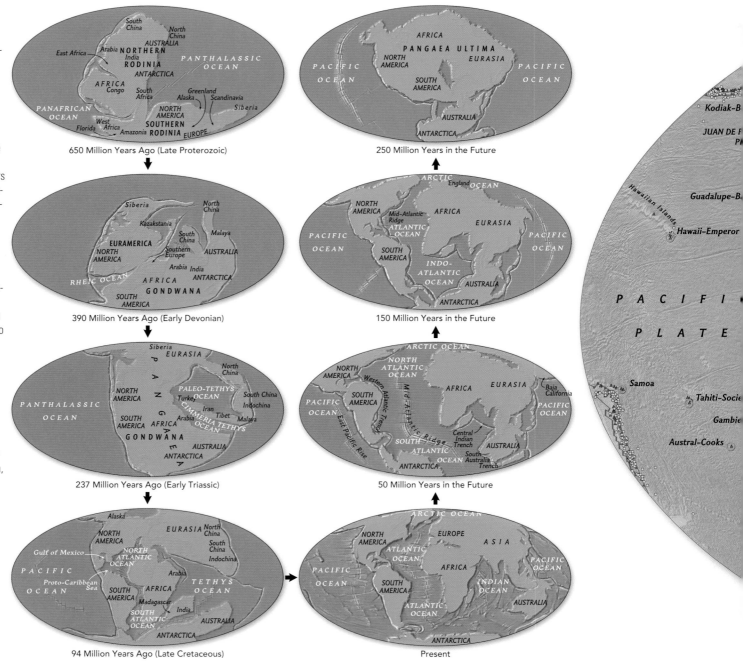

650 Million Years Ago (Late Proterozoic)

390 Million Years Ago (Early Devonian)

237 Million Years Ago (Early Triassic)

94 Million Years Ago (Late Cretaceous)

Present

50 Million Years in the Future

150 Million Years in the Future

250 Million Years in the Future

Geologic Time

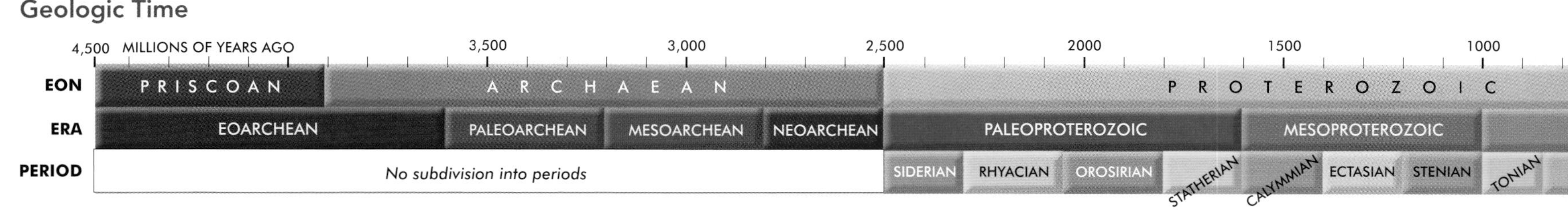

4,500 MILLIONS OF YEARS AGO
3,500
3,000
2,500
2000
1500
1000
EON
PRISCOAN
ARCHAEAN
PROTEROZOIC
ERA
EOARCHEAN
PALEOARCHEAN
MESOARCHEAN
NEOARCHEAN
PALEOPROTEROZOIC
MESOPROTEROZOIC
PERIOD
No subdivision into periods
SIDERIAN
RHYACIAN
OROSIRIAN
STATHERIAN
CALYMMIAN
ECTASIAN
STENIAN
TONIAN

Geologic Forces Change the Face of the Planet

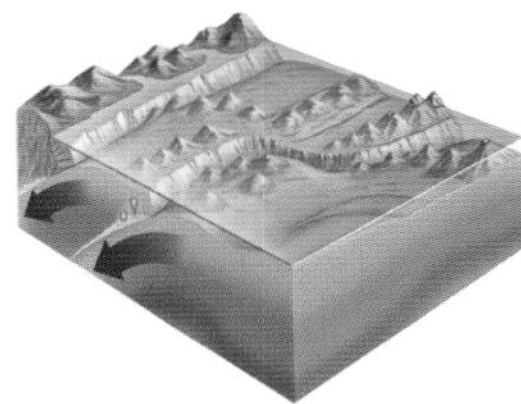

ACCRETION
As ocean plates move toward the edges of continents or island arcs and slide under them, seamounts are skimmed off and piled up in submarine trenches. The resulting buildup can cause continents to grow.

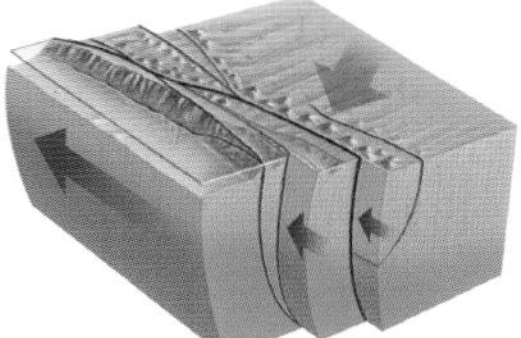

FAULTING
Enormous crustal plates do not slide smoothly. Strain built up along their edges may release in a series of small jumps, felt as minor tremors on land. Extended buildup can cause a sudden jump, producing an earthquake.

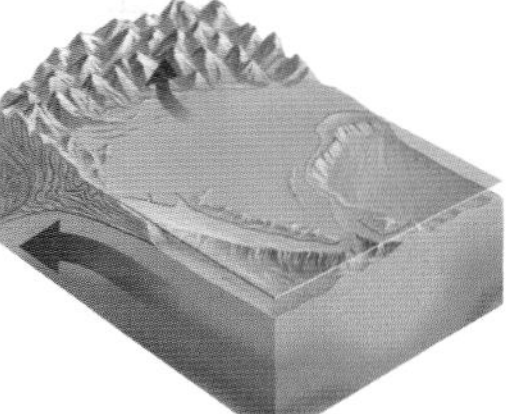

COLLISION
When two continental plates converge, the result can be the most dramatic mountain-building process on Earth. The Himalaya mountain range rose when the Indian subcontinent collided with Eurasia, driving the land upward.

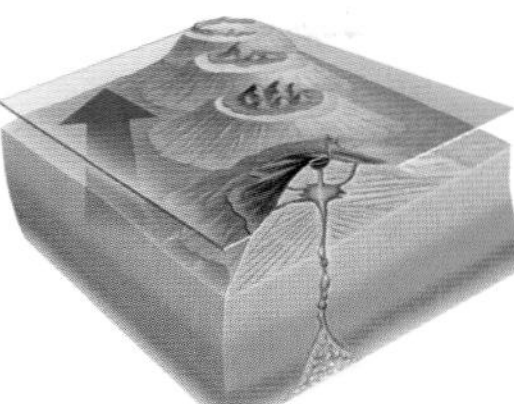

HOT SPOTS
In the cauldron of inner Earth, some areas burn hotter than others and periodically blast through their crustal covering as volcanoes. Such a "hot spot" built the Hawaiian Islands, leaving a string of oceanic protuberances.

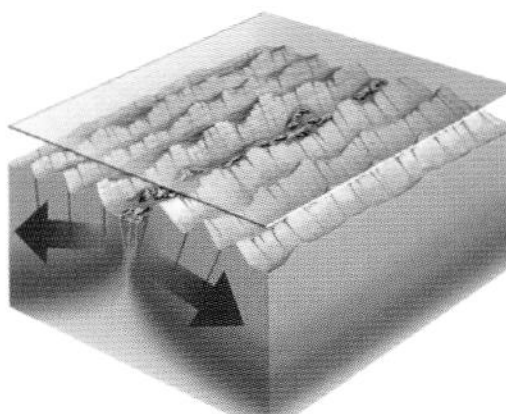

SPREADING
At the divergent boundary known as the Mid-Atlantic Ridge, oozing magma forces two plates apart by as much as eight inches a year. If that rate had been constant, the ocean could have reached its current width in 30 million years.

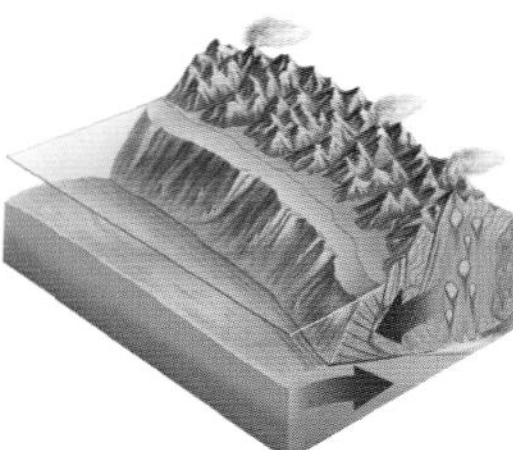

SUBDUCTION
When an oceanic plate and a continental plate converge, the older and heavier sea plate takes a dive. Plunging back into the interior of the Earth, it is transformed into molten material, only to rise again as magma.

Plate Tectonics

Tectonic boundaries mark areas of geologic change in ocean floors, on the margins of continents, and even within continents, as seen in the Great Rift Valley of East Africa. Clusters of volcanoes and frequent earthquakes indicate unstable areas.

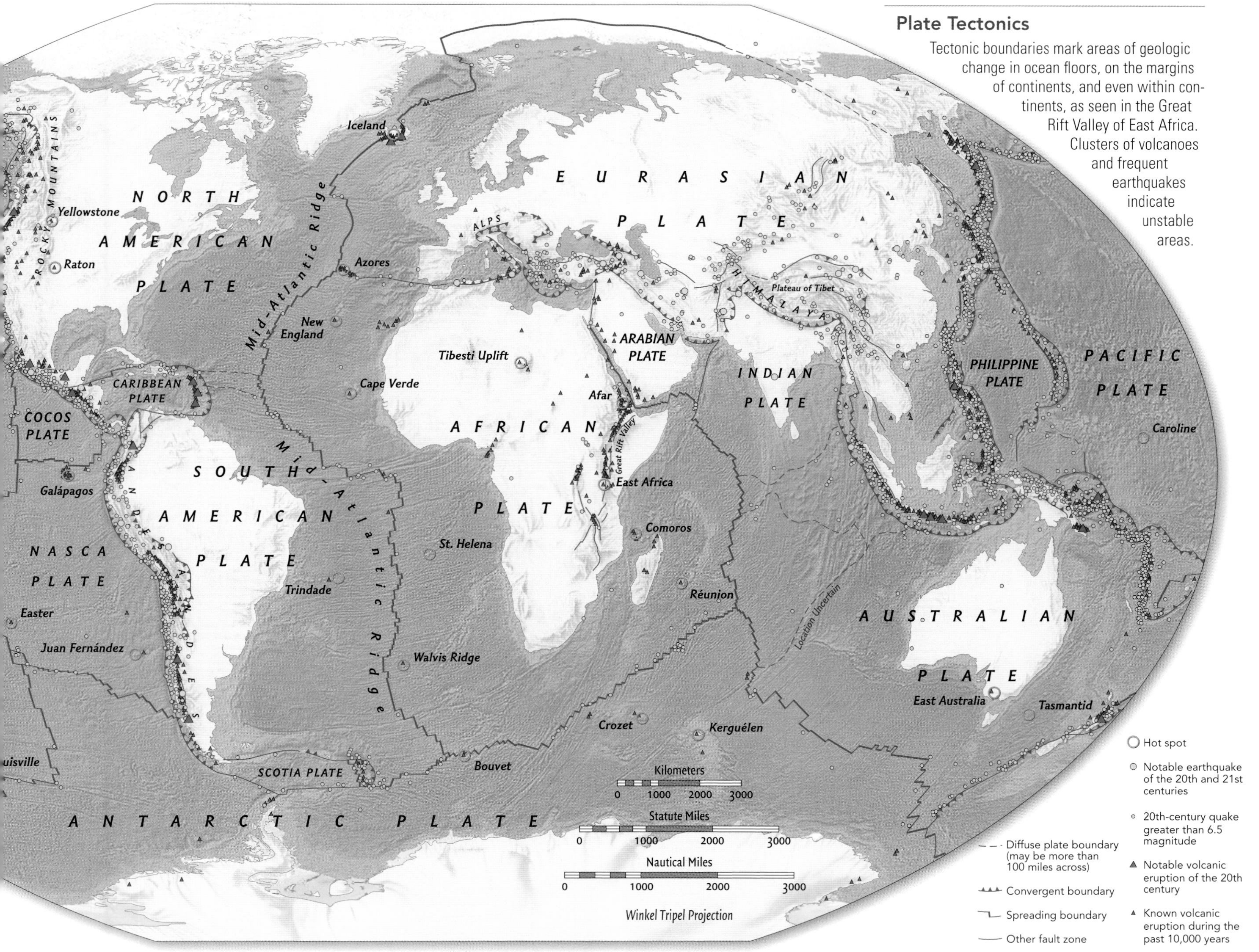

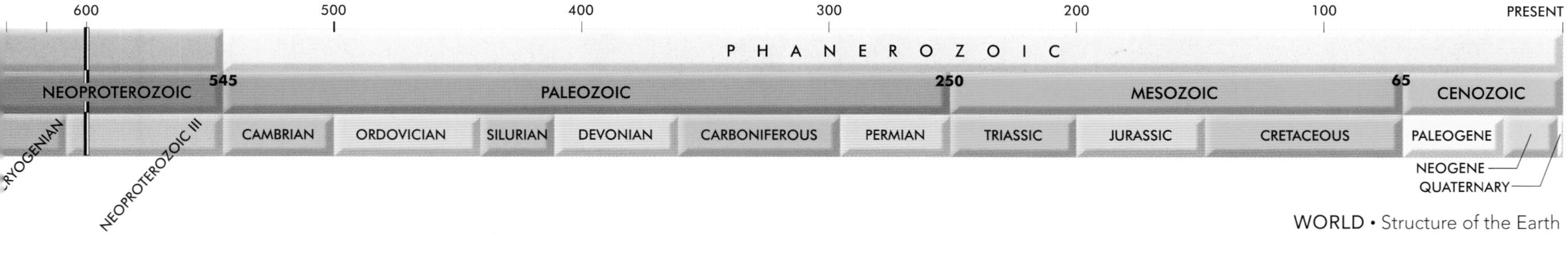

- Hot spot
- Notable earthquake of the 20th and 21st centuries
- 20th-century quake greater than 6.5 magnitude
- Notable volcanic eruption of the 20th century
- Known volcanic eruption during the past 10,000 years
- Diffuse plate boundary (may be more than 100 miles across)
- Convergent boundary
- Spreading boundary
- Other fault zone

Kilometers: 0 1000 2000 3000
Statute Miles: 0 1000 2000 3000
Nautical Miles: 0 1000 2000 3000

Winkel Tripel Projection

600	500	400	300	200	100	PRESENT

	PHANEROZOIC		
NEOPROTEROZOIC	545 PALEOZOIC	250 MESOZOIC	65 CENOZOIC

CRYOGENIAN · NEOPROTEROZOIC III · CAMBRIAN · ORDOVICIAN · SILURIAN · DEVONIAN · CARBONIFEROUS · PERMIAN · TRIASSIC · JURASSIC · CRETACEOUS · PALEOGENE · NEOGENE · QUATERNARY

EARTH'S OUTERMOST LAYER, the crust, ranges from 2 to 45 miles (3 to 70 km) thick and comprises a large variety of rocks that are aggregates of one or more types of minerals.

Scientists recognize three main classes of rock. Igneous rock forms when molten material cools and solidifies, either rapidly at the Earth's surface—as perhaps a lava flow—or more slowly underground, as an intrusion. Sedimentary rocks form from mineral or rock fragments, or from organic material that is eroded or dissolved, then deposited at Earth's surface. Metamorphic rocks form when rocks of any origin (igneous, sedimentary, or metamorphic) are subjected to very high temperature and pressure; this type also forms as rocks react with fluids deep within the crust. Igneous and metamorphic rocks make up 95 percent of the crust's volume. Sedimentary rocks make up only about 5 percent; even so, they cover a large percentage of Earth's surface.

As a result of plate tectonics, the crust is in constant slow motion; thus, rocks change positions over time. Their compositions also change as they are gradually modified by metamorphism and melting. Rocks form and re-form in a sequence known as the rock cycle (see below). Understanding their nature and origin is important because rocks contain materials that sustain modern civilization. For example, steel requires the processing of iron—mainly from ancient sedimentary rocks; copper is mined principally from slowly cooled igneous rocks called plutons; and fossil fuels (e.g., coal, oil, natural gas) derive from organic material trapped ages ago in relatively young sedimentary rocks.

Rock Classes

IGNEOUS

Igneous rocks form when molten rock (magma) originating from deep within the Earth solidifies. The chemical composition of the magma and its cooling rate determine the final rock type.

Type	Description	Examples
Intrusive (Plutonic)	Intrusive igneous rocks are formed from magma that cools and solidifies deep beneath the Earth's surface. The insulating effect of the surrounding rock allows the magma to solidify very slowly. Slow cooling means the individual mineral grains have a long time to grow, so they grow to a relatively large size. Intrusive rocks typically are coarser grained than volcanic rocks.	Examples: gabbro, diorite, granite
Extrusive (Volcanic)	Extrusive igneous rocks are formed from magma that cools and solidifies at or near the Earth's surface. Exposure to the relatively cool temperature of the atmosphere or water makes the erupted magma solidify very quickly. Rapid cooling means the individual mineral grains have only a short time to grow, so their final size is very tiny, or fine-grained. Sometimes the magma is quenched so rapidly that individual minerals have no time to grow. This is how volcanic glass forms.	Examples: basalt, andesite, and rhyolite

SEDIMENTARY

Sedimentary rocks are formed from preexisting rocks or pieces of once living organisms. They form deposits that accumulate on the Earth's surface, generally with distinctive layering or bedding.

Type	Description	Examples
Clastic	Clastic sedimentary rocks are made up of pieces (clasts) of preexisting rocks. Pieces of rock are loosened by weathering, then transported to a basin or depression where sediment is trapped. If the sediment is buried deeply, it becomes compacted and cemented, forming sedimentary rock. Clastic sedimentary rocks may have particles ranging in size from microscopic clay to huge boulders. Their names are based on their grain size.	Examples: sandstone, mudstone, conglomerate
Chemical	Chemical sedimentary rocks are formed by chemical precipitation. This process begins when water traveling through rock dissolves some of the minerals, carrying them away from their source. Eventually these minerals are redeposited when the water evaporates.	Examples: evaporite, dolomite
Biologic	Biologic sedimentary rocks form from once living organisms. They may comprise accumulated carbon-rich plant material or deposits of animal shells.	Examples: coal, chalk, limestone, chert

METAMORPHIC

Metamorphic rocks are those rocks that have been substantially changed from their original igneous, sedimentary, or earlier metamorphic form. They form when rocks are subjected to high heat; high pressure; hot, mineral-rich fluids; or, more commonly, some combination of these.

Type	Description	Examples
Foliated	Foliated rocks form when pressure deforms tabular minerals within a rock so they become aligned. These rocks develop a platy or sheetlike structure that reflects the directions from which pressure was applied.	Examples: schist, gneiss, slate
Massive (Nonfoliated)	Nonfoliated metamorphic rocks do not have a platy or sheetlike structure. There are several ways that nonfoliated rocks can be produced. Some rocks, such as limestone, are made of minerals that are not flat or elongated; no matter how much pressure is applied, the grains will not align despite recrystallization. Contact metamorphism occurs when hot igneous rock intrudes into preexisting rock. The preexisting rock is essentially baked by the heat, which changes mineral composition and texture primarily from heating rather than pressure effects.	Examples: marble, quartzite, hornfels

The Rock Cycle

To learn the origin and history of rocks, geologists study their mineralogy, texture, and fabric—characteristics that result from dynamic Earth-shaping processes driven by internal and external energy.

Internal energy is heat contained within the Earth. This intense heat creates convection currents in the mantle, which in turn cause tectonic plate movements and volcanism. External energy comes from the sun, which drives atmospheric processes that produce rain, snow, ice, and wind—powerful agents of weathering and erosion.

As internal energy builds and rebuilds Earth's rocky exterior, the forces of weathering and erosion break down surface materials and wear them away.

Ultimately, soil particles and rock fragments, called sediments, are carried by rivers into the oceans, where they may lithify, or harden into solid rock. In time, these sedimentary rocks may be subjected to heat and pressure at great depth. Mineral and structural changes occur as the rocks break and fold; they are transformed into metamorphic rocks.

Solid rocks subject to high heat and pressure during metamorphism can melt to form magma, which later can form igneous rocks, either intrusive or extrusive. The subsurface intrusive rocks (i.e., plutons) can later be uplifted by tectonic forces and (or) exposed by erosion. At the surface, the cycle continues as weathering and erosion break it down and wear it away.

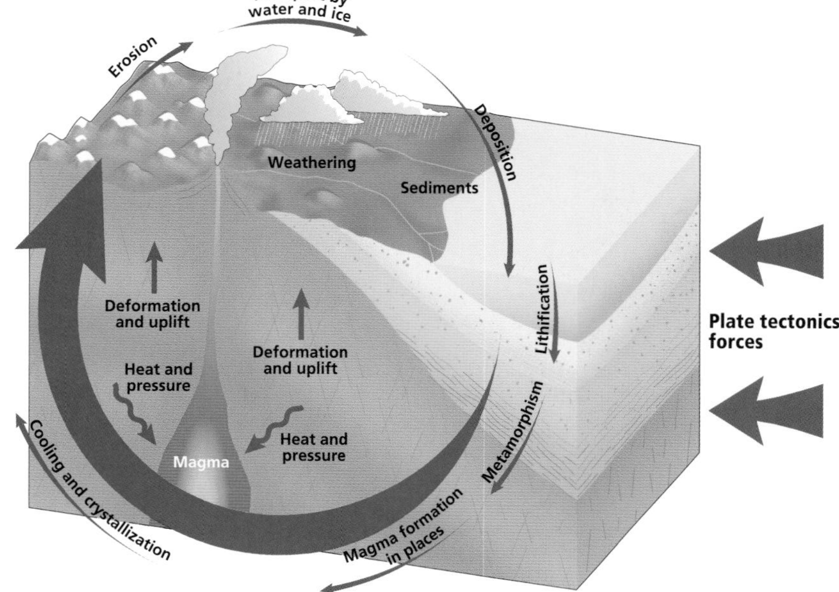

Transport by water and ice
Erosion
Deposition
Weathering
Sediments
Lithification
Deformation and uplift
Deformation and uplift
Heat and pressure
Heat and pressure
Magma
Metamorphism
Cooling and crystallization
Magma formation in places
Plate tectonics forces

Global Distribution of Rock Types

Age of Oceanic Crust

Million years ago (Ma)

0 | 5.3 | 23.8 | 33.7 | 53 | 65 | 98.9 | 144.2 | 170

Holocene | Miocene | Oligocene | Eocene | Paleocene | Upper Cretaceous | Lower Cretaceous | Upper to Middle Jurassic

Geologic period

In general, oceanic crust is much younger than surface rock.

- Continental shelf (primarily 550–170 Ma)
- Age uncertain

Global Distribution of Surface Rock

- Unconsolidated sediments
- Intrusive igneous or metamorphic rocks
- Extrusive igneous rocks
- Highly faulted or folded sedimentary, metamorphic, and igneous rocks
- Flat or gently dipping sedimentary rocks

Reading Earth History from Rocks

The Earth is 4.6 billion years old, with a long, complex history written in layers of rock.* By reading sequences of sedimentary rock, we can discover information about past environments and processes. The principle of superposition states that, provided rocks are not turned upside down by deformation, the oldest rocks are at the bottom of a sequence and younger rocks are found at the top. Unconformities tell us that uplift and erosion occurred before the deposition of younger sediments resumed. As an example, the rock sequence exposed in the Grand Canyon of Arizona indicates from oldest to youngest, the following major events:

DURING PRECAMBRIAN TIME:

1. Deposition of Vishnu sediment (about 2 billion years ago)
2. Mountain building, metamorphism of Vishnu sediment into Vishnu schist, and intrusion of Zoroaster granite (1.8 to 1.4 billion years ago)
3. Uplift and erosion resulting in an unconformity (1.4 to 1.2 billion years ago)
4. Deposition of Unkar Group sediments (1.2 to 1 billion years ago)
5. Tilting (1 billion years ago)
6. Erosion resulting in angular unconformity (1 billion to 543 million years ago)

DURING THE PHANEROZOIC (CAMBRIAN-RECENT) EON:

7. Deposition of Cambrian to Permian (and younger rocks not shown) sediments (543 to 520 million years ago), with disconformities indicating erosion and "missing" time where noted
8. Uplift and erosion of the Grand Canyon (20 million years ago to present)

The ages for these events are broadly defined by the radioisotopic dating of minerals in the metamorphic and igneous rocks, and by fossils and correlation to other rocks for the sedimentary rocks that are younger than the Precambrian-Cambrian boundary (543 million years ago).

Yavapai Point, Grand Canyon

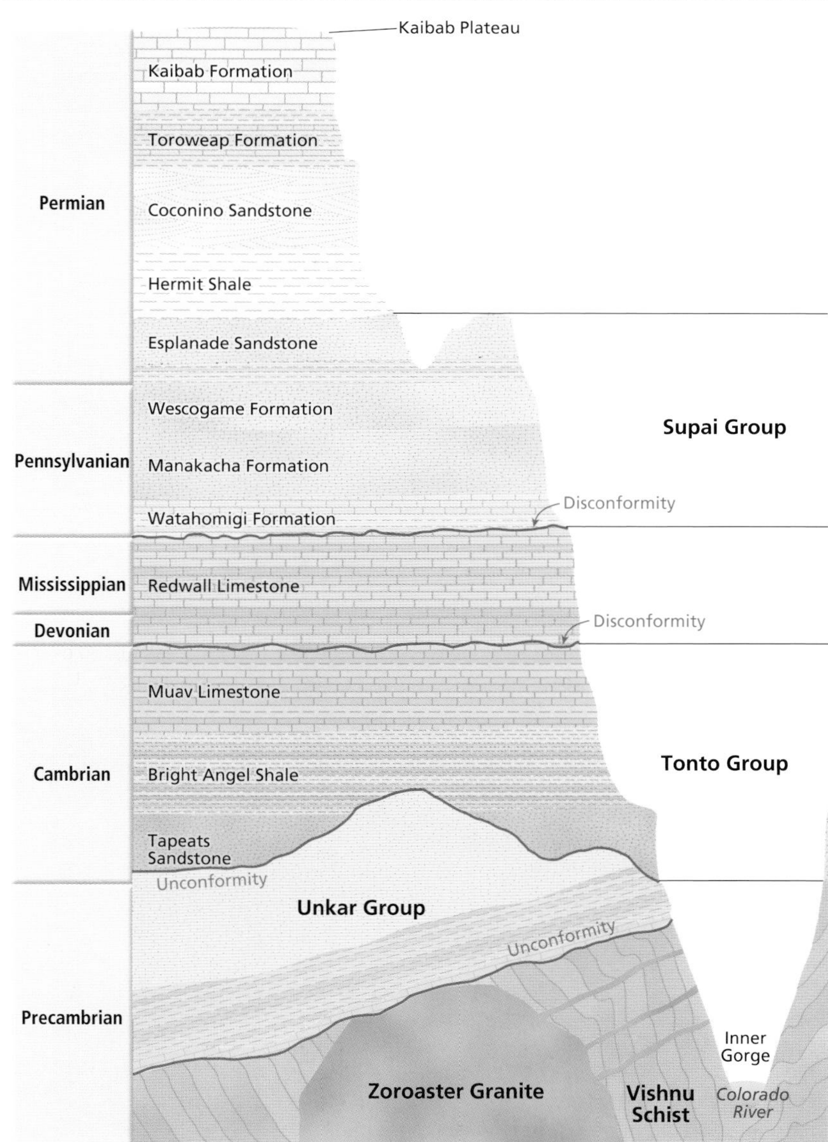
Kaibab Plateau
Permian
Kaibab Formation
Toroweap Formation
Coconino Sandstone
Hermit Shale
Esplanade Sandstone
Pennsylvanian
Wescogame Formation
Manakacha Formation
Watahomigi Formation
Supai Group
Disconformity
Mississippian
Redwall Limestone
Devonian
Disconformity
Cambrian
Muav Limestone
Bright Angel Shale
Tapeats Sandstone
Tonto Group
Unconformity
Precambrian
Unkar Group
Unconformity
Zoroaster Granite
Vishnu Schist
Inner Gorge
Colorado River

The oldest known, dated rocks on Earth go back to 4 billion years ago; geologic records of older rocks have been destroyed by more recent geologic events.

SEVEN MAJOR LANDFORM types are found on Earth's surface (see map); except for ice caps, all result from tectonic movements and denudational forces.

The loftiest landforms, mountains, often define the edges of tectonic plates. In places where continental plates converge, Earth's crust crumples into high ranges such as the Himalaya. Where oceanic plates dive beneath continental ones, volcanic mountains can rise. Volcanoes are common along the west coast of South America, which is part of the so-called Pacific Ring of Fire, the world's most active mountain-building zone.

Widely spaced mountains are another type, and examples of this landform are seen in the Basin and Range province of the western United States. These features are actually the tops of heavily eroded, faulted mountains. The eroded material filled adjacent valleys, giving these old summits the look of widely spaced mountains.

Extensive, relatively flat lands that are higher than surrounding areas are called plateaus. Formed by uplift, they include the Guiana Highlands of South America. Hills and low plateaus are rounded natural elevations of land with some local relief. The Canadian Shield and Ozarks of North America provide good examples. Depressions are large basins delimited by higher lands, an example of which is the Tarim Basin in western China. Plains are extensive areas of level or rolling treeless country. Examples include the steppes of Russia, the Ganges River plains, and the outback of Australia.

Brooks Ra.
Alaska Ra.
Rocky Mountains
Canadian Shield
Great Plains
NORTH AMERICA
Cascade Ra.
Great Basin
Ozark Plateau
Appalachian Mts.
Coastal Plain
Sa. Madre Occidental
Sa. Madre Oriental
ATLANTIC OCEAN
PACIFIC OCEAN
Guiana Highlands
Amazon Basin
SOUTH AMERICA
Andes
Brazilian Highlands
ATLANTIC OCEAN
Major Landform Types
Mountains
Widely spaced mountains
High plateaus
Hills and low plateaus
Depressions
Plains
Ice caps

Endogenic Landforms

LANDFORMS THAT RESULT FROM "INTERNAL" PROCESSES

Forces deep within the Earth give rise to mountains and other endogenic landforms. Some mountains (e.g., the Himalaya) were born when continental plates collided. Others rose in the form of volcanoes (the Cascades of North America, Mount Fuji of Japan) as sea plates subducted beneath continental plates or as plates moved over hot spots in Earth's mantle (Hawai'i). Still others were thrust up by tectonic uplift (parts of the western United States). Rifting and faulting, which occur along plate boundaries and sometimes within the plates themselves, also generate vertical tectonic landforms; these can be seen in Africa's Rift Valley and along the San Andreas Fault of California.

Clockwise from above: The Wasatch Range in Utah, uplifted by tectonic forces; the San Andreas Fault in California, a fracture in Earth's crust marking a plate boundary; Mount Fuji in Japan, a volcanic peak; Crater Lake in Oregon, a deep lake inside the caldera of Mount Mazama.

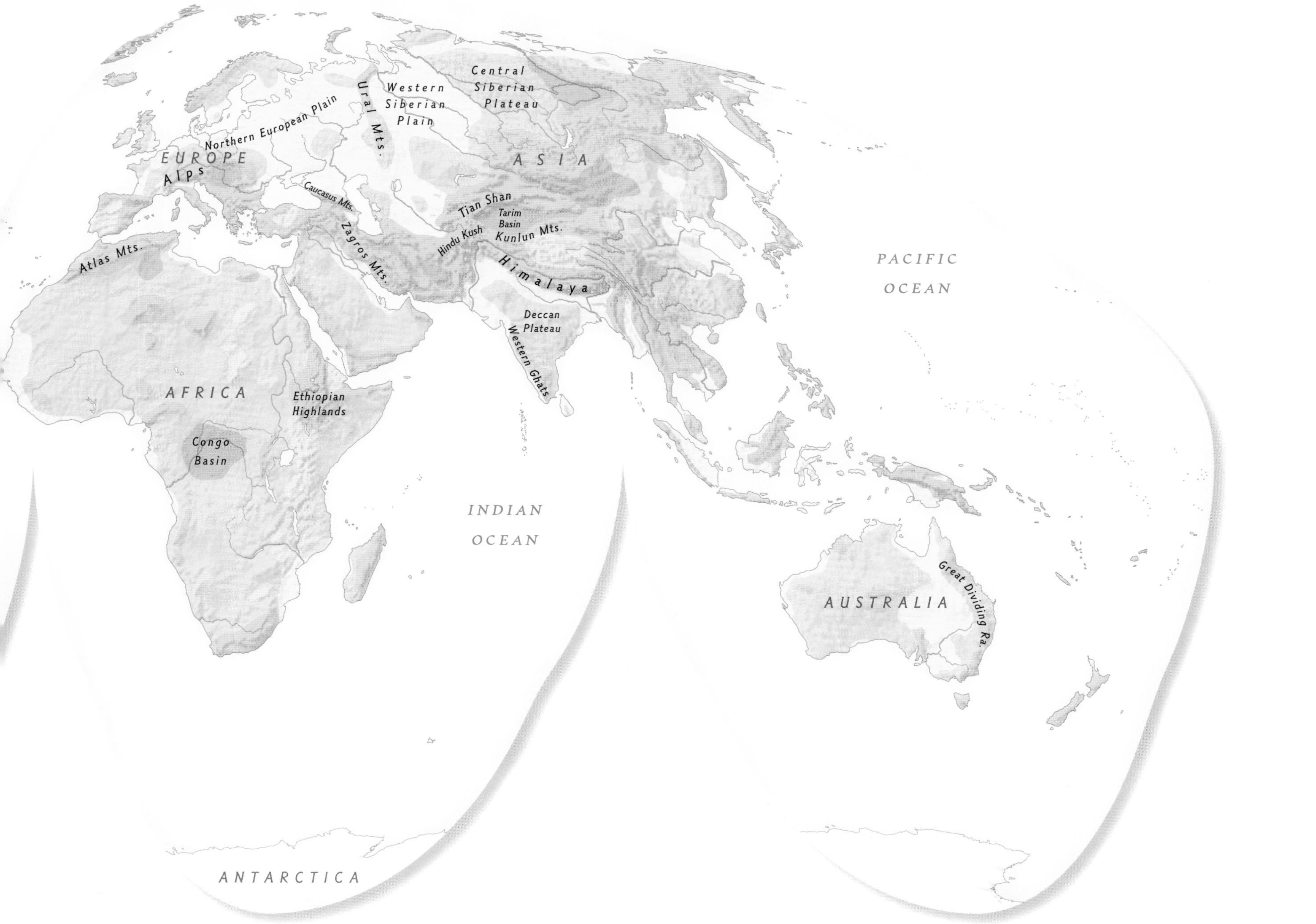

EUROPE
Alps
Northern European Plain
Ural Mts.
Western Siberian Plain
Central Siberian Plateau
ASIA
Caucasus Mts.
Tian Shan
Tarim Basin
Hindu Kush
Kunlun Mts.
Zagros Mts.
Himalaya
Atlas Mts.
PACIFIC OCEAN
Deccan Plateau
Western Ghats
AFRICA
Ethiopian Highlands
Congo Basin
INDIAN OCEAN
AUSTRALIA
Great Dividing Ra.
ANTARCTICA

Exogenic Landforms

LANDFORMS THAT RESULT FROM "EXTERNAL" PROCESSES

External agents create exogenic landforms. Weathering by rain, groundwater, and other natural elements slowly breaks down rocks, such as the limestone in karst landscapes or the granite in an exfoliation dome (Yosemite's Half Dome). Erosion removes weathered material and transports it from place to place. In the American Southwest, erosion continues to shape the spires of Bryce Canyon and the walls of slot canyons.

Clockwise from above: tower karst in Thailand, weathered limestone in humid climate; Bryce Canyon in Utah, eroded sedimentary rocks in arid climate; slot canyon in the American Southwest, sedimentary rock eroded by water; Half Dome in Yosemite, California, weathered granite batholith.

Other Landforms

Some landforms are the impact sites (or craters) of asteroids, comets, and meteorites. The most readily observable are Meteor Crater in Arizona and New Quebec Crater in eastern Canada. Other landforms include man-made dams and open-pit mines, as well as biogenic features such as coral reefs made by coral polyps and giant mounds built by termites.

Meteor Crater, Arizona

Termite mound, Cape York Peninsula, Australia

All of Earth's features are created and continually reshaped by such factors as wind, water, ice, tectonics, and humans. This painting brings together 34 natural and man-made features to show typical locations and relationships of landforms; it does not depict an actual region. Definitions of most landforms can be found in the glossary.

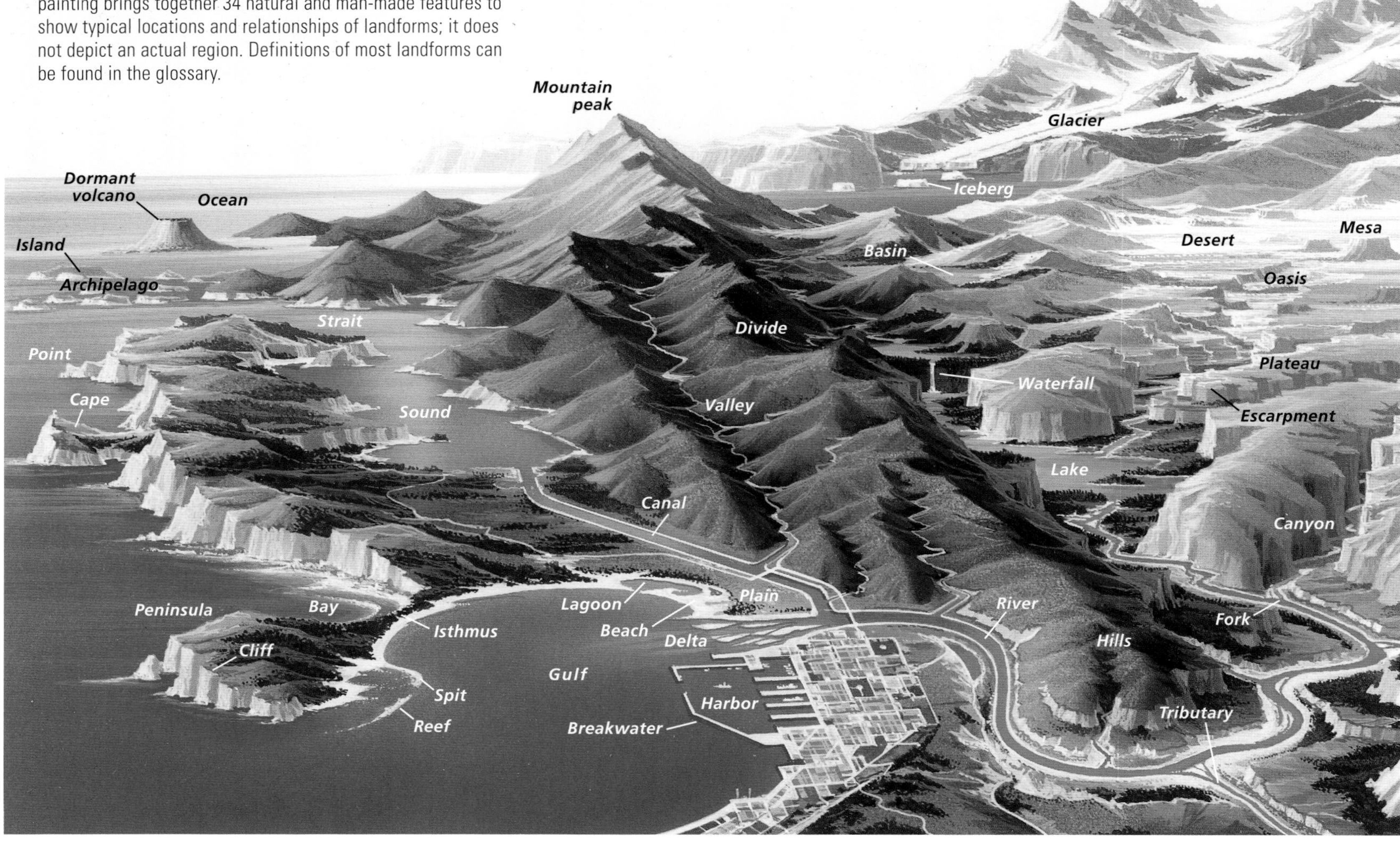
Mountain range
Mountain peak
Glacier
Dormant volcano
Ocean
Iceberg
Island
Mesa
Desert
Basin
Archipelago
Oasis
Strait
Divide
Point
Waterfall
Plateau
Cape
Sound
Valley
Escarpment
Lake
Canal
Canyon
Plain
Lagoon
River
Peninsula
Bay
Fork
Isthmus
Beach
Delta
Hills
Cliff
Gulf
Spit
Harbor
Tributary
Reef
Breakwater

Landforms Created by Wind

The term "eolian" (from Aeolus, the Greek god of the winds) describes landforms shaped by the wind. The erosive action of wind is characterized by deflation, or the removal of dust and sand from dry soil; sandblasting, the erosion of rock by wind-borne sand; and deposition, the laying down of sediments. The effects of wind erosion are evident in many parts of the world (see map), particularly where there are large deposits of sand or loess (dust and silt dropped by wind). Among desert landforms, sand dunes may be the most spectacular. They come in several types (below): **Barchan dunes** are crescents with arms pointing downwind; **transverse dunes** are "waves," with crests perpendicular to the wind; **star dunes** have curving ridges radiating from their centers; **parabolic dunes** are crescents with arms that point upwind; and **longitudinal dunes** lie parallel to the wind.

ASIA
EUROPE
NORTH AMERICA
AFRICA
SOUTH AMERICA
AUSTRALIA
ANTARCTICA
Desert
Loess deposit
See Land Cover pp. 32-33

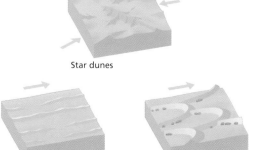

Wind direction

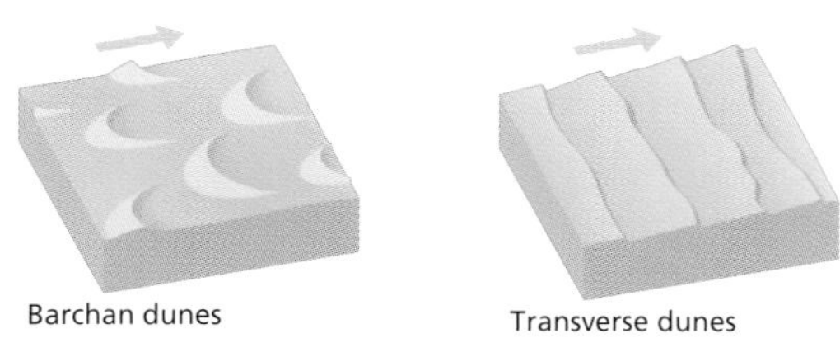

Barchan dunes

Transverse dunes

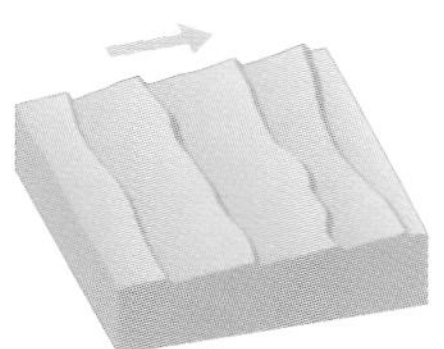

Star dunes

Longitudinal (seif) dunes

Parabolic dunes

EOLIAN LANDFORMS

Desert dunes, which actually cover only a small portion of desert areas, range in height from just a few feet to more than a thousand feet. Coastal dunes form when wind and waves deposit sediments along the shores of oceans and other large bodies of water. Loess hills are large deposits of wind-borne silt, the most extensive of which are found in North America and Asia.

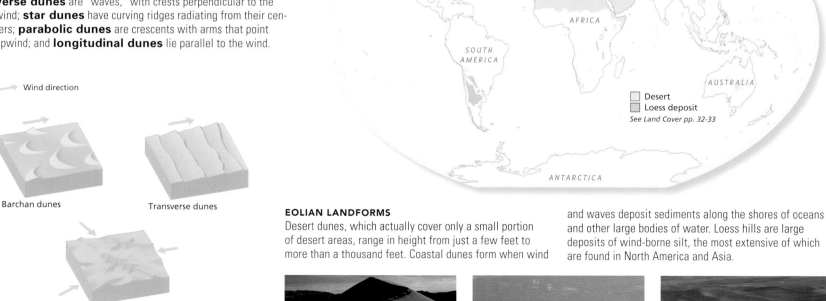

Desert dunes: Death Valley National Park, California

Coastal dunes: Dune du Nord, Quebec

Loess deposits: Palouse Hills, Washington

Landforms Created by Water

Highlighted on the map at right are Earth's major watersheds. These are drainage basins for rivers, which create fluvial (from a Latin word meaning "river") landforms. Wave action and groundwater also produce characteristic landforms.

RIVERS

Some rivers form broad loops called meanders (below) as faster currents erode their outer banks and slower currents deposit materials along inner banks. When a river breaks through the narrow neck of a meander, the abandoned curve becomes an oxbow lake.

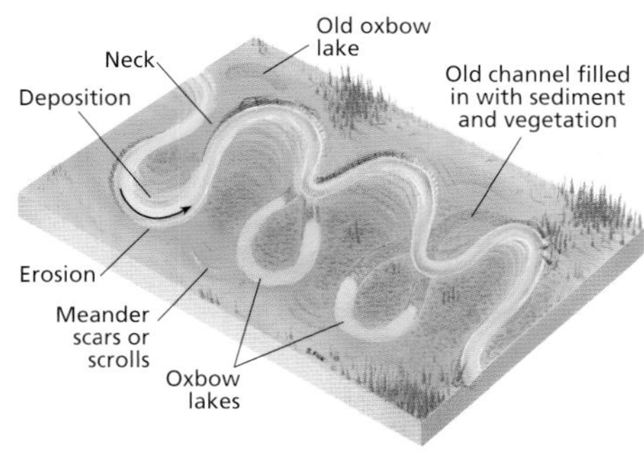

Old oxbow lake
Neck
Deposition
Old channel filled in with sediment and vegetation
Erosion
Meander scars or scrolls
Oxbow lakes

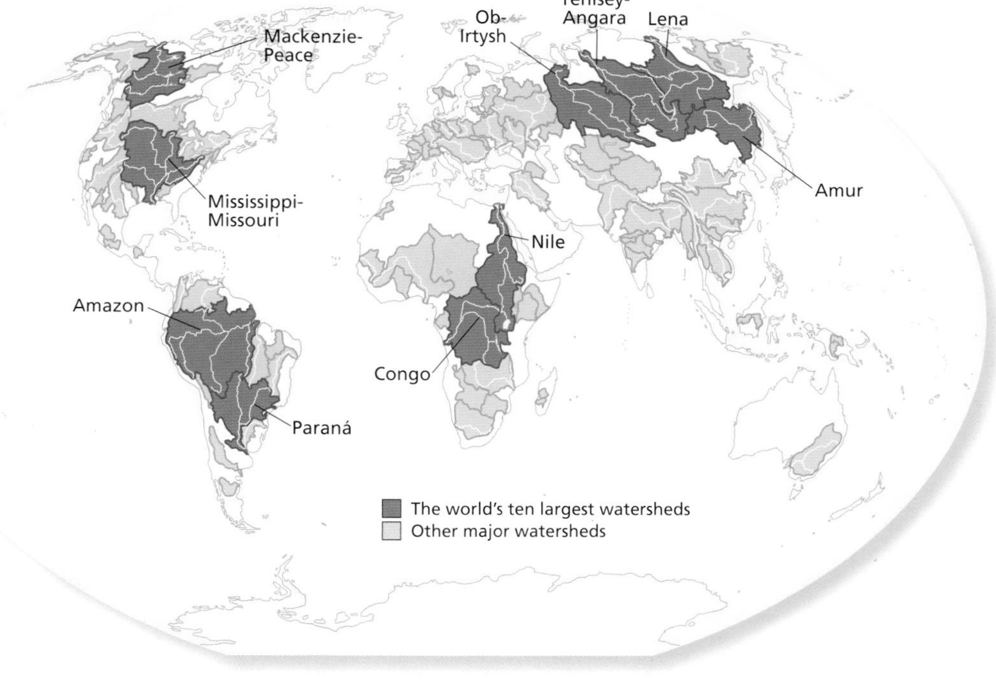

Mackenzie-Peace
Ob-Irtysh
Yenisey-Angara
Lena
Amur
Mississippi-Missouri
Nile
Amazon
Congo
Paraná
The world's ten largest watersheds
Other major watersheds

RIVER DELTAS

Sediment deposited at a river's mouth builds a delta, a term first used by the ancient Greeks to describe the Nile Delta; its triangular shape resembles the fourth letter of the Greek alphabet. Not all deltas have that classic shape: The Mississippi River forms a bird's-foot delta.

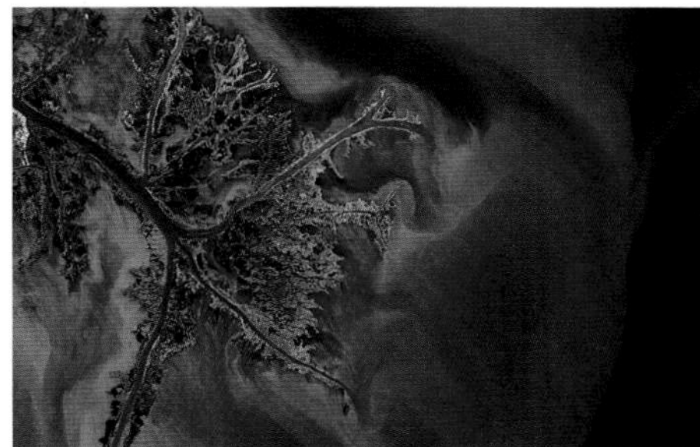

Mississippi River Delta

COASTAL AREAS

Through erosion and deposition, tides and wave action continually reshape the coastlines of the world. Ocean currents transport sand and gravel from one part of a shore to another, sometimes building beach extensions called spits, long ridges that project into open water. Relentless waves undercut coastal cliffs, eroding volumes of material and leaving behind sea stacks and sea arches, remnants made of more resistant rock. As ocean levels rise, narrow arms of the sea (fjords) may reach inland for miles, filling deep valleys once occupied by glaciers flowing to the sea.

Sea stacks: Victoria, Australia

GROUNDWATER

Water in the ground slowly dissolves limestone, a highly soluble rock. Over time, caves form and underground streams flow through the rock; sinkholes develop at the surface as underlying rock gives way. Karst landscapes, named for the rugged Karst region of the former Yugoslavia, are large areas of unusual landforms created by weathered and eroded limestone.

Karst cave: Kickapoo Cave, Texas

Landforms Created by Ice

Among the legacies of Earth's most recent ice age (see map) are landforms shaped by glaciers. There are two kinds of glaciers: valley, or alpine, and continental ice sheets. These large, slow-moving masses of ice can crush or topple anything in their paths; they even stop rivers in their tracks, creating ice-dammed lakes. Glaciers are also powerful agents of erosion, grinding against the ground and picking up and carrying huge amounts of rock and soil, which they deposit at their margins when they begin to melt; these deposits are called lateral and terminal moraines. The paintings below show how an ice sheet (upper) leaves a lasting imprint on the land (lower).

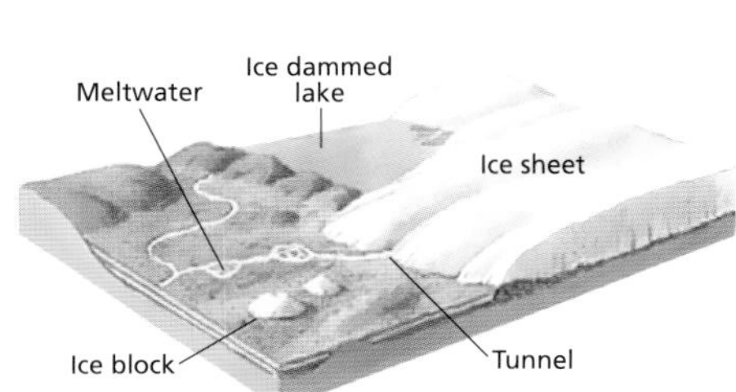

Meltwater
Ice dammed lake
Ice sheet
Ice block
Tunnel

BEFORE AND AFTER (LEFT)

Meltwater deposits material in long, narrow ridges (eskers). Ice embedded in the ground melts and forms lakes (kettles). Ice overruns unconsolidated materials and shapes them into hills (drumlins).

NORTH AMERICA
EUROPE
ASIA
AFRICA
SOUTH AMERICA
AUSTRALIA
ANTARCTICA
Greatest extent of ice during last ice age

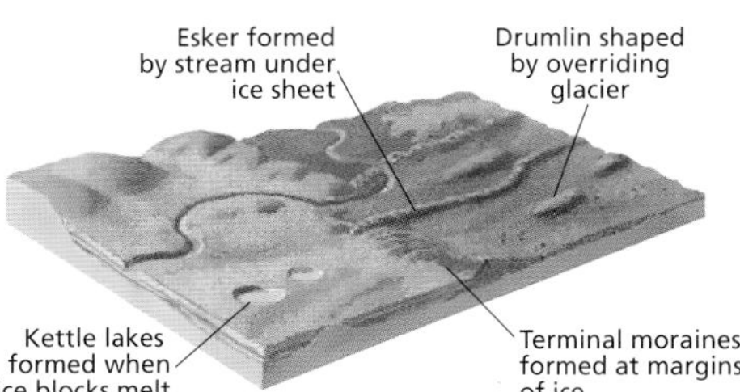

Esker formed by stream under ice sheet
Drumlin shaped by overriding glacier
Kettle lakes formed when ice blocks melt
Terminal moraines formed at margins of ice

Glacial valley: Sierra Nevada, California

POSTGLACIAL LANDFORMS

As they move, alpine glaciers widen their V-shaped valleys, often leaving behind U-shaped ones when they withdraw (left). Ice sheets leave an even larger legacy simply because they cover more territory. Among their creations are drumlin fields (right) and lake basins, including the ones now filled by the Great Lakes of North America.

Drumlins: Kejimkujik Lake, Nova Scotia

EARTH'S LARGEST FEATURES—oceans and continents—can be seen from thousands of miles out in space. So can some of its relatively smaller ones: vast plains and long mountain chains, huge lakes and great ice sheets. The sizes, shapes, locations, and interrelationships of these and innumerable other features, large and small, give Earth its unique appearance.

Mountains, plateaus, and plains give texture to the land. In North and South America, the Rockies and Andes rise above great basins and plains, while in Asia the Himalaya and Plateau of Tibet form the rugged core of Earth's largest continent. All are the result of powerful forces within the planet pushing up the land. Other features, such as valleys and canyons, were created when weathering and erosion wore down parts of the surface. Landmasses are not the only places with dramatic features: Lying beneath the oceans are enormous mountains and towering volcanoes, high plateaus and seemingly bottomless trenches.

Around most continents are shallow seas concealing gently sloping continental shelves. From the margins of these shelves, steeper continental slopes lead ever deeper into the abyss. Although scientists use different terms to describe their studies of the ocean depths (bathymetry) and the lay of the land (topography), Earth's surface is a continuum, with similar features giving texture to lands both above and below the sea level.

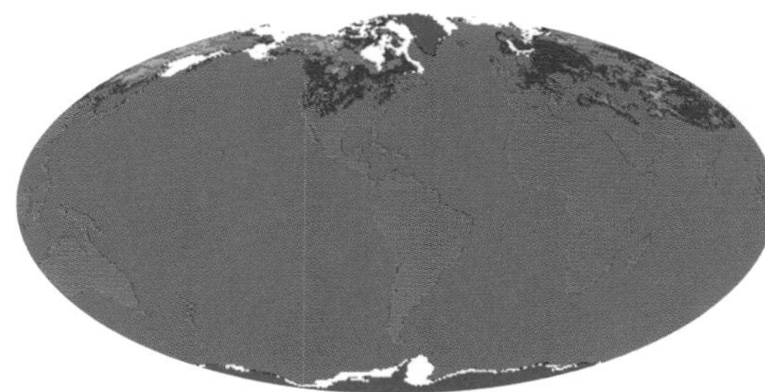

SNOW AND ICE **Just over 2 percent of Earth's water is locked in ice, snow, and glaciers. Ice and snow reflect solar energy back into space, thus regulating the temperature. Ocean levels can also be affected, rising or falling as polar ice sheets shrink or grow.**

Distribution of Earth's Elevations and Depths (Hypsometry)

Hypsometry measures the distribution of elevation and depth as a function of the area covered. At right, the "Raw %" curve shows two concentrations of average elevation: about 4,000 meters (13,000 ft) below sea level and about 800 meters (2,600 ft) above sea level. The "peaks" in the curve reflect the large, nearly flat areas of ocean floor, and vast land areas of Asia, Greenland, and Antarctica. The "Cumulative %" curve shows that about 72 percent of Earth's surface is below sea level, based on a worldwide two-minute (latitude-longitude) grid and a 200-meter (650-ft) grouping of vertical data.

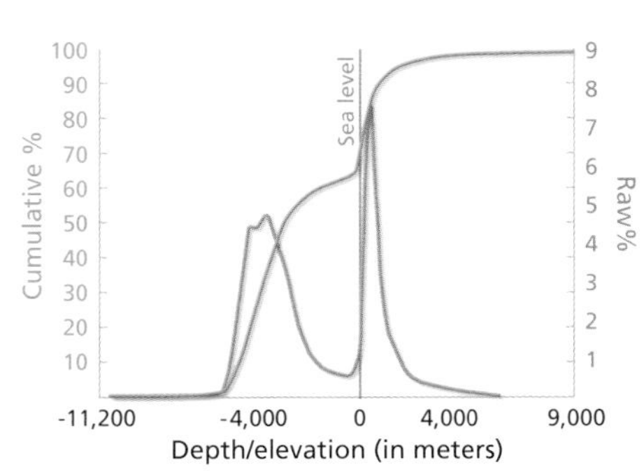
Cumulative %
100
90
80
70
60
50
40
30
20
10
Sea level
Raw%
9
8
7
6
5
4
3
2
1
-11,200
-4,000
0
4,000
9,000
Depth/elevation (in meters)

Surface by the Numbers

AREA

TOTAL SURFACE AREA: 196,938,000 square miles (510,066,000 sq km)

LAND AREA: 57,393,000 square miles (148,647,000 sq km), 29.1 percent of total surface area

WATER AREA: 139,545,000 square miles (361,419,000 sq km), 70.9 percent of total surface area

SURFACE FEATURES

HIGHEST LAND: Mount Everest, 29,035 feet (8,850 m) above sea level

LOWEST LAND: shore of Dead Sea, 1,365 feet (416 m) below sea level

OCEAN DEPTHS

DEEPEST PART OF OCEAN: Challenger Deep, in the Pacific Ocean southwest of Guam, 35,827 feet (10,920 m) below the surface

AVERAGE OCEAN DEPTH: 12,205 feet (3,720 m)

CHEMICAL MAKEUP OF EARTH'S CRUST

As a percentage of the crust's weight: oxygen 46.6, silicon 27.7, aluminum 8.1, iron 5.0, calcium 3.6, sodium 2.8, potassium 2.6, magnesium 2.1, and other elements totaling 1.5.

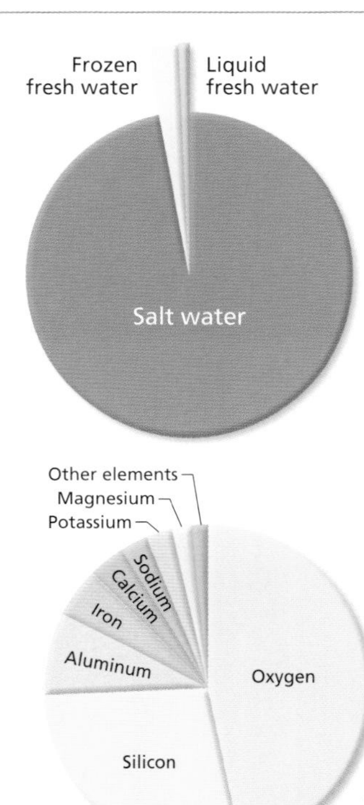
Frozen fresh water
Liquid fresh water
Salt water
Other elements
Magnesium
Potassium
Sodium
Calcium
Iron
Aluminum
Oxygen
Silicon

Earth Surface Elevations and Depths

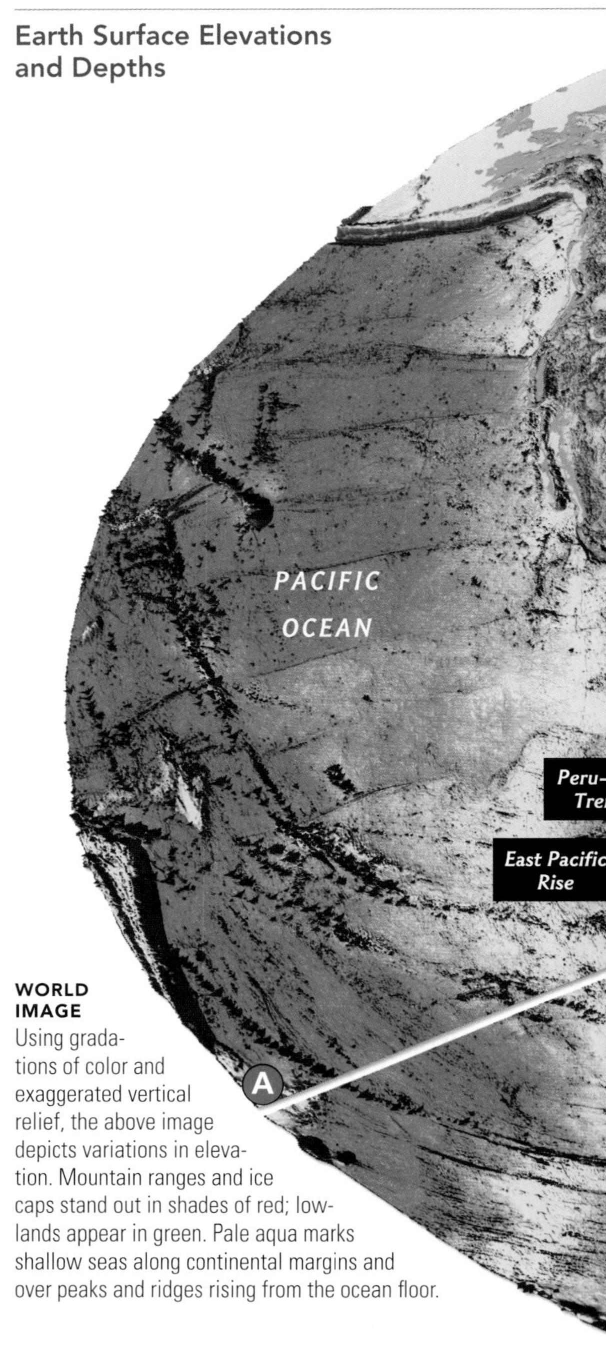
PACIFIC OCEAN
Peru-Cl
Trenc
East Pacific Rise
A

WORLD IMAGE
Using gradations of color and exaggerated vertical relief, the above image depicts variations in elevation. Mountain ranges and ice caps stand out in shades of red; lowlands appear in green. Pale aqua marks shallow seas along continental margins and over peaks and ridges rising from the ocean floor.

A Slice of Earth

Combining bathymetric and topographic data, this profile shows details of the Earth's crust—from the western Pacific Basin (A) to the Atlantic Basin; across Africa, the Himalaya, and the Japan Trench; then back to the western Pacific margin (B).

SOUTH AMERICA
NORTH AMERICA
PACIFIC OCEAN
ATLANTIC OCEAN
A
Andes
East Pacific Rise
Peru-Chile Trench
Mid-A
Ric

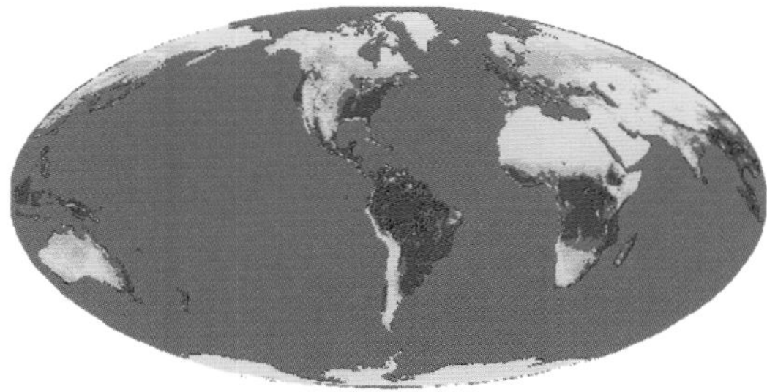

VEGETATIVE COVER Forests and woodlands cover 28 percent of Earth's land areas, helping those regions retain heat and thus playing a major role in the shaping of climate. Vast grasslands hold grains that are an important element in the world food supply.

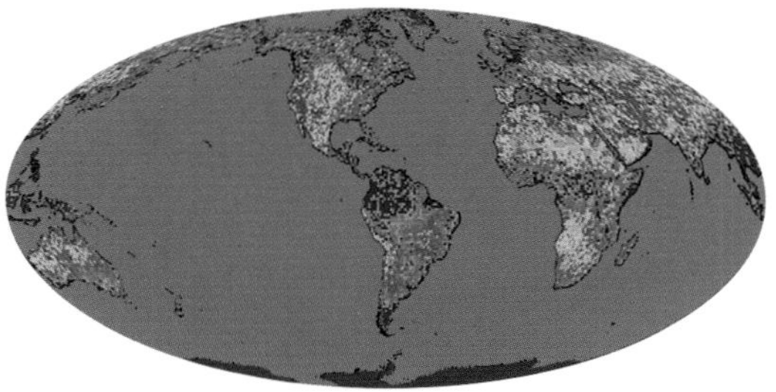

DAY AND NIGHT TEMPERATURE DIFFERENCES Vegetative cover influences variations between day and night temperatures in an area. Rain forests and other heavily vegetated regions retain heat well and experience relatively small changes, whereas deserts (in red) are subject to extreme variations.

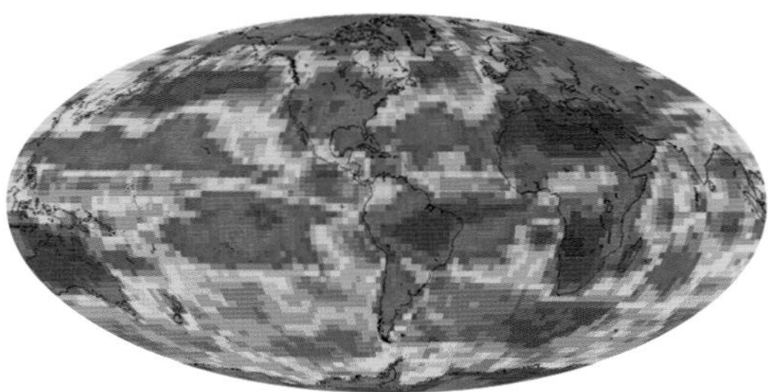

CLOUD COVER This composite image shows the regions with the heaviest cloud cover (red) on a typical June day. The gradation to blue signifies decreasing cover. Clouds contain moisture, affect temperatures, and on any given day cover 50 to 70 percent of Earth's surface.

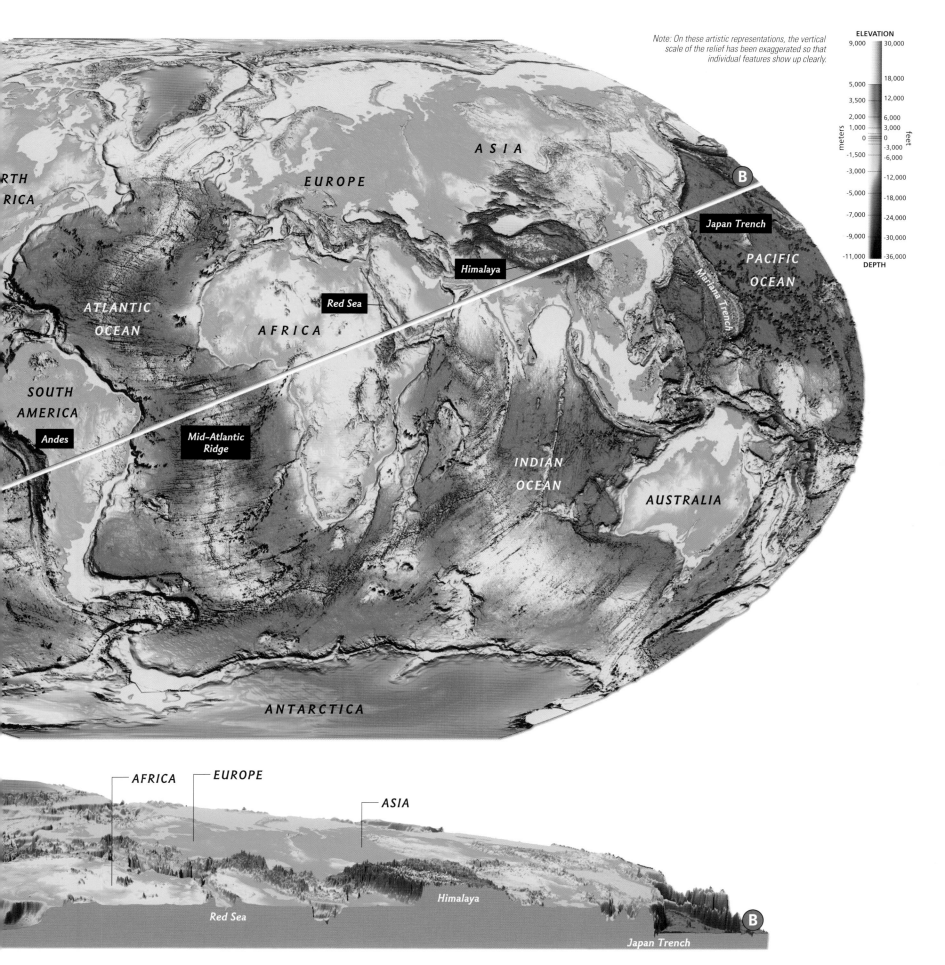

Note: On these artistic representations, the vertical scale of the relief has been exaggerated so that individual features show up clearly.

ELEVATION
meters: 9,000; 5,000; 3,500; 2,000; 1,000; 0; -1,500; -3,000; -5,000; -7,000; -9,000; -11,000
feet: 30,000; 18,000; 12,000; 6,000; 3,000; 0; -3,000; -6,000; -12,000; -18,000; -24,000; -30,000; -36,000
DEPTH

RTH
RICA
EUROPE
ASIA
B
Japan Trench
PACIFIC OCEAN
Mariana Trench
Himalaya
Red Sea
ATLANTIC OCEAN
AFRICA
SOUTH AMERICA
Andes
Mid-Atlantic Ridge
INDIAN OCEAN
AUSTRALIA
ANTARCTICA

AFRICA
EUROPE
ASIA
Himalaya
Red Sea
B
Japan Trench

RELIABLE INFORMATION on global vegetative cover is an important requirement for many Earth-system studies, and the best source for an overall view of the planet is satellite data. Such data allow for the creation of internally consistent, reproducible, and accurate land cover maps like the one at right, which is based on a year of global satellite imagery from the Advanced Very High Resolution Radiometer (AVHRR) at a spatial resolution of one kilometer.

The change of vegetation through time, or its phenology, is captured in the satellite record and used to differentiate classes of vegetative cover. By recording the data at different wavelengths of the electromagnetic spectrum, scientists can derive land cover types through spectral variation. Maps made from this information help identify places undergoing changes. Descriptions of the various land cover types are provided below.

Global Land Cover Composition

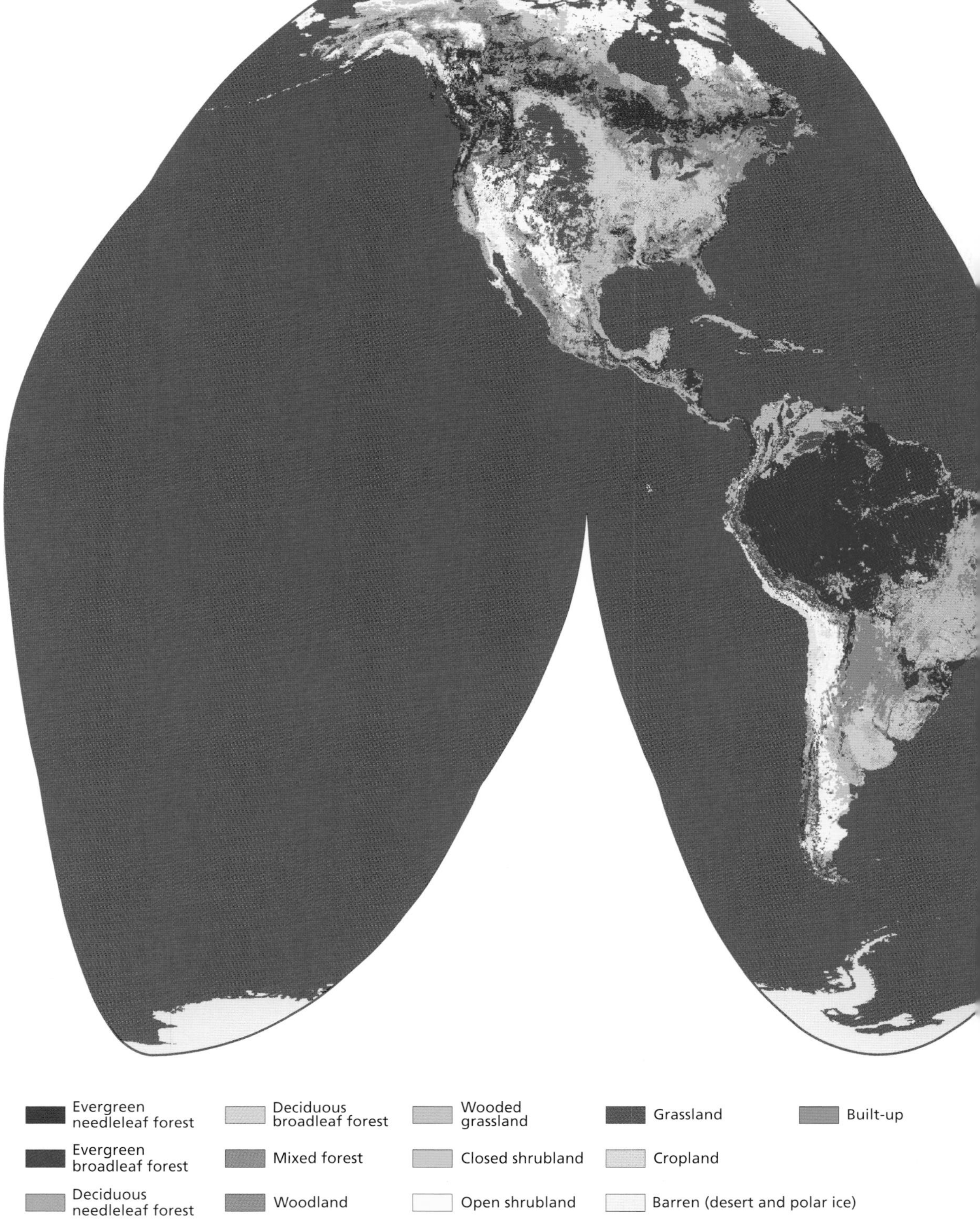

Evergreen needleleaf forest
Evergreen broadleaf forest
Deciduous needleleaf forest
Deciduous broadleaf forest
Mixed forest
Woodland
Wooded grassland
Closed shrubland
Open shrubland
Grassland
Cropland
Barren (desert and polar ice)
Built-up

EVERGREEN NEEDLELEAF FOREST
In this land cover type, more than 60 percent of the land is covered by a forest canopy; tree height exceeds 5 meters. Evergreen needleleaf forests are typical of the boreal (northern subarctic) region. In many of these areas, trees are grown on plantations and logged for the making of paper and building products.

EVERGREEN BROADLEAF FOREST
More than 60 percent of the land is covered by a forest canopy; tree height exceeds 5 meters. Such forests, which include tropical rain forests, dominate in the tropics and contain the greatest concentrations of biodiversity. In many areas, mechanized farms, ranches, and tree plantations are replacing this land cover.

DECIDUOUS NEEDLELEAF FOREST
More than 60 percent of the land is covered by a forest canopy; tree height exceeds 5 meters. Trees respond to cold seasons by shedding their leaves simultaneously. This class is dominant only in Siberia, taking the form of larch forests with a short June-to-August growing season.

DECIDUOUS BROADLEAF FOREST
More than 60 percent of the land is covered by a forest canopy; tree height exceeds 5 meters. In dry or cold seasons, trees shed their leaves simultaneously. Much of this forest has been converted to cropland in temperate regions, with large remnants found only on steep slopes.

MIXED FOREST
More than 60 percent of the land is covered by a forest canopy; tree height exceeds 5 meters. Both needleleaf and deciduous types appear, with neither having coverage of less than 25 percent or more than 75 percent. This type is largely found between temperate deciduous and boreal evergreen forests.

WOODLAND
Land has herbaceous or woody understories and tree canopy cover of 40 to 60 percent; trees exceed 5 meters and may be evergreen or deciduous. This type is common in the tropics and is most highly degraded in areas with long histories of human habitation, such as West Africa.

WOODED GRASSLAND
Land has herbaceous or woody understories and tree canopy cover of 10 to 40 percent; trees exceed 5 meters and may be evergreen or deciduous. This type includes classic African savanna, as well as open boreal woodlands that demarcate tree lines and the beginning of tundra ecosystems.

CLOSED SHRUBLAND
Bushes or shrubs dominate, with a canopy coverage of more than 40 percent. Bushes do not exceed 5 meters in height; shrubs or bushes can be evergreen or deciduous. Tree canopy is less than 10 percent. This land cover can be found where prolonged cold or dry seasons limit plant growth.

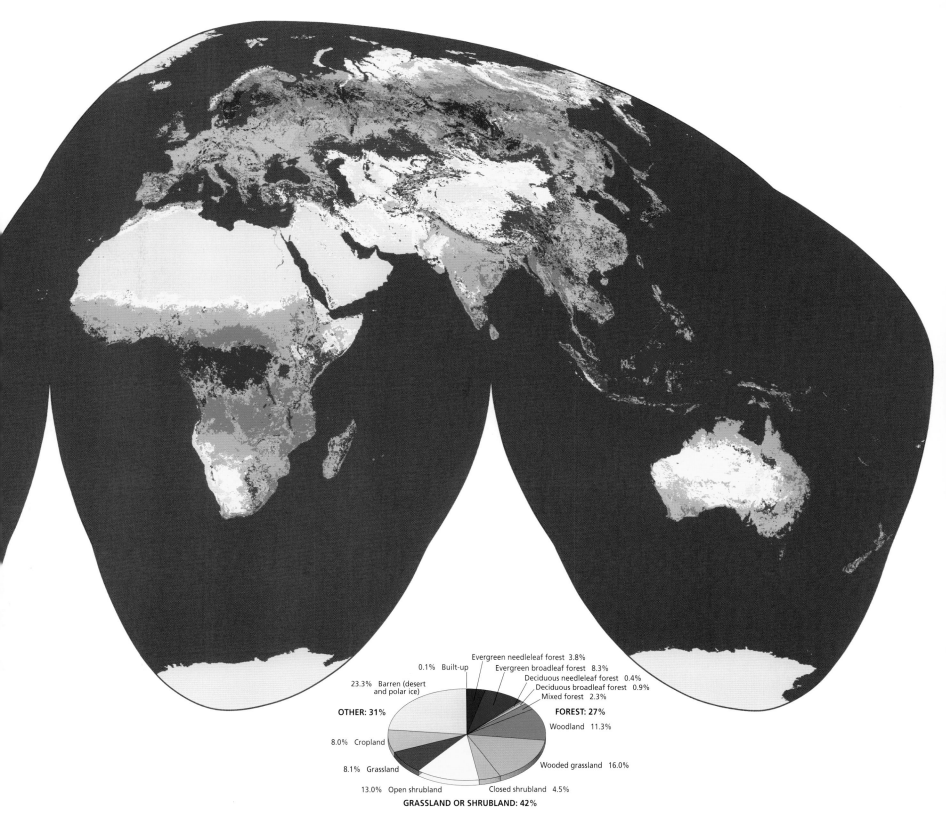

0.1% Built-up
Evergreen needleleaf forest 3.8%
Evergreen broadleaf forest 8.3%
Deciduous needleleaf forest 0.4%
Deciduous broadleaf forest 0.9%
Mixed forest 2.3%
23.3% Barren (desert and polar ice)
OTHER: 31%
FOREST: 27%
Woodland 11.3%
8.0% Cropland
8.1% Grassland
Wooded grassland 16.0%
13.0% Open shrubland
Closed shrubland 4.5%
GRASSLAND OR SHRUBLAND: 42%

OPEN SHRUBLAND
Shrubs are dominant, with a canopy cover between 10 and 40 percent; they do not exceed 2 meters in height and can be evergreen or deciduous. The remaining land is either barren or characterized by annual herbaceous cover. This land cover type occurs in semiarid or severely cold regions.

GRASSLAND
Land has continuous herbaceous cover and less than 10 percent tree or shrub canopy cover. This type occurs in a wide range of habitats. Perennial grasslands in the central United States and Russia, for example, are the most extensive and mark a line of decreased precipitation that limits agriculture.

CROPLAND
Crop-producing fields make up more than 80 percent of the landscape. Areas of high-intensity agriculture, including mechanized farming, stretch across temperate regions. Much agriculture in the developing world is fragmented, however, and occurs on small plots of land.

BARREN AND DESERT
Exposed soil, sand, or rocks are typical; the land never has more than 10 percent vegetated cover during any time of year. This class includes true deserts, such as the Sahara in Africa. Desertification, the expansion of deserts due to land degradation or climate change, is a problem in areas.

URBAN AND BUILT-UP
Land cover includes buildings and other man-made structures. This class was mapped using the populated places layer that is part of the "Digital Chart of the World" (Danko, 1992). Urban and built-up cover represents the most densely developed areas of human habitation.

SNOW AND ICE
Land has permanent snow and ice; it never has more than 10 percent vegetated cover at any time of year. The greatest expanses of this class can be seen in Greenland, on other Arctic islands, and in Antarctica. Glaciers at high elevations form significant examples in Alaska, the Himalaya, and Iceland.

THE TERM "CLIMATE" describes the average "weather" conditions, as measured over many years, that prevail at any given point around the world at a given time of the year. Daily weather may differ dramatically from that expected on the basis of climatic statistics.

Energy from the sun drives the global climate system. Much of this incoming energy is absorbed in the tropics. Outgoing heat radiation, much of which exits at high latitudes, balances the absorbed incoming solar energy. To achieve a balance across the globe, huge amounts of heat are moved from the tropics to polar regions by both the atmosphere and the oceans.

The tilt of Earth's axis leads to shifting patterns of incoming solar energy throughout the year. More energy is transported to higher latitudes in winter than in summer, and hence the contrast in temperatures between the tropics and polar regions is greatest at this time of year—especially in the Northern Hemisphere.

Scientists present this data in many ways, using climographs (see page 36), which show information about specific places. Alternatively, they produce maps, which show regional and worldwide data.

The effects of the climatic contrasts are seen in the distribution of Earth's lifeforms. Temperature, precipitation, and the amount of sunlight all determine what plants can grow in a region and the animals that live there. People are more adaptable, but climate exerts powerful constraints on where we live.

Climatic conditions define planning decisions, such as how much heating oil we need for the winter, and the necessary rainfall for agriculture in the summer. Fluctuations from year to year (e.g., cold winters or summer droughts) make planning more difficult.

In the longer term, continued global warming may change climatic conditions around the world, which could dramatically alter temperature and precipitation patterns and lead to more frequent heat waves, floods, and droughts.

JANUARY SOLAR ENERGY

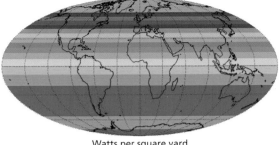

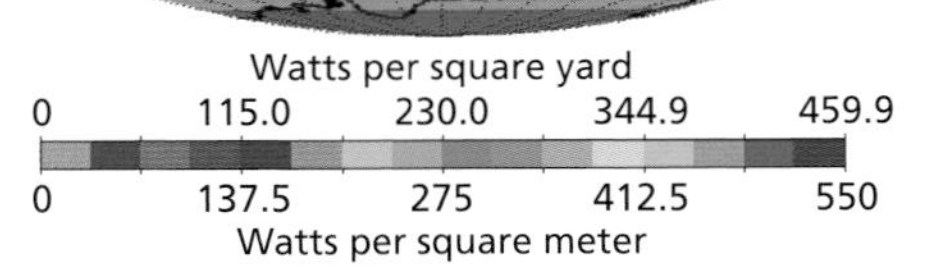
Watts per square yard
0 115.0 230.0 344.9 459.9
0 137.5 275 412.5 550
Watts per square meter

JULY SOLAR ENERGY

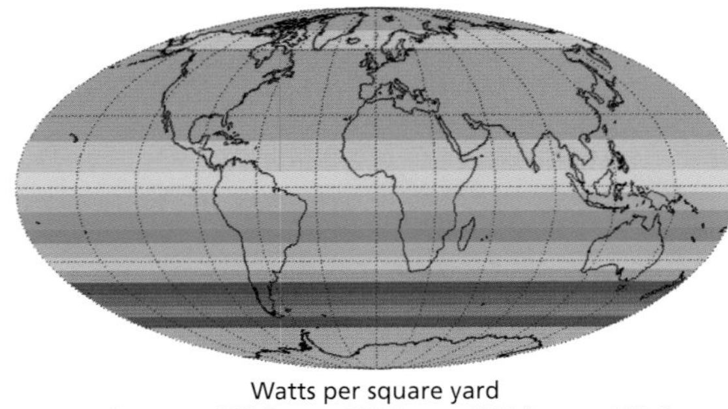

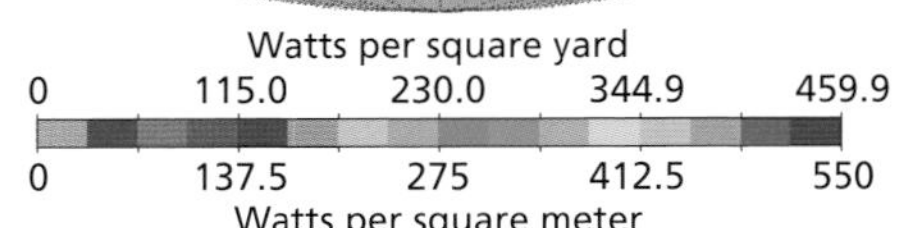
Watts per square yard
0 115.0 230.0 344.9 459.9
0 137.5 275 412.5 550
Watts per square meter

JANUARY AVERAGE TEMPERATURE

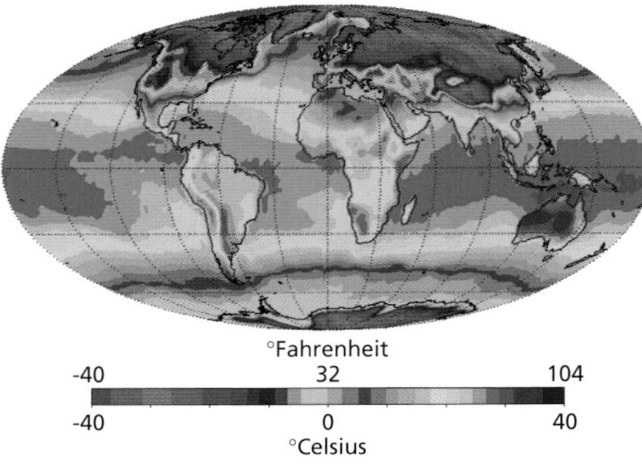
°Fahrenheit
-40 32 104
-40 0 40
°Celsius

JULY AVERAGE TEMPERATURE

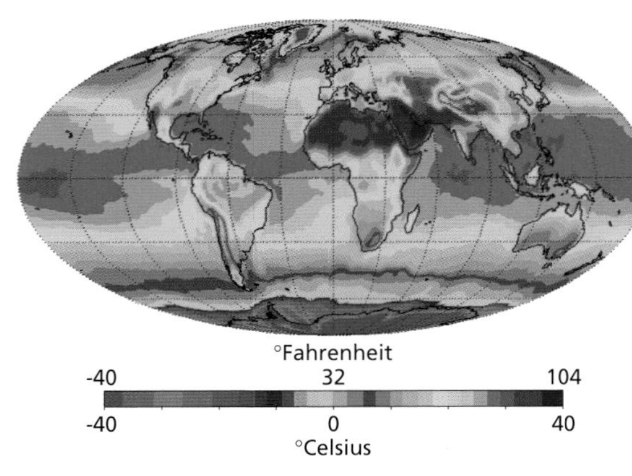
°Fahrenheit
-40 32 104
-40 0 40
°Celsius

JANUARY CLOUD COVER

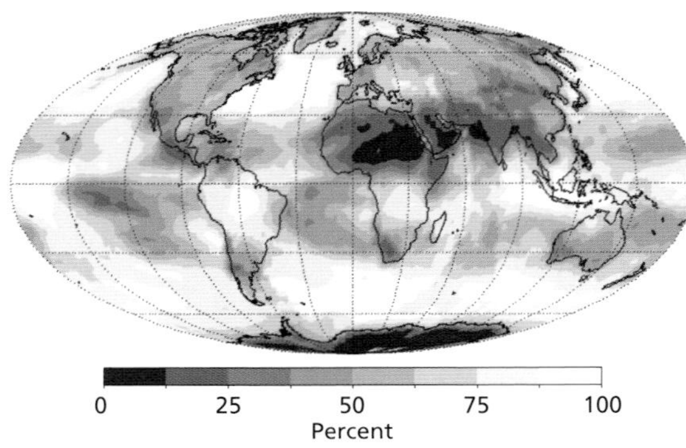
0 25 50 75 100
Percent

JULY CLOUD COVER

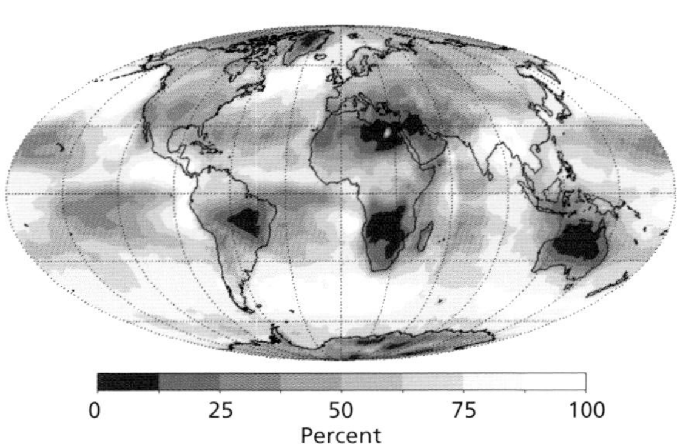
0 25 50 75 100
Percent

JANUARY PRECIPITATION

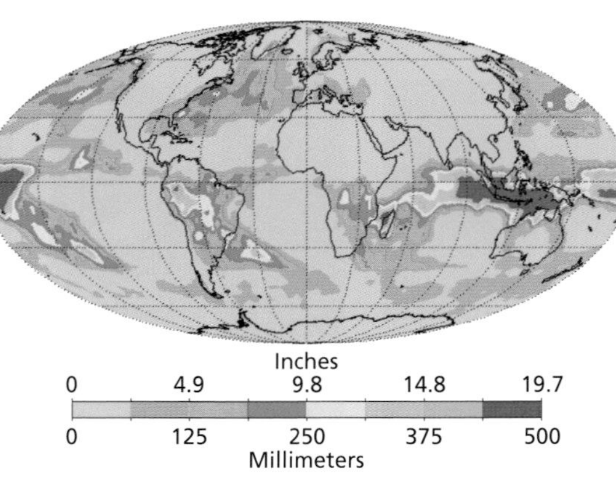
Inches
0 4.9 9.8 14.8 19.7
0 125 250 375 500
Millimeters

JULY PRECIPITATION

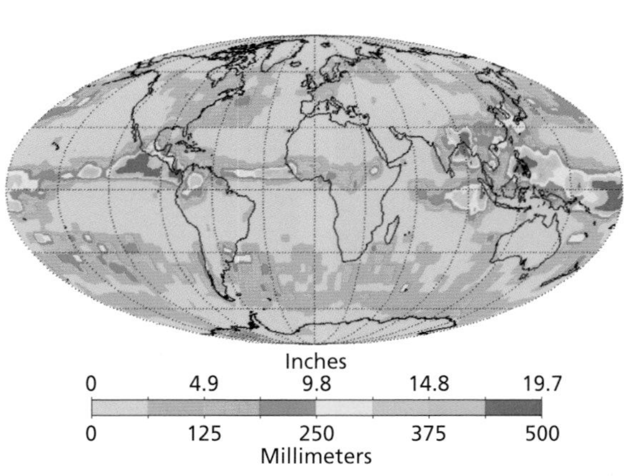
Inches
0 4.9 9.8 14.8 19.7
0 125 250 375 500
Millimeters

COOL TO WARM
10 MILLION YEARS AGO
1 MILLION YEARS AGO
100,000 YEARS AGO

Major Factors that Influence Climate

LATITUDE AND ANGLE OF THE SUN'S RAYS

As Earth circles the sun, the tilt of its axis causes changes in the angle of the sun's rays and in the periods of daylight at different latitudes. Polar regions experience the greatest variation, with long periods of limited or no sunlight in winter and sometimes 24 hours of daylight in the summer.

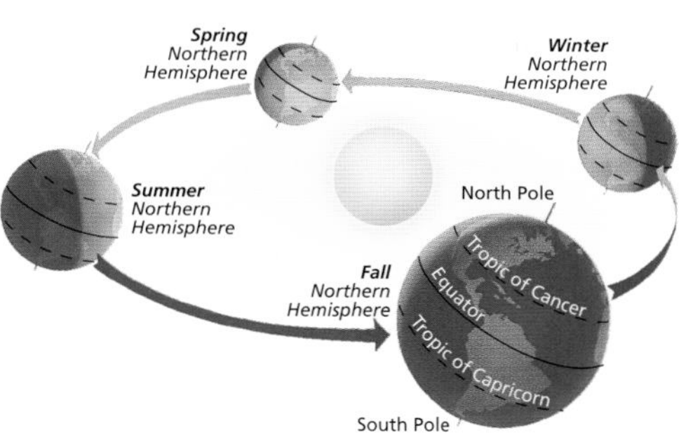

Spring Northern Hemisphere
Winter Northern Hemisphere
Summer Northern Hemisphere
Fall Northern Hemisphere
North Pole
Tropic of Cancer
Equator
Tropic of Capricorn
South Pole

ELEVATION (ALTITUDE)

In general, climatic conditions become colder as elevation increases, just as they do when latitude increases. "Life zones" on a high mountain reflect the changes: Plants at the base are the same as those in surrounding countryside. Farther up, treed vegetation distinctly ends at the tree line; at the highest elevations, snow covers the mountain.

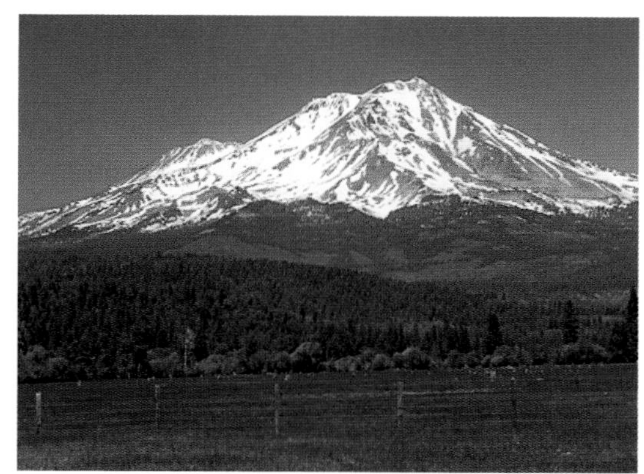

Mount Shasta, California

TOPOGRAPHY

Mountain ranges are natural barriers to air movement. In California (see diagram at right), winds off the Pacific carry moisture-laden air toward the coast. The Coast Ranges allow for some condensation and light precipitation. Inland, the taller Sierra Nevada range wrings more significant precipitation from the air. On the leeward slopes of the Sierra Nevada, sinking air warms from compression, clouds evaporate, and dry conditions prevail.

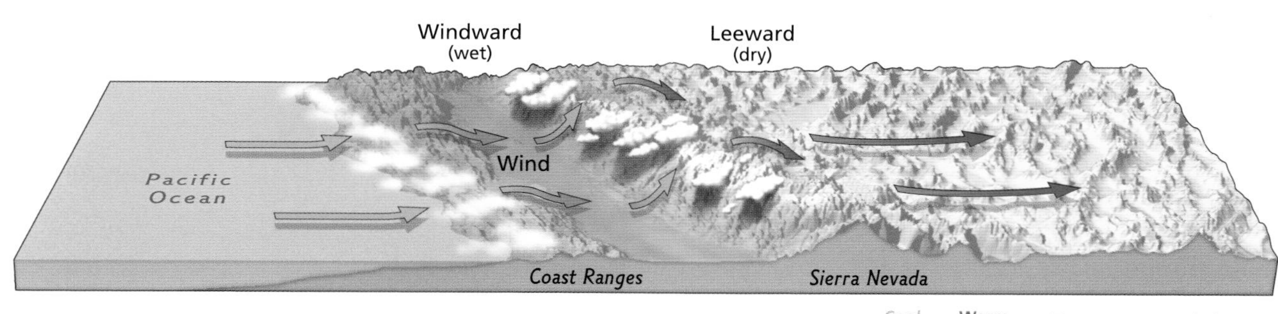

Windward (wet)
Leeward (dry)
Pacific Ocean
Wind
Coast Ranges
Sierra Nevada
Cool
Warm
Temperature variations as air moves over mountains

EFFECTS OF GEOGRAPHY

The location of a place and its distance from mountains and bodies of water help determine its prevailing wind patterns and what types of air masses affect it. Coastal areas may enjoy refreshing breezes in summer, when cooler ocean air moves ashore. Places south and east of the Great Lakes can expect "lake effect" snow in winter, when cold air travels over relatively warmer waters. In spring and summer, people living in "Tornado Alley" in the central United States watch for thunderstorms. Here, three types of air masses often converge: cold and dry from the north, warm and dry from the southwest, and warm and moist from the Gulf of Mexico. The colliding air masses often spawn tornadic storms.

Rocky Mountains
Great Plains
Great Lakes
Cascade Ra.
Sierra Nevada
Coast Ranges
Appalachian Mountains
ATLANTIC OCEAN
Gulf Stream Current
California Current
PACIFIC OCEAN
Gulf of Mexico
Cold winds over warm water
Cool onshore ocean winds
Desert winds
Warm onshore ocean winds
50°N
40°N
30°N
20°N
120°W
110°W
90°W
70°W

PREVAILING GLOBAL WIND PATTERNS

As shown at right, three large-scale wind patterns are found in the Northern Hemisphere and three are found in the Southern Hemisphere. These are average conditions and do not necessarily reflect conditions on a particular day. As seasons change, the wind patterns shift north or south. So does the intertropical convergence zone, which moves back and forth across the Equator. Sailors called this zone the doldrums because its winds are typically weak.

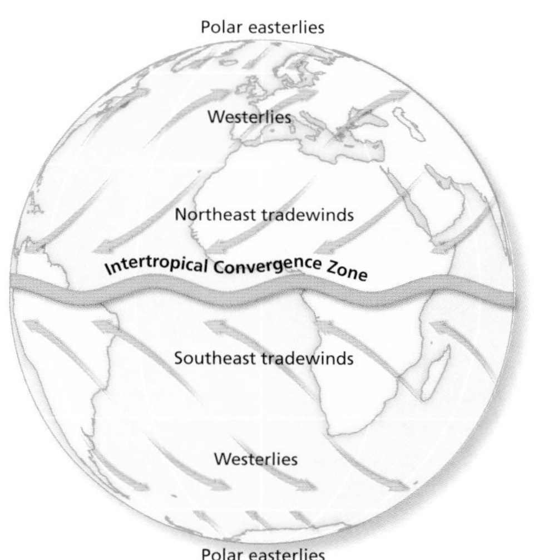

Polar easterlies
Westerlies
Northeast tradewinds
Intertropical Convergence Zone
Southeast tradewinds
Westerlies
Polar easterlies

SURFACE OF THE EARTH

Just look at any globe or a world map showing land cover, and you will see another important influence on climate: Earth's surface. The amount of sunlight that is absorbed or reflected by the surface determines how much atmospheric heating occurs. Darker areas, such as heavily vegetated regions, tend to be good absorbers; lighter areas, such as snow- and ice-covered regions, tend to be good reflectors. Oceans absorb a high proportion of the solar energy falling upon them, but release it more slowly. Both the oceans and the atmosphere distribute heat around the globe.

Temperature Change over Time

Cold and warm periods punctuate Earth's long history. Some were fairly short (perhaps hundreds of years); others spanned hundreds of thousands of years. In some cold periods, glaciers grew and spread over large regions. In subsequent warm periods, the ice retreated. Each period profoundly affected plant and animal life. The most recent cool period, often called the little ice age, ended in western Europe around the year 1850.

Since the turn of the 20th century, temperatures have been rising steadily throughout the world. But it is not yet clear how much of this warming is due to natural causes and how much derives from human activities, such as the burning of fossil fuels and the clearing of forests.

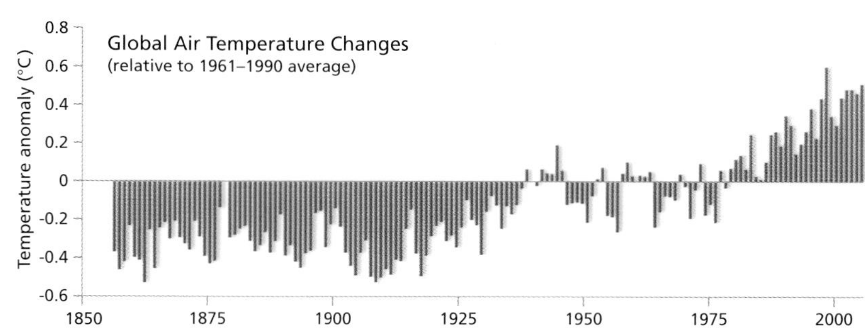

Global Air Temperature Changes
(relative to 1961–1990 average)
Temperature anomaly (°C)
0.8
0.6
0.4
0.2
0
-0.2
-0.4
-0.6
1850
1875
1900
1925
1950
1975
2000

10,000 YEARS AGO

1,000 YEARS AGO

PRESENT

Climate

CLIMATE ZONES ARE PRIMARILY CONTROLLED by latitude—which governs the prevailing winds, the angle of the sun's rays, and the length of day throughout the year—and by geographical location with respect to mountains and oceans. Elevation, surface attributes, and other variables modify the primary controlling factors. Latitudinal banding of climate zones is most pronounced over Africa and Asia, where fewer north-south mountain ranges mean less disruption of prevailing winds. In the Western Hemisphere, the high, almost continuous mountain range that extends from western Canada to southern South America helps create dry regions on its leeward slopes. Over the United States, where westerly winds prevail, areas to the east of the range lie in a "rain shadow" and are therefore drier. In northern parts of South America, where easterly trade winds prevail, the rain shadow lies west of the mountains. Ocean effects dominate much of western Europe and southern parts of Australia.

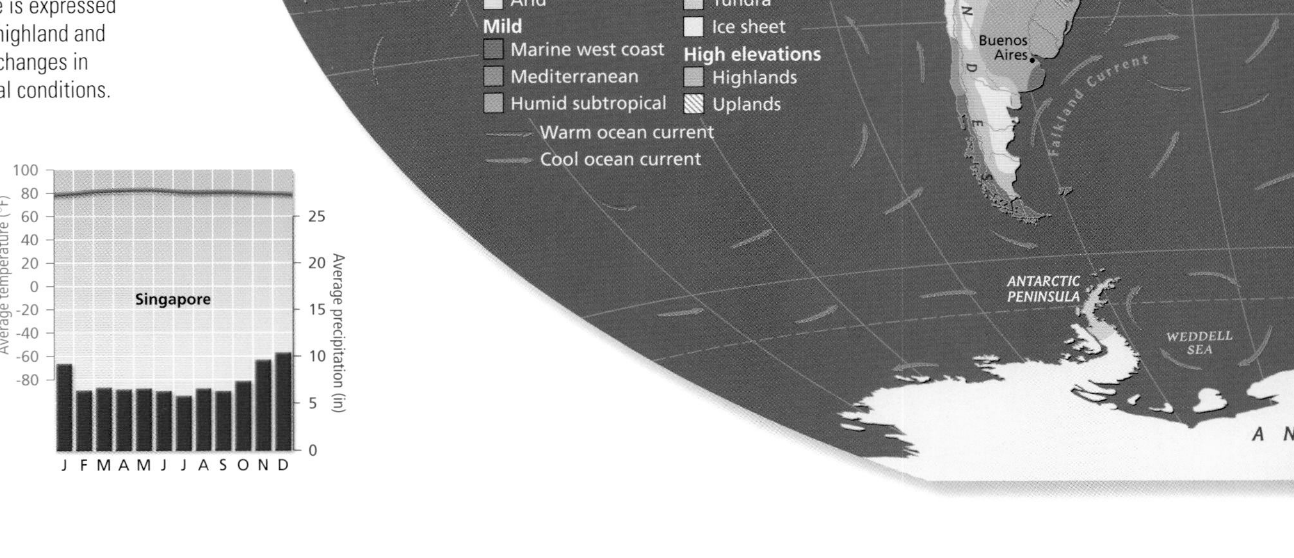

Barrow
Fairbanks
GREENLAND
ROCKY MOUNTAINS
NORTH AMERICA
Chicago
Denver
Mississippi
Subarctic Current
North Pacific Drift
California Current
Hawaiian Islands
GULF OF MEXICO
Gulf Stream
North Atlantic Drift
Labrador Current
North Equatorial Current
PACIFIC OCEAN
ATLANTIC OCEAN
Equatorial Countercurrent
South Equatorial Current
Amazon
AMAZONIA
SOUTH AMERICA
ANDES
Peru Current
Brazil Current
Buenos Aires
Falkland Current
ANTARCTIC PENINSULA
WEDDELL SEA
Climate Zones
(based on modified Köppen system)
Tropical
Tropical wet
Tropical wet & dry
Dry
Semiarid
Arid
Mild
Marine west coast
Mediterranean
Humid subtropical
Continental
Warm summer
Cool summer
Subarctic
Polar
Tundra
Ice sheet
High elevations
Highlands
Uplands
Warm ocean current
Cool ocean current

Climographs

The map at right shows the global distribution of climate zones, while the following 12 climographs (graphs of monthly temperature and precipitation) provide snapshots of the climate at specific places. Each place has a different climate type, which is described in general terms. Rainfall is shown in a bar graph format (scale on right side of the graph); temperature is expressed with a line graph (scale on left side). Places with highland and upland climates were not included because local changes in elevation can produce significant variations in local conditions.

TROPICAL WET

This climate type has the most predictable conditions. Warm and rainy year-round, regions with a tropical wet climate experience little variation from month to month. This type is mainly found within a zone extending about 10 degrees on either side of the Equator. With as much as 60 inches (152 cm) of rain each year, the tropical wet climate supports lush vegetation.

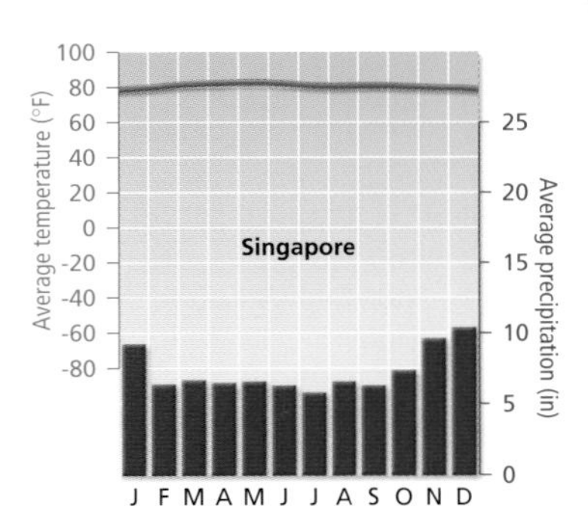

Singapore
Average temperature (°F)
Average precipitation (in)
J F M A M J J A S O N D

TROPICAL WET AND DRY

Because of seasonal reversals in wind direction (monsoons), this climate type is characterized by a slightly cooler dry season and a warmer, very moist wet season. The highest temperatures usually occur just before the wet season. Although average annual conditions may be similar to a tropical wet climate, the rainy season brings much more rain.

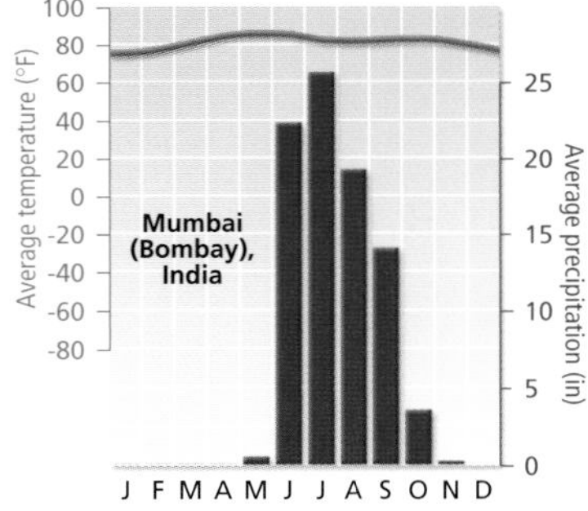

Mumbai (Bombay), India
Average temperature (°F)
Average precipitation (in)
J F M A M J J A S O N D

ARID

Centered between 20° and 30° north and south latitude, this climate type is the result of a persistent high-pressure area and, along the western margins of continents, a cold ocean current. Rainfall amounts in regions with this climate type are negligible, and there is some seasonal variation in temperature. Desert vegetation is typically sparse.

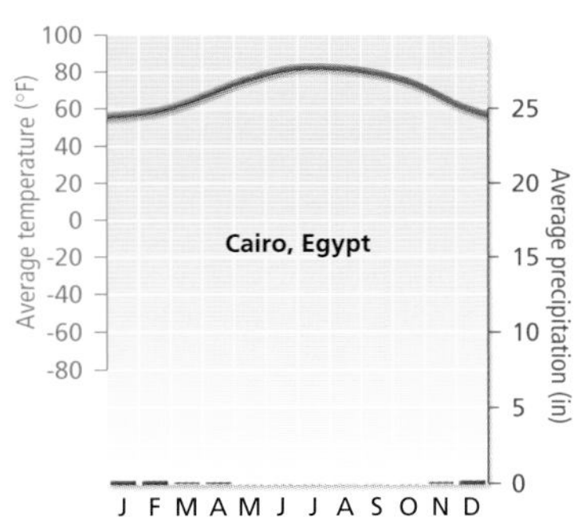

Cairo, Egypt
Average temperature (°F)
Average precipitation (in)
J F M A M J J A S O N D

SEMIARID

Regions with a semiarid climate lie poleward of areas with a desert (arid) climate; they have a much greater range in monthly temperatures and receive significantly more rainfall than deserts. This climate type is often found in inland regions, in the rain shadow of mountain ranges. Annual rainfall amounts support mainly grasses and small shrubs.

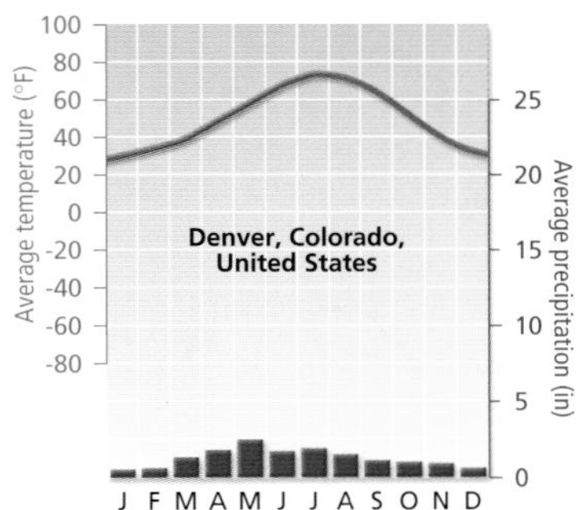

Denver, Colorado, United States
Average temperature (°F)
Average precipitation (in)
J F M A M J J A S O N D

MARINE WEST COAST

This climate type is primarily found between 40 and 60 degrees latitude; it occurs on the west coasts of continents and across much of Europe. Prevailing westerly winds bring milder ocean air ashore, but sunny days are limited and precipitation is frequent. Except in the highest elevations, most precipitation falls as rain. This climate supports extensive forests.

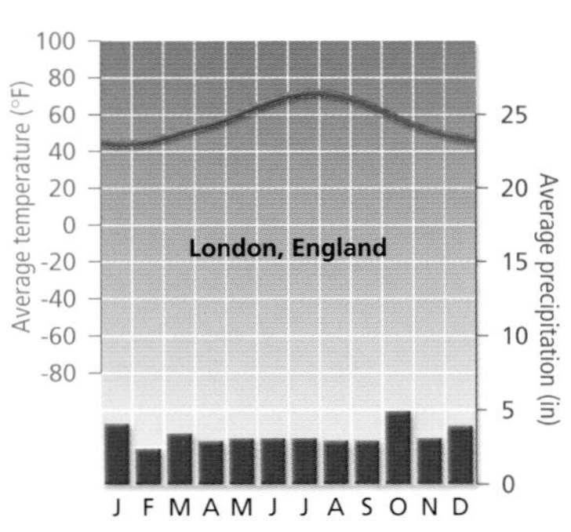

London, England
Average temperature (°F)
Average precipitation (in)
J F M A M J J A S O N D

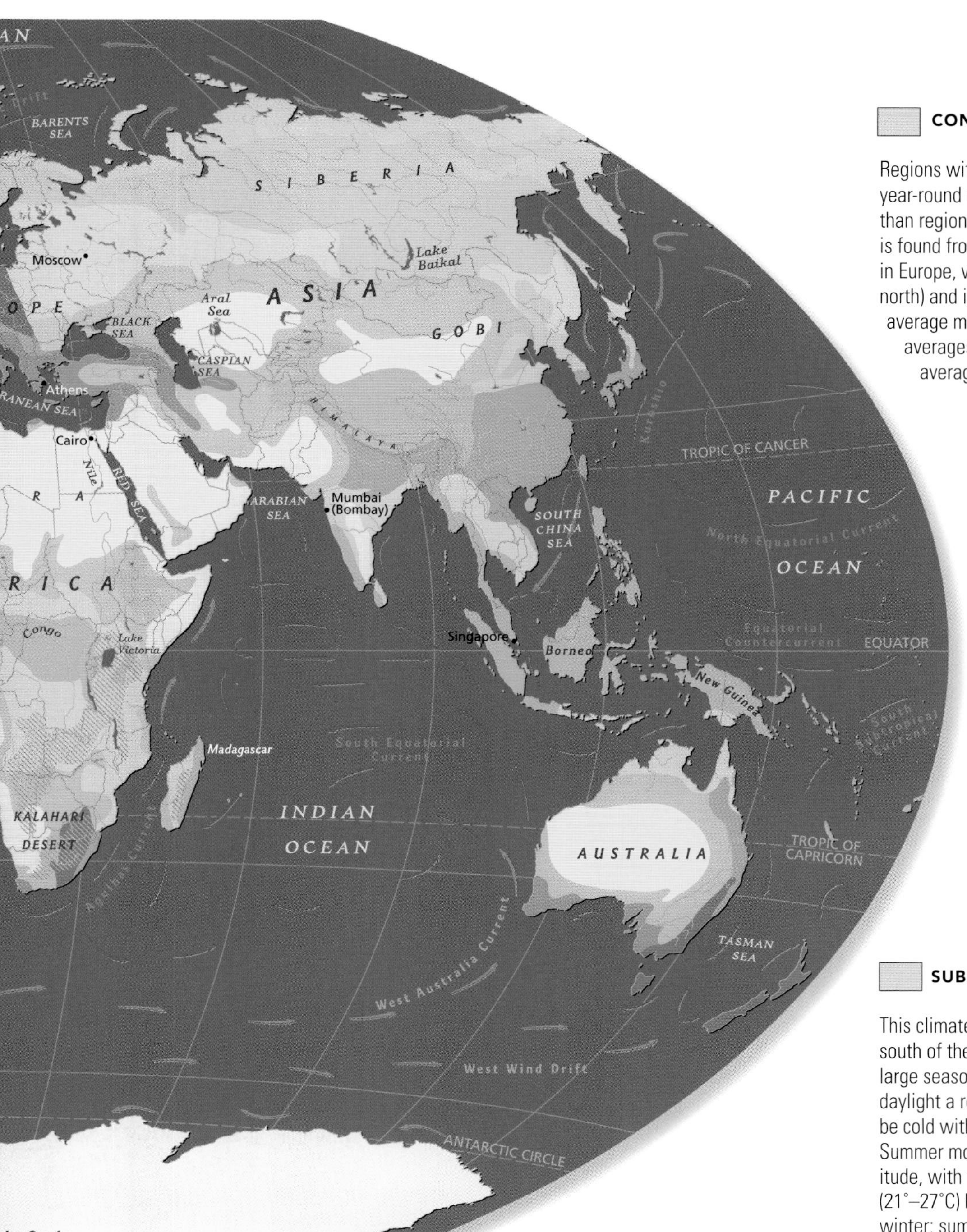
BARENTS SEA
S I B E R I A
Moscow
Lake Baikal
Aral Sea
A S I A
BLACK SEA
G O B I
CASPIAN SEA
Athens
Cairo
Nile
RED SEA
H I M A L A Y A
Kuroshio
TROPIC OF CANCER
PACIFIC
OCEAN
ARABIAN SEA
Mumbai (Bombay)
SOUTH CHINA SEA
North Equatorial Current
Congo
Lake Victoria
Singapore
Borneo
Equatorial Countercurrent
EQUATOR
New Guinea
South Subtropical Current
Madagascar
South Equatorial Current
KALAHARI DESERT
INDIAN
OCEAN
AUSTRALIA
TROPIC OF CAPRICORN
Agulhas Current
West Australia Current
TASMAN SEA
West Wind Drift
ANTARCTIC CIRCLE

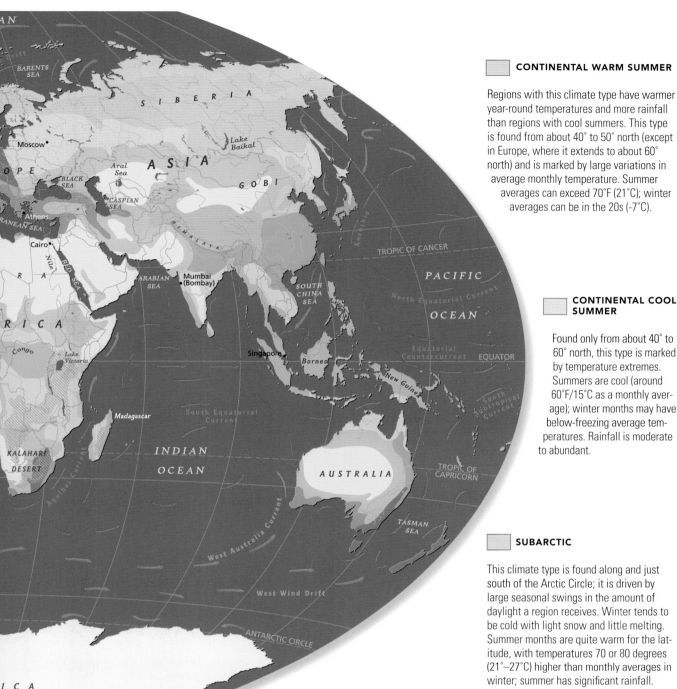

CONTINENTAL WARM SUMMER

Regions with this climate type have warmer year-round temperatures and more rainfall than regions with cool summers. This type is found from about 40° to 50° north (except in Europe, where it extends to about 60° north) and is marked by large variations in average monthly temperature. Summer averages can exceed 70°F (21°C); winter averages can be in the 20s (-7°C).

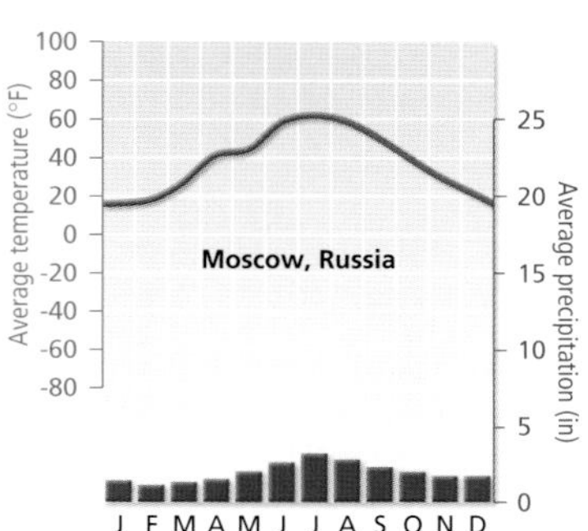
Average temperature (°F)
100
80
60
40
20
0
-20
-40
-60
-80
Chicago, Illinois, United States
Average precipitation (in)
25
20
15
10
5
0
J F M A M J J A S O N D

CONTINENTAL COOL SUMMER

Found only from about 40° to 60° north, this type is marked by temperature extremes. Summers are cool (around 60°F/15°C as a monthly average); winter months may have below-freezing average temperatures. Rainfall is moderate to abundant.

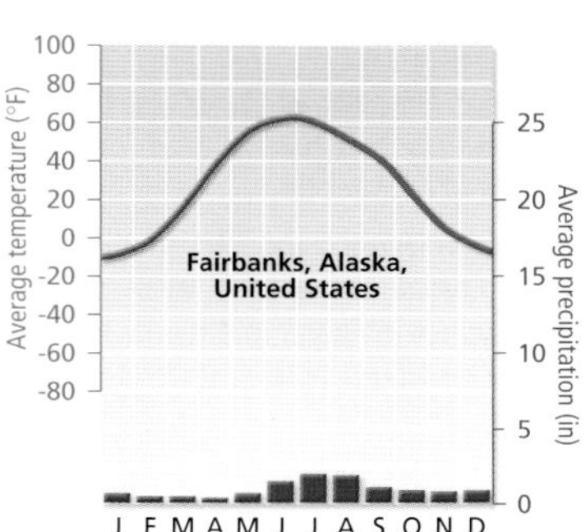
Average temperature (°F)
100
80
60
40
20
0
-20
-40
-60
-80
Moscow, Russia
Average precipitation (in)
25
20
15
10
5
0
J F M A M J J A S O N D

SUBARCTIC

This climate type is found along and just south of the Arctic Circle; it is driven by large seasonal swings in the amount of daylight a region receives. Winter tends to be cold with light snow and little melting. Summer months are quite warm for the latitude, with temperatures 70 or 80 degrees (21°–27°C) higher than monthly averages in winter; summer has significant rainfall.

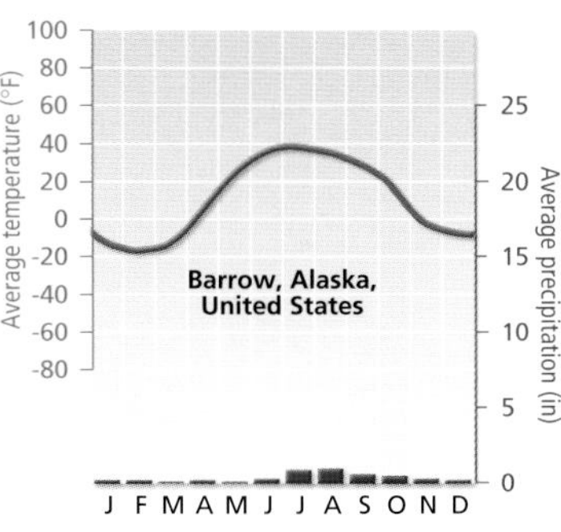
Average temperature (°F)
100
80
60
40
20
0
-20
-40
-60
-80
Fairbanks, Alaska, United States
Average precipitation (in)
25
20
15
10
5
0
J F M A M J J A S O N D

MEDITERRANEAN

This term describes the climate of much of the Mediterranean region. Such a climate is also found in narrow bands along the west coasts of continents that lie around 30 to 35 degrees poleward from the Equator. Summer months are typically warm to hot with dry conditions, while winter months are cool (but not cold) and provide modest precipitation.

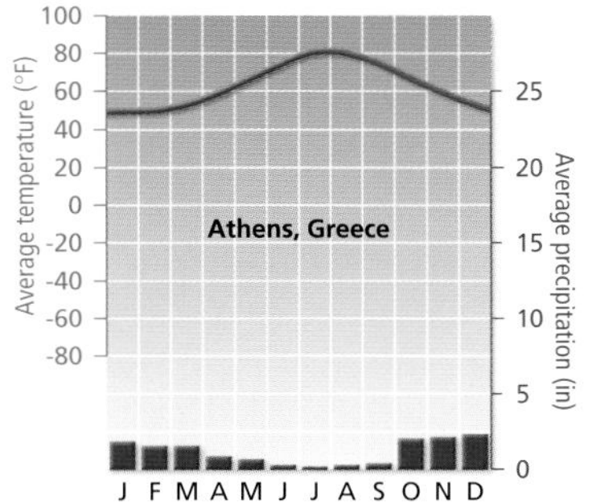
Average temperature (°F)
100
80
60
40
20
0
-20
-40
-60
-80
Athens, Greece
Average precipitation (in)
25
20
15
10
5
0
J F M A M J J A S O N D

TUNDRA

Along the southern boundary of this climatic zone, ground-hugging plants meet the northernmost trees (the tree line). Here, the warmest average monthly temperature is below 50°F (10°C), with only one to four months having an average monthly temperature that is above freezing. Precipitation amounts are low, typically about 10 inches (25 cm) or less annually.

Average temperature (°F)
100
80
60
40
20
0
-20
-40
-60
-80
Barrow, Alaska, United States
Average precipitation (in)
25
20
15
10
5
0
J F M A M J J A S O N D

HUMID SUBTROPICAL

This climate type dominates eastern regions of continents at 30 to 35 degrees latitude. Here, warm ocean waters lead to warm and humid summers. Rainfall is greatest near the coast, supporting forest growth; precipitation is less farther west, supporting grasslands. Winter can bring cold waves and snowy periods, except in areas right on the coast.

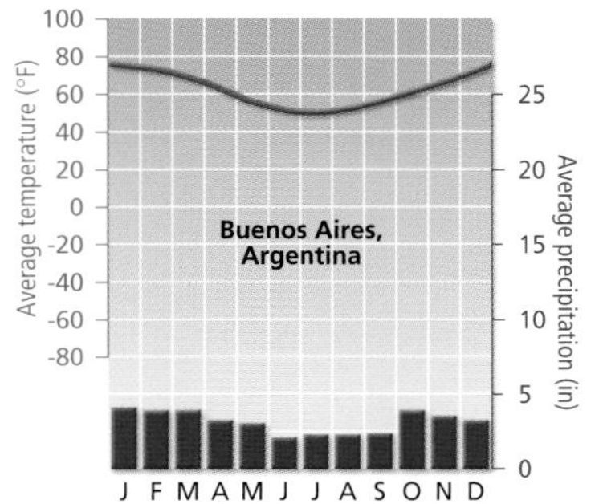
Average temperature (°F)
100
80
60
40
20
0
-20
-40
-60
-80
Buenos Aires, Argentina
Average precipitation (in)
25
20
15
10
5
0
J F M A M J J A S O N D

ICE SHEET

This climate type is found at high latitudes in interior Greenland and across most of Antarctica; average monthly temperatures are around zero degrees Fahrenheit (-18°C) and below. Snow defines the landscape, but precipitation is only about 5 inches (13 cm) or less annually. The combined effects of cold and dryness produce desert-like conditions.

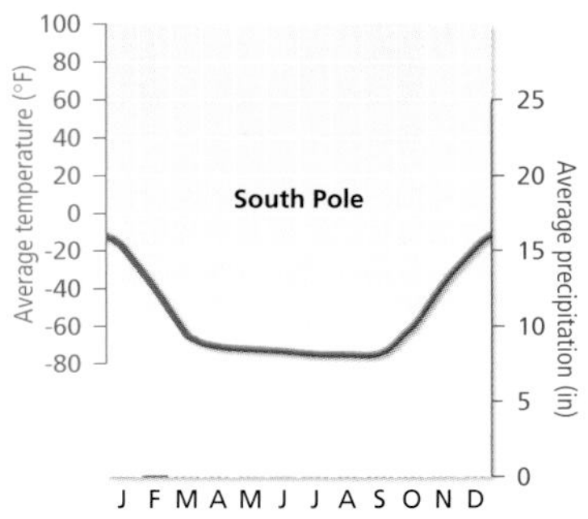
Average temperature (°F)
100
80
60
40
20
0
-20
-40
-60
-80
South Pole
Average precipitation (in)
25
20
15
10
5
0
J F M A M J J A S O N D

STEP OUTSIDE AND YOU EXPERIENCE many facets of weather. Humidity, air temperature and pressure, wind speed and direction, cloud cover and type, and the amount and form of precipitation are all atmospheric characteristics of the momentary conditions we call weather.

The sun is ultimately responsible for the weather. Its rays are absorbed differently by land and water surfaces (equal amounts of solar radiation heat the ground more quickly than they heat water). Differential warming, in turn, causes variations in the temperature and pressure of overlying air masses.

As an air mass warms, it becomes lighter and rises higher into the atmosphere. As an air mass cools, it becomes heavier and sinks. Pressure differences between masses of air generate winds, which tend to blow from high-pressure areas to areas of low pressure. Fast-moving, upper-atmosphere winds known as jet streams help move weather systems around the world.

Large weather systems called cyclones rotate counterclockwise in the Northern Hemisphere (clockwise in the Southern Hemisphere); they are also called "lows," because their centers are low-pressure areas. Clouds and precipitation are usually associated with these systems. Anticyclones, or "highs," rotate in the opposite direction and are high-pressure areas. They usually bring clearer skies and more settled weather.

The boundary between two air masses is called a front. Here, wind, temperature, and humidity change abruptly, producing atmospheric instability. When things get "out of balance" in the atmosphere, storms may develop, bringing rain or snow and sometimes thunder and lightning as well. Storms are among nature's great equalizers.

The weather you experience is influenced by many factors, including your location's latitude, elevation, and proximity to water bodies. Even the degree of urban development, which creates "heat islands," and the amount of snow cover, which chills an overlying air mass, play important roles. The next time you watch a weather report on television, think about the many factors, some thousands of miles away, that help make the weather what it is.

The swirling cloud pattern and well-formed eye of Hurricane Katrina stand out in this NOAA satellite image from late morning on August 29, 2005. At the time, Katrina was making its third landfall near the Louisiana-Mississippi border, and was by now a weakening Category Two storm. (The other two landfalls were near Miami, Florida, as a strong tropical storm, and just south of New Orleans as a hurricane.) Its storm surge, flooding, and high winds caused incredible destruction from Louisiana eastward to Alabama, and Katrina ranks as the costliest—and also one of the deadliest—hurricanes ever to strike the U.S.

Hurricanes (defined as tropical low-pressure systems with sustained winds of at least 74 miles an hour) can also be prolific rainmakers. In 1972, Agnes dropped torrents of rain on the northeast U.S., causing severe flooding in several states. Despite the dramatic rainfall sometimes brought by hurricanes, nontropical (or extratropical) low-pressure systems actually bring most of the precipitation that falls in the middle latitudes (30° to 60° latitude).

Major Factors that Influence Weather

THE WATER CYCLE

As the sun warms the surface of Earth, water rises in the form of water vapor from lakes, rivers, oceans, plants, the ground, and other sources. This process is called evaporation. Water vapor provides the moisture that forms clouds; it eventually returns to Earth in the form of precipitation, and the cycle continues.

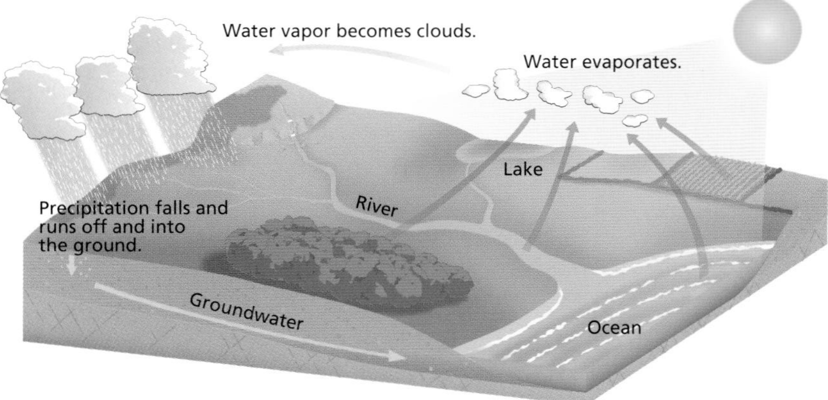
Water vapor becomes clouds.
Water evaporates.
Lake
River
Precipitation falls and runs off and into the ground.
Groundwater
Ocean

AIR MASSES

When air hovers for a while over a surface area with uniform humidity and temperature, it takes on the characteristics of the area below. For example, an air mass over the tropical Atlantic Ocean would become warm and humid; an air mass over the winter snow and ice of northern Canada would become cold and dry. These massive volumes of air often cover thousands of miles and reach to the stratosphere. Over time, mid-latitude cyclonic storms and global wind patterns move them to locations far from their source regions.

JET STREAM

A meandering current of high-speed wind, a jet stream is usually found around five to ten miles above Earth's surface. It generally flows west to east, often in a noncontinuous wavy fashion, with cold, Equatorward dips (called troughs) and warm, Poleward bulges (called ridges). The polar jet separates cold and warm masses of air; the subtropical jet is less likely to be related to temperature differences. Fronts and low-pressure areas are typically located near a jet stream.

WEATHER FRONTS

The transition zone between two air masses of different humidity and temperature is called a front. Along a cold front, cold air displaces warm air; along a warm front, warm air displaces cold air. When neither air mass displaces the other, a stationary front develops. Towering clouds and intense storms may form along cold fronts, while widespread clouds and rain, snow, sleet, or drizzle may accompany warm fronts.

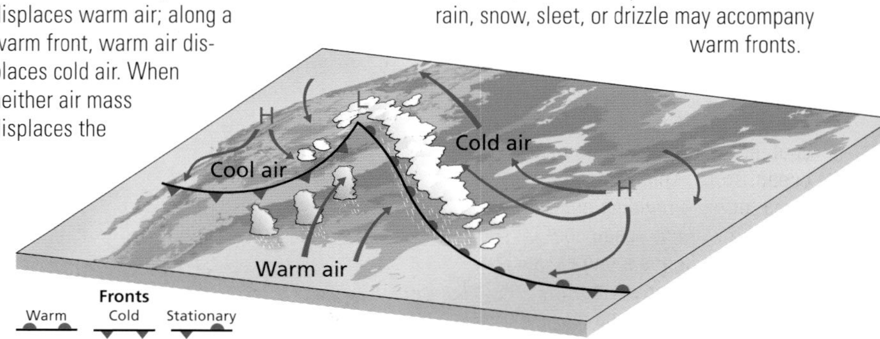
H
Cool air
Cold air
H
Warm air
Fronts
Warm
Cold
Stationary

Cloud Types

Clouds are the visible collections of water droplets or ice particles in the atmosphere. Meteorologists classify them according to shape and altitude.

Stratus are low-level clouds that are flat or layered; they are much longer and wider than they are tall. Fog is a stratus cloud that touches the ground. Altostratus (alto means "high") is a stratus cloud about two miles above Earth. When these clouds rain or snow, they are called nimbostratus. Cirrostratus clouds lie at an altitude of about four miles.

Cumulus clouds have flat bottoms and puffy tops. The flat bottoms mark the altitude at which rising air reaches its condensation level (typically about a mile above Earth's surface); the puffy tops show how the cloud "bubbles up." Cumulus often develop as sunlight heats the ground and the ground, in turn, heats the air. If cumulus tower, they can transform into cumulonimbus (thunderstorm) clouds, with their tops reaching an altitude of seven miles or more.

Cumulus clouds can also develop in layers. Stratocumulus is a layered cumulus cloud about a mile above the ground. Altocumulus is a similar cloud at an altitude of two miles. Its greater distance from the ground makes the cumulus puffs appear smaller than those of stratocumulus clouds. The cirrocumulus type (with still smaller puffs) is found about four to five miles higher.

Cirrus clouds occur at an altitude of four miles or more, where the temperature is always below freezing; hence, these clouds are always filled with ice crystals.

As a general forecasting rule, dry weather is most likely when cumulus clouds remain flat and/or when mid-level (altocumulus) clouds are not present. Precipitation is most likely when two or more clouds occur at the same time, and/or when cumulus clouds tower to great heights or turn into cumulonimbus clouds.

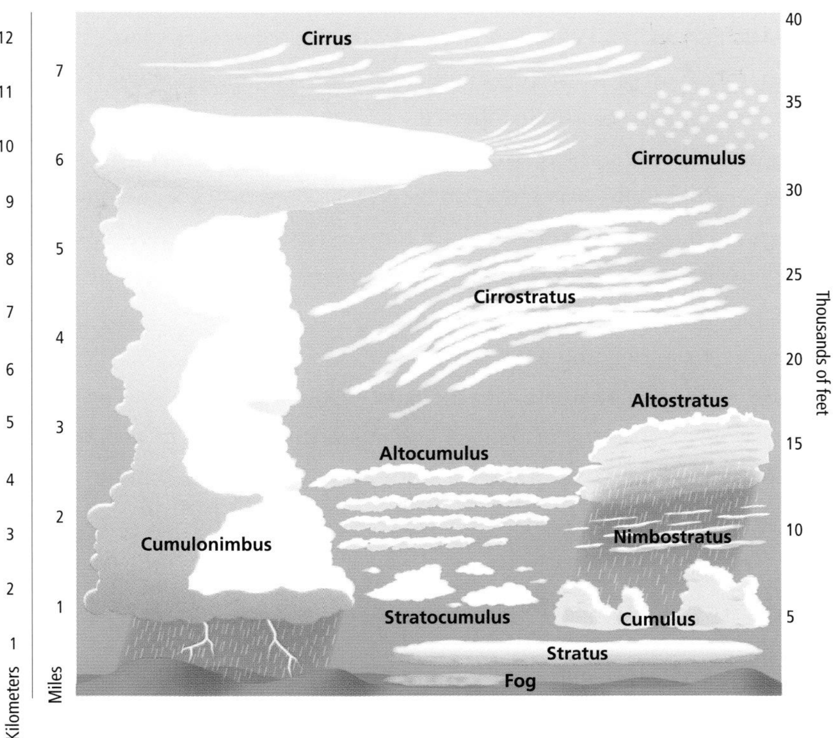
Cirrus
Cirrocumulus
Cirrostratus
Altostratus
Altocumulus
Nimbostratus
Cumulonimbus
Stratocumulus
Cumulus
Stratus
Fog
Kilometers
Miles
Thousands of feet
1
2
3
4
5
6
7
8
9
10
11
12
5
10
15
20
25
30
35
40

Tropical Cyclones

Hurricanes and their counterparts in other places (typhoons near Japan and cyclones off India and Australia) are moderately large low-pressure systems that form most often during the warmer months of the year. They occur mainly near the Equator, in regions with prevailing easterly winds. These systems develop winds between 75 and 150 miles an hour and, on some rare occasions, even stronger winds. As the storms move toward the middle latitudes, where the prevailing winds are mainly westerly, they can "recurve" (move toward the east). Some hurricanes have stayed nearly stationary at times, while others have made loops and spirals along their paths.

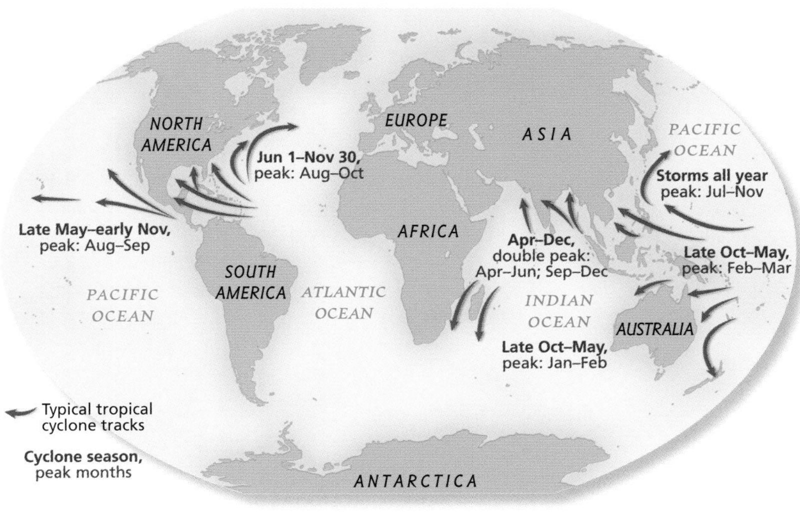
NORTH AMERICA
EUROPE
ASIA
PACIFIC OCEAN
Jun 1–Nov 30, peak: Aug–Oct
Storms all year peak: Jul–Nov
Late May–early Nov, peak: Aug–Sep
AFRICA
Apr–Dec, double peak: Apr–Jun; Sep–Dec
Late Oct–May, peak: Feb–Mar
SOUTH AMERICA
ATLANTIC OCEAN
PACIFIC OCEAN
INDIAN OCEAN
AUSTRALIA
Late Oct–May, peak: Jan–Feb
Typical tropical cyclone tracks
Cyclone season, peak months
ANTARCTICA

Lightning

In order to estimate the mean annual distribution of lightning (more than 1.2 billion intracloud and cloud-to-ground flashes), NASA scientists used five years of data taken from a satellite orbiting 460 miles above Earth. Lightning distribution is directly linked to climate, with maximal occurrence in areas that see frequent thunderstorms (the red areas on the map below).

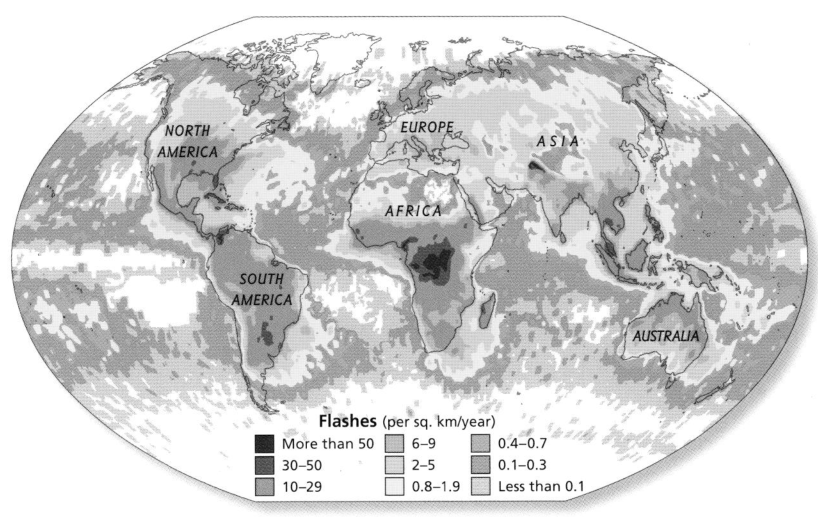
NORTH AMERICA
EUROPE
ASIA
AFRICA
SOUTH AMERICA
AUSTRALIA
Flashes (per sq. km/year)
More than 50
30–50
10–29
6–9
2–5
0.8–1.9
0.4–0.7
0.1–0.3
Less than 0.1

El Niño and La Niña

Periodic shifts in wind speed and direction in the tropical eastern Pacific can lead to changes in sea-surface temperatures. In what scientists call El Niño events, prevailing easterly winds weaken or give way to westerly winds, and the normal upwelling process, which brings cool, nutrient-rich waters up from lower levels of the ocean, stops. This stoppage causes sea-surface temperatures to rise, providing an unfavorable habitat for many fish. The warmer ocean conditions can also lead to more rainfall and floods along the west coast of the Americas. A stronger easterly wind flow, on the other hand, can increase upwelling and make the sea-surface temperatures even colder, producing La Niña. Both phenomena can have far-reaching weather effects. For example, strong El Niño events often result in a weak Atlantic Ocean hurricane season but produce plentiful precipitation in the normally dry southwestern United States. La Niña events favor more Atlantic hurricanes, but can spell drought in the southwestern U.S., even for normally dry southern California.

From left to right, the above image sequence shows how temperatures in the Pacific Ocean changed as the 1997 to 1998 El Niño event evolved. The first image, from March 10, 1997, shows a mostly cool ocean (blue shades). By mid-June, sea-surface temperatures (red shades) were above average from South America across much of the tropical Pacific. By mid-September, the warmth had extended from California southward to Chile and westward across most of the tropical Pacific. The final image, from late December 1997, shows a major El Niño, with sea-surface temperatures measuring six to eight degrees above average on the Fahrenheit scale.

To learn about weather extremes, see Geographic Comparisons on page 264.

HOME TO ALL LIVING THINGS, the biosphere is an intricate system made up of constantly interacting realms that support life: parts of the atmosphere (air), lithosphere (land), and hydrosphere (water in the ground, at the surface, and in the air).

As a result of the interaction between realms of the biosphere and changes in the distance of Earth's rotation around the sun, Earth's flora and fauna have changed over the eons, sometimes slowly and sometimes rapidly. Some species have continued to evolve; others, like the dinosaurs, have become extinct.

Life, of course, interacts with the land, water, and air, playing a significant role in shaping Earth's face and influencing its natural processes. Billions of years ago one of the smallest life-forms, photosynthetic bacteria (organisms that produce oxygen as a by-product of their metabolism), helped provide the oxygen in the air we breathe.

Human beings are currently Earth's dominant life-form. Through the ages, we have evolved the means to affect the planet in ways both positive and negative. At present, we are introducing changes to the biosphere at greater rates than natural processes may be able to accommodate, as societies make ever increasing demands on Earth's resources.

It is now clear that human beings are able to greatly influence the fate of the biosphere. It is also clear that developing a better understanding of how the biosphere functions, and how its realms interact, is fundamental to sustaining it. This requires a multi- and interdisciplinary perspective that brings together different worldviews from each of the physical, biological, and social sciences.

The Biosphere from Space

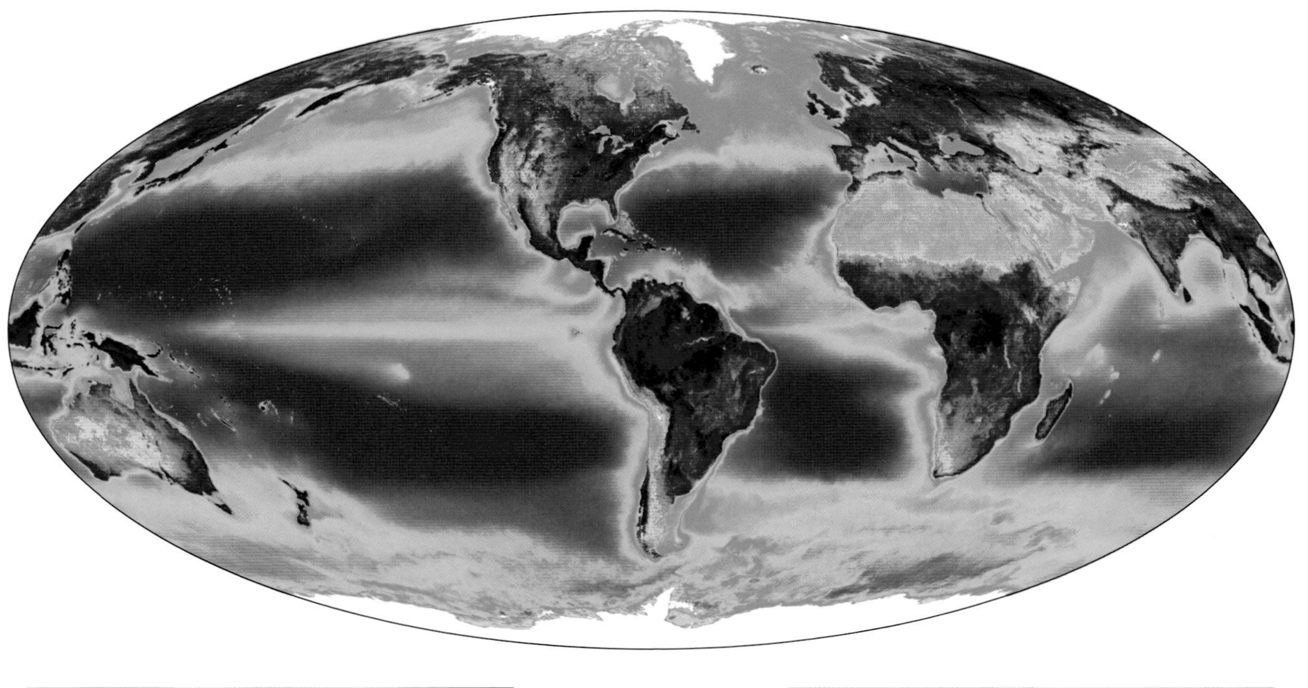

>.01 .05 .2 1 2 5 20 50
OCEAN: CHLOROPHYLL a CONCENTRATION (mg/m^3)

Maximum Minimum
LAND: NORMALIZED DIFFERENCE VEGETATION INDEX

Satellite technology enables us to monitor life on Earth. For example, satellite sensors help us measure the amount of chlorophyll—the green pigment used by plants during photosynthesis—on land and in masses of water. Satellite measurements can also provide an estimate of the distribution and abundance of both terrestrial vegetation and aquatic phytoplankton. By color-coding data (see the color scales for the world map), we can actually quantify changes in vegetation on land and in the oceans from season to season and from year to year. The map reveals an unequal distribution of life for the June-to-August period. Most of the Northern Hemisphere has become green, except in areas of low rainfall or poor soil. Spectacular phytoplankton blooms are evident in the equatorial Pacific. Vegetation has lightened in the southern winter, as the rays of the sun provide less energy.

Biosphere Dynamics

A fundamental characteristic of the biosphere is the interconnectivity among all of its components. Known as holoceonosis, this interrelationship means that when one part of the biosphere changes, so will others. The biosphere is a dynamic system where interactions are occurring all the time between and within living and nonliving components.

The main fuel that keeps the biosphere dynamic is the sun's energy, which is captured by Earth's surface and later harvested by plants and other photosynthetic organisms. The energy flows from these organisms through a living web that includes herbivores (plant feeders), carnivores (flesh feeders), and decomposers (detritus feeders). Energy from the sun also drives the recycling of water and all chemical elements necessary for life. The flow of energy and the continuous recycling of matter are two key processes of the biosphere.

Humans are part of this web of life. We have evolved, we interact with other living organisms, and we may become extinct. We have also developed large-scale organizations (societies, for example) that constitute the "sociosphere." Human interactions within this sphere occur through a diverse array of technologies and cultural frameworks and include activities such as fishing, agriculture, forestry, mining, and urban development. All are resource-utilization processes that can affect the biosphere on a global scale.

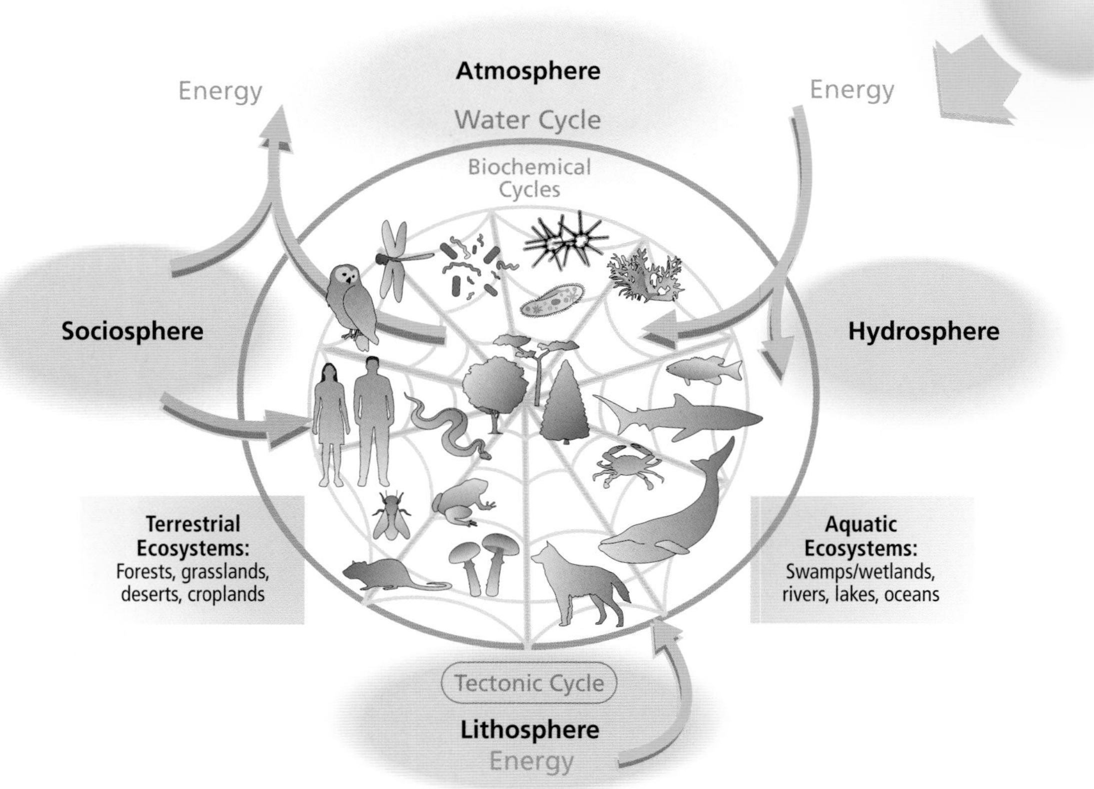
Energy
Atmosphere
Water Cycle
Energy
Biochemical Cycles
Sociosphere
Hydrosphere
Terrestrial Ecosystems:
Forests, grasslands, deserts, croplands
Aquatic Ecosystems:
Swamps/wetlands, rivers, lakes, oceans
Tectonic Cycle
Lithosphere
Energy

Earth System Dynamics

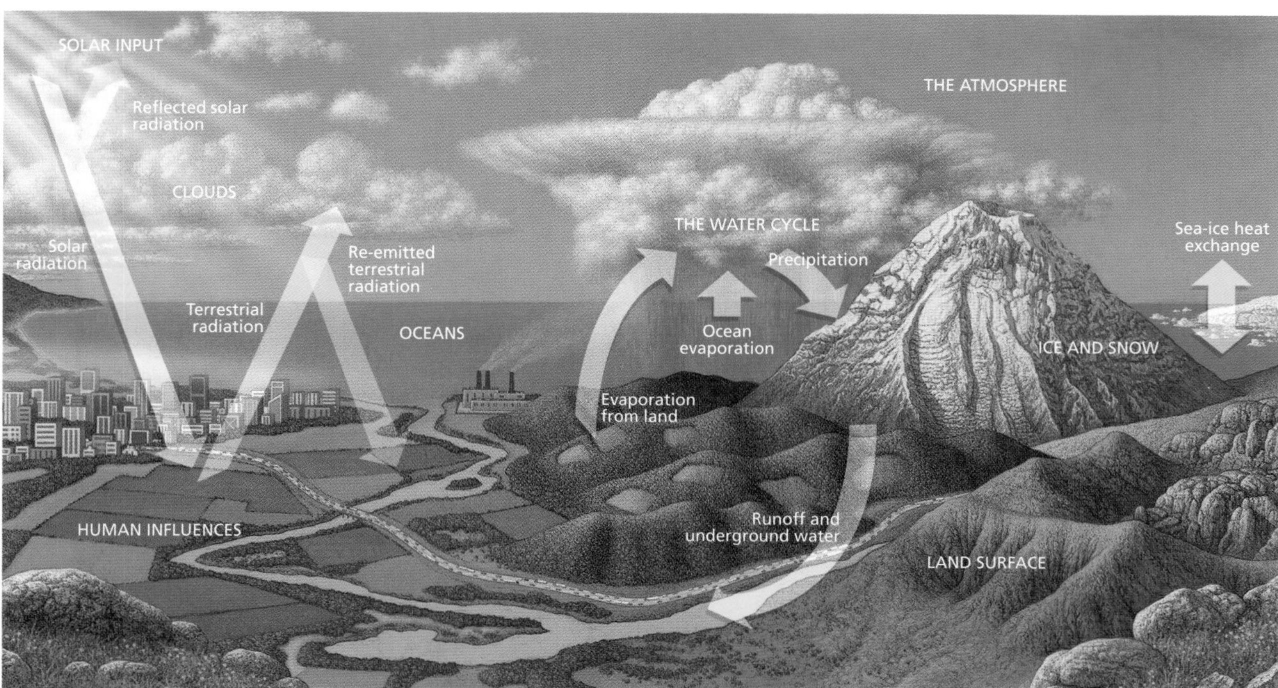
SOLAR INPUT
Reflected solar radiation
CLOUDS
Solar radiation
Re-emitted terrestrial radiation
Terrestrial radiation
OCEANS
THE ATMOSPHERE
THE WATER CYCLE
Precipitation
Ocean evaporation
Evaporation from land
Sea-ice heat exchange
ICE AND SNOW
HUMAN INFLUENCES
Runoff and underground water
LAND SURFACE

Earth is a dynamic system driven by energy flow from the sun and the planet's interior. Electromagnetic energy from the sun is converted to heat energy in the atmosphere (the greenhouse effect). Energy imbalances cause atmospheric and oceanic currents and drive the water cycle—a result of which is the wearing down of landscapes. Energy flow from Earth's interior drives the tectonic cycle, which builds landscapes. The cycles vary because they derive from independent forces that operate on different time scales and with changing intensities. Variations in these cycles keep the complex interactions among the biosphere, lithosphere, hydrosphere, and atmosphere from reaching a balance; the tendency of Earth processes to reach a balance causes natural global change. People can influence these interactions: By modifying the chemical composition of the atmosphere, for example, humans can cause changes in the greenhouse effect.

Size of the Biosphere

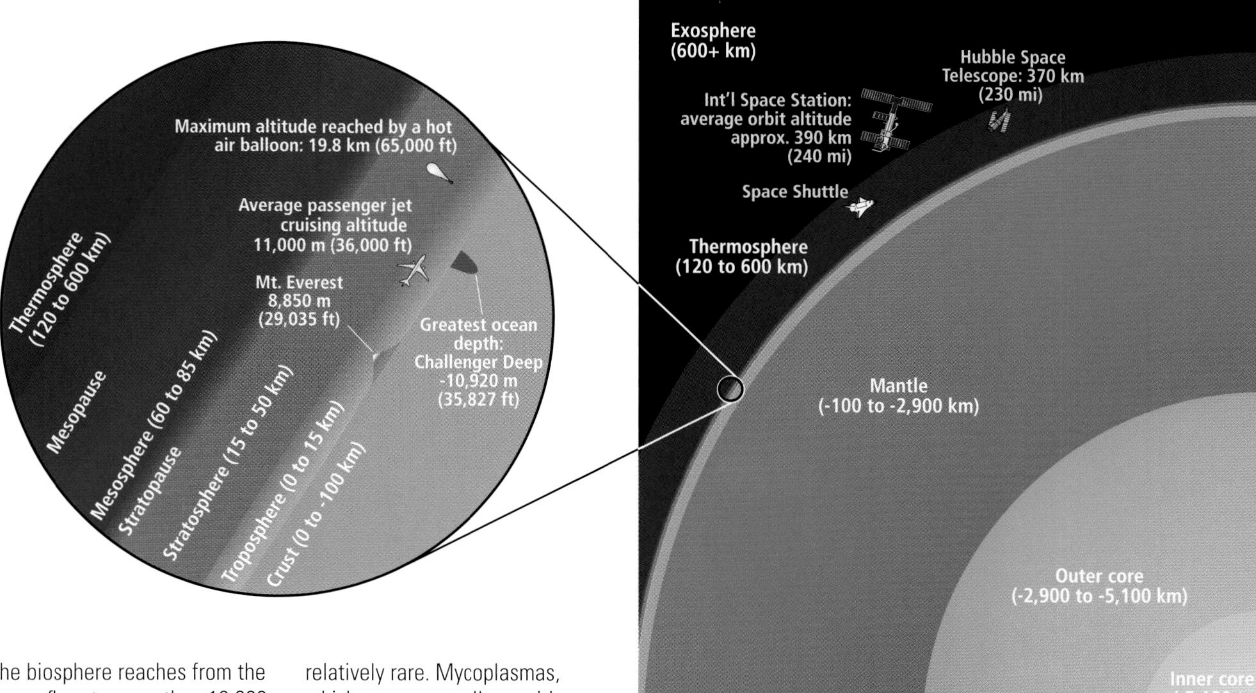
Maximum altitude reached by a hot air balloon: 19.8 km (65,000 ft)
Average passenger jet cruising altitude 11,000 m (36,000 ft)
Mt. Everest 8,850 m (29,035 ft)
Greatest ocean depth: Challenger Deep -10,920 m (35,827 ft)
Thermosphere (120 to 600 km)
Mesopause
Mesosphere (60 to 85 km)
Stratopause
Stratosphere (15 to 50 km)
Troposphere (0 to 15 km)
Crust (0 to -100 km)
Exosphere (600+ km)
Hubble Space Telescope: 370 km (230 mi)
Int'l Space Station: average orbit altitude approx. 390 km (240 mi)
Space Shuttle
Thermosphere (120 to 600 km)
Mantle (-100 to -2,900 km)
Outer core (-2,900 to -5,100 km)
Inner core (-5,100 to -6,378 km)

The biosphere reaches from the ocean floor to more than 10,000 meters (33,000 ft) above sea level. Most life, however, occurs in a zone extending from about 200 meters (650 ft) below the surface of the ocean to 6,000 meters (20,000 ft) above sea level. Humans can occupy much of the biosphere and exert influence on all of its regions.

Organisms that make up the biosphere vary greatly in size and number. Small life-forms generally reach very high numbers, while large ones may be relatively rare. Mycoplasmas, which are very small parasitic bacteria, can measure 0.2 to 0.3 micrometers (one micrometer is one-millionth of a meter, or three-millionths of a foot). Other organisms can be very large: Blue whales weigh about 110,000 kilograms (240,000 lbs) and reach a length of more than 25 meters (80 ft); they are the largest animals on Earth. Dinosaurs weighed as much as 80,000 kilograms (175,000 lbs) and measured up to 33 meters (108 ft) long.

The Biosphere over Time

Ever since life arose on Earth more than three billion years ago, the biosphere has gone through many changes (see time line at right). These have been driven, in part, by drifting continents, ice ages, shifting sea levels, and the consequences of activities in the biosphere itself.

Over millions of years, the addition of oxygen to the atmosphere allowed for the development of terrestrial ecosystems. But in fairly rapid fashion, humans have had a significant effect on the world's ecosystems; our ability to modify species through gene manipulation will further increase our impact.

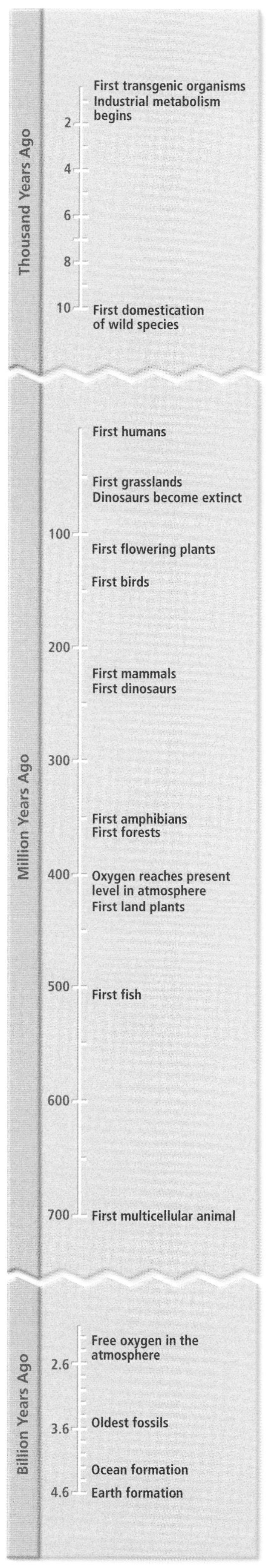
Thousand Years Ago
First transgenic organisms
Industrial metabolism begins
2
4
6
8
10
First domestication of wild species
Million Years Ago
First humans
First grasslands
Dinosaurs become extinct
100
First flowering plants
First birds
200
First mammals
First dinosaurs
300
First amphibians
First forests
400
Oxygen reaches present level in atmosphere
First land plants
500
First fish
600
700
First multicellular animal
Billion Years Ago
Free oxygen in the atmosphere
2.6
3.6
Oldest fossils
Ocean formation
4.6
Earth formation

BIODIVERSITY REFERS TO THREE MEASURES of Earth's intricate web of life: the number of different species, the genetic diversity within a species, and the variety of ecosystems in which species live. Greatest in the wet tropics, biodiversity is important for many reasons, including helping to provide food and medicine, breathable air, drinkable water, livable climates, protection from pests and diseases, and ecosystem stability.

Humankind is only one species in a vast array of life-forms. It is, however, an especially influential and increasingly disruptive actor in the huge cast of characters on the stage of planet Earth. Estimates of the total number of plant and animal species range from ten million to a hundred million; of these, fewer than two million have been described. Yet a substantial number of those species may be gone before we even have a chance to understand their value.

For most of human history, people have often looked at plants and animals simply as resources for meeting their own basic needs. Scientists today count more than a quarter million plant species, of which just nine provide three-quarters of all our food; in that respect, biodiversity has been an unimaginable luxury. It is ironic that as humankind's power to destroy other species grows, so does our ingenuity in finding new and beneficial uses for them.

Sometimes the benefits of preserving a species may have nothing to do with food or medicine. Before a worldwide ban on exports of elephant ivory, the estimated value of such exports was 40 million dollars a year for all of Africa. Now, in Kenya alone, the viewing value of elephants by tourists is thought to be 25 million dollars a year.

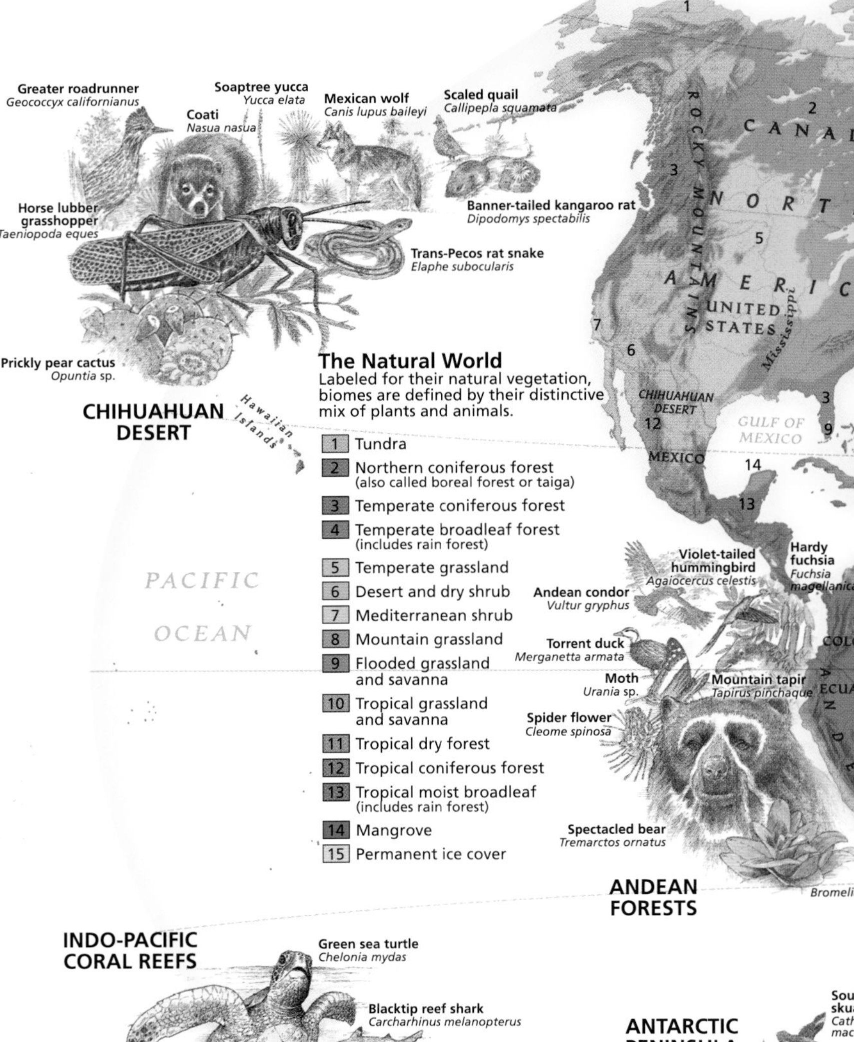

Greater roadrunner
Geococcyx californianus
Soaptree yucca
Yucca elata
Coati
Nasua nasua
Mexican wolf
Canis lupus baileyi
Scaled quail
Callipepla squamata
Horse lubber grasshopper
Taeniopoda eques
Banner-tailed kangaroo rat
Dipodomys spectabilis
Trans-Pecos rat snake
Elaphe subocularis
Prickly pear cactus
Opuntia sp.
CHIHUAHUAN DESERT
Hawaiian Islands
ROCKY MOUNTAINS
CANADA
NORTH AMERICA
UNITED STATES
Mississippi
CHIHUAHUAN DESERT
GULF OF MEXICO
MEXICO
PACIFIC OCEAN
The Natural World
Labeled for their natural vegetation, biomes are defined by their distinctive mix of plants and animals.
1 Tundra
2 Northern coniferous forest (also called boreal forest or taiga)
3 Temperate coniferous forest
4 Temperate broadleaf forest (includes rain forest)
5 Temperate grassland
6 Desert and dry shrub
7 Mediterranean shrub
8 Mountain grassland
9 Flooded grassland and savanna
10 Tropical grassland and savanna
11 Tropical dry forest
12 Tropical coniferous forest
13 Tropical moist broadleaf (includes rain forest)
14 Mangrove
15 Permanent ice cover
Violet-tailed hummingbird
Aglaiocercus celestis
Hardy fuchsia
Fuchsia magellanica
Andean condor
Vultur gryphus
Torrent duck
Merganetta armata
Moth
Urania sp.
Mountain tapir
Tapirus pinchaque
Spider flower
Cleome spinosa
Spectacled bear
Tremarctos ornatus
ANDEAN FORESTS
INDO-PACIFIC CORAL REEFS
Green sea turtle
Chelonia mydas
Blacktip reef shark
Carcharhinus melanopterus
Mushroom coral
Fungia sp.
Neon fusilier
Pterocaesio tile
Coral cod
Cephalopholis miniata
Coral
Porites sp.
Whitemouth moray
Gymnothorax meleagris
Staghorn coral
Acropora sp.
Humpback whale
Megaptera novaeangliae
Whitecheek surgeonfish
Acanthurus nigricauds
Giant clam
Tridacna gigas
ANTARCTIC PENINSULA
Adélie penguin
Pygoscelis adeliae
Weddell seal
Leptonychotes weddelli
Lichen
Octopus
Pareledone sp.

Species Diversity

Among fauna and flora, insects make up the largest classification in terms of sheer number of species, with fungi ranked a distant second. At the other extreme, the categories with the smallest numbers—mammals, birds, and mollusks—also happen to be the classes with the greatest percentage of threatened species (see middle graph, below). This is not just a matter of proportion: These groups include the most at-risk species in terms of absolute numbers as well.

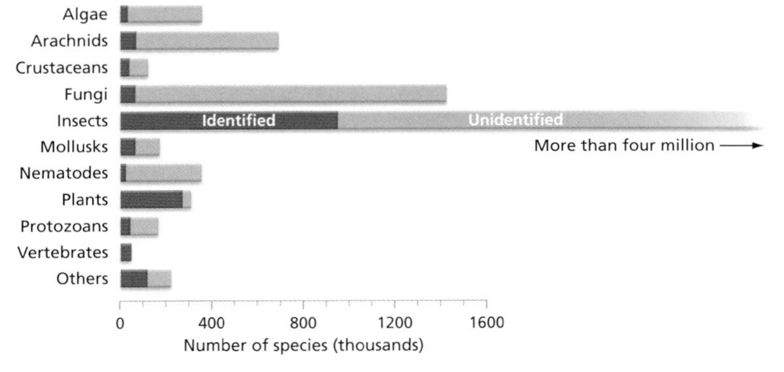

Algae
Arachnids
Crustaceans
Fungi
Insects
Identified
Unidentified
More than four million
Mollusks
Nematodes
Plants
Protozoans
Vertebrates
Others
0
400
800
1200
1600
Number of species (thousands)

Threatened Ecoregions

British ecologist Norman Myers defined the "biodiversity hotspot" concept in 1988 to help address the dilemma of identifying conservation priorities. The biodiversity hotspots hold especially high numbers of endemic species, yet their combined area of remaining habitat covers only 2.3 percent of the Earth's land surface. Each hotspot faces extreme threats and has already lost at least 70 percent of its original natural vegetation. Of particular concern to scientists is that 75 percent of all threatened terrestrial vertebrates occur only in the hotspots.

NORTH AMERICA
California Floristic Province
Madrean Pine-Oak Woodlands
Caribbean Islands
Mesoamerica
Polynesia-Micronesia
PACIFIC OCEAN
Tumbes-Chocó-Magdalena
SOUTH AMERICA
Tropical Andes
Cerrado
Atlantic Forest
Chilean Winter Rainfall-Valdivian Forests
New Zealand
ATLANTIC OCEAN
EUROPE
Caucasus
Mediterranean Basin
Irano-Anatolian
Mountains of Central Asia
ASIA
Mountains of Southwest China
Japan
Himalaya
Indo-Burma
Philippines
PACIFIC OCEAN
AFRICA
Guinean Forests of West Africa
Eastern Afromontane
Horn of Africa
Coastal Forests of Eastern Africa
Succulent Karoo
Cape Floristic Region
Maputaland-Pondoland-Albany
Madagascar and the Indian Ocean Islands
Western Ghats and Sri Lanka
INDIAN OCEAN
Sundaland
Wallacea
Polynesia-Micronesia
East Melanesian Islands
New Caledonia
AUSTRALIA
Southwest Australia
New Zealand
ANTARCTICA
Biodiversity "Hotspots"
Hotspot regions

Threatened Species

Africa · Australia/Ocea · Asia · Europe

Number of species threatened: 0, 300, 600, 900, 1,200

Mammals *(90%) · Birds *(100%) · Reptiles *(6%)

*Percent assessed

ARCTIC OCEAN

BARENTS SEA
RUSSIA
SIBERIA
ASIA
EUROPE
FRANCE
PORTUGAL
MOROCCO
Lake Baikal
Aral Sea
BLACK SEA
CASPIAN SEA
MEDITERRANEAN SEA
GOBI
CHINA
HIMALAYA
JORDAN
SAHARA
Nile
RED SEA
ARABIAN SEA
INDIA
Western Ghats
SOUTH CHINA SEA
AFRICA
Congo
Lake Victoria
ATLANTIC OCEAN
KALAHARI DESERT
SOUTH AFRICA
Madagascar
INDIAN OCEAN
INDONESIA
Borneo
New Guinea
PAPUA NEW GUINEA
PACIFIC OCEAN
AUSTRALIA
New Caledonia
TASMAN SEA
NEW ZEALAND
ANTARCTIC PENINSULA
WEDDELL SEA
ANTARCTICA

SIBERIAN TAIGA

Wood wasp *Urocerus gigas*
Pacific golden plover *Pluvialis fulva*
Sable *Martes zibellina*
Mazarine blue butterfly *Cyaniris semiargus*
Pacific diver *Gavia pacifica*
Ross's gull *Rhodostethia rosea*
Orange stump mushroom *Naematoloma capnoides*
Caesar's mushroom *Amanita caesarea*
Short-billed dowitcher *Limnodromus griseus*
Reindeer *Rangifer tarandus*
Lichen
Yellow-brown boletus *Suillus luteus*
Radiola sp.
Siberian crane *Grus leucogeranus*
Goshawk *Accipiter gentilis*
Peacock butterfly *Inachis io*

MEDITERRANEAN REGION

Spectacled warbler *Sylvia conspicillata*
Hermann's tortoise *Testudo hermanni*
Cedar of Lebanon *Cedrus libani*
European mouflon *Ovis orientalis musimon*
Petromarula *Petromarula pinnata*
Moussier's redstart *Phoenicurus moussieri*
Spiny mullein *Verbascum spinosum*
Corsican red deer *Cervus elaphus corsicanus*
Scarab (beetle) *Scarabaeus laticollis*
Ruin lizard *Lacerta sicula*
Cork oak *Quercus suber*

NEW GUINEA FORESTS

King bird of paradise *Cicinnurus regius*
Victoria crowned pigeon *Goura victoria*
Tree frog *Litoria* sp.
Rhododendron alticolum
Goodfellow's tree-kangaroo *Dendrolagus goodfellowi*
D'Albertis's python *Liasis albertisii*
Spotted cuscus *Spilocuscus maculatus*
Papuan tiger orchid *Grammatophyllum papuanum*
Common birdwing *Ornithoptera priamus*

WESTERN GHATS

Great pied hornbill *Buceros bicornis*
Asian elephant *Elephas maximus*
Lion-tailed macaque *Macaca silenus*
Orchid *Dendrobium nanum*
Mugger crocodile *Crocodylus palustris*
Nilgiri tahr (wild goat) *Hemitragus hylocrius*
Dragonfly *Trithemis aurora*
Rhodomyrtus sp.
Tiger *Panthera tigris*
Gaur *Bos gaurus*
Jumping spider *Chrysilla* sp.

ATLANTIC FORESTS

Black hawk-eagle *Spizaetus tyrannus*
Butterfly *Dismorphia amphione*
Maned sloth *Bradypus torquatus*
Emerald pit viper *Bothriopsis bilineata*
Jequitiranabóia *Fulgora lanternaria*
Black Jacobin *Melanotrochilus fuscus*
Golden lion tamarin *Leontopithecus rosalia*
Common tegu *Tupinambis teguixin*
Tree fern *Alsophila armata*
Seven-colored tanager *Tangara fastuosa*
Orchid *Cattleya forbesii*
Vriesea sp.

CAPE FLORISTIC REGION

Cape mountain zebra *Equus zebra zebra*
Table Mountain ghost frog *Heleophryne rosei*
Cape grysbok *Raphicerus melanotis*
Chacma baboon *Papio cynocephalus*
Silver tree *Leucadendron argenteum*
Geometric tortoise *Psammobates geometricus*
King protea *Protea cynaroides*
King cricket *Maxentius* sp.

NEW ZEALAND

Southern rata *Metrosideros umbellata*
Flax weevil *Anagotus fairburni*
Fiordland crested penguin *Eudyptes pachyrhynchus*
Snail *Paryphanta lignaria*
Kakapo (parrot) *Strigops habroptilus*
Tree weta *Hemideina* sp.
Lancewood *Pseudopanax crassifolius*
Wild spaniard *Aciphylla* sp.
Takahe *Porphyrio mantelli*
Snowberry *Gaultheria* sp.

p penguin
s antarctica
h
opsis macropterus
tic krill
sia superba

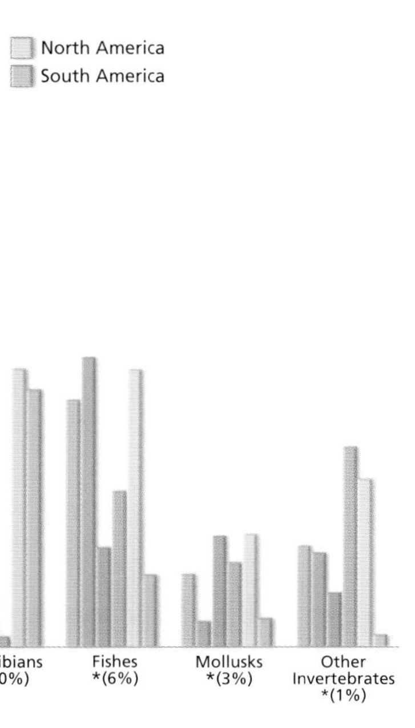

North America
South America
ibians 0%)
Fishes *(6%)
Mollusks *(3%)
Other Invertebrates *(1%)

Projected Biodiversity Status

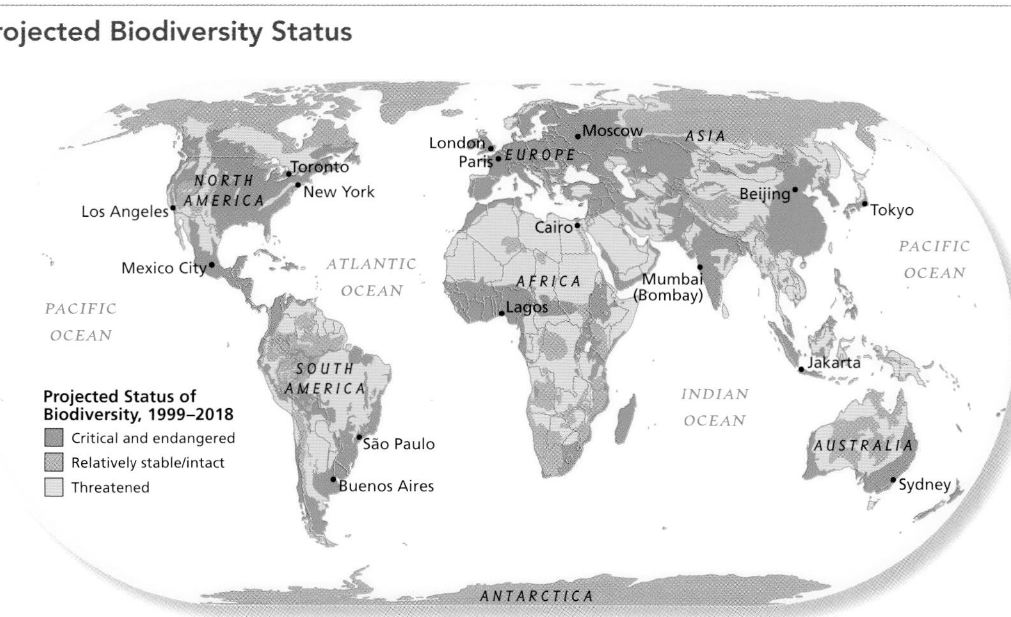

Moscow
London
Paris
EUROPE
ASIA
NORTH AMERICA
Toronto
New York
Los Angeles
Beijing
Tokyo
Cairo
Mexico City
ATLANTIC OCEAN
PACIFIC OCEAN
AFRICA
Mumbai (Bombay)
Lagos
PACIFIC OCEAN
SOUTH AMERICA
Jakarta
INDIAN OCEAN
São Paulo
AUSTRALIA
Buenos Aires
Sydney
ANTARCTICA
Projected Status of Biodiversity, 1999–2018
Critical and endangered
Relatively stable/intact
Threatened

Biodiversity is decreasing at a rapidly increasing rate. According to scientists, current extinction rates are a hundred to a thousand times greater than the normal rate of extinction; furthermore, the number of species threatened with extinction continues to increase (with, for example, one in three amphibians and one in four mammals at risk in the wild). Species are not being killed off directly: The two leading causes of extinction are loss of habitats and the impact of invasive species, although other threats include overexploitation, pollution, disease, and climate change.

WHILE POPULATIONS IN MANY PARTS of the world are expanding, those of Europe—along with some other rich industrial areas such as Japan—show little to no growth, or may actually be shrinking. Many such countries must bring in immigrant workers to keep their economies thriving. A clear correlation exists between wealth and low fertility: the higher the incomes and educational levels, the lower the rates of reproduction.

Many governments keep vital statistics, recording births and deaths, and count their populations regularly to try to plan ahead. The United States has taken a census every ten years since 1790, recording the ages, the occupations, and other important facts about its people. The United Nations helps less developed countries carry out censuses and improve their demographic information.

Governments of some poor countries may find that half their populations are under the age of 20. They are faced with the overwhelming tasks of providing adequate education and jobs while encouraging better family-planning programs. Governments of nations with low birthrates find themselves with growing numbers of elderly people but fewer workers able to provide tax money for health care and pensions.

In a mere 150 years, world population has grown fivefold, at an ever increasing pace. The industrial revolution helped bring about improvements in food supplies and advances in both medicine and public health, which allowed people to live longer and to have more healthy babies. Today, 15,000 people are born into the world every hour, and nearly all of them are in poor African, Asian, and South American nations. This situation concerns planners, who look to demographers (professionals who study all aspects of population) for important data.

Lights of the World

Satellite imagery offers a surprising view of the world at night. Bright lights in Europe, Asia, and the United States give a clear picture of densely populated areas with ample electricity. Reading this map requires great care, however. Some totally dark areas, like most of Australia, do in fact have very small populations, but other light-free areas—in China and Africa, for example—may simply hide dense populations with not enough electricity to be seen by a satellite. Wealthy areas with fewer people, such as Florida, may be using their energy wastefully. Ever since the 1970s, demographers have supplemented census data with information from satellite imagery.

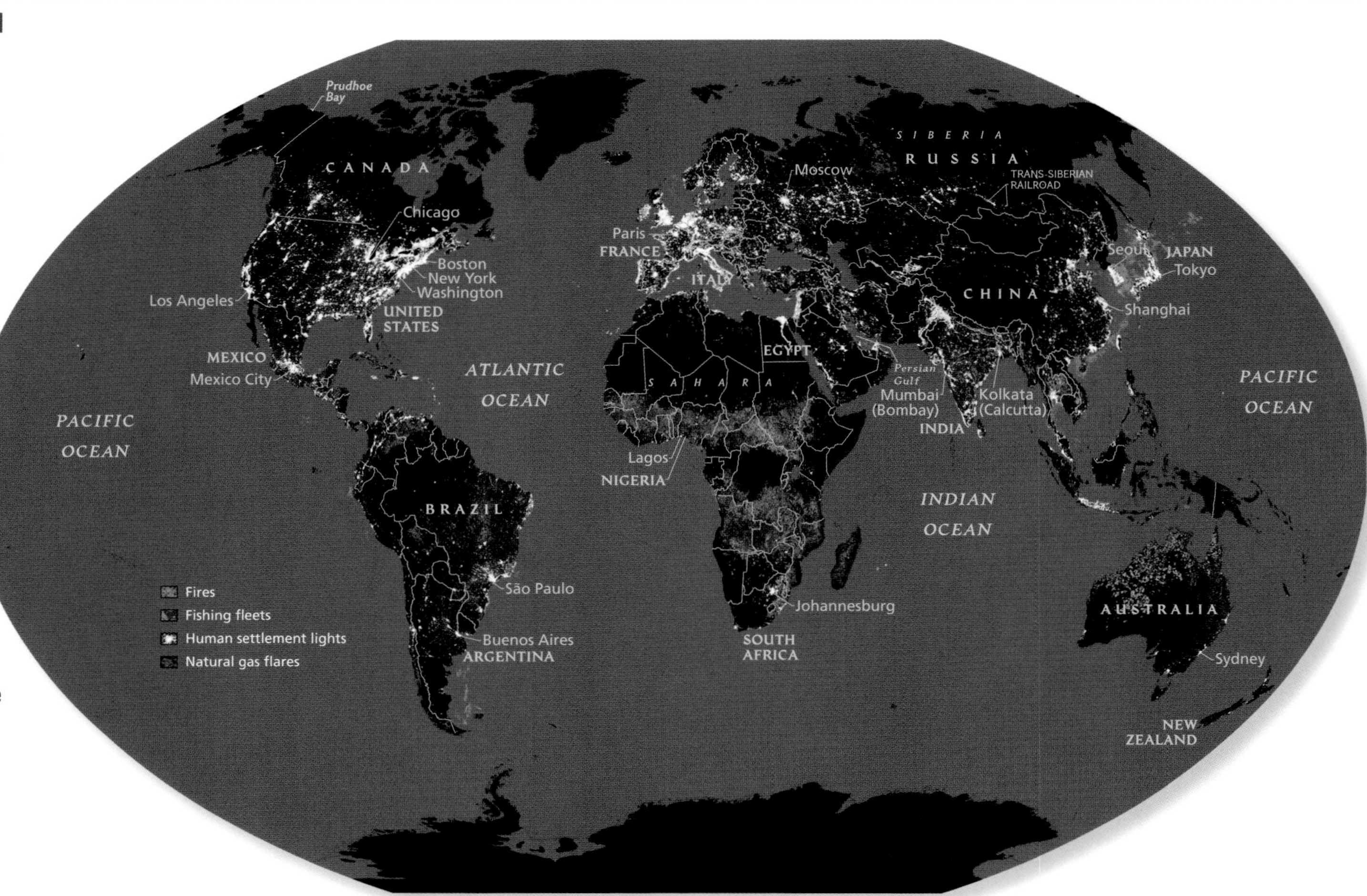

Prudhoe Bay
CANADA
Chicago
Boston
New York
Washington
UNITED STATES
Los Angeles
MEXICO
Mexico City
ATLANTIC OCEAN
PACIFIC OCEAN
BRAZIL
São Paulo
Buenos Aires
ARGENTINA
Fires
Fishing fleets
Human settlement lights
Natural gas flares
Paris
FRANCE
ITALY
Moscow
SIBERIA
RUSSIA
TRANS-SIBERIAN RAILROAD
CHINA
Seoul
JAPAN
Tokyo
Shanghai
EGYPT
SAHARA
Persian Gulf
Mumbai (Bombay)
Kolkata (Calcutta)
INDIA
Lagos
NIGERIA
INDIAN OCEAN
Johannesburg
SOUTH AFRICA
PACIFIC OCEAN
AUSTRALIA
Sydney
NEW ZEALAND

Population Pyramids

A population pyramid shows the number of males and females in every age group of a population. A pyramid for Nigeria reveals that over half—about 55 percent—of the population is under 20, while only 19 percent of Italy's population is younger than 20.

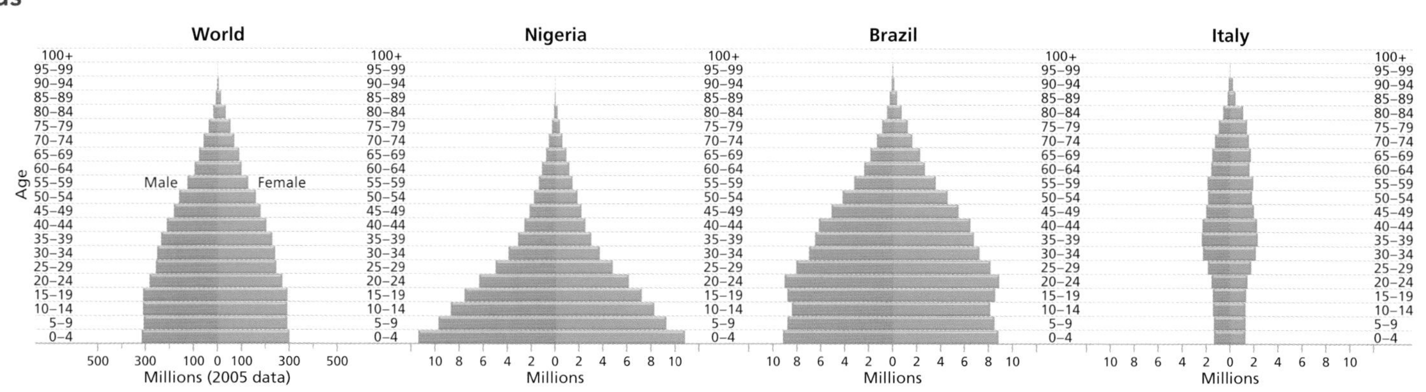

World
Nigeria
Brazil
Italy
Age
Male
Female
100+
95–99
90–94
85–89
80–84
75–79
70–74
65–69
60–64
55–59
50–54
45–49
40–44
35–39
30–34
25–29
20–24
15–19
10–14
5–9
0–4
500 300 100 0 100 300 500
Millions (2005 data)
10 8 6 4 2 0 2 4 6 8 10
Millions

14 50 100 150 200 250 300 350 400 450 500 550 600 650 700 750 800 850 900 950 1000
Year

Population Growth

The population of the world is not distributed evenly. In this cartogram Canada is almost invisible, while India looks enormous because its population is 34 times greater than Canada's. In reality, Canada is 3 times larger than India, in size. The shape of almost every country looks distorted when populations are compared in this way.

Population sizes are constantly changing, however. In countries that are experiencing many more births than deaths, population totals are ballooning. In others, too few babies are born to replace the number of people who die, and populations are shrinking. A cartogram devoted solely to growth rates around the world would look quite different from this one.

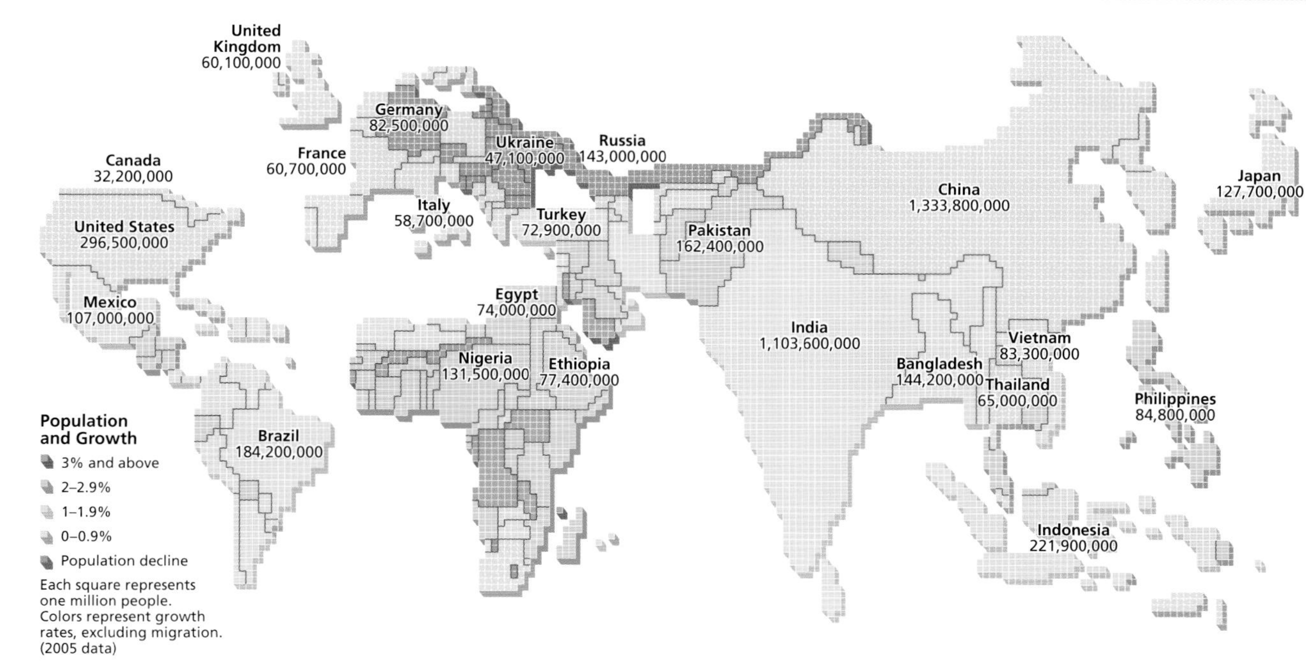

United Kingdom 60,100,000
Germany 82,500,000
France 60,700,000
Ukraine 47,100,000
Russia 143,000,000
Canada 32,200,000
Italy 58,700,000
Turkey 72,900,000
Pakistan 162,400,000
China 1,333,800,000
Japan 127,700,000
United States 296,500,000
Mexico 107,000,000
Egypt 74,000,000
India 1,103,600,000
Vietnam 83,300,000
Nigeria 131,500,000
Ethiopia 77,400,000
Bangladesh 144,200,000
Thailand 65,000,000
Philippines 84,800,000
Brazil 184,200,000
Indonesia 221,900,000
Population and Growth
3% and above
2–2.9%
1–1.9%
0–0.9%
Population decline
Each square represents one million people. Colors represent growth rates, excluding migration. (2005 data)

Population Density

A country's population density is estimated by figuring out how many people would occupy one square mile if they were all spread out evenly. In reality, people live together most closely in cities, on seacoasts, and in river valleys. Singapore, a tiny country largely composed of a single city, has a high population density—more than 17,000 people per square mile. Greenland, by comparison, has less than one person per square mile because it is mostly covered by ice. Its people mainly fish for a living and dwell in small groups near the shore.

NORTH AMERICA · Chicago · New York · Philadelphia · Los Angeles · Miami · Mexico City · PACIFIC OCEAN · ATLANTIC OCEAN · Bogotá · Lima · SOUTH AMERICA · Belo Horizonte · Rio de Janeiro · São Paulo · Santiago · Buenos Aires · St. Petersburg · Moscow · London · Paris · EUROPE · Madrid · Istanbul · Baghdad · Cairo · Riyadh · Tehran · Lahore · Karachi · Delhi · AFRICA · Lagos · Kinshasa · ASIA · Beijing · Tianjin · Seoul · Tokyo · Osaka · Wuhan · Shanghai · Dhaka · Kolkata (Calcutta) · Mumbai (Bombay) · Hyderabad · Bangalore · Chennai · Bangkok · Hong Kong · Manila · Ho Chi Minh City · INDIAN OCEAN · Jakarta · AUSTRALIA · ANTARCTICA

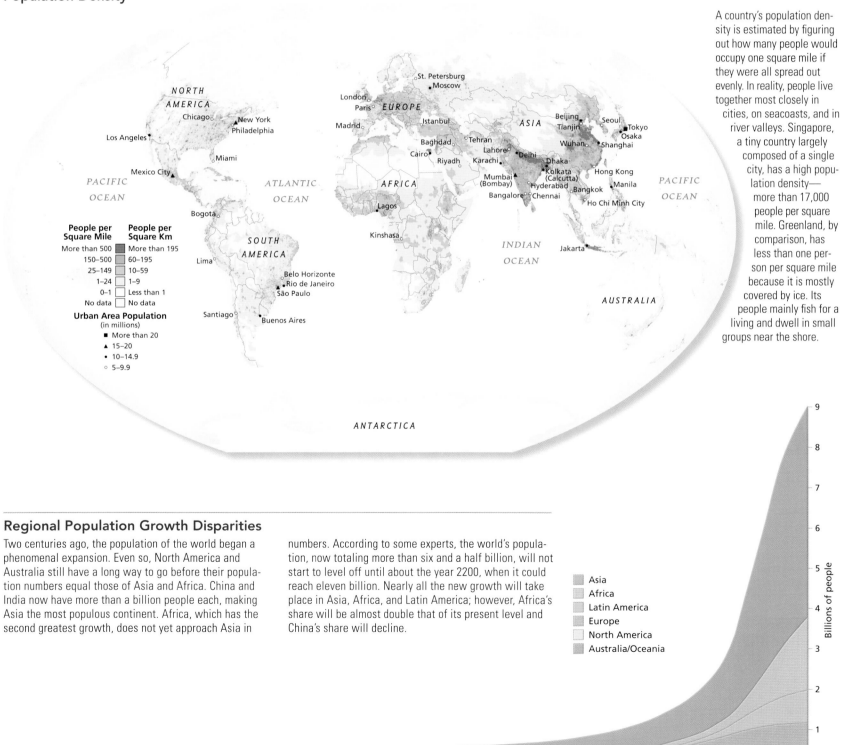

People per Square Mile	People per Square Km
More than 500	More than 195
150–500	60–195
25–149	10–59
1–24	1–9
0–1	Less than 1
No data	No data

Urban Area Population (in millions)
- More than 20
- 15–20
- 10–14.9
- 5–9.9

Regional Population Growth Disparities

Two centuries ago, the population of the world began a phenomenal expansion. Even so, North America and Australia still have a long way to go before their population numbers equal those of Asia and Africa. China and India now have more than a billion people each, making Asia the most populous continent. Africa, which has the second greatest growth, does not yet approach Asia in numbers. According to some experts, the world's population, now totaling more than six and a half billion, will not start to level off until about the year 2200, when it could reach eleven billion. Nearly all the new growth will take place in Asia, Africa, and Latin America; however, Africa's share will be almost double that of its present level and China's share will decline.

Asia · Africa · Latin America · Europe · North America · Australia/Oceania

Billions of people: 0 1 2 3 4 5 6 7 8 9

Year: 1100 1150 1200 1250 1300 1350 1400 1450 1500 1550 1600 1650 1700 1750 1800 1850 1900 1950 2000 2050

Fertility

Fertility, or birthrate, measures the average number of children born to women in a given population. It can also be expressed as the number of live births per thousand people in a population per year. In low-income countries with limited educational opportunities for girls and women, birthrates reach their highest levels.

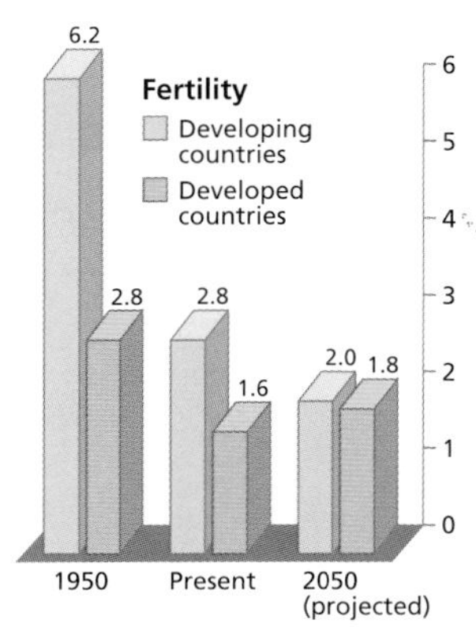
Fertility
Developing countries
Developed countries
6.2
2.8
2.8
1.6
2.0
1.8
1950
Present
2050 (projected)

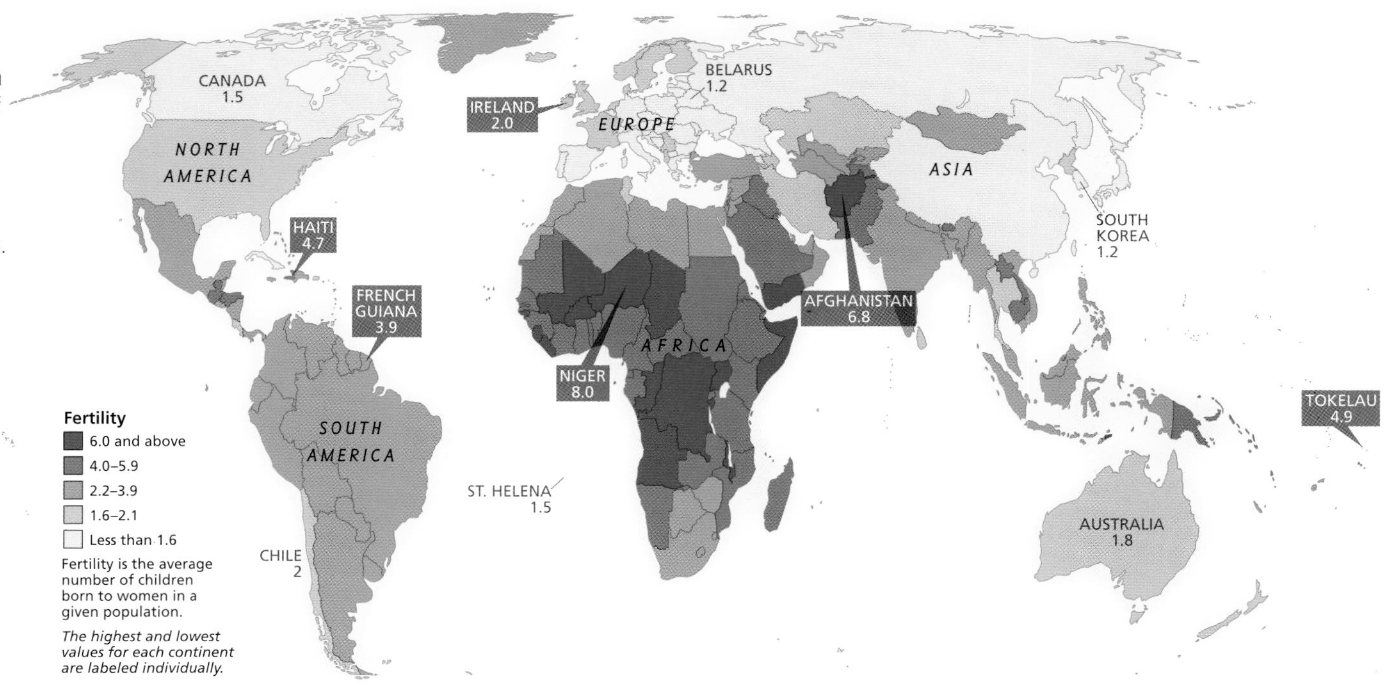
CANADA 1.5
NORTH AMERICA
IRELAND 2.0
BELARUS 1.2
EUROPE
ASIA
HAITI 4.7
FRENCH GUIANA 3.9
SOUTH KOREA 1.2
AFGHANISTAN 6.8
AFRICA
NIGER 8.0
TOKELAU 4.9
SOUTH AMERICA
ST. HELENA 1.5
AUSTRALIA 1.8
CHILE 2
Fertility
6.0 and above
4.0–5.9
2.2–3.9
1.6–2.1
Less than 1.6
Fertility is the average number of children born to women in a given population.
The highest and lowest values for each continent are labeled individually.

Urban Population Densities

People around the world are leaving farms and moving to cities, where jobs and opportunities are better. In 2000 almost half the world's people lived in towns or cities. The shift of population from the countryside to urban centers will probably continue in less developed countries for many years to come.

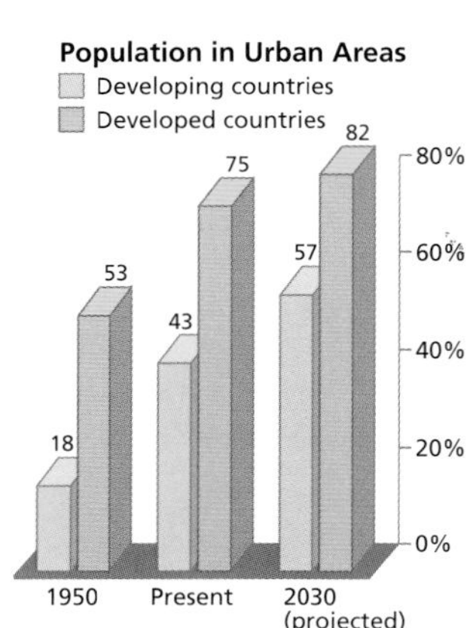
Population in Urban Areas
Developing countries
Developed countries
18
53
43
75
57
82
80%
60%
40%
20%
0%
1950
Present
2030 (projected)

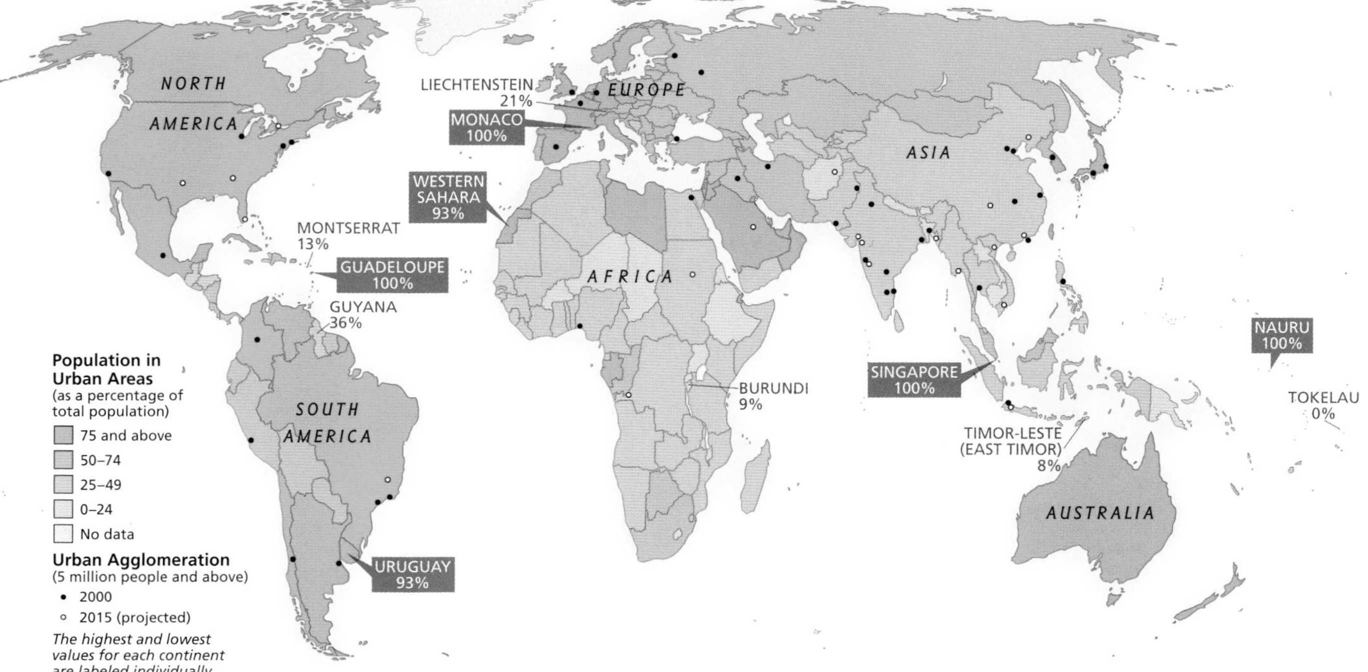
NORTH AMERICA
LIECHTENSTEIN 21%
EUROPE
MONACO 100%
ASIA
WESTERN SAHARA 93%
MONTSERRAT 13%
GUADELOUPE 100%
AFRICA
GUYANA 36%
NAURU 100%
SINGAPORE 100%
BURUNDI 9%
TOKELAU 0%
SOUTH AMERICA
TIMOR-LESTE (EAST TIMOR) 8%
AUSTRALIA
URUGUAY 93%
Population in Urban Areas (as a percentage of total population)
75 and above
50–74
25–49
0–24
No data
Urban Agglomeration (5 million people and above)
2000
2015 (projected)
The highest and lowest values for each continent are labeled individually.

Urban Population Growth

Urban populations are growing more than twice as fast as populations as a whole. Soon, the world's city dwellers will outnumber its rural inhabitants as towns become cities and cities merge into megacities with more than ten million people. Globalization speeds the process. Although cities generate wealth and provide better health care along with electricity, clean water, sewage treatment, and other benefits, they can also cause great ecological damage. Squatter settlements and slums may develop if cities cannot keep up with millions of new arrivals. Smog, congestion, pollution, and crime are other dangers. Good city management is a key to future prosperity.

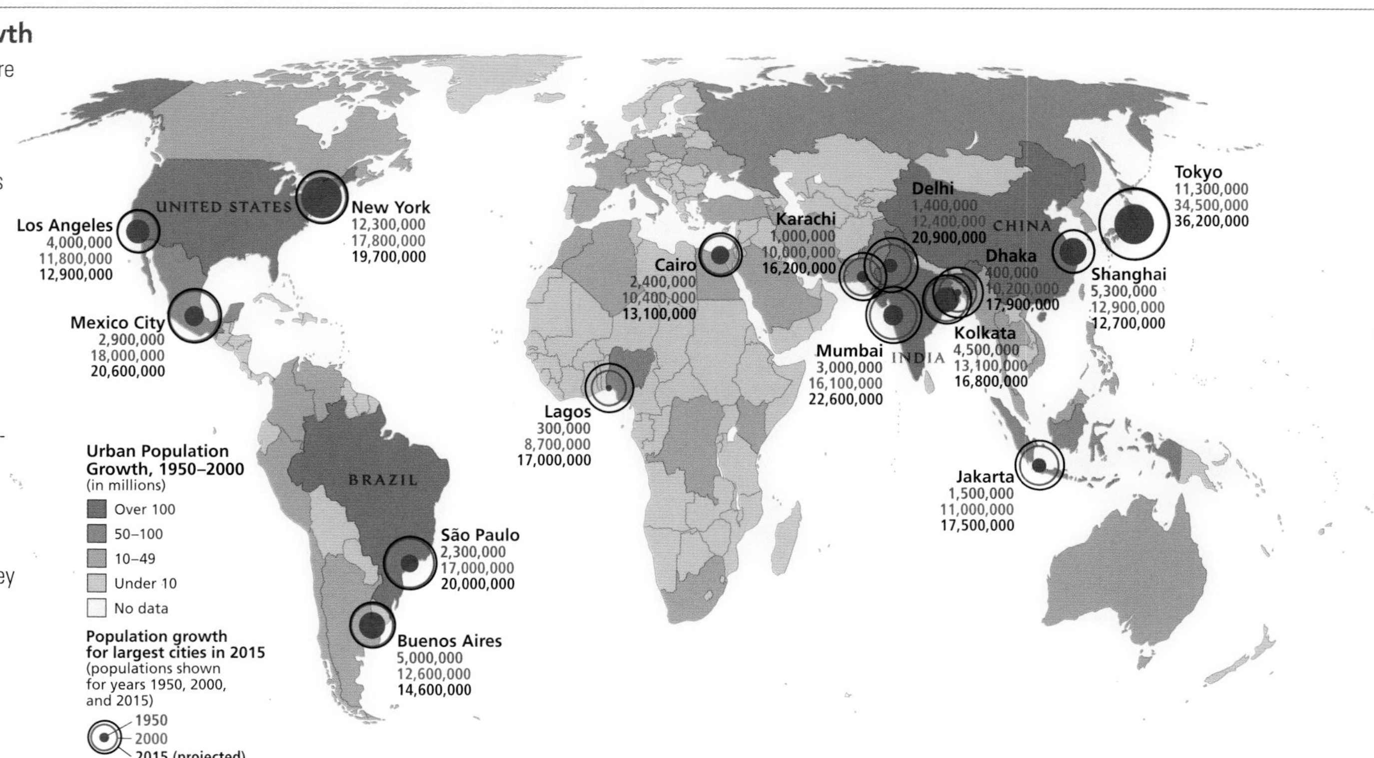
UNITED STATES
New York 12,300,000 17,800,000 19,700,000
Los Angeles 4,000,000 11,800,000 12,900,000
Mexico City 2,900,000 18,000,000 20,600,000
Delhi 1,400,000 12,400,000 20,900,000
Karachi 1,000,000 10,000,000 16,200,000
CHINA
Tokyo 11,300,000 34,500,000 36,200,000
Cairo 2,400,000 10,400,000 13,100,000
Dhaka 400,000 10,200,000 17,900,000
Shanghai 5,300,000 12,900,000 12,700,000
Mumbai 3,000,000 16,100,000 22,600,000
INDIA
Kolkata 4,500,000 13,100,000 16,800,000
Lagos 300,000 8,700,000 17,000,000
BRAZIL
Jakarta 1,500,000 11,000,000 17,500,000
São Paulo 2,300,000 17,000,000 20,000,000
Buenos Aires 5,000,000 12,600,000 14,600,000
Urban Population Growth, 1950–2000 (in millions)
Over 100
50–100
10–49
Under 10
No data
Population growth for largest cities in 2015 (populations shown for years 1950, 2000, and 2015)
1950
2000
2015 (projected)

Life Expectancy

Life expectancy for population groups does not mean that all people die by a certain age. It is an average of death statistics. High infant mortality results in low life expectancy: People who live to adulthood will probably reach old age; there are just fewer of them.

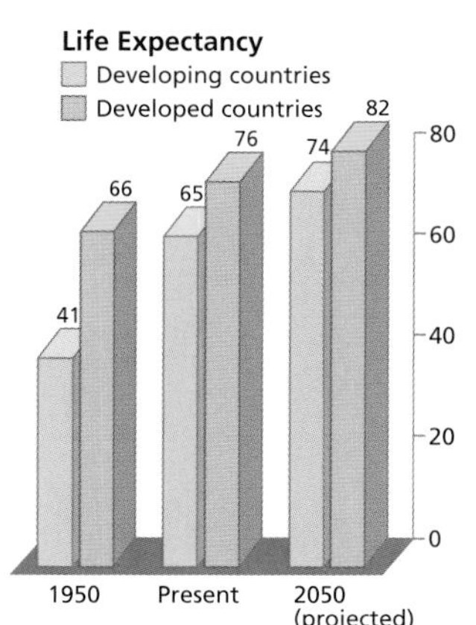

Life Expectancy
Developing countries
Developed countries
41
66
65
76
74
82
80
60
40
20
0
1950
Present
2050 (projected)

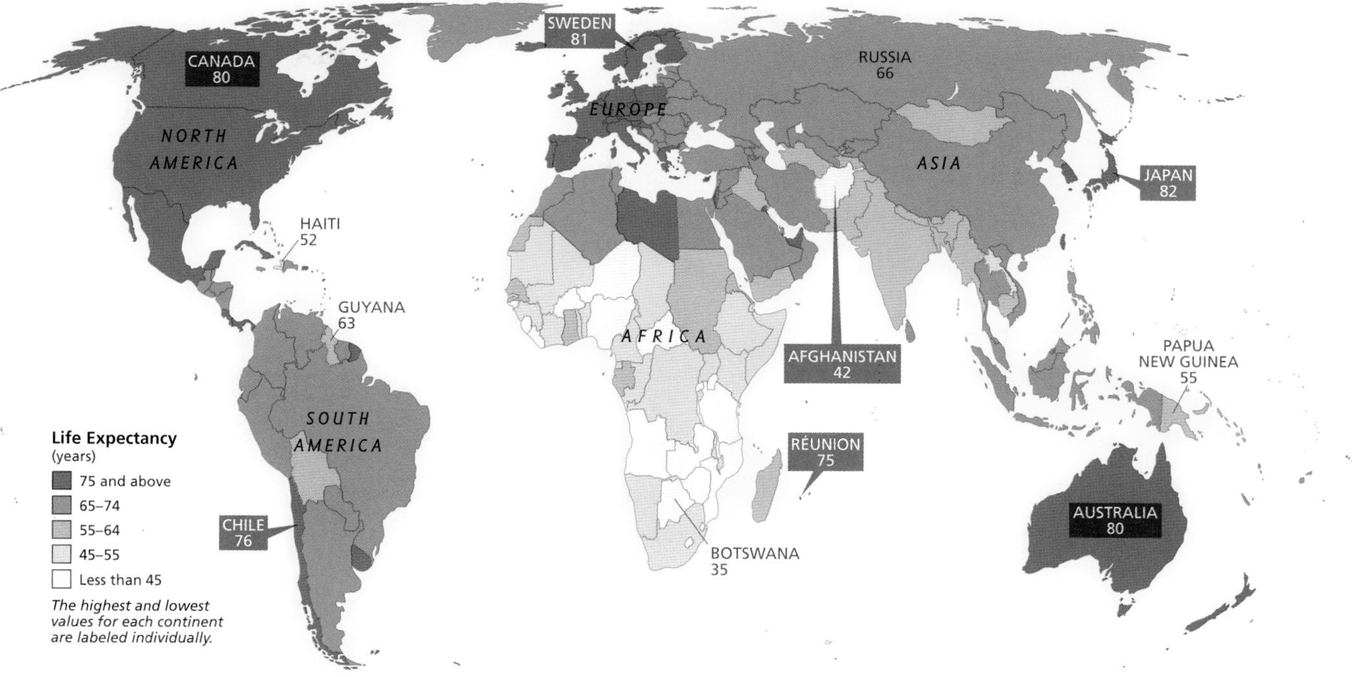

CANADA 80
SWEDEN 81
RUSSIA 66
NORTH AMERICA
EUROPE
ASIA
JAPAN 82
HAITI 52
GUYANA 63
AFRICA
AFGHANISTAN 42
PAPUA NEW GUINEA 55
SOUTH AMERICA
RÉUNION 75
CHILE 76
AUSTRALIA 80
BOTSWANA 35
Life Expectancy (years)
75 and above
65–74
55–64
45–55
Less than 45
The highest and lowest values for each continent are labeled individually.

Migration

International migration has reached its highest level, with foreign workers now providing the labor in several Middle Eastern nations and immigrant workers proving essential to rich countries with low birthrates. Refugees continue to escape grim political and environmental conditions, while businesspeople and tourists keep many economies spinning.

Migrant Population
(percentage of regional population)

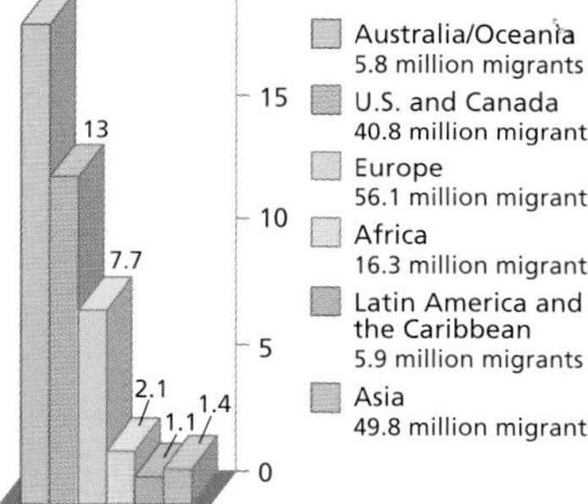

19.1
13
7.7
2.1
1.1
1.4
20
15
10
5
0
Australia/Oceania 5.8 million migrants
U.S. and Canada 40.8 million migrants
Europe 56.1 million migrants
Africa 16.3 million migrants
Latin America and the Caribbean 5.9 million migrants
Asia 49.8 million migrants

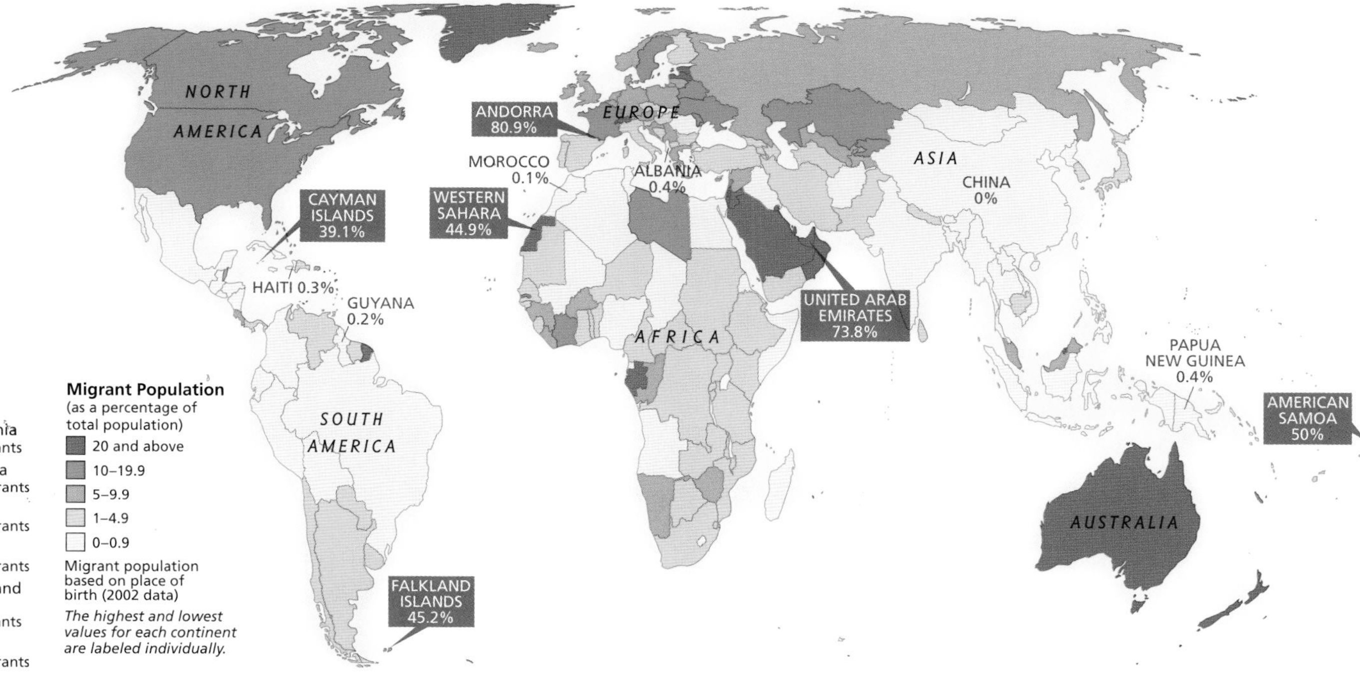

NORTH AMERICA
ANDORRA 80.9%
EUROPE
MOROCCO 0.1%
ALBANIA 0.4%
ASIA
CHINA 0%
CAYMAN ISLANDS 39.1%
WESTERN SAHARA 44.9%
HAITI 0.3%
GUYANA 0.2%
UNITED ARAB EMIRATES 73.8%
AFRICA
PAPUA NEW GUINEA 0.4%
SOUTH AMERICA
AMERICAN SAMOA 50%
AUSTRALIA
FALKLAND ISLANDS 45.2%
Migrant Population (as a percentage of total population)
20 and above
10–19.9
5–9.9
1–4.9
0–0.9
Migrant population based on place of birth (2002 data)
The highest and lowest values for each continent are labeled individually.

Most Populous Places

(MID-2005 DATA)

1. China 1,333,827,000
2. India 1,103,596,000
3. United States 296,483,000
4. Indonesia 221,932,000
5. Brazil 184,184,000
6. Pakistan 162,420,000
7. Bangladesh 144,233,000
8. Russia 143,025,000
9. Nigeria 131,530,000
10. Japan 127,728,000
11. Mexico 107,029,000
12. Philippines 84,765,000
13. Vietnam 83,305,000
14. Germany 82,490,000
15. Ethiopia 77,431,000
16. Egypt 74,033,000
17. Turkey 72,907,000
18. Iran 69,515,000
19. Thailand 65,002,000
20. Dem. Rep. of Congo 60,764,000

Most Crowded Places

POPULATION DENSITY (POP/SQ. MI.)

1. Monaco 41,250
2. Singapore 17,946
3. Gibraltar (U.K.) 7,511
4. Malta 3,278
5. Bermuda (U.K.) 3,212
6. Bahrain 2,744
7. Bangladesh 2,594
8. Maldives 2,538
9. Channel Islands 1,987
10. Taiwan 1,627
11. Mauritius 1,578
12. Palestinian Areas 1,556
13. Barbados 1,554
14. Nauru 1,529
15. Aruba 1,322
16. San Marino 1,295
17. South Korea 1,260
18. Mayotte (Fr.) 1,249
19. Puerto Rico (U.S.) 1,132
20. Netherlands 1,033

Demographic Extremes

LIFE EXPECTANCY

LOWEST (FEMALE, IN YEARS):

35 Botswana, Lesotho
37 Swaziland, Zambia
41 Zimbabwe
42 Afghanistan, Angola, Sierra Leone

LOWEST (MALE, IN YEARS):

34 Botswana, Swaziland
36 Lesotho
38 Zambia
39 Angola, Sierra Leone

HIGHEST (FEMALE, IN YEARS):

85 Japan
84 France, San Marino, Spain
83 Australia, Iceland, Italy, Sweden, Switzerland

HIGHEST (MALE, IN YEARS):

79 Iceland, Liechtenstein
78 Anguilla , Australia, Israel, Japan, Norway, San Marino, Sweden, Switzerland
77 Canada, Cayman Islands (U.K.), Faroe Islands (Den.), France, Italy, Kuwait, Singapore, Spain

POPULATION AGE STRUCTURE

HIGHEST % POPULATION UNDER AGE 15

51% Uganda
48% Chad, Dem. Rep. of Congo , Niger
47% Burundi, Mali
46% Angola, Burkina Faso, Congo, Guinea-Bissau, Liberia, Malawi, Palestinian Areas, Yemen

HIGHEST % POPULATION OVER AGE 65

22% Monaco
20% Japan
19% Italy
18% Germany, Greece

A PERSON'S NATIONALITY AND LANGUAGE are often assumed to be the same: A German speaks German, for example. The ability to use a specific language has often been viewed as a defining characteristic of a citizen. But there are only about 200 countries, while there are some 5,000 living languages. In a quarter of all nations, no single language is spoken by a majority of the inhabitants. Canada is legally bilingual; India has 22 official languages; and French, Spanish, English, Portuguese, and German are each the official language of at least two nations.

Most languages are spoken by only a few hundred or a few thousand people. Over 200 languages are spoken by more than a million people; 23 languages have 50 million or more speakers.

How we define language makes it difficult to determine the exact number of languages. A dialect, for instance, is a variety of language used by a specific group of persons, with its own rules of grammar or pronunciation. Other linguistic systems that fail to attain the full status of languages are pidgins (contact languages used by groups with different native languages to communicate) and creoles (what pidgins are called when they are adopted as native languages).

Voices of the World

ESKIMO-ALEUT

Of this family's dozen languages in Asia and North America, only Greenlandic, Greenland's official language, may outlive this century.

AMERICAN INDIAN (NORTH)

More than 300 native languages were once spoken in the United States and Canada. Two-thirds survive, but the few speakers left are aging. Even as native languages fade, their sounds echo in place-names such as Chicago and Massachusetts.

1 Algonquian-Ritwan
2 Caddoan
3 Hokan
4 Iroquoian
5 Kiowa-Tanoan
6 Muskogean
7 Nadene
8 Penutian
9 Salishan
10 Siouan
11 Uto-Aztecan
12 Wakashan
13 Undetermined

AMERICAN INDIAN (MESO-)

Quiché and Yucatec, Mayan languages, are the region's strongest indigenous tongues. Most languages faded after European contact, but a few were documented by missionaries. Alonso de Molina recorded Nahuatl, the Aztec language, in the mid-1500s.

1 Macro-Chibchan
2 Mayan
3 Mixe-Zoquean
4 Oto-Manguean
5 Totonacan
6 Uto-Aztecan

ISOLATES

Dozens of rare languages—such as Basque in Spain and France, Burushaski in Pakistan—persist as linguistic islands. Despite decades of research, links to known language groups have yet to be verified. Chukchi, spoken in Siberia, is an example of a member of an isolated small language family.

Isolates and isolated small families

AMERICAN INDIAN (SOUTH)

Perhaps a thousand Indian languages that once had a voice here have disappeared. Two modest success stories: Quechua, the language of the Inca, has ten million speakers; Guaraní is the major language of Paraguay.

1 Arawakan
2 Kariban
3 Macro-Chibchan
4 Macro-Ge
5 Pano-Takanan
6 Quechumaran
7 Tukánoan
8 Tupían
9 Other
10 Undetermined

AFRO-ASIATIC

The languages of ancier lon, Assyria, Egypt, and tine belonged to this far Still thriving, the largest Afro-Asiatic language, A spreads in tandem with

1 Berber
2 Chadic
3 Cushitic
4 Omot
5 Semit

Hawaiian Islands

PACIFIC OCEAN

CANADA

NORTH AMERICA

UNITED STATES

MEXICO

PERU

SOUTH AMERICA

PARAGUAY

Uninhabited

Vanishing Languages

Some 10,000 languages—or more—are thought to have once existed (see graph at right). This is an estimate; unlike extinct animals, dead languages rarely left traces, as most lacked a written form. About 5,000 still exist, but linguists fear that the rate of loss is quickening.

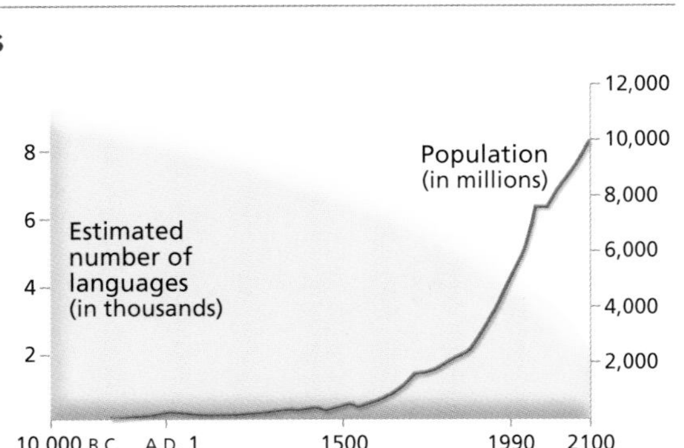
Estimated number of languages (in thousands)
Population (in millions)
8
6
4
2
12,000
10,000
8,000
6,000
4,000
2,000
10,000 B.C.
A.D. 1
1500
1990
2100

Evolution of Languages

Even as many languages have disappeared, a few dominant linguistic groups have spawned numerous related tongues. Thus, the Germanic language, which derived from Proto-Indo-European and was spoken by tribes that settled in northern and western Europe, has diversified into several major languages today.

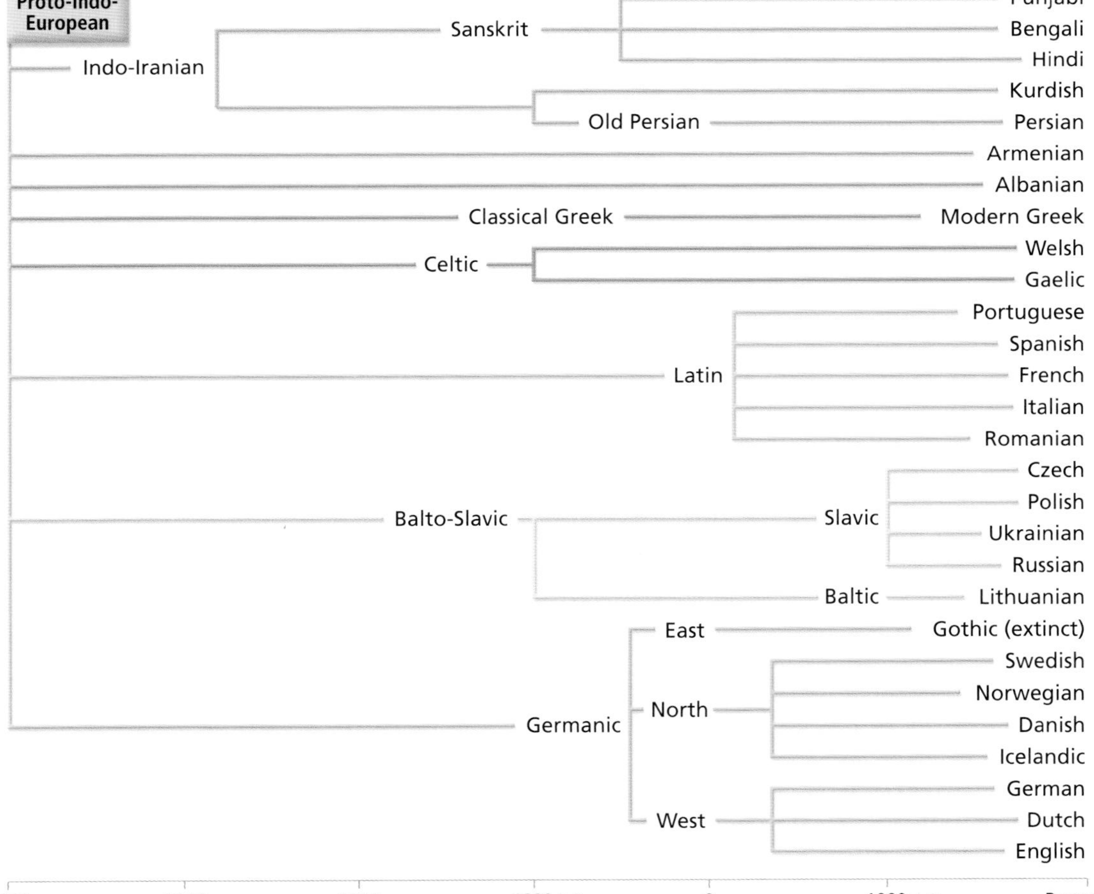
Proto-Indo-European
Indo-Iranian
Sanskrit
Punjabi
Bengali
Hindi
Old Persian
Kurdish
Persian
Armenian
Albanian
Classical Greek
Modern Greek
Celtic
Welsh
Gaelic
Latin
Portuguese
Spanish
French
Italian
Romanian
Balto-Slavic
Slavic
Czech
Polish
Ukrainian
Russian
Baltic
Lithuanian
Germanic
East
Gothic (extinct)
North
Swedish
Norwegian
Danish
Icelandic
West
German
Dutch
English
4000
3000
2000
1000 B.C.
0
1000 A.D.
Present

How Many Speak What?

Languages can paint vivid historical pictures of migration and colonization. English, Spanish, and Portuguese, for example, originated in parts of Europe with only a tenth of China's population and area; yet they rival Mandarin Chinese in total number of speakers. They spread because England, Spain, and Portugal built large overseas empires. India, which has been a part of several empires, currently has 22 official languages (in addition to English) and a population of one billion; only a fifth of its people speak Hindi.

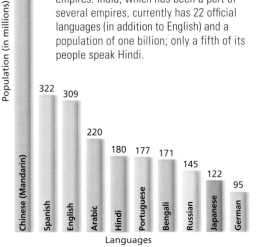

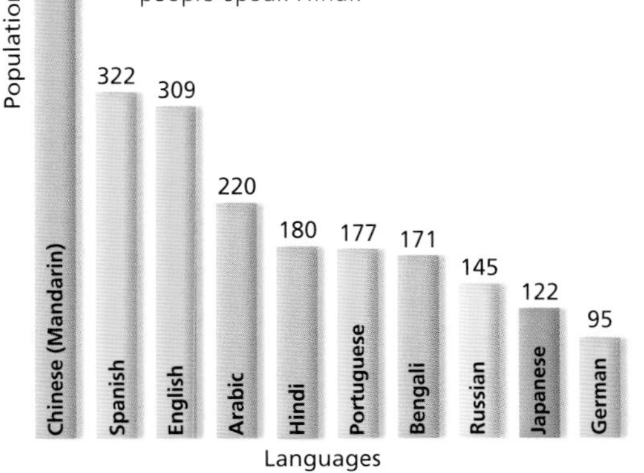
Population (in millions)
873
Chinese (Mandarin)
322
Spanish
309
English
220
Arabic
180
Hindi
177
Portuguese
171
Bengali
145
Russian
122
Japanese
95
German
Languages

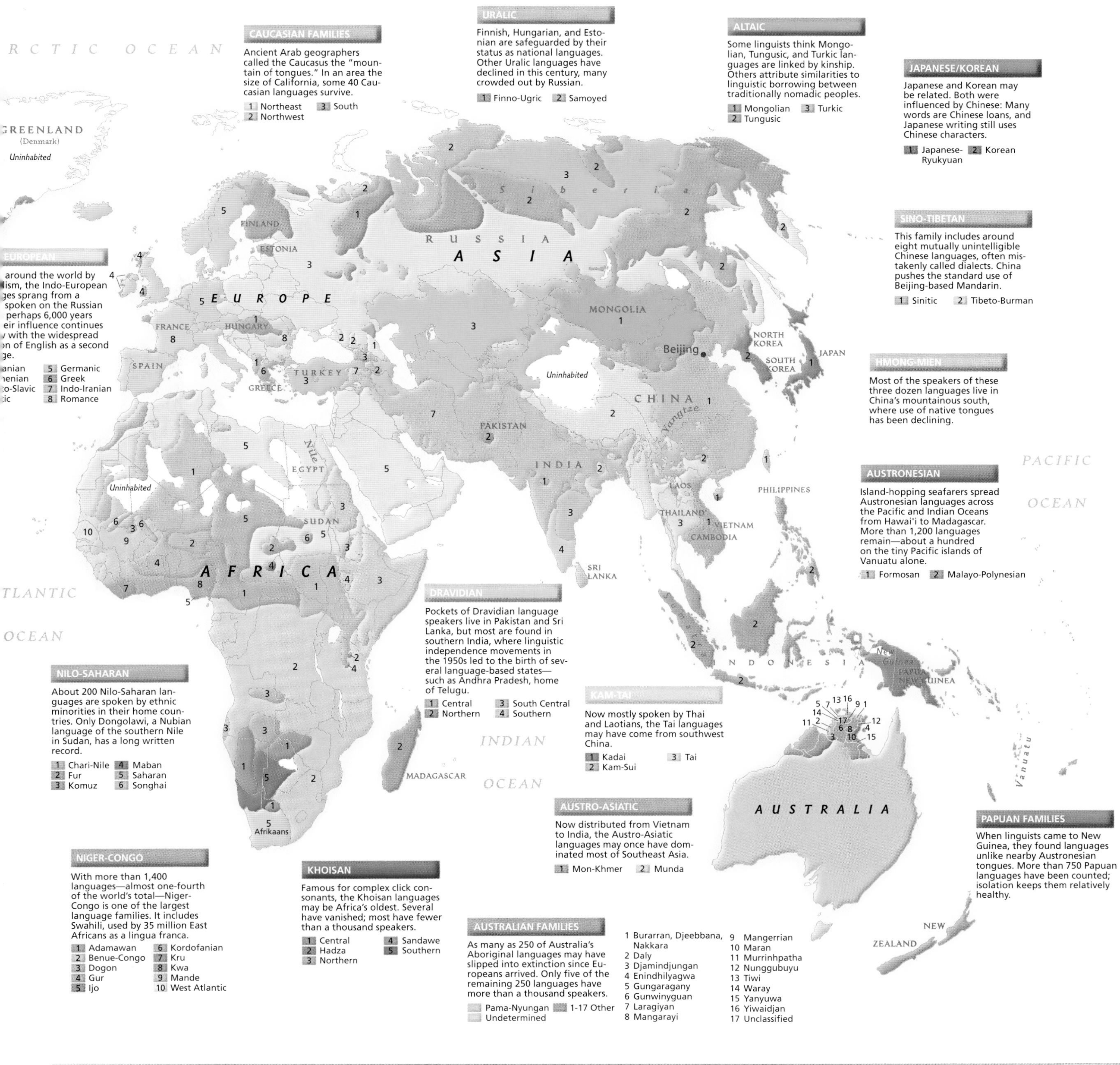

CAUCASIAN FAMILIES
Ancient Arab geographers called the Caucasus the "mountain of tongues." In an area the size of California, some 40 Caucasian languages survive.
1 Northeast 2 Northwest 3 South
URALIC
Finnish, Hungarian, and Estonian are safeguarded by their status as national languages. Other Uralic languages have declined in this century, many crowded out by Russian.
1 Finno-Ugric 2 Samoyed
ALTAIC
Some linguists think Mongolian, Tungusic, and Turkic languages are linked by kinship. Others attribute similarities to linguistic borrowing between traditionally nomadic peoples.
1 Mongolian 2 Tungusic 3 Turkic
JAPANESE/KOREAN
Japanese and Korean may be related. Both were influenced by Chinese: Many words are Chinese loans, and Japanese writing still uses Chinese characters.
1 Japanese-Ryukyuan 2 Korean
SINO-TIBETAN
This family includes around eight mutually unintelligible Chinese languages, often mistakenly called dialects. China pushes the standard use of Beijing-based Mandarin.
1 Sinitic 2 Tibeto-Burman
HMONG-MIEN
Most of the speakers of these three dozen languages live in China's mountainous south, where use of native tongues has been declining.
AUSTRONESIAN
Island-hopping seafarers spread Austronesian languages across the Pacific and Indian Oceans from Hawai'i to Madagascar. More than 1,200 languages remain—about a hundred on the tiny Pacific islands of Vanuatu alone.
1 Formosan 2 Malayo-Polynesian
EUROPEAN
5 Germanic
6 Greek
7 Indo-Iranian
8 Romance
GREENLAND
(Denmark)
Uninhabited
EUROPE
ASIA
RUSSIA
Siberia
FINLAND
ESTONIA
FRANCE
HUNGARY
SPAIN
TURKEY
GREECE
MONGOLIA
NORTH KOREA
SOUTH KOREA
JAPAN
Beijing
CHINA
Yangtze
Uninhabited
PAKISTAN
INDIA
EGYPT
Nile
SUDAN
AFRICA
LAOS
THAILAND
VIETNAM
CAMBODIA
PHILIPPINES
SRI LANKA
Sumatra
INDONESIA
New Guinea
PAPUA NEW GUINEA
PACIFIC OCEAN
ATLANTIC OCEAN
INDIAN OCEAN
MADAGASCAR
Afrikaans
AUSTRALIA
Vanuatu
NEW ZEALAND
DRAVIDIAN
Pockets of Dravidian language speakers live in Pakistan and Sri Lanka, but most are found in southern India, where linguistic independence movements in the 1950s led to the birth of several language-based states—such as Andhra Pradesh, home of Telugu.
1 Central 2 Northern 3 South Central 4 Southern
KAM-TAI
Now mostly spoken by Thai and Laotians, the Tai languages may have come from southwest China.
1 Kadai 2 Kam-Sui 3 Tai
NILO-SAHARAN
About 200 Nilo-Saharan languages are spoken by ethnic minorities in their home countries. Only Dongolawi, a Nubian language of the southern Nile in Sudan, has a long written record.
1 Chari-Nile 2 Fur 3 Komuz 4 Maban 5 Saharan 6 Songhai
AUSTRO-ASIATIC
Now distributed from Vietnam to India, the Austro-Asiatic languages may once have dominated most of Southeast Asia.
1 Mon-Khmer 2 Munda
PAPUAN FAMILIES
When linguists came to New Guinea, they found languages unlike nearby Austronesian tongues. More than 750 Papuan languages have been counted; isolation keeps them relatively healthy.
NIGER-CONGO
With more than 1,400 languages—almost one-fourth of the world's total—Niger-Congo is one of the largest language families. It includes Swahili, used by 35 million East Africans as a lingua franca.
1 Adamawan 2 Benue-Congo 3 Dogon 4 Gur 5 Ijo 6 Kordofanian 7 Kru 8 Kwa 9 Mande 10 West Atlantic
KHOISAN
Famous for complex click consonants, the Khoisan languages may be Africa's oldest. Several have vanished; most have fewer than a thousand speakers.
1 Central 2 Hadza 3 Northern 4 Sandawe 5 Southern
AUSTRALIAN FAMILIES
As many as 250 of Australia's Aboriginal languages may have slipped into extinction since Europeans arrived. Only five of the remaining 250 languages have more than a thousand speakers.
Pama-Nyungan 1-17 Other Undetermined
1 Burarran, Djeebbana, Nakkara
2 Daly
3 Djamindjungan
4 Enindhilyagwa
5 Gungaragany
6 Gunwinyguan
7 Laragiyan
8 Mangarayi
9 Mangerrian
10 Maran
11 Murrinhpatha
12 Nunggubuyu
13 Tiwi
14 Waray
15 Yanyuwa
16 Yiwaidjan
17 Unclassified

Major Language Families Today

Many of the world's languages belong to the Indo-European language group, which is thought to have ancient roots in the Russian Steppes. The map at right illustrates how far members of this group—and others—have spread over the millennia. The map locates languages by territory; it does not indicate the number of speakers. For example, the Altaic group covers a vast area, but it has only about 145 million speakers. Austronesian, on the other hand, is spoken within a much smaller area, but it has 312 million speakers.

Major Language Families Today

- Afro-Asiatic
- Altaic
- Austro-Asiatic
- Austronesian
- Dravidian
- Indo-European
- Japanese/Korean
- Kam-Tai
- Niger-Congo
- Nilo-Saharan
- Sino-Tibetan
- Uralic
- Other

NORTH AMERICA
Toronto
New York
Los Angeles
Mexico City
ATLANTIC OCEAN
PACIFIC OCEAN
SOUTH AMERICA
São Paulo
Buenos Aires
London
Paris
EUROPE
Moscow
ASIA
Beijing
Tokyo
Cairo
AFRICA
Lagos
Mumbai (Bombay)
INDIAN OCEAN
PACIFIC OCEAN
Jakarta
AUSTRALIA
Sydney
ANTARCTICA

THE GREAT POWER OF RELIGION comes from its ability to speak to the heart of individuals and societies. Since earliest human times, honoring nature spirits or the belief in a supreme being has brought comfort and security in the face of fundamental questions of life and death.

Billions of people are now adherents of Hinduism, Buddhism, Judaism, Christianity, and Islam, all of which began in Asia. Universal elements of these faiths include ritual and prayer, sacred sites and pilgrimage, saints and martyrs, ritual clothing and implements, dietary laws and fasting, festivals and holy days, and special ceremonies for life's major moments. Sometimes otherworldly, most religions have moral and ethical guidelines that attempt to make life better on Earth as well. Their tenets and goals are taught not only at the church, synagogue, mosque, or temple but also through schools, storytelling, parables, painting, sculpture, and even dance and drama.

The world's major religions blossomed from the teachings and revelations of individuals who heeded and transmitted the voice of God or discovered a way to salvation that could be understood by others. Abraham and Moses for Jews, the Buddha for Buddhists, Jesus Christ for Christians, and Muhammad for Muslims fulfilled the roles of divine teachers who experienced essential truths of existence.

Throughout history, priests, rabbis, clergymen, and imams have recited, interpreted, and preached the holy words of sacred texts and writings to the faithful. Today the world's religions, with their guidance here on Earth and hopes and promises for the afterlife, continue to exert an extraordinary force on billions of people.

NORTH AMERICA
Toronto
New York
Los Angeles
PACIFIC OCEAN
Mexico City
ATLANTIC OCEAN
SOUTH AMERICA
São Paulo
Buenos Aires
Major Religions
Eastern Orthodox
Protestant
Roman Catholic
Other Christian
Jewish
Shia Muslim
Sunni Muslim
Hindu
Tibetan Buddhist
Southeast Asian Buddhist
East Asian Buddhist, Confucianist, Shintoist
East Asian Buddhist, Confucianist, Daoist
Sikh
Indigenous

BUDDHISM
Founded about 2,500 years ago by Shakyamuni Buddha (or Gautama Buddha), Buddhism teaches liberation from suffering through the threefold cultivation of morality, meditation, and wisdom. Buddhists revere the Three Jewels: Buddha (the Awakened One), Dharma (the Truth), and Sangha (the community of monks and nuns).

CHRISTIANITY
Christian belief in eternal life is based on the example of Jesus Christ, a Jew born some 2,000 years ago. The New Testament tells of his teaching, persecution, crucifixion, and resurrection. Today Christianity is found around the world in three main forms: Roman Catholicism, Eastern Orthodox, and Protestantism.

HINDUISM
Hinduism began in India more than 4,000 years ago and is still flourishing. Sacred texts known as the Vedas form the basis of Hindu faith and ritual

Adherents Worldwide

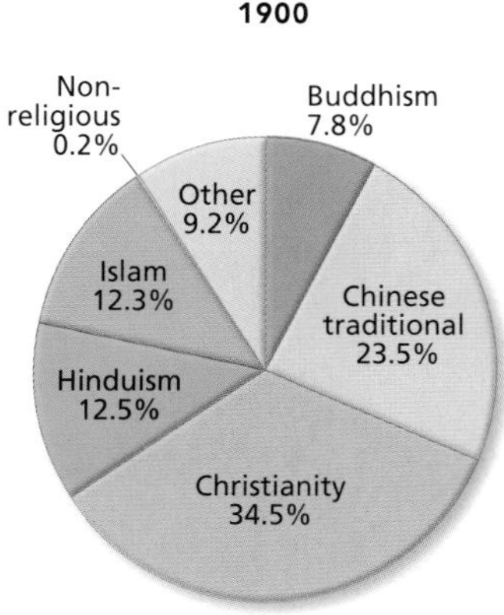
1900
Non-religious 0.2%
Buddhism 7.8%
Other 9.2%
Islam 12.3%
Chinese traditional 23.5%
Hinduism 12.5%
Christianity 34.5%

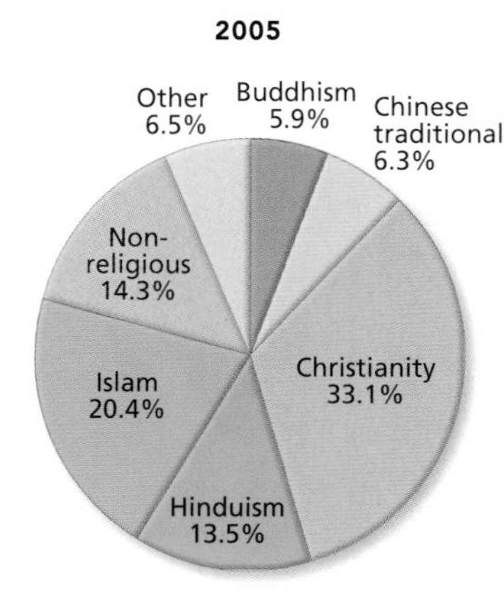
2005
Other 6.5%
Buddhism 5.9%
Chinese traditional 6.3%
Non-religious 14.3%
Islam 20.4%
Christianity 33.1%
Hinduism 13.5%

The growth of Islam and the decline of Chinese traditional religion stand out as significant changes over the past hundred years. Christianity, the largest of the world's main faiths, has remained fairly stable in its number of adherents. Today more than one in six people claim to be atheistic or nonreligious.

Adherents by Continent

In terms of the total number of religious adherents, Asia ranks first. This is not only because half the world's people live on that continent, but also because three of the five major faiths are practiced there: Hinduism in South Asia; Buddhism in East and Southeast Asia; and Islam from Indonesia to the Central Asian republics to Turkey. Oceania, Europe, North America, and South America are overwhelmingly Christian. Africa, with many millions of Muslims and Christians,also retains large numbers of animists.

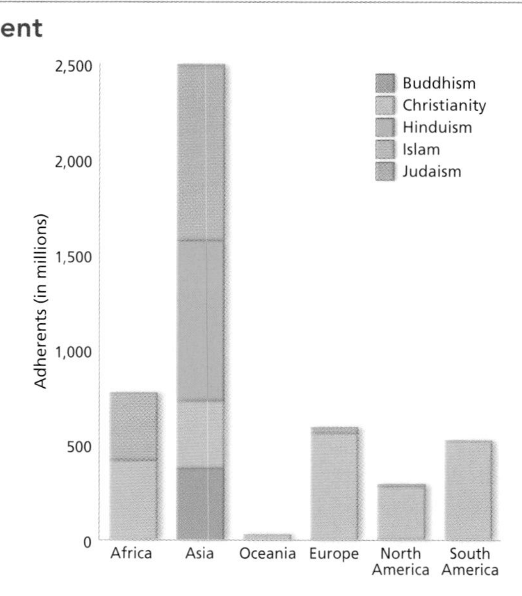
Adherents (in millions)
2,500
2,000
1,500
1,000
500
0
Africa
Asia
Oceania
Europe
North America
South America
Buddhism
Christianity
Hinduism
Islam
Judaism

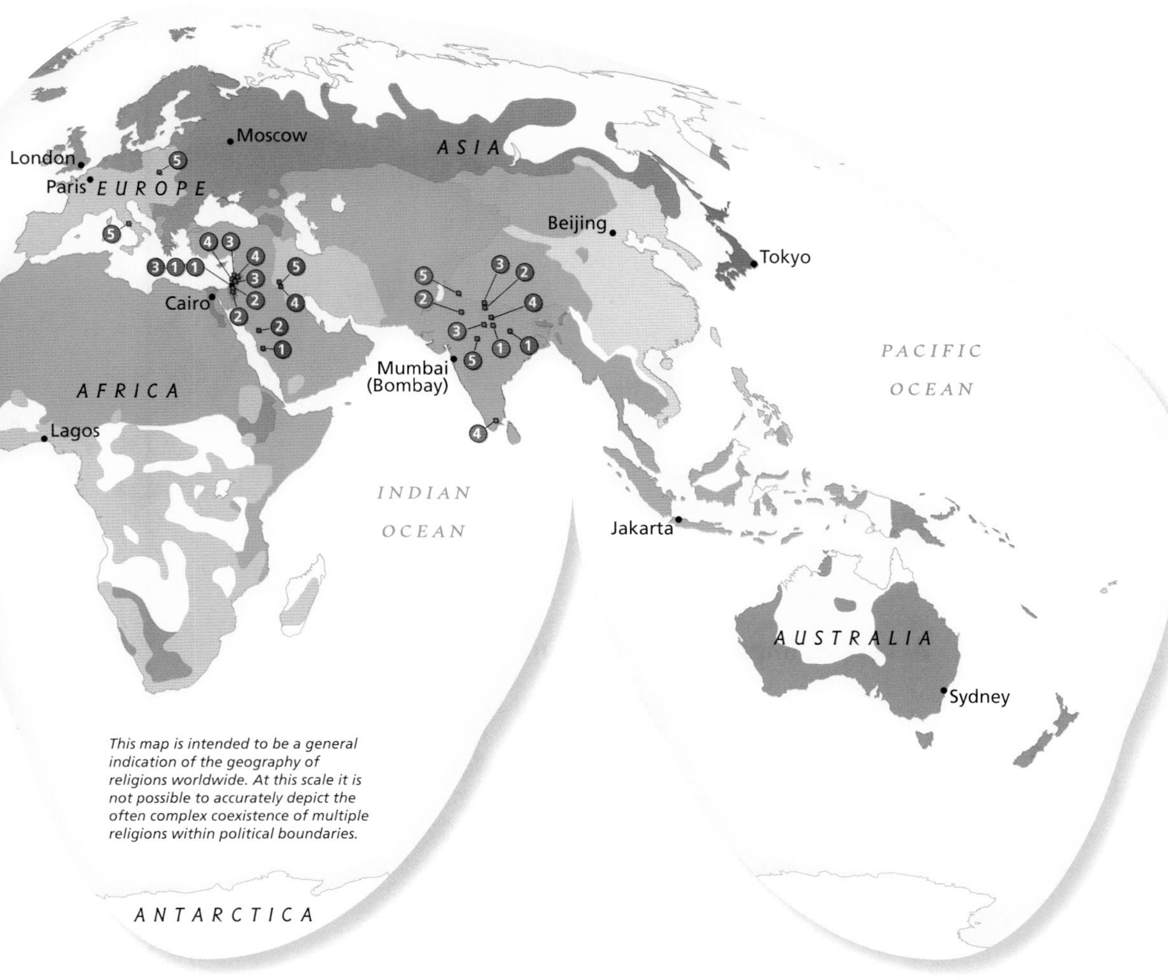
London
Paris
EUROPE
Moscow
ASIA
Beijing
Tokyo
Cairo
AFRICA
Lagos
Mumbai (Bombay)
PACIFIC OCEAN
INDIAN OCEAN
Jakarta
AUSTRALIA
Sydney
ANTARCTICA
This map is intended to be a general indication of the geography of religions worldwide. At this scale it is not possible to accurately depict the often complex coexistence of multiple religions within political boundaries.

Sacred Places

BUDDHISM
1. Bodhgaya: Where Buddha attained awakening
2. Kusinagara: Where Buddha entered nirvana
3. Lumbini: Place of Buddha's last human birth
4. Sarnath: Place where Buddha delivered his first sermon
5. Sanchi: Location of famous stupa containing relics of Buddha

CHRISTIANITY
1. Jerusalem: Church of the Holy Sepulchre, Jesus's crucifixion
2. Bethlehem: Jesus's birthplace
3. Nazareth: Where Jesus grew up
4. Shore of the Sea of Galilee: Where Jesus gave the Sermon on the Mount
5. Rome and the Vatican: Tombs of St. Peter and St. Paul

HINDUISM
1. Varanasi (Banaras): Most holy Hindu site, home of Shiva
2. Vrindavan: Krishna's birthplace
3. Allahabad: At confluence of Ganges and Yamuna rivers, purest place to bathe
4. Madurai: Temple of Minakshi, great goddess of the south
5. Badrinath: Vishnu's shrine

ISLAM
1. Mecca: Muhammad's birthplace
2. Medina: City of Muhammad's flight, or hegira
3. Jerusalem: Dome of the Rock, Muhammad's stepping-stone to heaven
4. Najaf (Shiite): Tomb of Imam Ali
5. Kerbala (Shiite): Tomb of Imam Hoseyn

JUDAISM
1. Jerusalem: Location of the Western Wall and first and second temples
2. Hebron: Tomb of the patriarchs and their wives
3. Safed: Where Kabbalah (Jewish mysticism) flourished
4. Tiberias: Where Talmud (source of Jewish law) first composed
5. Auschwitz: Symbol of six million Jews who perished in the Holocaust

ıe main trinity of gods com-ˈises Brahma the creator, ishnu the preserver, and ıiva the destroyer. Hindus ɜlieve in reincarnation.

ISLAM
Muslims believe that the Koran, Islam's sacred book, accurately records the spoken word of God (Allah) as revealed to the Prophet Muhammad, born in Mecca around A.D. 570. Strict adherents pray five times a day, fast during the holy month of Ramadan, and make at least one pilgrimage to Mecca, Islam's holiest city.

JUDAISM
The 4,000-year-old religion of the Jews stands as the oldest of the major faiths that believe in a single god. Judaism's traditions, customs, laws, and beliefs date back to Abraham, the founder, and to the Torah, the first five books of the Old Testament, believed to have been handed down to Moses on Mount Sinai.

Adherents by Country

COUNTRIES WITH THE MOST BUDDHISTS

COUNTRY	BUDDHISTS
1. China	111,359,000
2. Japan	70,723,000
3. Thailand	53,294,000
4. Vietnam	40,781,000
5. Myanmar	37,152,000
6. Sri Lanka	13,235,000
7. Cambodia	12,698,000
8. India	7,597,000
9. South Korea	7,281,000
10. Taiwan*	4,823,000

COUNTRIES WITH THE MOST CHRISTIANS

COUNTRY	CHRISTIANS
1. United States	252,394,000
2. Brazil	166,847,000
3. China	110,956,000
4. Mexico	102,012,000
5. Russia	84,495,000
6. Philippines	73,987,000
7. India	68,190,000
8. Germany	61,833,000
9. Nigeria	61,438,000
10. Congo, Dem. Rep.	53,371,000

COUNTRIES WITH THE MOST HINDUS

COUNTRY	HINDUS
1. India	810,387,000
2. Nepal	19,020,000
3. Bangladesh	17,029,000
4. Indonesia	7,633,000
5. Sri Lanka	2,173,000
6. Pakistan	2,100,000
7. Malaysia	1,855,000
8. United States	1,144,000
9. South Africa	1,079,000
10. Myanmar	1,007,000

COUNTRIES WITH THE MOST MUSLIMS

COUNTRY	MUSLIMS
1. Indonesia	171,569,000
2. Pakistan	154,563,000
3. India	134,150,000
4. Bangladesh	132,868,000
5. Turkey	71,323,000
6. Iran	67,724,000
7. Egypt	63,503,000
8. Nigeria	54,666,000
9. Algeria	31,859,000
10. Morocco	31,001,000

COUNTRIES WITH THE MOST JEWS

COUNTRY	JEWS
1. United States	5,764,000
2. Israel	4,772,000
3. France	607,000
4. Argentina	520,000
5. Palestine*	451,000
6. Canada	414,000
7. Brazil	384,000
8. United Kingdom	312,000
9. Russia	245,000
10. Germany	226,000

**Non-sovereign nation*

All figures are estimates based on data for the year 2005.
Countries with the highest reported nonreligious populations include China, Russia, United States, Germany, India, Japan, North Korea, Vietnam, France, and Italy.

IN THE PAST 50 YEARS, health conditions have improved dramatically. With better economic and living conditions and access to immunization and other basic health services, global life expectancy has risen from 40 to 65 years; the death rate for children under five years old has fallen by half; and diseases that once killed and disabled millions have been eradicated, eliminated, or greatly reduced in impact. Today, fully three-quarters of the world's children benefit from protection against six infectious diseases that were responsible in the past for many millions of infant and child deaths.

Current efforts to improve health face new and daunting challenges, however. Infant and child mortality from infectious diseases remains relatively high in many poor countries. Each year, more than ten million children under five years old die—41 percent of them in sub-Saharan Africa and 34 percent in South Asia. Improvement in children's health has slowed dramatically in the past 20 years, particularly where child death rates have historically been highest.

The HIV/AIDS pandemic has erased decades of steady improvements in sub-Saharan Africa. An estimated 25 million people are HIV-positive in Africa alone—and AIDS is taking a toll in India, China, and Eastern Europe. The death toll in Africa is contributing to reversals in life expectancy—just 47 years instead of the estimated 62 years without AIDS. An estimated 15 million children have lost one or both their parents to the disease.

Vast gaps in health outcomes between rich and poor persist. About 99 percent of global childhood deaths occur in poor countries, with the poorest within those countries having the highest child-mortality rates. In Indonesia, for example, a child born in a poor household is four times as likely to die by her fifth birthday than a child born to a well-off family.

In many high- and middle-income countries, chronic, lifestyle-related diseases such as cardiovascular disease, diabetes, and others are becoming the predominant cause of disability and death. Because the focus of policymakers has been on treatment rather than prevention, the costs of dealing with these ailments contributes to high (and rapidly increasing) health-care spending. Tobacco-related illnesses are major problems worldwide. In developed countries, smoking is the cause of more than one-third of male deaths in middle age, and about one in eight female deaths. It is estimated that due to trends of increasing tobacco use, of all the people aged under 20 alive today in China, 50 million will die prematurely from tobacco.

Health-Care Availability

Regional differences in health-care resources are striking. While countries in Europe and the Americas have relatively large numbers of physicians and nurses, nations with far higher burdens of disease (particularly African countries) are experiencing severe deficits in both health workers and health facilities.

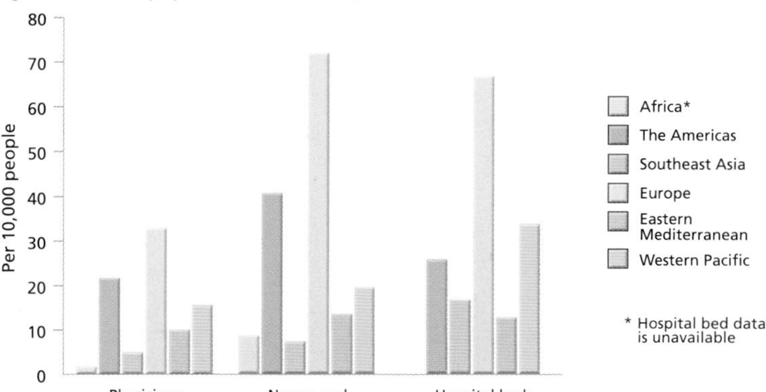
Per 10,000 people
0
10
20
30
40
50
60
70
80
Physicians
Nurses and midwives
Hospital beds
Africa*
The Americas
Southeast Asia
Europe
Eastern Mediterranean
Western Pacific
* Hospital bed data is unavailable

Income Levels: Indicators of Health and Literacy

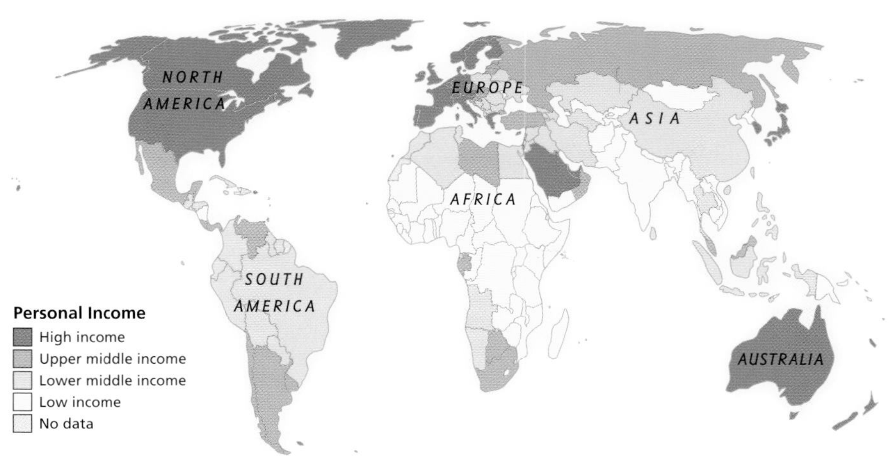
NORTH AMERICA
EUROPE
ASIA
AFRICA
SOUTH AMERICA
AUSTRALIA
Personal Income
High income
Upper middle income
Lower middle income
Low income
No data

Access to Improved Sanitation

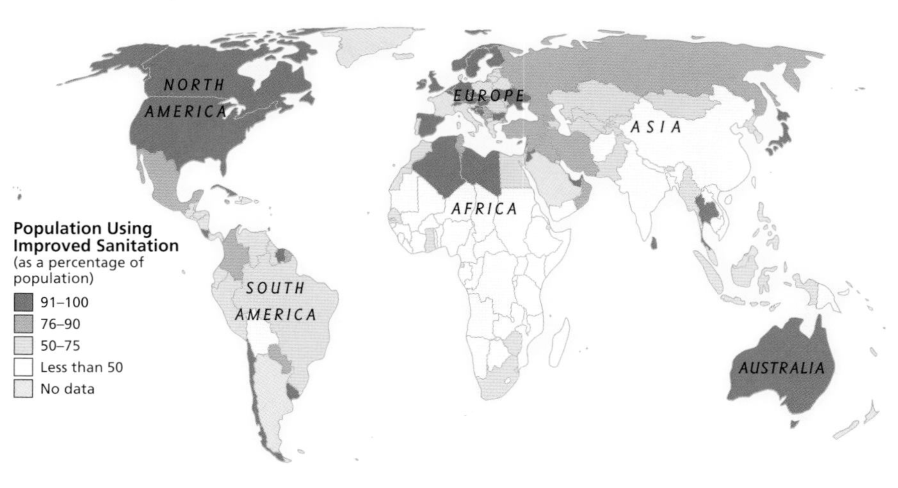
NORTH AMERICA
EUROPE
ASIA
AFRICA
SOUTH AMERICA
AUSTRALIA
Population Using Improved Sanitation
(as a percentage of population)
91–100
76–90
50–75
Less than 50
No data

Nutrition

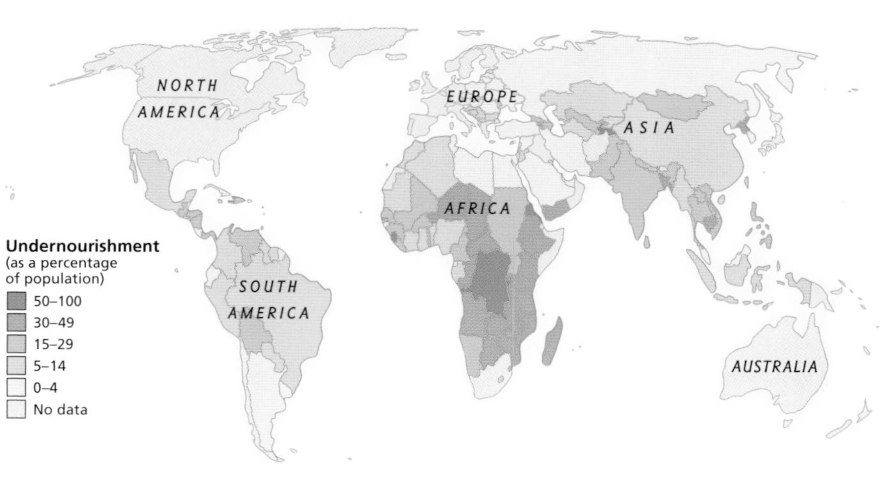
NORTH AMERICA
EUROPE
ASIA
AFRICA
SOUTH AMERICA
AUSTRALIA
Undernourishment
(as a percentage of population)
50–100
30–49
15–29
5–14
0–4
No data

HIV

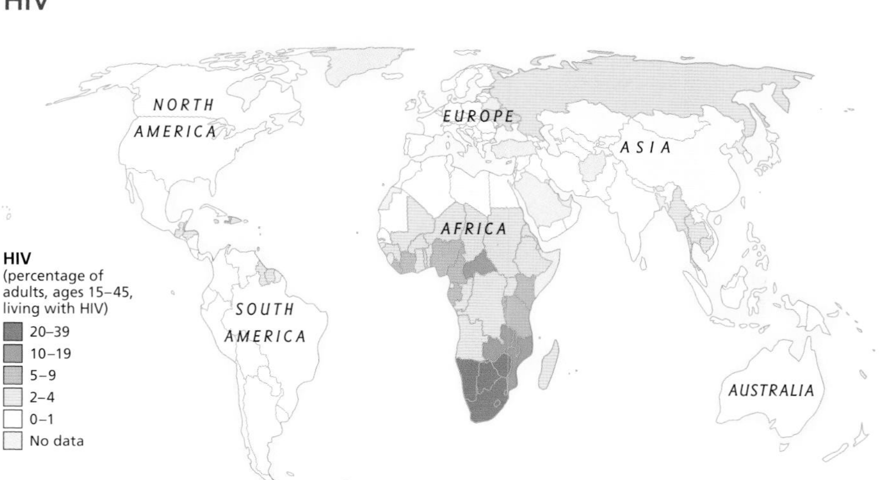
NORTH AMERICA
EUROPE
ASIA
AFRICA
SOUTH AMERICA
AUSTRALIA
HIV
(percentage of adults, ages 15–45, living with HIV)
20–39
10–19
5–9
2–4
0–1
No data

Global Disease Burden

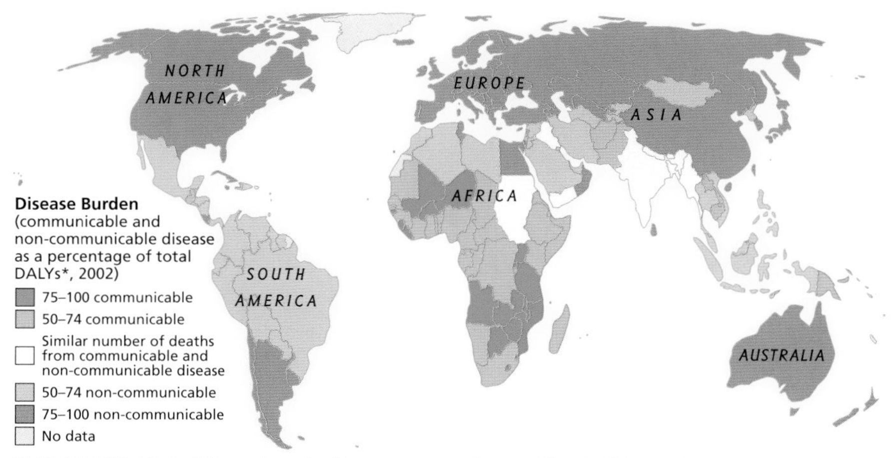
NORTH AMERICA
EUROPE
ASIA
AFRICA
SOUTH AMERICA
AUSTRALIA
Disease Burden (communicable and non-communicable disease as a percentage of total DALYs*, 2002)
75–100 communicable
50–74 communicable
Similar number of deaths from communicable and non-communicable disease
50–74 non-communicable
75–100 non-communicable
No data

*DALYs (disability adjusted life years) are a health gap measure used to quantify potential years of life lost to illness or premature death. One DALY can be thought of as one lost year of "healthy" life.

While infectious and parasitic diseases account for nearly one-quarter of total deaths in developing countries, they result in relatively few deaths in wealthier nations. In contrast, cardiovascular diseases and cancer are more significant causes of death in industrialized countries. Over time, as fertility rates fall, social and living conditions improve, the population ages, and further advances are made against infectious diseases in poorer countries, the distribution of causes of death between developed and developing nations may converge.

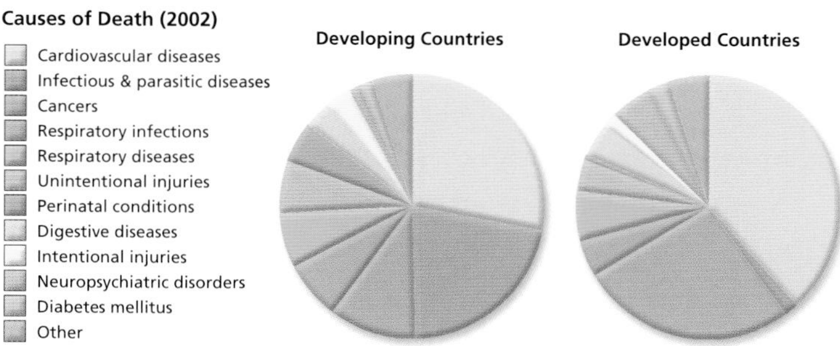
Causes of Death (2002)
Cardiovascular diseases
Infectious & parasitic diseases
Cancers
Respiratory infections
Respiratory diseases
Unintentional injuries
Perinatal conditions
Digestive diseases
Intentional injuries
Neuropsychiatric disorders
Diabetes mellitus
Other
Developing Countries
Developed Countries

Under-Five Mortality

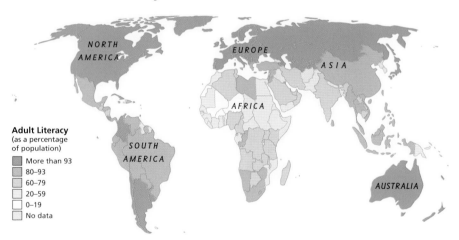

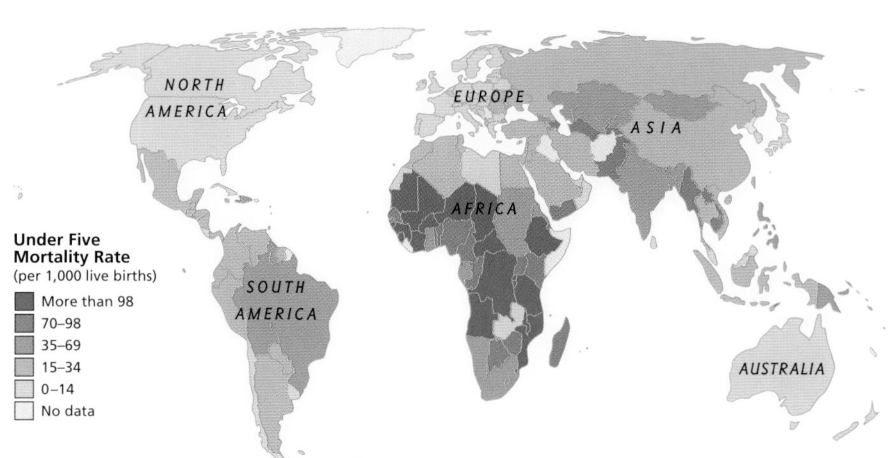
NORTH AMERICA
EUROPE
ASIA
AFRICA
SOUTH AMERICA
AUSTRALIA
Under Five Mortality Rate (per 1,000 live births)
More than 98
70–98
35–69
15–34
0–14
No data

Maternal Mortality

MATERNAL MORTALITY RATIO PER 100,000 LIVE BIRTHS*

COUNTRIES WITH THE HIGHEST MATERNAL MORTALITY RATES:

1.	Sierra Leone	2,000
2.	Malawi	1,800
3.	Angola	1,700
4.	Niger	1,600
5.	Tanzania	1,500
6.	Rwanda	1,400
7.	Mali	1,200
8.	Zimbabwe	1,100
9.	Central African Republic	1,100
10.	Guinea-Bissau	1,100

COUNTRIES WITH THE LOWEST MATERNAL MORTALITY RATES:

1.	Iceland	0
2.	Sweden	2
3.	Slovakia	3
4.	Spain	4
5.	Austria	4
6.	Kuwait	5
7.	Portugal	5
8.	Italy	5
9.	Denmark	5
10.	Ireland	5

Adjusted for underreporting and misclassification

Education and Literacy

NORTH AMERICA
EUROPE
ASIA
AFRICA
SOUTH AMERICA
AUSTRALIA

Adult Literacy
(as a percentage of population)
- More than 93
- 80–93
- 60–79
- 20–59
- 0–19
- No data

Basic education is an investment for the long-term prosperity of a nation, generating individual, household, and social benefits. Some countries (e.g., Eastern and Western Europe, the U.S.) have long traditions of high educational attainment among both genders, and now have well-educated populations of all ages. In contrast, many low-income countries have only recently expanded access to primary education; girls still lag behind boys in enrollment and completion of primary school, and then in making the transition to secondary school. These countries will have to wait many years before most individuals in the productive ages have even minimal levels of reading, writing, and basic arithmetic skills.

The expansion of secondary schooling tends to lag even further behind, so countries with low educational attainment will likely be at a disadvantage for at least a generation. Although no one doubts that the key to long-term economic growth and poverty reduction lies in greater education opportunities for all, many poor countries face the tremendous challenge of paying for schools and teachers today, while having to wait 20 years for the economic returns to those investments.

School Enrollment for Girls

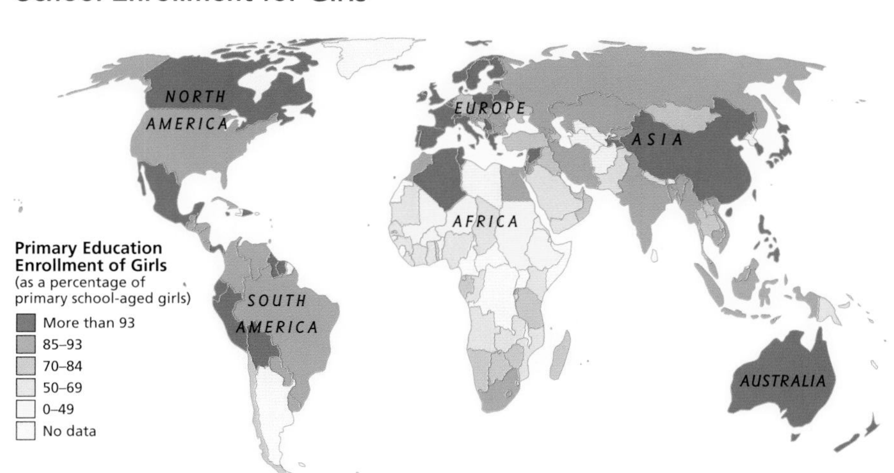
NORTH AMERICA
EUROPE
ASIA
AFRICA
SOUTH AMERICA
AUSTRALIA
Primary Education Enrollment of Girls (as a percentage of primary school-aged girls)
More than 93
85–93
70–84
50–69
0–49
No data

Developing Human Capital

In the pyramids below, more red and blue in the bars indicates a higher level of educational attainment, or "human capital," which contributes greatly to a country's ability for future economic growth. These two countries are similar in population size, but their human capital measures are significantly different.

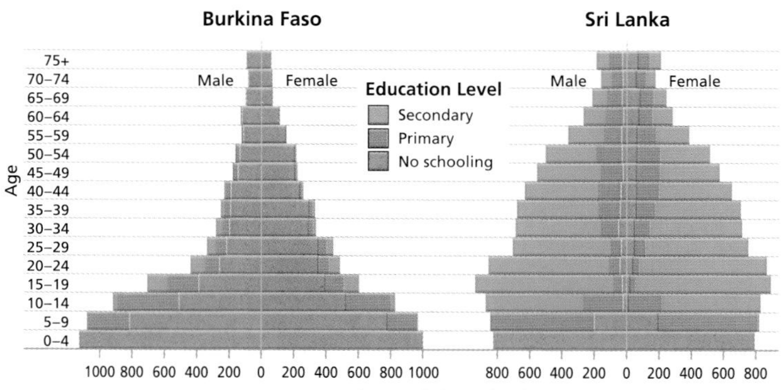
Burkina Faso
Sri Lanka
Male
Female
Education Level
Secondary
Primary
No schooling
Age
75+
70–74
65–69
60–64
55–59
50–54
45–49
40–44
35–39
30–34
25–29
20–24
15–19
10–14
5–9
0–4
1000 800 600 400 200 0 200 400 600 800 1000
800 600 400 200 0 200 400 600 800
Thousands (2000 data)

POLITICAL VIOLENCE, WAR, AND TERROR continue to plague many areas of the world in the early 21st century, despite dramatic decreases in major armed conflict since 1991. The 20th century is often described as the century of "total war" as modern weapons technologies made every facet of society a potential target in warfare. The globe was rocked by two world wars, self-determination wars in developing countries, and the threat of nuclear annihilation during the Cold War. Whereas the first half of the century was torn by interstate wars among the most powerful states, the latter half was consumed by protracted civil wars in the weakest states. The end of the Cold War emboldened international engagement, and concerted efforts toward peace had reduced armed conflicts more than half by early 2006.

While long-standing wars still smolder in Africa and Asia in the early 21st century, global apprehension is riveted on super-powerful states, super-empowered individuals, and the proliferation of "weapons of mass disruption." Globalization is both bringing people closer together and making us ever more vulnerable. Though violence is generally subsiding and democracy spreading, tensions appear to be increasing across the world's oil-producing regions. A little-understood "war on terror" punctuates the hard-won peace and prods us toward an uncertain future. Prospects for an ever more peaceful world are good, yet much work remains.

Political Violence

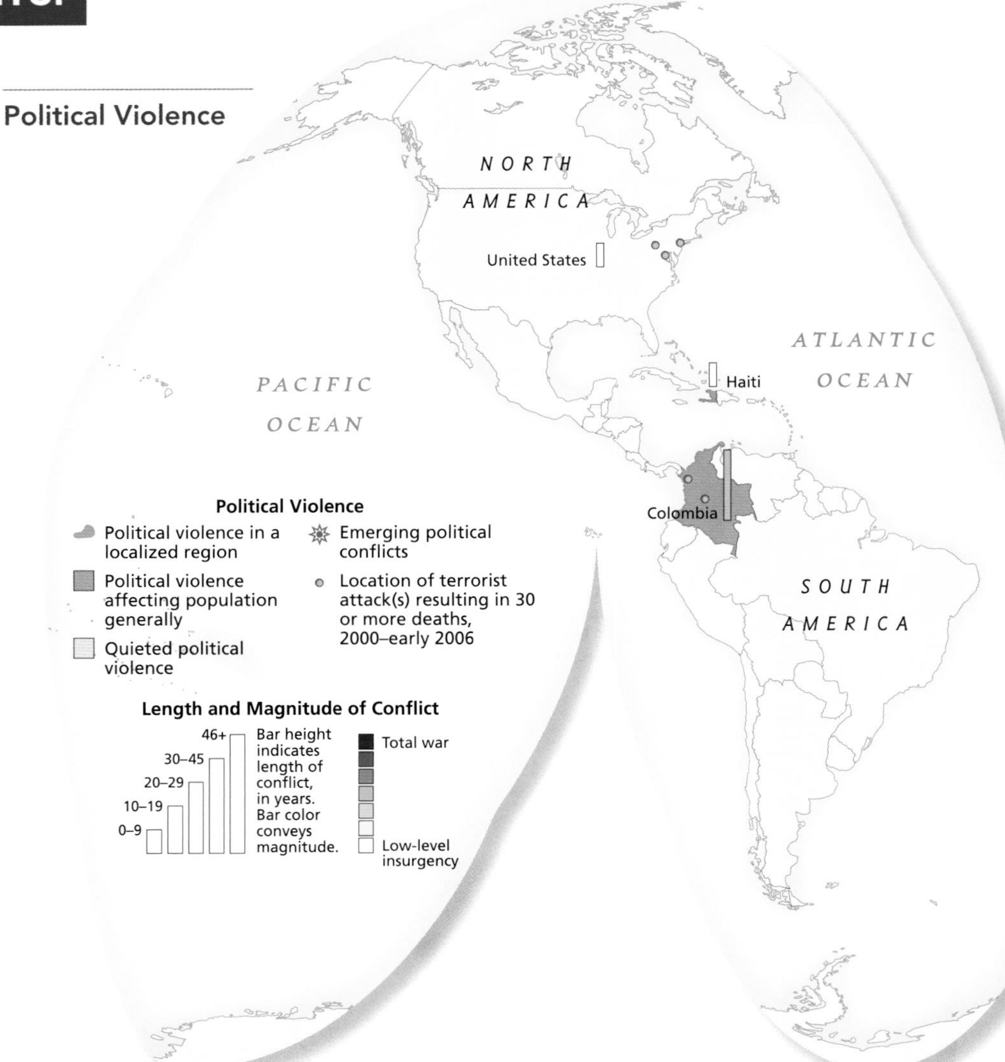

NORTH AMERICA
United States
PACIFIC OCEAN
ATLANTIC OCEAN
Haiti
Colombia
SOUTH AMERICA
Political Violence
Political violence in a localized region
Political violence affecting population generally
Quieted political violence
Emerging political conflicts
Location of terrorist attack(s) resulting in 30 or more deaths, 2000–early 2006
Length and Magnitude of Conflict
46+
30–45
20–29
10–19
0–9
Bar height indicates length of conflict, in years. Bar color conveys magnitude.
Total war
Low-level insurgency

Peace-Building Capacities

The quality of a government's response to rising tensions is the most crucial factor in the management of political conflict. "Peace-building capacity" gauges a country's ability to manage emerging conflicts successfully and avoid outbreaks of serious violence. This capacity is greatest when a government provides reasonable levels of human security; does not condone policies of political or economic discrimination; has a successful track record of managing self-determination movements; maintains stable, democratic institutions; has attained substantial human and material resources; and is free of serious threats from neighboring countries. Peace-building capacities have generally improved since the end of the Cold War; they remain weakest in African and Muslim countries.

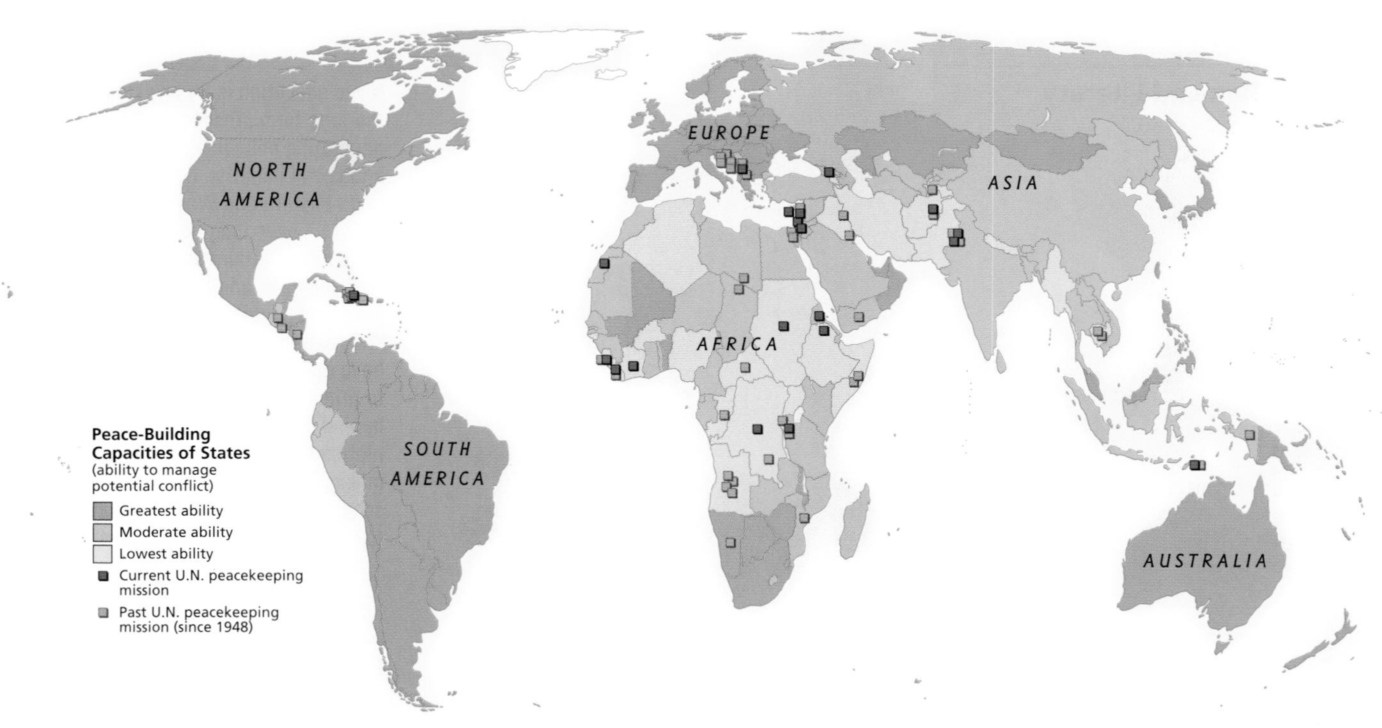

NORTH AMERICA
EUROPE
ASIA
AFRICA
SOUTH AMERICA
AUSTRALIA
Peace-Building Capacities of States (ability to manage potential conflict)
Greatest ability
Moderate ability
Lowest ability
Current U.N. peacekeeping mission
Past U.N. peacekeeping mission (since 1948)

Change in Magnitude of Ongoing Conflicts

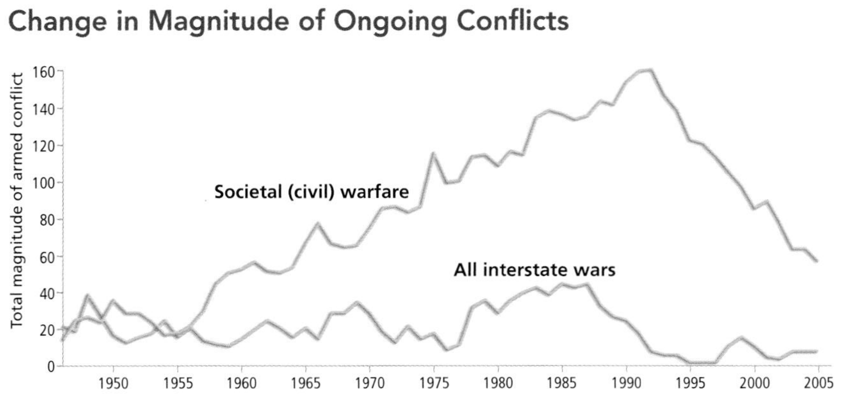

Total magnitude of armed conflict
160
140
120
100
80
60
40
20
0
Societal (civil) warfare
All interstate wars
1950
1955
1960
1965
1970
1975
1980
1985
1990
1995
2000
2005

Global Regimes by Type

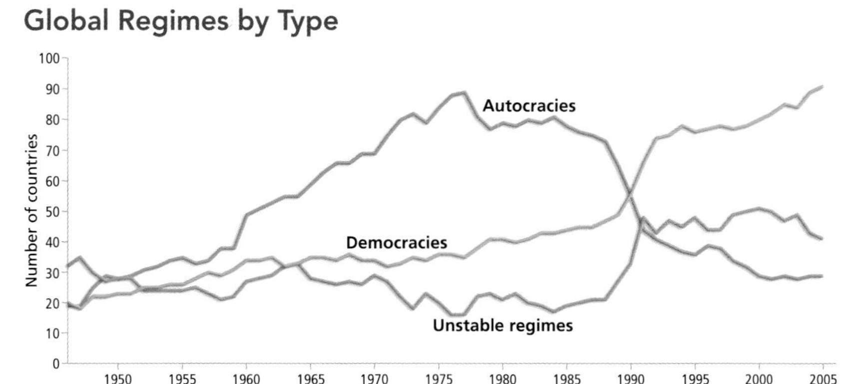

Number of countries
100
90
80
70
60
50
40
30
20
10
0
Autocracies
Democracies
Unstable regimes
1950
1955
1960
1965
1970
1975
1980
1985
1990
1995
2000
2005

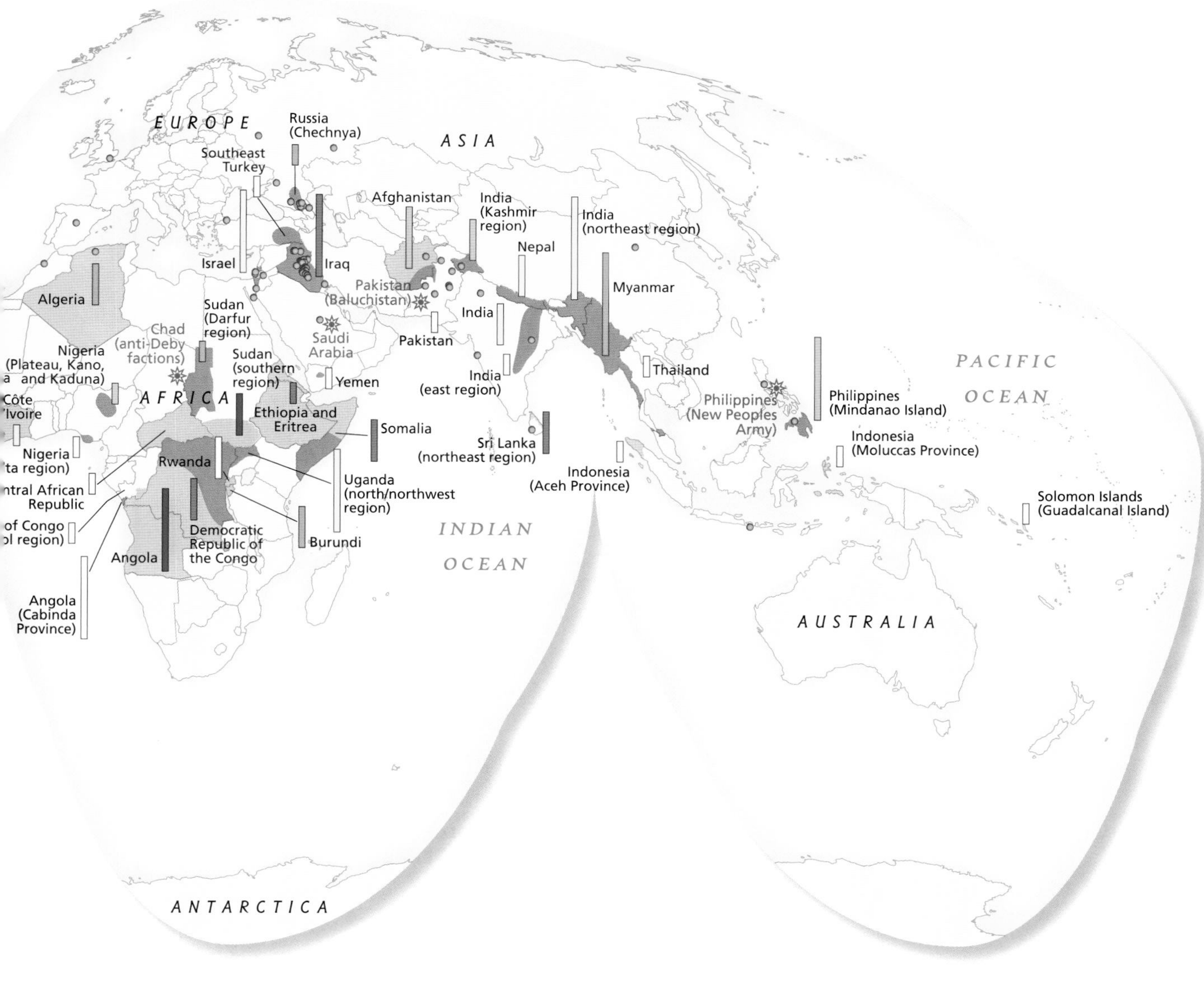
EUROPE
Russia (Chechnya)
ASIA
Southeast Turkey
Afghanistan
India (Kashmir region)
India (northeast region)
Nepal
Israel
Iraq
Algeria
Pakistan (Baluchistan)
Myanmar
Sudan (Darfur region)
Chad (anti-Deby factions)
Saudi Arabia
India
Pakistan
Nigeria (Plateau, Kano, and Kaduna)
Sudan (southern region)
Yemen
India (east region)
Thailand
PACIFIC OCEAN
AFRICA
Ethiopia and Eritrea
Philippines (New Peoples Army)
Philippines (Mindanao Island)
Somalia
Sri Lanka (northeast region)
Indonesia (Moluccas Province)
Rwanda
Uganda (north/northwest region)
Indonesia (Aceh Province)
Solomon Islands (Guadalcanal Island)
Democratic Republic of the Congo
Burundi
INDIAN OCEAN
Angola
Angola (Cabinda Province)
AUSTRALIA
ANTARCTICA

Terrorist Attacks

"Terrorism" has a special connotation with violent attacks on civilians. The vast majority of such attacks are domestic. "International terrorism" is a special subset of attacks linked to globalization in which militants go abroad to strike their targets, select domestic targets linked to a foreign state, or attack international transports such as planes or ships. The numbers of victims are quite low compared with other forms of violence and terrorism but have doubled since the dramatic 9/11 attacks on the United States.

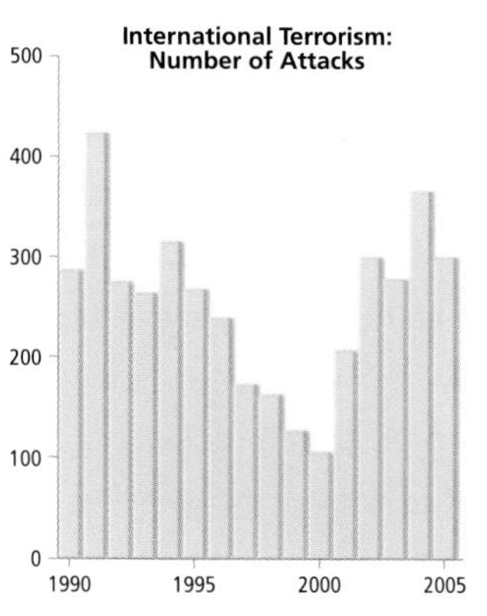
International Terrorism: Number of Attacks
500
400
300
200
100
0
1990
1995
2000
2005

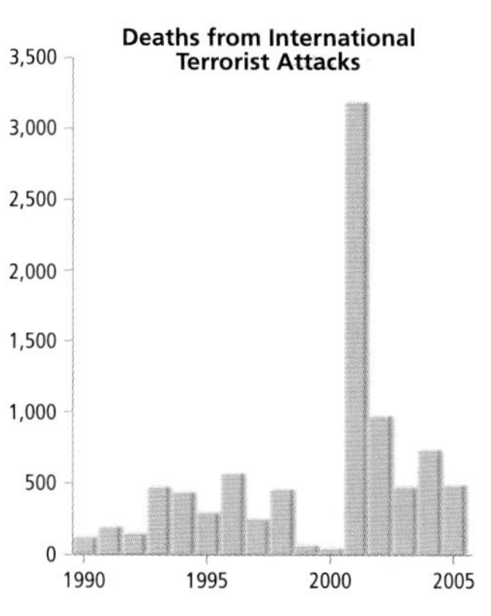
Deaths from International Terrorist Attacks
3,500
3,000
2,500
2,000
1,500
1,000
500
0
1990
1995
2000
2005

Genocides and Politicides Since 1955

Our worst fears are realized when governments are directly involved in killing their own, unarmed citizens. Lethal repression is most often associated with autocratic regimes; its most extreme forms are termed genocide and politicide. These policies involve the intentional destruction, in whole or in part, of a communal or ethnic group (genocide) or opposition group (politicide). "Death squads" and "ethnic cleansing" have brutalized populations in 29 countries at various times since 1955.

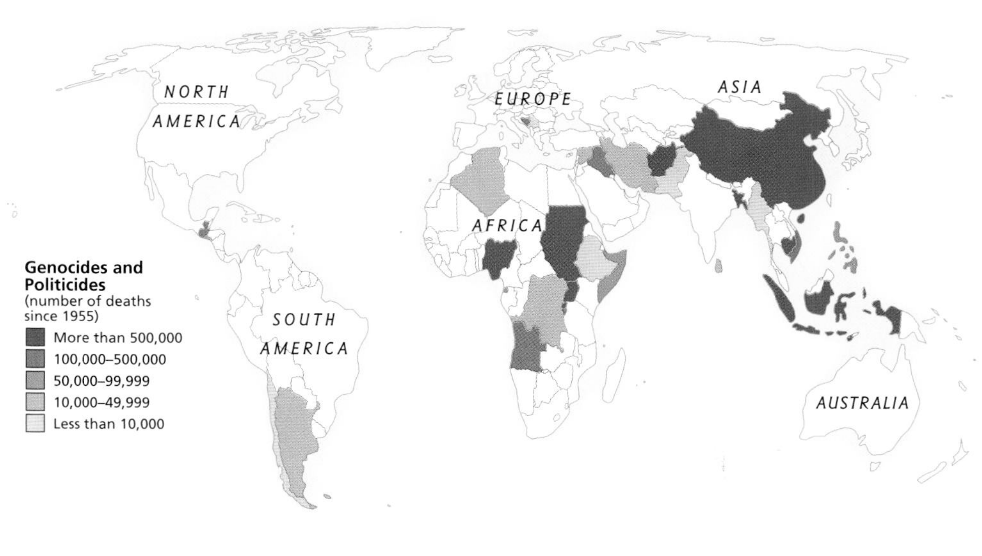
NORTH AMERICA
EUROPE
ASIA
AFRICA
SOUTH AMERICA
AUSTRALIA
Genocides and Politicides
(number of deaths since 1955)
More than 500,000
100,000–500,000
50,000–99,999
10,000–49,999
Less than 10,000

Weapons Possessions

	Nuclear: Declared stockpile	Nuclear: Suspected or undeclared program	Chemical: Declared stockpile now being destroyed	Chemical: Undeclared stockpile or development program	Biological: Suspected offensive development program
Albania			●		
China	●			●	●
Egypt				●	●
France	●				
India	●		●		
Iran		●		●	●
Israel	●			●	●
Libya			●		
North Korea		●		●	●
Pakistan	●				
Russia	●		●		●
South Korea			●		
Syria				●	●
United Kingdom	●				
United States	●		●		

The proliferation of weapons of mass destruction (WMD) is a principal concern in the 21st century. State weakness and official corruption increase the possibilities that these modern technologies might fall into the wrong hands and be a source of terror, extortion, or war.

Refugees

Refugees are persons who have fled their country of origin due to fear of persecution for reasons of, for example, race, religion, or political opinion. IDPs (internally displaced persons) are often displaced for the same reasons as refugees, but they still reside in their country of origin. By the end of 2004, the global number of refugees was 9.2 million persons. The most recent estimate of IDPs worldwide (December 2005) was just under 24 million.

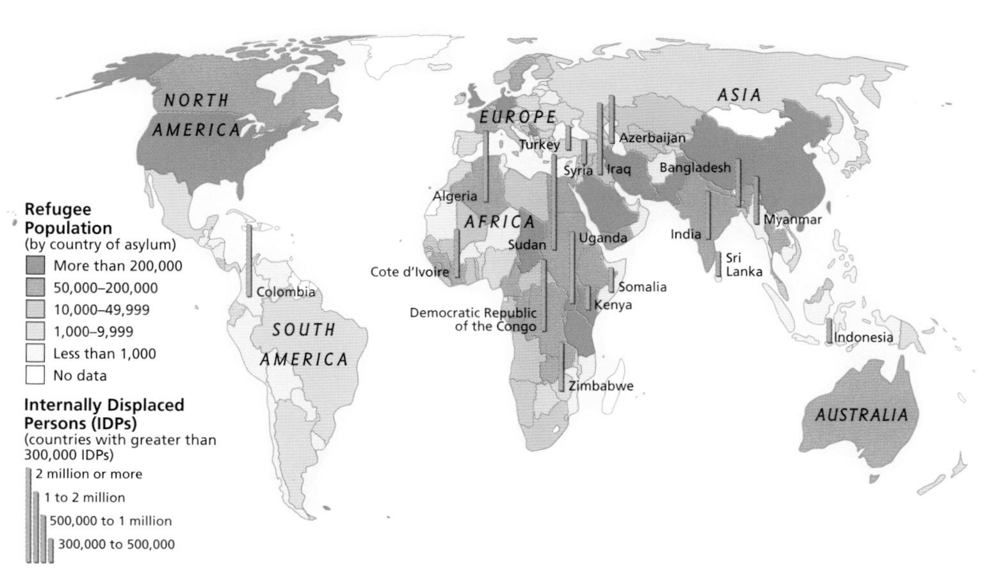
NORTH AMERICA
EUROPE
ASIA
Turkey
Azerbaijan
Syria
Iraq
Bangladesh
Algeria
AFRICA
Myanmar
Sudan
Uganda
India
Cote d'Ivoire
Sri Lanka
Colombia
Somalia
Kenya
Democratic Republic of the Congo
SOUTH AMERICA
Indonesia
Zimbabwe
AUSTRALIA
Refugee Population
(by country of asylum)
More than 200,000
50,000–200,000
10,000–49,999
1,000–9,999
Less than 1,000
No data
Internally Displaced Persons (IDPs)
(countries with greater than 300,000 IDPs)
2 million or more
1 to 2 million
500,000 to 1 million
300,000 to 500,000

A GLOBAL ECONOMIC ACTIVITY MAP (right) reveals striking differences in the composition of output in advanced economies (such as the United States, Japan, and western Europe) compared with less developed countries (such as Nigeria and China). Advanced economies tend to have high proportions of their GDP in services, while developing economies have relatively high proportions in agriculture and industry.

There are different ways of looking at the distribution of manufacturing industry activity. When examined by country, the United States leads in production in many industries, but Western European countries are also a major manufacturing force. Western Europe outpaces the U.S. in the production of cars, chemicals, and food.

The world's sixth largest economy is found in China, and it has been growing quite rapidly. Chinese workers take home only a fraction of the cash pocketed each week by their economic rivals in the West, but are quickly catching up to the global economy with their purchase of cell phones and motor vehicles—two basic consumer products of the modern age.

The Middle East—a number of whose countries enjoy relatively high per-capita GDP values—produces more fuel than any other region, but it has virtually no other economic output besides that single commodity.

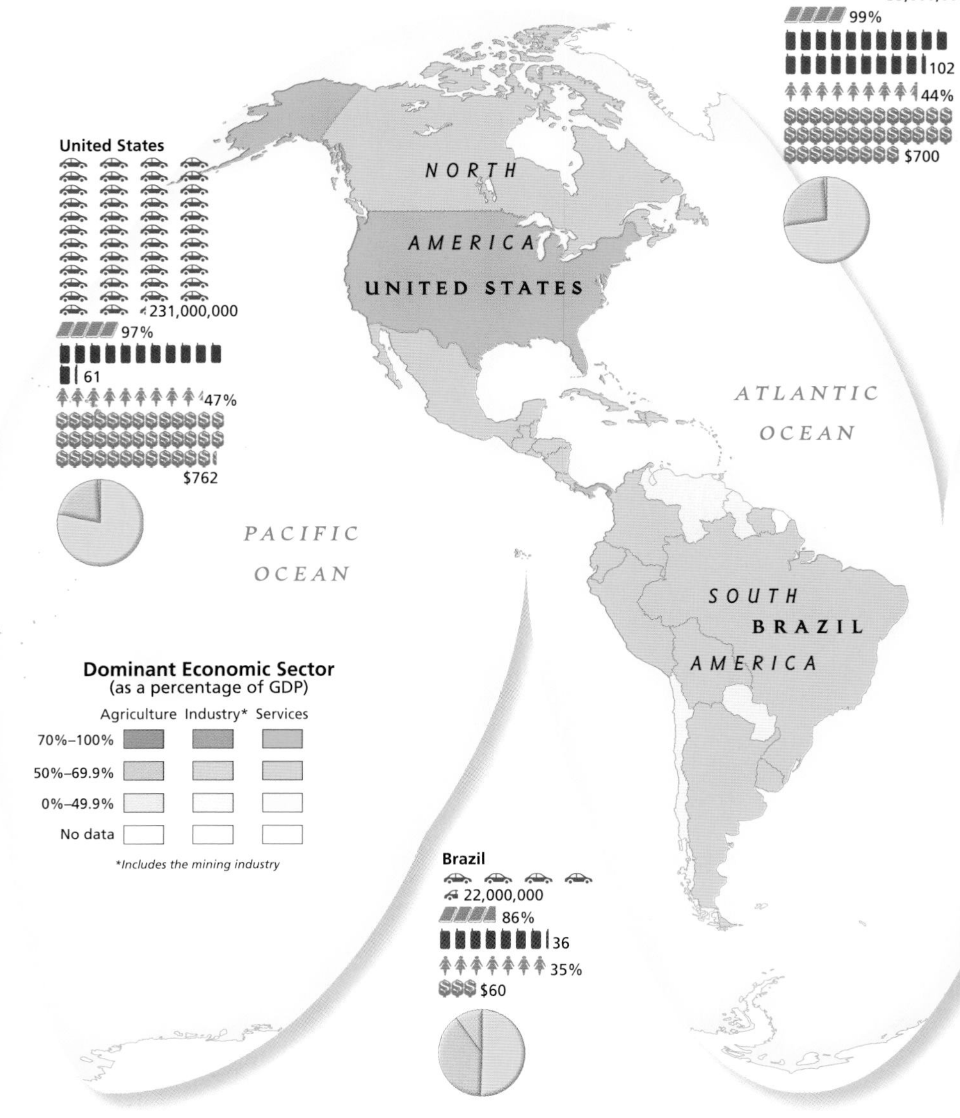
United Kingdom
33,000,000
99%
102
44%
$700
United States
231,000,000
97%
61
47%
$762
NORTH
AMERICA
UNITED STATES
ATLANTIC
OCEAN
PACIFIC
OCEAN
SOUTH
BRAZIL
AMERICA
Dominant Economic Sector
(as a percentage of GDP)
Agriculture Industry* Services
70%–100%
50%–69.9%
0%–49.9%
No data
*Includes the mining industry
Brazil
22,000,000
86%
36
35%
$60

Labor Migration

People in search of jobs gravitate toward the higher-income economies, unless immigration policies prevent them from doing so. Japan, for instance, has one of the world's most restrictive immigration policies and a population that is more than 99 percent Japanese. Some nations are "labor importers," while others are "labor exporters." In the mid-1990s, Malaysia was the largest Asian importer (close to a million workers) and the Philippines was the largest Asian exporter (4.2 million). The largest share of foreign workers in domestic employment is found in the Persian Gulf and Singapore.

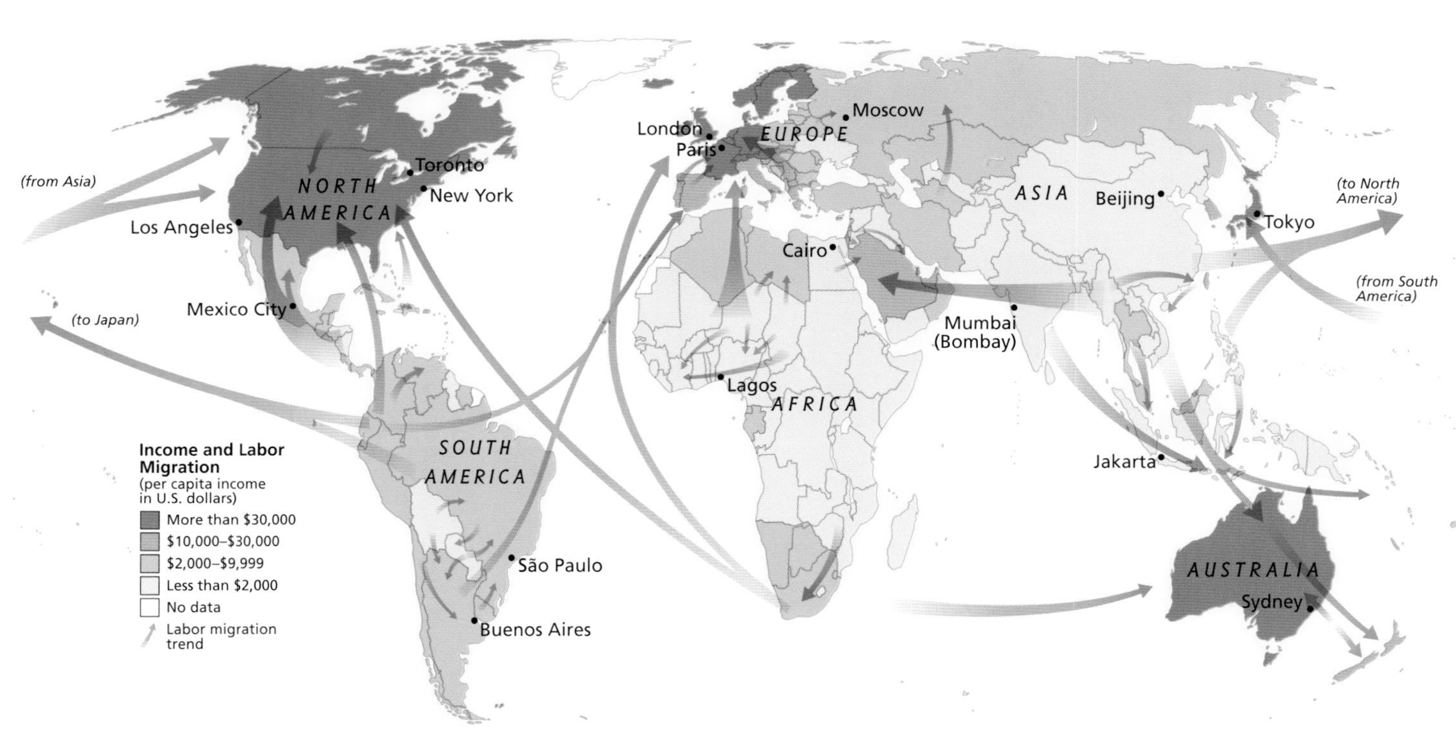
(from Asia)
(to Japan)
Los Angeles
Toronto
New York
NORTH
AMERICA
Mexico City
London
Paris
EUROPE
Moscow
ASIA
Beijing
Tokyo
(to North America)
(from South America)
Cairo
Mumbai
(Bombay)
Lagos
AFRICA
Jakarta
SOUTH
AMERICA
São Paulo
Buenos Aires
AUSTRALIA
Sydney
Income and Labor Migration
(per capita income in U.S. dollars)
More than $30,000
$10,000–$30,000
$2,000–$9,999
Less than $2,000
No data
Labor migration trend

Top GDP Growth Rates
(based on PPP, or purchasing power parity)*

(2000–2005 AVERAGE)	
1. Equatorial Guinea	13%
2. Turkmenistan	12%
3. Sierra Leone	12%
4. Chad	12%
5. Armenia	11%
6. Azerbaijan	11%
7. Kazakhstan	11%
8. Tajikistan	11%
9. China	11%
10. Myanmar	11%

*For more information on PPP, please see map on page 57.

The World's Richest and Poorest Countries

RICHEST	GDP PER CAPITA (PPP) (2005)
1. Luxembourg	$64,900
2. Norway	$40,800
3. United States	$39,700
4. Ireland	$38,200
5. Qatar	$33,800
6. Denmark	$33,300
7. Canada	$33,000
8. Iceland	$32,800
9. Austria	$32,100
10. Equatorial Guinea	$30,800

POOREST	GDP PER CAPITA (PPP) (2005)
1. Sierra Leone	$630
2. Democratic Rep. of the Congo	$640
3. Tanzania	$670
4. Malawi	$680
5. Yemen	$700
6. Ethiopia	$750
7. Burundi	$760
8. Guinea-Bissau	$820
9. Madagascar	$850
10. Niger	$860

Figures are listed in U.S. dollars.

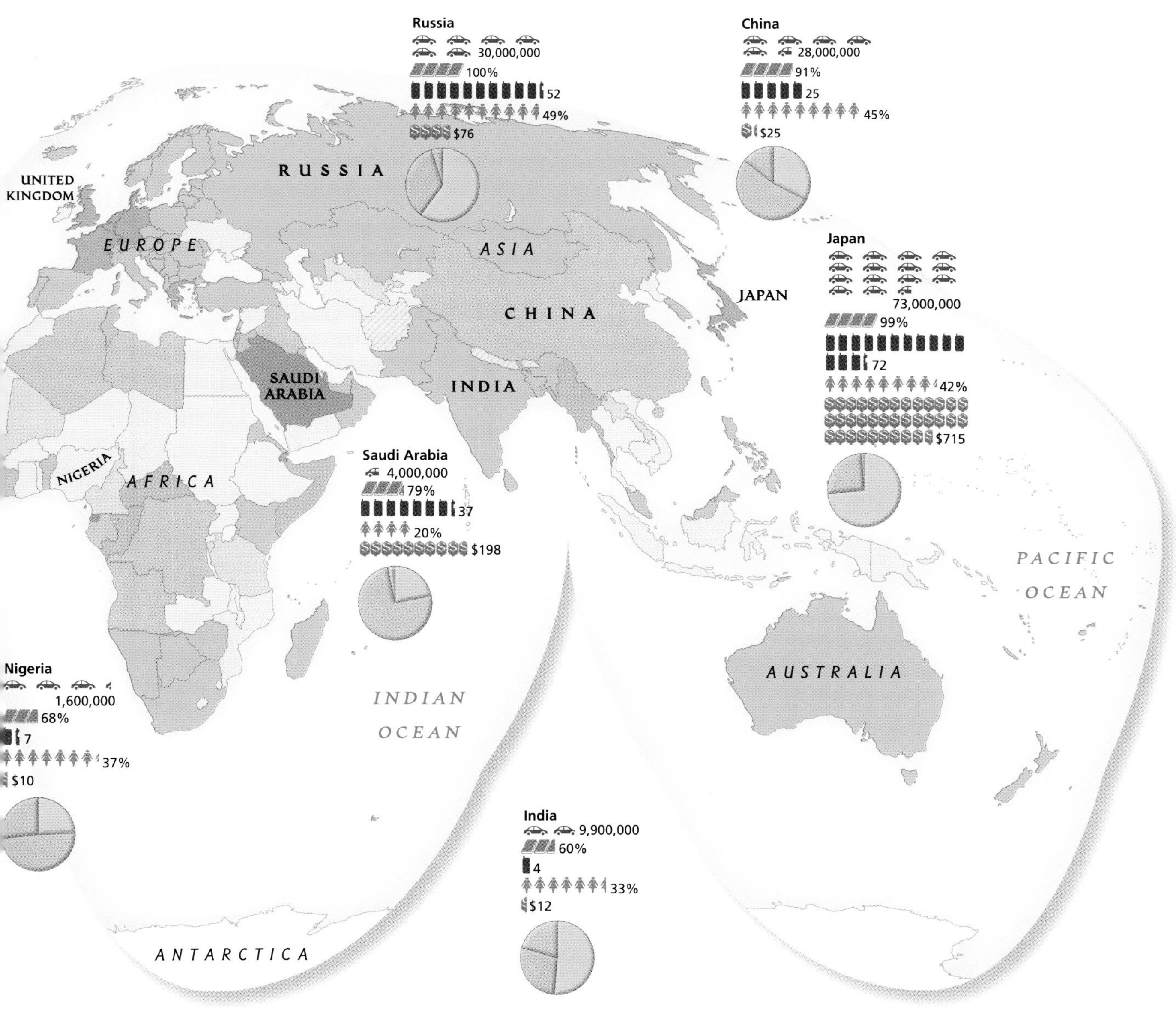
Russia
30,000,000
100%
52
49%
$76
China
28,000,000
91%
25
45%
$25
Japan
73,000,000
99%
72
42%
$715
Saudi Arabia
4,000,000
79%
37
20%
$198
Nigeria
1,600,000
68%
7
37%
$10
India
9,900,000
60%
4
33%
$12
UNITED KINGDOM
EUROPE
RUSSIA
ASIA
CHINA
JAPAN
INDIA
SAUDI ARABIA
NIGERIA
AFRICA
INDIAN OCEAN
PACIFIC OCEAN
AUSTRALIA
ANTARCTICA

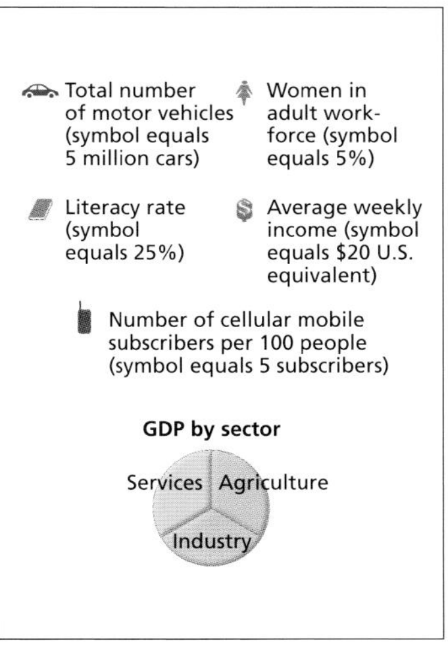
Total number of motor vehicles (symbol equals 5 million cars)
Women in adult work-force (symbol equals 5%)
Literacy rate (symbol equals 25%)
Average weekly income (symbol equals $20 U.S. equivalent)
Number of cellular mobile subscribers per 100 people (symbol equals 5 subscribers)
GDP by sector
Services
Agriculture
Industry

Gross Domestic Product

The gross domestic product (GDP) is the total market value of goods and services produced by a nation's economy in a given year using global currency exchange rates. It is a convenient way of calculating the level of a nation's international purchasing power and economic strength, but it does not show average wealth of individuals or measure standard of living. For example, a country could have high exports in products, but still have a low standard of living.

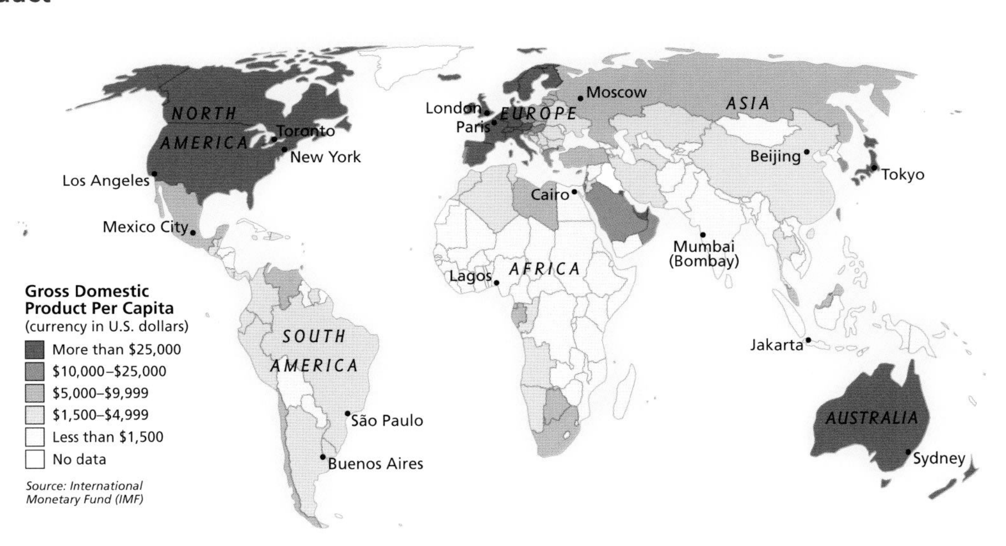
NORTH AMERICA
Toronto
New York
Los Angeles
Mexico City
London
Paris
EUROPE
Moscow
ASIA
Beijing
Tokyo
Cairo
Mumbai (Bombay)
Lagos
AFRICA
SOUTH AMERICA
Jakarta
São Paulo
Buenos Aires
AUSTRALIA
Sydney
Gross Domestic Product Per Capita
(currency in U.S. dollars)
More than $25,000
$10,000–$25,000
$5,000–$9,999
$1,500–$4,999
Less than $1,500
No data
Source: International Monetary Fund (IMF)

Gross Domestic Product: Purchasing Power Parity (PPP)

The PPP method calculates the relative value of currencies based on what each currency will buy in its country of origin–providing a good comparison between national economies. Per capita GDP at PPP is a very good but not perfect indicator of living standards. For instance, although workers in China earn only a fraction of the wage of American workers, (measured at current dollar rates) they also spend it in a lower-cost environment.

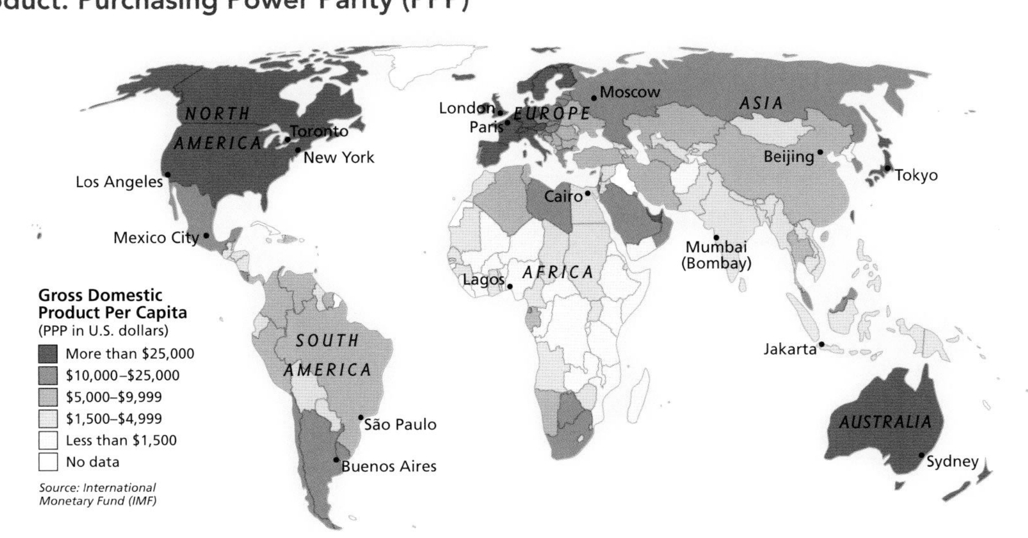
NORTH AMERICA
Toronto
New York
Los Angeles
Mexico City
London
Paris
EUROPE
Moscow
ASIA
Beijing
Tokyo
Cairo
Mumbai (Bombay)
Lagos
AFRICA
SOUTH AMERICA
Jakarta
São Paulo
Buenos Aires
AUSTRALIA
Sydney
Gross Domestic Product Per Capita
(PPP in U.S. dollars)
More than $25,000
$10,000–$25,000
$5,000–$9,999
$1,500–$4,999
Less than $1,500
No data
Source: International Monetary Fund (IMF)

Major Manufacturers

(All figures in billions of U.S. dollars, 2004)

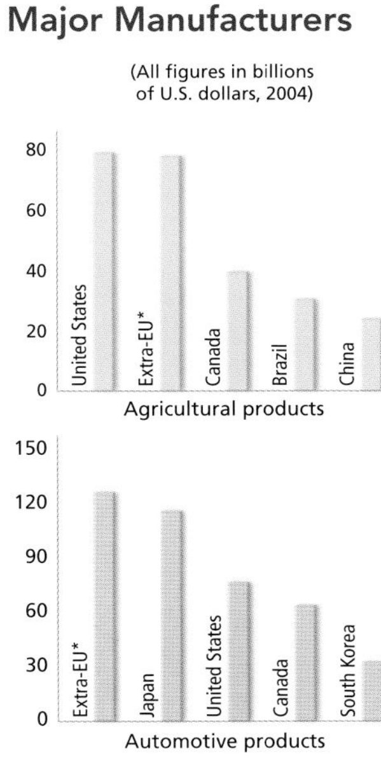
United States
Extra-EU*
Canada
Brazil
China
Agricultural products
Extra-EU*
Japan
United States
Canada
South Korea
Automotive products

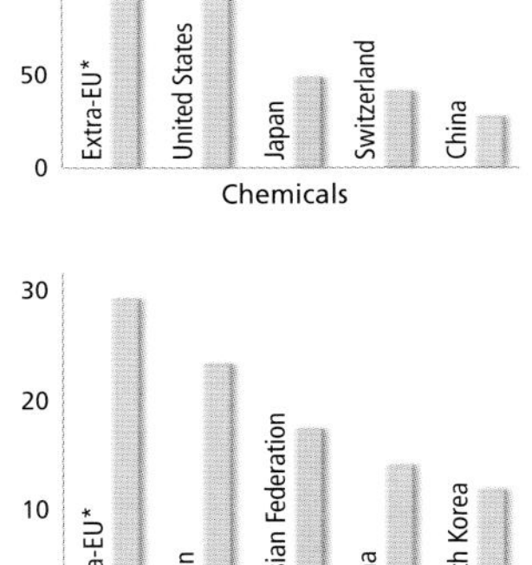
Extra-EU*
United States
Japan
Switzerland
China
Chemicals

Extra-EU*, Japan, Russian Federation, China, South Korea — Iron and steel

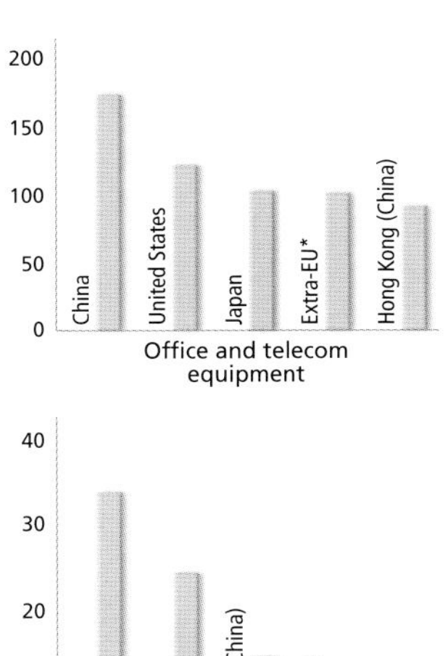
China
United States
Japan
Extra-EU*
Hong Kong (China)
Office and telecom equipment

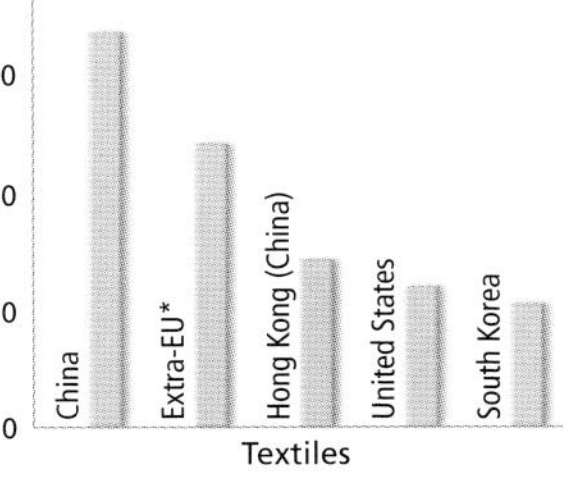
China
Extra-EU*
Hong Kong (China)
United States
South Korea
Textiles

*Extra-EU trade statistics record goods imported and exported between European Union members and non-European Union members.

WORLD TRADE HAS EXPANDED at a dizzying pace in the decades following World War II. The dollar value of world merchandise exports rose from $61 billion in 1950 to $10.1 trillion in 2005. Adjusted for price changes, world trade grew 30 times over the last 55 years, much faster than world output. Trade in manufactures expanded much faster than that of mining products (including fuels) and agricultural products. In the last decades many developing countries have become important exporters of manufactures (e.g. China, South Korea, Mexico). However, there are still many less-developed countries—primarily in Africa and the Middle East—that are dependent on a few primary commodities for their export earnings. Commercial services exports have expanded rapidly over the past two decades, and amounted to $2.4 trillion in 2005. While developed countries account for more than two-thirds of world services trade, some developing countries now gain most of their export earnings from services exports. Earnings from tourism in the Caribbean and that from software exports in India are prominent examples of developing countries' dynamic services exports.

Capital flows and worker remittances have gained in importance worldwide and are another important aspect of globalization. The stock of worldwide foreign direct investment was estimated to be close to $9 trillion at the end of 2004, $2.2 trillion of which was invested in developing countries. Capital markets in many developing countries remain small, fragile, and underdeveloped, which hampers household savings and the funding of local enterprises.

NORTH AMERICA
EUROPE
ASIA
MIDDLE EAST
AFRICA
SOUTH AMERICA
AUSTRALIA
Single-Commodity-Dependent Economy
(single commodity comprises greater than 40 percent of exports)
Cotton or wool
Crude oil & petroleum products
Fishing
Machinery & Equipment
Metals & minerals
Other agriculture
World Economies
(GNI per capita in U.S. dollars)
High income
Upper middle income
Lower middle income
Low income
No data
Stock exchange
World Merchandise Trade
(in billions of U.S. dollars)
Greater than 300
100–300
50–99
10–49
Less than 10

Growth of World Trade

After World War II the export growth of manufactured goods greatly outstripped other exports. This graph shows the volume growth on a semi-log scale (a straight line represents constant growth) rather than a standard scale (a straight line indicates a constant increase in the absolute values in each year).

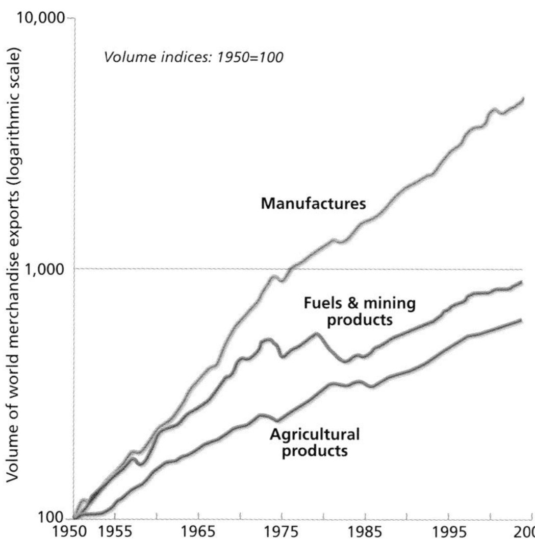
10,000
1,000
100
Volume indices: 1950=100
Volume of world merchandise exports (logarithmic scale)
Manufactures
Fuels & mining products
Agricultural products
1950 1955 1965 1975 1985 1995 2005

Merchandise Exports

Manufactured goods account for three-quarters of world merchandise exports. Export values of two subtypes—machinery and office/telecom equipment—exceed the total export value of mining products; world exports in chemicals and automotive products exceed the export value of all agricultural products.

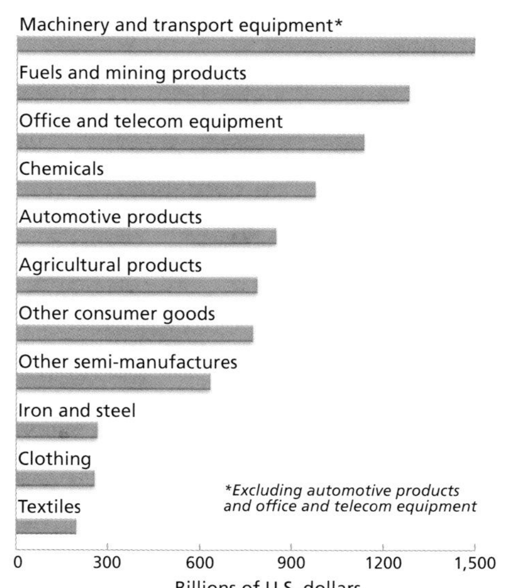
Machinery and transport equipment*
Fuels and mining products
Office and telecom equipment
Chemicals
Automotive products
Agricultural products
Other consumer goods
Other semi-manufactures
Iron and steel
Clothing
Textiles
*Excluding automotive products and office and telecom equipment
0 300 600 900 1200 1,500
Billions of U.S. dollars

Main Trading Nations

The U.S., Germany, and Japan account for nearly 30 percent of total world merchandise trade. Ongoing negotiations among the 144 member nations of the World Trade Organization are tackling market-access barriers in agriculture, textiles, and clothing—areas where many developing countries hope to compete.

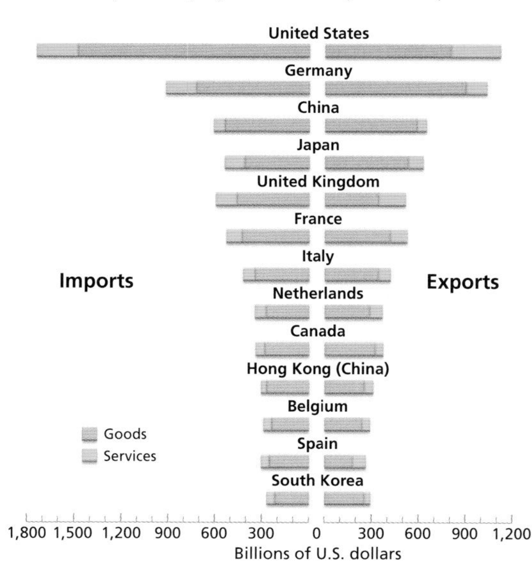
United States
Germany
China
Japan
United Kingdom
France
Italy
Netherlands
Canada
Hong Kong (China)
Belgium
Spain
South Korea
Imports
Exports
Goods
Services
1,800 1,500 1,200 900 600 300 0 300 600 900 1,200
Billions of U.S. dollars

World Debt

Measuring a nation's outstanding foreign debt in relation to its GDP indicates the size of future income needed to pay back the debt; it also shows how much a nation has relied in the past on foreign savings to finance investment and consumption expenditures. A high external debt ratio can pose a financial risk if debt service payments are not assured.

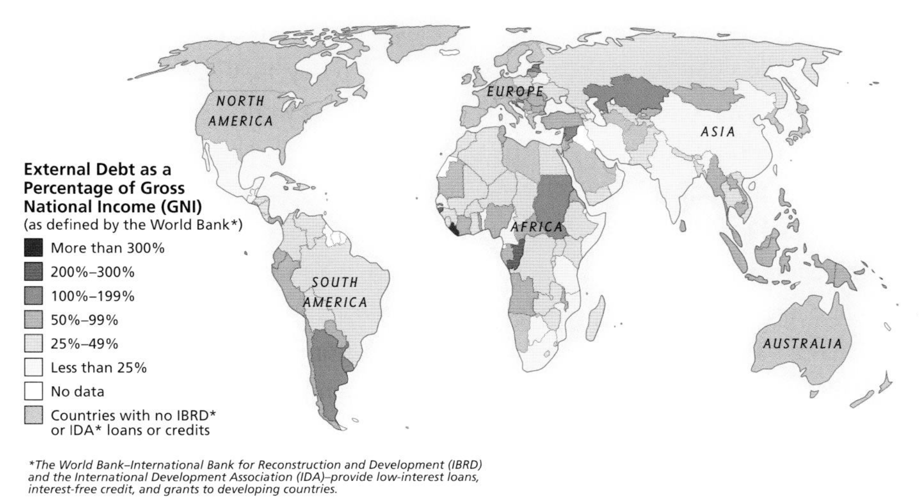
NORTH AMERICA
EUROPE
ASIA
AFRICA
SOUTH AMERICA
AUSTRALIA
External Debt as a Percentage of Gross National Income (GNI)
(as defined by the World Bank*)
More than 300%
200%–300%
100%–199%
50%–99%
25%–49%
Less than 25%
No data
Countries with no IBRD* or IDA* loans or credits
*The World Bank–International Bank for Reconstruction and Development (IBRD) and the International Development Association (IDA)–provide low-interest loans, interest-free credit, and grants to developing countries.

Trade Blocs

Regional trade is on the rise. Agreements between neighboring countries to offer each other trade benefits can create larger markets and improve the economy of the region as a whole. But they can also lead to discrimination, especially when more efficient suppliers outside the regional agreements are prevented from supplying their goods and services.

Major Regional Trade Agreements
APEC - Asia-Pacific Economic Cooperation
ASEAN - Association of Southeast Asian Nations
COMESA - Common Market for Eastern and Southern Africa
ECOWAS - Economic Community of West African States
EU - European Union
MERCOSUR - Southern Common Market
SAPTA - South Asian Preferential Trade Arrangement
APEC & NAFTA - North American Free Trade Agreement
APEC & ASEAN
NORTH AMERICA
EUROPE
ASIA
AFRICA
SOUTH AMERICA
AUSTRALIA

Top Merchandise Exporters and Importers

	PERCENTAGE OF WORLD TOTAL	VALUE (BILLIONS)
TOP EXPORTERS		
Germany	9.3	$971
United States	8.7	$904
China	7.3	$762
Japan	5.7	$596
France	4.4	$459
Netherlands	3.9	$401
United Kingdom	3.6	$378
Italy	3.5	$367
Canada	3.5	$360
Belgium	3.2	$330
Hong Kong (China)	2.8	$292
South Korea	2.7	$285
Russia	2.4	$245
Singapore	2.2	$230
Mexico	2.1	$214
TOP IMPORTERS		
United States	16.1	$1,733
Germany	7.2	$774
China	6.1	$660
Japan	4.8	$516
United Kingdom	4.7	$501
France	4.6	$496
Italy	3.5	$380
Netherlands	3.3	$358
Belgium	3.0	$320
Canada	3.0	$320
Hong Kong (China)	2.8	$301
Spain	2.6	$278
South Korea	2.4	$261
Mexico	2.2	$232
Singapore	1.9	$200

Trade Flow: Fuels

The leading exporters of fuel products are countries in the Middle East, Africa, Russia, and central and western Asia; all export more fuel than they consume. But intraregional energy trade is growing, with some of the key producers—Canada, Indonesia, Norway, and the United Kingdom, for example—located in regions that are net energy importers.

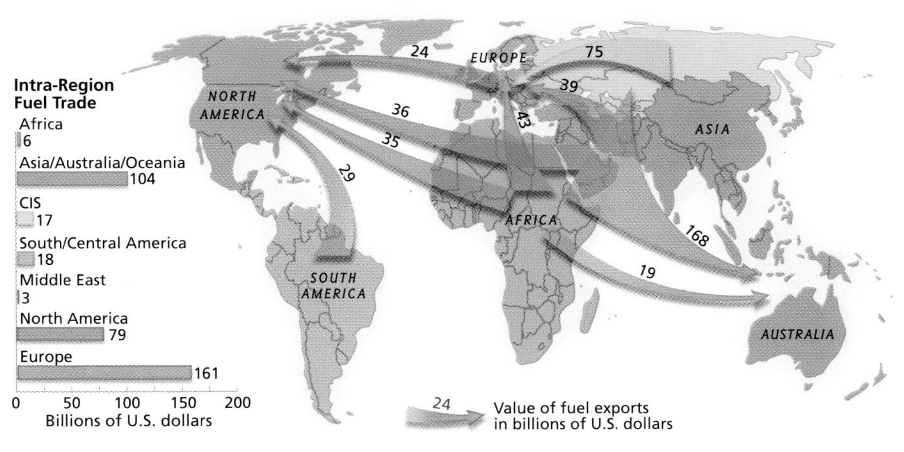
Intra-Region Fuel Trade
Africa
6
Asia/Australia/Oceania
104
CIS
17
South/Central America
18
Middle East
3
North America
79
Europe
161
0 50 100 150 200
Billions of U.S. dollars
24 Value of fuel exports in billions of U.S. dollars
NORTH AMERICA
EUROPE
ASIA
AFRICA
SOUTH AMERICA
AUSTRALIA
24
75
39
36
35
43
29
168
19

Trade Flow: Agricultural Products

The world trade in agricultural products is less concentrated than trade in fuels, with processed goods making up the majority. Agricultural products encounter high export barriers, which limit the opportunities for some exporters to expand into foreign markets. Reducing such barriers is a major challenge for governments that are engaged in agricultural trade negotiations.

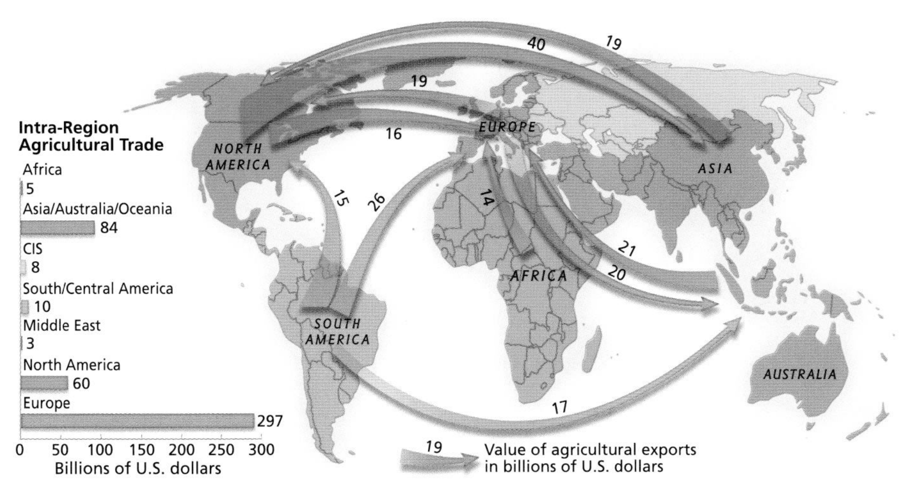
Intra-Region Agricultural Trade
Africa
5
Asia/Australia/Oceania
84
CIS
8
South/Central America
10
Middle East
3
North America
60
Europe
297
0 50 100 150 200 250 300
Billions of U.S. dollars
19 Value of agricultural exports in billions of U.S. dollars
NORTH AMERICA
EUROPE
ASIA
AFRICA
SOUTH AMERICA
AUSTRALIA
40
19
19
16
15
26
14
21
20
17

Top Commercial Services Exporters and Importers

(includes transportation, travel, and other services)

	PERCENTAGE OF WORLD TOTAL	VALUE (BILLIONS)
TOP EXPORTERS		
United States	14.6	$353
United Kingdom	7.6	$183
Germany	5.9	$143
France	4.7	$114
Japan	4.4	$107
Italy	3.9	$93
Spain	3.8	$91
China	3.4	$81
Netherlands	3.1	$75
India	2.8	$68
Hong Kong (China)	2.5	$60
Ireland	2.3	$55
Austria	2.2	$54
Belgium	2.2	$53
Canada	2.1	$51
TOP IMPORTERS		
United States	12.2	$289
Germany	8.4	$199
United Kingdom	6.4	$150
Japan	5.8	$136
France	4.4	$103
Italy	3.9	$92
China	3.6	$85
Netherlands	2.9	$69
Ireland	2.9	$68
India	2.9	$67
Spain	2.8	$65
Canada	2.6	$62
South Korea	2.5	$58
Austria	2.2	$52
Belgium	2.2	$51

THE POPULATION OF THE PLANET, which nearly tops six and a half billion, continues to increase by 230,000 new mouths a day. What will they eat? Where will the additional food come from?

Worldwide, agricultural production also continues to grow, but the food-producing regions are unevenly distributed around the globe. And though efforts to raise the levels of production even more (while relying less on chemical applications that damage the environment) are vitally important, they can go only so far in solving a great dilemma: How can we get more food to the millions of people who do not have enough to eat? Invariably, it is the economic situation of nations—which ones have food surpluses to sell; which ones need food and have or don't have enough money to buy it—that determines who goes hungry.

For people in the world's poorest regions, the situation is grim. The United Nations Food and Agriculture Organization reports that every night 815 million people in the developing world go to bed hungry and that malnourishment contributes to at least one-third of all child deaths. It also says that 13 million people in southern Africa face famine. Most cases of malnutrition are found in the developing countries of the tropics, where rapid population growth and other factors are depleting agricultural and financial resources.

Land Use and Commercial Agriculture

At various times and in various places, people began to till the land. The beginning of agriculture—cultivating soil, producing crops, and raising livestock—created a generally reliable food supply. Many historians believe that the planting and tending of crops also led to the first fixed settlements. Over thousands of years, the human population has grown in number, occupying more land and producing more food. Today most of the world's potential cropland is being cultivated. The challenge now is to balance population and land use. Human occupation, commercial agriculture, and Earth's ecosystems (including woodlands, forests, and deserts, which feed far fewer people per acre than croplands) all have to be sustained. People must eat, but they also need viable ecosystems in which to live.

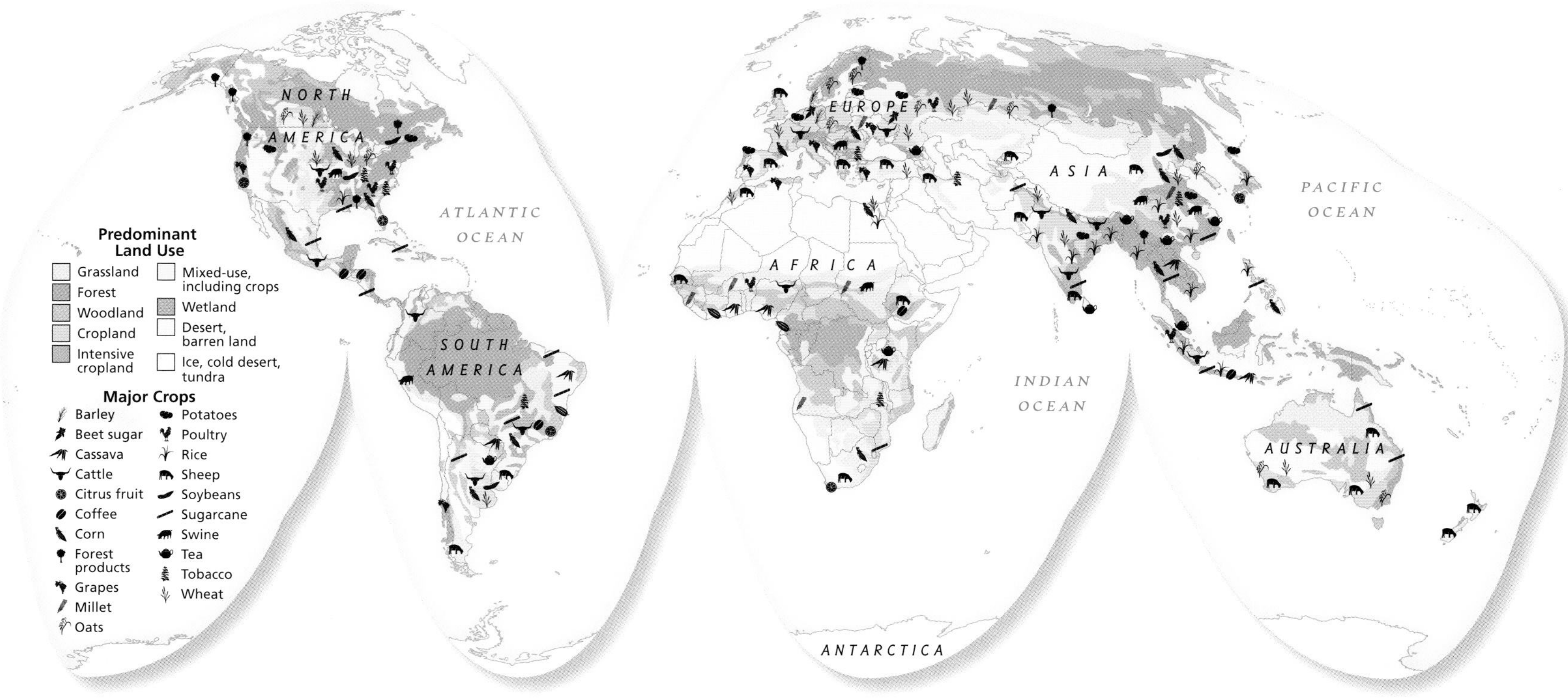
NORTH AMERICA
SOUTH AMERICA
EUROPE
ASIA
AFRICA
AUSTRALIA
ANTARCTICA
ATLANTIC OCEAN
PACIFIC OCEAN
INDIAN OCEAN
Predominant Land Use
Grassland
Forest
Woodland
Cropland
Intensive cropland
Mixed-use, including crops
Wetland
Desert, barren land
Ice, cold desert, tundra
Major Crops
Barley
Beet sugar
Cassava
Cattle
Citrus fruit
Coffee
Corn
Forest products
Grapes
Millet
Oats
Potatoes
Poultry
Rice
Sheep
Soybeans
Sugarcane
Swine
Tea
Tobacco
Wheat

Fishing and Aquaculture

Fish, a low-cost source of protein, is assuming a more central role in the human diet. Since 1950, the world's yearly catch of ocean fish has more than quadrupled. And an increase in fish-farming ponds and commercial production of seaweed, collectively called aquaculture, has spawned one of the fastest-growing areas of food production; it now accounts for 40 percent of the fish people eat. About 90 percent of aquaculture occurs in developing countries, with China (where the technique began some 4,000 years ago) accounting for a bit more than two-thirds of total output. Experts project that by 2010, fish farming may overtake cattle ranching as a world food source.

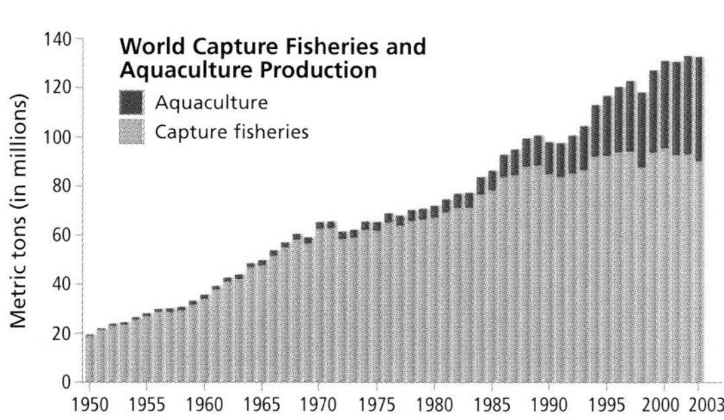
World Capture Fisheries and Aquaculture Production
Aquaculture
Capture fisheries
Metric tons (in millions)
0
20
40
60
80
100
120
140
1950 1955 1960 1965 1970 1975 1980 1985 1990 1995 2000 2003

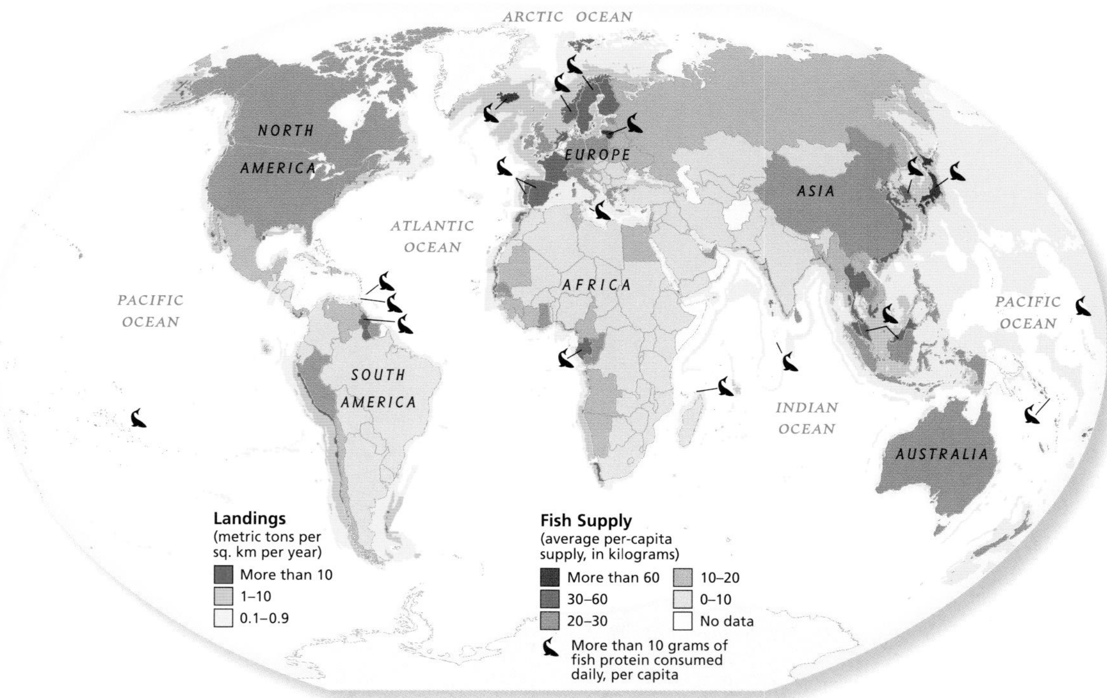
ARCTIC OCEAN
NORTH AMERICA
SOUTH AMERICA
EUROPE
ASIA
AFRICA
AUSTRALIA
ATLANTIC OCEAN
PACIFIC OCEAN
PACIFIC OCEAN
INDIAN OCEAN
Landings
(metric tons per sq. km per year)
More than 10
1–10
0.1–0.9
Fish Supply
(average per-capita supply, in kilograms)
More than 60
30–60
20–30
10–20
0–10
No data
More than 10 grams of fish protein consumed daily, per capita

World Agricultural Production

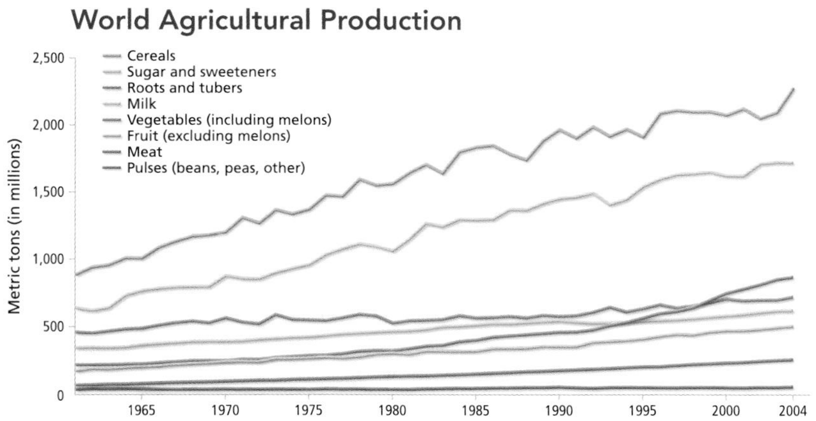

Cereals
Sugar and sweeteners
Roots and tubers
Milk
Vegetables (including melons)
Fruit (excluding melons)
Meat
Pulses (beans, peas, other)
Metric tons (in millions)
2,500
2,000
1,500
1,000
500
0
1965
1970
1975
1980
1985
1990
1995
2000
2004

In the past few decades, world food production has more than kept pace with the burgeoning global population. Meat and cereals account for the most dramatic increases. New high-yield crops, additional irrigated land, and fertilizers have contributed to the rise in production. But there are related problems: Scientists warn that overuse of fertilizers causes nitrogen overload in Earth's waters. Insufficient use, in particular in Africa, has long-term adverse consequences for food security.

Undernourishment in the Developing World

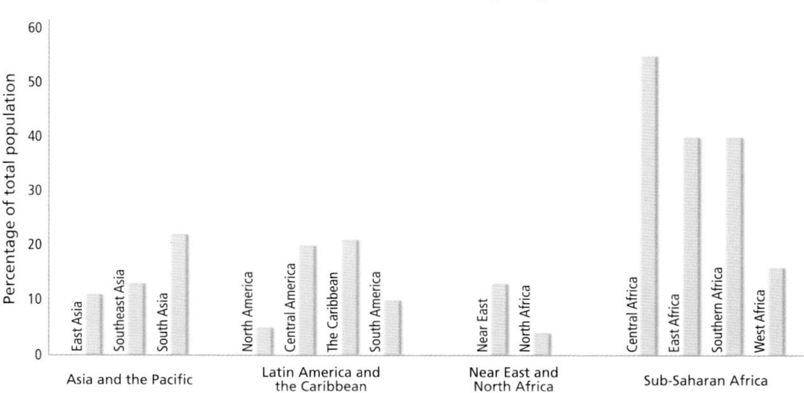

Percentage of total population
60
50
40
30
20
10
0
East Asia
Southeast Asia
South Asia
North America
Central America
The Caribbean
South America
Near East
North Africa
Central Africa
East Africa
Southern Africa
West Africa
Asia and the Pacific
Latin America and the Caribbean
Near East and North Africa
Sub-Saharan Africa

More food than ever is produced, but its distribution is uneven. Africa, in particular, is a continent of contrasts: Almost half the people in central, eastern, and southern Africa are undernourished, while a much lower percentage of people in the north and west are undernourished. The United Nations estimates that more than three-quarters of a billion people suffer from persistent malnourishment. Without access to adequate food, these populations cannot lead healthy, productive lives.

Caloric Supply

As shown at right, cereals (grains) dominate the caloric supply of people in Africa and Asia. Sugars, oils, and proteins comprise a much higher portion in other parts of the world, and the increasing consumption rates of these foods leads to obesity problems in many countries.

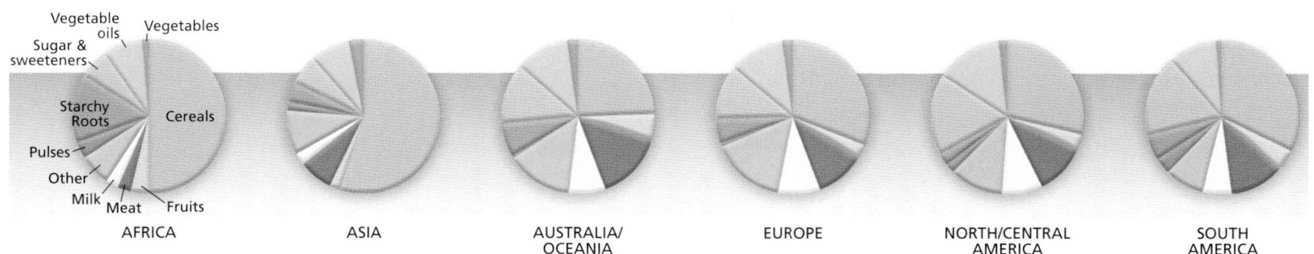

Vegetable oils
Vegetables
Sugar & sweeteners
Starchy Roots
Cereals
Pulses
Other
Milk
Meat
Fruits
AFRICA
ASIA
AUSTRALIA/ OCEANIA
EUROPE
NORTH/CENTRAL AMERICA
SOUTH AMERICA

Indicates breakdown of per-capita calorie supply

World Grain Production

Humans rely on plant sources for carbohydrates, with grains (the edible parts of cereal plants) providing 80 percent of the food energy (calorie) supply. This means that the major grains—corn, wheat, and rice—are the foods that fuel humanity. Most cereal grains are grown in the Northern Hemisphere (see map), with the United States and France producing enough to be the largest exporters. Many parts of the world cannot grow cereal grains because they do not have productive farmland or the needed technology. Again and again throughout history, the actions of nations have been shaped by disparities in the supply and demand of grains, and by the knowledge that grains equal survival. Waverley Root, a food historian, once wrote: "[p]ossession of wheat or lack of it sways the destinies of nations; nor is it rare to find wheat being used as a political weapon.... [I]t is difficult to foresee any future in which it will not still exert a powerful influence on human history."

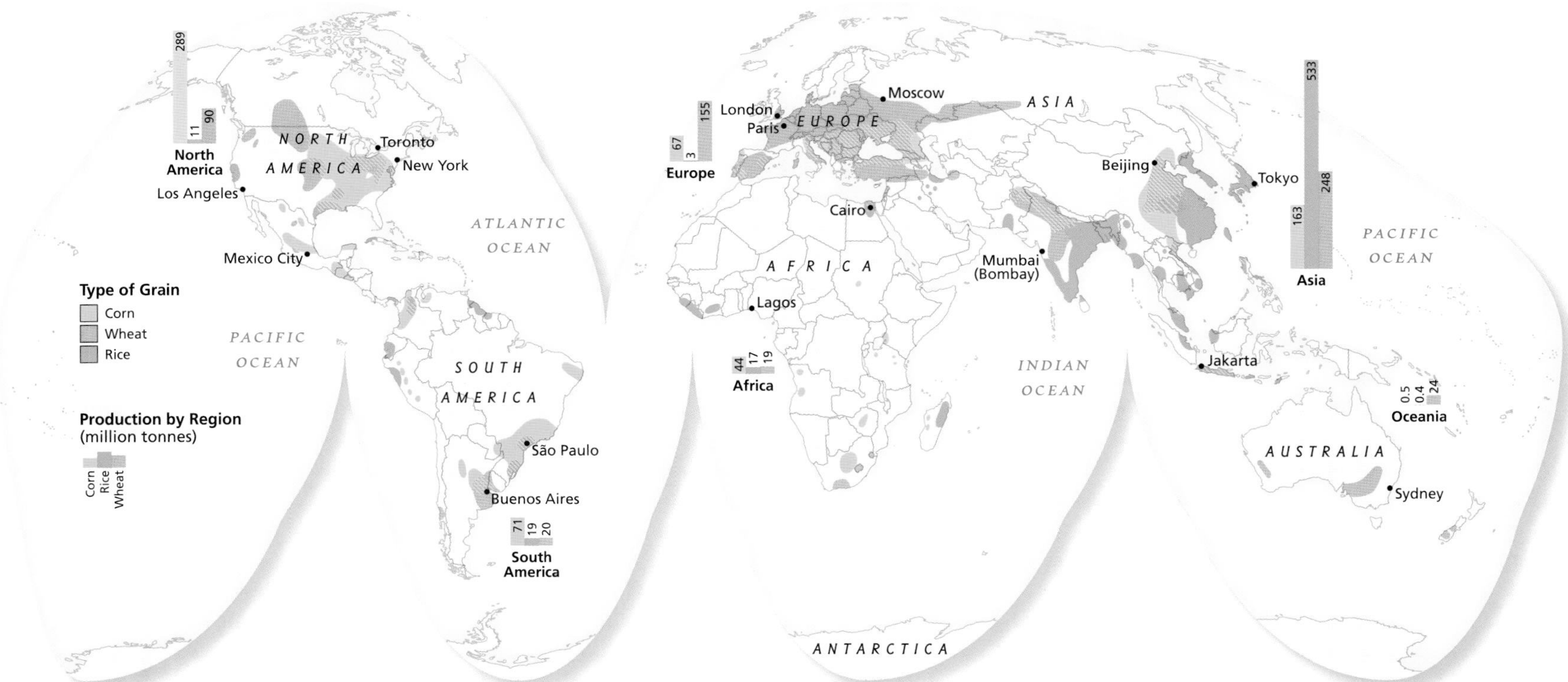

289
11
90
North America
NORTH AMERICA
Toronto
New York
Los Angeles
Mexico City
ATLANTIC OCEAN
Type of Grain
Corn
Wheat
Rice
PACIFIC OCEAN
SOUTH AMERICA
Production by Region (million tonnes)
Corn
Rice
Wheat
São Paulo
Buenos Aires
71
19
20
South America
155
67
3
Europe
London
Paris
EUROPE
Moscow
ASIA
Cairo
AFRICA
Lagos
44
17
19
Africa
Mumbai (Bombay)
INDIAN OCEAN
Beijing
Tokyo
533
163
248
Asia
PACIFIC OCEAN
Jakarta
0.5
0.4
24
Oceania
AUSTRALIA
Sydney
ANTARCTICA

CORN
A staple in prehistoric Mexico and Peru, corn (or maize) is native to the New World. By the time Columbus's crew first tasted it, corn already was a hardy crop in much of North and South America.

WHEAT
Among the two oldest foods (barley is the other), wheat was important in ancient Mediterranean civilizations; today it is the most widely cultivated grain. Wheat grows best in temperate climates.

RICE
Originating in Asia many millennia ago, rice is the staple grain for about half the world's people. It is a labor-intensive plant that grows primarily in paddies (wet land) and thrives in the hot, humid tropics.

PRIMARY ENERGY comes in many different forms. Some fuels, such as animal dung and fuelwood, have a low energy content, while coal, natural gas, and oil contain much more. By adopting a common measurement that takes these differences into account, we can compare energy usage around the world. Today, the international standard is the "metric ton of oil equivalent" (toe), which translates all forms of energy (solid, liquid, or gas) to a common baseline. On this basis, global energy consumption is currently about 10.2 billion tons of oil equivalent a year.

The world's chief sources of energy are oil, natural gas, and coal, in that order. In each case, however, the major consuming countries are becoming increasingly dependent on imports. While oil has been shipped from producing countries to consumers for many years, increasing amounts of coal—mainly used for generating electricity—are on the move. Western Europe and countries like the United States and Japan are also beginning to import liquified natural gas, adding to their reliance on energy from elsewhere.

Production and consumption patterns show major differences worldwide. North America, with less than one-tenth of the world's population, uses about one-quarter of its energy. Countries with rapidly developing economies, like China and India, need more. As demand for energy grows, prices rise and alternative sources become more attractive.

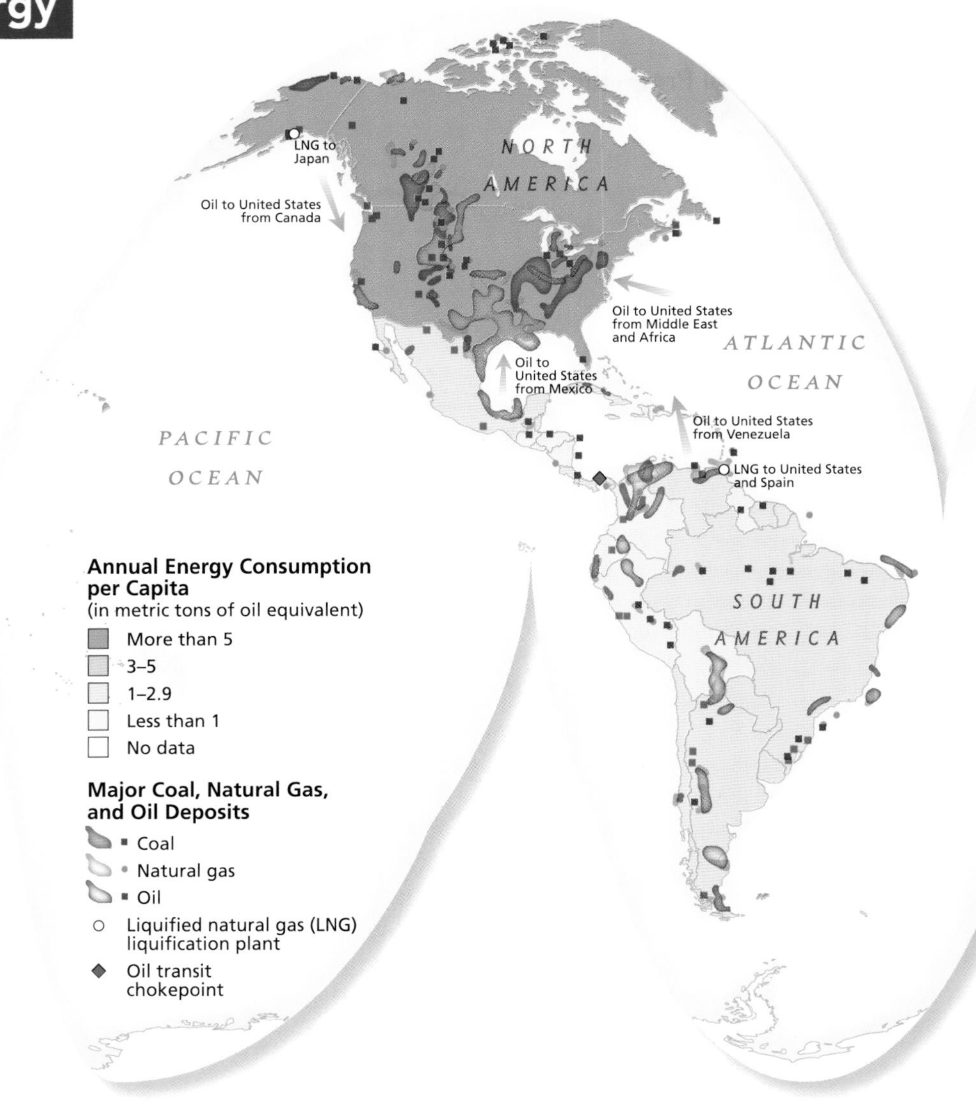
LNG to Japan
Oil to United States from Canada
NORTH AMERICA
Oil to United States from Middle East and Africa
ATLANTIC OCEAN
Oil to United States from Mexico
PACIFIC OCEAN
Oil to United States from Venezuela
LNG to United States and Spain
SOUTH AMERICA
Annual Energy Consumption per Capita
(in metric tons of oil equivalent)
More than 5
3–5
1–2.9
Less than 1
No data
Major Coal, Natural Gas, and Oil Deposits
Coal
Natural gas
Oil
Liquified natural gas (LNG) liquification plant
Oil transit chokepoint

Energy Production

WORLD ENERGY PRODUCTION BY TYPE

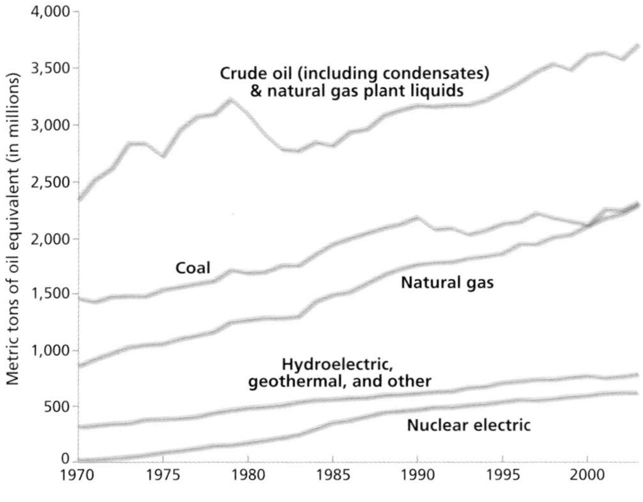
Metric tons of oil equivalent (in millions)
4,000
3,500
3,000
2,500
2,000
1,500
1,000
500
0
1970
1975
1980
1985
1990
1995
2000
Crude oil (including condensates) & natural gas plant liquids
Coal
Natural gas
Hydroelectric, geothermal, and other
Nuclear electric

WORLD ENERGY PRODUCTION BY REGION

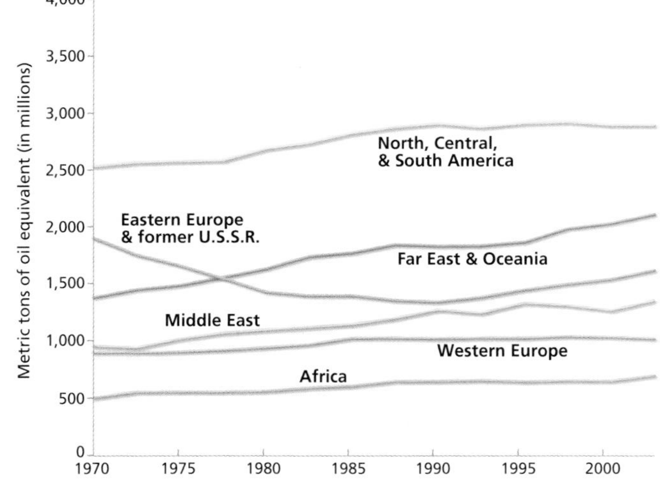
Metric tons of oil equivalent (in millions)
4,000
3,500
3,000
2,500
2,000
1,500
1,000
500
0
1970
1975
1980
1985
1990
1995
2000
North, Central, & South America
Eastern Europe & former U.S.S.R.
Far East & Oceania
Middle East
Western Europe
Africa

Fossil Fuel Extraction

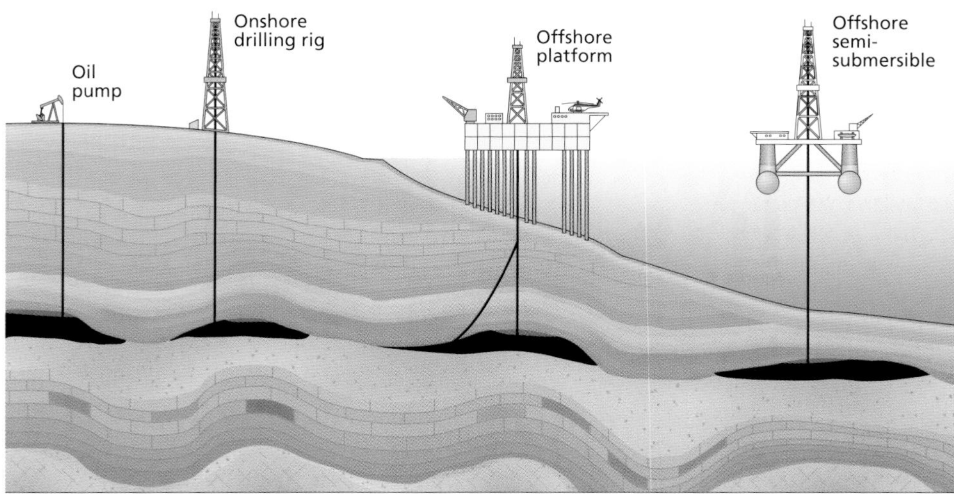
Oil pump
Onshore drilling rig
Offshore platform
Offshore semi-submersible

OIL EXTRACTION
Drilling-operation types depend on whether oil is in the ground or under the ocean. An onshore drilling rig uses a basic derrick; off-shore drilling is done with platform or semisubmersible designs (as shown above).

GAS EXTRACTION
Natural gas occurs in many of the same types of geologic structures as oil, and it is generally thought to have the same organic origins as oil. Gas-drilling and oil-drilling operations are essentially the same.

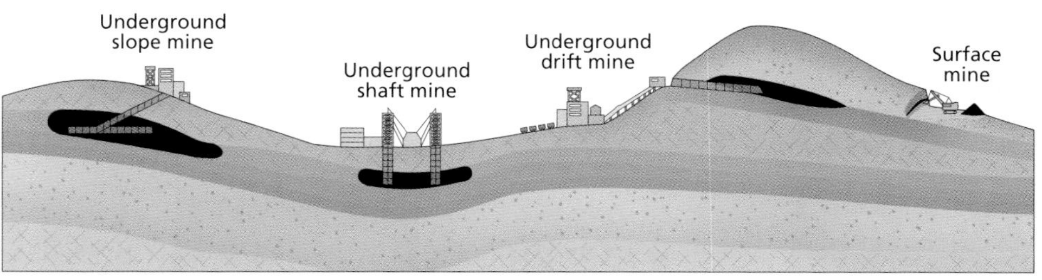
Underground slope mine
Underground shaft mine
Underground drift mine
Surface mine

COAL MINING
The mining of coal made the industrial revolution possible, and coal still provides a major energy source. Once a labor-intensive process, coal mining is now heavily mechanized. An underground slope mine allows coal to be transported to the surface by a conveyor rather than an elevator. Underground drift mines and surface mines allow the easiest use of coal-cutting machinery.

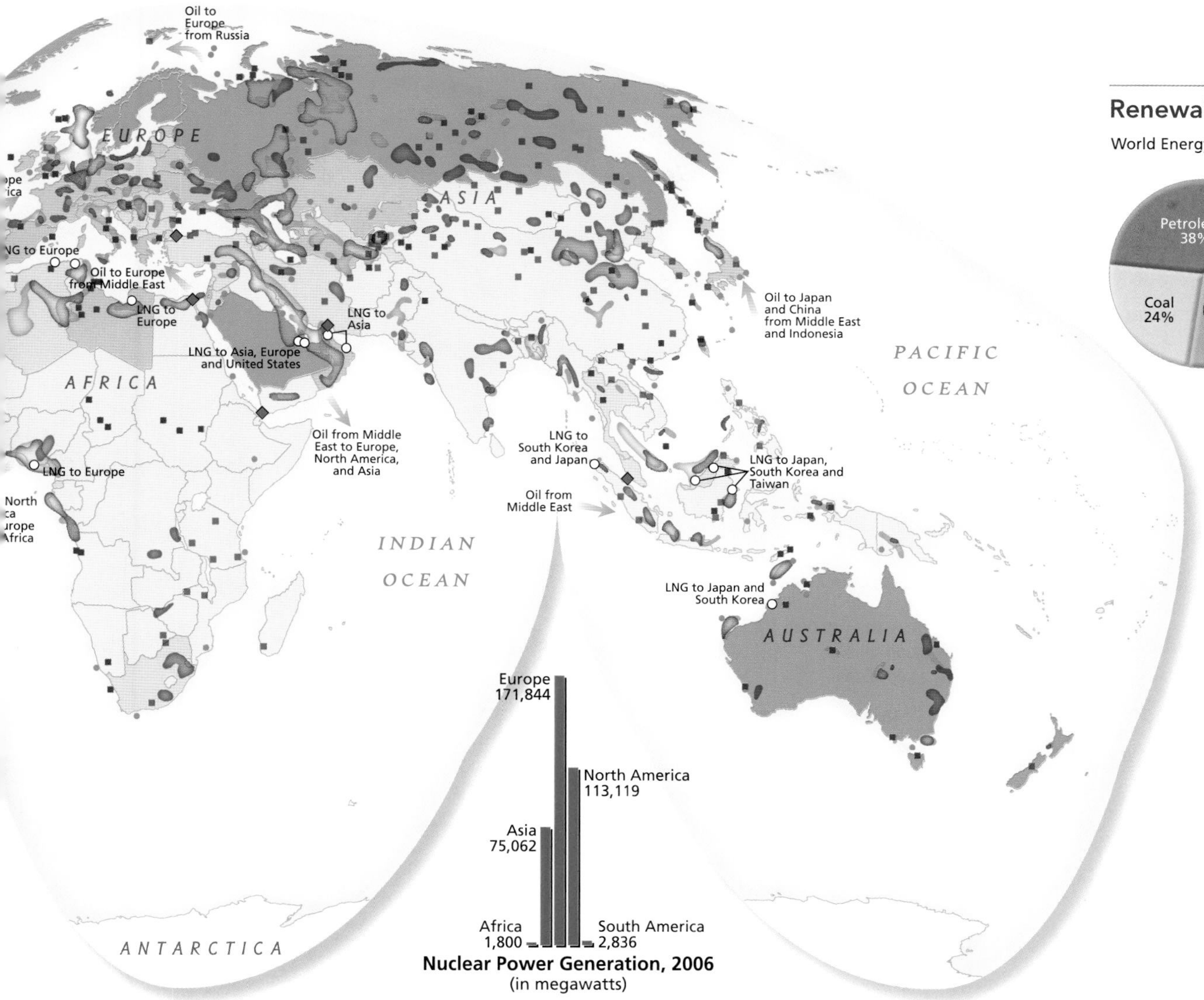

Nuclear Power Generation, 2006
(in megawatts)

Europe	171,844
North America	113,119
Asia	75,062
Africa	1,800
South America	2,836

Renewable Resources

World Energy Production

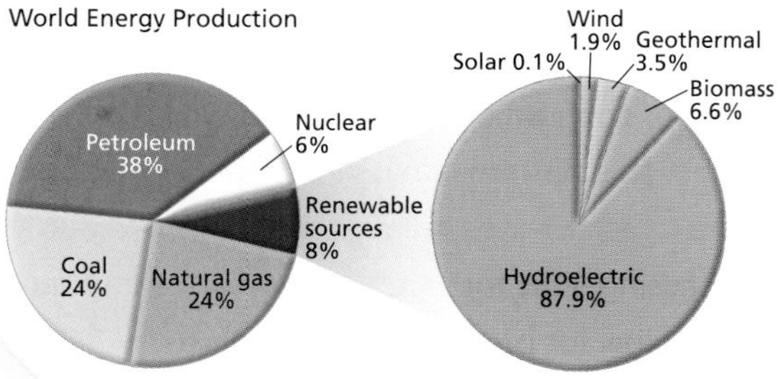

Petroleum	38%
Coal	24%
Natural gas	24%
Nuclear	6%
Renewable sources	8%

Renewable source	Share
Hydroelectric	87.9%
Biomass	6.6%
Geothermal	3.5%
Wind	1.9%
Solar	0.1%

HYDROELECTRIC POWER
Hydroelectric plants in South America and the United States (Grand Coulee, in Washington State) are among the largest in the world. China has the greatest hydroelectric potential.

Biomass, Hydroelectric, and Geothermal Power

Burning biomass to release energy is a carbon-neutral process (i.e., it does not cause a net increase in carbon dioxide); the carbon is already part of the cycle. Biomass would require extensive conversion, however. Hydroelectric power is potentially the major renewable energy source, and more than 30 percent of the potential sites around the world have not yet been developed. In many geothermal sites it is possible to drill wells for a steady supply of steam, which can then be used to run turbines to generate electricity.

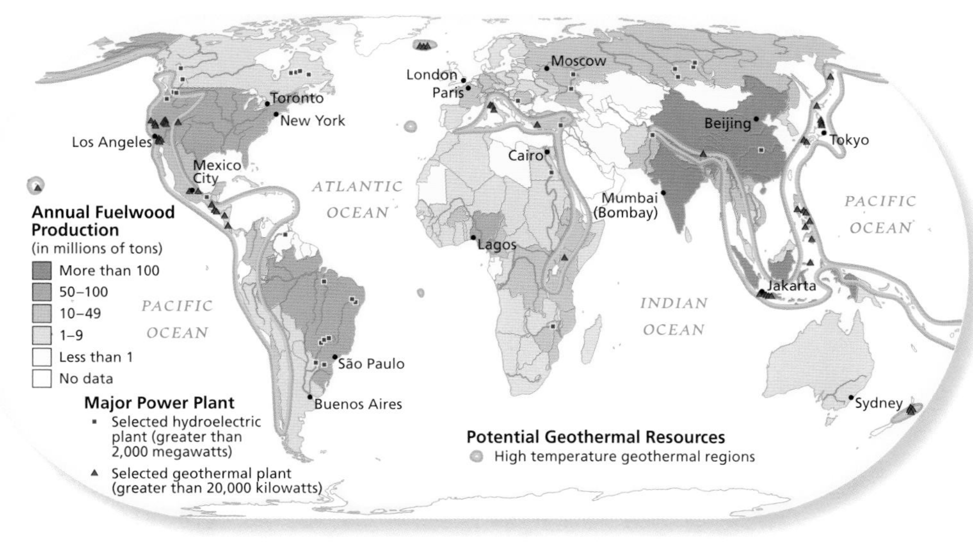
Annual Fuelwood Production
(in millions of tons)
More than 100
50–100
10–49
1–9
Less than 1
No data
Major Power Plant
Selected hydroelectric plant (greater than 2,000 megawatts)
Selected geothermal plant (greater than 20,000 kilowatts)
Potential Geothermal Resources
High temperature geothermal regions
ATLANTIC OCEAN
PACIFIC OCEAN
INDIAN OCEAN

GEOTHERMAL POWER
Geothermal power plants pipe steam and hot water from the ground to make electricity. The world's largest installation—The Geysers—is in California.

Wind and Solar Power

Wind, solar, tidal, wave, and other technologies are promising sources of natural, renewable energy. As the technology and economics of wind power improve, certain regions of the world could become "Saudi Arabias of wind." Solar radiation received on Earth each year corresponds to 3,000 times global energy consumption, but the problem with solar energy, just as with many other renewable energy resources, is their intermittent nature and the lack of storage technologies.

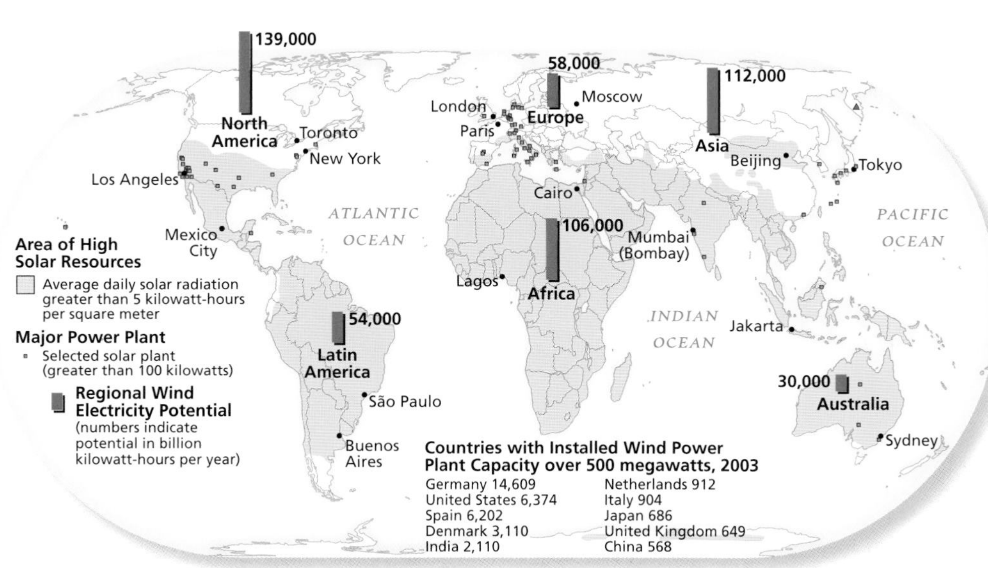
Area of High Solar Resources
Average daily solar radiation greater than 5 kilowatt-hours per square meter
Major Power Plant
Selected solar plant (greater than 100 kilowatts)
Regional Wind Electricity Potential
(numbers indicate potential in billion kilowatt-hours per year)
North America 139,000
Europe 58,000
Asia 112,000
Africa 106,000
Latin America 54,000
Australia 30,000
Countries with Installed Wind Power Plant Capacity over 500 megawatts, 2003
Germany 14,609
United States 6,374
Spain 6,202
Denmark 3,110
India 2,110
Netherlands 912
Italy 904
Japan 686
United Kingdom 649
China 568

SOLAR POWER
California holds the Earth's largest solar power arrays, one of which helps provide 160 megawatts of electric power.

WIND POWER
Harnessing the wind is the goal of the fastest-growing energy technology. In the U.S., the wind industry generates enough power each year to meet the electricity needs of one million people.

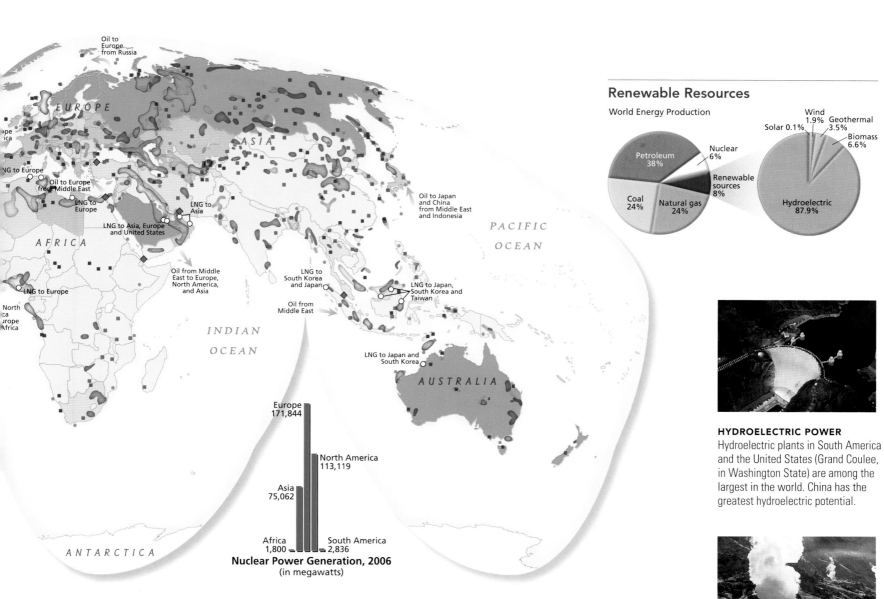

THE SPATIAL PATTERN of world mineral production is the result of several factors: geology, climate, economic systems, and social preferences. This pattern can be seen on the map at right, which locates major production and processing sites for various mineral commodities (see below for profiles on 18 important minerals).

Plate movements, volcanism, and sedimentation are geologic processes that form valuable concentrations of minerals. The same geologic forces that formed the Andes, for example, are responsible for the porphyry copper deposits along South America's Pacific coast. Other processes concentrate copper in sedimentary basins and in volcanic arcs. Climatic factors, such as the tropical conditions that contribute to bauxite formation, are also important.

Mineral consumption by industries is positively correlated with income and differs greatly among countries. Developed nations use larger volumes of materials and a wider variety of mineral commodities than less developed countries. In developed nations, annual copper use is typically 5 to 10 kilograms per person; for less developed ones, usage is only a few kilograms per person. Recent economic growth has led to greater demand for many mineral resources. Meeting that need without causing harm to the environment will be one of the major challenges for societies in the 21st century.

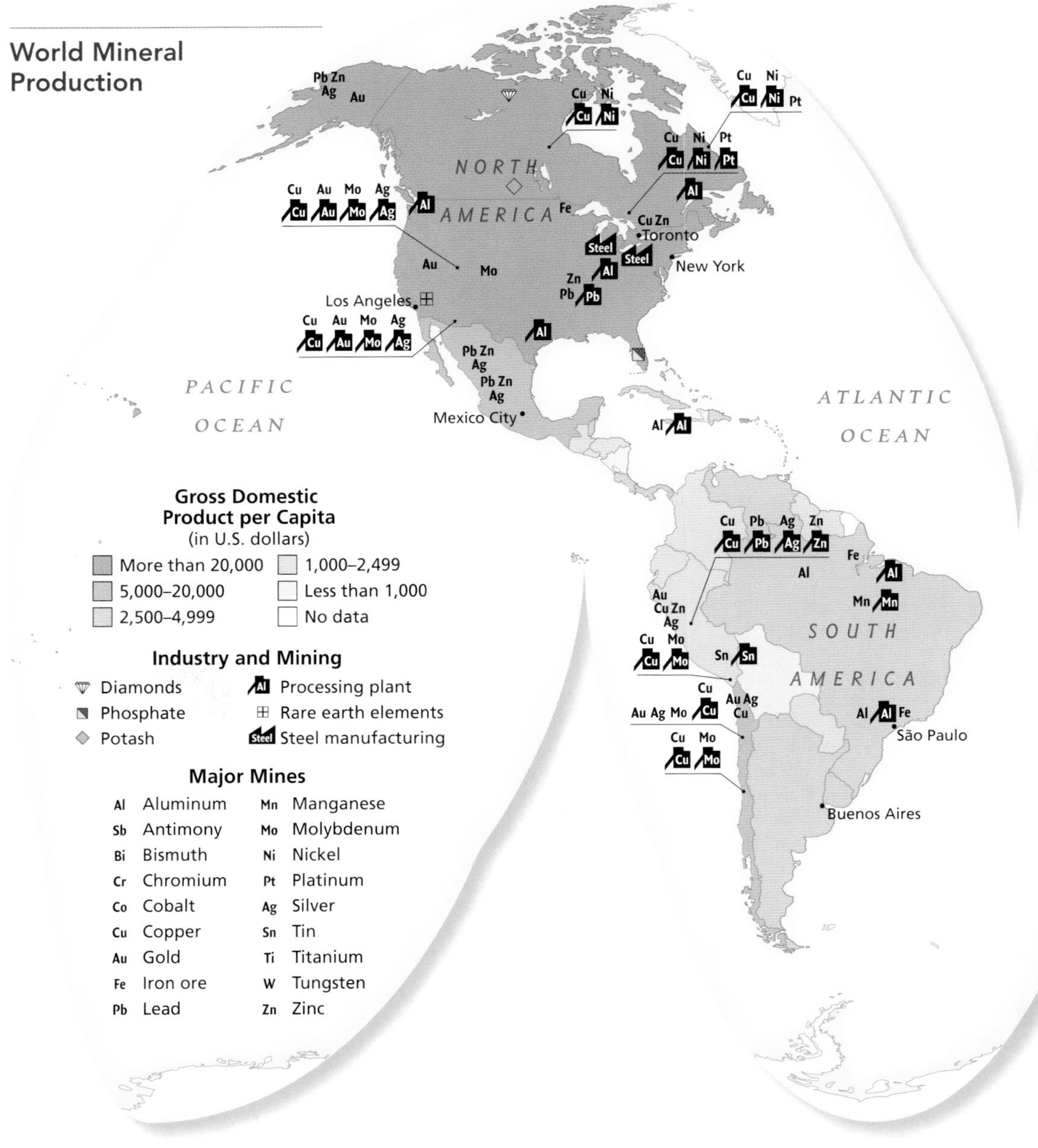
World Mineral Production
NORTH AMERICA
SOUTH AMERICA
PACIFIC OCEAN
ATLANTIC OCEAN
Toronto
New York
Los Angeles
Mexico City
São Paulo
Buenos Aires
Gross Domestic Product per Capita (in U.S. dollars)
More than 20,000
5,000–20,000
2,500–4,999
1,000–2,499
Less than 1,000
No data
Industry and Mining
Diamonds
Phosphate
Potash
Processing plant
Rare earth elements
Steel manufacturing
Major Mines
Al Aluminum
Sb Antimony
Bi Bismuth
Cr Chromium
Co Cobalt
Cu Copper
Au Gold
Fe Iron ore
Pb Lead
Mn Manganese
Mo Molybdenum
Ni Nickel
Pt Platinum
Ag Silver
Sn Tin
Ti Titanium
W Tungsten
Zn Zinc

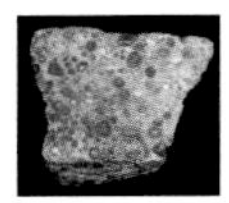

Aluminum (Al) Bauxite, the principal ore of aluminum, is an aggregate of millimeter- to centimeter-size oval structures, composed of aluminum hydroxide, that form in areas of deep and prolonged tropical weathering of aluminum-rich parent materials. World production of bauxite was 156 million tons in 2004. Australia was the largest producer (56 million), followed by Brazil, Guinea, and China. Alumina (Al_2O_3), an intermediate product, is made by refining bauxite and then smelting to make aluminum metal; both of these steps are very energy intensive. China, the United States, and Russia have the largest aluminum smelting capacities. In 2004, the world production of aluminum was estimated at 28.9 million tons.

Chromium (Cr) Chromite ($FeCr_2O_4$) is the principal ore mineral of chromium. Black chromite forms in layered, iron- and magnesium-rich igneous deposits (as in this photo), which contributed nearly half the world's 2004 production, estimated at more than 17 million tons. South Africa has long been the largest producer on the planet. Kazakhstan and India together produced another 33 percent. The main use of chromium is in the manufacture of stainless and heat-resistant steels. Chromite is also used in the production of chromium chemicals and in acid-resistant refractories.

Copper (Cu) Chalcopyrite ($CuFeS_2$), the principal ore of copper, occurs as veins and disseminations in igneous and sedimentary host rocks. Copper is also mined as other sulfides, the native metal, and oxides. In 2004, world mine production of copper metal was 14.5 million tons. Chile was the leading producer (5.4 million tons), followed by the U.S. (1.2 million), and Peru (1 million). Copper is used for electric and electronic products, in construction of buildings, and as an alloy metal.

Diamond (gem and industrial) Diamonds are used both as gems and as materials to increase the hardness of cutting tools. Natural diamonds are generally brought to the Earth's surface by unusual volcanic eruptions, gas-charged igneous melts that originate at depths of 150+ km in the Earth. The map locates the major producers of natural gems and industrial diamonds. Diamonds can also be produced synthetically, and about 88 percent of industrial diamonds now have this origin. Industrial diamond mining produced 70 million carats in 2004, more than 90 percent of which came from the Congo, Australia, Russia, Botswana, and South Africa.

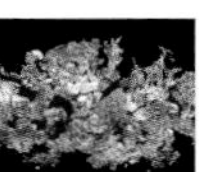

Gold (Au) Native gold and electrum, an alloy with silver, are the most common forms and precipitate from hot, water-rich fluids in the Earth. Historically, gold was used as money or as a backup for paper money. Today, no major country backs its currency with gold, but private investors may hold gold as a hedge against economic uncertainty. Gold is also used in jewelry, as a dental material, and in electronic equipment. South Africa was the largest producer of mined gold in 2004 (344 tons), followed by the U.S., Australia, and China. Total world production in 2004 was estimated at 2,470 tons.

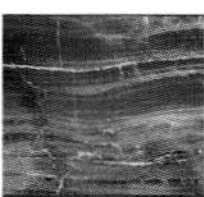

Iron Ore and Steel Iron (Fe) is the 4th most abundant element in the Earth's crust and occurs in a wide variety of oxide (magnetite and hematite), hydroxide (goethite), sulfide (pyrite, pyrrhotite), carbonate (siderite), and silicate minerals found in sedimentary rocks. Nearly all the 2004 world production of 1.25 billion tons came from iron oxide and hydroxide deposits. The largest producers were China, Brazil, and Australia. In 2004, world crude steel production was over one billion tons. China, the EU countries, and Japan were the main producers.

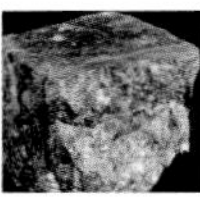

Lead (Pb) Galena (PbS) is the principal ore mineral of lead. In 2004, world mine production of lead was 3.1 million tons. China was the largest producer (950,000 tons), followed by Australia and the United States. Due to lead's toxicity, the number of lead-containing products has been reduced in recent years, and automobile lead-acid batteries are effectively recycled. This effort has reduced the consumption of primary (new) lead in the United States and Europe, but China's use continues to expand. Lead is also used in ammunition, solder, in television glass, and in the radiation shields for x-ray equipment.

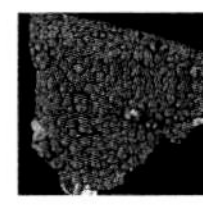

Manganese (Mn) This element is essential to steel making as an additive to remove sulfur and excess oxygen. It is also employed as an alloying element and is used in dry-cell batteries. Mn geochemistry is similar to iron's; however, it is never mined from the same deposits. World production was 11 million tons in 2004. The largest producers are South Africa and Gabon. Australia comes in third, followed by Brazil, Ghana, and India. China does not produce much, and must import manganese.

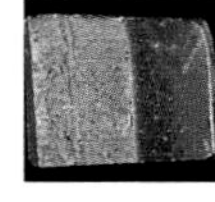

Nickel (Ni) Two very different types of deposits are the sources for nickel. In sulfide deposits found in ultramafic rock complexes, nickel occurs primarily in the mineral pentlandite ($(Fe,Ni)_9S_8$). It is also produced from oxide and silicate minerals in thick soils that form over certain rock types in tropical environments. World mine production was 1.4 million tons in 2004. Russia (the top producer, at 315,000 tons) and Canada produce nickel from sulfide ores; Australia, Indonesia, and New Caledonia rely on the deeply weathered soils. Nickel is used to make stainless steel and in electroplating.

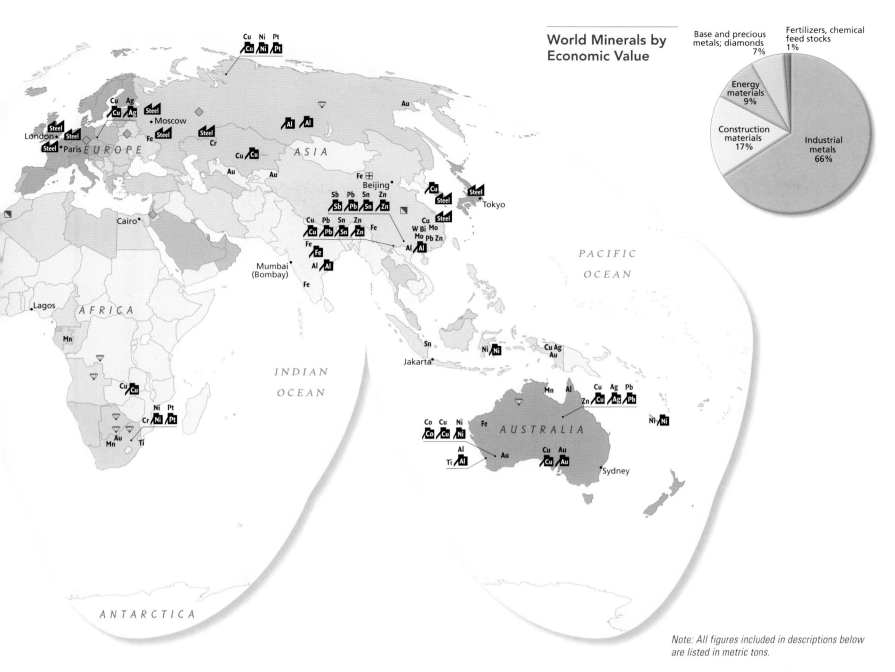

World Minerals by Economic Value

Industrial metals 66%
Construction materials 17%
Energy materials 9%
Base and precious metals; diamonds 7%
Fertilizers, chemical feed stocks 1%

Note: All figures included in descriptions below are listed in metric tons.

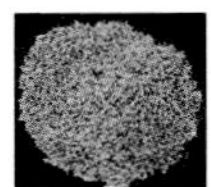

Phosphate Rock (P) This substance is the primary ore needed to make phosphoric acid, which is used in the production of certain fertilizers. Most phosphate deposits initially formed when phosphorus-rich deep-ocean waters upwelled onto tropical continental shelves, and phosphate-rich sediments were deposited through biologic activity. In 2004, the world production of phosphate rock was 138 million tons; the United States was the leading producer (37 million tons). China (25 million) was second, while Morocco and Western Sahara together accounted for 23 million tons.

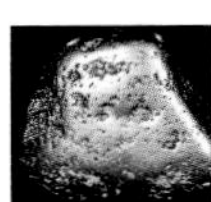

Platinum-Group Metals (Pt, Pd, Ru, Rh, Ir, Os) These substances are used in catalytic converters that clean the exhaust from cars; they are also used in jewelry and in chemotherapy for cancer. World mine production of platinum and palladium in 2004 was 218 tons and 190 tons, respectively, and came from mafic igneous rock complexes, usually of Precambrian age. South Africa was the leading producer of platinum (163 tons), followed by Russia (36 tons). Russia produced 74 tons of palladium, while South Africa mined 78 tons. Other important producers of platinum-group metals are the U.S. and Canada.

Potash (K) This term is the industrial name for a group of water-soluble salts that contain potassium. The main sources are deposits that include mixtures of the minerals halite (NaCl), sylvite (KCl), and carnallite (KMgCl3•6H2O), along with other potassium-, magnesium-, and bromine-bearing minerals and saline brines. Most is used in fertilizer, while the remainder is employed in the production of chemicals. Total 2004 production of 30 million tons came mainly from Canada (9.5), Russia (4.7), Belarus (4.65), and Germany (3.67 million). Israel and Jordan produce significant amounts of potash from the Dead Sea.

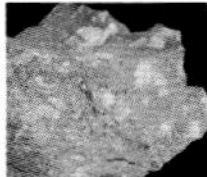

Rare Earths (REE) This group of 17 metals ranges from lanthanum (La) to lutetium (Lu) in the periodic table of elements. Rare earth metals are used in the making of a wide variety of products, including chemical catalysts for petroleum refining, rechargeable batteries, phosphors for TV and computer screens, and superalloys. These elements are indeed "rare," and concentrated only in unusual igneous bodies. World mine production of rare earth oxides was 102,000 tons in 2004 with China producing the great majority (95,000) of these.

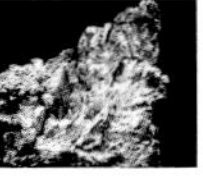

Silver (Ag) This substance has the highest electrical conductivity of all elements. It occurs in native form; mixed with native gold in electrum; as simple sulfides (argentite, Ag_2S); as complex antimony- and arsenic-bearing minerals; and as a trace constituent in galena. Silver is used for coins, electrical and electronic components, jewelry, tableware, and in film photography (digital cameras are causing a reduced demand). In 2004, world mine production was 19,500 tons. Mexico, which mined 2,850 tons of silver, was the largest producer; it was followed by Peru (2,800 tons) and China (2,600 tons).

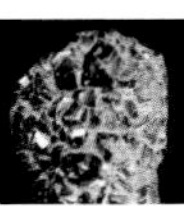

Tin (Sn) The most common use of tin is as a coating to prevent oxidation of a covered metal, such as steel in "tin cans." When alloyed with other metals, tin makes solder, pewter, and bronze. Window glass is manufactured by floating molten glass on molten tin. Organo-tin chemicals are used as pesticides, fungicides, and wood preservatives. The major ore mineral of tin is cassiterite (SnO_2). China, which mined 100,000 tons in 2004, was the world's largest producer that year. Indonesia (70,000 tons) and Peru (40,000 tons) were the second and third largest producers. Total world production in 2004 was 250,000 tons.

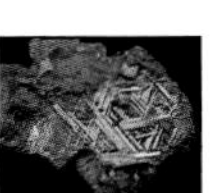

Titanium (Ti) More than 95 percent of titanium is consumed as TiO_2 pigment; the rest is processed to make titanium metal or sponge. Because titanium metal is light, has high strength, and resists corrosion, it is used in aerospace, marine, medical, and military applications. Russia, Japan, and Kazakhstan were the largest makers of titanium sponge in 2004. The titanium-bearing minerals ilmenite ($FeTiO_3$) and rutile (TiO_2), originally formed in igneous rocks, are common components in beach and dune sands and are processed into TiO_2 pigment used in paints and plastics. Australia (1.1 million tons) and South Africa (also 1.1 million) were the largest producers of titanium-bearing mineral concentrates in 2004.

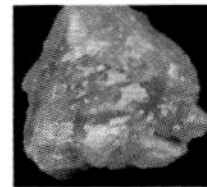

Tungsten (formerly wolfram) (W) The main use of tungsten is in tungsten-carbide cutting tools. Because of its high melting point, this substance is added to certain steels to give them strength at high temperatures. It is also used in lightbulb filaments. Tungsten mainly occurs in two types of deposits—either in skarns than contain scheelite (CaWO4), or in veins that contain wolframite (Fe,Mn(WO_4). In 2004, China produced 53,000 tons of tungsten, followed by Russia, with 3,500 tons. World production was 60,000 tons.

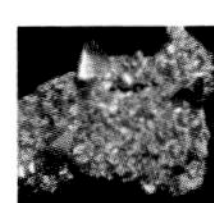

Zinc (Zn) The largest use of zinc is as a coating for steel; zinc-coated, "galvanized" steel resists rust and corrosion. Zinc is also used to make brass, solder, and batteries, and it is added to soil, rubber, and cosmetics. In 2004, world mine production was 9.1 million tons. The largest producers were China (2 million), Peru (1.4 million), and Australia (1.3 million). Canada and the United States were also significant producers, with 90 percent of U.S. production coming from a single mine in Alaska. Sphalerite (ZnS) is the principal ore mineral of zinc.

MOST ENVIRONMENTAL DAMAGE is due to human activity. Some harmful actions are inadvertent—the release, for example, of chlorofluorocarbons (CFCs), once thought to be inert gases, into the atmosphere. Others are deliberate and include such acts as the disposal of sewage into rivers.

Among the root causes of human-induced damage are excessive consumption (mainly in industrialized countries) and rapid population growth (primarily in the developing nations). So, even though scientists may develop products and technologies that have no adverse effects on the environment, their efforts will be muted if both population and consumption continue to increase worldwide.

Socioeconomic and environmental indicators can reveal much about long-term trends; unfortunately, such data are not collected routinely in many countries. With respect to urban environmental quality, suitable indicators would include electricity consumption, numbers of automobiles, and rates of land conversion from rural to urban. The rapid conversion of countryside to built-up areas during the last 25 to 50 years is a strong indicator that change is occurring at an ever quickening pace.

Many types of environmental stress are interrelated and may have far-reaching consequences. Global warming, for one, will likely increase water scarcity, desertification, deforestation, and coastal flooding (due to rising sea level)—all of which can have a significant impact on human populations.

NORTH AMERICA
SOUTH AMERICA
PACIFIC OCEAN
ATLANTIC OCEAN
Chicago
New York
Philadelphia
Los Angeles
Miami
Mexico City
Bogotá
Lima
Belo Horizonte
Rio de Janeiro
São Paulo
Santiago
Buenos Aires
Cities
Megacity, over 10 million
5 to 10 million
Pollution
Major industrial accident
Major oil rig explosion
Major oil spill
Dead zone (water persistently oxygen-starved)
Areas most sensitive to acid rain
Frequent pollution from shipping
Desertification
Areas at highest risk of desertification
Deforestation
Current tropical forest
Cleared tropical forest
Current temperate forest
Cleared temperate forest

Global Climate Change

The world's climate is constantly changing—over decades, centuries, and millennia. Currently, several lines of reasoning support the idea that humans are likely to live in a much warmer world before the end of this century. Atmospheric concentrations of carbon dioxide and other "greenhouse gases" are now well above historical levels, and simulation models predict that these gases will result in a warming of the lower atmosphere (particularly in polar regions) but a cooling of the stratosphere. Experimental evidence supports these predictions.

Indeed, throughout the last decade the globally averaged annual surface temperature was higher than the hundred-year mean. Model simulations of the impacts of this warming—and studies indicating significant reductions already occurring in polar permafrost and sea ice cover—are so alarming that most scientists and many policy people believe that immediate action must be taken to slow the changes.

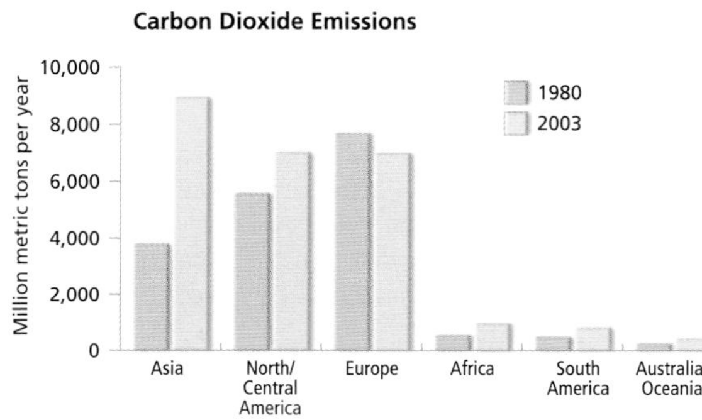
Carbon Dioxide Emissions
Million metric tons per year
10,000
8,000
6,000
4,000
2,000
0
1980
2003
Asia
North/Central America
Europe
Africa
South America
Australia/Oceania

Depletion of the Ozone Layer

The ozone layer in the stratosphere has long shielded the biosphere from harmful solar ultraviolet radiation. Since the 1970s, however, the layer has been thinning over Antarctica—and more recently elsewhere. If the process continues, there will be significant effects on human health, including more cases of skin cancer and eye cataracts, and on biological systems. Fortunately, scientific understanding of the phenomenon came rather quickly.

Beginning in the 1950s, increasing amounts of CFCs (and other gases with similar properties) were released into the atmosphere. CFCs are chemically inert in the lower atmosphere but decompose in the stratosphere, subsequently destroying ozone. This understanding provided the basis for successful United Nations actions (Vienna Convention, 1985; Montréal Protocol, 1987) to phase out these gases.

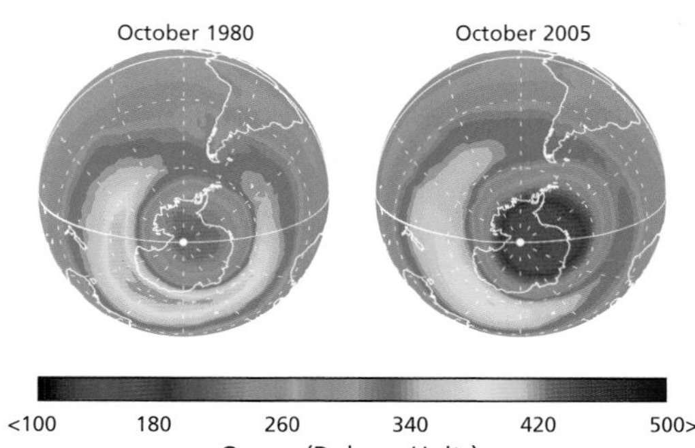
October 1980
October 2005
<100
180
260
340
420
500>
Ozone (Dobson Units)

Pollution

People know that water is not always pure and that beaches may be closed to bathers due to raw sewage. An example of serious contamination is the Minamata, Japan, disaster of the 1950s. More than a hundred people died and thousands were paralyzed after they ate fish containing mercury discharged from a local factory. Examples of water and soil pollution also include the contamination of groundwater, salinization of irrigated lands in semiarid regions, and the so-called chemical time bomb issue, where accumulated toxins are suddenly mobilized following a change in external conditions. Preventing and mitigating such problems requires the modernization of industrial plants, additional staff training, a better understanding of the problems, the development of more effective policies, and greater public support.

Urban air quality remains a serious problem, particularly in developing countries. In some developed countries, successful control measures have improved air quality over the past 50 years; in others, trends have actually reversed, with brown haze often hanging over metropolitan areas.

Solid and hazardous waste disposal is a universal urban problem, and the issue is on many political agendas. In the world's poorest countries, "garbage pickers" (usually women and children) are symbols of abject poverty. In North America, toxic wastes are frequently transported long distances. But transport introduces the risk of highway and rail accidents, causing serious local contamination.

Human Footprint
Highest Lowest

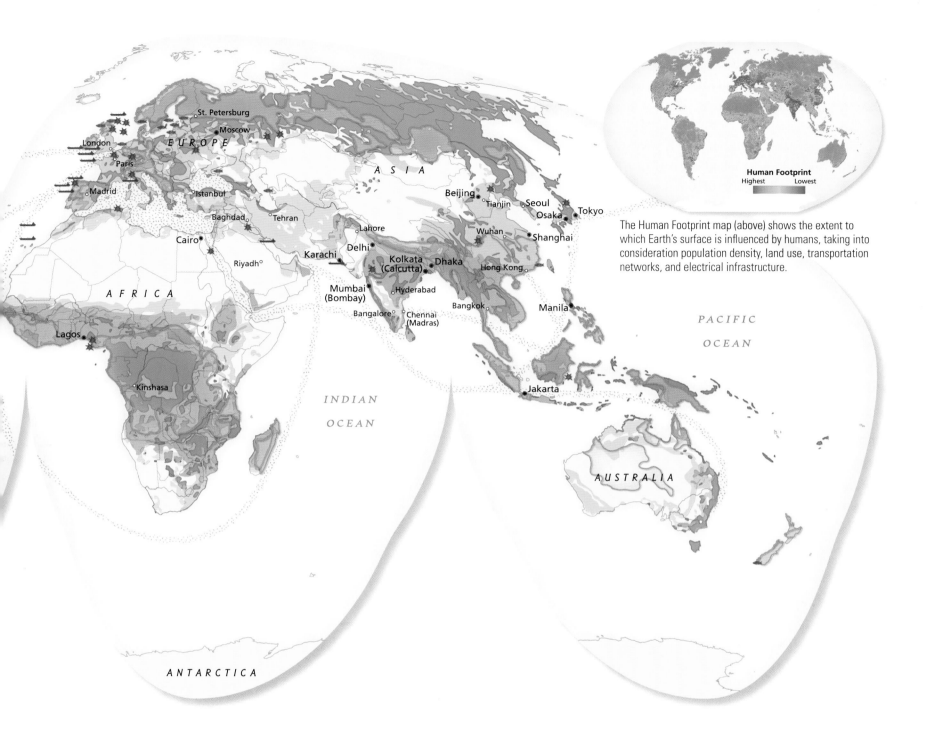

The Human Footprint map (above) shows the extent to which Earth's surface is influenced by humans, taking into consideration population density, land use, transportation networks, and electrical infrastructure.

Water Scarcity

Shortages of drinking water are increasing in many parts of the world, and studies indicate that by the year 2025, one billion people in northern China, Afghanistan, Pakistan, Iraq, Egypt, Tunisia, and other areas will face "absolute drinking water scarcity." But water is also needed by industry and agriculture, in hydroelectric-power production, and for transport. With increasing population, industrialization, and global warming, the situation can only worsen.

Water scarcity has already become a major brake on development in many countries, including Poland, Singapore, and parts of North America. In countries where artesian wells are pumping groundwater more rapidly than it can be replaced, water is actually being mined. In river basins where water is shared by several jurisdictions, social tensions will increase. This is particularly so in the Middle East, North Africa, and East Africa, where the availability of fresh water is less than 1,300 cubic yards (1,000 cu m) per capita per annum; water-rich countries such as Iceland, New Zealand, and Canada enjoy more than a hundred times as much.

Irrigation can be a particularly wasteful use of water. Some citrus-growing nations, for example, are exporting not only fruit but also so-called virtual water, which includes the water inside the fruit as well as the wasted irrigation water that drains away from the orchards. Many individuals and organizations believe that water scarcity is the major environmental issue of the 21st century.

Soil Degradation and Desertification

Deserts exist where rainfall is too little and too erratic to support life except in a few favored localities. Even in these "oases," occasional sandstorms may inhibit agricultural activity. In semiarid zones, lands can easily become degraded or desert-like if they are overused or subject to long or frequent drought. The Sahel of Africa faced this situation in the 1970s and early 1980s, but rainfall subsequently returned to normal, and some of the land recovered.

Often, an extended drought over a wide area can trigger desertification if the land has already been degraded by human actions. Causes of degradation include overgrazing, overcultivation, deforestation, soil erosion, overconsumption of groundwater, and the salinization/waterlogging of irrigated lands.

An emerging issue is the effect of climate warming on desertification. Warming will probably lead to more drought in more parts of the world. Glaciers would begin to disappear, and the meltwater flowing through semiarid downstream areas would diminish.

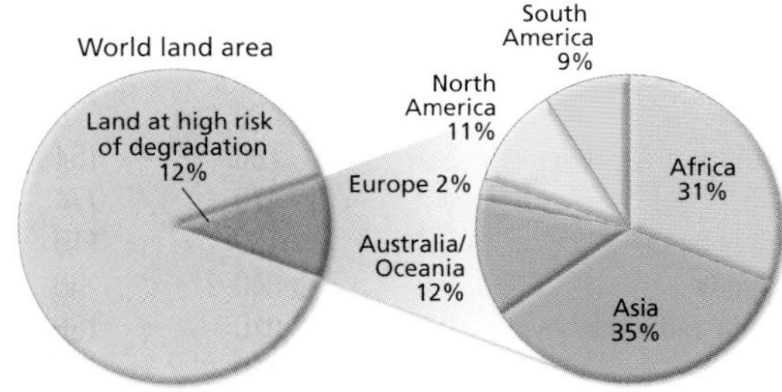
World land area
Land at high risk of degradation 12%
South America 9%
North America 11%
Europe 2%
Australia/ Oceania 12%
Africa 31%
Asia 35%

Deforestation

Widespread deforestation in the wet tropics is largely the result of short-term and unsustainable uses. In Mexico, Brazil, and Peru, only 30, 42, and 45 percent (respectively) of the total land still has a closed forest cover. International agencies such as FAO, UNEP, UNESCO, WWF/IUCN, and others are working to improve the situation through education, restoration, and land protection. Venezuela enjoys a very high level of forest protection (63 percent); by comparison, Russia protects just 2 percent.

The loss of forests has contributed to the atmospheric buildup of carbon dioxide (a greenhouse gas), changes in rainfall patterns (in Brazil at least), soil erosion, and soil nutrient losses. Deforestation in the wet tropics, where more than half of the world's species live, is the main cause of biodiversity loss.

In contrast to the tropics, the forest cover in the temperate zones has increased slightly in the last 50 years because of the adoption of conservation practices and because abandoned farmland has been replaced by forest.

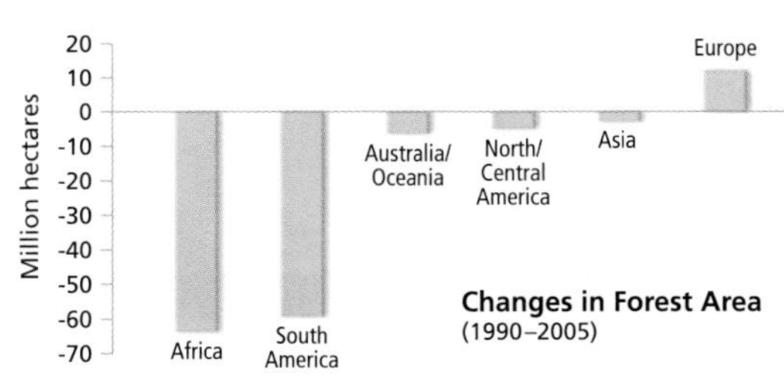
Million hectares
20
10
0
-10
-20
-30
-40
-50
-60
-70
Africa
South America
Australia/ Oceania
North/ Central America
Asia
Europe
Changes in Forest Area (1990–2005)

IN RECENT YEARS, environmental groups and world organizations have identified certain sites and land areas whose value is so great, and status so critical, that they require special protection.

This protection takes various forms. UNESCO's World Heritage Committee has identified more than 800 sites that are of great cultural or natural value. Some are very famous: Stonehenge, the Great Wall of China, the Taj Mahal, the Great Barrier Reef, and the Grand Canyon, for example. Others are monuments to important and sometimes tragic chapters in history: Auschwitz in Poland and the Senegalese island of Gorée, which was for 400 years the largest slaving station on the African coast. Some sites are threatened natural features of great value: the Danube Delta in Romania, for instance, and Lake Baikal in Russia.

Conservationists have identified 34 "biodiversity hotspots" (see World Biodiversity, pp. 42-43) that make up less than 2.5 percent of Earth's land surface but are the only remaining habitats for 50 percent of all plant species and 42 percent of all nonfish vertebrates. Currently, the average protected area coverage of hotspots is 10 percent of their original extent.

Though "protected areas" vary greatly in their objectives, the extent to which they are integrated into the wider landscape, and the effectiveness with which they are managed, provide powerful evidence of a nation's commitment to conservation.

NORTH AMERICA
Toronto
New York
Los Angeles
Mexico City
ATLANTIC OCEAN
World Heritage Sites
Cultural
Natural
Mixed site (site with both cultural and natural value)
SOUTH AMERICA
São Paulo
PACIFIC OCEAN
Buenos Aires

Designated Protected Areas

An array of overlapping conventions designed to preserve everything from wetlands, seas, and wilderness to birds and biogenetic reserves protects approximately 11.5 percent of Earth's land area. In contrast, less than one percent of the total ocean area is protected.

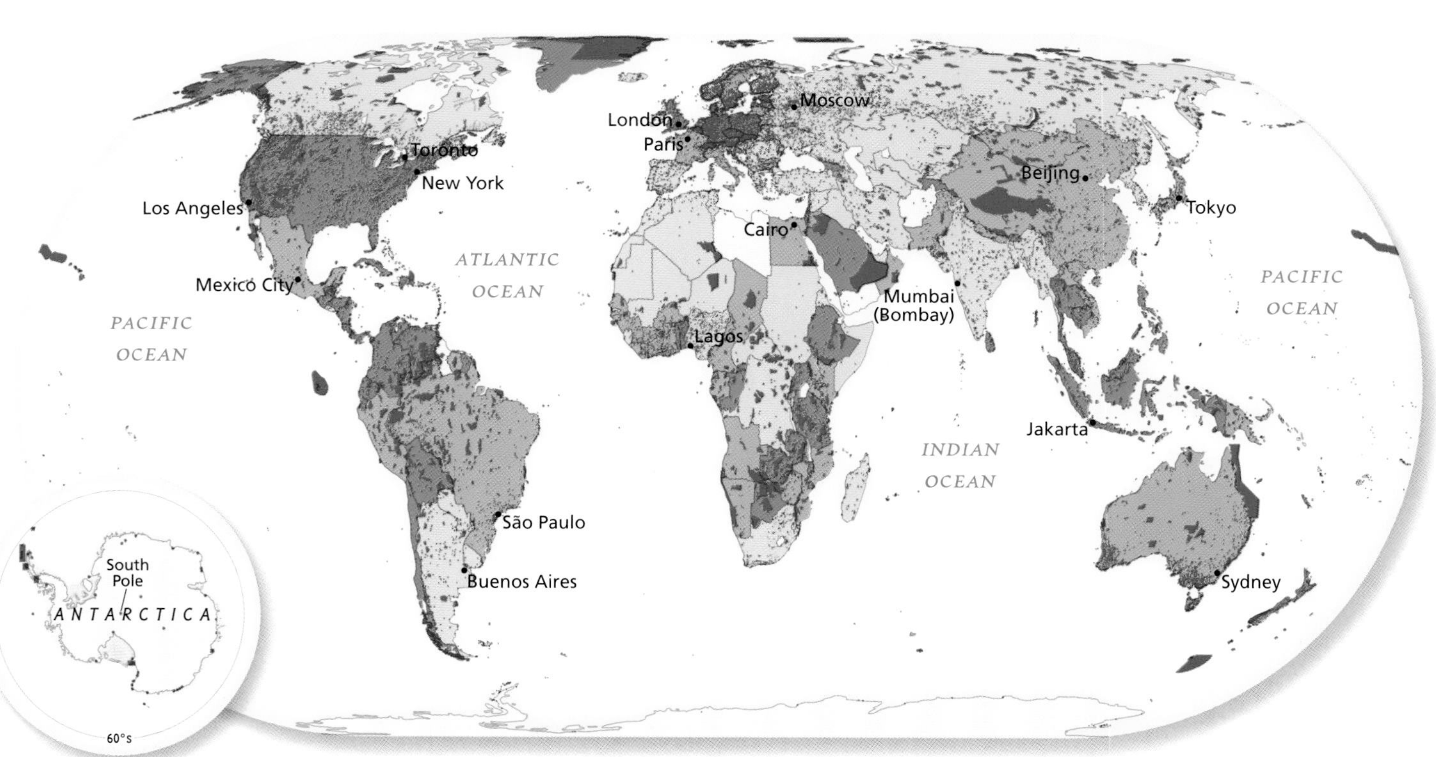
London
Paris
Moscow
Toronto
New York
Beijing
Los Angeles
Tokyo
Cairo
ATLANTIC OCEAN
Mexico City
Mumbai (Bombay)
PACIFIC OCEAN
PACIFIC OCEAN
Lagos
Jakarta
INDIAN OCEAN
São Paulo
Buenos Aires
Sydney

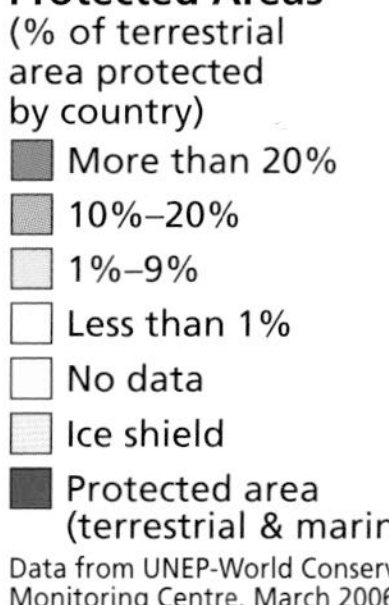
South Pole
ANTARCTICA
60°S

Protected Areas
(% of terrestrial area protected by country)
- More than 20%
- 10%–20%
- 1%–9%
- Less than 1%
- No data
- Ice shield
- Protected area (terrestrial & marine)

Data from UNEP-World Conservation Monitoring Centre, March 2006

COUNTRIES WITH HIGHEST % PROTECTED AREA

COUNTRY (WITH TOTAL AREA >11,000 SQ. MI.)	PERCENTAGE OF LAND PROTECTED	GDP PER CAPITA (U.S. $)	POP. DENSITY (SQ. MI.)
Venezuela	70.3	4,260	76
Zambia	41.5	460	39
Tanzania	39.7	300	100
Saudi Arabia	38.5	10,200	30
Panama	37.2	4,270	111
Guatemala	32.6	2,160	302
Colombia	32.6	2,130	105
New Zealand	32.1	24,500	39
Germany	31.5	33,160	598
Estonia	31.4	8,230	77

COUNTRIES WITH LOWEST % PROTECTED AREA

COUNTRY (WITH TOTAL AREA >11,000 SQ. MI.)	PERCENTAGE OF LAND PROTECTED	GDP PER CAPITA (U.S. $)	POP. DENSITY (SQ. MI.)
Iraq	0.0	950	170
Yemen	0.0	640	102
Libya	0.1	3,400	8
Lesotho	0.2	760	154
Haiti	0.3	470	774
Afghanistan	0.3	180	119
Uruguay	0.4	3,840	50
Bosnia and Herzegovina	0.5	2,020	185
Somalia	0.8	260	35
Mauritania	1.1	420	8

PROTECTED LAND AREAS BY REGION

CONTINENT OR REGION	SQUARE MILES PROTECTED	AS PERCENTAGE OF TOTAL LAND AREA
North America	1,249,049	16.5
South America	1,370,046	19.8
Europe	877,583	9.0
Africa	1,187,394	10.2
Asia	1,193,905	12.0
Australia/Oceania	382,786	12.3
Antarctica	1,749	0.03
WORLD	**6,653,720**	**11.5**

London
Paris
EUROPE
Moscow
ASIA
Beijing
Tokyo
Cairo
Mumbai (Bombay)
AFRICA
Lagos
PACIFIC OCEAN
INDIAN OCEAN
Jakarta
AUSTRALIA
Sydney
ANTARCTICA

Endemism

Regional Share of Plant Endemism

South America 24%
Africa 10%
North America 17%
Europe 2%
Asia 35%
Australia/Oceania 12%

Endemism—the presence of species found nowhere else—is a key criterion for determining conservation priorities, as areas with high levels of endemism are the most vulnerable to biodiversity loss. The highest levels of endemism occur on oceanic islands and in montane regions.

Ouratea dependens is one of thousands of plants unique to Madagascar.

The World Heritage Site System

NATURAL HERITAGE SITE
Canada's Tatshenshini-Alsek Provincial Wilderness holds a portion of the largest nonpolar ice cap and hundreds of valley glaciers; it is the last major stronghold for North America's grizzly bears. The park designation averted what would have been an enormous open-pit mine.

CULTURAL HERITAGE SITE
Site of some of the most important monuments of ancient Greece, the Acropolis illustrates the civilizations, myths, and religions that flourished there for a period of over a thousand years. Europe claims about half of the world's cultural heritage sites, with over 300.

MIXED HERITAGE SITE
The town of Ohrid, on the shores of Lake Ohrid in the former Yugoslav Republic of Macedonia, exemplifies a mixed heritage site. The ten-million-year-old lake may be the oldest in Europe, and the town is one of the continent's oldest continuously inhabited sites.

WORLD HERITAGE LIST

The World Heritage List was established under the terms of the 1972 UNESCO "Convention Concerning the Protection of the World Cultural and Natural Heritage."

The first 12 World Heritage Sites were named in 1978; among them were L'Anse aux Meadows in Canada, the site of the first Viking settlement in North America; the Galápagos Islands; the cathedral of Aachen, Germany; the historic city center of Krakow, Poland; the island of Gorée, off Senegal; and Mesa Verde and Yellowstone National Parks in the United States.

New sites are added annually. In December 2005, the list comprised 812 sites, with 628 cultural, 160 natural, and 24 mixed sites, located in 137 countries. On average, 30 newly designated sites are added to the list each year, but 2000 must have been considered an auspicious time for listings; 61 sites were added that year, the largest number ever.

MOST VISITED NATURAL HERITAGE SITES

NAME	SIZE OF SITE (SQ. MI.)	COUNTRY	VISITORS PER YEAR
Great Smoky Mountains National Park	805	United States	9,205,037
Wet Tropics of Queensland	3,453	Australia	5,000,000
Canadian Rocky Mountain Parks	8,907	Canada	6,017,221
Grand Canyon National Park	1,880	United States	4,308,549
Yosemite National Park	1,176	United States	3,272,155
Olympic National Park	1,425	United States	3,047,234
Yellowstone National Park	3,428	United States	2,866,785
Glacier/Waterton National Park	1,767	U.S./Canada	2,399,161
Great Barrier Reef	134,633	Australia	1,971,945

THERE IS A GROWING CONSENSUS that globalization is defined by increasing levels of interdependence over vast distances, not just in the economic dimension, but along the lines of person-to-person contact, technological connectivity, and political ties. In many important ways, global integration is continuing to deepen over the years, and ties between countries have continued to strengthen despite deterrents such as acts of terror, stalling of trade talks, and divisions over international peace and security issues.

The A.T. Kearney/Foreign Policy magazine Globalization Index "reverse-engineers" the globalization phenomenon and quantifies its most important component indicators—spanning trade, finance, political engagement, information technology, and personal contact—to determine the rankings of 62 countries. These countries together account for 96 percent of the world's gross domestic product (GDP) and 85 percent of the world's population. The index measures 12 variables, which are divided into four "baskets": economic integration, technological connectivity, personal contact, and political engagement.

In years past, Western European countries have claimed many of the top spots as engaged participants in the international system. Small trading nations like Singapore and Ireland have tended to take top places in the index due in part to their particular reliance on other countries for trade, investment, and tourism.

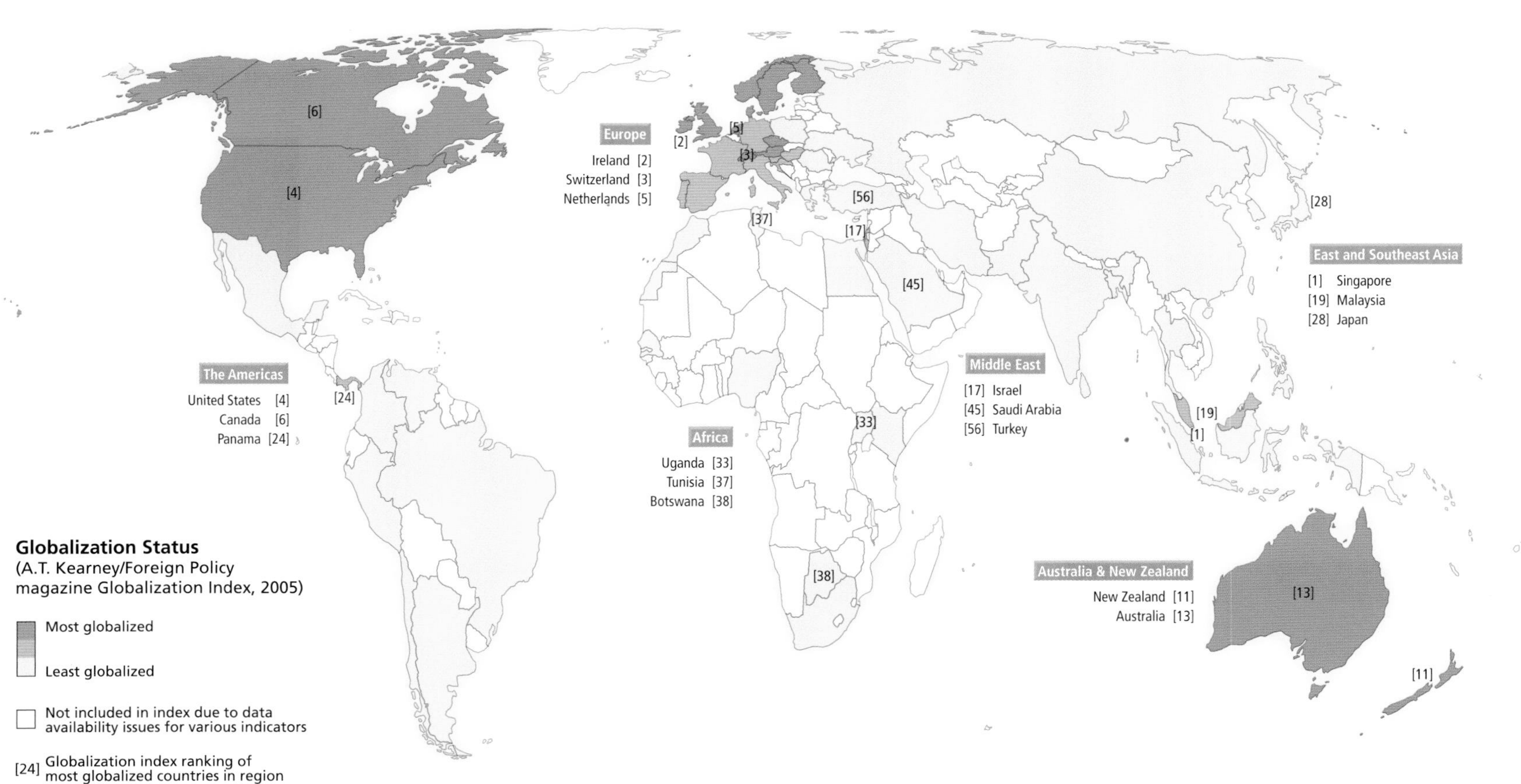
[6]
[4]
Europe
Ireland [2]
Switzerland [3]
Netherlands [5]
[2]
[5]
[3]
[56]
[37]
[17]
[45]
[28]
East and Southeast Asia
[1] Singapore
[19] Malaysia
[28] Japan
The Americas
United States [4]
Canada [6]
Panama [24]
[24]
Middle East
[17] Israel
[45] Saudi Arabia
[56] Turkey
Africa
Uganda [33]
Tunisia [37]
Botswana [38]
[33]
[19]
[1]
[38]
Australia & New Zealand
New Zealand [11]
Australia [13]
[13]
[11]
Globalization Status
(A.T. Kearney/Foreign Policy magazine Globalization Index, 2005)
Most globalized
Least globalized
Not included in index due to data availability issues for various indicators
[24] Globalization index ranking of most globalized countries in region

Transnational Corporations

Transnational corporations have played an important role in global economic integration, through sales, investments, and operations in countries around the world. In fact, a number of them have assets equivalent to or larger than the nominal GDPs of some nations. Many of these companies have also made their non-economic influence felt as their products and services shape consumption habits, business practices, and local cultures.

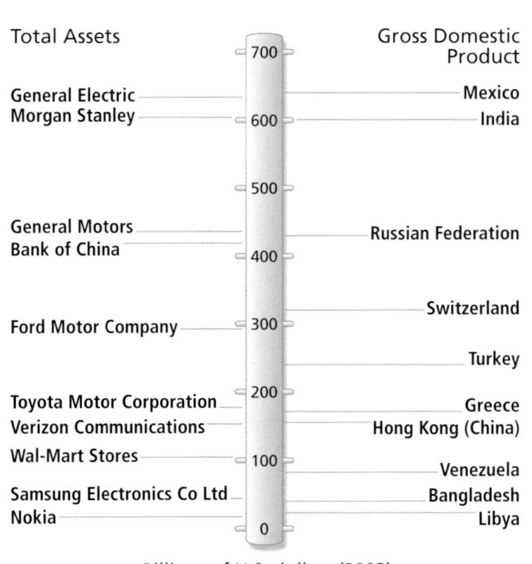
Total Assets
Gross Domestic Product
General Electric
Morgan Stanley
General Motors
Bank of China
Ford Motor Company
Toyota Motor Corporation
Verizon Communications
Wal-Mart Stores
Samsung Electronics Co Ltd
Nokia
Mexico
India
Russian Federation
Switzerland
Turkey
Greece
Hong Kong (China)
Venezuela
Bangladesh
Libya
700
600
500
400
300
200
100
0
Billions of U.S. dollars (2003)

Extremes of Globalization

In the 2005 Globalization Index, Singapore took the top spot on the strength of its foreign trade ties and increased political engagement. Ireland came second, with moderate gains in investment inflows and services trade, as well as an increase in non-economic ties such as international travel and continued participation in the United Nations' peacekeeping efforts. The strong United States showing is primarily a result of its remarkable technological prowess, evidenced by the growth in Internet hosts and secure servers, which are enabling factors for continued technological integration.

Yet a glance at this year's index suggests that those who seek to expand globalization's benefits have their work cut out for them. The bottom ten countries in the index account for more than 50 percent of the world's population. As many indicators are measured on a per-capita basis, gains from globalization may be slow to reach the massive populations of these nations.

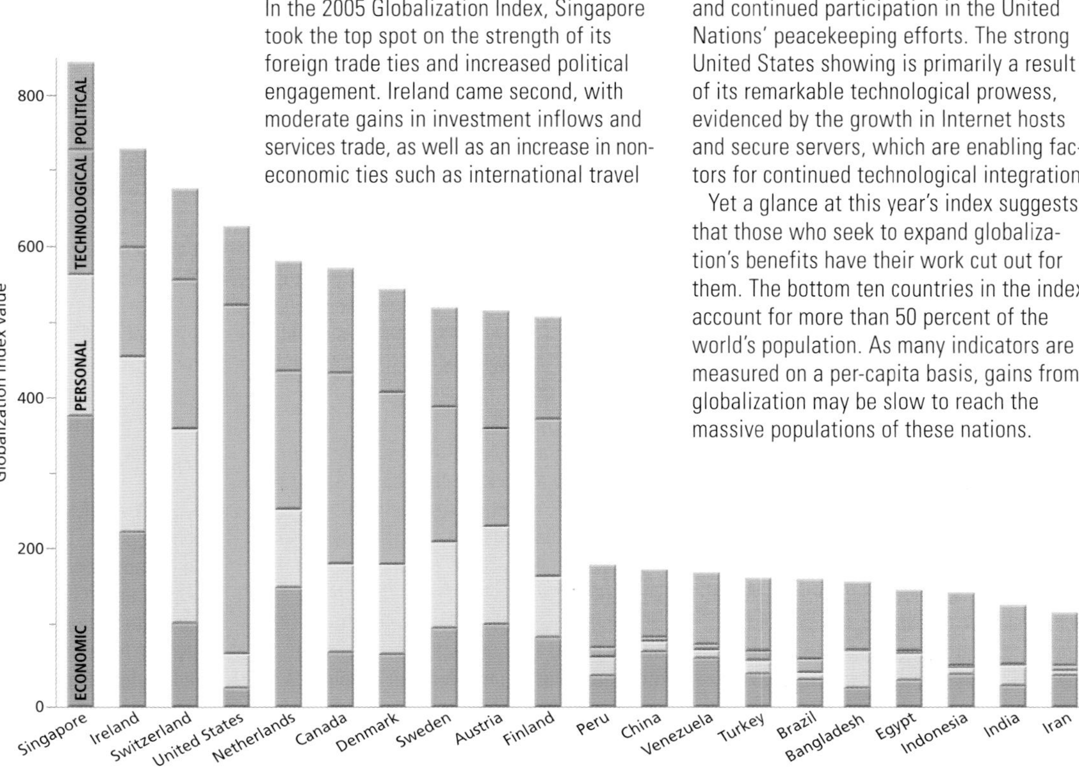
Globalization index value
800
600
400
200
0
ECONOMIC
PERSONAL
TECHNOLOGICAL
POLITICAL
Singapore
Ireland
Switzerland
United States
Netherlands
Canada
Denmark
Sweden
Austria
Finland
Peru
China
Venezuela
Turkey
Brazil
Bangladesh
Egypt
Indonesia
India
Iran
Most Globalized Countries
Least Globalized Countries

Economic Integration

Economic integration combines data on trade and foreign direct investment. Measured as a percentage of gross domestic product (GDP), foreign direct investment flows include investments in physical assets, such as plant and equipment, both into and out of a country. These measures reflect a country's dependence on global trade and investment; however, they do not necessarily reflect economic strength.

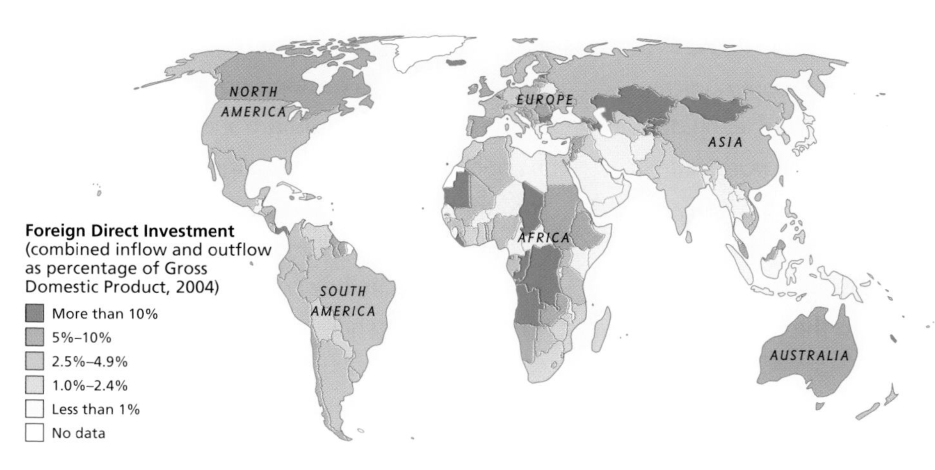
NORTH AMERICA
EUROPE
ASIA
AFRICA
SOUTH AMERICA
AUSTRALIA
Foreign Direct Investment
(combined inflow and outflow as percentage of Gross Domestic Product, 2004)
More than 10%
5%–10%
2.5%–4.9%
1.0%–2.4%
Less than 1%
No data

Personal Contact

Personal contact tracks international travel and tourism, international telephone traffic, and cross-border remittances and personal transfers (including worker remittances, compensation to employees, and other person-to-person and nongovernmental transfers). International telephone calls sum up the total number of minutes of telephone traffic into and out of a country on a per-capita basis.

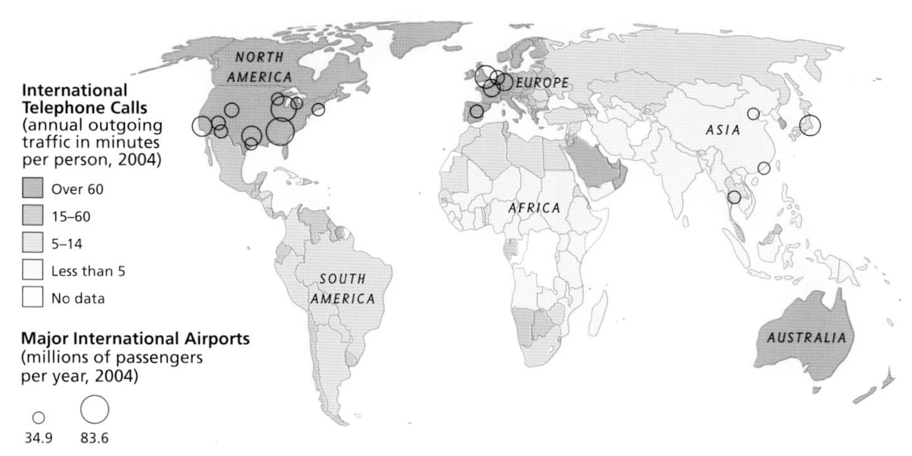
NORTH AMERICA
EUROPE
ASIA
AFRICA
SOUTH AMERICA
AUSTRALIA
International Telephone Calls
(annual outgoing traffic in minutes per person, 2004)
Over 60
15–60
5–14
Less than 5
No data
Major International Airports
(millions of passengers per year, 2004)
34.9
83.6

Technological Connectivity

Technological connectivity counts the number of Internet users, hosts, and secure servers through which transactions are carried out. These indicators measure penetration—that is, how many users there are, as well as how widespread the infrastructure is, for each country. The Internet has broken down physical borders, bridging continents and multiplying networks between businesses, governments, and citizens at a faster pace than ever.

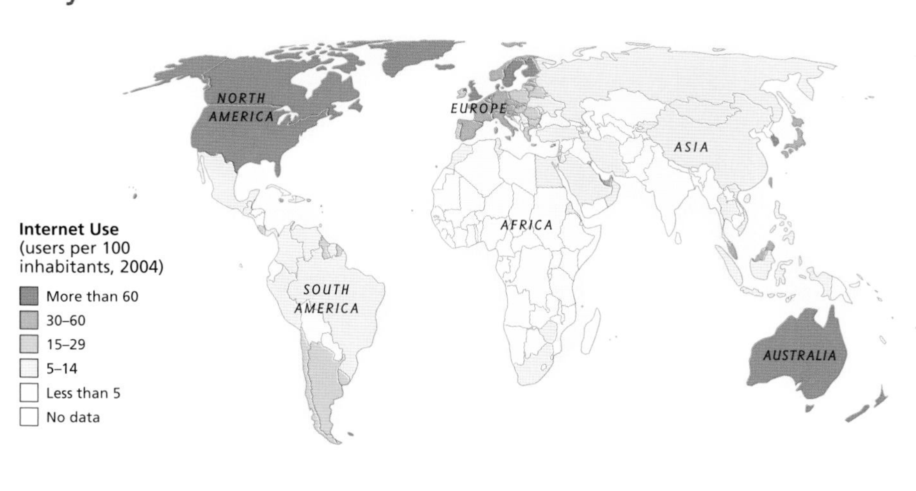
NORTH AMERICA
EUROPE
ASIA
AFRICA
SOUTH AMERICA
AUSTRALIA
Internet Use
(users per 100 inhabitants, 2004)
More than 60
30–60
15–29
5–14
Less than 5
No data

Political Engagement

Political engagement includes each country's memberships in a variety of representative international organizations, personnel and financial contributions to UN peacekeeping missions, ratification of selected multilateral treaties, and amounts of governmental transfer payments and receipts. The measures provide an indication of how various countries rank as participants of international arrangements relative to their economic and population sizes.

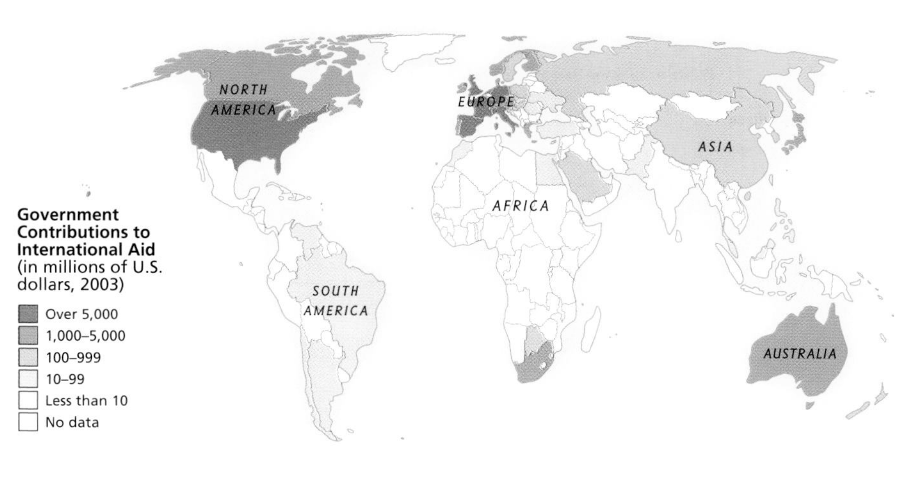
NORTH AMERICA
EUROPE
ASIA
AFRICA
SOUTH AMERICA
AUSTRALIA
Government Contributions to International Aid
(in millions of U.S. dollars, 2003)
Over 5,000
1,000–5,000
100–999
10–99
Less than 10
No data

International Outsourcing

Improvements in communication technologies, such as the Internet and digital telephone lines, are making it increasingly possible for firms to source their service inputs from suppliers abroad. Recent examples include call centers and computer software development services provided by India to the rest of the world. Until recently, global production networks mostly involved the offshoring of manufactured intermediate inputs, whereas now many services, as well, can be produced in one country and utilized in another.

TRENDS IN OUTSOURCING

International outsourcing of services has been steadily increasing but it is still at relatively low levels. Although U.S. business service imports have roughly doubled in each of the past several decades, they remained at less than one-half of one percent of total GDP in 2003. India, reported to be the recipient of significant outsourcing, itself outsources a large amount of services.

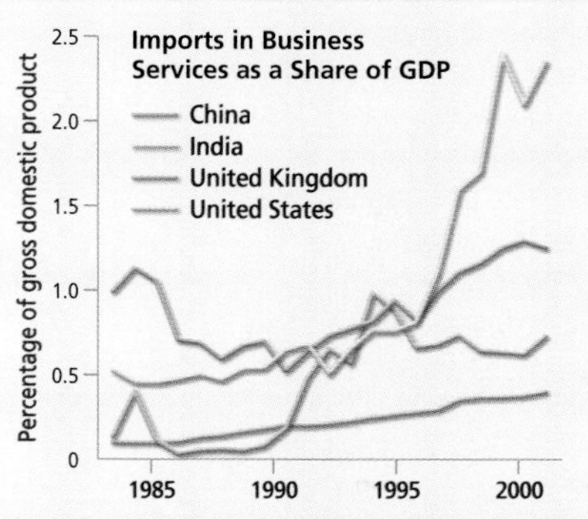
Imports in Business Services as a Share of GDP
China
India
United Kingdom
United States
Percentage of gross domestic product
2.5
2.0
1.5
1.0
0.5
0
1985
1990
1995
2000

As shown in the graph below, the U.K. and the U.S. have the largest net surpluses in business services. But this is not true for all industrialized countries. The data reveal no clear pattern of developing or industrial countries either being net exporters or net importers. For example, in addition to the U.K. and the U.S. having a net surplus in business services, India also does. Yet, Indonesia has a large net deficit in business services, as do Germany and Ireland.

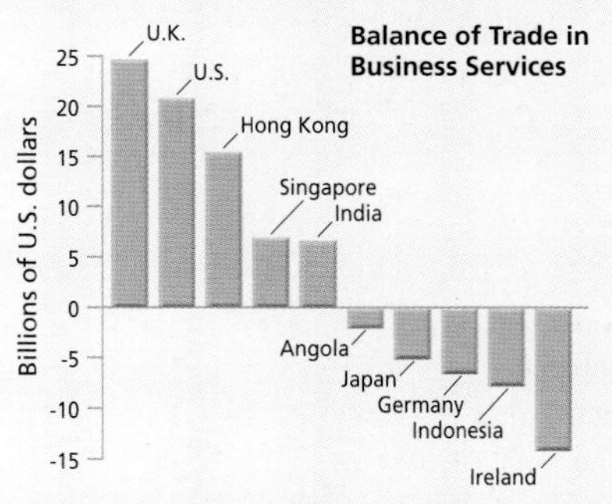
Balance of Trade in Business Services
Billions of U.S. dollars
25
20
15
10
5
0
-5
-10
-15
U.K.
U.S.
Hong Kong
Singapore
India
Angola
Japan
Germany
Indonesia
Ireland

TOP OUTSOURCERS OF BUSINESS SERVICES

VALUE (BILLIONS OF U.S. DOLLARS)	
United States	44
Germany	40
Italy	24
Netherlands	24
France	23
Japan	23
United Kingdom	22
Ireland	22

In dollar value terms, the U.S. ranks highest in outsourcing of business services, but as a share of the country's overall GDP, its value is comparatively low (0.4 percent at the end of 2003). In smaller countries, trade generally accounts for a larger percentage of GDP. Among the top relative outsourcers of business services are several small developing countries, such as Angola (16 percent of GDP), Lebanon (12 percent), Congo (10 percent), Azerbaijan (9 percent), and Seychelles (8 percent).

THE TECHNOLOGICAL REVOLUTION that began in the 1950s has given rise to a new Information Age in which global communications networks underpin virtually every facet of modern life. Each day, trillions of dollars worth of goods and services are traded worldwide in the form of bits and bytes, zipping through space, under the seas, beneath our feet, and in the air around us. Information has never been so plentiful, or so cheap. The first mass-produced book, the Gutenberg Bible, took up to two years to print and was beyond the means of all but a wealthy few. Today, a copy of the Bible can be downloaded over the Internet for free in seconds.

The Net itself has quickly evolved into a ubiquitous "network of networks" carrying everything from financial data to phone calls, entertainment to e-shopping, messaging to multimedia. Now the stage is set for a paradigm shift that will see inanimate objects around us become part of an intelligent "Internet of things," exchanging information spontaneously without the need for human intervention.

Already, tiny radio-frequency tags track goods from manufacturer to consumer; soon they could be providing information about a person's identity, buying habits, medical history, and more. Work is also underway on networks of miniscule wireless sensors capable of measuring a huge range of environmental variables, from temperature, pressure, and movement to whether a refrigerator needs restocking.

Centers of Technological Innovation

With access to information technology (IT) now a major determinant of economic growth and social development, researchers are working on ways to measure and map the distribution of technology.

The Technological Achievement Index aims to provide a country-by-country snapshot of IT penetration by measuring local levels of innovation, access to newer technologies like the Internet, the availability of old technology (e.g., telephones and electricity), and the potential for future skills development via schools and training.

The Technological Innovation Index, meanwhile, shines a spotlight on the centers of innovation that are driving today's technological revolution. Each country is assigned an innovation score based on the number of patents generated by its residents, which is then weighted against national population figures to provide a global perspective. The results can be surprising, with some of the world's smaller nations easily outstripping the industrial giants.

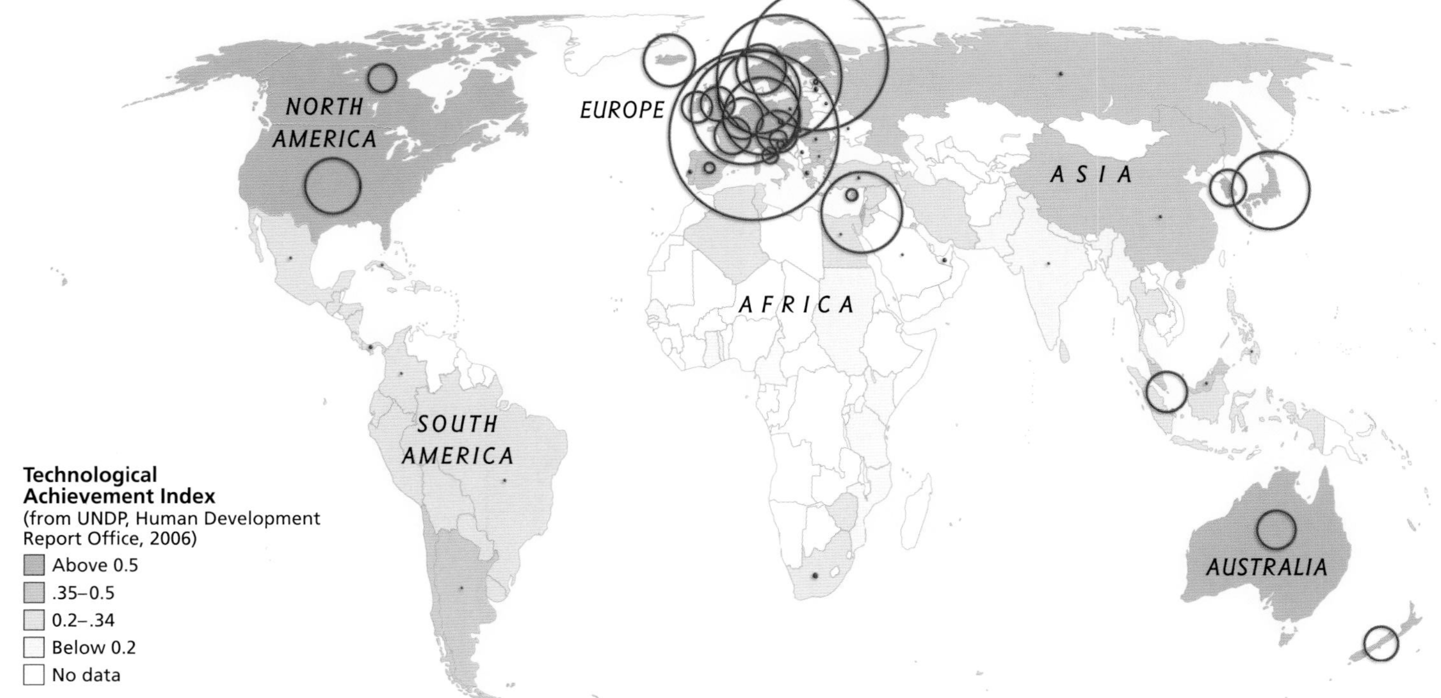
NORTH AMERICA
EUROPE
ASIA
AFRICA
SOUTH AMERICA
AUSTRALIA
Technological Achievement Index
(from UNDP, Human Development Report Office, 2006)
Above 0.5
.35–0.5
0.2–.34
Below 0.2
No data

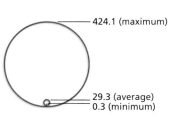

Technological Innovation Index
(international patent applications per 1 million people)

424.1 (maximum)
29.3 (average)
0.3 (minimum)

Data from World Intellectual Property Organization, 2006

424.1	Switzerland	100.9	Belgium	10.5	Czech Republic	2.3	Belarus
354.4	Finland	95.8	Australia	9.7	Estonia	1.9	China
311.4	Sweden	90.9	South Korea	7.6	South Africa	1.4	Malaysia
269.6	Netherlands	90.9	France	6.5	Latvia	1.4	Brazil
229.8	Luxembourg	85.0	New Zealand	5.9	Slovakia	1.3	Saudi Arabia
204.9	Denmark	84.4	United Kingdom	5.0	Portugal	1.3	Mexico
202.1	Israel	76.6	Ireland	5.0	Greece	1.1	Ukraine
193.7	Japan	70.1	Canada	5.0	United Arab Emirates	1.0	Cuba
191.6	Germany	43.0	Slovenia	4.0	Panama	0.7	Egypt
138.4	United States	39.4	Italy	3.8	Russia	0.6	Romania
128.8	Iceland	28.0	Cyprus	3.3	Serbia & Montenegro	0.6	India
124.5	Norway	25.4	Spain	2.7	Bulgaria	0.5	Colombia
103.8	Austria	16.0	Croatia	2.5	Poland	0.5	Argentina
101.0	Singapore	15.6	Hungary	2.3	Turkey	0.3	Philippines

Milestones in Technology

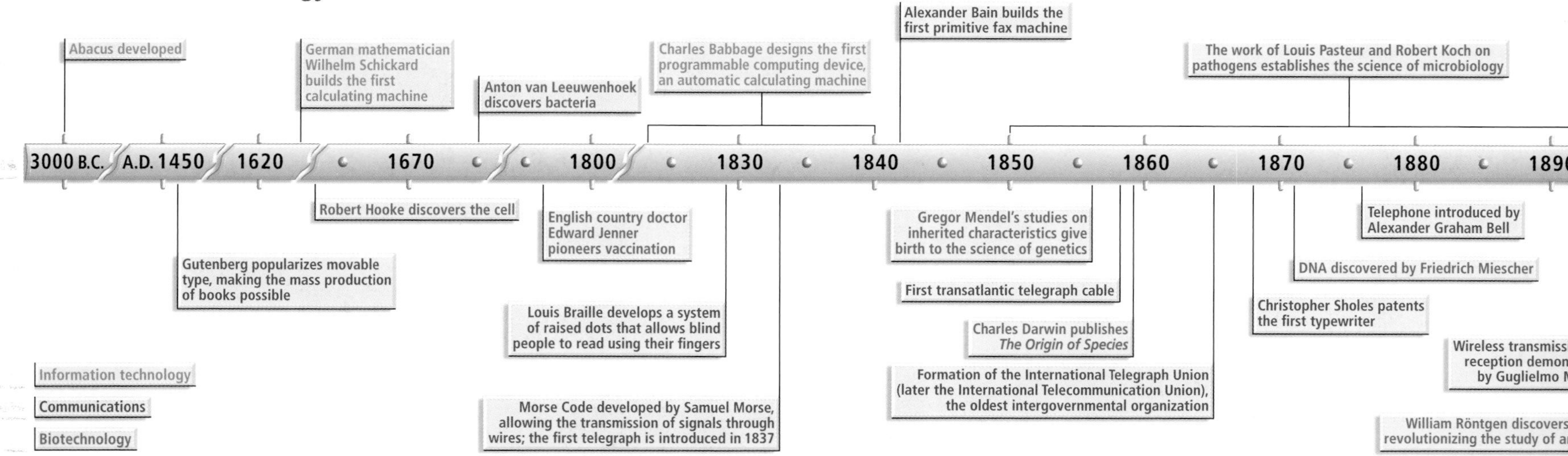
Abacus developed
German mathematician Wilhelm Schickard builds the first calculating machine
Anton van Leeuwenhoek discovers bacteria
Charles Babbage designs the first programmable computing device, an automatic calculating machine
Alexander Bain builds the first primitive fax machine
The work of Louis Pasteur and Robert Koch on pathogens establishes the science of microbiology
3000 B.C.
A.D. 1450
1620
1670
1800
1830
1840
1850
1860
1870
1880
1890
Gutenberg popularizes movable type, making the mass production of books possible
Robert Hooke discovers the cell
English country doctor Edward Jenner pioneers vaccination
Louis Braille develops a system of raised dots that allows blind people to read using their fingers
Morse Code developed by Samuel Morse, allowing the transmission of signals through wires; the first telegraph is introduced in 1837
Gregor Mendel's studies on inherited characteristics give birth to the science of genetics
First transatlantic telegraph cable
Charles Darwin publishes The Origin of Species
Formation of the International Telegraph Union (later the International Telecommunication Union), the oldest intergovernmental organization
Telephone introduced by Alexander Graham Bell
DNA discovered by Friedrich Miescher
Christopher Sholes patents the first typewriter
Wireless transmission reception demonstra by Guglielmo Mar
William Röntgen discovers x-r revolutionizing the study of anat
Information technology
Communications
Biotechnology

The Digital Divide

If access to digital information is taken for granted in industrialized nations, information and communication technologies (ICTs) remain far out of reach for millions living in the developing world. The result of widespread poverty and geographical challenges like mountainous terrain or widely dispersed, isolated communities, this "digital divide" threatens to further entrench global economic imbalances. Connecting the estimated one billion still unconnected means finding ways to measure differences in ICT access within and between economies worldwide. The International Telecommunication Union's Digital Opportunity Index is a composite model based on 11 different indicators of opportunity, infrastructure, and utilization. Among the information-rich, South Korea, Japan, and Denmark score the highest; at the thin end of the scale, sub-Saharan Africa fares the worst. The fastest improvement is taking place in the Asia-Pacific region—especially China, which now has the world's largest number of mobile cellular subscribers.

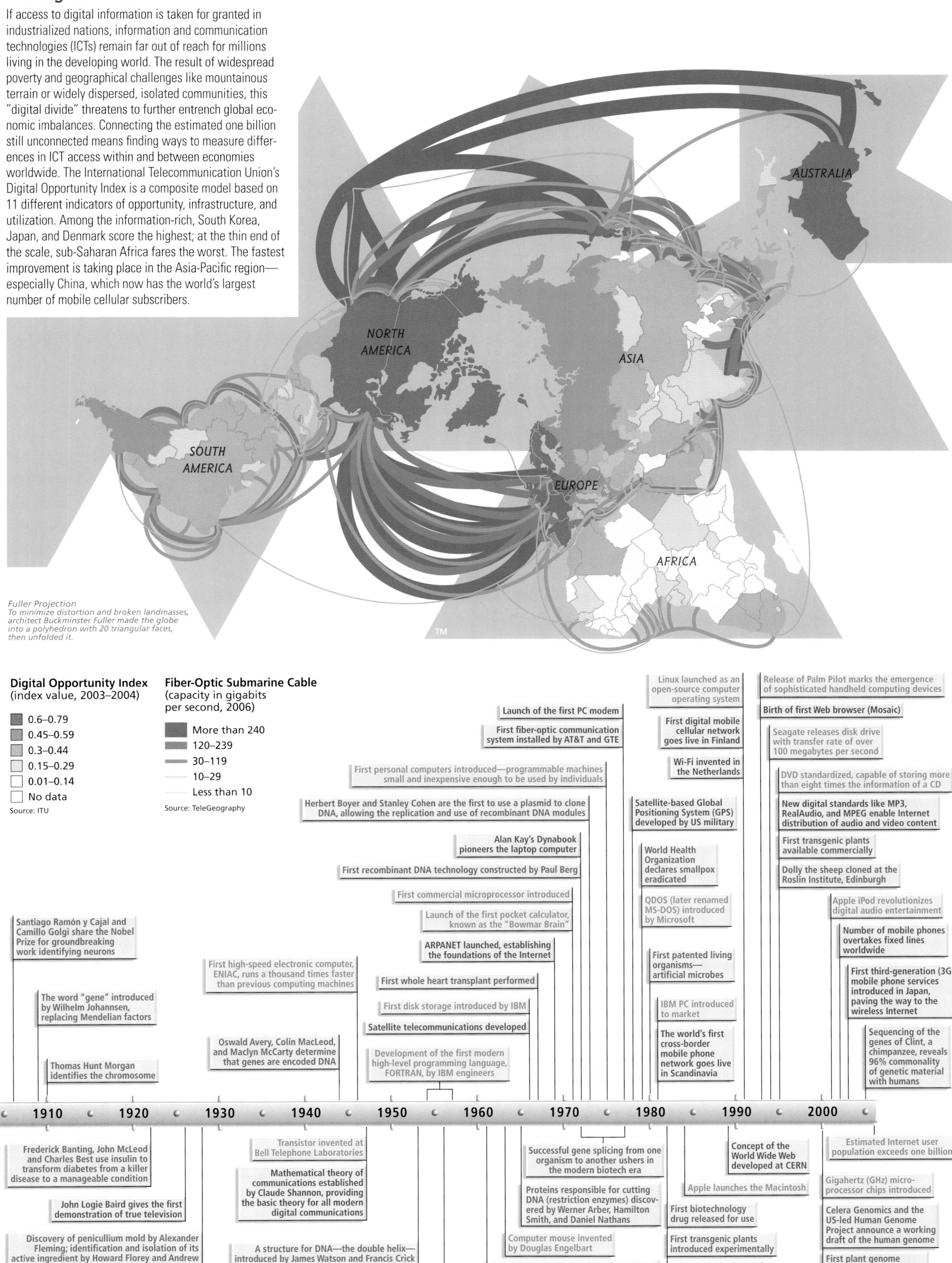

AUSTRALIA
NORTH AMERICA
ASIA
SOUTH AMERICA
EUROPE
AFRICA
TM
Fuller Projection
To minimize distortion and broken landmasses, architect Buckminster Fuller made the globe into a polyhedron with 20 triangular faces, then unfolded it.
Digital Opportunity Index (index value, 2003–2004)
0.6–0.79
0.45–0.59
0.3–0.44
0.15–0.29
0.01–0.14
No data
Source: ITU
Fiber-Optic Submarine Cable (capacity in gigabits per second, 2006)
More than 240
120–239
30–119
10–29
Less than 10
Source: TeleGeography
Santiago Ramón y Cajal and Camillo Golgi share the Nobel Prize for groundbreaking work identifying neurons
The word "gene" introduced by Wilhelm Johannsen, replacing Mendelian factors
Thomas Hunt Morgan identifies the chromosome
First high-speed electronic computer, ENIAC, runs a thousand times faster than previous computing machines
Oswald Avery, Colin MacLeod, and Maclyn McCarty determine that genes are encoded DNA
First personal computers introduced—programmable machines small and inexpensive enough to be used by individuals
Herbert Boyer and Stanley Cohen are the first to use a plasmid to clone DNA, allowing the replication and use of recombinant DNA modules
Alan Kay's Dynabook pioneers the laptop computer
First recombinant DNA technology constructed by Paul Berg
First commercial microprocessor introduced
Launch of the first pocket calculator, known as the "Bowmar Brain"
ARPANET launched, establishing the foundations of the Internet
First whole heart transplant performed
First disk storage introduced by IBM
Satellite telecommunications developed
Development of the first modern high-level programming language, FORTRAN, by IBM engineers
Launch of the first PC modem
First fiber-optic communication system installed by AT&T and GTE
Linux launched as an open-source computer operating system
First digital mobile cellular network goes live in Finland
Wi-Fi invented in the Netherlands
Satellite-based Global Positioning System (GPS) developed by US military
World Health Organization declares smallpox eradicated
QDOS (later renamed MS-DOS) introduced by Microsoft
First patented living organisms—artificial microbes
IBM PC introduced to market
The world's first cross-border mobile phone network goes live in Scandinavia
Release of Palm Pilot marks the emergence of sophisticated handheld computing devices
Birth of first Web browser (Mosaic)
Seagate releases disk drive with transfer rate of over 100 megabytes per second
DVD standardized, capable of storing more than eight times the information of a CD
New digital standards like MP3, RealAudio, and MPEG enable Internet distribution of audio and video content
First transgenic plants available commercially
Dolly the sheep cloned at the Roslin Institute, Edinburgh
Apple iPod revolutionizes digital audio entertainment
Number of mobile phones overtakes fixed lines worldwide
First third-generation (3G) mobile phone services introduced in Japan, paving the way to the wireless Internet
Sequencing of the genes of Clint, a chimpanzee, reveals 96% commonality of genetic material with humans
00
1910
1920
1930
1940
1950
1960
1970
1980
1990
2000
Frederick Banting, John McLeod and Charles Best use insulin to transform diabetes from a killer disease to a manageable condition
John Logie Baird gives the first demonstration of true television
Discovery of penicullium mold by Alexander Fleming; identification and isolation of its active ingredient by Howard Florey and Andrew Moyer leads to the first commercial antibiotic
Transistor invented at Bell Telephone Laboratories
Mathematical theory of communications established by Claude Shannon, providing the basic theory for all modern digital communications
A structure for DNA—the double helix—introduced by James Watson and Francis Crick
TAT-1, the first transatlantic submarine telephone cable, goes into service
Computer mouse invented by Douglas Engelbart
Integrated circuit, which puts an entire electronic circuit on a tiny silicon chip, developed by Jack Kilby and Robert Noyce
Successful gene splicing from one organism to another ushers in the modern biotech era
Proteins responsible for cutting DNA (restriction enzymes) discovered by Werner Arber, Hamilton Smith, and Daniel Nathans
Apple launches the Macintosh
First biotechnology drug released for use
First transgenic plants introduced experimentally
Mass market launch of the compact disc (CD)
Concept of the World Wide Web developed at CERN
Estimated Internet user population exceeds one billion
Gigahertz (GHz) microprocessor chips introduced
Celera Genomics and the US-led Human Genome Project announce a working draft of the human genome
First plant genome sequenced— Arabidopsis thaliana (mousear cress)

THE "COOPERATIVE ANARCHY" of the global Internet, a vast collection of interconnected computer networks communicating through specific protocols (information exchange rules), defies easy characterization or measurement of its behavior. Still, a lack of understanding has not stalled development of technologies that enable and support Internet growth.

Old behavior models for telephone networks no longer apply to packet delivery (data sent over a network) and to application support over multiple links, routers, and Internet Service Providers (ISPs). The sheer volume of traffic and the high capacity of electronic pathways have made Internet monitoring and analysis a more challenging endeavor. Users and providers both benefit from measurements that detect and isolate problems, but watching every link is not practical or particularly effective.

Each ISP monitors its own infrastructure and quality of service; however, business and policy concerns often keep ISPs from sharing such information. Common sense supports creation of a measurement infrastructure that would yield maximal Internet coverage for a reasonable price. But dynamically changing network configurations, as well as complex business and geopolitical concerns, make it difficult to acquire a worldwide view of the Internet.

A BRIEF HISTORY

1960s: ARPANET, a system designed to promote the sharing of supercomputers by researchers in the United States, is commissioned by the Department of Defense.

1970s: People begin to use ARPANET to collaborate on research projects and discuss common interests. In **1974**, a commercial version goes online for the first time.

1980s: Corporations begin to use the Internet for e-mail. As the Internet grows in importance, viruses start to create concerns about online privacy and security. New terms such as "hacker" come into use.

1990s: After the introduction of browsers for navigating the World Wide Web, Internet use expands rapidly (see graph below). By the late 1990s, 200 million people are connected, with online consumer spending totaling in the tens of billions of dollars. During this time, Internet-related companies attract enormous amounts of money from investors.

EARLY 2000s: Internet stock values take a deep plunge following the "dotcom" crash of April 2000. But rapid Internet growth continues, with more than 100 million new users each year. Satellite communications technology allows people to easily access the Internet with handheld devices.

Mapping the Spread of a Computer Virus

The graphics below detail the spread of the Nyxem E-mail Virus during early 2006. This virus operates in much the same way other viruses do, running as an e-mail attachment that attempts to disable antivirus software and harvest e-mail addresses to automatically spread itself. However, the Nyxem virus stands out because it exhibits the rare behavior of reporting its progress to a single web site, thus allowing researchers to undertake a detailed analysis of its activity.

These images, generated with a geographic visualization tool called Cuttlefish, highlight the correlation between human activity at certain times of the day (e.g., booting computers and reading e-mail), the spread of the virus, and the corresponding geographical locations of the infected computers.

The image at upper left includes a key that maps colors to the number of infected hosts. Circles of varying diameter and color depict the number of infected hosts in each region. At top right is a histogram showing the number of infected hosts over the roughly two-week period of analysis.

Newly Infected Nyxem Hosts
(per location, in thousands)

329–1,399 | 77–328 | 18–76 | 5–17 | 2–4 | 1

Circle diameter represents a logarithmic scale of the number of hosts affected per location at a given time.

**Coordinated Universal Time (UTC) is the international time standard. It is the current term for what was commonly referred to as Greenwich Meridian Time (GMT). Zero (0) hours UTC is midnight in Greenwich England, which lies on the zero longitudinal meridian. Universal Time is based on a 24-hour clock; therefore, afternoon hours such as 5 pm UTC are expressed as 17:00 UTC (seventeen hours, zero minutes).*

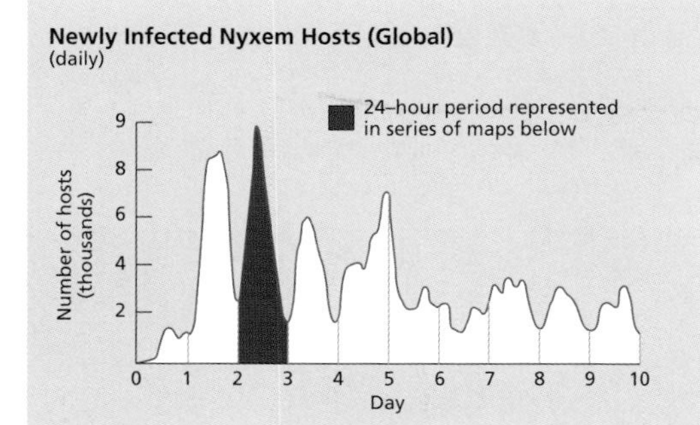
Newly Infected Nyxem Hosts (Global)
(daily)
24-hour period represented in series of maps below
Number of hosts (thousands)
9
8
6
4
2
0 1 2 3 4 5 6 7 8 9 10
Day

00:00 UTC

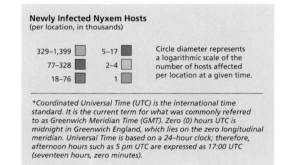

12:00 UTC

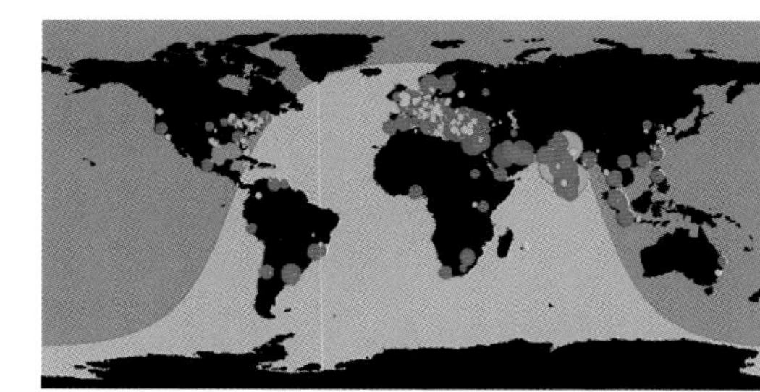

03:00 UTC

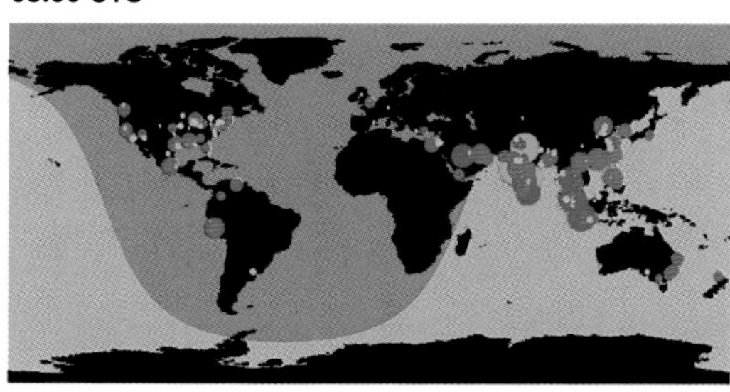

15:00 UTC

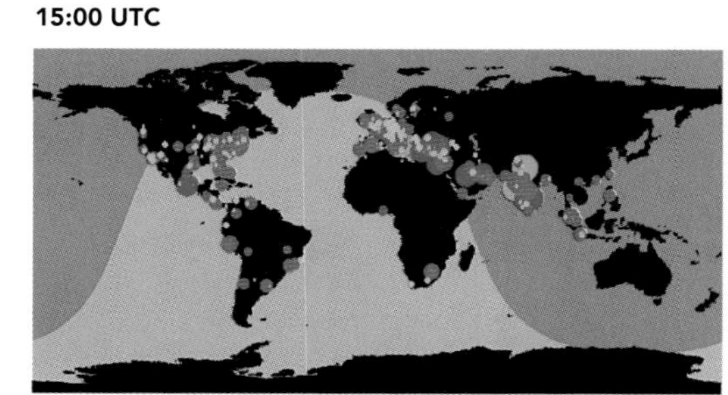

06:00 UTC

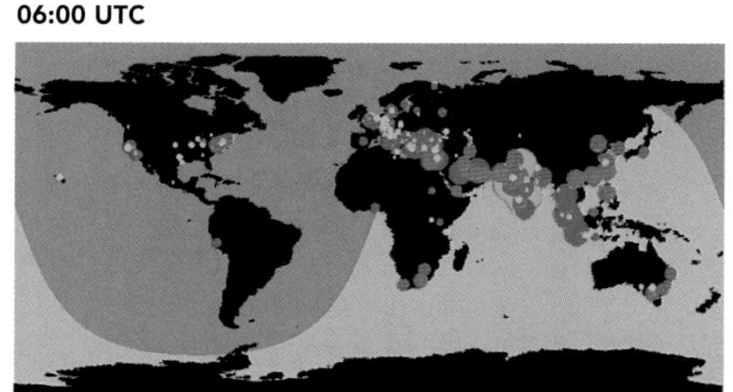

18:00 UTC

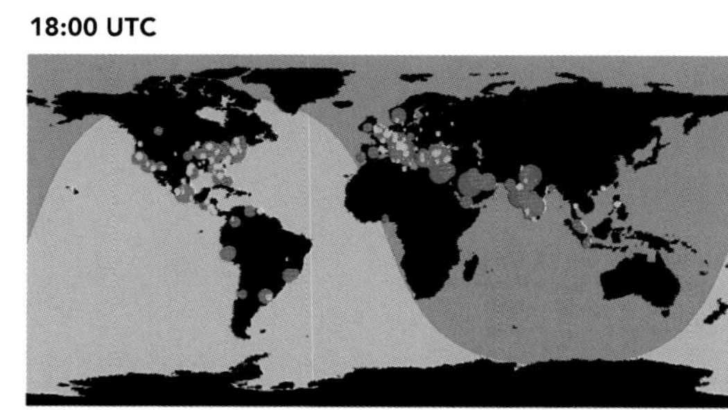

09:00 UTC

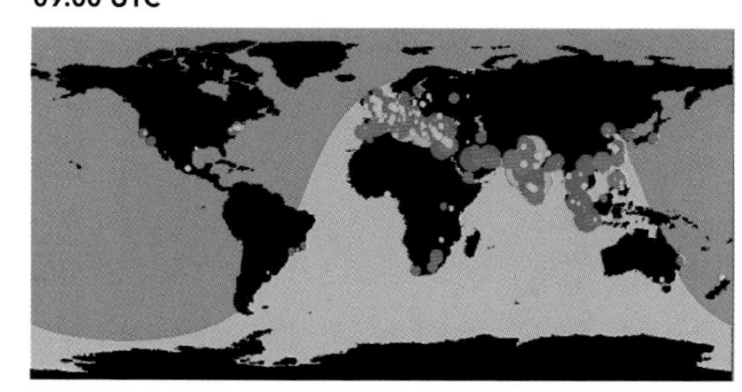

21:00 UTC

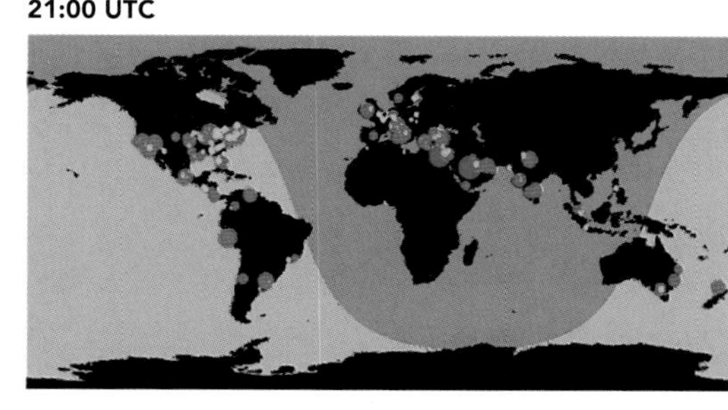

Internet Users Worldwide (estimated), 1995–2005

December 1995: 40 million

December 2000: 400 million

Jakarta, ID
Singapore, SG
Bangkok, TH
Delhi, IN
Bombay, IN
Abu Dhabi, AE
Beijing, CN
Taipei, TW
Seoul, KR
Vladivostok, RU
Tokyo, JP
Sydney, AU
Moscow, RU
Tel Aviv, IL
Ankara, TR
Kiev, UA
Pretoria, ZA
Helsinki, FI
Sofia, BG
Warsaw, PL
Stockholm, SE
Vienna, AT
Berlin, DE
Oslo, NO
Frankfurt, DE
Brussels, BE
Paris, FR
London, UK
Dublin, IE
Alges, PT
Honolulu, US
Rio de Janeiro, BR
Buenos Aires, AR
San Jose, US
San Diego, US
Phoenix, US
Denver, US
Houston, US
Chicago, US
Toronto, CA
Washington, US
Ottawa, CA
Boston, US

100E 110E 90E 80E 70E 60E 50E 40E 30E 20E 10E 0 120E 130E 140E 150E 160E 170E 180E/W 170W 160W 150W 140W 130W 120W 110W 100W 90W 80W 70W 60W 50W 40W 30W 20W 10W

ASIA OCEANIA AFRICA EUROPE NORTH AMERICA SOUTH AMERICA

7473(SINGTEL)
4637(HKT)
10026(ANC)
4766(KIX)
3786(DACOMNET)
2497(IIJ)
2516(KDDI)
7474(OPTUSCOM)
8342(ROSTELECOM)
3320(DeutscheTelekom)
1299(TELIANET)
3257(TISCALI)
1273(CW)
5459(LINX)
701(UUNET)
1239(SprintLink)
3356(LEVEL3)
7018(AT&T)
209(QWEST)
3549(GBIX)
174(Cogent)
6461(ABOVENET)
2914(VERIO)
3561(CWUSA)
2828(XO)
702(UUNET)
4323(TimeWarner)
7911(WCG)
7132(SBIS)
6453(TELEGLOBE)
6395(Broadwing)
5650(ELIX)
703(UUNET)
3491(BTN)
2152(CSUNET)
6539(GROUPTLCOM)

Global Internet Connectivity

The above graph is a macroscopic snapshot of the Internet core, based on data collected from April 4 to April 17, 2005. Internet Service Providers (ISPs) are represented by squares, with better-connected ISPs found toward the center. The colors indicate "outdegree" (the number of "next-hop" systems that were observed accepting traffic from a link), from lowest (blue) to highest (yellow).

The top 11 network nodes observed in this data set are based in the United States, and one of the European ISPs in the top 15 observed networks is the European branch of an American company. While ISPs in Europe and Asia have many links with ISPs in the United States, there are few direct links between ISPs in Asia and Europe. Both technical (cabling and router placement and management) and policy factors (business and cost models, geopolitical considerations) contribute to the ISP associations represented in this graph.

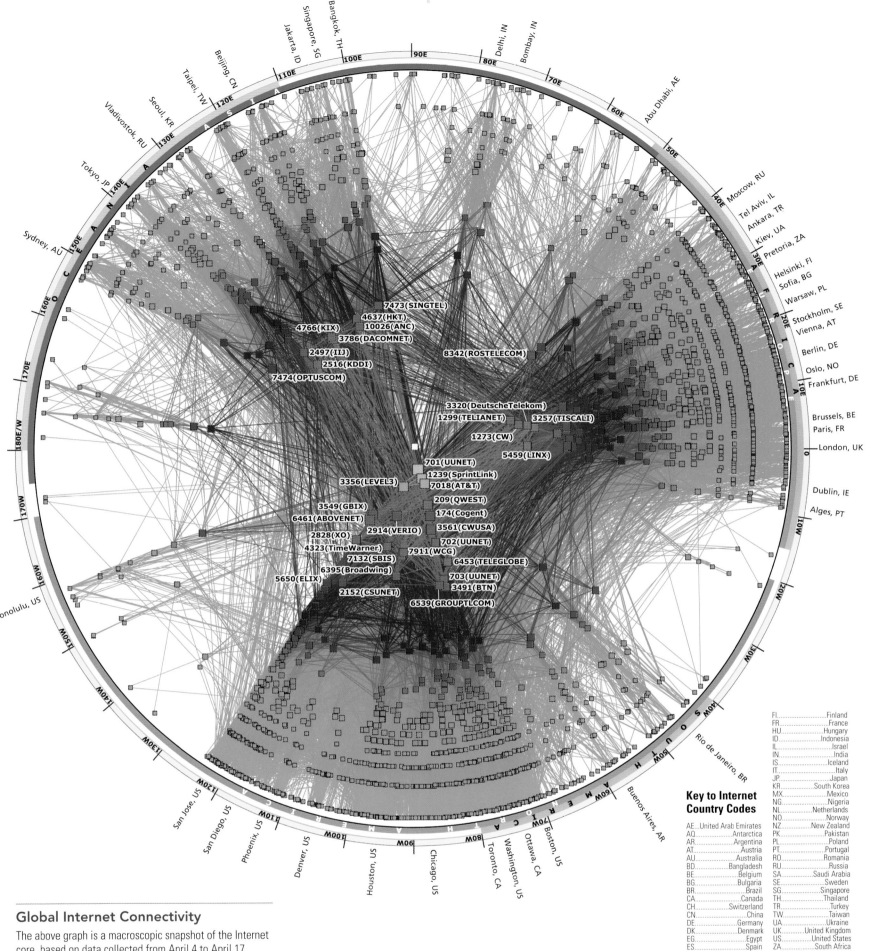

Key to Internet Country Codes

Code	Country	Code	Country
AE	United Arab Emirates	FI	Finland
AQ	Antarctica	FR	France
AR	Argentina	HU	Hungary
AT	Austria	ID	Indonesia
AU	Australia	IL	Israel
BD	Bangladesh	IN	India
BE	Belgium	IS	Iceland
BG	Bulgaria	IT	Italy
BR	Brazil	JP	Japan
CA	Canada	KR	South Korea
CH	Switzerland	MX	Mexico
CN	China	NG	Nigeria
DE	Germany	NL	Netherlands
DK	Denmark	NO	Norway
EG	Egypt	NZ	New Zealand
ES	Spain	PK	Pakistan
		PL	Poland
		PT	Portugal
		RO	Romania
		RU	Russia
		SA	Saudi Arabia
		SE	Sweden
		SG	Singapore
		TH	Thailand
		TR	Turkey
		TW	Taiwan
		UA	Ukraine
		UK	United Kingdom
		US	United States
		ZA	South Africa

Worldwide Distribution of Internet Resources

The worldwide distribution of Internet resources—ISPs, Autonomous System (AS) routers, address space—is highly nonuniform and is unrelated to a region's size or population. For this graph, Internet addresses of routable paths announced on March 21, 2006, were mapped to physical locations and compared with public demographic data.

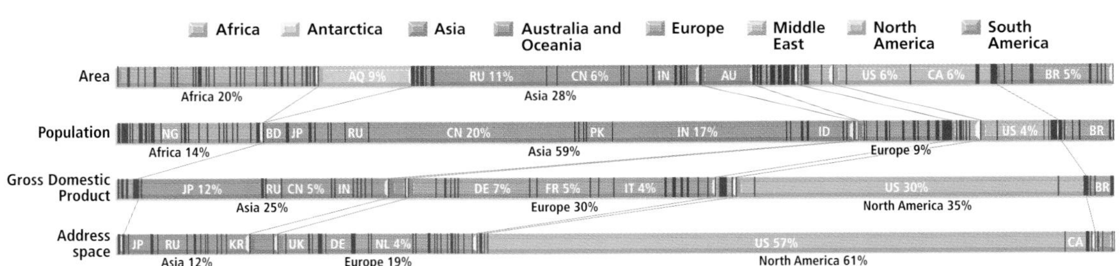
Africa
Antarctica
Asia
Australia and Oceania
Europe
Middle East
North America
South America
Area
AQ 9%
RU 11%
CN 6%
IN
AU
US 6%
CA 6%
BR 5%
Africa 20%
Asia 28%
Population
NG
BD
JP
RU
CN 20%
PK
IN 17%
ID
US 4%
BR
Africa 14%
Asia 59%
Europe 9%
Gross Domestic Product
JP 12%
RU
CN 5%
IN
DE 7%
FR 5%
IT 4%
US 30%
BR
Asia 25%
Europe 30%
North America 35%
Address space
JP
RU
KR
UK
DE
NL 4%
US 57%
CA
Asia 12%
Europe 19%
North America 61%

December 2005: 940 million

North America

Millions of years of weathering and erosion, in the form of wind, rain, snow, heat, cold, and the Colorado River, have shaped the Grand Canyon into one of North America's geographic icons.

North America is both incredibly old, geologically speaking, and relatively young, when viewed in terms of its human history.

About 200 million years ago, North America separated from Africa when the supercontinent Pangaea began to break apart. For a while, it was attached to Europe, but in time that connection was broken and the North American landmass began roughly assuming its current shape and size. Meanwhile, the other continents were still separating from one another and jockeying for position on the face of the planet.

Some of the oldest stones in the world are found in North America. Dating from nearly four billion years ago, they form the stout underbelly of Canada's frozen tundra. In the east, an ancient mountain system—the Appalachians—runs from the United States into Canada. But not everything is so utterly ancient: North America's human history is only thousands of years old, while that of Africa, the birthplace of humankind, dates back millions of years. Just in the past couple of centuries, North America has experienced dramatic changes in its population, landscapes, and environment, an incredible transformation brought about by waves of immigration, booming economies, and relentless development.

PHYSICAL GEOGRAPHY From the world's largest island (Greenland) and greatest concentration of fresh water (the Great Lakes) to such spectacular features as the Grand Canyon and Niagara Falls, North America holds a wealth of superlatives. It is also home to Earth's largest and tallest trees (the redwoods of California) and many of its biggest animals (grizzly bears, moose, and bison). The continent is known as well for dramatic extremes of climate—from the sauna-like 134°F (57°C) recorded in California's Death Valley to the brutally cold minus 87°F (-66°C) logged on Greenland's windswept ice cap.

Third largest of the continents, after Asia and Africa, North America encompasses 9.45 million square miles (24.5 million sq km); its northernmost tip is in Greenland (Cape Morris Jesup), and its southernmost point is in Panama (Península de Azuero).

Deeply indented with inlets and bays, North America claims the longest coastline when compared with other continents. Its land is surrounded by vast oceans and sizable seas: the Atlantic in the east, the Pacific in the west, the Arctic in the north, and the Gulf of Mexico and Caribbean Sea in the south. This geographic circumstance kept the continent isolated for millions of years, greatly influencing the development of its flora and fauna, as well as its human history. Into North America's coastal waters pour a number of mighty rivers, including the Saint Lawrence, Rio Grande, Yukon, Columbia, and Mississippi.

Three significant geologic features dominate the continental landmass: the Canadian (Laurentian) Shield; the great Western Cordillera, which includes the Rocky Mountains, Sierra Nevada, and Sierra Madre; and a colossal flatland that embraces the Great Plains, the Mississippi-Missouri River basin, and most of the Great Lakes region. Other major components include the ancient Appalachian Mountains and the predominantly volcanic islands of the Caribbean Sea. The continent peaks out at 20,320 feet (6,194 m) on the summit of Mount McKinley (Denali), in Alaska, and drops to 282 feet (86 m) below sea level in Death Valley.

The climates of North America range from the frigid conditions of the Arctic ice cap to the steamy tropics of Central America (considered part of North America) and the Caribbean; in between are variations of dry, mild, and continental climes.

The continent has an equally diverse biological heritage, ranging from seemingly endless tundra and coniferous forests in the north to vast deserts and dense rain forests in the south. North America once held huge herds of bison, antelope, elk, and other large wildlife, but such populations declined as the human population grew and spread across the continent.

HISTORY Although the exact date will probably never be determined, North America's human history began sometime between 12,000 and 30,000 years ago, when Asiatic nomads crossed the Bering Strait into Alaska. The descendants of these people spread throughout the continent, evolving into distinct tribes with their own lifestyles and more than 550 different languages.

Most of these original Americans were still hunting and gathering when Europeans arrived in North America; however, several groups had already developed sophisticated cultures. By 1200 B.C., the Olmec of Mexico had created what is generally deemed the first "civilization" in the Western Hemisphere; theirs was a highly advanced society with a calendar, writing system, and stonework architecture. About a hundred years later, the Maya took root in Mexico and Central America, reaching an apex around A.D. 700 with the creation of an elaborate religion and sprawling temple cities. In central Mexico, the highly militaristic Toltec and Aztec forged sprawling empires that drew cultural inspiration from both the Olmec and Maya.

One of the most significant moments for North America—indeed, it was among the most influential events in world history—came in 1492, when a Spanish expedition under Christopher Columbus set foot on an island in the Bahamas. This initial landing ushered in an era of European exploration and settlement that would alter the social fabric of the entire continent. In the next few decades, Hernán Cortés vanquished the Aztec, and Spain claimed virtually the whole Caribbean region and Central America. Other Europeans soon followed—English, French, Dutch, Russians, and even Danes—the leading edge of a migration that would become one of the greatest in human history (more than 70 million people and still counting).

The Native American cultures were unable to compete: They were plagued by European diseases, against which they had little or no resistance; unable to counter the superior firepower of the invaders; and relentlessly driven from their lands. The continent's rich tribal mosaic gradually melted away, replaced by myriad European colonies. By the end of the 19th century, these colonies had been superseded by autonomous nation-states, such as Canada, Mexico, and the United States. Since 1960, many of the Caribbean isles have gained independence, yet quite a few remain colonial possessions under the British, French, Dutch, and U.S. flags.

During the past century, both the U.S. and Canada managed to propel themselves into the ranks of the world's richest nations. But the rest of the continent failed to keep pace, plagued by poverty, despotic governments, and social unrest. In the decades since World War II, many of the Spanish-speaking nations—Cuba, the Dominican

Republic, Nicaragua, El Salvador, and Guatemala—have been racked by bloody revolution. The U.S., on the other hand, ended the 20th century as the only true superpower, with a military presence and political, economic, and cultural influences that extend around the globe.

CULTURE North America's cultural landscape has changed profoundly over the past 500 years. Before the 16th century, the continent was fragmented into hundreds of different cultures developed along tribal lines. From the Inuit people of the Arctic to the Cuña Indians of the Panama jungle, a majority of North America's people had barely risen above Stone Age cultural levels. Noteworthy exceptions included the great civilizations of Mexico and Central America, the pueblo builders of the southwestern U.S., and the highly organized cultivators of the Great Lakes region and the Mississippi Valley. But for the most part, the average North American was migratory, had no concept of written language, and used stone or wooden tools.

The arrival of the Europeans brought permanent settlements, metal tools (and weapons), and written languages. The newcomers founded towns based on Old World models, some of which would evolve into world-class cities—New York, Los Angeles, Chicago, Toronto, and Mexico City among them. Native tongues gave way to a trio of European languages—English, Spanish, and French—now spoken by most of North America's 515 million people. And ancient beliefs yielded to new religions, like Roman Catholicism and Protestantism, which now dominate the continent's spiritual life. The Europeans brought ideas—concepts like democracy, capitalism, religious choice, and free speech—that continue to shape political, intellectual, and economic life.

Despite common historical threads, the coat that comprises today's North America is one of many colors. Mexico and Central America are dominated by Hispano-Indian culture and tend to have more in common with South America than with their neighbors north of the Rio Grande. Although Anglo-Saxon ways still hold sway in the U.S. and Canada, a surge of immigration from Latin America, Asia, and Pacific islands has introduced new cultural traditions. From the Rastafarians of Jamaica to the Creoles of Martinique, the Caribbean islands have fostered myriad microcultures that blend European, African, and Latin traditions.

ECONOMY When it comes to business and industry, North America—and especially the U.S.—is the envy of the world. No other continent produces such an abundance of merchandise or profusion of crops, and no other major region comes close to North America's per capita resource and product consumption. From the high-tech citadels of Silicon Valley to the dream factories of Hollywood, the continent is a world leader in dozens of fields and industries, including computers, entertainment, aerospace, finance, medicine, defense, and agriculture.

The quest for monetary and material success can be traced all the way back to early European immigrants and the tireless work ethic they brought with them. These people, and their cultural descendants,

The ceremonial core of Tikal, a major Maya cultural and population center in Guatemala's Petén region, covers approximately one square mile (2.5 sq km). From its early beginnings as a small village (900–300 B.C.), Tikal grew in stature and size to house some 50,000 people at its peak (A.D. 600–800). Even in ruins, its massive Temple I (left) and Temple II (right) remain impressive structures amid myriad palaces, plazas, and ball courts.

sought to improve their standard of living by exploiting the natural wealth of the land. North America's forests, minerals, and farmlands stoked an industrial revolution that by the end of the 19th century had propelled the U.S. into the ranks of the richest and most powerful nations. Indeed, the continent has an abundance of natural resources: vast petroleum reserves in Alaska and around the Gulf of Mexico, huge coal deposits in the Appalachian and Rocky Mountains, swift-flowing rivers to produce hydropower, and fertile soils that lead to copious harvests.

But the most important product has always been ideas—the ability of its inhabitants to imagine. Next is the ability to transform those ideas into reality through experimentation and hard work. Many of the innovations that revolutionized modern life—the telephone, electric lighting, motor vehicles, airplanes, computers, shopping malls, television, the Internet—were either invented or first mass-produced in the U.S.

Globalization has spread U.S. goods—and by extension, American ideas and culture—around the planet. To a large extent the U.S. dollar has become the world currency, and the financial wizards of New York's Wall Street now control a lion's share of global investment funds. The creation of the North American Free Trade Association (NAFTA) in 1994 drew Canada and Mexico into the same economic web. But success has brought a host of concerns, not the least of which involves the continued exploitation of natural resources. North America is home to only roughly 8 percent of the planet's people, yet its per capita consumption of energy is almost six times as great as the average for all other continents. Its appetite for timber, metals, and water resources is just as voracious.

Other parts of the continent continue to lag in terms of economic vitality. Most Caribbean nations—along with Costa Rica and Belize—now rely on the tourist industry to generate the bulk of their gross national product, while most Central American countries continue to bank on agricultural commodities such as bananas and coffee. Poverty has spurred millions of Mexicans, Central Americans, and Caribbean islanders to migrate northward (legally and illegally) in search of better lives. Finding ways to integrate these disenfranchised masses into the continent's economic miracle is one of the greatest challenges facing North America in the 21st century.

North America: **Physical and Political**

ARCTIC OCEAN
North Magnetic Pole 2006
North Geomagnetic Pole 2008
QUEEN ELIZABETH ISLANDS
PARRY ISLANDS
GREENLAND
GREENLAND SEA
NORWEGIAN SEA
ARCTIC CIRCLE
ICELAND
Faroe Islands
Jan Mayen
Meridian of Greenwich (London)
Denmark Strait
Davis Strait
BAFFIN BAY
Baffin Island
BEAUFORT SEA
BERING SEA
Bering Str.
Brooks Range
Mt. McKinley (Denali) 6194 (20320 ft)
Highest point in North America
Alaska Range
GULF OF ALASKA
PACIFIC OCEAN
YUKON PLATEAU
COAST MOUNTAINS
ROCKY MOUNTAINS
CANADIAN SHIELD
GREAT PLAINS
HUDSON BAY
Hudson Strait
LABRADOR SEA
Labrador
Laurentide Scarp
ISLAND OF NEWFOUNDLAND
NOVA SCOTIA
ATLANTIC OCEAN
CENTRAL LOWLAND
Geographical Center of the 48 Contiguous United States
APPALACHIAN MOUNTAINS
Piedmont
COASTAL PLAIN
Great Basin
Lowest point in North America -86 (-282 ft)
Death Valley
Colorado Plateau
Sonoran Desert
CASCADE RANGE
Sierra Nevada
BAJA CALIFORNIA
GULF OF CALIFORNIA
TROPIC OF CANCER
SIERRA MADRE OCCIDENTAL
SIERRA MADRE ORIENTAL
GULF OF MEXICO
Mississippi River Delta
Florida
BAHAMAS
CUBA
GREATER ANTILLES
LESSER ANTILLES
HISPANIOLA
JAMAICA
PUERTO RICO
CARIBBEAN SEA
Yucatan Peninsula
Isthmus of Tehuantepec
CENTRAL AMERICA
Isthmus of Panama
SOUTH AMERICA
ANDES
Bermuda Is.
Azimuthal Equidistant Projection
SCALE 1:28,768,000
1 CENTIMETER = 288 KILOMETERS; 1 INCH = 454 MILES
0 200 400 600 800 1000
KILOMETERS
0 200 400 600 800
STATUTE MILES
International boundary
Elevations in meters
Longitude West 90° of Greenwich
BERING SEA AND THE ALEUTIAN ISLANDS
Same Scale as Main Map
SIBERIA
Koryak Range
Kamchatka Peninsula
ALASKA
ALEUTIAN ISLANDS
Alaska Peninsula
Longitude East of Greenwich
Longitude West of Greenwich

ASIA
RUSSIA
ARCTIC OCEAN
North Magnetic Pole 2006
CHUKCHI SEA
QUEEN ELIZABETH ISLANDS
PARRY ISLANDS
GREENLAND (KALAALLIT NUNAAT) Denmark
KNUD RASMUSSEN LAND
GREENLAND SEA
NORWEGIAN SEA
UNITED KINGDOM
ICELAND
Reykjavík
Jan Mayen Norway
Denmark Strait
ARCTIC CIRCLE
Lincoln Sea
Alert
Eureka
Ellesmere Island
North Geomagnetic Pole 2005
Siorapaluk
THULE AIR BASE
Qaanaaq
Savissivik
Kullorsuaq
Upernavik
Uummannaq
Ilulissat
Qeqertarsuaq (Godhavn)
Kangerlussuaq
Kangaamiut
Nuuk (Godthåb)
Paamiut
Qeqertarsuatsiaat
Narsarsuaq
Nanortalik
Nunap Isua (Cape Farewell)
Ittoqqortoormiit
Tasiilaq
Danmark Havn
Daneborg
Ittuarmiit
Timmiarmiut
BAFFIN BAY
Baffin Island
Davis Strait
Devon Island
Bylot Island
Arctic Bay
Pond Inlet
Clyde River
Qikiqtarjuaq
Pangnirtung
Iqaluit
Cape Dorset
Resolute
Somerset Island
Prince of Wales Island
Victoria Island
Banks Island
Viscount Melville Sound
BEAUFORT SEA
Sachs Harbour
Holman
Cambridge Bay
Boothia Peninsula
Taloyoak
Gjoa Haven
Kugluktuk
Perry Island
Igloolik
Hall Beach
Foxe Basin
Repulse Bay
Southampton Island
Coral Harbour
Hudson Strait
Ivujivik
Salluit
Kangirsuk
Ungava Bay
Resolution Island
Port Burwell
LABRADOR SEA
NUNAVUT
ARCTIC CIRCLE
Mould Bay
ALASKA
Barrow
Wainwright
Point Hope
Point Lay
Prudhoe Bay
North Slope
Brooks Range
Kaktovik
Kotzebue
Kobuk
Nome
Teller
Seward Peninsula
Bering Str.
St. Lawrence Island
Norton Sound
Unalakleet
Galena
Hughes
Tanana
Allakaket
Wiseman
Fort Yukon
Circle
Fairbanks
Big Delta
Tok
Gulkana
Healy
Cantwell
McGrath
Anchorage
Palmer
Kenai
Homer
Seward
Valdez
Whittier
Bethel
Aniak
Anvik
St. Michael
Kodiak
GULF OF ALASKA
King Salmon
Tuktoyaktuk
Inuvik
Fort McPherson
Old Crow
Paulatuk
YUKON
Dawson
Mayo
Pelly Crossing
Haines Junction
Whitehorse
Ross River
Watson Lake
Yakutat
Haines
Juneau
Sitka
Dease Lake
Alexander Archipelago
Wrangell
Ketchikan
Prince Rupert
Stewart
Smithers
Kitimat
Terrace
Queen Charlotte Islands
NORTHWEST TERRITORIES
Norman Wells
Fort Good Hope
Déline
Great Bear Lake
Echo Bay
Lupin
Rae Lakes
Yellowknife
Fort Simpson
Great Slave Lake
Fort Resolution
Lutselk'e
Hay River
Fort Liard
Fort Smith
Fort Nelson
Uranium City
Lake Athabasca
Fort Chipewyan
Fort Vermilion
Meander River
Keg River
Baker Lake
Chesterfield Inlet
Rankin Inlet
Arviat
CANADA
HUDSON BAY
Churchill
Brochet
Reindeer Lake
Lynn Lake
Split Lake
Shamattawa
Fort Severn
Belcher Islands
Inukjuak
Kuujjuaq
NOUVEAU QUÉBEC
Kuujjuarapik
Schefferville
Nain
Davis Inlet
Makkovik
Cartwright
Happy Valley-Goose Bay
Churchill Falls
LABRADOR
NEWFOUNDLAND AND LABRADOR
Esker
Labrador City
Radisson
Chisasibi
James Bay
Akimiski I.
Eastmain
Nemiscau
Waskaganish
Moosonee
QUEBEC
BRITISH COLUMBIA
ALBERTA
SASKATCHEWAN
MANITOBA
ONTARIO
Dawson Creek
Fort St. John
Grande Prairie
Peace River
Fort McMurray
Fort Fraser
Prince George
Bella Bella
Bella Coola
Williams Lake
Edmonton
Lac La Biche
Jasper
Wetaskiwin
N. Battleford
Red Deer
Calgary
Lethbridge
Medicine Hat
Swift Current
Moose Jaw
Regina
Saskatoon
Prince Albert
Kerrobert
Yorkton
Dauphin
Melfort
Île-à-la-Crosse
La Ronge
Flin Flon
The Pas
Nelson House
Thompson
Norway House
Gods Lake
Island Lake
Big Trout Lake
Sandy Lake
Grand Rapids
Berens River
Lake Winnipeg
Lake Winnipegosis
Cat Lake
Pickle Lake
Attawapiskat
Lansdowne House
Ogoki
Red Lake
Winnipeg
Brandon
Minnedosa
Kenora
Sioux Lookout
Lake of the Woods
Lake Nipigon
Nipigon
Hearst
Thunder Bay
Kapuskasing
Timmins
Matagami
Chibougamau
Val-d'Or
Amos
Rouyn-Noranda
Chicoutimi
Dolbeau
Québec
Trois-Rivières
MONTRÉAL
Ottawa
Kingston
Cornwall
Peterborough
Sudbury
North Bay
Sault Ste. Marie
Chapleau
Oba
Sept-Îles
Baie-Comeau
Rimouski
Matane
Gaspé
Natashquan
Port-Menier
Harrington Harbour
Blanc-Sablon
Lourdes-de-Blanc-Sablon
L'Anse aux Meadows
St. Anthony
Roddickton
Corner Brook
Gander
Grand Falls-Windsor
St. John's
Avalon Pen.
Trepassey
Newfoundland
Island of Newfoundland
Channel-Port aux Basques
St.-Pierre & Miquelon France
Sydney
Cape Breton Island
Charlottetown
P.E.I.
Chatham
Edmundston
N.B.
Moncton
Fredericton
Saint John
New Glasgow
Dartmouth
Halifax
NOVA SCOTIA
Shelburne
Yarmouth
Revelstoke
Kamloops
Kelowna
Lillooet
Lytton
Vancouver
Vancouver I.
Nanaimo
Victoria
Port Hardy
Campbell River
Powell River
Cranbrook
Banff
Louise
UNITED STATES
WASH.
Seattle
Everett
Bellingham
Olympia
Tacoma
Longview
Vancouver
Yakima
Spokane
Coeur d'Alene
Kalispell
Richland
Portland
Salem
Corvallis
Eugene
Coos Bay
Medford
Crescent City
OREGON
Klamath Falls
Ontario
Baker City
Lewiston
Missoula
Helena
Butte
Bozeman
Great Falls
Havre
Glasgow
MONTANA
Billings
Miles City
Livingston
Salmon
IDAHO
Boise
Idaho Falls
Pocatello
Twin Falls
Cody
Sheridan
WYOMING
Riverton
Casper
Rock Springs
Cheyenne
Laramie
Rapid City
Pierre
SOUTH DAKOTA
NORTH DAKOTA
Minot
Williston
Dickinson
Bismarck
Fargo
Grand Forks
Moorhead
Aberdeen
Mitchell
Sioux Falls
Hot Springs
Sioux City
Scottsbluff
NEBR.
North Platte
Grand Island
Omaha
Lincoln
International Falls
Ely
Duluth
Superior
MINN.
St. Cloud
Minneapolis
St. Paul
Mankato
Rochester
IOWA
Des Moines
Fort Dodge
Cedar Rapids
Dubuque
Davenport
WIS.
Green Bay
Milwaukee
Madison
Kenosha
CHICAGO
Aurora
ILL.
Springfield
Indianapolis
Rhinelander
Marquette
L. Superior
MICHIGAN
L. Michigan
Lansing
Flint
Detroit
Toledo
Lake Huron
TORONTO
Hamilton
Oshawa
Lake Ontario
Buffalo
Rochester
Cleveland
PA.
Pittsburgh
OHIO
Dayton
Columbus
Cincinnati
Harrisburg
NEW YORK
PHILADELPHIA
Trenton
N.J.
Baltimore
Annapolis MD.
Dover DEL.
Washington, D.C.
W.VA.
Charleston
Charlottesville
VA.
Richmond
Norfolk
Virginia Beach
Albany
N.Y.
Hartford CONN.
Providence R.I.
Boston
MASS.
Manchester
Concord
N.H.
VT.
Montpelier
ME.
Augusta
Bangor
Portland
Redding
Yreka
Eureka
Winnemucca
Elko
NEVADA
Reno
Carson City
Ely
Sacramento
Oakland
San Francisco
San Jose
Stockton
Monterey
Fresno
Tonopah
San Luis Obispo
Santa Maria
Santa Barbara
Bakersfield
LOS ANGELES
Long Beach
SAN DIEGO
TIJUANA
Ensenada
Mexicali
San Bernardino
Las Vegas
Kingman
Flagstaff
ARIZONA
PHOENIX
Scottsdale
Mesa
Tucson
Yuma
Nogales
Douglas
Ogden
Salt Lake City
Provo
UTAH
Moab
Cedar City
St. George
Grand Jct.
Craig
Boulder
Fort Collins
Denver
Colorado Sprs.
COLO.
Pueblo
Alamosa
Cortez
Trinidad
Santa Fe
Albuquerque
NEW MEXICO
Las Vegas
Amarillo
Clovis
Lubbock
Roswell
Truth or Consequences
Las Cruces
Carlsbad
Hobbs
El Paso
CIUDAD JUÁREZ
Odessa
Midland
Abilene
TEXAS
Wichita Falls
Fort Worth
DALLAS
Tyler
Waco
San Angelo
Austin
SAN ANTONIO
HOUSTON
Galveston
Corpus Christi
Laredo
Brownsville
Beaumont
Port Arthur
Lufkin
Lake Charles
Lafayette
Baton Rouge
LA.
Shreveport
Houma
New Orleans
Biloxi
Mobile
Pensacola
Tallahassee
Gainesville
Jacksonville
St. Augustine
Daytona Beach
Orlando
Tampa
St. Petersburg
Sarasota
Fort Myers
Fort Pierce
West Palm Beach
Freeport
Fort Lauderdale
Miami
Miami Beach
Key West
FLORIDA
Goodland
Manhattan
Topeka
KANS.
Kansas City
Hutchinson
Wichita
Dodge City
Jefferson City
MO.
St. Louis
IND.
Evansville
Springfield
Louisville
KY.
Frankfort
Lexington
Cape Girardeau
Clarksville
Nashville
TENN.
Knoxville
Asheville
Winston-Salem
Raleigh
N.C.
Fayetteville
Wilmington
Charlotte
Spartanburg
S.C.
Columbia
Myrtle Beach
Charleston
Augusta
Savannah
Atlanta
GA.
Macon
Columbus
Albany
Valdosta
Dothan
Montgomery
ALA.
Birmingham
Tuscaloosa
Huntsville
Chattanooga
Memphis
MISS.
Jackson
Selma
Little Rock
ARK.
Pine Bluff
Texarkana
Fayetteville
Ft. Smith
Hot Springs
Tulsa
Enid
OKLAHOMA
Oklahoma City
Lawton
Azimuthal Equidistant Projection
SCALE 1:28,768,000
1 CENTIMETER = 288 KILOMETERS; 1 INCH = 454 MILES
KILOMETERS
STATUTE MILES
Bermuda Is. U.K.
ATLANTIC OCEAN
PACIFIC OCEAN
GULF OF MEXICO
TROPIC OF CANCER
BAHAMAS
Nassau
Andros I.
Turks & Caicos Is. U.K.
LA HABANA (Havana)
Pinar del Río
Matanzas
Artemisa
Colón
Santa Clara
Cienfuegos
Sancti Spíritus
Ciego de Ávila
Camagüey
Las Tunas
Holguín
Manzanillo
Santiago de Cuba
Guantánamo
Cayman Is. U.K.
Montego Bay
JAMAICA
May Pen
Kingston
HAITI
Les Cayes
Cap-Haïtien
PORT-AU-PRINCE
DOMINICAN REPUBLIC
Puerto Plata
Santiago
SANTO DOMINGO
Barahona
San Juan
PUERTO RICO U.S.
Virgin Islands U.S. & U.K.
St. Thomas
St. Croix
Basseterre
ST. KITTS & NEVIS
ANTIGUA & BARBUDA
St. John's
Fr. Guadeloupe
DOMINICA
Roseau
Fr. Martinique
Castries
ST. LUCIA
Kingstown
ST. VINCENT AND THE GRENADINES
BARBADOS
Bridgetown
St. George's
GRENADA
Port-of-Spain
TRINIDAD AND TOBAGO
GREATER ANTILLES
LESSER ANTILLES
WEST INDIES
Neth. Aruba
Curaçao
Bonaire
Neth. Ant.
CARIBBEAN SEA
CARACAS
VENEZUELA
BOGOTÁ
COLOMBIA
SOUTH AMERICA
MEXICO
BAJA CALIFORNIA
Hermosillo
Guaymas
Santa Rosalía
Nuevo Casas Grandes
Moctezuma
Magdalena
Mazatlán
Cuauhtémoc
Chihuahua
Ciudad Obregón
Navojoa
Los Mochis
Delicias
Hidalgo del Parral
Guasave
Culiacán
La Paz
Cabo San Lucas
Durango
Torreón
Gómez Palacio
Monclova
Piedras Negras
Nuevo Laredo
Nueva Rosita
Reynosa
McAllen
Matamoros
MONTERREY
Saltillo
Linares
Matehuala
Ciudad Victoria
Mazatlán
Fresnillo
Zacatecas
Aguascalientes
San Luis Potosí
Ciudad Mante
Tampico
Ciudad Valles
Tepic
Puerto Vallarta
GUADALAJARA
LEÓN
Guanajuato
Querétaro
Tuxpan
Poza Rica
Salamanca
Morelia
Colima
Tecomán
Uruapan
Apatzingán
MÉXICO
Puebla
Veracruz
NETZAHUALCÓYOTL
Córdoba
Tehuacán
Coatzacoalcos
Chilpancingo
Tlaxiaco
Acapulco
Oaxaca
Juchitán
Tehuantepec
Puerto Ángel
Miahuatlán
Islas Revillagigedo Mexico
Mérida
Motul
Valladolid
Cancún
Cozumel
Yucatán Pen.
Campeche
Ciudad del Carmen
Felipe Carrillo Puerto
Chetumal
Villahermosa
Tuxtla Gutiérrez
Flores
Belize City
Belmopan
BELIZE
GUATEMALA
Cobán
Tapachula
Quetzaltenango
San Pedro Sula
La Ceiba
HONDURAS
Santa Ana
Juticalpa
Tegucigalpa
Sonsonate
San Salvador
EL SALVADOR
San Miguel
Choluteca
Chinandega
León
NICARAGUA
MANAGUA
Granada
Kukalaya
Bluefields
Puerto Cabezas
Cayos Miskitos
Isla de San Andrés Colombia
Liberia
Puntarenas
COSTA RICA
Alajuela
San José
Ciudad Cortés
Puerto Limón
Bocas del Toro
PANAMA
Colón
Panamá
Santiago
Chitré
David
Puerto Armuelles
BERING SEA AND THE ALEUTIAN ISLANDS
Same Scale as Main Map
Monday
Sunday
Longitude East 170° of Greenwich
Longitude West 170° of Greenwich
Date Line
Komandorskiye Ostrova Russia
Wales
Seward Pen.
Nome
Norton Sound
St. Michael
St. Lawrence Island Alaska
Anvik
Hooper Bay
Tununak
Nunivak Is.
St. Matthew Island Alaska
Bethel
Quinhagak
Goodnews Bay
Togiak
Dillingham
Bristol Bay
Pribilof Islands Alaska
Pilot Point
Alaska Peninsula
Chignik
Perryville
Cold Bay
Sand Point
Unimak
Unalaska
Nikolski
Atka
Andreanof Is.
Kiska
Rat Is.
Attu
Near Islands
ALEUTIAN ISLANDS
Longitude West 90° of Greenwich

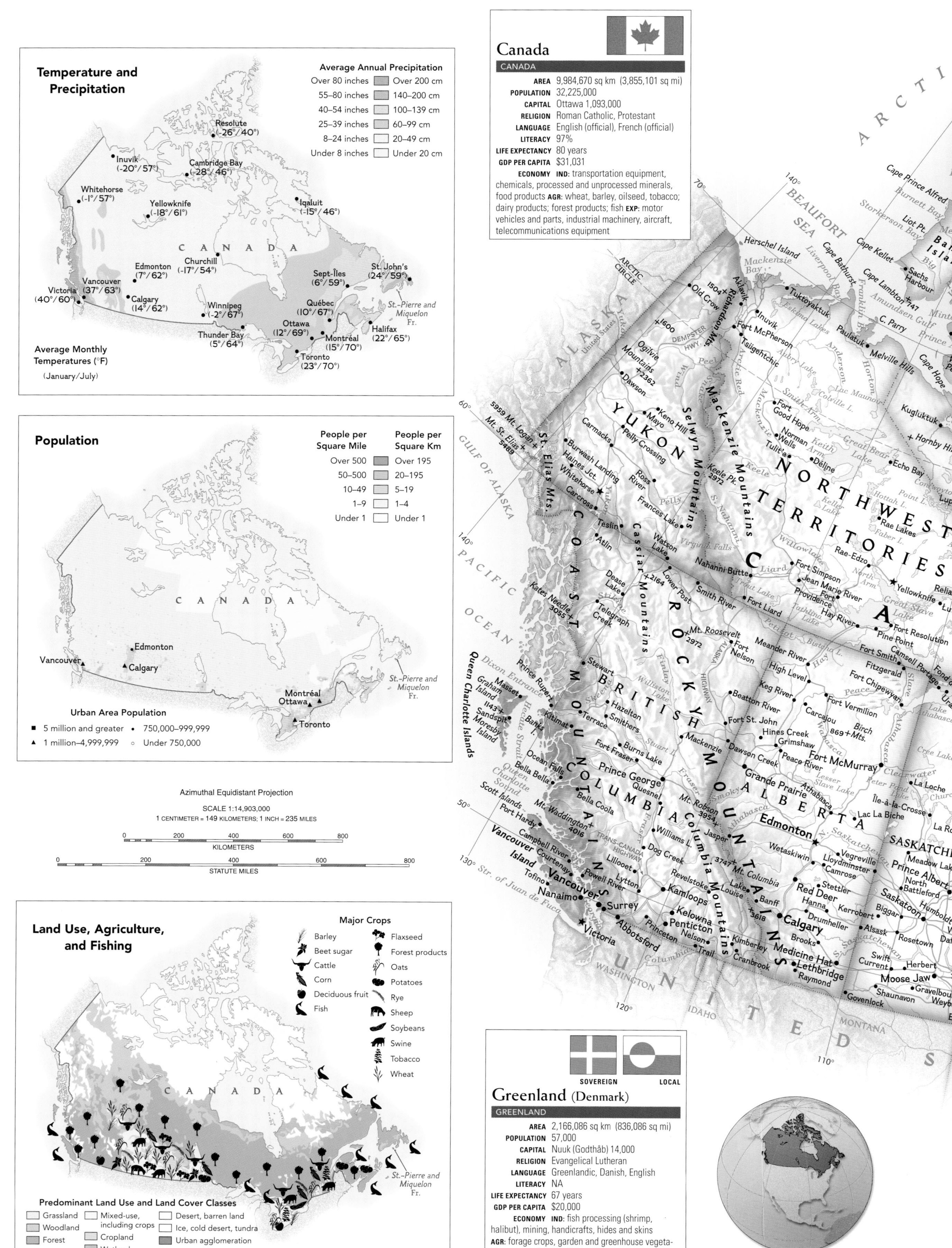
Canada
CANADA
AREA 9,984,670 sq km (3,855,101 sq mi)
POPULATION 32,225,000
CAPITAL Ottawa 1,093,000
RELIGION Roman Catholic, Protestant
LANGUAGE English (official), French (official)
LITERACY 97%
LIFE EXPECTANCY 80 years
GDP PER CAPITA $31,031
ECONOMY IND: transportation equipment, chemicals, processed and unprocessed minerals, food products AGR: wheat, barley, oilseed, tobacco; dairy products; forest products; fish EXP: motor vehicles and parts, industrial machinery, aircraft, telecommunications equipment
Temperature and Precipitation
Average Annual Precipitation
Over 80 inches Over 200 cm
55–80 inches 140–200 cm
40–54 inches 100–139 cm
25–39 inches 60–99 cm
8–24 inches 20–49 cm
Under 8 inches Under 20 cm
Resolute (-26°/40°)
Inuvik (-20°/57°)
Cambridge Bay (-28°/46°)
Whitehorse (-1°/57°)
Yellowknife (-18°/61°)
Iqaluit (-15°/46°)
CANADA
Churchill (-17°/54°)
Edmonton (7°/62°)
Vancouver (37°/63°)
Victoria (40°/60°)
Calgary (14°/62°)
Winnipeg (-2°/67°)
Sept-Îles (6°/59°)
St. John's (24°/59°)
Québec (10°/67°)
St.-Pierre and Miquelon Fr.
Ottawa (12°/69°)
Halifax (22°/65°)
Thunder Bay (5°/64°)
Montréal (15°/70°)
Toronto (23°/70°)
Average Monthly Temperatures (°F) (January/July)
Population
People per Square Mile
People per Square Km
Over 500 Over 195
50–500 20–195
10–49 5–19
1–9 1–4
Under 1 Under 1
CANADA
Edmonton
Vancouver
Calgary
St.-Pierre and Miquelon Fr.
Montréal
Ottawa
Toronto
Urban Area Population
5 million and greater
750,000–999,999
1 million–4,999,999
Under 750,000
Azimuthal Equidistant Projection
SCALE 1:14,903,000
1 CENTIMETER = 149 KILOMETERS; 1 INCH = 235 MILES
0 200 400 600 800 KILOMETERS
0 200 400 600 800 STATUTE MILES
Land Use, Agriculture, and Fishing
Major Crops
Barley
Beet sugar
Cattle
Corn
Deciduous fruit
Fish
Flaxseed
Forest products
Oats
Potatoes
Rye
Sheep
Soybeans
Swine
Tobacco
Wheat
CANADA
St.-Pierre and Miquelon Fr.
Predominant Land Use and Land Cover Classes
Grassland
Woodland
Forest
Mixed-use, including crops
Cropland
Wetland
Desert, barren land
Ice, cold desert, tundra
Urban agglomeration
BEAUFORT SEA
ARCTIC
ALASKA United States
YUKON
NORTHWEST TERRITORIES
BRITISH COLUMBIA
ALBERTA
SASKATCHEWAN
GULF OF ALASKA
PACIFIC OCEAN
UNITED STATES
WASHINGTON
IDAHO
MONTANA
Queen Charlotte Islands
Vancouver Island
COAST MOUNTAINS
ROCKY MOUNTAINS
Mackenzie Mountains
Selwyn Mountains
Cassiar Mountains
Columbia Mountains
St. Elias Mts.
Mt. Logan 5959
Mt. St. Elias 5489
Yellowknife
Whitehorse
Edmonton
Calgary
Vancouver
Victoria
Inuvik
Tuktoyaktuk
Aklavik
Dawson
Fort McMurray
Prince George
Kamloops
Kelowna
Lethbridge
Medicine Hat
Red Deer
Grande Prairie
Saskatoon
Moose Jaw
Prince Albert
Hay River
Fort Smith
Fort Simpson
Nanaimo
Surrey
Abbotsford
Prince Rupert
Greenland (Denmark)
SOVEREIGN
LOCAL
GREENLAND
AREA 2,166,086 sq km (836,086 sq mi)
POPULATION 57,000
CAPITAL Nuuk (Godthåb) 14,000
RELIGION Evangelical Lutheran
LANGUAGE Greenlandic, Danish, English
LITERACY NA
LIFE EXPECTANCY 67 years
GDP PER CAPITA $20,000
ECONOMY IND: fish processing (shrimp, halibut), mining, handicrafts, hides and skins AGR: forage crops, garden and greenhouse vegetables; sheep; fish EXP: fish and fish products

Industry and Mining
Major Mines
Al Aluminum
Co Cobalt
Cu Copper
Au Gold
Pb Lead
Mi Molybdenum
Ni Nickel
Pt Platinum
Ag Silver
U Uranium
Zn Zinc
Gross Domestic Product per Capita (in U.S. dollars)
20,000–43,400
10,000–19,999
3,500–9,999
400–3,499
Coal
Diamonds
Manufacturing center
Petroleum
Potash
Processing plant
C A N A D A
Vancouver
Edmonton
Calgary
Winnipeg
Toronto
Windsor
Montréal
St.-Pierre and Miquelon Fr.
SOVEREIGN
LOCAL
St.-Pierre and Miquelon (France)
TERR. COLL. OF ST.-PIERRE AND MIQUELON
AREA 242 sq km (93 sq mi)
POPULATION 7,000
CAPITAL St.-Pierre 6,000
RELIGION Roman Catholic
LANGUAGE French (official)
LITERACY 99%
LIFE EXPECTANCY 78 years
GDP PER CAPITA $7,000
ECONOMY IND: fish processing and supply base for fishing fleets, tourism AGR: vegetables; poultry; fish EXP: fish and fish products, soybeans, animal feed, mollusks and crustaceans
QUEEN ELIZABETH ISLANDS
SVERDRUP ISLANDS
PARRY ISLANDS
NUNAVUT
Baffin Island
Ellesmere Island
Axel Heiberg Island
Devon Island
Somerset Island
Prince of Wales Island
Boothia Peninsula
Southampton Island
GREENLAND (KALAALLIT NUNAAT) Denmark
North Magnetic Pole 2006
North Geomagnetic Pole 2005
BAFFIN BAY
DAVIS STRAIT
HUDSON STRAIT
HUDSON BAY
FOXE BASIN
Ungava Bay
PÉNINSULE D'UNGAVA
NOUVEAU-QUÉBEC
LABRADOR
LABRADOR SEA
NEWFOUNDLAND AND LABRADOR
QUÉBEC
ONTARIO
MANITOBA
NEW BRUNSWICK
PRINCE EDWARD ISLAND
NOVA SCOTIA
ISLAND OF NEWFOUNDLAND
GULF OF ST. LAWRENCE
ATLANTIC OCEAN
Alert
Eureka
Grise Fiord
Resolute
Pond Inlet
Clyde River
Iqaluit
Pangnirtung
Kimmirut
Igloolik
Hall Beach
Repulse Bay
Rankin Inlet
Arviat
Baker Lake
Chesterfield Inlet
Churchill
Thompson
Winnipeg
Brandon
Kenora
Thunder Bay
Sault Ste. Marie
Sudbury
North Bay
Timmins
Moosonee
Ottawa
MONTRÉAL
Québec
Sherbrooke
Trois-Rivières
Chicoutimi
Kingston
Peterborough
Barrie
Oshawa
TORONTO
Hamilton
Kitchener
London
Windsor
Kuujjuaq
Kuujjuarapik
Inukjuak
Schefferville
Labrador City
Nain
Sept-Îles
Rimouski
Gaspé
Fredericton
Moncton
Saint John
Charlottetown
Halifax
Dartmouth
Sydney
Corner Brook
Gander
St. John's
Avalon Pen.
Lake Superior
Lake Huron
Lake Ontario
Lake Erie
MINNESOTA
WIS.
MICHIGAN
NEW YORK
PENNSYLVANIA
OHIO
MAINE
VT.
N.H.
ARCTIC CIRCLE

PACIFIC OCEAN
ROCKY MOUNTAINS
GREAT PLAINS
GREAT BASIN
CASCADE RANGE
SIERRA NEVADA
COLORADO PLATEAU
Columbia Plateau
Mojave Desert
Sonoran Desert
Llano Estacado
Edwards Plateau
ALASKA
BROOKS RANGE
ALASKA RANGE
COAST MOUNTAINS
GULF OF ALASKA
BEAUFORT SEA
BERING SEA
ARCTIC CIRCLE
Mt. McKinley (Denali) 20320 (6194 m)
Mt. Whitney 14494 (4418 m)
Death Valley -282 (-86 m)

ATLANTIC OCEAN
GULF OF MEXICO
GULF OF MAINE
CENTRAL LOWLAND
APPALACHIAN MOUNTAINS
Appalachian Plateau
Cumberland Plateau
Allegheny Mountains
Blue Ridge
Piedmont
Ozark Plateau
Black Belt
Sea Islands
Lake Superior
Lake Michigan
Lake Huron
Lake Erie
Lake Ontario
Upper Peninsula
Lower Peninsula
Isle Royale
Keweenaw Peninsula
Eagle Mt. 2301
Mt. Arvon 1979
Timms Hill 1951
Charles Mound 1235
Campbell Hill 1550
Mt. Katahdin 5268
Mt. Washington 6288
Mt. Mansfield 4393
Mt. Marcy 5344
Adirondack Mts.
Catskill Mts.
Slide Mt. 4180
Mt. Greylock 3491
Mt. Frissell 2380
Jerimoth Hill 812
High Pt. 1803
Mt. Davis 3213
Backbone Mt. 3360
Spruce Knob 4863
Black Mt. 4145
Mt. Rogers 5729
Clingmans Dome 6643
Mt. Mitchell 6684
Sassafras Mt. 3560
Brasstown Bald 4784
Taum Sauk Mt. 1772
Woodall Mt. 806
Cheaha Mt. 2407
Britton Hill 345
Driskill Mt. 535
Boston Mts.
Magazine Mt. 2753
Ouachita Mts.
Great Smoky Mts.
White Mts.
Green Mts.
Niagara Falls
Finger Lakes
Pine Barrens
Cape Cod
Cape Ann
Martha's Vineyard
Nantucket I.
Long Island Sd.
Long I.
Cape May
Delaware Bay
Chesapeake Bay
Cape Charles
Great Dismal Swamp
Albemarle Sound
Pamlico Sd.
Cape Hatteras
Cape Lookout
Cape Fear
Okefenokee Swamp
Cape Canaveral
Lake Okeechobee
The Everglades
Biscayne Bay
Florida Keys
Straits of Florida
Cape Sable
Cape Romano
Tampa Bay
Charlotte Harbor
Dry Tortugas
Marquesas Keys
Apalachee Bay
Cape San Blas
Pensacola Bay
Mobile Bay
Mississippi Sd.
Breton Sd.
Mississippi River Delta
Lake Pontchartrain
Barataria Bay
Timbalier Bay
Terrebonne Bay
Atchafalaya Bay
Marsh Island
Galveston Bay
TROPIC OF CANCER
CUBA
HAITI
Mississippi
Ohio
Tennessee
Missouri
St. Lawrence
Hudson
Delaware
Susquehanna
Potomac
10,000
9,000
8,000
7,000
6,000
5,000
4,000
3,000
2,000
1,000
250
0 (sea level)
elevations in feet
Albers Conic Equal-Area Projection
SCALE 1:10,824,000
1 CENTIMETER = 108 KILOMETERS; 1 INCH = 171 MILES
KILOMETERS
STATUTE MILES
PRINCIPAL HAWAIIAN ISLANDS
Longitude West 159° of Greenwich
PACIFIC OCEAN
KAUA'I
Kawaikini 5243
NI'IHAU
O'AHU
MOLOKA'I
LĀNA'I
MAUI
Kaho'olawe
HAWAI'I
Mauna Kea 13796
Mauna Loa 13679
Kilauea 4077
Ka Lae (South Cape)

C A N A
ALBERTA
SASKATCHEWAN
MANITO
BRITISH COLUMBIA
Str. of Juan de Fuca
Bellingham
Mt. Olympus 7980
Bremerton
Everett
Seattle
Aberdeen
WASHINGTON
Tacoma
Olympia
Mt. Rainier 14411
Centralia
Longview
Astoria
Kelso
Mt. St. Helens 8366
Vancouver
Yakima
Richland
Wenatchee
Spokane
Coeur d'Alene
Colville
Sandpoint
Pullman
Walla Walla
Lewiston
Wallace
Columbia
Portland
Mt. Hood 11239
The Dalles
Newport
Salem
Albany
Corvallis
Eugene
Springfield
OREGON
North Bend
Coos Bay
Roseburg
Pendleton
La Grande
Baker City
John Day
Ontario
Burns
Grants Pass
Medford
Ashland
Klamath Falls
Crescent City
Crane
Bonners Ferry
Kalispell
Polson
Cut Bank
Shelby
Havre
Turner
Malta
Glasgow
Fort Peck Lake
Wolf Point
Williston
Sidney
Great Falls
Fort Benton
Lewistown
MONTANA
Missoula
Deer Lodge
Helena
Butte
Bozeman
Livingston
Billings
Laurel
Dillon
Roundup
Miles City
Forsyth
Glendive
Baker
Hardin
IDAHO
Salmon
Payette
Caldwell
Boise
Nampa
Sun Valley
Mountain Home
Borah Pk. 12662
Idaho Falls
Pocatello
Blackfoot
Jerome
Twin Falls
Rupert
Burley
Montpelier
Preston
Powell
Cody
Sheridan
Buffalo
Worland
Thermopolis
Gillette
Newcastle
Grand Teton 13770
Gannett Pk. 13804
WYOMING
Riverton
Lander
Casper
Douglas
Lusk
Kemmerer
Green River
Rock Springs
Rawlins
Evanston
Laramie
Cheyenne
Portal
St. John
Stanley
Minot
Rugby
Devils Lake
Lake Sakakawea
Harvey
Grand Forks
NORTH DAKOTA
Dickinson
Mandan
Bismarck
Jamestown
Valley City
Mott
Fort Yates
Ashley
Lemmon
Mobridge
Aberdeen
Faith
Lake Oahe
Belle Fourche
SOUTH DAKOTA
Lead
Rapid City
Pierre
Huron
Hot Springs
Martin
Mitchell
Lake Francis Case
Sioux Falls
Yankton
Chadron
Valentine
Ainsworth
Alliance
Scottsbluff
NEBRASKA
Sidney
North Platte
Grand Island
Kearney
Hastings
McCook
Columbus
Platte
Norfolk
P A C I F I C   O C E A N
Yreka
Mt. Shasta 14162
Goose L.
Eureka
Redding
Susanville
Red Bluff
Fort Bragg
Ukiah
Yuba City
Sacramento
Santa Rosa
Vallejo
Oakland
San Francisco
San Mateo
Stockton
Palo Alto
Modesto
Santa Cruz
San Jose
Monterey
Salinas
Fresno
Coalinga
Visalia
Paso Robles
Delano
San Luis Obispo
Bakersfield
Santa Maria
Lompoc
Santa Barbara
Glendale
Pasadena
LOS ANGELES
Long Beach
Santa Ana
San Bernardino
Palm Springs
Riverside
Salton Sea
SAN DIEGO
National City
El Centro
Mojave
Ridgecrest
Bishop
CALIFORNIA
SIERRA NEVADA
Denio
McDermitt
Winnemucca
Lovelock
Carlin
Elko
Wells
Reno
Carson City
NEVADA
GREAT BASIN
McGill
Ely
Hawthorne
Mt. Jefferson 11949
Tonopah
Goldfield
Pioche
Caliente
Beatty
Death Valley
-282
Las Vegas
Boulder City
Lake Mead
Needles
Great Salt Lake
Logan
Ogden
Salt Lake City
Tooele
Provo
Utah L.
Kings Pk. 13528
Vernal
Nephi
Price
Sevier Lake
Fillmore
Manti
Richfield
UTAH
Moab
Parowan
Cedar City
Panguitch
St. George
Kanab
Monticello
Lake Powell
Craig
Fort Collins
Greeley
Longmont
Boulder
Fort Morgan
Denver
Aurora
Glenwood Springs
Grand Junction
COLORADO
Delta
Gunnison
Montrose
Pikes Pk. 14110
Colorado Springs
Pueblo
Salida
Canon City
Lamar
La Junta
Silverton
Cortez
Durango
Alamosa
Walsenburg
Trinidad
ROCKY MOUNTAINS
COLORADO PLATEAU
Farmington
Grand Canyon
Kingman
Williams
Flagstaff
Prescott
Winslow
Holbrook
ARIZONA
Wickenburg
Scottsdale
PHOENIX
Mesa
Baldy Peak 11403
Globe
Gila Bend
Casa Grande
Morenci
Eloy
Safford
Ajo
Tucson
Willcox
Benson
Tombstone
Nogales
Bisbee
Douglas
Yuma
Wheeler Peak 13161
Raton
Clayton
Los Alamos
Springer
Gallup
Grants
Santa Fe
Las Vegas
Albuquerque
NEW MEXICO
Belen
Tucumcari
Vaughn
Magdalena
Fort Sumner
Clovis
Socorro
Roswell
Truth or Consequences
Alamogordo
Artesia
Silver City
Lordsburg
Deming
Las Cruces
Carlsbad
Hobbs
El Paso
Colby
Goodland
Russell
Salina
Hays
Great Bend
Garden City
KANSAS
Hutchinson
Arkansas
Dodge City
Liberal
Guymon
Woodward
Ponca City
Enid
Stillwater
Dalhart
Dumas
Borger
Pampa
Amarillo
Oklahoma City
OKLA
Chickasha
Hereford
Lawton
Childress
Red
Plainview
Vernon
Wichita Falls
Lubbock
Brownfield
Lamesa
Snyder
Sweetwater
Abilene
Big Spring
Midland
Odessa
Brownwood
Pecos
Van Horn
TEXAS
San Angelo
Fort Stockton
Temple
Marfa
Alpine
Ozona
Sonora
Sanderson
Amistad Reservoir
Rio Grande
Del Rio
New Braunfels
SAN ANTONIO
Uvalde
Eagle Pass
Beeville
Aransas
Alice
Laredo
Falfurrias
Raymondville
Edinburg
McAllen
Brownsville
MEXICO
ARCTIC OCEAN
BEAUFORT SEA
CHUKCHI SEA
Barrow
Wainwright
Atqasuk
Point Lay
Prudhoe Bay
Kaktovik
Point Hope
Umiat
North Slope
BROOKS RANGE
Noatak
Kivalina
ARCTIC CIRCLE
RUSSIA
Shishmaref
Kotzebue
Kiana
Shungnak
Kobuk
Wiseman
CANADA
U.S.
Selawik
Bering Str.
Wales
Teller
Deering
Allakaket
Fort Yukon
Hughes
Beaver
Circle
Yukon
Gambell
Savoonga
Nome
Koyuk
Golovin
Nulato
Galena
Tanana
Rampart
Fairbanks
Eagle
ALASKA
Ruby
Kaltag
Unalakleet
St. Lawrence Island
Lake Minchumina
Nenana
Big Delta
St. Michael
Alakanuk
Kotlik
ALASKA RANGE
Tanacross
Mountain Village
McGrath
Cantwell
Mt. McKinley (Denali) 20320
Northway
Hooper Bay
Anvik
Holy Cross
Flat
Farewell
Gulkana
Tununak
Aniak
Red Devil
Skwentna
Palmer
Valdez
Mekoryuk
Bethel
Nyac
Kashegelok
Anchorage
Whittier
Cordova
Nunivak Island
Quinhagak
Kenai
Seward
Cape Yakataga
Goodnews Bay
Newhalen
Iliamna Lake
Homer
Seldovia
Yakutat
Togiak
Dillingham
Naknek
King Salmon
BERING SEA
GULF OF ALASKA
Egegik
Kodiak
Kodiak Island
Pilot Point
Karluk
Chignik
Cold Bay
Sand Point
YUKON
NORTHWEST TERRITORIES
BRITISH COLUMBIA
Skagway
Haines
Juneau
Gustavus
Hoonah
Sitka
Petersburg
Wrangell
Ketchikan
Hydaburg
PACIFIC OCEAN
ALASKA
0 100 200 300 km
0 50 100 150 statute mi

United States
UNITED STATES OF AMERICA
AREA 9,826,630 sq km (3,794,083 sq mi)
POPULATION 296,483,000
CAPITAL Washington, D.C. 4,098,000
RELIGION Protestant, Roman Catholic
LANGUAGE English, Spanish
LITERACY 97%
LIFE EXPECTANCY 78 years
GDP PER CAPITA $39,650
ECONOMY IND: petroleum, steel, motor vehicles, aerospace AGR: wheat, corn, other grains, fruits; beef; forest products; fish EXP: capital goods, industrial supplies, consumer goods, agricultural products
Albers Conic Equal-Area Projection
SCALE 1:10,824,000
1 CENTIMETER = 108 KILOMETERS; 1 INCH = 171 MILES
0 100 200 300 400 500
KILOMETERS
0 100 200 300 400 500
STATUTE MILES
ONTARIO
QUEBEC
PRINCE EDWARD ISLAND
NEW BRUNSWICK
NOVA SCOTIA
GULF OF MAINE
ATLANTIC OCEAN
GULF OF MEXICO
BAHAMAS
CUBA
HAITI
TROPIC OF CANCER
Straits of Florida
Lake Superior
Lake Michigan
Lake Huron
Lake Erie
Lake Ontario
Georgian Bay
Lake of the Woods
St. Lawrence
Bay of Fundy
Chesapeake Bay
Delaware Bay
Pamlico Sound
Albemarle Sound
Port Royal Sound
Mobile Bay
Tampa Bay
L. Okeechobee
MINNESOTA
WISCONSIN
MICHIGAN
IOWA
ILLINOIS
INDIANA
OHIO
MISSOURI
KENTUCKY
TENNESSEE
ARKANSAS
MISSISSIPPI
ALABAMA
GEORGIA
FLORIDA
LOUISIANA
SOUTH CAROLINA
NORTH CAROLINA
VIRGINIA
WEST VIRGINIA
MARYLAND
DELAWARE
PENNSYLVANIA
NEW JERSEY
NEW YORK
CONN.
RHODE ISLAND
MASSACHUSETTS
VERMONT
NEW HAMPSHIRE
MAINE
APPALACHIAN MOUNTAINS
Duluth
St. Paul
Milwaukee
Madison
Green Bay
Des Moines
CHICAGO
Detroit
Lansing
Grand Rapids
Indianapolis
Columbus
Cleveland
Cincinnati
Pittsburgh
Louisville
Frankfort
Lexington
St. Louis
Jefferson City
Kansas City
Springfield
Nashville
Memphis
Knoxville
Chattanooga
Little Rock
Jackson
Birmingham
Montgomery
Atlanta
Tallahassee
Jacksonville
Orlando
Tampa
St. Petersburg
Miami
Key West
Baton Rouge
New Orleans
Mobile
Columbia
Charleston
Savannah
Raleigh
Durham
Charlotte
Greensboro
Richmond
Norfolk
Virginia Beach
Washington, D.C.
Baltimore
Annapolis
Dover
PHILADELPHIA
Harrisburg
Trenton
NEW YORK
Hartford
Providence
Boston
Concord
Montpelier
Augusta
Albany
Buffalo
Rochester
Syracuse
Portland
Bangor
Mt. Katahdin 5268
Mt. Washington 6288
Mt. Marcy 5344
Longitude West 90° of Greenwich
PRINCIPAL HAWAIIAN ISLANDS
Longitude West 159° of Greenwich
PACIFIC OCEAN
KAUA'I
NI'IHAU
O'AHU
MOLOKA'I
LĀNA'I
MAUI
KAHO'OLAWE
HAWAI'I
Honolulu
Hilo
Mauna Loa 13679
Kīlauea 4077
13796
10023
0 100 km
0 100 statute mi

Temperature and Precipitation

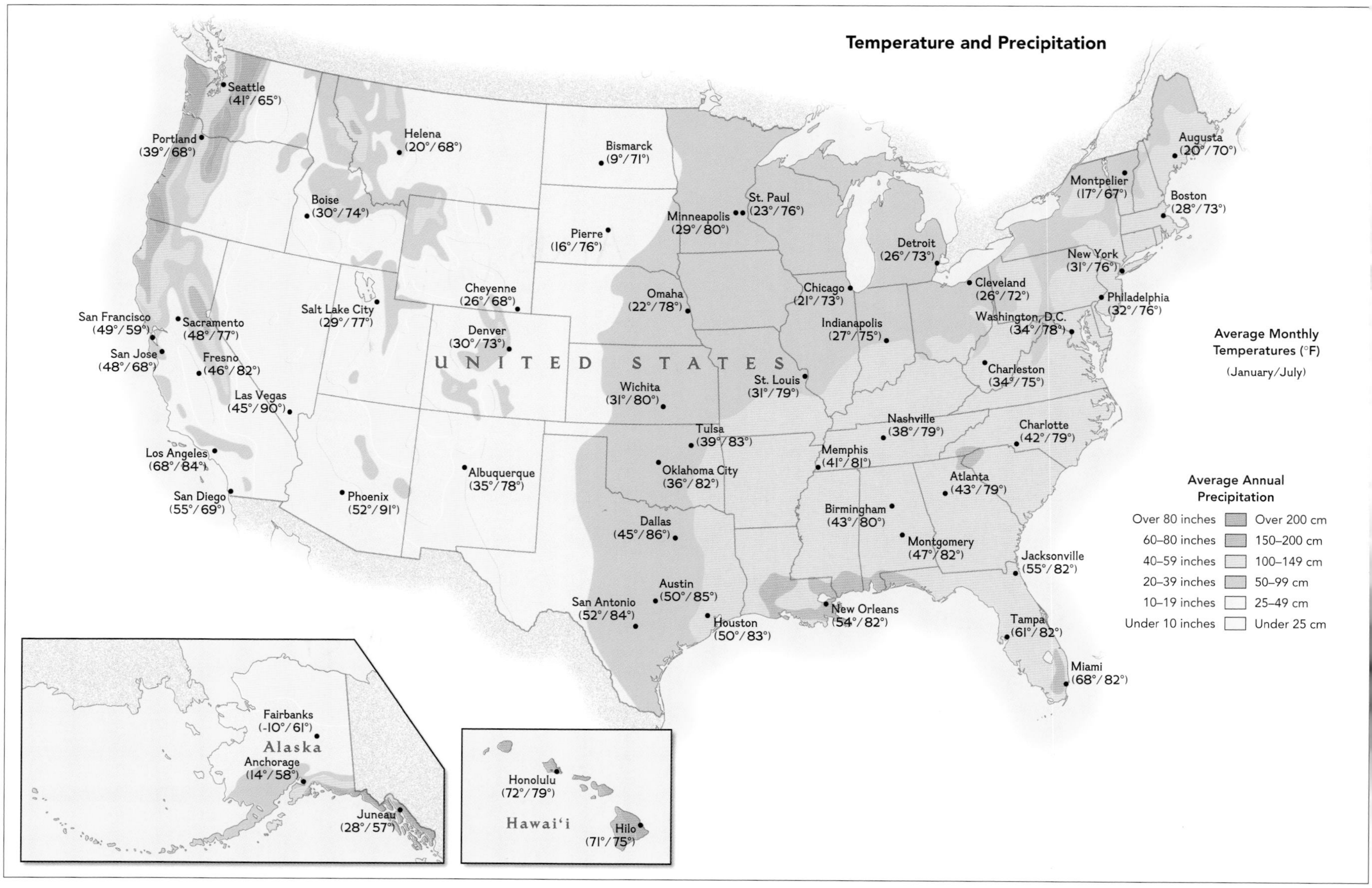

Seattle (41°/65°)
Portland (39°/68°)
Helena (20°/68°)
Bismarck (9°/71°)
Boise (30°/74°)
Pierre (16°/76°)
Minneapolis (29°/80°)
St. Paul (23°/76°)
Augusta (20°/70°)
Montpelier (17°/67°)
Boston (28°/73°)
Detroit (26°/73°)
New York (31°/76°)
San Francisco (49°/59°)
Sacramento (48°/77°)
Salt Lake City (29°/77°)
Cheyenne (26°/68°)
Omaha (22°/78°)
Chicago (21°/73°)
Cleveland (26°/72°)
Philadelphia (32°/76°)
Washington, D.C. (34°/78°)
San Jose (48°/68°)
Fresno (46°/82°)
Denver (30°/73°)
Indianapolis (27°/75°)
Las Vegas (45°/90°)
Wichita (31°/80°)
St. Louis (31°/79°)
Charleston (34°/75°)
UNITED STATES
Nashville (38°/79°)
Charlotte (42°/79°)
Tulsa (39°/83°)
Memphis (41°/81°)
Los Angeles (68°/84°)
Albuquerque (35°/78°)
Oklahoma City (36°/82°)
Atlanta (43°/79°)
San Diego (55°/69°)
Phoenix (52°/91°)
Birmingham (43°/80°)
Dallas (45°/86°)
Montgomery (47°/82°)
Jacksonville (55°/82°)
Austin (50°/85°)
San Antonio (52°/84°)
New Orleans (54°/82°)
Houston (50°/83°)
Tampa (61°/82°)
Miami (68°/82°)
Fairbanks (-10°/61°)
Alaska
Anchorage (14°/58°)
Juneau (28°/57°)
Honolulu (72°/79°)
Hawai'i
Hilo (71°/75°)

Average Monthly Temperatures (°F)
(January/July)

Average Annual Precipitation

Over 80 inches	Over 200 cm
60–80 inches	150–200 cm
40–59 inches	100–149 cm
20–39 inches	50–99 cm
10–19 inches	25–49 cm
Under 10 inches	Under 25 cm

Land Use, Agriculture, and Fishing

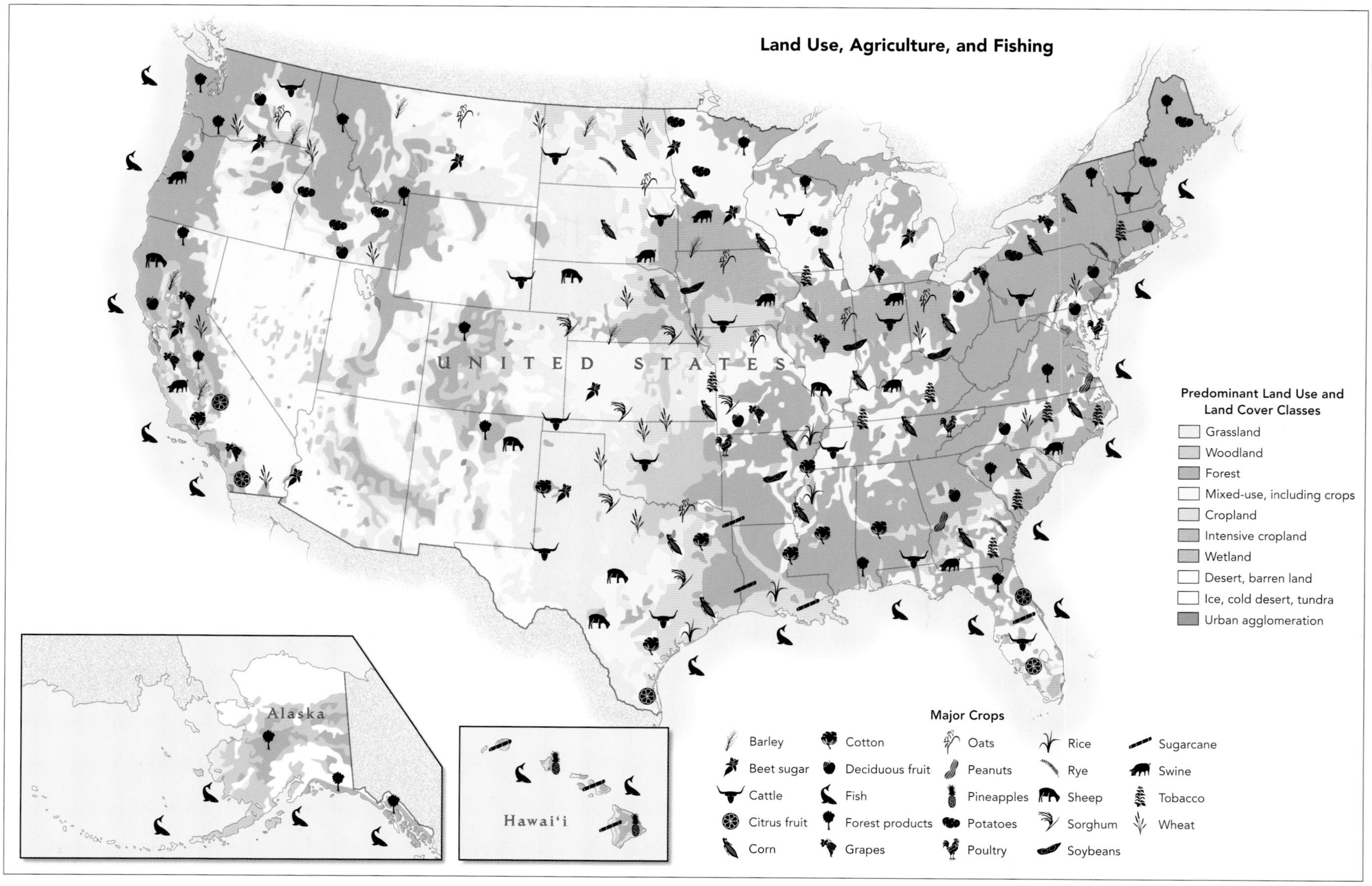

UNITED STATES
Alaska
Hawai'i

Predominant Land Use and Land Cover Classes

- Grassland
- Woodland
- Forest
- Mixed-use, including crops
- Cropland
- Intensive cropland
- Wetland
- Desert, barren land
- Ice, cold desert, tundra
- Urban agglomeration

Major Crops

Barley	Cotton	Oats	Rice	Sugarcane
Beet sugar	Deciduous fruit	Peanuts	Rye	Swine
Cattle	Fish	Pineapples	Sheep	Tobacco
Citrus fruit	Forest products	Potatoes	Sorghum	Wheat
Corn	Grapes	Poultry	Soybeans	

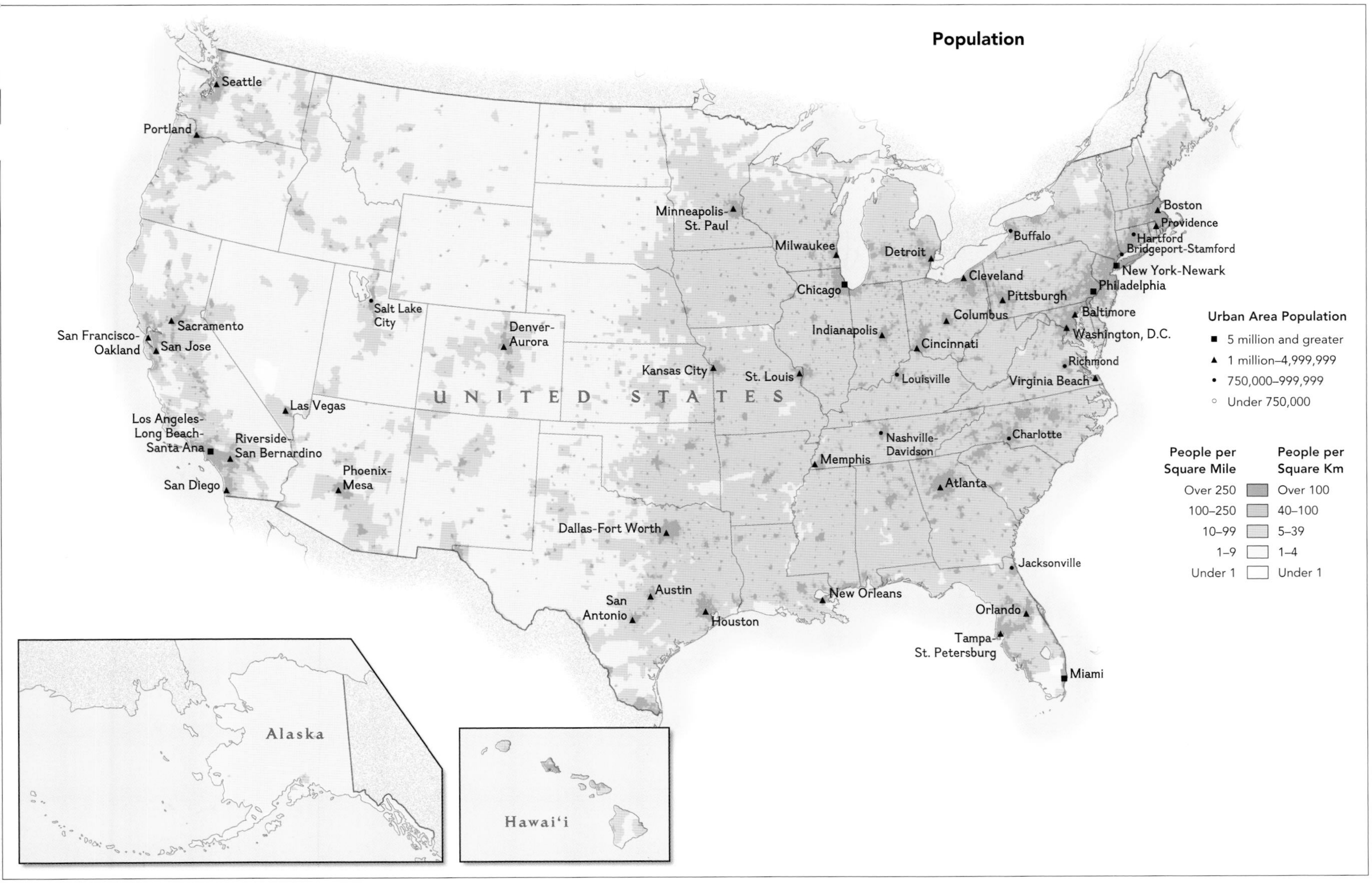

Population

Seattle
Portland
Minneapolis-St. Paul
Boston
Providence
Hartford
Bridgeport-Stamford
Buffalo
Milwaukee
Detroit
New York-Newark
Cleveland
Philadelphia
Chicago
Pittsburgh
Baltimore
Salt Lake City
Columbus
Washington, D.C.
Sacramento
Indianapolis
Cincinnati
San Francisco-Oakland
San Jose
Denver-Aurora
Richmond
Kansas City
St. Louis
Louisville
Virginia Beach
UNITED STATES
Las Vegas
Los Angeles-Long Beach-Santa Ana
Riverside-San Bernardino
Nashville-Davidson
Charlotte
Memphis
Phoenix-Mesa
San Diego
Atlanta
Dallas-Fort Worth
Jacksonville
Austin
New Orleans
San Antonio
Houston
Orlando
Tampa-St. Petersburg
Miami
Alaska
Hawai'i

Urban Area Population

- ■ 5 million and greater
- ▲ 1 million–4,999,999
- • 750,000–999,999
- ○ Under 750,000

People per Square Mile	People per Square Km
Over 250	Over 100
100–250	40–100
10–99	5–39
1–9	1–4
Under 1	Under 1

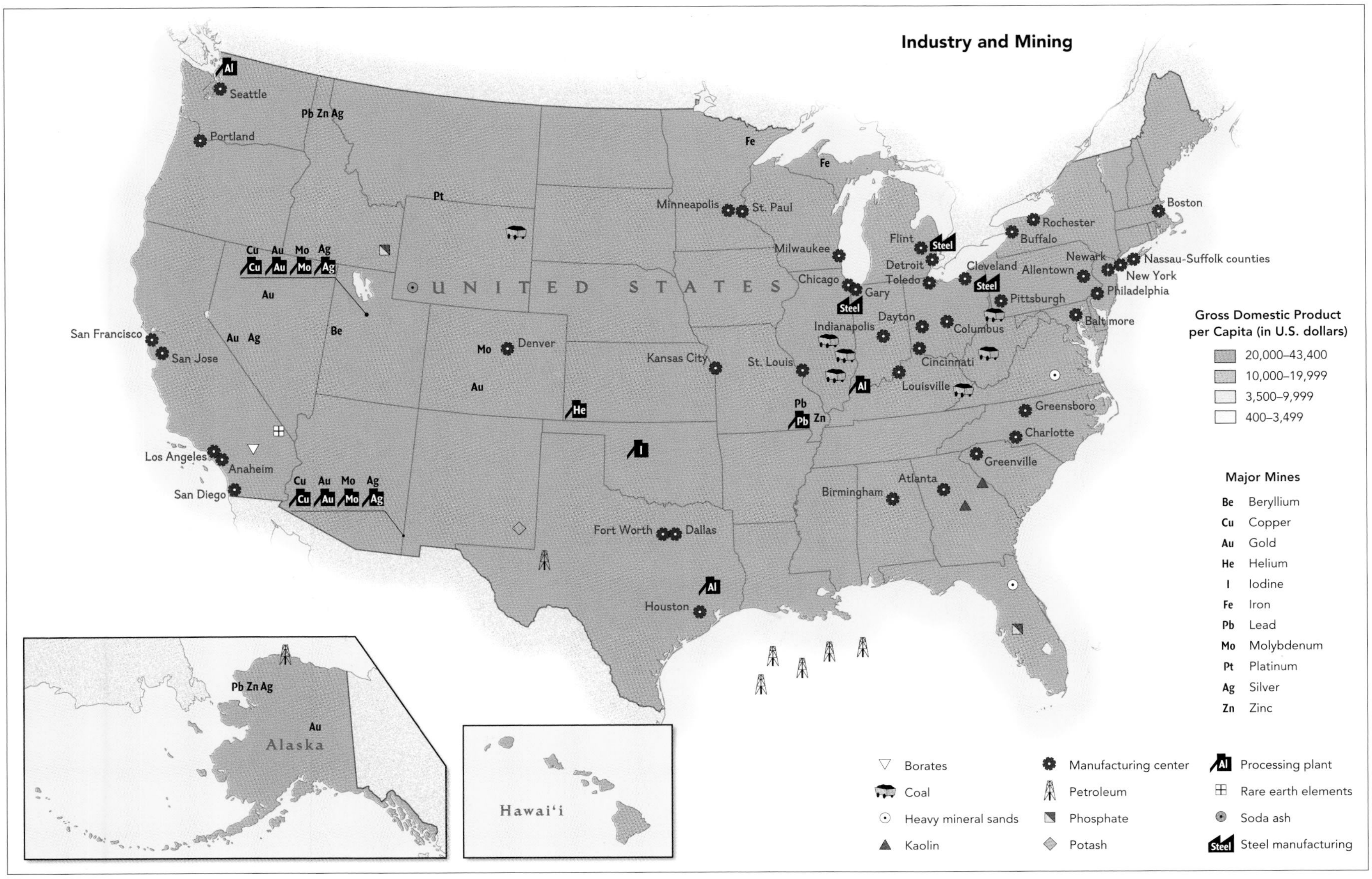

Industry and Mining

Al
Seattle
Pb Zn Ag
Portland
Fe
Fe
Pt
Minneapolis
St. Paul
Boston
Rochester
Buffalo
Flint
Steel
Milwaukee
Cu Au Mo Ag
Cu Au Mo Ag
Detroit
Newark
Nassau-Suffolk counties
Cleveland
Allentown
New York
Toledo
Steel
Chicago
Gary
Steel
Philadelphia
Pittsburgh
Au
UNITED STATES
Baltimore
Indianapolis
Dayton
Columbus
San Francisco
Be
Au Ag
San Jose
Mo
Denver
Kansas City
St. Louis
Cincinnati
Au
Louisville
Al
He
Greensboro
Pb
Pb Zn
Charlotte
I
Greenville
Los Angeles
Anaheim
Atlanta
Birmingham
Cu Au Mo Ag
Cu Au Mo Ag
San Diego
Fort Worth
Dallas
Al
Houston
Pb Zn Ag
Au
Alaska
Hawai'i

Gross Domestic Product per Capita (in U.S. dollars)

- 20,000–43,400
- 10,000–19,999
- 3,500–9,999
- 400–3,499

Major Mines

Be	Beryllium
Cu	Copper
Au	Gold
He	Helium
I	Iodine
Fe	Iron
Pb	Lead
Mo	Molybdenum
Pt	Platinum
Ag	Silver
Zn	Zinc

- Borates
- Coal
- Heavy mineral sands
- Kaolin
- Manufacturing center
- Petroleum
- Phosphate
- Potash
- Al Processing plant
- Rare earth elements
- Soda ash
- Steel Steel manufacturing

PACIFIC OCEAN
CANADA
ALBERTA
SASKATCHEWAN
MANITOBA
BRITISH COLUMBIA
WASHINGTON
OREGON
CALIFORNIA
NEVADA
IDAHO
MONTANA
WYOMING
UTAH
COLORADO
ARIZONA
NEW MEXICO
NORTH DAKOTA
SOUTH DAKOTA
NEBRASKA
KANSAS
OKLAHOMA
TEXAS
MEXICO
ROCKY MOUNTAINS
GREAT BASIN
COLORADO PLATEAU
SIERRA NEVADA
COAST RANGES
CASCADE RANGE
Bellingham
Seattle
Aberdeen
Olympia
Spokane
Yakima
Coeur d'Alene
Kalispell
Havre
Williston
Minot
Grand Forks
Bismarck
Portland
Richland
Lewiston
Missoula
Great Falls
Glendive
Newport
Salem
Helena
Butte
Bozeman
Billings
Miles City
Hardin
Bowman
Burns
Boise
Crescent City
Klamath Falls
Eureka
Idaho Falls
Pocatello
Montpelier
Buffalo
Gillette
Rapid City
Pierre
Sioux Falls
Casper
Winnemucca
Elko
Salt Lake City
Rock Springs
Laramie
Cheyenne
North Platte
Grand Island
Valentine
Reno
Carson City
Sacramento
Oakland
San Francisco
San Jose
Provo
Ely
Tonopah
Pioche
Cedar City
Grand Junction
Denver
Colorado Springs
Pueblo
Salina
Garden City
Wichita
Las Vegas
Lake Mead
Bakersfield
LOS ANGELES
San Bernardino
SAN DIEGO
Yuma
PHOENIX
Kingman
Flagstaff
Gallup
Farmington
Durango
Taos
Santa Fe
Albuquerque
Amarillo
Enid
Oklahoma City
Clovis
Lubbock
Wichita Falls
Roswell
Alamogordo
Las Cruces
Carlsbad
Tucson
Safford
Nogales
Douglas
El Paso
Odessa
Midland
Abilene
San Angelo
Fort Worth
Van Horn
Pecos
Fort Stockton
Del Rio
Austin
SAN ANTONIO
Laredo
Corpus Christi
McAllen
Brownsville
Rio Grande
Great Salt Lake
Lake Powell
Salton Sea
ALASKA
ARCTIC OCEAN
BEAUFORT SEA
CHUKCHI SEA
BERING SEA
GULF OF ALASKA
PACIFIC OCEAN
RUSSIA
ARCTIC CIRCLE
Bering Str.
North Slope
BROOKS RANGE
ALASKA RANGE
YUKON
NORTHWEST TERRITORIES
BRITISH COLUMBIA
CANADA
U.S.
Prudhoe Bay
Circle
Manley Hot Springs
Fairbanks
Eagle
Nenana
Big Delta
Tok
Cantwell
Gulkana
Palmer
Anchorage
Valdez
Whittier
Seward
Homer
Skagway
Haines
Juneau
St. Lawrence Island
Nunivak Island
Kodiak Island
Iliamna Lake
0 100 200 300 km
0 50 100 150 statute mi

ATLANTIC OCEAN
GULF OF MEXICO
Albers Conic Equal-Area Projection
SCALE 1:10,824,000
1 CENTIMETER = 108 KILOMETERS; 1 INCH = 171 MILES
KILOMETERS
STATUTE MILES
TROPIC OF CANCER
PRINCIPAL HAWAIIAN ISLANDS
Longitude West 90° of Greenwich
Longitude West 159° of Greenwich
PACIFIC OCEAN
NEW YORK
PHILADELPHIA
CHICAGO
HOUSTON
Washington, D.C.

PACIFIC OCEAN
WASHINGTON
OREGON
CALIFORNIA
NEVADA
IDAHO
MONTANA
WYOMING
UTAH
COLORADO
ARIZONA
NEW MEXICO
NORTH DAKOT
SOUTH DAKOT
NEBRASK
KANS
OK
TEX
CAN
MEXICO
OLYMPIC COAST NATIONAL MARINE SANCTUARY
OLYMPIC N.P.
NORTH CASCADES N.P.
MT. RAINIER N.P.
GLACIER N.P.
CRATER LAKE N.P.
REDWOOD N.P.
LASSEN VOLCANIC N.P.
CORDELL BANK N.M.S.
GULF OF THE FARALLONES N.M.S.
MONTEREY BAY N.M.S.
YOSEMITE N.P.
KINGS CANYON N.P.
SEQUOIA N.P.
DEATH VALLEY N.P.
CHANNEL ISLANDS N.M.S.
CHANNEL ISLANDS N.P.
JOSHUA TREE N.P.
GREAT BASIN N.P.
BRYCE CANYON N.P.
CAPITOL REEF N.P.
ARCHES N.P.
CANYONLANDS N.P.
ZION N.P.
GRAND CANYON N.P.
PETRIFIED FOREST N.P.
SAGUARO N.P.
MESA VERDE N.P.
BLACK CANYON OF THE GUNNISON N.P.
GREAT SAND DUNES N.P.
ROCKY MOUNTAIN N.P.
YELLOWSTONE N.P.
GRAND TETON N.P.
WIND CAVE N.P.
BADLANDS N.P.
THEODORE ROOSEVELT N.P.
CARLSBAD CAVERNS N.P.
GUADALUPE MOUNTAINS N.P.
BIG BEND N.P.
Columbia
Snake
Missouri
Yellowstone
Great Salt Lake
Platte
Arkansas
Colorado
Rio Grande
Pecos
Red
ARCTIC OCEAN
RUSSIA
BERING SEA
GULF OF ALASKA
CANADA
ALASKA
Noatak
Yukon
KOBUK VALLEY N.P.
GATES OF THE ARCTIC N.P. AND PRESERVE
DENALI N.P. AND PRESERVE
WRANGELL-ST. ELIAS N.P. AND PRESERVE
LAKE CLARK N.P. AND PRESERVE
KATMAI N.P. AND PRESERVE
KENAI FJORDS N.P.
GLACIER BAY N.P. AND PRESERVE
0 200 km
0 200 statute mi
MAP KEY
National Park System
National Forest
National Wildlife Refuge
National Grassland
Bureau of Land Management
Indian Reservation
Military Reservation
Department of Energy
National Marine Sanctuary
Only national parks and marine sanctuaries are labeled.

MINNESOTA
WISCONSIN
MICHIGAN
IOWA
ILLINOIS
INDIANA
OHIO
PENNSYLVANIA
NEW YORK
VERMONT
NEW HAMPSHIRE
MAINE
MASSACHUSETTS
CONN.
RHODE ISLAND
NEW JERSEY
DELAWARE
MARYLAND
Washington, D.C.
WEST VIRGINIA
VIRGINIA
KENTUCKY
MISSOURI
ARKANSAS
TENNESSEE
NORTH CAROLINA
SOUTH CAROLINA
GEORGIA
ALABAMA
MISSISSIPPI
LOUISIANA
FLORIDA
ATLANTIC OCEAN
GULF OF MEXICO
BAHAMAS
CUBA
VOYAGEURS N.P.
ISLE ROYALE N.P.
THUNDER BAY N.M.S.
STELLWAGEN BANK N.M.S.
ACADIA N.P.
CUYAHOGA VALLEY N.P.
SHENANDOAH N.P.
MAMMOTH CAVE N.P.
GREAT SMOKY MOUNTAINS N.P.
MONITOR N.M.S.
CONGAREE N.P.
HOT SPRINGS N.P.
GRAY'S REEF N.M.S.
FLOWER GARDEN BANKS N.M.S.
EVERGLADES N.P.
BISCAYNE N.P.
DRY TORTUGAS N.P.
FLORIDA KEYS N.M.S.
Lake of the Woods
Lake Superior
Lake Michigan
Lake Huron
Georgian Bay
Lake Erie
Lake Ontario
Lake Champlain
St. Lawrence
Hudson
Mississippi
Missouri
Ohio
Savannah
Lake Okeechobee
Albers Conic Projection
SCALE 1:9,683,000
1 CENTIMETER = 97 KILOMETERS; 1 INCH = 153 MILES
KILOMETERS
STATUTE MILES
Longitude West 90° of Greenwich
Longitude West 159° of Greenwich
PACIFIC OCEAN
KAUA'I
O'AHU
MOLOKA'I
MAUI
LĀNA'I
HAWAI'I
HALEAKALĀ N.P
HAWAIIAN ISLANDS HUMPBACK WHALE NATIONAL MARINE SANCTUARY
HAWAI'I VOLCANOES NATIONAL PARK
PRINCIPAL HAWAIIAN ISLANDS
100 km
100 statute mi

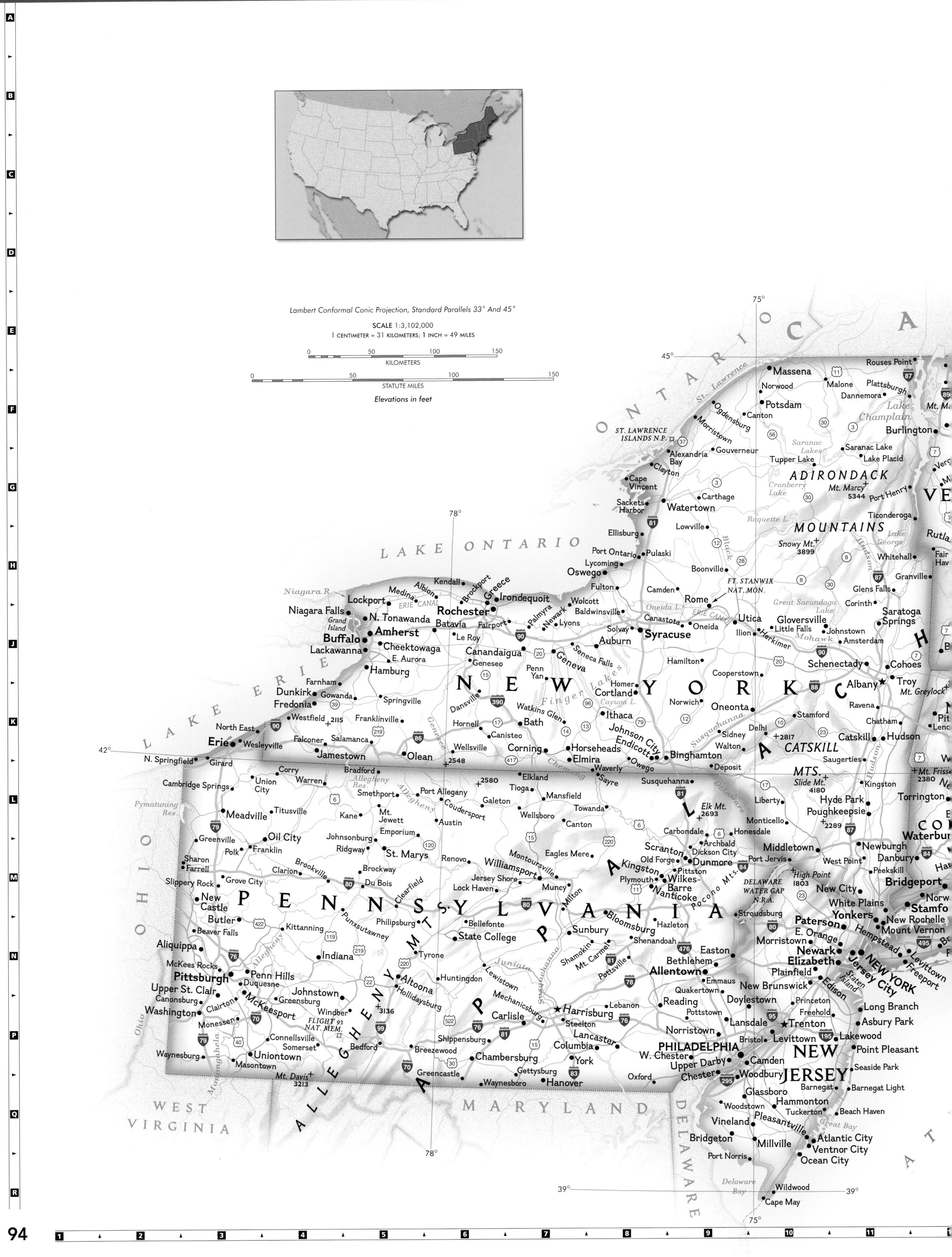

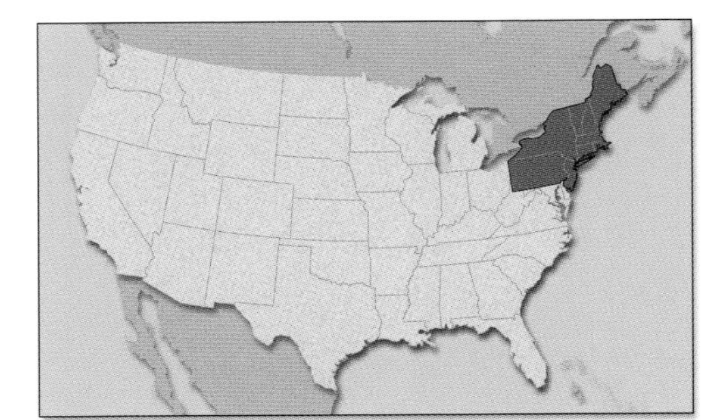

Lambert Conformal Conic Projection, Standard Parallels 33° And 45°

SCALE 1:3,102,000
1 CENTIMETER = 31 KILOMETERS; 1 INCH = 49 MILES

0 50 100 150
KILOMETERS

0 50 100 150
STATUTE MILES

Elevations in feet

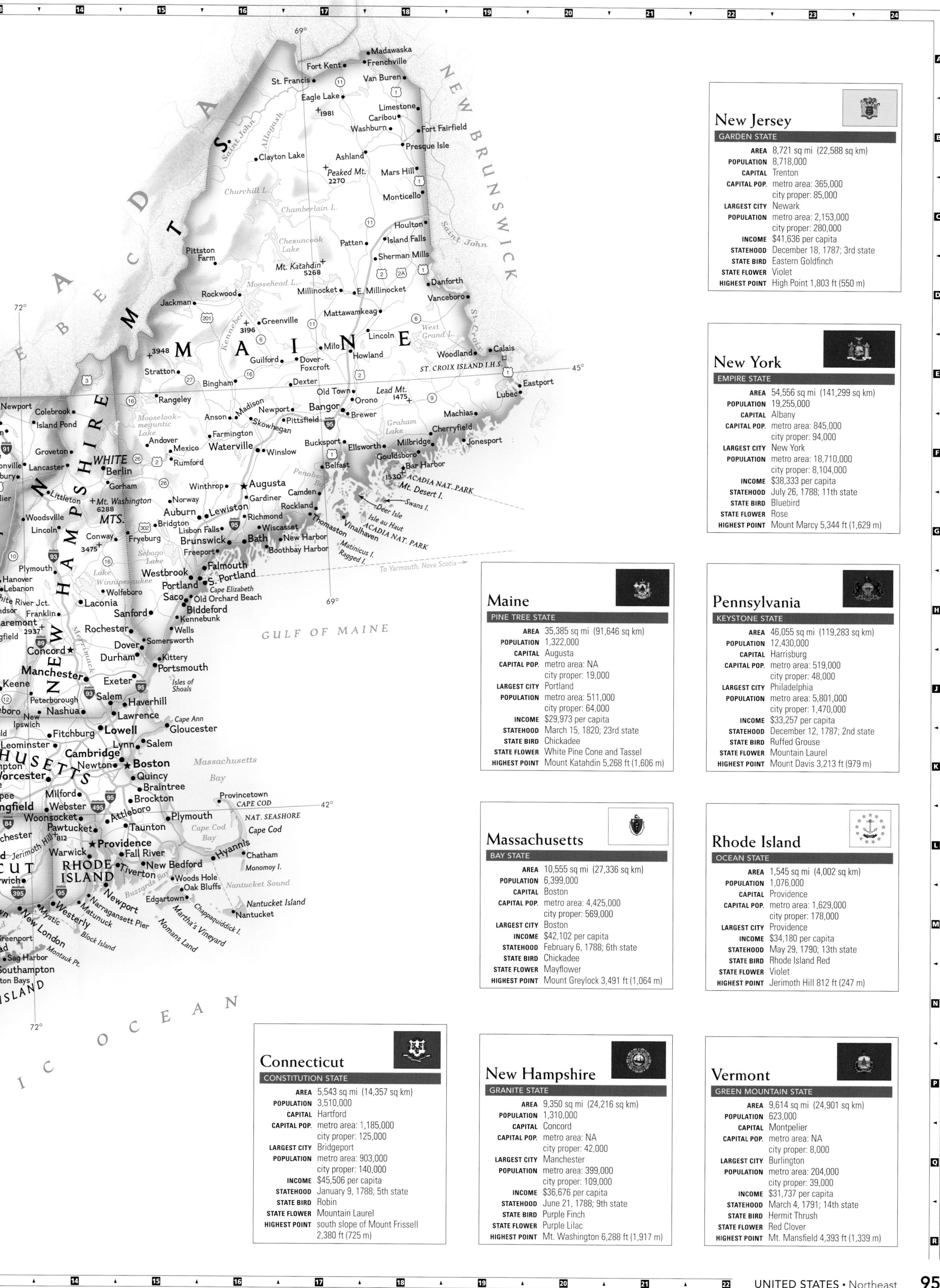

69°
Madawaska
Frenchville
Fort Kent
St. Francis
Van Buren
Eagle Lake
1981
Limestone
Caribou
Washburn
Fort Fairfield
Presque Isle
NEW BRUNSWICK
Saint John
Allagash
Clayton Lake
Ashland
Peaked Mt.
2270
Mars Hill
Churchill L.
Monticello
Chamberlain L.
Houlton
Chesuncook Lake
Patten
Island Falls
Sherman Mills
Pittston Farm
Mt. Katahdin
5268
Moosehead L.
Danforth
Rockwood
Millinocket
E. Millinocket
Vanceboro
Jackman
QUEBEC
Greenville
3196
Mattawamkeag
West Grand L.
St. Croix
Lincoln
Howland
Milo
Woodland
Calais
3948
MAINE
Guilford
Dover-Foxcroft
ST. CROIX ISLAND I.H.S.
45°
Stratton
Bingham
Dexter
Old Town
Lead Mt.
1475
Orono
Eastport
Lubec
Newport
Colebrook
Island Pond
Rangeley
Madison
Newport
Bangor
Brewer
Pittsfield
Skowhegan
Anson
Mooselookmeguntic Lake
Graham Lake
Machias
Farmington
Cherryfield
Andover
Mexico
Waterville
Winslow
Bucksport
Milbridge
Jonesport
Groveton
Ellsworth
Gouldsboro
Lancaster
WHITE
Berlin
Rumford
Belfast
Penobscot Bay
Bar Harbor
1530
ACADIA NAT. PARK
Mt. Desert I.
Gorham
Winthrop
Augusta
Camden
Littleton
Mt. Washington
6288
Norway
Gardiner
Swans I.
Deer Isle
Rockland
Auburn
Lewiston
Richmond
Isle au Haut
Woodsville
MTS.
Bridgton
Thomaston
Vinalhaven
Wiscasset
ACADIA NAT. PARK
Lincoln
Lisbon Falls
Conway
Fryeburg
Brunswick
Bath
New Harbor
3475
Sebago Lake
Freeport
Boothbay Harbor
Matinicus I.
Ragged I.
Plymouth
Falmouth
To Yarmouth, Nova Scotia
Westbrook
Hanover
Lebanon
Lake Winnipesaukee
S. Portland
Portland
Wolfeboro
Cape Elizabeth
White River Jct.
Laconia
Saco
Old Orchard Beach
69°
Franklin
Biddeford
Claremont
Sanford
Kennebunk
2937
Rochester
Wells
GULF OF MAINE
Somersworth
Merrimack
Dover
Concord
Kittery
Durham
Portsmouth
Manchester
NEW HAMPSHIRE
Exeter
Isles of Shoals
Keene
Salem
Haverhill
Peterborough
Nashua
Lawrence
Cape Ann
New Ipswich
Gloucester
Fitchburg
Lowell
Leominster
Lynn
Salem
Cambridge
Newton
Boston
Massachusetts Bay
Worcester
MASSACHUSETTS
Quincy
Braintree
Provincetown
Milford
Brockton
CAPE COD
42°
Webster
Springfield
Attleboro
Plymouth
NAT. SEASHORE
Woonsocket
Pawtucket
Taunton
Cape Cod Bay
Cape Cod
Jerimoth Hill
812
Providence
Warwick
Fall River
Hyannis
Chatham
RHODE ISLAND
New Bedford
Tiverton
Buzzards Bay
Monomoy I.
CONNECTICUT
Norwich
Woods Hole
Oak Bluffs
Nantucket Sound
Newport
Edgartown
Nantucket Island
Nantucket
Narragansett Pier
Martha's Vineyard
Chappaquiddick I.
Mystic
Westerly
Matunuck
New London
Block Island
Nomans Land
Greenport
Montauk Pt.
Sag Harbor
Southampton
Hampton Bays
LONG ISLAND
72°
ATLANTIC OCEAN

New Jersey

GARDEN STATE

AREA	8,721 sq mi (22,588 sq km)
POPULATION	8,718,000
CAPITAL	Trenton
CAPITAL POP.	metro area: 365,000 city proper: 85,000
LARGEST CITY	Newark
POPULATION	metro area: 2,153,000 city proper: 280,000
INCOME	$41,636 per capita
STATEHOOD	December 18, 1787; 3rd state
STATE BIRD	Eastern Goldfinch
STATE FLOWER	Violet
HIGHEST POINT	High Point 1,803 ft (550 m)

New York

EMPIRE STATE

AREA	54,556 sq mi (141,299 sq km)
POPULATION	19,255,000
CAPITAL	Albany
CAPITAL POP.	metro area: 845,000 city proper: 94,000
LARGEST CITY	New York
POPULATION	metro area: 18,710,000 city proper: 8,104,000
INCOME	$38,333 per capita
STATEHOOD	July 26, 1788; 11th state
STATE BIRD	Bluebird
STATE FLOWER	Rose
HIGHEST POINT	Mount Marcy 5,344 ft (1,629 m)

Maine

PINE TREE STATE

AREA	35,385 sq mi (91,646 sq km)
POPULATION	1,322,000
CAPITAL	Augusta
CAPITAL POP.	metro area: NA city proper: 19,000
LARGEST CITY	Portland
POPULATION	metro area: 511,000 city proper: 64,000
INCOME	$29,973 per capita
STATEHOOD	March 15, 1820; 23rd state
STATE BIRD	Chickadee
STATE FLOWER	White Pine Cone and Tassel
HIGHEST POINT	Mount Katahdin 5,268 ft (1,606 m)

Pennsylvania

KEYSTONE STATE

AREA	46,055 sq mi (119,283 sq km)
POPULATION	12,430,000
CAPITAL	Harrisburg
CAPITAL POP.	metro area: 519,000 city proper: 48,000
LARGEST CITY	Philadelphia
POPULATION	metro area: 5,801,000 city proper: 1,470,000
INCOME	$33,257 per capita
STATEHOOD	December 12, 1787; 2nd state
STATE BIRD	Ruffed Grouse
STATE FLOWER	Mountain Laurel
HIGHEST POINT	Mount Davis 3,213 ft (979 m)

Massachusetts

BAY STATE

AREA	10,555 sq mi (27,336 sq km)
POPULATION	6,399,000
CAPITAL	Boston
CAPITAL POP.	metro area: 4,425,000 city proper: 569,000
LARGEST CITY	Boston
INCOME	$42,102 per capita
STATEHOOD	February 6, 1788; 6th state
STATE BIRD	Chickadee
STATE FLOWER	Mayflower
HIGHEST POINT	Mount Greylock 3,491 ft (1,064 m)

Rhode Island

OCEAN STATE

AREA	1,545 sq mi (4,002 sq km)
POPULATION	1,076,000
CAPITAL	Providence
CAPITAL POP.	metro area: 1,629,000 city proper: 178,000
LARGEST CITY	Providence
INCOME	$34,180 per capita
STATEHOOD	May 29, 1790; 13th state
STATE BIRD	Rhode Island Red
STATE FLOWER	Violet
HIGHEST POINT	Jerimoth Hill 812 ft (247 m)

Connecticut

CONSTITUTION STATE

AREA	5,543 sq mi (14,357 sq km)
POPULATION	3,510,000
CAPITAL	Hartford
CAPITAL POP.	metro area: 1,185,000 city proper: 125,000
LARGEST CITY	Bridgeport
POPULATION	metro area: 903,000 city proper: 140,000
INCOME	$45,506 per capita
STATEHOOD	January 9, 1788; 5th state
STATE BIRD	Robin
STATE FLOWER	Mountain Laurel
HIGHEST POINT	south slope of Mount Frissell 2,380 ft (725 m)

New Hampshire

GRANITE STATE

AREA	9,350 sq mi (24,216 sq km)
POPULATION	1,310,000
CAPITAL	Concord
CAPITAL POP.	metro area: NA city proper: 42,000
LARGEST CITY	Manchester
POPULATION	metro area: 399,000 city proper: 109,000
INCOME	$36,676 per capita
STATEHOOD	June 21, 1788; 9th state
STATE BIRD	Purple Finch
STATE FLOWER	Purple Lilac
HIGHEST POINT	Mt. Washington 6,288 ft (1,917 m)

Vermont

GREEN MOUNTAIN STATE

AREA	9,614 sq mi (24,901 sq km)
POPULATION	623,000
CAPITAL	Montpelier
CAPITAL POP.	metro area: NA city proper: 8,000
LARGEST CITY	Burlington
POPULATION	metro area: 204,000 city proper: 39,000
INCOME	$31,737 per capita
STATEHOOD	March 4, 1791; 14th state
STATE BIRD	Hermit Thrush
STATE FLOWER	Red Clover
HIGHEST POINT	Mt. Mansfield 4,393 ft (1,339 m)

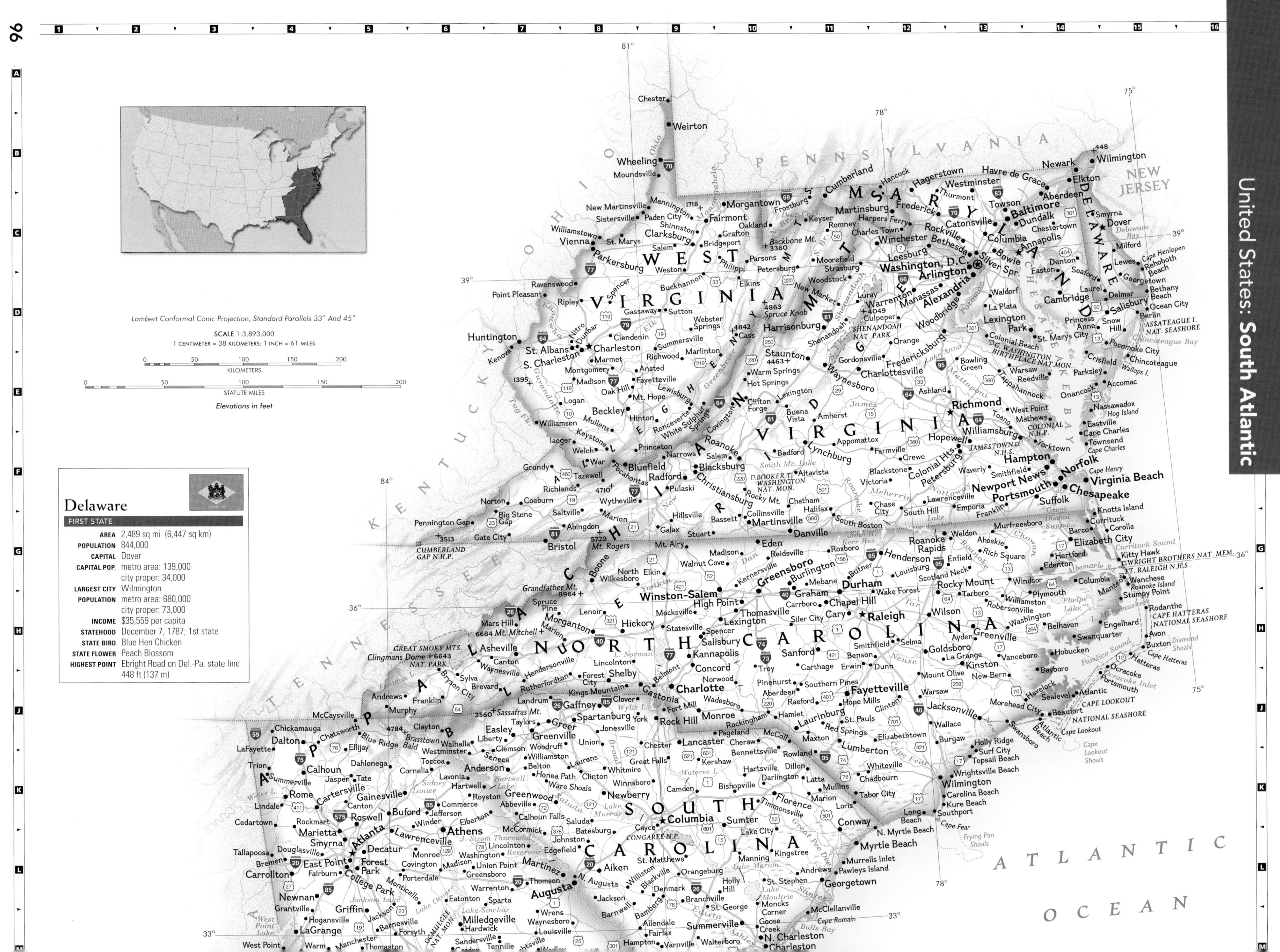
ATLANTIC OCEAN
Lambert Conformal Conic Projection, Standard Parallels 33° And 45°
SCALE 1:3,893,000
1 CENTIMETER = 38 KILOMETERS; 1 INCH = 61 MILES
KILOMETERS
STATUTE MILES
Elevations in feet
Delaware
FIRST STATE
AREA 2,489 sq mi (6,447 sq km)
POPULATION 844,000
CAPITAL Dover
CAPITAL POP. metro area: 139,000
city proper: 34,000
LARGEST CITY Wilmington
POPULATION metro area: 680,000
city proper: 73,000
INCOME $35,559 per capita
STATEHOOD December 7, 1787; 1st state
STATE BIRD Blue Hen Chicken
STATE FLOWER Peach Blossom
HIGHEST POINT Ebright Road on Del.-Pa. state line
448 ft (137 m)

GULF OF MEXICO
FLORIDA
Straits of Florida
Florida Keys
Tallahassee
Jacksonville
Orlando
Tampa
St. Petersburg
Clearwater
Miami
Hialeah
Fort Lauderdale
Hollywood
Pensacola
Panama City
Gainesville
Ocala
Daytona Beach
St. Augustine
Savannah
Brunswick
Valdosta
Albany
Thomasville
Bainbridge
Fernandina Beach
Palm Bay
Melbourne
Fort Pierce
Port St. Lucie
West Palm Beach
Boca Raton
Fort Myers
Cape Coral
Naples
Sarasota
Bradenton
Lakeland
Kissimmee
Key West
Key Largo
Marathon
EVERGLADES NATIONAL PARK
BISCAYNE N.P.
BIG CYPRESS NAT. PRESERVE
CANAVERAL N.S.
JOHN F. KENNEDY SPACE CENTER
CASTILLO DE SAN MARCOS NAT. MON.
FORT MATANZAS NAT. MON.
FORT CAROLINE NAT. MEM.
CUMBERLAND ISLAND NAT. SEASHORE
FORT FREDERICA NAT. MON.
FT. PULASKI NAT. MON.
GULF ISLANDS N.S.
DRY TORTUGAS NAT. PARK
345 + Britton Hill
Lake Okeechobee
30°
27°
87°
84°
81°

Maryland

OLD LINE STATE

AREA	12,407 sq mi (32,133 sq km)
POPULATION	5,600,000
CAPITAL	Annapolis
CAPITAL POP.	metro area: 2,639,000 city proper: 36,000
LARGEST CITY	Baltimore
POPULATION	metro area: 2,639,000 city proper: 636,000
INCOME	$39,629 per capita
STATEHOOD	April 28, 1788; 7th state
STATE BIRD	Baltimore Oriole
STATE FLOWER	Black-eyed Susan
HIGHEST POINT	Backbone Mt. 3,360 ft (1,024 m)

North Carolina

TAR HEEL STATE

AREA	53,819 sq mi (139,389 sq km)
POPULATION	8,683,000
CAPITAL	Raleigh
CAPITAL POP.	metro area: 915,000 city proper: 327,000
LARGEST CITY	Charlotte
POPULATION	metro area: 1,475,000 city proper: 594,000
INCOME	$29,303 per capita
STATEHOOD	November 21, 1789; 12th state
STATE BIRD	Cardinal
STATE FLOWER	American Dogwood
HIGHEST POINT	Mount Mitchell 6,684 ft (2,037 m)

South Carolina

PALMETTO STATE

AREA	32,020 sq mi (82,932 sq km)
POPULATION	4,255,000
CAPITAL	Columbia
CAPITAL POP.	metro area: 679,000 city proper: 116,000
LARGEST CITY	Columbia
INCOME	$27,153 per capita
STATEHOOD	May 23, 1788; 8th state
STATE BIRD	Carolina Wren
STATE FLOWER	Yellow Jessamine
HIGHEST POINT	Sassafras Mt. 3,560 ft (1,085 m)

Virginia

OLD DOMINION

AREA	42,774 sq mi (110,785 sq km)
POPULATION	7,567,000
CAPITAL	Richmond
CAPITAL POP.	metro area: 1,154,000 city proper: 192,000
LARGEST CITY	Virginia Beach
POPULATION	metro area: 1,644,000 city proper: 440,000
INCOME	$36,175 per capita
STATEHOOD	June 25, 1788; 10th state
STATE BIRD	Cardinal
STATE FLOWER	American Dogwood
HIGHEST POINT	Mount Rogers 5,729 ft (1,746 m)

District of Columbia

THE NATION'S CAPITAL

AREA	68 sq mi (177 sq km)
POPULATION	551,000
CAPITAL POP.	metro area: 5,140,000 city proper: 551,000
INCOME	$52,101 per capita
STATEHOOD	1790-1791 (Site of capital chosen by George Washington, Maryland and Virginia then ceded a ten mile by ten mile area that included land from both states)
STATE BIRD	Wood Thrush
STATE FLOWER	American Beauty Rose
HIGHEST POINT	Tenleytown at Reno Reservoir 410 ft (125 m)

Florida

SUNSHINE STATE

AREA	65,755 sq mi (170,304 sq km)
POPULATION	17,790,000
CAPITAL	Tallahassee
CAPITAL POP.	metro area: 332,000 city proper: 157,000
LARGEST CITY	Jacksonville
POPULATION	metro area: 1,225,000 city proper: 778,000
INCOME	$31,460 per capita
STATEHOOD	March 3, 1845; 27th state
STATE BIRD	Mockingbird
STATE FLOWER	Orange Blossom
HIGHEST POINT	Britton Hill 345 ft (105 m)

Georgia

PEACH STATE

AREA	59,425 sq mi (153,909 sq km)
POPULATION	9,073,000
CAPITAL	Atlanta
CAPITAL POP.	metro area: 4,708,000 city proper: 419,000
LARGEST CITY	Atlanta
INCOME	$30,074 per capita
STATEHOOD	January 2, 1788; 4th state
STATE BIRD	Brown Thrasher
STATE FLOWER	Cherokee Rose
HIGHEST POINT	Brasstown Bald 4,784 ft (1,458 m)

West Virginia

MOUNTAIN STATE

AREA	24,230 sq mi (62,755 sq km)
POPULATION	1,817,000
CAPITAL	Charleston
CAPITAL POP.	metro area: 308,000 city proper: 52,000
LARGEST CITY	Charleston
INCOME	$25,681 per capita
STATEHOOD	June 20, 1863; 35th state
STATE BIRD	Cardinal
STATE FLOWER	Rhododendron (Big Laurel)
HIGHEST POINT	Spruce Knob 4,863 ft (1,482 m)

CANADA
ONTARIO
LAKE SUPERIOR
LAKE HURON
LAKE MICHIGAN
MINNESOTA
WISCONSIN
MICHIGAN
UPPER PENINSULA
ISLE ROYALE NATIONAL PARK
APOSTLE ISLANDS NAT. LAKESHORE
PICTURED ROCKS NAT. LAKESHORE
SLEEPING BEAR DUNES NAT. LAKESHORE
ST. CROIX NAT. SCENIC RIVERWAY
KEWEENAW N.H.P.
Keweenaw Peninsula
Sault Ste. Marie
Marquette
Green Bay
Milwaukee
Madison
Lansing
Grand Rapids
Flint
Saginaw
Escanaba
Superior
Eau Claire
La Crosse
Wausau
Oshkosh
Appleton
Alpena
Traverse City
Muskegon
Kenosha
Racine
Sheboygan
Manitowoc

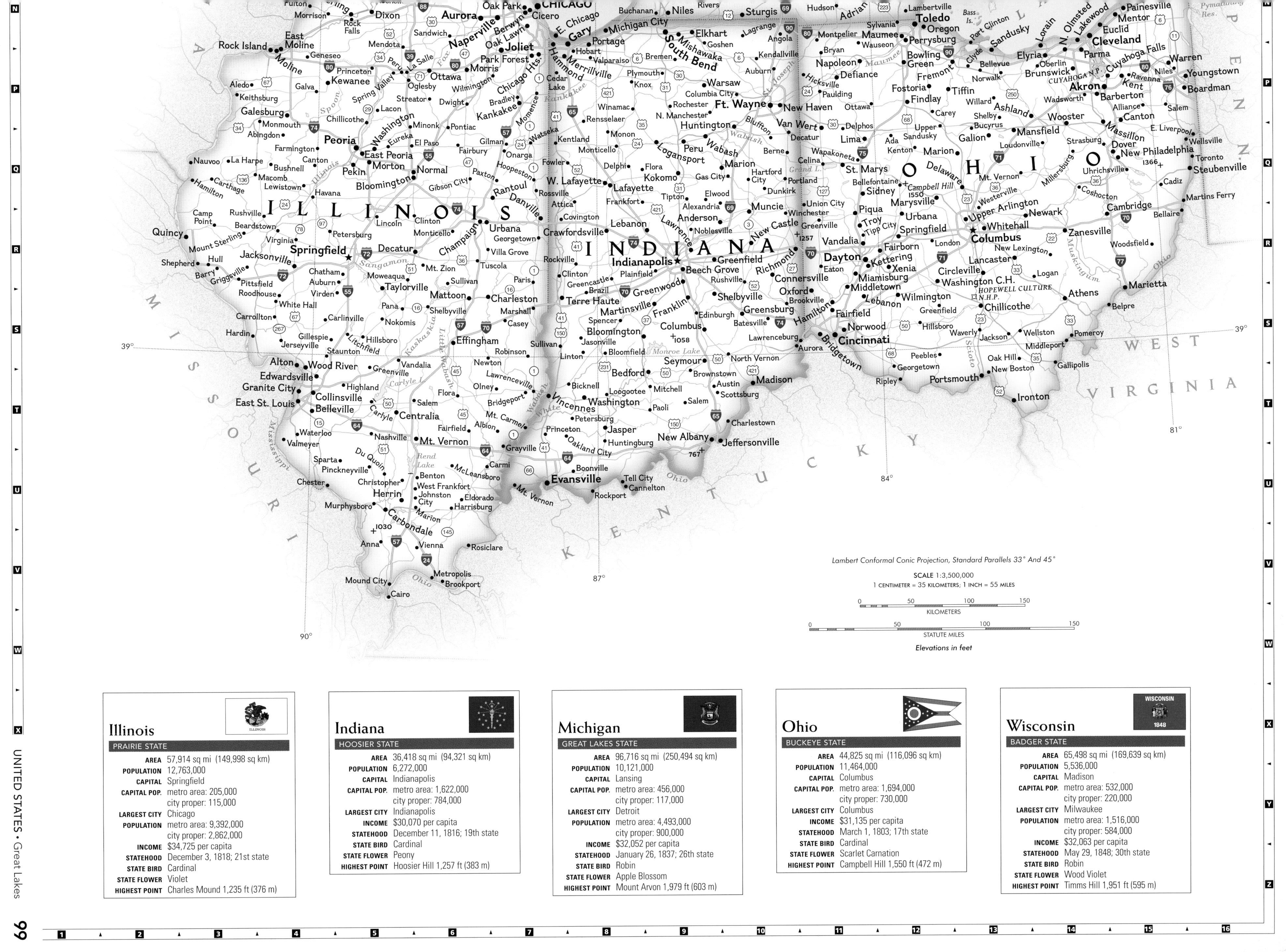
ILLINOIS
INDIANA
OHIO
MISSOURI
KENTUCKY
WEST VIRGINIA
Lambert Conformal Conic Projection, Standard Parallels 33° And 45°
SCALE 1:3,500,000
1 CENTIMETER = 35 KILOMETERS; 1 INCH = 55 MILES
KILOMETERS
STATUTE MILES
Elevations in feet

Illinois
PRAIRIE STATE

AREA	57,914 sq mi (149,998 sq km)
POPULATION	12,763,000
CAPITAL	Springfield
CAPITAL POP.	metro area: 205,000 city proper: 115,000
LARGEST CITY	Chicago
POPULATION	metro area: 9,392,000 city proper: 2,862,000
INCOME	$34,725 per capita
STATEHOOD	December 3, 1818; 21st state
STATE BIRD	Cardinal
STATE FLOWER	Violet
HIGHEST POINT	Charles Mound 1,235 ft (376 m)

Indiana
HOOSIER STATE

AREA	36,418 sq mi (94,321 sq km)
POPULATION	6,272,000
CAPITAL	Indianapolis
CAPITAL POP.	metro area: 1,622,000 city proper: 784,000
LARGEST CITY	Indianapolis
INCOME	$30,070 per capita
STATEHOOD	December 11, 1816; 19th state
STATE BIRD	Cardinal
STATE FLOWER	Peony
HIGHEST POINT	Hoosier Hill 1,257 ft (383 m)

Michigan
GREAT LAKES STATE

AREA	96,716 sq mi (250,494 sq km)
POPULATION	10,121,000
CAPITAL	Lansing
CAPITAL POP.	metro area: 456,000 city proper: 117,000
LARGEST CITY	Detroit
POPULATION	metro area: 4,493,000 city proper: 900,000
INCOME	$32,052 per capita
STATEHOOD	January 26, 1837; 26th state
STATE BIRD	Robin
STATE FLOWER	Apple Blossom
HIGHEST POINT	Mount Arvon 1,979 ft (603 m)

Ohio
BUCKEYE STATE

AREA	44,825 sq mi (116,096 sq km)
POPULATION	11,464,000
CAPITAL	Columbus
CAPITAL POP.	metro area: 1,694,000 city proper: 730,000
LARGEST CITY	Columbus
INCOME	$31,135 per capita
STATEHOOD	March 1, 1803; 17th state
STATE BIRD	Cardinal
STATE FLOWER	Scarlet Carnation
HIGHEST POINT	Campbell Hill 1,550 ft (472 m)

Wisconsin
BADGER STATE

AREA	65,498 sq mi (169,639 sq km)
POPULATION	5,536,000
CAPITAL	Madison
CAPITAL POP.	metro area: 532,000 city proper: 220,000
LARGEST CITY	Milwaukee
POPULATION	metro area: 1,516,000 city proper: 584,000
INCOME	$32,063 per capita
STATEHOOD	May 29, 1848; 30th state
STATE BIRD	Robin
STATE FLOWER	Wood Violet
HIGHEST POINT	Timms Hill 1,951 ft (595 m)

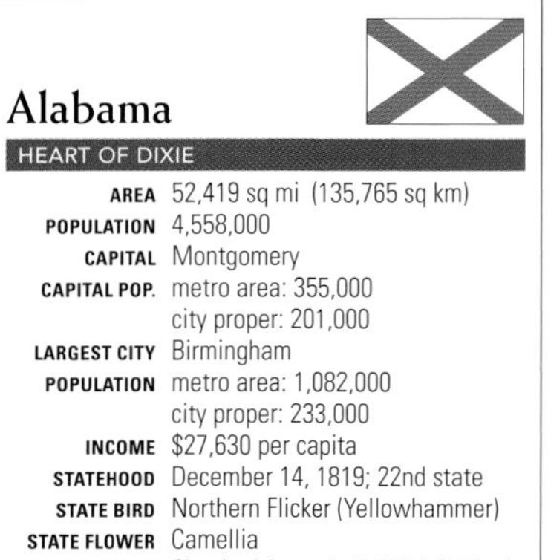

Alabama

HEART OF DIXIE

AREA	52,419 sq mi (135,765 sq km)
POPULATION	4,558,000
CAPITAL	Montgomery
CAPITAL POP.	metro area: 355,000 city proper: 201,000
LARGEST CITY	Birmingham
POPULATION	metro area: 1,082,000 city proper: 233,000
INCOME	$27,630 per capita
STATEHOOD	December 14, 1819; 22nd state
STATE BIRD	Northern Flicker (Yellowhammer)
STATE FLOWER	Camellia
HIGHEST POINT	Cheaha Mountain 2,407 ft (734 m)

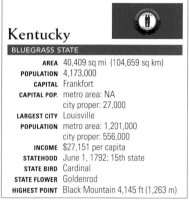

Arkansas

NATURAL STATE

AREA	53,179 sq mi (137,732 sq km)
POPULATION	2,779,000
CAPITAL	Little Rock
CAPITAL POP.	metro area: 637,000 city proper: 184,000
LARGEST CITY	Little Rock
INCOME	$25,724 per capita
STATEHOOD	June 15, 1836; 25th state
STATE BIRD	Mockingbird
STATE FLOWER	Apple Blossom
HIGHEST POINT	Magazine Mt. 2,753 ft (839 m)

Kentucky

BLUEGRASS STATE

AREA	40,409 sq mi (104,659 sq km)
POPULATION	4,173,000
CAPITAL	Frankfort
CAPITAL POP.	metro area: NA city proper: 27,000
LARGEST CITY	Louisville
POPULATION	metro area: 1,201,000 city proper: 556,000
INCOME	$27,151 per capita
STATEHOOD	June 1, 1792; 15th state
STATE BIRD	Cardinal
STATE FLOWER	Goldenrod
HIGHEST POINT	Black Mountain 4,145 ft (1,263 m)

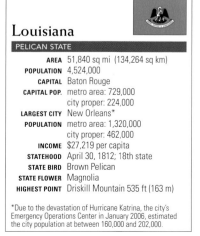

Louisiana

PELICAN STATE

AREA	51,840 sq mi (134,264 sq km)
POPULATION	4,524,000
CAPITAL	Baton Rouge
CAPITAL POP.	metro area: 729,000 city proper: 224,000
LARGEST CITY	New Orleans*
POPULATION	metro area: 1,320,000 city proper: 462,000
INCOME	$27,219 per capita
STATEHOOD	April 30, 1812; 18th state
STATE BIRD	Brown Pelican
STATE FLOWER	Magnolia
HIGHEST POINT	Driskill Mountain 535 ft (163 m)

*Due to the devastation of Hurricane Katrina, the city's Emergency Operations Center in January 2006, estimated the city population at between 160,000 and 202,000.

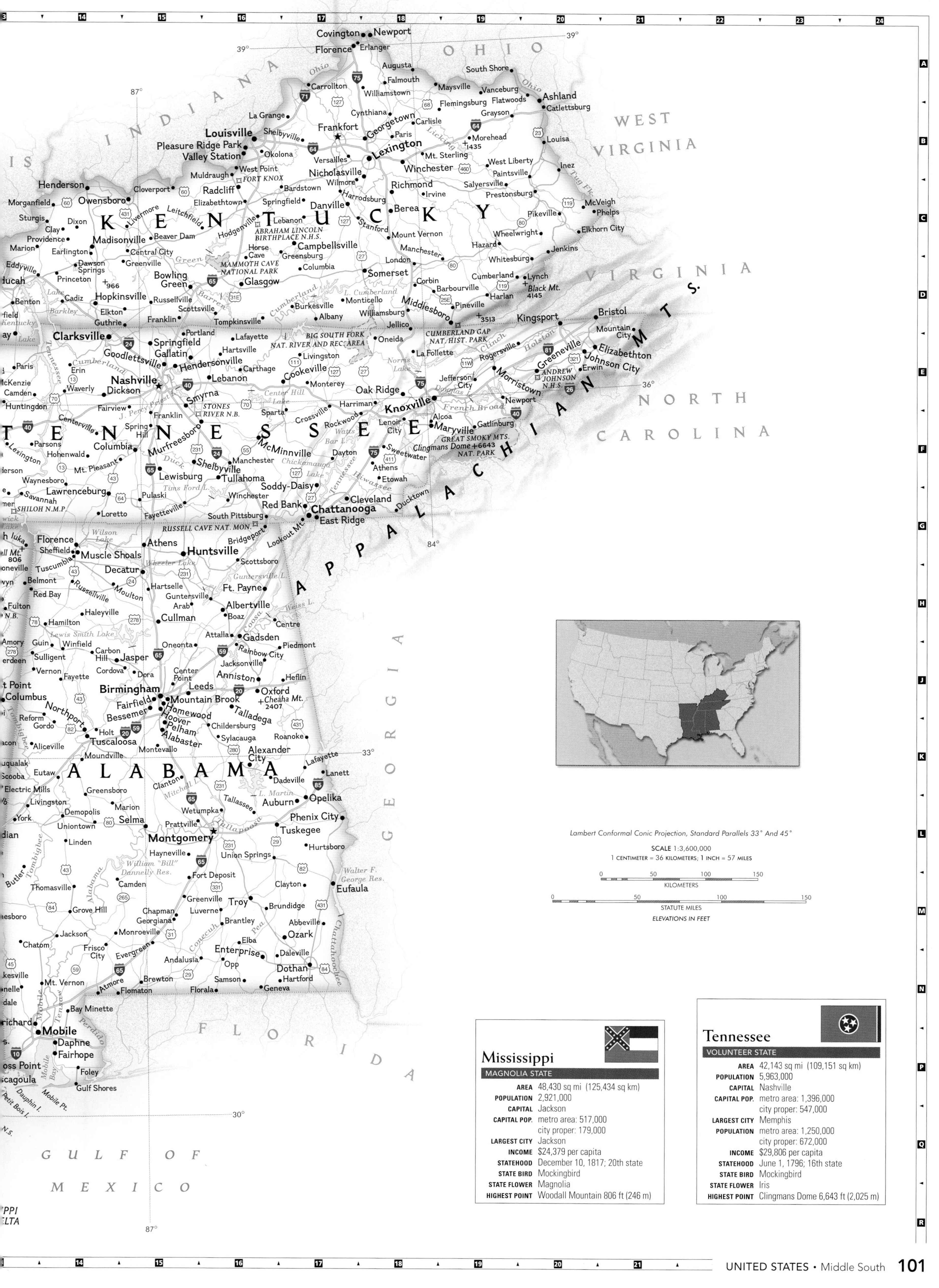

OHIO
INDIANA
WEST VIRGINIA
VIRGINIA
NORTH CAROLINA
KENTUCKY
TENNESSEE
ALABAMA
GEORGIA
FLORIDA
APPALACHIAN MTS.
GULF OF MEXICO
Covington
Newport
Florence
Erlanger
Louisville
Frankfort
Lexington
Ashland
Owensboro
Bowling Green
Clarksville
Nashville
Knoxville
Chattanooga
Kingsport
Bristol
Johnson City
Murfreesboro
Huntsville
Birmingham
Tuscaloosa
Montgomery
Mobile
Dothan
Gadsden
Anniston
Auburn
Opelika
Decatur
Florence
Muscle Shoals
FORT KNOX
ABRAHAM LINCOLN BIRTHPLACE N.H.S.
MAMMOTH CAVE NATIONAL PARK
BIG SOUTH FORK NAT. RIVER AND REC. AREA
CUMBERLAND GAP NAT. HIST. PARK
STONES RIVER N.B.
GREAT SMOKY MTS. NAT. PARK
Clingmans Dome 6643
Black Mt. 4145
Cheaha Mt. 2407
SHILOH N.M.P.
RUSSELL CAVE NAT. MON.
ANDREW JOHNSON N.H.S.
Lambert Conformal Conic Projection, Standard Parallels 33° And 45°
SCALE 1:3,600,000
1 CENTIMETER = 36 KILOMETERS; 1 INCH = 57 MILES
0 50 100 150
KILOMETERS
0 50 100 150
STATUTE MILES
ELEVATIONS IN FEET

Mississippi

MAGNOLIA STATE

AREA	48,430 sq mi (125,434 sq km)
POPULATION	2,921,000
CAPITAL	Jackson
CAPITAL POP.	metro area: 517,000 city proper: 179,000
LARGEST CITY	Jackson
INCOME	$24,379 per capita
STATEHOOD	December 10, 1817; 20th state
STATE BIRD	Mockingbird
STATE FLOWER	Magnolia
HIGHEST POINT	Woodall Mountain 806 ft (246 m)

Tennessee

VOLUNTEER STATE

AREA	42,143 sq mi (109,151 sq km)
POPULATION	5,963,000
CAPITAL	Nashville
CAPITAL POP.	metro area: 1,396,000 city proper: 547,000
LARGEST CITY	Memphis
POPULATION	metro area: 1,250,000 city proper: 672,000
INCOME	$29,806 per capita
STATEHOOD	June 1, 1796; 16th state
STATE BIRD	Mockingbird
STATE FLOWER	Iris
HIGHEST POINT	Clingmans Dome 6,643 ft (2,025 m)

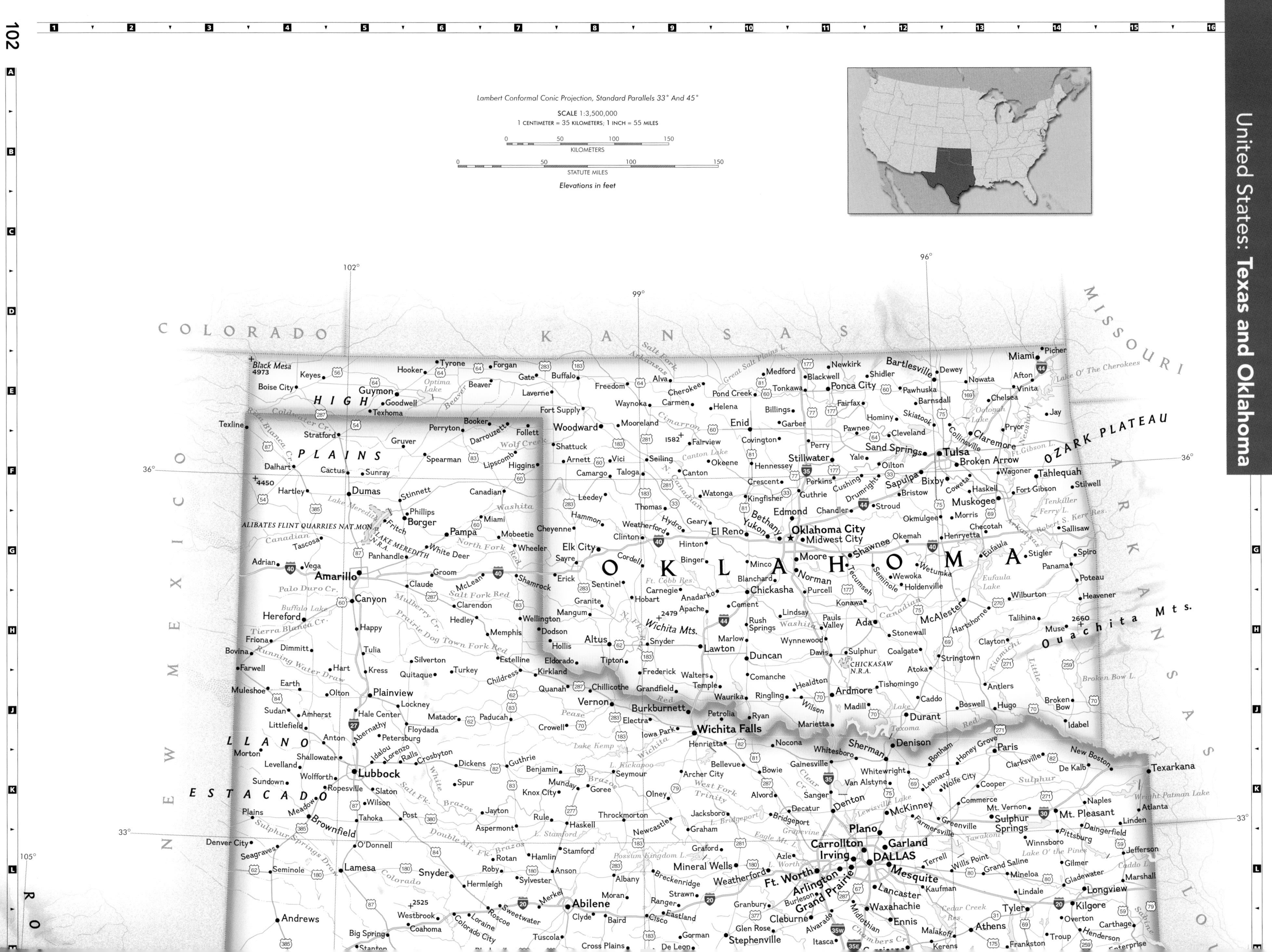
Lambert Conformal Conic Projection, Standard Parallels 33° And 45°
SCALE 1:3,500,000
1 CENTIMETER = 35 KILOMETERS; 1 INCH = 55 MILES
KILOMETERS
STATUTE MILES
Elevations in feet
OKLAHOMA
KANSAS
MISSOURI
ARKANSAS
COLORADO
NEW MEXICO
OZARK PLATEAU
Ouachita Mts.
HIGH PLAINS
LLANO ESTACADO
Oklahoma City
Tulsa
DALLAS
Ft. Worth
Amarillo
Lubbock
Wichita Falls
Abilene
Texarkana
Black Mesa 4973

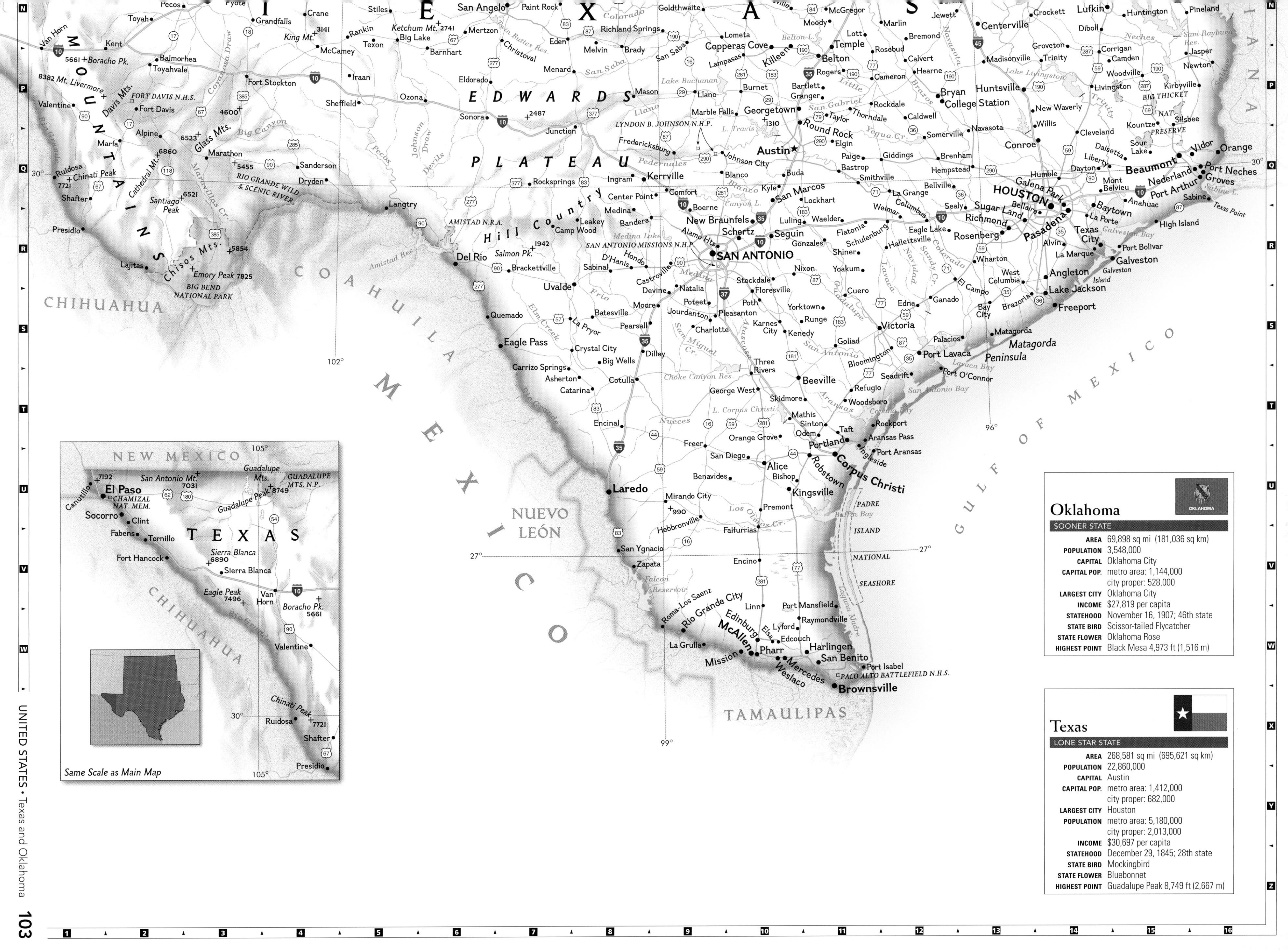
TEXAS
EDWARDS PLATEAU
MOUNTAINS
Hill Country
COAHUILA
MEXICO
NUEVO LEÓN
TAMAULIPAS
CHIHUAHUA
GULF OF MEXICO
BIG BEND NATIONAL PARK
RIO GRANDE WILD & SCENIC RIVER
AMISTAD N.R.A.
FORT DAVIS N.H.S.
LYNDON B. JOHNSON N.H.P.
SAN ANTONIO MISSIONS N.H.P.
BIG THICKET NAT. PRESERVE
PADRE ISLAND NATIONAL SEASHORE
PALO ALTO BATTLEFIELD N.H.S.
SAN ANTONIO
HOUSTON
Austin
Corpus Christi
Laredo
Brownsville
Galveston
Beaumont
NEW MEXICO
TEXAS
CHIHUAHUA
El Paso
CHAMIZAL NAT. MEM.
GUADALUPE MTS. N.P.
Guadalupe Peak 8749
Same Scale as Main Map
Oklahoma
SOONER STATE
AREA 69,898 sq mi (181,036 sq km)
POPULATION 3,548,000
CAPITAL Oklahoma City
CAPITAL POP. metro area: 1,144,000
city proper: 528,000
LARGEST CITY Oklahoma City
INCOME $27,819 per capita
STATEHOOD November 16, 1907; 46th state
STATE BIRD Scissor-tailed Flycatcher
STATE FLOWER Oklahoma Rose
HIGHEST POINT Black Mesa 4,973 ft (1,516 m)
Texas
LONE STAR STATE
AREA 268,581 sq mi (695,621 sq km)
POPULATION 22,860,000
CAPITAL Austin
CAPITAL POP. metro area: 1,412,000
city proper: 682,000
LARGEST CITY Houston
POPULATION metro area: 5,180,000
city proper: 2,013,000
INCOME $30,697 per capita
STATEHOOD December 29, 1845; 28th state
STATE BIRD Mockingbird
STATE FLOWER Bluebonnet
HIGHEST POINT Guadalupe Peak 8,749 ft (2,667 m)

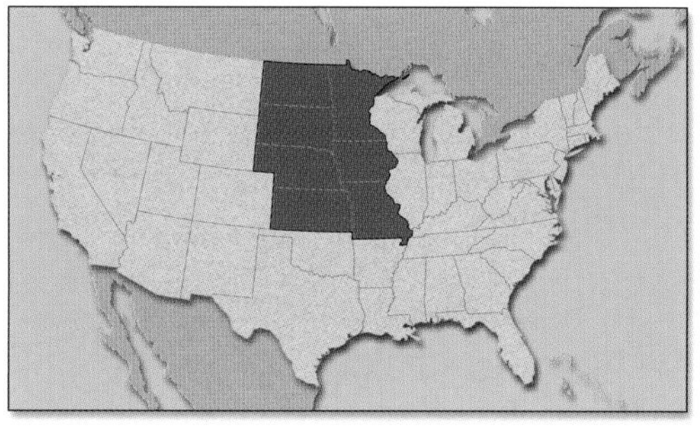

Lambert Conformal Conic Projection, Standard Parallels 33° And 45°

SCALE 1:4,100,000
1 CENTIMETER = 41 KILOMETERS; 1 INCH = 65 MILES

KILOMETERS: 0 · 50 · 100 · 150

STATUTE MILES: 0 · 50 · 100 · 150

Elevations in feet

Iowa

HAWKEYE STATE

AREA	56,272 sq mi (145,743 sq km)
POPULATION	2,966,000
CAPITAL	Des Moines
CAPITAL POP.	metro area: 512,000 city proper: 194,000
LARGEST CITY	Des Moines
INCOME	$30,970 per capita
STATEHOOD	December 28, 1846; 29th state
STATE BIRD	Eastern Goldfinch
STATE FLOWER	Wild Prairie Rose
HIGHEST POINT	Hawkeye Point 1,670 ft (509 m)

Kansas

SUNFLOWER STATE

AREA	82,277 sq mi (213,096 sq km)
POPULATION	2,745,000
CAPITAL	Topeka
CAPITAL POP.	metro area: 228,000 city proper: 122,000
LARGEST CITY	Wichita
POPULATION	metro area: 585,000 city proper: 354,000
INCOME	$31,003 per capita
STATEHOOD	January 29, 1861; 34th state
STATE BIRD	Western Meadowlark
STATE FLOWER	Sunflower
HIGHEST POINT	Mt. Sunflower 4,039 ft (1,231 m)

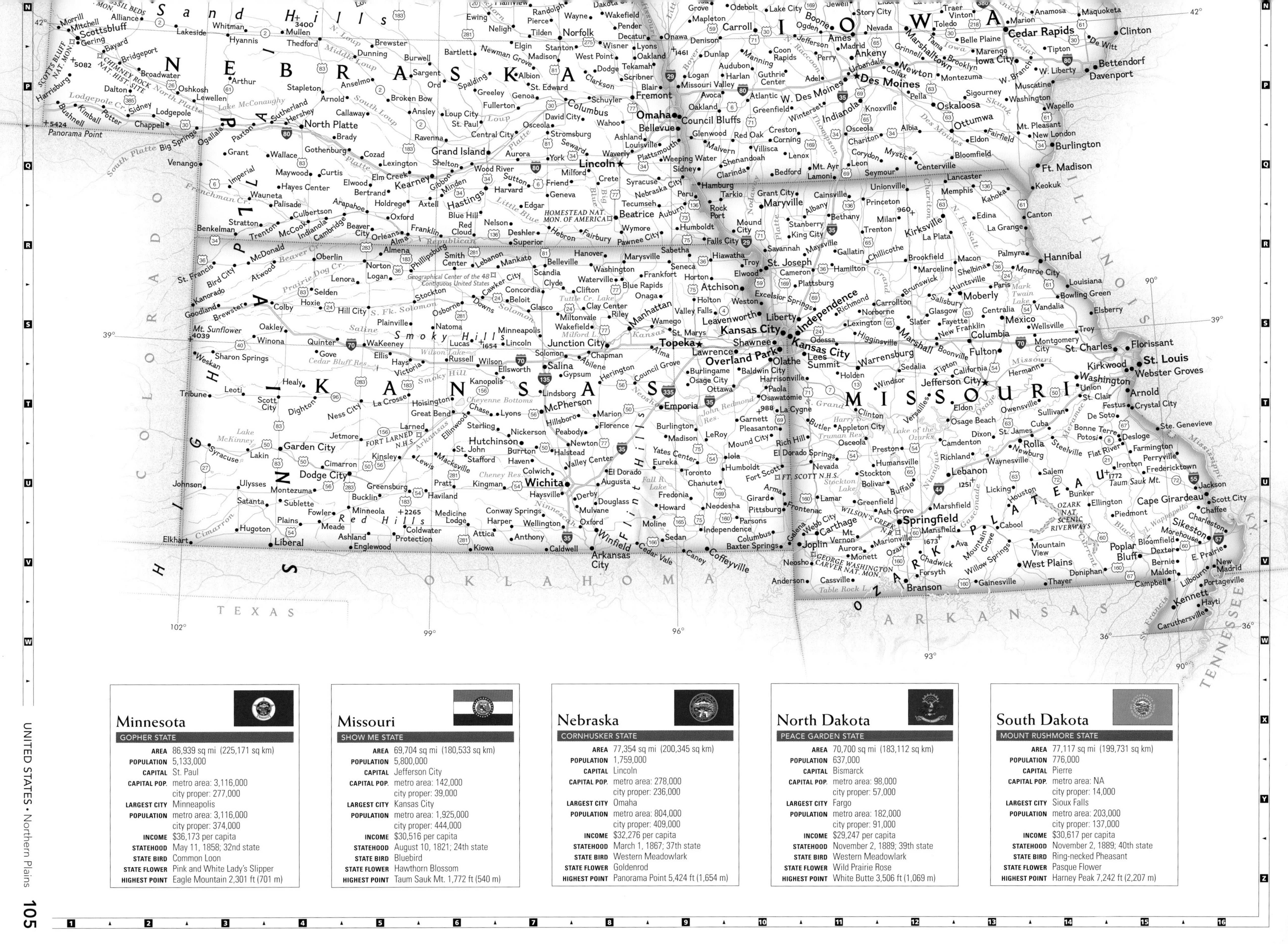
NEBRASKA
KANSAS
MISSOURI
IOWA
ILLINOIS
TENNESSEE
KY.
OKLAHOMA
TEXAS
COLORADO
ARKANSAS
OZARK PLATEAU
Sand Hills
Smoky Hills
Red Hills
Flint Hills
High Plains
Lincoln
Omaha
Topeka
Jefferson City
Kansas City
St. Louis
Des Moines
Wichita
Springfield
Council Bluffs
Cedar Rapids
Davenport
Grand Island
North Platte
Scottsbluff
Dodge City
Garden City
Salina
Hutchinson
Emporia
Joplin
Columbia
St. Joseph
Cape Girardeau
Taum Sauk Mt.
Panorama Point
Mt. Sunflower 4039
Minnesota
GOPHER STATE
AREA 86,939 sq mi (225,171 sq km)
POPULATION 5,133,000
CAPITAL St. Paul
CAPITAL POP. metro area: 3,116,000
city proper: 277,000
LARGEST CITY Minneapolis
POPULATION metro area: 3,116,000
city proper: 374,000
INCOME $36,173 per capita
STATEHOOD May 11, 1858; 32nd state
STATE BIRD Common Loon
STATE FLOWER Pink and White Lady's Slipper
HIGHEST POINT Eagle Mountain 2,301 ft (701 m)
Missouri
SHOW ME STATE
AREA 69,704 sq mi (180,533 sq km)
POPULATION 5,800,000
CAPITAL Jefferson City
CAPITAL POP. metro area: 142,000
city proper: 39,000
LARGEST CITY Kansas City
POPULATION metro area: 1,925,000
city proper: 444,000
INCOME $30,516 per capita
STATEHOOD August 10, 1821; 24th state
STATE BIRD Bluebird
STATE FLOWER Hawthorn Blossom
HIGHEST POINT Taum Sauk Mt. 1,772 ft (540 m)
Nebraska
CORNHUSKER STATE
AREA 77,354 sq mi (200,345 sq km)
POPULATION 1,759,000
CAPITAL Lincoln
CAPITAL POP. metro area: 278,000
city proper: 236,000
LARGEST CITY Omaha
POPULATION metro area: 804,000
city proper: 409,000
INCOME $32,276 per capita
STATEHOOD March 1, 1867; 37th state
STATE BIRD Western Meadowlark
STATE FLOWER Goldenrod
HIGHEST POINT Panorama Point 5,424 ft (1,654 m)
North Dakota
PEACE GARDEN STATE
AREA 70,700 sq mi (183,112 sq km)
POPULATION 637,000
CAPITAL Bismarck
CAPITAL POP. metro area: 98,000
city proper: 57,000
LARGEST CITY Fargo
POPULATION metro area: 182,000
city proper: 91,000
INCOME $29,247 per capita
STATEHOOD November 2, 1889; 39th state
STATE BIRD Western Meadowlark
STATE FLOWER Wild Prairie Rose
HIGHEST POINT White Butte 3,506 ft (1,069 m)
South Dakota
MOUNT RUSHMORE STATE
AREA 77,117 sq mi (199,731 sq km)
POPULATION 776,000
CAPITAL Pierre
CAPITAL POP. metro area: NA
city proper: 14,000
LARGEST CITY Sioux Falls
POPULATION metro area: 203,000
city proper: 137,000
INCOME $30,617 per capita
STATEHOOD November 2, 1889; 40th state
STATE BIRD Ring-necked Pheasant
STATE FLOWER Pasque Flower
HIGHEST POINT Harney Peak 7,242 ft (2,207 m)

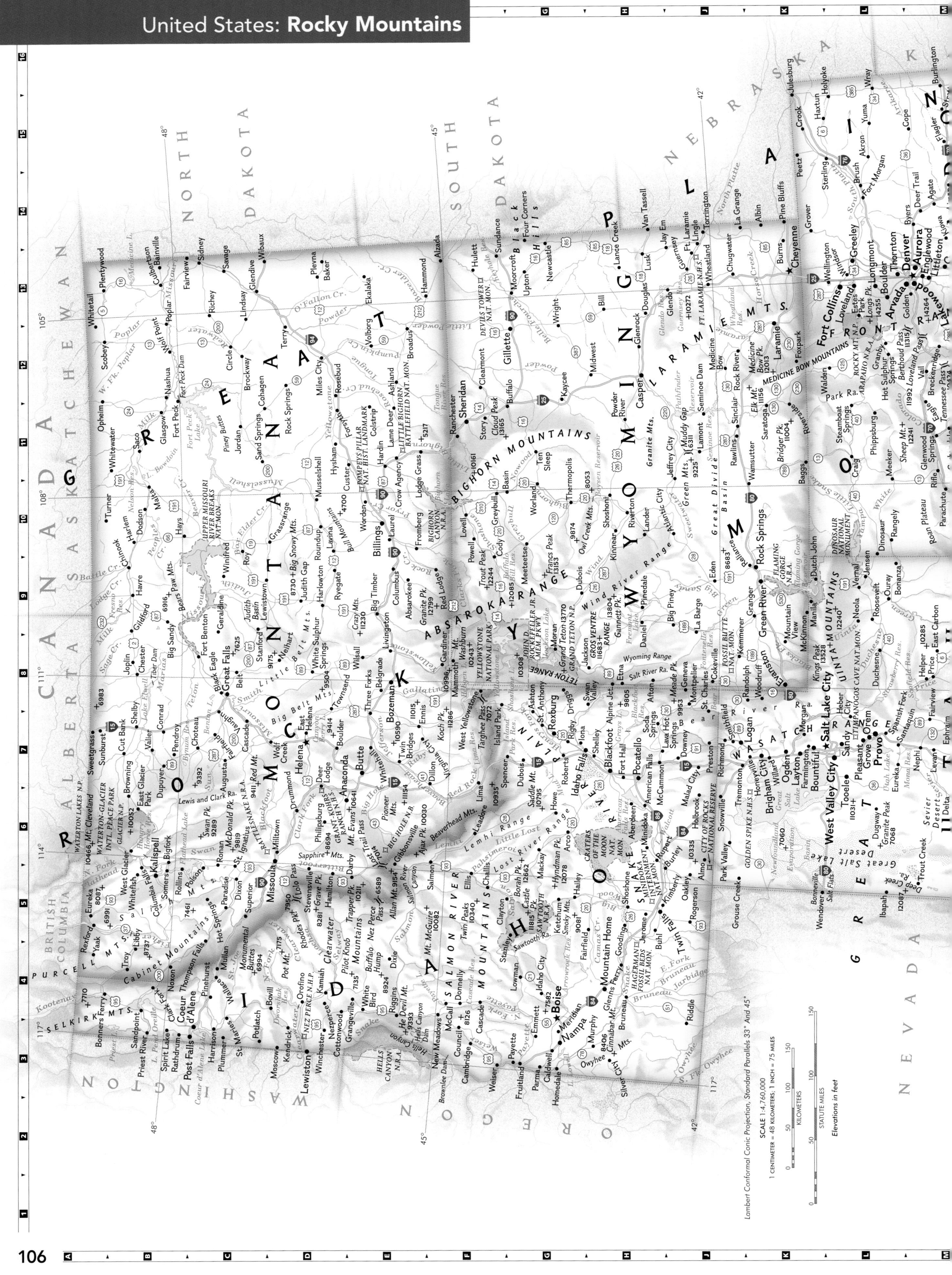
MONTANA
IDAHO
WYOMING
GREAT PLAINS
NORTH DAKOTA
SOUTH DAKOTA
NEBRASKA
WASHINGTON
OREGON
NEVADA
CANADA
ALBERTA
SASKATCHEWAN
BRITISH COLUMBIA
BIGHORN MOUNTAINS
ABSAROKA RANGE
LARAMIE MTS.
UINTA MOUNTAINS
SALMON RIVER MOUNTAINS
Wind River Range
YELLOWSTONE NATIONAL PARK
Helena
Boise
Cheyenne
Salt Lake City
Denver
Lambert Conformal Conic Projection, Standard Parallels 33° And 45°
SCALE 1:4,760,000
1 CENTIMETER = 48 KILOMETERS; 1 INCH = 75 MILES
KILOMETERS
STATUTE MILES
Elevations in feet

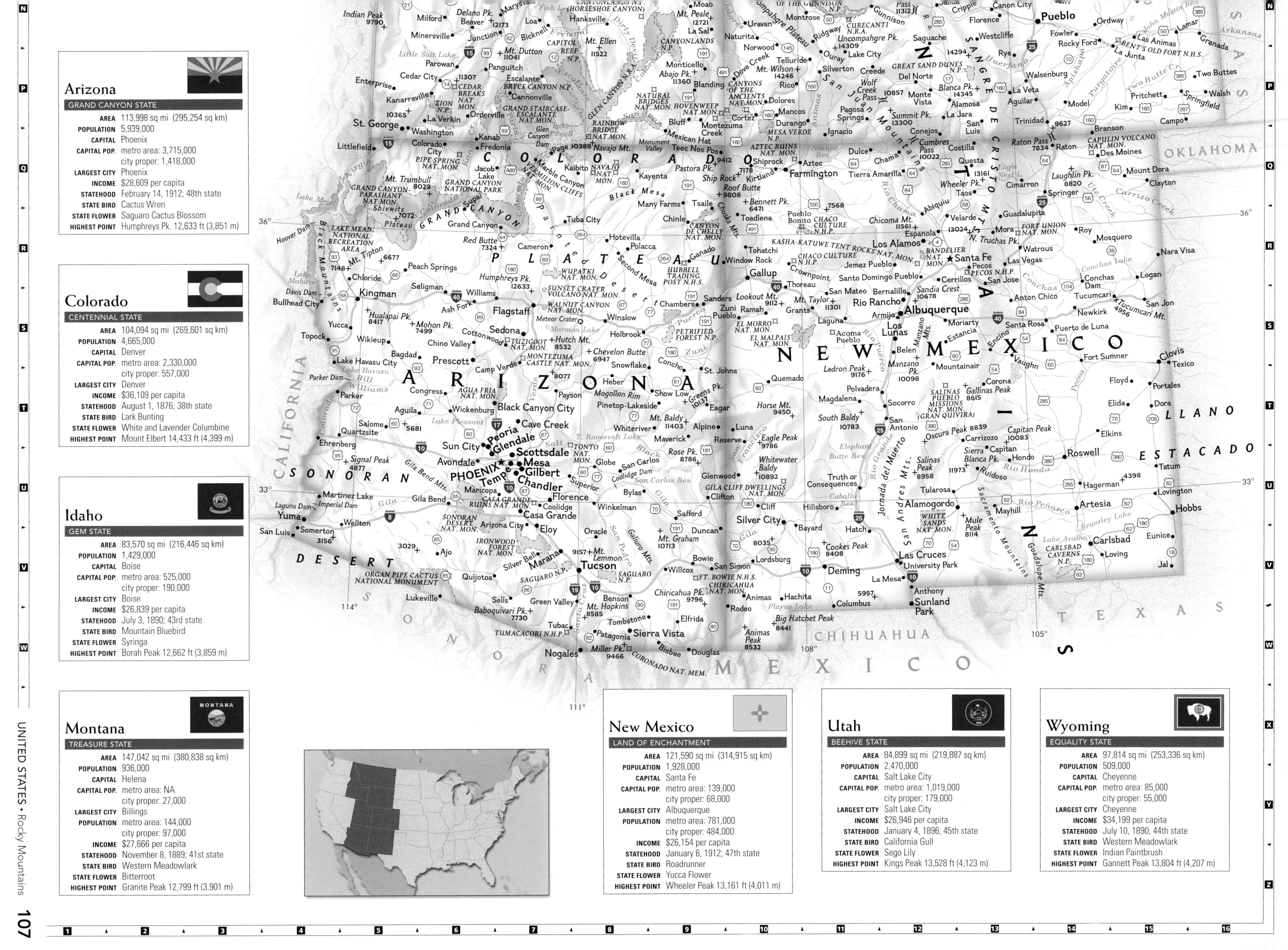
ARIZONA
NEW MEXICO
COLORADO PLATEAU
SONORAN DESERT
LLANO ESTACADO
SANGRE DE CRISTO MTS.
SAN JUAN MOUNTAINS
GRAND CANYON
OKLAHOMA
TEXAS
CALIFORNIA
SONORA
CHIHUAHUA
MEXICO
PHOENIX
Santa Fe
Albuquerque
Tucson
Flagstaff
Pueblo
Las Cruces
Gallup
Farmington
Roswell
Yuma
Nogales
Kingman
St. George
Mesa
Scottsdale
Glendale
Chandler
Gilbert
Tempe
Peoria
Sun City
Rio Rancho
Los Alamos
Carlsbad
Hobbs
Clovis
Deming
Alamogordo
Silver City
Prescott
Sedona
Page
Durango
Trinidad
Raton
Tucumcari
Santa Rosa
Socorro
Truth or Consequences
Lake Havasu City
Bullhead City
Sierra Vista
Douglas
Bisbee
Tombstone
Casa Grande
Florence
Winslow
Holbrook
Show Low
Black Canyon City
Cave Creek
Humphreys Pk. 12633
Wheeler Pk. 13161
Guadalupe Mts.
Sacramento Mountains
San Andres Mts.
Jornada del Muerto
Black Mesa
Chuska Mts.
Black Mountains
36°
33°
105°
108°
111°
114°

Arizona

GRAND CANYON STATE

AREA	113,998 sq mi (295,254 sq km)
POPULATION	5,939,000
CAPITAL	Phoenix
CAPITAL POP.	metro area: 3,715,000 city proper: 1,418,000
LARGEST CITY	Phoenix
INCOME	$28,609 per capita
STATEHOOD	February 14, 1912; 48th state
STATE BIRD	Cactus Wren
STATE FLOWER	Saguaro Cactus Blossom
HIGHEST POINT	Humphreys Pk. 12,633 ft (3,851 m)

Colorado

CENTENNIAL STATE

AREA	104,094 sq mi (269,601 sq km)
POPULATION	4,665,000
CAPITAL	Denver
CAPITAL POP.	metro area: 2,330,000 city proper: 557,000
LARGEST CITY	Denver
INCOME	$36,109 per capita
STATEHOOD	August 1, 1876; 38th state
STATE BIRD	Lark Bunting
STATE FLOWER	White and Lavender Columbine
HIGHEST POINT	Mount Elbert 14,433 ft (4,399 m)

Idaho

GEM STATE

AREA	83,570 sq mi (216,446 sq km)
POPULATION	1,429,000
CAPITAL	Boise
CAPITAL POP.	metro area: 525,000 city proper: 190,000
LARGEST CITY	Boise
INCOME	$26,839 per capita
STATEHOOD	July 3, 1890; 43rd state
STATE BIRD	Mountain Bluebird
STATE FLOWER	Syringa
HIGHEST POINT	Borah Peak 12,662 ft (3,859 m)

Montana

TREASURE STATE

AREA	147,042 sq mi (380,838 sq km)
POPULATION	936,000
CAPITAL	Helena
CAPITAL POP.	metro area: NA city proper: 27,000
LARGEST CITY	Billings
POPULATION	metro area: 144,000 city proper: 97,000
INCOME	$27,666 per capita
STATEHOOD	November 8, 1889; 41st state
STATE BIRD	Western Meadowlark
STATE FLOWER	Bitterroot
HIGHEST POINT	Granite Peak 12,799 ft (3,901 m)

New Mexico

LAND OF ENCHANTMENT

AREA	121,590 sq mi (314,915 sq km)
POPULATION	1,928,000
CAPITAL	Santa Fe
CAPITAL POP.	metro area: 139,000 city proper: 68,000
LARGEST CITY	Albuquerque
POPULATION	metro area: 781,000 city proper: 484,000
INCOME	$26,154 per capita
STATEHOOD	January 6, 1912; 47th state
STATE BIRD	Roadrunner
STATE FLOWER	Yucca Flower
HIGHEST POINT	Wheeler Peak 13,161 ft (4,011 m)

Utah

BEEHIVE STATE

AREA	84,899 sq mi (219,887 sq km)
POPULATION	2,470,000
CAPITAL	Salt Lake City
CAPITAL POP.	metro area: 1,019,000 city proper: 179,000
LARGEST CITY	Salt Lake City
INCOME	$26,946 per capita
STATEHOOD	January 4, 1896; 45th state
STATE BIRD	California Gull
STATE FLOWER	Sego Lily
HIGHEST POINT	Kings Peak 13,528 ft (4,123 m)

Wyoming

EQUALITY STATE

AREA	97,814 sq mi (253,336 sq km)
POPULATION	509,000
CAPITAL	Cheyenne
CAPITAL POP.	metro area: 85,000 city proper: 55,000
LARGEST CITY	Cheyenne
INCOME	$34,199 per capita
STATEHOOD	July 10, 1890; 44th state
STATE BIRD	Western Meadowlark
STATE FLOWER	Indian Paintbrush
HIGHEST POINT	Gannett Peak 13,804 ft (4,207 m)

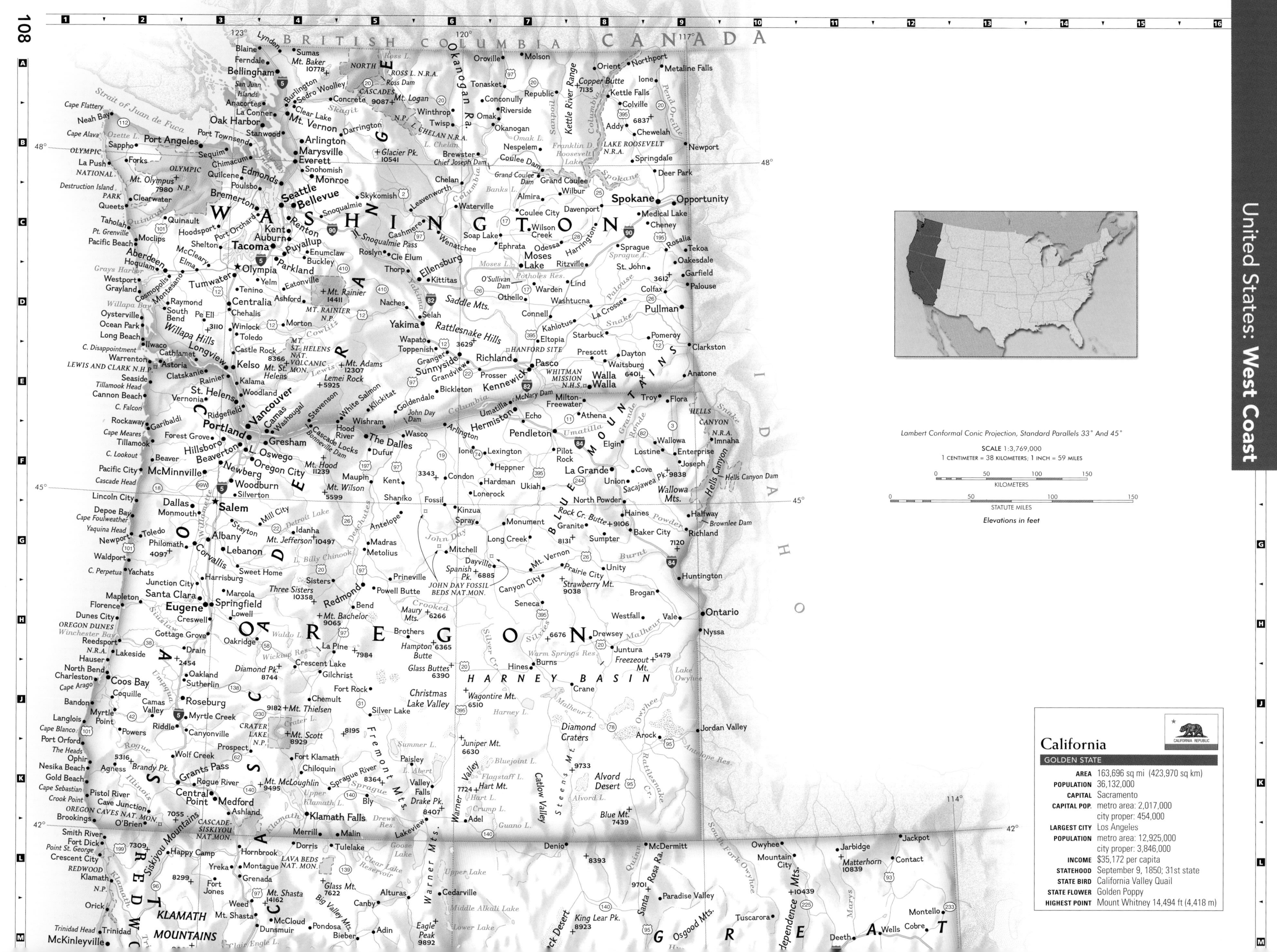
California
GOLDEN STATE
AREA 163,696 sq mi (423,970 sq km)
POPULATION 36,132,000
CAPITAL Sacramento
CAPITAL POP. metro area: 2,017,000
city proper: 454,000
LARGEST CITY Los Angeles
POPULATION metro area: 12,925,000
city proper: 3,846,000
INCOME $35,172 per capita
STATEHOOD September 9, 1850; 31st state
STATE BIRD California Valley Quail
STATE FLOWER Golden Poppy
HIGHEST POINT Mount Whitney 14,494 ft (4,418 m)
Lambert Conformal Conic Projection, Standard Parallels 33° And 45°
SCALE 1:3,769,000
1 CENTIMETER = 38 KILOMETERS; 1 INCH = 59 MILES
KILOMETERS
STATUTE MILES
Elevations in feet
BRITISH COLUMBIA
CANADA
WASHINGTON
OREGON
IDAHO
Seattle
Tacoma
Olympia
Spokane
Portland
Salem
Eugene
Vancouver
Bellingham
Yakima
Walla Walla
Pendleton
Medford
Klamath Falls
Bend
HARNEY BASIN
BLUE MOUNTAINS
KLAMATH MOUNTAINS
CRATER LAKE N.P.
Mt. Rainier 14411
Mt. Hood 11239
Mt. Shasta 14162
Okanogan Ra.
Strait of Juan de Fuca

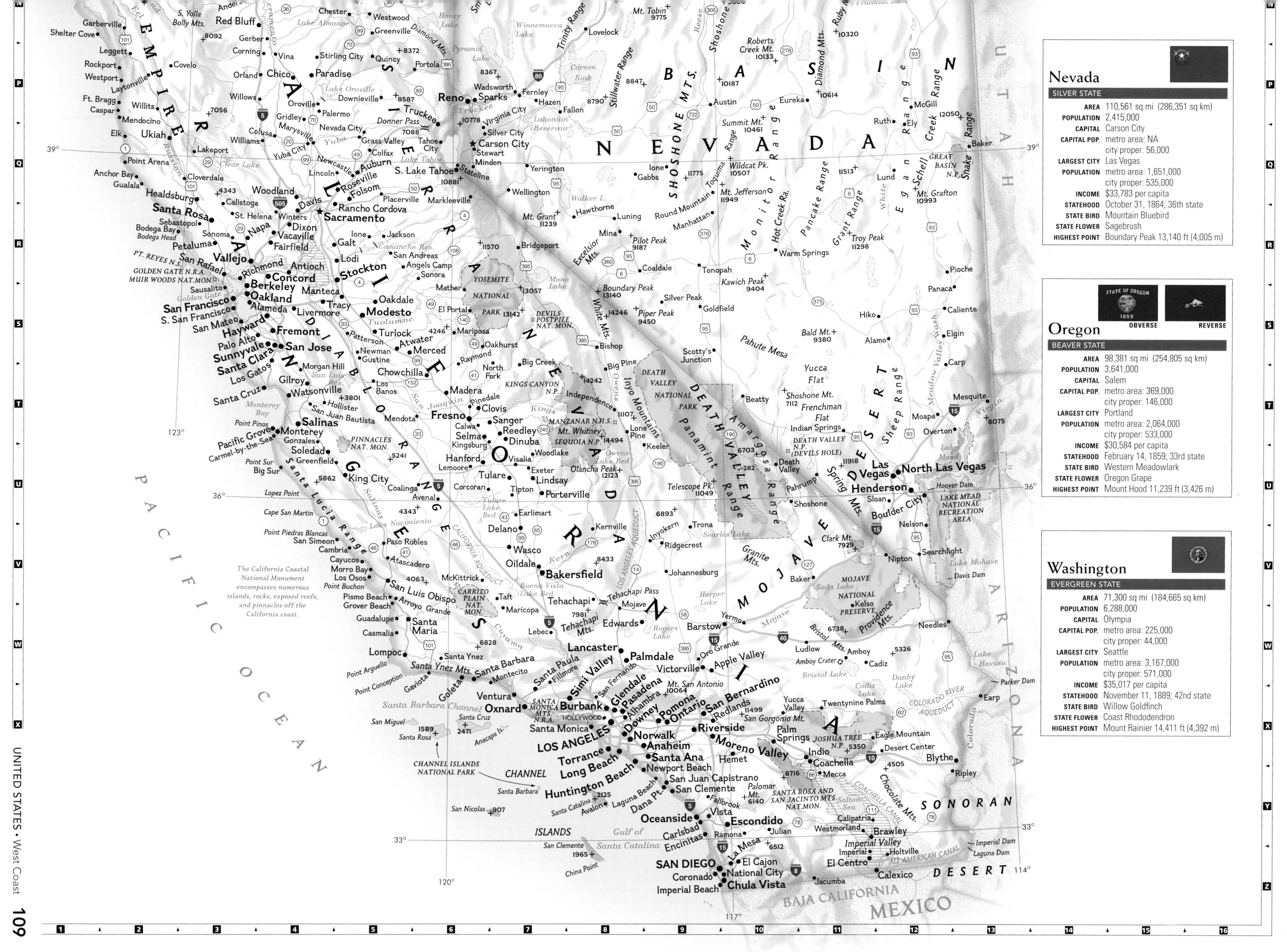
NEVADA
GREAT BASIN
SIERRA NEVADA
DIABLO RANGE
EMPIRE
MOJAVE
SONORAN DESERT
PACIFIC OCEAN
UTAH
ARIZONA
BAJA CALIFORNIA
MEXICO
DEATH VALLEY NATIONAL PARK
YOSEMITE NATIONAL PARK
KINGS CANYON N.P.
SEQUOIA N.P.
JOSHUA TREE N.P.
GREAT BASIN N.P.
LAKE MEAD NATIONAL RECREATION AREA
MOJAVE NATIONAL PRESERVE
PINNACLES NAT. MON.
DEVILS POSTPILE NAT. MON.
CARRIZO PLAIN NAT. MON.
SANTA MONICA MTS. N.R.A.
GOLDEN GATE N.R.A.
MUIR WOODS NAT. MON.
PT. REYES N.S.
MANZANAR N.H.S.
SANTA ROSA AND SAN JACINTO MTS. NAT. MON.
CHANNEL ISLANDS NATIONAL PARK
CHANNEL ISLANDS
SHOSHONE MTS.
Panamint Range
Amargosa Range
Inyo Mountains
White Mts.
Santa Lucia Range
Sheep Range
Spring Mts.
Providence Mts.
Chocolate Mts.
Sacramento
Carson City
San Francisco
Oakland
San Jose
Fresno
Bakersfield
Reno
Las Vegas
North Las Vegas
Henderson
LOS ANGELES
Long Beach
Santa Ana
Anaheim
Riverside
San Bernardino
SAN DIEGO
Chula Vista
Oceanside
Escondido
Santa Barbara
Oxnard
Ventura
Salinas
Monterey
Stockton
Modesto
Santa Rosa
Redding
Red Bluff
Chico
Eureka
Ely
Tonopah
Pahrump
Barstow
Palm Springs
El Centro
Calexico
Needles
Blythe
Lake Tahoe
Salton Sea
Colorado River
California Coastal National Monument
The California Coastal National Monument encompasses numerous islands, rocks, exposed reefs, and pinnacles off the California coast.
39°
36°
33°
123°
120°
117°
114°

Nevada

SILVER STATE

AREA	110,561 sq mi (286,351 sq km)
POPULATION	2,415,000
CAPITAL	Carson City
CAPITAL POP.	metro area: NA
	city proper: 56,000
LARGEST CITY	Las Vegas
POPULATION	metro area: 1,651,000
	city proper: 535,000
INCOME	$33,783 per capita
STATEHOOD	October 31, 1864; 36th state
STATE BIRD	Mountain Bluebird
STATE FLOWER	Sagebrush
HIGHEST POINT	Boundary Peak 13,140 ft (4,005 m)

Oregon

STATE OF OREGON 1859

OBVERSE REVERSE

BEAVER STATE

AREA	98,381 sq mi (254,805 sq km)
POPULATION	3,641,000
CAPITAL	Salem
CAPITAL POP.	metro area: 369,000
	city proper: 146,000
LARGEST CITY	Portland
POPULATION	metro area: 2,064,000
	city proper: 533,000
INCOME	$30,584 per capita
STATEHOOD	February 14, 1859; 33rd state
STATE BIRD	Western Meadowlark
STATE FLOWER	Oregon Grape
HIGHEST POINT	Mount Hood 11,239 ft (3,426 m)

Washington

EVERGREEN STATE

AREA	71,300 sq mi (184,665 sq km)
POPULATION	6,288,000
CAPITAL	Olympia
CAPITAL POP.	metro area: 225,000
	city proper: 44,000
LARGEST CITY	Seattle
POPULATION	metro area: 3,167,000
	city proper: 571,000
INCOME	$35,017 per capita
STATEHOOD	November 11, 1889; 42nd state
STATE BIRD	Willow Goldfinch
STATE FLOWER	Coast Rhododendron
HIGHEST POINT	Mount Rainier 14,411 ft (4,392 m)

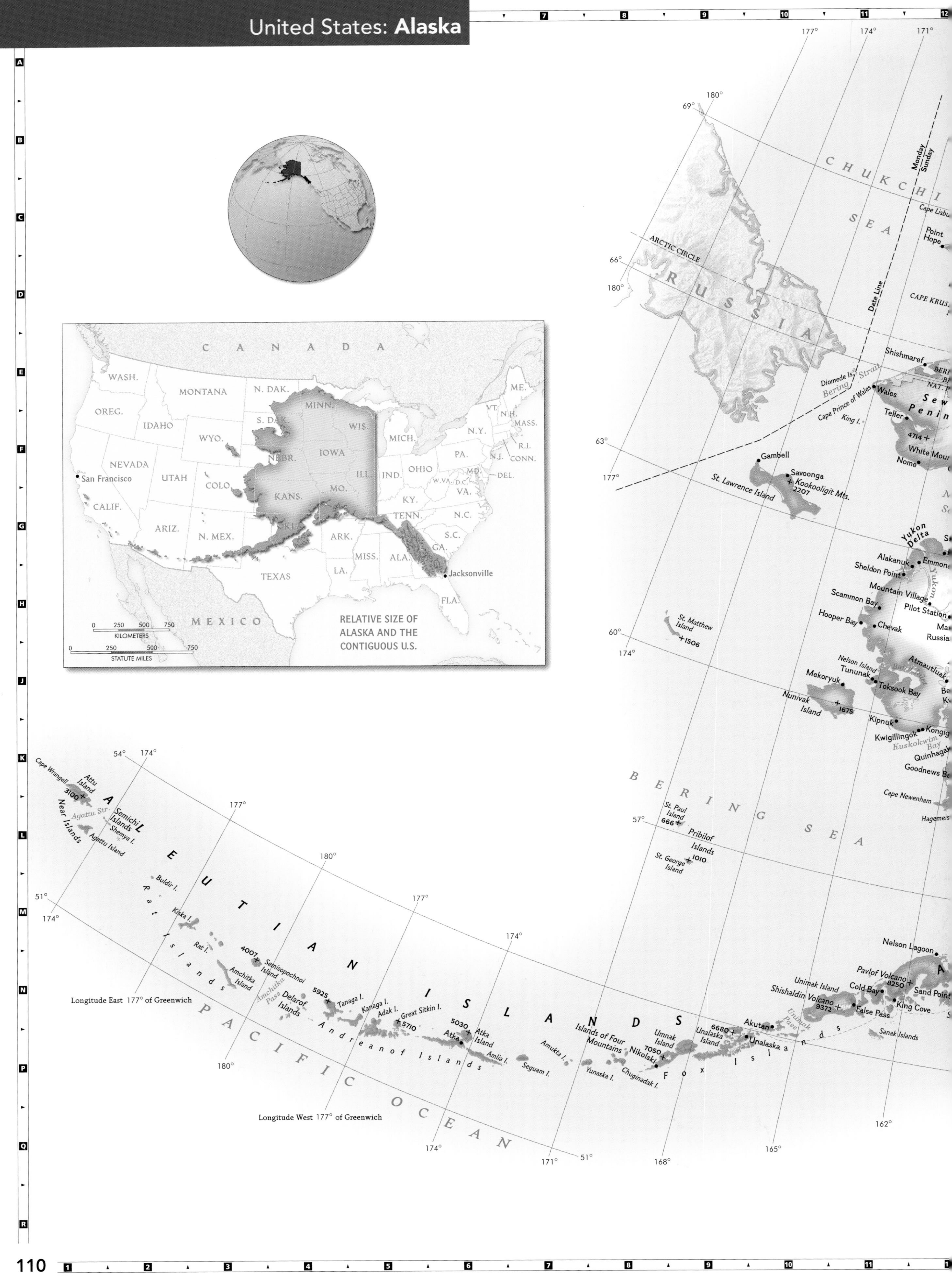
C A N A D A
WASH.
OREG.
IDAHO
MONTANA
N. DAK.
S. DAK.
WYO.
NEVADA
UTAH
COLO.
CALIF.
ARIZ.
N. MEX.
NEBR.
KANS.
OKLA.
TEXAS
MINN.
IOWA
MO.
ARK.
LA.
WIS.
ILL.
MICH.
IND.
OHIO
KY.
TENN.
MISS.
ALA.
GA.
FLA.
S.C.
N.C.
VA.
W.VA.
PA.
N.Y.
VT.
N.H.
ME.
MASS.
R.I.
CONN.
N.J.
MD.
D.C.
DEL.
San Francisco
Jacksonville
M E X I C O
KILOMETERS
STATUTE MILES
RELATIVE SIZE OF ALASKA AND THE CONTIGUOUS U.S.
C H U K C H I
S E A
R U S S I A
ARCTIC CIRCLE
Date Line
Monday
Sunday
Cape Lisbu
Point Hope
CAPE KRUS
Shishmaref
Diomede Is.
Bering Strait
Cape Prince of Wales
Wales
King I.
Teller
4714
White Mour
Nome
Gambell
Savoonga
Kookooligit Mts.
2207
St. Lawrence Island
Yukon Delta
Alakanuk
Emmonak
Sheldon Point
Mountain Village
Scammon Bay
Pilot Station
Hooper Bay
Chevak
St. Matthew Island
1506
Nelson Island
Tununak
Atmautluak
Toksook Bay
Mekoryuk
Nunivak Island
1675
Kipnuk
Kwigillingok
Kongig
Kuskokwim Bay
Quinhagak
Goodnews Ba
Cape Newenham
Hagemeis
B E R I N G S E A
St. Paul Island
666
Pribilof Islands
St. George Island
1010
Cape Wrangell
Attu Island
3100
Near Islands
Agattu Str.
Agattu Island
Semichi Islands
Shemya I.
A L E U T I A N I S L A N D S
Buldir I.
Rat Islands
Kiska I.
Rat I.
Amchitka Island
Amchitka Pass
4007
Semisopochnoi Island
Delarof Islands
5925
Tanaga I.
Kanaga I.
Adak I.
Great Sitkin I.
5710
Andreanof Islands
5030
Atka Island
Atka
Amlia I.
Seguam I.
Amukta I.
Yunaska I.
Islands of Four Mountains
Chuginadak I.
Umnak Island
7050
Nikolski
Fox Islands
6680
Unalaska Island
Unalaska
Akutan
Unimak Pass
Unimak Island
Shishaldin Volcano
9372
False Pass
Pavlof Volcano
8250
Cold Bay
King Cove
Sand Point
Sanak Islands
Nelson Lagoon
Longitude East 177° of Greenwich
Longitude West 177° of Greenwich
P A C I F I C O C E A N

Alaska
LAST FRONTIER
AREA 663,267 sq mi (1,717,854 sq km)
POPULATION 664,000
CAPITAL Juneau
CAPITAL POP. metro area: NA
city proper: 31,000
LARGEST CITY Anchorage
POPULATION metro area: 345,000
city proper: 273,000
INCOME $34,085 per capita
STATEHOOD January 3, 1959; 49th state
STATE BIRD Willow Ptarmigan
STATE FLOWER Forget-me-not
HIGHEST POINT Mt. McKinley 20,320 ft (6,194 m)
ARCTIC OCEAN
BEAUFORT SEA
NORTH SLOPE
BROOKS RANGE
ALASKA
ALASKA RANGE
ALEUTIAN RANGE
ALASKA PENINSULA
GULF OF ALASKA
PACIFIC OCEAN
YUKON
NORTHWEST TERRITORIES
NUNAVUT
BRITISH COLUMBIA
CANADA
ALEXANDER ARCHIPELAGO
COAST MTS.
St. Elias Mountains
Chugach Mountains
Kuskokwim Mountains
Endicott Mts.
Philip Smith Mts.
Davidson Mts.
Baird Mountains
Kaiyuh Mts.
Talkeetna Mts.
Kiokluk Mts. 4093
Barrow
Point Barrow
Wainwright
Icy Cape
Peard Bay
Dease Inlet
Smith Bay
Cape Halkett
Harrison Bay
Teshekpuk Lake
Prudhoe Bay
Deadhorse
Kaktovik
Lookout Ridge 2344
Mt. Chamberlin 9020
Mt. Isto 9060
NOATAK NAT. PRESERVE
Anaktuvuk Pass
7420
8025
GATES OF THE ARCTIC N.P. AND PRESERVE
KOBUK VALLEY N.P.
Mt. Igikpak 8510
Arctic Village
Wiseman
Kiana
Ambler
Noorvik
Shungnak
Kobuk
Selawik
Evansville
Venetie
Fort Yukon
Chalkyitsik
ARCTIC CIRCLE
Allakaket
Beaver
Hughes
Stevens Village
Circle
Huslia
Rampart
Central
WHITE MTS. N.R.A.
STEESE HWY.
YUKON-CHARLEY RIVERS NATIONAL PRESERVE
Eagle
Koyukuk
Nulato
Galena
Tanana
Manley Hot Springs
College
Fairbanks
Ruby
Kaltag
Unalakleet
Nenana
Anderson
Delta Junction
DENALI NATIONAL PARK AND PRESERVE
Healy
Denali Park
Mt. Hayes 13832
ALASKA HWY.
TAYLOR HWY.
Tok
Tanacross
Tetlin
Northway Junction
4508
Mt. McKinley (Denali) 20320 (6194m)
Nikolai
McGrath
Cantwell
DENALI HWY.
RICHARDSON HWY.
Mentasta Lake
Shageluk
Holy Cross
Aniak
Red Devil
Sleetmute
Talkeetna
Gulkana
Gakona
Glennallen
Copper Center
GLENN HWY.
WRANGELL-ST. ELIAS NATIONAL PARK AND PRESERVE
Mt. Blackburn 16390
Mt. Bona 16421
Wasilla
Palmer
Mt. Marcus Baker 13176
Mt. Torbert 11413
Birchwood
Anchorage
Tyonek
Valdez
LAKE CLARK N.P. AND PRESERVE
Redoubt Volcano 10197
Kenai
Soldotna
Whittier
Mt. Tom White 11210
Cordova
Mt. St. Elias 18008
Kenai Peninsula
Nilnilchik
Seward
Nondalton
Koliganek
New Stuyahok
Iliamna Lake
Homer
Seldovia
Port Graham
KENAI FJORDS N.P.
Montague Island
Hinchinbrook Island
Yakutat
Malaspina Glacier
Mt. Foster 7127
KLONDIKE GOLD RUSH N.H.P.
Skagway
Haines
Devils Paw 8584
Juneau
Mt. Fairweather 15300
GLACIER BAY N.P. AND PRESERVE
Dillingham
Manokotak
Naknek
King Salmon
KATMAI N.P. AND PRESERVE
Mount Katmai 6715
Egegik
Becharof Lake
Shuyak I.
Afognak Island
Port Lions
Kodiak
Kodiak Island
Larsen Bay
Old Harbor
Akhiok
ANIAKCHAK N.M. AND PRESERVE
Sutwik I.
Chignik Lagoon
Trinity Islands
Chirikof Island
Hoonah
Pelican
Chichagof Island
ADMIRALTY ISLAND N.M.
Angoon
Kates Needle 10023
Sitka
SITKA N.H.P.
Baranof Island
Kake
Kupreanof Island
Petersburg
Wrangell
Thorne Bay
Prince of Wales Island
Revillagigedo Island
MISTY FIORDS N.M.
Klawock
Craig
Ketchikan
Metlakatla
Dixon Entrance
Azimutal Eqidistant Projection
SCALE 1:7,650,000
1 CENTIMETER = 76 KILOMETERS; 1 INCH = 120 MILES
0 100 200 300
KILOMETERS
0 100 200 300
STATUTE MILES
Elevations in feet

Hawai'i

ALOHA STATE

AREA	10,931 sq mi (28,311 sq km)
POPULATION	1,275,000
CAPITAL	Honolulu
CAPITAL POP.	metro area: 900,000 city proper: 377,000
LARGEST CITY	Honolulu
INCOME	$32,606 per capita
STATEHOOD	August 21, 1959; 50th state
STATE BIRD	Nene (Hawaiian Goose)
STATE FLOWER	Yellow Hibiscus
HIGHEST POINT	Mauna Kea (Pu'u Wekiu) 13,796 ft (4,205 m)

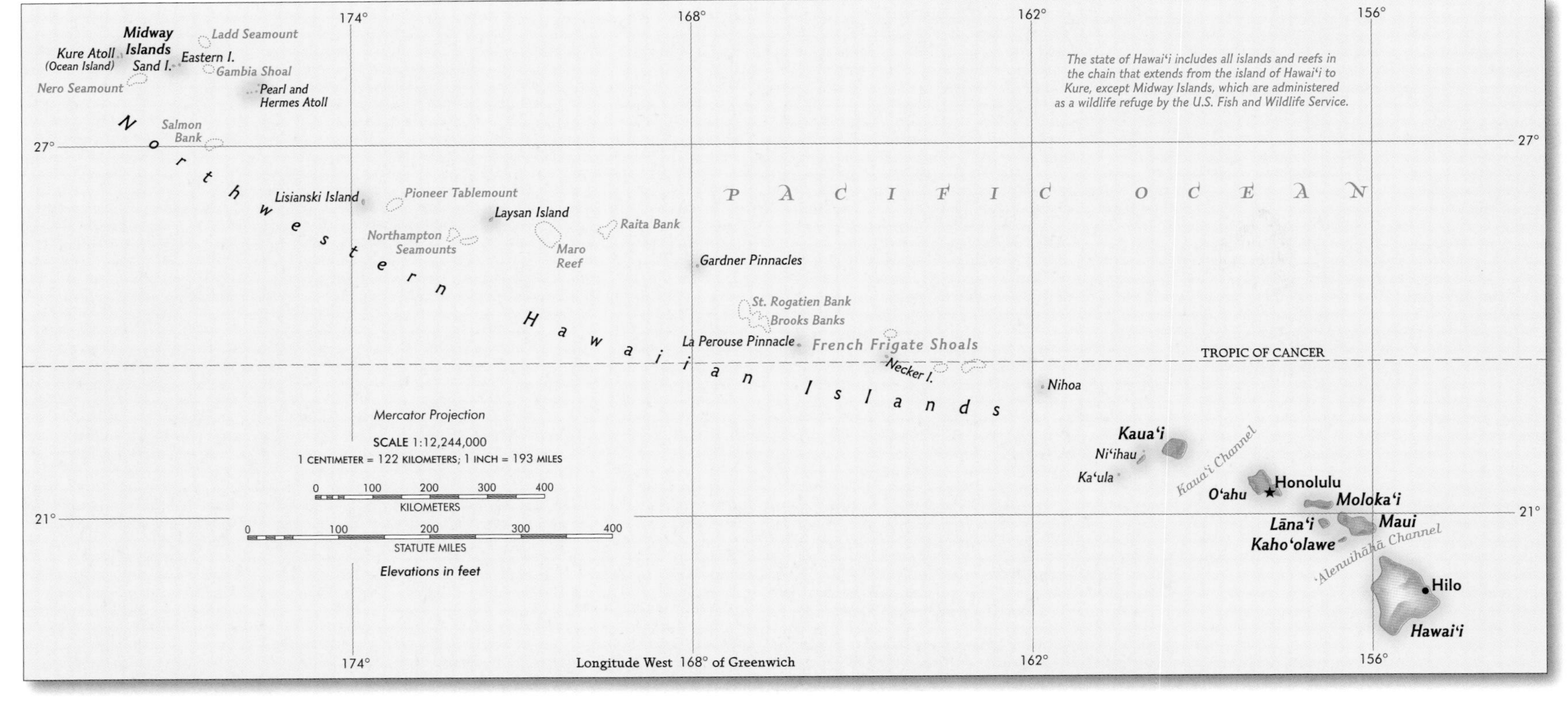

Midway Islands
Kure Atoll (Ocean Island)
Sand I.
Eastern I.
Ladd Seamount
Gambia Shoal
Nero Seamount
Pearl and Hermes Atoll
Salmon Bank
Northwestern Hawaiian Islands
Lisianski Island
Pioneer Tablemount
Laysan Island
Northampton Seamounts
Maro Reef
Raita Bank
Gardner Pinnacles
St. Rogatien Bank
Brooks Banks
La Perouse Pinnacle
French Frigate Shoals
Necker I.
Nihoa
PACIFIC OCEAN
TROPIC OF CANCER
The state of Hawai'i includes all islands and reefs in the chain that extends from the island of Hawai'i to Kure, except Midway Islands, which are administered as a wildlife refuge by the U.S. Fish and Wildlife Service.
Kaua'i
Ni'ihau
Ka'ula
Kaua'i Channel
O'ahu
Honolulu
Moloka'i
Lāna'i
Maui
Kaho'olawe
'Alenuihāhā Channel
Hilo
Hawai'i
Mercator Projection
SCALE 1:12,244,000
1 CENTIMETER = 122 KILOMETERS; 1 INCH = 193 MILES
KILOMETERS
STATUTE MILES
Elevations in feet
Longitude West 168° of Greenwich

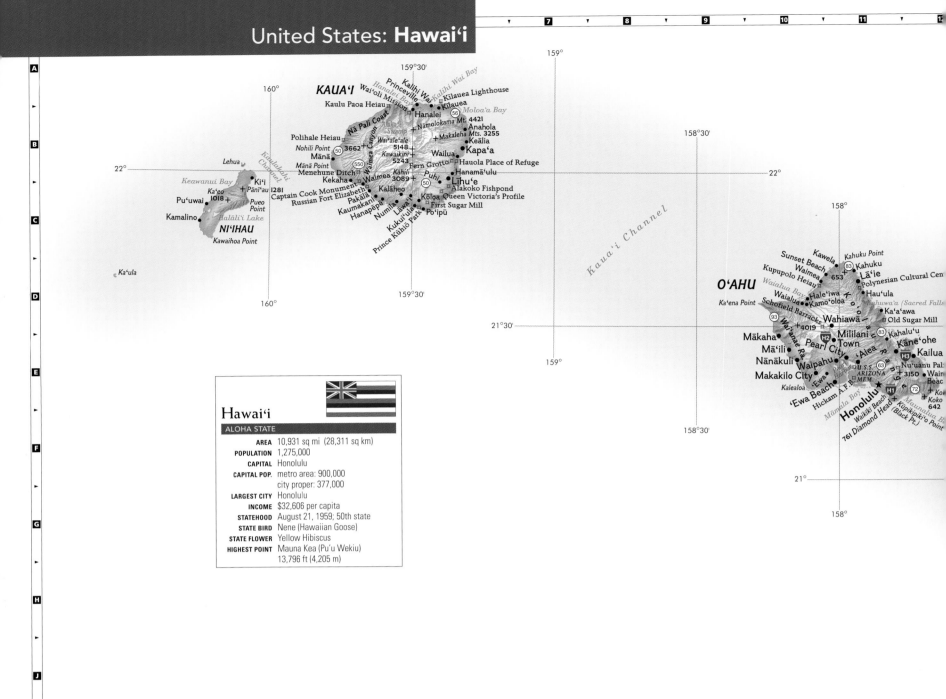

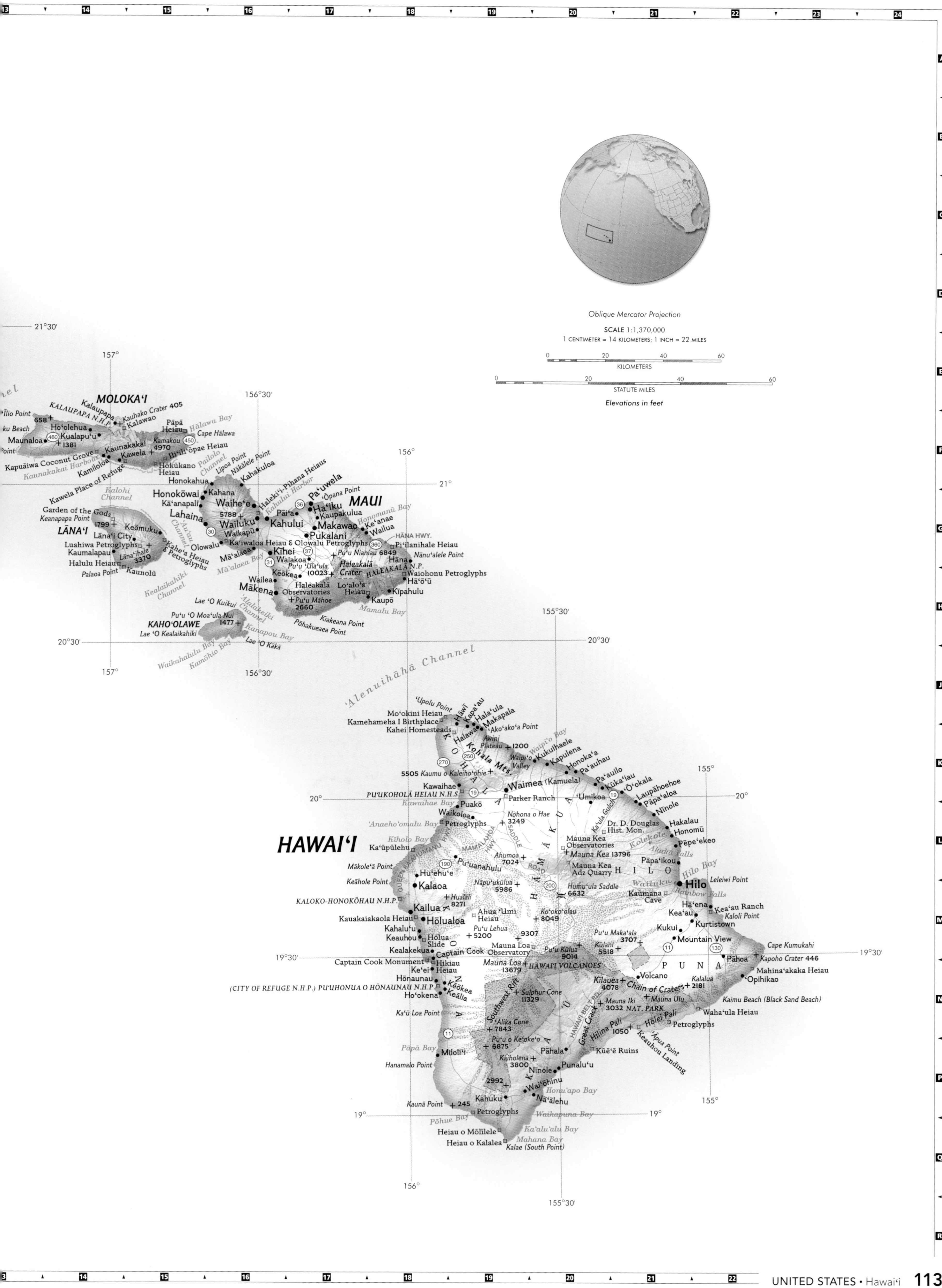

Oblique Mercator Projection
SCALE 1:1,370,000
1 CENTIMETER = 14 KILOMETERS; 1 INCH = 22 MILES
KILOMETERS
STATUTE MILES
Elevations in feet
MOLOKA‘I
KALAUPAPA N.H.P.
Kalaupapa
Kauhako Crater 405
Kalawao
Hālawa Bay
Pāpā Heiau
Cape Hālawa
Ho‘olehua
Kualapu‘u
Maunaloa
1381
Kamakou 4970
Kaunakakai
Kawela
Ili‘ili‘ōpae Heiau
Kapuāiwa Coconut Grove
Kaunakakai Harbor
Kamiloloa
Kawela Place of Refuge
Hōkūkano Heiau
Pailolo Channel
Lipoa Point
Nākālele Point
Kalohi Channel
Garden of the Gods
Keanapapa Point
LĀNA‘I
Lāna‘i City
Keōmuku
Luahiwa Petroglyphs
Kaumalapau
Halulu Heiau
Palaoa Point
Kaunolū
Lāna‘ihale 3370
Kahe‘a Heiau & Petroglyphs
Kealaikahiki Channel
Honokahua
Kahana
Honokōwai
Kā‘anapali
Lahaina
Waihe‘e
5788
Wailuku
Waikapū
Olowalu
Mā‘alaea
Mā‘alaea Bay
Kahakuloa
Haleki‘i-Pihana Heiaus
Kahului Harbor
Kahului
Pā‘ia
Pa‘uwela
‘Ōpana Point
Ha‘iku
Kaupakulua
MAUI
Makawao
Pukalani
Honomanū Bay
Ke‘anae
Wailua
HĀNA HWY.
Ka‘iwaloa Heiau & Olowalu Petroglyphs
Pi‘ilanihale Heiau
Kīhei
Waiakoa
Pu‘u Nianiau 6849
Nānu‘alele Point
Hāna
Kēōkea
Pu‘u ‘Ula‘ula 10023
Haleakalā Crater
HALEAKALĀ N.P.
Waiohonu Petroglyphs
Hā‘ō‘ū
Wailea
Mākena
Haleakalā Observatories
Lo‘alo‘a Heiau
Kīpahulu
Pu‘u Māhoe 2660
Kaupō
Mamalu Bay
Lae ‘O Kuikui
Pu‘u ‘O Moa‘ula Nui 1477
KAHO‘OLAWE
Lae ‘O Kealaikahiki
‘Alalākeiki Channel
Kīakeana Point
Pōhakueaea Point
Kanapou Bay
Lae ‘O Kākā
Waikahalulu Bay
Kamōhio Bay
‘Alenuihāhā Channel
HAWAI‘I
‘Upolu Point
Hāwī
Kapa‘au
Hala‘ula
Makapala
Mo‘okini Heiau
Kamehameha I Birthplace
Kahei Homesteads
Halawa
‘Ako‘ako‘a Point
‘Awini Plateau
1200
Waipi‘o Bay
Kukuihaele
Kohala Mts.
Waipi‘o Valley
Kapulena
Honoka‘a
Pa‘auhau
KOHALA
5505 Kaumu o Kaleiho‘ohie
Kawaihae
PU‘UKOHOLĀ HEIAU N.H.S.
Waimea (Kamuela)
Parker Ranch
Pa‘auilo
Kūka‘iau
‘Ō‘ōkala
Laupāhoehoe
Pāpa‘aloa
Nīnole
‘Umikoa
Kawaihae Bay
Puakō
Waikoloa
Petroglyphs
‘Anaeho‘omalu Bay
Nohona o Hae 3249
Kīholo Bay
Ka‘ūpūlehu
Dr. D. Douglas Hist. Mon.
Hakalau
Honomū
Pēpē‘ekeo
Mauna Kea Observatories
Mauna Kea 13796
Kolekole
‘Akaka Falls
Ahumoa 7024
Pu‘uanahulu
Mauna Kea Adz Quarry
HILO
Pāpa‘ikou
Hilo Bay
Mākole‘ā Point
Hu‘ehu‘e
Keāhole Point
Kalaoa
Napu‘ukulua 5986
Humu‘ula Saddle 6632
Wailuku
Hilo
Leleiwi Point
Rainbow Falls
Kaūmana Cave
KALOKO-HONOKŌHAU N.H.P.
Hualālai 8271
Kailua
Hā‘ena
Kea‘au Ranch
Kaloli Point
Kauakaiakaola Heiau
Hōlualoa
Ahu a ‘Umi Heiau
Ko‘oko‘olau 8049
Kea‘au
Kurtistown
Kahalu‘u
Keauhou
Hōlua Slide
Pu‘u Lehua 5200
9307
Pu‘u Maka‘ala 3707
Kukui
Mountain View
Kealakekua
Captain Cook
Mauna Loa Observatory
Kūlani 5518
Cape Kumukahi
Kapoho Crater 446
Pāhoa
Captain Cook Monument
Hikiau Heiau
Ke‘ei
Pu‘u Kūlua 9014
Mauna Loa 13679
HAWAI‘I VOLCANOES
PUNA
Mahina‘akaka Heiau
‘Ōpihikao
Hōnaunau
(CITY OF REFUGE N.H.P.) PU‘UHONUA O HŌNAUNAU N.H.P.
Kēōkea
Ho‘okena
Ke‘ālia
Sulphur Cone 11329
Southwest Rift
Kīlauea 4078
Volcano
Chain of Craters
Kalalua 2181
Mauna Ulu
Kaimu Beach (Black Sand Beach)
Mauna Iki 3032
NAT. PARK
Waha‘ula Heiau
Ka‘ū Loa Point
‘Ālika Cone 7843
Hōlei Pali
Petroglyphs
Hilina Pali
Great Crack
1050
‘Āpua Point
Keauhou Landing
Pu‘u o Ke‘oke‘o 6875
Pāpā Bay
Miloli‘i
Pāhala
Kūē‘ē Ruins
Hanamalo Point
Kaiholena 3800
Nīnole
Punalu‘u
2992
Wai‘ōhinu
Honu‘apo Bay
Kahuku
Nā‘ālehu
Kaunā Point
245
Petroglyphs
Pōhue Bay
Waikapuna Bay
Ka‘alu‘alu Bay
Heiau o Mōlīlele
Mahana Bay
Heiau o Kalalea
Kalae (South Point)
21°30′
21°
20°30′
20°
19°30′
19°
157°
156°30′
156°
155°30′
155°

UNITED STATES
CALIFORNIA
ARIZONA
NEW MEXICO
TEXAS
TIJUANA
Mexicali
Laguna Salada
San Luis Río Colorado
B. de Todos Santos
Ensenada
Cabo Colonet
Vicente Guerrero
San Felipe
Puerto Peñasco
San Quintín
El Rosario
Punta San Antonio
Isla de Guadalupe
BAJA CALIFORNIA
Golfo de California
Punta Prieta
Bahía Sebastián Vizcaíno
Isla Cedros
Isla Natividad
Punta Eugenia
Laguna Ojo de Liebre
Desierto de Vizcaíno
San Ignacio
Santa Rosalía
Mulegé
Bahía Ballenas
La Purísima
Comondú
Loreto
I. Carmen
Rocas Alijos
Isla Magdalena
Cabo San Lázaro
Bahía Magdalena
Isla Santa Margarita
Llano de la Magdalena
I. San José
I. Espíritu Santo
La Paz
I. Cerralvo
Todos Santos
Cabo Falso
Cabo San Lucas
TROPIC OF CANCER
Islas Revillagigedo
Mexico
I. Roca Partida
I. San Benedicto
I. Clarión
I. Socorro
PACIFIC OCEAN
Nogáles
Caborca
CIUDAD JUÁREZ
Agua Prieta
Cananea
Magdalena
Ascensión
Benjamín Hill
La Libertad
Cúmpas
Nacozari Viejo
Villa Ahumada
Nuevo Casas Grandes
Moctezuma
I. Ángel de la Guarda
Hermosillo
Isla Tiburón
Guadalupe
Namiquipa
Buenaventura
Mazatán
Sahuaripa
Guaymas
Ciudad Obregón
Navojoa
Huatabampo
Ahome
Los Mochis
Topolobampo
Guasave
Guamúchil
El Fuerte
San Blas
Francisco del Oro
SIERRA MADRE OCCIDENTAL
Ciudad Guerrero
Aldama
Chihuahua
Cuauhtémoc
Delicias
Ciudad Camargo
Ojinaga
Río Grande (Río Bravo del Norte)
Presa de la Amistad
Ciudad Acuña
Piedras Negras
Allende
Nueva Rosita
Nuevo Laredo
Frontera
Monclova
Sabinas Hidalgo
Presa Falcon
Matamoros
Reynosa
MONTERREY
Paredón
Montemorelos
San Fernando
Saltillo
Linares
Jiménez
Sierra Mojada
Hidalgo del Parral
Santa Bárbara
Gómez Palacio
San Pedro de las Colonias
Torreón
Parras
Nazas
Conception del Oro
Santiago Papasquiaro
Culiacán
Altata
Eldorado
Quilá
La Cruz
Dimas
Durango
Canatlán
Cuencamé
Juan Aldama
El Salto
Mazatlán
Villa Unión
Rosario
Escuinapa
Acaponeta
Tecuala
Tuxpan
Santiago Ixcuintla
Islas Marías
Tepic
Compostela
Puerto Vallarta
Cabo Corrientes
Fresnillo
Zacatecas
Guadalupe
Valparaíso
Villanueva
La Paz
Matehuala
Santander Jiménez
Ciudad Victoria
Ciudad Mante
Tula
San Luis Potosí
Cárdenas
Río Verde
Aguascalientes
Lagos de Moreno
LEÓN
Guanajuato
Irapuato
GUADALAJARA
Ameca
Lago de Chapala
Tampico
Ciudad Valles
Tamazunchale
Querétaro
Celaya
Salamanca
La Barca
Pachuca
Autlán
Ciudad Guzmán
Uruapan
Morelia
Pátzcuaro
MÉXICO
Toluca
Manzanillo
Colima
Tecomán
Coalcomán
Apatzingán
NETZAHUALCÓYOTL
Cuernavaca
Ciudad Altamirano
Taxco
Iguala
Popocatépetl
Lázaro Cárdenas
Bahía Petacalco
Ixtapa
Petatlán
Sierra Madre del Sur
Tecpan
Atoyac
Acapulco
Ayutla
Punta Maldonado
Chilpancingo
Huajuapan de León
Balsas
SIERRA MADRE ORIENTAL
MEXICO
Conchos
Yaqui
110°
100°
30°
20°

Belize

BELIZE

AREA 22,965 sq km (8,867 sq mi)
POPULATION 292,000
CAPITAL Belmopan 9,000
RELIGION Roman Catholic, Protestant
LANGUAGE English (official), Spanish, Mayan, Garifuna (Carib), Creole
LITERACY 94%
LIFE EXPECTANCY 70 years
GDP PER CAPITA $3,594
ECONOMY **IND:** garment production, food processing, tourism, construction **AGR:** bananas, coca, citrus, sugar; lumber; fish **EXP:** sugar, bananas, citrus, clothing

Costa Rica

REPUBLIC OF COSTA RICA

AREA 51,100 sq km (19,730 sq mi)
POPULATION 4,331,000
CAPITAL San José 1,085,000
RELIGION Roman Catholic, Evangelical
LANGUAGE Spanish (official), English
LITERACY 96%
LIFE EXPECTANCY 79 years
GDP PER CAPITA $4,325
ECONOMY **IND:** microprocessors, food processing, textiles and clothing, construction materials **AGR:** coffee, pineapples, bananas, sugar; beef; timber **EXP:** coffee, bananas, sugar, pineapples

El Salvador

REPUBLIC OF EL SALVADOR

AREA 21,041 sq km (8,124 sq mi)
POPULATION 6,881,000
CAPITAL San Salvador 1,424,000
RELIGION Roman Catholic, Protestant
LANGUAGE Spanish, Nahua
LITERACY 80%
LIFE EXPECTANCY 70 years
GDP PER CAPITA $2,301
ECONOMY **IND:** food processing, beverages, petroleum, chemicals **AGR:** coffee, sugar, corn, rice; beef; shrimp **EXP:** offshore assembly exports, coffee, sugar, shrimp

Guatemala

REPUBLIC OF GUATEMALA

AREA 108,889 sq km (42,042 sq mi)
POPULATION 12,701,000
CAPITAL Guatemala City 951,000
RELIGION Roman Catholic, Protestant, indigenous Mayan beliefs
LANGUAGE Spanish, 23 officially recognized Amerindian languages
LITERACY 71%
LIFE EXPECTANCY 66 years
GDP PER CAPITA $2,157
ECONOMY **IND:** sugar, textiles and clothing, furniture, chemicals **AGR:** sugarcane, corn, bananas, coffee; cattle **EXP:** coffee, sugar, petroleum, apparel

Honduras

REPUBLIC OF HONDURAS

AREA 112,492 sq km (43,433 sq mi)
POPULATION 7,212,000
CAPITAL Tegucigalpa 1,007,000
RELIGION Roman Catholic
LANGUAGE Spanish, Amerindian dialects
LITERACY 76%
LIFE EXPECTANCY 71 years
GDP PER CAPITA $1,046
ECONOMY **IND:** sugar, coffee, textiles, clothing **AGR:** bananas, coffee, citrus; beef; timber; shrimp **EXP:** coffee, shrimp, bananas, gold

Mexico

UNITED MEXICAN STATES

AREA 1,964,375 sq km (758,449 sq mi)
POPULATION 107,029,000
CAPITAL Mexico City 18,660,000
RELIGION Roman Catholic, Protestant
LANGUAGE Spanish, various Mayan, Nahuatl, and other indigenous languages
LITERACY 92%
LIFE EXPECTANCY 75 years
GDP PER CAPITA $6,397
ECONOMY **IND:** food and beverages, tobacco, chemicals, iron and steel **AGR:** corn, wheat, soybeans, rice; beef; wood products **EXP:** manufactured goods, oil and oil products, silver, fruits

Nicaragua

REPUBLIC OF NICARAGUA

AREA 130,000 sq km (50,193 sq mi)
POPULATION 5,774,000
CAPITAL Managua 1,098,000
RELIGION Roman Catholic, Evangelical
LANGUAGE Spanish (official), English, indigenous languages
LITERACY 68%
LIFE EXPECTANCY 69 years
GDP PER CAPITA $820
ECONOMY **IND:** food processing, chemicals, machinery and metal products, textiles **AGR:** coffee, bananas, sugarcane, cotton; beef **EXP:** coffee, beef, shrimp and lobster, tobacco

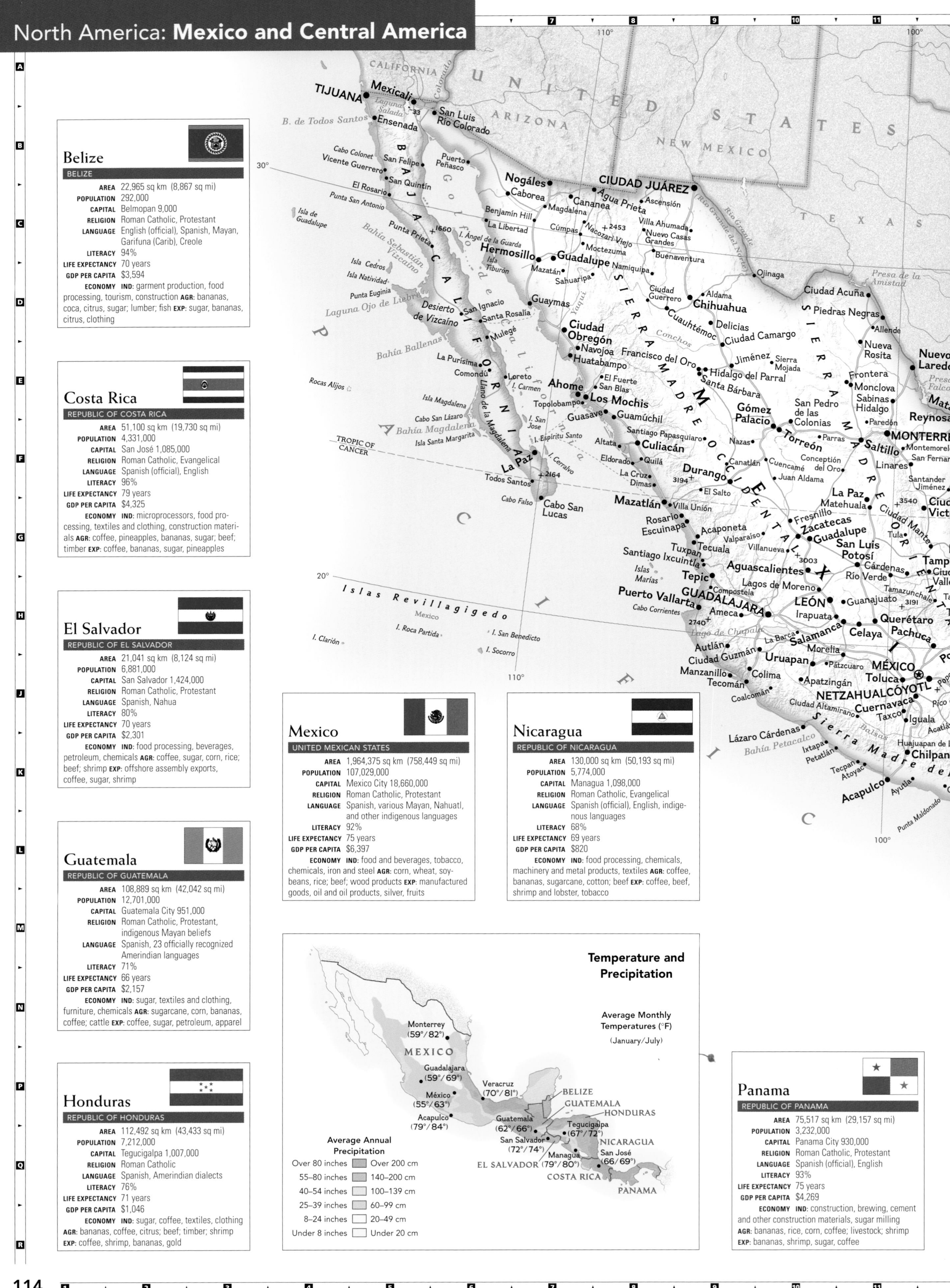

Temperature and Precipitation

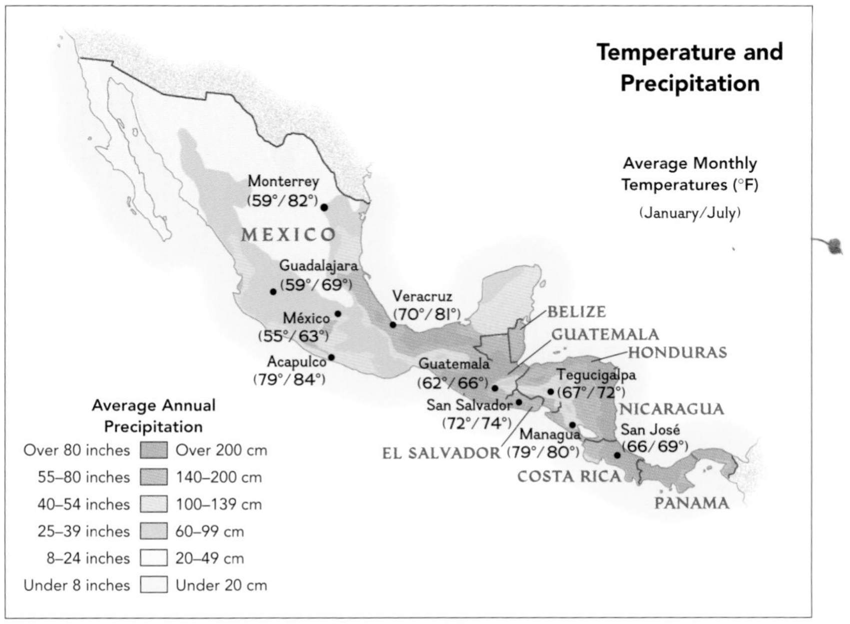

Average Monthly Temperatures (°F)
(January/July)
MEXICO
Monterrey (59°/82°)
Guadalajara (59°/69°)
México (55°/63°)
Acapulco (79°/84°)
Veracruz (70°/81°)
BELIZE
GUATEMALA
HONDURAS
Guatemala (62°/66°)
Tegucigalpa (67°/72°)
San Salvador (72°/74°)
NICARAGUA
Managua (79°/80°)
San José (66/69°)
EL SALVADOR
COSTA RICA
PANAMA
Average Annual Precipitation
Over 80 inches | Over 200 cm
55–80 inches | 140–200 cm
40–54 inches | 100–139 cm
25–39 inches | 60–99 cm
8–24 inches | 20–49 cm
Under 8 inches | Under 20 cm

Panama

REPUBLIC OF PANAMA

AREA 75,517 sq km (29,157 sq mi)
POPULATION 3,232,000
CAPITAL Panama City 930,000
RELIGION Roman Catholic, Protestant
LANGUAGE Spanish (official), English
LITERACY 93%
LIFE EXPECTANCY 75 years
GDP PER CAPITA $4,269
ECONOMY **IND:** construction, brewing, cement and other construction materials, sugar milling **AGR:** bananas, rice, corn, coffee; livestock; shrimp **EXP:** bananas, shrimp, sugar, coffee

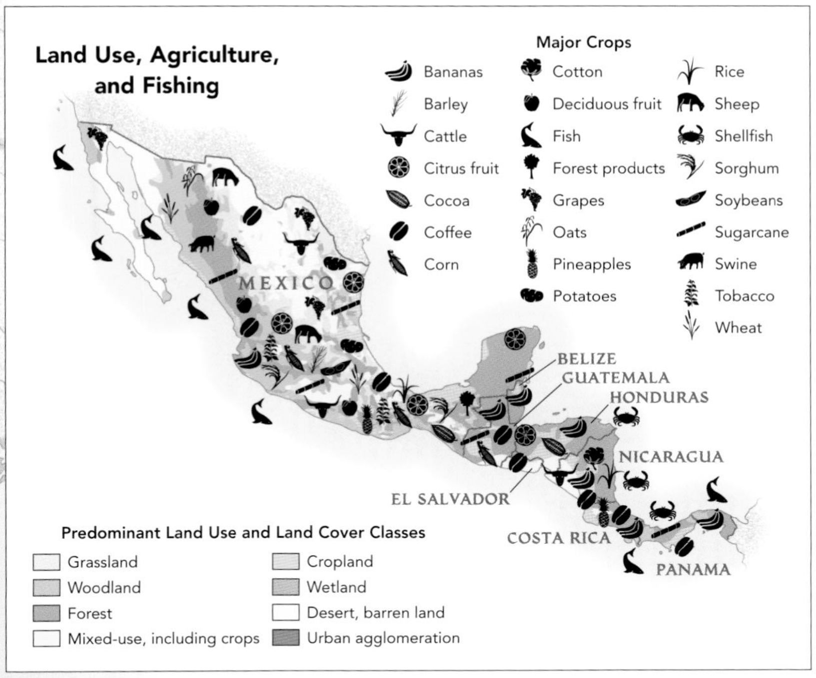

Land Use, Agriculture, and Fishing
Major Crops
Bananas
Barley
Cattle
Citrus fruit
Cocoa
Coffee
Corn
Cotton
Deciduous fruit
Fish
Forest products
Grapes
Oats
Pineapples
Potatoes
Rice
Sheep
Shellfish
Sorghum
Soybeans
Sugarcane
Swine
Tobacco
Wheat
MEXICO
BELIZE
GUATEMALA
HONDURAS
NICARAGUA
EL SALVADOR
COSTA RICA
PANAMA
Predominant Land Use and Land Cover Classes
Grassland
Woodland
Forest
Mixed-use, including crops
Cropland
Wetland
Desert, barren land
Urban agglomeration

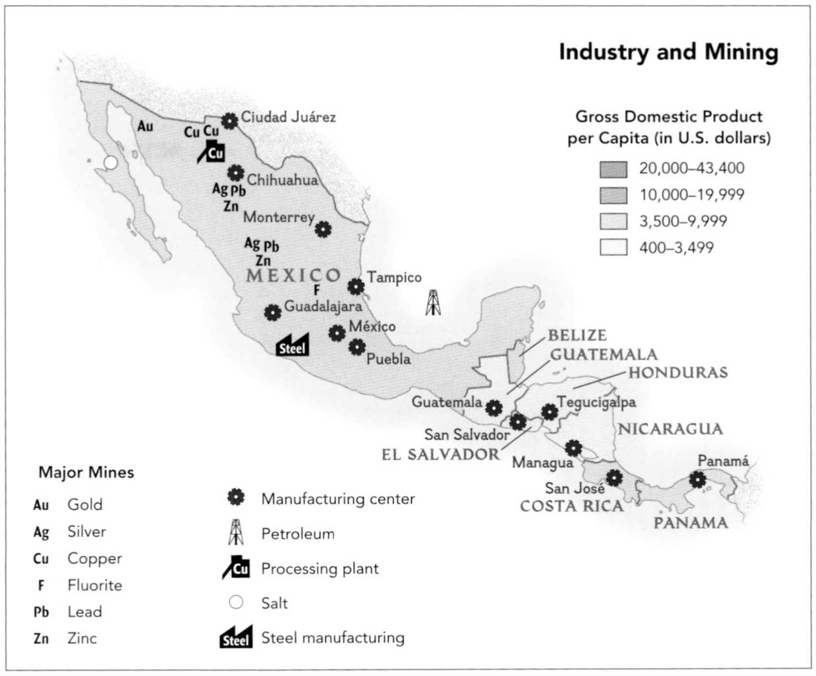

Industry and Mining
Gross Domestic Product per Capita (in U.S. dollars)
20,000–43,400
10,000–19,999
3,500–9,999
400–3,499
Ciudad Juárez
Au
Cu Cu
Cu
Chihuahua
Ag Pb Zn
Monterrey
Ag Pb Zn
MEXICO
F
Tampico
Guadalajara
México
Steel
Puebla
BELIZE
GUATEMALA
HONDURAS
Guatemala
Tegucigalpa
San Salvador
NICARAGUA
EL SALVADOR
Managua
Panamá
San José
COSTA RICA
PANAMA
Major Mines
Au Gold
Ag Silver
Cu Copper
F Fluorite
Pb Lead
Zn Zinc
Manufacturing center
Petroleum
Processing plant
Salt
Steel manufacturing

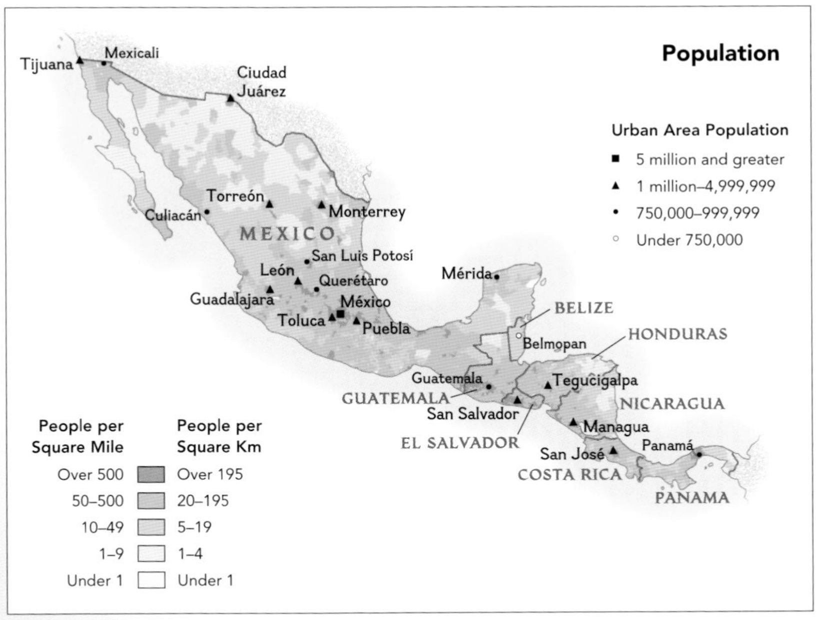

Population
Tijuana
Mexicali
Ciudad Juárez
Urban Area Population
5 million and greater
1 million–4,999,999
750,000–999,999
Under 750,000
Torreón
Culiacán
Monterrey
MEXICO
San Luis Potosí
León
Querétaro
Mérida
Guadalajara
México
Toluca
Puebla
BELIZE
Belmopan
HONDURAS
Guatemala
Tegucigalpa
GUATEMALA
San Salvador
NICARAGUA
Managua
EL SALVADOR
San José
Panamá
COSTA RICA
PANAMA
People per Square Mile
Over 500
50–500
10–49
1–9
Under 1
People per Square Km
Over 195
20–195
5–19
1–4
Under 1

GULF OF MEXICO
TROPIC OF CANCER
Madre
90°
20°
80°
10°
30°
Yucatan Channel
Arrecife Alacránes
Cayo Arenas
Campeche Bank
Bajo Nuevo
Arrecifes Triángulos
Dzibilchaltún
El Ceibo
Hunucmá
Motul
Izamal
El Cuyo
Cancún
Isla Mujeres
Tizimín
Puerto Morelos
Mérida
Valladolid
Cozumel
Halachó
Ticul
Tekax
Chichén Itzá
I. Cozumel
Uxmal
YUCATÁN
Vigía Chico
Campeche
Hopelchén
Felipe Carrillo Puerto
Laguna de Términos
Ciudad del Carmen
Champotón
PENINSULA
Chetumal
Veracruz
Tres Zapotes
San Andrés Tuxtla
Coatzacoalcos
Paraíso
Frontera
Escárcego
Corozal
Ambergris Cay
Jonuta
Balancán
Monclava
Orange Walk
Islas Santanilla Honduras
Jáltipan
La Venta
Villahermosa
Belmopan
Belize City
Minatitlán
Tenosique
El Ceibo
BELIZE
Istmo de Tehuantepec
Flores
Dangriga
La Libertad
Golfo de Honduras
Tuxtla Gutiérrez
PETÉN
Punta Gorda
Is. de la Bahía
San Cristóbal de Las Casas
San Luis
Puerto Barrios
Trujillo
Brus Laguna
Laguna de Caratasca
Juchitán
Presa de la Angostura
Lívingston
Puerto Cortés
La Ceiba
MOSQUITIA
Tonalá
GUATEMALA
San Pedro Sula
Patuca
Cabo Gracias a Dios
Tehuantepec
Pijijiapan
Cobán
HONDURAS
Coco
Cayos Miskitos
Golfo de Tehuantepec
Escuintla
Negro
Zacapa
Chiquimula
Santa Rosa
Comayagua
Juticalpa
Dákura
Huehuetenango
Sang Sang
Puerto Cabezas
Tapachula
Ciudad Hidalgo
GUATEMALA
Tegucigalpa
Bocay
I. de Providencia Colombia
Quetzaltenango
Mazatenango
Santa Ana
Kilambe 1750
3976 Vol. de Acatenango
Jutiapa
Sensuntepeque
Kuikuina
Escuintla
San José
Sonsonate
Estelí
Matagalpa
I. de San Andrés Colombia
San Salvador
Nacaome
EL SALVADOR
Choluteca
NICARAGUA
Laguna de Perlas
San Miguel
Golfo de Fonseca
Boaco
Islas del Maíz
Costa de Miskitos
Chinandega
León
Masaya
Bluefields
Juigalpa
Punta Mono
L. de Managua
MANAGUA
Granada
1610
Lago de Nicaragua
719
Rivas
San Juan del Norte
La Cruz
San Juan del Sur
Cabo Santa Elena
Cañas
Quesada
Liberia
Volcán Irazú 3432
Puerto Limón
COSTA RICA
Puntarenas
Cartago
Sixaola
Almirante
Bocas del Toro
Golfo de los Mosquitos
PANAMA CANAL
Portobelo
Punta San Blas
Arch. de San Blas
Lago Bayano
Península de Nicoya
Alajuela
San José
Cerro Chirripó 3819
Volcán Barú 3475
Colón
Panamá
Puerto Obaldía
Penonomé
I. del Rey
La Palma
1875
Yaviza
Ciudad Cortés
Golfito
Península de Osa
Puerto Jiménez
Golfo Dulce
Puerto Armuelles
Punta Burica
David
Santiago
Chitré
Golfo de Panamá
Golfo de Chiriquí
Las Tablas
Isla de Coiba
416
Península de Azuero
PANAMA
CARIBBEAN SEA
PACIFIC OCEAN
COLOMBIA
I. del Coco Costa Rica
Azimuthal Equidistant Projection
SCALE 1:10,006,000
1 CENTIMETER = 100 KILOMETERS; 1 INCH = 158 MILES
0 100 200 300 400 KILOMETERS
0 100 200 300 400 STATUTE MILES

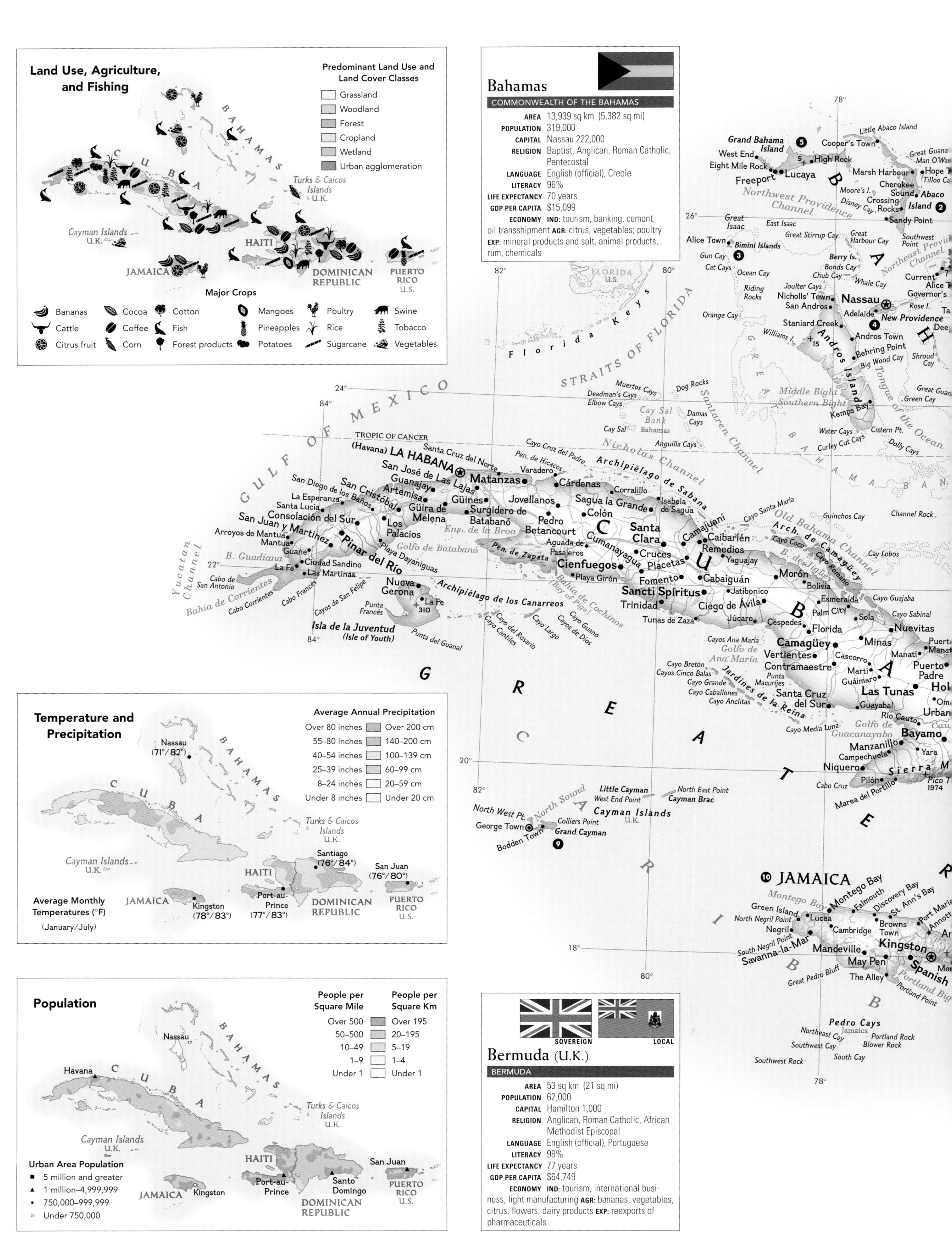
Land Use, Agriculture, and Fishing
Predominant Land Use and Land Cover Classes
Grassland
Woodland
Forest
Cropland
Wetland
Urban agglomeration
Major Crops
Bananas
Cocoa
Cotton
Mangoes
Poultry
Swine
Cattle
Coffee
Fish
Pineapples
Rice
Tobacco
Citrus fruit
Corn
Forest products
Potatoes
Sugarcane
Vegetables
Temperature and Precipitation
Average Annual Precipitation
Over 80 inches / Over 200 cm
55–80 inches / 140–200 cm
40–54 inches / 100–139 cm
25–39 inches / 60–99 cm
8–24 inches / 20–59 cm
Under 8 inches / Under 20 cm
Average Monthly Temperatures (°F) (January/July)
Nassau (71°/82°)
Santiago (76°/84°)
San Juan (76°/80°)
Kingston (78°/83°)
Port-au-Prince (77°/83°)
Population
People per Square Mile / People per Square Km
Over 500 / Over 195
50–500 / 20–195
10–49 / 5–19
1–9 / 1–4
Under 1 / Under 1
Urban Area Population
5 million and greater
1 million–4,999,999
750,000–999,999
Under 750,000
BAHAMAS
CUBA
HAITI
DOMINICAN REPUBLIC
PUERTO RICO U.S.
JAMAICA
Cayman Islands U.K.
Turks & Caicos Islands U.K.
GULF OF MEXICO
STRAITS OF FLORIDA
TROPIC OF CANCER
(Havana) LA HABANA
Isla de la Juventud (Isle of Youth)
Cayman Islands U.K.
JAMAICA
Kingston
Nassau
Grand Bahama Island
Andros Island
Yucatan Channel
Old Bahama Channel
Nicholas Channel
Northwest Providence Channel
GREATER

Bahamas

COMMONWEALTH OF THE BAHAMAS

AREA 13,939 sq km (5,382 sq mi)
POPULATION 319,000
CAPITAL Nassau 222,000
RELIGION Baptist, Anglican, Roman Catholic, Pentecostal
LANGUAGE English (official), Creole
LITERACY 96%
LIFE EXPECTANCY 70 years
GDP PER CAPITA $15,099
ECONOMY **IND:** tourism, banking, cement, oil transshipment **AGR:** citrus, vegetables; poultry **EXP:** mineral products and salt, animal products, rum, chemicals

Bermuda (U.K.)

SOVEREIGN · LOCAL

BERMUDA

AREA 53 sq km (21 sq mi)
POPULATION 62,000
CAPITAL Hamilton 1,000
RELIGION Anglican, Roman Catholic, African Methodist Episcopal
LANGUAGE English (official), Portuguese
LITERACY 98%
LIFE EXPECTANCY 77 years
GDP PER CAPITA $64,749
ECONOMY **IND:** tourism, international business, light manufacturing **AGR:** bananas, vegetables, citrus, flowers; dairy products **EXP:** reexports of pharmaceuticals

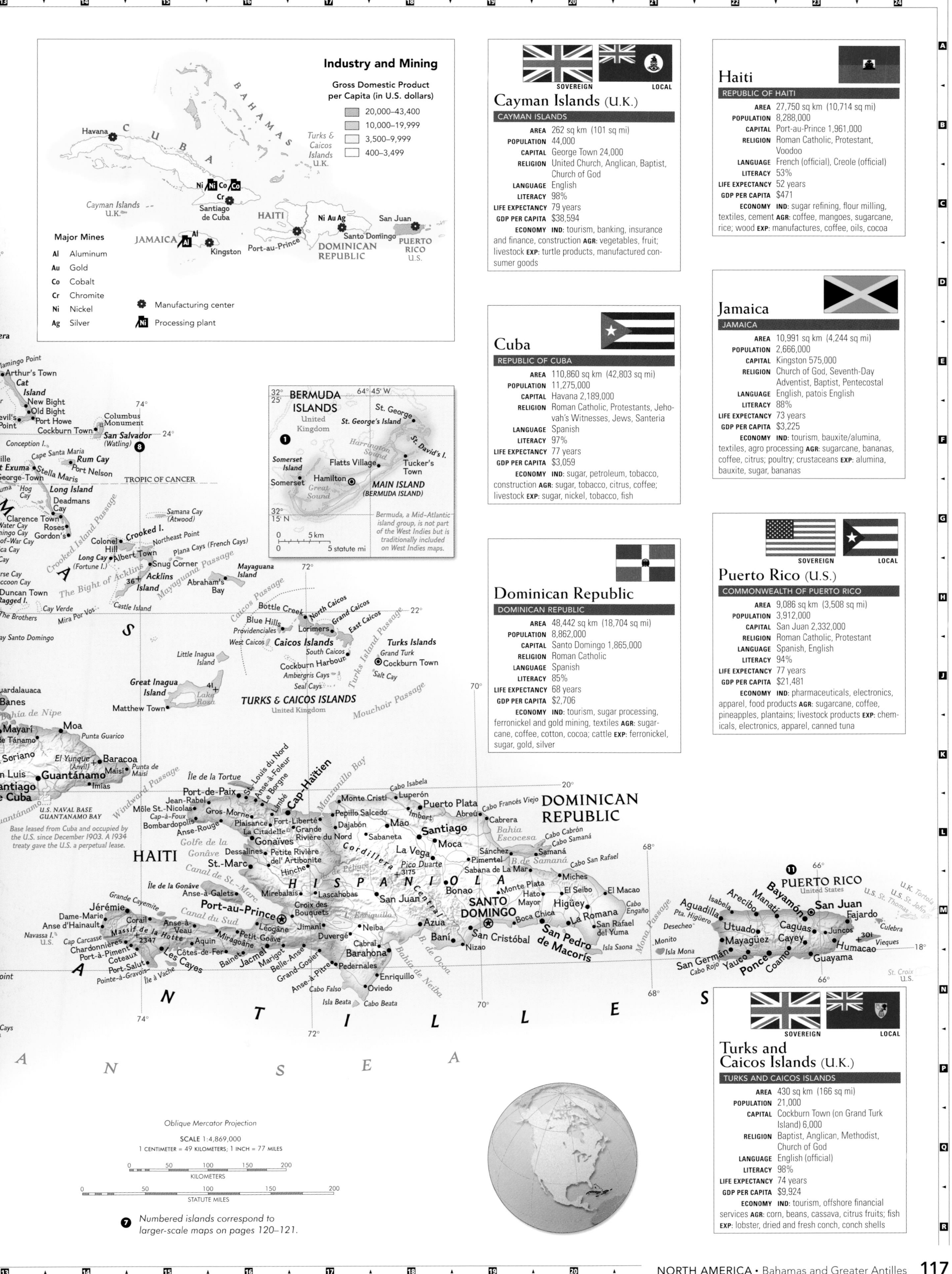

Industry and Mining
Gross Domestic Product per Capita (in U.S. dollars)
20,000–43,400
10,000–19,999
3,500–9,999
400–3,499
Major Mines
Al Aluminum
Au Gold
Co Cobalt
Cr Chromite
Ni Nickel
Ag Silver
Manufacturing center
Processing plant
BERMUDA ISLANDS
United Kingdom
Bermuda, a Mid-Atlantic island group, is not part of the West Indies but is traditionally included on West Indies maps.
TURKS & CAICOS ISLANDS
United Kingdom
U.S. NAVAL BASE GUANTANAMO BAY
Base leased from Cuba and occupied by the U.S. since December 1903. A 1934 treaty gave the U.S. a perpetual lease.
HAITI
DOMINICAN REPUBLIC
PUERTO RICO
United States
HISPANIOLA
ANTILLES
CARIBBEAN SEA
Oblique Mercator Projection
SCALE 1:4,869,000
1 CENTIMETER = 49 KILOMETERS; 1 INCH = 77 MILES
KILOMETERS
STATUTE MILES
Numbered islands correspond to larger-scale maps on pages 120–121.

Cayman Islands (U.K.)

SOVEREIGN LOCAL

CAYMAN ISLANDS

AREA 262 sq km (101 sq mi)
POPULATION 44,000
CAPITAL George Town 24,000
RELIGION United Church, Anglican, Baptist, Church of God
LANGUAGE English
LITERACY 98%
LIFE EXPECTANCY 79 years
GDP PER CAPITA $38,594
ECONOMY **IND:** tourism, banking, insurance and finance, construction **AGR:** vegetables, fruit; livestock **EXP:** turtle products, manufactured consumer goods

Haiti

REPUBLIC OF HAITI

AREA 27,750 sq km (10,714 sq mi)
POPULATION 8,288,000
CAPITAL Port-au-Prince 1,961,000
RELIGION Roman Catholic, Protestant, Voodoo
LANGUAGE French (official), Creole (official)
LITERACY 53%
LIFE EXPECTANCY 52 years
GDP PER CAPITA $471
ECONOMY **IND:** sugar refining, flour milling, textiles, cement **AGR:** coffee, mangoes, sugarcane, rice; wood **EXP:** manufactures, coffee, oils, cocoa

Cuba

REPUBLIC OF CUBA

AREA 110,860 sq km (42,803 sq mi)
POPULATION 11,275,000
CAPITAL Havana 2,189,000
RELIGION Roman Catholic, Protestants, Jehovah's Witnesses, Jews, Santeria
LANGUAGE Spanish
LITERACY 97%
LIFE EXPECTANCY 77 years
GDP PER CAPITA $3,059
ECONOMY **IND:** sugar, petroleum, tobacco, construction **AGR:** sugar, tobacco, citrus, coffee; livestock **EXP:** sugar, nickel, tobacco, fish

Jamaica

JAMAICA

AREA 10,991 sq km (4,244 sq mi)
POPULATION 2,666,000
CAPITAL Kingston 575,000
RELIGION Church of God, Seventh-Day Adventist, Baptist, Pentecostal
LANGUAGE English, patois English
LITERACY 88%
LIFE EXPECTANCY 73 years
GDP PER CAPITA $3,225
ECONOMY **IND:** tourism, bauxite/alumina, textiles, agro processing **AGR:** sugarcane, bananas, coffee, citrus; poultry; crustaceans **EXP:** alumina, bauxite, sugar, bananas

Dominican Republic

DOMINICAN REPUBLIC

AREA 48,442 sq km (18,704 sq mi)
POPULATION 8,862,000
CAPITAL Santo Domingo 1,865,000
RELIGION Roman Catholic
LANGUAGE Spanish
LITERACY 85%
LIFE EXPECTANCY 68 years
GDP PER CAPITA $2,706
ECONOMY **IND:** tourism, sugar processing, ferronickel and gold mining, textiles **AGR:** sugarcane, coffee, cotton, cocoa; cattle **EXP:** ferronickel, sugar, gold, silver

Puerto Rico (U.S.)

SOVEREIGN LOCAL

COMMONWEALTH OF PUERTO RICO

AREA 9,086 sq km (3,508 sq mi)
POPULATION 3,912,000
CAPITAL San Juan 2,332,000
RELIGION Roman Catholic, Protestant
LANGUAGE Spanish, English
LITERACY 94%
LIFE EXPECTANCY 77 years
GDP PER CAPITA $21,481
ECONOMY **IND:** pharmaceuticals, electronics, apparel, food products **AGR:** sugarcane, coffee, pineapples, plantains; livestock products **EXP:** chemicals, electronics, apparel, canned tuna

Turks and Caicos Islands (U.K.)

SOVEREIGN LOCAL

TURKS AND CAICOS ISLANDS

AREA 430 sq km (166 sq mi)
POPULATION 21,000
CAPITAL Cockburn Town (on Grand Turk Island) 6,000
RELIGION Baptist, Anglican, Methodist, Church of God
LANGUAGE English (official)
LITERACY 98%
LIFE EXPECTANCY 74 years
GDP PER CAPITA $9,924
ECONOMY **IND:** tourism, offshore financial services **AGR:** corn, beans, cassava, citrus fruits; fish **EXP:** lobster, dried and fresh conch, conch shells

SOVEREIGN LOCAL

Anguilla (U.K.)

ANGUILLA

AREA 96 sq km (37 sq mi)
POPULATION 13,000
CAPITAL The Valley 1,000
RELIGION Anglican, Methodist, other Protestant, Roman Catholic
LANGUAGE English (official)
LITERACY 95%
LIFE EXPECTANCY 78 years
GDP PER CAPITA $10,811
ECONOMY **IND:** tourism, boat building, offshore financial services **AGR:** small quantities of tobacco, vegetables; cattle raising **EXP:** lobster, fish, livestock, salt

Antigua and Barbuda

ANTIGUA AND BARBUDA

AREA 442 sq km (171 sq mi)
POPULATION 80,000
CAPITAL St. John's 28,000
RELIGION Anglican, other Protestant, Roman Catholic
LANGUAGE English (official), local dialects
LITERACY 89%
LIFE EXPECTANCY 71 years
GDP PER CAPITA $8,595
ECONOMY **IND:** tourism, construction, light manufacturing (clothing, alcohol, household appliances) **AGR:** cotton, fruits, vegetables, bananas; livestock **EXP:** petroleum products, manufactures, machinery and transport equipment, food and live animals

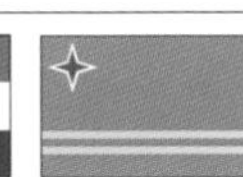

SOVEREIGN LOCAL

Aruba (Netherlands)

ARUBA

AREA 193 sq km (75 sq mi)
POPULATION 97,000
CAPITAL Oranjestad 29,000
RELIGION Roman Catholic, Protestant
LANGUAGE Dutch (official), Papiamento, English, Spanish
LITERACY 97%
LIFE EXPECTANCY 79 years
GDP PER CAPITA $21,131
ECONOMY **IND:** tourism, transshipment facilities, oil refining **AGR:** aloes; livestock; fish **EXP:** live animals and animal products, art and collectibles, machinery and electrical equipment, transport equipment

Barbados

BARBADOS

AREA 430 sq km (166 sq mi)
POPULATION 258,000
CAPITAL Bridgetown 140,000
RELIGION Anglican, Pentecostal, Methodist
LANGUAGE English
LITERACY 100%
LIFE EXPECTANCY 72 years
GDP PER CAPITA $10,538
ECONOMY **IND:** tourism, sugar, light manufacturing, component assembly for export **AGR:** sugarcane, vegetables, cotton **EXP:** sugar and molasses, rum, other foods and beverages, chemicals

SOVEREIGN LOCAL

British Virgin Islands (U.K.)

BRITISH VIRGIN ISLANDS

AREA 153 sq km (59 sq mi)
POPULATION 22,000
CAPITAL Road Town 12,000
RELIGION Protestant, Roman Catholic
LANGUAGE English (official)
LITERACY 98%
LIFE EXPECTANCY 74 years
GDP PER CAPITA $43,366
ECONOMY **IND:** tourism, light industry, construction, rum **AGR:** fruits, vegetables; livestock; fish **EXP:** rum, fresh fish, fruits, animals

Dominica

COMMONWEALTH OF DOMINICA

AREA 751 sq km (290 sq mi)
POPULATION 70,000
CAPITAL Roseau 27,000
RELIGION Roman Catholic, Protestant
LANGUAGE English (official), French patois
LITERACY 94%
LIFE EXPECTANCY 74 years
GDP PER CAPITA $3,466
ECONOMY **IND:** soap, coconut oil, tourism, copra **AGR:** bananas, citrus, mangoes, root crops; forest and fishery potential not exploited **EXP:** bananas, soap, bay oil, vegetables

Grenada

GRENADA

AREA 344 sq km (133 sq mi)
POPULATION 101,000
CAPITAL St. George's 33,000
RELIGION Roman Catholic, Anglican, other Protestant
LANGUAGE English (official), French patois
LITERACY 98%
LIFE EXPECTANCY 71 years
GDP PER CAPITA $3,872
ECONOMY **IND:** food and beverages, textiles, light assembly operations, tourism **AGR:** bananas, cocoa, nutmeg, mace **EXP:** bananas, cocoa, nutmeg, fruit and vegetables

Guadeloupe (France)

OVERSEAS DEPARTMENT OF FRANCE

AREA 1,705 sq km (658 sq mi)
POPULATION 450,000
CAPITAL Basse-Terre 11,000
RELIGION Roman Catholic
LANGUAGE French (official)
LITERACY 90%
LIFE EXPECTANCY 78 years
GDP PER CAPITA $7,900
ECONOMY **IND:** construction, cement, rum, sugar **AGR:** bananas, sugarcane, tropical fruits and vegetables; cattle **EXP:** bananas, sugar, rum

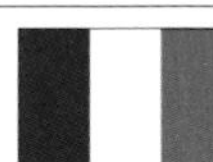

Martinique (France)

OVERSEAS DEPARTMENT OF FRANCE

AREA 1,100 sq km (425 sq mi)
POPULATION 397,000
CAPITAL Fort-de-France 93,000
RELIGION Roman Catholic, Protestant
LANGUAGE French, Creole patois
LITERACY 98%
LIFE EXPECTANCY 79 years
GDP PER CAPITA $14,400
ECONOMY **IND:** construction, rum, cement, oil refining **AGR:** pineapples, avocados, bananas, flowers **EXP:** refined petroleum products, bananas, rum, pineapples

SOVEREIGN LOCAL

Montserrat (U.K.)

MONTSERRAT

AREA 102 sq km (39 sq mi)
POPULATION 5,000
CAPITAL Plymouth (abandoned)
RELIGION Anglican, Methodist, Roman Catholic, Pentecostal, Seventh-Day Adventist, other Christian denominations
LANGUAGE English
LITERACY 97%
LIFE EXPECTANCY 79 years
GDP PER CAPITA $12,067
ECONOMY **IND:** tourism, rum, textiles, electronic appliances **AGR:** cabbages, carrots, cucumbers, tomatoes; livestock products **EXP:** electronic components, plastic bags, apparel, hot peppers

SOVEREIGN LOCAL

Netherlands Antilles (Neth.)

NETHERLANDS ANTILLES

AREA 800 sq km (309 sq mi)
POPULATION 187,000
CAPITAL Willemstad 134,000
RELIGION Roman Catholic
LANGUAGE Papiamento, English, Dutch (official), Spanish
LITERACY 97%
LIFE EXPECTANCY 76 years
GDP PER CAPITA $17,164
ECONOMY **IND:** tourism, petroleum refining, petroleum transshipment facilities, light manufacturing **AGR:** aloes, sorghum, peanuts, vegetables **EXP:** petroleum products

St. Kitts and Nevis

FEDERATION OF SAINT KITTS AND NEVIS

AREA 269 sq km (104 sq mi)
POPULATION 48,000
CAPITAL Basseterre 13,000
RELIGION Anglican, other Protestant, Roman Catholic
LANGUAGE English
LITERACY 97%
LIFE EXPECTANCY 70 years
GDP PER CAPITA $9,269
ECONOMY **IND:** sugar processing, tourism, cotton, salt **AGR:** sugarcane, rice, yams, vegetables; fish **EXP:** machinery, food, electronics, beverages

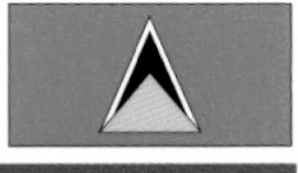

St. Lucia

SAINT LUCIA

AREA 616 sq km (238 sq mi)
POPULATION 163,000
CAPITAL Castries 14,000
RELIGION Roman Catholic, Seventh-Day Adventist, Pentecostal
LANGUAGE English (official), French patois
LITERACY 90%
LIFE EXPECTANCY 74 years
GDP PER CAPITA $4,506
ECONOMY **IND:** clothing, assembly of electronic components, beverages, corrugated cardboard boxes **AGR:** bananas, coconuts, vegetables, citrus **EXP:** bananas, clothing, cocoa, vegetables

St. Vincent and the Grenadines

SAINT VINCENT AND THE GRENADINES

AREA 389 sq km (150 sq mi)
POPULATION 111,000
CAPITAL Kingstown 29,000
RELIGION Anglican, Methodist, Roman Catholic
LANGUAGE English, French patois
LITERACY 96%
LIFE EXPECTANCY 72 years
GDP PER CAPITA $3,357
ECONOMY **IND:** food processing, cement, furniture, clothing **AGR:** bananas, coconuts, sweet potatoes, spices; cattle; fish **EXP:** bananas, eddoes and dasheen (taro), arrowroot starch, tennis racquets

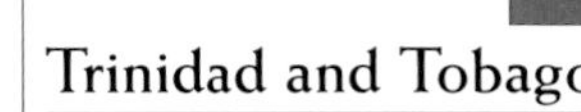

Trinidad and Tobago

REPUBLIC OF TRINIDAD AND TOBAGO

AREA 5,128 sq km (1,980 sq mi)
POPULATION 1,305,000
CAPITAL Port-of-Spain 55,000
RELIGION Roman Catholic, Hindu, Anglican, Baptist, Pentecostal, Muslim
LANGUAGE English (official), Hindi, French, Spanish, Chinese
LITERACY 99%
LIFE EXPECTANCY 71 years
GDP PER CAPITA $8,772
ECONOMY **IND:** petroleum, chemicals, tourism, food processing **AGR:** cocoa, rice, citrus, coffee; poultry **EXP:** petroleum and petroleum products, chemicals, steel products, fertilizer

SOVEREIGN LOCAL

Virgin Islands (U.S.)

UNITED STATES VIRGIN ISLANDS

AREA 386 sq km (149 sq mi)
POPULATION 109,000
CAPITAL Charlotte Amalie 51,000
RELIGION Baptist, Roman Catholic, Episcopalian
LANGUAGE English, Spanish or Spanish Creole, French or French Creole
LITERACY NA
LIFE EXPECTANCY 79 years
GDP PER CAPITA $17,200
ECONOMY **IND:** tourism, petroleum refining, watch assembly, rum distilling **AGR:** fruit, vegetables, sorghum; Senepol cattle **EXP:** refined petroleum products

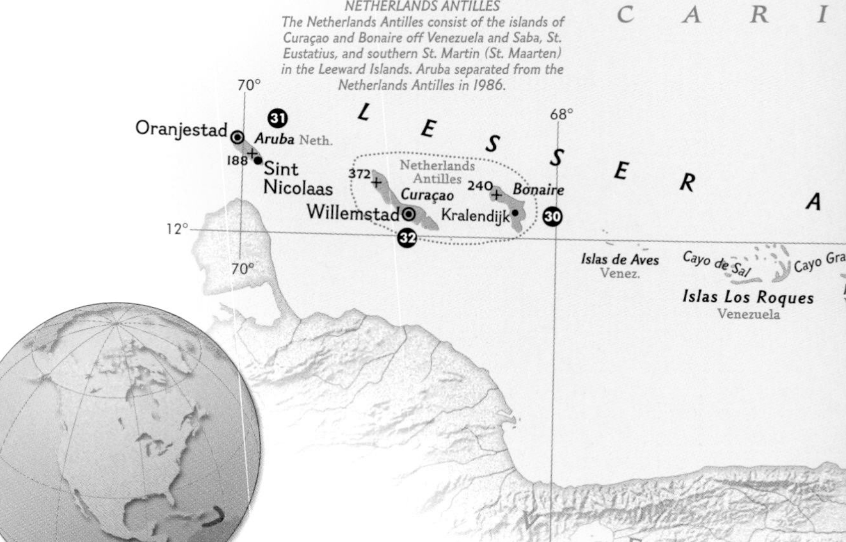
NETHERLANDS ANTILLES
The Netherlands Antilles consist of the islands of Curaçao and Bonaire off Venezuela and Saba, St. Eustatius, and southern St. Martin (St. Maarten) in the Leeward Islands. Aruba separated from the Netherlands Antilles in 1986.
C A R I
L E S S E R A
Oranjestad
31
Aruba Neth.
188
Sint Nicolaas
372
Netherlands Antilles
Curaçao
240
Bonaire
Willemstad
Kralendijk
30
32
70°
68°
12°
10°
Islas de Aves Venez.
Cayo de Sal
Cayo Gran
Islas Los Roques Venezuela
Oblique Mercator Projection

SCALE 1:5,237,000
1 CENTIMETER = 52 KILOMETERS; 1 INCH = 83 MILES

0 50 100 150 200 KILOMETERS

0 50 100 150 200 STATUTE MILES

21 *Numbered islands correspond to larger-scale maps on pages 120–121.*

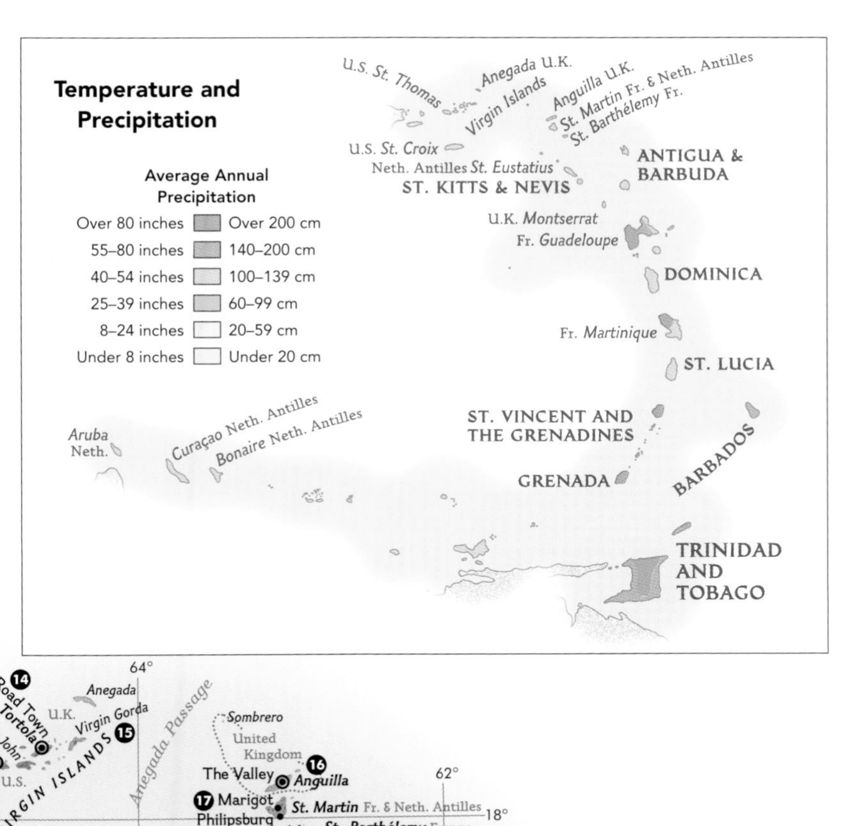

Temperature and Precipitation
Average Annual Precipitation
Over 80 inches Over 200 cm
55–80 inches 140–200 cm
40–54 inches 100–139 cm
25–39 inches 60–99 cm
8–24 inches 20–59 cm
Under 8 inches Under 20 cm
U.S. St. Thomas
Anegada U.K.
Virgin Islands
Anguilla U.K.
St. Martin Fr. & Neth. Antilles
St. Barthélemy Fr.
U.S. St. Croix
Neth. Antilles St. Eustatius
ST. KITTS & NEVIS
ANTIGUA & BARBUDA
U.K. Montserrat
Fr. Guadeloupe
DOMINICA
Fr. Martinique
ST. LUCIA
ST. VINCENT AND THE GRENADINES
GRENADA
BARBADOS
Aruba Neth.
Curaçao Neth. Antilles
Bonaire Neth. Antilles
TRINIDAD AND TOBAGO

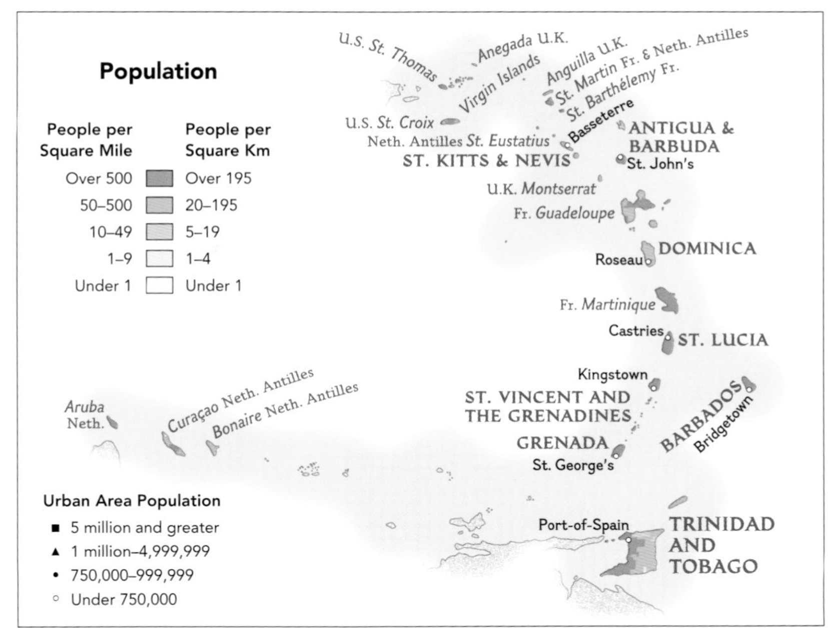

Population
People per Square Mile
Over 500
50–500
10–49
1–9
Under 1
People per Square Km
Over 195
20–195
5–19
1–4
Under 1
Urban Area Population
■ 5 million and greater
▲ 1 million–4,999,999
• 750,000–999,999
○ Under 750,000
Basseterre
St. John's
Roseau
Castries
Kingstown
Bridgetown
St. George's
Port-of-Spain

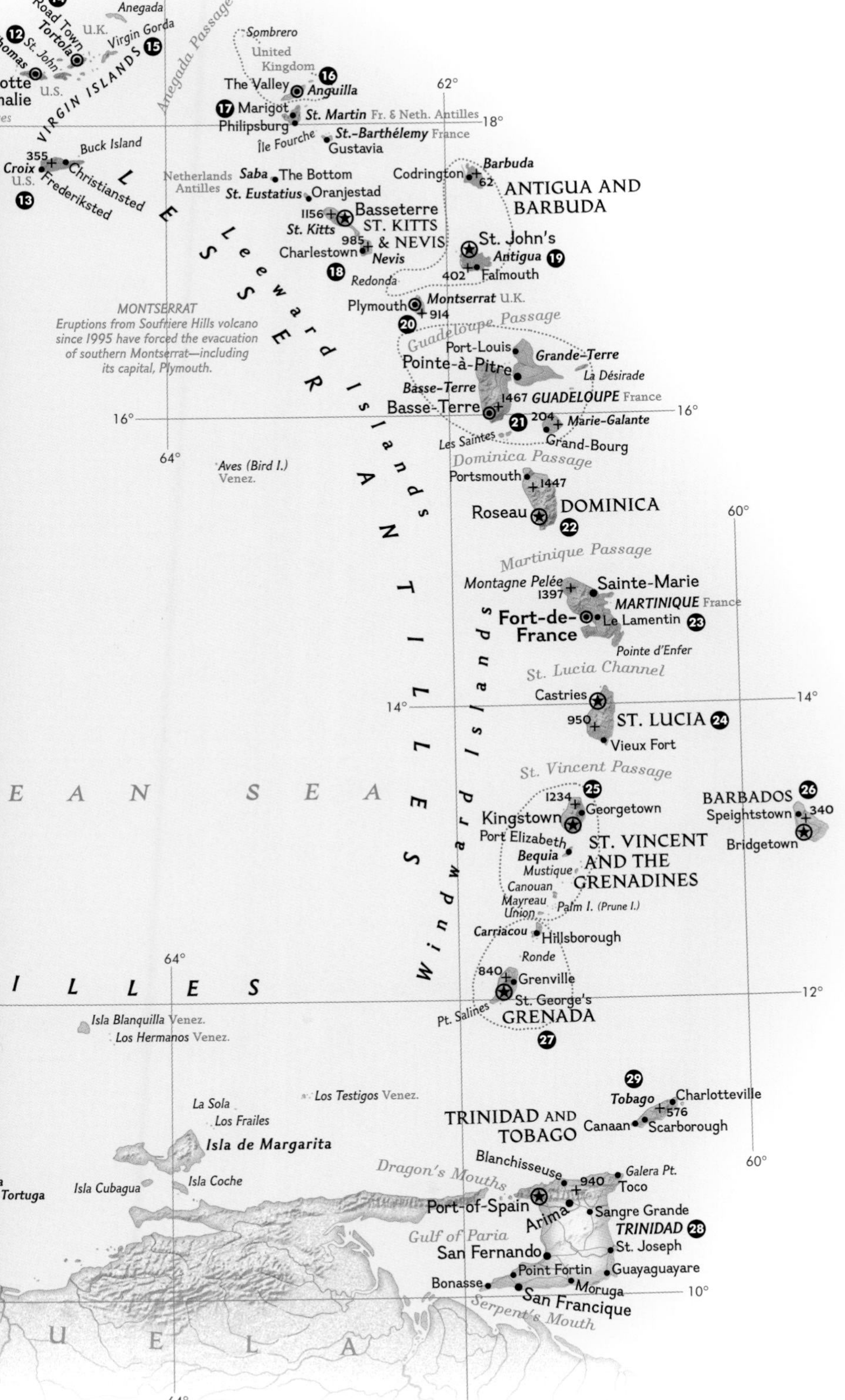

Road Town
Tortola
St. John
St. Thomas
Anegada
Virgin Gorda
U.K.
VIRGIN ISLANDS
Anegada Passage
Sombrero
United Kingdom
The Valley
Anguilla
Marigot
Philipsburg
St. Martin Fr. & Neth. Antilles
Île Fourche
St.-Barthélemy France
Gustavia
Buck Island
Christiansted
Frederiksted
Netherlands Antilles
Saba
The Bottom
St. Eustatius
Oranjestad
Barbuda
Codrington
ANTIGUA AND BARBUDA
Basseterre
ST. KITTS & NEVIS
St. Kitts
Charlestown
Nevis
Redonda
St. John's
Antigua
Falmouth
Plymouth
Montserrat U.K.
MONTSERRAT
Eruptions from Soufrière Hills volcano since 1995 have forced the evacuation of southern Montserrat—including its capital, Plymouth.
Leeward Islands
LESSER ANTILLES
Guadeloupe Passage
Port-Louis
Grande-Terre
Pointe-à-Pitre
La Désirade
Basse-Terre
GUADELOUPE France
Marie-Galante
Les Saintes
Grand-Bourg
Aves (Bird I.) Venez.
Dominica Passage
Portsmouth
Roseau
DOMINICA
Martinique Passage
Montagne Pelée
Sainte-Marie
MARTINIQUE France
Fort-de-France
Le Lamentin
Pointe d'Enfer
St. Lucia Channel
Castries
ST. LUCIA
Vieux Fort
St. Vincent Passage
Windward Islands
CARIBBEAN SEA
Kingstown
Georgetown
Port Elizabeth
Bequia
Mustique
Canouan
Mayreau
Union
Palm I. (Prune I.)
ST. VINCENT AND THE GRENADINES
BARBADOS
Speightstown
Bridgetown
Carriacou
Hillsborough
Ronde
Grenville
St. George's
Pt. Salines
GRENADA
Isla Blanquilla Venez.
Los Hermanos Venez.
Los Testigos Venez.
La Sola
Los Frailes
Isla de Margarita
Isla Coche
Isla Cubagua
La Tortuga
Tobago
Charlotteville
Scarborough
Canaan
TRINIDAD AND TOBAGO
Dragon's Mouths
Blanchisseuse
Galera Pt.
Toco
Port-of-Spain
Arima
Sangre Grande
TRINIDAD
Gulf of Paria
San Fernando
St. Joseph
Point Fortin
Guayaguayare
Bonasse
Moruga
San Francique
Serpent's Mouth
VENEZUELA

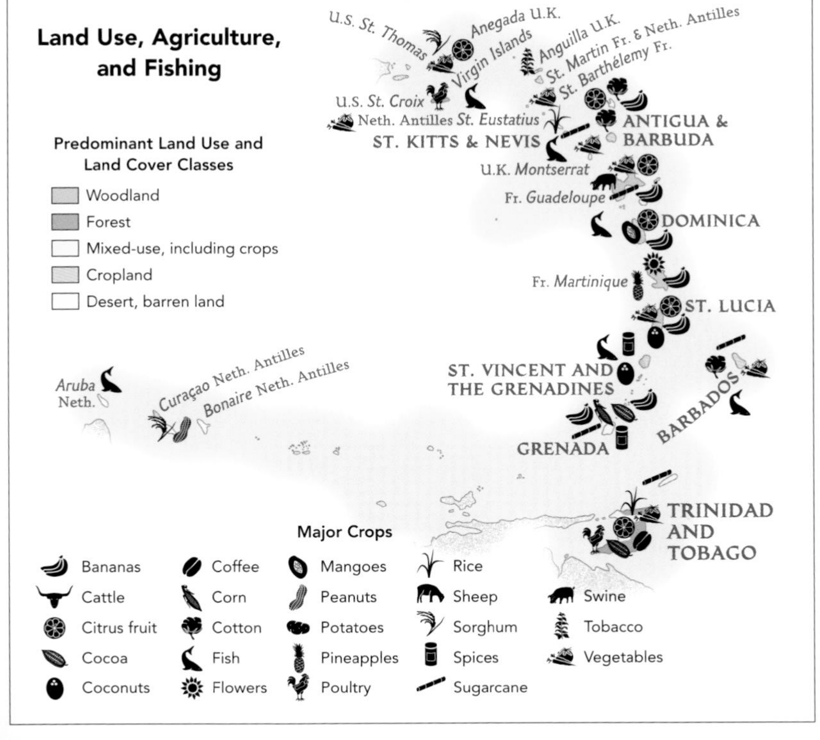

Land Use, Agriculture, and Fishing
Predominant Land Use and Land Cover Classes
Woodland
Forest
Mixed-use, including crops
Cropland
Desert, barren land
Major Crops
Bananas
Cattle
Citrus fruit
Cocoa
Coconuts
Coffee
Corn
Cotton
Fish
Flowers
Mangoes
Peanuts
Potatoes
Pineapples
Poultry
Rice
Sheep
Sorghum
Spices
Sugarcane
Swine
Tobacco
Vegetables

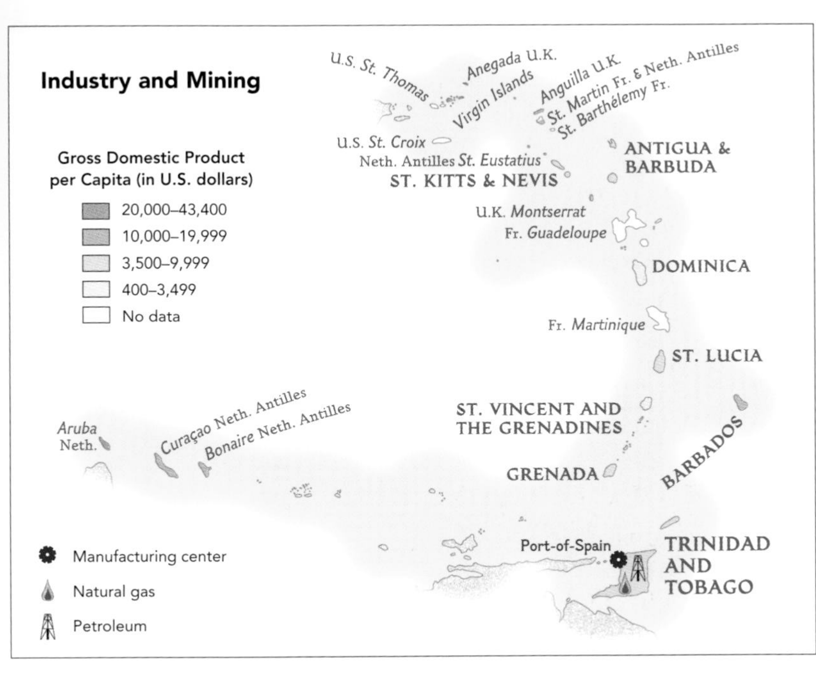

Industry and Mining
Gross Domestic Product per Capita (in U.S. dollars)
20,000–43,400
10,000–19,999
3,500–9,999
400–3,499
No data
Manufacturing center
Natural gas
Petroleum
Port-of-Spain

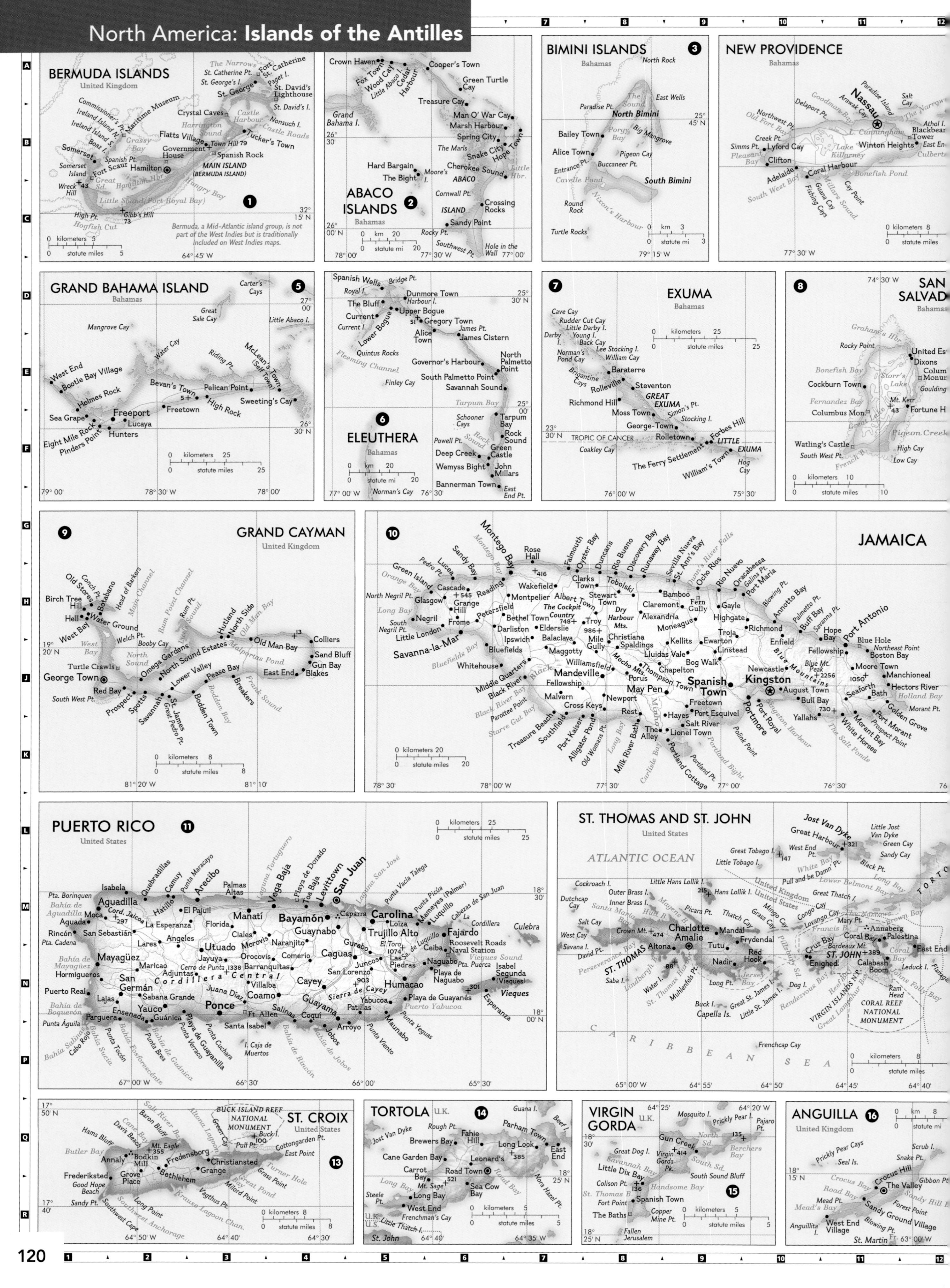

BERMUDA ISLANDS
United Kingdom
St. Catherine Pt.
Fort St. Catherine
St. George's I.
St. George
St. David's Lighthouse
St. David's I.
Crystal Caves
Castle Harbour
Nonsuch I.
Castle Roads
Tucker's Town
Flatts Village
Harrington Sound
Government House
Town Hill 79
Spanish Rock
Commissioner's Pt.
Ireland Island N.
Ireland Island S.
Maritime Museum
Boaz I.
Somerset
Spanish Pt.
Fort Scaur
Hamilton
Somerset Island
MAIN ISLAND (BERMUDA ISLAND)
Wreck Hill
Great Sd.
Little Sound
Port Royal Bay
Hungry Bay
High Pt.
Gibb's Hill
Hogfish Cut
Bermuda, a Mid-Atlantic island group, is not part of the West Indies but is traditionally included on West Indies maps.
ABACO ISLANDS
Bahamas
Crown Haven
Fox Town
Wood Cay
Little Abaco I.
Cedar Harbour
Cooper's Town
Green Turtle Cay
Treasure Cay
Grand Bahama I.
Man O' War Cay
Marsh Harbour
Spring City
The Marls
Snake City
Hope Town
Hard Bargain
Moore's I.
The Bight
Cherokee Sound
Little Hbr.
ABACO
Cornwall Pt.
Crossing Rocks
ISLAND
Sandy Point
Rocky Pt.
Southwest Pt.
Hole in the Wall
BIMINI ISLANDS
Bahamas
North Rock
East Wells
Paradise Pt.
North Bimini
Bailey Town
Porgy Bay
Big Mangrove
Alice Town
Pigeon Cay
Entrance Pt.
Buccaneer Pt.
South Bimini
Round Rock
Nixon's Harbour
Turtle Rocks
NEW PROVIDENCE
Bahamas
Nassau
Paradise Island
Salt Cay
Delaport Pt.
Goodman's Bay
Arawak Cay
Northwest Pt.
Old Fort Bay
Athol I.
Blackbeard Tower
Creek Pt.
Simms Pt.
Lyford Cay
Lake Killarney
Winton Heights
East End
Pleasant Bay
Clifton
Adelaide
Coral Harbour
Bonefish Pond
South West Bay
Guana Cay
Fishing Cays
Cay Point
GRAND BAHAMA ISLAND
Bahamas
Carter's Cays
Great Sale Cay
Mangrove Cay
Little Abaco I.
Water Cay
Riding Pt.
McLean's Town (Self Town)
West End
Bootle Bay Village
Bevan's Town
Pelican Point
Holmes Rock
Freeport
Freetown
High Rock
Sweeting's Cay
Sea Grape
Lucaya
Eight Mile Rock
Pinders Point
Hunters
ELEUTHERA
Bahamas
Spanish Wells
Bridge Pt.
Royal I.
Dunmore Town
Harbour I.
The Bluff
Upper Bogue
Current
Current I.
Lower Bogue
Gregory Town
Alice Town
James Pt.
James Cistern
Quintus Rocks
Fleeming Channel
Governor's Harbour
North Palmetto Point
Finley Cay
South Palmetto Point
Savannah Sound
Tarpum Bay
Schooner Cays
Rock Sound
Powell Pt.
Deep Creek
Green Castle
Wemyss Bight
John Millars
Bannerman Town
East End Pt.
Norman's Cay
EXUMA
Bahamas
Cave Cay
Rudder Cut Cay
Little Darby I.
Darby I.
Young I.
Back Cay
Lee Stocking I.
Norman's Pond Cay
William Cay
Brigantine Cays
Barraterre
Rolleville
Steventon
GREAT EXUMA
Richmond Hill
Simon's Pt.
Moss Town
Stocking I.
George Town
TROPIC OF CANCER
Rolletown
Forbes Hill
Coakley Cay
LITTLE EXUMA
The Ferry Settlement
William's Town
Hog Cay
SAN SALVADOR
Bahamas
Graham's Hbr.
Rocky Point
United Estates
Dixons
Columbus Monument
Bonefish Bay
Storr's Lake
Cockburn Town
Goulding
Fernandez Bay
Mt. Kerr
Columbus Mon.
Great Lake
Fortune Hill
Pigeon Creek
Watling's Castle
High Cay
South West Pt.
French Bay
Low Cay
GRAND CAYMAN
United Kingdom
Conch Pt.
Old Stores
Botabano
Head of Barkers
Main Channel
Rum Point Channel
Rum Pt.
Birch Tree Hill
Hell
Water Ground
North Sound
West Bay
Welch Pt.
Booby Cay
Hutland
North Side
Old Man Bay
Colliers
Omega Gardens
North Sound Estates
Malportas Pond
Sand Bluff
Turtle Crawls
Gun Bay
George Town
Lower Valley
Pease Bay
East End
Blakes
Red Bay
South West Pt.
Prospect
Spotts
Savannah
St. James
Great Pedro Pt.
Bodden Town
Breakers
Frank Sound
JAMAICA
Montego Bay
Rose Hall
Falmouth
Oyster Bay
Duncans
Rio Bueno
Discovery Bay
Runaway Bay
Sevilla Nueva
St. Ann's Bay
Dunn's River Falls
Ocho Rios
Rio Nuevo
Oracabessa
Galina Pt.
Port Maria
Green Island
Pedro Pt.
Lucea
Sandy Bay
Cascade
Reading
Wakefield
Clarks Town
Tobolski
Bamboo
North Negril Pt.
Glasgow
Grange Hill
Montpelier
Albert Town
Stewart Town
The Cockpit Country
Claremont
Fern Gully
Gayle
Blowing Pt.
Annotto Bay
Long Bay
Negril
Petersfield
Bethel Town
Dry Harbour Mts.
Alexandria
Highgate
Buff Bay
South Negril Pt.
Frome
Darliston
Elderslie
Troy
Moneague
Richmond
Hope Bay
Port Antonio
Little London
Ipswich
Balaclava
Christiana
Kellits
Ewarton
Troja
Enfield
Blue Hole
Savanna-la-Mar
Bluefields
Mile Gully
Spaldings
Linstead
Fellowship
Northeast Point
Boston Bay
Bluefields Bay
Maggotty
Lluidas Vale
Blue Mountains
Blue Mt. Peak
Whitehouse
Williamsfield
Bog Walk
Moore Town
Manchioneal
Middle Quarters
Mandeville
Chapelton
Newcastle
Black River
Fellowship
Porus
Spanish Town
Kingston
Hectors River
May Pen
August Town
Seaforth
Bath
Holland Bay
Malvern
Newport
Freetown
Bull Bay
Morant Pt.
Cross Keys
Port Esquivel
Yallahs
Golden Grove
Rest
Hayes
Salt River
Lionel Town
Portmore
Port Royal
Port Morant
Treasure Beach
Southfield
The Alley
Morant Bay
Prospect Point
Port Kaiser
Alligator Pond
Old Womans Pt.
Long Bay
Milk River Bath
Carlisle Bay
Portland Cottage
Portland Pt.
Portland Bight
Polink Point
White Horses
Kingston Harbour
The Salt Ponds
PUERTO RICO
United States
Isabela
Quebradillas
Camuy
Punta Maracayo
Arecibo
Palmas Altas
Laguna Tortuguero
Vega Baja
Playa de Dorado
Toa Baja
Levittown
San Juan
Punta Vacía Talega
Pta. Borinquen
Aguadilla
Hatillo
El Pajuil
Manatí
Bayamón
Caparra
Carolina
Loíza
Punta Picúa
Mameyes (Palmer)
Luquillo
Cabezas de San Juan
Bahía de Aguadilla
Moca
Cord. Jaicoa
Aguada
La Esperanza
Florida
Ciales
Guaynabo
Trujillo Alto
Fajardo
Culebra
Rincón
San Sebastián
Morovis
Naranjito
Gurabo
El Toro
Roosevelt Roads Naval Station
Pta. Cadena
Lares
Angeles
Utuado
Comerío
Caguas
Juncos
Ceiba
Vieques Sound
Bahía de Mayagüez
Mayagüez
Jayuya
Orocovis
Las Piedras
Naguabo
Pta. Puerca
Maricao
Cerro de Punta
Barranquitas
San Lorenzo
Playa de Naguabo
Isabel Segunda (Vieques)
Hormigueros
Adjuntas
Cordillera Central
Villalba
Cayey
Humacao
Vieques
San Germán
Sierra de Cayey
Puerto Real
Lajas
Sabana Grande
Juana Díaz
Coamo
Yabucoa
Playa de Guayanés
Puerto Yabucoa
Esperanza
Bahía de Boquerón
Yauco
Ponce
Guayama
Patillas
Ensenada
Guánica
Ft. Allen
Salinas
Coquí
Punta Águila
Parguera
Santa Isabel
Arroyo
Maunabo
Punta Yeguas
Cabo Rojo
Punta Tocón
Punta Brea
Bahía de Guánica
Playa de Guayanilla
Punta Cucharas
I. Caja de Muertos
Bahía de Rincón
Bahía de Jobos
Jobos
Punta Viento
ST. THOMAS AND ST. JOHN
United States
Jost Van Dyke
Little Jost Van Dyke
Great Harbour
Green Cay
Sandy Cay
ATLANTIC OCEAN
Great Tobago I.
Little Tobago I.
West End Pt.
White Bay
Black Pt.
Pull and be Damn' Pt.
Lower Belmont Bay
Long Bay
TORTOLA
Cockroach I.
Little Hans Lollik I.
Outer Brass I.
Hans Lollik I.
United Kingdom
United States
Great Thatch I.
Dutchcap Cay
Inner Brass I.
Santa Maria Bay
Hull B.
Magens B.
Picara Pt.
Thatch Cay
Grass Cay
Mingo Cay
Congo Cay
Lovango Cay
The Narrows
Mary Pt.
Brown Bay
Salt Cay
Crown Mt.
Charlotte Amalie
Mandal
Francis B.
Annaberg
West Cay
Savana I.
Altona
Tutu
Frydendal
Cruz Bay
Coral Bay
Palestina
David Pt.
Perseverance Bay
ST. THOMAS
Nadir
Red Hook
Pillsbury Sd.
Bordeaux Mt.
ST. JOHN
East End
Enighed
Leduck I.
Calabash Boom
Flanagan I.
Saba I.
Lindbergh B.
Water I.
St. Thomas Hbr.
Muhlenfels Pt.
Long Pt.
Jersey Bay
Great St. James I.
Little St. James I.
Dog I.
Rendezvous Bay
Reef Bay
Great Lameshur Bay
Ram Head
Johns Folly Bay
CORAL REEF NATIONAL MONUMENT
Buck I.
Capella Is.
VIRGIN ISLANDS N.P.
Frenchcap Cay
CARIBBEAN SEA
ST. CROIX
BUCK ISLAND REEF NATIONAL MONUMENT
Buck I.
Salt River Bay
Baron Bluff
Green Cay
Altona Lagoon
Cane Bay
Davis Beach
Hams Bluff
Mt. Eagle
Pull Pt.
Cottongarden Pt.
East Point
Butler Bay
Annaly
Bodkin Mill
Fredensborg
Christiansted
Turner Hole
Frederiksted
Grove Place
Grange
Grass Point
Good Hope Beach
Bethlehem
Great Pond
Great Pond Bay
Sandy Pt.
Southwest Cape
Long Point
Southwest Anchorage
Krause Lagoon Chan.
Vagthus Pt.
Milord Point
TORTOLA
U.K.
Guana I.
Beef I.
Rough Pt.
Jost Van Dyke
Brewers Bay
Fahie Hill
Parham Town
Long Look
East End
Cane Garden Bay
Leonard's
Carrot Bay
Road Town
Road Bay
Nora Hazel Pt.
Long Bay
Mt. Sage
Sea Cow Bay
Steele Pt.
Long Bay
West End
Frenchman's Cay
Little Thatch I.
St. John
U.K.
U.S.
VIRGIN GORDA
U.K.
Mosquito I.
Prickly Pear I.
Pajaro Pt.
Gun Creek
North Sd.
Berchers Bay
Great Dog I.
Virgin Gorda Pk.
Savannah Bay
South Sd.
Little Dix Bay
South Sound Bluff
Colison Pt.
Handsome Bay
St. Thomas B.
Spanish Town
Fort Point
The Baths
Copper Mine Pt.
Fallen Jerusalem
ANGUILLA
United Kingdom
Prickly Pear Cays
Scrub I.
Seal Is.
Snake Pt.
Crocus Hill
Crocus Bay
The Valley
Gibbon Pt.
Sandy Hill
Road Bay
Forest Point
Mead Pt.
Sandy Ground Village
Mead's Bay
Blowing Pt.
West End Village
Anguillita I.
St. Martin

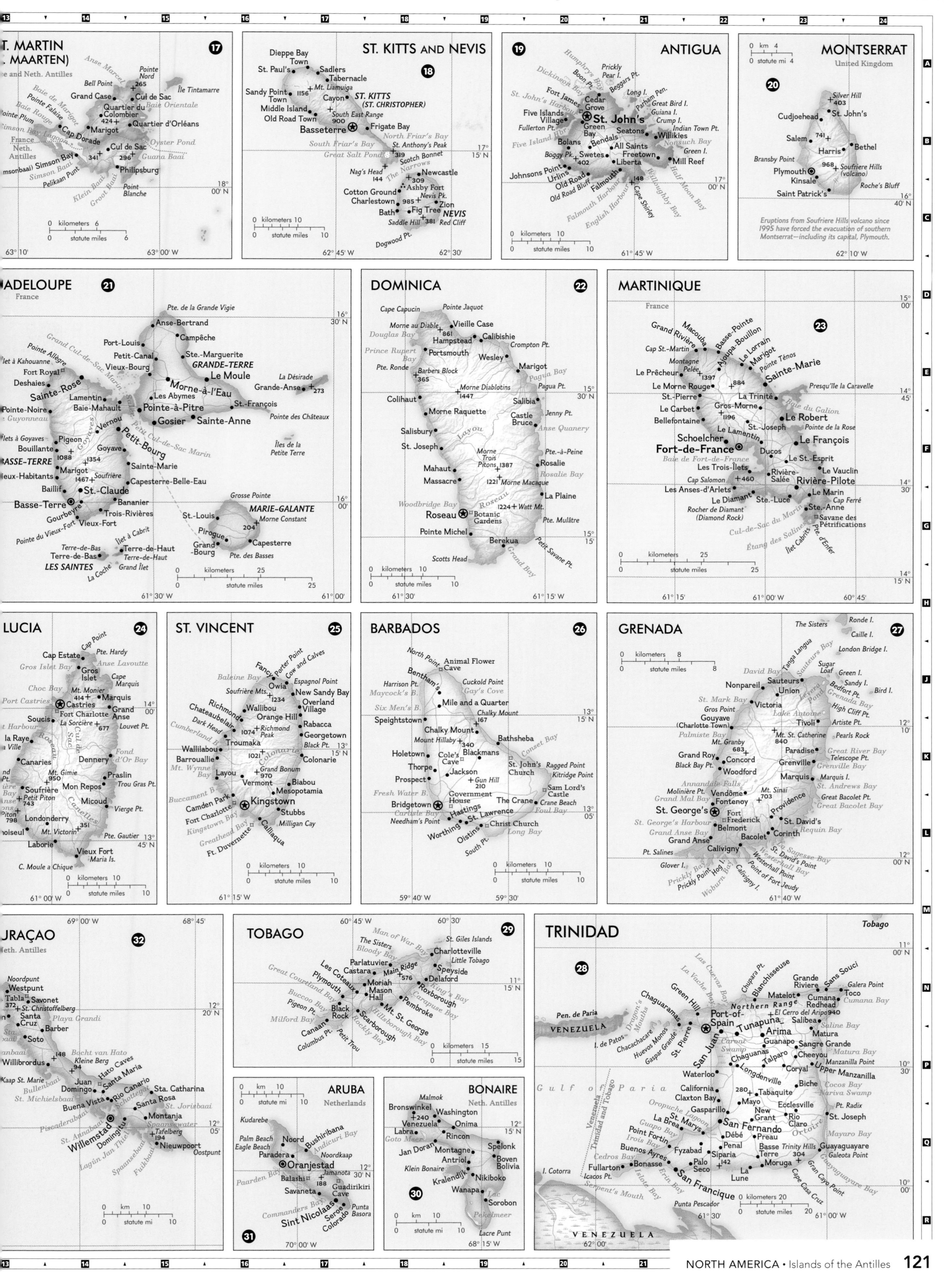

T. MARTIN
. MAARTEN)
e and Neth. Antilles
17
Pointe Nord
Île Tintamarre
Bell Point
Grand Case
Cul de Sac
Baie Orientale
Quartier du Colombier
Quartier d'Orléans
Marigot
Cap Dorade
Oyster Pond
Cul de Sac
Guana Baai
France
Neth. Antilles
Simpson Bay
Philipsburg
Pelikaan Punt
Point Blanche
ST. KITTS AND NEVIS
18
Dieppe Bay Town
St. Paul's
Sadlers
Tabernacle
Mt. Liamuiga
Sandy Point Town
Cayon
ST. KITTS (ST. CHRISTOPHER)
Middle Island
South East Range
Old Road Town
Basseterre
Frigate Bay
North Friar's Bay
South Friar's Bay
St. Anthony's Peak
Great Salt Pond
Scotch Bonnet
Nag's Head
The Narrows
Newcastle
Ashby Fort
Cotton Ground
Nevis Pk.
Charlestown
Zion
Bath
Fig Tree
NEVIS
Saddle Hill
Red Cliff
Dogwood Pt.
ANTIGUA
19
Prickly Pear I.
Beggars Pt.
Long I.
Parham Pen.
Great Bird I.
Guiana I.
Crump I.
Cedar Grove
St. John's
Five Islands Village
Fullerton Pt.
Green Bay
Seatons
Indian Town Pt.
Willikies
Nonsuch Bay
Bolans
Bendals
All Saints
Freetown
Green I.
Boggy Pk.
Swetes
Liberta
Mill Reef
Johnsons Point
Urlins
Old Road
Falmouth
Falmouth Harbour
English Harbour
Cape Shirley
Willoughby Bay
Half Moon Bay
MONTSERRAT
United Kingdom
20
Silver Hill
St. John's
Cudjoehead
Salem
Harris
Bethel
Bransby Point
Plymouth
Soufriere Hills (volcano)
Kinsale
Roche's Bluff
Saint Patrick's
Eruptions from Soufriere Hills volcano since 1995 have forced the evacuation of southern Montserrat—including its capital, Plymouth.
ADELOUPE
France
21
Pte. de la Grande Vigie
Anse-Bertrand
Campêche
Port-Louis
Petit-Canal
Ste.-Marguerite
GRANDE-TERRE
Vieux-Bourg
Le Moule
La Désirade
Grande-Anse
Fort Royal
Deshaies
Sainte-Rose
Lamentin
Morne-à-l'Eau
Les Abymes
Pointe-Noire
Baie-Mahault
Pointe-à-Pitre
St.-François
Pointe des Châteaux
Gosier
Sainte-Anne
Vernou
Pigeon
Goyave
Petit-Bourg
Îles de la Petite Terre
Bouillante
ASSE-TERRE
Marigot
Soufrière
Sainte-Marie
Capesterre-Belle-Eau
Baillif
St.-Claude
Basse-Terre
Bananier
Trois-Rivières
Gourbeyre
Vieux-Fort
Grosse Pointe
MARIE-GALANTE
St.-Louis
Morne Constant
Pirogue
Capesterre
Grand-Bourg
Pte. des Basses
Terre-de-Bas
Terre-de-Haut
LES SAINTES
Grand Îlet
DOMINICA
22
Cape Capucin
Pointe Jaquot
Morne au Diable
Vieille Case
Calibishie
Hampstead
Crompton Pt.
Portsmouth
Wesley
Marigot
Pagua Bay
Pte. Ronde
Barbers Block
Morne Diablotins
Pagua Pt.
Colihaut
Salibia
Morne Raquette
Castle Bruce
Salisbury
St. Joseph
Rosalie
Mahaut
Massacre
Morne Macaque
La Plaine
Roseau
Botanic Gardens
Watt Mt.
Pte. Mulâtre
Pointe Michel
Berekua
Scotts Head
MARTINIQUE
France
23
Grand Rivière
Macouba
Basse-Pointe
Ajoupa-Bouillon
Le Lorrain
Marigot
Cap St.-Martin
Montagne Pelée
Sainte-Marie
Le Prêcheur
Le Morne Rouge
Presqu'île la Caravelle
St.-Pierre
La Trinité
Le Carbet
Gros-Morne
Le Robert
Bellefontaine
St.-Joseph
Le Lamentin
Schoelcher
Le François
Fort-de-France
Ducos
Le St.-Esprit
Le Vauclin
Les Trois-Îlets
Rivière-Salée
Rivière-Pilote
Cap Salomon
Les Anses-d'Arlets
Le Marin
Le Diamant
Ste.-Luce
Ste.-Anne
Rocher de Diamant (Diamond Rock)
Savane des Pétrifications
LUCIA
24
Cap Point
Pte. Hardy
Cap Estate
Gros Islet
Castries
Marquis
Fort Charlotte
Grand Anse
Soucis
Louvet Pt.
Dennery
Canaries
Mt. Gimie
Praslin
Soufrière
Mon Repos
Petit Piton
Micoud
Londonderry
Vierge Pt.
Mt. Victorin
Pte. Gautier
Laborie
Vieux Fort
Maria Is.
C. Moule a Chique
ST. VINCENT
25
Fancy
Owia
Espagnol Point
Soufrière Mts.
New Sandy Bay
Overland Village
Richmond
Wallibou
Orange Hill
Chateaubelair
Rabacca
Richmond Peak
Georgetown
Troumaka
Black Pt.
Wallilabou
Barrouallie
Colonarie
Grand Bonum
Layou
Vermont
Biabou
Mesopotamia
Camden Park
Kingstown
Fort Charlotte
Stubbs
Milligan Cay
Calliaqua
Ft. Duvernette
BARBADOS
26
North Point
Animal Flower Cave
Harrison Pt.
Cuckold Point
Mile and a Quarter
Speightstown
Chalky Mount
Bathsheba
Mount Hillaby
Holetown
Blackmans
Cole's Cave
St. John's Church
Ragged Point
Thorpe
Jackson
Prospect
Gun Hill
Sam Lord's Castle
Government House
The Crane
Crane Beach
Bridgetown
Hastings
St. Lawrence
Christ Church
Needham's Point
Worthing
Oistins
South Pt.
GRENADA
27
The Sisters
Ronde I.
Caille I.
London Bridge I.
Sugar Loaf
Green I.
Sandy I.
Bird I.
Nonpareil
Sauteurs
Union
Victoria
Gros Point
Gouyave (Charlotte Town)
Tivoli
Artiste Pt.
Mt. St. Catherine
Pearls Rock
Mt. Granby
Paradise
Grand Roy
Concord
Telescope Pt.
Grenville
Woodford
Marquis
Molinière Pt.
Vendôme
Mt. Sinai
Fontenoy
St. George's
Fort Frederick
Belmont
St. David's
Corinth
Grand Anse
Bacolet
Pt. Salines
Calivigny
Glover I.
Prickly Point
URAÇAO
eth. Antilles
32
Noordpunt
Westpunt
Tabla
Savonet
St. Christoffelberg
Santa Cruz
Barber
Soto
Willibrordus
Kaap St. Marie
Hato Caves
Juan Domingo
Santa Maria
Sta. Catharina
Rio Canario
Buena Vista
Santa Rosa
Willemstad
Montanja
Tafelberg
Nieuwpoort
Oostpunt
TOBAGO
29
Man of War Bay
St. Giles Islands
Charlotteville
Little Tobago
Parlatuvier
Castara
Main Ridge
Speyside
Delaford
Moriah
Mason Hall
Roxborough
Plymouth
Black Rock
Pembroke
Mt. St. George
Canaan
Scarborough
Columbus Pt.
Petit Trou
TRINIDAD
Tobago
28
Chupara Pt.
Blanchisseuse
Grande Riviere
Sans Souci
Galera Point
Toco
Matelot
Cumana
Redhead
El Cerro del Aripo
Northern Range
Pen. de Paria
VENEZUELA
Chaguaramas
Green Hill
Port-of-Spain
Tunapuna
Arima
Salibea
Matura
Guanapo
Sangre Grande
Caroni Swamp
Chaguanas
Talparo
Cheeyou
Manzanilla Point
Upper Manzanilla
Waterloo
Longdenville
Coryal
Gulf of Paria
California
Claxton Bay
Tabaquite
Biche
Mayo
Ecclesville
Pt. Radix
Gasparillo
New Grant
Rio Claro
St. Joseph
San Fernando
Débé
Preau
Point Fortin
Penal
Basse Terre
Guayaguayare
Galeota Point
Fyzabad
Siparia
Moruga
Fullarton
Bonasse
Palo Seco
La Lune
Icacos Pt.
San Francique
Serpent's Mouth
Punta Pescador
VENEZUELA
ARUBA
Netherlands
31
Kudarebe
Palm Beach
Eagle Beach
Noord
Bushiribana
Paradera
Oranjestad
Jamanota
Balashi
Savaneta
Guadirikiri Cave
Sint Nicolaas
Seroe Colorado
Punta Basora
BONAIRE
Neth. Antilles
30
Malmok
Bronswinkel
Washington
Venezuela
Onima
Labra
Rincon
Spelonk
Jan Doran
Montagne
Boven Bolivia
Antriol
Klein Bonaire
Kralendijk
Nikiboko
Wanapa
Sorobon
Pekelmeer
Lacre Punt

South America

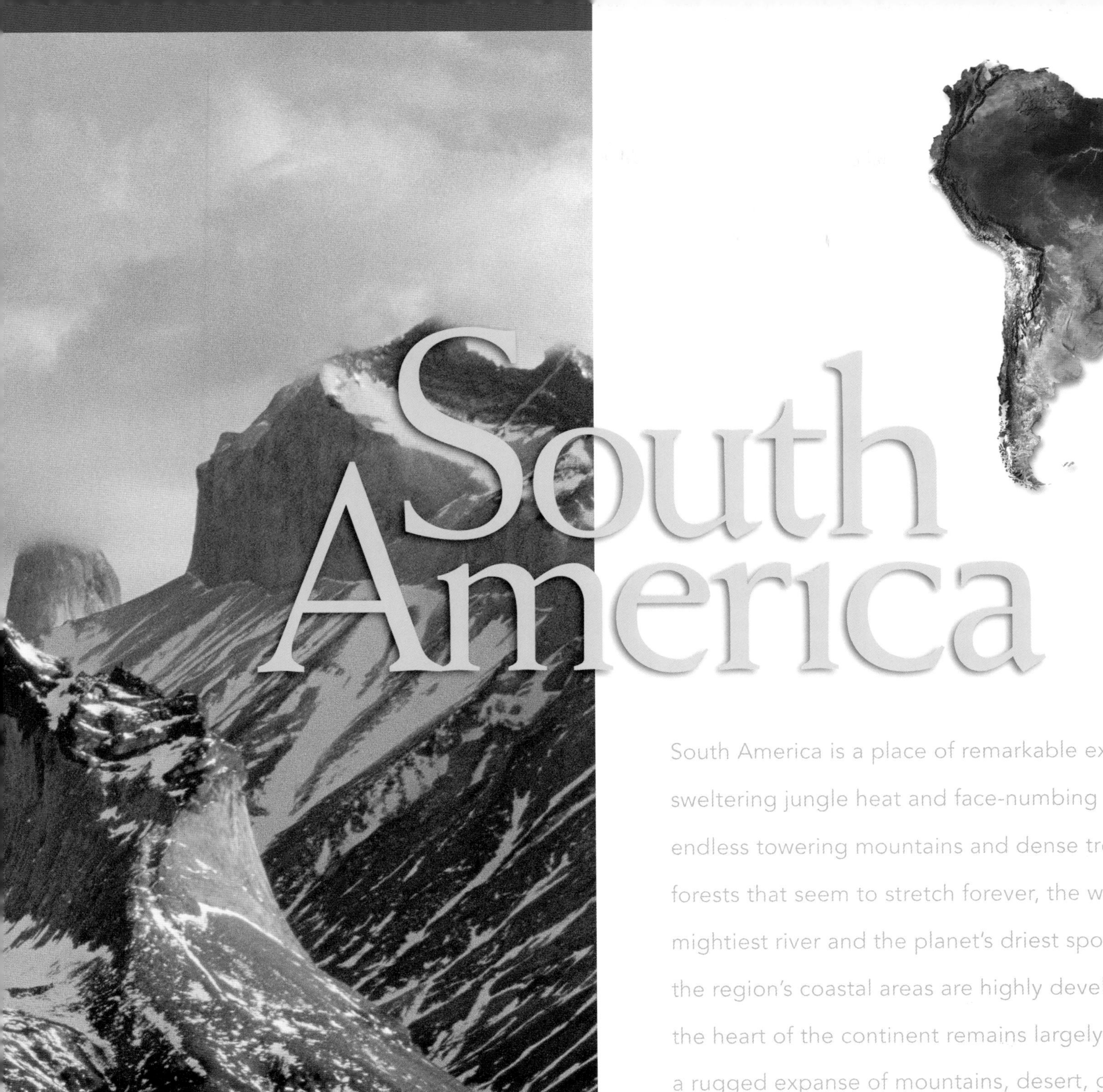

The ice-shrouded Torres del Paine Mountains take pride of place in Chile's harsh Patagonia region. Home to indigenous populations and endemic flora and fauna, Patagonia, which also encompasses a large swath of Argentina, has often been described as "the last place on Earth."

South America is a place of remarkable extremes—sweltering jungle heat and face-numbing cold, endless towering mountains and dense tropical forests that seem to stretch forever, the world's mightiest river and the planet's driest spot. While the region's coastal areas are highly developed, the heart of the continent remains largely vacant, a rugged expanse of mountains, desert, grassland, and forest that constitutes one of the world's last great wilderness treasures.

Although much of the continent remains wild and untamed, South America has its refined side. It provided a cradle for several ancient civilizations and in modern times has given birth to some of the world's biggest metropolises. Yet indigenous communities, though only a small percentage of the population, still exist—high in the mountains of Ecuador, deep in the Amazon jungle of Brazil, scattered in the forested hinterlands of Suriname, and elsewhere.

South America has also afforded us some of the great cultural highlights of the past hundred years—the astonishing discovery of the lost city of Machu Picchu in the Peruvian Andes, Evita Perón rousing crowds in Argentina, the alluring "Girl from Ipanema" on the beach in Brazil, and Pele's magic with a soccer ball.

PHYSICAL GEOGRAPHY With a base along the Caribbean coast and an apex at Cape Horn, South America is shaped rather like an elongated triangle. Embracing a total area of nearly 6.9 million square miles (17.8 million sq km), it's the fourth largest continent, bounded by the Atlantic Ocean in the east, the Pacific Ocean in the west, and the Caribbean Sea in the north. Its only connection to another landmass (North America) is the narrow Isthmus of Panama between Colombia and Panama. In the deep south, only the stormy Drake Passage separates South America from the Antarctic continent.

Despite its hefty size, South America has a relatively short coastline and few islands. However its offshore elements are distinctive: frigid Tierra del Fuego, the battle-torn Falklands (Malvinas), the biologically wondrous Galápagos, the spectacular fiord country of southern Chile, and untamed Marajó Island in the Amazon delta.

Three huge physical features dominate the South American mainland: the Andes mountains, the Amazon Basin, and a wide southern plain that encompasses the Pampas, the Gran Chaco, and much of Patagonia. The Andes cordillera, which runs all the way from northern Colombia to southern Chile and Argentina, is the world's longest mountain range. It's also one of the highest—more than 50 peaks over 20,000 feet (6,100 m)—and one of the most active in terms of volcanism and earthquakes.

South America's hydrology is perhaps the most astounding of any continent. Rainwater spilling off the Andes creates the mighty Amazon River and its thousand-plus tributaries, which in turn sustain the world's largest rain forest and greatest diversity of flora and fauna. Although the Amazon itself is not the planet's longest watercourse, it carries more liquid than the next ten biggest rivers combined. Spilling off a tabletop mountain in the northern Amazon is Angel Falls, the world's highest cascade at 3,212 feet (979 m), and tumbling off an ancient lava cliff between Brazil and Argentina is thunderous Iguazú Falls.

Among the continent's other geographic oddities are windswept Patagonia at the continent's southern tip and the extremely arid Atacama Desert, which often goes without rain for hundreds of years. The endless Pampas prairie of Argentina and Uruguay was the birthplace of gaucho culture, while the Pantanal region of southern Brazil is among the Earth's great wetlands.

HISTORY Like its continental cousin to the north, South America was first inhabited by nomads whose Asiatic ancestors crossed the Bering Strait during the last great ice age, sometime between 12,000 and 30,000 years ago. After crossing the Isthmus of Panama, they diffused throughout the continent and evolved into hundreds of different tribal groups with their own languages, customs, and traditions.

Starting around 3000 B.C., Amerindians living in the Andes region began to cultivate beans, squash, cotton, and potatoes. By 1000 B.C., villages along Peru's northern coastal plain had evolved into the Chavin culture, the continent's first true civilization. With a religion based on worship of the jaguar god, the Chavin built great ceremonial centers with mud-brick temples and pyramids. They also developed polychrome pottery, intricate weaving, and South America's first metallurgy. By the sixth century A.D., the Chavin had been eclipsed by other sophisticated Peruvian cultures such as the Moche, Nasca, and Tiwanaku. The last of the region's great Amerindian cultures was the Inca; master stonemasons and soldiers, the Inca forged an empire that stretched from present-day southern Colombia to northern Chile and Argentina.

Christopher Columbus "discovered" South America in 1498 on his third voyage to the New World, but the landmass (and adjacent North America) didn't receive its current name until Italian mariner Amerigo Vespucci explored its coast (1499–1502) and first postulated that it was a continent unto itself rather than part of Asia. In their quest for riches, the Spanish conquistadors came into violent contact with local Amerindian groups, climaxing in Francisco Pizarro's invasion of the Andes and bloody triumph over the Inca Empire in the 1530s. While the Spaniards were busy conquering the west coast, the Portuguese were claiming the continent's eastern shore, an area they called Brazil after a local dyewood tree. Driven off their land, decimated by disease, and pressed into slavery, South America's native population quickly declined in all but the most remote regions. Within half a century of first contact, European hegemony over the entire continent was assured.

Three distinct groups—the military, wealthy families, and the Roman Catholic Church—came to dominate South America's new Iberian colonies by the end of the 16th century. Using Indian labor and millions of slaves imported from Africa, they developed a society based on sprawling ranches and European-style cities such as Lima and Bogotá. Missions under the direction of the Jesuits and Franciscans were used to convert and control Indians in frontier areas. By the dawn of the 19th century—inspired by popular uprisings in the United States and France—South America's colonies had hatched their own revolutions. Between 1810 and 1824, Simón Bolívar and José de San Martín liberated all of the region's Spanish-speaking lands. Brazil declared its independence from Portugal in 1822.

Despite impressive economic gains in some countries—most notably Argentina—most of South America's independent states were stagnant by the early 20th century, struggling beneath a twin yoke of brutal military rule and neocolonial economic exploitation. This status quo endured until the late 1990s, when democracy flowered across the continent.

One of the most dramatic ruins in South America, the Inca ceremonial center of Machu Picchu hovers 2,000 feet (610 m) above the Urubamba River in the Peruvian Andes. It was built in the mid- to late 1400s at the behest of Pachacuti, the ruler who greatly enlarged the Inca Empire through conquest and colonization.

CULTURE A rich blend of Iberian, African, and Amerindian traditions, South America has some of the world's most lively and distinctive cultures. These cultures are also among the most urban. Despite romantic images of the Amazon and Machu Picchu, the vast majority of South Americans live in cities rather than the rain forest or mountains. A massive rural exodus since the 1950s has transformed South America into the most urbanized continent after Australia, a region that now boasts three of the world's 15 largest cities: São Paulo (18 million), Buenos Aires (13 million), and Rio de Janeiro (11 million). Ninety percent of these people live within 200 miles (320 km) of the coast, leaving huge expanses of the interior virtually unpopulated.

Several common threads bind the continent's more than 370 million people. Iberian languages dominate, with about half speaking Spanish and the other half Portuguese. There are several linguistic anomalies—French, Dutch, and English in the Guianas, and Amerindian dialects in the remote Amazon and Andes—but most South Americans don't need a translator when talking to one another. And despite recent inroads by Protestant missionaries—especially among remote Indian tribes and the urban poor—nearly 90 percent of South Americans adhere to the Roman Catholic faith.

Yet the continent also flaunts an amazing ethnic diversity. Although the majority of people can still trace their ancestors back to Spain or Portugal, waves of immigration have transformed South America into an ethnic smorgasbord. Amerindians and mixed-blood mestizos make up more than 80 percent of the population in Bolivia, Ecuador, and Peru. More than one-third of Argentines can boast Italian roots. Blond-haired, blue-eyed Germans populate many parts of Chile, Uruguay, and southern Brazil. Almost 40 percent of Brazilians and a high percentage of the residents of coastal Colombia and Venezuela are the descendants of African slaves. Asian Indians comprise the largest ethnic groups in both Suriname and Guyana.

This blend has produced a vibrant modern culture with influence far beyond the bounds of its South American cradle. Argentina's beloved tango—music, lyrics, and dance steps born of the Buenos Aires ghettos—is now an icon of romance all around the world. Brazil's steamy port cities hatched sensual Afro-Latino rhythms such as samba and bossa nova, Peruvian pipe music has become synonymous with the Andes, while Colombia has produced a rousing Latino rock. South America's rich literary map includes everything from the magical realism of Gabriel García Márquez and Mario Vargas Llosa to the sensual poems of Pablo Neruda and the poignant prose of Jorge Luis Borges. A similar passion flows through soccer, the region's favorite game, where the likes of Pele and Maradona have led their respective national teams (Brazil and Argentina) to multiple World Cup titles.

ECONOMICS Even though South America's colonies gained their independence at a relatively early stage, they were not able to achieve economic autonomy to any large extent. By the early 20th century, nearly all of them were dependent on commodity exports to Europe or the United States: bananas, rubber, sugar, coffee, timber, emeralds, copper, oil, and beef. In the short term some countries did very well with exports, especially Argentina, which counted itself among the world's richest nations until the 1950s. But failure to make a full transition from resource extraction into modern business and industry spelled economic doom for the entire continent.

By the 1960s, most of South America was mired in negative or neutral economic growth, increasingly dependent on overseas aid, and plagued by unemployment and poverty. Corruption, military rule, and mismanagement augmented an already dire situation. Hyperinflation of several hundred percent per annum battered Brazil and Argentina in the 1980s, nearly crippling the continent's two largest economies. During the same era, narcotics became one of South America's most important money spinners—cocaine exported in great quantities from Colombia, Bolivia, and Peru. Yet by the 1990s, most countries saw light at the end of their dim economic tunnels. In the early years of the 21st century, although fundamental problems remain—like huge foreign debt—the region's nouvelle democracy spurred an era of relative prosperity, raising the GDP per capita in many countries.

South America still relies, to a large extent, on commodity exports: oil from Venezuela, coffee from Colombia, and copper from Chile. But recent decades have seen a dramatic shift toward manufacturing and niche agriculture. Brazil now earns more money from making automobiles and aircraft than from shipping rubber overseas. Chile has earned a worldwide market for its wine, fruit, and salmon.

Despite protests from indigenous tribes and environmental groups, South American governments have tried to spur even more growth by opening up the Amazon region to economic exploitation—the extraction of oil and timber and the transformation of rain forest into cattle ranches. But this practice is already wreaking widespread ecological havoc. The Amazon could very well be the key to the region's economic future—not by the decimation of the world's richest forest, but by the sustainable management and commercial development of its largely untapped biodiversity into medical, chemical, and nutritional products. Many researchers believe that potential treatments for cancer and other ailments may lie hidden in South America's shadowy rain forest.

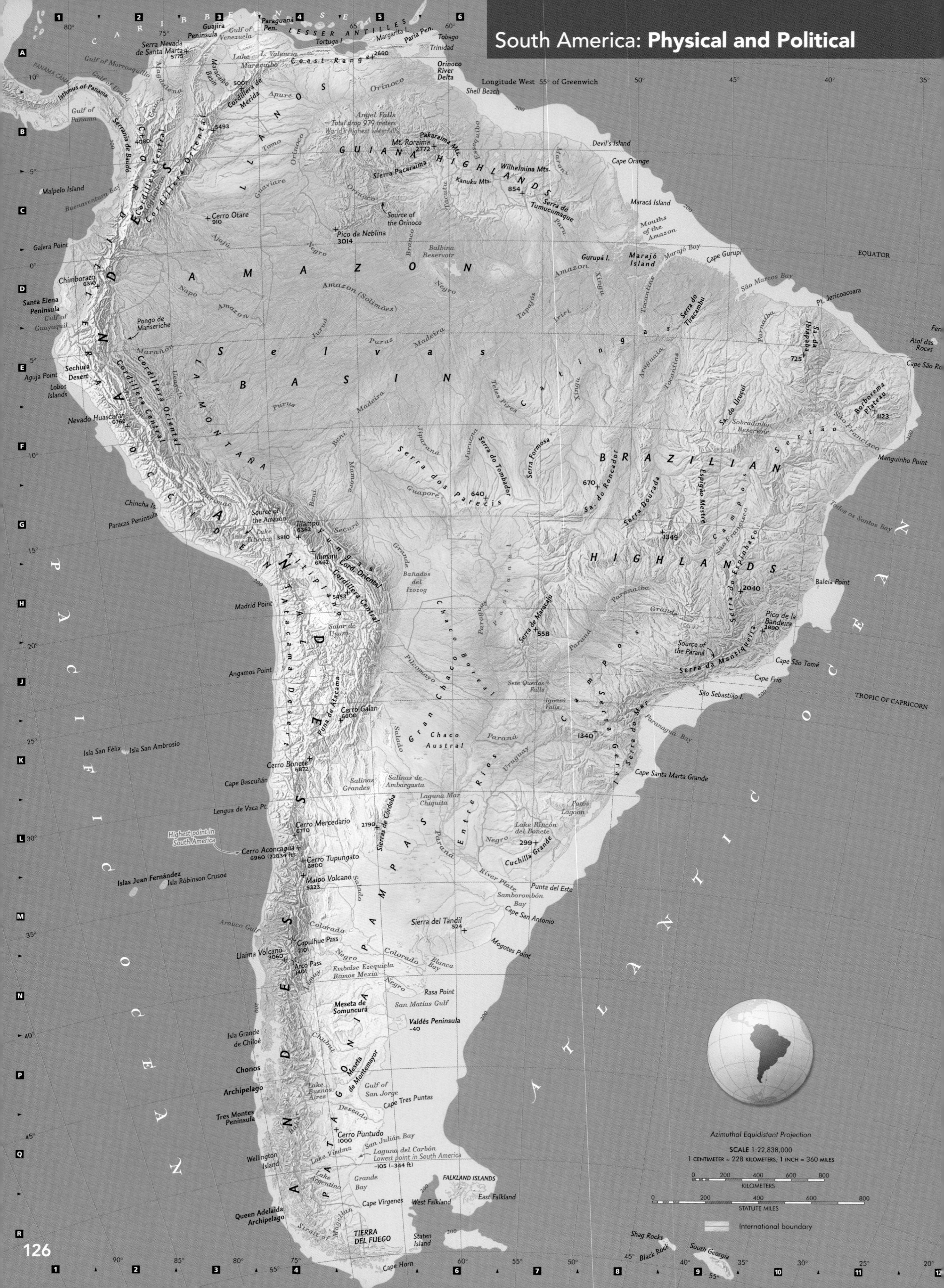

South America: Physical and Political
Longitude West 55° of Greenwich
EQUATOR
TROPIC OF CAPRICORN
PACIFIC OCEAN
ATLANTIC OCEAN
LESSER ANTILLES
Guajira Peninsula
Gulf of Venezuela
Paraguaná Pen.
Tortuga I.
Margarita I.
Paria Pen.
Tobago
Trinidad
Serra Nevada de Santa Marta
5775
Lake Maracaibo
L. Valencia
Coast Range
2660
Orinoco River Delta
Shell Beach
Gulf of Morrosquillo
Gulf of Urabá
PANAMA CANAL
Isthmus of Panama
Gulf of Panama
Maracaibo Basin
Cordillera de Mérida
5007
Apure
Orinoco
LLANOS
Angel Falls
Total drop 979 meters
World's highest waterfall
Mt. Roraima
2772
Pakaraima Mts.
GUIANA HIGHLANDS
Sierra Pacaraima
Wilhelmina Mts.
Kanuku Mts.
854
Serra de Tumucumaque
Devil's Island
Cape Orange
Serranía de Baudó
Cordillera Central
Cordillera Oriental
5493
4080
Tomo
Guaviare
Malpelo Island
Buenaventura Bay
Cerro Otare
910
Source of the Orinoco
Pico da Neblina
3014
Maracá Island
Mouths of the Amazon
Galera Point
Chimborazo
6310
Santa Elena Peninsula
Gulf of Guayaquil
Napo
Amazon
AMAZON BASIN
Amazon (Solimões)
Negro
Branco
Balbina Reservoir
Gurupá I.
Marajó Island
Marajó Bay
Cape Gurupi
São Marcos Bay
Pt. Jericoacoara
Xingu
Tocantins
Serra do Tiracambu
Pongo de Manseriche
Marañón
Selvas
Purus
Madeira
Juruá
Tapajós
Iriri
Caatinga
Araguaia
Parnaíba
Sa. da Ibiapaba
725
Atol das Rocas
Cape São Roque
Sechura Desert
Aguja Point
Lobos Islands
Cordillera Central
Cordillera Oriental
LA MONTAÑA
Ucayali
Teles Pires
Sa. do Uruçuí
Sobradinho Reservoir
Borborema Plateau
1123
São Francisco
Sertão
Nevado Huascarán
6768
Beni
Mamoré
Jiparaná
Juruena
Serra dos Parecis
640
Serra do Tombador
Serra Formosa
BRAZILIAN HIGHLANDS
670
Sa. do Roncador
Serra Dourada
Espigão Mestre
Campos
Manguinho Point
Guaporé
Chincha Is.
Paracas Peninsula
Source of the Amazon
Lake Titicaca
3810
Illampu
6362
Illimani
6462
Yungas
Cord. Oriental
Cordillera Central
Altiplano
5453
Grande
Bañados del Izozog
1349
São Francisco
Serra do Espinhaço
2040
Todos os Santos Bay
Baleia Point
Madrid Point
Salar de Uyuni
Chaco Boreal
Paraguay
Pantanal
Serra de Maracaju
558
Paraná
Paranaíba
Grande
Pico da Bandeira
2890
Source of the Paraná
Serra da Mantiqueira
Cape São Tomé
Cape Frio
São Sebastião I.
Angamos Point
Atacama Desert
Puna de Atacama
Pilcomayo
Sete Quedas Falls
Iguaçu Falls
Serra Geral
Serra do Mar
Paranaguá Bay
Cerro Galan
6600
Salado
Gran Chaco
Chaco Austral
Paraná
1340
Isla San Félix
Isla San Ambrosio
Cerro Bonete
6872
Uruguay
Cape Santa Marta Grande
Cape Bascuñán
Salinas Grandes
Salinas de Ambargasta
Laguna Mar Chiquita
Entre Ríos
Patos Lagoon
Lengua de Vaca Pt.
Highest point in South America
Cerro Mercedario
6770
Sierras de Córdoba
2790
Lake Rincón del Bonete
Negro
299
Cuchilla Grande
Cerro Aconcagua
6960 (22834 ft)
Cerro Tupungato
6800
Maipo Volcano
5323
Islas Juan Fernández
Isla Róbinson Crusoe
River Plate
Punta del Este
Samborombón Bay
Cape San Antonio
PAMPAS
Arauco Gulf
Colorado
Sierra del Tandil
524
Copulhue Pass
2101
Llaima Volcano
3060
Arco Pass
1401
Embalse Ezequiela Ramos Mexía
Colorado
Blanca Bay
Mogotes Point
Limay
Rasa Point
San Matías Gulf
Meseta de Somuncurá
Valdés Peninsula
-40
Isla Grande de Chiloé
Chubut
Chonos Archipelago
PATAGONIA
Meseta de Montemayor
Lake Buenos Aires
Gulf of San Jorge
Cape Tres Puntas
Tres Montes Peninsula
Deseado
Cerro Puntudo
1000
San Julián Bay
Wellington Island
Lake Viedma
Laguna del Carbón
Lowest point in South America
-105 (-344 ft)
Lake Argentino
Grande Bay
FALKLAND ISLANDS
East Falkland
West Falkland
Cape Vírgenes
Queen Adelaida Archipelago
Strait of Magellan
TIERRA DEL FUEGO
Staten Island
Cape Horn
Shag Rocks
Black Rock
South Georgia
Azimuthal Equidistant Projection
SCALE 1:22,838,000
1 CENTIMETER = 228 KILOMETERS; 1 INCH = 360 MILES
KILOMETERS
STATUTE MILES
International boundary

Longitude West 55° of Greenwich
Azimuthal Equidistant Projection
SCALE 1:22,838,000
1 CENTIMETER = 228 KILOMETERS; 1 INCH = 360 MILES
KILOMETERS
STATUTE MILES
EQUATOR
TROPIC OF CAPRICORN
TRINIDAD AND TOBAGO
Port-of-Spain
Trinidad
Tobago
VENEZUELA
CARACAS
Maracaibo
Barquisimeto
Valencia
Maracay
Barcelona
Maturín
Ciudad Bolívar
Ciudad Guayana
COLOMBIA
BOGOTÁ
MEDELLÍN
CALI
BARRANQUILLA
CARTAGENA
Santa Marta
Cúcuta
Bucaramanga
Manizales
Pereira
Armenia
Villavicencio
Neiva
Pasto
Popayán
PANAMA
Panamá
ECUADOR
QUITO
GUAYAQUIL
Cuenca
Machala
Manta
Esmeraldas
PERU
LIMA
Callao
Arequipa
Trujillo
Chiclayo
Piura
Iquitos
Cusco
Chimbote
Huancayo
Tacna
Pucallpa
Juliaca
BOLIVIA
La Paz
Sucre
Santa Cruz
Cochabamba
Oruro
Potosí
Tarija
Trinidad
GUYANA
Georgetown
SURINAME
Paramaribo
FRENCH GUIANA
France
Cayenne
BRAZIL
BRASÍLIA
SÃO PAULO
RIO DE JANEIRO
SALVADOR (Bahia)
FORTALEZA
BELO HORIZONTE
MANAUS
CURITIBA
RECIFE
PORTO ALEGRE
BELÉM
GOIÂNIA
Campinas
Santos
Natal
João Pessoa
Maceió
Aracaju
Teresina
São Luís
Florianópolis
Vitória
Vila Velha
Porto Velho
Rio Branco
Macapá
Boa Vista
Cuiabá
Campo Grande
Santarém
Marabá
Uberlândia
Ribeirão Prêto
Juiz de Fora
Londrina
Maringá
Joinville
Feira de Santana
PARAGUAY
Asunción
Ciudad del Este
Encarnación
URUGUAY
MONTEVIDEO
Salto
Paysandú
Rivera
ARGENTINA
BUENOS AIRES
SAN JUSTO
CÓRDOBA
ROSARIO
La Plata
Mar del Plata
Bahía Blanca
Santa Fe
Paraná
Mendoza
San Juan
Salta
San Miguel de Tucumán
Resistencia
Corrientes
Posadas
Neuquén
Comodoro Rivadavia
Río Gallegos
Ushuaia
CHILE
SANTIAGO
Valparaíso
Antofagasta
Concepción
Arica
Iquique
Calama
La Serena
Coquimbo
Temuco
Valdivia
Puerto Montt
Punta Arenas
Talca
Chillán
Osorno
ISLA GRANDE DE CHILOÉ
ARCHIPIÉLAGO DE LOS CHONOS
ARCHIPIÉLAGO REINA ADELAIDA
ISLA GRANDE DE TIERRA DEL FUEGO
Isla de los Estados (Staten Island)
Cabo de Hornos (Cape Horn)
FALKLAND ISLANDS (ISLAS MALVINAS) U.K.
West Falkland
East Falkland
Stanley
Administered by United Kingdom (claimed by Argentina)
South Georgia U.K.
PENÍNSULA VALDÉS
Golfo San Jorge
Golfo San Matías
Isla San Félix
Isla San Ambrosio
Chile
Islas Juan Fernández
Chile
Isla de Malpelo
Colombia
I. de San Andrés
Colombia
Arquipélago de Fernando de Noronha
Brazil
Atol das Rocas
Brazil
PACIFIC OCEAN
ATLANTIC OCEAN
ANDES
Amazonas (Amazon)
Solimões (Amazonas)
Orinoco
Negro
Madeira
Paraná
Paraguay
Uruguay
Tocantins
Xingu
Tapajós
São Francisco

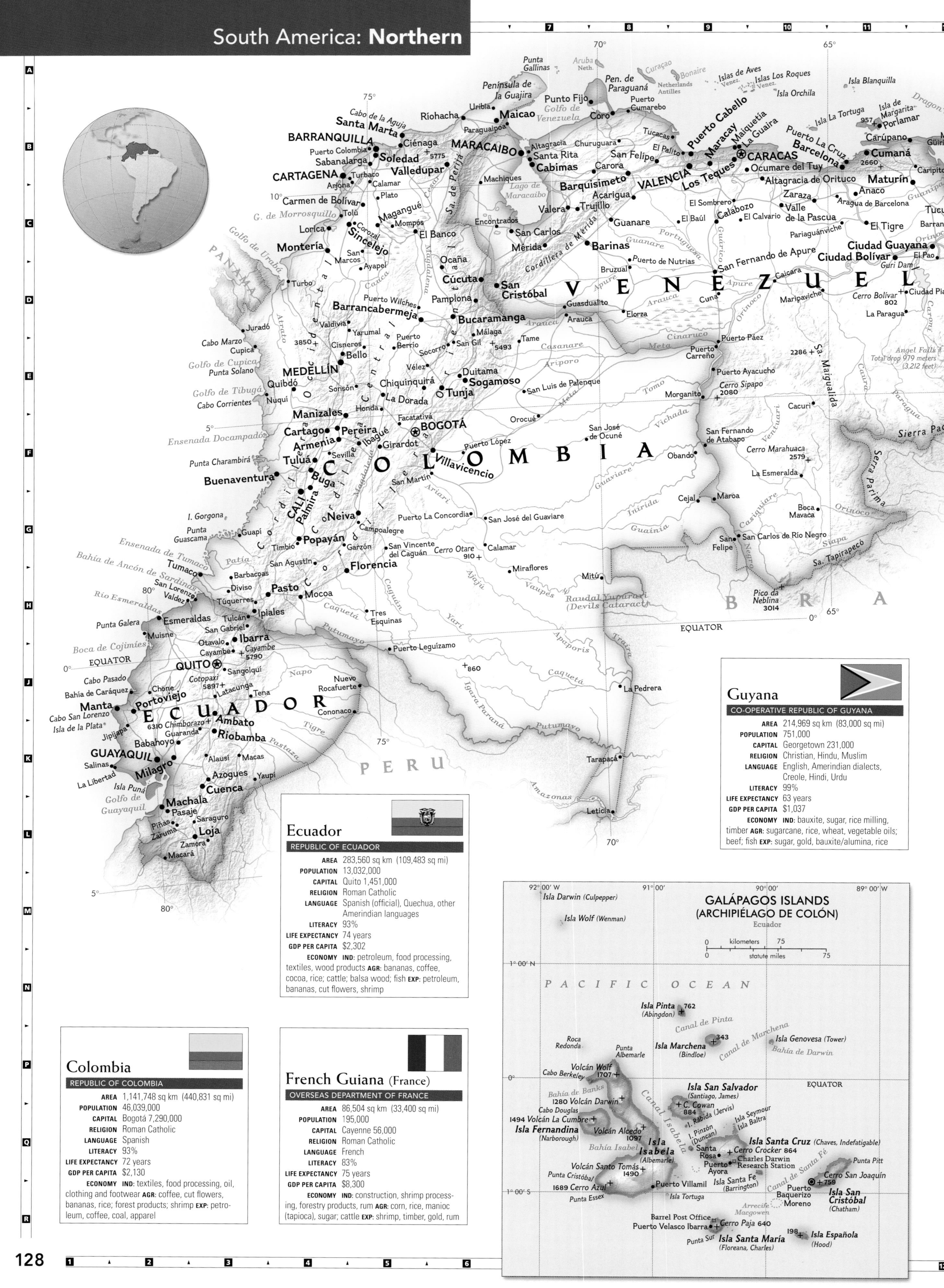

COLOMBIA
VENEZUELA
ECUADOR
PERU
BRAZIL
BOGOTÁ
CARACAS
QUITO
MEDELLÍN
CALI
BARRANQUILLA
CARTAGENA
MARACAIBO
VALENCIA
GUAYAQUIL
Galápagos Islands (Archipiélago de Colón)
Ecuador
PACIFIC OCEAN
EQUATOR
Guyana
CO-OPERATIVE REPUBLIC OF GUYANA
AREA 214,969 sq km (83,000 sq mi)
POPULATION 751,000
CAPITAL Georgetown 231,000
RELIGION Christian, Hindu, Muslim
LANGUAGE English, Amerindian dialects, Creole, Hindi, Urdu
LITERACY 99%
LIFE EXPECTANCY 63 years
GDP PER CAPITA $1,037
ECONOMY IND: bauxite, sugar, rice milling, timber AGR: sugarcane, rice, wheat, vegetable oils; beef; fish EXP: sugar, gold, bauxite/alumina, rice
Ecuador
REPUBLIC OF ECUADOR
AREA 283,560 sq km (109,483 sq mi)
POPULATION 13,032,000
CAPITAL Quito 1,451,000
RELIGION Roman Catholic
LANGUAGE Spanish (official), Quechua, other Amerindian languages
LITERACY 93%
LIFE EXPECTANCY 74 years
GDP PER CAPITA $2,302
ECONOMY IND: petroleum, food processing, textiles, wood products AGR: bananas, coffee, cocoa, rice; cattle; balsa wood; fish EXP: petroleum, bananas, cut flowers, shrimp
Colombia
REPUBLIC OF COLOMBIA
AREA 1,141,748 sq km (440,831 sq mi)
POPULATION 46,039,000
CAPITAL Bogotá 7,290,000
RELIGION Roman Catholic
LANGUAGE Spanish
LITERACY 93%
LIFE EXPECTANCY 72 years
GDP PER CAPITA $2,130
ECONOMY IND: textiles, food processing, oil, clothing and footwear AGR: coffee, cut flowers, bananas, rice; forest products; shrimp EXP: petroleum, coffee, coal, apparel
French Guiana (France)
OVERSEAS DEPARTMENT OF FRANCE
AREA 86,504 sq km (33,400 sq mi)
POPULATION 195,000
CAPITAL Cayenne 56,000
RELIGION Roman Catholic
LANGUAGE French
LITERACY 83%
LIFE EXPECTANCY 75 years
GDP PER CAPITA $8,300
ECONOMY IND: construction, shrimp processing, forestry products, rum AGR: corn, rice, manioc (tapioca), sugar; cattle EXP: shrimp, timber, gold, rum

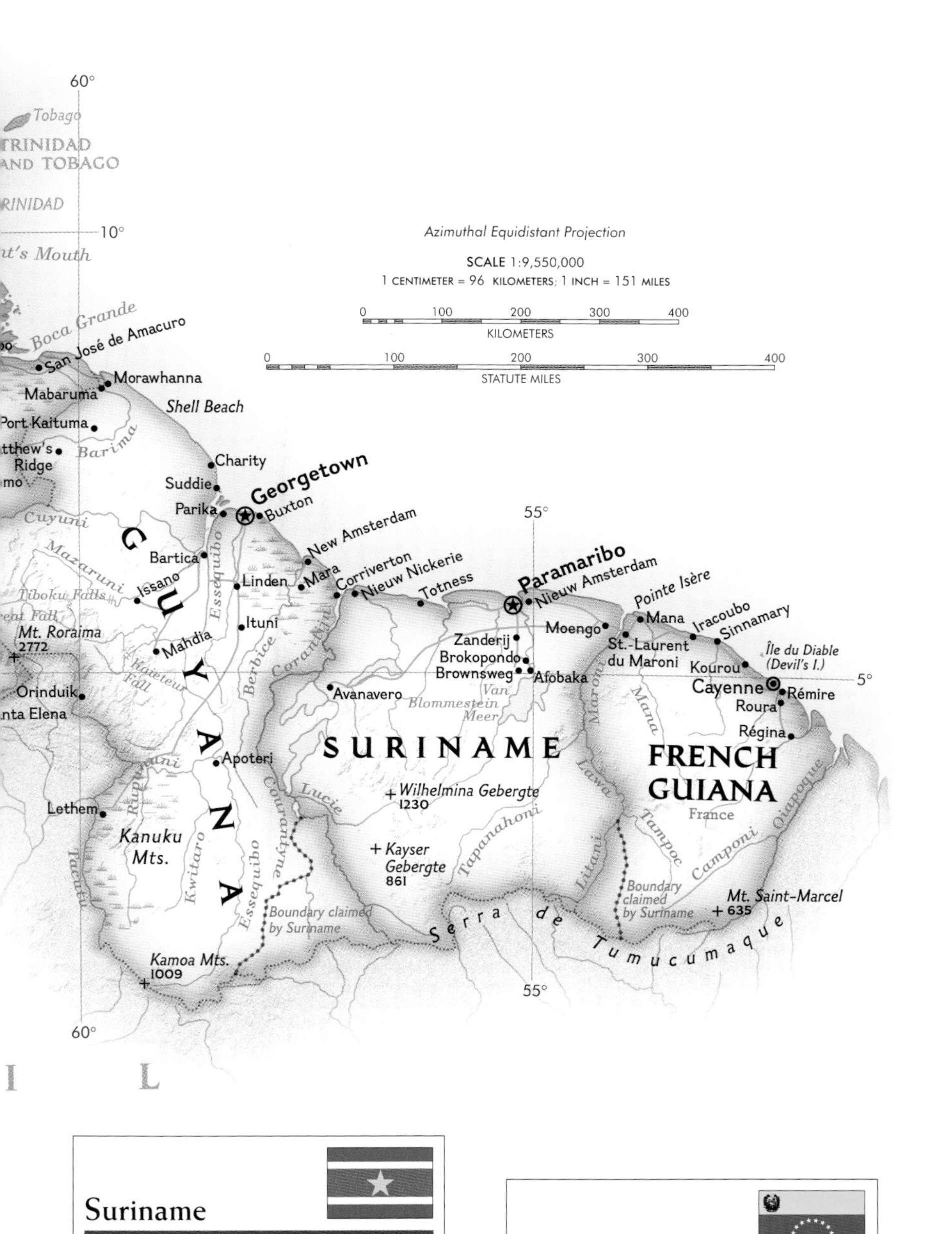

60°
Tobago
TRINIDAD AND TOBAGO
TRINIDAD
10°
Azimuthal Equidistant Projection
SCALE 1:9,550,000
1 CENTIMETER = 96 KILOMETERS; 1 INCH = 151 MILES
KILOMETERS
STATUTE MILES
Boca Grande
San José de Amacuro
Morawhanna
Mabaruma
Shell Beach
Port Kaituma
Barima
Charity
Suddie
Georgetown
Parika
Buxton
Cuyuni
Mazaruni
GUYANA
Bartica
Issano
Linden
Mara
New Amsterdam
Corriverton
Nieuw Nickerie
Totness
Paramaribo
Nieuw Amsterdam
Pointe Isère
Mana
Iracoubo
Sinnamary
55°
Ituni
Mahdia
Mt. Roraima
2772
Essequibo
Berbice
Corantijn
Zanderij
Brokopondo
Brownsweg
Afobaka
Moengo
St.-Laurent du Maroni
Kourou
Île du Diable (Devil's I.)
Cayenne
Rémire
Roura
Régina
5°
Orinduik
Avanavero
Van Blommestein Meer
SURINAME
FRENCH GUIANA
France
Apoteri
Lethem
Rupununi
Kanuku Mts.
Kwitaro
Wilhelmina Gebergte
1230
Kayser Gebergte
861
Tapanahoni
Litani
Lawa
Marowijne
Tampoc
Camopi
Oiapoque
Boundary claimed by Suriname
Mt. Saint-Marcel
635
Serra de Tumucumaque
Kamoa Mts.
1009
55°
60°

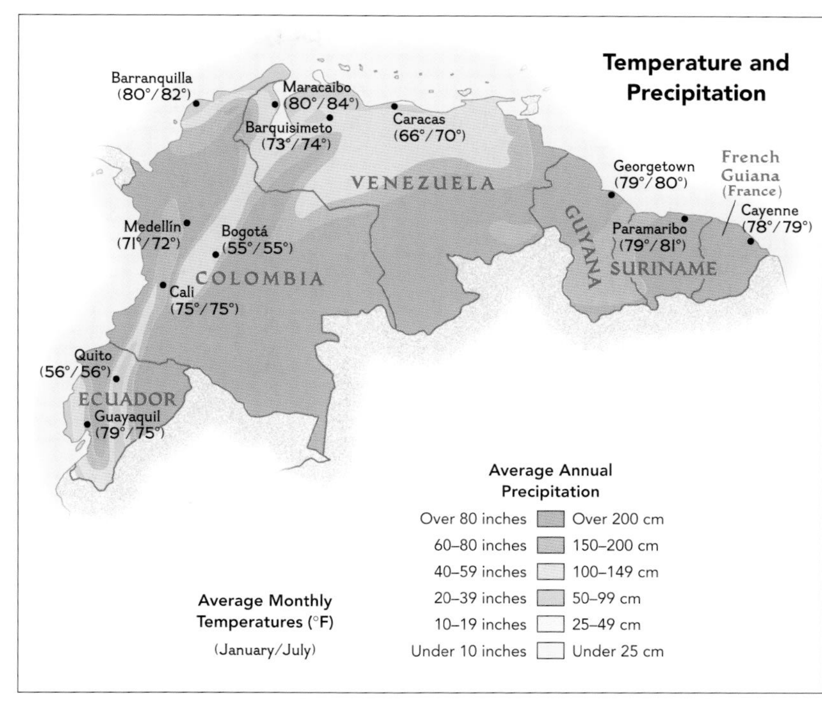

Temperature and Precipitation
Barranquilla (80°/82°)
Maracaibo (80°/84°)
Barquisimeto (73°/74°)
Caracas (66°/70°)
VENEZUELA
Georgetown (79°/80°)
French Guiana (France)
Cayenne (78°/79°)
Paramaribo (79°/81°)
GUYANA
SURINAME
Medellín (71°/72°)
Bogotá (55°/55°)
COLOMBIA
Cali (75°/75°)
Quito (56°/56°)
ECUADOR
Guayaquil (79°/75°)
Average Monthly Temperatures (°F) (January/July)
Average Annual Precipitation
Over 80 inches | Over 200 cm
60–80 inches | 150–200 cm
40–59 inches | 100–149 cm
20–39 inches | 50–99 cm
10–19 inches | 25–49 cm
Under 10 inches | Under 25 cm

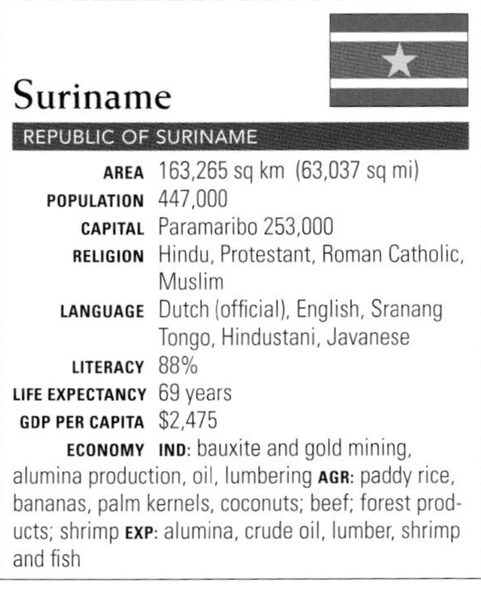

Suriname

REPUBLIC OF SURINAME

AREA 163,265 sq km (63,037 sq mi)
POPULATION 447,000
CAPITAL Paramaribo 253,000
RELIGION Hindu, Protestant, Roman Catholic, Muslim
LANGUAGE Dutch (official), English, Sranang Tongo, Hindustani, Javanese
LITERACY 88%
LIFE EXPECTANCY 69 years
GDP PER CAPITA $2,475
ECONOMY **IND:** bauxite and gold mining, alumina production, oil, lumbering **AGR:** paddy rice, bananas, palm kernels, coconuts; beef; forest products; shrimp **EXP:** alumina, crude oil, lumber, shrimp and fish

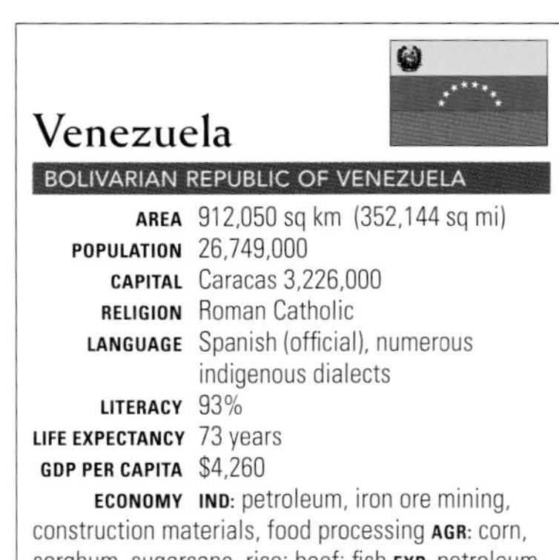

Venezuela

BOLIVARIAN REPUBLIC OF VENEZUELA

AREA 912,050 sq km (352,144 sq mi)
POPULATION 26,749,000
CAPITAL Caracas 3,226,000
RELIGION Roman Catholic
LANGUAGE Spanish (official), numerous indigenous dialects
LITERACY 93%
LIFE EXPECTANCY 73 years
GDP PER CAPITA $4,260
ECONOMY **IND:** petroleum, iron ore mining, construction materials, food processing **AGR:** corn, sorghum, sugarcane, rice; beef; fish **EXP:** petroleum, bauxite and aluminum, steel, chemicals

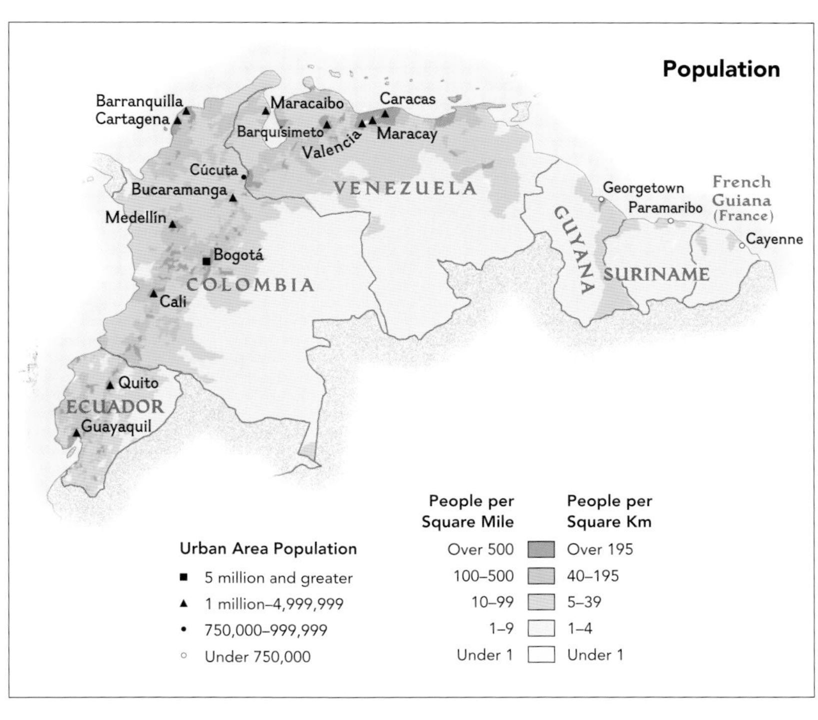

Population
Barranquilla
Cartagena
Maracaibo
Caracas
Barquisimeto
Valencia
Maracay
Cúcuta
Bucaramanga
VENEZUELA
Georgetown
Paramaribo
French Guiana (France)
Cayenne
Medellín
Bogotá
COLOMBIA
GUYANA
SURINAME
Cali
Quito
ECUADOR
Guayaquil
Urban Area Population
5 million and greater
1 million–4,999,999
750,000–999,999
Under 750,000
People per Square Mile | People per Square Km
Over 500 | Over 195
100–500 | 40–195
10–99 | 5–39
1–9 | 1–4
Under 1 | Under 1

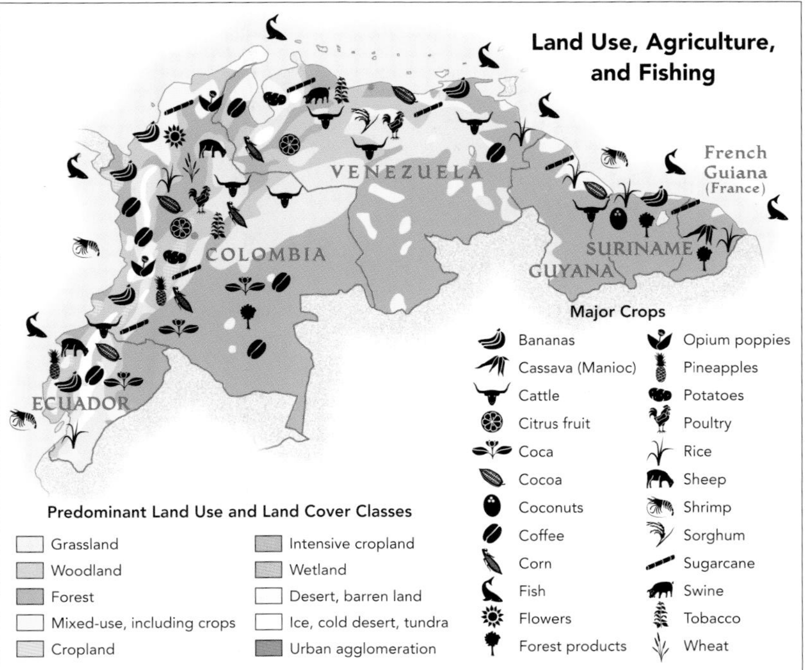

Land Use, Agriculture, and Fishing
VENEZUELA
French Guiana (France)
COLOMBIA
SURINAME
GUYANA
ECUADOR
Major Crops
Bananas
Cassava (Manioc)
Cattle
Citrus fruit
Coca
Cocoa
Coconuts
Coffee
Corn
Fish
Flowers
Forest products
Opium poppies
Pineapples
Potatoes
Poultry
Rice
Sheep
Shrimp
Sorghum
Sugarcane
Swine
Tobacco
Wheat
Predominant Land Use and Land Cover Classes
Grassland
Woodland
Forest
Mixed-use, including crops
Cropland
Intensive cropland
Wetland
Desert, barren land
Ice, cold desert, tundra
Urban agglomeration

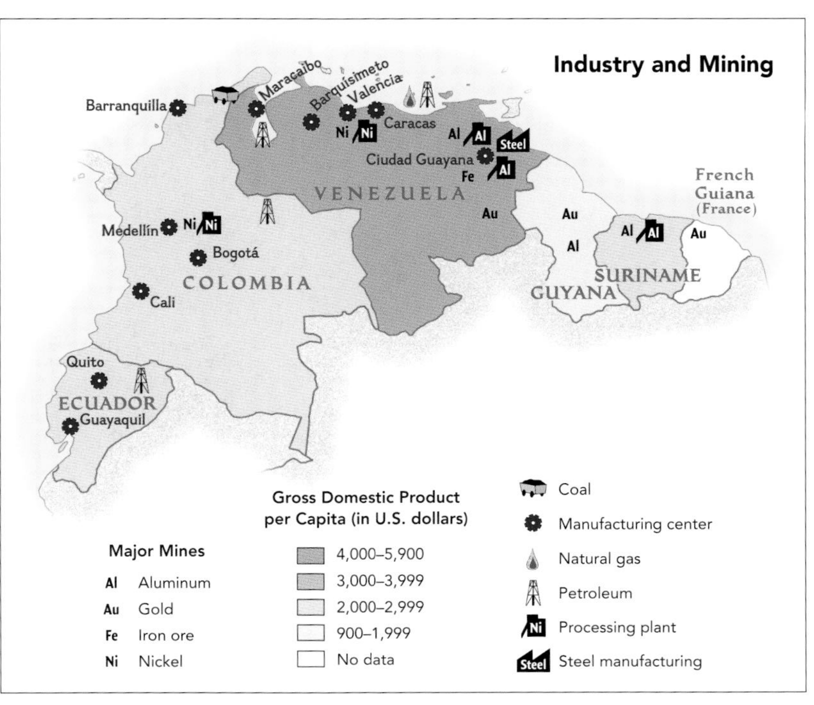

Industry and Mining
Barranquilla
Maracaibo
Barquisimeto
Valencia
Caracas
Ni
Al
Steel
Ciudad Guayana
Fe
VENEZUELA
Au
French Guiana (France)
Medellín
Bogotá
COLOMBIA
SURINAME
GUYANA
Cali
Quito
ECUADOR
Guayaquil
Gross Domestic Product per Capita (in U.S. dollars)
4,000–5,900
3,000–3,999
2,000–2,999
900–1,999
No data
Major Mines
Al Aluminum
Au Gold
Fe Iron ore
Ni Nickel
Coal
Manufacturing center
Natural gas
Petroleum
Processing plant
Steel manufacturing

VENEZUELA
COLOMBIA
ECUADOR
PERU
BOLIVIA
BRAZIL
PARAGUAY
CHILE
ARGENTINA
URUGUAY
SURINAME
FRENCH GUIANA
EQUATOR
TROPIC OF CAPRICORN
MANAUS
LIMA
La Paz
Sucre
Asunción
Iquitos
Porto Velho
Rio Branco
Santarém
Cuiabá
Campo Grande
Santa Cruz
Cochabamba
Arequipa
Cusco
Boa Vista
NORTHERN PERIMETER HIGHWAY
TRANS-AMAZON HIGHWAY
Pico da Neblina 3014
Mt. Roraima 2772
Nevado Sajama 6542
Temperature and Precipitation
Manaus (79°/80°)
Belém (78°/79°)
Fortaleza (81°/79°)
Recife (80°/75°)
Salvador (Bahia) (79°/74°)
Brasília (70°/65°)
Belo Horizonte (73°/65°)
Rio de Janeiro (79°/69°)
São Paulo (70°/59°)
Curitiba (68°/54°)
Porto Alegre (76°/58°)
Asunción (82°/64°)
Santa Cruz (80°/69°)
Sucre (61°/57°)
La Paz (50°/44°)
Lima (72°/61°)
BRAZIL
PERU
BOLIVIA
PARAGUAY
Average Annual Precipitation
Over 80 inches Over 200 cm
60–80 inches 150–200 cm
40–59 inches 100–149 cm
20–39 inches 50–99 cm
10–19 inches 25–49 cm
Under 10 inches Under 25 cm
Average Monthly Temperatures (°F) (January/July)

Bolivia

REPUBLIC OF BOLIVIA

AREA 1,098,581 sq km (424,164 sq mi)
POPULATION 8,922,000
CAPITAL La Paz (administrative) 1,477,000; Sucre (constitutional) 212,000
RELIGION Roman Catholic
LANGUAGE Spanish (official), Quechua (official), Aymara (official)
LITERACY 87%
LIFE EXPECTANCY 64 years
GDP PER CAPITA $935
ECONOMY **IND**: mining, smelting, petroleum, food and beverages **AGR**: soybeans, coffee, coca, cotton; timber **EXP**: natural gas, soybeans and soy products, crude petroleum, zinc ore

Brazil

FEDERATIVE REPUBLIC OF BRAZIL

AREA 8,547,403 sq km (3,300,169 sq mi)
POPULATION 184,184,000
CAPITAL Brasília 3,099,000
RELIGION Roman Catholic, Protestant
LANGUAGE Portuguese (official)
LITERACY 86%
LIFE EXPECTANCY 71 years
GDP PER CAPITA $3,225
ECONOMY **IND**: textiles, shoes, chemicals, cement **AGR**: coffee, soybeans, wheat, rice; beef **EXP**: transport equipment, iron ore, soybeans, footwear

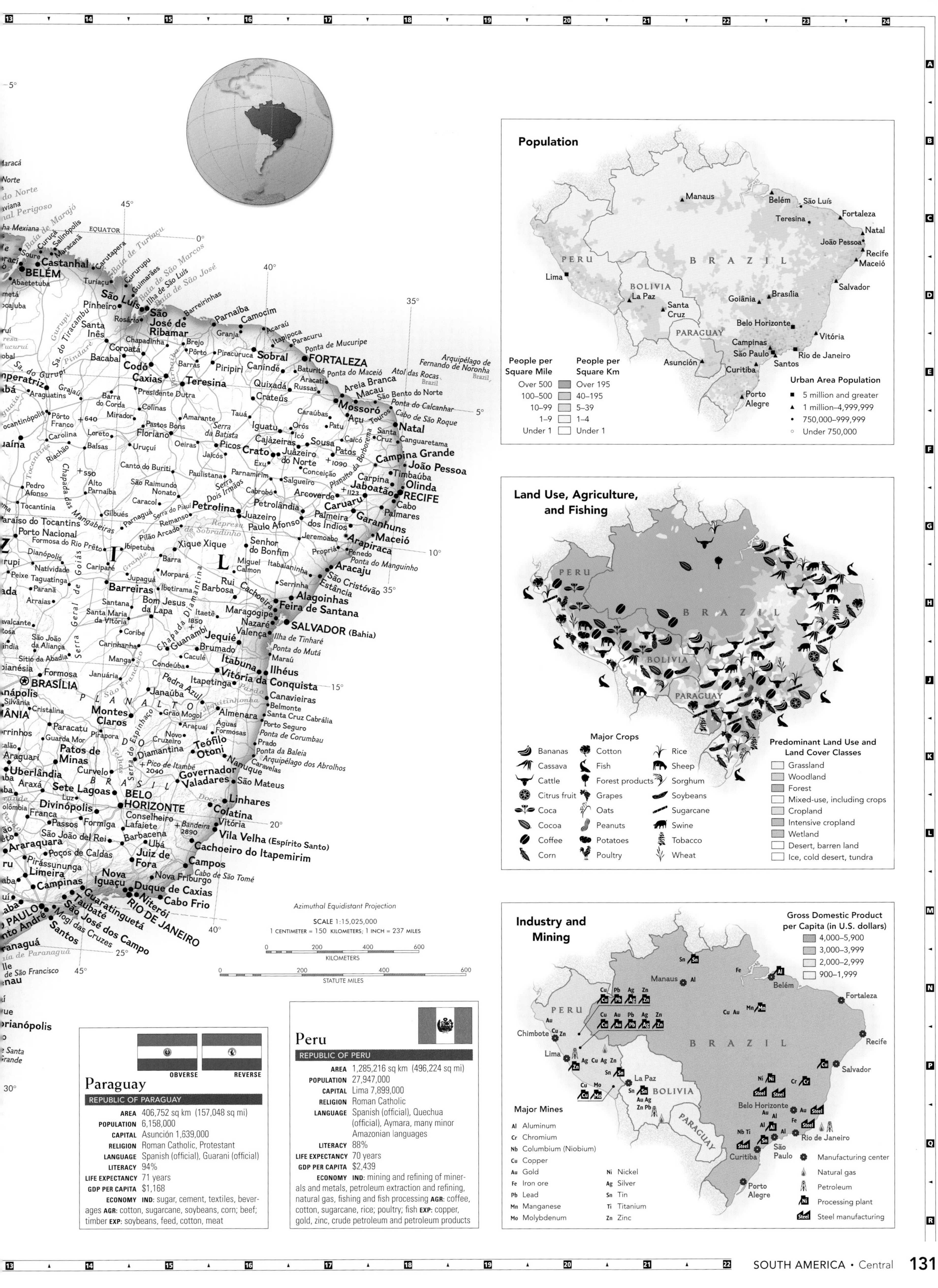
Population
People per Square Mile
Over 500
100–500
10–99
1–9
Under 1
People per Square Km
Over 195
40–195
5–39
1–4
Under 1
Urban Area Population
5 million and greater
1 million–4,999,999
750,000–999,999
Under 750,000
Land Use, Agriculture, and Fishing
Major Crops
Bananas
Cassava
Cattle
Citrus fruit
Coca
Cocoa
Coffee
Corn
Cotton
Fish
Forest products
Grapes
Oats
Peanuts
Potatoes
Poultry
Rice
Sheep
Sorghum
Soybeans
Sugarcane
Swine
Tobacco
Wheat
Predominant Land Use and Land Cover Classes
Grassland
Woodland
Forest
Mixed-use, including crops
Cropland
Intensive cropland
Wetland
Desert, barren land
Ice, cold desert, tundra
Industry and Mining
Gross Domestic Product per Capita (in U.S. dollars)
4,000–5,900
3,000–3,999
2,000–2,999
900–1,999
Major Mines
Al Aluminum
Cr Chromium
Nb Columbium (Niobium)
Cu Copper
Au Gold
Fe Iron ore
Pb Lead
Mn Manganese
Mo Molybdenum
Ni Nickel
Ag Silver
Sn Tin
Ti Titanium
Zn Zinc
Manufacturing center
Natural gas
Petroleum
Processing plant
Steel manufacturing
Azimuthal Equidistant Projection
SCALE 1:15,025,000
1 CENTIMETER = 150 KILOMETERS; 1 INCH = 237 MILES
KILOMETERS
STATUTE MILES
Paraguay
OBVERSE
REVERSE
REPUBLIC OF PARAGUAY
AREA 406,752 sq km (157,048 sq mi)
POPULATION 6,158,000
CAPITAL Asunción 1,639,000
RELIGION Roman Catholic, Protestant
LANGUAGE Spanish (official), Guarani (official)
LITERACY 94%
LIFE EXPECTANCY 71 years
GDP PER CAPITA $1,168
ECONOMY IND: sugar, cement, textiles, beverages AGR: cotton, sugarcane, soybeans, corn; beef; timber EXP: soybeans, feed, cotton, meat
Peru
REPUBLIC OF PERU
AREA 1,285,216 sq km (496,224 sq mi)
POPULATION 27,947,000
CAPITAL Lima 7,899,000
RELIGION Roman Catholic
LANGUAGE Spanish (official), Quechua (official), Aymara, many minor Amazonian languages
LITERACY 88%
LIFE EXPECTANCY 70 years
GDP PER CAPITA $2,439
ECONOMY IND: mining and refining of minerals and metals, petroleum extraction and refining, natural gas, fishing and fish processing AGR: coffee, cotton, sugarcane, rice; poultry; fish EXP: copper, gold, zinc, crude petroleum and petroleum products

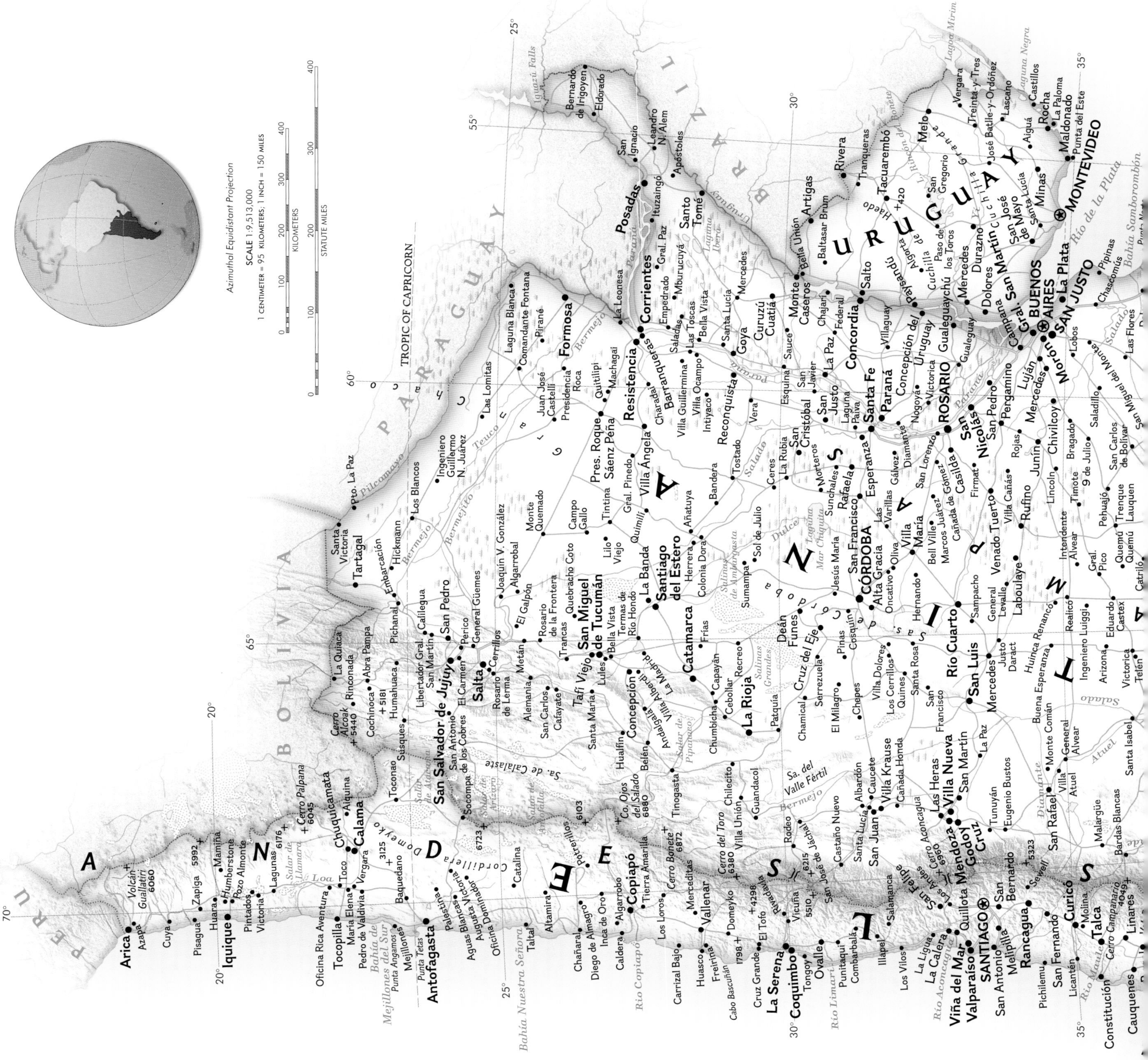

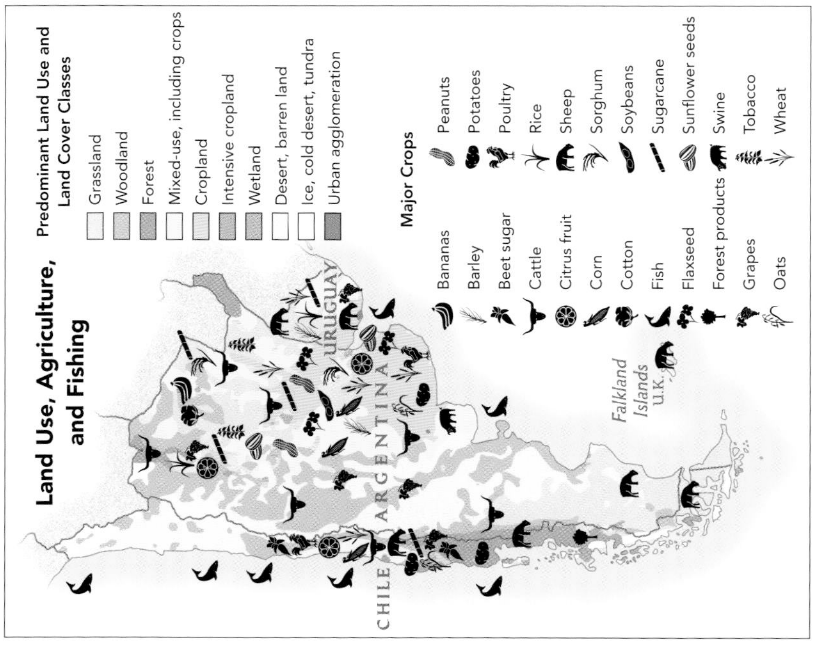

Land Use, Agriculture, and Fishing

Predominant Land Use and Land Cover Classes

- Grassland
- Woodland
- Forest
- Mixed-use, including crops
- Cropland
- Intensive cropland
- Wetland
- Desert, barren land
- Ice, cold desert, tundra
- Urban agglomeration

Major Crops

Bananas	Peanuts
Barley	Potatoes
Beet sugar	Poultry
Cattle	Rice
Citrus fruit	Sheep
Corn	Sorghum
Cotton	Soybeans
Fish	Sugarcane
Flaxseed	Sunflower seeds
Forest products	Swine
Grapes	Tobacco
Oats	Wheat

CHILE ARGENTINA URUGUAY Falkland Islands U.K.

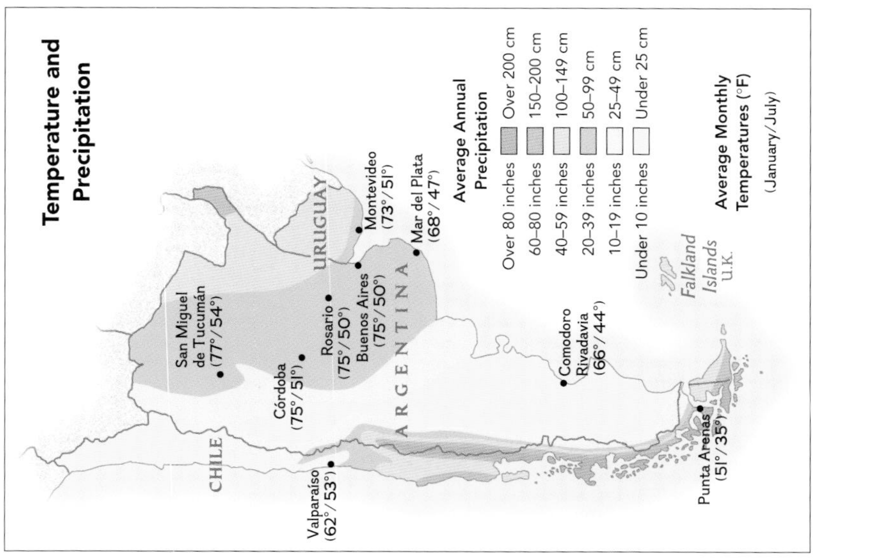

Temperature and Precipitation

CHILE ARGENTINA URUGUAY

San Miguel de Tucumán (77°/54°)
Córdoba (75°/51°)
Valparaíso (62°/53°)
Rosario (75°/50°)
Buenos Aires (75°/50°)
Montevideo (73°/51°)
Mar del Plata (68°/47°)
Comodoro Rivadavia (66°/44°)
Punta Arenas (51°/35°)
Falkland Islands U.K.

Average Annual Precipitation

Over 80 inches	Over 200 cm
60–80 inches	150–200 cm
40–59 inches	100–149 cm
20–39 inches	50–99 cm
10–19 inches	25–49 cm
Under 10 inches	Under 25 cm

Average Monthly Temperatures (°F) (January/July)

Azimuthal Equidistant Projection

SCALE 1:9,513,000
1 CENTIMETER = 95 KILOMETERS; 1 INCH = 150 MILES

KILOMETERS 0 100 200 300 400
STATUTE MILES 0 100 200 300 400

PERU BOLIVIA PARAGUAY BRAZIL URUGUAY ARGENTINA CHILE
TROPIC OF CAPRICORN

Arica, Iquique, Tocopilla, Antofagasta, Calama, Chuquicamata, Taltal, Copiapó, Vallenar, La Serena, Coquimbo, Ovalle, Viña del Mar, Valparaíso, SANTIAGO, Rancagua, Curicó, Talca, San Fernando, Constitución, Cauquenes, Linares
San Salvador de Jujuy, Salta, San Miguel de Tucumán, Santiago del Estero, Catamarca, La Rioja, San Juan, Mendoza, Godoy Cruz, San Luis, Río Cuarto, CÓRDOBA, Santa Fe, Paraná, ROSARIO, BUENOS AIRES, La Plata, SAN JUSTO, Morón, Resistencia, Corrientes, Formosa, Posadas, Reconquista, Concordia, Santo Tomé
Salto, Paysandú, Rivera, Tacuarembó, Melo, MONTEVIDEO, Maldonado, Rocha, Minas
Río de la Plata, Bahía Samborombón, Gran Chaco, Sa. de Córdoba, Cordillera Domeyko, Pilcomayo, Bermejo, Salado, Paraná, Uruguay

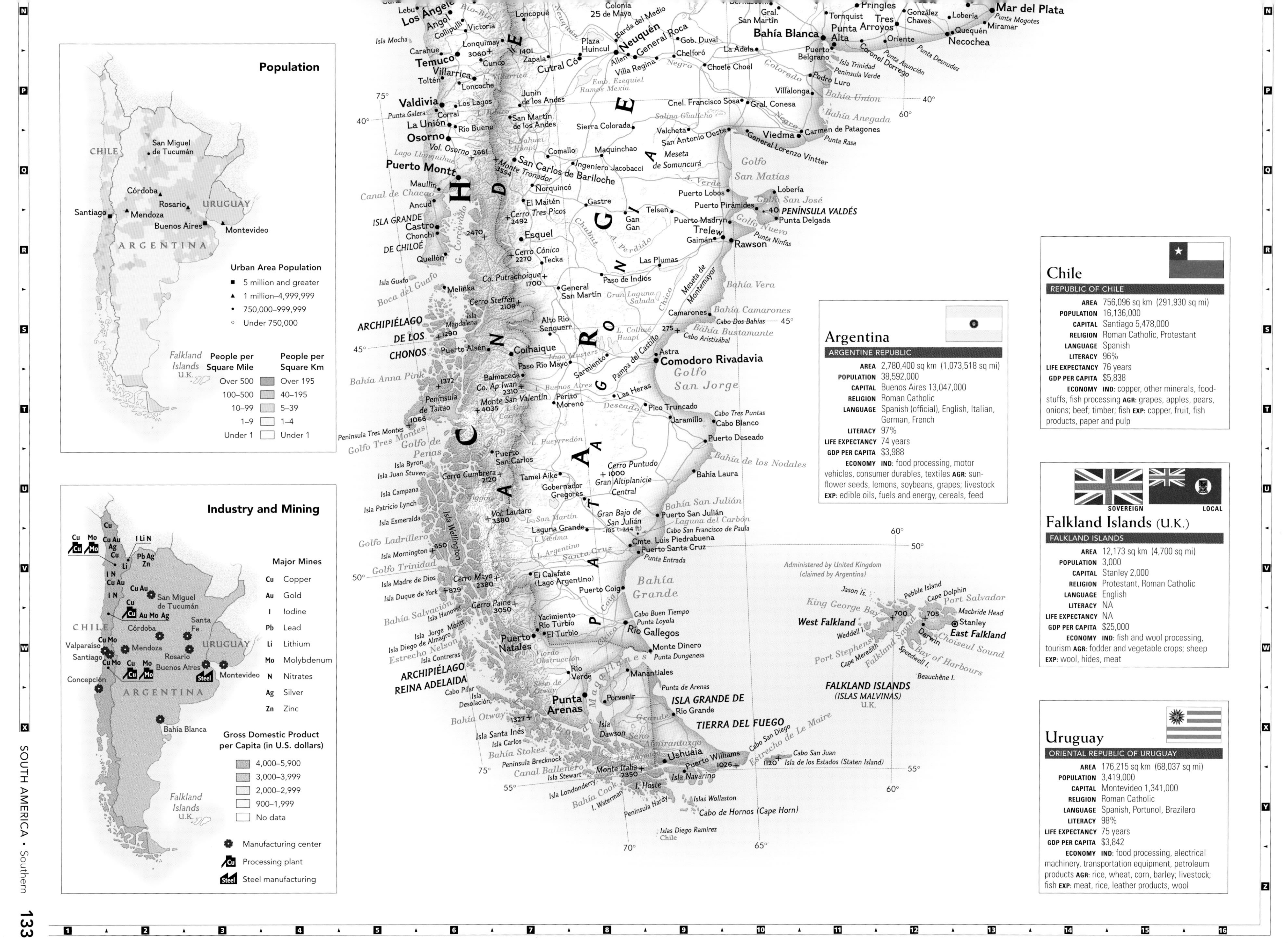
Population
CHILE
San Miguel de Tucumán
Córdoba
Santiago
Mendoza
Rosario
URUGUAY
Buenos Aires
Montevideo
ARGENTINA
Falkland Islands U.K.
Urban Area Population
5 million and greater
1 million–4,999,999
750,000–999,999
Under 750,000
People per Square Mile
Over 500
100–500
10–99
1–9
Under 1
People per Square Km
Over 195
40–195
5–39
1–4
Under 1
Industry and Mining
Major Mines
Cu Copper
Au Gold
I Iodine
Pb Lead
Li Lithium
Mo Molybdenum
N Nitrates
Ag Silver
Zn Zinc
Gross Domestic Product per Capita (in U.S. dollars)
4,000–5,900
3,000–3,999
2,000–2,999
900–1,999
No data
Manufacturing center
Processing plant
Steel manufacturing
Valparaíso
Concepción
Bahía Blanca
Santa Fe
PATAGONIA
Mar del Plata
Bahía Blanca
Neuquén
Valdivia
Temuco
Osorno
Puerto Montt
San Carlos de Bariloche
Esquel
Coihaique
Comodoro Rivadavia
Golfo San Jorge
Golfo San Matías
PENÍNSULA VALDÉS
Rawson
Trelew
Viedma
Puerto Deseado
Puerto San Julián
Puerto Santa Cruz
Río Gallegos
Puerto Natales
Punta Arenas
ISLA GRANDE DE TIERRA DEL FUEGO
Ushuaia
Puerto Williams
Isla Wellington
ARCHIPIÉLAGO DE LOS CHONOS
ARCHIPIÉLAGO REINA ADELAIDA
ISLA GRANDE DE CHILOÉ
Cabo de Hornos (Cape Horn)
Isla de los Estados (Staten Island)
Estrecho de Le Maire
Islas Diego Ramírez Chile
FALKLAND ISLANDS (ISLAS MALVINAS) U.K.
Administered by United Kingdom (claimed by Argentina)
West Falkland
East Falkland
Stanley
Falkland Sound
Bahía Grande
40°
45°
50°
55°
60°
65°
70°
75°

Chile

REPUBLIC OF CHILE

AREA 756,096 sq km (291,930 sq mi)
POPULATION 16,136,000
CAPITAL Santiago 5,478,000
RELIGION Roman Catholic, Protestant
LANGUAGE Spanish
LITERACY 96%
LIFE EXPECTANCY 76 years
GDP PER CAPITA $5,838
ECONOMY **IND:** copper, other minerals, foodstuffs, fish processing **AGR:** grapes, apples, pears, onions; beef; timber; fish **EXP:** copper, fruit, fish products, paper and pulp

Argentina

ARGENTINE REPUBLIC

AREA 2,780,400 sq km (1,073,518 sq mi)
POPULATION 38,592,000
CAPITAL Buenos Aires 13,047,000
RELIGION Roman Catholic
LANGUAGE Spanish (official), English, Italian, German, French
LITERACY 97%
LIFE EXPECTANCY 74 years
GDP PER CAPITA $3,988
ECONOMY **IND:** food processing, motor vehicles, consumer durables, textiles **AGR:** sunflower seeds, lemons, soybeans, grapes; livestock **EXP:** edible oils, fuels and energy, cereals, feed

SOVEREIGN LOCAL

Falkland Islands (U.K.)

FALKLAND ISLANDS

AREA 12,173 sq km (4,700 sq mi)
POPULATION 3,000
CAPITAL Stanley 2,000
RELIGION Protestant, Roman Catholic
LANGUAGE English
LITERACY NA
LIFE EXPECTANCY NA
GDP PER CAPITA $25,000
ECONOMY **IND:** fish and wool processing, tourism **AGR:** fodder and vegetable crops; sheep **EXP:** wool, hides, meat

Uruguay

ORIENTAL REPUBLIC OF URUGUAY

AREA 176,215 sq km (68,037 sq mi)
POPULATION 3,419,000
CAPITAL Montevideo 1,341,000
RELIGION Roman Catholic
LANGUAGE Spanish, Portunol, Brazilero
LITERACY 98%
LIFE EXPECTANCY 75 years
GDP PER CAPITA $3,842
ECONOMY **IND:** food processing, electrical machinery, transportation equipment, petroleum products **AGR:** rice, wheat, corn, barley; livestock; fish **EXP:** meat, rice, leather products, wool

Europe

The fantastical Neuschwanstein Castle, built in the late 1800s and later the model for Disneyland's iconic fairy-tale castle, sits high above the Alpsee in the Bavarian Alps. Although "Mad King Ludwig" intended his creation to be a paean to medieval architecture, he actually incorporated running water, automatic flush toilets, and other revolutionary conveniences of the day.

Europe is the world's second smallest continent, after Australia. A cluster of peninsulas and islands extending from northwestern Asia, Europe comprises more than 40 countries. Despite its northern location, most of its population enjoys a mild climate tempered by warm ocean currents such as the Gulf Stream.

Europe has been inhabited for some 40,000 years. During the past millennium Europeans explored the planet and established far-flung empires. Europe led the world in science and invention, and launched the industrial revolution. By the end of the 19th century, it dominated world commerce, spreading European ideas, languages, legal systems, and political patterns around the globe.

The 20th century brought unprecedented changes. Germany and its neighbors ignited two world wars. The Russian Revolution introduced communism. And Europe, weakened by war, lost its dominant position in the world along with its empires.

In 1947, the United States and the Soviet Union entered into a Cold War, pitting capitalism and democracy against communism and state control. Western Europe, backed by the U.S., prospered with market economies, democracy, and free speech; Eastern and Central European countries, their centrally planned economies closely tied to the Soviet Union's, fell behind and, despite full employment and social benefits, people suffered the lack of personal freedom.

In Western Europe, age-old enemies started cooperating. In 1952 six countries founded a common market for coal and steel; it soon included more countries and more commodities until, in 1991, the European Union was formed. Border controls were eliminated between 15 member countries (in 1999, 12 members introduced a common European currency). Also in 1991, the Soviet Union collapsed. Germany, which had been split by the Cold War, was reunified. Eastern and Central Europe started the difficult transition toward Western-style democracy and privatization.

When chaos overtook the Balkans, Yugoslavia shattered into five countries. But other forces are working toward a cohesive Europe. People move freely throughout the continent; they share the same pop culture, pursue similar urban lifestyles, and rely heavily on cell phones and the Internet.

Environmental problems are often international. Acid rain from England kills life in Swedish lakes. A nuclear accident in Ukraine damages dozens of countries. The Danube and Rhine Rivers spread industrial pollution downstream. Wherever possible, regional solutions hold the most promise, like the projected cleanup of the Baltic Sea involving nine surrounding countries.

Although the European Union enforces strict environmental laws, Eastern Europe understood little about the environment until the 1990s. Some countries still contain toxic waste dumps, untreated sewage, and other hazards, but they have insufficient funds to meet the high costs of cleanup.

A political United States of Europe will probably never happen, but the economic advantages of the European Union have greatly benefitted its member countries (currently numbering 25, with 4 more waiting for membership) as they enter a new era of history.

PHYSICAL GEOGRAPHY Europe is bounded by the Arctic Ocean in the north, the Atlantic Ocean in the west, the Mediterranean and Black Seas in the south, and the Caspian Sea in the southeast. The traditional land boundary is a line following the Ural Mountains south across Russia from the Arctic Ocean, via the Ural River to the Caspian Sea. The line then continues west along the crest of the Caucasus Mountains between the Caspian and Black Seas, making Mount El'brus (18,510 ft; 5,642 m), on the northern side, the highest mountain in Europe. Waterways linking the Black Sea to the Mediterranean place a small part of Turkey in Europe.

Two mountain systems lie between icy tundra and boreal forest in the far north and the warm, dry, hilly Mediterranean coast in the south. Ancient, rugged highlands, worn down by successive Ice Age glaciers, arc southwestward from Scandinavia, through the British Isles, to the Iberian Peninsula, while an active Alpine system spreads east to west across southern Europe. Still rising from a collision of tectonic plates, these mountains include the Carpathians, the Alps, the Pyrenees, and their many spurs. The high point is Mont Blanc (15,781 ft; 4,810 m), shared by France and Italy. Three major navigable rivers—the Danube, the Rhine, and the Rhône—rise in the Alps. Europe's longest river, however, is the Volga, flowing southeast across Russia to the Caspian Sea. Movements in Earth's crust cause earthquakes and volcanic eruptions in southern Europe and in Iceland. The best known volcanoes are Vesuvius, Etna, and Stromboli, all three in Italy.

Between Europe's two mountain systems, a rolling, fertile plain stretches across the continent from the Pyrenees to the Urals, well drained by several rivers. Some of the world's greatest cities are located here, including Paris, Berlin, and Moscow. Huge industrial areas on this plain are home to much of Europe's dense population.

HISTORY Named for King Minos, the first civilization in Europe appeared in Crete about 2000 B.C. Minoans traded with Egypt and western Asia, produced impressive art and architecture, and developed a unique form of writing. Around 1450 B.C., their culture disappeared, probably after a major volcanic eruption or an invasion by warlike Mycenaeans. Homer's *Iliad* and *Odyssey* describe the Mycenaean era that followed.

Classical Greek civilization began in the eighth century B.C. The great achievements of the Greeks in philosophy, mathematics, natural sciences, political thought, and the arts have influenced European civilization ever since. Greece bequeathed its legacy to Rome, known for its builders, engineers, military strategists, and lawmakers. The Roman Empire eventually reached from Britain to Persia and lasted roughly 500 years, until invasions by Germanic tribes from the north destroyed it.

During Roman times a new religion, Christianity, entered Europe from western Asia. As Rome declined, the Christian Church became the common thread binding Europeans together. It maintained schools and learning in its monasteries through the Middle Ages. In the 11th century, theological differences split Christianity into Orthodoxy in the east, led by patriarchs, and Roman Catholicism in the west, under popes.

Ottoman Turks introduced Islam to the Balkans through conquest during the 14th and 15th centuries. A hundred years later, the Protestant Reformation in northern Europe broke the unity of the Roman Catholic Church and provoked a century of wars.

In the 15th and 16th centuries, the Renaissance—a rebirth of arts, science, and culture—spread northward throughout the continent. Political power shifted to Western Europe, where strong nations emerged, notably England, France, Spain, and Portugal. Under powerful kings, worldwide explorations created mercantile empires, even as ideas of democracy and equality started circulating.

In the 18th century, Britain's American colonies became independent and, in the wake of the French Revolution that toppled the monarchy, Napoleon tried, but failed, to seize all of Europe. In 1815, a balance of power was reestablished among European countries until the forces of nationalism, socialism, and democracy exploded into two world wars a century later.

Following World War II, the Cold War between the U.S. and the Soviet Union replaced the old balance of power with a deadly balance of nuclear armaments, reducing Europe to lesser status. But by the time the Cold War came to an end in the 1990s, Western Europe had coalesced into the European Union. A large number of countries were also allied with the North Atlantic Treaty Organization (NATO), and Europe was embarking on a new era of economic and military cooperation.

CULTURE Next to Asia, Europe has the world's densest population. Scores of distinct ethnic groups, speaking some 40 languages, inhabit more than 40 countries, which vary in size from vast European Russia to tiny Vatican City, each with its own history and traditions. Yet Europe has a more uniform culture than any other continent. Its population is overwhelmingly of one race, Caucasian, despite the recent arrival of immigrants from Africa and Asia. Most of its languages fall into three groups with Indo-European roots: Germanic, Romance, or Slavic. One religion, Christianity, predominates in various forms, and social structures nearly everywhere are based on economic classes.

Great periods of creativity in the arts have occurred at various times all over the continent and shape its collective culture. Classical Greek sculpture and architecture are widely seen as paradigms of beauty. Gothic cathedrals of medieval France still inspire awe. Renaissance works of art, from paintings by Leonardo da Vinci in Florence to plays by Shakespeare in England, are famous worldwide. Music composed by Mozart of Austria, Beethoven of Germany, and Tchaikovsky of Russia has passed far beyond Europe. Spanish artist Pablo Picasso transformed the Western world's concept of art. By the 20th century, European culture had penetrated everywhere.

The success of America's multibillion-dollar entertainment industry makes some Europeans feel culturally threatened. American movies flood the continent; American products and lifestyles are aggressively marketed. English is becoming the preferred second language for students all over Europe. Others see the blending of cultures as an inevitable aspect of globalization and a chance to export their own pop music, plays, architecture, fashions, and gourmet foods to other countries. A more imminent worry focuses on immigrant groups established as legitimate and illegal workers, refugees, and asylum seekers, who cling to their own habits, religions, and languages. Every European society is becoming multicultural, with political as well as cultural consequences.

Rome's greatest landmark, the Colosseum, was completed in A.D. 80; it held 50,000 spectators during gladiator fights and other events. Four stories high, this structure combines Greek esthetics with Roman building techniques.

ECONOMY Europe is fortunate in having fertile soil, a temperate climate, ample natural resources, and a long, irregular coastline that gives most countries access to the sea and foreign trade. Navigable rivers often help the 13 landlocked countries.

Europe is currently undertaking two of the most far-reaching economic experiments in its history. While some countries in Eastern and Central Europe are still converting centrally planned, communist-style economies to the democratic market system, 25 highly developed European nations have created a powerful "eurozone" by replacing their national money with the euro, a shared currency.

The progress of many ex-Soviet bloc countries has been slower than anticipated due, in part, to a need for laws preventing corruption and abuse of the new system, and for institutions to assure sound financial management. Poland and Slovenia have been among the most successful. Russia and Belarus, on the other hand, have slipped into worsening poverty, causing some people to clamor for a return to the safety nets of communism.

The eurozone countries did not have a totally smooth transition to the single currency. The new European Central Bank could not keep the euro from losing a quarter of its value against the U.S. dollar in its first three years; however, in recent years, the euro has strengthened considerably and the advantages of a shared currency are increasingly tangible: Banking has become faster and easier, and the newly enlarged bond market has led to many corporate reforms and important mergers. A majority of voters in Britain, Sweden, and Denmark, called "euroskeptics," refused to adopt the euro in 1999 like other European Union members. But they will probably vote to do so as the eurozone grows in strength and influence.

Meanwhile, the advantages offered by the European Union encourage outside countries to practice the tough economic and fiscal policies that are prerequisites for membership. Ten countries were admitted in 2004: Estonia, Latvia, Lithuania, Cyprus, Malta, the Czech Republic, Hungary, Poland, Slovakia, and Slovenia. With the anticipated addition of Bulgaria and Romania in 2007, the European Union will have a population of nearly half a billion, firmly cementing it as one of the largest economies in the world. Many Europeans speculate that in time the euro may rival the U.S. dollar as the principal global currency.

Europe: Physical and Political

A commonly accepted division between Asia and Europe–here marked by a green line–is formed by the Ural Mountains, Ural River, Caspian Sea, Caucasus Mountains, and the Black Sea with its outlets, the Bosporus and Dardanelles.
Azimuthal Equidistant Projection
SCALE 1:18,036,000
1 CENTIMETER = 180 KILOMETERS; 1 INCH = 284 MILES
KILOMETERS
STATUTE MILES
International boundary
ARCTIC CIRCLE
NORWEGIAN SEA
ATLANTIC OCEAN
NORTH SEA
BALTIC SEA
GULF OF BOTHNIA
GULF OF FINLAND
BARENTS SEA
WHITE SEA
BLACK SEA
CASPIAN SEA
ARAL SEA
MEDITERRANEAN SEA
ADRIATIC SEA
TYRRHENIAN SEA
IONIAN SEA
AEGEAN SEA
SEA OF CRETE
SEA OF AZOV
LIGURIAN SEA
BALEARIC SEA
ALBORAN SEA
CELTIC SEA
IRISH SEA
BAY OF BISCAY
PERSIAN GULF
Gulf of Sidra
English Channel
Strait of Gibraltar
Strait of Otranto
ICELAND
BRITISH ISLES
GREAT BRITAIN
IRELAND
SCANDINAVIA
KOLA PENINSULA
IBERIAN PENINSULA
BALKAN PENINSULA
APENNINES
ALPS
PYRENEES
URAL MOUNTAINS
CAUCASUS MOUNTAINS
CARPATHIAN MOUNTAINS
DINARIC ALPS
Balkan Mountains
Rhodope Mts.
Pindus Mts.
Transylvanian Alps
Cantabrian Mountains
Iberian Mountains
Sierra Morena
Baetic Mountains
Mulhacén 3481
Er Rif
ATLAS MOUNTAINS
SAHARA
AFRICA
ASIA
ANATOLIA (ASIA MINOR)
Kuzey Anadolu Dağlari
MESOPOTAMIA
SYRIAN DESERT
Dead Sea –416 (–1365 ft) World's lowest point
Levant Coast
SUEZ CANAL
CYPRUS
CRETE
RHODES
Dodecanese
Cyclades
PELOPONNESUS
IONIAN ISLANDS
SICILY
Etna 3322
Malta
MALTESE ISLANDS
SARDINIA
CORSICA
BALEARIC ISLANDS
Majorca
Minorca
Ibiza
Vesuvius 1281
Corno Grande 2912
Mont Blanc 4810
Matterhorn 4478
Grossglockner 3798
Gerlach 2655
Olympus 2917
El'brus 5642 (18,510 ft) Highest point in Europe
Mount Ararat 5137
Caspian Sea: Surface elevation –28 m (–92 ft) Lowest point in Europe
Caspian Depression
Volga Upland
Central Russian Upland
EAST EUROPEAN PLAIN
NORTHERN EUROPEAN PLAIN
Valdai Hills
Smolensk-Moscow Upland
Dnieper Lowland
Dnieper Upland
Volyn-Podolian Upland
Black Sea Lowland
Danube River Delta
Volga River Delta
Great Hungarian Plain
Pripyat Marshes
Timan Ridge
Northern Uvals
Maan Ridge
Salpaus Ridge
Suomen Ridge
Lake Region
Finnmark Plateau
North Cape
Kebnekaise 2111
Galdhøpiggen 2469
Lofoten
Vesterålen
Shetland Islands
Orkney Islands
Faroe Islands
Outer Hebrides
Inner Hebrides
Grampian Mts.
Highlands
Ben Nevis 1343
Southern Uplands
The Pennines
Cambrian Mts.
Snowdon 1085
Carrantuohill 1041
Isle of Man
Land's End
Channel Islands
Point St.-Mathieu
Normandy
Armorican Massif
Paris Basin
Aquitaine Basin
Massif Central
Puy de Sancy 1886
Cévennes
Pico de Aneto 3404
Jura Mts.
Vosges
Black Forest
Bohemian Forest
Ore Mts.
Sudeten
Harz
Ardennes
Frisian Islands
JUTLAND
ZEALAND
FYN
Gotland
Öland
Saaremaa
Hiiumaa
Åland Is.
Gulf of Riga
Gulf of Gdańsk
Kattegat
Skagerrak
Lake Ladoga
Lake Onega
White Sea–Baltic Canal
Murman Coast
Kanin Pen.
Kolguyev Island
Malozemel'skaya Tundra
Bol'shezemel'skaya Tundra
Pechora Basin
Narodnaya 1895
Upper Kama Upland
Mugodzhar Hills
Obshchiy Syrt
THE STEPPES
Ryn Peski
Yergeni Hills
Stavropol' Plateau
Ciscaucasia
Transcaucasia
Lesser Caucasus
Kuban Lowland
Donets Ridge
Azov Upland
CRIMEA
Crimean Mts.
Absheron Pen.
Bosporus
Dardanelles
Sea of Marmara
Iron Gate
Volga
Danube
Dnieper
Don
Ural
Rhine
Elbe
Oder
Vistula
Loire
Seine
Garonne
Ebro
Tagus
Douro
Guadalquivir
Tigris
Euphrates
Shatt al Arab
Amu Darya
Tobol
WEST SIBERIAN PLAIN
Cape Finisterre
Cape St. Vincent

A commonly accepted division between Asia and Europe–here marked by a green line–is formed by the Ural Mountains, Ural River, Caspian Sea, Caucasus Mountains, and the Black Sea with its outlets, the Bosporus and Dardanelles.
Azimuthal Equidistant Projection
SCALE 1:18,036,000
1 CENTIMETER = 180 KILOMETERS; 1 INCH = 284 MILES
KILOMETERS
STATUTE MILES
Small country
Meridian of Greenwich (London)
Longitude East 5° of Greenwich
5° Longitude West of Greenwich
ARCTIC CIRCLE
NORWEGIAN SEA
NORTH SEA
ATLANTIC OCEAN
BAY OF BISCAY
MEDITERRANEAN SEA
BLACK SEA
CASPIAN SEA
ICELAND
NORWAY
SWEDEN
FINLAND
RUSSIA
KAZAKHSTAN
UNITED KINGDOM
IRELAND
FRANCE
SPAIN
PORTUGAL
GERMANY
POLAND
UKRAINE
ROMANIA
ITALY
GREECE
TURKEY
LIBYA
ALGERIA
MOROCCO
TUNISIA
EGYPT
SYRIA
IRAQ
IRAN
SAUDIA ARABIA

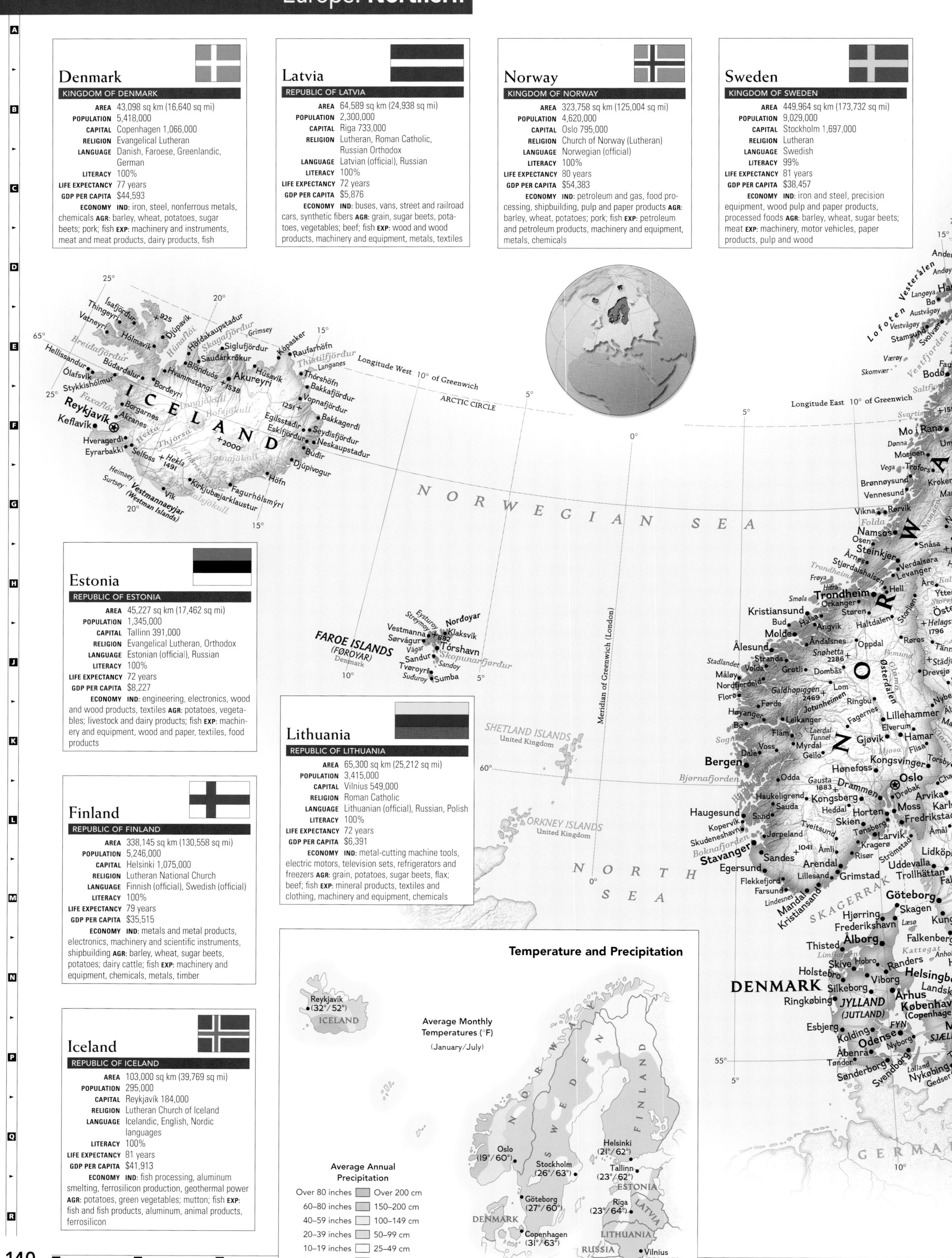

Denmark
KINGDOM OF DENMARK

AREA 43,098 sq km (16,640 sq mi)
POPULATION 5,418,000
CAPITAL Copenhagen 1,066,000
RELIGION Evangelical Lutheran
LANGUAGE Danish, Faroese, Greenlandic, German
LITERACY 100%
LIFE EXPECTANCY 77 years
GDP PER CAPITA $44,593
ECONOMY **IND:** iron, steel, nonferrous metals, chemicals **AGR:** barley, wheat, potatoes, sugar beets; pork; fish **EXP:** machinery and instruments, meat and meat products, dairy products, fish

Latvia
REPUBLIC OF LATVIA

AREA 64,589 sq km (24,938 sq mi)
POPULATION 2,300,000
CAPITAL Riga 733,000
RELIGION Lutheran, Roman Catholic, Russian Orthodox
LANGUAGE Latvian (official), Russian
LITERACY 100%
LIFE EXPECTANCY 72 years
GDP PER CAPITA $5,876
ECONOMY **IND:** buses, vans, street and railroad cars, synthetic fibers **AGR:** grain, sugar beets, potatoes, vegetables; beef; fish **EXP:** wood and wood products, machinery and equipment, metals, textiles

Norway
KINGDOM OF NORWAY

AREA 323,758 sq km (125,004 sq mi)
POPULATION 4,620,000
CAPITAL Oslo 795,000
RELIGION Church of Norway (Lutheran)
LANGUAGE Norwegian (official)
LITERACY 100%
LIFE EXPECTANCY 80 years
GDP PER CAPITA $54,383
ECONOMY **IND:** petroleum and gas, food processing, shipbuilding, pulp and paper products **AGR:** barley, wheat, potatoes; pork; fish **EXP:** petroleum and petroleum products, machinery and equipment, metals, chemicals

Sweden
KINGDOM OF SWEDEN

AREA 449,964 sq km (173,732 sq mi)
POPULATION 9,029,000
CAPITAL Stockholm 1,697,000
RELIGION Lutheran
LANGUAGE Swedish
LITERACY 99%
LIFE EXPECTANCY 81 years
GDP PER CAPITA $38,457
ECONOMY **IND:** iron and steel, precision equipment, wood pulp and paper products, processed foods **AGR:** barley, wheat, sugar beets; meat **EXP:** machinery, motor vehicles, paper products, pulp and wood

Estonia
REPUBLIC OF ESTONIA

AREA 45,227 sq km (17,462 sq mi)
POPULATION 1,345,000
CAPITAL Tallinn 391,000
RELIGION Evangelical Lutheran, Orthodox
LANGUAGE Estonian (official), Russian
LITERACY 100%
LIFE EXPECTANCY 72 years
GDP PER CAPITA $8,227
ECONOMY **IND:** engineering, electronics, wood and wood products, textiles **AGR:** potatoes, vegetables; livestock and dairy products; fish **EXP:** machinery and equipment, wood and paper, textiles, food products

Lithuania
REPUBLIC OF LITHUANIA

AREA 65,300 sq km (25,212 sq mi)
POPULATION 3,415,000
CAPITAL Vilnius 549,000
RELIGION Roman Catholic
LANGUAGE Lithuanian (official), Russian, Polish
LITERACY 100%
LIFE EXPECTANCY 72 years
GDP PER CAPITA $6,391
ECONOMY **IND:** metal-cutting machine tools, electric motors, television sets, refrigerators and freezers **AGR:** grain, potatoes, sugar beets, flax; beef; fish **EXP:** mineral products, textiles and clothing, machinery and equipment, chemicals

Finland
REPUBLIC OF FINLAND

AREA 338,145 sq km (130,558 sq mi)
POPULATION 5,246,000
CAPITAL Helsinki 1,075,000
RELIGION Lutheran National Church
LANGUAGE Finnish (official), Swedish (official)
LITERACY 100%
LIFE EXPECTANCY 79 years
GDP PER CAPITA $35,515
ECONOMY **IND:** metals and metal products, electronics, machinery and scientific instruments, shipbuilding **AGR:** barley, wheat, sugar beets, potatoes; dairy cattle; fish **EXP:** machinery and equipment, chemicals, metals, timber

Iceland
REPUBLIC OF ICELAND

AREA 103,000 sq km (39,769 sq mi)
POPULATION 295,000
CAPITAL Reykjavík 184,000
RELIGION Lutheran Church of Iceland
LANGUAGE Icelandic, English, Nordic languages
LITERACY 100%
LIFE EXPECTANCY 81 years
GDP PER CAPITA $41,913
ECONOMY **IND:** fish processing, aluminum smelting, ferrosilicon production, geothermal power **AGR:** potatoes, green vegetables; mutton; fish **EXP:** fish and fish products, aluminum, animal products, ferrosilicon

ICELAND
Reykjavík
Akureyri
NORWEGIAN SEA
FAROE ISLANDS (FØROYAR) Denmark
Tórshavn
SHETLAND ISLANDS United Kingdom
ORKNEY ISLANDS United Kingdom
NORTH SEA
ARCTIC CIRCLE
Longitude West 10° of Greenwich
Longitude East 10° of Greenwich
Meridian of Greenwich (London)
NORWAY
Trondheim
Bergen
Oslo
Stavanger
SKAGERRAK
DENMARK
København (Copenhagen)
Göteborg
Temperature and Precipitation
Average Monthly Temperatures (°F) (January/July)
Reykjavík (32°/52°)
Oslo (19°/60°)
Stockholm (26°/63°)
Helsinki (21°/62°)
Tallinn (23°/62°)
Göteborg (27°/60°)
Riga (23°/64°)
Copenhagen (31°/63°)
Vilnius (22°/65°)
Average Annual Precipitation
Over 80 inches / Over 200 cm
60–80 inches / 150–200 cm
40–59 inches / 100–149 cm
20–39 inches / 50–99 cm
10–19 inches / 25–49 cm
Under 10 inches / Under 25 cm

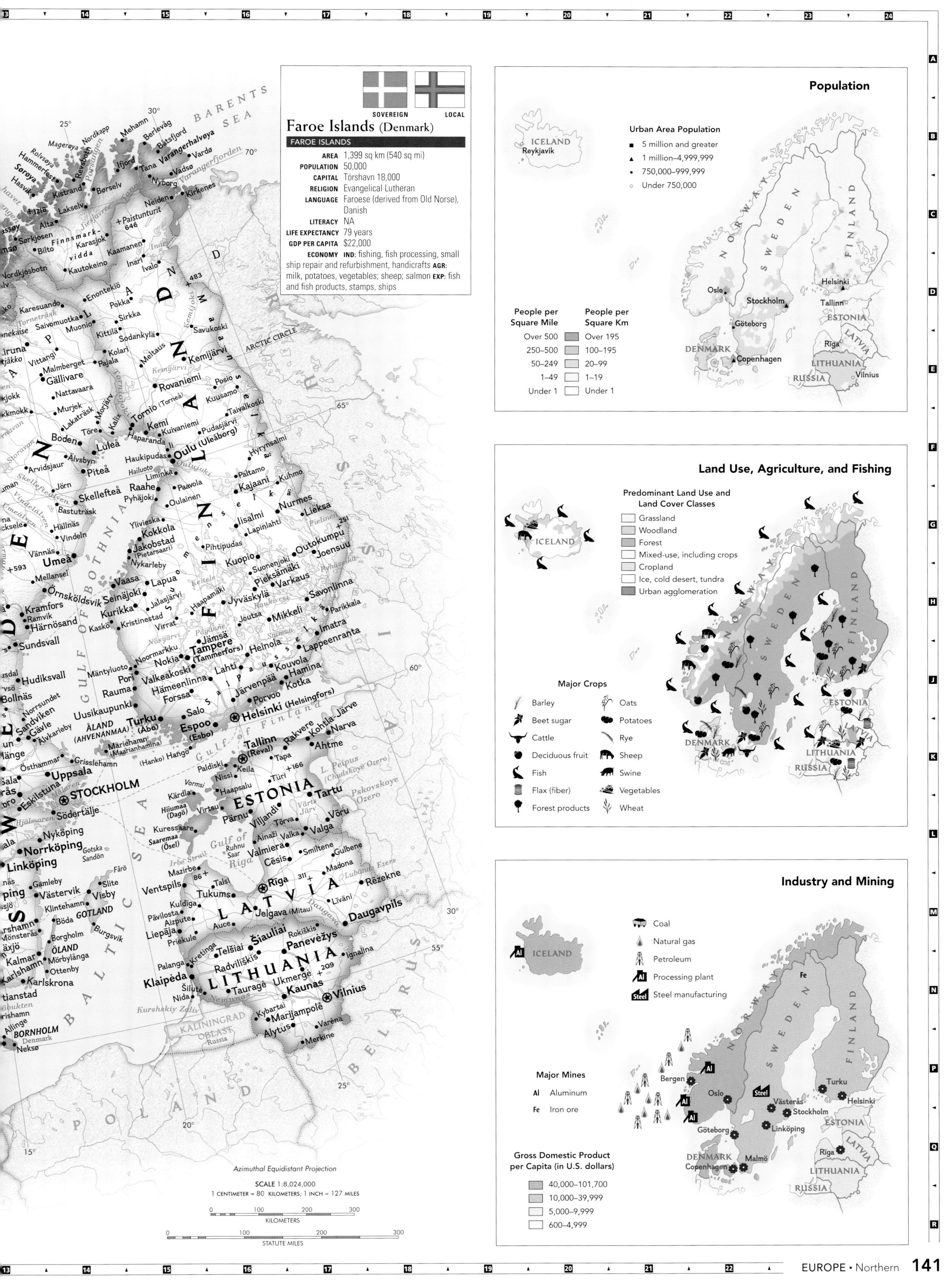

SOVEREIGN
LOCAL
Faroe Islands (Denmark)
FAROE ISLANDS
AREA 1,399 sq km (540 sq mi)
POPULATION 50,000
CAPITAL Tórshavn 18,000
RELIGION Evangelical Lutheran
LANGUAGE Faroese (derived from Old Norse), Danish
LITERACY NA
LIFE EXPECTANCY 79 years
GDP PER CAPITA $22,000
ECONOMY IND: fishing, fish processing, small ship repair and refurbishment, handicrafts AGR: milk, potatoes, vegetables; sheep; salmon EXP: fish and fish products, stamps, ships
Population
Urban Area Population
5 million and greater
1 million–4,999,999
750,000–999,999
Under 750,000
People per Square Mile
People per Square Km
Over 500 | Over 195
250–500 | 100–195
50–249 | 20–99
1–49 | 1–19
Under 1 | Under 1
Land Use, Agriculture, and Fishing
Predominant Land Use and Land Cover Classes
Grassland
Woodland
Forest
Mixed-use, including crops
Cropland
Ice, cold desert, tundra
Urban agglomeration
Major Crops
Barley
Beet sugar
Cattle
Deciduous fruit
Fish
Flax (fiber)
Forest products
Oats
Potatoes
Rye
Sheep
Swine
Vegetables
Wheat
Industry and Mining
Coal
Natural gas
Petroleum
Processing plant
Steel manufacturing
Major Mines
Al Aluminum
Fe Iron ore
Gross Domestic Product per Capita (in U.S. dollars)
40,000–101,700
10,000–39,999
5,000–9,999
600–4,999
Azimuthal Equidistant Projection
SCALE 1:8,024,000
1 CENTIMETER = 80 KILOMETERS; 1 INCH = 127 MILES
KILOMETERS
STATUTE MILES
BARENTS SEA
GULF OF BOTHNIA
BALTIC SEA
Gulf of Finland
Gulf of Riga
FINLAND
ESTONIA
LATVIA
LITHUANIA
RUSSIA
BELARUS
POLAND
KALININGRAD OBLAST Russia
STOCKHOLM
Helsinki (Helsingfors)
Tallinn (Reval)
Rīga
Vilnius

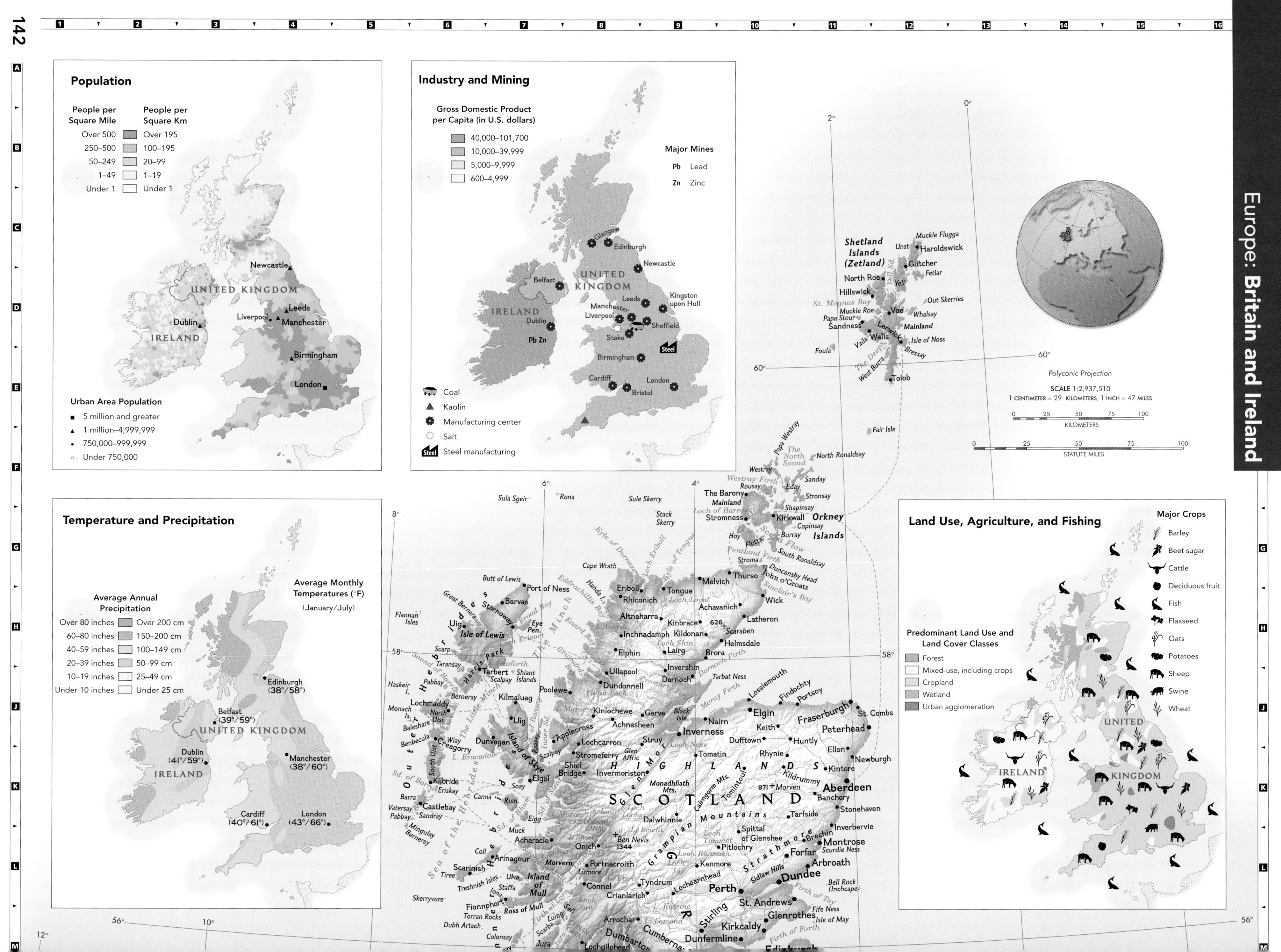
Population
People per Square Mile
Over 500
250–500
50–249
1–49
Under 1
People per Square Km
Over 195
100–195
20–99
1–19
Under 1
Urban Area Population
5 million and greater
1 million–4,999,999
750,000–999,999
Under 750,000
Industry and Mining
Gross Domestic Product per Capita (in U.S. dollars)
40,000–101,700
10,000–39,999
5,000–9,999
600–4,999
Major Mines
Pb Lead
Zn Zinc
Coal
Kaolin
Manufacturing center
Salt
Steel manufacturing
Temperature and Precipitation
Average Annual Precipitation
Over 80 inches
60–80 inches
40–59 inches
20–39 inches
10–19 inches
Under 10 inches
Over 200 cm
150–200 cm
100–149 cm
50–99 cm
25–49 cm
Under 25 cm
Average Monthly Temperatures (°F) (January/July)
Edinburgh (38°/58°)
Belfast (39°/59°)
Dublin (41°/59°)
Manchester (38°/60°)
Cardiff (40°/61°)
London (43°/66°)
Land Use, Agriculture, and Fishing
Predominant Land Use and Land Cover Classes
Forest
Mixed-use, including crops
Cropland
Wetland
Urban agglomeration
Major Crops
Barley
Beet sugar
Cattle
Deciduous fruit
Fish
Flaxseed
Oats
Potatoes
Sheep
Swine
Wheat
Polyconic Projection
SCALE 1:2,937,510
1 CENTIMETER = 29 KILOMETERS; 1 INCH = 47 MILES
KILOMETERS
STATUTE MILES
Shetland Islands (Zetland)
Orkney Islands
SCOTLAND
Aberdeen
Dundee
Inverness
Perth
Grampian Mountains
Isle of Lewis
Island of Skye
UNITED KINGDOM
IRELAND

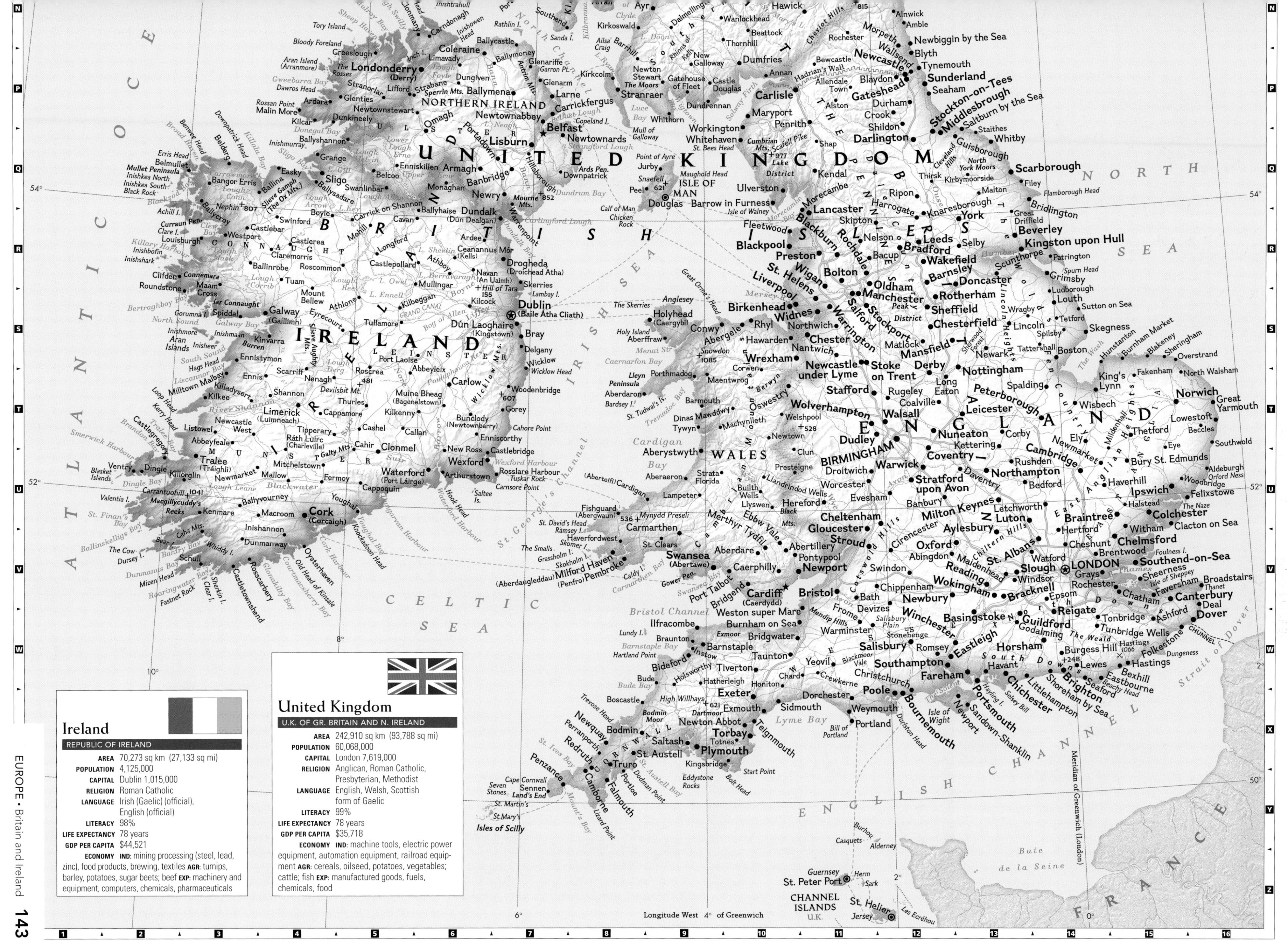

ATLANTIC OCEAN
NORTH SEA
IRISH SEA
CELTIC SEA
ENGLISH CHANNEL
St. George's Channel
North Channel
Bristol Channel
Strait of Dover
Baie de la Seine
BRITISH ISLES
UNITED KINGDOM
IRELAND
NORTHERN IRELAND
ENGLAND
WALES
ISLE OF MAN
CHANNEL ISLANDS U.K.
FRANCE
Dublin (Baile Átha Cliath)
Belfast
LONDON
Cardiff (Caerdydd)
Douglas
Cork (Corcaigh)
Galway (Gaillimh)
Limerick (Luimneach)
Waterford (Port Láirge)
Londonderry (Derry)
BIRMINGHAM
Manchester
Liverpool
Leeds
Sheffield
Bristol
Newcastle
Kingston upon Hull
Plymouth
Southampton
Norwich
Isles of Scilly
St. Peter Port
St. Helier
Meridian of Greenwich (London)
Longitude West 4° of Greenwich

Ireland

REPUBLIC OF IRELAND

AREA 70,273 sq km (27,133 sq mi)
POPULATION 4,125,000
CAPITAL Dublin 1,015,000
RELIGION Roman Catholic
LANGUAGE Irish (Gaelic) (official), English (official)
LITERACY 98%
LIFE EXPECTANCY 78 years
GDP PER CAPITA $44,521
ECONOMY **IND:** mining processing (steel, lead, zinc), food products, brewing, textiles **AGR:** turnips, barley, potatoes, sugar beets; beef **EXP:** machinery and equipment, computers, chemicals, pharmaceuticals

United Kingdom

U.K. OF GR. BRITAIN AND N. IRELAND

AREA 242,910 sq km (93,788 sq mi)
POPULATION 60,068,000
CAPITAL London 7,619,000
RELIGION Anglican, Roman Catholic, Presbyterian, Methodist
LANGUAGE English, Welsh, Scottish form of Gaelic
LITERACY 99%
LIFE EXPECTANCY 78 years
GDP PER CAPITA $35,718
ECONOMY **IND:** machine tools, electric power equipment, automation equipment, railroad equipment **AGR:** cereals, oilseed, potatoes, vegetables; cattle; fish **EXP:** manufactured goods, fuels, chemicals, food

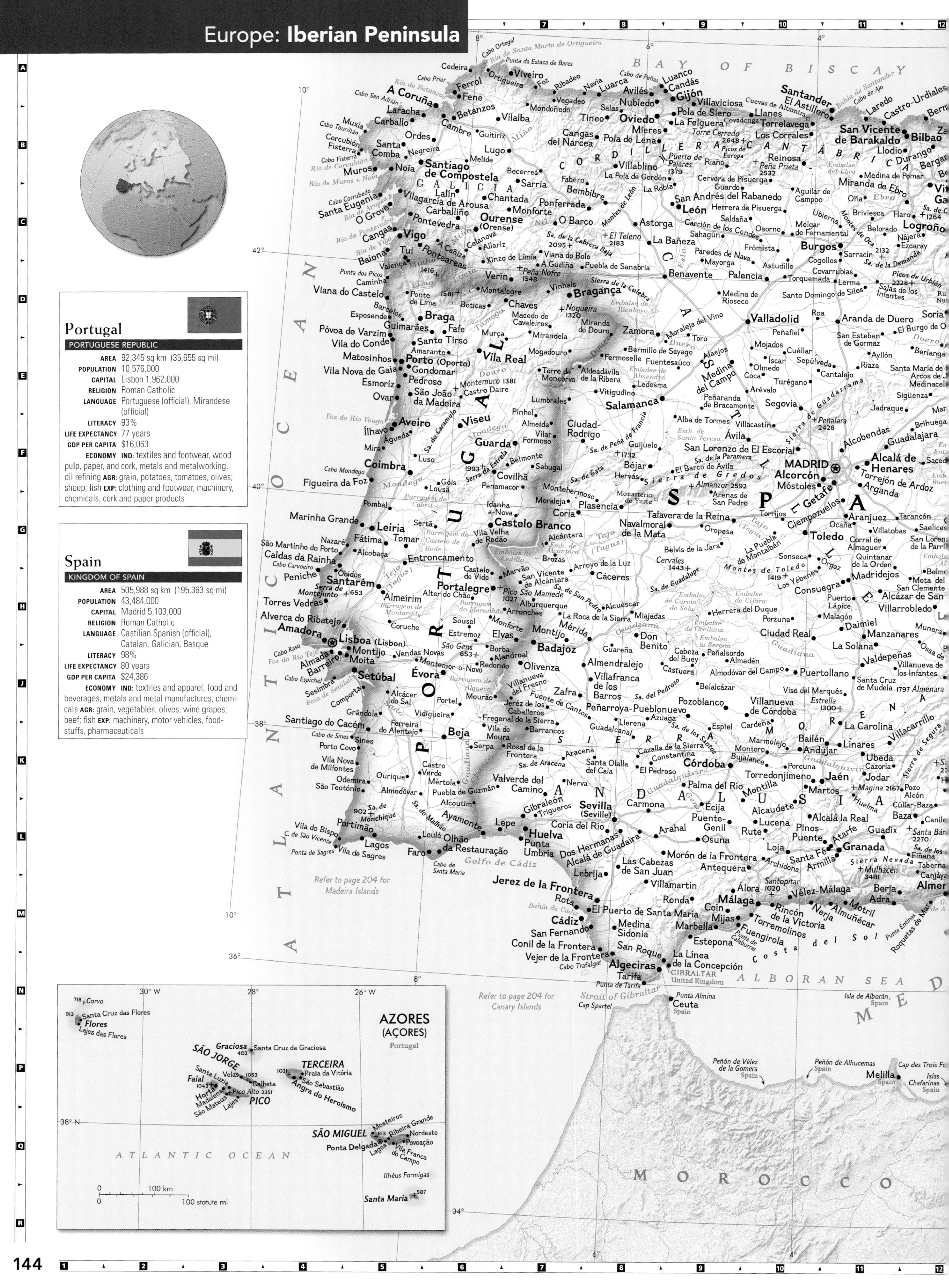
Portugal
PORTUGUESE REPUBLIC
AREA 92,345 sq km (35,655 sq mi)
POPULATION 10,576,000
CAPITAL Lisbon 1,962,000
RELIGION Roman Catholic
LANGUAGE Portuguese (official), Mirandese (official)
LITERACY 93%
LIFE EXPECTANCY 77 years
GDP PER CAPITA $16,063
ECONOMY IND: textiles and footwear, wood pulp, paper, and cork, metals and metalworking, oil refining AGR: grain, potatoes, tomatoes, olives; sheep; fish EXP: clothing and footwear, machinery, chemicals, cork and paper products
Spain
KINGDOM OF SPAIN
AREA 505,988 sq km (195,363 sq mi)
POPULATION 43,484,000
CAPITAL Madrid 5,103,000
RELIGION Roman Catholic
LANGUAGE Castilian Spanish (official), Catalan, Galician, Basque
LITERACY 98%
LIFE EXPECTANCY 80 years
GDP PER CAPITA $24,386
ECONOMY IND: textiles and apparel, food and beverages, metals and metal manufactures, chemicals AGR: grain, vegetables, olives, wine grapes; beef; fish EXP: machinery, motor vehicles, foodstuffs, pharmaceuticals
BAY OF BISCAY
ATLANTIC OCEAN
PORTUGAL
SPAIN
MOROCCO
ALBORAN SEA
CORDILLERA CANTÁBRICA
GALICIA
CASTILLA Y LEÓN
CASTILLA-LA MANCHA
ANDALUSIA
SIERRA MORENA
MADRID
Lisboa (Lisbon)
Porto (Oporto)
Sevilla (Seville)
Refer to page 204 for Madeira Islands
Refer to page 204 for Canary Islands
Strait of Gibraltar
GIBRALTAR United Kingdom
Ceuta Spain
Melilla Spain
AZORES (AÇORES) Portugal
SÃO JORGE
TERCEIRA
PICO
SÃO MIGUEL
Santa Maria
Flores
Faial
Graciosa
Ponta Delgada
Angra do Heroísmo
ATLANTIC OCEAN
100 km
100 statute mi

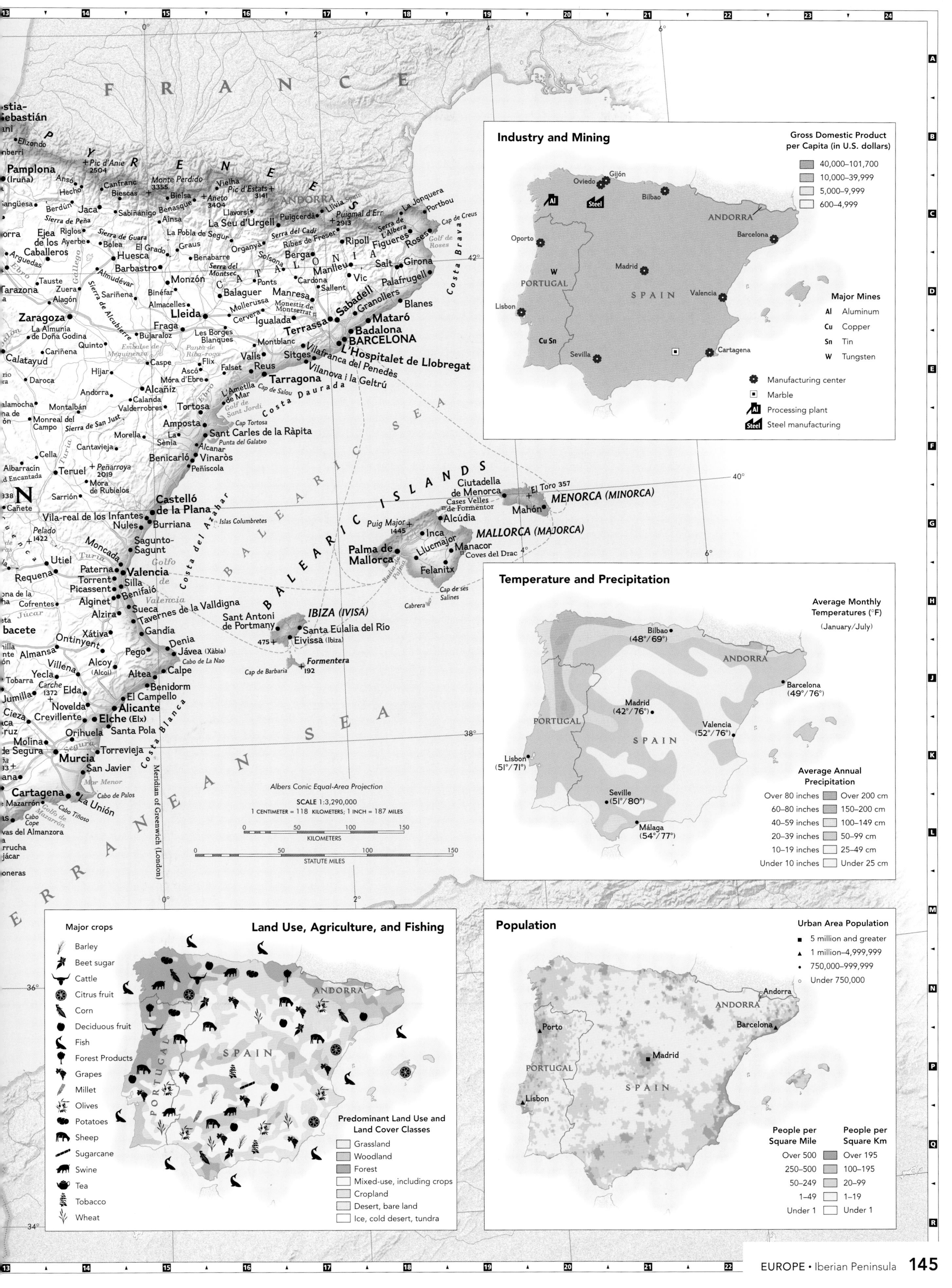

F R A N C E
P Y R E N E E S
C A T A L O N I A
BALEARIC ISLANDS
B A L E A R I C S E A
MEDITERRANEAN SEA
Pamplona (Iruña)
Zaragoza
Lleida
BARCELONA
L'Hospitalet de Llobregat
Badalona
Sabadell
Terrassa
Mataró
Girona
Tarragona
Reus
Tortosa
Castelló de la Plana
Valencia
Alicante
Elche (Elx)
Murcia
Cartagena
Teruel
Huesca
Andorra
ANDORRA
Costa Brava
Costa Daurada
Costa del Azahar
Costa Blanca
Palma de Mallorca
MALLORCA (MAJORCA)
MENORCA (MINORCA)
IBIZA (IVISA)
Formentera
Eivissa (Ibiza)
Mahón
Ciutadella de Menorca
Meridian of Greenwich (London)
Albers Conic Equal-Area Projection
SCALE 1:3,290,000
1 CENTIMETER = 118 KILOMETERS; 1 INCH = 187 MILES
KILOMETERS
STATUTE MILES
Industry and Mining
Gross Domestic Product per Capita (in U.S. dollars)
40,000–101,700
10,000–39,999
5,000–9,999
600–4,999
Major Mines
Al Aluminum
Cu Copper
Sn Tin
W Tungsten
Manufacturing center
Marble
Processing plant
Steel manufacturing
Temperature and Precipitation
Average Monthly Temperatures (°F) (January/July)
Bilbao (48°/69°)
Barcelona (49°/76°)
Madrid (42°/76°)
Valencia (52°/76°)
Lisbon (51°/71°)
Seville (51°/80°)
Málaga (54°/77°)
Average Annual Precipitation
Over 80 inches Over 200 cm
60–80 inches 150–200 cm
40–59 inches 100–149 cm
20–39 inches 50–99 cm
10–19 inches 25–49 cm
Under 10 inches Under 25 cm
Land Use, Agriculture, and Fishing
Major crops
Barley
Beet sugar
Cattle
Citrus fruit
Corn
Deciduous fruit
Fish
Forest Products
Grapes
Millet
Olives
Potatoes
Sheep
Sugarcane
Swine
Tea
Tobacco
Wheat
Predominant Land Use and Land Cover Classes
Grassland
Woodland
Forest
Mixed-use, including crops
Cropland
Desert, bare land
Ice, cold desert, tundra
Population
Urban Area Population
5 million and greater
1 million–4,999,999
750,000–999,999
Under 750,000
People per Square Mile / People per Square Km
Over 500 Over 195
250–500 100–195
50–249 20–99
1–49 1–19
Under 1 Under 1
SPAIN
PORTUGAL

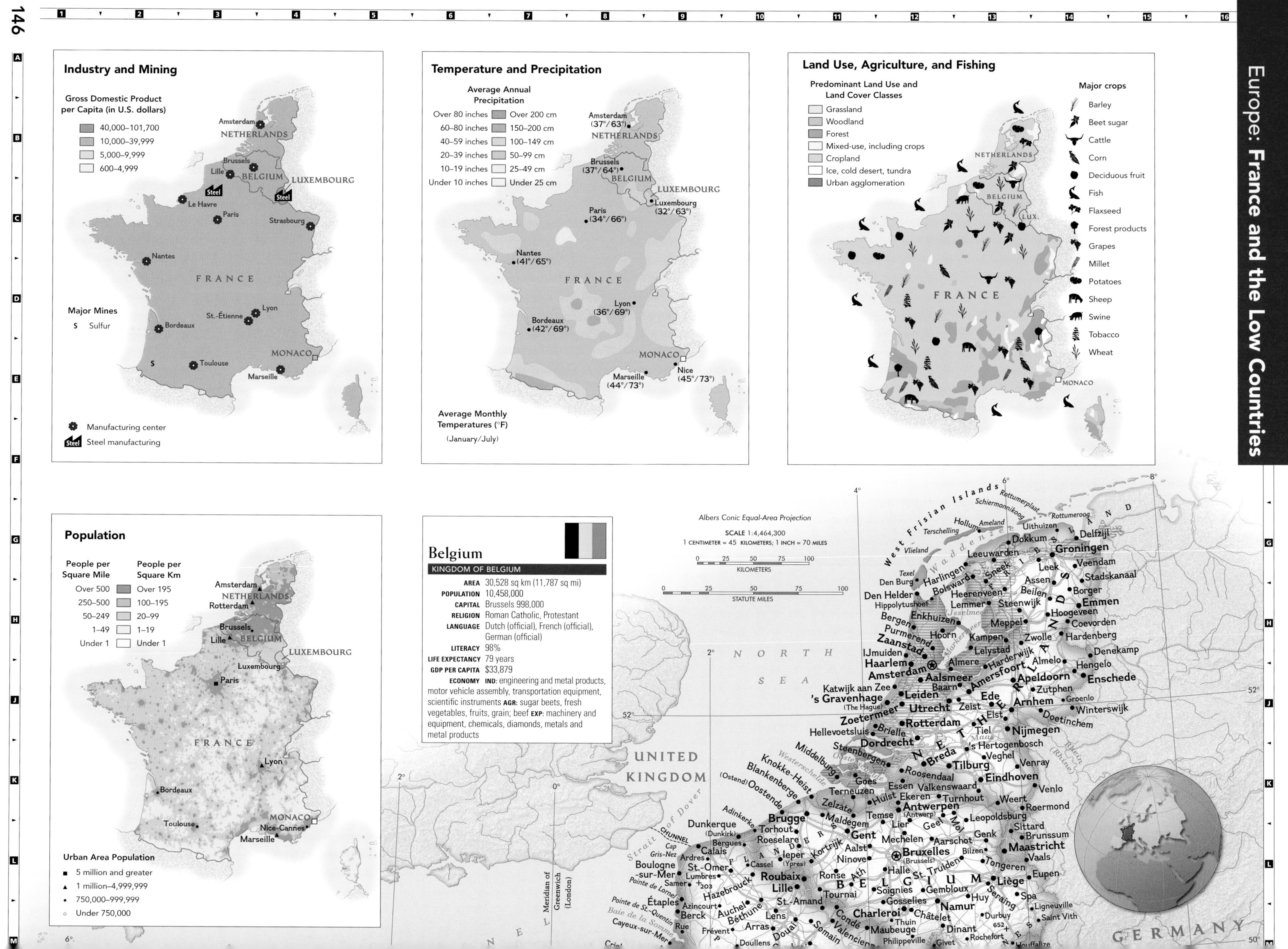
Industry and Mining
Gross Domestic Product per Capita (in U.S. dollars)
40,000–101,700
10,000–39,999
5,000–9,999
600–4,999
Major Mines
S Sulfur
Manufacturing center
Steel manufacturing
Amsterdam
NETHERLANDS
Brussels
Lille
BELGIUM
LUXEMBOURG
Le Havre
Paris
Strasbourg
Nantes
FRANCE
St.-Étienne
Lyon
Bordeaux
Toulouse
MONACO
Marseille
Temperature and Precipitation
Average Annual Precipitation
Over 80 inches | Over 200 cm
60–80 inches | 150–200 cm
40–59 inches | 100–149 cm
20–39 inches | 50–99 cm
10–19 inches | 25–49 cm
Under 10 inches | Under 25 cm
Average Monthly Temperatures (°F) (January/July)
Amsterdam (37°/63°)
Brussels (37°/64°)
Luxembourg (32°/63°)
Paris (34°/66°)
Nantes (41°/65°)
Lyon (36°/69°)
Bordeaux (42°/69°)
Marseille (44°/73°)
Nice (45°/73°)
Land Use, Agriculture, and Fishing
Predominant Land Use and Land Cover Classes
Grassland
Woodland
Forest
Mixed-use, including crops
Cropland
Ice, cold desert, tundra
Urban agglomeration
Major crops
Barley
Beet sugar
Cattle
Corn
Deciduous fruit
Fish
Flaxseed
Forest products
Grapes
Millet
Potatoes
Sheep
Swine
Tobacco
Wheat
Population
People per Square Mile | People per Square Km
Over 500 | Over 195
250–500 | 100–195
50–249 | 20–99
1–49 | 1–19
Under 1 | Under 1
Urban Area Population
5 million and greater
1 million–4,999,999
750,000–999,999
Under 750,000
Amsterdam
Rotterdam
Brussels
Lille
Luxembourg
Paris
Lyon
Bordeaux
Toulouse
Nice-Cannes
Marseille
Belgium
KINGDOM OF BELGIUM
AREA 30,528 sq km (11,787 sq mi)
POPULATION 10,458,000
CAPITAL Brussels 998,000
RELIGION Roman Catholic, Protestant
LANGUAGE Dutch (official), French (official), German (official)
LITERACY 98%
LIFE EXPECTANCY 79 years
GDP PER CAPITA $33,879
ECONOMY IND: engineering and metal products, motor vehicle assembly, transportation equipment, scientific instruments AGR: sugar beets, fresh vegetables, fruits, grain; beef EXP: machinery and equipment, chemicals, diamonds, metals and metal products
Albers Conic Equal-Area Projection
SCALE 1:4,464,300
1 CENTIMETER = 45 KILOMETERS; 1 INCH = 70 MILES
KILOMETERS
STATUTE MILES
NORTH SEA
UNITED KINGDOM
West Frisian Islands
NETHERLANDS
BELGIUM
GERMANY
Meridian of Greenwich (London)
Amsterdam
Rotterdam
's Gravenhage (The Hague)
Utrecht
Haarlem
Leiden
Groningen
Eindhoven
Tilburg
Breda
Nijmegen
Arnhem
Apeldoorn
Enschede
Maastricht
Antwerpen (Antwerp)
Gent
Brugge
Bruxelles (Brussels)
Liège
Namur
Charleroi
Lille
Roubaix
Dunkerque (Dunkirk)
Calais
Boulogne-sur-Mer

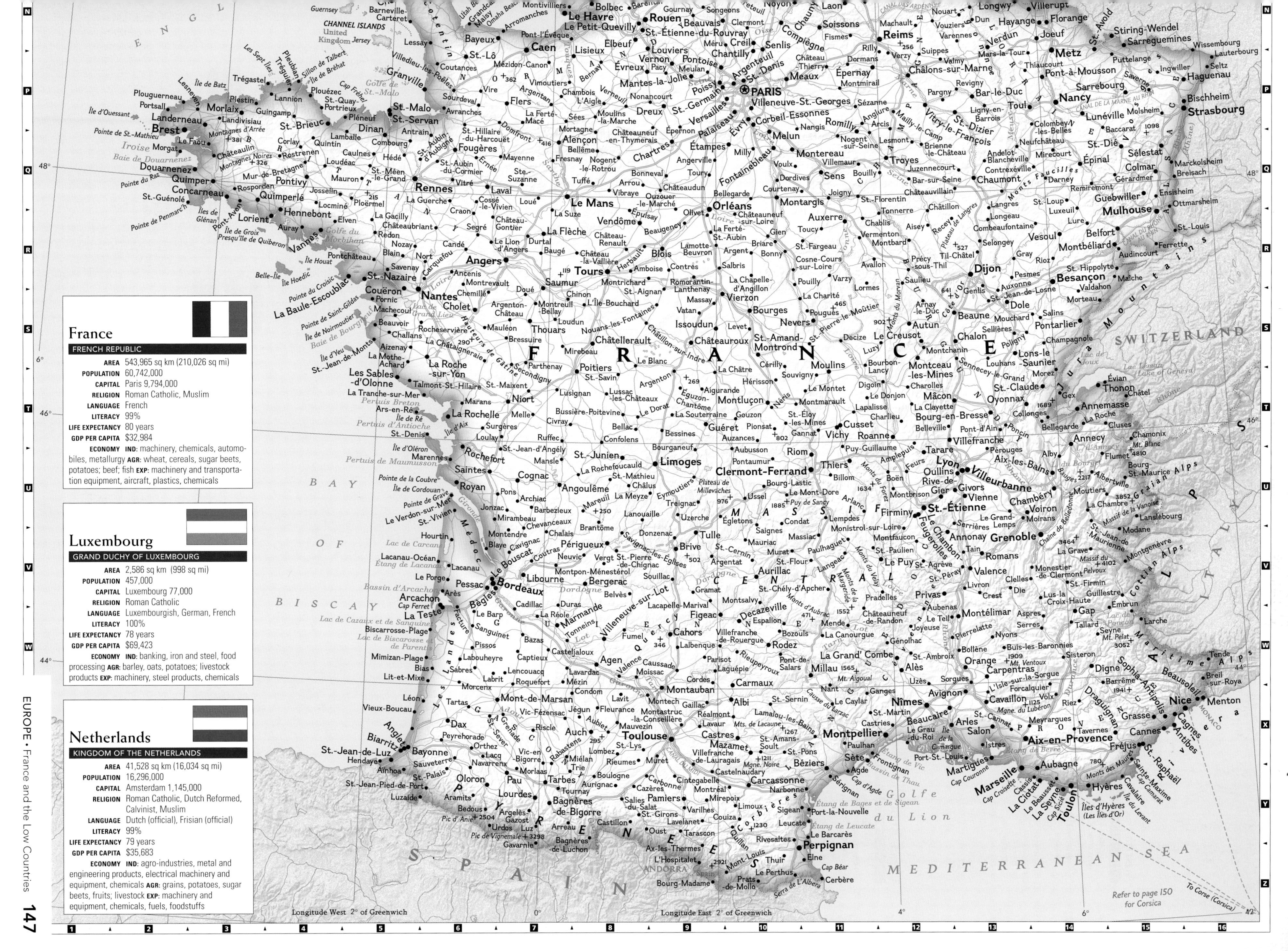
FRANCE
SWITZERLAND
ITALY
SPAIN
ANDORRA
BAY OF BISCAY
MEDITERRANEAN SEA
Golfe du Lion
PARIS
Le Havre
Rouen
Caen
Brest
Rennes
Nantes
Le Mans
Orléans
Tours
Angers
Reims
Metz
Nancy
Strasbourg
Mulhouse
Dijon
Besançon
Lyon
Villeurbanne
St.-Étienne
Grenoble
Clermont-Ferrand
Limoges
Poitiers
Bordeaux
Toulouse
Montpellier
Nîmes
Marseille
Toulon
Nice
Perpignan
Massif Central
Pyrenees
Jura Mountains
Alps
Refer to page 150 for Corsica
To Corse (Corsica)
Longitude West 2° of Greenwich
Longitude East 2° of Greenwich

France

FRENCH REPUBLIC

AREA 543,965 sq km (210,026 sq mi)
POPULATION 60,742,000
CAPITAL Paris 9,794,000
RELIGION Roman Catholic, Muslim
LANGUAGE French
LITERACY 99%
LIFE EXPECTANCY 80 years
GDP PER CAPITA $32,984
ECONOMY **IND:** machinery, chemicals, automobiles, metallurgy **AGR:** wheat, cereals, sugar beets, potatoes; beef; fish **EXP:** machinery and transportation equipment, aircraft, plastics, chemicals

Luxembourg

GRAND DUCHY OF LUXEMBOURG

AREA 2,586 sq km (998 sq mi)
POPULATION 457,000
CAPITAL Luxembourg 77,000
RELIGION Roman Catholic
LANGUAGE Luxembourgish, German, French
LITERACY 100%
LIFE EXPECTANCY 78 years
GDP PER CAPITA $69,423
ECONOMY **IND:** banking, iron and steel, food processing **AGR:** barley, oats, potatoes; livestock products **EXP:** machinery, steel products, chemicals

Netherlands

KINGDOM OF THE NETHERLANDS

AREA 41,528 sq km (16,034 sq mi)
POPULATION 16,296,000
CAPITAL Amsterdam 1,145,000
RELIGION Roman Catholic, Dutch Reformed, Calvinist, Muslim
LANGUAGE Dutch (official), Frisian (official)
LITERACY 99%
LIFE EXPECTANCY 79 years
GDP PER CAPITA $35,683
ECONOMY **IND:** agro-industries, metal and engineering products, electrical machinery and equipment, chemicals **AGR:** grains, potatoes, sugar beets, fruits; livestock **EXP:** machinery and equipment, chemicals, fuels, foodstuffs

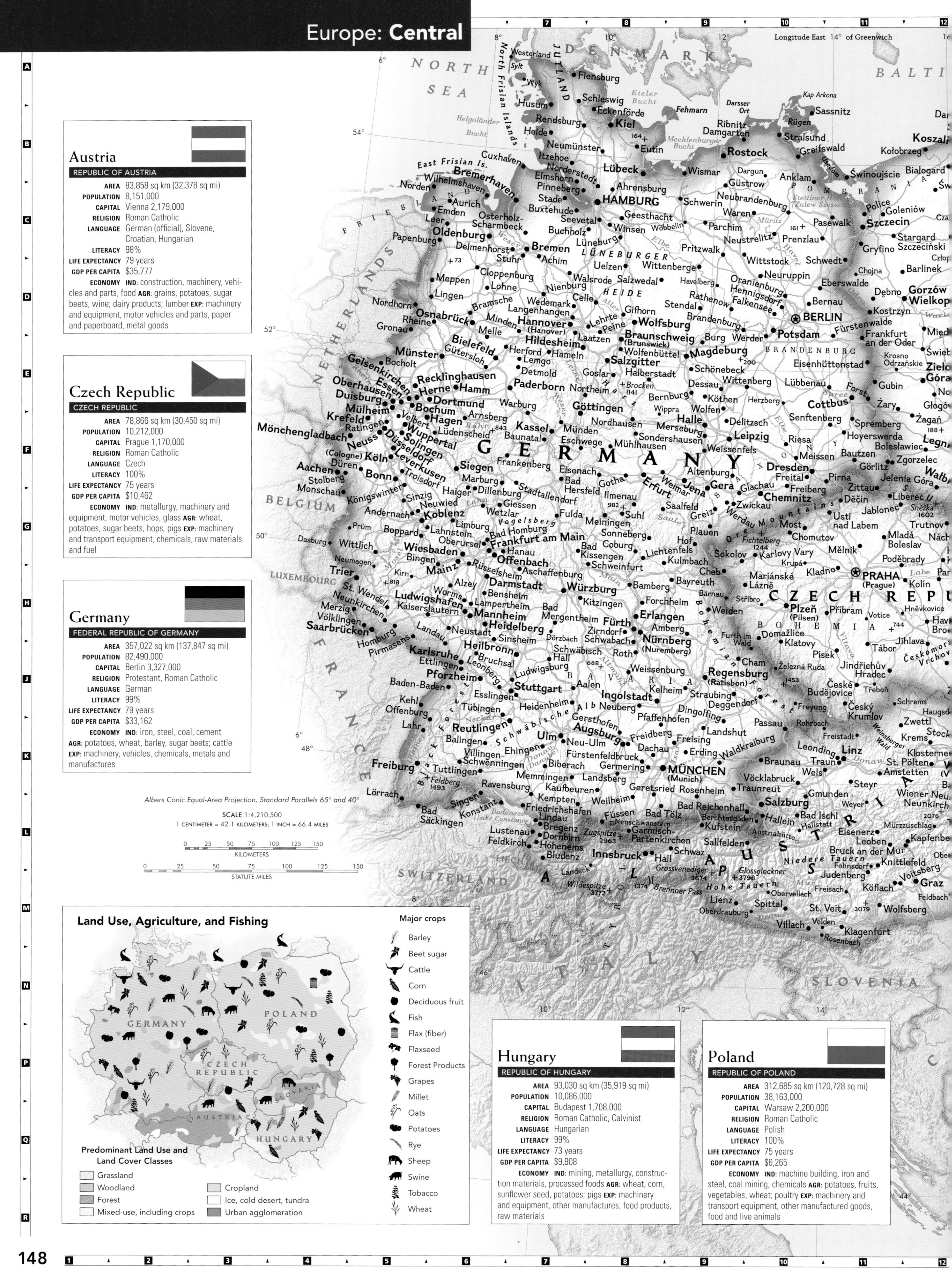

Austria

REPUBLIC OF AUSTRIA

AREA 83,858 sq km (32,378 sq mi)
POPULATION 8,151,000
CAPITAL Vienna 2,179,000
RELIGION Roman Catholic
LANGUAGE German (official), Slovene, Croatian, Hungarian
LITERACY 98%
LIFE EXPECTANCY 79 years
GDP PER CAPITA $35,777
ECONOMY **IND:** construction, machinery, vehicles and parts, food **AGR:** grains, potatoes, sugar beets, wine; dairy products; lumber **EXP:** machinery and equipment, motor vehicles and parts, paper and paperboard, metal goods

Czech Republic

CZECH REPUBLIC

AREA 78,866 sq km (30,450 sq mi)
POPULATION 10,212,000
CAPITAL Prague 1,170,000
RELIGION Roman Catholic
LANGUAGE Czech
LITERACY 100%
LIFE EXPECTANCY 75 years
GDP PER CAPITA $10,462
ECONOMY **IND:** metallurgy, machinery and equipment, motor vehicles, glass **AGR:** wheat, potatoes, sugar beets, hops; pigs **EXP:** machinery and transport equipment, chemicals, raw materials and fuel

Germany

FEDERAL REPUBLIC OF GERMANY

AREA 357,022 sq km (137,847 sq mi)
POPULATION 82,490,000
CAPITAL Berlin 3,327,000
RELIGION Protestant, Roman Catholic
LANGUAGE German
LITERACY 99%
LIFE EXPECTANCY 79 years
GDP PER CAPITA $33,162
ECONOMY **IND:** iron, steel, coal, cement **AGR:** potatoes, wheat, barley, sugar beets; cattle **EXP:** machinery, vehicles, chemicals, metals and manufactures

Albers Conic Equal-Area Projection, Standard Parallels 65° and 40°

SCALE 1:4,210,500
1 CENTIMETER = 42.1 KILOMETERS; 1 INCH = 66.4 MILES

Land Use, Agriculture, and Fishing

GERMANY
POLAND
CZECH REPUBLIC
SLOVAKIA
AUSTRIA
HUNGARY
Major crops
Barley
Beet sugar
Cattle
Corn
Deciduous fruit
Fish
Flax (fiber)
Flaxseed
Forest Products
Grapes
Millet
Oats
Potatoes
Rye
Sheep
Swine
Tobacco
Wheat
Predominant Land Use and Land Cover Classes
Grassland
Woodland
Forest
Mixed-use, including crops
Cropland
Ice, cold desert, tundra
Urban agglomeration

Hungary

REPUBLIC OF HUNGARY

AREA 93,030 sq km (35,919 sq mi)
POPULATION 10,086,000
CAPITAL Budapest 1,708,000
RELIGION Roman Catholic, Calvinist
LANGUAGE Hungarian
LITERACY 99%
LIFE EXPECTANCY 73 years
GDP PER CAPITA $9,908
ECONOMY **IND:** mining, metallurgy, construction materials, processed foods **AGR:** wheat, corn, sunflower seed, potatoes; pigs **EXP:** machinery and equipment, other manufactures, food products, raw materials

Poland

REPUBLIC OF POLAND

AREA 312,685 sq km (120,728 sq mi)
POPULATION 38,163,000
CAPITAL Warsaw 2,200,000
RELIGION Roman Catholic
LANGUAGE Polish
LITERACY 100%
LIFE EXPECTANCY 75 years
GDP PER CAPITA $6,265
ECONOMY **IND:** machine building, iron and steel, coal mining, chemicals **AGR:** potatoes, fruits, vegetables, wheat; poultry **EXP:** machinery and transport equipment, other manufactured goods, food and live animals

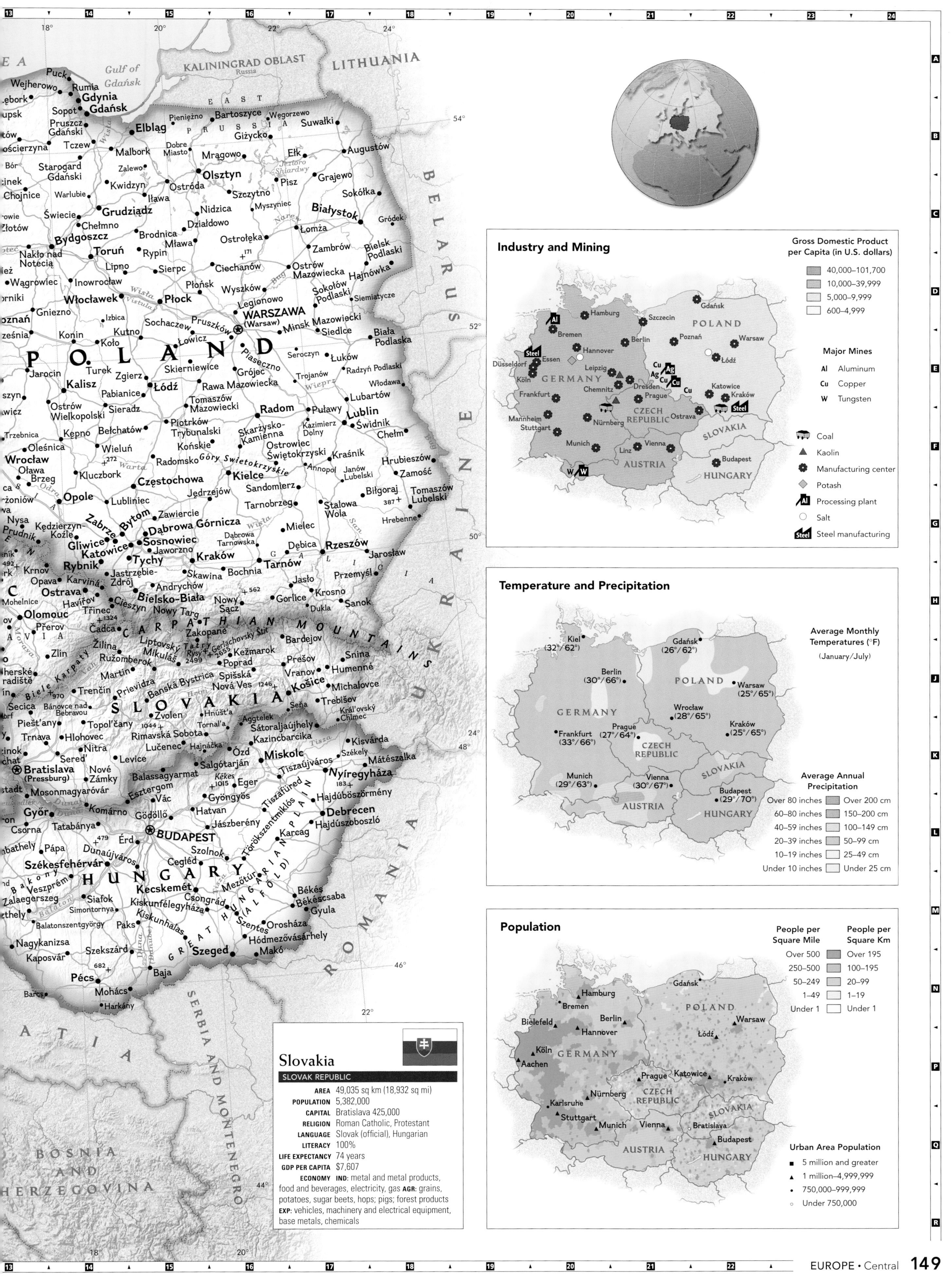

Gulf of Gdańsk
KALININGRAD OBLAST
Russia
LITHUANIA
BELARUS
UKRAINE
ROMANIA
SERBIA AND MONTENEGRO
BOSNIA AND HERZEGOVINA
POLAND
SLOVAKIA
HUNGARY
CARPATHIAN MOUNTAINS
GREAT HUNGARIAN PLAIN (ALFÖLD)
EAST PRUSSIA
Puck
Wejherowo
Rumia
Gdynia
Sopot
Gdańsk
Pruszcz Gdański
Tczew
Malbork
Elbląg
Pieniężno
Bartoszyce
Węgorzewo
Suwałki
Giżycko
Dobre Miasto
Mrągowo
Ełk
Augustów
Starogard Gdański
Zalewo
Olsztyn
Grajewo
Chojnice
Kwidzyn
Ostróda
Pisz
Sokółka
Iława
Szczytno
Grudziądz
Nidzica
Myszyniec
Białystok
Świecie
Chełmno
Działdowo
Gródek
Łomża
Bydgoszcz
Brodnica
Ostrołęka
Toruń
Mława
Zambrów
Bielsk Podlaski
Nakło nad Notecią
Rypin
Lipno
Sierpc
Ciechanów
Ostrów Mazowiecka
Hajnówka
Wągrowiec
Inowrocław
Płońsk
Wyszków
Sokołów Podlaski
Siemiatycze
Włocławek
Płock
Legionowo
Gniezno
WARSZAWA (Warsaw)
Izbica
Sochaczew
Pruszków
Mińsk Mazowiecki
Siedlce
Kutno
Biała Podlaska
Konin
Koło
Łowicz
Piaseczno
Seroczyn
Łuków
Jarocin
Turek
Zgierz
Skierniewice
Grójec
Trojanów
Radzyń Podlaski
Kalisz
Pabianice
Łódź
Rawa Mazowiecka
Włodawa
Tomaszów Mazowiecki
Lubartów
Ostrów Wielkopolski
Sieradz
Radom
Puławy
Lublin
Piotrków Trybunalski
Kazimierz Dolny
Świdnik
Kępno
Bełchatów
Skarżysko-Kamienna
Chełm
Trzebnica
Ostrowiec Świętokrzyski
Oleśnica
Wieluń
Końskie
Kraśnik
Wrocław
Oława
Radomsko
Góry Świętokrzyskie
Hrubieszów
Brzeg
Kluczbork
Kielce
Annopol
Janów Lubelski
Zamość
Częstochowa
Sandomierz
Biłgoraj
Tomaszów Lubelski
Jędrzejów
Opole
Lubliniec
Tarnobrzeg
Stalowa Wola
Zawiercie
Hrebenne
Nysa
Kędzierzyn-Koźle
Zabrze
Bytom
Dąbrowa Górnicza
Mielec
Prudnik
Gliwice
Sosnowiec
Dąbrowa Tarnowska
Dębica
Rzeszów
Katowice
Jaworzno
Jarosław
Rybnik
Tychy
Kraków
Tarnów
Krnov
Jastrzębie-Zdrój
Skawina
Bochnia
Przemyśl
Opava
Karviná
Andrychów
Jasło
Krosno
Ostrava
Bielsko-Biała
Nowy Sącz
Gorlice
Sanok
Mohelnice
Havířov
Cieszyn
Dukla
Olomouc
Třinec
Nowy Targ
Přerov
Čadca
Zakopané
Gerlachovský štít
Bardejov
Žilina
Tatry
Rysy
Kežmarok
Zlín
Ružomberok
Liptovský Mikuláš
Prešov
Snina
Poprad
Martin
Vranov
Humenné
Uherské Hradiště
Biele Karpaty
Banská Bystrica
Spišská Nová Ves
Košice
Michalovce
Trenčín
Prievidza
Šaca
Trebišov
Šecica
Bánovce nad Bebravou
Zvolen
Hnúšťa
Král'ovský Chlmec
Piešťany
Topoľčany
Tornaľa
Aggtelek
Sátoraljaújhely
Trnava
Hlohovec
Rimavská Sobota
Kazincbarcika
Kisvárda
Nitra
Lučenec
Hajnáčka
Ózd
Miskolc
Székely
Mátészalka
Bratislava (Pressburg)
Sereď
Levice
Salgótarján
Tiszaújváros
Nyíregyháza
Nové Zámky
Balassagyarmat
Kékes
Eger
Tiszafüred
Hajdúböszörmény
Mosonmagyaróvár
Esztergom
Vác
Gyöngyös
Győr
Komárno
Gödöllő
Hatvan
Debrecen
Törökszentmiklós
Hajdúszoboszló
Csorna
Tatabánya
Jászberény
Karcag
Pápa
Érd
BUDAPEST
Szolnok
Dunaújváros
Székesfehérvár
Cegléd
Bakony
Veszprém
Kecskemét
Mezőtúr
Békés
Békéscsaba
Zalaegerszeg
Siófok
Kiskunfélegyháza
Csongrád
Gyula
Simontornya
Balaton
Kiskunhalas
Balatonszentgyörgy
Paks
Szentes
Orosháza
Hódmezővásárhely
Nagykanizsa
Szekszárd
Szeged
Makó
Kaposvár
Baja
Pécs
Mohács
Barcs
Harkány
Industry and Mining
Gross Domestic Product per Capita (in U.S. dollars)
40,000–101,700
10,000–39,999
5,000–9,999
600–4,999
Major Mines
Al Aluminum
Cu Copper
W Tungsten
Coal
Kaolin
Manufacturing center
Potash
Processing plant
Salt
Steel manufacturing
Hamburg
Bremen
Szczecin
Berlin
Poznań
Warsaw
Hannover
Düsseldorf
Essen
Köln
Leipzig
Chemnitz
Dresden
Frankfurt
Prague
Katowice
Kraków
Ostrava
Mannheim
Stuttgart
Nürnberg
Munich
Linz
Vienna
Budapest
GERMANY
CZECH REPUBLIC
AUSTRIA
Temperature and Precipitation
Average Monthly Temperatures (°F) (January/July)
Kiel (32°/62°)
Gdańsk (26°/62°)
Berlin (30°/66°)
Warsaw (25°/65°)
Wrocław (28°/65°)
Frankfurt (33°/66°)
Prague (27°/64°)
Kraków (25°/65°)
Munich (29°/63°)
Vienna (30°/67°)
Budapest (29°/70°)
Average Annual Precipitation
Over 80 inches Over 200 cm
60–80 inches 150–200 cm
40–59 inches 100–149 cm
20–39 inches 50–99 cm
10–19 inches 25–49 cm
Under 10 inches Under 25 cm
Population
People per Square Mile
Over 500
250–500
50–249
1–49
Under 1
People per Square Km
Over 195
100–195
20–99
1–19
Under 1
Bielefeld
Aachen
Karlsruhe
Bratislava
Urban Area Population
5 million and greater
1 million–4,999,999
750,000–999,999
Under 750,000

Slovakia

SLOVAK REPUBLIC

AREA 49,035 sq km (18,932 sq mi)
POPULATION 5,382,000
CAPITAL Bratislava 425,000
RELIGION Roman Catholic, Protestant
LANGUAGE Slovak (official), Hungarian
LITERACY 100%
LIFE EXPECTANCY 74 years
GDP PER CAPITA $7,607
ECONOMY **IND:** metal and metal products, food and beverages, electricity, gas **AGR:** grains, potatoes, sugar beets, hops; pigs; forest products **EXP:** vehicles, machinery and electrical equipment, base metals, chemicals

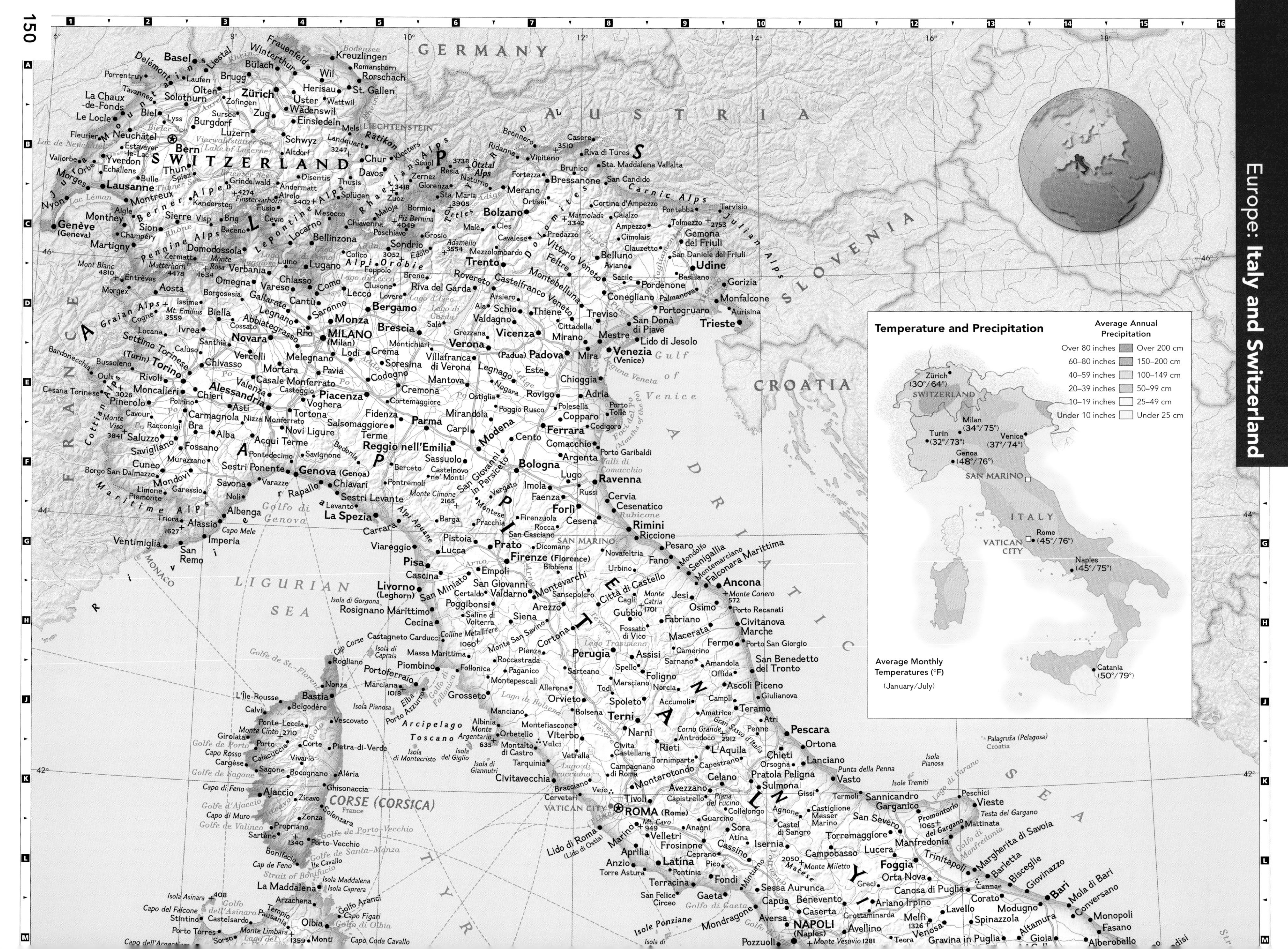
Temperature and Precipitation
Average Annual Precipitation
Over 80 inches Over 200 cm
60–80 inches 150–200 cm
40–59 inches 100–149 cm
20–39 inches 50–99 cm
10–19 inches 25–49 cm
Under 10 inches Under 25 cm
Average Monthly Temperatures (°F)
(January/July)
Zürich (30°/64°)
SWITZERLAND
Milan (34°/75°)
Turin (32°/73°)
Venice (37°/74°)
Genoa (48°/76°)
SAN MARINO
ITALY
VATICAN CITY
Rome (45°/76°)
Naples (45°/75°)
Catania (50°/79°)
GERMANY
AUSTRIA
SLOVENIA
CROATIA
FRANCE
LIECHTENSTEIN
MONACO
SWITZERLAND
Gulf of Venice
LIGURIAN SEA
CORSE (CORSICA)
ROMA (Rome)
MILANO (Milan)
NAPOLI (Naples)
Bern
Torino (Turin)
Genova (Genoa)
Firenze (Florence)
Venezia (Venice)
Bologna
Trieste
Ancona
Pescara
Bari
Foggia
Zürich
Basel
Genève (Geneva)
Lausanne
Luzern
Pisa
Livorno (Leghorn)
Perugia
Ajaccio
Bastia

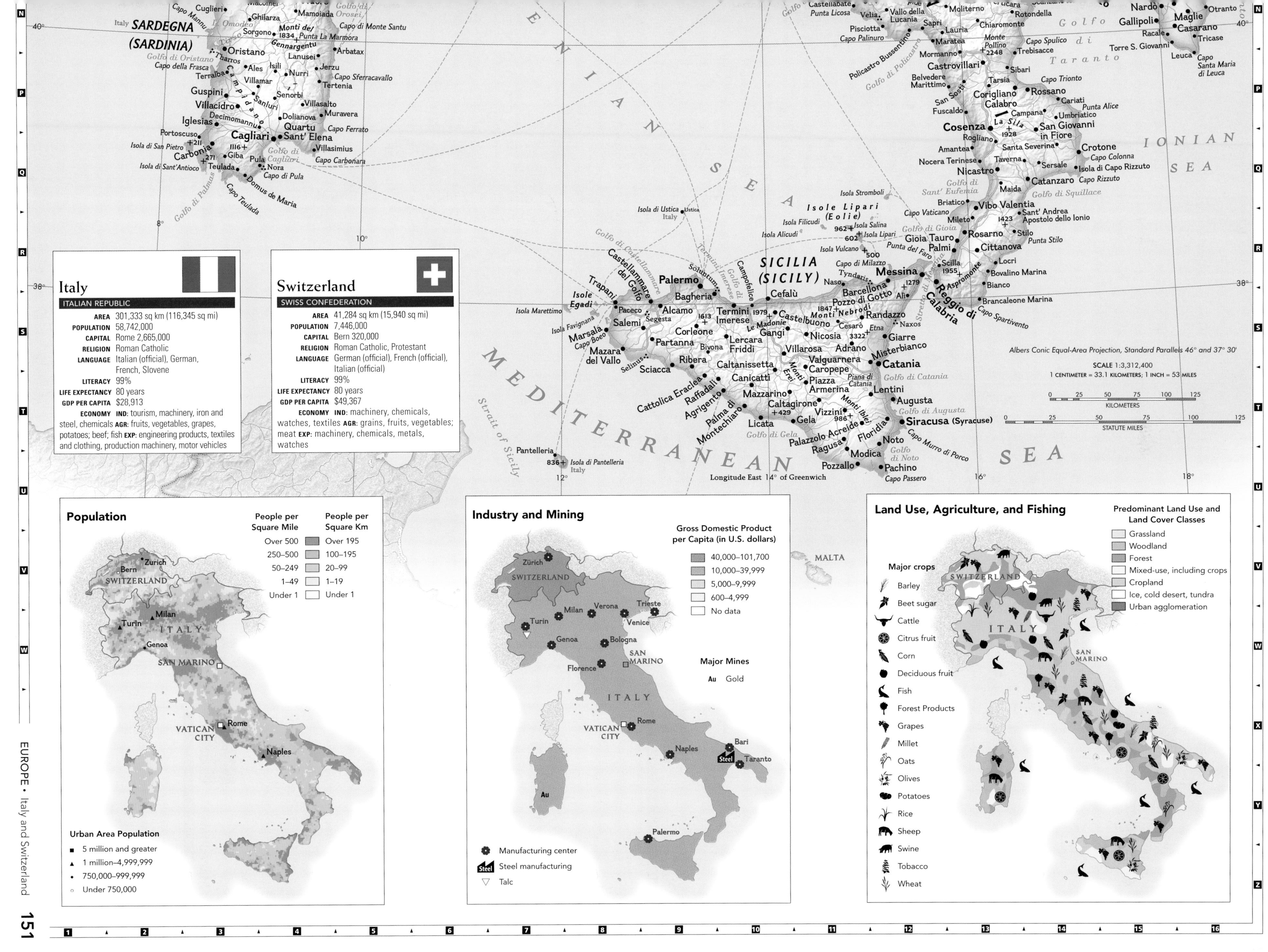
SARDEGNA (SARDINIA)
SICILIA (SICILY)
MEDITERRANEAN SEA
IONIAN SEA
Strait of Sicily
MALTA
Albers Conic Equal-Area Projection, Standard Parallels 46° and 37° 30'
SCALE 1:3,312,400
1 CENTIMETER = 33.1 KILOMETERS; 1 INCH = 53 MILES
KILOMETERS
STATUTE MILES
Longitude East 14° of Greenwich
Population
People per Square Mile
People per Square Km
Over 500
Over 195
250–500
100–195
50–249
20–99
1–49
1–19
Under 1
Under 1
Urban Area Population
5 million and greater
1 million–4,999,999
750,000–999,999
Under 750,000
Industry and Mining
Gross Domestic Product per Capita (in U.S. dollars)
40,000–101,700
10,000–39,999
5,000–9,999
600–4,999
No data
Major Mines
Au Gold
Manufacturing center
Steel manufacturing
Talc
Land Use, Agriculture, and Fishing
Predominant Land Use and Land Cover Classes
Grassland
Woodland
Forest
Mixed-use, including crops
Cropland
Ice, cold desert, tundra
Urban agglomeration
Major crops
Barley
Beet sugar
Cattle
Citrus fruit
Corn
Deciduous fruit
Fish
Forest Products
Grapes
Millet
Oats
Olives
Potatoes
Rice
Sheep
Swine
Tobacco
Wheat

Italy

ITALIAN REPUBLIC

AREA 301,333 sq km (116,345 sq mi)
POPULATION 58,742,000
CAPITAL Rome 2,665,000
RELIGION Roman Catholic
LANGUAGE Italian (official), German, French, Slovene
LITERACY 99%
LIFE EXPECTANCY 80 years
GDP PER CAPITA $28,913
ECONOMY **IND:** tourism, machinery, iron and steel, chemicals **AGR:** fruits, vegetables, grapes, potatoes; beef; fish **EXP:** engineering products, textiles and clothing, production machinery, motor vehicles

Switzerland

SWISS CONFEDERATION

AREA 41,284 sq km (15,940 sq mi)
POPULATION 7,446,000
CAPITAL Bern 320,000
RELIGION Roman Catholic, Protestant
LANGUAGE German (official), French (official), Italian (official)
LITERACY 99%
LIFE EXPECTANCY 80 years
GDP PER CAPITA $49,367
ECONOMY **IND:** machinery, chemicals, watches, textiles **AGR:** grains, fruits, vegetables; meat **EXP:** machinery, chemicals, metals, watches

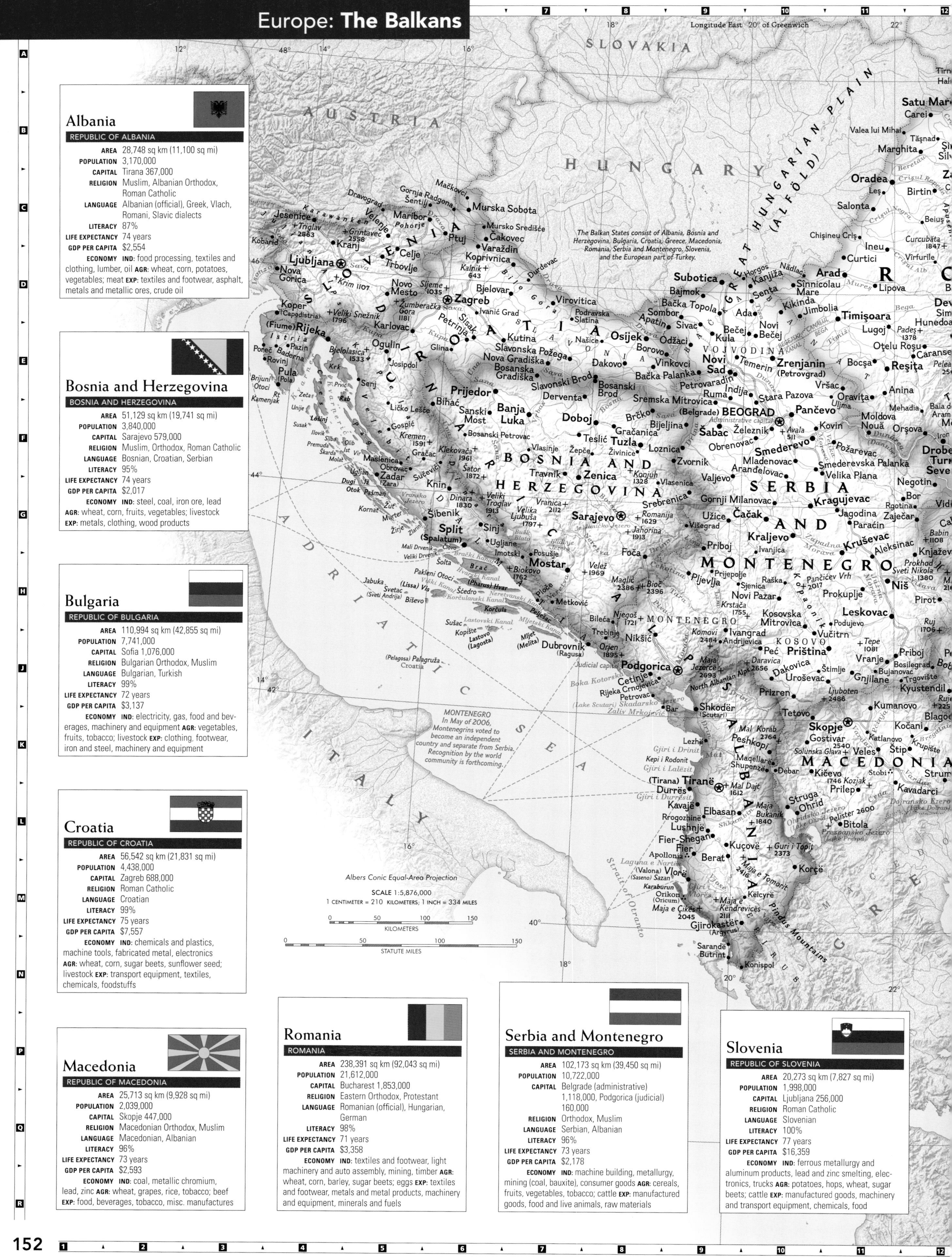
SLOVAKIA
AUSTRIA
HUNGARY
GREAT HUNGARIAN PLAIN (ALFÖLD)
SLOVENIA
CROATIA
BOSNIA AND HERZEGOVINA
SERBIA AND MONTENEGRO
MACEDONIA
ALBANIA
ITALY
ADRIATIC SEA
VOJVODINA
KOSOVO
MONTENEGRO
Longitude East 20° of Greenwich
The Balkan States consist of Albania, Bosnia and Herzegovina, Bulgaria, Croatia, Greece, Macedonia, Romania, Serbia and Montenegro, Slovenia, and the European part of Turkey.
MONTENEGRO In May of 2006, Montenegrins voted to become an independent country and separate from Serbia. Recognition by the world community is forthcoming.
Albers Conic Equal-Area Projection
SCALE 1:5,876,000
1 CENTIMETER = 210 KILOMETERS; 1 INCH = 334 MILES
KILOMETERS
STATUTE MILES
Strait of Otranto
Pindus Mountains
North Albanian Alps

Albania

REPUBLIC OF ALBANIA

AREA 28,748 sq km (11,100 sq mi)
POPULATION 3,170,000
CAPITAL Tirana 367,000
RELIGION Muslim, Albanian Orthodox, Roman Catholic
LANGUAGE Albanian (official), Greek, Vlach, Romani, Slavic dialects
LITERACY 87%
LIFE EXPECTANCY 74 years
GDP PER CAPITA $2,554
ECONOMY **IND:** food processing, textiles and clothing, lumber, oil **AGR:** wheat, corn, potatoes, vegetables; meat **EXP:** textiles and footwear, asphalt, metals and metallic ores, crude oil

Bosnia and Herzegovina

BOSNIA AND HERZEGOVINA

AREA 51,129 sq km (19,741 sq mi)
POPULATION 3,840,000
CAPITAL Sarajevo 579,000
RELIGION Muslim, Orthodox, Roman Catholic
LANGUAGE Bosnian, Croatian, Serbian
LITERACY 95%
LIFE EXPECTANCY 74 years
GDP PER CAPITA $2,017
ECONOMY **IND:** steel, coal, iron ore, lead **AGR:** wheat, corn, fruits, vegetables; livestock **EXP:** metals, clothing, wood products

Bulgaria

REPUBLIC OF BULGARIA

AREA 110,994 sq km (42,855 sq mi)
POPULATION 7,741,000
CAPITAL Sofia 1,076,000
RELIGION Bulgarian Orthodox, Muslim
LANGUAGE Bulgarian, Turkish
LITERACY 99%
LIFE EXPECTANCY 72 years
GDP PER CAPITA $3,137
ECONOMY **IND:** electricity, gas, food and beverages, machinery and equipment **AGR:** vegetables, fruits, tobacco; livestock **EXP:** clothing, footwear, iron and steel, machinery and equipment

Croatia

REPUBLIC OF CROATIA

AREA 56,542 sq km (21,831 sq mi)
POPULATION 4,438,000
CAPITAL Zagreb 688,000
RELIGION Roman Catholic
LANGUAGE Croatian
LITERACY 99%
LIFE EXPECTANCY 75 years
GDP PER CAPITA $7,557
ECONOMY **IND:** chemicals and plastics, machine tools, fabricated metal, electronics **AGR:** wheat, corn, sugar beets, sunflower seed; livestock **EXP:** transport equipment, textiles, chemicals, foodstuffs

Macedonia

REPUBLIC OF MACEDONIA

AREA 25,713 sq km (9,928 sq mi)
POPULATION 2,039,000
CAPITAL Skopje 447,000
RELIGION Macedonian Orthodox, Muslim
LANGUAGE Macedonian, Albanian
LITERACY 96%
LIFE EXPECTANCY 73 years
GDP PER CAPITA $2,593
ECONOMY **IND:** coal, metallic chromium, lead, zinc **AGR:** wheat, grapes, rice, tobacco; beef **EXP:** food, beverages, tobacco, misc. manufactures

Romania

ROMANIA

AREA 238,391 sq km (92,043 sq mi)
POPULATION 21,612,000
CAPITAL Bucharest 1,853,000
RELIGION Eastern Orthodox, Protestant
LANGUAGE Romanian (official), Hungarian, German
LITERACY 98%
LIFE EXPECTANCY 71 years
GDP PER CAPITA $3,358
ECONOMY **IND:** textiles and footwear, light machinery and auto assembly, mining, timber **AGR:** wheat, corn, barley, sugar beets; eggs **EXP:** textiles and footwear, metals and metal products, machinery and equipment, minerals and fuels

Serbia and Montenegro

SERBIA AND MONTENEGRO

AREA 102,173 sq km (39,450 sq mi)
POPULATION 10,722,000
CAPITAL Belgrade (administrative) 1,118,000, Podgorica (judicial) 160,000
RELIGION Orthodox, Muslim
LANGUAGE Serbian, Albanian
LITERACY 96%
LIFE EXPECTANCY 73 years
GDP PER CAPITA $2,178
ECONOMY **IND:** machine building, metallurgy, mining (coal, bauxite), consumer goods **AGR:** cereals, fruits, vegetables, tobacco; cattle **EXP:** manufactured goods, food and live animals, raw materials

Slovenia

REPUBLIC OF SLOVENIA

AREA 20,273 sq km (7,827 sq mi)
POPULATION 1,998,000
CAPITAL Ljubljana 256,000
RELIGION Roman Catholic
LANGUAGE Slovenian
LITERACY 100%
LIFE EXPECTANCY 77 years
GDP PER CAPITA $16,359
ECONOMY **IND:** ferrous metallurgy and aluminum products, lead and zinc smelting, electronics, trucks **AGR:** potatoes, hops, wheat, sugar beets; cattle **EXP:** manufactured goods, machinery and transport equipment, chemicals, food

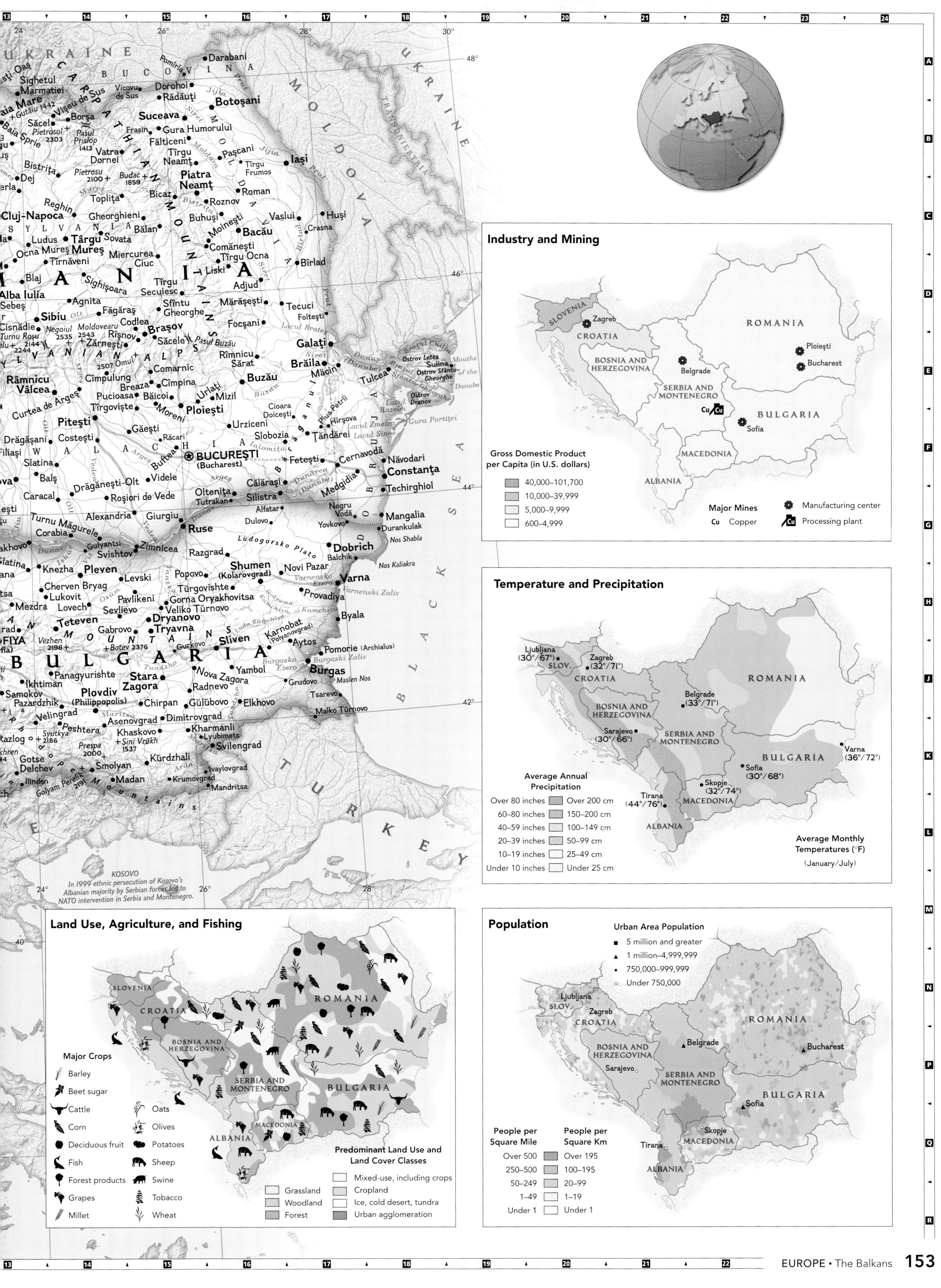

UKRAINE
MOLDOVA
ROMANIA
BULGARIA
TURKEY
BLACK SEA
CARPATHIAN MOUNTAINS
TRANSNISTRIA
BUCOVINA
MOLDOVA
TRANSYLVANIA
WALLACHIA
DOBRUJA
BALKAN MOUNTAINS
Rhodope Mountains
Ludogorsko Plato
BUCUREȘTI (Bucharest)
Cluj-Napoca
Iași
Brașov
Constanța
Galați
Brăila
Ploiești
Sibiu
Suceava
Botoșani
Bacău
Piatra Neamț
Pitești
Craiova
Tulcea
Sofia
Plovdiv
Varna
Burgas
Ruse
Stara Zagora
Pleven
Shumen (Kolarovgrad)
Dobrich
Sliven
Yambol
Haskovo
Veliko Tŭrnovo
Gabrovo
Kŭrdzhali
Smolyan
KOSOVO
In 1999 ethnic persecution of Kosovo's Albanian majority by Serbian forces led to NATO intervention in Serbia and Montenegro.
Industry and Mining
SLOVENIA
CROATIA
BOSNIA AND HERZEGOVINA
SERBIA AND MONTENEGRO
ROMANIA
BULGARIA
MACEDONIA
ALBANIA
Zagreb
Belgrade
Ploiești
Bucharest
Sofia
Gross Domestic Product per Capita (in U.S. dollars)
40,000–101,700
10,000–39,999
5,000–9,999
600–4,999
Major Mines
Cu Copper
Manufacturing center
Processing plant
Temperature and Precipitation
Ljubljana (30°/67°)
Zagreb (32°/71°)
Belgrade (33°/71°)
Sarajevo (30°/66°)
Varna (36°/72°)
Sofia (30°/68°)
Skopje (32°/74°)
Tirana (44°/76°)
Average Annual Precipitation
Over 80 inches | Over 200 cm
60–80 inches | 150–200 cm
40–59 inches | 100–149 cm
20–39 inches | 50–99 cm
10–19 inches | 25–49 cm
Under 10 inches | Under 25 cm
Average Monthly Temperatures (°F) (January/July)
Land Use, Agriculture, and Fishing
Major Crops
Barley
Beet sugar
Cattle
Corn
Deciduous fruit
Fish
Forest products
Grapes
Millet
Oats
Olives
Potatoes
Sheep
Swine
Tobacco
Wheat
Predominant Land Use and Land Cover Classes
Grassland
Woodland
Forest
Mixed-use, including crops
Cropland
Ice, cold desert, tundra
Urban agglomeration
Population
Urban Area Population
5 million and greater
1 million–4,999,999
750,000–999,999
Under 750,000
Ljubljana
Zagreb
Belgrade
Bucharest
Sarajevo
Sofia
Skopje
Tirana
People per Square Mile | People per Square Km
Over 500 | Over 195
250–500 | 100–195
50–249 | 20–99
1–49 | 1–19
Under 1 | Under 1

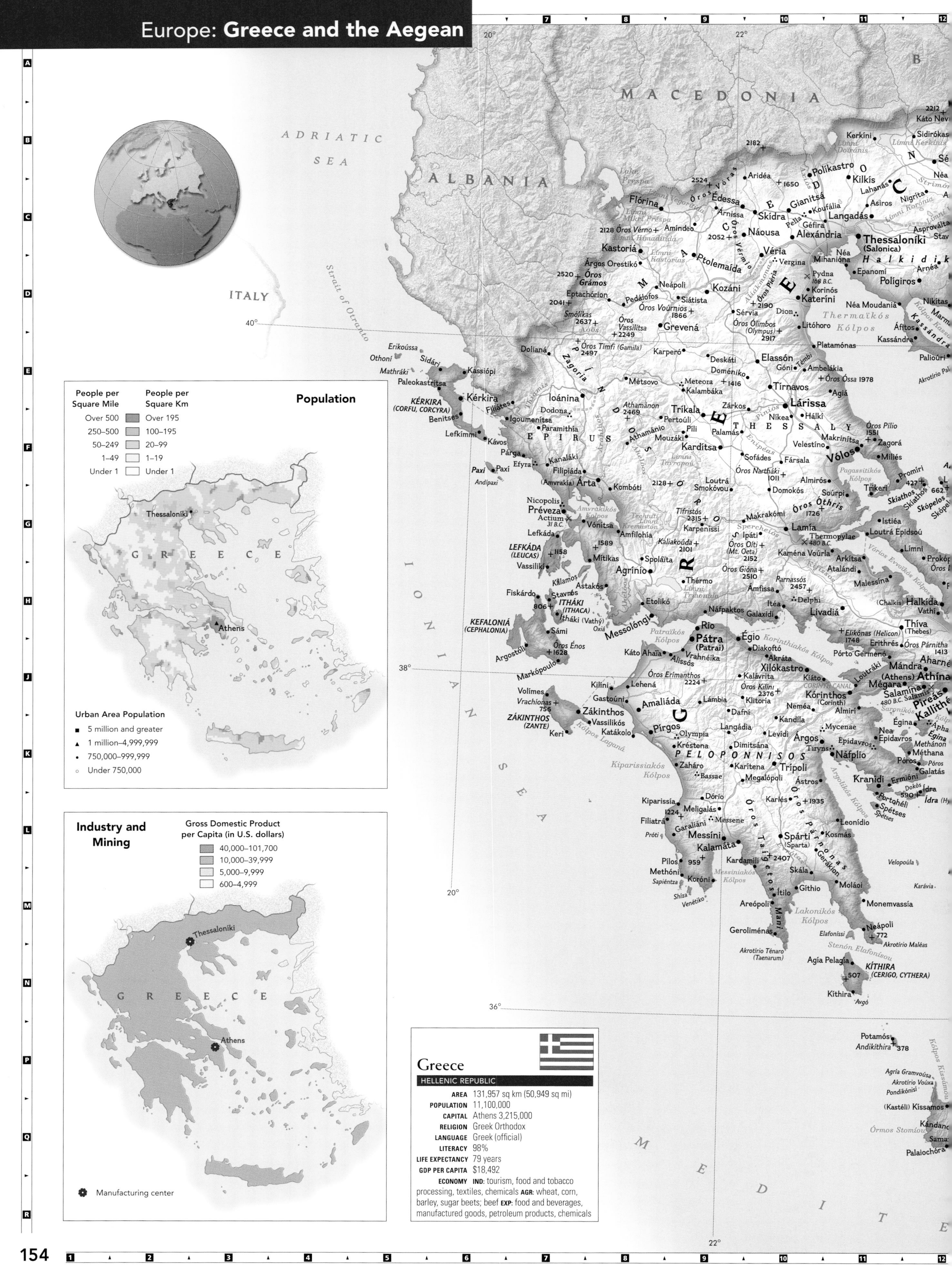
ADRIATIC SEA
ITALY
ALBANIA
MACEDONIA
Strait of Otranto
IONIAN SEA
EPIRUS
THESSALY
PELOPONNISOS
Thermaïkós Kólpos
Halkidikí
Thessaloníki (Salonica)
Lárissa
Vólos
Lamía
Pátra (Patrai)
Kórinthos (Corinth)
Athína (Athens)
Pireás
Tripoli
Kalamáta
Spárti (Sparta)
Ioánina
Kérkira
KÉRKIRA (CORFU, CORCYRA)
LEFKÁDA (LEUCAS)
ITHÁKI (ITHACA)
KEFALONIÁ (CEPHALONIA)
ZÁKINTHOS (ZANTE)
KÍTHIRA (CERIGO, CYTHERA)
Óros Ólimbos (Olympus) 2917
Population
People per Square Mile
People per Square Km
Over 500 — Over 195
250–500 — 100–195
50–249 — 20–99
1–49 — 1–19
Under 1 — Under 1
Thessaloníki
GREECE
Athens
Urban Area Population
5 million and greater
1 million–4,999,999
750,000–999,999
Under 750,000
Industry and Mining
Gross Domestic Product per Capita (in U.S. dollars)
40,000–101,700
10,000–39,999
5,000–9,999
600–4,999
Thessaloníki
GREECE
Athens
Manufacturing center

Greece

HELLENIC REPUBLIC

AREA 131,957 sq km (50,949 sq mi)
POPULATION 11,100,000
CAPITAL Athens 3,215,000
RELIGION Greek Orthodox
LANGUAGE Greek (official)
LITERACY 98%
LIFE EXPECTANCY 79 years
GDP PER CAPITA $18,492
ECONOMY **IND:** tourism, food and tobacco processing, textiles, chemicals **AGR:** wheat, corn, barley, sugar beets; beef **EXP:** food and beverages, manufactured goods, petroleum products, chemicals

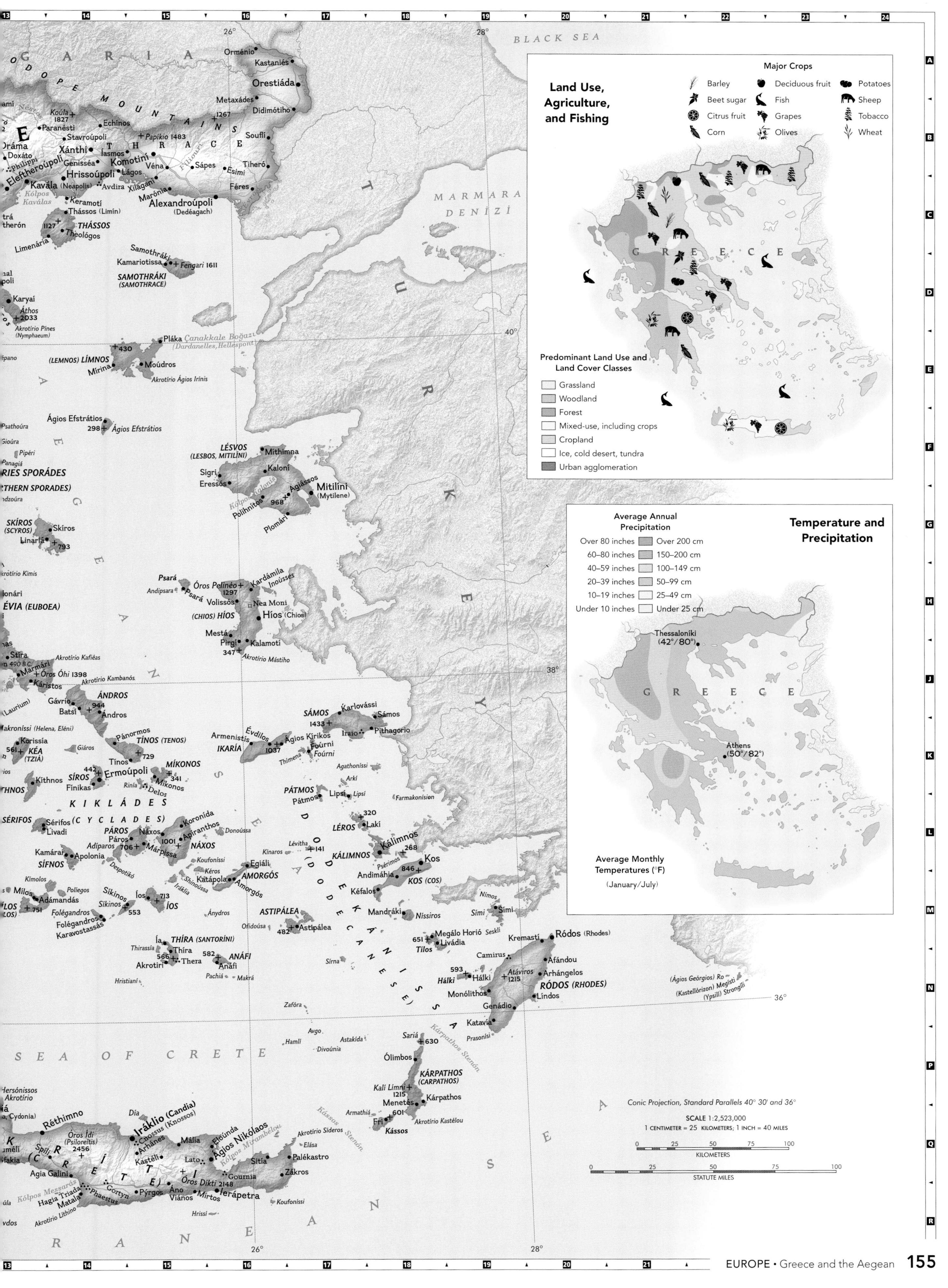

BLACK SEA
MARMARA DENİZİ
TURKEY
SEA OF CRETE
AEGEAN SEA
RODOPE MOUNTAINS
THRACE
Land Use, Agriculture, and Fishing
Major Crops
Barley
Beet sugar
Citrus fruit
Corn
Deciduous fruit
Fish
Grapes
Olives
Potatoes
Sheep
Tobacco
Wheat
GREECE
Predominant Land Use and Land Cover Classes
Grassland
Woodland
Forest
Mixed-use, including crops
Cropland
Ice, cold desert, tundra
Urban agglomeration
Temperature and Precipitation
Average Annual Precipitation
Over 80 inches
60–80 inches
40–59 inches
20–39 inches
10–19 inches
Under 10 inches
Over 200 cm
150–200 cm
100–149 cm
50–99 cm
25–49 cm
Under 25 cm
Thessaloníki (42°/80°)
Athens (50°/82°)
Average Monthly Temperatures (°F)
(January/July)
Orménio
Kastaniés
Orestiáda
Metaxádes
Didimótiho
Soufli
Xánthi
Komotiní
Alexandroúpoli (Dedéagach)
Kavála (Neapolis)
Féres
Tiheró
THÁSSOS
SAMOTHRÁKI (SAMOTHRACE)
Fengari 1611
Çanakkale Boğazı (Dardanelles, Hellespont)
(LEMNOS) LÍMNOS
Mírina
Moúdros
Ágios Efstrátios
LÉSVOS (LESBOS, MITILÍNI)
Mithimna
Mitilíni (Mytilene)
Plomári
SKÍROS (SCYROS)
VÓRIES SPORÁDES (NORTHERN SPORADES)
ÉVIA (EUBOEA)
Psará
(CHIOS) HÍOS
Híos (Chios)
Nea Moni
Inoússes
ÁNDROS
TÍNOS (TENOS)
MÍKONOS
Ermoúpoli
SÍROS
KÍTHNOS
SÉRIFOS
SÍFNOS
PÁROS
NÁXOS
KIKLÁDES (CYCLADES)
AMORGÓS
ÍOS
THÍRA (SANTORÍNI)
ANÁFI
ASTIPÁLEA
SÁMOS
Karlovássi
Pithagório
IKARÍA
PÁTMOS
LÉROS
KÁLIMNOS
KOS (COS)
DODEKÁNISSA (DODECANESE)
Nissiros
Sími
Tílos
Hálki
RÓDOS (RHODES)
Ródos (Rhodes)
Líndos
KÁRPATHOS (CARPATHOS)
Kárpathos
Kássos
Káspathos Stenón
Kássos Stenón
KRÍTI (CRETE)
Réthimno
Iráklio (Candia)
Cnossus (Knossos)
Mália
Ágios Nikólaos
Ierápetra
Sitía
Zákros
Oros Dikti 2148
Oros Idi (Psiloreitis) 2456
Conic Projection, Standard Parallels 40° 30′ and 36°
SCALE 1:2,523,000
1 CENTIMETER = 25 KILOMETERS; 1 INCH = 40 MILES
KILOMETERS
STATUTE MILES

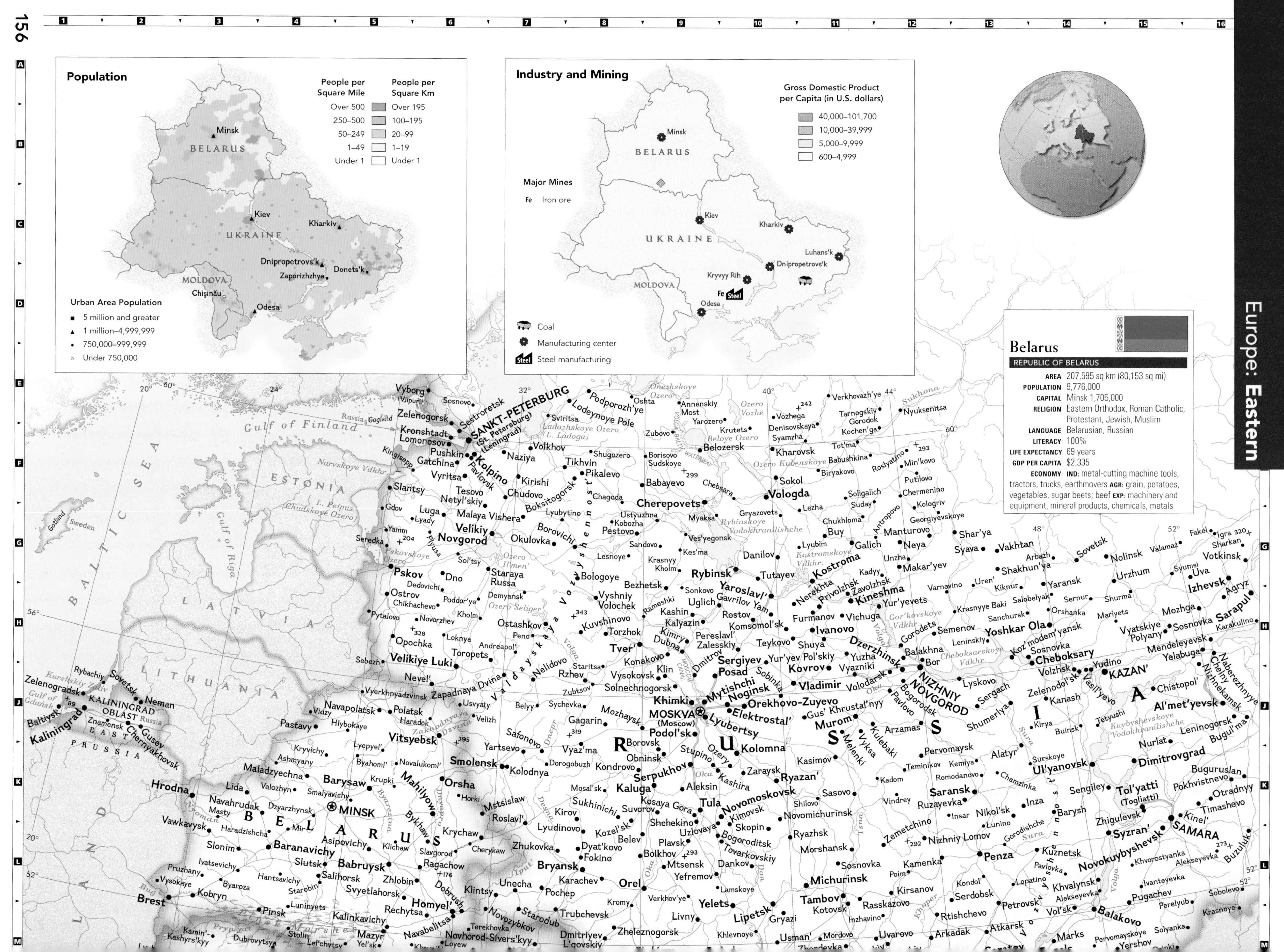
Population
People per Square Mile
Over 500
250–500
50–249
1–49
Under 1
People per Square Km
Over 195
100–195
20–99
1–19
Under 1
Minsk
BELARUS
Kiev
UKRAINE
Kharkiv
Dnipropetrovs'k
Donets'k
Zaporizhzhya
MOLDOVA
Chişinău
Odesa
Urban Area Population
5 million and greater
1 million–4,999,999
750,000–999,999
Under 750,000
Industry and Mining
Gross Domestic Product per Capita (in U.S. dollars)
40,000–101,700
10,000–39,999
5,000–9,999
600–4,999
Major Mines
Fe Iron ore
Luhans'k
Kryvyy Rih
Coal
Manufacturing center
Steel manufacturing
Belarus
REPUBLIC OF BELARUS
AREA 207,595 sq km (80,153 sq mi)
POPULATION 9,776,000
CAPITAL Minsk 1,705,000
RELIGION Eastern Orthodox, Roman Catholic, Protestant, Jewish, Muslim
LANGUAGE Belarusian, Russian
LITERACY 100%
LIFE EXPECTANCY 69 years
GDP PER CAPITA $2,335
ECONOMY IND: metal-cutting machine tools, tractors, trucks, earthmovers AGR: grain, potatoes, vegetables, sugar beets; beef EXP: machinery and equipment, mineral products, chemicals, metals
BALTIC SEA
Gulf of Finland
Gulf of Riga
ESTONIA
LATVIA
LITHUANIA
KALININGRAD OBLAST Russia
EAST PRUSSIA
POLAND
BELARUS
RUSSIA
SANKT-PETERBURG (St. Petersburg) (Leningrad)
MOSKVA (Moscow)
NIZHNIY NOVGOROD
KAZAN'
SAMARA
MINSK
Kaliningrad
Hrodna
Brest
Vitsyebsk
Mahilyow
Homyel'
Smolensk
Pskov
Velikiy Novgorod
Tver'
Yaroslavl'
Vologda
Cherepovets
Kostroma
Ivanovo
Vladimir
Kaluga
Tula
Ryazan'
Orel
Bryansk
Lipetsk
Tambov
Penza
Saransk
Cheboksary
Ul'yanovsk
Tol'yatti
Izhevsk
Sweden
Gotland

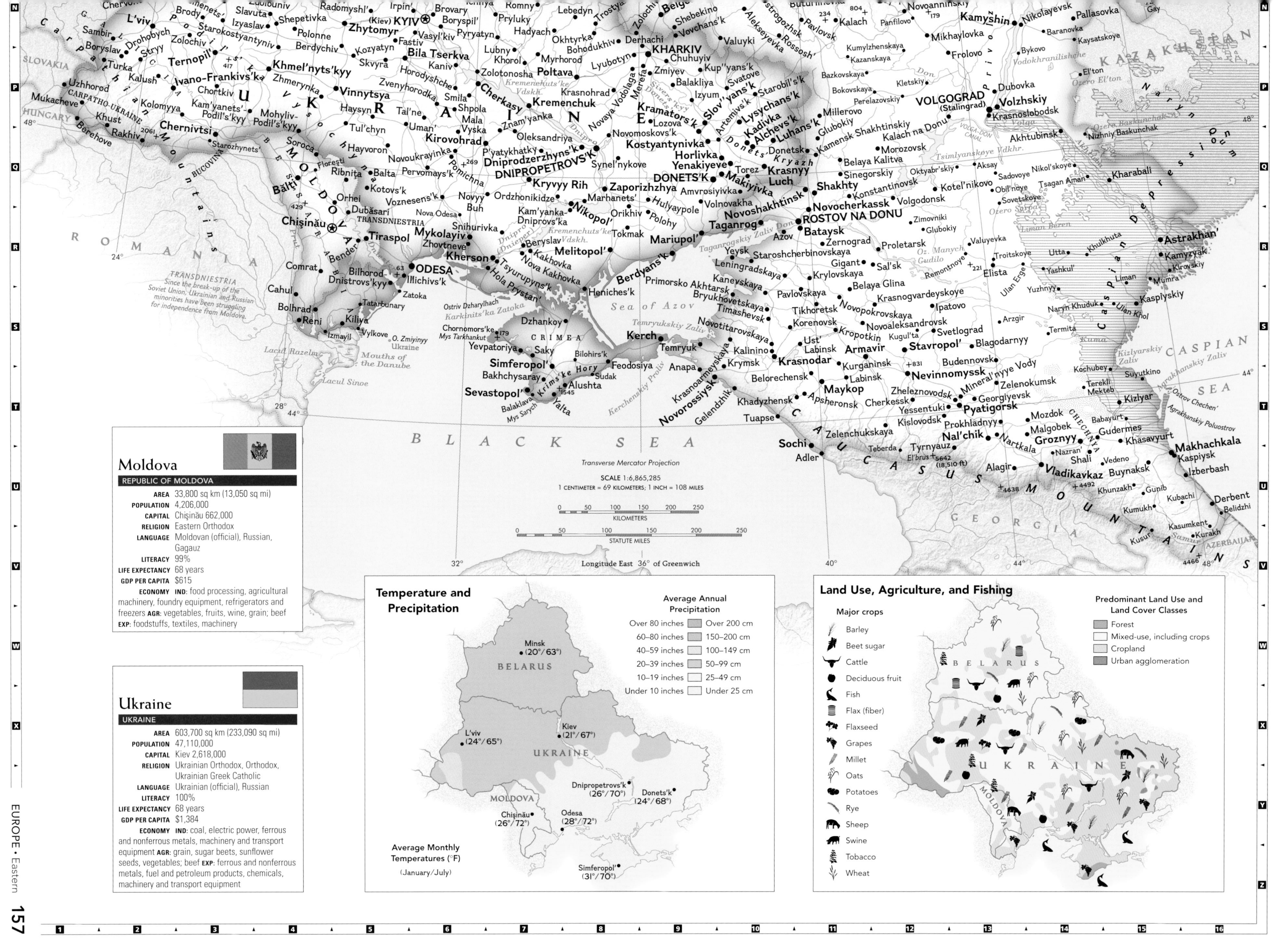

Moldova
REPUBLIC OF MOLDOVA
AREA 33,800 sq km (13,050 sq mi)
POPULATION 4,206,000
CAPITAL Chişinău 662,000
RELIGION Eastern Orthodox
LANGUAGE Moldovan (official), Russian, Gagauz
LITERACY 99%
LIFE EXPECTANCY 68 years
GDP PER CAPITA $615
ECONOMY IND: food processing, agricultural machinery, foundry equipment, refrigerators and freezers AGR: vegetables, fruits, wine, grain; beef EXP: foodstuffs, textiles, machinery
Ukraine
UKRAINE
AREA 603,700 sq km (233,090 sq mi)
POPULATION 47,110,000
CAPITAL Kiev 2,618,000
RELIGION Ukrainian Orthodox, Orthodox, Ukrainian Greek Catholic
LANGUAGE Ukrainian (official), Russian
LITERACY 100%
LIFE EXPECTANCY 68 years
GDP PER CAPITA $1,384
ECONOMY IND: coal, electric power, ferrous and nonferrous metals, machinery and transport equipment AGR: grain, sugar beets, sunflower seeds, vegetables; beef EXP: ferrous and nonferrous metals, fuel and petroleum products, chemicals, machinery and transport equipment
Temperature and Precipitation
Average Annual Precipitation
Over 80 inches Over 200 cm
60–80 inches 150–200 cm
40–59 inches 100–149 cm
20–39 inches 50–99 cm
10–19 inches 25–49 cm
Under 10 inches Under 25 cm
Minsk (20°/63°)
BELARUS
L'viv (24°/65°)
Kiev (21°/67°)
UKRAINE
Dnipropetrovs'k (26°/70°)
Donets'k (24°/68°)
MOLDOVA
Chişinău (26°/72°)
Odesa (28°/72°)
Simferopol' (31°/70°)
Average Monthly Temperatures (°F) (January/July)
Land Use, Agriculture, and Fishing
Major crops
Barley
Beet sugar
Cattle
Deciduous fruit
Fish
Flax (fiber)
Flaxseed
Grapes
Millet
Oats
Potatoes
Rye
Sheep
Swine
Tobacco
Wheat
Predominant Land Use and Land Cover Classes
Forest
Mixed-use, including crops
Cropland
Urban agglomeration
BELARUS
UKRAINE
MOLDOVA
Transverse Mercator Projection
SCALE 1:6,865,285
1 CENTIMETER = 69 KILOMETERS; 1 INCH = 108 MILES
KILOMETERS
STATUTE MILES
Longitude East 36° of Greenwich
BLACK SEA
Sea of Azov
CRIMEA
CASPIAN SEA
Caspian Depression
CAUCASUS MOUNTAINS
Carpathian Mountains
UKRAINE
MOLDOVA
ROMANIA
GEORGIA
KAZAKHSTAN
SLOVAKIA
HUNGARY
TRANSDNIESTRIA
TRANSDNIESTRIA Since the break-up of the Soviet Union, Ukrainian and Russian minorities have been struggling for independence from Moldova.
KYIV
(Kiev)
KHARKIV
DNIPROPETROVS'K
DONETS'K
ODESA
ROSTOV NA DONU
VOLGOGRAD (Stalingrad)
Chişinău
L'viv
Zhytomyr
Vinnytsya
Kirovohrad
Zaporizhzhya
Kryvyy Rih
Mykolayiv
Kherson
Simferopol'
Sevastopol'
Kerch
Mariupol'
Luhans'k
Krasnodar
Stavropol'
Astrakhan'
Makhachkala
Groznyy
Vladikavkaz
Nal'chik
Sochi
Novorossiysk
Taganrog
Shakhty
Tiraspol
Bălţi

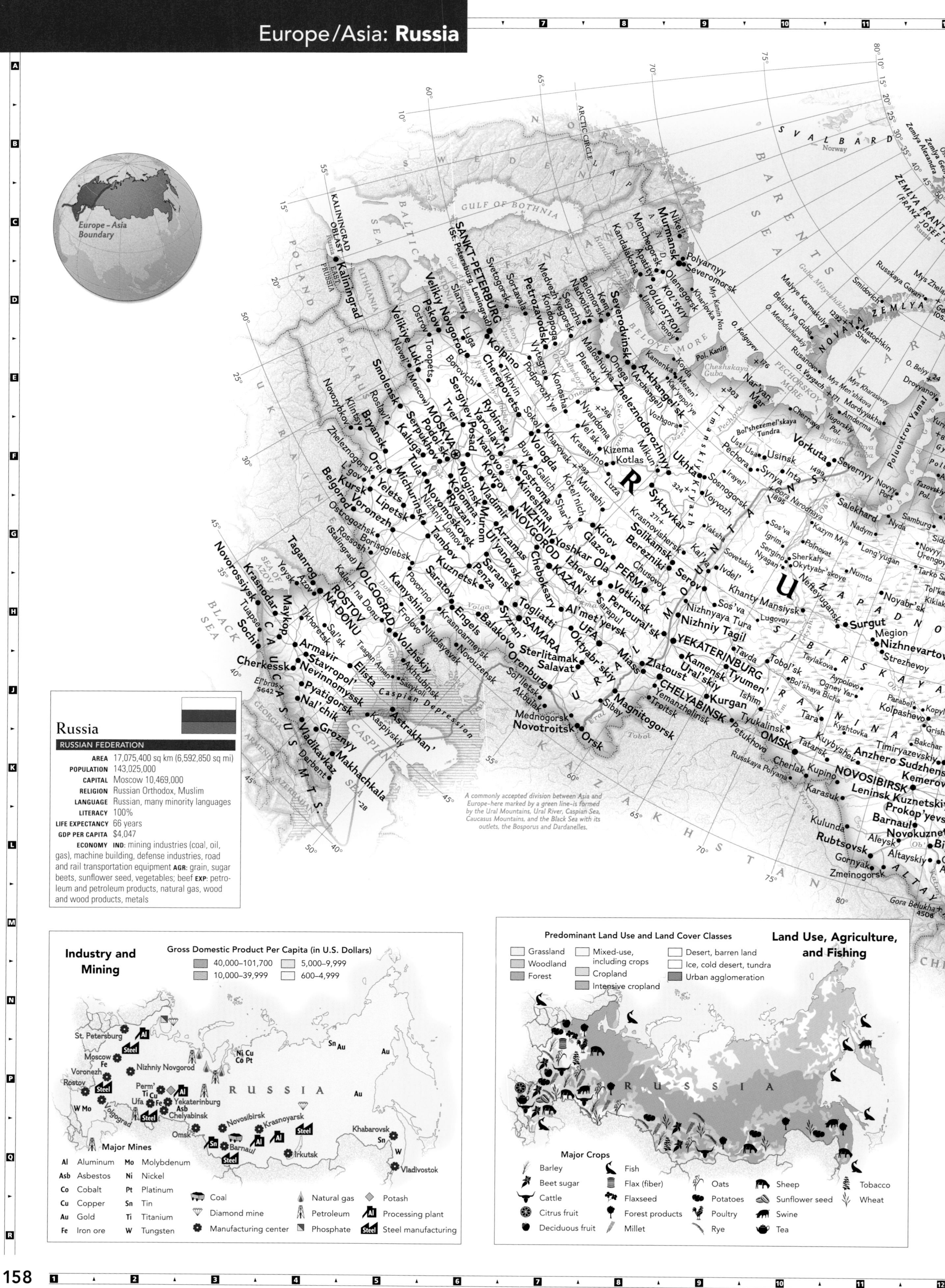
Europe - Asia Boundary
Russia
RUSSIAN FEDERATION
AREA 17,075,400 sq km (6,592,850 sq mi)
POPULATION 143,025,000
CAPITAL Moscow 10,469,000
RELIGION Russian Orthodox, Muslim
LANGUAGE Russian, many minority languages
LITERACY 100%
LIFE EXPECTANCY 66 years
GDP PER CAPITA $4,047
ECONOMY IND: mining industries (coal, oil, gas), machine building, defense industries, road and rail transportation equipment AGR: grain, sugar beets, sunflower seed, vegetables; beef EXP: petroleum and petroleum products, natural gas, wood and wood products, metals
A commonly accepted division between Asia and Europe–here marked by a green line–is formed by the Ural Mountains, Ural River, Caspian Sea, Caucasus Mountains, and the Black Sea with its outlets, the Bosporus and Dardanelles.
Industry and Mining
Gross Domestic Product Per Capita (in U.S. Dollars)
40,000–101,700
10,000–39,999
5,000–9,999
600–4,999
Major Mines
Al Aluminum
Asb Asbestos
Co Cobalt
Cu Copper
Au Gold
Fe Iron ore
Mo Molybdenum
Ni Nickel
Pt Platinum
Sn Tin
Ti Titanium
W Tungsten
Coal
Diamond mine
Manufacturing center
Natural gas
Petroleum
Phosphate
Potash
Processing plant
Steel manufacturing
Land Use, Agriculture, and Fishing
Predominant Land Use and Land Cover Classes
Grassland
Woodland
Forest
Mixed-use, including crops
Cropland
Intensive cropland
Desert, barren land
Ice, cold desert, tundra
Urban agglomeration
Major Crops
Barley
Beet sugar
Cattle
Citrus fruit
Deciduous fruit
Fish
Flax (fiber)
Flaxseed
Forest products
Millet
Oats
Potatoes
Poultry
Rye
Sheep
Sunflower seed
Swine
Tea
Tobacco
Wheat

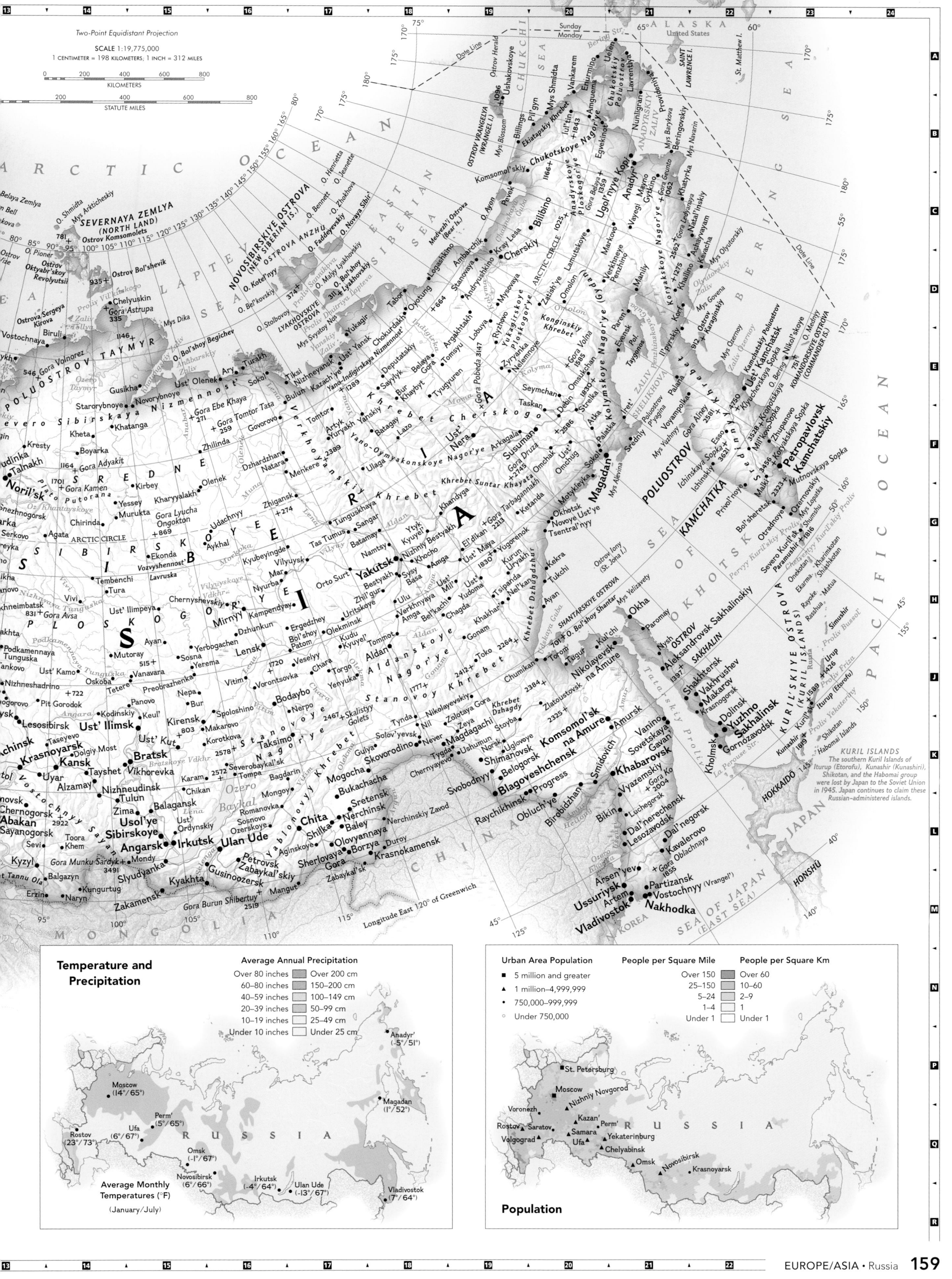
Two-Point Equidistant Projection
SCALE 1:19,775,000
1 CENTIMETER = 198 KILOMETERS; 1 INCH = 312 MILES
0 200 400 600 800
KILOMETERS
200 400 600 800
STATUTE MILES
ARCTIC OCEAN
SEVERNAYA ZEMLYA (NORTH LAND)
NOVOSIBIRSKIYE OSTROVA (NEW SIBERIAN IS.)
LAPTEV SEA
EAST SIBERIAN SEA
CHUKCHI SEA
BERING SEA
SEA OF OKHOTSK
PACIFIC OCEAN
SEA OF JAPAN (EAST SEA)
ALASKA
United States
Bering Str.
Date Line
Sunday
Monday
ARCTIC CIRCLE
POLUOSTROV TAYMYR
SREDNE SIBIRSKOYE PLOSKOGOR'YE
SIBERIA
Khrebet Cherskogo
Verkhoyanskiy Khrebet
Stanovoy Khrebet
Aldanskoye Nagor'ye
Chukotskoye Nagor'ye
Koryakskoye Nagor'ye
Kolymskoye Nagor'ye
POLUOSTROV KAMCHATKA
SAKHALIN
KURIL'SKIYE OSTROVA (KURIL ISLANDS)
KOMANDORSKIYE OSTROVA (COMMANDER IS.)
OSTROV VRANGELYA (WRANGEL I.)
SHANTARSKIYE OSTROVA
HOKKAIDŌ
HONSHŪ
JAPAN
CHINA
MONGOLIA
KOREA
Noril'sk
Krasnoyarsk
Bratsk
Irkutsk
Ulan Ude
Chita
Yakutsk
Magadan
Anadyr'
Petropavlovsk Kamchatskiy
Khabarovsk
Komsomol'sk na Amure
Blagoveshchensk
Vladivostok
Nakhodka
Yuzhno Sakhalinsk
Ozero Baykal
Longitude East 120° of Greenwich
KURIL ISLANDS
The southern Kuril Islands of Iturup (Etorofu), Kunashir (Kunashiri), Shikotan, and the Habomai group were lost by Japan to the Soviet Union in 1945. Japan continues to claim these Russian-administered islands.
Temperature and Precipitation
Average Annual Precipitation
Over 80 inches | Over 200 cm
60–80 inches | 150–200 cm
40–59 inches | 100–149 cm
20–39 inches | 50–99 cm
10–19 inches | 25–49 cm
Under 10 inches | Under 25 cm
Moscow (14°/65°)
Perm' (5°/65°)
Ufa (6°/67°)
Rostov (23°/73°)
Omsk (-1°/67°)
Novosibirsk (6°/66°)
Irkutsk (-4°/64°)
Ulan Ude (-13°/67°)
Anadyr' (-5°/51°)
Magadan (1°/52°)
Vladivostok (7°/64°)
RUSSIA
Average Monthly Temperatures (°F) (January/July)
Urban Area Population
5 million and greater
1 million–4,999,999
750,000–999,999
Under 750,000
People per Square Mile
Over 150
25–150
5–24
1–4
Under 1
People per Square Km
Over 60
10–60
2–9
1
Under 1
St. Petersburg
Moscow
Nizhniy Novgorod
Voronezh
Kazan'
Perm'
Rostov
Saratov
Samara
Volgograd
Ufa
Yekaterinburg
Chelyabinsk
Omsk
Novosibirsk
Krasnoyarsk
Population

ATLANTIC OCEAN
NORTH SEA
BALTIC SEA
BLACK SEA
MEDITERRANEAN SEA
LUXEMBOURG
LIECHTENSTEIN
MONACO
SAN MARINO
ANDORRA
VATICAN CITY
Gibraltar
United Kingdom
MALTA
CYPRUS
0 kilometers 900
0 statute miles 600

Independent Nations

Andorra

PRINCIPALITY OF ANDORRA

AREA 468 sq km (181 sq mi)
POPULATION 74,000
CAPITAL Andorra la Vella 21,000
RELIGION Roman Catholic
LANGUAGE Catalan (official), French, Castilian, Portuguese
LITERACY 100%
LIFE EXPECTANCY 84 years
GDP PER CAPITA $33,335
ECONOMY **IND:** tourism (particularly skiing), cattle raising, timber, banking **AGR:** rye, wheat, barley, oats; sheep **EXP:** tobacco products, furniture

Cyprus

REPUBLIC OF CYPRUS

AREA 9,251 sq km (3,572 sq mi)
POPULATION 965,000
CAPITAL Nicosia 205,000
RELIGION Greek Orthodox, Muslim
LANGUAGE Greek, Turkish, English
LITERACY 98%
LIFE EXPECTANCY 77 years
GDP PER CAPITA $18,562
ECONOMY **IND:** tourism, food and beverage processing, cement and gypsum production, ship repair **AGR:** citrus, vegetables, barley, grapes; poultry **EXP:** citrus, potatoes, pharmaceuticals, cement

Liechtenstein

PRINCIPALITY OF LIECHTENSTEIN

AREA 160 sq km (62 sq mi)
POPULATION 35,000
CAPITAL Vaduz 5,000
RELIGION Roman Catholic, Protestant
LANGUAGE German (official)
LITERACY 100%
LIFE EXPECTANCY 80 years
GDP PER CAPITA $101,654
ECONOMY **IND:** electronics, metal manufacturing, dental products **AGR:** wheat, barley, corn; livestock **EXP:** small machinery, audio/video connectors

Luxembourg

GRAND DUCHY OF LUXEMBOURG

AREA 2,586 sq km (998 sq mi)
POPULATION 457,000
CAPITAL Luxembourg 77,000
RELIGION Roman Catholic
LANGUAGE Luxembourgish, German, French
LITERACY 100%
LIFE EXPECTANCY 78 years
GDP PER CAPITA $69,423
ECONOMY **IND:** banking, iron and steel, food processing **AGR:** barley, oats, potatoes; livestock products **EXP:** machinery, steel products, chemicals

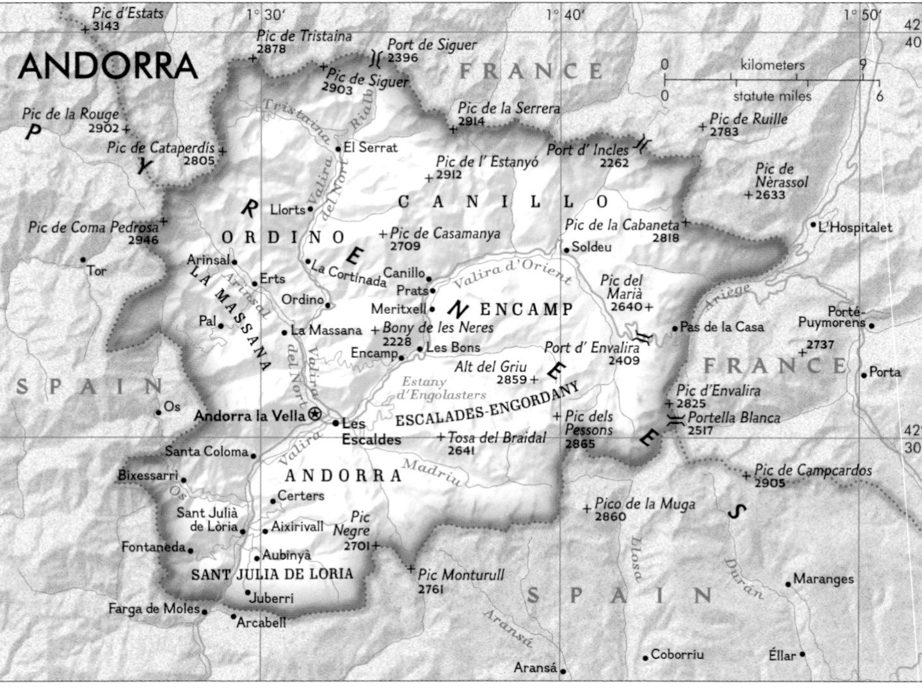
ANDORRA
FRANCE
SPAIN
PYRENEES
CANILLO
ORDINO
LA MASSANA
ENCAMP
ESCALDES-ENGORDANY
ANDORRA
SANT JULIÀ DE LÒRIA
Andorra la Vella
Pic d'Estats 3143
Pic de Tristaina 2878
Port de Siguer 2396
Pic de Siguer 2903
Pic de la Serrera 2914
Pic de Ruille 2783
Port d'Incles 2262
Pic de l'Estanyó 2912
Pic de Nérassol 2633
Pic de Coma Pedrosa 2946
Pic de Casamanya 2709
Pic de la Cabaneta 2818
Pic del Maià 2640
Pic d'Envalira 2825
Port d'Envalira 2409
Pic dels Pessons 2865
Portella Blanca 2517
Pic de Campcardos 2905
Pico de la Muga 2860
Pic Negre 2701
Pic Monturull 2761
Tosa del Braidal 2641
Alt del Griu 2859
El Serrat
Llorts
Soldeu
L'Hospitalet
Arinsal
Erts
La Cortinada
Canillo
Prats
Ordino
Meritxell
Pal
La Massana
Encamp
Les Bons
Pas de la Casa
Porta
Os
Les Escaldes
Santa Coloma
Bixessarri
Certers
Aixirivall
Aubinyà
Juberri
Arcabell
Farga de Moles
Fontaneda
Maranges
Coborriu
Éllar
Aransá
Tor
0 kilometers 9
0 statute miles 6

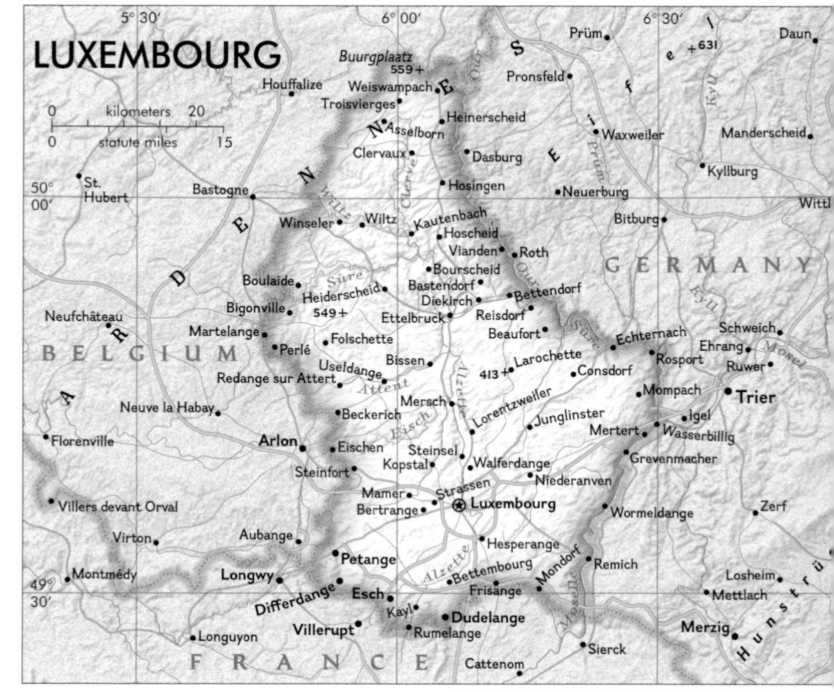
LUXEMBOURG
BELGIUM
GERMANY
FRANCE
ARDENNES
EIFEL
HUNSRÜCK
Burgplaatz 559
Houffalize
Weiswampach
Troisvierges
Heinerscheid
Asselborn
Clervaux
Dasburg
Hosingen
Bastogne
Wiltz
Kautenbach
Hoscheid
Vianden
Roth
Boulaide
Bourscheid
Bastendorf
Diekirch
Bettendorf
Heiderscheid
Bigonville
Ettelbruck
Reisdorf
Beaufort
Echternach
Martelange
Perlé
Folschette
Useldange
Bissen
Larochette
Consdorf
Redange sur Attert
Mersch
Mompach
Trier
Beckerich
Arlon
Eischen
Steinfort
Kopstal
Steinsel
Walferdange
Junglinster
Mertert
Wasserbillig
Grevenmacher
Niederanven
Mamer
Bertrange
Strassen
Luxembourg
Hesperange
Petange
Bettembourg
Mondorf
Remich
Esch
Kayl
Dudelange
Rumelange
Differdange
Villerupt
Longwy
Aubange
Virton
Montmédy
Longuyon
Cattenom
Sierck
Merzig
Losheim
Mettlach
Zerf
Wormeldange
Frisange
Prüm
Pronsfeld
Waxweiler
Manderscheid
Daun
Kyllburg
Neuerburg
Bitburg
Schweich
Ehrang
Ruwer
Rosport
Igel
St. Hubert
Neufchâteau
Neuve la Habay
Florenville
Villers devant Orval
0 kilometers 20
0 statute miles 15

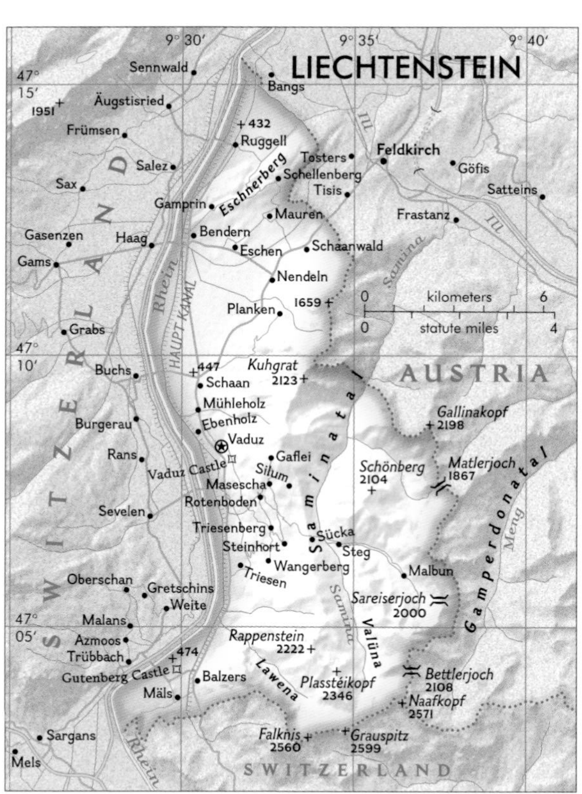
LIECHTENSTEIN
AUSTRIA
SWITZERLAND
Sennwald
Bangs
Ruggell
Feldkirch
Gisingen
Tosters
Schellenberg
Tisis
Gofis
Satteins
Frümsen
Salez
Sax
Mauren
Gamprin
Eschen
Frastanz
Bendern
Schaanwald
Haag
Gasenzen
Gams
Nendeln
Planken
Grabs
Buchs
Schaan
Kuhgrat 2123
Mühleholz
Ebenholz
Gallinakopf 2198
Burgerau
Vaduz
Vaduz Castle
Gaflei
Silum
Rans
Schönberg 2104
Matlerjoch 1867
Masescha
Rotenboden
Sevelen
Triesenberg
Steinhort
Sücka
Steg
Malbun
Triesen
Wangerberg
Oberschan
Gretschins
Weite
Sareiserjoch 2000
Malans
Azmoos
Trübbach
Rappenstein 2222
Gutenberg Castle
Balzers
Mäls
Plassteikopf 2346
Bettlerjoch 2108
Naafkopf 2571
Falknis 2560
Grauspitz 2599
Sargans
Mels
0 kilometers 6
0 statute miles 4

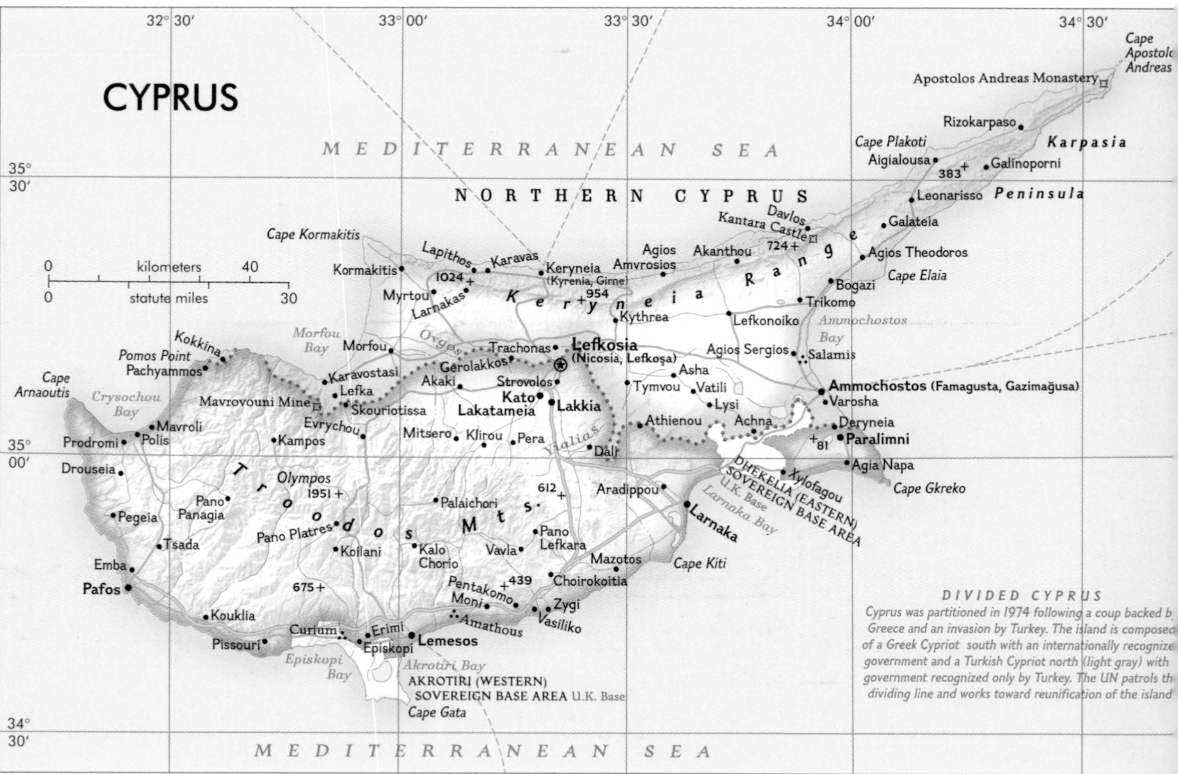
CYPRUS
MEDITERRANEAN SEA
NORTHERN CYPRUS
Cape Apostolos Andreas
Apostolos Andreas Monastery
Rizokarpaso
Cape Plakoti
Karpasia Peninsula
Aigialousa
Galinoporni
Leonarisso
Davlos
Kantara Castle
Galateia
Agios Theodoros
Cape Elaia
Cape Kormakitis
Lapithos
Karavas
Keryneia (Kyrenia, Girne)
Agios Amvrosios
Akanthou
Kormakitis
Myrtou
Larnakas
Kerynia Range
Kythrea
Lefkoniko
Bogazi
Trikomo
Ammochostos Bay
Morfou Bay
Morfou
Trachonas
Lefkosia (Nicosia, Lefkoşa)
Agios Sergios
Salamis
Pomos Point
Pachyammos
Kokkina
Karavostasi
Gerolakkos
Strovolos
Asha
Tymvou
Vatili
Ammochostos (Famagusta, Gazimağusa)
Varosha
Cape Arnaoutis
Chrysochou Bay
Mavrovouni Mine
Lefka
Skouriotissa
Akaki
Kato Lakatameia
Lakkia
Lysi
Athienou
Achna
Deryneia
Paralimni
Polis
Mavroli
Prodromi
Evrychou
Kampos
Mitsero
Klirou
Pera
Dali
Agia Napa
Cape Gkreko
Drouseia
Olympos 1951
Troodos Mts
DHEKELIA (EASTERN) SOVEREIGN BASE AREA
Aradippou
Palaichori
Pano Panagia
Pegeia
Tsada
Pano Platres
Kalo Chorio
Kollani
Vavla
Pano Lefkara
Larnaka
Larnaka Bay
Mazotos
Cape Kiti
Emba
Pafos
Pentakomo
Moni
Choirokoitia
Zygi
Vasiliko
Amathous
Kouklia
Pissouri
Curium
Erimi
Episkopi
Lemesos
Episkopi Bay
Akrotiri Bay
AKROTIRI (WESTERN) SOVEREIGN BASE AREA U.K. Base
Cape Gata
0 kilometers 40
0 statute miles 30
DIVIDED CYPRUS
Cyprus was partitioned in 1974 following a coup backed b
Greece and an invasion by Turkey. The island is composed
of a Greek Cypriot south with an internationally recognize
government and a Turkish Cypriot north (light gray) with
government recognized only by Turkey. The UN patrols th
dividing line and works toward reunification of the island

Malta

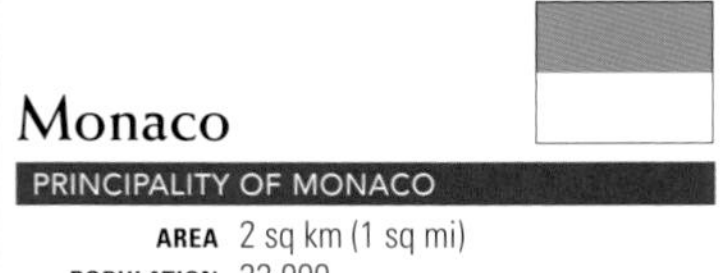

REPUBLIC OF MALTA

AREA 316 sq km (122 sq mi)
POPULATION 405,000
CAPITAL Valletta 83,000
RELIGION Roman Catholic
LANGUAGE Maltese (official), English (official)
LITERACY 93%
LIFE EXPECTANCY 78 years
GDP PER CAPITA $14,074
ECONOMY **IND:** tourism, electronics, ship building and repair, construction **AGR:** potatoes, cauliflower, grapes, wheat; pork **EXP:** machinery and transport equipment, manufactures

Monaco

PRINCIPALITY OF MONACO

AREA 2 sq km (1 sq mi)
POPULATION 33,000
CAPITAL Monaco 34,000
RELIGION Roman Catholic
LANGUAGE French (official), English, Italian, Monegasque
LITERACY 99%
LIFE EXPECTANCY 80 years
GDP PER CAPITA $32,984
ECONOMY **IND:** tourism, construction, small-scale industrial and consumer products **AGR:** NA **EXP:** Full customs integration with France

San Marino

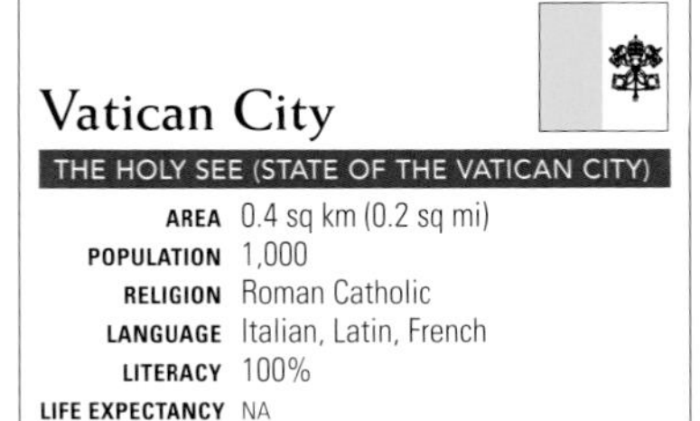

REPUBLIC OF SAN MARINO

AREA 61 sq km (24 sq mi)
POPULATION 30,000
CAPITAL San Marino 5,000
RELIGION Roman Catholic
LANGUAGE Italian
LITERACY 96%
LIFE EXPECTANCY 81 years
GDP PER CAPITA $44,607
ECONOMY **IND:** tourism, banking, textiles, electronics **AGR:** wheat, grapes, corn, olives; cattle **EXP:** building stone, lime, wood, chestnuts

Vatican City

THE HOLY SEE (STATE OF THE VATICAN CITY)

AREA 0.4 sq km (0.2 sq mi)
POPULATION 1,000
RELIGION Roman Catholic
LANGUAGE Italian, Latin, French
LITERACY 100%
LIFE EXPECTANCY NA
GDP PER CAPITA NA
ECONOMY **IND:** printing, production of coins, medals, and postage stamps, a small amount of mosaics and staff uniforms, worldwide banking and financial activities **AGR:** NA **EXP:** NA

MONACO
FRANCE
MEDITERRANEAN SEA
LA ROUSSE
ST. ROMAN
LA NOIX
TENAO
LARVOTTO
BEAUSOLEIL
MONTE CARLO
LA CONDAMINE
MONACO-VILLE
FONTVIEILLE
CAP D'AIL
Port of Monaco
Port of Fontvieille
Larvotto Beach
Monte Carlo Country Club
Monte Carlo Beach Hotel
Cinéma d'Été
Sea Club
Monte-Carlo Sporting Club d'Été
Saint Joseph's Church
Grimaldi Forum
Town Hall of Beausoleil
Saint Charles' Church
Office of Tourism
Hotel Metropole
National Museum of Fine Arts
Monte Carlo Radio and Television Station
Casino Gardens
Sporting Club
Casino of Monte Carlo
Hotel Hermitage
Hotel de Paris
Convention Center and Auditorium
Ste. Dévote's Church
Municipal Administrative Center
Princess Antoinette Park
Museum of Prehistoric Anthropology
Covered Market
Monaco R.R. Station
Exotic Garden
Zoo
Palace of Monaco
Palace Square
Palace of Justice
Fort Antoine
Government House
Town Hall
Oceanographic Museum
Princess Grace Hospital Center
Grotto of the Observatory
Cathedral of Monaco
St. Martin's Gardens
Louis II Stadium
Princess Grace Rose Garden
Heliport
kilometer
statute mile

SAN MARINO
ITALY
Ceriano
Torriana
Verucchio
Falciano
Cerasolo
La Dogana
Bruciato
Serravalle
Torello
Monte Olivo
Mulazzano
Fiorina
Monte Ventoso
Ventoso
Sorazzeco
Cailungo
Gualdicciolo
Domagnano
Monte Cerreto
Acquaviva
Borgo Maggiore
Valdragone
Corianino
San Marino
La Rocca o Guaita
Monte Titano
San Giovanni
Castello di Montemaggio
Faetano
Albereto
Murata
Montescudo
Castellaccio
Fiorentino
Monte Giardino
Chiesanuova
Montemaggio
Teglio
Monte San Cristoforo
Gesso
Castello
Sassofeltrio
Monteliccians
kilometers
statute miles

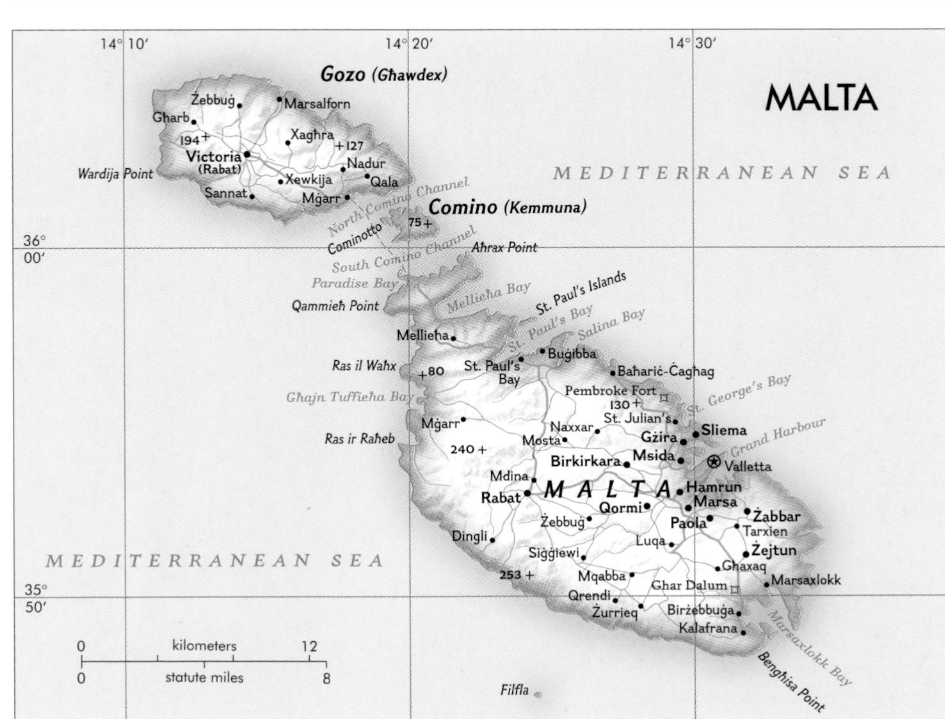
MALTA
Gozo (Ghawdex)
Comino (Kemmuna)
MEDITERRANEAN SEA
Żebbuġ
Marsalforn
Gharb
Xaghra
Victoria (Rabat)
Nadur
Wardija Point
Xewkija
Qala
Sannat
Mġarr
North Comino Channel
Cominotto
South Comino Channel
Ahrax Point
Paradise Bay
Qammieh Point
Mellieha Bay
St. Paul's Islands
Mellieha
St. Paul's Bay
Salina Bay
Ras il Wahx
Buġibba
Bahariċ-Ċaghaq
Ghajn Tuffieha Bay
Pembroke Fort
St. Julian's
St. George's Bay
Mġarr
Naxxar
Mosta
Gżira
Sliema
Ras ir Raheb
Msida
Grand Harbour
Birkirkara
Valletta
Mdina
MALTA
Hamrun
Rabat
Qormi
Marsa
Żabbar
Żebbuġ
Paola
Tarxien
Dingli
Luqa
Żejtun
Siġġiewi
Ghaxaq
Mqabba
Marsaxlokk
Qrendi
Ghar Dalam
Żurrieq
Birżebbuġa
Kalafrana
Marsaxlokk Bay
Benghisa Point
Filfla
kilometers
statute miles

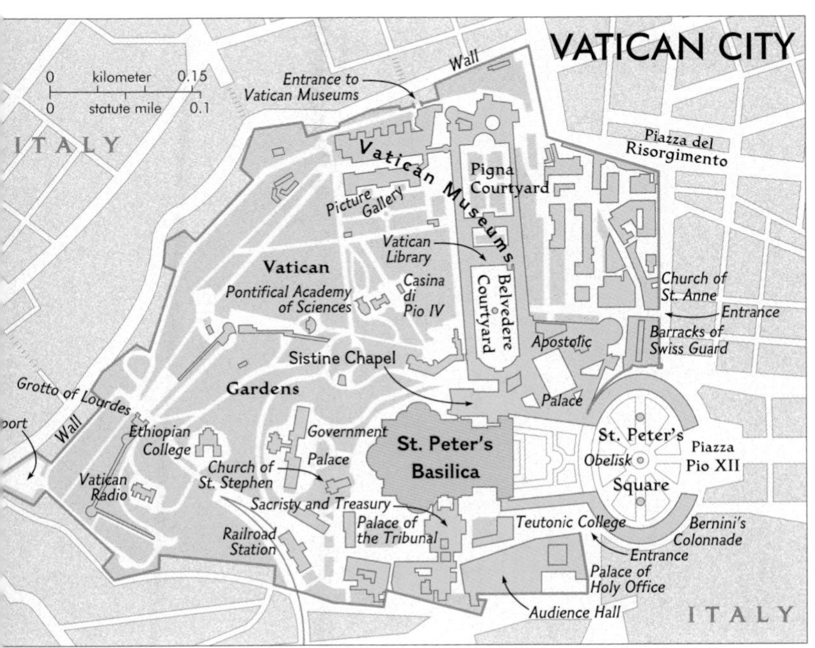
VATICAN CITY
ITALY
kilometer
statute mile
Wall
Entrance to Vatican Museums
Piazza del Risorgimento
Vatican Museums
Pigna Courtyard
Picture Gallery
Vatican Library
Vatican
Casina di Pio IV
Belvedere Courtyard
Church of St. Anne
Entrance
Pontifical Academy of Sciences
Barracks of Swiss Guard
Apostolic
Sistine Chapel
Gardens
Palace
Grotto of Lourdes
Government Palace
St. Peter's Basilica
St. Peter's Square
Obelisk
Piazza Pio XII
Ethiopian College
Church of St. Stephen
Vatican Radio
Sacristy and Treasury
Palace of the Tribunal
Teutonic College
Bernini's Colonnade
Railroad Station
Entrance
Palace of Holy Office
Audience Hall

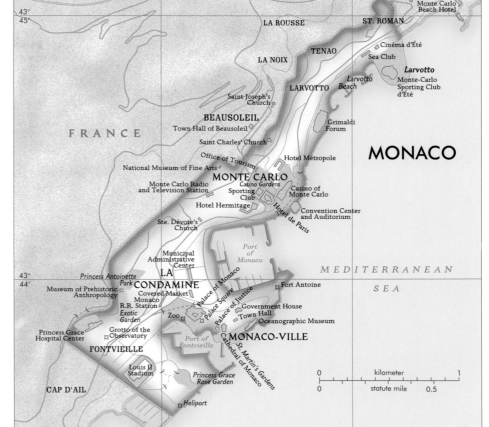

Dependency

SOVEREIGN LOCAL

Gibraltar (U.K.)

GIBRALTAR

AREA 7 sq km (3 sq mi)
POPULATION 29,000
CAPITAL Gibraltar 27,000
RELIGION Roman Catholic, Church of England
LANGUAGE English, Spanish, Italian, Portuguese
LITERACY NA
LIFE EXPECTANCY 80 years
GDP PER CAPITA $27,900
ECONOMY **IND:** tourism, banking and finance, ship repairing, tobacco **AGR:** NA **EXP:** petroleum, manufactured goods

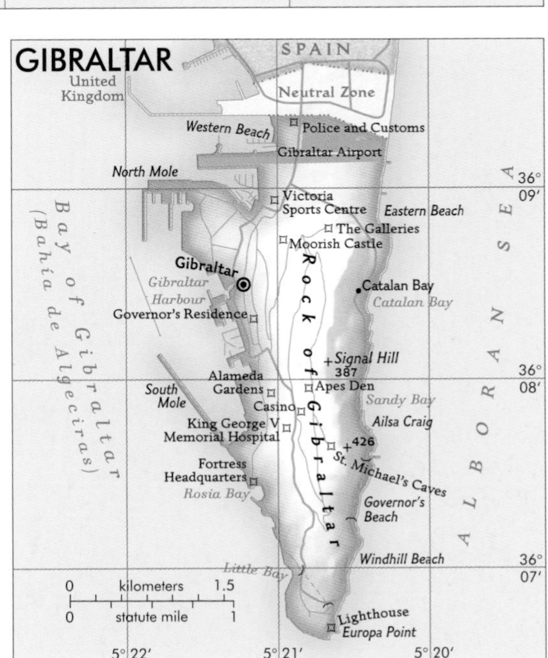
GIBRALTAR
United Kingdom
SPAIN
Neutral Zone
Western Beach
Police and Customs
Gibraltar Airport
North Mole
Victoria Sports Centre
Eastern Beach
The Galleries
Moorish Castle
Bay of Gibraltar (Bahía de Algeciras)
Gibraltar
Gibraltar Harbour
Rock of Gibraltar
Catalan Bay
Governor's Residence
Signal Hill
Alameda Gardens
Apes Den
South Mole
Casino
Sandy Bay
King George V Memorial Hospital
Ailsa Craig
St. Michael's Caves
Fortress Headquarters
Rosia Bay
Governor's Beach
ALBORAN SEA
Little Bay
Windhill Beach
Lighthouse
Europa Point
kilometers
statute mile

Asia

The continent of Asia, occupying four-fifths of the giant Eurasian landmass, stretches across ten time zones from the Pacific Ocean in the east to the Ural Mountains and Black Sea in the west. It is the largest of continents, with dazzling geographic diversity and 30 percent of the Earth's land surface. Asia includes numerous island nations, such as Japan, the Philippines, Indonesia, and Sri Lanka, as well as many of the world's major islands: Borneo, Sumatra, Honshu, Celebes, Java, and half of New Guinea.

Siberia, the huge Asian section of Russia, reaches deep inside the Arctic Circle and fills the continent's northern quarter. To its south lie the large countries of Kazakhstan, Mongolia, and China. In all, Asia contains 46 nations, accounting for 60 percent of the Earth's population—more than 3.9 billion people—yet deserts, mountains, jungles, and other inhospitable zones render much of Asia empty or underpopulated.

Immortalized in art and verse, the beautiful Li River in China's northeastern Guangxi Province meanders 105 miles (169 km) through a landscape of towering limestone peaks clad with verdant bamboo forests, rushing waterfalls, and precariously perched villages, where traditional ways of life such as night fishing still hold sway.

Asia

For millennia, people have lived near the seas and along great rivers. Early civilizations arose in China along the Yellow River, in South Asia on the Indus, and in the Middle East along the Tigris and Euphrates. Today, Asia's large populations continue to thrive near inland waterways and coastal regions.

India and China, historically isolated from each other by the Himalaya Mountains and Myanmar's jungles, developed rich, vibrant cultures with art, literature, and philosophy of the highest order. China's 1.3 billion people and India's billion make up nearly two-thirds of Asia's population. These countries stand as rivals, each trying to modernize and assert itself while struggling with formidable problems of poverty, pollution, urbanization, and illiteracy.

Breakup of the Soviet Union in 1991 allowed for the creation of eight new Asian countries, five in Central Asia—Kazakhstan, Kyrgyzstan, Uzbekistan, Turkmenistan, and Tajikistan—and three in the Caucasus region—Georgia, Armenia, and Azerbaijan.

Asia's few democracies, including Israel, India, and Japan, contrast with much more authoritarian governments or military regimes, which are numerous and widespread. Monarchies in Bhutan, Nepal, Jordan, Saudi Arabia, and Brunei (a sultanate) pass rulership through family lines.

Events at the start of the 21st century have put new focus on the Middle East, the role of Islam, and control of religious extremism. More than half of Asia's countries are Muslim, yet they possess very different languages, climates, economies, and ethnic groups. But all share emotional links with their co-religionists and care deeply about the development of Islam in the decades ahead.

PHYSICAL GEOGRAPHY Asia, the planet's youngest continent, displays continuing geologic activity. Volcanoes form a chain known as the Ring of Fire along the entire Pacific edge, from Siberia's Kamchatka Peninsula to the islands of the Philippines and Indonesia. The Indian subcontinent pushes into the heart of Asia, raising and contorting the towering Karakoram and Himalaya ranges. Earthquakes rattle China, Japan, and West Asia.

Geographic extremes allow Asia to claim many world records. Mount Everest, monarch of the Himalaya, is the planet's highest point at 29,035 feet (8,850 m). The super-salty Dead Sea lies 1,365 feet (416 m) below sea level—the lowest point. A site in Assam, India, receives an astonishing 39 feet (12 m) of rain each year, making it the wettest spot on Earth, and Siberia's ancient Lake Baikal, arcing 395 miles (636 km), plunges over a mile (5,371 ft; 1,637 m) as the world's deepest lake. It harbors many unique plant and animal species, including tens of thousands of freshwater seals.

The Caspian Sea, salty and isolated on the border of Europe and Asia, is the largest lake, measuring more than four times the area of Lake Superior. A 39,000-mile (62,800 km) coastline, longest of any continent's, allows all but 12 Asian nations direct access to the sea.

These landlocked countries, mostly in Central Asia (excepting Laos), form part of a great band across the middle latitudes comprised of deserts, mountains, and arid plateaus. The vast Tibetan Plateau, home to the yak, snow leopard, wild ass, and migrating antelope, gives rise to Asia's vital rivers: the Yellow, Yangtze, Indus, Ganges, Salween, and Mekong. At the heart of the continent exists a convergence of the world's mighty mountains: Himalaya, Karakoram, Hindu Kush, Pamir, and Kunlun.

Flowing sand dunes of the Arabian Peninsula contrast with steppes that extend for thousands of grassy miles from Europe to Mongolia. To the north, girdling Asia's northern latitudes, grow boreal forests made up of conifers—the taiga—largest unbroken woodlands in the world. Beyond the taiga lie frozen expanses of tundra.

Far to the south, monsoon winds bring annual rains to thickly populated regions of South and Southeast Asia. These wet, green domains support some of the world's last rain forests and amazing numbers of plants. Human impact through agriculture, animal grazing, and forestry has altered much of Asia's landscape and continues to threaten the natural realm.

HISTORY Asia's great historical breadth encompasses thousands of years, vast distances, and a kaleidoscope of peoples. From China to Lebanon, from Siberia to Sri Lanka, Asia has more ethnic and national groups than any other continent. Their histories have evolved through peaceful growth and migration, but more often through military conquest.

The Fertile Crescent region of the Middle East saw the emergence of agriculture and early settlements some 10,000 years ago. Later, successful irrigation helped bring forth the first civilization in Sumer, today's southern Iraq; Sumerians invented the first wheeled vehicles, the potter's wheel, the first system of writing—cuneiform—and codes of law.

During the second millennium B.C., a pastoral people called Aryans, or Indo-Iranians, pushed into present-day Afghanistan and eastern Iran, then steadily occupied much of India, Western, and Central Asia.

Central Asia has always been a historic melting pot of flourishing cultures. More than 2,000 years ago a braid of ancient caravan tracks—the Silk Road—carried precious goods between East Asia and the rest of the world: sleek horses, exotic foods, medicines, jewels, birds, and perfume. More practical were gunpowder, the magnetic compass, the printing press, mathematics, ceramics, and silk. Trade flourished especially during China's Han dynasty (206 B.C.–A.D. 220), Tang dynasty (A.D. 618–907), and the Mongol period (13th and 14th centuries). Mongols at their height came closer than any other people to conquering all of Asia, threatening Europe in the west and twice trying to invade Japan.

Another great expansion was the conquest and settlement of Siberia and Central Asia by Russians. The Trans-Siberian Railway, built between 1891 and 1905, opened up Siberia for settlement. During the 19th century, Russian armies and colonizers spread through Central

Asia as well, claiming the khanates for an expanding Russian empire. Great Britain, France, and other European countries also laid claim to parts of Asia.

Today, colonial empires have ended and a seemingly stable community of nations with defined borders exists in Asia. Yet rivalries, threats, and war dominate many regions. Indochina is only now healing after decades of violence. The Korean Peninsula remains divided. Nuclear-armed India and Pakistan have fought three wars since independence in 1947. Religious and ethnic hostilities inflame many areas, nowhere more so than in the Middle East. Troubled Afghanistan, victim of almost continuous warfare since 1979, saw a U.S.-led invasion in 2001 to oust the Taliban government and destroy terrorist groups. Many claim peace will come to these areas only after economic stability, steps towards democracy, and recognition of human rights are achieved.

CULTURE Numerous cultural forces, each linked to broad geographic areas, have formed and influenced Asia's rich civilizations and hundreds of ethnic groups. The two oldest are the cultural milieus of India and China.

India's culture still reverberates throughout countries as varied as Sri Lanka, Pakistan, Afghanistan, Nepal, Bangladesh, Myanmar (Burma), and across seas to Thailand, Cambodia, Singapore, and Indonesia. The world religions of Hinduism and Buddhism originated in India and spread as traders, scholars, and priests sought distant footholds. The island of Bali in predominantly Muslim Indonesia remains Hindu today. Many regions of Asia first encountered writing in the form of Sanskrit, the holy script of Hinduism.

China's civilization, more than four thousand years old, has profoundly influenced the development of all of East Asia, much of Southeast Asia, and parts of Central Asia. Chinese institutions such as government, warfare, architecture, the arts and sciences, and even chopsticks reached to the heart of other lands and peoples. Most important of all were the Chinese written language, a complex script with thousands of characters, and Confucianism, an ethical world view that affected philosophy, politics, and relations within society. Japan, Korea, and Vietnam especially absorbed these cultural gifts.

Today, most Chinese call themselves "Han," a term that embraces more than 90 percent of the population—a billion people—and thus makes them the world's largest ethnic group. In addition, China's government recognizes 55 other ethnic minorities within its borders.

Islam, a third great cultural influence in Asia, proved formidable in its energy and creative genius. Arabs from the seventh century onward, spurred on by faith, moved rapidly into Southwest Asia. Their religion and culture, particularly Arabic writing, spread through Iran and Afghanistan to the Indian subcontinent. In time, shipping, commerce, and missionaries carried Islam on to the Malay Peninsula and Indonesian archipelago. Indonesia, the largest Muslim country with more than 200 million believers, and Pakistan and Bangladesh, each with more than 100 million Muslims, attest to Islam's success.

Europeans, too, have affected Asia's cultures, from the conquests of Alexander the Great to today's multinational corporations. Colonial powers, especially Britain in India, France in Indochina, Holland in the Indonesian archipelago, and numerous countries in China, left a lasting mark even after nationalist movements forced them out in the late 1940s and early 1950s.

In 1791, King Bodawapaya of Myanmar commissioned an enormous Buddhist pagoda in Mingun. Although construction stopped upon the king's death in 1819, the building still measures an astounding 256 feet square (78 m sq) at its base and is 150 feet (45.7 m) tall. Subsequent earthquakes cracked the structure.

ECONOMY Blessed with resources and teeming with energetic people, Asia still suffers from great disparities between rich and poor. The livelihood of most Asians rests on agriculture and age-old methods of production. Vietnamese women turn waterwheels by foot-power. Iranian farmers plow using buffaloes. Indian villagers, bent at the waist, plant rice seedlings by hand. Bangladeshi fishermen cast circular nets, hoping for a few small fish. Burmese lacquerwork, Chinese embroidery, Middle Eastern brassware, and Indonesian batik cloth represent local crafts.

Wet-rice cultivation from Japan southward has shaped life for hundreds of millions of Asians. To the west, across north China, Central Asia, and beyond to the Middle East, wheat growing has dominated. Plantation and cash crops, too, such as rubber, tea, palm oil, coconuts, sugarcane, and tobacco continue to sustain regional economies.

Across Asia, country dwellers have flocked in the millions to the cities, seeking jobs and a better life. From Jakarta to Baghdad, the growth of megacities represents a dramatic change over the past 50 years. In China, as many as 100 million people form a floating population, seeking work wherever it can be found.

The emergence of postwar Japan as Asia's strongest economy set a model for newly industrialized centers such as South Korea, Hong Kong, Singapore, and Taiwan. Japan, with few natural resources, imports oil, foodstuffs, and textiles, but succeeds by exporting cars, chemicals, and electronics. Central Asian nations of the former Soviet Union have industrialized but require further diversification to rise above poverty. Lands in the Persian Gulf region have flourished from petroleum, and many countries now use light industry as a motor for growth. Tourism, too, plays its part and has helped Thailand, Nepal, and parts of Indonesia and China, including Hong Kong.

India's liberalized economy has encouraged a large, growing middle class, and China—an economic dynamo with plentiful resources—may become the world's largest economy in 25 years.

Yet hunger for minerals, water, agricultural land, fuelwood, housing, and animal products poses great challenges for Asia as every nation tries to raise the standard of living of its people.

Asia: Physical and Political

Two-Point Equidistant Projection
SCALE 1:39,821,000
1 CENTIMETER = 398 KILOMETERS; 1 INCH = 629 MILES
KILOMETERS
STATUTE MILES
International boundary
Disputed or undefined boundary
A commonly accepted division between Asia and Europe–here marked by a green line–is formed by the Ural Mountains, Ural River, Caspian Sea, Caucasus Mountains, and the Black Sea with its outlets, the Bosporus and Dardanelles.
ARCTIC OCEAN
North Pole
GREENLAND
SVALBARD
FRANZ JOSEF LAND
NOVAYA ZEMLYA
BARENTS SEA
KARA SEA
Yamal Peninsula
Gulf of Ob
Gyda Pen.
Taymyr Peninsula
NORTH LAND
Bol'shevik I.
Komsomolets I.
October Revolution I.
NEW SIBERIAN IS.
Kotel'nyy I.
EAST SIBERIAN SEA
Wrangel I.
Kolyma Lowland
Chukchi Pen.
Bering Str.
East Cape
ARCTIC CIRCLE
Gulf of Anadyr
Cape Navarin
Cape Olyutorskiy
Koryak Range
Kolyma Range
Cherskiy Range
Verkhoyansk Range
KAMCHATKA PENINSULA
Klyuchevskaya Sopka 4750
Commander Islands
BERING SEA
ALEUTIAN ISLANDS
Cape Lopatka
KURIL ISLANDS
SEA OF OKHOTSK
Shantar Islands
SAKHALIN
Tatar Strait
HOKKAIDO
HONSHU
SHIKOKU
KYUSHU
JAPAN
SEA OF JAPAN (EAST SEA)
Fuji 3776
Izu Islands
Bonin Islands
Volcano Islands
MARIANA ISLANDS
TROPIC OF CANCER
Guam
CAROLINE ISLANDS
PACIFIC OCEAN
PHILIPPINE SEA
Babelthuap
RYUKYU ISLANDS
Okinawa
TAIWAN
Taiwan Strait
EAST CHINA SEA
YELLOW SEA
Bo Hai
Korea
Sikhote Alin' Range
Ussuri
Amur
Manchurian Plain
Lesser Khingan Range
Greater Khingan Range
Dzhugdzhur Range
Stanovoy Range
Yablonovyy Range
Source of the Amur–Onon
Mongolian Plateau
GOBI
Yin Shan
North China Plain
Luliang Shan
Qin Ling
Yangtze Gorges
Sichuan Basin
Dongting Hu
Poyang Hu
Wuyi Shan
Xi
Hainan
Gulf of Tonkin
Luzon Strait
Luzon
PHILIPPINE ISLANDS
Samar
Mindoro
Panay
Negros
Mindanao
Palawan
SULU SEA
CELEBES SEA
Kinabalu 4101
SOUTH CHINA SEA
BORNEO
CELEBES
Makassar Strait
MOLUCCAS
Halmahera
Ceram
Buru
BANDA SEA
Timor
Flores
Lombok
Bali
JAVA SEA
Java
GREATER SUNDA ISLANDS
Bangka
Billiton
Natuna Is.
NEW GUINEA
Maoke Mts.
Jaya Peak 4884
Aru Islands
Dolak
Tanimbar Islands
ARAFURA SEA
EQUATOR
INDOCHINA PENINSULA
Annam Cordillera
Mekong
Tonle Sap
Gulf of Thailand
MALAY PENINSULA
Strait of Malacca
SUMATRA
Barisan Mountains
Kerinci 3800
Nias
Mentawai Islands
ANDAMAN SEA
Andaman Islands
Nicobar Islands
Irrawaddy
Salween
Mt. Victoria 3053
Brahmaputra
CENTRAL SIBERIAN PLATEAU
North Siberian Lowland
Lena
Lower Tunguska
Angara
Yenisey
Eastern Sayan Mts.
Western Sayan Mountains
Lake Baikal
World's deepest lake 1620 m (5315 ft)
Source of the Yenisey-Angara
Source of the Ob-Irtysh
ALTAY MOUNTAINS
Belukha 4506
Dzungarian Basin
Bogda Shan
Turpan Depression
Lop Nur
Bei Shan
Qilian Shan
Qaidam Basin
Altun Shan
TARIM BASIN
Taklimakan Desert
TIAN SHAN
Victory Peak 7439
KUNLUN MOUNTAINS
Muztag 7282
PLATEAU OF TIBET
Tanggula Range
Nyainqentanglha Shan
Nganglong Range
Gangdise Ra.
Source of the Yangtze
Source of the Yellow
Bayan Har Shan
Daxue Mts.
Gongga Shan 7556
KARAKORAM RA.
K2 (Godwin Austen) 8611
KASHMIR
Hindu Kush
HIMALAYA
Mt. Everest 8850 (29035 ft)
World's highest point
Ganges Plain
Ganges
Chota Nagpur Plateau
Vindhya Range
Narmada
DECCAN PLATEAU
Eastern Ghats
Western Ghats
Krishna
Coromandel Coast
Malabar Coast
Cape Comorin
Sri Lanka
BAY OF BENGAL
LACCADIVE SEA
Lakshadweep
Maldive Islands
Great Indian Desert
Indus
Sutlej
Gulf of Kutch
Gulf of Khambhat
WEST SIBERIAN PLAIN
Ob
Irtysh
Tobol
Ishim Steppe
Kazakh Uplands
THE STEPPES
Betpaqdala
Lake Balkhash
Ili
Syr Darya
Amu Darya
Qizilqum
Turan Lowland
Garagum
Aral Sea
Ustyurt Plateau
Kopet Mts.
Garabogaz Bay
Caspian Depression
CASPIAN SEA
Elburz Mts. 5671
Dasht-e Lut
Helmand
Zagros Mountains
Ural
URAL MOUNTAINS
Narodnaya 1895
NORTHERN EUROPEAN PLAIN
EUROPE
Volga
Don
Lake Onega
Lake Ladoga
White Sea
Kola Peninsula
SCANDINAVIA
Gulf of Bothnia
BALTIC SEA
NORWEGIAN SEA
GREENLAND SEA
ARCTIC CIRCLE
NORTH SEA
BRITISH ISLES
Great Britain
Ireland
Meridian of Greenwich (London)
ATLANTIC OCEAN
ALPS
IBERIAN PENINSULA
BALKAN PENINSULA
ATLAS MOUNTAINS
MEDITERRANEAN SEA
Crimea
BLACK SEA
Caucasus Mountains
Elbrus 5642
Mt. Ararat 5137
Kura
ANATOLIA (ASIA MINOR)
Taurus Mts.
Cyprus
Levant Coast
Syrian Desert
Mesopotamia
Tigris
Euphrates
Dead Sea
World's lowest point
SINAI
SUEZ CANAL
Gulf of Aqaba
An Nafud
Ad Dahna
Hasa Plain
PERSIAN GULF
GULF OF OMAN
Ra's al Hadd
Gulf of Masira
ARABIAN PENINSULA
Rub al Khali
Tuwayq Mountains
Hejaz
Tihamah
Hadhramaut
RED SEA
GULF OF ADEN
Socotra
ARABIAN SEA
Somali Peninsula
ETHIOPIAN HIGHLANDS
SAHARA
AFRICA
TROPIC OF CANCER
INDIAN OCEAN
Seychelles
Comoro Is.
EQUATOR

Two-Point Equidistant Projection
SCALE 1:39,821,000
1 CENTIMETER = 398 KILOMETERS; 1 INCH = 629 MILES
KILOMETERS
STATUTE MILES
KURIL ISLANDS
The southern Kuril Islands of Iturup (Etorofu), Kunashir (Kunashiri), Shikotan, and the Habomai group were lost by Japan to the Soviet Union in 1945. Japan continues to claim these Russian-administered islands.
A commonly accepted division between Asia and Europe–here marked by a green line–is formed by the Ural Mountains, Ural River, Caspian Sea, Caucasus Mountains, and the Black Sea with its outlets, the Bosporus and Dardanelles.
Turkey, Cyprus, Syria, Lebanon, Israel, Jordan, Egypt, Iraq, Iran, and the countries of the Arabian Peninsula form the heart of the Middle East region.
ARCTIC OCEAN
PACIFIC OCEAN
INDIAN OCEAN
RUSSIA
SIBERIA
KAZAKHSTAN
MONGOLIA
CHINA
INDIA
JAPAN
SAUDI ARABIA
IRAN
INDONESIA
Longitude East 90° of Greenwich
TROPIC OF CANCER
EQUATOR
ARCTIC CIRCLE

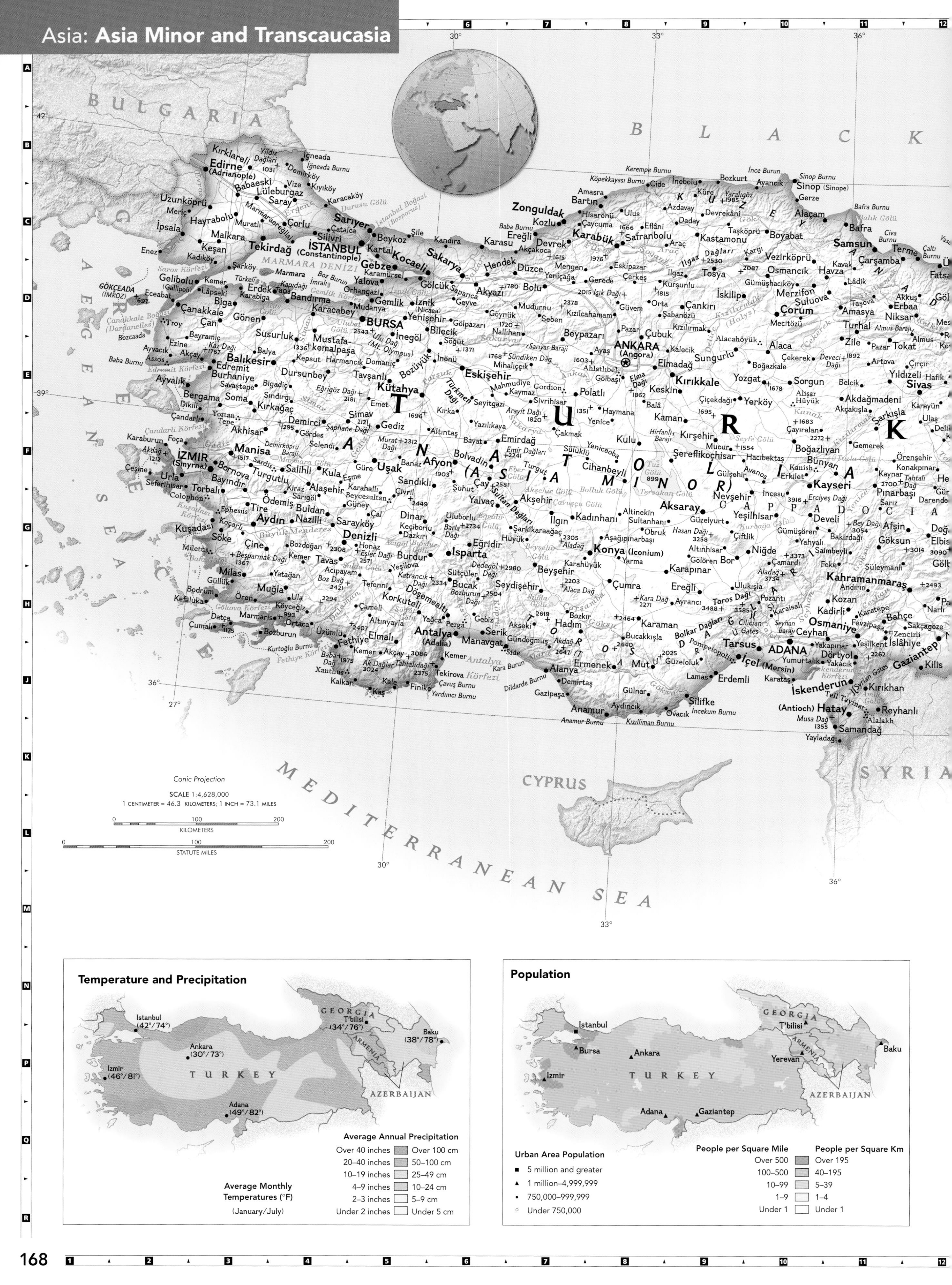
BULGARIA
BLACK
AEGEAN SEA
MEDITERRANEAN SEA
CYPRUS
SYRIA
TURKEY
ANATOLIA
(ASIA MINOR)
CAPPADOCIA
MARMARA DENİZİ
ANKARA (Angora)
İSTANBUL (Constantinople)
Edirne (Adrianople)
İZMİR (Smyrna)
BURSA
ADANA
Konya (Iconium)
Antalya (Adalia)
Eskişehir
Kayseri
Samsun
Gaziantep
Kahramanmaraş
Malatya
Sivas
Tokat
Çorum
Zonguldak
Sinop (Sinope)
Kastamonu
Karabük
Tekirdağ
Gelibolu (Gallipoli)
Çanakkale
Balıkesir
Manisa
Aydın
Denizli
Muğla
Uşak
Afyon
Kütahya
Isparta
Burdur
Niğde
Nevşehir
Aksaray
Kırşehir
Kırıkkale
Yozgat
Osmaniye
İskenderun
Hatay (Antioch)
İçel (Mersin)
Tarsus
Karaman
Bolkar Dağları
TOROS DAĞLARI
Tuz Gölü
Conic Projection
SCALE 1:4,628,000
1 CENTIMETER = 46.3 KILOMETERS; 1 INCH = 73.1 MILES
0 100 200
KILOMETERS
0 100 200
STATUTE MILES
42°
39°
36°
27°
30°
33°
Temperature and Precipitation
Istanbul (42°/74°)
Ankara (30°/73°)
Izmir (46°/81°)
Adana (49°/82°)
T'bilisi (34°/76°)
Baku (38°/78°)
GEORGIA
ARMENIA
AZERBAIJAN
TURKEY
Average Annual Precipitation
Over 40 inches | Over 100 cm
20–40 inches | 50–100 cm
10–19 inches | 25–49 cm
4–9 inches | 10–24 cm
2–3 inches | 5–9 cm
Under 2 inches | Under 5 cm
Average Monthly Temperatures (°F)
(January/July)
Population
Istanbul
Bursa
Ankara
Izmir
Adana
Gaziantep
T'bilisi
Yerevan
Baku
GEORGIA
ARMENIA
AZERBAIJAN
TURKEY
Urban Area Population
5 million and greater
1 million–4,999,999
750,000–999,999
Under 750,000
People per Square Mile | People per Square Km
Over 500 | Over 195
100–500 | 40–195
10–99 | 5–39
1–9 | 1–4
Under 1 | Under 1

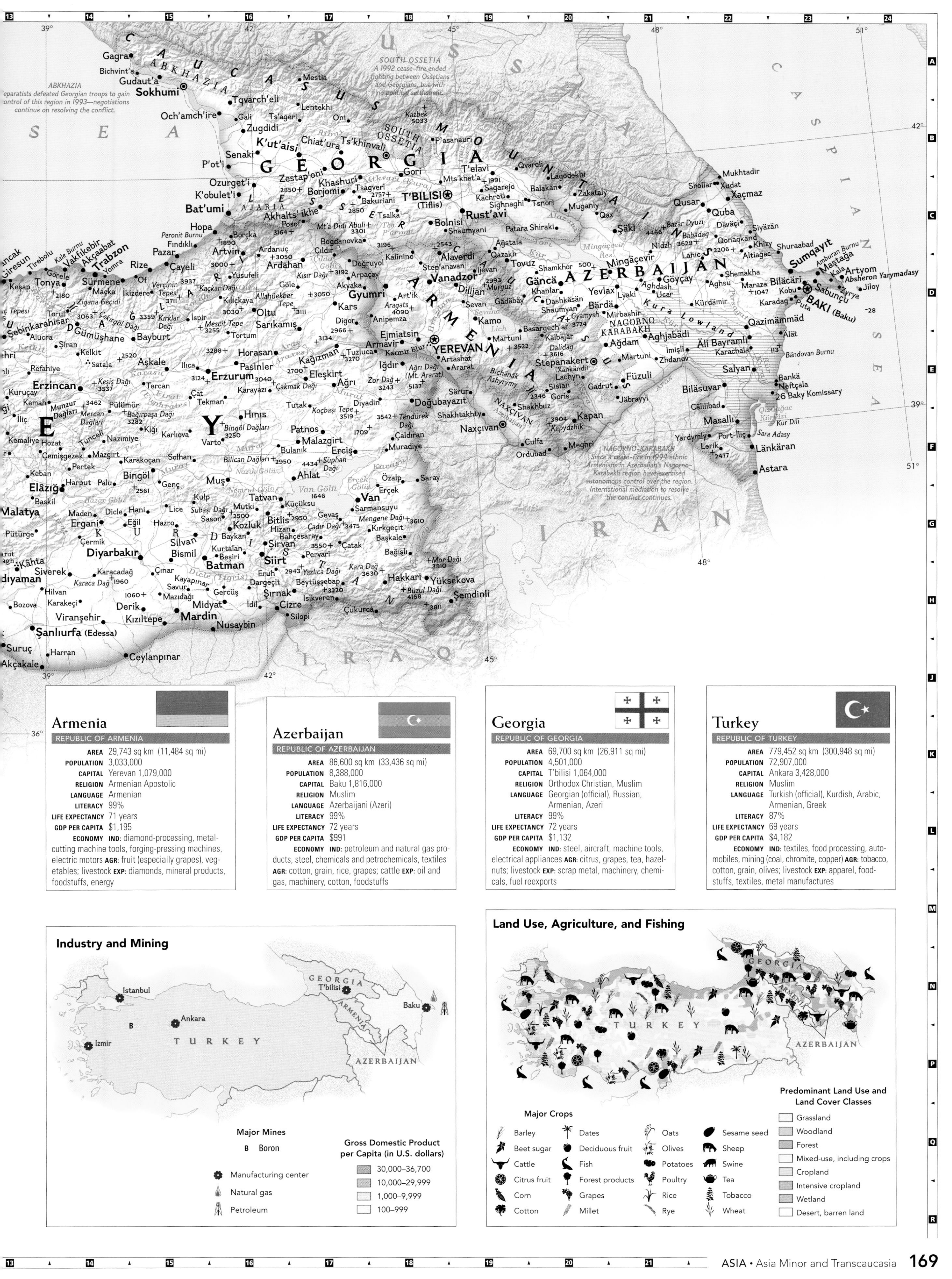

GEORGIA
ARMENIA
AZERBAIJAN
TURKEY
IRAN
IRAQ
RUSSIA
CASPIAN SEA
CAUCASUS MOUNTAINS
T'BILISI (Tiflis)
YEREVAN
BAKI (Baku)
ABKHAZIA
Separatists defeated Georgian troops to gain control of this region in 1993—negotiations continue on resolving the conflict.
SOUTH OSSETIA
A 1992 cease-fire ended fighting between Ossetians and Georgians, but with no political settlement.
NAGORNO-KARABAKH
Since a cease-fire in 1994 ethnic Armenians in Azerbaijan's Nagorno-Karabakh region have exercised autonomous control over the region. International mediation to resolve the conflict continues.
Armenia
REPUBLIC OF ARMENIA
AREA 29,743 sq km (11,484 sq mi)
POPULATION 3,033,000
CAPITAL Yerevan 1,079,000
RELIGION Armenian Apostolic
LANGUAGE Armenian
LITERACY 99%
LIFE EXPECTANCY 71 years
GDP PER CAPITA $1,195
ECONOMY IND: diamond-processing, metal-cutting machine tools, forging-pressing machines, electric motors AGR: fruit (especially grapes), vegetables; livestock EXP: diamonds, mineral products, foodstuffs, energy
Azerbaijan
REPUBLIC OF AZERBAIJAN
AREA 86,600 sq km (33,436 sq mi)
POPULATION 8,388,000
CAPITAL Baku 1,816,000
RELIGION Muslim
LANGUAGE Azerbaijani (Azeri)
LITERACY 99%
LIFE EXPECTANCY 72 years
GDP PER CAPITA $991
ECONOMY IND: petroleum and natural gas products, steel, chemicals and petrochemicals, textiles AGR: cotton, grain, rice, grapes; cattle EXP: oil and gas, machinery, cotton, foodstuffs
Georgia
REPUBLIC OF GEORGIA
AREA 69,700 sq km (26,911 sq mi)
POPULATION 4,501,000
CAPITAL T'bilisi 1,064,000
RELIGION Orthodox Christian, Muslim
LANGUAGE Georgian (official), Russian, Armenian, Azeri
LITERACY 99%
LIFE EXPECTANCY 72 years
GDP PER CAPITA $1,132
ECONOMY IND: steel, aircraft, machine tools, electrical appliances AGR: citrus, grapes, tea, hazelnuts; livestock EXP: scrap metal, machinery, chemicals, fuel reexports
Turkey
REPUBLIC OF TURKEY
AREA 779,452 sq km (300,948 sq mi)
POPULATION 72,907,000
CAPITAL Ankara 3,428,000
RELIGION Muslim
LANGUAGE Turkish (official), Kurdish, Arabic, Armenian, Greek
LITERACY 87%
LIFE EXPECTANCY 69 years
GDP PER CAPITA $4,182
ECONOMY IND: textiles, food processing, automobiles, mining (coal, chromite, copper) AGR: tobacco, cotton, grain, olives; livestock EXP: apparel, foodstuffs, textiles, metal manufactures
Industry and Mining
Istanbul
Ankara
İzmir
T'bilisi
Baku
Major Mines
B Boron
Manufacturing center
Natural gas
Petroleum
Gross Domestic Product per Capita (in U.S. dollars)
30,000–36,700
10,000–29,999
1,000–9,999
100–999
Land Use, Agriculture, and Fishing
Major Crops
Barley
Beet sugar
Cattle
Citrus fruit
Corn
Cotton
Dates
Deciduous fruit
Fish
Forest products
Grapes
Millet
Oats
Olives
Potatoes
Poultry
Rice
Rye
Sesame seed
Sheep
Swine
Tea
Tobacco
Wheat
Predominant Land Use and Land Cover Classes
Grassland
Woodland
Forest
Mixed-use, including crops
Cropland
Intensive cropland
Wetland
Desert, barren land

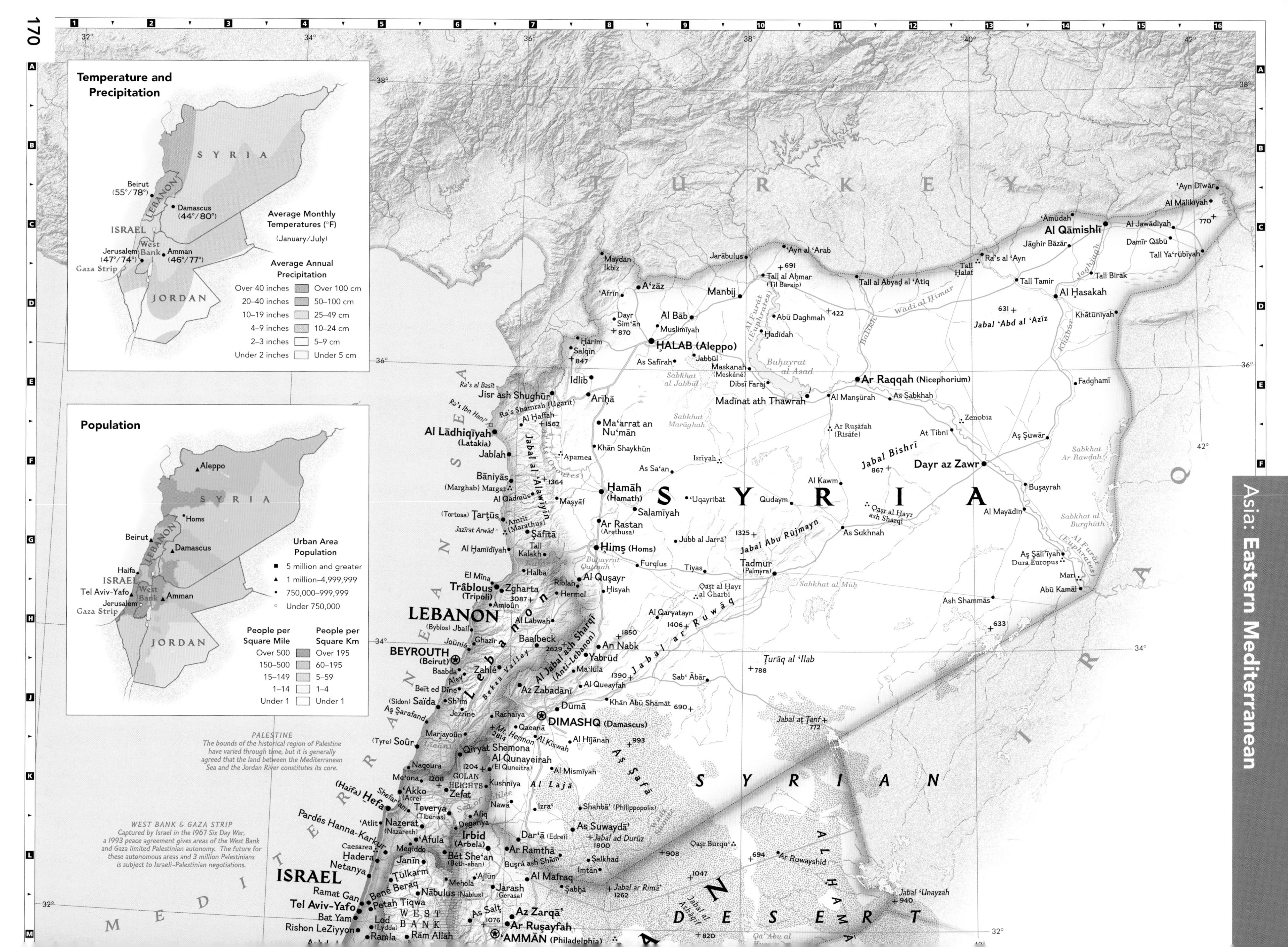
Temperature and Precipitation
SYRIA
LEBANON
ISRAEL
JORDAN
Beirut (55°/78°)
Damascus (44°/80°)
Jerusalem (47°/74°)
Amman (46°/77°)
West Bank
Gaza Strip
Average Monthly Temperatures (°F) (January/July)
Average Annual Precipitation
Over 40 inches | Over 100 cm
20–40 inches | 50–100 cm
10–19 inches | 25–49 cm
4–9 inches | 10–24 cm
2–3 inches | 5–9 cm
Under 2 inches | Under 5 cm
Population
Aleppo
Homs
Beirut
Damascus
Haifa
Tel Aviv-Yafo
Jerusalem
Amman
Urban Area Population
5 million and greater
1 million–4,999,999
750,000–999,999
Under 750,000
People per Square Mile | People per Square Km
Over 500 | Over 195
150–500 | 60–195
15–149 | 5–59
1–14 | 1–4
Under 1 | Under 1
PALESTINE
The bounds of the historical region of Palestine have varied through time, but it is generally agreed that the land between the Mediterranean Sea and the Jordan River constitutes its core.
WEST BANK & GAZA STRIP
Captured by Israel in the 1967 Six Day War, a 1993 peace agreement gives areas of the West Bank and Gaza limited Palestinian autonomy. The future for these autonomous areas and 3 million Palestinians is subject to Israeli-Palestinian negotiations.
TURKEY
SYRIA
IRAQ
SYRIAN DESERT
MEDITERRANEAN SEA
LEBANON
ISRAEL
WEST BANK
AL ḨAMĀD
Al Qāmishlī
Al Ḩasakah
Ḩalab (Aleppo)
Ar Raqqah (Nicephorium)
Madīnat ath Thawrah
Buḩayrat al Asad
Al Furāt (Euphrates)
Tigris
Dayr az Zawr
Jabal Bishrī
Jabal 'Abd al 'Azīz
Al Lādhiqīyah (Latakia)
Jabal al 'Alawīyīn
Ḩamāh (Hamath)
Ḩimş (Homs)
Tadmur (Palmyra)
Jabal Abu Rujmayn
Jabal ar Ruwāq
Ţarţūs (Tortosa)
Trâblous (Tripoli)
Lebanon
Al Jabal ash Sharqī (Anti-Lebanon)
Bekaa Valley
Baalbeck
BEYROUTH (Beirut)
Saïda (Sidon)
Soûr (Tyre)
DIMASHQ (Damascus)
Mt. Hermon 2814
GOLAN HEIGHTS
Aş Şafā
Al Lajā
Jabal ad Durūz 1800
As Suwaydā'
Irbid (Arbela)
Az Zarqā'
AMMĀN (Philadelphia)
Ḩefa (Haifa)
Tel Aviv-Yafo
Ţurāq al 'Ilab
Jabal aţ Ţanf 772
Ar Ruwayshid

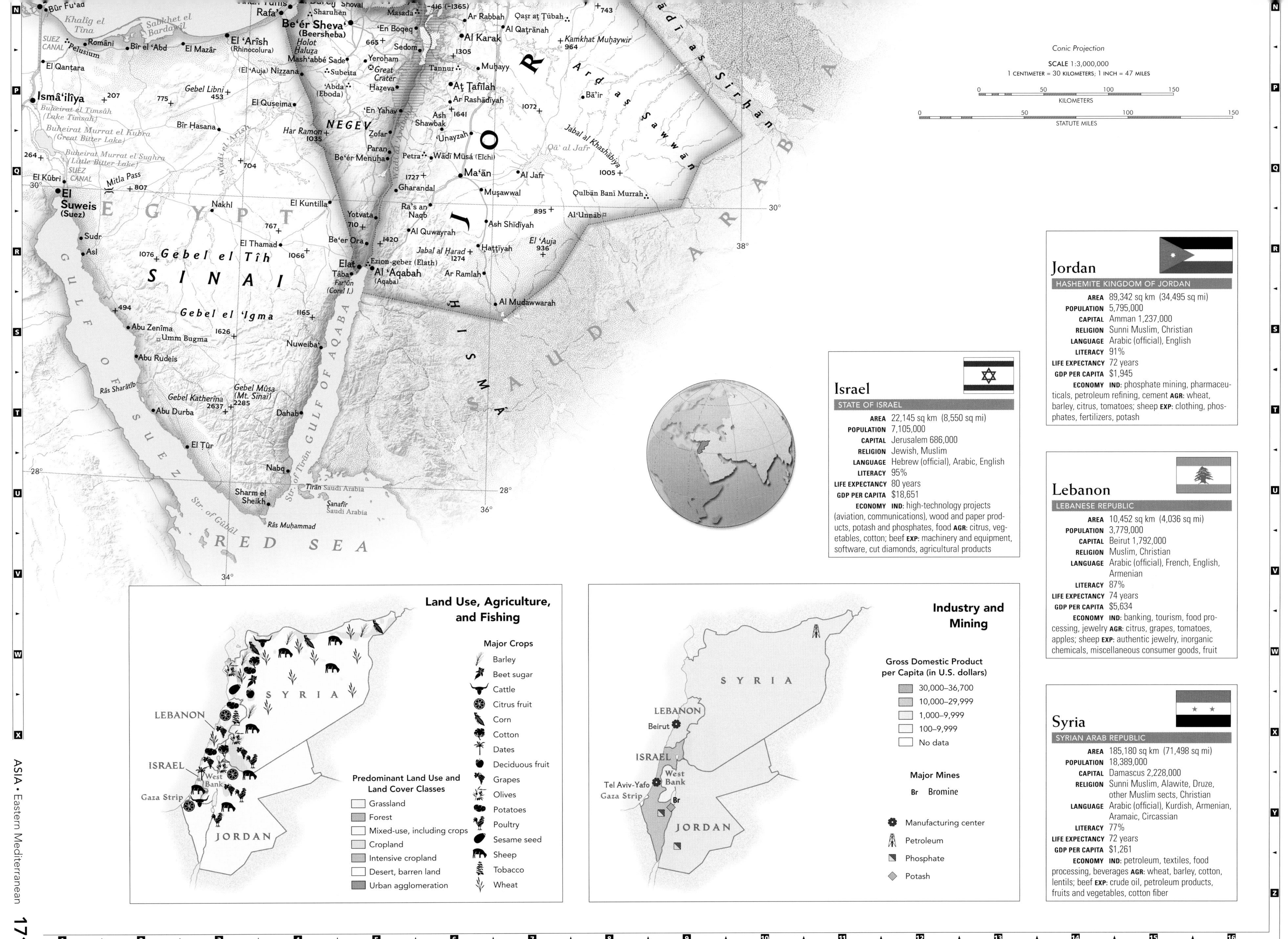
Conic Projection
SCALE 1:3,000,000
1 CENTIMETER = 30 KILOMETERS; 1 INCH = 47 MILES
KILOMETERS
STATUTE MILES
EGYPT
SINAI
NEGEV
JORDAN
SAUDI ARABIA
HISMĀ
Ard as Şawwān
Wādī as Sirḩān
RED SEA
GULF OF SUEZ
GULF OF AQABA
Str. of Tīrān
Str. of Gûbâl
Gebel el Tîh
Gebel el 'Igma
El Suweis (Suez)
Ismâ'ilîya
Bûr Fu'ad
El Qantara
El 'Arîsh (Rhinocolura)
Nakhl
El Tûr
Sharm el Sheikh
Dahab
Nuweiba'
Elat
Al 'Aqabah (Aqaba)
Be'ér Sheva (Beersheba)
Ma'ān
Aṭ Ṭafīlah
Al Karak
Petra
Wādī Mūsá (Elchi)
Al Mudawwarah
Gebel Katherîna 2637
Gebel Mûsa (Mt. Sinai) 2285
Land Use, Agriculture, and Fishing
Major Crops
Barley
Beet sugar
Cattle
Citrus fruit
Corn
Cotton
Dates
Deciduous fruit
Grapes
Olives
Potatoes
Poultry
Sesame seed
Sheep
Tobacco
Wheat
Predominant Land Use and Land Cover Classes
Grassland
Forest
Mixed-use, including crops
Cropland
Intensive cropland
Desert, barren land
Urban agglomeration
SYRIA
LEBANON
ISRAEL
West Bank
Gaza Strip
JORDAN
Industry and Mining
Gross Domestic Product per Capita (in U.S. dollars)
30,000–36,700
10,000–29,999
1,000–9,999
100–9,999
No data
Major Mines
Br Bromine
Manufacturing center
Petroleum
Phosphate
Potash
Beirut
Tel Aviv-Yafo

Jordan

HASHEMITE KINGDOM OF JORDAN

AREA 89,342 sq km (34,495 sq mi)
POPULATION 5,795,000
CAPITAL Amman 1,237,000
RELIGION Sunni Muslim, Christian
LANGUAGE Arabic (official), English
LITERACY 91%
LIFE EXPECTANCY 72 years
GDP PER CAPITA $1,945
ECONOMY **IND:** phosphate mining, pharmaceuticals, petroleum refining, cement **AGR:** wheat, barley, citrus, tomatoes; sheep **EXP:** clothing, phosphates, fertilizers, potash

Israel

STATE OF ISRAEL

AREA 22,145 sq km (8,550 sq mi)
POPULATION 7,105,000
CAPITAL Jerusalem 686,000
RELIGION Jewish, Muslim
LANGUAGE Hebrew (official), Arabic, English
LITERACY 95%
LIFE EXPECTANCY 80 years
GDP PER CAPITA $18,651
ECONOMY **IND:** high-technology projects (aviation, communications), wood and paper products, potash and phosphates, food **AGR:** citrus, vegetables, cotton; beef **EXP:** machinery and equipment, software, cut diamonds, agricultural products

Lebanon

LEBANESE REPUBLIC

AREA 10,452 sq km (4,036 sq mi)
POPULATION 3,779,000
CAPITAL Beirut 1,792,000
RELIGION Muslim, Christian
LANGUAGE Arabic (official), French, English, Armenian
LITERACY 87%
LIFE EXPECTANCY 74 years
GDP PER CAPITA $5,634
ECONOMY **IND:** banking, tourism, food processing, jewelry **AGR:** citrus, grapes, tomatoes, apples; sheep **EXP:** authentic jewelry, inorganic chemicals, miscellaneous consumer goods, fruit

Syria

SYRIAN ARAB REPUBLIC

AREA 185,180 sq km (71,498 sq mi)
POPULATION 18,389,000
CAPITAL Damascus 2,228,000
RELIGION Sunni Muslim, Alawite, Druze, other Muslim sects, Christian
LANGUAGE Arabic (official), Kurdish, Armenian, Aramaic, Circassian
LITERACY 77%
LIFE EXPECTANCY 72 years
GDP PER CAPITA $1,261
ECONOMY **IND:** petroleum, textiles, food processing, beverages **AGR:** wheat, barley, cotton, lentils; beef **EXP:** crude oil, petroleum products, fruits and vegetables, cotton fiber

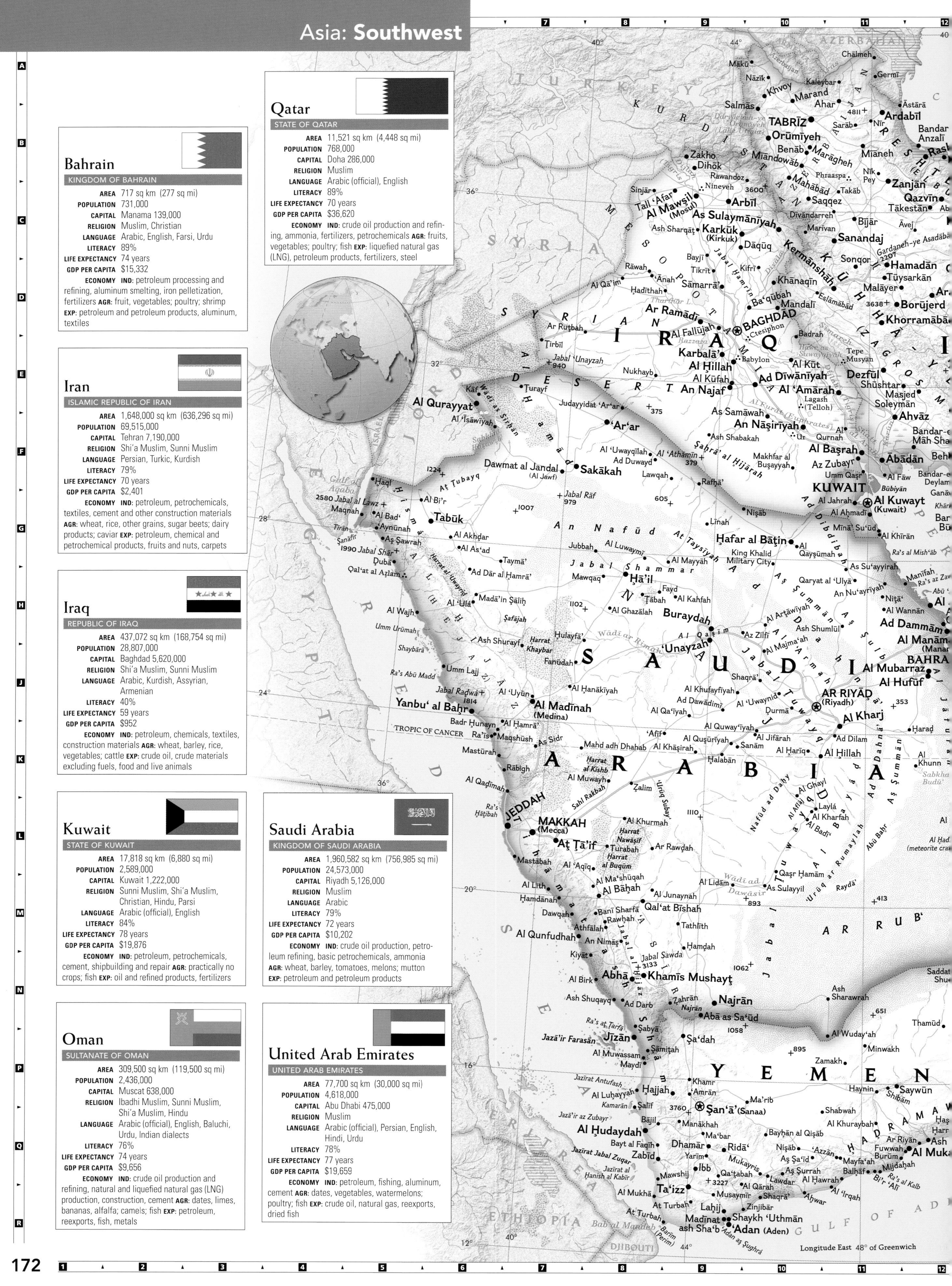
TURKEY
SYRIA
JORDAN
ISRAEL
IRAQ
KUWAIT
SAUDI ARABIA
YEMEN
ERITREA
ETHIOPIA
DJIBOUTI
EGYPT
KURDISTAN
MESOPOTAMIA
SYRIAN DESERT
An Nafūd
RED SEA
GULF OF ADEN
AR RUB' AL KHALI
TROPIC OF CANCER
BAGHDAD
AR RIYĀD (Riyadh)
AL KUWAYT (Kuwait)
ŞAN'Ā' (Sanaa)
MAKKAH (Mecca)
Al Madīnah (Medina)
JEDDAH
Al Başrah
Al Mawşil (Mosul)
TABRĪZ
Orūmīyeh
Kermānshāh
Hamadān
Ahvāz
Tabūk
Ḩā'il
Buraydah
Aţ Ţā'if
Abhā
Khamīs Mushayţ
Najrān
Jīzān
Al Ḩudaydah
Ta'izz
'Adan (Aden)
Yanbu' al Baḩr
Al Hufūf
Ad Dammām
Al Manāmah
Longitude East 48° of Greenwich

Qatar

STATE OF QATAR

AREA 11,521 sq km (4,448 sq mi)
POPULATION 768,000
CAPITAL Doha 286,000
RELIGION Muslim
LANGUAGE Arabic (official), English
LITERACY 89%
LIFE EXPECTANCY 70 years
GDP PER CAPITA $36,620
ECONOMY **IND:** crude oil production and refining, ammonia, fertilizers, petrochemicals **AGR:** fruits, vegetables; poultry; fish **EXP:** liquefied natural gas (LNG), petroleum products, fertilizers, steel

Bahrain

KINGDOM OF BAHRAIN

AREA 717 sq km (277 sq mi)
POPULATION 731,000
CAPITAL Manama 139,000
RELIGION Muslim, Christian
LANGUAGE Arabic, English, Farsi, Urdu
LITERACY 89%
LIFE EXPECTANCY 74 years
GDP PER CAPITA $15,332
ECONOMY **IND:** petroleum processing and refining, aluminum smelting, iron pelletization, fertilizers **AGR:** fruit, vegetables; poultry; shrimp **EXP:** petroleum and petroleum products, aluminum, textiles

Iran

ISLAMIC REPUBLIC OF IRAN

AREA 1,648,000 sq km (636,296 sq mi)
POPULATION 69,515,000
CAPITAL Tehran 7,190,000
RELIGION Shi'a Muslim, Sunni Muslim
LANGUAGE Persian, Turkic, Kurdish
LITERACY 79%
LIFE EXPECTANCY 70 years
GDP PER CAPITA $2,401
ECONOMY **IND:** petroleum, petrochemicals, textiles, cement and other construction materials **AGR:** wheat, rice, other grains, sugar beets; dairy products; caviar **EXP:** petroleum, chemical and petrochemical products, fruits and nuts, carpets

Iraq

REPUBLIC OF IRAQ

AREA 437,072 sq km (168,754 sq mi)
POPULATION 28,807,000
CAPITAL Baghdad 5,620,000
RELIGION Shi'a Muslim, Sunni Muslim
LANGUAGE Arabic, Kurdish, Assyrian, Armenian
LITERACY 40%
LIFE EXPECTANCY 59 years
GDP PER CAPITA $952
ECONOMY **IND:** petroleum, chemicals, textiles, construction materials **AGR:** wheat, barley, rice, vegetables; cattle **EXP:** crude oil, crude materials excluding fuels, food and live animals

Kuwait

STATE OF KUWAIT

AREA 17,818 sq km (6,880 sq mi)
POPULATION 2,589,000
CAPITAL Kuwait 1,222,000
RELIGION Sunni Muslim, Shi'a Muslim, Christian, Hindu, Parsi
LANGUAGE Arabic (official), English
LITERACY 84%
LIFE EXPECTANCY 78 years
GDP PER CAPITA $19,876
ECONOMY **IND:** petroleum, petrochemicals, cement, shipbuilding and repair **AGR:** practically no crops; fish **EXP:** oil and refined products, fertilizers

Saudi Arabia

KINGDOM OF SAUDI ARABIA

AREA 1,960,582 sq km (756,985 sq mi)
POPULATION 24,573,000
CAPITAL Riyadh 5,126,000
RELIGION Muslim
LANGUAGE Arabic
LITERACY 79%
LIFE EXPECTANCY 72 years
GDP PER CAPITA $10,202
ECONOMY **IND:** crude oil production, petroleum refining, basic petrochemicals, ammonia **AGR:** wheat, barley, tomatoes, melons; mutton **EXP:** petroleum and petroleum products

Oman

SULTANATE OF OMAN

AREA 309,500 sq km (119,500 sq mi)
POPULATION 2,436,000
CAPITAL Muscat 638,000
RELIGION Ibadhi Muslim, Sunni Muslim, Shi'a Muslim, Hindu
LANGUAGE Arabic (official), English, Baluchi, Urdu, Indian dialects
LITERACY 76%
LIFE EXPECTANCY 74 years
GDP PER CAPITA $9,656
ECONOMY **IND:** crude oil production and refining, natural and liquefied natural gas (LNG) production, construction, cement **AGR:** dates, limes, bananas, alfalfa; camels; fish **EXP:** petroleum, reexports, fish, metals

United Arab Emirates

UNITED ARAB EMIRATES

AREA 77,700 sq km (30,000 sq mi)
POPULATION 4,618,000
CAPITAL Abu Dhabi 475,000
RELIGION Muslim
LANGUAGE Arabic (official), Persian, English, Hindi, Urdu
LITERACY 78%
LIFE EXPECTANCY 77 years
GDP PER CAPITA $19,659
ECONOMY **IND:** petroleum, fishing, aluminum, cement **AGR:** dates, vegetables, watermelons; poultry; fish **EXP:** crude oil, natural gas, reexports, dried fish

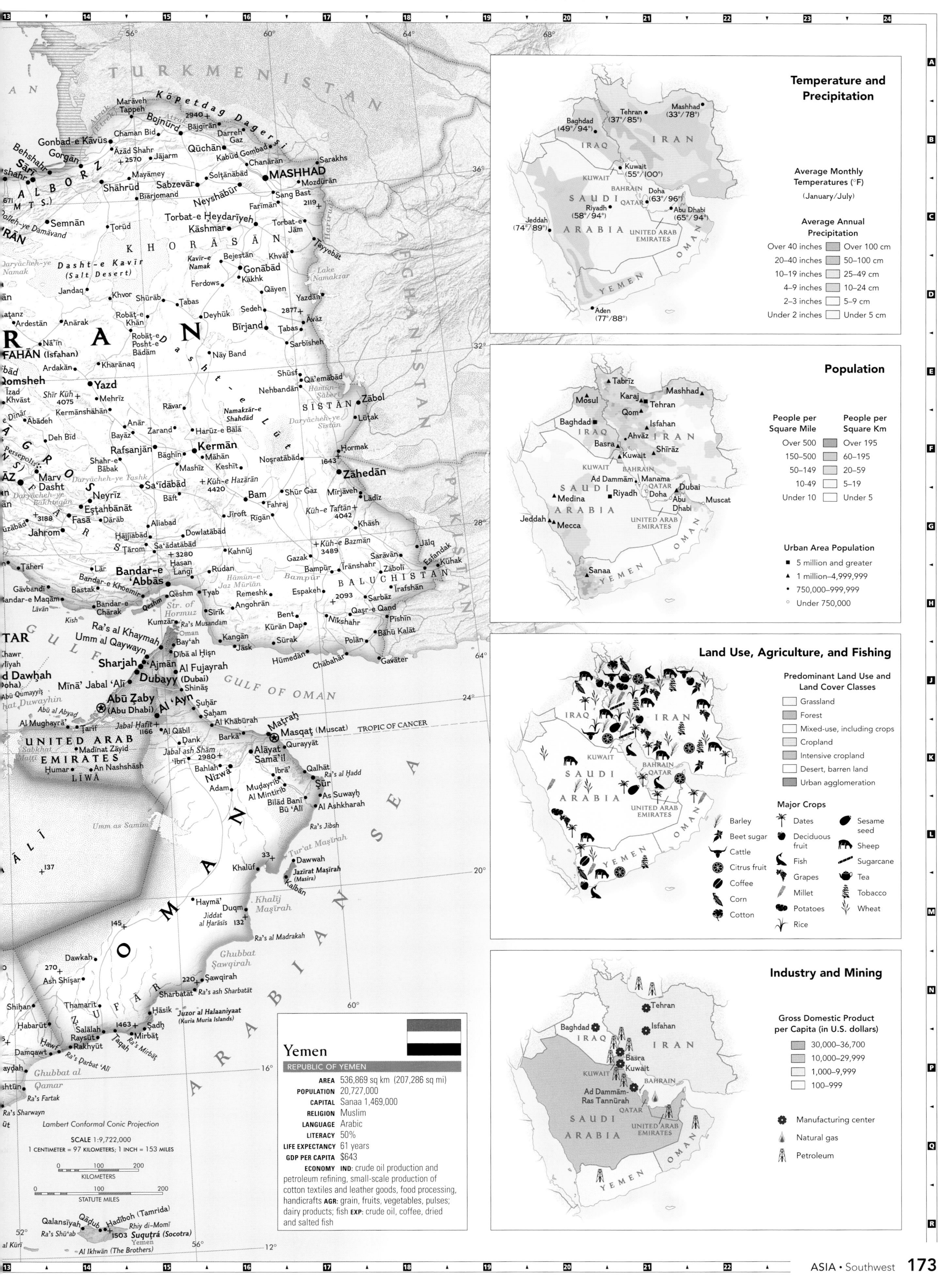
TURKMENISTAN
Köpetdag Dagerі
Maraveh Tappeh
2940
Bojnūrd
Bājgīrān
Chaman Bīd
Darreh Gaz
Gonbad-e Kāvūs
Gorgān
Behshahr
Sārī
Āzād Shahr
2570
Jājarm
Qūchān
Kabūd Gonbad
Chanārān
Sarakhs
MASHHAD
Mozdūrān
ALBORZ
Mayāmey
Shāhrūd
Sabzevār
Solṭānābād
Neyshābūr
Sang Bast
2119
Bīārjomand
Farīmān
Semnān
Ţorūd
Torbat-e Ḩeydarīyeh
Torbat-e Jām
Kāshmar
Damāvand
KHORĀSĀN
Dasht-e Kavīr (Salt Desert)
Kavīr-e Namak
Bejestān
Khvāf
Gonābād
Kākhk
Taybād
Lake Namakzar
Ferdows
Qāyen
Jandaq
Khvor
Shūrāb
Ţabas
Yazdān
Robāţ-e Khān
Deyhūk
Sedeh
2877
Āvāz
Ardestān
Anārak
Bīrjand
Ţabas
Robāţ-e Posht-e Bādām
Sarbīsheh
IRAN
Nā'īn
EŞFAHĀN (Isfahan)
Nāy Band
Ardakān
Kharānaq
Dasht-e Lūt
Shūsf
Qa'emābād
Hāmūn-e Şāberī
Qomsheh
Yazd
Nehbandān
Shīr Kūh 4075
Mehrīz
Ravar
Namakzār-e Shahdād
SĪSTĀN
Zābol
Kermānshāhān
Ābādeh
Anār
Harūz-e Bālā
Daryācheh-ye Sīstān
Lūţak
Deh Bīd
Bayāz
Zarand
Rafsanjān
Kermān
Hormak
Persepolis
Shahr-e Bābak
Bāghīn
Māhān
Noşratābād
1643
Mashīz
Keshīt
Zāhedān
Marv Dasht
Daryācheh-ye Tashk
Sa'īdābād
Kūh-e Hazārān 4420
Bam
Shūr Gaz
Mīrjāveh
Lādīz
Daryācheh-ye Bakhtegān
Neyrīz
Bāft
Fahraj
Eşţahbānāt
Jīroft
Rīgān
Kūh-e Taftān 4042
Fasā
Dārāb
3188
Aliabad
Khāsh
Jahrom
Ḩājjīābād
Dowlatābād
Jālq
Ţārom
Sa'ādatābād
3280
Kahnūj
Kūh-e Bazmān 3489
Esfandak
Hasan Langī
Gazak
Sarāvān
Kūhak
Ţāherī
Lār
Bandar-e 'Abbās
Rudan
Bampūr
Īrānshahr
Zābolī
Hāmūn-e Jaz Mūrīān
Bampūr
BALUCHISTAN
Gāvbandī
Bastak
Bandar-e Khoemir
Qeshm
Tyab
Remeshk
Espakeh
Īrafshān
Bandar-e Maqām
Bandar-e Chārak
2093
Sarbāz
Angohrān
Qaşr-e Qand
Lāvān
Str. of Hormuz
Sīrīk
Bent
Pīshīn
Kish
Kumzār
Ra's Musandam
Kūrān Dap
Nīkshahr
QATAR
Ra's al Khaymah
Kangān
Bāhū Kalāt
Umm al Qaywayn
Bay'ah
Jāsk
Sūrak
Polān
PERSIAN GULF
Sharjah
'Ajmān
Dibā al Ḩişn
Al Fujayrah
Hūmedān
Chābahār
Gavāter
Ad Dawḩah (Doha)
Mīnā' Jabal 'Alī
Dubayy (Dubai)
Shināş
GULF OF OMAN
Abū Qumayyiş
Abū Z̧aby (Abu Dhabi)
Al 'Ayn
Şuḩār
Khawr al Duwayhin
Abū al Abyad
Şaḩam
Al Khābūrah
Al Mughayrā'
Ţarīf
Jabal Ḩafīt 1166
Al Qābil
Barkā'
Maţraḩ
Masqaţ (Muscat)
TROPIC OF CANCER
UNITED ARAB EMIRATES
Sabkhat Maţţī
Madīnat Zāyid
Dank
Jabal ash Shām 2980
Qurayyāt
'Ibrī
Ālayat Samā'il
An Nashhāsh
Ḩumar
LĪWĀ
Bahlah
Nizwá
Ibrā'
Qalhāt
Ra's al Ḩadd
Şūr
Adam
Mudayrib
Al Mintirib
As Suwayḩ
Bilād Banī Bū 'Alī
Al Ashkharah
Umm as Samīm
Ra's Jibsh
RUB' AL KHĀLĪ
137
Tur'at Maşīrah
33
Khalūf
Dawwah
Jazīrat Maşīrah (Masira)
Kalban
Haymā'
Duqm
Jiddat al Ḩarāsīs
132
Khalīj Maşīrah
145
OMAN
Ra's al Madrakah
Ghubbat Şawqirah
Dawkah
270
Ash Shişar
220
Şawqirah
Sharbatāt
Ra's ash Sharbatāt
ARABIAN SEA
Shihan
Thamarīt
ZUFĀR
Ḩāsik
Juzor al Halaaniyaat (Kuria Muria Islands)
Ḩabarūt
Şalālah
1463
Şadḩ
Raysūt
Rakhyūt
Mirbāţ
Ḩawf
Damqawt
Taqah
Ra's Mirbāţ
Ra's Darbat 'Alī
Ghubbat al Qamar
Ra's Fartak
Ra's Sharwayn
Lambert Conformal Conic Projection
SCALE 1:9,722,000
1 CENTIMETER = 97 KILOMETERS; 1 INCH = 153 MILES
0 100 200 KILOMETERS
0 100 200 STATUTE MILES
Qalansīyah
Qādub
Ḩadiboh (Tamrida)
Rhiy di-Momī
Ra's Shū'ab
1503
Suquţrá (Socotra)
Yemen
Al Ikhwān (The Brothers)
Temperature and Precipitation
Mashhad (33°/78°)
Tehran (37°/85°)
Baghdad (49°/94°)
IRAQ
IRAN
Kuwait (55°/100°)
KUWAIT
BAHRAIN
Doha (63°/96°)
QATAR
SAUDI ARABIA
Riyadh (58°/94°)
Abu Dhabi (65°/94°)
Jeddah (74°/89°)
UNITED ARAB EMIRATES
OMAN
YEMEN
Aden (77°/88°)
Average Monthly Temperatures (°F) (January/July)
Average Annual Precipitation
Over 40 inches / Over 100 cm
20–40 inches / 50–100 cm
10–19 inches / 25–49 cm
4–9 inches / 10–24 cm
2–3 inches / 5–9 cm
Under 2 inches / Under 5 cm
Population
Tabrīz
Mashhad
Mosul
Karaj
Tehran
Qom
Baghdad
Isfahan
Ahvāz
Basra
Shīrāz
Kuwait
Ad Dammām
Manama
Dubai
Medina
Riyadh
Doha
Abu Dhabi
Muscat
Jeddah
Mecca
Sanaa
People per Square Mile / People per Square Km
Over 500 / Over 195
150–500 / 60–195
50–149 / 20–59
10–49 / 5–19
Under 10 / Under 5
Urban Area Population
5 million and greater
1 million–4,999,999
750,000–999,999
Under 750,000
Land Use, Agriculture, and Fishing
Predominant Land Use and Land Cover Classes
Grassland
Forest
Mixed-use, including crops
Cropland
Intensive cropland
Desert, barren land
Urban agglomeration
Major Crops
Barley
Beet sugar
Cattle
Citrus fruit
Coffee
Corn
Cotton
Dates
Deciduous fruit
Fish
Grapes
Millet
Potatoes
Rice
Sesame seed
Sheep
Sugarcane
Tea
Tobacco
Wheat
Industry and Mining
Tehran
Isfahan
Baghdad
Basra
Kuwait
Ad Dammām-Ras Tannūrah
Gross Domestic Product per Capita (in U.S. dollars)
30,000–36,700
10,000–29,999
1,000–9,999
100–999
Manufacturing center
Natural gas
Petroleum

Yemen

REPUBLIC OF YEMEN

AREA 536,869 sq km (207,286 sq mi)
POPULATION 20,727,000
CAPITAL Sanaa 1,469,000
RELIGION Muslim
LANGUAGE Arabic
LITERACY 50%
LIFE EXPECTANCY 61 years
GDP PER CAPITA $643
ECONOMY **IND:** crude oil production and petroleum refining, small-scale production of cotton textiles and leather goods, food processing, handicrafts **AGR:** grain, fruits, vegetables, pulses; dairy products; fish **EXP:** crude oil, coffee, dried and salted fish

Kazakhstan
REPUBLIC OF KAZAKHSTAN
AREA 2,717,300 sq km (1,049,155 sq mi)
POPULATION 15,079,000
CAPITAL Astana 332,000
RELIGION Muslim, Russian Orthodox
LANGUAGE Kazakh (Qazaq), Russian (official)
LITERACY 98%
LIFE EXPECTANCY 66 years
GDP PER CAPITA $2,746
ECONOMY IND: oil, coal, iron ore, manganese AGR: grain (mostly spring wheat), cotton; livestock EXP: oil and oil products, ferrous metals, chemicals, machinery
Turkmenistan
TURKMENISTAN
AREA 488,100 sq km (188,456 sq mi)
POPULATION 5,240,000
CAPITAL Ashgabat 574,000
RELIGION Muslim, Eastern Orthodox
LANGUAGE Turkmen, Russian, Uzbek
LITERACY 99%
LIFE EXPECTANCY 63 years
GDP PER CAPITA $2,596
ECONOMY IND: natural gas, oil, petroleum products, textiles AGR: cotton, grain; livestock EXP: gas, crude oil, petrochemicals, cotton fiber
Uzbekistan
REPUBLIC OF UZBEKISTAN
AREA 447,400 sq km (172,742 sq mi)
POPULATION 26,444,000
CAPITAL Tashkent 2,155,000
RELIGION Muslim, Eastern Orthodox
LANGUAGE Uzbek, Russian
LITERACY 99%
LIFE EXPECTANCY 67 years
GDP PER CAPITA $450
ECONOMY IND: textiles, food processing, machine building, metallurgy AGR: cotton, vegetables, fruits, grain; livestock EXP: cotton, gold, energy products, mineral fertilizers
Temperature and Precipitation
KAZAKHSTAN
UZBEKISTAN
TURKMENISTAN
Almaty (19°/74°)
Tashkent (32°/81°)
Samarqand (33°/78°)
Average Monthly Temperatures (°F) (January/July)
Average Annual Precipitation
Over 40 inches | Over 100 cm
20–40 inches | 50–100 cm
10–19 inches | 25–49 cm
4–9 inches | 10–24 cm
2–3 inches | 5–9 cm
Under 2 inches | Under 5 cm
RUSSIA
KAZAKHSTAN
UZBEKISTAN
TURKMENISTAN
IRAN
AFGHANISTAN
AZERBAIJAN
CASPIAN SEA
ARAL SEA
Caspian Depression
Naryn Qum
USTYURT PLATEAU
Qoraqalpog'iston
Qizilqum
Garagum
Köpetdag Mountains
Garabil Plateau
Volga River Delta
Aral Mangy Qaraqumy
BAYKONUR COSMODROME Russian-administered
ARAL SEA Once the world's fourth largest lake, the Aral Sea today is less than half its 1960 extent. Soviet-era irrigation canals divert river water—causing the sea to shrink and changing the former lake bed into desert. A UN study predicts the Aral Sea could disappear by 2016.
GARAGUM CANAL
Oral
Aqtöbe
Atyraū
Qostanay
Rūdnyy
Qyzylorda
Aqtaū
Nukus
Urganch
Daşoguz
Buxoro (Bukhara)
Navoiy
Samarqand
Qarshi
Türkmenabat (Chärjew)
Mary
Aşgabat (Ashgabat)
Balkanabat
Türkmenbaşy
Bayqongyr (Baykonur) (Leninsk)
Zhezqazgan
Aral
Beyneu
Kazakh localities, rivers and other minor labels

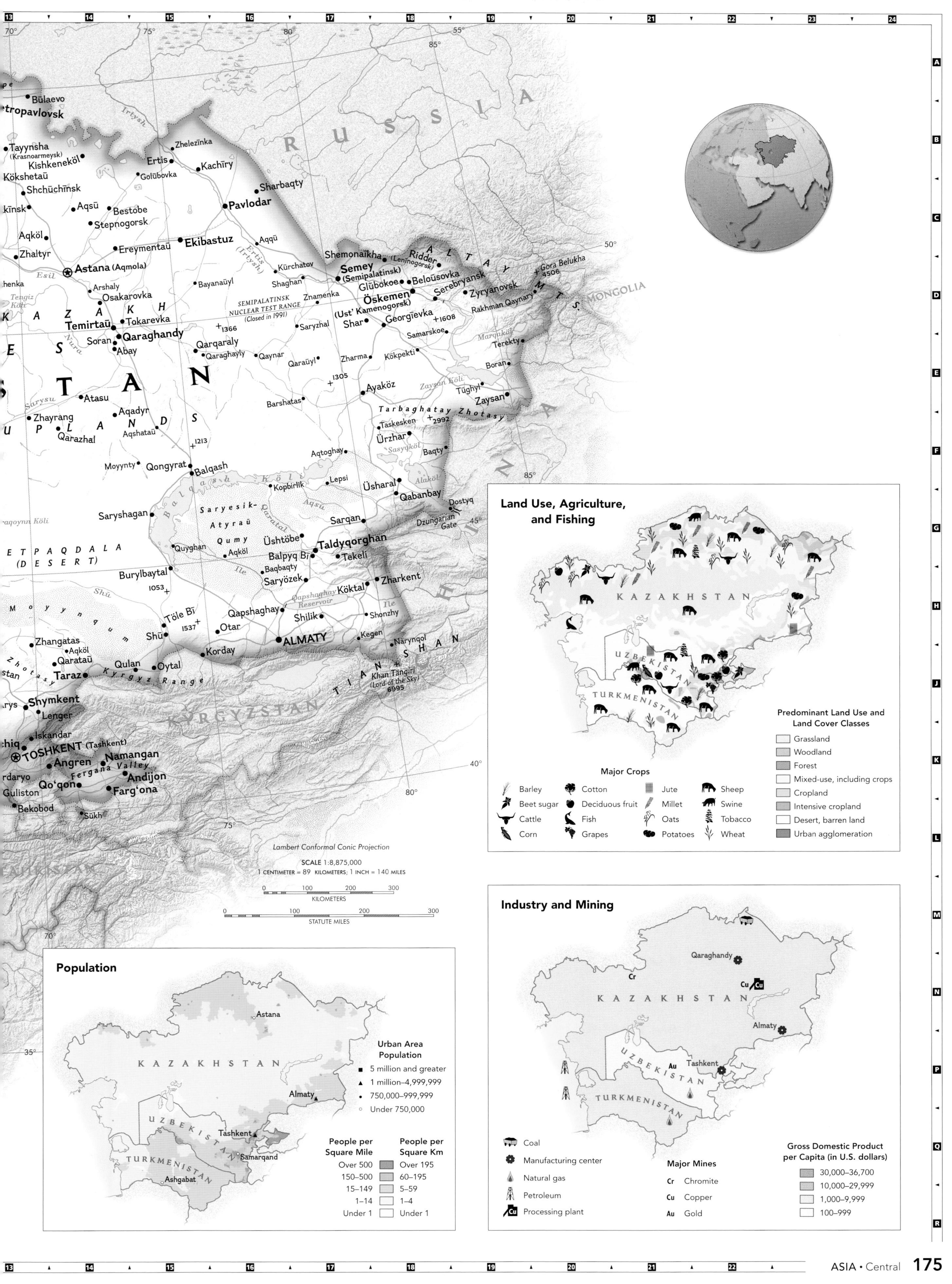
R U S S I A
K A Z A K H S T A N
K A Z A K H U P L A N D S
MONGOLIA
KYRGYZSTAN
Bŭlaevo
Petropavlovsk
Tayynsha (Krasnoarmeysk)
Kishkeneköl
Kökshetaū
Shchūchīnsk
Aqsū
Bestobe
Stepnogorsk
Aqköl
Zhaltyr
Ereymentaū
Ekibastuz
Astana (Aqmola)
Arshaly
Osakarovka
Temirtaū
Tokarevka
Soran
Qaraghandy
Abay
Zhelezīnka
Ertis
Kachīry
Golūbovka
Sharbaqty
Pavlodar
Aqqū
Bayanaūyl
Kūrchatov
Shaghan
Semey (Semipalatinsk)
SEMIPALATINSK NUCLEAR TEST RANGE (Closed in 1991)
Znamenka
Shemonaīkha
Ridder (Leninogorsk)
Glūbokoe
Beloūsovka
Serebryansk
Zyryanovsk
Gora Belukha 4506
Rakhman Qaynary
Öskemen (Ust' Kamenogorsk)
Shar
Georgīevka
Samarskoe
Saryzhal
Qarqaraly
Qaraghayly
Qaynar
Qaraūyl
Zharma
Kökpekti
Terekty
Boran
Markaköl
Zaysan Köli
Tūghyl
Zaysan
Ayaköz
Barshatas
Tarbaghatay Zhotasy
Taskesken
Ürzhar
Sasyqköl
Baqty
Alaköl
Üsharal
Qabanbay
Dostyq
Dzungarian Gate
Aqtoghay
Lepsi
Kopbirlik
Balqash Köli
Balqash
Qongyrat
Moyynty
Atasu
Aqadyr
Zhayrang
Qarazhal
Aqshataū
Saryshagan
Saryesik-Atyraū
Qumy
Quyghan
Aqköl
Üshtöbe
Taldyqorghan
Sarqan
Balpyq Bī
Tekeli
Baqbaqty
Saryözek
Burylbaytal
Köktal
Zharkent
Kapshaghay Reservoir
Qapshaghay
Shilik
Shonzhy
Tōle Bī
Otar
Shū
ALMATY
Kegen
Naryngol
Korday
Betpaqdala (Desert)
Moyynqum
Zhangatas
Qarataū
Zhotasy
Taraz
Qulan
Oytal
Kyrgyz Range
TIAN SHAN
Khan Tängiri (Lord of the Sky) 6995
Shymkent
Lenger
Iskandar
TOSHKENT (Tashkent)
Angren
Namangan
Fergana Valley
Andijon
Qo'qon
Farg'ona
Guliston
Bekobod
Sūkh
Lambert Conformal Conic Projection
SCALE 1:8,875,000
1 CENTIMETER = 89 KILOMETERS; 1 INCH = 140 MILES
KILOMETERS
STATUTE MILES
Land Use, Agriculture, and Fishing
KAZAKHSTAN
UZBEKISTAN
TURKMENISTAN
Major Crops
Barley
Beet sugar
Cattle
Corn
Cotton
Deciduous fruit
Fish
Grapes
Jute
Millet
Oats
Potatoes
Sheep
Swine
Tobacco
Wheat
Predominant Land Use and Land Cover Classes
Grassland
Woodland
Forest
Mixed-use, including crops
Cropland
Intensive cropland
Desert, barren land
Urban agglomeration
Industry and Mining
Qaraghandy
Almaty
Tashkent
Coal
Manufacturing center
Natural gas
Petroleum
Processing plant
Major Mines
Cr Chromite
Cu Copper
Au Gold
Gross Domestic Product per Capita (in U.S. dollars)
30,000–36,700
10,000–29,999
1,000–9,999
100–999
Population
Astana
Almaty
Tashkent
Samarqand
Ashgabat
Urban Area Population
5 million and greater
1 million–4,999,999
750,000–999,999
Under 750,000
People per Square Mile
Over 500
150–500
15–149
1–14
Under 1
People per Square Km
Over 195
60–195
5–59
1–4
Under 1

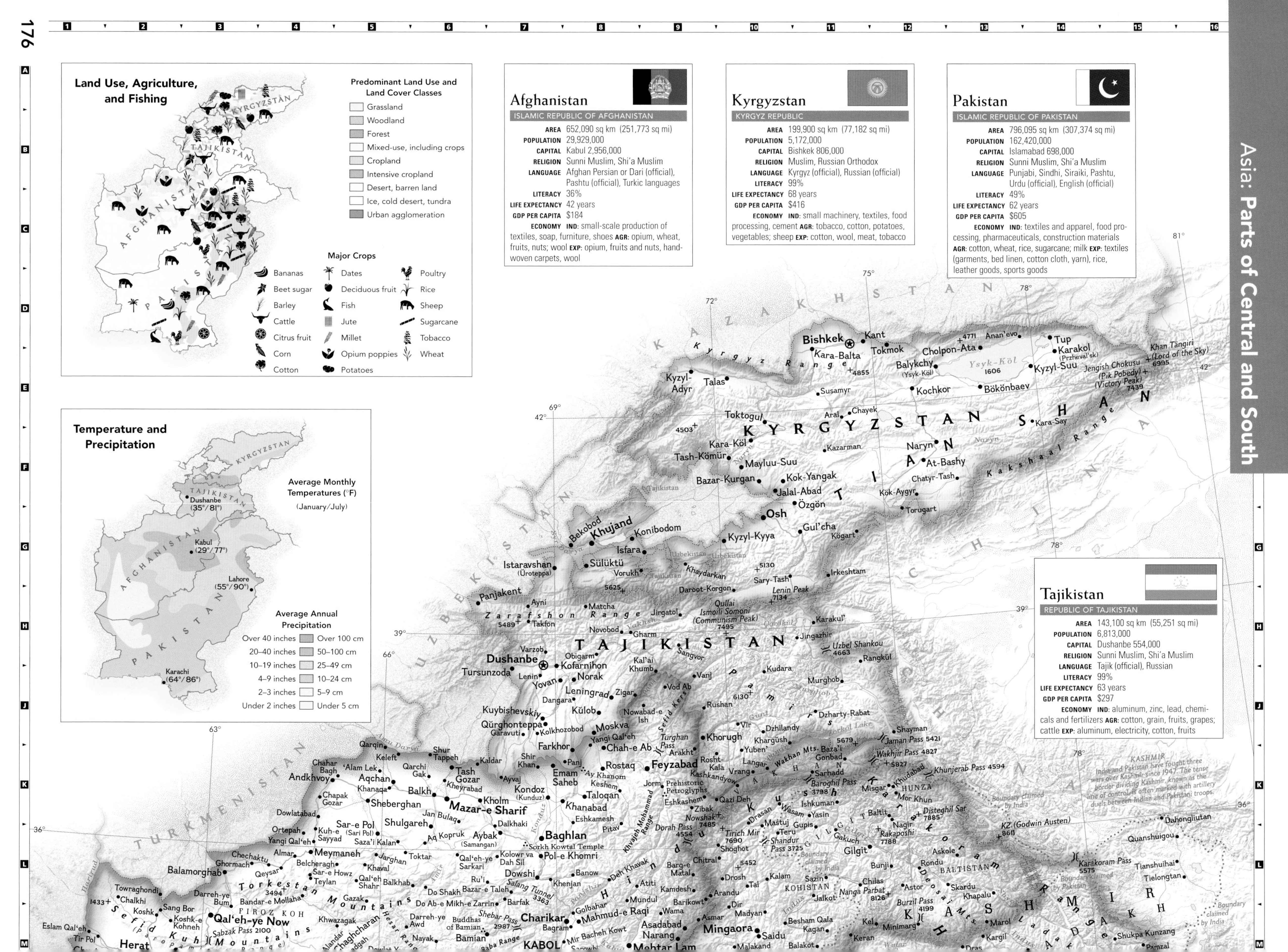
Land Use, Agriculture, and Fishing
Predominant Land Use and Land Cover Classes
Grassland
Woodland
Forest
Mixed-use, including crops
Cropland
Intensive cropland
Desert, barren land
Ice, cold desert, tundra
Urban agglomeration
Major Crops
Bananas
Beet sugar
Barley
Cattle
Citrus fruit
Corn
Cotton
Dates
Deciduous fruit
Fish
Jute
Millet
Opium poppies
Potatoes
Poultry
Rice
Sheep
Sugarcane
Tobacco
Wheat
Temperature and Precipitation
Average Monthly Temperatures (°F) (January/July)
Dushanbe (35°/81°)
Kabul (29°/77°)
Lahore (55°/90°)
Karachi (64°/86°)
Average Annual Precipitation
Over 40 inches — Over 100 cm
20–40 inches — 50–100 cm
10–19 inches — 25–49 cm
4–9 inches — 10–24 cm
2–3 inches — 5–9 cm
Under 2 inches — Under 5 cm
Afghanistan
ISLAMIC REPUBLIC OF AFGHANISTAN
AREA 652,090 sq km (251,773 sq mi)
POPULATION 29,929,000
CAPITAL Kabul 2,956,000
RELIGION Sunni Muslim, Shi'a Muslim
LANGUAGE Afghan Persian or Dari (official), Pashtu (official), Turkic languages
LITERACY 36%
LIFE EXPECTANCY 42 years
GDP PER CAPITA $184
ECONOMY IND: small-scale production of textiles, soap, furniture, shoes AGR: opium, wheat, fruits, nuts; wool EXP: opium, fruits and nuts, hand-woven carpets, wool
Kyrgyzstan
KYRGYZ REPUBLIC
AREA 199,900 sq km (77,182 sq mi)
POPULATION 5,172,000
CAPITAL Bishkek 806,000
RELIGION Muslim, Russian Orthodox
LANGUAGE Kyrgyz (official), Russian (official)
LITERACY 99%
LIFE EXPECTANCY 68 years
GDP PER CAPITA $416
ECONOMY IND: small machinery, textiles, food processing, cement AGR: tobacco, cotton, potatoes, vegetables; sheep EXP: cotton, wool, meat, tobacco
Pakistan
ISLAMIC REPUBLIC OF PAKISTAN
AREA 796,095 sq km (307,374 sq mi)
POPULATION 162,420,000
CAPITAL Islamabad 698,000
RELIGION Sunni Muslim, Shi'a Muslim
LANGUAGE Punjabi, Sindhi, Siraiki, Pashtu, Urdu (official), English (official)
LITERACY 49%
LIFE EXPECTANCY 62 years
GDP PER CAPITA $605
ECONOMY IND: textiles and apparel, food processing, pharmaceuticals, construction materials AGR: cotton, wheat, rice, sugarcane; milk EXP: textiles (garments, bed linen, cotton cloth, yarn), rice, leather goods, sports goods
Tajikistan
REPUBLIC OF TAJIKISTAN
AREA 143,100 sq km (55,251 sq mi)
POPULATION 6,813,000
CAPITAL Dushanbe 554,000
RELIGION Sunni Muslim, Shi'a Muslim
LANGUAGE Tajik (official), Russian
LITERACY 99%
LIFE EXPECTANCY 63 years
GDP PER CAPITA $297
ECONOMY IND: aluminum, zinc, lead, chemicals and fertilizers AGR: cotton, grain, fruits, grapes; cattle EXP: aluminum, electricity, cotton, fruits
KAZAKHSTAN
KYRGYZSTAN
TAJIKISTAN
UZBEKISTAN
TURKMENISTAN
TIAN SHAN
CHINA
KASHMIR
India and Pakistan have fought three wars over Kashmir since 1947. The tense border dividing Kashmir, known as the line of control, is often marked with artillery duels between Indian and Pakistani troops.

Population
Urban Area Population
5 million and greater
1 million–4,999,999
750,000–999,999
Under 750,000
People per Square Mile
Over 500
150–500
50–149
10–49
Under 10
People per Square Km
Over 195
60–195
20–59
5–19
Under 5
Industry and Mining
Gross Domestic Product per Capita (in U.S. dollars)
30,000–36,700
10,000–29,999
1,000–9,999
100–999
Major Mines
Au Gold
Aluminum processing plant
Manufacturing center
Polyconic Projection
SCALE 1:5,877,000
1 CENTIMETER = 59 KILOMETERS; 1 INCH = 93 MILES
KILOMETERS
STATUTE MILES
TROPIC OF CANCER
ARABIAN SEA
IRAN
PAKISTAN
BALUCHISTAN
KARACHI
HYDERABAD
MULTAN
LAHORE
FAISALABAD
RAWALPINDI
GUJRANWALA
Quetta

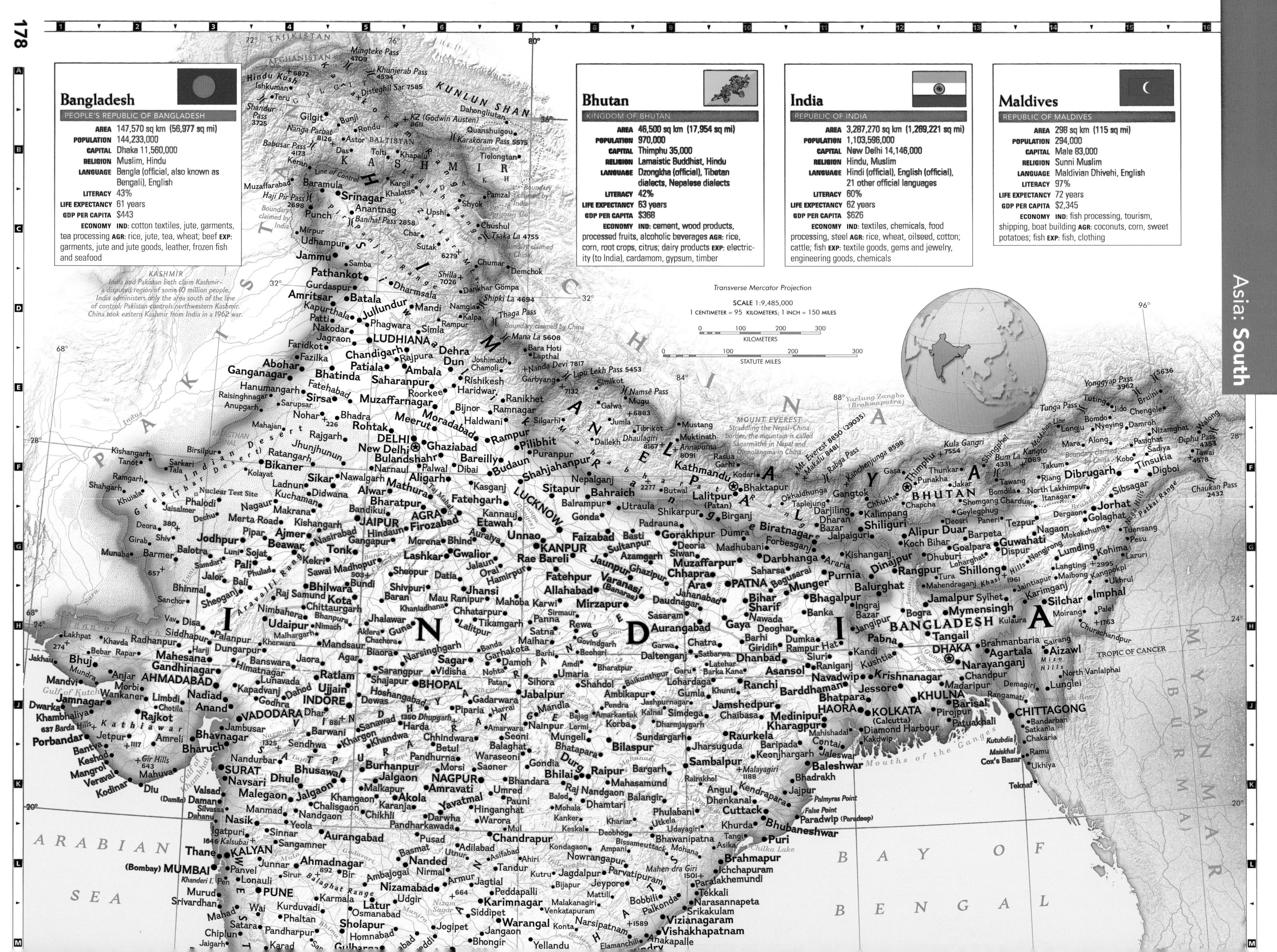
Transverse Mercator Projection
SCALE 1:9,485,000
1 CENTIMETER = 95 KILOMETERS; 1 INCH = 150 MILES
KILOMETERS
STATUTE MILES
KASHMIR
India and Pakistan both claim Kashmir–a disputed region of some 10 million people. India administers only the area south of the line of control; Pakistan controls northwestern Kashmir. China took eastern Kashmir from India in a 1962 war.
MOUNT EVEREST
Straddling the Nepal-China border, the mountain is called Sagarmatha in Nepal and Qomolangma in China.
PAKISTAN
INDIA
CHINA
NEPAL
BHUTAN
BANGLADESH
MYANMAR (BURMA)
HIMALAYA
KUNLUN SHAN
KASHMIR
ARABIAN SEA
BAY OF BENGAL
TROPIC OF CANCER
Great Indian Desert (Thar Desert)
DELHI
New Delhi
Kathmandu
Thimphu
DHAKA
KOLKATA (Calcutta)
(Bombay) MUMBAI
CHITTAGONG
Mt. Everest 8850 (29035)
AFGHANISTAN
TAJIKISTAN

Bangladesh

PEOPLE'S REPUBLIC OF BANGLADESH

AREA 147,570 sq km (56,977 sq mi)
POPULATION 144,233,000
CAPITAL Dhaka 11,560,000
RELIGION Muslim, Hindu
LANGUAGE Bangla (official, also known as Bengali), English
LITERACY 43%
LIFE EXPECTANCY 61 years
GDP PER CAPITA $443
ECONOMY **IND:** cotton textiles, jute, garments, tea processing **AGR:** rice, jute, tea, wheat; beef **EXP:** garments, jute and jute goods, leather, frozen fish and seafood

Bhutan

KINGDOM OF BHUTAN

AREA 46,500 sq km (17,954 sq mi)
POPULATION 970,000
CAPITAL Thimphu 35,000
RELIGION Lamaistic Buddhist, Hindu
LANGUAGE Dzongkha (official), Tibetan dialects, Nepalese dialects
LITERACY 42%
LIFE EXPECTANCY 63 years
GDP PER CAPITA $368
ECONOMY **IND:** cement, wood products, processed fruits, alcoholic beverages **AGR:** rice, corn, root crops, citrus; dairy products **EXP:** electricity (to India), cardamom, gypsum, timber

India

REPUBLIC OF INDIA

AREA 3,287,270 sq km (1,269,221 sq mi)
POPULATION 1,103,596,000
CAPITAL New Delhi 14,146,000
RELIGION Hindu, Muslim
LANGUAGE Hindi (official), English (official), 21 other official languages
LITERACY 60%
LIFE EXPECTANCY 62 years
GDP PER CAPITA $626
ECONOMY **IND:** textiles, chemicals, food processing, steel **AGR:** rice, wheat, oilseed, cotton; cattle; fish **EXP:** textile goods, gems and jewelry, engineering goods, chemicals

Maldives

REPUBLIC OF MALDIVES

AREA 298 sq km (115 sq mi)
POPULATION 294,000
CAPITAL Male 83,000
RELIGION Sunni Muslim
LANGUAGE Maldivian Dhivehi, English
LITERACY 97%
LIFE EXPECTANCY 72 years
GDP PER CAPITA $2,345
ECONOMY **IND:** fish processing, tourism, shipping, boat building **AGR:** coconuts, corn, sweet potatoes; fish **EXP:** fish, clothing

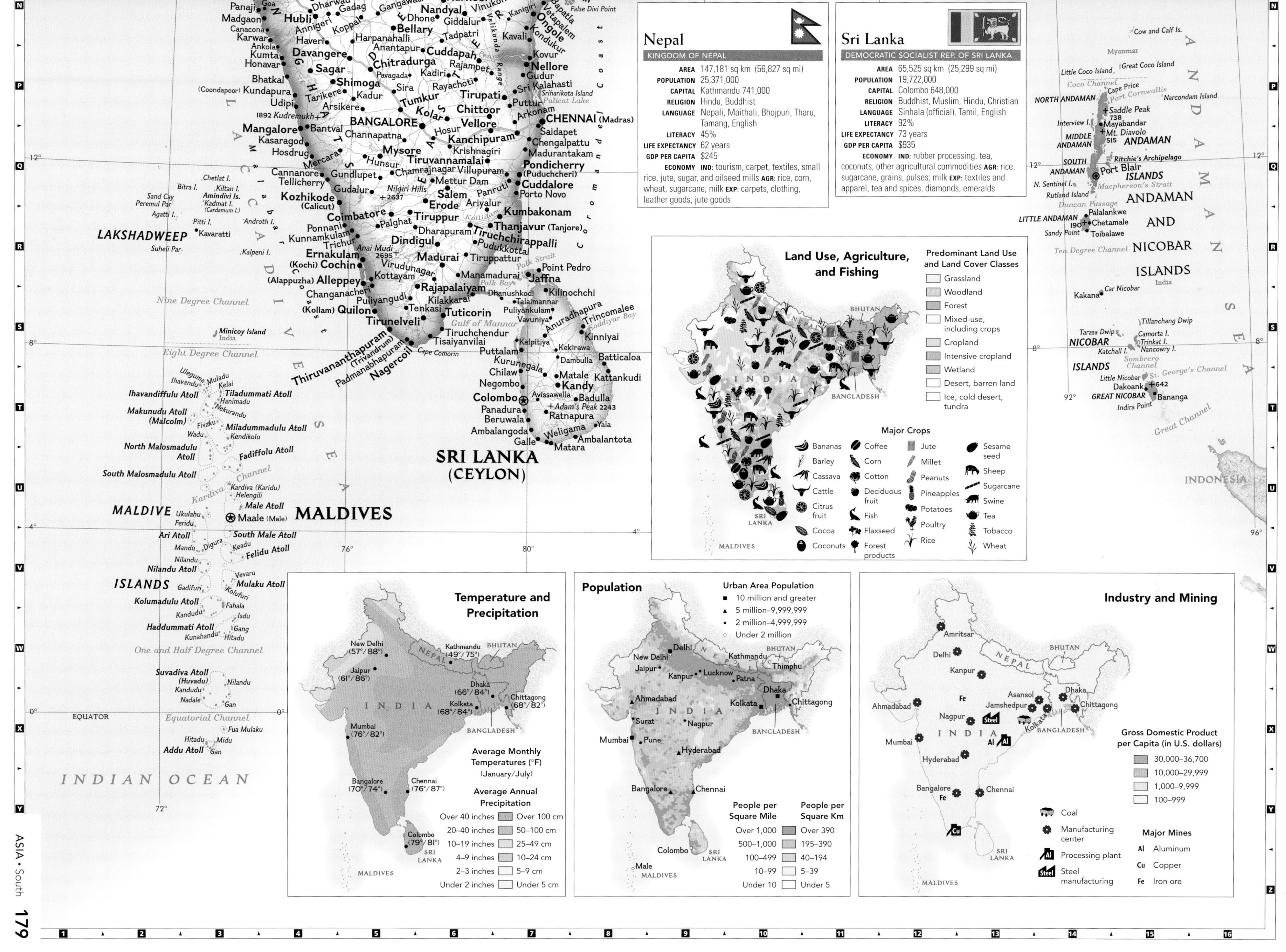

Nepal
KINGDOM OF NEPAL
AREA 147,181 sq km (56,827 sq mi)
POPULATION 25,371,000
CAPITAL Kathmandu 741,000
RELIGION Hindu, Buddhist
LANGUAGE Nepali, Maithali, Bhojpuri, Tharu, Tamang, English
LITERACY 45%
LIFE EXPECTANCY 62 years
GDP PER CAPITA $245
ECONOMY IND: tourism, carpet, textiles, small rice, jute, sugar, and oilseed mills AGR: rice, corn, wheat, sugarcane; milk EXP: carpets, clothing, leather goods, jute goods
Sri Lanka
DEMOCRATIC SOCIALIST REP. OF SRI LANKA
AREA 65,525 sq km (25,299 sq mi)
POPULATION 19,722,000
CAPITAL Colombo 648,000
RELIGION Buddhist, Muslim, Hindu, Christian
LANGUAGE Sinhala (official), Tamil, English
LITERACY 92%
LIFE EXPECTANCY 73 years
GDP PER CAPITA $935
ECONOMY IND: rubber processing, tea, coconuts, other agricultural commodities AGR: rice, sugarcane, grains, pulses; milk EXP: textiles and apparel, tea and spices, diamonds, emeralds
Land Use, Agriculture, and Fishing
Predominant Land Use and Land Cover Classes
Grassland
Woodland
Forest
Mixed-use, including crops
Cropland
Intensive cropland
Wetland
Desert, barren land
Ice, cold desert, tundra
Major Crops
Bananas
Barley
Cassava
Cattle
Citrus fruit
Cocoa
Coconuts
Coffee
Corn
Cotton
Deciduous fruit
Fish
Flaxseed
Forest products
Jute
Millet
Peanuts
Pineapples
Potatoes
Poultry
Rice
Sesame seed
Sheep
Sugarcane
Swine
Tea
Tobacco
Wheat
Temperature and Precipitation
New Delhi (57°/88°)
Jaipur (61°/86°)
Kathmandu (49°/75°)
Dhaka (66°/84°)
Kolkata (68°/84°)
Chittagong (68°/82°)
Mumbai (76°/82°)
Bangalore (70°/74°)
Chennai (76°/87°)
Colombo (79°/81°)
Average Monthly Temperatures (°F) (January/July)
Average Annual Precipitation
Over 40 inches | Over 100 cm
20–40 inches | 50–100 cm
10–19 inches | 25–49 cm
4–9 inches | 10–24 cm
2–3 inches | 5–9 cm
Under 2 inches | Under 5 cm
Population
Urban Area Population
10 million and greater
5 million–9,999,999
2 million–4,999,999
Under 2 million
People per Square Mile | People per Square Km
Over 1,000 | Over 390
500–1,000 | 195–390
100–499 | 40–194
10–99 | 5–39
Under 10 | Under 5
Industry and Mining
Coal
Manufacturing center
Processing plant
Steel manufacturing
Gross Domestic Product per Capita (in U.S. dollars)
30,000–36,700
10,000–29,999
1,000–9,999
100–999
Major Mines
Al Aluminum
Cu Copper
Fe Iron ore
SRI LANKA (CEYLON)
MALDIVES
MALDIVE ISLANDS
LAKSHADWEEP
ANDAMAN AND NICOBAR ISLANDS
INDIAN OCEAN
ANDAMAN SEA
LACCADIVE SEA
Coromandel Coast
Malabar Coast
Nine Degree Channel
Eight Degree Channel
One and Half Degree Channel
Equatorial Channel
Ten Degree Channel
EQUATOR
INDONESIA

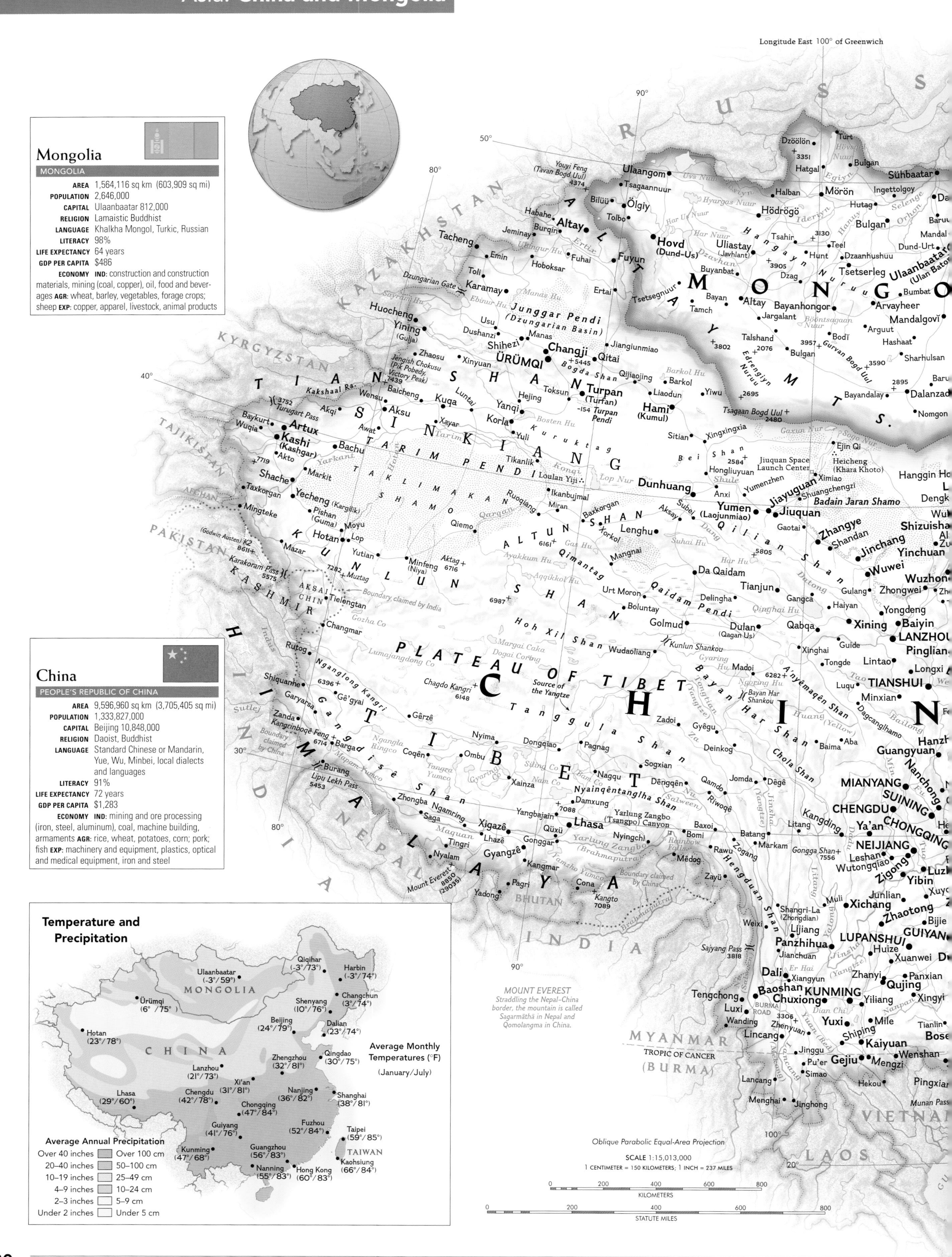
Mongolia
MONGOLIA
AREA 1,564,116 sq km (603,909 sq mi)
POPULATION 2,646,000
CAPITAL Ulaanbaatar 812,000
RELIGION Lamaistic Buddhist
LANGUAGE Khalkha Mongol, Turkic, Russian
LITERACY 98%
LIFE EXPECTANCY 64 years
GDP PER CAPITA $486
ECONOMY IND: construction and construction materials, mining (coal, copper), oil, food and beverages AGR: wheat, barley, vegetables, forage crops; sheep EXP: copper, apparel, livestock, animal products
China
PEOPLE'S REPUBLIC OF CHINA
AREA 9,596,960 sq km (3,705,405 sq mi)
POPULATION 1,333,827,000
CAPITAL Beijing 10,848,000
RELIGION Daoist, Buddhist
LANGUAGE Standard Chinese or Mandarin, Yue, Wu, Minbei, local dialects and languages
LITERACY 91%
LIFE EXPECTANCY 72 years
GDP PER CAPITA $1,283
ECONOMY IND: mining and ore processing (iron, steel, aluminum), coal, machine building, armaments AGR: rice, wheat, potatoes, corn; pork; fish EXP: machinery and equipment, plastics, optical and medical equipment, iron and steel
Temperature and Precipitation
Average Monthly Temperatures (°F) (January/July)
Ulaanbaatar (-3°/59°)
Qiqihar (-3°/73°)
Harbin (-3°/74°)
Ürümqi (6°/75°)
Changchun (3°/74°)
Shenyang (10°/76°)
Dalian (23°/74°)
Beijing (24°/79°)
Hotan (23°/78°)
Qingdao (30°/75°)
Zhengzhou (32°/81°)
Lanzhou (21°/73°)
Xi'an (31°/81°)
Nanjing (36°/82°)
Lhasa (29°/60°)
Chengdu (42°/78°)
Shanghai (38°/81°)
Chongqing (47°/84°)
Guiyang (41°/76°)
Fuzhou (52°/84°)
Taipei (59°/85°)
Kunming (47°/68°)
Guangzhou (56°/83°)
Kaohsiung (66°/84°)
Nanning (55°/83°)
Hong Kong (60°/83°)
MONGOLIA
CHINA
TAIWAN
Average Annual Precipitation
Over 40 inches — Over 100 cm
20–40 inches — 50–100 cm
10–19 inches — 25–49 cm
4–9 inches — 10–24 cm
2–3 inches — 5–9 cm
Under 2 inches — Under 5 cm
MOUNT EVEREST
Straddling the Nepal-China border, the mountain is called Sagarmāthā in Nepal and Qomolangma in China.
Longitude East 100° of Greenwich
Oblique Parabolic Equal-Area Projection
SCALE 1:15,013,000
1 CENTIMETER = 150 KILOMETERS; 1 INCH = 237 MILES
KILOMETERS 0 200 400 600 800
STATUTE MILES 0 200 400 600 800
RUSSIA
KAZAKHSTAN
KYRGYZSTAN
TAJIKISTAN
AFGHAN.
PAKISTAN
KASHMIR
INDIA
NEPAL
BHUTAN
MYANMAR (BURMA)
LAOS
VIETNAM
MONGOLIA
CHINA
TROPIC OF CANCER
PLATEAU OF TIBET
TIAN SHAN
KUNLUN SHAN
ALTUN SHAN
HIMALAYA
TARIM PENDI
TAKLIMAKAN SHAMO
Junggar Pendi (Dzungarian Basin)
Qaidam Pendi
Badain Jaran Shamo
Tanggula Shan
Gangdisê Shan
Hengduan Shan
Qilian Shan
Bayan Har Shan
Hangayn Nuruu
ALTAY
Mount Everest 8850 (29035)
Ulaangom
Ölgiy
Hovd (Dund-Us)
Uliastay (Javhlant)
Mörön
Bulgan
Ulaanbaatar (Ulan Bator)
Altay
Tacheng
Altay
Karamay
Yining (Gulja)
Shihezi
ÜRÜMQI
Changji
Turpan (Turfan)
Hami (Kumul)
Aksu
Kuqa
Korla
Artux
Kashi (Kashgar)
Shache
Yecheng (Kargilik)
Hotan
Minfeng (Niya)
Qiemo
Ruoqiang
Dunhuang
Yumen (Laojunmiao)
Jiayuguan
Jiuquan
Zhangye
Jinchang
Wuwei
Golmud
Xining
LANZHOU
TIANSHUI
Da Qaidam
Lhasa
Xigazê
Gyangzê
Nagqu
Qamdo
Dali
KUNMING
Panzhihua
Xichang
CHENGDU
CHONGQING
MIANYANG
SUINING
NEIJIANG
Zigong
Yibin
GUIYANG
LUPANSHUI
Ya'an
Kangding
Gejiu
Mengzi
Kaiyuan

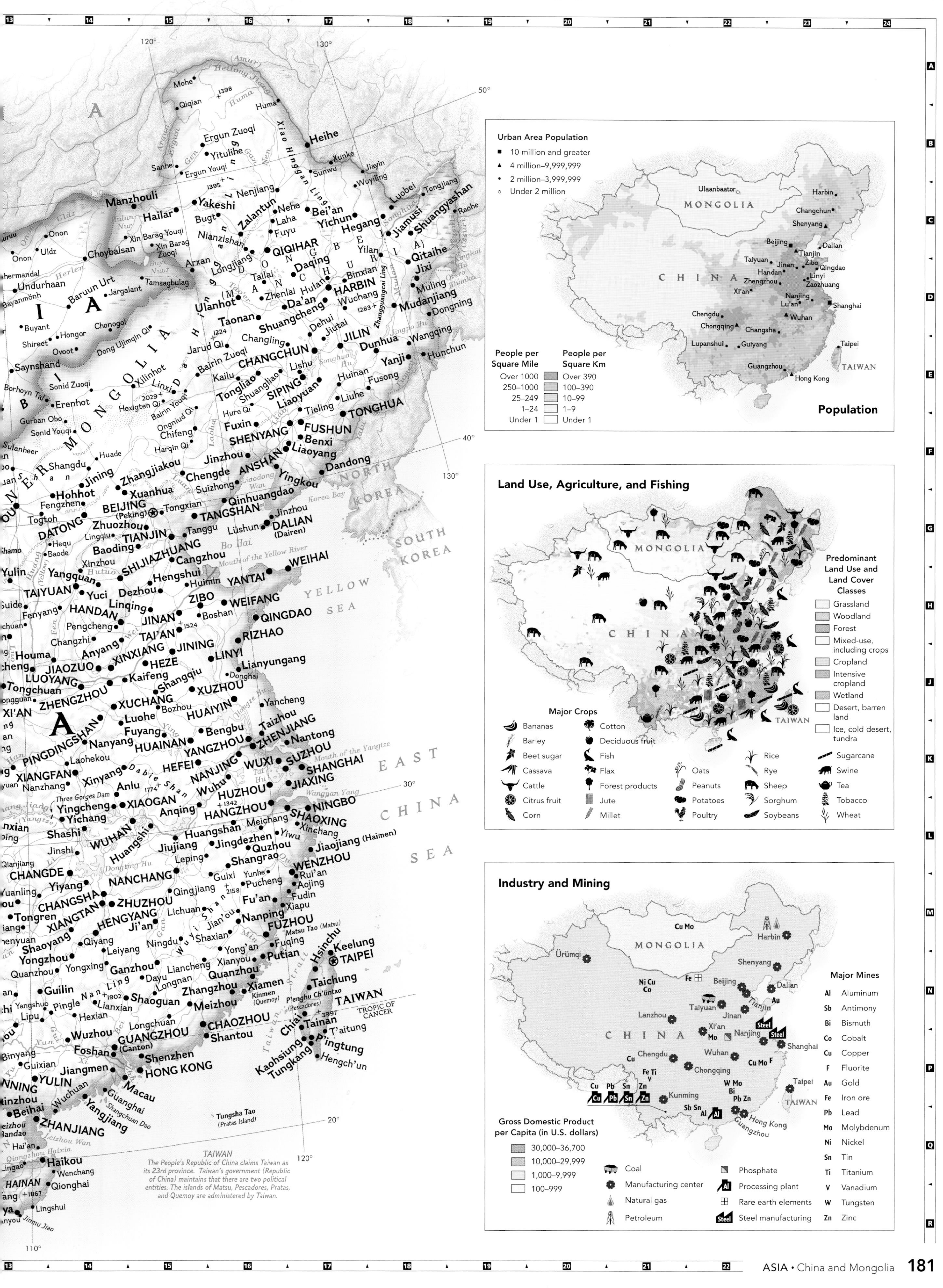

Urban Area Population
10 million and greater
4 million–9,999,999
2 million–3,999,999
Under 2 million
People per Square Mile
Over 1000
250–1000
25–249
1–24
Under 1
People per Square Km
Over 390
100–390
10–99
1–9
Under 1
Population
MONGOLIA
CHINA
TAIWAN
Ulaanbaatar
Harbin
Changchun
Shenyang
Beijing
Tianjin
Dalian
Taiyuan
Jinan
Zibo
Qingdao
Handan
Linyi
Zhengzhou
Zaozhuang
Xi'an
Nanjing
Lu'an
Shanghai
Wuhan
Chengdu
Chongqing
Changsha
Lupanshui
Guiyang
Taipei
Guangzhou
Hong Kong
Land Use, Agriculture, and Fishing
Predominant Land Use and Land Cover Classes
Grassland
Woodland
Forest
Mixed-use, including crops
Cropland
Intensive cropland
Wetland
Desert, barren land
Ice, cold desert, tundra
Major Crops
Bananas
Barley
Beet sugar
Cassava
Cattle
Citrus fruit
Corn
Cotton
Deciduous fruit
Fish
Flax
Forest products
Jute
Millet
Oats
Peanuts
Potatoes
Poultry
Rice
Rye
Sheep
Sorghum
Soybeans
Sugarcane
Swine
Tea
Tobacco
Wheat
Industry and Mining
Cu Mo
Harbin
Ürümqi
Shenyang
Fe
Beijing
Dalian
Ni Cu Co
Au
Taiyuan
Tianjin
Jinan
Lanzhou
Xi'an
Mo
Nanjing
Steel
Shanghai
Chengdu
Cu
Wuhan
Cu Mo F
Fe Ti V
Chongqing
Taipei
Cu Pb Sn Zn
Kunming
W Mo Bi
Pb Zn
Sb Sn
Al
Hong Kong
Guangzhou
Gross Domestic Product per Capita (in U.S. dollars)
30,000–36,700
10,000–29,999
1,000–9,999
100–999
Coal
Manufacturing center
Natural gas
Petroleum
Phosphate
Processing plant
Rare earth elements
Steel manufacturing
Major Mines
Al Aluminum
Sb Antimony
Bi Bismuth
Co Cobalt
Cu Copper
F Fluorite
Au Gold
Fe Iron ore
Pb Lead
Mo Molybdenum
Ni Nickel
Sn Tin
Ti Titanium
V Vanadium
W Tungsten
Zn Zinc
TAIWAN
The People's Republic of China claims Taiwan as its 23rd province. Taiwan's government (Republic of China) maintains that there are two political entities. The islands of Matsu, Pescadores, Pratas, and Quemoy are administered by Taiwan.
Mohe
Qiqian
Heihe
Ergun Zuoqi
Yitulihe
Sanhe
Ergun Youqi
Xunke
Sunwu
Jiayin
Wuyiling
Manzhouli
Hailar
Yakeshi
Nenjiang
Bei'an
Yichun
Hegang
Jiamusi
Shuangyashan
Tongjiang
Raohe
Choybalsan
QIQIHAR
Daqing
HARBIN
Qitaihe
Jixi
Mudanjiang
Dongning
Ulanhot
Taonan
Shuangcheng
JILIN
Dunhua
Wangqing
Hunchun
Yanji
CHANGCHUN
SIPING
Tonghua
Tieling
FUSHUN
SHENYANG
Benxi
Liaoyang
Fuxin
Chifeng
Jinzhou
ANSHAN
Yingkou
Dandong
Chengde
Zhangjiakou
Hohhot
Jining
BEIJING (Peking)
Tongxian
TANGSHAN
Qinhuangdao
DALIAN (Dairen)
Jinzhou
Lüshun
TIANJIN
Tanggu
DATONG
Baoding
SHIJIAZHUANG
Cangzhou
TAIYUAN
Yangquan
Yuci
Dezhou
Hengshui
YANTAI
WEIHAI
ZIBO
WEIFANG
QINGDAO
HANDAN
JINAN
TAI'AN
RIZHAO
LINYI
Lianyungang
JINING
XINXIANG
JIAOZUO
LUOYANG
HEZE
Kaifeng
Shangqiu
XUZHOU
ZHENGZHOU
XI'AN
XUCHANG
HUAIYIN
Yancheng
PINGDINGSHAN
Nanyang
HUAINAN
Bengbu
YANGZHOU
ZHENJIANG
Taizhou
Nantong
XIANGFAN
HEFEI
NANJING
WUXI
SUZHOU
SHANGHAI
JIAXING
HUZHOU
HANGZHOU
NINGBO
SHAOXING
Yichang
WUHAN
Huangshi
XIAOGAN
Anqing
Huangshan
Jingdezhen
Jiujiang
NANCHANG
Shangrao
WENZHOU
CHANGDE
Yiyang
CHANGSHA
ZHUZHOU
XIANGTAN
HENGYANG
Nanping
FUZHOU
Fuqing
Putian
Quanzhou
Xiamen
Zhangzhou
Keelung
TAIPEI
Hsinchu
Taichung
TAIWAN
Tainan
Kaohsiung
P'ingtung
T'aitung
Hengch'un
Shaoguan
Meizhou
CHAOZHOU
Shantou
GUANGZHOU (Canton)
Shenzhen
HONG KONG
Macau
Foshan
Jiangmen
Wuzhou
Guilin
YULIN
ZHANJIANG
Haikou
Qionghai
Wenchang
HAINAN
Lingshui
Tungsha Tao (Pratas Island)
Matsu Tao (Matsu)
Kinmen (Quemoy)
P'enghu Ch'üntao (Pescadores)
TROPIC OF CANCER
NORTH KOREA
SOUTH KOREA
Korea Bay
Bo Hai
YELLOW SEA
EAST CHINA SEA
MONGOLIA
120°
130°
50°
40°
30°
20°
110°

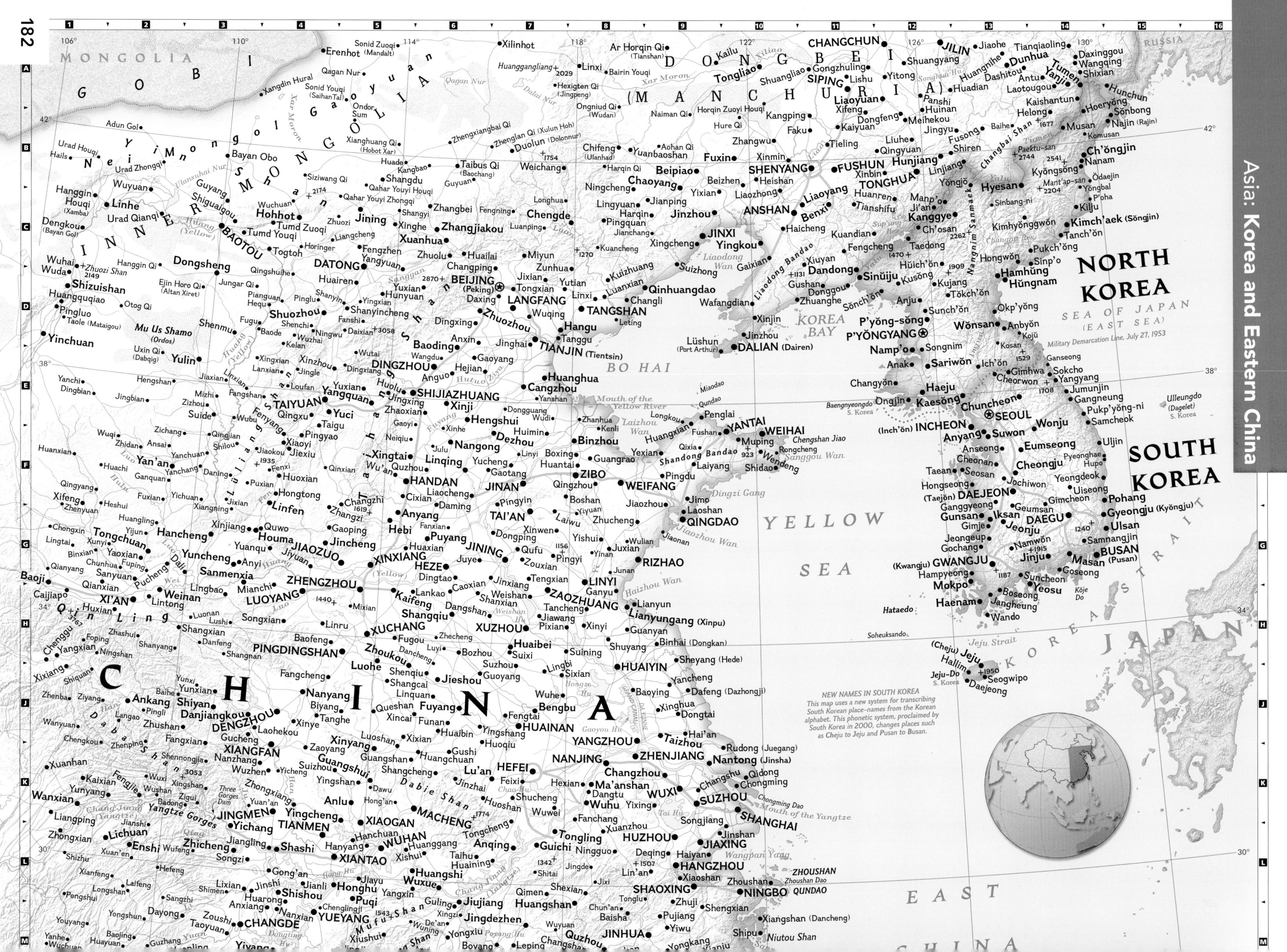
NORTH KOREA
SOUTH KOREA
CHINA
MONGOLIA
RUSSIA
JAPAN
SEA OF JAPAN (EAST SEA)
YELLOW SEA
EAST CHINA
BO HAI
KOREA BAY
KOREA STRAIT
Military Demarcation Line, July 27, 1953
NEW NAMES IN SOUTH KOREA
This map uses a new system for transcribing South Korean place-names from the Korean alphabet. This phonetic system, proclaimed by South Korea in 2000, changes places such as Cheju to Jeju and Pusan to Busan.
P'YŎNGYANG
SEOUL
BEIJING (Peking)
TIANJIN (Tientsin)
SHANGHAI
DALIAN (Dairen)
SHENYANG
CHANGCHUN
JILIN
QINGDAO
JINAN
ZHENGZHOU
TAIYUAN
SHIJIAZHUANG
NANJING
HEFEI
WUHAN
XI'AN
HANGZHOU
BUSAN (Pusan)
INCHEON
DAEGU
GWANGJU
DAEJEON
Jeju
Jeju-Do
Ulleungdo (Dagelet) S. Korea
Liaodong Bandao
Shandong Bandao
Jeju Strait
Mouth of the Yellow River
Mouth of the Yangtze
Yangtze Gorges
Three Gorges Dam
Mu Us Shamo (Ordos)
Qin Ling
Dabie Shan
Changbai Shan
Paektu-san 2744
Nangnim Sanmaek
MANCHURIA
NEI MONGOL
DONGBEI
GOBI
GRAND CANAL

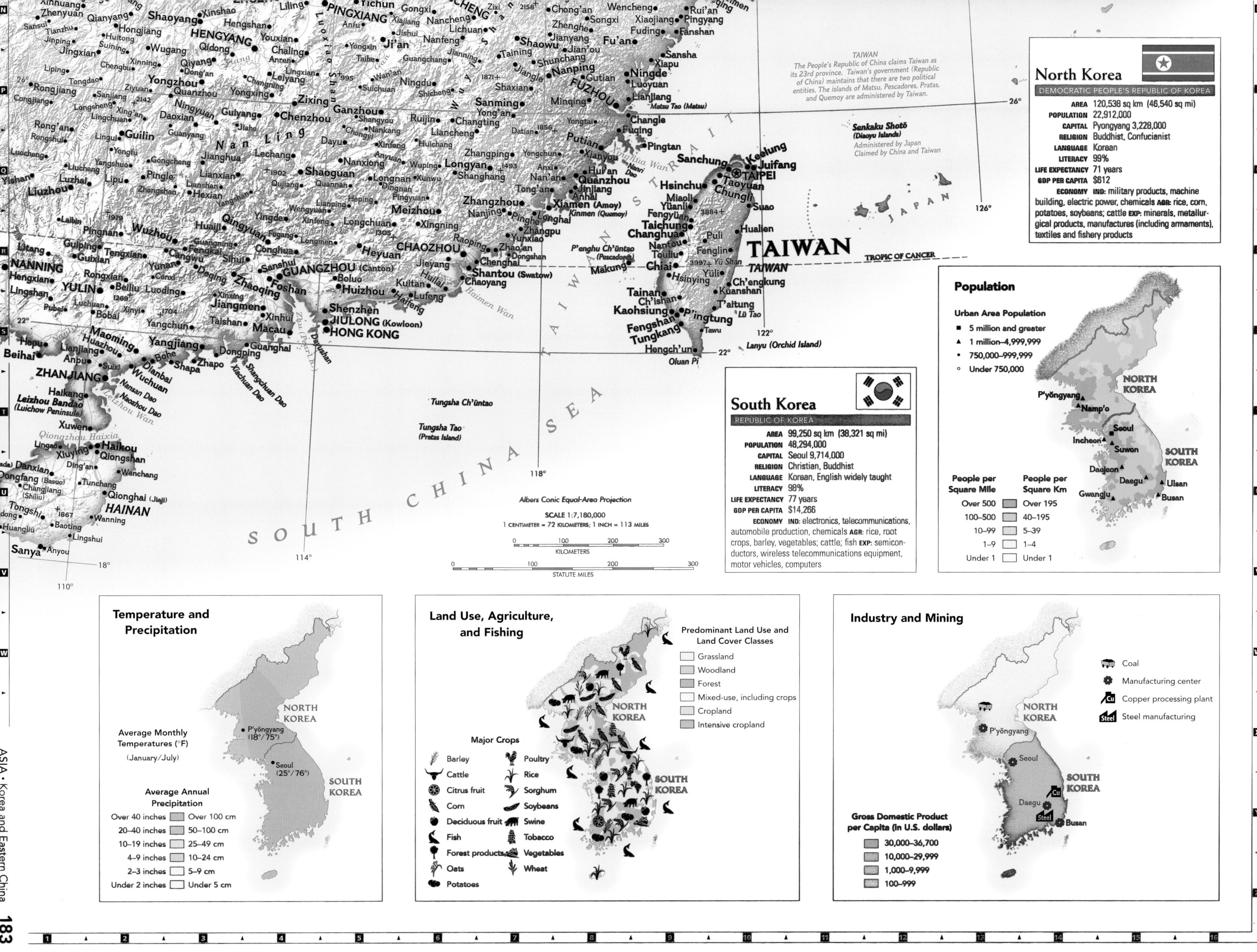

TAIWAN
The People's Republic of China claims Taiwan as its 23rd province. Taiwan's government (Republic of China) maintains that there are two political entities. The islands of Matsu, Pescadores, Pratas, and Quemoy are administered by Taiwan.
Senkaku Shotō (Diaoyu Islands)
Administered by Japan
Claimed by China and Taiwan
North Korea
DEMOCRATIC PEOPLE'S REPUBLIC OF KOREA
AREA 120,538 sq km (46,540 sq mi)
POPULATION 22,912,000
CAPITAL Pyongyang 3,228,000
RELIGION Buddhist, Confucianist
LANGUAGE Korean
LITERACY 99%
LIFE EXPECTANCY 71 years
GDP PER CAPITA $612
ECONOMY IND: military products, machine building, electric power, chemicals AGR: rice, corn, potatoes, soybeans; cattle EXP: minerals, metallurgical products, manufactures (including armaments), textiles and fishery products
TAIWAN STRAIT
TROPIC OF CANCER
SOUTH CHINA SEA
South Korea
REPUBLIC OF KOREA
AREA 99,250 sq km (38,321 sq mi)
POPULATION 48,294,000
CAPITAL Seoul 9,714,000
RELIGION Christian, Buddhist
LANGUAGE Korean, English widely taught
LITERACY 98%
LIFE EXPECTANCY 77 years
GDP PER CAPITA $14,266
ECONOMY IND: electronics, telecommunications, automobile production, chemicals AGR: rice, root crops, barley, vegetables; cattle; fish EXP: semiconductors, wireless telecommunications equipment, motor vehicles, computers
Albers Conic Equal-Area Projection
SCALE 1:7,180,000
1 CENTIMETER = 72 KILOMETERS; 1 INCH = 113 MILES
KILOMETERS
STATUTE MILES
Population
Urban Area Population
5 million and greater
1 million–4,999,999
750,000–999,999
Under 750,000
People per Square Mile
Over 500
100–500
10–99
1–9
Under 1
People per Square Km
Over 195
40–195
5–39
1–4
Under 1
Temperature and Precipitation
Average Monthly Temperatures (°F) (January/July)
P'yŏngyang (18°/75°)
Seoul (25°/76°)
Average Annual Precipitation
Over 40 inches | Over 100 cm
20–40 inches | 50–100 cm
10–19 inches | 25–49 cm
4–9 inches | 10–24 cm
2–3 inches | 5–9 cm
Under 2 inches | Under 5 cm
Land Use, Agriculture, and Fishing
Predominant Land Use and Land Cover Classes
Grassland
Woodland
Forest
Mixed-use, including crops
Cropland
Intensive cropland
Major Crops
Barley
Cattle
Citrus fruit
Corn
Deciduous fruit
Fish
Forest products
Oats
Potatoes
Poultry
Rice
Sorghum
Soybeans
Swine
Tobacco
Vegetables
Wheat
Industry and Mining
Coal
Manufacturing center
Copper processing plant
Steel manufacturing
Gross Domestic Product per Capita (in U.S. dollars)
30,000–36,700
10,000–29,999
1,000–9,999
100–999
NORTH KOREA
SOUTH KOREA

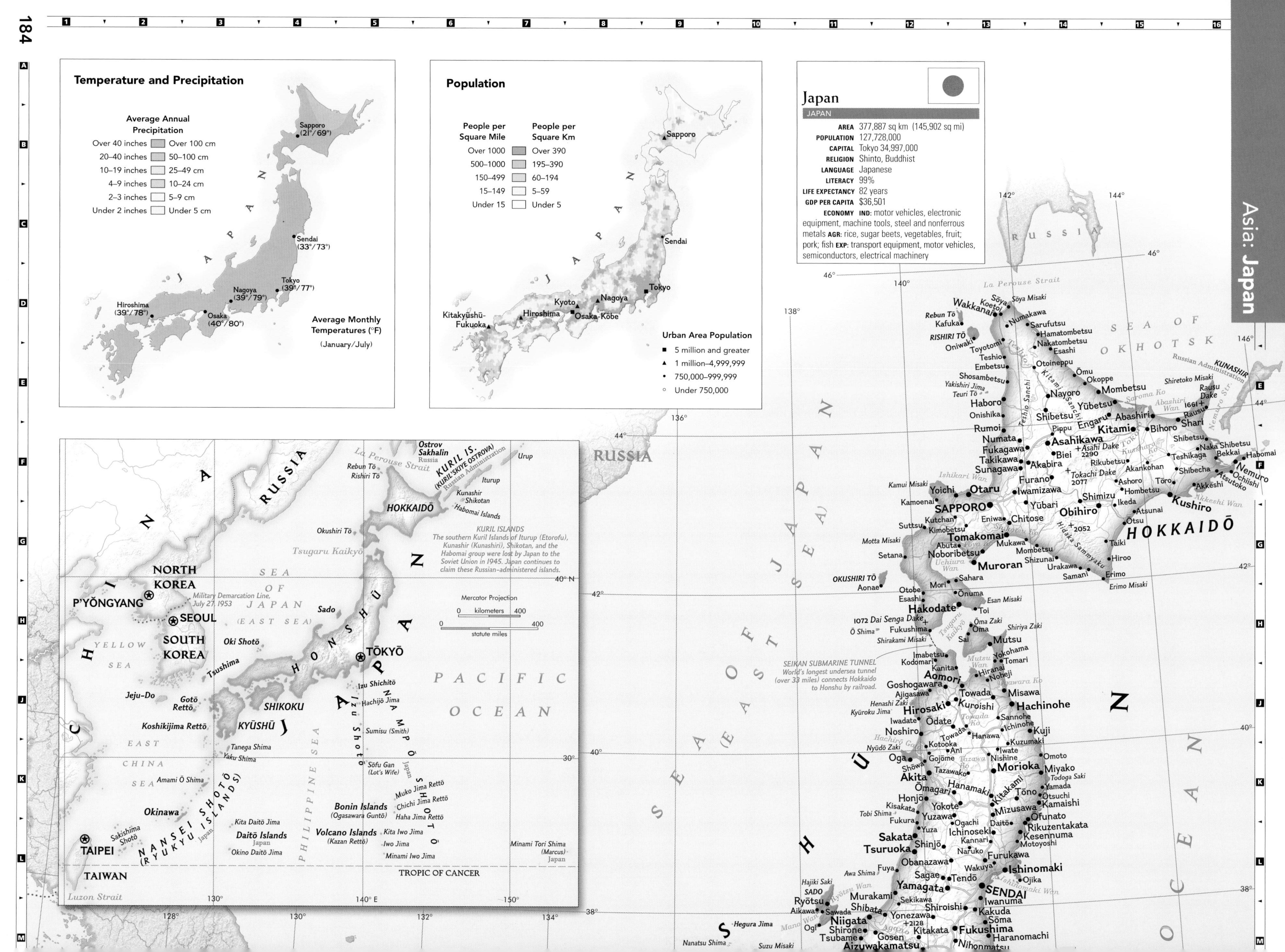
Temperature and Precipitation
Average Annual Precipitation
Over 40 inches | Over 100 cm
20–40 inches | 50–100 cm
10–19 inches | 25–49 cm
4–9 inches | 10–24 cm
2–3 inches | 5–9 cm
Under 2 inches | Under 5 cm
Sapporo (21°/69°)
Sendai (33°/73°)
Tokyo (39°/77°)
Nagoya (39°/79°)
Osaka (40°/80°)
Hiroshima (39°/78°)
JAPAN
Average Monthly Temperatures (°F)
(January/July)
Population
People per Square Mile | People per Square Km
Over 1000 | Over 390
500–1000 | 195–390
150–499 | 60–194
15–149 | 5–59
Under 15 | Under 5
Sapporo
Sendai
Tokyo
Nagoya
Kyoto
Osaka-Kobe
Hiroshima
Kitakyūshū-Fukuoka
Urban Area Population
5 million and greater
1 million–4,999,999
750,000–999,999
Under 750,000
Ostrov Sakhalin
Russia
KURIL IS. (KURIL'SKIYE OSTROVA)
Russian Administration
Urup
Iturup
Kunashir
Shikotan
Habomai Islands
La Perouse Strait
Rebun Tō
Rishiri Tō
HOKKAIDŌ
Okushiri Tō
Tsugaru Kaikyō
KURIL ISLANDS
The southern Kuril Islands of Iturup (Etorofu), Kunashir (Kunashiri), Shikotan, and the Habomai group were lost by Japan to the Soviet Union in 1945. Japan continues to claim these Russian-administered islands.
Mercator Projection
0 kilometers 400
0 statute miles 400
RUSSIA
CHINA
NORTH KOREA
P'YŎNGYANG
SOUTH KOREA
SEOUL
Military Demarcation Line, July 27, 1953
YELLOW SEA
SEA OF JAPAN (EAST SEA)
Sado
Oki Shotō
Tsushima
Jeju-Do
Gotō Rettō
Koshikijima Rettō
HONSHŪ
TŌKYŌ
SHIKOKU
KYŪSHŪ
Tanega Shima
Yaku Shima
EAST CHINA SEA
Amami Ō Shima
Okinawa
NANSEI SHOTŌ (RYUKYU ISLANDS)
Japan
Sakishima Shotō
TAIPEI
TAIWAN
Luzon Strait
Izu Shichitō
Hachijō Jima
Izu Shotō
NAMPŌ SHOTŌ
Sumisu (Smith)
Sōfu Gan (Lot's Wife)
Muko Jima Rettō
Chichi Jima Rettō
Haha Jima Rettō
Bonin Islands (Ogasawara Guntō)
Volcano Islands (Kazan Rettō)
Kita Iwo Jima
Iwo Jima
Minami Iwo Jima
Kita Daitō Jima
Daitō Islands
Okino Daitō Jima
PHILIPPINE SEA
PACIFIC OCEAN
Minami Tori Shima (Marcus) Japan
TROPIC OF CANCER
40° N
30°
130°
140° E
150°
SEA OF OKHOTSK
HOKKAIDŌ
SEA OF JAPAN (EAST SEA)
PACIFIC OCEAN
SEIKAN SUBMARINE TUNNEL
World's longest undersea tunnel (over 33 miles) connects Hokkaido to Honshu by railroad.
KUNASHIR
Russian Administration
Wakkanai
Sōya Misaki
Rebun Tō
RISHIRI TŌ
Asahikawa
Asahi Dake 2290
Tokachi Dake 2077
SAPPORO
Otaru
Obihiro
Kushiro
Nemuro
Tomakomai
Muroran
Hakodate
OKUSHIRI TŌ
Aomori
Hirosaki
Hachinohe
Morioka
Akita
SENDAI
Yamagata
Fukushima
Niigata
Sakata
Tsuruoka
Ishinomaki
SADO
Ryōtsu
Hegura Jima
Nanatsu Shima
Suzu Misaki
Erimo Misaki
Shiretoko Misaki
Rausu Dake 1661

Japan

JAPAN

AREA 377,887 sq km (145,902 sq mi)
POPULATION 127,728,000
CAPITAL Tokyo 34,997,000
RELIGION Shinto, Buddhist
LANGUAGE Japanese
LITERACY 99%
LIFE EXPECTANCY 82 years
GDP PER CAPITA $36,501
ECONOMY IND: motor vehicles, electronic equipment, machine tools, steel and nonferrous metals AGR: rice, sugar beets, vegetables, fruit; pork; fish EXP: transport equipment, motor vehicles, semiconductors, electrical machinery

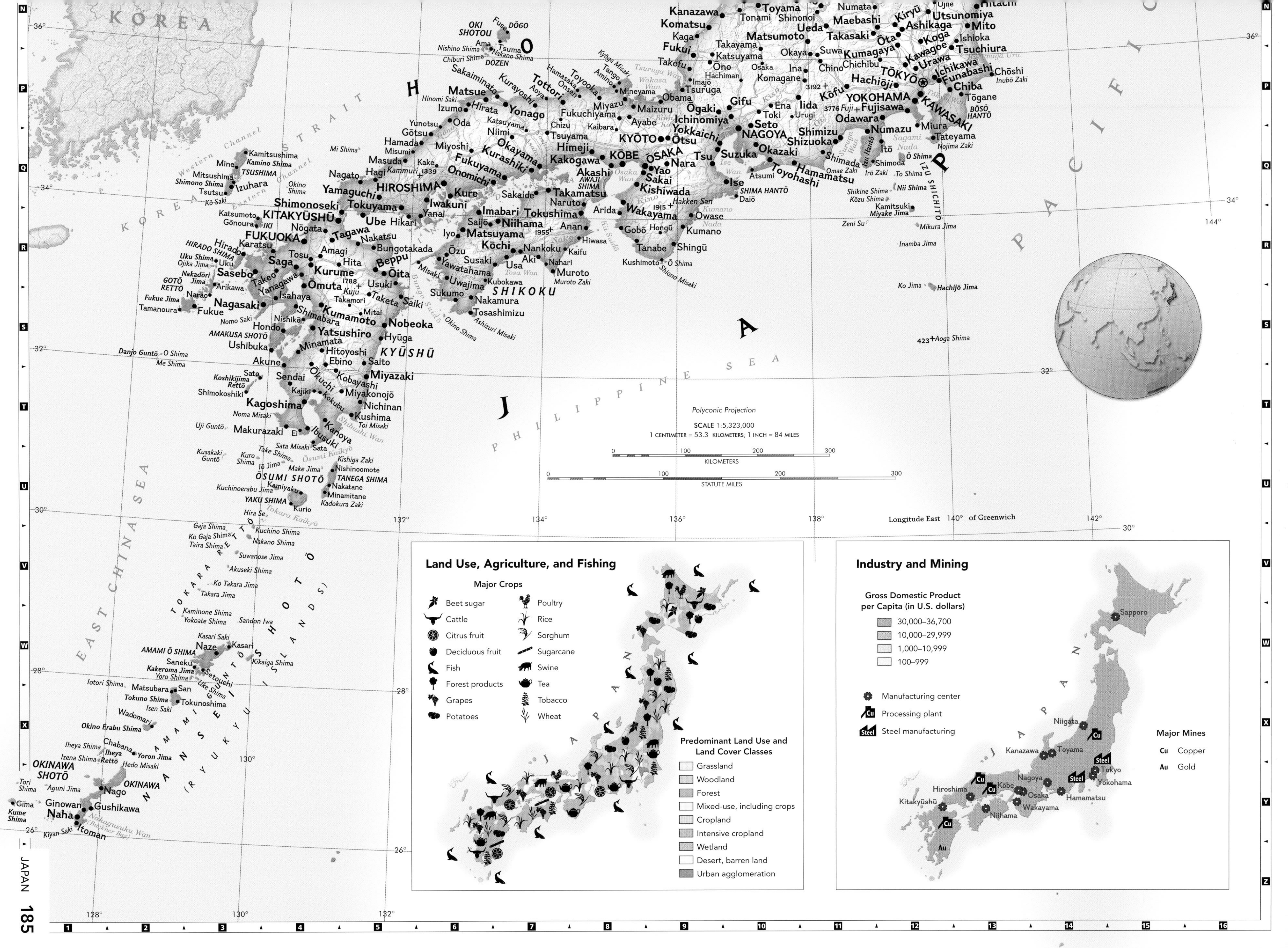

Land Use, Agriculture, and Fishing
Major Crops
Beet sugar
Cattle
Citrus fruit
Deciduous fruit
Fish
Forest products
Grapes
Potatoes
Poultry
Rice
Sorghum
Sugarcane
Swine
Tea
Tobacco
Wheat
Predominant Land Use and Land Cover Classes
Grassland
Woodland
Forest
Mixed-use, including crops
Cropland
Intensive cropland
Wetland
Desert, barren land
Urban agglomeration
Industry and Mining
Gross Domestic Product per Capita (in U.S. dollars)
30,000–36,700
10,000–29,999
1,000–10,999
100–999
Manufacturing center
Processing plant
Steel manufacturing
Major Mines
Cu Copper
Au Gold
Polyconic Projection
SCALE 1:5,323,000
1 CENTIMETER = 53.3 KILOMETERS; 1 INCH = 84 MILES
KILOMETERS
STATUTE MILES
Longitude East 140° of Greenwich
KOREA
KOREA STRAIT
EAST CHINA SEA
PHILIPPINE SEA
HONSHU
SHIKOKU
KYŪSHŪ
NANSEI SHOTŌ (RYUKYU ISLANDS)
TOKARA RETTŌ
ŌSUMI SHOTŌ
OKINAWA SHOTŌ
OKINAWA
TŌKYŌ
YOKOHAMA
KAWASAKI
NAGOYA
KYŌTO
ŌSAKA
KŌBE
HIROSHIMA
FUKUOKA
KITAKYŪSHŪ

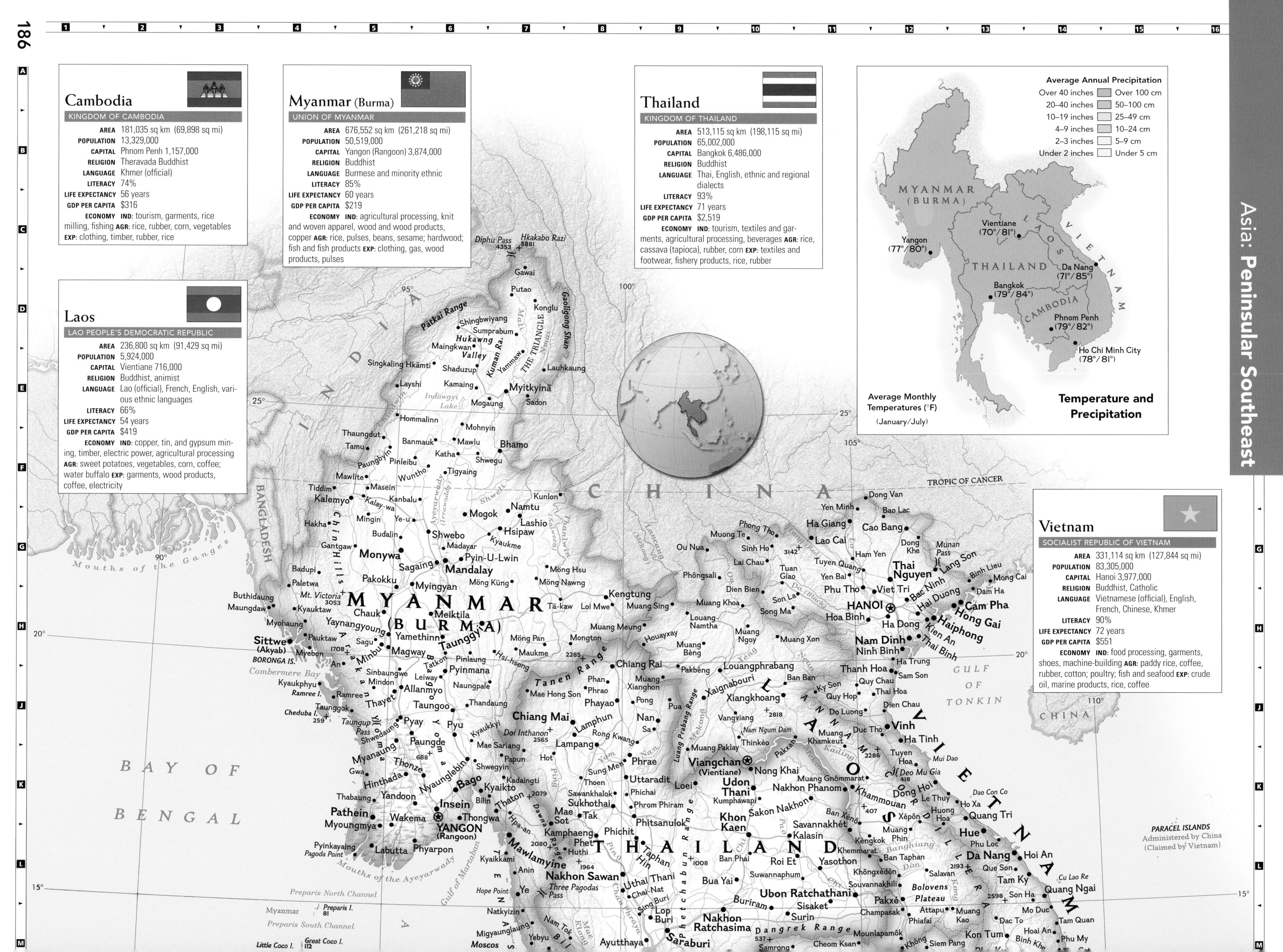
Cambodia
KINGDOM OF CAMBODIA
AREA 181,035 sq km (69,898 sq mi)
POPULATION 13,329,000
CAPITAL Phnom Penh 1,157,000
RELIGION Theravada Buddhist
LANGUAGE Khmer (official)
LITERACY 74%
LIFE EXPECTANCY 56 years
GDP PER CAPITA $316
ECONOMY IND: tourism, garments, rice milling, fishing AGR: rice, rubber, corn, vegetables EXP: clothing, timber, rubber, rice
Myanmar (Burma)
UNION OF MYANMAR
AREA 676,552 sq km (261,218 sq mi)
POPULATION 50,519,000
CAPITAL Yangon (Rangoon) 3,874,000
RELIGION Buddhist
LANGUAGE Burmese and minority ethnic
LITERACY 85%
LIFE EXPECTANCY 60 years
GDP PER CAPITA $219
ECONOMY IND: agricultural processing, knit and woven apparel, wood and wood products, copper AGR: rice, pulses, beans, sesame; hardwood; fish and fish products EXP: clothing, gas, wood products, pulses
Thailand
KINGDOM OF THAILAND
AREA 513,115 sq km (198,115 sq mi)
POPULATION 65,002,000
CAPITAL Bangkok 6,486,000
RELIGION Buddhist
LANGUAGE Thai, English, ethnic and regional dialects
LITERACY 93%
LIFE EXPECTANCY 71 years
GDP PER CAPITA $2,519
ECONOMY IND: tourism, textiles and garments, agricultural processing, beverages AGR: rice, cassava (tapioca), rubber, corn EXP: textiles and footwear, fishery products, rice, rubber
Laos
LAO PEOPLE'S DEMOCRATIC REPUBLIC
AREA 236,800 sq km (91,429 sq mi)
POPULATION 5,924,000
CAPITAL Vientiane 716,000
RELIGION Buddhist, animist
LANGUAGE Lao (official), French, English, various ethnic languages
LITERACY 66%
LIFE EXPECTANCY 54 years
GDP PER CAPITA $419
ECONOMY IND: copper, tin, and gypsum mining, timber, electric power, agricultural processing AGR: sweet potatoes, vegetables, corn, coffee; water buffalo EXP: garments, wood products, coffee, electricity
Vietnam
SOCIALIST REPUBLIC OF VIETNAM
AREA 331,114 sq km (127,844 sq mi)
POPULATION 83,305,000
CAPITAL Hanoi 3,977,000
RELIGION Buddhist, Catholic
LANGUAGE Vietnamese (official), English, French, Chinese, Khmer
LITERACY 90%
LIFE EXPECTANCY 72 years
GDP PER CAPITA $551
ECONOMY IND: food processing, garments, shoes, machine-building AGR: paddy rice, coffee, rubber, cotton; poultry; fish and seafood EXP: crude oil, marine products, rice, coffee
Average Annual Precipitation
Over 40 inches Over 100 cm
20–40 inches 50–100 cm
10–19 inches 25–49 cm
4–9 inches 10–24 cm
2–3 inches 5–9 cm
Under 2 inches Under 5 cm
MYANMAR (BURMA)
LAOS
VIETNAM
THAILAND
CAMBODIA
Yangon (77°/80°)
Vientiane (70°/81°)
Da Nang (71°/85°)
Bangkok (79°/84°)
Phnom Penh (79°/82°)
Ho Chi Minh City (78°/81°)
Average Monthly Temperatures (°F)
(January/July)
Temperature and Precipitation
CHINA
INDIA
BANGLADESH
MYANMAR (BURMA)
THAILAND
LAOS
VIETNAM
BAY OF BENGAL
GULF OF TONKIN
TROPIC OF CANCER
PARACEL ISLANDS
Administered by China
(Claimed by Vietnam)
HANOI
YANGON (Rangoon)
Viangchan (Vientiane)
Mandalay
Chiang Mai
Haiphong
Sittwe (Akyab)
Mouths of the Ganges
Mouths of the Ayeyarwady
Gulf of Martaban
Preparis North Channel
Preparis South Channel
Hkakabo Razi 5881
Diphu Pass 4353
Patkai Range
Gaoligong Shan
Chin Hills
Dangrek Range
Luang Prabang Range
Tanen Range
Bolovens Plateau

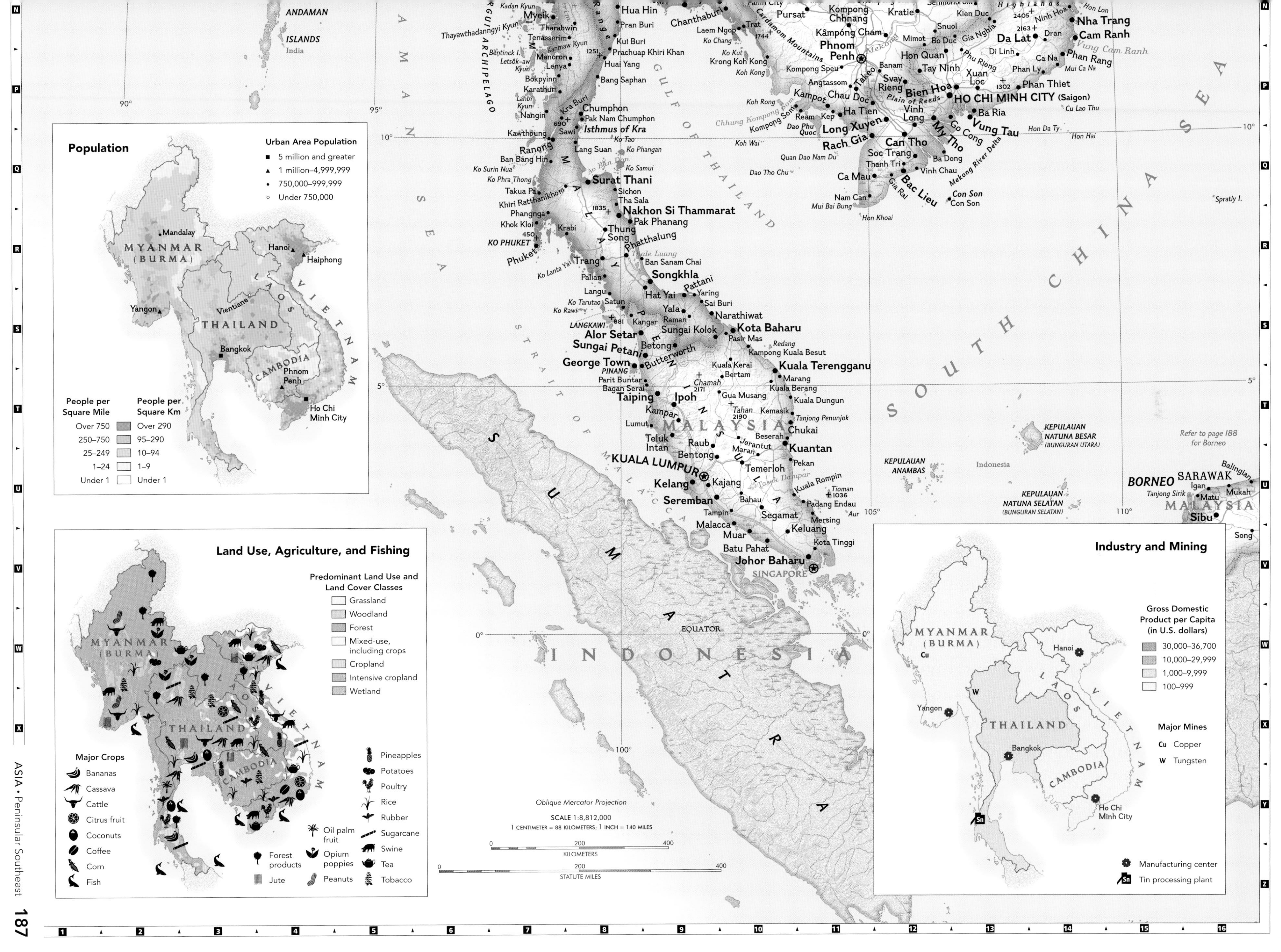
Population
Urban Area Population
5 million and greater
1 million–4,999,999
750,000–999,999
Under 750,000
People per Square Mile
Over 750
250–750
25–249
1–24
Under 1
People per Square Km
Over 290
95–290
10–94
1–9
Under 1
Land Use, Agriculture, and Fishing
Predominant Land Use and Land Cover Classes
Grassland
Woodland
Forest
Mixed-use, including crops
Cropland
Intensive cropland
Wetland
Major Crops
Bananas
Cassava
Cattle
Citrus fruit
Coconuts
Coffee
Corn
Fish
Forest products
Jute
Oil palm fruit
Opium poppies
Peanuts
Pineapples
Potatoes
Poultry
Rice
Rubber
Sugarcane
Swine
Tea
Tobacco
Industry and Mining
Gross Domestic Product per Capita (in U.S. dollars)
30,000–36,700
10,000–29,999
1,000–9,999
100–999
Major Mines
Cu Copper
W Tungsten
Manufacturing center
Tin processing plant
Oblique Mercator Projection
SCALE 1:8,812,000
1 CENTIMETER = 88 KILOMETERS; 1 INCH = 140 MILES
KILOMETERS
STATUTE MILES
Refer to page 188 for Borneo
SOUTH CHINA SEA
GULF OF THAILAND
STRAIT OF MALACCA
ANDAMAN SEA
ANDAMAN ISLANDS
MERGUI ARCHIPELAGO
SUMATRA
INDONESIA
MALAY PENINSULA
MALAYSIA
SINGAPORE
BORNEO
SARAWAK
EQUATOR
KUALA LUMPUR
HO CHI MINH CITY (Saigon)
Phnom Penh
Johor Baharu
George Town
Kota Baharu
Kuala Terengganu
Kuantan
Ipoh
Nha Trang
Cam Ranh
Da Lat
Can Tho
Surat Thani
Nakhon Si Thammarat
Songkhla
Hat Yai
Phuket
KEPULAUAN NATUNA BESAR (BUNGURAN UTARA)
KEPULAUAN NATUNA SELATAN (BUNGURAN SELATAN)
KEPULAUAN ANAMBAS

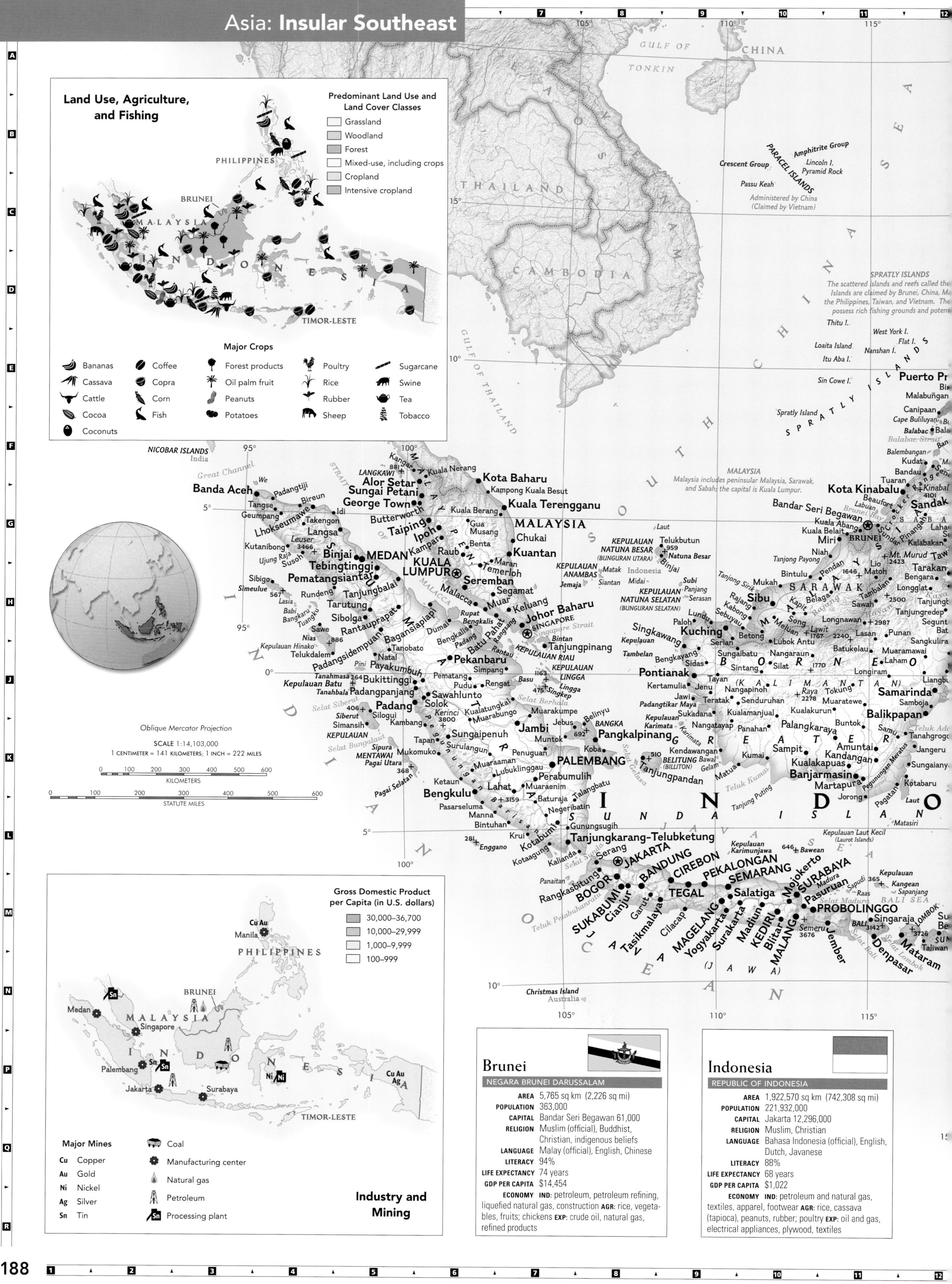
Land Use, Agriculture, and Fishing
Predominant Land Use and Land Cover Classes
Grassland
Woodland
Forest
Mixed-use, including crops
Cropland
Intensive cropland
PHILIPPINES
BRUNEI
MALAYSIA
INDONESIA
TIMOR-LESTE
Major Crops
Bananas
Cassava
Cattle
Cocoa
Coconuts
Coffee
Copra
Corn
Fish
Forest products
Oil palm fruit
Peanuts
Potatoes
Poultry
Rice
Rubber
Sheep
Sugarcane
Swine
Tea
Tobacco
Oblique Mercator Projection
SCALE 1:14,103,000
1 CENTIMETER = 141 KILOMETERS; 1 INCH = 222 MILES
0 100 200 300 400 500 600
KILOMETERS
0 100 200 300 400 500 600
STATUTE MILES
Gross Domestic Product per Capita (in U.S. dollars)
30,000–36,700
10,000–29,999
1,000–9,999
100–999
Manila
PHILIPPINES
BRUNEI
Medan
MALAYSIA
Singapore
Palembang
Jakarta
Surabaya
INDONESIA
TIMOR-LESTE
Major Mines
Cu Copper
Au Gold
Ni Nickel
Ag Silver
Sn Tin
Coal
Manufacturing center
Natural gas
Petroleum
Processing plant
Industry and Mining
GULF OF TONKIN
CHINA
THAILAND
CAMBODIA
GULF OF THAILAND
Amphitrite Group
Crescent Group
PARACEL ISLANDS
Lincoln I.
Pyramid Rock
Passu Keah
Administered by China (Claimed by Vietnam)
SPRATLY ISLANDS
The scattered islands and reefs called the Spratly Islands are claimed by Brunei, China, Malaysia, the Philippines, Taiwan, and Vietnam. They possess rich fishing grounds and potential...
Thitu I.
West York I.
Flat I.
Nanshan I.
Loaita Island
Itu Aba I.
Sin Cowe I.
Spratly Island
SOUTH CHINA SEA
MALAYSIA
Malaysia includes peninsular Malaysia, Sarawak, and Sabah; the capital is Kuala Lumpur.
NICOBAR ISLANDS
India
Great Channel
Banda Aceh
Kota Baharu
Alor Setar
Sungai Petani
George Town
Kuala Terengganu
Taiping
Ipoh
MEDAN
Binjai
KUALA LUMPUR
Kuantan
Seremban
Malacca
Johor Baharu
SINGAPORE
Pekanbaru
Padang
Jambi
Pangkalpinang
PALEMBANG
Bengkulu
Tanjungkarang-Telubketung
JAKARTA
BANDUNG
CIREBON
SEMARANG
SURABAYA
PROBOLINGGO
Denpasar
Mataram
Kota Kinabalu
Bandar Seri Begawan
Sandakan
Kuching
Sibu
Pontianak
Samarinda
Balikpapan
Banjarmasin
SARAWAK
KALIMANTAN (BORNEO)
KEPULAUAN NATUNA BESAR
KEPULAUAN ANAMBAS
KEPULAUAN NATUNA SELATAN
KEPULAUAN RIAU
KEPULAUAN LINGGA
BANGKA
BELITUNG
INDIAN OCEAN
JAVA SEA
INDONESIA
(JAWA)
Christmas Island
Australia
MALAYSIA

Brunei
NEGARA BRUNEI DARUSSALAM

AREA 5,765 sq km (2,226 sq mi)
POPULATION 363,000
CAPITAL Bandar Seri Begawan 61,000
RELIGION Muslim (official), Buddhist, Christian, indigenous beliefs
LANGUAGE Malay (official), English, Chinese
LITERACY 94%
LIFE EXPECTANCY 74 years
GDP PER CAPITA $14,454
ECONOMY **IND:** petroleum, petroleum refining, liquefied natural gas, construction **AGR:** rice, vegetables, fruits; chickens **EXP:** crude oil, natural gas, refined products

Indonesia
REPUBLIC OF INDONESIA

AREA 1,922,570 sq km (742,308 sq mi)
POPULATION 221,932,000
CAPITAL Jakarta 12,296,000
RELIGION Muslim, Christian
LANGUAGE Bahasa Indonesia (official), English, Dutch, Javanese
LITERACY 88%
LIFE EXPECTANCY 68 years
GDP PER CAPITA $1,022
ECONOMY **IND:** petroleum and natural gas, textiles, apparel, footwear **AGR:** rice, cassava (tapioca), peanuts, rubber; poultry **EXP:** oil and gas, electrical appliances, plywood, textiles

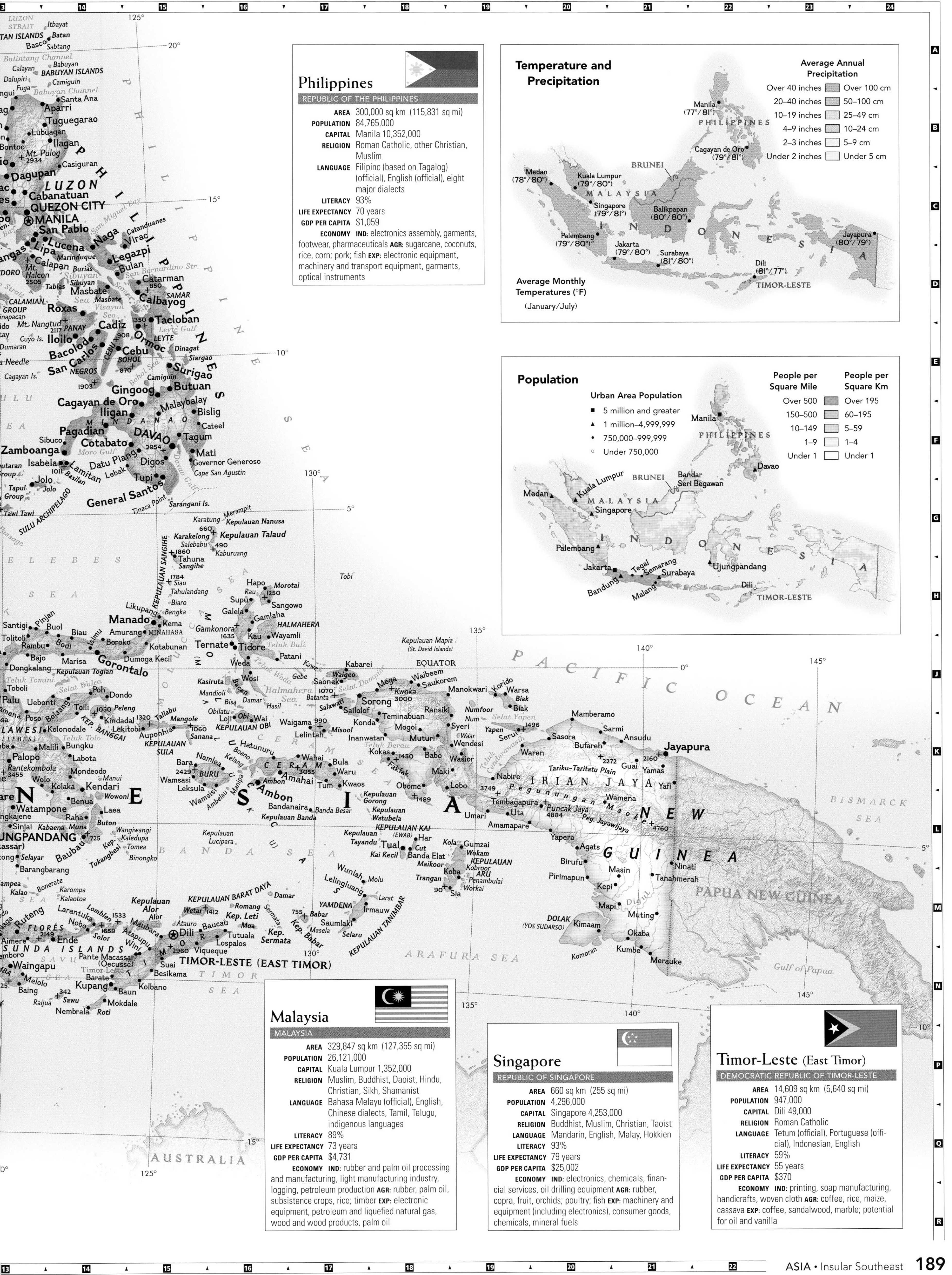
Temperature and Precipitation
Average Annual Precipitation
Over 40 inches | Over 100 cm
20–40 inches | 50–100 cm
10–19 inches | 25–49 cm
4–9 inches | 10–24 cm
2–3 inches | 5–9 cm
Under 2 inches | Under 5 cm
Average Monthly Temperatures (°F)
(January/July)
Manila (77°/81°)
Cagayan de Oro (79°/81°)
Medan (78°/80°)
Kuala Lumpur (79°/80°)
Singapore (79°/81°)
Balikpapan (80°/80°)
Palembang (79°/80°)
Jakarta (79°/80°)
Surabaya (81°/80°)
Dili (81°/77°)
Jayapura (80°/79°)
Population
Urban Area Population
5 million and greater
1 million–4,999,999
750,000–999,999
Under 750,000
People per Square Mile | People per Square Km
Over 500 | Over 195
150–500 | 60–195
10–149 | 5–59
1–9 | 1–4
Under 1 | Under 1
PACIFIC OCEAN
PHILIPPINES
LUZON
MANILA
QUEZON CITY
MINDANAO
CELEBES SEA
MOLUCCA SEA
HALMAHERA
BANDA SEA
ARAFURA SEA
TIMOR SEA
TIMOR-LESTE (EAST TIMOR)
NEW GUINEA
PAPUA NEW GUINEA
AUSTRALIA
BISMARCK SEA
Gulf of Papua
EQUATOR

Philippines

REPUBLIC OF THE PHILIPPINES

AREA 300,000 sq km (115,831 sq mi)
POPULATION 84,765,000
CAPITAL Manila 10,352,000
RELIGION Roman Catholic, other Christian, Muslim
LANGUAGE Filipino (based on Tagalog) (official), English (official), eight major dialects
LITERACY 93%
LIFE EXPECTANCY 70 years
GDP PER CAPITA $1,059
ECONOMY **IND:** electronics assembly, garments, footwear, pharmaceuticals **AGR:** sugarcane, coconuts, rice, corn; pork; fish **EXP:** electronic equipment, machinery and transport equipment, garments, optical instruments

Malaysia

MALAYSIA

AREA 329,847 sq km (127,355 sq mi)
POPULATION 26,121,000
CAPITAL Kuala Lumpur 1,352,000
RELIGION Muslim, Buddhist, Daoist, Hindu, Christian, Sikh, Shamanist
LANGUAGE Bahasa Melayu (official), English, Chinese dialects, Tamil, Telugu, indigenous languages
LITERACY 89%
LIFE EXPECTANCY 73 years
GDP PER CAPITA $4,731
ECONOMY **IND:** rubber and palm oil processing and manufacturing, light manufacturing industry, logging, petroleum production **AGR:** rubber, palm oil, subsistence crops, rice; timber **EXP:** electronic equipment, petroleum and liquefied natural gas, wood and wood products, palm oil

Singapore

REPUBLIC OF SINGAPORE

AREA 660 sq km (255 sq mi)
POPULATION 4,296,000
CAPITAL Singapore 4,253,000
RELIGION Buddhist, Muslim, Christian, Taoist
LANGUAGE Mandarin, English, Malay, Hokkien
LITERACY 93%
LIFE EXPECTANCY 79 years
GDP PER CAPITA $25,002
ECONOMY **IND:** electronics, chemicals, financial services, oil drilling equipment **AGR:** rubber, copra, fruit, orchids; poultry; fish **EXP:** machinery and equipment (including electronics), consumer goods, chemicals, mineral fuels

Timor-Leste (East Timor)

DEMOCRATIC REPUBLIC OF TIMOR-LESTE

AREA 14,609 sq km (5,640 sq mi)
POPULATION 947,000
CAPITAL Dili 49,000
RELIGION Roman Catholic
LANGUAGE Tetum (official), Portuguese (official), Indonesian, English
LITERACY 59%
LIFE EXPECTANCY 55 years
GDP PER CAPITA $370
ECONOMY **IND:** printing, soap manufacturing, handicrafts, woven cloth **AGR:** coffee, rice, maize, cassava **EXP:** coffee, sandalwood, marble; potential for oil and vanilla

Africa

A lone African elephant drinks at a water hole in Chobe National Park, Botswana, where protected enclaves help support some 120,000 of the continent's 400,000 to 660,000 elephants. In the late 1970s, there were 1.3 million elephants in Africa; poaching and habitat loss contributed to the decline.

Africa is often called the continent of beginnings. Fossil and bone records of the earliest humans go back more than 4 million years, and perhaps 1.8 million years ago our early upright ancestor, *Homo erectus*, departed Africa on the long journey that eventually peopled the Earth. It now seems likely that every person today comes from a lineage that leads back to an ancient African. Innumerable cave paintings and petroglyphs, from the Sahara to South Africa, provide clues to the beliefs and way of life of these age-old hominids.

Second largest continent after Asia, Africa accounts for a fifth of the world's land surface. Its unforgettable form, bulging to the west, lies surrounded by oceans and seas and can be considered underpopulated because only slightly more than 13.5 percent of the world's population lives here. Yet Africa's 53 countries now contain more than 905 million people, two-thirds living in the countryside, mostly in coastal regions, near lakes, and along river courses.

The mighty Sahara, largest hot desert in the world, covers more than a quarter of Africa's surface and divides the continent. Desert zones—Sahara, Kalahari, Namib—contrast with immense tropical rain forests. Watered regions of lakes and rivers lie beyond the Sahel, a vast semiarid zone of short grasses that spans the continent south of the Sahara. Most of Africa is made up of savanna—high, rolling, grassy plains.

These savannas have been home since earliest times to people often called Bantu, a reference to both social groupings and their languages. Other distinct physical types exist around the continent as well: BaMbuti (Pygmies), San (Bushmen), Nilo-Saharans, and Hamito-Semitics (Berbers and Cushites). Africa's astonishing number of spoken languages—1,600, more than any other continent—reflect the great diversity of ethnic and social groups.

Near the Equator, perpetual ice and snow crown Mount Kilimanjaro, the continent's highest point at 19,340 feet (5,895 m). The Nile, longest river in the world at 4,241 miles (6,825 km), originates in mountains south of the Equator and flows north-northeast before finally delivering its life-giving waters into the Mediterranean Sea.

Africa, blessed with wondrous deserts, rivers, grasslands, forests, and multihued earth, and possessing huge reserves of mineral wealth and biodiversity, waits expectantly for a prosperous future.

Many obstacles, however, complicate the way forward. African countries experience great gaps in wealth between city and country, such as between Lagos and Nigeria and Cairo and Egypt.

Nearly 40 other African cities have populations numbering more than a million. Lack of clean water and the spread of diseases—malaria, tuberculosis, cholera, and AIDS among them—undermine people's health. In addition, war and huge concentrations of refugees displaced by fighting, persecution, and famine deter any chance of growth and stability. Africa today seems to stand between hope and hopelessness.

PHYSICAL Africa stretches an astounding 5,000 miles (8,047 km) from north to south and 4,600 miles (7,403 km) from east to west. The continent rises from generally narrow coastal strips to form a gigantic plateau, with portions over 2,000 feet (610 m) in height. It has limited harbors and a coastline with few bays and inlets. Though formed by a series of expansive uplands, Africa has few true mountain chains. Main ranges in the north are the Atlas in Morocco and the Ahaggar in the Sahara. To the southeast, the Ethiopian Highlands form a broad area of high topography. The massive volcanic peaks of Mount Kilimanjaro and Mount Kenya rise in dramatic isolation from surrounding plains. Between Uganda and Democratic Republic of the Congo, the Ruwenzori Range runs north to south and falls steeply in the west to the Rift Valley.

The East African Rift System is the continent's most dramatic geologic feature. This great rent actually begins in the Red Sea, then cuts southward to form the stunning landscape of lakes, volcanoes, and deep valleys that finally ends near the mouth of the Zambezi River. The Rift Valley, a region of active plate tectonics, marks the divide where East Africa is steadily being pulled away, eventually to become a mini-continent.

The Great Escarpment in southern Africa, a plateau edge that falls off to the coastal strip, is best represented by the stark, highly eroded Drakensberg Range, which reaches altitudes over 11,400 feet (3,482 m).

Madagascar, fourth largest island in the world, lies east of the main continent and is remarkable for its flora and fauna, including medicinal plants and lemur species.

Africa's great rivers include the Niger, Congo, and Zambezi, each regionally important for internal transport and fishing. The Nile drains 6 percent of the continent; its two main branches, the Blue Nile and the White Nile, meet at Khartoum, in Sudan.

Wildlife still abounds in eastern and southern Africa and supports ecotourism, but hundreds of plant and animal species live precariously close to extinction.

HISTORY After millions of years of human evolution, there arose along the Nile River the brilliant civilization of Egypt. Mastery of agriculture and the river's annual flooding led to a series of dynasties that lasted for some 3,000 years, creating an astounding legacy of tombs, statuary, pyramids, temples, and hieroglyphic writing.

The long-standing power of Carthage ruled the western Mediterranean, but was conquered by the Roman Empire in 146 B.C. Rome and Byzantium henceforth controlled all of North Africa's coastal strip until the Arab influx from the seventh century onward. The Arabs quickly took all of North Africa and spread their language and religion. Arabic and Islam have been unifying forces ever since. Trans-Sahara trade and contact converted many sub-Saharan people, such as the Hausa of Nigeria, to Islam.

Indigenous kingdoms have punctuated Africa's history. Finds from Great Zimbabwe, a massive fortress-city and inland empire that flourished from the 11th to 15th centuries, show contacts with places as far away as India and China.

Along the Niger River, regional empires rose and fell between A.D. 800 and 1600. Slaves, ivory, gold, and kola nuts, used for flavoring and medicine, formed the basis of trade. In the Niger Delta area, Yoruba, Ashanti, and Hausa states also had their periods of grandness. Longest lasting of all was Benin, a major African kingdom that survived from the 13th to 19th centuries.

The Swahili (literally, "coastal plain") culture arose from a mix of Arabs, local people, and others who from A.D. 900 onward spread to towns and cities of the east coast, along the Indian Ocean, from Somalia to Zanzibar. The Swahili language remains a major lingua franca in east, central, and southern Africa.

The magnificent Temple of Ramses II (circa 1279–1213 B.C.) at Abu Simbel is so revered that when the damming of the Nile at Aswan promised to submerge it, both it and the Temple of Nefertari (not shown) were meticulously dismantled and reassembled (1964–68) on higher ground 600 feet (184 m) to the west.

Colonialism's long period of domination, during which Portugal, Great Britain, France, Belgium, Germany, and Italy ruled the continent, spans from the mid-1500s to the mid-1900s. The Portuguese arrived first in search of riches and the sea route to India. In time, commerce and Christianity pushed Europe into Africa.

The terrible slave trade shipped millions of Africans to North and South America and Arab regions. European presence encouraged exploration to find the sources of Africa's main rivers and to fill in blank spots on the map.

In the late 19th century, Europe's powers embarked on a "scramble for Africa," which led to a partitioning of the entire continent by 1914. After the two World Wars colonialism weakened. Independence for some countries began in the 1950s and came to most in the 1960s, in power transfers ranging from peaceful (Ghana, Senegal) to bloody (Kenya, Algeria). Freedom arrived in Rhodesia, with the new name Zimbabwe, in 1980, and in Namibia in 1990. The end of white rule in South Africa culminated with the election of Nelson Mandela in 1994.

CULTURE Hunting, fishing, and gathering supported Africa's early humans. In time, agriculture led to permanent settlements and diversity in society, first along the Nile River and then in the south.

Village-based communities, resilient and lasting in their institutions, have formed the core of African life for thousands of years. With crop cultivation came domestication of animals—cattle, sheep, and goats. Ironworking reached sub-Saharan Africa from the north by about the fourth century B.C., allowing for new tools and weapons that accelerated change.

Kingdoms grew from the soil of village life. Kings and their courts resembled village elders in their roles as judges, mediators of disputes, and masters of trade. Early kingdoms in Mali, Ghana, and elsewhere conducted long-distance trade in gold, ivory, hides, jewels, feathers, and salt.

In some places, religious leaders became kings. Seen as divine, they assumed rights over land and cattle herds and in return took responsibility for the people's well-being.

Settled life allowed time and energy for arts, crafts, and other creative activities. In West Africa, artists, carvers, and bronze casters of the Ife (12th and 13th centuries) and Benin (16th and 17th centuries) kingdoms produced masterpieces in different mediums, culminating in terra-cotta heads and bronze statues and bas-reliefs of exquisite craftsmanship and naturalism. African art, especially sculpture, continues to hold a high place in world culture.

Rich traditions of oral narrative survive to preserve the history and collective memories of different tribes and groups. Bards known as griots tell tales and sing epic songs while accompanied by their instruments.

Traditional religion and ritual still have a powerful place in Africa, for health, wealth, good harvests, and to honor the forces of nature. The Dogon people retain a complex cosmology and perform a great ceremony every 60 years to mark the appearance of the star Sirius between two mountains.

Most major world religions are represented in Africa: Islam, Christianity, Judaism, even Hinduism. Islam predominates in the north, and south of the Sahara Christianity claims multitudes of followers—Islam and Christianity claim respectively 350 million and 400 million followers.

European languages and schooling, legacies of colonialism, have had lasting effects on modern Africa. Yet far from the cities one can still find blue-turbanned Tuareg wandering the Sahara, slender Masai on the savannas of East Africa, Pygmies in the rain forests, and San (Bushmen) adapted to the Kalahari Desert's harsh conditions. Color, exuberance, and diversity manage to shine through the clouds of trouble that beset the nations of Africa.

ECONOMY Africa ranks among the richest regions in the world in natural resources; it contains vast reserves of fossil fuels, precious metals, ores, and gems, including almost all of the world's chromium, much uranium, copper, tremendous underground gold reserves, and diamonds. West Africa exports major amounts of iron ore.

Yet Africa, the poorest continent, accounts for a mere one percent of world economic output. South Africa's economy alone nearly equals that of all other sub-Saharan countries combined.

With little history of refining and manufacturing (limited to parts of North and South Africa), small-scale agriculture dominates the activities of more than 60 percent of Africans: Main crops are corn, wheat, rice, yams, potatoes, and cassava. Economic life revolves around farmsteads and village markets. Important cash crops include cacao, coffee, tea, fruit, and palm and vegetable oils.

Even though food production is increasing, agriculture takes place on only 6 percent of Africa's land and fails to keep pace with population growth—six children is the average for every woman, and in many countries nearly half the people are under 15. Most countries rely on imported food and loans. A cycle of crushing debt repayment, unemployment, and instability repels much-needed foreign investment.

Tourism, while offering hope to numerous countries, mostly in north, east, and southern Africa, highlights the need for conservation and interdependence between humans and the varied ecosystems that support Africa's plants and wildlife. Stresses today include poaching, overgrazing, and deforestation.

The African Union (AU)—formerly the Organization of African Unity (OAU)—and numerous regional trading blocks try to encourage economic cooperation and political stability, essential for sustained growth. After decades of corruption, ruinous to many economies, Africans now realize that any hope for development lies with themselves and their leaders.

Africa: Physical and Political
Azimuthal Equidistant Projection
SCALE 1:30,268,000
1 CENTIMETER = 303 KILOMETERS; 1 INCH = 478 MILES
KILOMETERS
STATUTE MILES
International boundary
Disputed or undefined boundary
ATLANTIC OCEAN
INDIAN OCEAN
MEDITERRANEAN SEA
SAHARA
SAHEL
CONGO BASIN
KALAHARI DESERT

Longitude West 20° of Greenwich
Longitude East 20° of Greenwich
Azimuthal Equidistant Projection
SCALE 1:30,268,000
1 CENTIMETER = 303 KILOMETERS; 1 INCH = 478 MILES
KILOMETERS
STATUTE MILES
TROPIC OF CANCER
TROPIC OF CAPRICORN
EQUATOR
Meridian of Greenwich (London)
ATLANTIC OCEAN
INDIAN OCEAN
MEDITERRANEAN SEA
BLACK SEA
CASPIAN SEA
GULF OF GUINEA
GULF OF ADEN
PERSIAN GULF
Mozambique Channel
MOROCCO
ALGERIA
TUNISIA
LIBYA
EGYPT
WESTERN SAHARA
MAURITANIA
MALI
NIGER
CHAD
SUDAN
SENEGAL
GAMBIA
GUINEA-BISSAU
GUINEA
SIERRA LEONE
LIBERIA
CÔTE D'IVOIRE (IVORY COAST)
BURKINA FASO
GHANA
TOGO
BENIN
NIGERIA
CAMEROON
CENTRAL AFRICAN REPUBLIC
EQUATORIAL GUINEA
SAO TOME & PRINCIPE
GABON
CONGO
DEMOCRATIC REPUBLIC OF THE CONGO
ERITREA
DJIBOUTI
ETHIOPIA
SOMALIA
SOMALILAND
KENYA
UGANDA
RWANDA
BURUNDI
TANZANIA
ANGOLA
ZAMBIA
MALAWI
MOZAMBIQUE
ZIMBABWE
NAMIBIA
BOTSWANA
SOUTH AFRICA
LESOTHO
SWAZILAND
MADAGASCAR
COMOROS
SEYCHELLES
SAUDI ARABIA
YEMEN
SYRIA
IRAQ
IRAN
TURKEY
JORDAN
ISRAEL
LEBANON
CYPRUS
KUWAIT
QATAR
BAHRAIN
U.A.E.
GREECE
ITALY
SPAIN
PORTUGAL
FRANCE
SAHARA
Tristan da Cunha Group
Saint Helena U.K.
Ascension U.K.
CANARY ISLANDS (ISLAS CANARIAS) Spain
MADEIRA ISLANDS Portugal
Cape of Good Hope
CAIRO (EL QÂHIRA)
KHARTOUM
ADDIS ABABA (ĀDIS ĀBEBA)
NAIROBI
KINSHASA
LUANDA
PRETORIA
CAPE TOWN
DAKAR
ALGER (Algiers)
TUNIS
TARĀBULUS (Tripoli)
LAGOS
ABUJA
ANTANANARIVO
MUQDISHO (Mogadishu)
DAR ES SALAAM
HARARE
MAPUTO
JOHANNESBURG

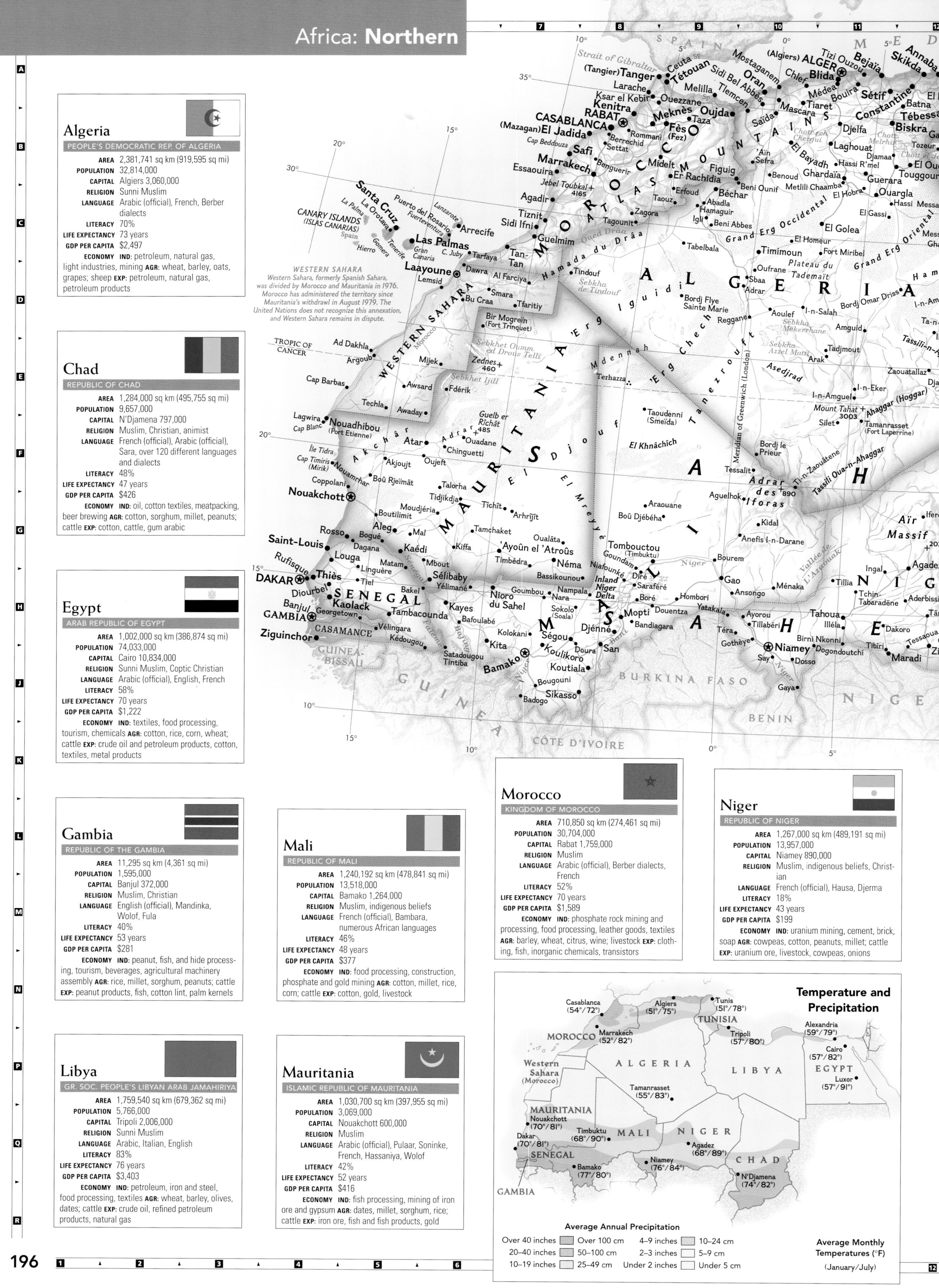

WESTERN SAHARA
Western Sahara, formerly Spanish Sahara, was divided by Morocco and Mauritania in 1976. Morocco has administered the territory since Mauritania's withdrawal in August 1979. The United Nations does not recognize this annexation, and Western Sahara remains in dispute.
Temperature and Precipitation
Casablanca (54°/72°)
Algiers (51°/75°)
Tunis (51°/78°)
Marrakech (52°/82°)
Tripoli (57°/80°)
Alexandria (59°/79°)
Cairo (57°/82°)
Luxor (57°/91°)
Tamanrasset (55°/83°)
Nouakchott (70°/81°)
Dakar (70°/81°)
Timbuktu (68°/90°)
Agadez (68°/89°)
Niamey (76°/84°)
Bamako (77°/80°)
N'Djamena (74°/82°)
MOROCCO
Western Sahara (Morocco)
ALGERIA
TUNISIA
LIBYA
EGYPT
MAURITANIA
MALI
NIGER
CHAD
SENEGAL
GAMBIA
Average Annual Precipitation
Over 40 inches Over 100 cm
20–40 inches 50–100 cm
10–19 inches 25–49 cm
4–9 inches 10–24 cm
2–3 inches 5–9 cm
Under 2 inches Under 5 cm
Average Monthly Temperatures (°F) (January/July)

Algeria

PEOPLE'S DEMOCRATIC REP. OF ALGERIA

AREA 2,381,741 sq km (919,595 sq mi)
POPULATION 32,814,000
CAPITAL Algiers 3,060,000
RELIGION Sunni Muslim
LANGUAGE Arabic (official), French, Berber dialects
LITERACY 70%
LIFE EXPECTANCY 73 years
GDP PER CAPITA $2,497
ECONOMY **IND:** petroleum, natural gas, light industries, mining **AGR:** wheat, barley, oats, grapes; sheep **EXP:** petroleum, natural gas, petroleum products

Chad

REPUBLIC OF CHAD

AREA 1,284,000 sq km (495,755 sq mi)
POPULATION 9,657,000
CAPITAL N'Djamena 797,000
RELIGION Muslim, Christian, animist
LANGUAGE French (official), Arabic (official), Sara, over 120 different languages and dialects
LITERACY 48%
LIFE EXPECTANCY 47 years
GDP PER CAPITA $426
ECONOMY **IND:** oil, cotton textiles, meatpacking, beer brewing **AGR:** cotton, sorghum, millet, peanuts; cattle **EXP:** cotton, cattle, gum arabic

Egypt

ARAB REPUBLIC OF EGYPT

AREA 1,002,000 sq km (386,874 sq mi)
POPULATION 74,033,000
CAPITAL Cairo 10,834,000
RELIGION Sunni Muslim, Coptic Christian
LANGUAGE Arabic (official), English, French
LITERACY 58%
LIFE EXPECTANCY 70 years
GDP PER CAPITA $1,222
ECONOMY **IND:** textiles, food processing, tourism, chemicals **AGR:** cotton, rice, corn, wheat; cattle **EXP:** crude oil and petroleum products, cotton, textiles, metal products

Gambia

REPUBLIC OF THE GAMBIA

AREA 11,295 sq km (4,361 sq mi)
POPULATION 1,595,000
CAPITAL Banjul 372,000
RELIGION Muslim, Christian
LANGUAGE English (official), Mandinka, Wolof, Fula
LITERACY 40%
LIFE EXPECTANCY 53 years
GDP PER CAPITA $281
ECONOMY **IND:** peanut, fish, and hide processing, tourism, beverages, agricultural machinery assembly **AGR:** rice, millet, sorghum, peanuts; cattle **EXP:** peanut products, fish, cotton lint, palm kernels

Libya

GR. SOC. PEOPLE'S LIBYAN ARAB JAMAHIRIYA

AREA 1,759,540 sq km (679,362 sq mi)
POPULATION 5,766,000
CAPITAL Tripoli 2,006,000
RELIGION Sunni Muslim
LANGUAGE Arabic, Italian, English
LITERACY 83%
LIFE EXPECTANCY 76 years
GDP PER CAPITA $3,403
ECONOMY **IND:** petroleum, iron and steel, food processing, textiles **AGR:** wheat, barley, olives, dates; cattle **EXP:** crude oil, refined petroleum products, natural gas

Mali

REPUBLIC OF MALI

AREA 1,240,192 sq km (478,841 sq mi)
POPULATION 13,518,000
CAPITAL Bamako 1,264,000
RELIGION Muslim, indigenous beliefs
LANGUAGE French (official), Bambara, numerous African languages
LITERACY 46%
LIFE EXPECTANCY 48 years
GDP PER CAPITA $377
ECONOMY **IND:** food processing, construction, phosphate and gold mining **AGR:** cotton, millet, rice, corn; cattle **EXP:** cotton, gold, livestock

Mauritania

ISLAMIC REPUBLIC OF MAURITANIA

AREA 1,030,700 sq km (397,955 sq mi)
POPULATION 3,069,000
CAPITAL Nouakchott 600,000
RELIGION Muslim
LANGUAGE Arabic (official), Pulaar, Soninke, French, Hassaniya, Wolof
LITERACY 42%
LIFE EXPECTANCY 52 years
GDP PER CAPITA $416
ECONOMY **IND:** fish processing, mining of iron ore and gypsum **AGR:** dates, millet, sorghum, rice; cattle **EXP:** iron ore, fish and fish products, gold

Morocco

KINGDOM OF MOROCCO

AREA 710,850 sq km (274,461 sq mi)
POPULATION 30,704,000
CAPITAL Rabat 1,759,000
RELIGION Muslim
LANGUAGE Arabic (official), Berber dialects, French
LITERACY 52%
LIFE EXPECTANCY 70 years
GDP PER CAPITA $1,589
ECONOMY **IND:** phosphate rock mining and processing, food processing, leather goods, textiles **AGR:** barley, wheat, citrus, wine; livestock **EXP:** clothing, fish, inorganic chemicals, transistors

Niger

REPUBLIC OF NIGER

AREA 1,267,000 sq km (489,191 sq mi)
POPULATION 13,957,000
CAPITAL Niamey 890,000
RELIGION Muslim, indigenous beliefs, Christian
LANGUAGE French (official), Hausa, Djerma
LITERACY 18%
LIFE EXPECTANCY 43 years
GDP PER CAPITA $199
ECONOMY **IND:** uranium mining, cement, brick, soap **AGR:** cowpeas, cotton, peanuts, millet; cattle **EXP:** uranium ore, livestock, cowpeas, onions

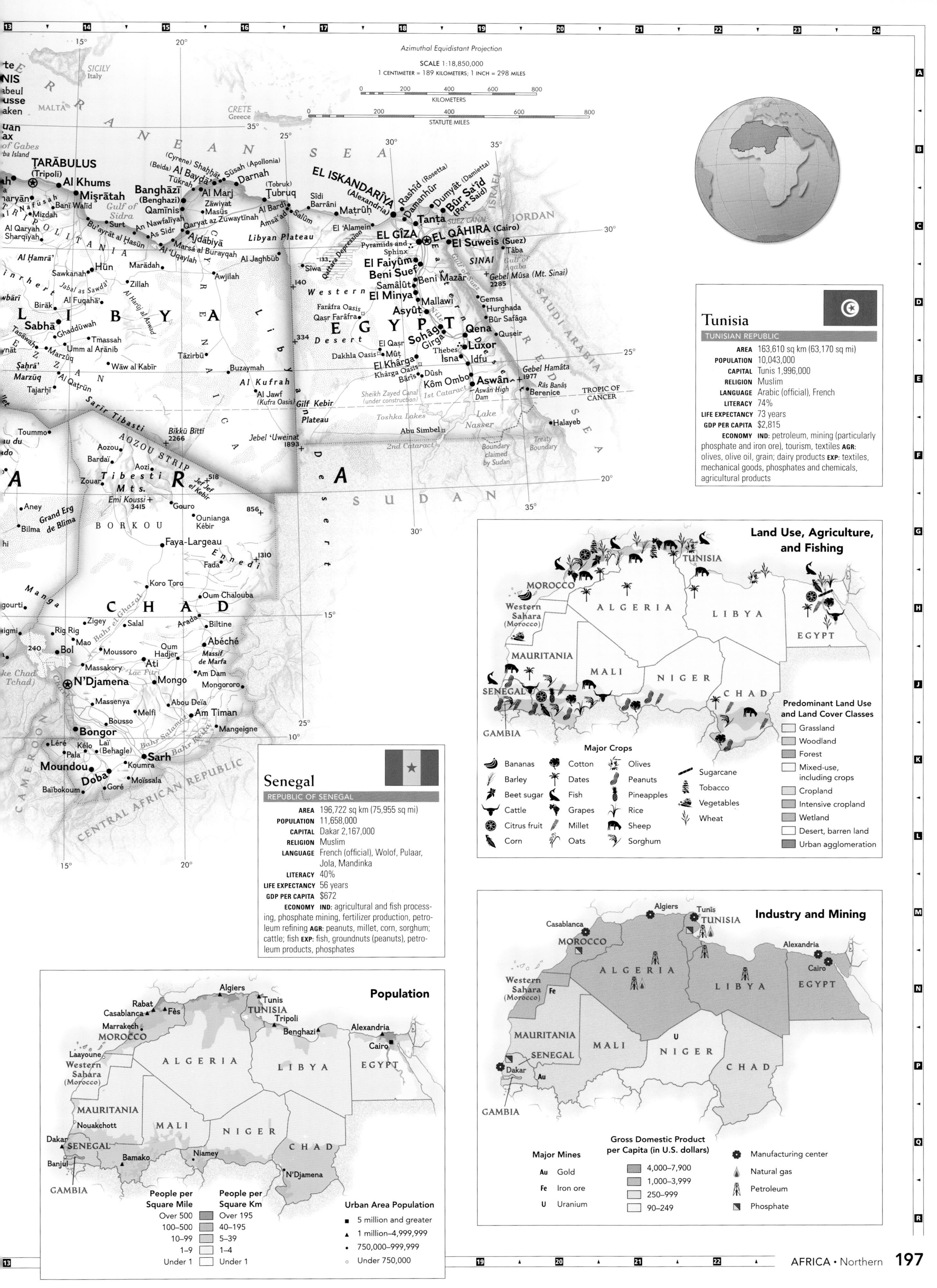

Azimuthal Equidistant Projection
SCALE 1:18,850,000
1 CENTIMETER = 189 KILOMETERS; 1 INCH = 298 MILES
KILOMETERS
STATUTE MILES
M E D I T E R R A N E A N S E A
SICILY Italy
MALTA
CRETE Greece
ṬARĀBULUS (Tripoli)
Al Khums
Miṣrātah
Banghāzī (Benghazi)
Al Bayḍā' (Beida)
Shaḥḥāt (Cyrene)
Sūsah (Apollonia)
Darnah
Ṭubruq (Tobruk)
Gulf of Sidra
L I B Y A
EL ISKANDARÎYA (Alexandria)
EL QÂHIRA (Cairo)
EL GÎZA
El Suweis (Suez)
Bûr Sa'îd (Port Said)
Libyan Plateau
Qattara Depression
Western Desert
E G Y P T
SINAI
Gebel Mûsa (Mt. Sinai) 2285
Aswân
Lake Nasser
Abu Simbel
TROPIC OF CANCER
RED SEA
SAUDI ARABIA
ISRAEL
JORDAN
S U D A N
AOZOU STRIP
Tibesti Mts.
Emi Koussi 3415
B O R K O U
C H A D
N'Djamena
Lake Chad (Lac Tchad)
CENTRAL AFRICAN REPUBLIC
CAMEROON
Land Use, Agriculture, and Fishing
Major Crops
Bananas, Barley, Beet sugar, Cattle, Citrus fruit, Corn, Cotton, Dates, Fish, Grapes, Millet, Oats, Olives, Peanuts, Pineapples, Rice, Sheep, Sorghum, Sugarcane, Tobacco, Vegetables, Wheat
Predominant Land Use and Land Cover Classes
Grassland
Woodland
Forest
Mixed-use, including crops
Cropland
Intensive cropland
Wetland
Desert, barren land
Urban agglomeration
Industry and Mining
Major Mines
Au Gold
Fe Iron ore
U Uranium
Gross Domestic Product per Capita (in U.S. dollars)
4,000–7,900
1,000–3,999
250–999
90–249
Manufacturing center
Natural gas
Petroleum
Phosphate
Population
People per Square Mile
Over 500
100–500
10–99
1–9
Under 1
People per Square Km
Over 195
40–195
5–39
1–4
Under 1
Urban Area Population
5 million and greater
1 million–4,999,999
750,000–999,999
Under 750,000

Tunisia

TUNISIAN REPUBLIC

AREA 163,610 sq km (63,170 sq mi)
POPULATION 10,043,000
CAPITAL Tunis 1,996,000
RELIGION Muslim
LANGUAGE Arabic (official), French
LITERACY 74%
LIFE EXPECTANCY 73 years
GDP PER CAPITA $2,815
ECONOMY **IND:** petroleum, mining (particularly phosphate and iron ore), tourism, textiles **AGR:** olives, olive oil, grain; dairy products **EXP:** textiles, mechanical goods, phosphates and chemicals, agricultural products

Senegal

REPUBLIC OF SENEGAL

AREA 196,722 sq km (75,955 sq mi)
POPULATION 11,658,000
CAPITAL Dakar 2,167,000
RELIGION Muslim
LANGUAGE French (official), Wolof, Pulaar, Jola, Mandinka
LITERACY 40%
LIFE EXPECTANCY 56 years
GDP PER CAPITA $672
ECONOMY **IND:** agricultural and fish processing, phosphate mining, fertilizer production, petroleum refining **AGR:** peanuts, millet, corn, sorghum; cattle; fish **EXP:** fish, groundnuts (peanuts), petroleum products, phosphates

Azimuthal Equidistant Projection

SCALE 1:18,454,000

1 CENTIMETER = 185 KILOMETERS; 1 INCH = 291 MILES

Burundi

REPUBLIC OF BURUNDI

AREA 27,834 sq km (10,747 sq mi)
POPULATION 7,795,000
CAPITAL Bujumbura 378,000
RELIGION Roman Catholic, indigenous beliefs, Muslim, Protestant
LANGUAGE Kirundi (official), French (official), Swahili
LITERACY 52%
LIFE EXPECTANCY 49 years
GDP PER CAPITA $93
ECONOMY **IND:** light consumer goods, assembly of imported components, public works construction, food processing **AGR:** coffee, cotton, tea, corn; beef **EXP:** coffee, tea, sugar, cotton

Central African Republic

CENTRAL AFRICAN REPUBLIC

AREA 622,984 sq km (240,535 sq mi)
POPULATION 4,238,000
CAPITAL Bangui 698,000
RELIGION indigenous beliefs, Protestant, Roman Catholic, Muslim
LANGUAGE French (official), Sangho, tribal languages
LITERACY 51%
LIFE EXPECTANCY 44 years
GDP PER CAPITA $330
ECONOMY **IND:** gold and diamond mining, logging, brewing, textiles **AGR:** cotton, coffee, tobacco, manioc (tapioca); timber **EXP:** diamonds, timber, cotton, coffee

Congo, Democratic Republic of the

DEMOCRATIC REPUBLIC OF THE CONGO

AREA 2,344,885 sq km (905,365 sq mi)
POPULATION 60,764,000
CAPITAL Kinshasa 5,277,000
RELIGION Roman Catholic, Protestant, Kimbanguist, Muslim
LANGUAGE French (official), Lingala, Kingwana, Kikongo, Tshiluba
LITERACY 66%
LIFE EXPECTANCY 50 years
GDP PER CAPITA $115
ECONOMY **IND:** mining (diamonds, copper, zinc), mineral processing, consumer products, cement **AGR:** coffee, sugar, palm oil, rubber; wood products **EXP:** diamonds, copper, crude oil, coffee

Djibouti

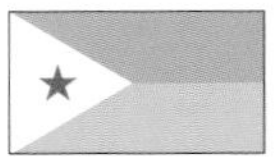

REPUBLIC OF DJIBOUTI

AREA 23,200 sq km (8,958 sq mi)
POPULATION 793,000
CAPITAL Djibouti 502,000
RELIGION Muslim, Christian
LANGUAGE French (official), Arabic (official), Somali, Afar
LITERACY 68%
LIFE EXPECTANCY 52 years
GDP PER CAPITA $852
ECONOMY **IND:** construction, agricultural processing, salt **AGR:** fruits, vegetables; goats **EXP:** reexports, hides and skins, coffee (in transit)

Eritrea

STATE OF ERITREA

AREA 121,144 sq km (46,774 sq mi)
POPULATION 4,670,000
CAPITAL Asmara 556,000
RELIGION Muslim, Coptic Christian, Roman Catholic, Protestant
LANGUAGE Afar, Arabic, Tigre, Kunama, Tigrinya, other Cushitic languages
LITERACY 59%
LIFE EXPECTANCY 58 years
GDP PER CAPITA $187
ECONOMY **IND:** food processing, beverages, clothing and textiles, salt **AGR:** sorghum, lentils, vegetables, corn; livestock; fish **EXP:** livestock, sorghum, textiles, food

Ethiopia

FEDERAL DEMOCRATIC REP. OF ETHIOPIA

AREA 1,133,380 sq km (437,600 sq mi)
POPULATION 77,431,000
CAPITAL Addis Ababa 2,723,000
RELIGION Muslim, Ethiopian Orthodox, animist
LANGUAGE Amharic, Oromigna, Tigrinya, Guaragigna, Somali
LITERACY 43%
LIFE EXPECTANCY 48 years
GDP PER CAPITA $106
ECONOMY **IND:** food processing, beverages, textiles, chemicals **AGR:** cereals, pulses, coffee, oilseed; hides **EXP:** coffee, qat, gold, leather products

Kenya

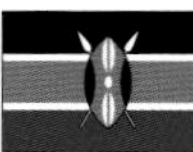

REPUBLIC OF KENYA

AREA 580,367 sq km (224,081 sq mi)
POPULATION 33,830,000
CAPITAL Nairobi 2,575,000
RELIGION Protestant, Roman Catholic, indigenous beliefs, Muslim
LANGUAGE English (official), Kiswahili (official), many indigenous languages
LITERACY 85%
LIFE EXPECTANCY 47 years
GDP PER CAPITA $443
ECONOMY **IND:** small-scale consumer goods (plastic, furniture), agricultural products, oil refining, aluminum **AGR:** tea, coffee, corn, wheat; dairy products **EXP:** tea, horticultural products, coffee, petroleum products

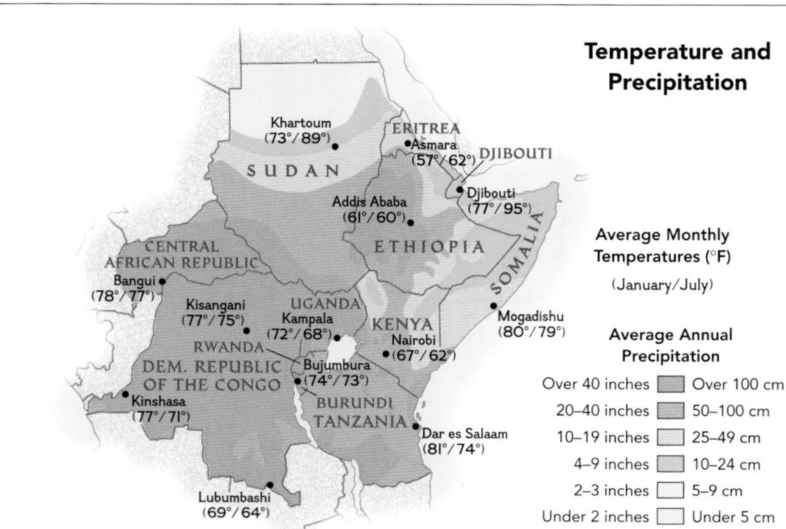
Temperature and Precipitation
Khartoum (73°/89°)
SUDAN
ERITREA
Asmara (57°/62°)
DJIBOUTI
Djibouti (77°/95°)
Addis Ababa (61°/60°)
ETHIOPIA
SOMALIA
CENTRAL AFRICAN REPUBLIC
Bangui (78°/77°)
Kisangani (77°/75°)
UGANDA
Kampala (72°/68°)
KENYA
Nairobi (67°/62°)
Mogadishu (80°/79°)
RWANDA
DEM. REPUBLIC OF THE CONGO
Bujumbura (74°/73°)
BURUNDI
TANZANIA
Kinshasa (77°/71°)
Dar es Salaam (81°/74°)
Lubumbashi (69°/64°)
Average Monthly Temperatures (°F)
(January/July)
Average Annual Precipitation
Over 40 inches Over 100 cm
20–40 inches 50–100 cm
10–19 inches 25–49 cm
4–9 inches 10–24 cm
2–3 inches 5–9 cm
Under 2 inches Under 5 cm

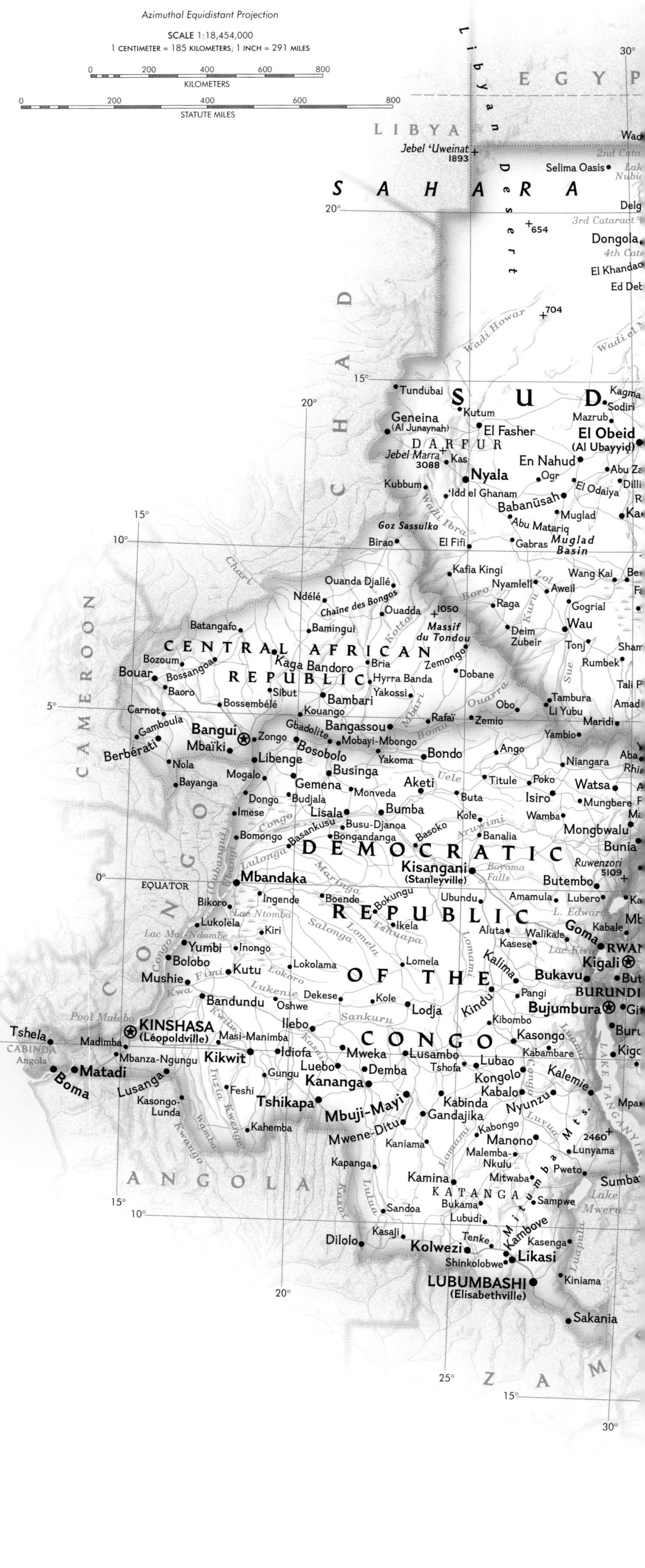

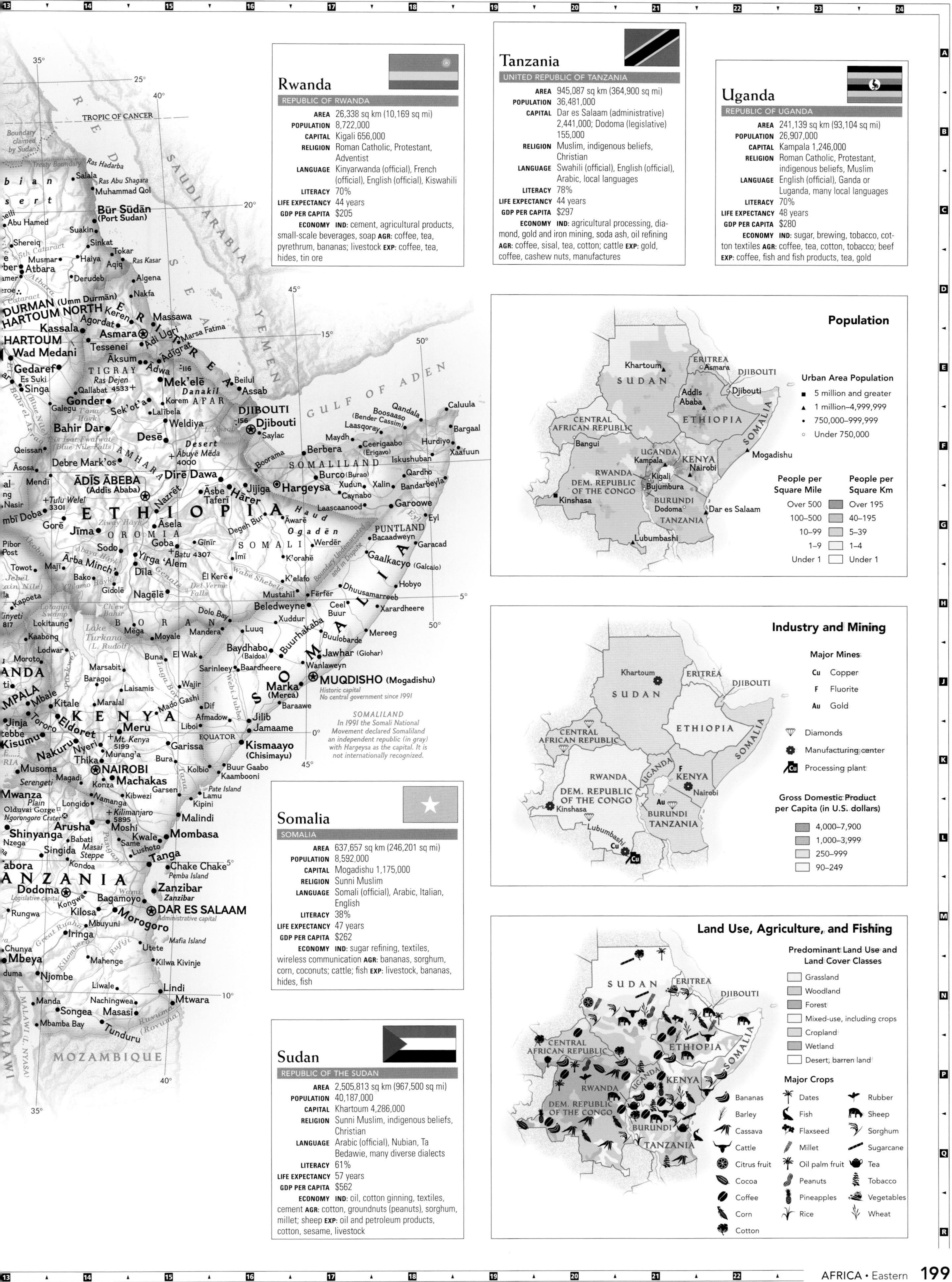

Rwanda
REPUBLIC OF RWANDA
AREA 26,338 sq km (10,169 sq mi)
POPULATION 8,722,000
CAPITAL Kigali 656,000
RELIGION Roman Catholic, Protestant, Adventist
LANGUAGE Kinyarwanda (official), French (official), English (official), Kiswahili
LITERACY 70%
LIFE EXPECTANCY 44 years
GDP PER CAPITA $205
ECONOMY IND: cement, agricultural products, small-scale beverages, soap AGR: coffee, tea, pyrethrum, bananas; livestock EXP: coffee, tea, hides, tin ore

Tanzania
UNITED REPUBLIC OF TANZANIA
AREA 945,087 sq km (364,900 sq mi)
POPULATION 36,481,000
CAPITAL Dar es Salaam (administrative) 2,441,000; Dodoma (legislative) 155,000
RELIGION Muslim, indigenous beliefs, Christian
LANGUAGE Swahili (official), English (official), Arabic, local languages
LITERACY 78%
LIFE EXPECTANCY 44 years
GDP PER CAPITA $297
ECONOMY IND: agricultural processing, diamond, gold and iron mining, soda ash, oil refining AGR: coffee, sisal, tea, cotton; cattle EXP: gold, coffee, cashew nuts, manufactures

Uganda
REPUBLIC OF UGANDA
AREA 241,139 sq km (93,104 sq mi)
POPULATION 26,907,000
CAPITAL Kampala 1,246,000
RELIGION Roman Catholic, Protestant, indigenous beliefs, Muslim
LANGUAGE English (official), Ganda or Luganda, many local languages
LITERACY 70%
LIFE EXPECTANCY 48 years
GDP PER CAPITA $280
ECONOMY IND: sugar, brewing, tobacco, cotton textiles AGR: coffee, tea, cotton, tobacco; beef EXP: coffee, fish and fish products, tea, gold

Somalia
SOMALIA
AREA 637,657 sq km (246,201 sq mi)
POPULATION 8,592,000
CAPITAL Mogadishu 1,175,000
RELIGION Sunni Muslim
LANGUAGE Somali (official), Arabic, Italian, English
LITERACY 38%
LIFE EXPECTANCY 47 years
GDP PER CAPITA $262
ECONOMY IND: sugar refining, textiles, wireless communication AGR: bananas, sorghum, corn, coconuts; cattle; fish EXP: livestock, bananas, hides, fish

Sudan
REPUBLIC OF THE SUDAN
AREA 2,505,813 sq km (967,500 sq mi)
POPULATION 40,187,000
CAPITAL Khartoum 4,286,000
RELIGION Sunni Muslim, indigenous beliefs, Christian
LANGUAGE Arabic (official), Nubian, Ta Bedawie, many diverse dialects
LITERACY 61%
LIFE EXPECTANCY 57 years
GDP PER CAPITA $562
ECONOMY IND: oil, cotton ginning, textiles, cement AGR: cotton, groundnuts (peanuts), sorghum, millet; sheep EXP: oil and petroleum products, cotton, sesame, livestock

SOMALILAND
In 1991 the Somali National Movement declared Somaliland an independent republic (in gray) with Hargeysa as the capital. It is not internationally recognized.
MUQDISHO (Mogadishu)
Historic capital
No central government since 1991

Population
Urban Area Population
5 million and greater
1 million–4,999,999
750,000–999,999
Under 750,000
People per Square Mile
Over 500
100–500
10–99
1–9
Under 1
People per Square Km
Over 195
40–195
5–39
1–4
Under 1

Industry and Mining
Major Mines
Cu Copper
F Fluorite
Au Gold
Diamonds
Manufacturing center
Processing plant
Gross Domestic Product per Capita (in U.S. dollars)
4,000–7,900
1,000–3,999
250–999
90–249

Land Use, Agriculture, and Fishing
Predominant Land Use and Land Cover Classes
Grassland
Woodland
Forest
Mixed-use, including crops
Cropland
Wetland
Desert, barren land
Major Crops
Bananas
Barley
Cassava
Cattle
Citrus fruit
Cocoa
Coffee
Corn
Cotton
Dates
Fish
Flaxseed
Millet
Oil palm fruit
Peanuts
Pineapples
Rice
Rubber
Sheep
Sorghum
Sugarcane
Tea
Tobacco
Vegetables
Wheat

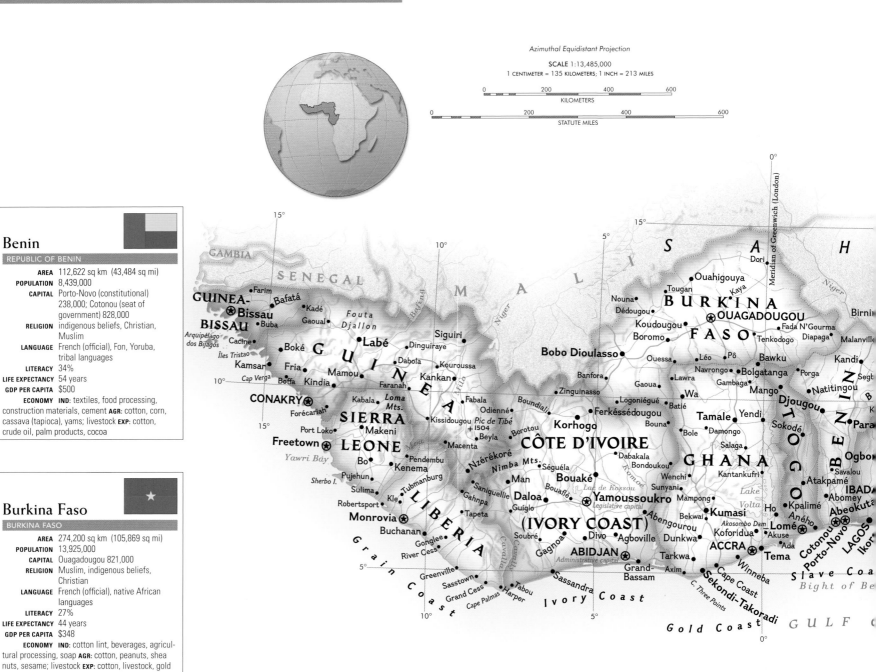

Azimuthal Equidistant Projection
SCALE 1:13,485,000
1 CENTIMETER = 135 KILOMETERS; 1 INCH = 213 MILES
0 200 400 600
KILOMETERS
0 200 400 600
STATUTE MILES
GAMBIA
SENEGAL
GUINEA-BISSAU
Bissau
Farim
Bafatá
Kadé
Gaoual
Buba
Fouta Djallon
Arquipélago dos Bijagós
Cacine
Îles Tristao
Labé
Boké
GUINEA
Siguiri
Dinguiraye
Kamsar
Fria
Mamou
Dabola
Kouroussa
Cap Verga
Boffa
Kindia
Faranah
Kankan
CONAKRY
Kabala
Loma Mts.
Forécariah
SIERRA LEONE
Makeni
Port Loko
Freetown
Kissidougou
Pic de Tibé
1504
Yawri Bay
Sherbo I.
Bo
Kenema
Pendembu
Macenta
Pujehun
Sulima
Robertsport
Monrovia
Buchanan
LIBERIA
Tubmanburg
Saniquellie
Gahnpa
Tapeta
Nzérékoré
Nimba Mts.
Kle
River Cess
Greenville
Sasstown
Grand Cess
Cape Palmas
Harper
Tabou
Grain Coast
MALI
Niger
Bafing
Bobo Dioulasso
Banfora
Zinguinasso
Fabala
Odienné
Boundiali
Korhogo
Ferkéssédougou
Beyla
Borotou
CÔTE D'IVOIRE
(IVORY COAST)
Séguéla
Man
Bouaké
Daloa
Bouaflé
Guiglo
Lac de Kossou
Yamoussoukro
Legislative capital
Soubré
Divo
Gagnoa
Agboville
ABIDJAN
Administrative capital
Grand-Bassam
Sassandra
Cavally
Ivory Coast
Dabakala
Bondoukou
Kaya
Ouahigouya
Dori
Tougan
Nouna
Dédougou
BURKINA FASO
OUAGADOUGOU
Koudougou
Boromo
Fada N'Gourma
Tenkodogo
Diapaga
Ouessa
Léo
Pô
Bawku
Navrongo
Bolgatanga
Gaoua
Lawra
Wa
Gambaga
Logoniégué
Batié
Bouna
Tamale
Yendi
Bole
Damongo
Salaga
GHANA
Wenchi
Kintampo
Sunyani
Mampong
Kumasi
Bekwai
Akosombo Dam
Lake Volta
Koforidua
Dunkwa
Abengourou
ACCRA
Tema
Tarkwa
Axim
Cape Coast
Winneba
Sekondi-Takoradi
C. Three Points
Gold Coast
Meridian of Greenwich (London)
Ho
Kpalimé
Lomé
Aného
Akuse
Ada
Mango
Sokodé
Djougou
TOGO
Kantankufri
Atakpamé
Savalou
Natitingou
Porga
Kandi
BENIN
Cotonou
Porto-Novo
LAGOS
Abeokuta
Abomey
Slave Coast
Bight of Benin
GULF
Birni
Malanville
Niger
SAHEL

Benin

REPUBLIC OF BENIN

AREA 112,622 sq km (43,484 sq mi)
POPULATION 8,439,000
CAPITAL Porto-Novo (constitutional) 238,000; Cotonou (seat of government) 828,000
RELIGION indigenous beliefs, Christian, Muslim
LANGUAGE French (official), Fon, Yoruba, tribal languages
LITERACY 34%
LIFE EXPECTANCY 54 years
GDP PER CAPITA $500
ECONOMY **IND:** textiles, food processing, construction materials, cement **AGR:** cotton, corn, cassava (tapioca), yams; livestock **EXP:** cotton, crude oil, palm products, cocoa

Burkina Faso

BURKINA FASO

AREA 274,200 sq km (105,869 sq mi)
POPULATION 13,925,000
CAPITAL Ouagadougou 821,000
RELIGION Muslim, indigenous beliefs, Christian
LANGUAGE French (official), native African languages
LITERACY 27%
LIFE EXPECTANCY 44 years
GDP PER CAPITA $348
ECONOMY **IND:** cotton lint, beverages, agricultural processing, soap **AGR:** cotton, peanuts, shea nuts, sesame; livestock **EXP:** cotton, livestock, gold

Cameroon

REPUBLIC OF CAMEROON

AREA 475,442 sq km (183,569 sq mi)
POPULATION 16,380,000
CAPITAL Yaoundé 1,616,000
RELIGION indigenous beliefs, Christian, Muslim
LANGUAGE 24 major African language groups, English (official), French (official)
LITERACY 79%
LIFE EXPECTANCY 48 years
GDP PER CAPITA $1,007
ECONOMY **IND:** petroleum production and refining, aluminum production, food processing, light consumer goods **AGR:** coffee, cocoa, cotton, rubber; livestock; timber **EXP:** crude oil and petroleum products, lumber, cocoa beans, aluminum

Congo

REPUBLIC OF THE CONGO

AREA 342,000 sq km (132,047 sq mi)
POPULATION 3,999,000
CAPITAL Brazzaville 1,080,000
RELIGION Christian, animist
LANGUAGE French (official), Lingala, Monokutuba, local languages
LITERACY 84%
LIFE EXPECTANCY 52 years
GDP PER CAPITA $1,129
ECONOMY **IND:** petroleum extraction, cement, lumber, brewing **AGR:** cassava (tapioca), sugar, rice, corn; forest products **EXP:** petroleum, lumber, plywood, sugar

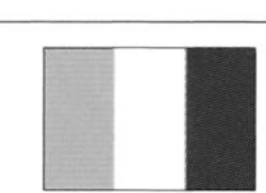

Côte d'Ivoire (Ivory Coast)

REPUBLIC OF CÔTE D'IVOIRE

AREA 322,462 sq km (124,503 sq mi)
POPULATION 18,154,000
CAPITAL Abidjan (administrative) 3,337,000; Yamoussoukro 416,000
RELIGION Muslim, indigenous beliefs, Christian
LANGUAGE French (official), Dioula, 60 native dialects
LITERACY 51%
LIFE EXPECTANCY 47 years
GDP PER CAPITA $908
ECONOMY **IND:** foodstuffs, beverages, wood products, oil refining **AGR:** coffee, cocoa beans, bananas, palm kernels; timber **EXP:** cocoa, coffee, timber, petroleum

Equatorial Guinea

REPUBLIC OF EQUATORIAL GUINEA

AREA 28,051 sq km (10,831 sq mi)
POPULATION 504,000
CAPITAL Malabo 95,000
RELIGION Roman Catholic, pagan practices
LANGUAGE Spanish (official), French (official), pidgin English, Fang, Bubi, Ibo
LITERACY 86%
LIFE EXPECTANCY 45 years
GDP PER CAPITA $7,845
ECONOMY **IND:** petroleum, fishing, sawmilling, natural gas **AGR:** coffee, cocoa, rice, yams; livestock; timber **EXP:** petroleum, methanol, timber, cocoa

Gabon

GABONESE REPUBLIC

AREA 267,667 sq km (103,347 sq mi)
POPULATION 1,384,000
CAPITAL Libreville 611,000
RELIGION Christian, animist
LANGUAGE French (official), Fang, Myene, Nzebi, Bapounou/Eschira
LITERACY 63%
LIFE EXPECTANCY 56 years
GDP PER CAPITA $4,710
ECONOMY **IND:** petroleum extraction and refining, manganese and gold mining, chemicals, ship repair **AGR:** cocoa, coffee, sugar, palm oil; okoume (a tropical softwood); fish **EXP:** crude oil, timber, manganese, uranium

Ghana

REPUBLIC OF GHANA

AREA 238,537 sq km (92,100 sq mi)
POPULATION 22,019,000
CAPITAL Accra 1,847,000
RELIGION Christian, indigenous beliefs, Muslim
LANGUAGE English (official), Akan, Moshi-Dagomba, Ewe, Ga
LITERACY 75%
LIFE EXPECTANCY 58 years
GDP PER CAPITA $403
ECONOMY **IND:** mining, lumbering, light manufacturing, aluminum smelting **AGR:** cocoa, rice, coffee, cassava (tapioca); timber **EXP:** gold, cocoa, timber, tuna

Guinea

REPUBLIC OF GUINEA

AREA 245,857 sq km (94,926 sq mi)
POPULATION 9,453,000
CAPITAL Conakry 1,366,000
RELIGION Muslim, Christian, indigenous beliefs
LANGUAGE French (official), ethnic languages
LITERACY 36%
LIFE EXPECTANCY 49 years
GDP PER CAPITA $421
ECONOMY **IND:** bauxite, gold, diamonds, alumina refining **AGR:** rice, coffee, pineapples, palm kernels; cattle; timber **EXP:** bauxite, alumina, gold, diamonds

Guinea-Bissau

REPUBLIC OF GUINEA-BISSAU

AREA 36,125 sq km (13,948 sq mi)
POPULATION 1,586,000
CAPITAL Bissau 336,000
RELIGION indigenous beliefs, Muslim
LANGUAGE Portuguese (official), Crioulo, African languages
LITERACY 42%
LIFE EXPECTANCY 44 years
GDP PER CAPITA $176
ECONOMY **IND:** agricultural products processing, beer, soft drinks **AGR:** rice, corn, beans, cassava (tapioca); timber; fish **EXP:** cashew nuts, shrimp, peanuts, palm kernels

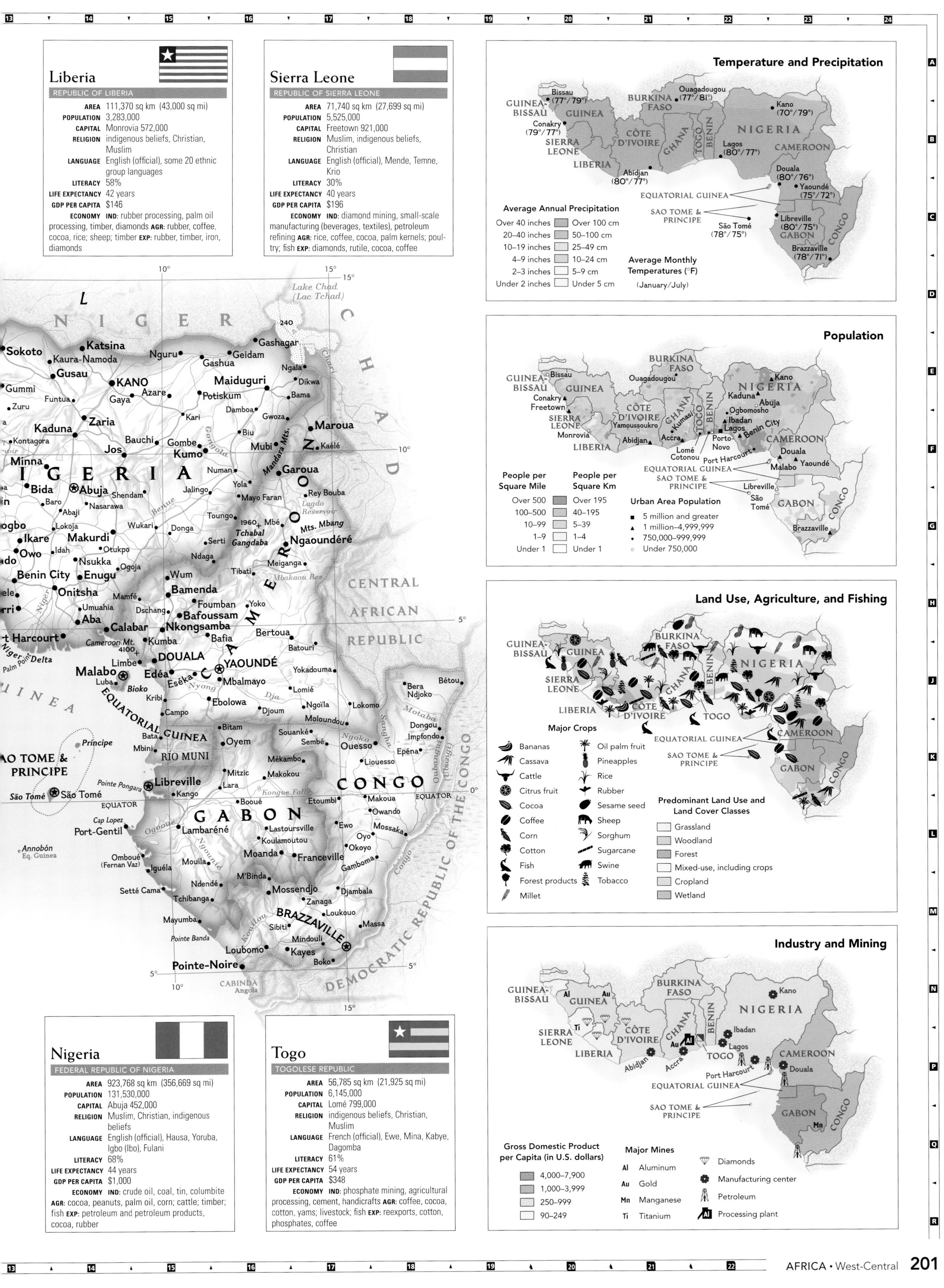
Temperature and Precipitation
Average Annual Precipitation
Over 40 inches — Over 100 cm
20–40 inches — 50–100 cm
10–19 inches — 25–49 cm
4–9 inches — 10–24 cm
2–3 inches — 5–9 cm
Under 2 inches — Under 5 cm
Average Monthly Temperatures (°F)
(January/July)
Population
People per Square Mile
Over 500
100–500
10–99
1–9
Under 1
People per Square Km
Over 195
40–195
5–39
1–4
Under 1
Urban Area Population
5 million and greater
1 million–4,999,999
750,000–999,999
Under 750,000
Land Use, Agriculture, and Fishing
Major Crops
Bananas
Cassava
Cattle
Citrus fruit
Cocoa
Coffee
Corn
Cotton
Fish
Forest products
Millet
Oil palm fruit
Pineapples
Rice
Rubber
Sesame seed
Sheep
Sorghum
Sugarcane
Swine
Tobacco
Predominant Land Use and Land Cover Classes
Grassland
Woodland
Forest
Mixed-use, including crops
Cropland
Wetland
Industry and Mining
Gross Domestic Product per Capita (in U.S. dollars)
4,000–7,900
1,000–3,999
250–999
90–249
Major Mines
Al Aluminum
Au Gold
Mn Manganese
Ti Titanium
Diamonds
Manufacturing center
Petroleum
Processing plant

Liberia

REPUBLIC OF LIBERIA

AREA 111,370 sq km (43,000 sq mi)
POPULATION 3,283,000
CAPITAL Monrovia 572,000
RELIGION indigenous beliefs, Christian, Muslim
LANGUAGE English (official), some 20 ethnic group languages
LITERACY 58%
LIFE EXPECTANCY 42 years
GDP PER CAPITA $146
ECONOMY **IND:** rubber processing, palm oil processing, timber, diamonds **AGR:** rubber, coffee, cocoa, rice; sheep; timber **EXP:** rubber, timber, iron, diamonds

Sierra Leone

REPUBLIC OF SIERRA LEONE

AREA 71,740 sq km (27,699 sq mi)
POPULATION 5,525,000
CAPITAL Freetown 921,000
RELIGION Muslim, indigenous beliefs, Christian
LANGUAGE English (official), Mende, Temne, Krio
LITERACY 30%
LIFE EXPECTANCY 40 years
GDP PER CAPITA $196
ECONOMY **IND:** diamond mining, small-scale manufacturing (beverages, textiles), petroleum refining **AGR:** rice, coffee, cocoa, palm kernels; poultry; fish **EXP:** diamonds, rutile, cocoa, coffee

Nigeria

FEDERAL REPUBLIC OF NIGERIA

AREA 923,768 sq km (356,669 sq mi)
POPULATION 131,530,000
CAPITAL Abuja 452,000
RELIGION Muslim, Christian, indigenous beliefs
LANGUAGE English (official), Hausa, Yoruba, Igbo (Ibo), Fulani
LITERACY 68%
LIFE EXPECTANCY 44 years
GDP PER CAPITA $1,000
ECONOMY **IND:** crude oil, coal, tin, columbite **AGR:** cocoa, peanuts, palm oil, corn; cattle; timber; fish **EXP:** petroleum and petroleum products, cocoa, rubber

Togo

TOGOLESE REPUBLIC

AREA 56,785 sq km (21,925 sq mi)
POPULATION 6,145,000
CAPITAL Lomé 799,000
RELIGION indigenous beliefs, Christian, Muslim
LANGUAGE French (official), Ewe, Mina, Kabye, Dagomba
LITERACY 61%
LIFE EXPECTANCY 54 years
GDP PER CAPITA $348
ECONOMY **IND:** phosphate mining, agricultural processing, cement, handicrafts **AGR:** coffee, cocoa, cotton, yams; livestock; fish **EXP:** reexports, cotton, phosphates, coffee

Angola

REPUBLIC OF ANGOLA

AREA 1,246,700 sq km (481,354 sq mi)
POPULATION 15,375,000
CAPITAL Luanda 2,623,000
RELIGION indigenous beliefs, Roman Catholic, Protestant
LANGUAGE Portuguese (official), Bantu and other African languages
LITERACY 67%
LIFE EXPECTANCY 40 years
GDP PER CAPITA $1,309
ECONOMY **IND:** petroleum, diamonds, iron ore, phosphates **AGR:** bananas, sugarcane, coffee, sisal; livestock; forest products; fish **EXP:** crude oil, diamonds, refined petroleum products, gas

Botswana

REPUBLIC OF BOTSWANA

AREA 581,730 sq km (224,607 sq mi)
POPULATION 1,640,000
CAPITAL Gaborone 199,000
RELIGION Christian, Badimo
LANGUAGE Setswana, Kalanga, Sekgalagadi, English (official)
LITERACY 80%
LIFE EXPECTANCY 35 years
GDP PER CAPITA $4,771
ECONOMY **IND:** diamonds, copper, nickel, salt **AGR:** livestock, sorghum, maize, millet **EXP:** diamonds, copper, nickel, soda ash

Lesotho

KINGDOM OF LESOTHO

AREA 30,355 sq km (11,720 sq mi)
POPULATION 1,804,000
CAPITAL Maseru 170,000
RELIGION Christian, indigenous beliefs
LANGUAGE Sesotho, English (official), Zulu, Xhosa
LITERACY 85%
LIFE EXPECTANCY 35 years
GDP PER CAPITA $764
ECONOMY **IND:** food, beverages, textiles, apparel assembly **AGR:** corn, wheat, pulses, sorghum; livestock **EXP:** clothing, footwear, road vehicles, wool and mohair

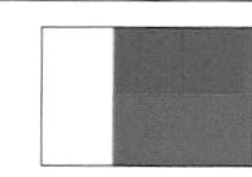

Madagascar

REPUBLIC OF MADAGASCAR

AREA 587,041 sq km (226,658 sq mi)
POPULATION 17,308,000
CAPITAL Antananarivo 1,678,000
RELIGION indigenous beliefs, Christian, Muslim
LANGUAGE French (official), Malagasy (official)
LITERACY 69%
LIFE EXPECTANCY 55 years
GDP PER CAPITA $222
ECONOMY **IND:** meat processing, soap, breweries, tanneries **AGR:** coffee, vanilla, sugarcane, cloves; livestock products **EXP:** coffee, vanilla, shellfish, sugar

Malawi

REPUBLIC OF MALAWI

AREA 118,484 sq km (45,747 sq mi)
POPULATION 12,341,000
CAPITAL Lilongwe 587,000
RELIGION Christian, Muslim
LANGUAGE Chichewa (official), Chinyanja, Chiyao, Chitumbuka
LITERACY 63%
LIFE EXPECTANCY 45 years
GDP PER CAPITA $165
ECONOMY **IND:** tobacco, tea, sugar, sawmill products **AGR:** tobacco, sugarcane, cotton, tea; cattle **EXP:** tobacco, tea, sugar, cotton

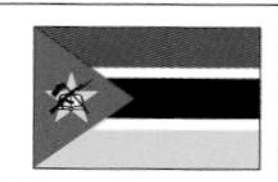

Mozambique

REPUBLIC OF MOZAMBIQUE

AREA 799,380 sq km (308,642 sq mi)
POPULATION 19,420,000
CAPITAL Maputo 1,221,000
RELIGION Catholic, Zionist Christian, Muslim
LANGUAGE Emakhuwa, Xichangana, Portuguese (official), Elomwe, Cisena, Echuwabo
LITERACY 48%
LIFE EXPECTANCY 42 years
GDP PER CAPITA $328
ECONOMY **IND:** food, beverages, chemicals (fertilizer, soap, paints), aluminum **AGR:** cotton, cashew nuts, sugarcane, tea; beef **EXP:** aluminum, prawns, cashews, cotton

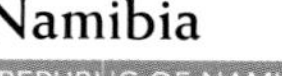

Namibia

REPUBLIC OF NAMIBIA

AREA 824,292 sq km (318,261 sq mi)
POPULATION 2,031,000
CAPITAL Windhoek 237,000
RELIGION Lutheran, other Christian, indigenous beliefs
LANGUAGE Afrikaans, German, English (official), indigenous languages
LITERACY 84%
LIFE EXPECTANCY 46 years
GDP PER CAPITA $2,661
ECONOMY **IND:** meatpacking, fish processing, dairy products, mining (diamonds, lead, zinc) **AGR:** millet, sorghum, peanuts; livestock; fish **EXP:** diamonds, copper, gold, zinc

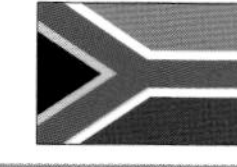

South Africa

REPUBLIC OF SOUTH AFRICA

AREA 1,219,090 sq km (470,693 sq mi)
POPULATION 46,923,000
CAPITAL Pretoria (administrative) 1,209,000; Bloemfontein (judicial) 381,000; Cape Town (legislative) 2,967,000
RELIGION Zion Christian, Pentecostal, Catholic, Methodist, Dutch Reformed
LANGUAGE IsiZulu, IsiXhosa, Afrikaans, Sepedi, English, Setswana
LITERACY 86%
LIFE EXPECTANCY 52 years
GDP PER CAPITA $4,507
ECONOMY **IND:** mining (platinum, gold, chromium), automobile assembly, metalworking, machinery **AGR:** corn, wheat, sugarcane, fruits; beef **EXP:** gold, diamonds, platinum, other metals and minerals

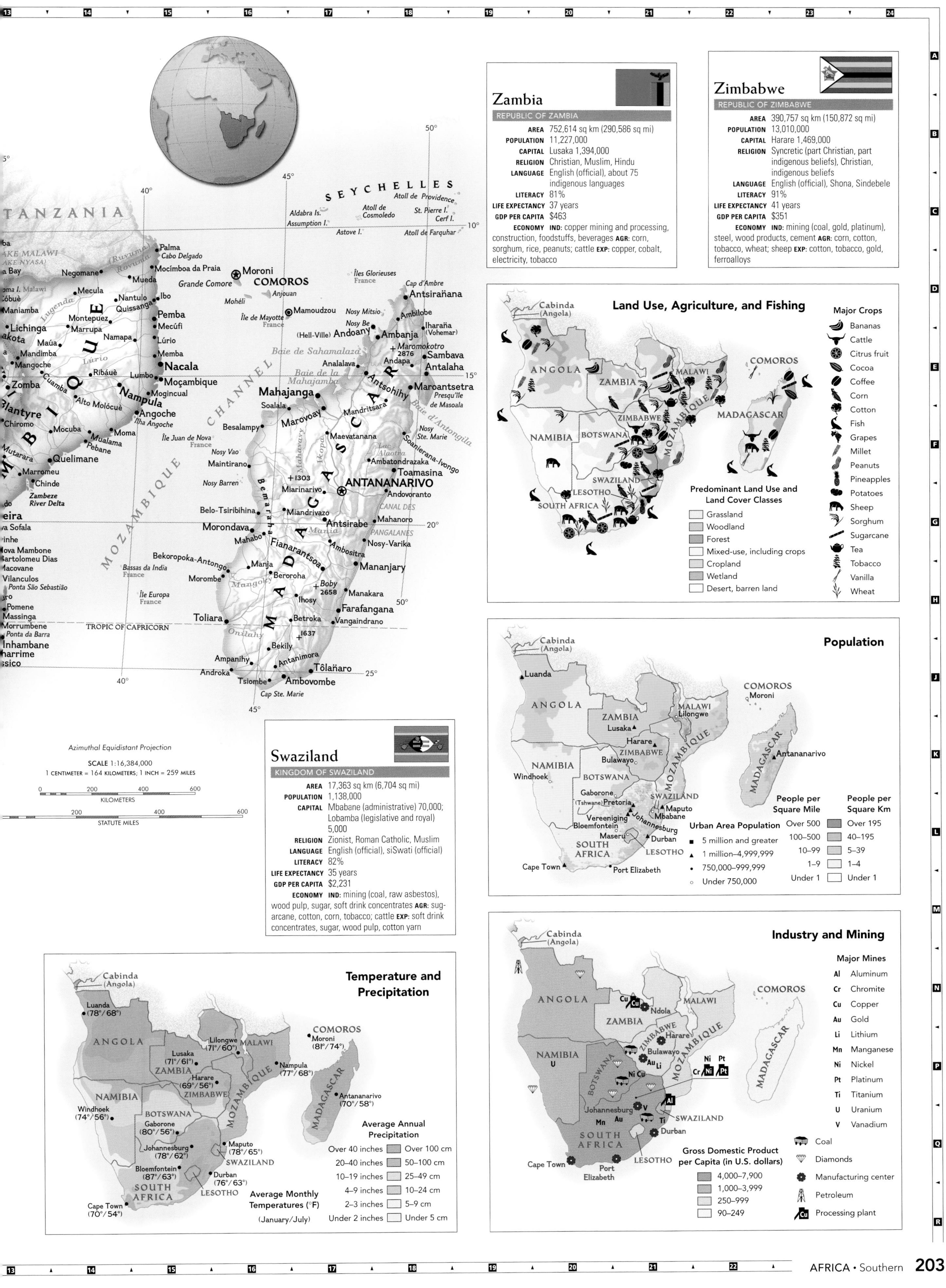

SEYCHELLES
Aldabra Is.
Assumption I.
Atoll de Cosmoledo
Astove I.
Atoll de Providence
St. Pierre I.
Cerf I.
Atoll de Farquhar
TANZANIA
COMOROS
Moroni
Grande Comore
Anjouan
Mohéli
Mamoudzou
Île de Mayotte
France
Îles Glorieuses
France
Cap d'Ambre
Antsirañana
Ambilobe
Iharaña (Vohemar)
Nosy Mitsio
Nosy Be
(Hell-Ville) Andoany
Ambanja
Maromokotro 2876
Sambava
Andapa
Antalaha
Baie de Sahamalaza
Analalava
Baie de la Mahajamba
Antsohihy
Maroantsetra
Presqu'île de Masoala
Baie d'Antongila
Mahajanga
Soalala
Marovoay
Mandritsara
Besalampy
Maevatanana
Nosy Sté. Marie
Soanierana-Ivongo
Île Juan de Nova
France
Nosy Vao
Maintirano
Lac Alaotra
Ambatondrazaka
Toamasina
Nosy Barren
Bemaraha
1303
Miarinarivo
ANTANANARIVO
Andovoranto
CANAL DES PANGALANES
Belo-Tsiribihina
Miandrivazo
Morondava
Antsirabe
Mahanoro
Mahabo
Mania
Fianarantsoa
Ambositra
Nosy-Varika
Bekoropoka-Antongo
Manja
Mananjary
Bassas da India
France
Morombe
Beroroha
Mangoky
Boby 2658
Manakara
Île Europa
France
Ihosy
Farafangana
Toliara
Betroka
Vangaindrano
TROPIC OF CAPRICORN
Onilahy
1637
Bekily
Ampanihy
Antanimora
Tôlañaro
Androka
Tsiombe
Ambovombe
Cap Ste. Marie
MADAGASCAR
MOZAMBIQUE CHANNEL
MOZAMBIQUE
Palma
Cabo Delgado
Mocímboa da Praia
Mueda
Negomane
Lake Malawi (Lake Nyasa)
Ruvuma
Rovuma
Mecula
Nantulo
Ibo
Quissanga
Lugenda
Pemba
Montepuez
Marrupa
Mecúfi
Lichinga
Maúa
Namapa
Lúrio
Memba
Mandimba
Mangoche
Lurio
Nacala
Ribáuè
Lumbo
Moçambique
Zomba
Cuamba
Nampula
Mogincual
Alto Molócuè
Angoche
Ilha Angoche
Blantyre
Chiromo
Mocuba
Moma
Mualama
Pebane
Quelimane
Marromeu
Chinde
Zambeze River Delta
Sofala
Inhambane
Massinga
Vilanculos
Ponta São Sebastião
Pomene
Morrumbene
Ponta da Barra
Azimuthal Equidistant Projection
SCALE 1:16,384,000
1 CENTIMETER = 164 KILOMETERS; 1 INCH = 259 MILES
0 200 400 600
KILOMETERS
200 400 600
STATUTE MILES

Zambia
REPUBLIC OF ZAMBIA
AREA 752,614 sq km (290,586 sq mi)
POPULATION 11,227,000
CAPITAL Lusaka 1,394,000
RELIGION Christian, Muslim, Hindu
LANGUAGE English (official), about 75 indigenous languages
LITERACY 81%
LIFE EXPECTANCY 37 years
GDP PER CAPITA $463
ECONOMY IND: copper mining and processing, construction, foodstuffs, beverages AGR: corn, sorghum, rice, peanuts; cattle EXP: copper, cobalt, electricity, tobacco

Zimbabwe
REPUBLIC OF ZIMBABWE
AREA 390,757 sq km (150,872 sq mi)
POPULATION 13,010,000
CAPITAL Harare 1,469,000
RELIGION Syncretic (part Christian, part indigenous beliefs), Christian, indigenous beliefs
LANGUAGE English (official), Shona, Sindebele
LITERACY 91%
LIFE EXPECTANCY 41 years
GDP PER CAPITA $351
ECONOMY IND: mining (coal, gold, platinum), steel, wood products, cement AGR: corn, cotton, tobacco, wheat; sheep EXP: cotton, tobacco, gold, ferroalloys

Swaziland
KINGDOM OF SWAZILAND
AREA 17,363 sq km (6,704 sq mi)
POPULATION 1,138,000
CAPITAL Mbabane (administrative) 70,000; Lobamba (legislative and royal) 5,000
RELIGION Zionist, Roman Catholic, Muslim
LANGUAGE English (official), siSwati (official)
LITERACY 82%
LIFE EXPECTANCY 35 years
GDP PER CAPITA $2,231
ECONOMY IND: mining (coal, raw asbestos), wood pulp, sugar, soft drink concentrates AGR: sugarcane, cotton, corn, tobacco; cattle EXP: soft drink concentrates, sugar, wood pulp, cotton yarn

Land Use, Agriculture, and Fishing
Cabinda (Angola)
ANGOLA
ZAMBIA
MALAWI
COMOROS
ZIMBABWE
MOZAMBIQUE
MADAGASCAR
NAMIBIA
BOTSWANA
SWAZILAND
LESOTHO
SOUTH AFRICA
Major Crops
Bananas
Cattle
Citrus fruit
Cocoa
Coffee
Corn
Cotton
Fish
Grapes
Millet
Peanuts
Pineapples
Potatoes
Sheep
Sorghum
Sugarcane
Tea
Tobacco
Vanilla
Wheat
Predominant Land Use and Land Cover Classes
Grassland
Woodland
Forest
Mixed-use, including crops
Cropland
Wetland
Desert, barren land

Population
Cabinda (Angola)
Luanda
ANGOLA
ZAMBIA
Lusaka
MALAWI
Lilongwe
COMOROS
Moroni
Harare
ZIMBABWE
Bulawayo
MOZAMBIQUE
MADAGASCAR
Antananarivo
NAMIBIA
Windhoek
BOTSWANA
Gaborone
(Tshwane) Pretoria
SWAZILAND
Maputo
Mbabane
Vereeniging
Johannesburg
Bloemfontein
Maseru
Durban
SOUTH AFRICA
LESOTHO
Cape Town
Port Elizabeth
Urban Area Population
5 million and greater
1 million–4,999,999
750,000–999,999
Under 750,000
People per Square Mile
Over 500
100–500
10–99
1–9
Under 1
People per Square Km
Over 195
40–195
5–39
1–4
Under 1

Temperature and Precipitation
Cabinda (Angola)
Luanda (78°/68°)
ANGOLA
Lilongwe (71°/60°)
MALAWI
COMOROS
Moroni (81°/74°)
Lusaka (71°/61°)
ZAMBIA
Nampula (77°/68°)
Harare (69°/56°)
ZIMBABWE
MOZAMBIQUE
MADAGASCAR
Antananarivo (70°/58°)
NAMIBIA
Windhoek (74°/56°)
BOTSWANA
Gaborone (80°/56°)
Johannesburg (78°/62°)
Maputo (78°/65°)
SWAZILAND
Bloemfontein (87°/63°)
Durban (76°/63°)
SOUTH AFRICA
LESOTHO
Cape Town (70°/54°)
Average Monthly Temperatures (°F) (January/July)
Average Annual Precipitation
Over 40 inches | Over 100 cm
20–40 inches | 50–100 cm
10–19 inches | 25–49 cm
4–9 inches | 10–24 cm
2–3 inches | 5–9 cm
Under 2 inches | Under 5 cm

Industry and Mining
Cabinda (Angola)
ANGOLA
ZAMBIA
Ndola
MALAWI
COMOROS
ZIMBABWE
Harare
Bulawayo
MOZAMBIQUE
MADAGASCAR
NAMIBIA
BOTSWANA
Johannesburg
SWAZILAND
Durban
SOUTH AFRICA
LESOTHO
Cape Town
Port Elizabeth
Major Mines
Al Aluminum
Cr Chromite
Cu Copper
Au Gold
Li Lithium
Mn Manganese
Ni Nickel
Pt Platinum
Ti Titanium
U Uranium
V Vanadium
Coal
Diamonds
Manufacturing center
Petroleum
Processing plant
Gross Domestic Product per Capita (in U.S. dollars)
4,000–7,900
1,000–3,999
250–999
90–249

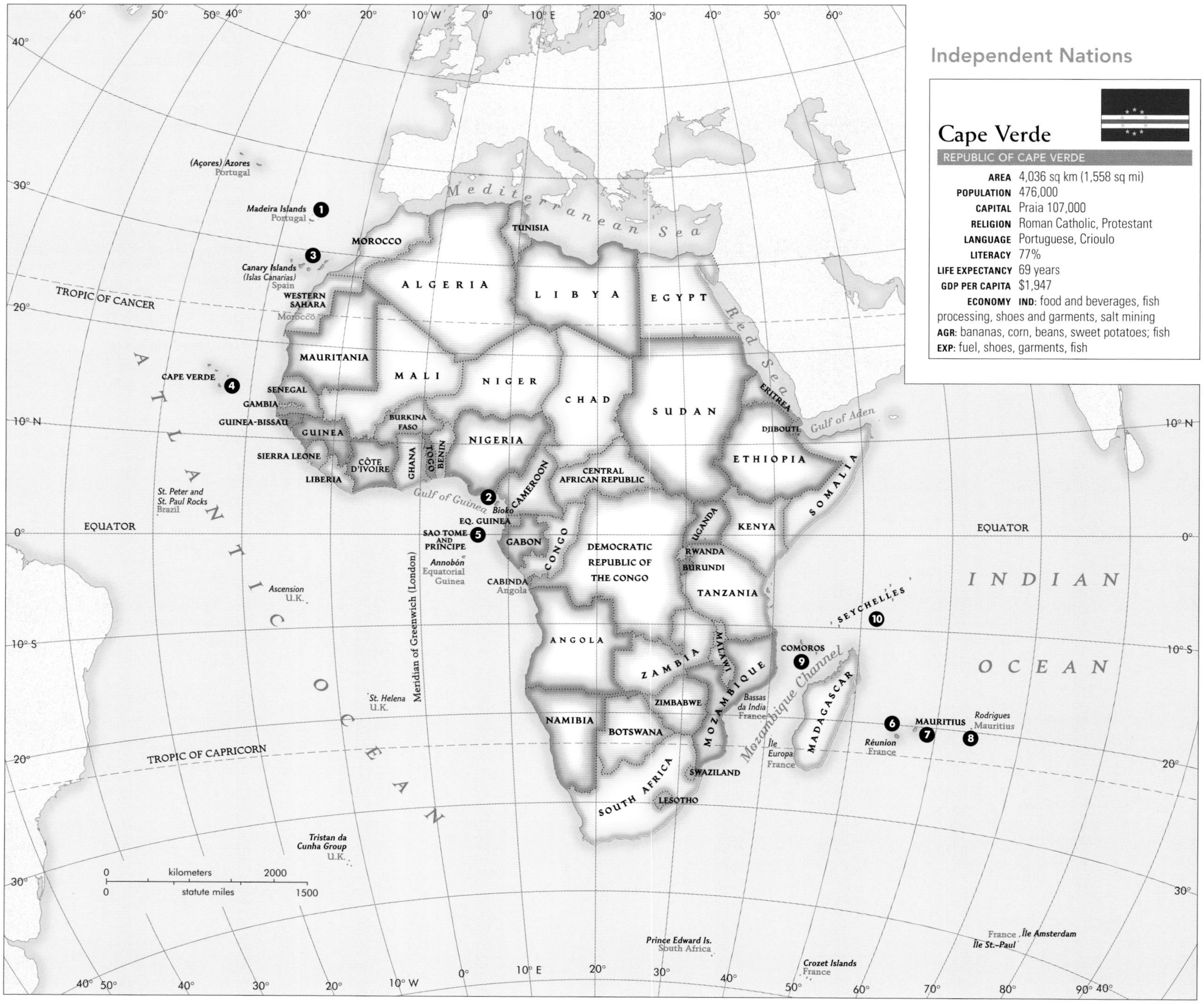

Independent Nations

TROPIC OF CANCER
EQUATOR
TROPIC OF CAPRICORN
Meridian of Greenwich (London)
ATLANTIC OCEAN
INDIAN OCEAN
Mediterranean Sea
Red Sea
Gulf of Aden
Gulf of Guinea
Mozambique Channel
(Açores) Azores Portugal
Madeira Islands Portugal 1
Canary Islands (Islas Canarias) Spain 3
CAPE VERDE 4
Bioko 2
SAO TOME AND PRINCIPE 5
Annobón Equatorial Guinea
St. Peter and St. Paul Rocks Brazil
Ascension U.K.
St. Helena U.K.
Tristan da Cunha Group U.K.
SEYCHELLES 10
COMOROS 9
Bassas da India France
Île Europa France
Réunion France 6
MAURITIUS 7
Rodrigues Mauritius 8
Prince Edward Is. South Africa
Crozet Islands France
France Île Amsterdam
Île St.-Paul
MOROCCO
ALGERIA
TUNISIA
LIBYA
EGYPT
WESTERN SAHARA Morocco
MAURITANIA
MALI
NIGER
CHAD
SUDAN
ERITREA
DJIBOUTI
ETHIOPIA
SOMALIA
SENEGAL
GAMBIA
GUINEA-BISSAU
GUINEA
SIERRA LEONE
LIBERIA
CÔTE D'IVOIRE
BURKINA FASO
GHANA
TOGO
BENIN
NIGERIA
CAMEROON
CENTRAL AFRICAN REPUBLIC
EQ. GUINEA
GABON
CONGO
DEMOCRATIC REPUBLIC OF THE CONGO
CABINDA Angola
UGANDA
KENYA
RWANDA
BURUNDI
TANZANIA
ANGOLA
ZAMBIA
MALAWI
MOZAMBIQUE
ZIMBABWE
NAMIBIA
BOTSWANA
MADAGASCAR
SOUTH AFRICA
SWAZILAND
LESOTHO
0 kilometers 2000
0 statute miles 1500

Cape Verde

REPUBLIC OF CAPE VERDE

AREA 4,036 sq km (1,558 sq mi)
POPULATION 476,000
CAPITAL Praia 107,000
RELIGION Roman Catholic, Protestant
LANGUAGE Portuguese, Crioulo
LITERACY 77%
LIFE EXPECTANCY 69 years
GDP PER CAPITA $1,947
ECONOMY **IND:** food and beverages, fish processing, shoes and garments, salt mining **AGR:** bananas, corn, beans, sweet potatoes; fish **EXP:** fuel, shoes, garments, fish

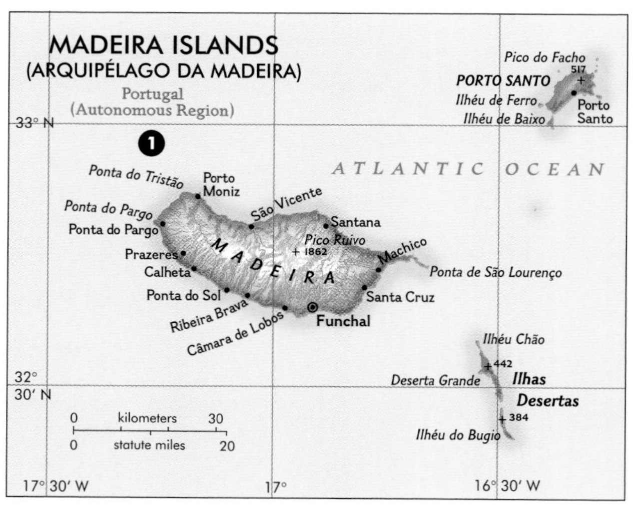

MADEIRA ISLANDS
(ARQUIPÉLAGO DA MADEIRA)
Portugal
(Autonomous Region)
ATLANTIC OCEAN
PORTO SANTO
Pico do Facho 517
Ilhéu de Ferro
Ilhéu de Baixo
Porto Santo
Ponta do Tristão
Porto Moniz
São Vicente
Santana
Pico Ruivo 1862
MADEIRA
Ponta do Pargo
Prazeres
Calheta
Ponta do Sol
Ribeira Brava
Câmara de Lobos
Funchal
Machico
Santa Cruz
Ponta de São Lourenço
Ilhéu Chão
442
Deserta Grande
Ilhas Desertas
384
Ilhéu do Bugio
0 kilometers 30
0 statute miles 20

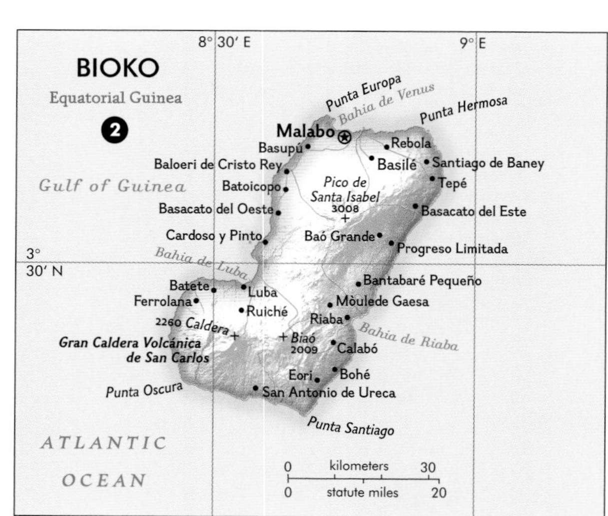

BIOKO
Equatorial Guinea
Gulf of Guinea
ATLANTIC OCEAN
Punta Europa
Bahía de Venus
Punta Hermosa
Malabo
Basupú
Rebola
Baloeri de Cristo Rey
Basilé
Santiago de Baney
Batoicopo
Tepé
Pico de Santa Isabel 3008
Basacato del Oeste
Basacato del Este
Cardoso y Pinto
Baó Grande
Progreso Limitada
Bahía de Luba
Batete
Luba
Bantabaré Pequeño
Ferrolana
Ruiché
Moulede Gaesa
2260 Caldera
Riaba
Gran Caldera Volcánica de San Carlos
Biaó 2009
Bahía de Riaba
Calabó
Eori
Bohé
Punta Oscura
San Antonio de Ureca
Punta Santiago
0 kilometers 30
0 statute miles 20

Comoros

UNION OF THE COMOROS

AREA 1,862 sq km (719 sq mi)
POPULATION 671,000
CAPITAL Moroni 53,000
RELIGION Sunni Muslim
LANGUAGE Arabic (official), French (official), Shikomoro
LITERACY 57%
LIFE EXPECTANCY 60 years
GDP PER CAPITA $427
ECONOMY **IND:** tourism, perfume distillation **AGR:** vanilla, cloves, perfume essences, copra **EXP:** vanilla, ylang-ylang, cloves, perfume oil

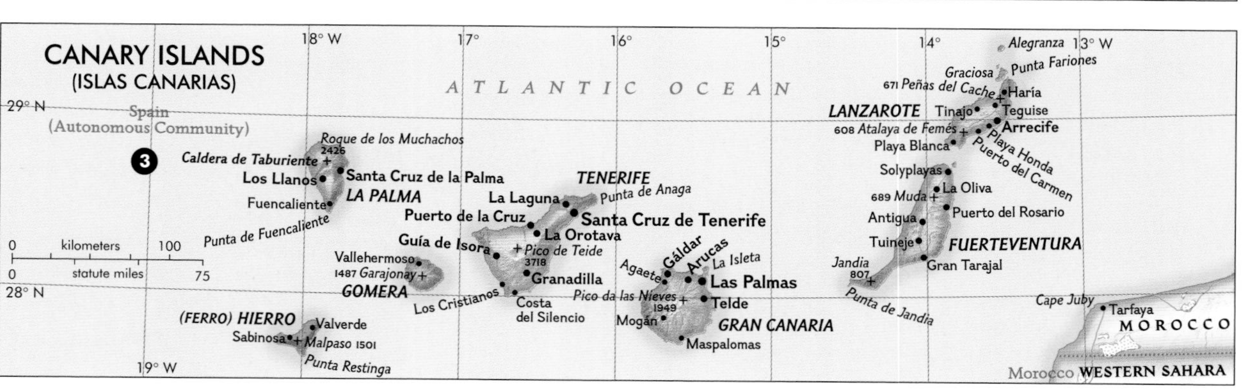

CANARY ISLANDS
(ISLAS CANARIAS)
Spain
(Autonomous Community)
ATLANTIC OCEAN
Roque de los Muchachos 2426
Caldera de Taburiente
Los Llanos
Santa Cruz de la Palma
LA PALMA
Fuencaliente
Punta de Fuencaliente
TENERIFE
La Laguna
Punta de Anaga
Puerto de la Cruz
Santa Cruz de Tenerife
La Orotava
Guía de Isora
Pico de Teide 3718
Granadilla
Los Cristianos
Vallehermoso
1487 Garajonay
GOMERA
(FERRO) HIERRO
Valverde
Sabinosa
Malpaso 1501
Punta Restinga
Agaete
Gáldar
Arucas
La Isleta
Las Palmas
Telde
Pico de las Nieves 1949
Mogán
GRAN CANARIA
Maspalomas
Costa del Silencio
Alegranza
Graciosa
Punta Fariones
671 Peñas del Cache
Haría
LANZAROTE
Tinajo
Teguise
608 Atalaya de Femés
Arrecife
Playa Blanca
Playa Honda
Puerto del Carmen
Solyplayas
La Oliva
689 Muda
Puerto del Rosario
Antigua
Tuineje
FUERTEVENTURA
Gran Tarajal
Jandía 807
Punta de Jandía
Cape Juby
Tarfaya
MOROCCO
Morocco WESTERN SAHARA
0 kilometers 100
0 statute miles 75

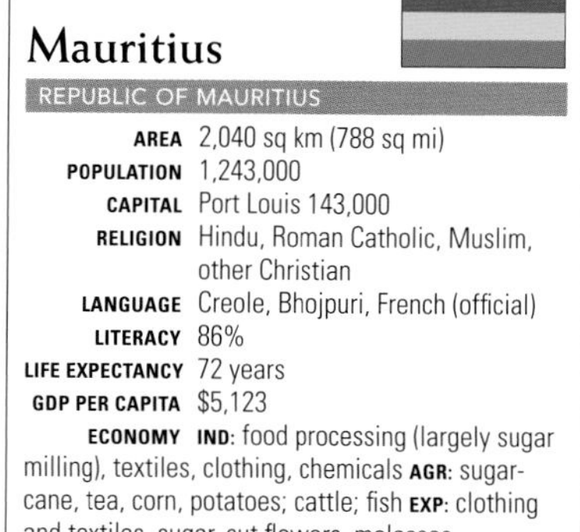

Mauritius

REPUBLIC OF MAURITIUS

AREA 2,040 sq km (788 sq mi)
POPULATION 1,243,000
CAPITAL Port Louis 143,000
RELIGION Hindu, Roman Catholic, Muslim, other Christian
LANGUAGE Creole, Bhojpuri, French (official)
LITERACY 86%
LIFE EXPECTANCY 72 years
GDP PER CAPITA $5,123
ECONOMY **IND:** food processing (largely sugar milling), textiles, clothing, chemicals **AGR:** sugarcane, tea, corn, potatoes; cattle; fish **EXP:** clothing and textiles, sugar, cut flowers, molasses

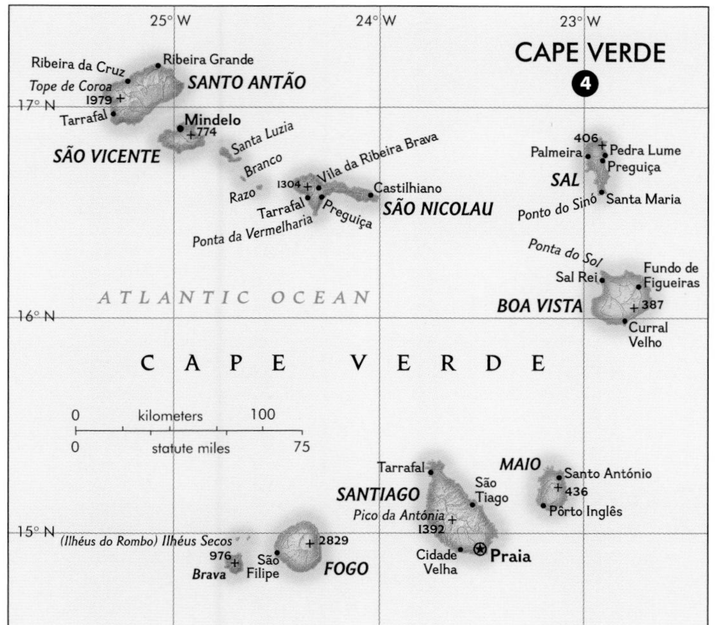
CAPE VERDE
4
SANTO ANTÃO
Ribeira da Cruz
Ribeira Grande
Tope de Coroa
1979
Tarrafal
Mindelo
774
SÃO VICENTE
Santa Luzia
Branco
Razo
1304
Vila da Ribeira Brava
Tarrafal
Castilhiano
Preguiça
SÃO NICOLAU
Ponta da Vermelharia
406
Palmeira
Pedra Lume
Preguiça
SAL
Ponto do Sinó
Santa Maria
Ponta do Sol
Sal Rei
Fundo de Figueiras
387
BOA VISTA
Curral Velho
ATLANTIC OCEAN
CAPE VERDE
kilometers 100
statute miles 75
Tarrafal
SANTIAGO
São Tiago
Pico da Antónia
1392
MAIO
Santo António
436
Pôrto Inglês
(Ilhéus do Rombo) Ilhéus Secos
976
Brava
São Filipe
2829
FOGO
Cidade Velha
Praia
25° W
24° W
23° W
17° N
16° N
15° N

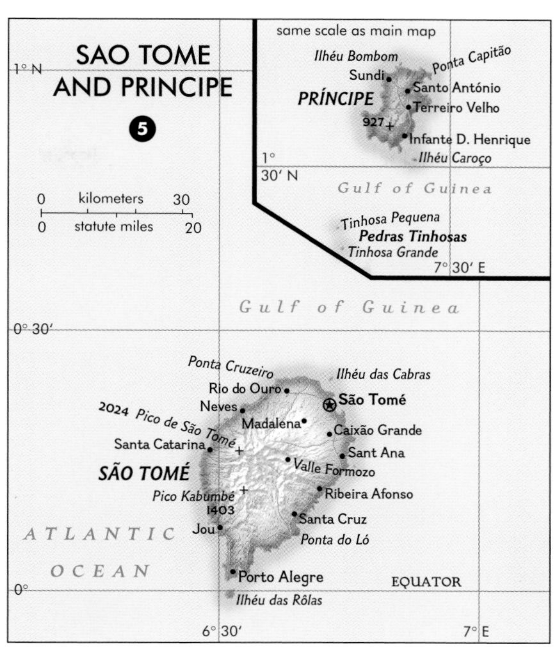
SAO TOME AND PRINCIPE
5
1° N
kilometers 30
statute miles 20
same scale as main map
Ilhéu Bombom
Sundi
Ponta Capitão
Santo António
Terreiro Velho
PRÍNCIPE
927
Infante D. Henrique
Ilhéu Caroço
1° 30′ N
Gulf of Guinea
Tinhosa Pequena
Pedras Tinhosas
Tinhosa Grande
7° 30′ E
Gulf of Guinea
0° 30′
Ponta Cruzeiro
Rio do Ouro
Ilhéu das Cabras
Neves
São Tomé
2024 Pico de São Tomé
Madalena
Caixão Grande
Santa Catarina
Sant Ana
SÃO TOMÉ
Valle Formozo
Pico Kabumbé
1403
Ribeira Afonso
Santa Cruz
Jou
Ponta do Ló
ATLANTIC OCEAN
Porto Alegre
Ilhéu das Rôlas
EQUATOR
0°
6° 30′
7° E

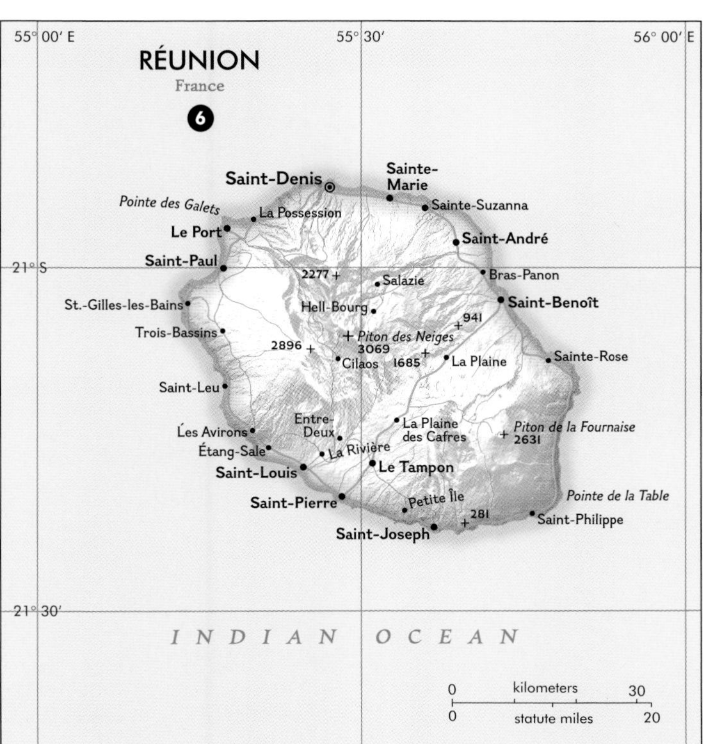
RÉUNION
France
6
55° 00′ E
55° 30′
56° 00′ E
Saint-Denis
Sainte-Marie
Pointe des Galets
La Possession
Sainte-Suzanna
Le Port
Saint-André
Saint-Paul
2277
Salazie
Bras-Panon
21° S
St.-Gilles-les-Bains
Hell-Bourg
Saint-Benoît
941
Trois-Bassins
2896
Piton des Neiges
3069
Cilaos
1685
La Plaine
Sainte-Rose
Saint-Leu
Entre-Deux
La Plaine des Cafres
Piton de la Fournaise
2631
Les Avirons
Étang-Salé
La Rivière
Le Tampon
Saint-Louis
Saint-Pierre
Petite Île
281
Pointe de la Table
Saint-Philippe
Saint-Joseph
21° 30′
INDIAN OCEAN
kilometers 30
statute miles 20

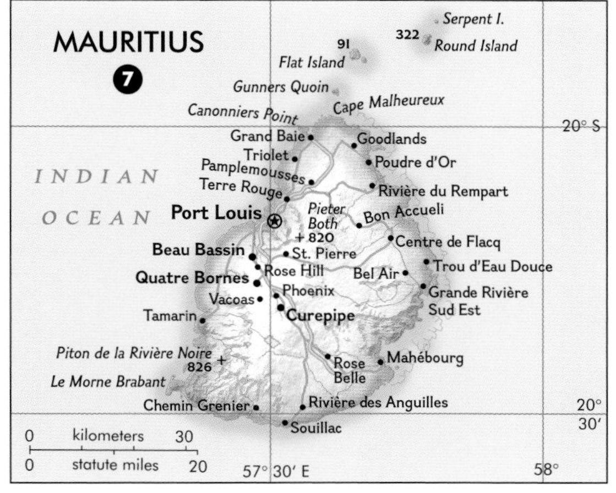
MAURITIUS
7
Serpent I.
91
322
Round Island
Flat Island
Gunners Quoin
Canonniers Point
Cape Malheureux
Grand Baie
Goodlands
Triolet
Poudre d'Or
Pamplemousses
Terre Rouge
Rivière du Rempart
INDIAN OCEAN
Port Louis
Pieter Both
820
Bon Accueil
Beau Bassin
St. Pierre
Centre de Flacq
Rose Hill
Bel Air
Trou d'Eau Douce
Quatre Bornes
Phoenix
Grande Rivière Sud Est
Vacoas
Tamarin
Curepipe
Piton de la Rivière Noire
826
Rose Belle
Mahébourg
Le Morne Brabant
Chemin Grenier
Rivière des Anguilles
Souillac
20° S
20° 30′
kilometers 30
statute miles 20
57° 30′ E
58°

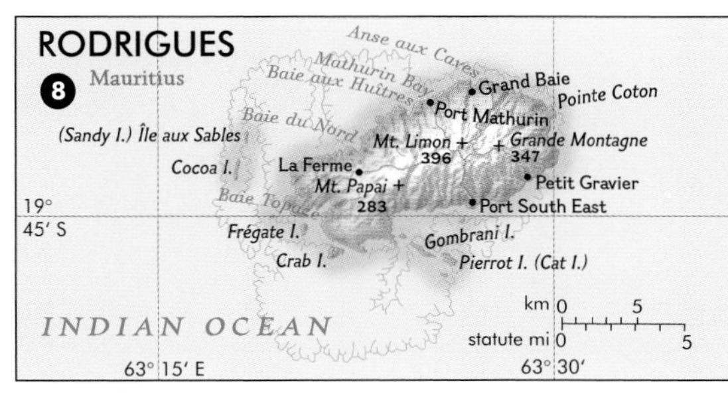
RODRIGUES
Mauritius
8
Anse aux Caves
Mathurin Bay
Baie aux Huîtres
Grand Baie
Pointe Coton
Port Mathurin
Baie du Nord
(Sandy I.) Île aux Sables
Mt. Limon
396
Grande Montagne
347
Cocoa I.
La Ferme
Mt. Papai
283
Petit Gravier
Baie Topaze
Port South East
19° 45′ S
Frégate I.
Gombrani I.
Crab I.
Pierrot I. (Cat I.)
INDIAN OCEAN
km 0 5
statute mi 0 5
63° 15′ E
63° 30′

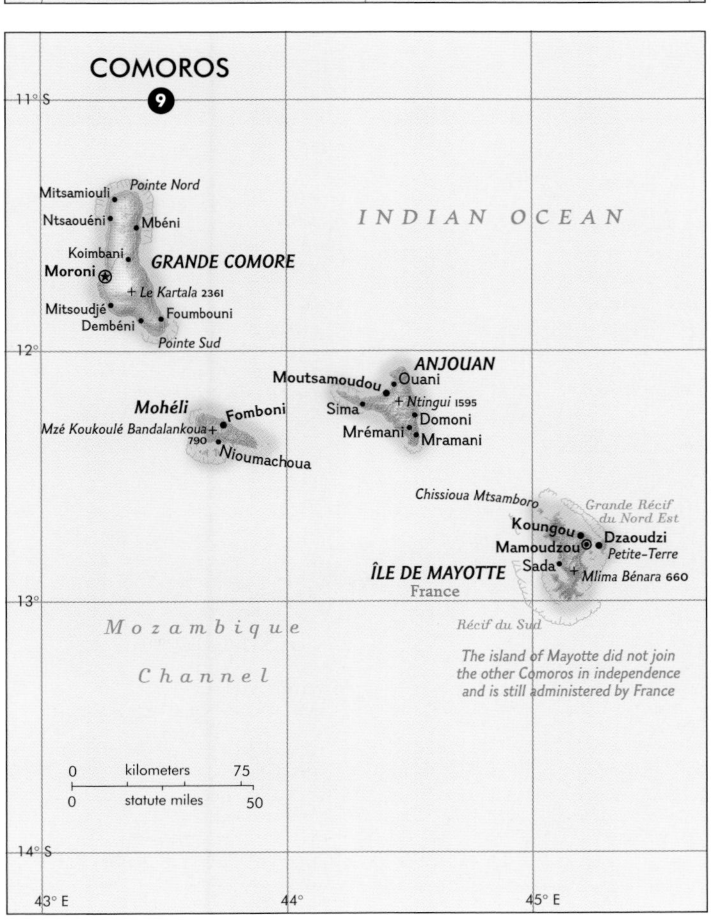
COMOROS
9
11° S
Pointe Nord
Mitsamiouli
Ntsaouéni
Mbéni
Koimbani
GRANDE COMORE
Moroni
Le Kartala 2361
Mitsoudjé
Foumbouni
Dembéni
Pointe Sud
12°
INDIAN OCEAN
ANJOUAN
Moutsamoudou
Ouani
Ntingui 1595
Mohéli
Fomboni
Sima
Domoni
Mzé Koukoulé Bandalankoua
790
Mrémani
Mramani
Nioumachoua
Chissioua Mtsamboro
Grande Récif du Nord Est
Koungou
Dzaoudzi
Mamoudzou
Petite-Terre
Sada
ÎLE DE MAYOTTE
France
Mlima Bénara 660
Récif du Sud
13°
Mozambique Channel
The island of Mayotte did not join the other Comoros in independence and is still administered by France
kilometers 75
statute miles 50
14° S
43° E
44°
45° E

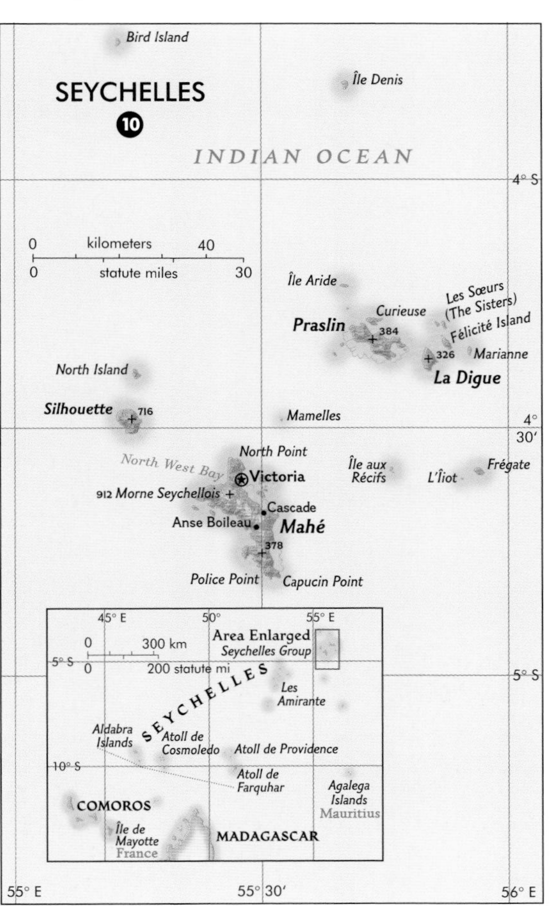
Bird Island
SEYCHELLES
10
Île Denis
INDIAN OCEAN
4° S
kilometers 40
statute miles 30
Île Aride
Les Sœurs (The Sisters)
Curieuse
Félicité Island
Praslin
384
326
Marianne
North Island
La Digue
Silhouette
716
Mamelles
4° 30′
North Point
North West Bay
Victoria
Île aux Récifs
L'Îlot
Frégate
912 Morne Seychellois
Cascade
Anse Boileau
Mahé
378
Police Point
Capucin Point
45° E
50°
55° E
300 km
200 statute mi
Area Enlarged
Seychelles Group
5° S
SEYCHELLES
Les Amirante
Aldabra Islands
Atoll de Cosmoledo
Atoll de Providence
10° S
Atoll de Farquhar
Agalega Islands
Mauritius
COMOROS
Île de Mayotte
France
MADAGASCAR
5° S
55° E
55° 30′
56° E

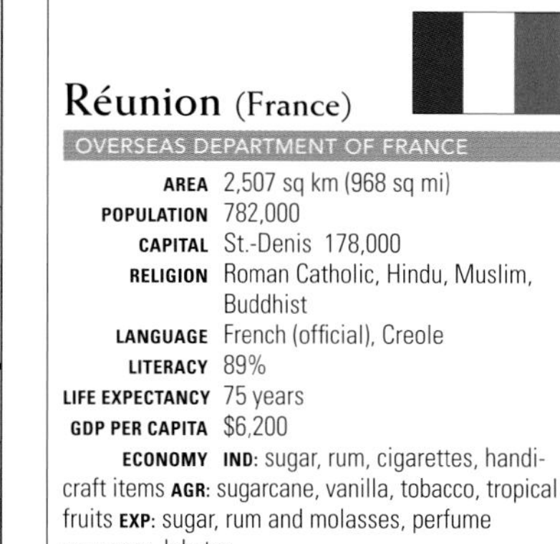

Réunion (France)

OVERSEAS DEPARTMENT OF FRANCE

AREA 2,507 sq km (968 sq mi)
POPULATION 782,000
CAPITAL St.-Denis 178,000
RELIGION Roman Catholic, Hindu, Muslim, Buddhist
LANGUAGE French (official), Creole
LITERACY 89%
LIFE EXPECTANCY 75 years
GDP PER CAPITA $6,200
ECONOMY **IND:** sugar, rum, cigarettes, handicraft items **AGR:** sugarcane, vanilla, tobacco, tropical fruits **EXP:** sugar, rum and molasses, perfume essences, lobster

Sao Tome and Principe

DEM. REP. OF SAO TOME AND PRINCIPE

AREA 1,001 sq km (386 sq mi)
POPULATION 153,000
CAPITAL São Tomé 54,000
RELIGION Roman Catholic, Protestant
LANGUAGE Portuguese (official)
LITERACY 79%
LIFE EXPECTANCY 63 years
GDP PER CAPITA $447
ECONOMY **IND:** light construction, textiles, soap, beer **AGR:** cocoa, coconuts, palm kernels, copra; poultry; fish **EXP:** cocoa, copra, coffee, palm oil

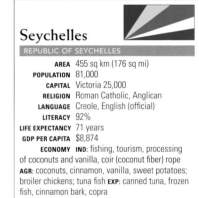

Seychelles

REPUBLIC OF SEYCHELLES

AREA 455 sq km (176 sq mi)
POPULATION 81,000
CAPITAL Victoria 25,000
RELIGION Roman Catholic, Anglican
LANGUAGE Creole, English (official)
LITERACY 92%
LIFE EXPECTANCY 71 years
GDP PER CAPITA $8,874
ECONOMY **IND:** fishing, tourism, processing of coconuts and vanilla, coir (coconut fiber) rope **AGR:** coconuts, cinnamon, vanilla, sweet potatoes; broiler chickens; tuna fish **EXP:** canned tuna, frozen fish, cinnamon bark, copra

Dependencies

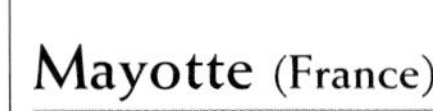

Mayotte (France)

TERRITORIAL COLLECTIVITY OF MAYOTTE

AREA 374 sq km (144 sq mi)
POPULATION 181,000
CAPITAL Mamoudzou 58,000
RELIGION Muslim
LANGUAGE Mahorian (a Swahili dialect), French (official)
LITERACY NA
LIFE EXPECTANCY 60 years
GDP PER CAPITA $2,600
ECONOMY **IND:** newly created lobster and shrimp industry, construction **AGR:** vanilla, ylang-ylang (perfume essence), coffee, copra **EXP:** ylang-ylang (perfume essence), vanilla, copra, coconuts

SOVEREIGN LOCAL

St. Helena (U.K.)

SAINT HELENA

AREA 411 sq km (159 sq mi)
POPULATION 6,000
CAPITAL Jamestown 2,000
RELIGION Anglican, Baptist, Seventh-Day Adventist, Roman Catholic
LANGUAGE English
LITERACY 97%
LIFE EXPECTANCY 77 years
GDP PER CAPITA $2,500
ECONOMY **IND:** construction, crafts (furniture, lacework, woodwork), fishing **AGR:** corn, potatoes, vegetables; timber; fish **EXP:** fish (frozen, canned, salt-dried skipjack, tuna), coffee, handicrafts

The largest structure ever built by living creatures, the Great Barrier Reef lies off Australia's northeast coast. Some 400 coral species and 1,500 species of fish inhabit its warm, shallow waters.

Australia
New Zealand and Oceania

Smallest of continents and sixth largest country in the world, Australia is the lowest, flattest, and, apart from Antarctica, the driest continent.

The Australian landmass is relatively arid, but varied climatic zones give it surprising diversity and a rich ecology. Unlike Europe and North America, where much of the landscape dates back 20,000 years to when great ice sheets retreated, Australia's land is many millions of years old; it retains an ancient feeling and distinctive geography and endures extremes of droughts, floods, tropical cyclones, severe storms, and bushfires.

Off the coast of northeast Queensland lies the Great Barrier Reef, the world's largest coral reef, which extends about 1,429 miles (2,300 km). The reef was formed and expanded over millions of years as tiny marine animals deposited their skeletons. Coral reefs, and the Great Barrier Reef especially, are considered the rain forests of the ocean for their complex life forms and multilayered biodiversity.

Australia, New Zealand and Oceania

The island of Tasmania lies off Australia's southeast coast. East from there, across the Tasman Sea, is the island nation of New Zealand, composed of South Island and North Island, respectively the 12th and 14th largest islands on Earth. North Island, unlike its southern neighbor, is riddled with geothermic activity.

Extending into the massive Pacific Ocean north and east of Australia and New Zealand are the thousands of islands—which include 12 independent nations and more than 20 territories—that make up greater Oceania. The term Oceania normally designates all the islands of the Central and South Pacific, including Australia, New Zealand, and specifically the islands of Melanesia, Micronesia, and Polynesia, including Hawai'i. Eons of isolation have allowed outstanding and bizarre life-forms to evolve, such as the duck-billed platypus—a monotreme, or egg-laying mammal native to Australia and Tasmania—and New Zealand's kiwi, a timid, nocturnal, wingless bird.

Oceania has many ethnic groups and layers and types of society, from sophisticated cosmopolitan cities to near-Stone Age people in the New Guinea highlands. Many became Christian converts in the 19th century; as a result, Christianity is widespread and dominant in many countries today. Excluding Australia, some 13 million people live in Oceania, three-fourths of whom are found in Papua New Guinea and New Zealand.

Polynesia, which means "many islands," is the most extensive of the ocean realms. It can be seen as a huge triangle in the central-south Pacific, with the points being New Zealand in the southwest, Easter Island in the southeast, and Hawai'i as the northern point. Other island groups include Tuvalu, Tokelau, Wallis and Futuna, Samoa, Tonga, Cook Islands, and French Polynesia.

Micronesia, north and west of Polynesia, includes the islands and island groups of Nauru, Marshall Islands, Palau, Mariana Islands, Kiribati, and Guam.

Melanesia, one of the three main divisions of Oceania, includes the Solomon Islands, Vanuatu, New Caledonia, the Bismarck Archipelago, and Fiji, and sometimes takes in Papua New Guinea, where more than 700 of the giant region's 1,200 languages are spoken.

PHYSICAL GEOGRAPHY The continent of Australia can be divided into three parts: the Western Plateau, Central Lowlands, and Eastern Highlands. The Western Plateau consists of very old rocks, some more than three billion years old. Much of the center of Australia is flat, but some ranges and the famous landmark Ayers Rock (Uluru) still rise up, everything around them having eroded away.

Much variety exists within the general context of a red, dusty, dry, flat continent, of which a third is desert and a third scrub and steppe. Sand dunes, mostly fixed and running north to south, and stony deserts mark the great tableland.

Many of Australia's rivers drain inland; though they erode their valleys near the highland sources, their lower courses are filling up with alluvium, and the rivers often end in salt lakes, dry for much of each year, when they become beds of salt and caked mud. Yet occasional spring rains in the outback can bring spectacular wildflowers.

Sparsely populated, Australia has nearly all its 20 million people along the east and southeast coasts, and of these about 40 percent live in the two cities of Sydney and Melbourne. Along the coasts are some fine harbors and long beaches and rocky headlands.

The Eastern Highlands rise gently from central Australia toward a series of high plateaus, the highest part around Mount Kosciuszko (7,310 ft; 2,228 m). The Great Escarpment runs from northern Queensland to the Victoria border in the south. Australia's highest waterfalls occur where rivers flow over the Great Escarpment.

The longest of all Australian river systems, the Murray River and its tributaries, including the long Darling River, drain part of Queensland, the major part of New South Wales, and a large part of Victoria before finally flowing into the Indian Ocean just east of Adelaide.

Most of the Great Dividing Range that separates rivers flowing to Central Australia from those flowing to the Pacific runs across remarkably flat country dotted with lakes and airstrips. In ancient times volcanoes erupted in eastern Australia, and lava plains covered large areas.

Australia is blessed with a fascinating mix of native flora and fauna. Its distinctive plants include the ubiquitous eucalyptus, sometimes called a gum tree, and acacia, which Australians call wattle, each with several hundred species. Other common plants include bottlebrushes, paperbarks, and tea trees. Animals include the iconic kangaroo, koala, wallaby, wombat, and dog-like dingo, also the echidna—a spiny anteater—and numerous beloved birds, such as parrots, cockatoos, and kookaburras, and the emu, second largest of all birds after the ostrich.

Foreign animals have been introduced. The rabbit and fox have proven to be particularly noxious pests, overgrazing the land and killing and driving out native species. A fence built in 1907, still maintained, runs a thousand miles from the north coast to the south to prevent rabbits from invading Western Australia.

New Zealand is mountainous compared to Australia; it has peaks over 10,000 feet in the Southern Alps and considerably more rain, making the climate cooler and more temperate. Among New Zealand's oddities is a fossil lizard species, the tuatara; individuals can live up to a hundred years.

The atolls, mountains, volcanoes, and sandy isles of greater Oceania, with limited land and small populations, have for most of history been isolated from the more settled parts of the world.

Peaks and promontories of the many islands of Polynesia form clouds and capture rain, making these islands very wet.

HISTORY Australia's first inhabitants, the Aborigines, migrated there some 50,000 or more years ago from Asia. Until the arrival of Europeans, the Aborigines had remained isolated from outside influences except for occasional trading in the north with Indonesian islanders.

Aboriginal pictographs, some repainted generation upon generation, grace the rock shelters and escarpment walls of Kakadu National Park in Australia's Northern Territory. Some paintings are considered *andjamun,* sacred and dangerous, and only may be viewed by tribal elders, while others may be looked upon by everyone.

In 1688 Englishman William Dampier landed on the northwest coast. Little interest was aroused, however, until Capt. James Cook noted the fertile east coast during his 1770 voyage, which stopped at Botany Bay, just south of today's Sydney. He claimed the entire continent for the British Empire and named it New South Wales.

Australia's formative moment came when Britain began colonizing the east coast in 1788 as a penal colony, so as to relieve overcrowded prisons in England. Altogether, 161,000 English, Irish, and other convicts were forced to settle there. Prison transports ended in 1868, and by that time regular emigrants had already begun settling down under, as Australia was called for being so far south of the Equator. By the mid-1800s systematic, permanent colonization had completely replaced the old penal settlements.

Introduction of sheep proved vital, and the wool industry flourished. A gold strike in Victoria in 1851 attracted prospectors from all over the world. Other strikes followed, and with minerals, sheep, and grain forming the base of the economy, Australia developed rapidly, expanding across the whole continent.

By 1861, Australians had established the straight-line boundaries between the colonies, and the Commonwealth of Australia was born January 1, 1901, relying on British parliamentary and U.S. federal traditions. Australia and New Zealand share a common British heritage and many similar characteristics, and both are democracies that continue to honor the British monarch.

The great seafaring navigators of Polynesia and Micronesia took part in the last phase of mankind's settlement of the globe, into the widely dispersed islands of the great Pacific. Their particular genius and contribution was the development of seafaring and navigation skills and canoe technology, which let them sail back and forth among islands across great distances. The more diverse, land-based Melanesians fished along the coasts and practiced horticulture farther inland.

CULTURE Australia's Aborigines were hunters and gatherers moving with the seasons, taking with them only those possessions necessary for hunting and preparing food. Perhaps 500 or more tribes lived in Australia at the time of Captain Cook in 1770.

Aboriginal society was based on a complex network of intricate kinship relationships. No formal government or authority existed, but social control was maintained by a system of beliefs called the Dreaming. These beliefs found expression in song, art, and dance. A rich oral tradition existed in which stories of the Dreamtime, the time of creation, or recent history were passed down. Aboriginal rock carvings and paintings date back at least 30,000 years.

Australia's Aborigines have faced two centuries and more of lost land, brutalization, and discrimination. In the 1960s an Aboriginal movement grew to press for full citizenship and improved education. Modern Aboriginal art has undergone a revival as Aboriginal artists have preserved their ancient values while learning from the contemporary world.

Most Australians are of British and Irish ancestry and the majority live in urban areas. The population has more than doubled since the end of World War II, spurred by an ambitious postwar immigration program, with many coming from Greece, Turkey, Italy, and Lebanon. In the 1970s Australia officially ended discriminatory immigration policies, and substantial Asian immigration followed. Today Asians make up some 7 percent of the population.

The largest church groups are the Anglican and Roman Catholic, though some say sport is the national religion; Australians are famous in cricket, rugby, and swimming.

The Maori—indigenous Polynesian people of New Zealand—arrived in different migrations starting around 1150, and a "great fleet" arrived in the 14th century, probably from Tahiti. Maori art is characterized by beautiful wood carvings that adorn houses and fish hooks carved out of whale bone. In the 1840 Treaty of Waitangi, the Maori gave formal control of their land to the British, though they kept all other rights of livelihood.

ECONOMY Australia dominates all of Oceania economically. Its connection to Asia grows more important as a supplier of raw material to other Pacific Rim countries and an importer of finished manufactured products. Japan is Australia's leading trade partner and thousands of children learn Japanese in Australian schools. The standard of living is high and people have considerable leisure time, a sign for Australians of a good life.

Most of the rich farmland and good ports are in the east, particularly the southeast, and the areas around Perth, in Western Australia. Melbourne, Sydney, Brisbane, and Adelaide are the leading industrial and commercial cities.

Australia is highly industrialized. Its chief industries include mining, food processing, and the manufacture of industrial and transportation equipment, chemicals, iron and steel, textiles, machinery, and motor vehicles. Some lumbering is done in the east and southeast. Tropical and subtropical produce are also important, as are vineyards, dairy farms, and tobacco farms.

Chief export commodities are coal, gold, beef, mutton, wool, minerals, cereals, and manufactured products. Australia's economic ties with Asia and the Pacific Rim are increasingly important. Air transport and modern communications have shrunk distances, with landing strips on isolated atolls, in the desert outback, and in Papuan jungles.

Australia: Physical and Political

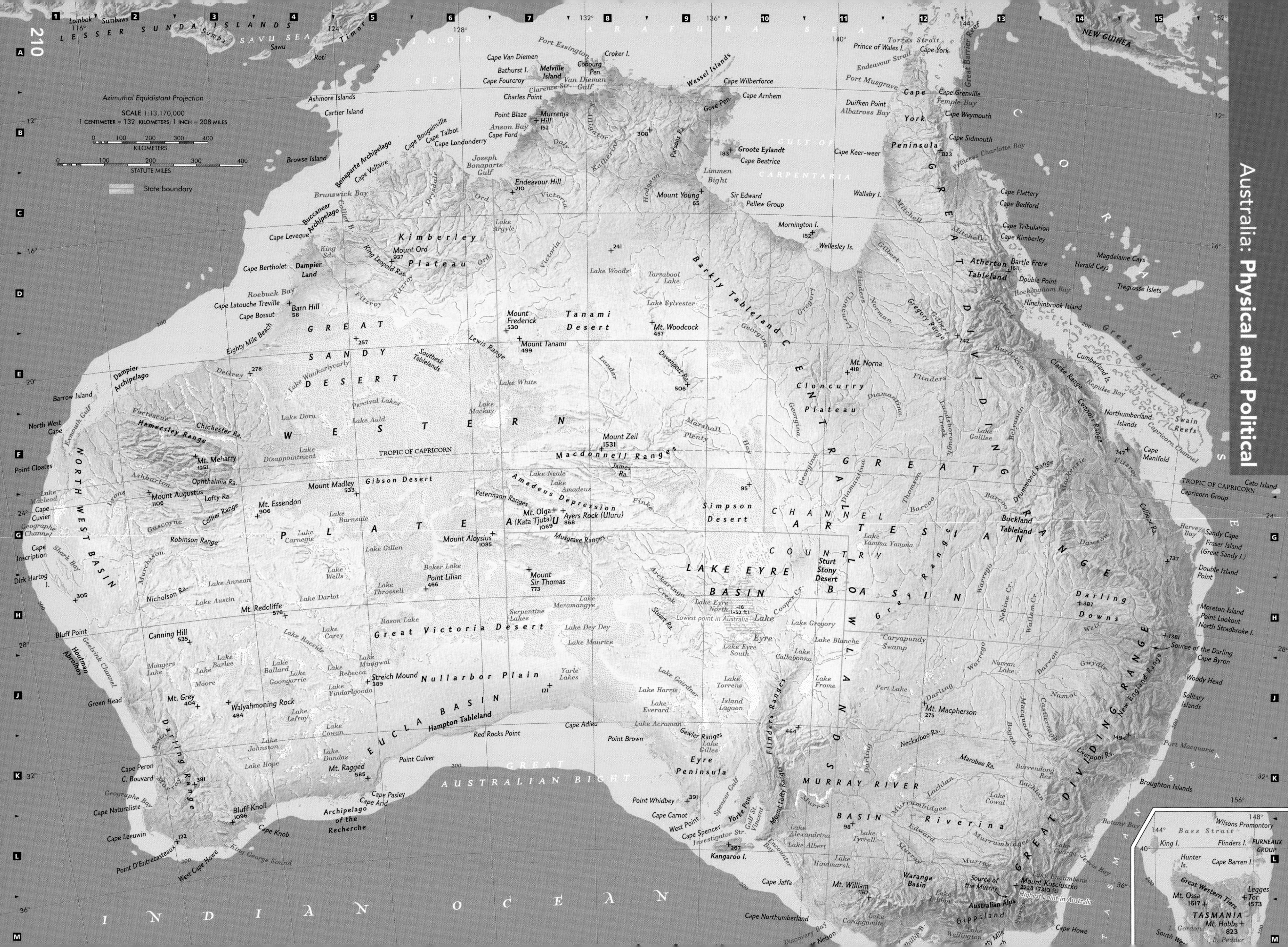
Azimuthal Equidistant Projection
SCALE 1:13,170,000
1 CENTIMETER = 132 KILOMETERS; 1 INCH = 208 MILES
KILOMETERS
STATUTE MILES
State boundary
CORAL SEA
ARAFURA SEA
TIMOR SEA
INDIAN OCEAN
TASMAN SEA
GULF OF CARPENTARIA
GREAT AUSTRALIAN BIGHT
LESSER SUNDA ISLANDS
NEW GUINEA
GREAT DIVIDING RANGE
Great Barrier Reef
Cape York Peninsula
Torres Strait
Atherton Tableland
CENTRAL LOWLANDS
GREAT ARTESIAN BASIN
LAKE EYRE BASIN
CHANNEL COUNTRY
MURRAY RIVER BASIN
Riverina
Darling Downs
Barkly Tableland
Tanami Desert
GREAT SANDY DESERT
Gibson Desert
Great Victoria Desert
Nullarbor Plain
Simpson Desert
Sturt Stony Desert
WESTERN PLATEAU
Kimberley Plateau
Macdonnell Ranges
Musgrave Ranges
Amadeus Depression
Ayers Rock (Uluru)
Mt. Olga (Kata Tjuta)
Hamersley Range
Mt. Meharry 1251
NORTH WEST BASIN
Darling Range
EUCLA BASIN
Flinders Ranges
Mount Lofty Ranges
Eyre Peninsula
Spencer Gulf
Kangaroo I.
Lake Eyre North -16 Lowest point in Australia
Mount Kosciuszko 2228 (7310 ft) Highest point in Australia
Australian Alps
TASMANIA
Bass Strait
Mt. Ossa 1617
Dampier Archipelago
Bonaparte Archipelago
Joseph Bonaparte Gulf
Cape Leeuwin
Cape Howe
Cape York
TROPIC OF CAPRICORN

Azimuthal Equidistant Projection
SCALE 1:13,170,000
1 CENTIMETER = 132 KILOMETERS; 1 INCH = 208 MILES
KILOMETERS
STATUTE MILES
Aboriginal Lands
Homesteads
PAPUA NEW GUINEA
TIMOR SEA
GULF OF CARPENTARIA
CORAL SEA
CORAL SEA ISLANDS TERRITORY
INDIAN OCEAN
GREAT AUSTRALIAN BIGHT
NORTHERN TERRITORY
QUEENSLAND
WESTERN AUSTRALIA
SOUTH AUSTRALIA
NEW SOUTH WALES
VICTORIA
AUSTRALIAN CAPITAL TERRITORY
TASMANIA
Same Scale as Main Map
GREAT SANDY DESERT
Gibson Desert
Great Victoria Desert
Tanami Desert
Simpson Desert
ARNHEM LAND
KIMBERLEY
GREAT DIVIDING RANGE
GREAT ARTESIAN BASIN
TROPIC OF CAPRICORN
Longitude East 136° of Greenwich
Darwin
Alice Springs
BRISBANE
SYDNEY
Canberra
MELBOURNE
ADELAIDE
PERTH
Hobart

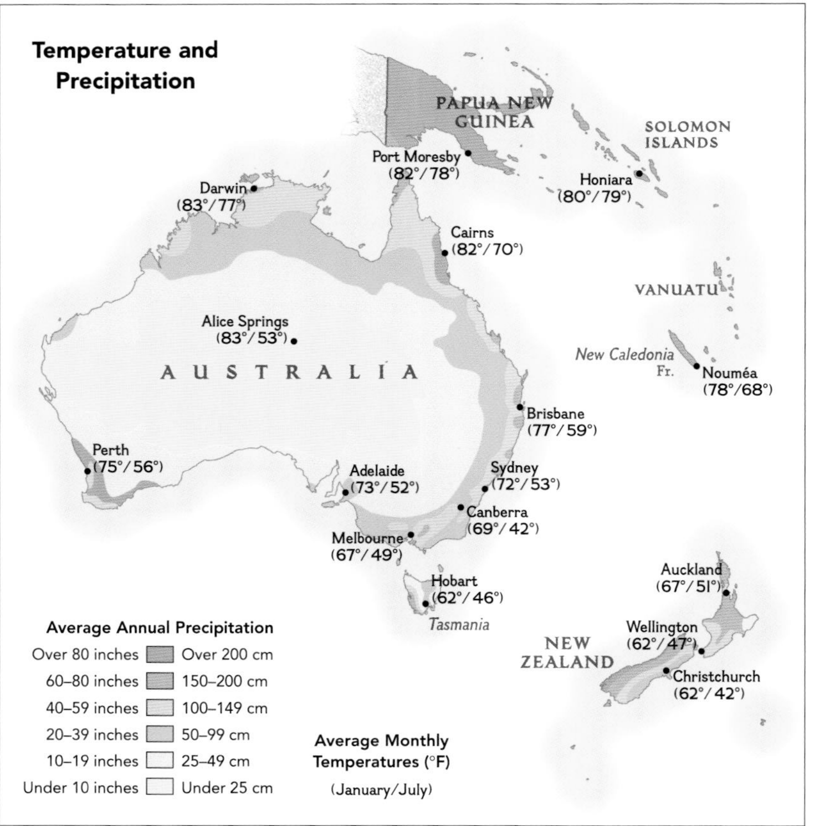
Temperature and Precipitation
PAPUA NEW GUINEA
SOLOMON ISLANDS
Port Moresby (82°/78°)
Honiara (80°/79°)
Darwin (83°/77°)
Cairns (82°/70°)
VANUATU
Alice Springs (83°/53°)
AUSTRALIA
New Caledonia Fr.
Nouméa (78°/68°)
Brisbane (77°/59°)
Perth (75°/56°)
Adelaide (73°/52°)
Sydney (72°/53°)
Canberra (69°/42°)
Melbourne (67°/49°)
Hobart (62°/46°)
Tasmania
Auckland (67°/51°)
Wellington (62°/47°)
NEW ZEALAND
Christchurch (62°/42°)
Average Annual Precipitation
Over 80 inches | Over 200 cm
60–80 inches | 150–200 cm
40–59 inches | 100–149 cm
20–39 inches | 50–99 cm
10–19 inches | 25–49 cm
Under 10 inches | Under 25 cm
Average Monthly Temperatures (°F)
(January/July)

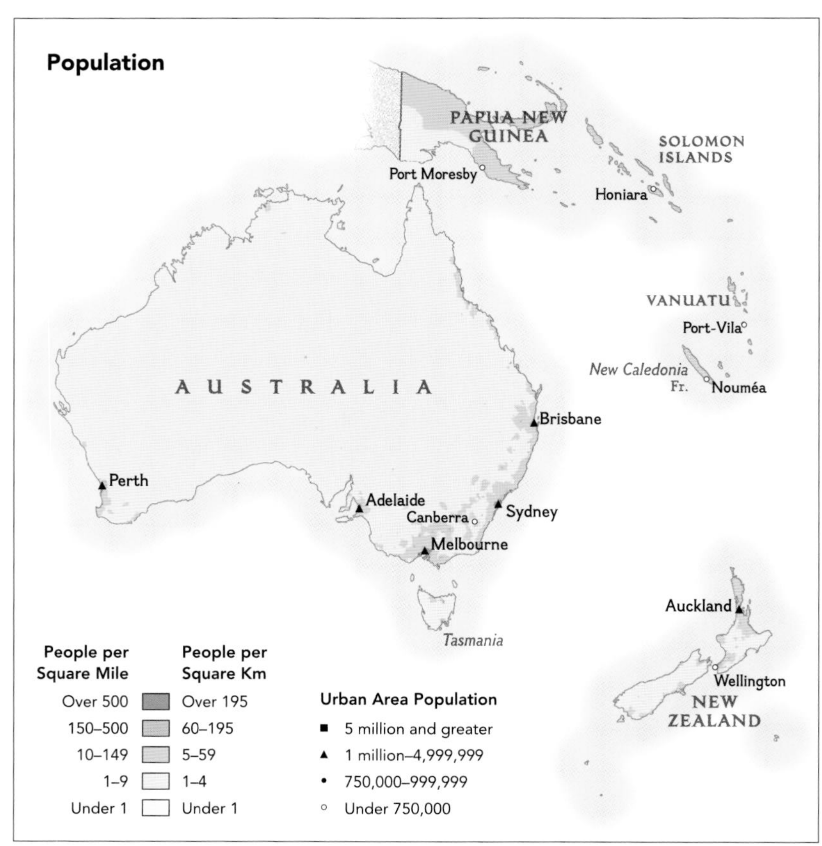
Population
PAPUA NEW GUINEA
SOLOMON ISLANDS
Port Moresby
Honiara
VANUATU
Port-Vila
New Caledonia Fr.
Nouméa
AUSTRALIA
Brisbane
Perth
Adelaide
Canberra
Sydney
Melbourne
Tasmania
Auckland
Wellington
NEW ZEALAND
People per Square Mile | People per Square Km
Over 500 | Over 195
150–500 | 60–195
10–149 | 5–59
1–9 | 1–4
Under 1 | Under 1
Urban Area Population
5 million and greater
1 million–4,999,999
750,000–999,999
Under 750,000

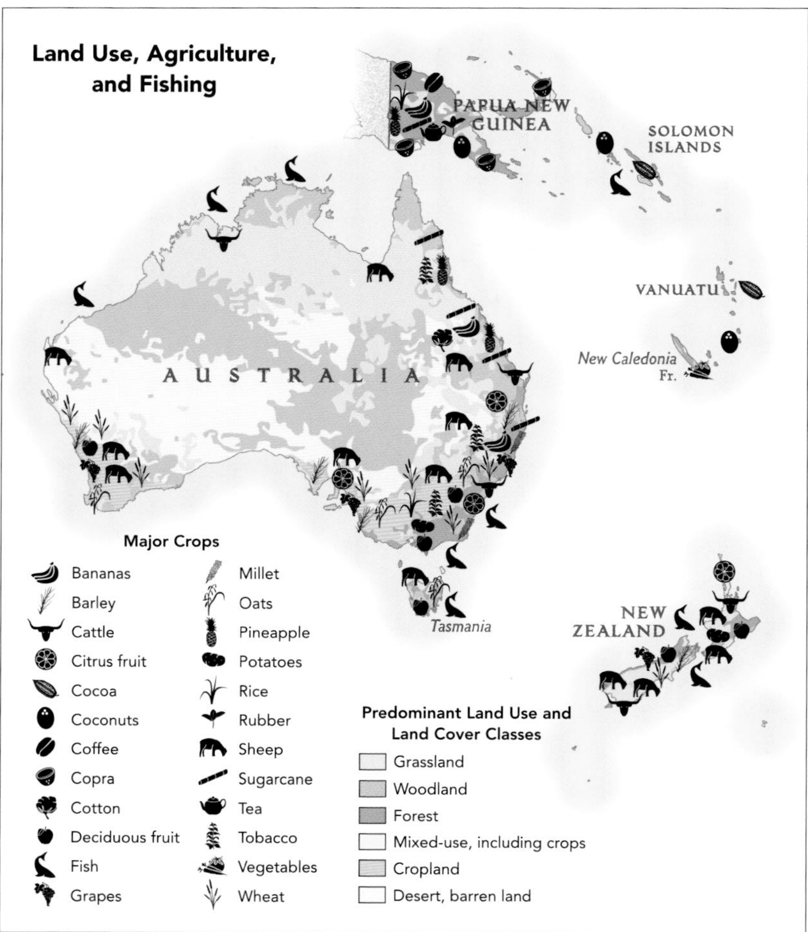
Land Use, Agriculture, and Fishing
PAPUA NEW GUINEA
SOLOMON ISLANDS
VANUATU
New Caledonia Fr.
AUSTRALIA
Tasmania
NEW ZEALAND
Major Crops
Bananas
Barley
Cattle
Citrus fruit
Cocoa
Coconuts
Coffee
Copra
Cotton
Deciduous fruit
Fish
Grapes
Millet
Oats
Pineapple
Potatoes
Rice
Rubber
Sheep
Sugarcane
Tea
Tobacco
Vegetables
Wheat
Predominant Land Use and Land Cover Classes
Grassland
Woodland
Forest
Mixed-use, including crops
Cropland
Desert, barren land

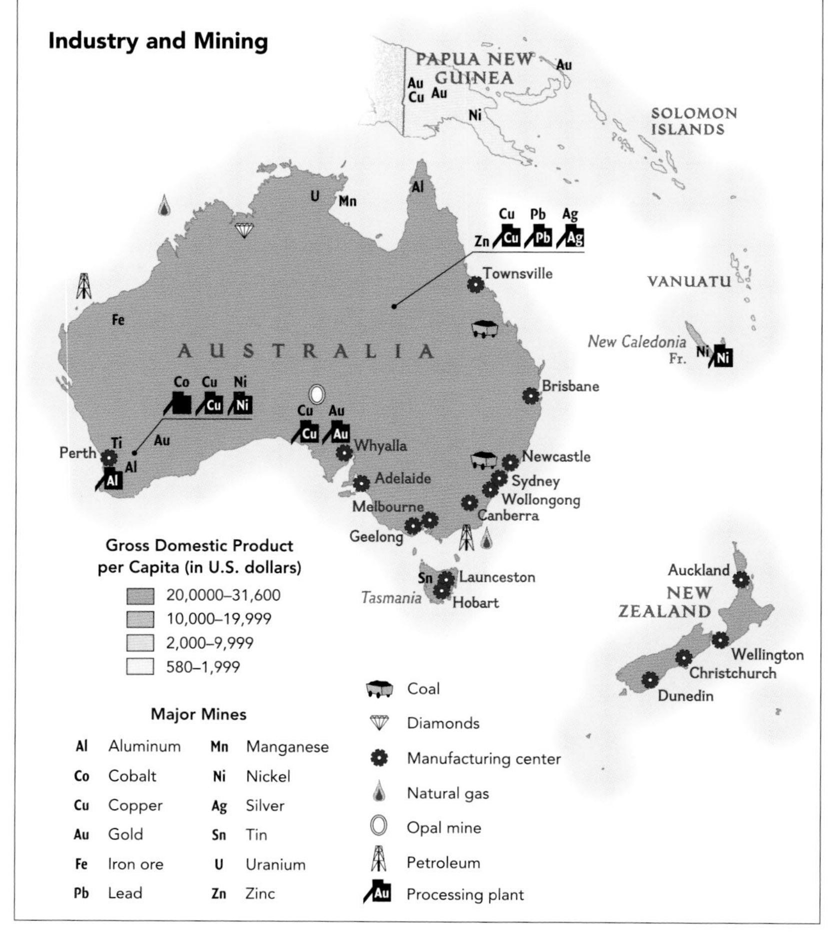
Industry and Mining
PAPUA NEW GUINEA
Au Cu Au Au Ni
SOLOMON ISLANDS
U Mn Al
Cu Pb Ag
Zn Cu Pb Ag
Townsville
VANUATU
Fe
AUSTRALIA
New Caledonia Fr.
Ni Ni
Co Cu Ni
Cu Ni
Cu Au
Cu Au
Brisbane
Perth
Ti
Al
Au
Al
Whyalla
Newcastle
Adelaide
Sydney
Wollongong
Melbourne
Canberra
Geelong
Sn
Launceston
Tasmania
Hobart
Auckland
NEW ZEALAND
Wellington
Christchurch
Dunedin
Gross Domestic Product per Capita (in U.S. dollars)
20,0000–31,600
10,000–19,999
2,000–9,999
580–1,999
Major Mines
Al Aluminum
Co Cobalt
Cu Copper
Au Gold
Fe Iron ore
Pb Lead
Mn Manganese
Ni Nickel
Ag Silver
Sn Tin
U Uranium
Zn Zinc
Coal
Diamonds
Manufacturing center
Natural gas
Opal mine
Petroleum
Au Processing plant

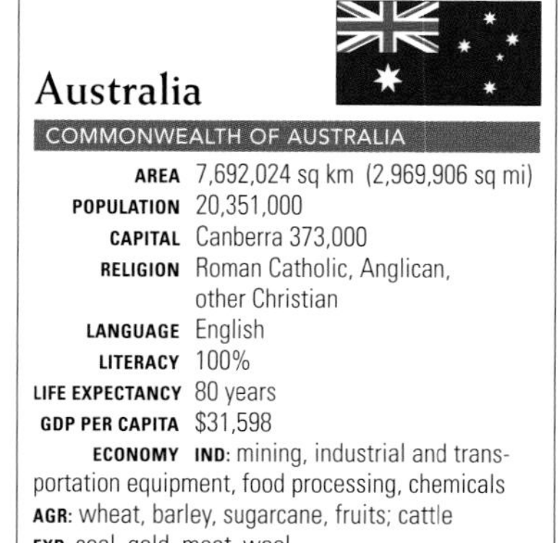

Australia

COMMONWEALTH OF AUSTRALIA

AREA 7,692,024 sq km (2,969,906 sq mi)
POPULATION 20,351,000
CAPITAL Canberra 373,000
RELIGION Roman Catholic, Anglican, other Christian
LANGUAGE English
LITERACY 100%
LIFE EXPECTANCY 80 years
GDP PER CAPITA $31,598
ECONOMY **IND:** mining, industrial and transportation equipment, food processing, chemicals **AGR:** wheat, barley, sugarcane, fruits; cattle **EXP:** coal, gold, meat, wool

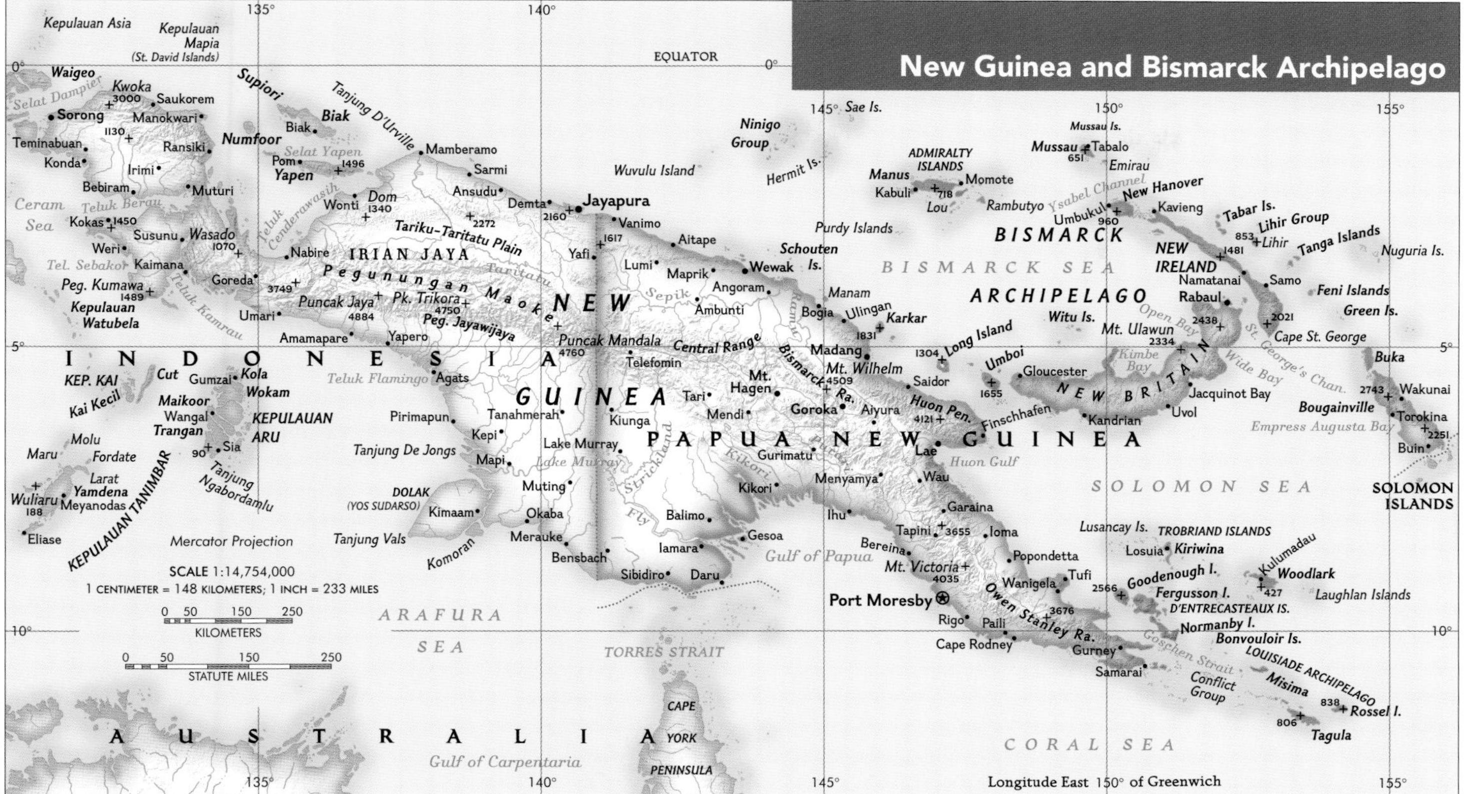
New Guinea and Bismarck Archipelago
EQUATOR
Kepulauan Asia
Kepulauan Mapia (St. David Islands)
Waigeo
Selat Dampier
Sorong
Kwoka 3000
Saukorem
Manokwari
Supiori
Biak
Numfoor
Yapen
Selat Yapen
Tanjung D'Urville
Mamberamo
Sarmi
Teminabuan
Konda
Ransiki
Irimi
Bebiram
Muturi
Ceram Sea
Teluk Berau
Teluk Cenderawasih
Kokas 1450
Wonti
Dom 1340
Susunu
Wasado 1070
Weri
Tel. Sebakor
Kaimana
Peg. Kumawa 1489
Kepulauan Watubela
Goreda
Umari
Teluk Kamrau
Nabire
IRIAN JAYA
Tariku-Taritatu Plain
2272
Pegunungan Maoke
Puncak Jaya 4884
Pk. Trikora 4750
Peg. Jayawijaya
Amamapare
Yapero
Demta
Jayapura
2160
Vanimo
Yafi
1617
Aitape
Lumi
Maprik
Wewak
Sepik
Angoram
Ambunti
NEW GUINEA
Puncak Mandala 4760
Central Range
Telefomin
INDONESIA
KEP. KAI
Kai Kecil
Cut
Gumzai
Kola
Wokam
Maikoor
Wangal
Trangan
KEPULAUAN ARU
Teluk Flamingo
Agats
Pirimapun
Tanahmerah
Kiunga
Tari
Mendi
Mt. Hagen
Molu
Fordate
Maru
Larat
Yamdena
Wuliaru
Meyanodas
188
Eliase
KEPULAUAN TANIMBAR
Sia
Tanjung Ngabordamlu
Tanjung De Jongs
DOLAK (YOS SUDARSO)
Kimaam
Kepi
Mapi
Lake Murray
Strickland
PAPUA NEW GUINEA
Muting
Okaba
Merauke
Bensbach
Fly
Balimo
Kikori
Iamara
Sibidiro
Daru
Gesoa
Gulf of Papua
Mercator Projection
SCALE 1:14,754,000
1 CENTIMETER = 148 KILOMETERS; 1 INCH = 233 MILES
KILOMETERS
STATUTE MILES
Tanjung Vals
Komoran
ARAFURA SEA
TORRES STRAIT
AUSTRALIA
CAPE YORK PENINSULA
Gulf of Carpentaria
Ninigo Group
Wuvulu Island
Hermit Is.
Sae Is.
ADMIRALTY ISLANDS
Manus
Kabuli
Lou
Momote
Mussau Is.
Mussau 651
Tabalo
Emirau
Purdy Islands
Schouten Is.
BISMARCK SEA
BISMARCK ARCHIPELAGO
Rambutyo
Ysabel Channel
Umbukul
New Hanover
Kavieng
Tabar Is.
Lihir Group
Lihir
Tanga Islands
Nuguria Is.
NEW IRELAND
Namatanai
Samo
Feni Islands
Green Is.
Rabaul
Witu Is.
Mt. Ulawun 2334
Open Bay
Cape St. George
St. George's Chan.
Manam
Bogia
Ulingan
Karkar
Madang
Mt. Wilhelm 4509
Bismarck Ra.
Long Island
Umboi
Gloucester
Kimbe Bay
Wide Bay
NEW BRITAIN
Buka
Wakunai
Torokina
Bougainville
Jacquinot Bay
Uvol
Empress Augusta Bay
Buin
Saidor
Huon Pen.
Finschhafen
Kandrian
Goroka
Aiyura
Lae
Huon Gulf
Gurimatu
Menyamya
Wau
Garaina
SOLOMON SEA
SOLOMON ISLANDS
Ihu
Bereina
Tapini
Ioma
Mt. Victoria 4035
Popondetta
Lusancay Is.
TROBRIAND ISLANDS
Losuia
Kiriwina
Kulumadau
Woodlark
Port Moresby
Owen Stanley Ra.
Wanigela
Tufi
Goodenough I.
Fergusson I.
D'ENTRECASTEAUX IS.
Laughlan Islands
Normanby I.
Bonvouloir Is.
Rigo
Paili
Cape Rodney
Gurney
Samarai
Goschen Strait
Conflict Group
LOUISIADE ARCHIPELAGO
Misima
Rossel I.
Tagula
CORAL SEA
Longitude East 150° of Greenwich

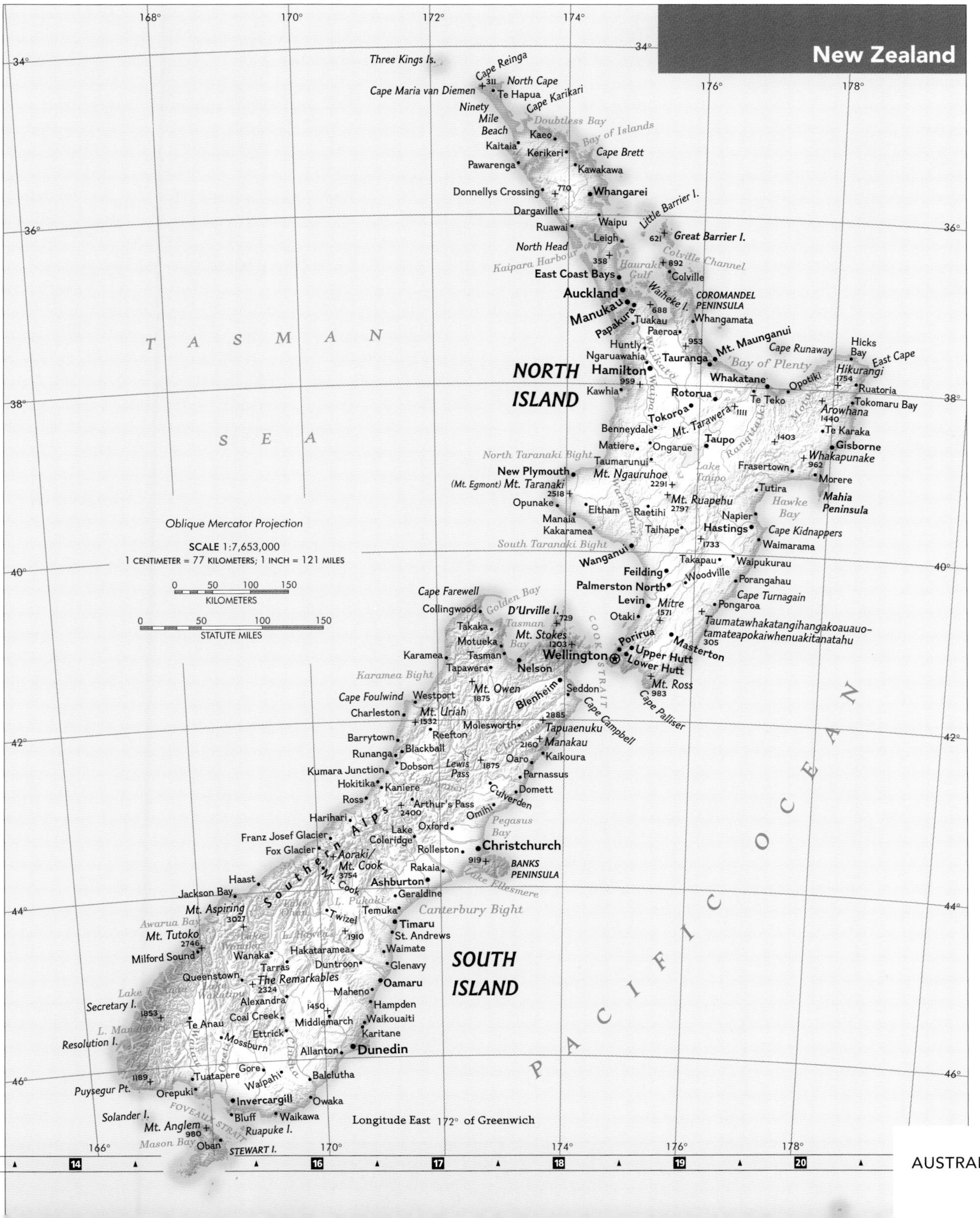

New Zealand

Three Kings Is.
Cape Reinga
North Cape
Cape Maria van Diemen
Te Hapua
Cape Karikari
Ninety Mile Beach
Doubtless Bay
Kaeo
Bay of Islands
Kaitaia
Kerikeri
Cape Brett
Pawarenga
Kawakawa
Donnellys Crossing
Whangarei
Dargaville
Little Barrier I.
Waipu
Ruawai
Leigh
Great Barrier I.
North Head
Kaipara Harbour
Hauraki Gulf
Colville Channel
Colville
East Coast Bays
Auckland
Manukau
Waiheke I.
COROMANDEL PENINSULA
Papakura
Tuakau
Whangamata
Paeroa
TASMAN SEA
Huntly
Ngaruawahia
Tauranga
Mt. Maunganui
Cape Runaway
Hicks Bay
East Cape
Bay of Plenty
Hikurangi
NORTH ISLAND
Hamilton
Whakatane
Opotiki
Ruatoria
Kawhia
Rotorua
Te Teko
Tokomaru Bay
Arowhana
Te Karaka
Tokoroa
Mt. Tarawera
Benneydale
Taupo
Gisborne
Matiere
Ongarue
Whakapunake
Taumarunui
Lake Taupo
Frasertown
Morere
North Taranaki Bight
New Plymouth
Mt. Ngauruhoe
(Mt. Egmont) Mt. Taranaki
Mt. Ruapehu
Tutira
Mahia Peninsula
Opunake
Eltham
Raetihi
Hawke Bay
Napier
Manaia
Taihape
Hastings
Cape Kidnappers
Kakaramea
Waimarama
South Taranaki Bight
Wanganui
Takapau
Waipukurau
Feilding
Woodville
Porangahau
Palmerston North
Cape Turnagain
Levin
Mitre
Pongaroa
Otaki
Taumatawhakatangihangakoauauotamateapokaiwhenuakitanatahu
Porirua
Masterton
Upper Hutt
Lower Hutt
Wellington
Mt. Ross
Cape Palliser
Cape Farewell
Golden Bay
Collingwood
D'Urville I.
Takaka
Tasman Bay
Mt. Stokes
Motueka
Tasman
Karamea
Nelson
Tapawera
Karamea Bight
COOK STRAIT
Cape Foulwind
Westport
Mt. Owen
Seddon
Blenheim
Charleston
Mt. Uriah
Cape Campbell
Molesworth
Tapuaenuku
Barrytown
Reefton
Manakau
Runanga
Blackball
Clarence
Kaikoura
Dobson
Oaro
Lewis Pass
Parnassus
Kumara Junction
Hokitika
Kaniere
Domett
Ross
Culverden
Arthur's Pass
Omihi
Harihari
Oxford
Pegasus Bay
Lake Coleridge
Franz Josef Glacier
Rolleston
Christchurch
Fox Glacier
Aoraki/Mt. Cook
Rakaia
BANKS PENINSULA
Haast
Southern Alps
Ashburton
Lake Ellesmere
Jackson Bay
Geraldine
Mt. Aspiring
Lake Pukaki
Temuka
Canterbury Bight
Awarua Bay
Twizel
Timaru
Mt. Tutoko
St. Andrews
Milford Sound
Waimate
Wanaka
Hakataramea
Glenavy
SOUTH ISLAND
Tarras
Duntroon
Queenstown
The Remarkables
Oamaru
Lake Wakatipu
Maheno
Secretary I.
Alexandra
Hampden
Coal Creek
Waikouaiti
Te Anau
Middlemarch
Karitane
Ettrick
Resolution I.
Mossburn
Allanton
Dunedin
Gore
Tuatapere
Waipahi
Balclutha
Puysegur Pt.
Orepuki
Owaka
Invercargill
FOVEAUX STRAIT
Bluff
Waikawa
Solander I.
Ruapuke I.
Mt. Anglem
Mason Bay
Oban
STEWART I.
PACIFIC OCEAN
Oblique Mercator Projection
SCALE 1:7,653,000
1 CENTIMETER = 77 KILOMETERS; 1 INCH = 121 MILES
KILOMETERS
STATUTE MILES
Longitude East 172° of Greenwich

New Zealand

NEW ZEALAND

AREA 270,534 sq km (104,454 sq mi)
POPULATION 4,107,000
CAPITAL Wellington 343,000
RELIGION Anglican, Roman Catholic, Presbyterian
LANGUAGE English (official), Maori (official)
LITERACY 99%
LIFE EXPECTANCY 79 years
GDP PER CAPITA $24,499
ECONOMY **IND:** food processing, wood and paper products, textiles, machinery **AGR:** wheat, barley, potatoes, pulses; wool; fish **EXP:** dairy products, meat, wood and wood products, fish

Papua New Guinea

IND. STATE OF PAPUA NEW GUINEA

AREA 462,840 sq km (178,703 sq mi)
POPULATION 5,887,000
CAPITAL Port Moresby 275,000
RELIGION indigenous beliefs, Roman Catholic, Lutheran, other Protestant
LANGUAGE Melanesian Pidgin, 715 indigenous languages
LITERACY 65%
LIFE EXPECTANCY 55 years
GDP PER CAPITA $824
ECONOMY **IND:** copra crushing, palm oil processing, plywood production, wood chip production **AGR:** coffee, cocoa, coconuts, palm kernels; poultry **EXP:** oil, gold, copper ore, logs

NORTH PACIFIC
AUSTRALIA
TASMAN SEA
CORAL SEA
PHILIPPINE SEA
INDIAN OCEAN
MICRONESIA
MELANESIA
POLYNESIA
NEW ZEALAND
PAPUA NEW GUINEA
SOLOMON ISLANDS
VANUATU
FIJI ISLANDS
TONGA
SAMOA
KIRIBATI
TUVALU
MARSHALL ISLANDS
FEDERATED STATES OF MICRONESIA
NAURU
PALAU
NEW CALEDONIA
JAPAN
CHINA
INDONESIA
PHILIPPINES
TROPIC OF CANCER
TROPIC OF CAPRICORN
EQUATOR
Date Line
Refer to pages 112–113 for large-scale map of Hawai'i
Longitude East 150° of Greenwich

UNITED STATES
Washington
San Francisco
Cape Mendocino
Sierra Nevada
LOS ANGELES
SAN DIEGO
TIJUANA
Baja California
Golfo de California
Isla de Guadalupe
Mexico
Isla Cedros
Punta Eugenia
Rocas Alijos
Mexico
TROPIC OF CANCER
Cabo Falso
Mazatlán
MEXICO
MÉXICO
Islas Revillagigedo
Mexico
Isla San Benedicto
Isla Socorro
Isla Clarión
Isla Roca Partida
Acapulco
GULF OF MEXICO
ATLANTIC OCEAN
BAHAMAS
CUBA
HAITI
JAMAICA
DOMINICAN REPUBLIC
Belmopan
BELIZE
GUATEMALA
GUATEMALA
HONDURAS
Tegucigalpa
San Salvador
EL SALVADOR
NICARAGUA
MANAGUA
CARIBBEAN SEA
Clipperton
France
San José
COSTA RICA
PANAMA
Panamá
CARACAS
VENEZUELA
Golfo de Panamá
Isla del Coco
Costa Rica
Isla de Malpelo
Colombia
BOGOTÁ
COLOMBIA
Isla Darwin
Ecuador
Galápagos Islands
(Archipiélago de Colón)
Isla Fernandina
Isla Isabela
Isla San Salvador
Isla Santa Cruz
Isla San Cristóbal
Isla Santa María
EQUATOR
QUITO
ECUADOR
GUAYAQUIL
Refer to page 120 for large-scale map of the Galápagos Islands
ANDES
BRAZIL
Trujillo
PERU
LIMA
BOLIVIA
La Paz
MARQUESAS ISLANDS
France
Eiao
Hatutu
Nuku Hiva
Ua Huka
51
Hiva Oa
50
Ua Pu
Tahuata
Mohotani (Motane)
Fatu Hiva
Caroline Island
TUAMOTU ARCHIPELAGO
44
43
46
Manihi
Takaroa
Napuka
Pukapuka
Makatea
Rangiroa
Tikei
45
Moorea
Makemo
Papeete
Anaa
Tatakoto
Tahiti
49
Hikueru
Hao
FRENCH POLYNESIA
France
Hereheretue
Îles Duc de Gloucester
Tureia
Tematagi
Moruroa
Marutea
Tubuai
Morane
Mangareva
47
Raivavae (Vavitu)
Îles Gambier
Temoe
52
United Kingdom
Oeno Island
Henderson Island
Ducie Island
Pitcairn Island
53
TROPIC OF CAPRICORN
Sala-y-Gómez
Chile
Isla de Pascua
(Easter Island)
Chile
Isla San Félix
Isla San Ambrosio
Chile
Rapa
Marotiri
(Îlots de Bass)
Chile
Islas Juan Fernández
Isla Santa Clara
Isla Alejandro Selkirk
Isla Róbinson Crusoe
Valparaíso
SANTIAGO
PACIFIC OCEAN
Concepción
CHILE
ARGENTINA
Isla Grande de Chiloé
Archipiélago de los Chonos
Golfo de Penas
Isla Campana
Isla Wellington
Isla Madre de Dios
Archipiélago Reina Adelaida
Isla Santa Inés
Mercator Projection
SCALE 1:39,295,000 AT THE EQUATOR
1 CENTIMETER = 392 KILOMETERS; 1 INCH = 620 MILES
0 500 1000 1500 2000
KILOMETERS
0 500 1000 1500 2000
STATUTE MILES
20 Numbered islands correspond to larger-scale maps on the following pages.
Major Pacific Island Groups
Mariana Islands
Marshall Islands
Caroline Islands
Society Islands and Tuamotu Archipelago
Other island
Longitude West of Greenwich

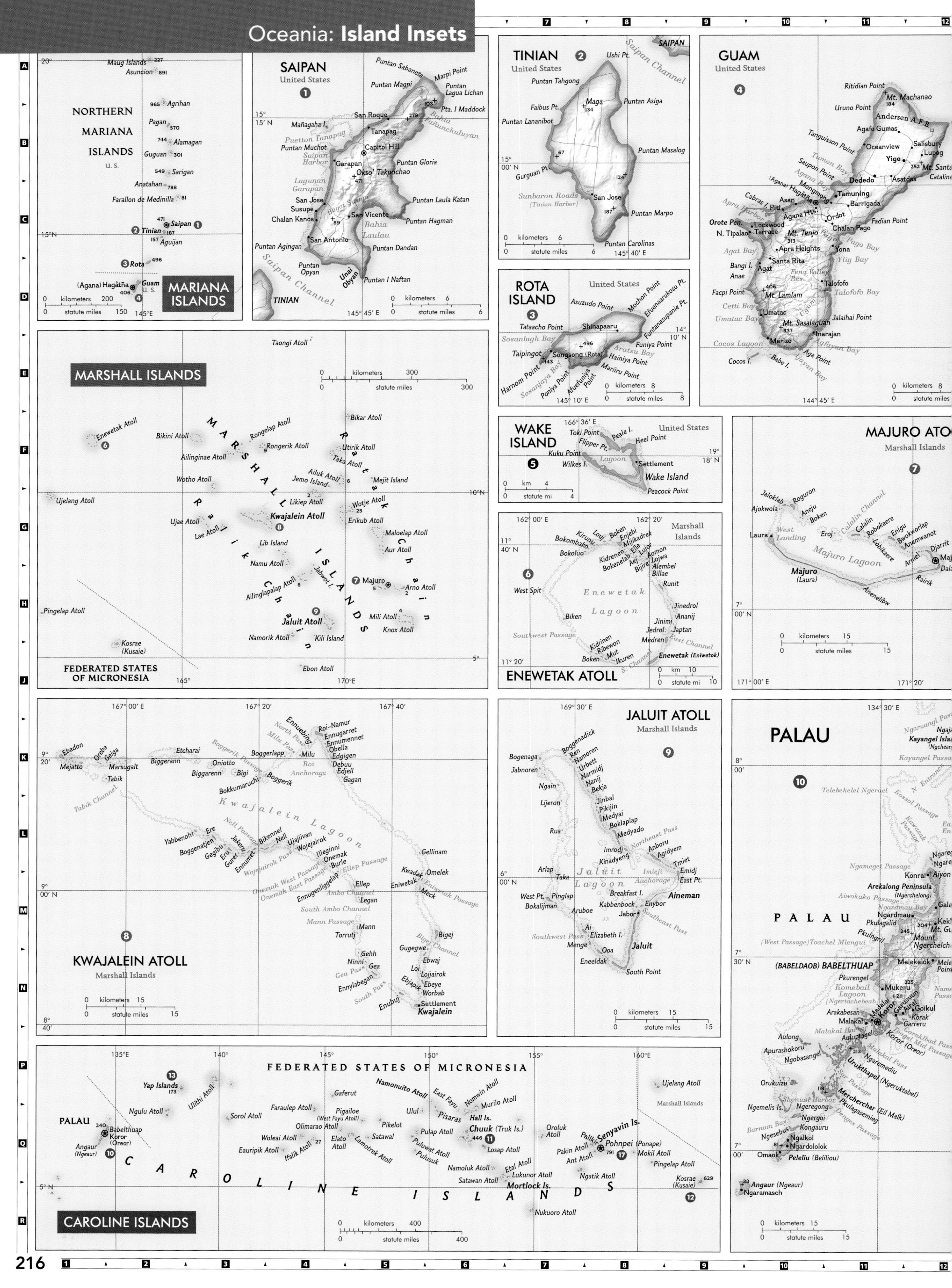
NORTHERN MARIANA ISLANDS
U. S.
MARIANA ISLANDS
Maug Islands
Asuncion
Agrihan
Pagan
Alamagan
Guguan
Sarigan
Anatahan
Farallon de Medinilla
Saipan
Tinian
Aguijan
Rota
(Agana) Hagåtña
Guam
SAIPAN
United States
Puntan Sabaneta
Marpi Point
Puntan Magpi
Puntan Lagua Lichan
Pta. I Maddock
Bahia Fañunchuluyan
San Roque
Mañagaha I.
Puetton Tanapag
Tanapag
Puntan Muchot
Capitol Hill
Saipan Harbor
Garapan
Puntan Gloria
Okso' Takpochao
Lagunan Garapan
San Jose
Susupe
Puntan Laula Katan
Chalan Kanoa
San Vicente
Bahia Laulau
Puntan Hagman
San Antonio
Puntan Agingan
Puntan Dandan
Puntan Opyan
Unai Obyan
Puntan I Naftan
Saipan Channel
TINIAN
TINIAN
United States
Ushi Pt.
Saipan Channel
Puntan Tahgong
Faibus Pt.
Maga
Puntan Asiga
Puntan Lananibot
Puntan Masalog
Gurguan Pt.
San Jose
Sunharon Roads (Tinian Harbor)
Puntan Marpo
Puntan Carolinas
GUAM
United States
Ritidian Point
Mt. Machanao
Uruno Point
Andersen A.F.B.
Agafo Gumas
Tanguisson Point
Oceanview
Salisbury
Lupog
Yigo
Mt. Santa Rosa
Catalina
Tumon Bay
Saupon Point
Dededo
Asatdas
Mongmong
Tamuning
Barrigada
Cabras I.
Piti
Asan
Orote Pen.
Agana Hts.
Ordot
Fadian Point
Lockwood Terrace
N. Tipalao
Mt. Tenjo
Chalan Pago
Apra Heights
Pago Bay
Agat Bay
Yona
Ylig Bay
Santa Rita
Bangi I.
Agat
Anae
Talofofo
Facpi Point
Mt. Lamlam
Talofofo Bay
Cetti Bay
Umatac
Umatac Bay
Jalaihai Point
Mt. Sasalaguan
Inarajan
Merizo
Cocos Lagoon
Achang Bay
Cocos I.
Babe I.
Aga Point
ROTA ISLAND
United States
Asuzudo Point
Mochon Point
Efuenaiarukosu Pt.
Funtanasupanie Pt.
Tataacho Point
Shinapaaru
Sosanlagh Bay
Funiya Point
Taipingot
Songsong (Rota)
Aratsu Bay
Hainiya Point
Mariiru Point
Harnom Point
Poniya Point
Afuefuniya Point
MARSHALL ISLANDS
Taongi Atoll
Bikar Atoll
Enewetak Atoll
Bikini Atoll
Rongelap Atoll
Rongerik Atoll
Utirik Atoll
Taka Atoll
Ailinginae Atoll
Wotho Atoll
Ailuk Atoll
Jemo Island
Mejit Island
Ujelang Atoll
Likiep Atoll
Wotje Atoll
Ujae Atoll
Kwajalein Atoll
Erikub Atoll
Lae Atoll
Maloelap Atoll
Lib Island
Aur Atoll
Namu Atoll
Jabwot I.
Majuro
Arno Atoll
Ailinglapalap Atoll
Pingelap Atoll
Jaluit Atoll
Mili Atoll
Namorik Atoll
Kili Island
Knox Atoll
Kosrae (Kusaie)
Ebon Atoll
FEDERATED STATES OF MICRONESIA
MARSHALL ISLANDS
Ralik Chain
Ratak Chain
WAKE ISLAND
United States
Toki Point
Peale I.
Heel Point
Flipper Pt.
Kuku Point
Lagoon
Wilkes I.
Settlement
Wake Island
Peacock Point
MAJURO ATOLL
Marshall Islands
Jaloklab
Rongron
Ajokwola
Aneju
Boken
Calalin Channel
Laura
West Landing
Eroj
Calalin
Robokaere
Enigu
Bwokwonlap
Anemwanot
Lobikaere
Djarrit
Majuro Lagoon
Arijiel
Majuro (Laura)
Rairik
Anenelibw
ENEWETAK ATOLL
Marshall Islands
Kirunu
Louj
Boken
Bokombako
Enjebi
Mijikadrek
Bokoluo
Kidrenen
Elle
Bokenelab
Aej
Lujor
Aomon
Bijire
Lojwa
Alembel
Billae
West Spit
Runit
Enewetak Lagoon
Jinedrol
Ananij
Biken
Jinimi
Jedrol
Japtan
Southwest Passage
Medren
East Channel
Kidrinen
Ribewon
Mut
Ikuren
Boken
S. Channel
Enewetak (Eniwetok)
KWAJALEIN ATOLL
Marshall Islands
Ennubing
Roi-Namur
North Pass
Ennugarret
Mlu Pass
Ennumennet
Obella
Ebadon
Oreba
Geiga
Etcharai
Boggerik Passage
Boggerlapp
Mlu
Edgigen
Mejatto
Marsugalt
Biggerann
Oniotto
Roi Anchorage
Debuu
Tabik
Biggarenn
Bigi
Edjell
Gagan
Bokkumaruchi
Boggerik
Tabik Channel
Kwajalein Lagoon
Nell Passage
Yabbenohr
Ere
Bikennel
Boggenatjen
Nell
Ujajiivan
Gegibu
Wojejairok
Eru
Illeginni
Jakeru
Onemak
Gellinam
Gurei
Burle
Ennumet
Wojejairok Pass
Ellep Passage
Onemak West Passage
Kwadak
Omelek
Onemak East Passage
Ennugenliggelap
Ellep
Eniwetak
Meck
Ambo Channel
Legan
South Ambo Channel
Mann Passage
Mann
Torrutj
Bigej
Bigej Channel
Gugegwe
Gehh
Ninni
Gea
Ebwaj
Loi
Gea Pass
Lojjairok
Ennylabegan
Ebeye
Ebjapik
Worbab
South Pass
Enubuj
Settlement
Kwajalein
JALUIT ATOLL
Marshall Islands
Boggenadick
Bogenaga
Ren
Namoren
Jabnoren
Urbett
Narmidj
Ngain
Nanij
Bekja
Lijeron
Jinbal
Pikijin
Medyai
Boklaplap
Rua
Medyado
Northeast Pass
Imrodj
Anboru
Kinadyeng
Agidyem
Arlap
Tmiet
Imieji Anchorage
Emidj
Taka
Jaluit Lagoon
East Pt.
West Pt.
Pinglap
Breakfast I.
Aineman
Bokalijman
Kabbenbock
Enybor
Aruboe
Jabor
Southeast Pass
Ai
Elizabeth I.
Southwest Pass
Menge
Jaluit
Ooa
Eneeldak
South Point
PALAU
Ngaruangl Passage
Kayangel Islands (Ngcheangel)
Kayangel Passage
Telebekelel Ngerael
N. Entrance
Kossol Passage
Kossol Reef
Kawasak Passage
Ngamegei Passage
Konrai
Aiyon
Arekalong Peninsula (Ngerchelong)
Aiwokako Passage
Ngardmau Bay
Ngardmau
Pkulagalid
Pkulngril
Mt. Gulitel
Mount Ngerchelch
(West Passage) Toachel Mlengui
(BABELDAOB) BABELTHUAP
Melekeiok
Pkurengel
Mukeru
Komebail Lagoon (Ngertachebeab)
Goikul
Arakabesan
Malakal
Koror (Oreor)
Korak
Garreru
Malakal Harbor
Aulptagel
Aulong
Apurashokoru
Ngobasangel
Malakal Pass
Ngaremediu
Orukuizu
Urukthapel (Ngeruktabel)
Mercherchar (Eil Malk)
Ngemelis Is.
Ngeregong
Ngergoi
Barnum Bay
Ngesebus
Kongauru
Ngalkol
Ngardololok
Omaok
Peleliu (Beliliou)
Angaur (Ngeaur)
Ngaramasch
CAROLINE ISLANDS
FEDERATED STATES OF MICRONESIA
Yap Islands
Ulithi Atoll
Ngulu Atoll
PALAU
Babelthuap
Koror (Oreor)
Angaur (Ngeaur)
Sorol Atoll
Faraulep Atoll
Gaferut
Namonuito Atoll
East Fayu
Nomwin Atoll
Murilo Atoll
Pigailoe (West Fayu Atoll)
Olimarao Atoll
Ulul
Pisaras
Hall Is.
Chuuk (Truk Is.)
Pikelot
Pulap Atoll
Woleai Atoll
Satawal
Elato Atoll
Eauripik Atoll
Ifalik Atoll
Lamotrek Atoll
Puluwat Atoll
Pulusuk
Losap Atoll
Namoluk Atoll
Etal Atoll
Satawan Atoll
Lukunor Atoll
Mortlock Is.
Nukuoro Atoll
Oroluk Atoll
Palikir
Senyavin Is.
Pohnpei (Ponape)
Pakin Atoll
Ant Atoll
Mokil Atoll
Pingelap Atoll
Ngatik Atoll
Ujelang Atoll
Marshall Islands
Kosrae (Kusaie)
CAROLINE ISLANDS

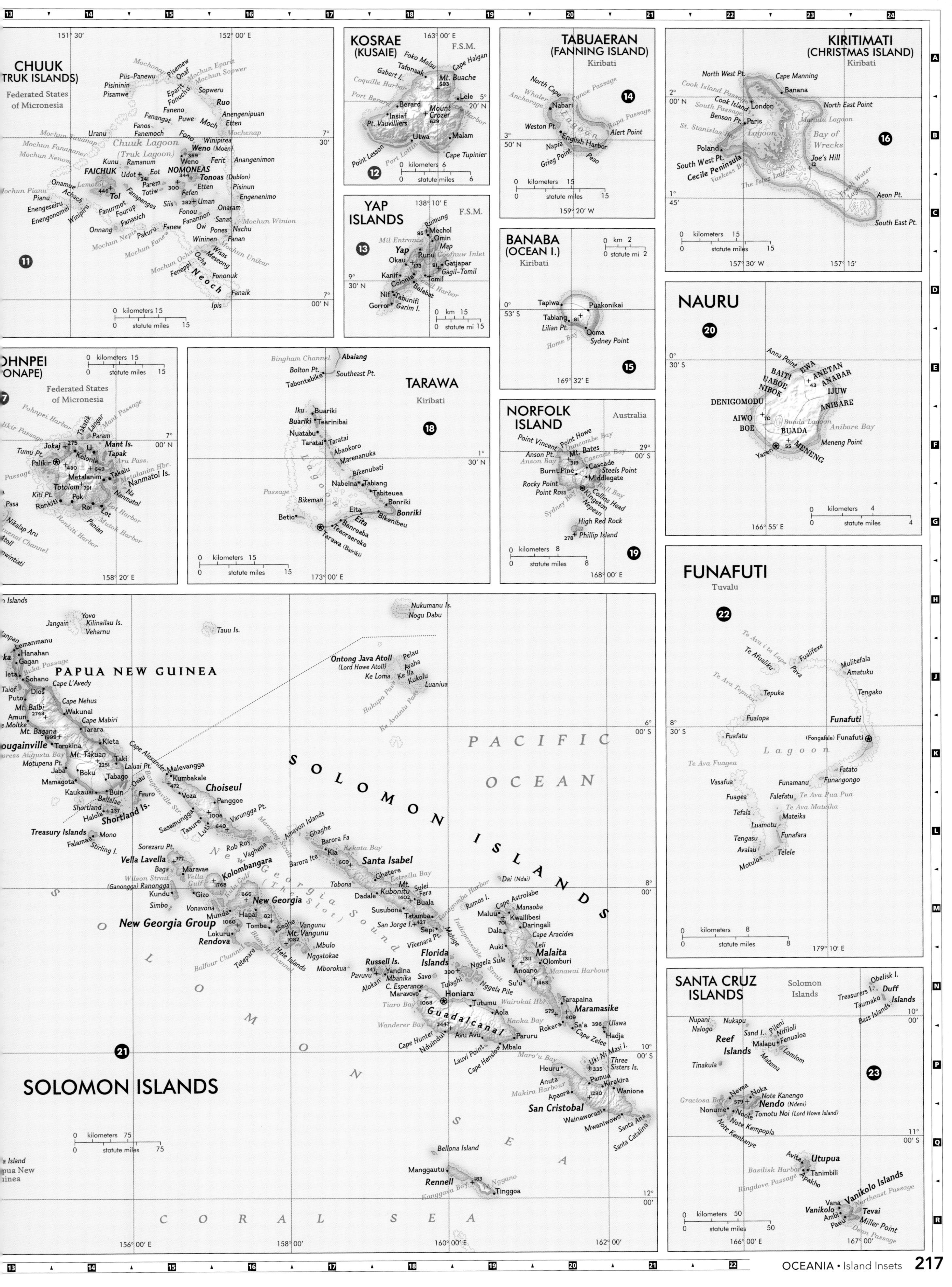
CHUUK
(TRUK ISLANDS)
Federated States of Micronesia
Chuuk Lagoon
(Truk Lagoon)
Weno (Moen)
FAICHUK
NOMONEAS
Tonoas (Dublon)
Tol
Fefen
Uman
Udot
Eot
Parem
Totiw
Fanapanges
Siis
Fonou
Onaram
Fanamnon
Sanat
Pones
Nachu
Wininen
Fanan
Ow
Fanew
Pakuru
Fanasich
Fourup
Fanurmot
Onnang
Winipiru
Enengenomei
Enengeseiru
Pianu
Onamue
Achach
Kunu
Ramanum
Fanamoch
Fanos
Uranu
Fanangat
Faneno
Puwe
Moch
Etten
Anengenipuan
Ruo
Sopweru
Eparit
Fonuchu
Pisemew
Onaf
Piis-Panewu
Pisininin
Pisamwe
Winipirea
Fono
Ferit
Anangenimon
Pisinun
Engenenimo
Neoch
Fononuk
Fanaik
Ipis
Fenepi
Wisas
Meseong
Ocha
Mochun Unikar
Mochun Winion
Mochun Nepis
Mochun Fanew
Mochun Ocha
Mochun Nenom
Mochun Fananan
Mochun Piaanu
Mochun Tauanap
Mochenap
Mochun Eparit
Mochun Sopweru
Mochonap
Lemolol
11
kilometers 15
statute miles 15
151° 30′
152° 00′ E
7° 30′
7° 00′ N
KOSRAE
(KUSAIE)
F.S.M.
Foko Malsu
Tafonsak
Gabert I.
Coquille Harbor
Port Berard
Berard
Insiaf
Pt. Vauvilliers
Mt. Buache
593
Cape Halgan
Lele
Mount Crozer
629
Utwa
Malam
Cape Tupinier
Point Lesson
Port Lottin
12
kilometers 6
statute miles 6
163° 00′ E
5° 20′ N
TABUAERAN
(FANNING ISLAND)
Kiribati
North Cape
Whaler Anchorage
Nabari
Weston Pt.
Napia
English Harbor
Grieg Point
Peao
Alert Point
Rapa Passage
Lagoon
14
kilometers 15
statute miles 15
3° 50′ N
159° 20′ W
KIRITIMATI
(CHRISTMAS ISLAND)
Kiribati
North West Pt.
Cape Manning
Banana
Cook Island Passage
Cook Island
London
South Passage
Benson Pt.
Paris
St. Stanislas Bay
Lagoon
North East Point
Manulu Lagoon
Bay of Wrecks
Poland
South West Pt.
Cecile Peninsula
Vaskess Bay
Joe's Hill
12
The Isles Lagoon
Fresh Water Lagoons
Aeon Pt.
South East Pt.
16
kilometers 15
statute miles 15
2° 00′ N
1° 45′
157° 30′ W
157° 15′
YAP
ISLANDS
F.S.M.
Rumung
Mechol
Omin
Map
Mil Entrance
Yap
Runu
Gofnuw Inlet
Okau
Gatjapar
Gagil-Tomil
Kanif
Tomil
Colonia
Balabat
Nif
Tabunifi
Gorror
Garim I.
Tomil Harbor
13
kilometers 15
statute mi 15
138° 10′ E
9° 30′ N
BANABA
(OCEAN I.)
Kiribati
Tapiwa
Tabiang
Lilian Pt.
Home Bay
Ooma
Sydney Point
Puakonikai
81
km 2
statute mi 2
0° 53′ S
169° 32′ E
15
NAURU
20
Anna Point
EWA
ANETAN
ANABAR
BAITI
UABOE
NIBOK
IJUW
DENIGOMODU
ANIBARE
AIWO
BOE
Buada Lagoon
BUADA
Anibare Bay
Meneng Point
Yaren
MENENG
kilometers 4
statute miles 4
0° 30′ S
166° 55′ E
POHNPEI
(PONAPE)
Federated States of Micronesia
Pohnpei Harbor
Mant Passage
Takatik
Langar
Param
Jokaj
Mant Is.
Tapak
Palikir
Kolonia
Metalanim
Metalanim Hbr.
Nanmatol Is.
Totolom
791
Kiti Pt.
Pok
Roi
Lot
Ronkiti
Pasa
Panian
Nikalap Aru
Na
Nanmatol
Tumu Pt.
Aru Pass.
Lot Harbor
Mutok Harbor
Ronkiti Harbor
7
kilometers 15
statute miles 15
7° 00′ N
158° 20′ E
TARAWA
Kiribati
Bingham Channel
Abaiang
Bolton Pt.
Southeast Pt.
Tabontebike
Iku
Buariki
Tearinibai
Nuatabu
Taratai
Abaokoro
Marenanuka
Bikenubati
Nabeina
Tabiang
Tabiteuea
Bonriki
Bikeman
Eita
Bikenibeu
Betio
Banreaba
Teaoraereke
Tarawa (Bairiki)
Lagoon
Passage
18
kilometers 15
statute miles 15
1° 30′ N
173° 00′ E
NORFOLK
ISLAND
Australia
Point Vincent
Point Howe
Duncombe Bay
Anson Pt.
Anson Bay
Mt. Bates
319
Cascade Bay
Cascade
Burnt Pine
Steels Point
Middlegate
Rocky Point
Point Ross
Kingston
Collins Head
Nepean
Sydney Bay
High Red Rock
Phillip Island
278
19
kilometers 8
statute miles 8
29° 00′ S
168° 00′ E
FUNAFUTI
Tuvalu
22
Te Ava i te Lape
Te Afualiku
Fualifeke
Pava
Mulitefala
Amatuku
Te Ava Tepuka
Tepuka
Tengako
Fualopa
Funafuti
(Fongafale) Funafuti
Fuafatu
Lagoon
Te Ava Fuagea
Fatato
Vasafua
Funamanu
Funangongo
Fuagea
Falefatu
Te Ava Pua Pua
Te Ava Mateika
Tefala
Mateika
Luamotu
Tengasu
Funafara
Avalau
Telele
Motuloa
kilometers 8
statute miles 8
8° 30′ S
179° 10′ E
SANTA CRUZ
ISLANDS
Solomon Islands
Obelisk I.
Duff Islands
Treasurers I.
Taumako
Bass Islands
Nupani
Nalogo
Nukapu
Pileni
Nifiloli
Fenualoa
Sand I.
Malapu
Reef Islands
Lomlom
Matema
Tinakula
Graciosa Bay
Nevea
Noka
579
Nete Kanengo
Nendo (Ndeni)
Nonume
Noole
Tomotu Noi (Lord Howe Island)
Nete Kempopla
Nete Kembanye
Avita
Utupua
Tanimbili
Basilisk Harbor
Apakho
Ringdove Passage
Vanikolo Islands
Northeast Passage
Vana
Vanikolo
Ambi
Paeu
Tevai
Miller Point
Dean Passage
23
kilometers 50
statute miles 50
10° 00′
11° 00′ S
166° 00′ E
167° 00′
SOLOMON ISLANDS
21
PAPUA NEW GUINEA
Nukumanu Is.
Nogu Dabu
Yovo
Kilinailau Is.
Veharnu
Jangain
Tauu Is.
Lemanmanu
Hanahan
Gagan
Buka Passage
Sohano
Cape L'Avedy
Dios
Puto
Cape Nehus
Wakunai
Mt. Balbi
2743
Cape Mabiri
Amun
Tarara
Mt. Bagana
1999
Kieta
Torokina
Bougainville
Empress Augusta Bay
Mt. Takuan
2251
Taki
Motupena Pt.
Jaba
Boku
Tabago
Mamagota
Kaukauai
Buin
Fauro
Ballalae
Shortland
Shortland Is.
Halola
237
Treasury Islands
Mono
Falamae
Stirling I.
Cape Alexander
Laluai Pt.
Bougainville Str.
Ovau
Malevangga
Kumbakale
472
Choiseul
Voza
Panggoe
Sasamungga
Tasure
Lutu
1006
640
Varunggo Pt.
Manning Strait
Ontong Java Atoll
(Lord Howe Atoll)
Pelau
Avaha
Ke Ila
Kukolu
Luaniua
Ke Loma
Hakupu Pass
Ke Avainiu Pass
PACIFIC
OCEAN
SOLOMON ISLANDS
Sorezaru Pt.
Vella Lavella
777
Baga
Maravae
Vella Gulf
Ranongga
(Ganongga)
Wilson Strait
Kolombangara
1768
Kula Gulf
Kundu
Gizo
Simbo
Vonavona
New Georgia
666
Munda
Hapai
821
New Georgia Group
1060
Tombe
Seghe
Vangunu
Mt. Vangunu
1082
Lokuru
Rendova
Mbulo
Nggatokae
Balfour Channel
Tetepare
Hele Islands
Blanche Channel
Mborokua
Rob Roy
Vaghena
Amavon Islands
Ghaghe
Barora Fa
Barora Ite
Kia
Rekata Bay
609
Santa Isabel
Estrella Bay
Ghatere
Tobona
Dadale
Kubonitu
1402
Sulei
Fera
Buala
Susubona
Tatamba
427
San Jorge I.
Sepi
New Georgia Sound
(The Slot)
Dai (Ndai)
Ramos I.
Cape Astrolabe
Manaoba
Maluu
Kwailibesi
701
Daringali
Cape Aracides
Dala
Auki
Leli
Malaita
Olomburi
1311
Anoano
Manawai Harbour
1463
Su'u
Nggela Sule
Nggela Pile
Indispensable Strait
Florida Islands
Vikenara Pt.
Mahige
Tulaghi
Savo
Russell Is.
Yandina
347
Pavuvu
Mbanika
Alokan
C. Esperance
Maravovo
390
Honiara
1068
Tutumu
Wairokai Hbr.
Tarapaina
Maramasike
579
Aola
Kaoka Bay
Tiaro Bay
Guadalcanal
2447
Wanderer Bay
Avu Avu
Paruru
Rokera
609
Sa'a
396
Ulawa
Hadja
Cape Zelee
Cape Hunter
Nduindui
Lauvi Point
Cape Henslow
Mbalo
Maro'u Bay
Uki Ni Masi I.
Three Sisters Is.
Heuru
335
Pamua
Kirakira
Anuta
Makira Harbour
Apaora
1280
Wanione
San Cristobal
Wainaworasi
Mwaniwowo
Santa Ana
Santa Catalina
Bellona Island
Manggautu
Rennell
183
Kanggava Bay
Nggano
Tinggoa
SOLOMON SEA
CORAL SEA
kilometers 75
statute miles 75
156° 00′ E
158° 00′
160° 00′ E
162° 00′
6° 00′ S
8° 00′
10° 00′ S
12° 00′

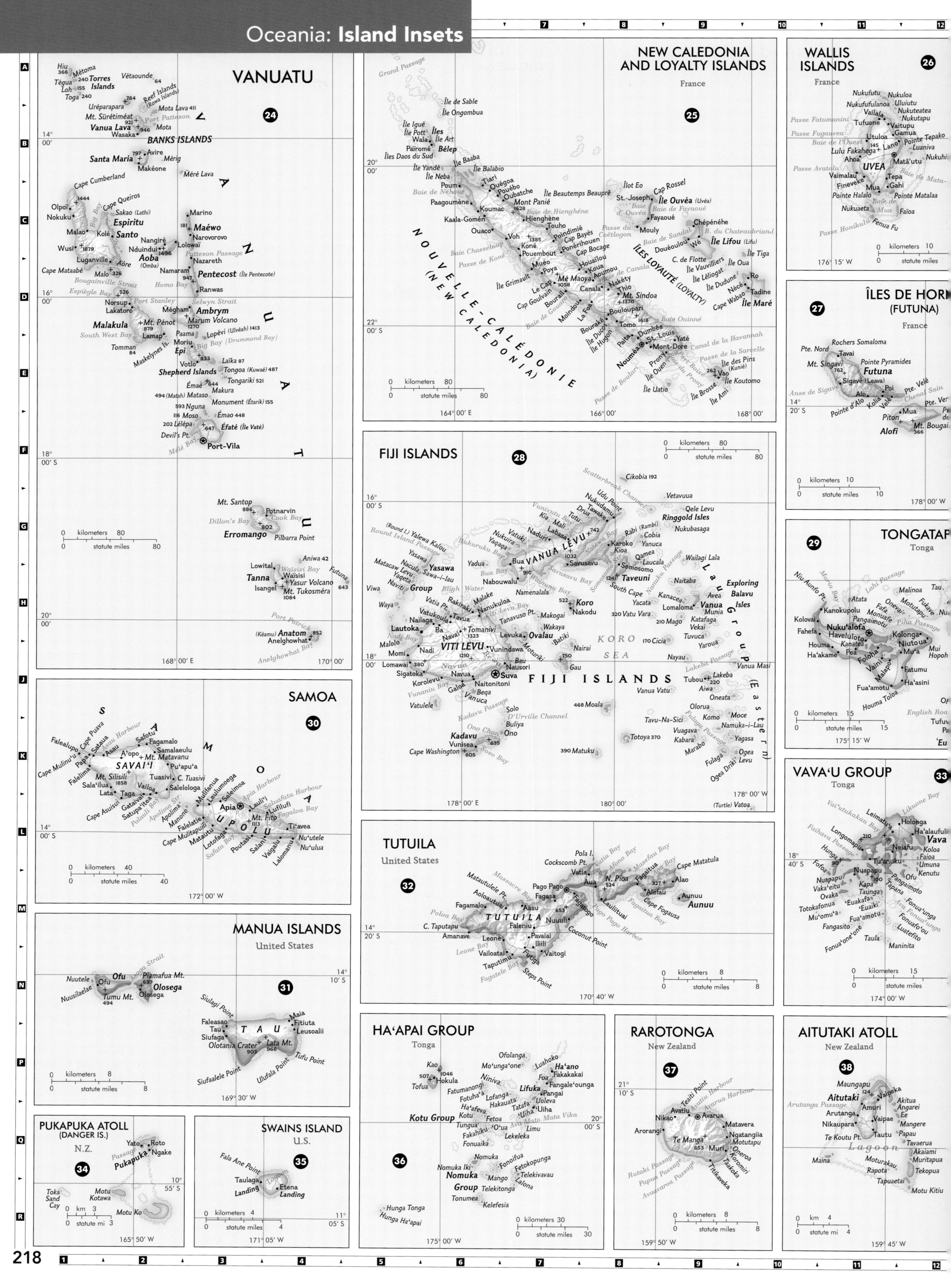

VANUATU
24
BANKS ISLANDS
Torres Islands
Vanua Lava
Santa Maria
Espiritu Santo
Aoba (Omba)
Maéwo
Pentecost (Île Pentecote)
Malakula
Ambrym
Epi
Shepherd Islands
Port-Vila
Erromango
Tanna
Anatom
NEW CALEDONIA AND LOYALTY ISLANDS
France
25
NOUVELLE-CALÉDONIE (NEW CALEDONIA)
ÎLES LOYAUTÉ (LOYALTY)
Nouméa
Île Ouvéa (Uvéa)
Île Lifou (Lifu)
Île Maré
WALLIS ISLANDS
France
26
UVEA
ÎLES DE HORN (FUTUNA)
France
27
Futuna
Alofi
FIJI ISLANDS
28
VITI LEVU
VANUA LEVU
Suva
KORO SEA
Lau Group (Eastern)
Kadavu
Taveuni
TONGATAPU
Tonga
29
Nuku'alofa
SAMOA
30
SAVAI'I
UPOLU
Apia
MANUA ISLANDS
United States
31
Ofu
Olosega
TAU
TUTUILA
United States
32
Pago Pago
Aunuu
VAVA'U GROUP
Tonga
33
PUKAPUKA ATOLL (DANGER IS.)
N.Z.
34
SWAINS ISLAND
U.S.
35
HA'APAI GROUP
Tonga
36
Kotu Group
Nomuka Group
RAROTONGA
New Zealand
37
Avarua
AITUTAKI ATOLL
New Zealand
38

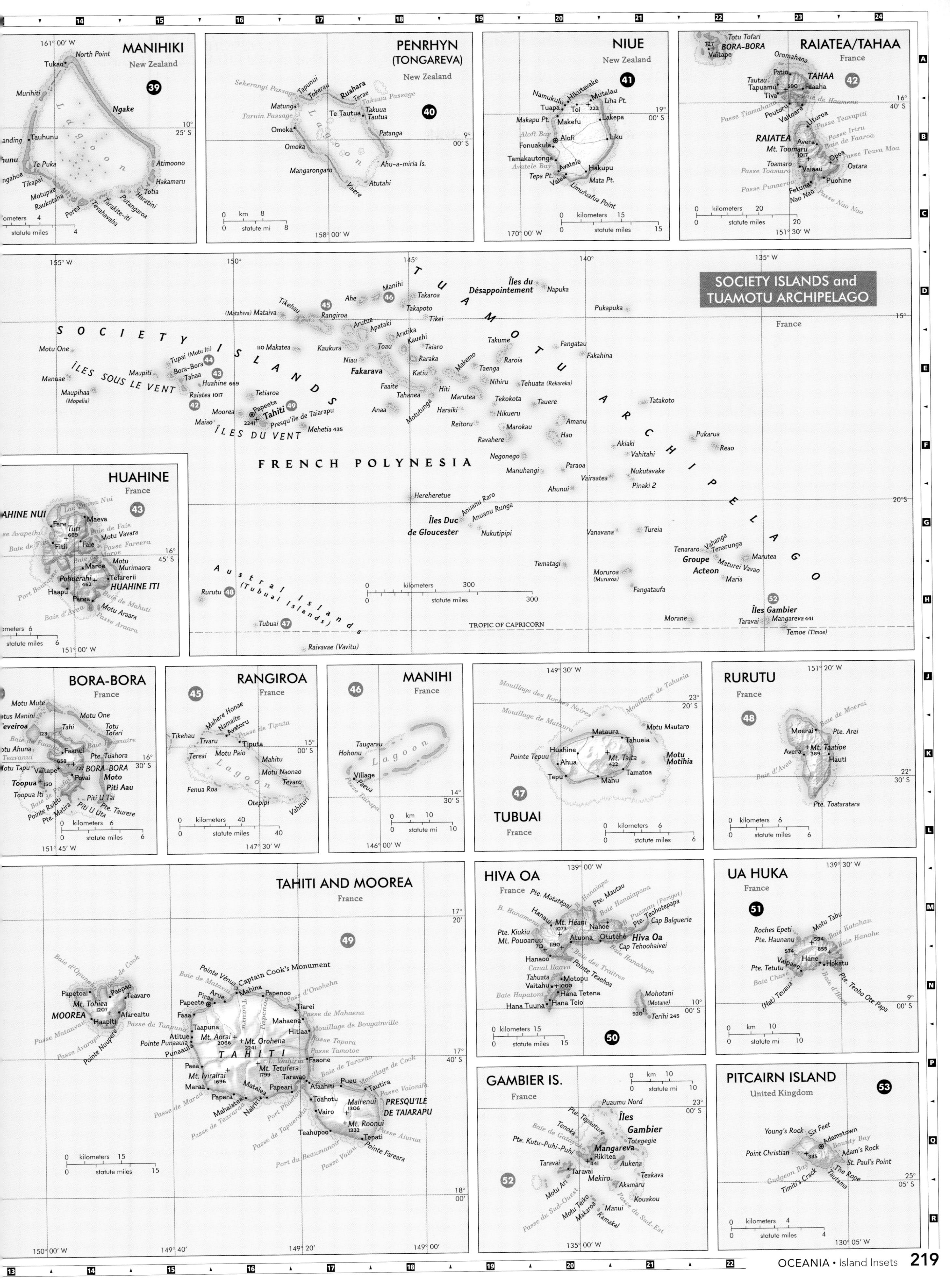

MANIHIKI
New Zealand
39
North Point
Tukao
Murihiti
Ngake
Lagoon
Tauhunu
Te Puka
Tikapai
Motupae
Raukotaha
Porea
Tevahavaha
Tarakite-iti
Putangaroa
Haratini
Totia
Hakamaru
Atimoono
161° 00′ W
10° 25′ S
PENRHYN (TONGAREVA)
New Zealand
40
Sekerangi Passage
Tarua Passage
Takuua Passage
Matunga
Tokerau
Tapunui
Ruahara
Terae
Te Tautua
Takuua
Tautua
Omoka
Patanga
Ahu-a-miria Is.
Mangarongaro
Vaiere
Atutahi
Lagoon
158° 00′ W
9° 00′ S
NIUE
New Zealand
41
Namukulu
Hikutavake
Mutalau
Liha Pt.
Tuapa
Toi
223
Makapu Pt.
Makefu
Lakepa
Alofi Bay
Alofi
Liku
Fonuakula
Tamakautonga
Avatele Bay
Avatele
Hakupu
Tepa Pt.
Vaiea
Mata Pt.
Limufuafua Point
170° 00′ W
19° 00′ S
RAIATEA/TAHAA
France
42
Totu Tofari
727
BORA-BORA
Vaitape
Oromahana
Patio
TAHAA
Tautau
Tapuamu
590
Faaaha
Tiva
Passe Tiamahana
Poutoru
Vaitoare
Uturoa
Passe Teavapiti
Passe Iriru
Baie de Faaroa
RAIATEA
Avera
Mt. Toomaru
1017
Opoa
Passe Teava Moa
Toamaro
Passe Toamaro
Vaiaau
Oatara
Passe Punaeroa
Puohine
Fetuna
Nao Nao
Passe Nao Nao
151° 30′ W
16° 40′ S
SOCIETY ISLANDS and TUAMOTU ARCHIPELAGO
France
SOCIETY ISLANDS
ÎLES SOUS LE VENT
ÎLES DU VENT
TUAMOTU ARCHIPELAGO
FRENCH POLYNESIA
Austral Islands (Tubuai Islands)
TROPIC OF CAPRICORN
Motu One
Manuae
Maupihaa (Mopelia)
Maupiti
Tupai (Motu Iti)
Bora-Bora
Tahaa
Huahine 669
Raiatea 1017
Tetiaroa
Moorea
Papeete
Tahiti
2241
Maiao
Presqu'île de Taiarapu
Mehetia 435
(Matahiva) Mataiva
Tikehau
Rangiroa
Ahe
Manihi
Takaroa
Takapoto
Tikei
Makatea
Arutua
Apataki
Kaukura
Aratika
Kauehi
Toau
Taiaro
Niau
Raraka
Fakarava
Katiu
Faaite
Tahanea
Hiti
Anaa
Motutunga
Haraiki
Marutea
Reitoru
Makemo
Taenga
Nihiru
Takume
Raroia
Fangatau
Fakahina
Îles du Désappointement
Napuka
Pukapuka
Tehuata (Rekareka)
Tekokota
Hikueru
Tauere
Marokau
Amanu
Hao
Ravahere
Negonego
Manuhangi
Paraoa
Vairaatea
Ahunui
Akiaki
Vahitahi
Nukutavake
Pinaki 2
Tatakoto
Pukarua
Reao
Hereheretue
Anuanu Raro
Anuanu Runga
Îles Duc de Gloucester
Nukutipipi
Vanavana
Tureia
Tenararo
Vahanga
Tenarunga
Groupe Acteon
Maturei Vavao
Marutea
Maria
Tematagi
Moruroa (Mururoa)
Fangataufa
Îles Gambier
Mangareva 441
Taravai
Temoe (Timoe)
Morane
Rurutu
Tubuai
Raivavae (Vavitu)
155° W
150°
145°
140°
135° W
15°
20°S
kilometers 300
statute miles 300
HUAHINE
France
43
HUAHINE NUI
Lac Fauna Nui
Maeva
Fare
Turi
669
Baie de Faie
Motu Vavara
Passe Avapeihi
Baie de Fitii
Fitii
Faie
Passe Fareera
Baie de Maroe
Motu Murimaora
Maroe
Tefarerii
Fare Pohuerahi
462
HUAHINE ITI
Port Bourayne
Haapu
Parea
Baie de Mahuti
Baie d'Avea
Motu Araara
Passe Araara
151° 00′ W
16° 45′ S
BORA-BORA
France
Motu Mute
Motu One
Tahi
Totu Tofari
Faanui
Baie de Faanui
Baie Hamaire
Pte. Tuahora
Vaitape
727
BORA-BORA
Povai
Moto
Piti Aau
Toopua
150
Toopua Iti
Piti U Tai
Piti U Uta
Pte. Taurere
Pointe Raititi
Pte. Matira
151° 45′ W
16° 30′ S
RANGIROA
France
45
Tikehau
Mahere Honae
Namaite
Avatoru
Passe de Tiputa
Tivaru
Tiputa
Tereai
Motu Paio
Mahitu
Motu Naonao
Tevaro
Fenua Roa
Otepipi
Vahituri
Lagoon
147° 30′ W
15° 00′ S
MANIHI
France
46
Taugarau
Hohonu
Lagoon
Village
Paeua
Passe Tairapa
146° 00′ W
14° 30′ S
TUBUAI
France
47
Mouillage des Roches Noires
Mouillage de Tahueia
Mouillage de Mataura
Mataura
Tahueia
Motu Mautaro
Huahine
Pointe Tepuu
Ahua
Mt. Taita
422
Motu Motihia
Tepu
Mahu
Tamatoa
149° 30′ W
23° 20′ S
RURUTU
France
48
Baie de Moerai
Moerai
Pte. Arei
Avera
Mt. Taatioe
389
Hauti
Baie d'Avera
Pte. Toataratara
151° 20′ W
22° 30′ S
TAHITI AND MOOREA
France
49
MOOREA
Baie d'Opunohu
Baie de Cook
Papetoai
Paopao
Teavaro
Mt. Tohiea
1207
Afareaitu
Haapiti
Passe Matauvau
Passe Avaroa
Pointe Nuupere
Passe de Taapuna
Pointe Vénus
Captain Cook's Monument
Baie de Matavai
Mahina
Papenoo
Pass d'Onoheha
Papeete
Pirae
Arue
Tiarei
Faaa
Passe de Mahaena
Mahaena
Mouillage de Bougainville
Taapuna
Mt. Aorai
2066
Mt. Orohena
2241
Hitiaa
Atitue
Pointe Punaauia
Punaauia
Passe Tapora
TAHITI
Passe Tamotoe
L. Vaihiria
Paea
Faaone
Mt. Tetufera
1799
Baie de Taravao
Mt. Ivirairai
1696
Taravao
Mouillage de Cook
Maraa
Papeari
Afaahiti
Pueu
Tautira
Passe de Maraa
Papara
Mataiea
Toahotu
Passe Vaionifa
Mahaiatea
Nahini
Port Phaeton
Mairenui
1306
PRESQU'ILE DE TAIARAPU
Passe de Teavaraa
Vairao
Passe de Tapuaeraha
Mt. Roonui
1332
Teahupoo
Tepati
Passe Aiurua
Port du Beaumanoir
Passe Vaiau
Pointe Fareara
150° 00′ W
149° 40′
149° 20′
149° 00′
17° 20′
17° 40′ S
18° 00′
HIVA OA
France
50
Pte. Matatepai
B. Hanaiapa
Pte. Mautau
Baie Hanaiapaoa
B. Hanamenu
Hanaui
Mt. Héani
1073
Nahoe
B. Puamau (Perigot)
Pte. Teohotepapa
Cap Balguerie
Pte. Kiukiu
Mt. Pouoanuu
Atuona
Otutéhé
Hiva Oa
Cap Tehoohaivei
713
1190
Baie Hanahupe
Hanaoo
Canal Haava
Baie des Traitres
Pointe Teaehoa
Tahuata
Motopu
Vaitahu
1000
Mohotani (Motane)
Baie Hapatoni
Hana Tetena
Hana Tuuna
Hana Teio
920
Terihi 245
139° 00′ W
10° 00′ S
UA HUKA
France
51
Motu Tabu
Baie Katohau
Roches Epeti
Baie Hanahe
Pte. Haunanu
594
855
574
Pte. Tetutu
Hane
Vaipaee
Hokatu
Baie Chavé
Baie d'Hane
(Hat) Teuaua
Pte. Teoho Ote Papa
139° 30′ W
9° 00′ S
GAMBIER IS.
France
52
Puaumu Nord
Îles Gambier
Pte. Tepaeture
Totegegie
Baie de Gatavake
Tenoka
Pte. Kutu-Puhi-Puhi
Mangareva
Rikitea
441
Aukena
Taravai
Tarava
Mekiro
Teakava
Akamaru
Motu Ari
Kouakou
Motu Teiko
Makaroa
Manui
Kamakal
Passe du Sud-Ouest
Passe du Sud-Est
135° 00′ W
23° 00′ S
PITCAIRN ISLAND
United Kingdom
53
Young's Rock
Six Feet
Adamstown
Bounty Bay
Point Christian
335
Adam's Rock
St. Paul's Point
Gudgeon Bay
Timiti's Crack
The Rope
Tautama
130° 05′ W
25° 05′ S

Independent Nations

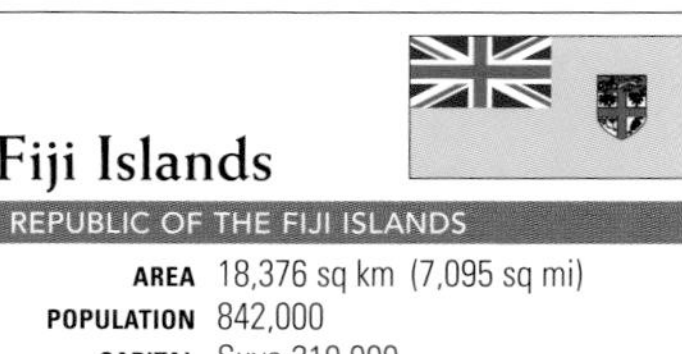

Fiji Islands

REPUBLIC OF THE FIJI ISLANDS

AREA 18,376 sq km (7,095 sq mi)
POPULATION 842,000
CAPITAL Suva 210,000
RELIGION Christian, Hindu, Muslim
LANGUAGE English (official), Fijian, Hindustani
LITERACY 94%
LIFE EXPECTANCY 68 years
GDP PER CAPITA $3,229
ECONOMY **IND:** tourism, sugar, clothing, copra **AGR:** sugarcane, coconuts, cassava (tapioca), rice; cattle; fish **EXP:** sugar, garments, gold, timber

Kiribati

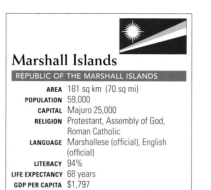

REPUBLIC OF KIRIBATI

AREA 811 sq km (313 sq mi)
POPULATION 92,000
CAPITAL Tarawa 42,000
RELIGION Roman Catholic, Protestant
LANGUAGE I-Kiribati, English (official)
LITERACY NA
LIFE EXPECTANCY 63 years
GDP PER CAPITA $815
ECONOMY **IND:** fishing, handicrafts **AGR:** copra, taro, breadfruit, sweet potatoes; fish **EXP:** copra, coconuts, seaweed, fish

Marshall Islands

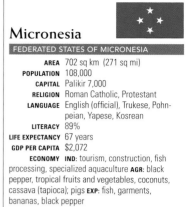

REPUBLIC OF THE MARSHALL ISLANDS

AREA 181 sq km (70 sq mi)
POPULATION 59,000
CAPITAL Majuro 25,000
RELIGION Protestant, Assembly of God, Roman Catholic
LANGUAGE Marshallese (official), English (official)
LITERACY 94%
LIFE EXPECTANCY 68 years
GDP PER CAPITA $1,797
ECONOMY **IND:** copra, tuna processing, tourism, craft items from shell, wood, and pearls **AGR:** coconuts, tomatoes, melons, taro; pigs **EXP:** copra cake, coconut oil, handicrafts, fish

Micronesia

FEDERATED STATES OF MICRONESIA

AREA 702 sq km (271 sq mi)
POPULATION 108,000
CAPITAL Palikir 7,000
RELIGION Roman Catholic, Protestant
LANGUAGE English (official), Trukese, Pohnpeian, Yapese, Kosrean
LITERACY 89%
LIFE EXPECTANCY 67 years
GDP PER CAPITA $2,072
ECONOMY **IND:** tourism, construction, fish processing, specialized aquaculture **AGR:** black pepper, tropical fruits and vegetables, coconuts, cassava (tapioca); pigs **EXP:** fish, garments, bananas, black pepper

Nauru

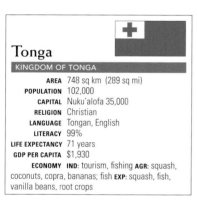

REPUBLIC OF NAURU

AREA 21 sq km (8 sq mi)
POPULATION 13,000
CAPITAL Yaren 5,000
RELIGION Protestant, Roman Catholic
LANGUAGE Nauruan (official), English
LITERACY NA
LIFE EXPECTANCY 61 years
GDP PER CAPITA $4,322
ECONOMY **IND:** phosphate mining, offshore banking, coconut products **AGR:** coconuts **EXP:** phosphates

Solomon Islands

SOLOMON ISLANDS

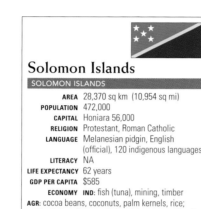

AREA 28,370 sq km (10,954 sq mi)
POPULATION 472,000
CAPITAL Honiara 56,000
RELIGION Protestant, Roman Catholic
LANGUAGE Melanesian pidgin, English (official), 120 indigenous languages
LITERACY NA
LIFE EXPECTANCY 62 years
GDP PER CAPITA $585
ECONOMY **IND:** fish (tuna), mining, timber **AGR:** cocoa beans, coconuts, palm kernels, rice; cattle; timber; fish **EXP:** timber, fish, copra, palm oil

Palau

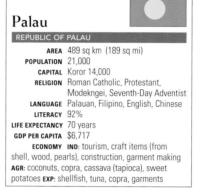

REPUBLIC OF PALAU

AREA 489 sq km (189 sq mi)
POPULATION 21,000
CAPITAL Koror 14,000
RELIGION Roman Catholic, Protestant, Modekngei, Seventh-Day Adventist
LANGUAGE Palauan, Filipino, English, Chinese
LITERACY 92%
LIFE EXPECTANCY 70 years
GDP PER CAPITA $6,717
ECONOMY **IND:** tourism, craft items (from shell, wood, pearls), construction, garment making **AGR:** coconuts, copra, cassava (tapioca), sweet potatoes **EXP:** shellfish, tuna, copra, garments

Samoa

INDEPENDENT STATE OF SAMOA

AREA 2,831 sq km (1,093 sq mi)
POPULATION 188,000
CAPITAL Apia 40,000
RELIGION Congregationalist, Roman Catholic, Methodist, Latter-Day Saints, Assembly of God
LANGUAGE Samoan (Polynesian), English
LITERACY 100%
LIFE EXPECTANCY 73 years
GDP PER CAPITA $1,968
ECONOMY **IND:** food processing, building materials, auto parts **AGR:** coconuts, bananas, taro, yams **EXP:** fish, coconut oil and cream, copra, taro

Tonga

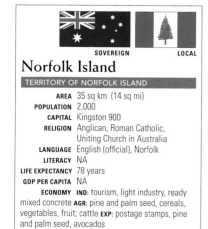

KINGDOM OF TONGA

AREA 748 sq km (289 sq mi)
POPULATION 102,000
CAPITAL Nuku'alofa 35,000
RELIGION Christian
LANGUAGE Tongan, English
LITERACY 99%
LIFE EXPECTANCY 71 years
GDP PER CAPITA $1,930
ECONOMY **IND:** tourism, fishing **AGR:** squash, coconuts, copra, bananas; fish **EXP:** squash, fish, vanilla beans, root crops

Tuvalu

TUVALU

AREA 26 sq km (10 sq mi)
POPULATION 10,000
CAPITAL Funafuti 6,000
RELIGION Church of Tuvalu (Congregationalist)
LANGUAGE Tuvaluan, English, Samoan, Kiribati
LITERACY NA
LIFE EXPECTANCY 64 years
GDP PER CAPITA $2,141
ECONOMY **IND:** fishing, tourism, copra **AGR:** coconuts; fish **EXP:** copra, fish

Vanuatu

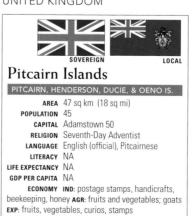

REPUBLIC OF VANUATU

AREA 12,190 sq km (4,707 sq mi)
POPULATION 218,000
CAPITAL Port-Vila 34,000
RELIGION Presbyterian, Anglican, Roman Catholic, Seventh-Day Adventist, indigenous beliefs
LANGUAGE over 100 local languages, pidgin (known as Bislama or Bichelama)
LITERACY 74%
LIFE EXPECTANCY 67 years
GDP PER CAPITA $1,405
ECONOMY **IND:** food and fish freezing, wood processing, meat canning **AGR:** copra, coconuts, cocoa, coffee; beef; fish **EXP:** copra, beef, cocoa, timber

Dependencies

AUSTRALIA

SOVEREIGN

LOCAL

Norfolk Island

TERRITORY OF NORFOLK ISLAND

AREA 35 sq km (14 sq mi)
POPULATION 2,000
CAPITAL Kingston 900
RELIGION Anglican, Roman Catholic, Uniting Church in Australia
LANGUAGE English (official), Norfolk
LITERACY NA
LIFE EXPECTANCY 78 years
GDP PER CAPITA NA
ECONOMY **IND:** tourism, light industry, ready mixed concrete **AGR:** pine and palm seed, cereals, vegetables, fruit; cattle **EXP:** postage stamps, pine and palm seed, avocados

Coral Sea Islands

CORAL SEA ISLANDS TERRITORY

AREA Less than 3 sq km (1 sq mi)
POPULATION none

UNITED KINGDOM

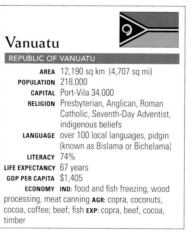

SOVEREIGN

LOCAL

Pitcairn Islands

PITCAIRN, HENDERSON, DUCIE, & OENO IS.

AREA 47 sq km (18 sq mi)
POPULATION 45
CAPITAL Adamstown 50
RELIGION Seventh-Day Adventist
LANGUAGE English (official), Pitcairnese
LITERACY NA
LIFE EXPECTANCY NA
GDP PER CAPITA NA
ECONOMY **IND:** postage stamps, handicrafts, beekeeping, honey **AGR:** fruits and vegetables; goats **EXP:** fruits, vegetables, curios, stamps

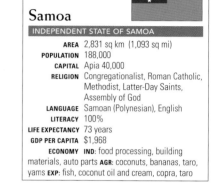

Dependencies

FRANCE

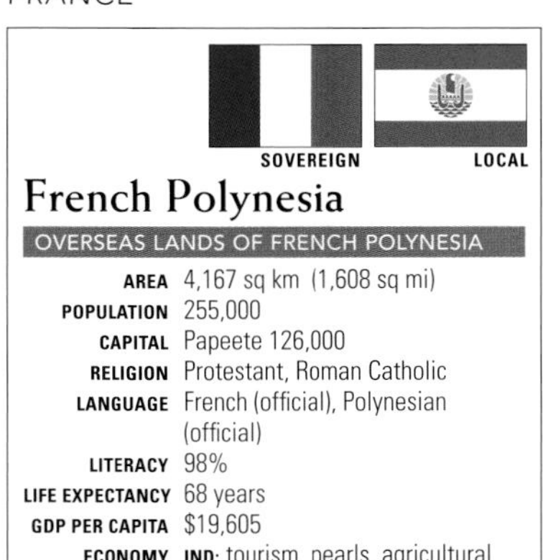

SOVEREIGN LOCAL

French Polynesia

OVERSEAS LANDS OF FRENCH POLYNESIA

AREA 4,167 sq km (1,608 sq mi)
POPULATION 255,000
CAPITAL Papeete 126,000
RELIGION Protestant, Roman Catholic
LANGUAGE French (official), Polynesian (official)
LITERACY 98%
LIFE EXPECTANCY 68 years
GDP PER CAPITA $19,605
ECONOMY **IND:** tourism, pearls, agricultural processing, handicrafts **AGR:** coconuts, vanilla, vegetables, fruits; poultry **EXP:** cultured pearls, coconut products, mother-of-pearl, vanilla

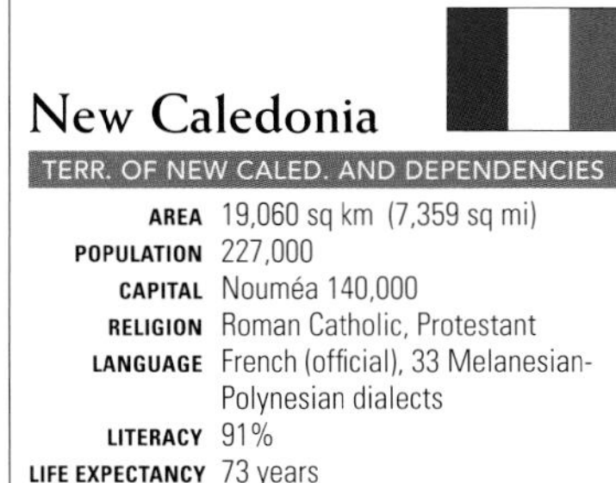

New Caledonia

TERR. OF NEW CALED. AND DEPENDENCIES

AREA 19,060 sq km (7,359 sq mi)
POPULATION 227,000
CAPITAL Nouméa 140,000
RELIGION Roman Catholic, Protestant
LANGUAGE French (official), 33 Melanesian-Polynesian dialects
LITERACY 91%
LIFE EXPECTANCY 73 years
GDP PER CAPITA $17,538
ECONOMY **IND:** nickel mining and smelting **AGR:** vegetables; beef **EXP:** ferronickels, nickel ore, fish

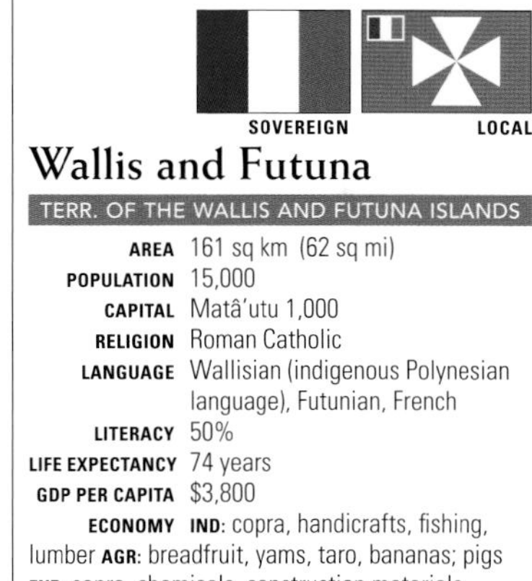

SOVEREIGN LOCAL

Wallis and Futuna

TERR. OF THE WALLIS AND FUTUNA ISLANDS

AREA 161 sq km (62 sq mi)
POPULATION 15,000
CAPITAL Matâ'utu 1,000
RELIGION Roman Catholic
LANGUAGE Wallisian (indigenous Polynesian language), Futunian, French
LITERACY 50%
LIFE EXPECTANCY 74 years
GDP PER CAPITA $3,800
ECONOMY **IND:** copra, handicrafts, fishing, lumber **AGR:** breadfruit, yams, taro, bananas; pigs **EXP:** copra, chemicals, construction materials

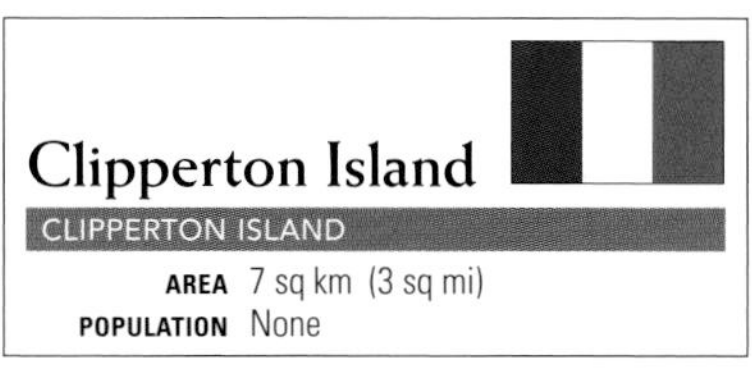

Clipperton Island

CLIPPERTON ISLAND

AREA 7 sq km (3 sq mi)
POPULATION None

NEW ZEALAND

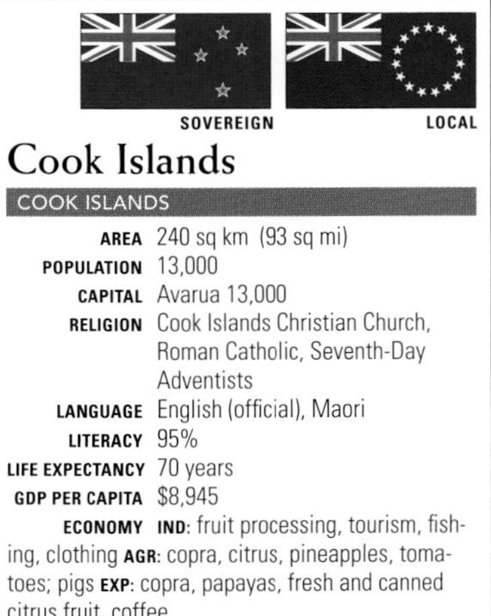

SOVEREIGN LOCAL

Cook Islands

COOK ISLANDS

AREA 240 sq km (93 sq mi)
POPULATION 13,000
CAPITAL Avarua 13,000
RELIGION Cook Islands Christian Church, Roman Catholic, Seventh-Day Adventists
LANGUAGE English (official), Maori
LITERACY 95%
LIFE EXPECTANCY 70 years
GDP PER CAPITA $8,945
ECONOMY **IND:** fruit processing, tourism, fishing, clothing **AGR:** copra, citrus, pineapples, tomatoes; pigs **EXP:** copra, papayas, fresh and canned citrus fruit, coffee

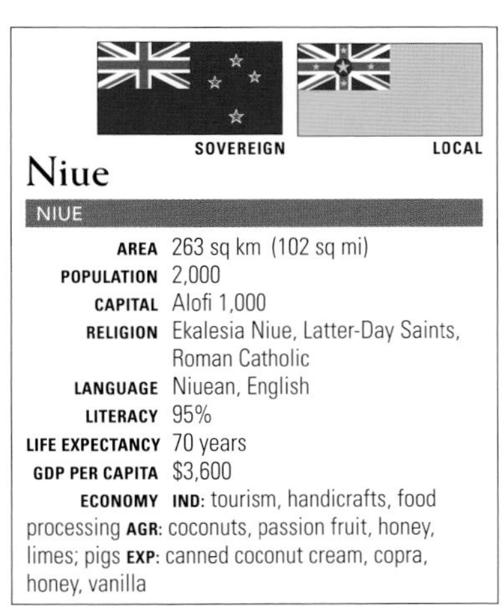

SOVEREIGN LOCAL

Niue

NIUE

AREA 263 sq km (102 sq mi)
POPULATION 2,000
CAPITAL Alofi 1,000
RELIGION Ekalesia Niue, Latter-Day Saints, Roman Catholic
LANGUAGE Niuean, English
LITERACY 95%
LIFE EXPECTANCY 70 years
GDP PER CAPITA $3,600
ECONOMY **IND:** tourism, handicrafts, food processing **AGR:** coconuts, passion fruit, honey, limes; pigs **EXP:** canned coconut cream, copra, honey, vanilla

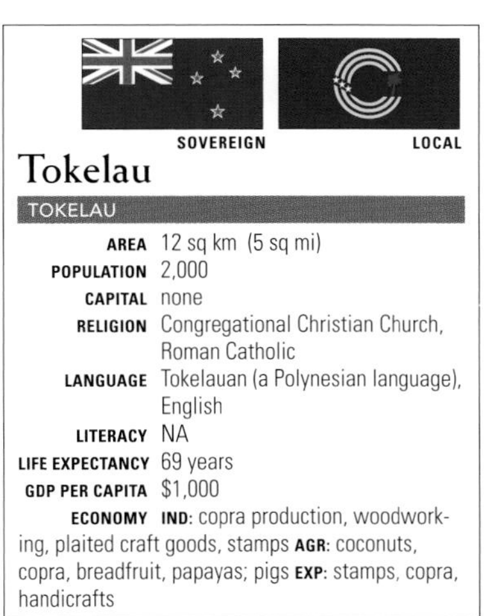

SOVEREIGN LOCAL

Tokelau

TOKELAU

AREA 12 sq km (5 sq mi)
POPULATION 2,000
CAPITAL none
RELIGION Congregational Christian Church, Roman Catholic
LANGUAGE Tokelauan (a Polynesian language), English
LITERACY NA
LIFE EXPECTANCY 69 years
GDP PER CAPITA $1,000
ECONOMY **IND:** copra production, woodworking, plaited craft goods, stamps **AGR:** coconuts, copra, breadfruit, papayas; pigs **EXP:** stamps, copra, handicrafts

UNITED STATES

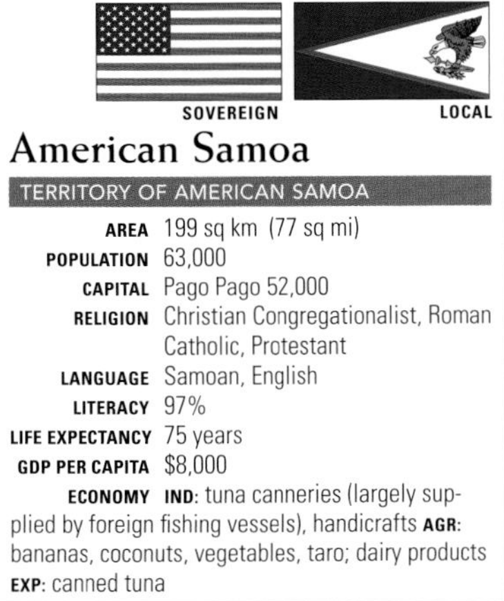

SOVEREIGN LOCAL

American Samoa

TERRITORY OF AMERICAN SAMOA

AREA 199 sq km (77 sq mi)
POPULATION 63,000
CAPITAL Pago Pago 52,000
RELIGION Christian Congregationalist, Roman Catholic, Protestant
LANGUAGE Samoan, English
LITERACY 97%
LIFE EXPECTANCY 75 years
GDP PER CAPITA $8,000
ECONOMY **IND:** tuna canneries (largely supplied by foreign fishing vessels), handicrafts **AGR:** bananas, coconuts, vegetables, taro; dairy products **EXP:** canned tuna

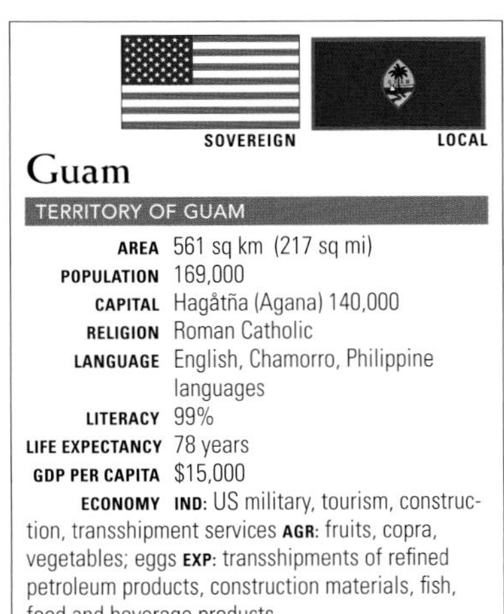

SOVEREIGN LOCAL

Guam

TERRITORY OF GUAM

AREA 561 sq km (217 sq mi)
POPULATION 169,000
CAPITAL Hagåtña (Agana) 140,000
RELIGION Roman Catholic
LANGUAGE English, Chamorro, Philippine languages
LITERACY 99%
LIFE EXPECTANCY 78 years
GDP PER CAPITA $15,000
ECONOMY **IND:** US military, tourism, construction, transshipment services **AGR:** fruits, copra, vegetables; eggs **EXP:** transshipments of refined petroleum products, construction materials, fish, food and beverage products

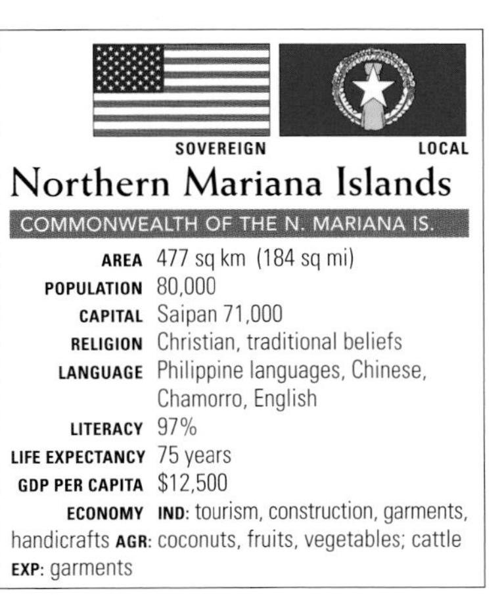

SOVEREIGN LOCAL

Northern Mariana Islands

COMMONWEALTH OF THE N. MARIANA IS.

AREA 477 sq km (184 sq mi)
POPULATION 80,000
CAPITAL Saipan 71,000
RELIGION Christian, traditional beliefs
LANGUAGE Philippine languages, Chinese, Chamorro, English
LITERACY 97%
LIFE EXPECTANCY 75 years
GDP PER CAPITA $12,500
ECONOMY **IND:** tourism, construction, garments, handicrafts **AGR:** coconuts, fruits, vegetables; cattle **EXP:** garments

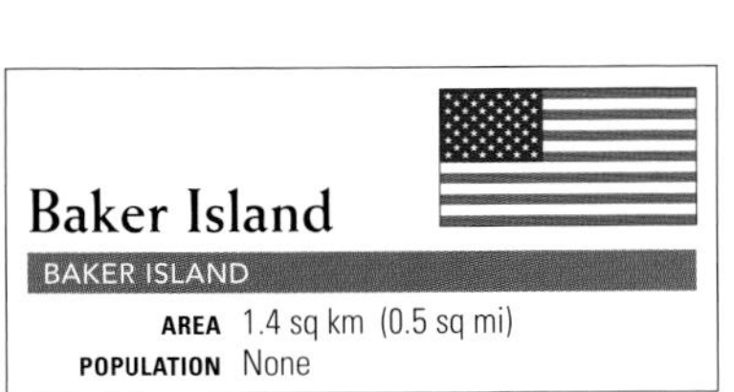

Baker Island

BAKER ISLAND

AREA 1.4 sq km (0.5 sq mi)
POPULATION None

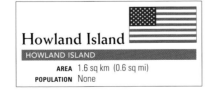

Howland Island

HOWLAND ISLAND

AREA 1.6 sq km (0.6 sq mi)
POPULATION None

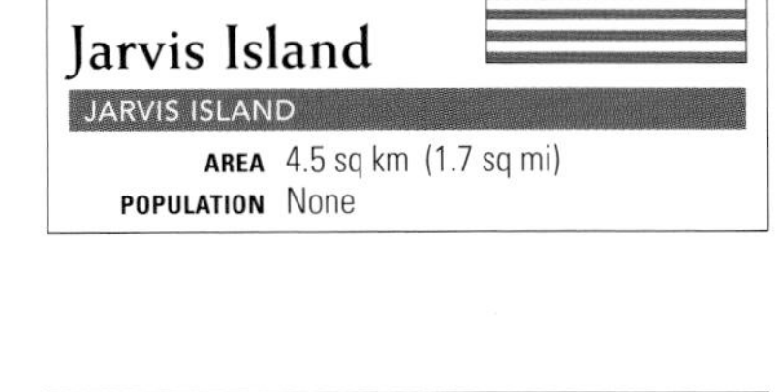

Jarvis Island

JARVIS ISLAND

AREA 4.5 sq km (1.7 sq mi)
POPULATION None

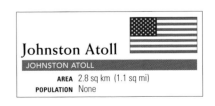

Johnston Atoll

JOHNSTON ATOLL

AREA 2.8 sq km (1.1 sq mi)
POPULATION None

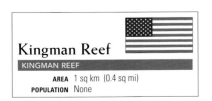

Kingman Reef

KINGMAN REEF

AREA 1 sq km (0.4 sq mi)
POPULATION None

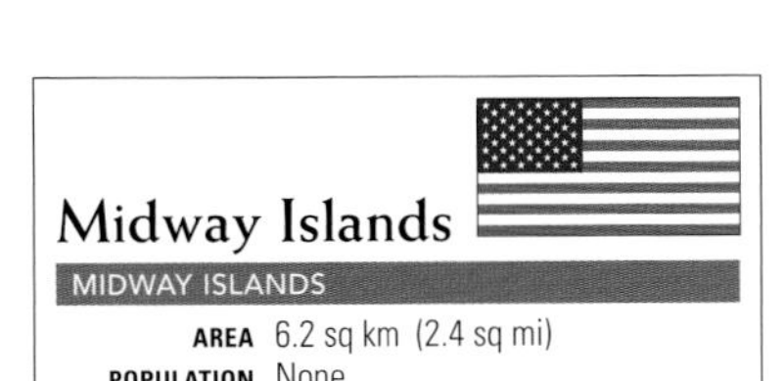

Midway Islands

MIDWAY ISLANDS

AREA 6.2 sq km (2.4 sq mi)
POPULATION None

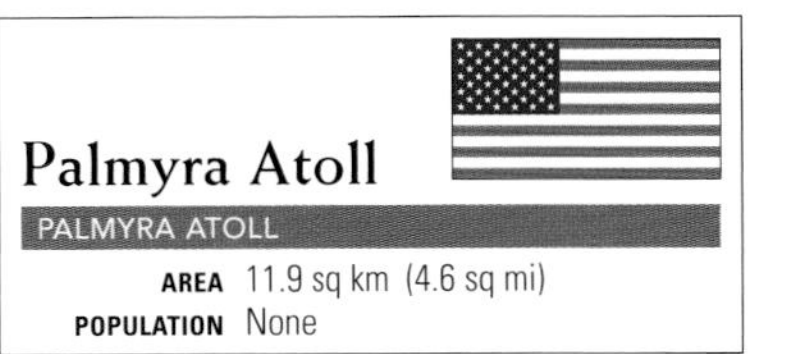

Palmyra Atoll

PALMYRA ATOLL

AREA 11.9 sq km (4.6 sq mi)
POPULATION None

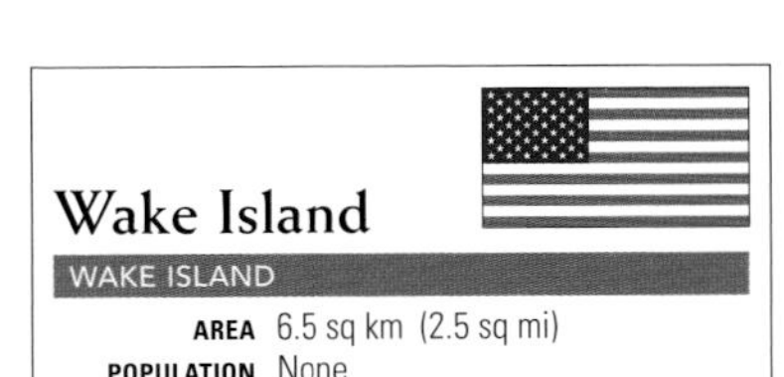

Wake Island

WAKE ISLAND

AREA 6.5 sq km (2.5 sq mi)
POPULATION None

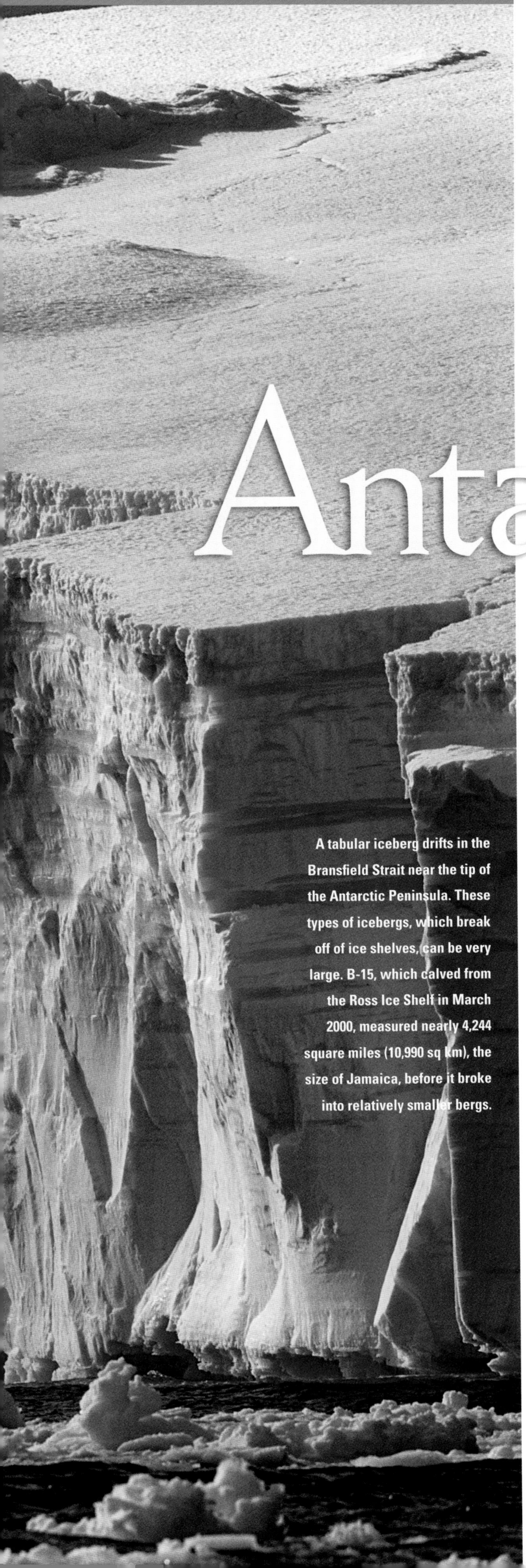

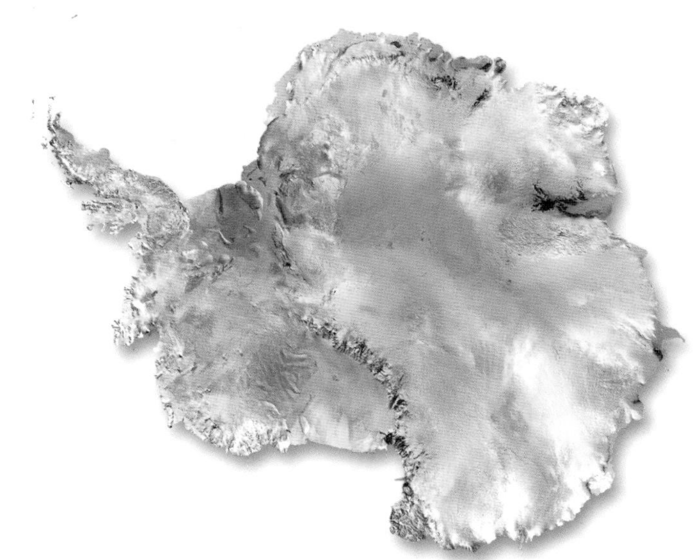

Antarctica

A tabular iceberg drifts in the Bransfield Strait near the tip of the Antarctic Peninsula. These types of icebergs, which break off of ice shelves, can be very large. B-15, which calved from the Ross Ice Shelf in March 2000, measured nearly 4,244 square miles (10,990 sq km), the size of Jamaica, before it broke into relatively smaller bergs.

Often called the last wilderness on Earth, Antarctica's unspoiled expanses of austere frozen beauty remain largely untouched by humans. Antarctica is the driest, coldest, windiest, and least populated of Earth's seven continents, and an average elevation of 8,000 ft (2,438 m) makes it the highest as well. It is larger than Europe or Australia; its 5.1 million square miles (13.2 million sq km) of ice-shrouded land sit at the bottom of the world.

Antarctica's ice cap, the greatest body of ice in the world, holds some 70 percent of Earth's fresh water. Yet despite all this ice and water, the Antarctic interior averages only two inches of precipitation per year, making it the largest ice desert in the world; the little snow that does fall, however, almost never melts.

The immensely heavy ice sheet, averaging over a mile (1.6 km) thick and reaching almost three miles (4.8 km) thick in places, compresses much of the continent's surface to below sea level. The weight actually deforms the South Pole, creating a slightly pear-shaped Earth.

Beneath the ice exists a continent of valleys, lakes, islands, and mountains, little dreamed of until the compilation of more than 2.5 million ice-thickness measurements revealed startling topography below. Less than 2 percent of Antarctica actually breaks through the ice cover to reveal stretches of coastline, islands, and features such as the outstanding Transantarctic Mountains, which extend for 1,800 miles (2,898 km) and separate East and West Antarctica.

In spite of perpetual light during the Antarctic summer (December to March), little heat accumulates because the white, snowy landscape reflects as much as 90 percent of the sun's incoming rays. During the half year of darkness, terrible cold and storms buffet the continent. The winter of 1983 saw the lowest temperature ever recorded on Earth—minus 128.6°F (-89.2°C).

Annual winter temperatures over the elevated central plateau average minus 80°F (-62.2°C), and this cold season causes the ice around Antarctica to grow quickly. Sea ice averaging six feet (2 m) deep more than doubles the size of the continent, extending outward to create a belt ranging from 300 miles to more than 1,000 miles (483–1,610 km) wide.

In spring, melting ice coincides with calving of huge white and blue-green icebergs from the Antarctic glaciers. The largest iceberg ever spotted, in 1956, measured 208 miles (335 km) long by 60 miles (97 km) wide, slightly larger than Belgium.

Antarctica's Southern Ocean, which holds 10 percent of the world's seawater, swirls in rhythm with the Antarctic Circumpolar Current, the largest, fastest current in the world, which sweeps clockwise around the globe unimpeded by any land. These high southern latitudes experience extremes of wind and weather. At around 60° south latitude, a remarkable interface of relatively warm waters from the southern Atlantic, Indian, and Pacific Oceans and the cold Southern Ocean creates conditions for an eruption of rich nutrients, phytoplankton, and zooplankton. These form the base for a flourishing marine ecosystem. Though limited in numbers of species—for example, only about 120 kinds of the world's 20,000 fish swim here—Antarctica's animal life has adapted extremely well to so harsh a climate. Seasonal feeding and energy storage in fats exemplify this specialization. Well-known animals of the far south include seals, whales, and distinctive birds such as flightless penguins, albatrosses, terns, and petrels.

PHYSICAL GEOGRAPHY Every summer thousands of scientists travel to Antarctica to obtain vital information about Earth's weather and ecology and the state of the southernmost continent. This interest attests to the region's role as a pristine laboratory, where measurements and rates of change in numerous scientific fields can point to larger issues of the world's environmental health.

Antarctica's oceanic and atmospheric system—indicator and element of climate change—is a main area of focus. Oceanographers attempt to understand more fully the global exchange of heat, sea-ice dynamics, salt and trace elements, and the entire marine biosphere. Other important research has included the 1985 discovery of a hole in Earth's protective ozone layer by scientists at the British Halley research station. This find brought to prominence a major ecological threat.

Ice and sediment cores provide insight into the world's ancient climate and allow for comparison with conditions today. Studies of the Antarctic ice sheet help predict future sea levels, important news for the three billion people who live in coastal areas. If the Antarctic ice sheet were to melt, global seas would rise by an estimated 200 feet, inundating many oceanic islands and gravely altering the world's coastlines.

Three basic water masses comprise the Southern Ocean: Antarctic Surface Water, Circumpolar Deep Water, and Antarctic Bottom Water. Sharp boundaries separate the water masses, each with its own characteristics. These differences drive circulation around the continent and contribute to the global heat engine and overall transfer of energy around the world.

Prominent physical features include the Vinson Massif, Antarctica's highest mountain at 16,067 feet (4,897 m). Discovered only in 1958 by U.S. Navy aircraft, it was first climbed by an American team in 1966.

The Antarctic Peninsula, reaching like a long arm 800 miles (1,288 km) into the Southern Ocean toward the tip of South America, is made up of a mountain range and many islands linked together by ice. Seals, penguins, and other sea birds find it particularly suitable, and the peninsula's relative accessibility makes it the Antarctic area most visited by humans.

The continent's only sizable river, the Onyx, arises from a coastal glacier near McMurdo Sound. Every summer its waters flow inland for some 20 miles (32 km), replenishing and raising the surface level of Lake Vanda, one of several lakes in the Dry Valleys. These valleys, free of snow and ice unlike the rest of Antarctica, were created by ancient glaciers. They stretch to the coast from the Transantarctic Mountains, a range high enough here to prevent the great Polar Plateau ice sheet from flowing down to the sea through the Dry Valleys, perhaps the driest places on Earth.

Immense ice shelves, produced by the main plateau disgorging masses of ice, rim much of the continent's coast and extend far into the sea. Largest are the Ross Ice Shelf, the size of France, and the Ronne Ice Shelf.

Special names exist for the many different types of ice: frazil ice, an early stage of sea-ice growth in which crystals below the surface form an unstructured slush; nilas, a thin sheen of ice on the sea surface that bends but does not break with wave action; pancake ice, named for its flattened circular shape; pack ice, frozen sea water and floating ice driven together to form a continuous mass; and fast ice, that part of the sea-ice cover attached to land.

Scientists seeking to understand sea ice are suspended above the icescape. Pancake ice forms when a thin surface film of ice crystals breaks up and thickens into irregular disks. These disks can measure from 1 to 10 feet (0.3–3 m) in diameter. Constant battering of the disks against one another causes the turned-up rims.

CULTURE, HISTORY, AND EXPLORATION The search for Antarctica represented the last great adventure of global exploration. British Capt. James Cook crossed three times into Antarctic waters between 1772 and 1775 and was probably the first to cross the Antarctic Circle. Though he never saw the continent, he believed in "a tract of land at the Pole that is the source of all the ice that is spread over this vast Southern Ocean."

His observations of marine mammals in great numbers lured whalers and sealers into the freezing southern waters in search of skins and oil. First sightings of the continent then followed in 1820.

Scientists seeking the south magnetic pole included British naval officer James Clark Ross, who between 1839–43 charted unknown territory, including a giant ice shelf later named after him, and located the approximate position of the south magnetic pole—the point toward which a compass needle points from any direction throughout surrounding areas.

In 1895 Norwegian whalers landed on the continent beyond the Antarctic Peninsula for the first time, and in 1898 a major Belgian scientific expedition overwintered in the Antarctic when their ship became stuck in pack ice for almost 13 months.

Douglas Mawson reached the south magnetic pole as part of Ernest Shackleton's 1907 Nimrod expedition. Later, Mawson led the Australasian Antarctic Expedition (1911–14), which produced observations in magnetism, geology, biology, and meteorology.

A race to reach the South Geographic Pole came to a climax in 1911–12. Norwegian Roald Amundsen's expedition reached the South Pole on December 14, 1911, after 97 days on the move, relying on husky dogs to pull their sleds. Simultaneously, the British team of Robert Falcon Scott and four companions set off unaware of Amundsen's swifter, better-managed effort. Scott's use of Manchurian ponies proved a mistake; his team reached the Pole 34 days later, only to find the Norwegian flag flying. The five men began the bitter return trip, but succumbed to cold, hunger, exhaustion, and bad weather, just 11 miles (18 km) from supplies. All died.

Another epic adventure involved Ernest Shackleton, whose British expedition aimed to traverse the entire continent. In 1915 Shackleton's main party of 28 men became stranded when sea ice trapped and crushed their ship. After more than a year on drifting ice, they sailed in lifeboats to Elephant Island at the tip of the Antarctic Peninsula. Shackleton and five others then embarked on an astonishing 800-mile (1,288 km) journey in a small boat to South Georgia, from where he eventually rescued his other men.

In 1935 Caroline Mikkelsen, wife of a Norwegian whaling captain, became the first woman to stand on Antarctica. Almost a dozen years later the U.S. Navy brought 4,700 men, 13 ships, and 23 aircraft to the continent, using icebreakers for the first time. The vast enterprise mapped large areas of the coastline and interior and took 70,000 aerial photographs.

The modern scientific era arrived with the 18-month-long International Geophysical Year (IGY, 1957–58), when many nations advanced knowledge of the continent. The Antarctic Treaty, signed in 1959 by 12 leading IGY participants, has done much to protect Antarctica.

Today about 50 research stations stand at many sites around Antarctica, and an ever shifting population, including tourists, can reach as high as 23,000 people in the summer. Tourism brings its own troubles. Recently, species of non-native grasses, presumably carried on visitors' clothing, have been found on the continent. Further unintentional aliens, such as algae, crustaceans, and parasites arrive on floating plastic bottles and other man-made debris.

MINERALS AND ECONOMY Many believe Antarctica has great resource wealth, but the harsh climate, short work season, and need to drill through thick ice make the recovery of these resources difficult.

Minerals under the ice include gold, uranium, cobalt, chromium, nickel, copper, iron, and platinum, as well as potentially large deposits of diamonds. Oil probably exists below the ocean floor, and coal deposits have been detected along the coast and throughout the Transantarctic Mountains.

A pressing reason to limit mineral exploration and drilling is Antarctica's extreme fragility. Sensitive plants, including rare moss beds on the Antarctic Peninsula, take three to four hundred years to grow, and a single human boot can cause tremendous damage.

In January 1998 an addition to the Antarctic Treaty, known as the Madrid Protocol, went into force, deeming Antarctica a natural reserve devoted to peace and science. It specifically banned mining and mineral exploitation of any kind until 2048.

But pressure builds yearly to find new mineral and petroleum deposits. Despite the ban, Russia and other countries appear to be actively exploring Antarctic oil, gas, and mineral resources. Also significant is the growing commercialization of Southern Ocean fisheries. Particularly vulnerable are the tiny shrimp-like krill that form a vital part of Antarctica's food chain. The collapse of fish and krill species might be analogous to the wholesale slaughter of fur seal populations in the late 1700s and early 1800s and the near destruction of the Southern Ocean's whales in the 20th century.

Antarctica already witnesses vehicle pollution; dumping of plastics, solid wastes, food, and batteries; burning of fossil fuels; and construction of roads and airstrips at the many scientific bases.

Even the most obvious resource of all—ice—may one day serve to relieve thirsty nations. Ships towing icebergs from Antarctica to all parts of the world could deliver this huge potential of fresh water, but at present such a project is simply too expensive.

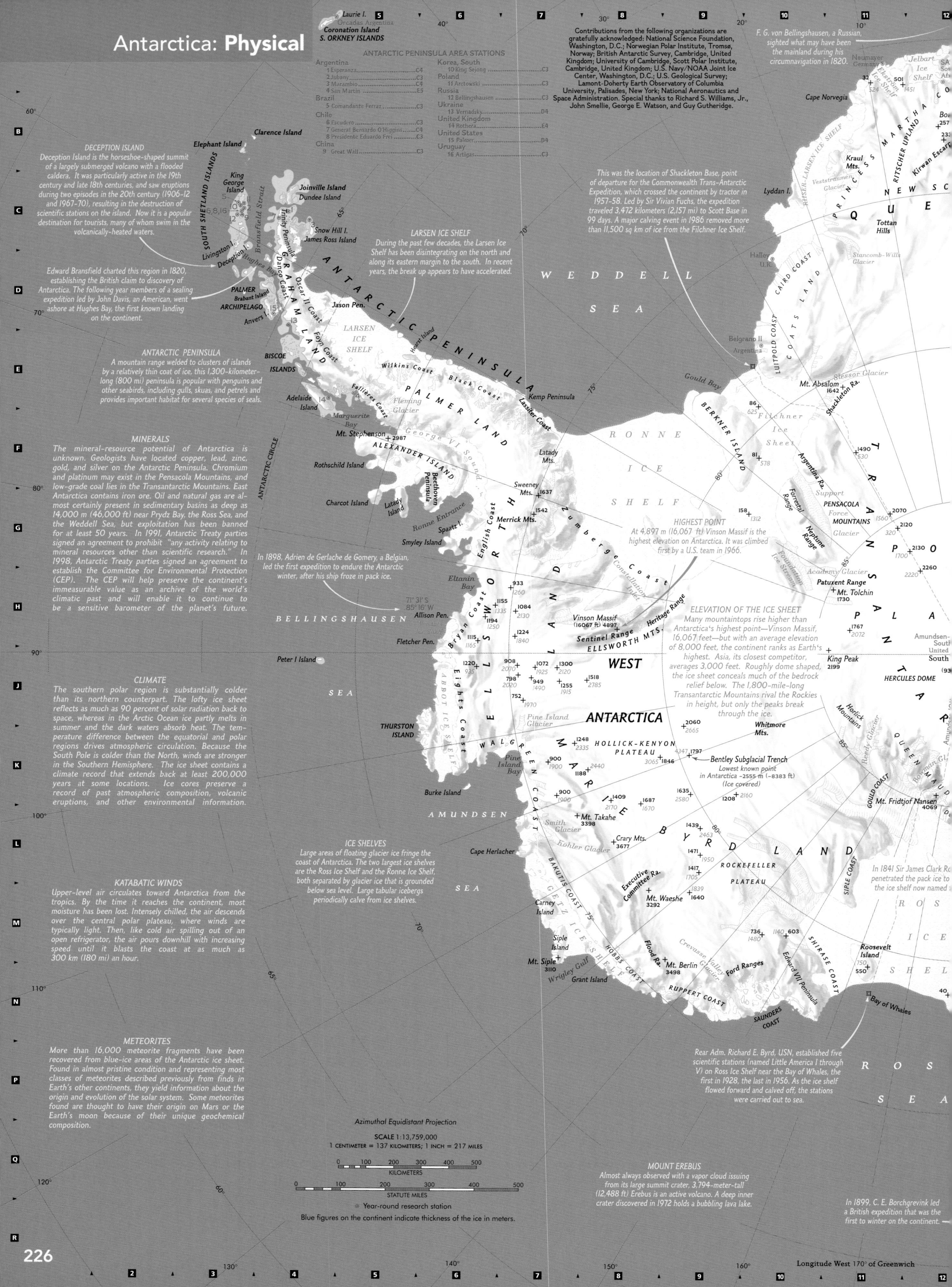

Antarctica: Physical
Laurie I.
Orcadas Argentina
Coronation Island
S. ORKNEY ISLANDS
ANTARCTIC PENINSULA AREA STATIONS
Argentina
1 Esperanza C4
2 Jubany C3
3 Marambio C4
4 San Martin E5
Brazil
5 Comandante Ferraz C3
Chile
6 Escudero C3
7 General Bernardo O'Higgins C4
8 Presidente Eduardo Frei C3
China
9 Great Wall C3
Korea, South
10 King Sejong C3
Poland
11 Arctowski C3
Russia
12 Bellingshausen C3
Ukraine
13 Vernadsky D4
United Kingdom
14 Rothera E4
United States
15 Palmer D4
Uruguay
16 Artigas C3
Contributions from the following organizations are gratefully acknowledged: National Science Foundation, Washington, D.C.; Norwegian Polar Institute, Tromsø, Norway; British Antarctic Survey, Cambridge, United Kingdom; University of Cambridge, Scott Polar Institute, Cambridge, United Kingdom; U.S. Navy/NOAA Joint Ice Center, Washington, D.C.; U.S. Geological Survey; Lamont-Doherty Earth Observatory of Columbia University, Palisades, New York; National Aeronautics and Space Administration. Special thanks to Richard S. Williams, Jr., John Smellie, George E. Watson, and Guy Gutheridge.
F. G. von Bellingshausen, a Russian, sighted what may have been the mainland during his circumnavigation in 1820.
DECEPTION ISLAND
Deception Island is the horseshoe-shaped summit of a largely submerged volcano with a flooded caldera. It was particularly active in the 19th century and late 18th centuries, and saw eruptions during two episodes in the 20th century (1906-12 and 1967-70), resulting in the destruction of scientific stations on the island. Now it is a popular destination for tourists, many of whom swim in the volcanically-heated waters.
Edward Bransfield charted this region in 1820, establishing the British claim to discovery of Antarctica. The following year members of a sealing expedition led by John Davis, an American, went ashore at Hughes Bay, the first known landing on the continent.
This was the location of Shackleton Base, point of departure for the Commonwealth Trans-Antarctic Expedition, which crossed the continent by tractor in 1957-58. Led by Sir Vivian Fuchs, the expedition traveled 3,472 kilometers (2,157 mi) to Scott Base in 99 days. A major calving event in 1986 removed more than 11,500 sq km of ice from the Filchner Ice Shelf.
LARSEN ICE SHELF
During the past few decades, the Larsen Ice Shelf has been disintegrating on the north and along its eastern margin to the south. In recent years, the break up appears to have accelerated.
ANTARCTIC PENINSULA
A mountain range welded to clusters of islands by a relatively thin coat of ice, this 1,300-kilometer-long (800 mi) peninsula is popular with penguins and other seabirds, including gulls, skuas, and petrels and provides important habitat for several species of seals.
MINERALS
The mineral-resource potential of Antarctica is unknown. Geologists have located copper, lead, zinc, gold, and silver on the Antarctic Peninsula. Chromium and platinum may exist in the Pensacola Mountains, and low-grade coal lies in the Transantarctic Mountains. East Antarctica contains iron ore. Oil and natural gas are almost certainly present in sedimentary basins as deep as 14,000 m (46,000 ft) near Prydz Bay, the Ross Sea, and the Weddell Sea, but exploitation has been banned for at least 50 years. In 1991, Antarctic Treaty parties signed an agreement to prohibit "any activity relating to mineral resources other than scientific research." In 1998, Antarctic Treaty parties signed an agreement to establish the Committee for Environmental Protection (CEP). The CEP will help preserve the continent's immeasurable value as an archive of the world's climatic past and will enable it to continue to be a sensitive barometer of the planet's future.
HIGHEST POINT
At 4,897 m (16,067 ft) Vinson Massif is the highest elevation on Antarctica. It was climbed first by a U.S. team in 1966.
In 1898, Adrien de Gerlache de Gomery, a Belgian, led the first expedition to endure the Antarctic winter, after his ship froze in pack ice.
71° 31' S
85° 16' W
ELEVATION OF THE ICE SHEET
Many mountaintops rise higher than Antarctica's highest point—Vinson Massif, 16,067 feet—but with an average elevation of 8,000 feet, the continent ranks as Earth's highest. Asia, its closest competitor, averages 3,000 feet. Roughly dome shaped, the ice sheet conceals much of the bedrock relief below. The 1,800-mile-long Transantarctic Mountains rival the Rockies in height, but only the peaks break through the ice.
CLIMATE
The southern polar region is substantially colder than its northern counterpart. The lofty ice sheet reflects as much as 90 percent of solar radiation back to space, whereas in the Arctic Ocean ice partly melts in summer and the dark waters absorb heat. The temperature difference between the equatorial and polar regions drives atmospheric circulation. Because the South Pole is colder than the North, winds are stronger in the Southern Hemisphere. The ice sheet contains a climate record that extends back at least 200,000 years at some locations. Ice cores preserve a record of past atmospheric composition, volcanic eruptions, and other environmental information.
Bentley Subglacial Trench
Lowest known point in Antarctica -2555 m (-8383 ft) (Ice covered)
ICE SHELVES
Large areas of floating glacier ice fringe the coast of Antarctica. The two largest ice shelves are the Ross Ice Shelf and the Ronne Ice Shelf, both separated by glacier ice that is grounded below sea level. Large tabular icebergs periodically calve from ice shelves.
KATABATIC WINDS
Upper-level air circulates toward Antarctica from the tropics. By the time it reaches the continent, most moisture has been lost. Intensely chilled, the air descends over the central polar plateau, where winds are typically light. Then, like cold air spilling out of an open refrigerator, the air pours downhill with increasing speed until it blasts the coast at as much as 300 km (180 mi) an hour.
In 1841 Sir James Clark Ross penetrated the pack ice to the ice shelf now named
METEORITES
More than 16,000 meteorite fragments have been recovered from blue-ice areas of the Antarctic ice sheet. Found in almost pristine condition and representing most classes of meteorites described previously from finds in Earth's other continents, they yield information about the origin and evolution of the solar system. Some meteorites found are thought to have their origin on Mars or the Earth's moon because of their unique geochemical composition.
Rear Adm. Richard E. Byrd, USN, established five scientific stations (named Little America I through V) on Ross Ice Shelf near the Bay of Whales, the first in 1928, the last in 1956. As the ice shelf flowed forward and calved off, the stations were carried out to sea.
Azimuthal Equidistant Projection
SCALE 1:13,759,000
1 CENTIMETER = 137 KILOMETERS; 1 INCH = 217 MILES
KILOMETERS
STATUTE MILES
Year-round research station
Blue figures on the continent indicate thickness of the ice in meters.
MOUNT EREBUS
Almost always observed with a vapor cloud issuing from its large summit crater, 3,794-meter-tall (12,488 ft) Erebus is an active volcano. A deep inner crater discovered in 1972 holds a bubbling lava lake.
In 1899, C. E. Borchgrevink led a British expedition that was the first to winter on the continent.
Longitude West 170° of Greenwich
WEDDELL SEA
BELLINGSHAUSEN SEA
AMUNDSEN SEA
ROSS SEA
ANTARCTIC PENINSULA
WEST ANTARCTICA
RONNE ICE SHELF
ELLSWORTH LAND
MARIE BYRD LAND
PALMER LAND
GRAHAM LAND
COATS LAND
ELLSWORTH MTS.
HOLLICK-KENYON PLATEAU
ROCKEFELLER PLATEAU
PENSACOLA MOUNTAINS
HERCULES DOME
Vinson Massif (16067 ft) 4897
Sentinel Range
Heritage Range
Mt. Takahe 3398
Crary Mts. 3677
Mt. Waeshe 3292
Mt. Berlin 3498
Mt. Siple 3110
Mt. Stephenson 2987
Mt. Fridtjof Nansen 4069
King Peak 2199
Mt. Tolchin 1730
Mt. Absalom 1642
Elephant Island
Clarence Island
King George Island
Livingston I.
Deception I.
Joinville Island
Dundee Island
Snow Hill I.
James Ross Island
Anvers I.
Adelaide Island
Alexander Island
Charcot Island
Rothschild Island
Peter I Island
Thurston Island
Burke Island
Carney Island
Siple Island
Grant Island
Roosevelt Island
Berkner Island
Bay of Whales

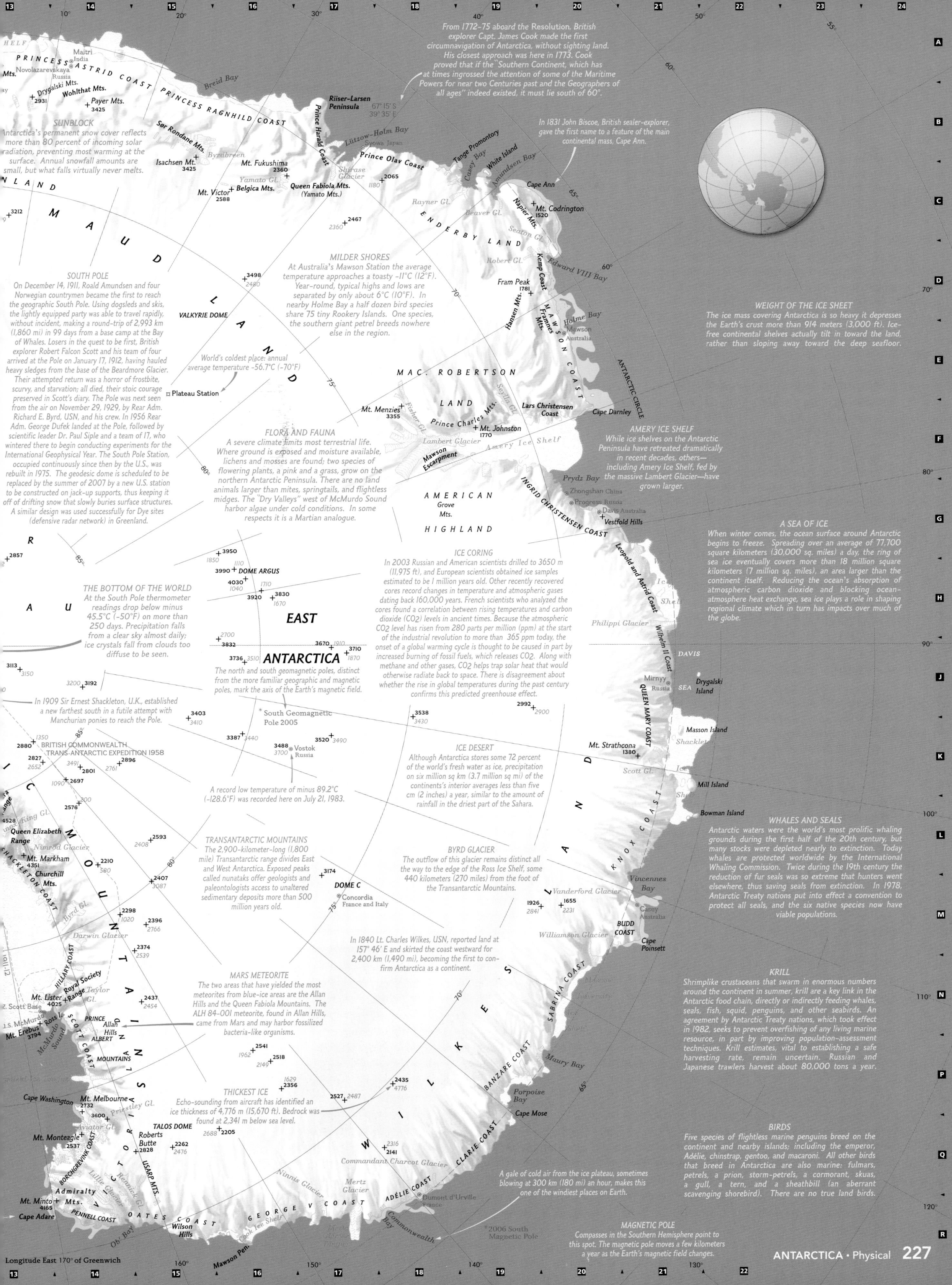

From 1772–75 aboard the Resolution, British explorer Capt. James Cook made the first circumnavigation of Antarctica, without sighting land. His closest approach was here in 1773. Cook proved that if the "Southern Continent, which has at times ingrossed the attention of some of the Maritime Powers for near two Centuries past and the Geographers of all ages" indeed existed, it must lie south of 60°.
In 1831 John Biscoe, British sealer-explorer, gave the first name to a feature of the main continental mass, Cape Ann.
SUNBLOCK
Antarctica's permanent snow cover reflects more than 80 percent of incoming solar radiation, preventing most warming at the surface. Annual snowfall amounts are small, but what falls virtually never melts.
SOUTH POLE
On December 14, 1911, Roald Amundsen and four Norwegian countrymen became the first to reach the geographic South Pole. Using dogsleds and skis, the lightly equipped party was able to travel rapidly, without incident, making a round-trip of 2,993 km (1,860 mi) in 99 days from a base camp at the Bay of Whales. Losers in the quest to be first, British explorer Robert Falcon Scott and his team of four arrived at the Pole on January 17, 1912, having hauled heavy sledges from the base of the Beardmore Glacier. Their attempted return was a horror of frostbite, scurvy, and starvation; all died, their stoic courage preserved in Scott's diary. The Pole was next seen from the air on November 29, 1929, by Rear Adm. Richard E. Byrd, USN, and his crew. In 1956 Rear Adm. George Dufek landed at the Pole, followed by scientific leader Dr. Paul Siple and a team of 17, who wintered there to begin conducting experiments for the International Geophysical Year. The South Pole Station, occupied continuously since then by the U.S., was rebuilt in 1975. The geodesic dome is scheduled to be replaced by the summer of 2007 by a new U.S. station to be constructed on jack-up supports, thus keeping it off of drifting snow that slowly buries surface structures. A similar design was used successfully for Dye sites (defensive radar network) in Greenland.
MILDER SHORES
At Australia's Mawson Station the average temperature approaches a toasty -11°C (12°F). Year-round, typical highs and lows are separated by only about 6°C (10°F). In nearby Holme Bay a half dozen bird species share 75 tiny Rookery Islands. One species, the southern giant petrel breeds nowhere else in the region.
World's coldest place: annual average temperature -56.7°C (-70°F)
Plateau Station
WEIGHT OF THE ICE SHEET
The ice mass covering Antarctica is so heavy it depresses the Earth's crust more than 914 meters (3,000 ft). Ice-free continental shelves actually tilt in toward the land, rather than sloping away toward the deep seafloor.
FLORA AND FAUNA
A severe climate limits most terrestrial life. Where ground is exposed and moisture available, lichens and mosses are found; two species of flowering plants, a pink and a grass, grow on the northern Antarctic Peninsula. There are no land animals larger than mites, springtails, and flightless midges. The "Dry Valleys" west of McMurdo Sound harbor algae under cold conditions. In some respects it is a Martian analogue.
AMERY ICE SHELF
While ice shelves on the Antarctic Peninsula have retreated dramatically in recent decades, others—including Amery Ice Shelf, fed by the massive Lambert Glacier—have grown larger.
A SEA OF ICE
When winter comes, the ocean surface around Antarctic begins to freeze. Spreading over an average of 77,700 square kilometers (30,000 sq. miles) a day, the ring of sea ice eventually covers more than 18 million square kilometers (7 million sq. miles), an area larger than the continent itself. Reducing the ocean's absorption of atmospheric carbon dioxide and blocking ocean-atmosphere heat exchange, sea ice plays a role in shaping regional climate which in turn has impacts over much of the globe.
ICE CORING
In 2003 Russian and American scientists drilled to 3650 m (11,975 ft), and European scientists obtained ice samples estimated to be 1 million years old. Other recently recovered cores record changes in temperature and atmospheric gases dating back 160,000 years. French scientists who analyzed the cores found a correlation between rising temperatures and carbon dioxide (CO2) levels in ancient times. Because the atmospheric CO2 level has risen from 280 parts per million (ppm) at the start of the industrial revolution to more than 365 ppm today, the onset of a global warming cycle is thought to be caused in part by increased burning of fossil fuels, which releases CO2. Along with methane and other gases, CO2 helps trap solar heat that would otherwise radiate back to space. There is disagreement about whether the rise in global temperatures during the past century confirms this predicted greenhouse effect.
THE BOTTOM OF THE WORLD
At the South Pole thermometer readings drop below minus 45.5°C (-50°F) on more than 250 days. Precipitation falls from a clear sky almost daily; ice crystals fall from clouds too diffuse to be seen.
EAST ANTARCTICA
The north and south geomagnetic poles, distinct from the more familiar geographic and magnetic poles, mark the axis of the Earth's magnetic field.
In 1909 Sir Ernest Shackleton, U.K., established a new farthest south in a futile attempt with Manchurian ponies to reach the Pole.
South Geomagnetic Pole 2005
BRITISH COMMONWEALTH TRANS-ANTARCTIC EXPEDITION 1958
Vostok Russia
ICE DESERT
Although Antarctica stores some 72 percent of the world's fresh water as ice, precipitation on six million sq km (3.7 million sq mi) of the continents's interior averages less than five cm (2 inches) a year, similar to the amount of rainfall in the driest part of the Sahara.
A record low temperature of minus 89.2°C (-128.6°F) was recorded here on July 21, 1983.
WHALES AND SEALS
Antarctic waters were the world's most prolific whaling grounds during the first half of the 20th century, but many stocks were depleted nearly to extinction. Today whales are protected worldwide by the International Whaling Commission. Twice during the 19th century the reduction of fur seals was so extreme that hunters went elsewhere, thus saving seals from extinction. In 1978, Antarctic Treaty nations put into effect a convention to protect all seals, and the six native species now have viable populations.
TRANSANTARCTIC MOUNTAINS
The 2,900-kilometer-long (1,800 mile) Transantarctic range divides East and West Antarctica. Exposed peaks called nunataks offer geologists and paleontologists access to unaltered sedimentary deposits more than 500 million years old.
BYRD GLACIER
The outflow of this glacier remains distinct all the way to the edge of the Ross Ice Shelf, some 440 kilometers (270 miles) from the foot of the Transantarctic Mountains.
DOME C
Concordia France and Italy
In 1840 Lt. Charles Wilkes, USN, reported land at 157° 46′ E and skirted the coast westward for 2,400 km (1,490 mi), becoming the first to confirm Antarctica as a continent.
KRILL
Shrimplike crustaceans that swarm in enormous numbers around the continent in summer, krill are a key link in the Antarctic food chain, directly or indirectly feeding whales, seals, fish, squid, penguins, and other seabirds. An agreement by Antarctic Treaty nations, which took effect in 1982, seeks to prevent overfishing of any living marine resource, in part by improving population-assessment techniques. Krill estimates, vital to establishing a safe harvesting rate, remain uncertain. Russian and Japanese trawlers harvest about 80,000 tons a year.
MARS METEORITE
The two areas that have yielded the most meteorites from blue-ice areas are the Allan Hills and the Queen Fabiola Mountains. The ALH 84-001 meteorite, found in Allan Hills, came from Mars and may harbor fossilized bacteria-like organisms.
THICKEST ICE
Echo-sounding from aircraft has identified an ice thickness of 4,776 m (15,670 ft). Bedrock was found at 2,341 m below sea level.
BIRDS
Five species of flightless marine penguins breed on the continent and nearby islands; including the emperor, Adélie, chinstrap, gentoo, and macaroni. All other birds that breed in Antarctica are also marine: fulmars, petrels, a prion, storm-petrels, a cormorant, skuas, a gull, a tern, and a sheathbill (an aberrant scavenging shorebird). There are no true land birds.
A gale of cold air from the ice plateau, sometimes blowing at 300 km (180 mi) an hour, makes this one of the windiest places on Earth.
MAGNETIC POLE
Compasses in the Southern Hemisphere point to this spot. The magnetic pole moves a few kilometers a year as the Earth's magnetic field changes.
*2006 South Magnetic Pole
QUEEN MAUD LAND
ENDERBY LAND
MAC. ROBERTSON LAND
AMERICAN HIGHLAND
WILKES LAND
TRANSANTARCTIC MOUNTAINS
VICTORIA LAND
Longitude East 170° of Greenwich

Elevation of the Ice Sheet

Antarctica is Earth's coldest, driest, and on average highest continent (about 8,000 ft; 2,438 m). The continent is covered by a vast ice sheet that blankets over 96 percent of the land mass. The highest point, located in East Antarctica, rises to 13,222 feet (4,030 m). The ice sheet is interrupted only by occasional mountain peaks that pierce the ice. One such peak is the Vinson Massif, Antarctica's highest point, which reaches an elevation of 16,067 feet (4,897 m) and is located in West Antarctica. Otherwise the icy surface is smooth (surface slopes rarely exceed more than 1 or 2 degrees). The shape of the ice sheet is determined in part by the weight of the ice itself, which causes the ice to flow outward. It is also determined in part by forces acting at the base of the ice sheet that tend to restrain it. The balance of these forces leads to a characteristically parabola-like shape. Departures from this simple shape occur as the ice from the interior domes spreads slowly over hills and valleys in the rocky base and where coastal mountain ranges channel the flow into outlet glaciers. Ice shelves form where there is sufficient ice to spread over the ocean. Ice shelves are the lowest and flattest parts of the ice sheet and are the source of the huge tabular icebergs that intermittently calve into the coastal ocean.

Surface Elevation

Vinson Massif
4897 m (16,067 ft)
Highest elevation on Antarctica
5,000 16,405
0 meters 0 feet

Measurements of a Paradox

Ninety percent of the world's ice and 70 percent of the world's fresh water are found here, yet most of Antarctica is truly a desert. The snow equivalent of less than three inches of rain falls over the high interior of the continent each year. But snow and ice have been slowly accumulating on Antarctica for millions of years. More than 15,600 feet (4,755 m) deep at its thickest, the mean depth of the ice exceeds 6,600 feet (2,012 m). Ice is generally much thicker on the interior of the ice sheet than at edges. This is because ice flows from the interior to edges, where it eventually returns to the ocean either in the form of icebergs or by melting directly into the ocean. The few areas of thin ice on the interior lie over chains of subglacial mountains. Glaciologists measure ice thickness with either a downward-pointing radar or by seismic sounding, which records the echo from an explosive shot buried just beneath the surface of the ice sheet. The thickness measurements used for this map were collected by scientists from 15 nations over the last 50 years. Although in theory the amount of ice in the ice sheet is sufficient to raise global sea levels by approximately 187 feet (57 m), it is extremely unlikely that the entire ice sheet could be lost in the foreseeable future.

Ice Sheet Thickness
5,000
16,405
0
meters
0
feet

Ice on the Move

Glaciologists once thought that ice motion in Antarctica's interior was slow and relatively uniform, with just a few fast-moving outlet glaciers and some ice streams (in West Antarctica) drawing ice from the interior down to the ice shelves and the sea. A computer model of ice flow, based on new satellite elevation measurements, suggests a more intricate ice-movement pattern. Like rivers, coastal ice flows appear to be fed by complex systems of tributaries that penetrate hundreds of miles into major drainage basins, and the major streams identified in East Antarctica dwarf those of the West. New satellite-based radar images agree with this more dynamic view. Ice velocities in the streams can be ten times greater than the flow of the adjacent slow-moving ice, and the resulting stream boundaries are often heavily crevassed and detectable from space.The computer model combines measurements of surface elevation, ice sheet thickness, and snowfall to calculate the pattern of ice flow that would keep Antarctica in balance at its present shape. The resulting continent-wide baseline picture of this "balanced" flow generally resembles the actual situation, and detailed observations can be compared against it to uncover any changes occurring in the size and shape of the ice sheet.

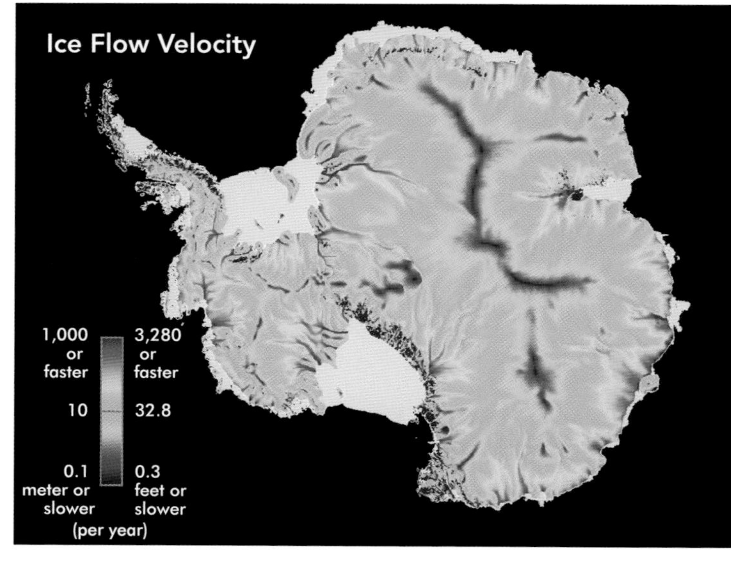
Ice Flow Velocity
1,000 or faster
3,280 or faster
10
32.8
0.1 meter or slower
0.3 feet or slower
(per year)

Ultimate Winds

Katabatic winds—cold air pouring down glacial slopes—often blow at 80 miles (129 km) per hour and can exceed 180 miles (290 km) per hour. These winds, which drain cold air masses from central Antarctica under the influence of gravity, are funnelled down valleys outward towards the coast, as indicated by the streamline arrows (right) on the white background of the Antarctic continent. When katabatic winds reach the coastline they often turn westward to blow counterclockwise around the continent. Offshore, circumpolar winds and currents push against the sea ice that grows to surround Antarctica each winter, leading to drift distances of up to several miles per day. The resulting near-shore movement of the sea ice is known as the East Wind drift, due to the dominant winds from the east. In some locations, such as the Weddell Sea, the drift is forced northward along the Antarctic Peninsula. In this case, and in the Bellingshausen, Amundsen, and Ross Seas, the combination of winds, currents, bathymetry, and topography leads to clockwise circulations known as gyres. In this image, the average sea-ice drift was determined from meteorological satellites. It illustrates the monthly average drift during the austral mid-winter, when sea-ice cover is at its maximum extent.

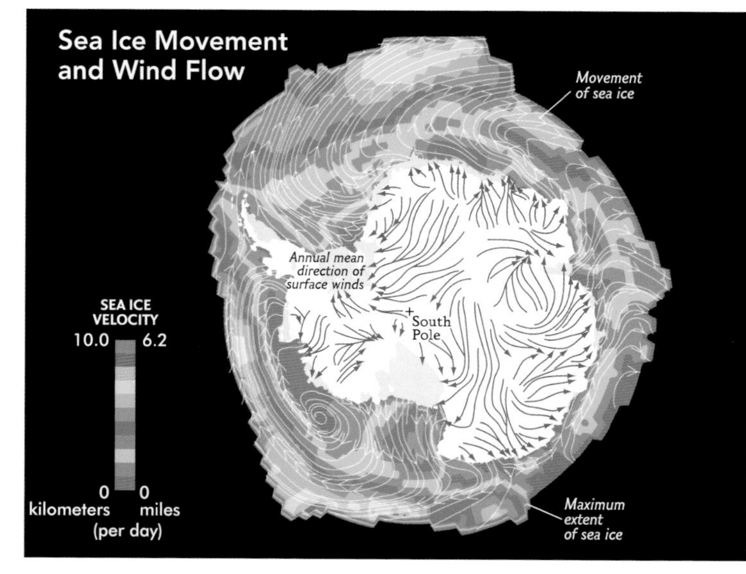
Sea Ice Movement and Wind Flow
Movement of sea ice
Annual mean direction of surface winds
South Pole
SEA ICE VELOCITY
10.0
6.2
0
kilometers
0
miles
(per day)
Maximum extent of sea ice

Antarctic Treaty

On December 1, 1959, after a decade of secret meetings, 12 nations—Argentina, Australia, Belgium, Chile, France, Japan, New Zealand, Norway, South Africa, the Soviet Union (Russia), the United Kingdom, and the United States—signed the Antarctic Treaty to preserve the frozen continent for peaceful scientific use only, a major feat during the height of Cold War rivalries. Since then, 32 other nations have joined.

The treaty includes all land, islands, and ice shelves south of 60° south latitude and enshrines the principles of peace, freedom of scientific research and exchange, and total banning of all military activity, nuclear testing, or disposal of radioactive waste. In addition, research stations are fully open to inspection, scientists may travel anywhere on the continent at any time, and countries can carry out aerial observations over any area.

A 1991 meeting prohibited mining in Antarctica. Other gatherings have asserted the importance of protecting wildlife, such as the Ross and fur seals, conserving unique biological habitats, and limiting human impact on sensitive ecological zones.The Antarctic Treaty made static all territorial claims held by 7 of the original 12 countries and prohibits any new claims. The treaty affirms that no country "rules the continent." For more than four decades it has proven to be an unprecedented example of international cooperation.

NORWEGIAN CLAIM
ARGENTINE CLAIM
BRITISH CLAIM
CHILEAN CLAIM
AUSTRALIAN CLAIM
FRENCH CLAIM
AUSTRALIAN CLAIM
NEW ZEALAND CLAIM
ATLANTIC OCEAN
INDIAN OCEAN
PACIFIC OCEAN
South Pole
Year-round research station
Seasonal research station
0 km 1500
0 mi 1000
Seaward extent of claims not delimited

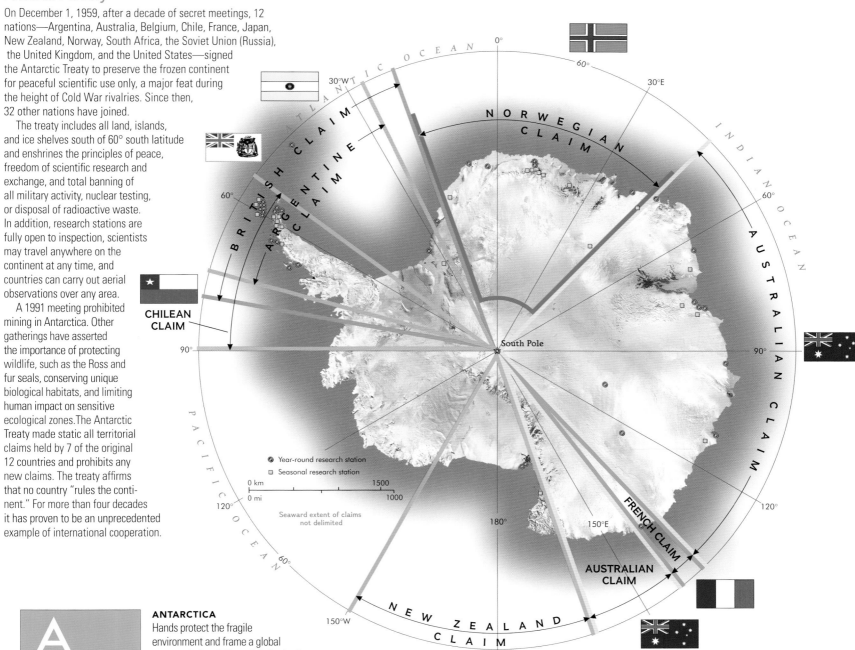

ANTARCTICA
Hands protect the fragile environment and frame a global segment below 60° south latitude; the dove of peace is between them. The A and the segment form a scale of justice.

Antarctic Convergence

The Antarctic Convergence refers to an undulating boundary in the seas that rings Antarctica roughly 950 miles (1,529 km) off the continental coast, between 50° and 60° south latitude. This narrow zone marks the meeting place of relatively warm waters from the southern Atlantic, Indian, and Pacific Oceans and the cold Antarctic Circumpolar Current. Because cold water sinks, it slips under the more buoyant warmer water and acts to power the great oceanic conveyor belt that affects life and weather around the world. The Antarctic Convergence also generates one of Earth's richest marine ecosystems. Mist and fog often rise at the interface of blended warm and cold waters. Immediately air becomes brisker and marine life alters. Water temperatures can plummet a dozen degrees (Fahrenheit) or more upon entering the Southern Ocean. The Antarctic Convergence functions as a barrier and forms Antarctica's biological extent. It delimits the Southern Ocean, which holds 10 percent of the world's seawater, and thus creates a largely closed ecosystem and isolates the continent from warmer waters. Deep, cold waters permit the proliferation of diatoms—single-celled algae—that in turn support krill, shrimp-like organisms that exist in enormous numbers. Krill form a vital part of the food chain, directly or indirectly providing nutrition for Antarctica's amazing wildlife, particularly fish, seals, whales, and birds, including five species of flightless penguins. Losses of this food source through over-harvesting by humans would seriously affect marine life.

As one travels north into warmer regions beyond the Antarctic Convergence, krill—the basis of Antarctica's life—perish and disappear. The Southern Ocean's rich waters, full of plant and animal life, stand apart from the continent itself, frozen and incredibly harsh, where vegetation is limited to lichens, mosses, and a mere two species of flowering plants. A small insect known as the wingless midge represents the largest land animal. In contrast, large body size and slow growth mark many marine animals, all of which have adapted magnificently to the cold environment.

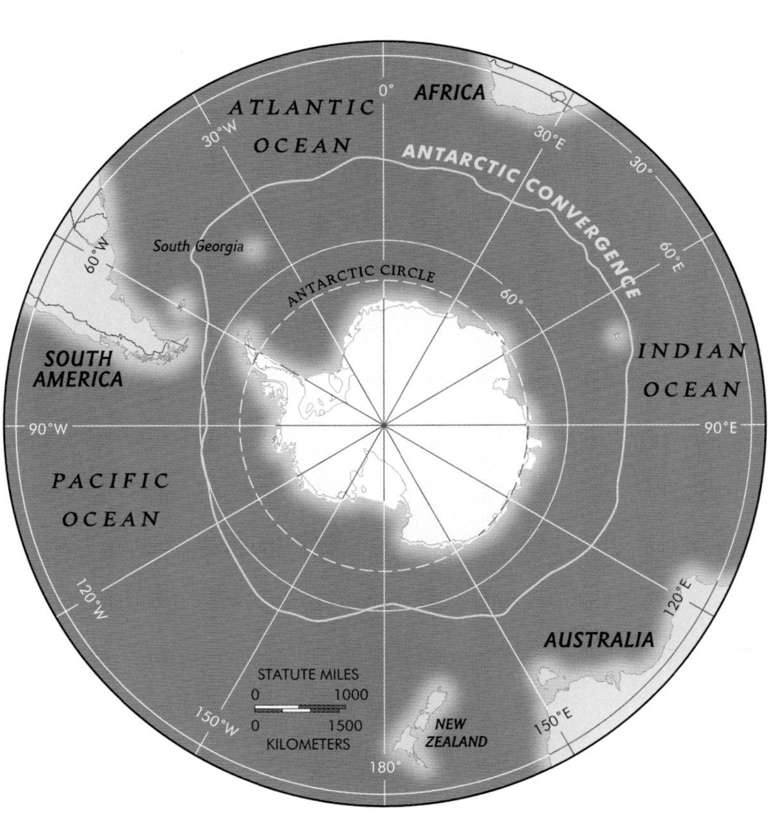
ATLANTIC OCEAN
AFRICA
ANTARCTIC CONVERGENCE
South Georgia
ANTARCTIC CIRCLE
SOUTH AMERICA
INDIAN OCEAN
PACIFIC OCEAN
AUSTRALIA
NEW ZEALAND
STATUTE MILES
0 1000
0 1500
KILOMETERS

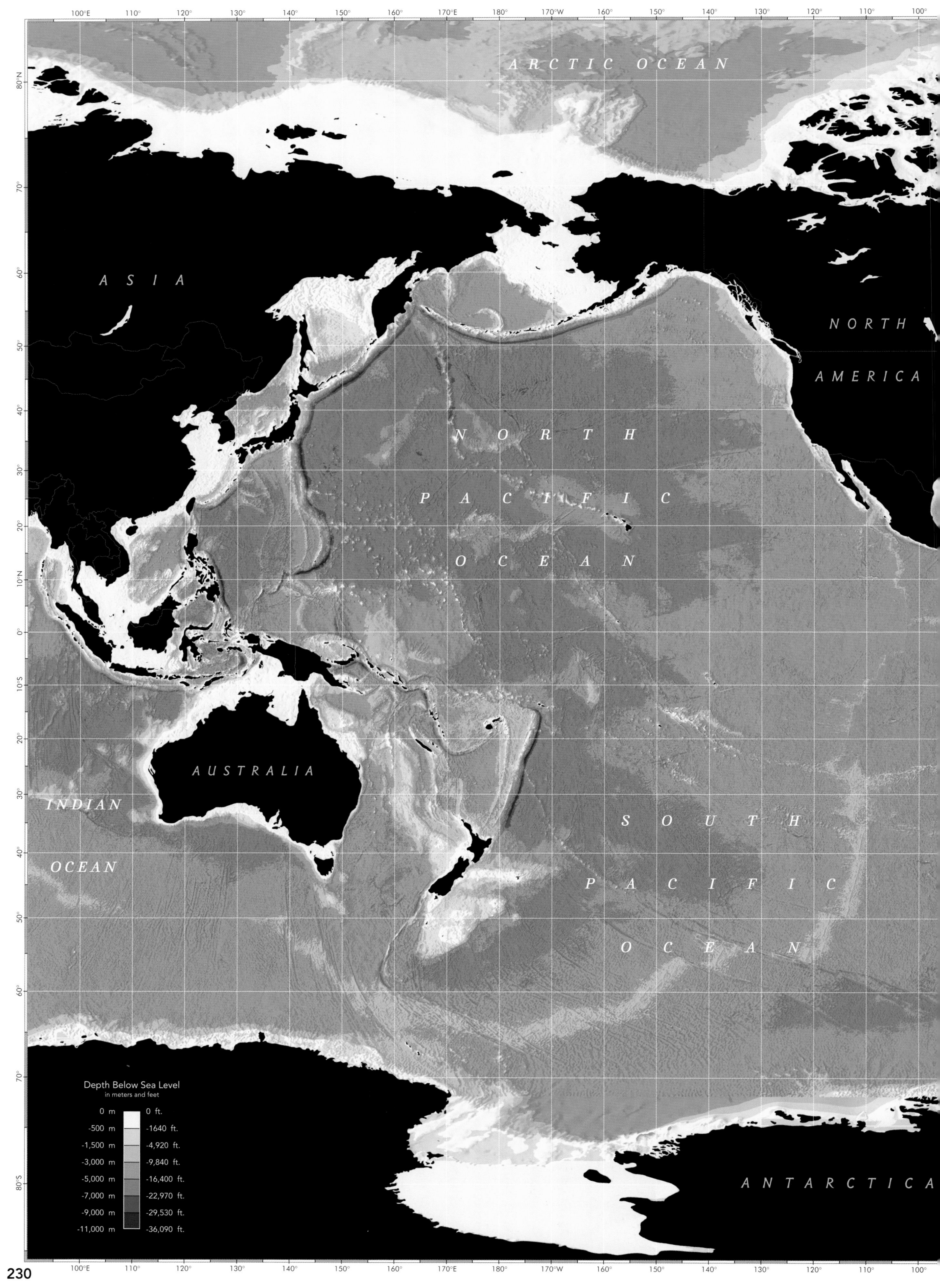

ARCTIC OCEAN
ASIA
NORTH AMERICA
NORTH PACIFIC OCEAN
AUSTRALIA
INDIAN OCEAN
SOUTH PACIFIC OCEAN
ANTARCTICA
Depth Below Sea Level
in meters and feet
0 m 0 ft.
-500 m -1640 ft.
-1,500 m -4,920 ft.
-3,000 m -9,840 ft.
-5,000 m -16,400 ft.
-7,000 m -22,970 ft.
-9,000 m -29,530 ft.
-11,000 m -36,090 ft.
100°E 110° 120° 130° 140° 150° 160° 170°E 180° 170°W 160° 150° 140° 130° 120° 110° 100°
80°N 70° 60° 50° 40° 30° 20° 10°N 0° 10°S 20° 30° 40° 50° 60° 70° 80°S

ARCTIC OCEAN
Greenland
EUROPE
ASIA
NORTH
ATLANTIC
OCEAN
Oceans
AFRICA
SOUTH
AMERICA
SOUTH
ATLANTIC
OCEAN
INDIAN
OCEAN
World Bathymetry
Kilometers
0 1,000 2,000 3,000
Statute Miles
0 1,000 2,000 3,000
Nautical Miles
0 1,000 2,000 3,000
Scale at the Equator
Miller Cylindrical Projection

EARTH IS A WATERY PLANET: More than 70 percent of its surface is covered by interconnected bodies of salt water that together make up a continuous, global ocean. Over the centuries, people have created artificial boundaries that divide this great water body into smaller oceans with numerous seas, gulfs, bays, straits, and channels.

The global ocean is a dynamic participant in Earth's physical, chemical, and biological processes. Millions of years ago, life itself most likely evolved in its waters. These are restless waters, always in motion. Tidal movement—the regular rise and fall of the ocean surface—results from gravitational forces exerted by the sun and the moon. The spin of Earth on its axis, coupled with wind, generates surface currents that redistribute warm and cold water around the planet. Variations in the temperature and salinity of water keep the thermohaline circulation system moving; this enormous system of interconnected currents, at the surface and deep in the ocean, influences climate patterns and circulates nutrients.

Where marine and terrestrial realms meet, one may find reefs built by tiny coral polyps or see cliffs and sea stacks shaped by countless waves. Many coastal zones are threatened, however, by overdevelopment, pollution, and overfishing. Farther out, in the deep ocean, lie vast untouched plains, high mountains and ridges, and valleys with floors lying as much as seven miles (11 km) below the sea surface. Teeming with life, the ocean includes "rain forests of the sea" and a host of marine species—even creatures who dwell in superhot waters near hydrothermal vents.

New technology is helping scientists to explore ever deeper and farther and to create more accurate maps of the ocean. Some of this underwater world has been explored with diving vessels and satellite imagery, but so much more remains to be discovered.

The Ocean Floor

The ocean floor is dynamic and varied. From the edge of the continental shelf (the shelf break), the continental slope plunges to the continental rise, which reaches to the abyssal plain. Periodically, terrestrial rocks and sediment flow through submarine canyons and form alluvial fans. The Mid-Ocean Ridge builds new seafloor; erosion and subsidence create atolls and guyots; and subducting tectonic plates form deep trenches in the ocean floor.

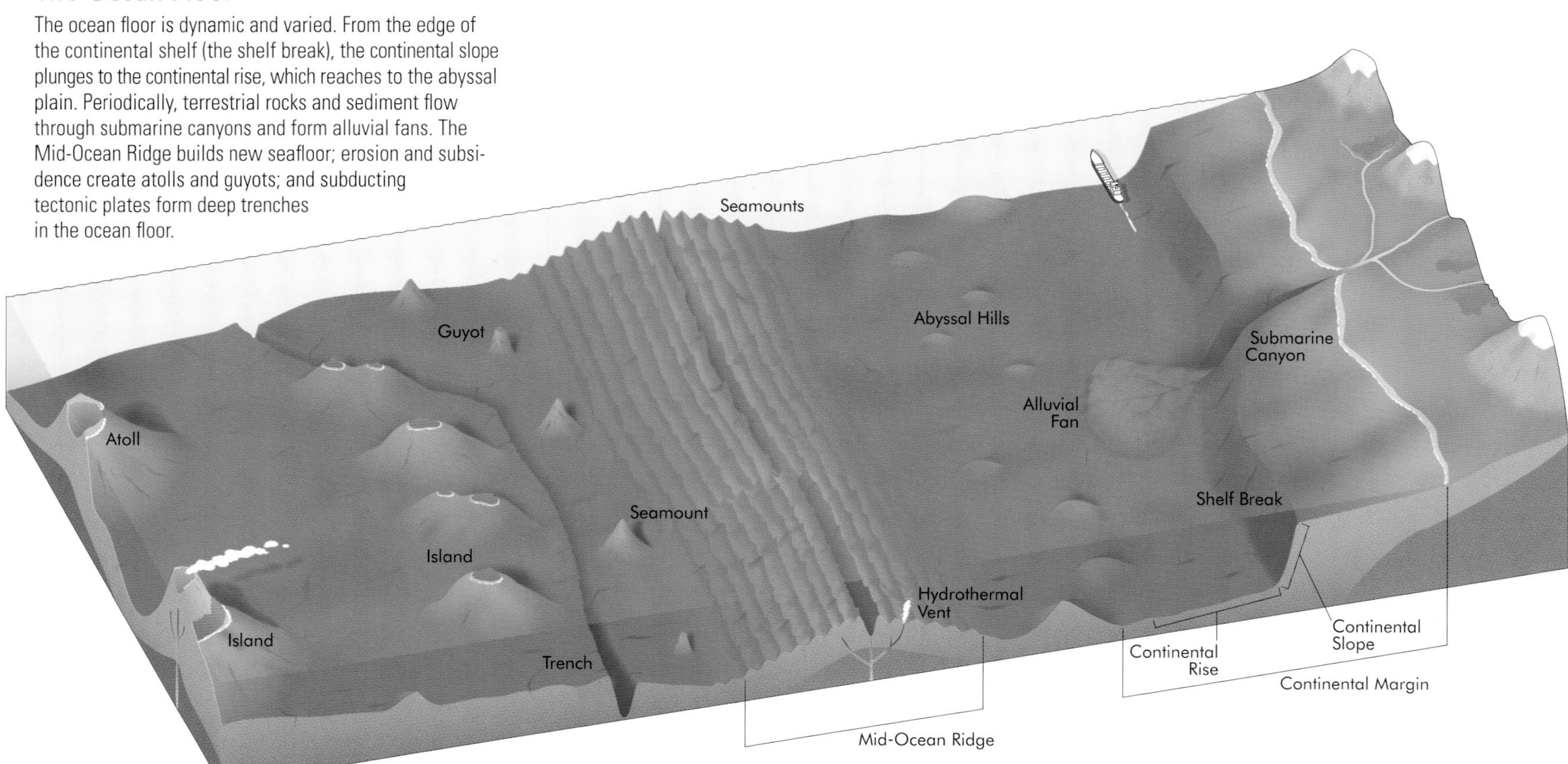
Seamounts
Guyot
Abyssal Hills
Submarine Canyon
Atoll
Alluvial Fan
Seamount
Shelf Break
Island
Hydrothermal Vent
Island
Trench
Continental Slope
Continental Rise
Continental Margin
Mid-Ocean Ridge

OCEAN WAVES

Waves may be born thousands of miles from shore, a result of large storms churning over the ocean. Wind pushing on the sea surface forms unorganized groups of waves that travel in all directions. In time, they organize into swell—groups of waves that can carry energy over thousands of miles of ocean. As the waves approach a surf zone, they steepen until their crests curl forward and break upon the beach.

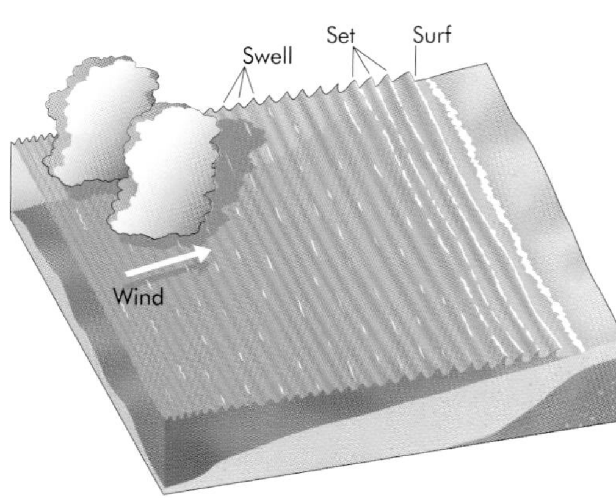
Swell
Set
Surf
Wind

CORAL MORPHOLOGY

Coral reefs—Earth's largest structures with biological origins—form primarily in the tropics, where water is clear and warm. They begin as fringing reefs, colonies built along coastlines by tiny organisms known as coral polyps. As a coastal area subsides, a fringing reef becomes a barrier reef enclosing a protected lagoon. Corals on a reef's seaward side rely on spur and groove formations to withstand powerful waves.

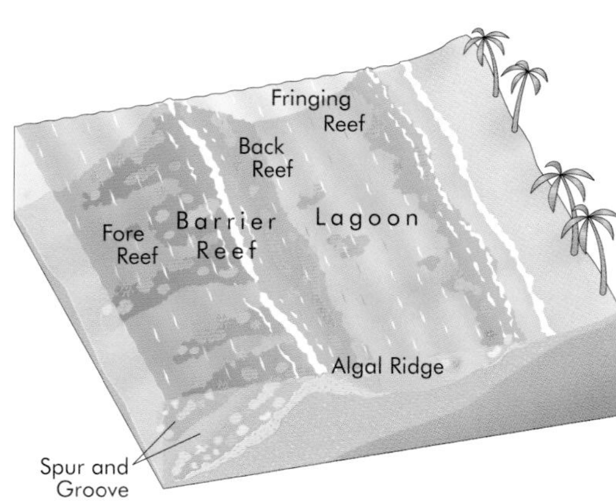
Fringing Reef
Back Reef
Fore Reef
Barrier Reef
Lagoon
Algal Ridge
Spur and Groove

COASTAL MORPHOLOGY

The contours of a coast determine how approaching ocean waves release their energy. In bays, wave energy is dispersed; at headlands, it is concentrated. Waves approaching at an angle produce longshore currents, which flow parallel to shore and transport sediment. Rip currents, generated by wind and the return flow of water, move outward. Over time, waves and currents reshape the coastlines of the world.

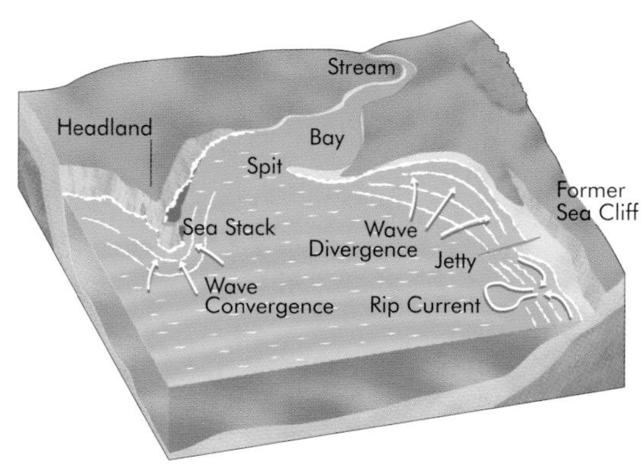
Stream
Headland
Bay
Spit
Former Sea Cliff
Sea Stack
Wave Divergence
Jetty
Wave Convergence
Rip Current

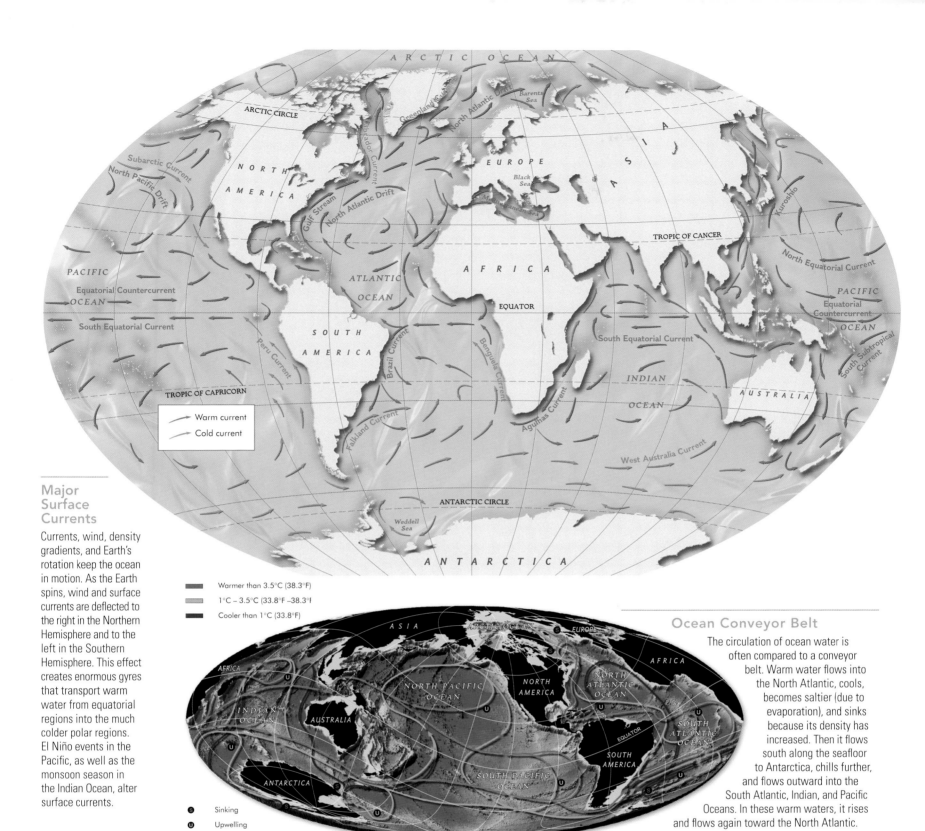

Major Surface Currents

Currents, wind, density gradients, and Earth's rotation keep the ocean in motion. As the Earth spins, wind and surface currents are deflected to the right in the Northern Hemisphere and to the left in the Southern Hemisphere. This effect creates enormous gyres that transport warm water from equatorial regions into the much colder polar regions. El Niño events in the Pacific, as well as the monsoon season in the Indian Ocean, alter surface currents.

Ocean Conveyor Belt

The circulation of ocean water is often compared to a conveyor belt. Warm water flows into the North Atlantic, cools, becomes saltier (due to evaporation), and sinks because its density has increased. Then it flows south along the seafloor to Antarctica, chills further, and flows outward into the South Atlantic, Indian, and Pacific Oceans. In these warm waters, it rises and flows again toward the North Atlantic.

TIDES

Both the sun and moon exert gravitational force on the Earth's ocean, creating tides. But because the moon is closer, its tug is much greater. During spring tides, when the moon is new or full, the combined pull of the sun and moon causes very high and low tides. Neap tides occur during the first and third quarters of the moon; at those times, the difference between tides is much smaller.

MAPPING THE OCEAN

Mapping the ocean requires myriad devices. In space, some satellites carry microwave radars to record data on wind speed and sea height; others use visible and infrared radiometers to collect biological productivity data. Radar altimetry and scatterometry are also used to record wind speed and direction. Out in the ocean, profiling floats collect temperature and salinity data. Ships use acoustics to map the sea floor.

THERMOHALINE CIRCULATION SYSTEM

Differences in the relative densities of volumes of water—determined by temperature (thermo) and salinity (haline)—drive thermohaline circulation. In polar regions, density increases as water cools and as evaporation makes it saltier; the mass of water sinks and flows along the ocean floor. Near the Equator, water warms and rises to the surface. If this system shut down, significant climate effects could occur.

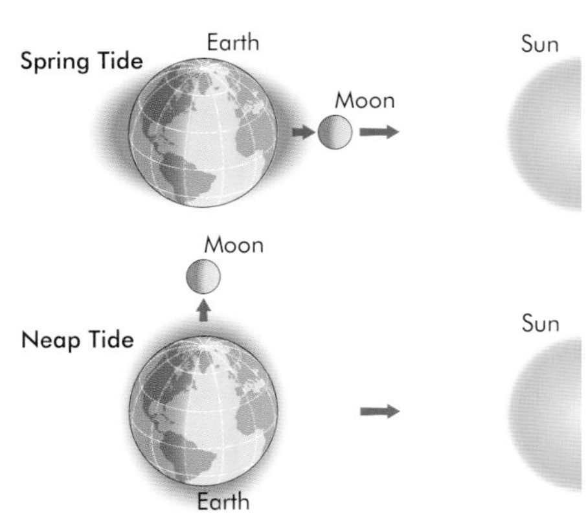
Spring Tide
Earth
Moon
Sun
Moon
Neap Tide
Sun
Earth

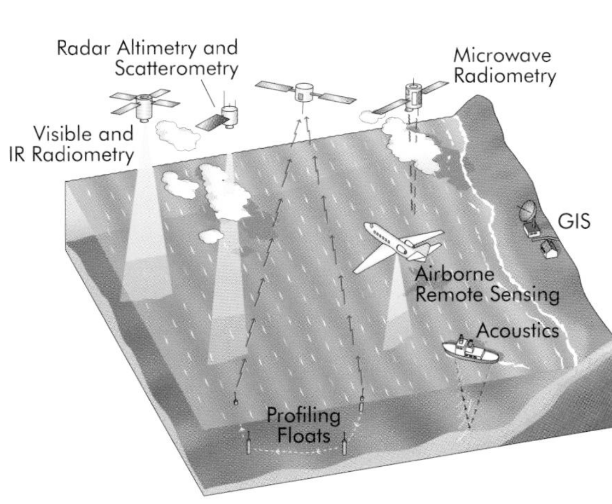
Radar Altimetry and Scatterometry
Microwave Radiometry
Visible and IR Radiometry
GIS
Airborne Remote Sensing
Acoustics
Profiling Floats

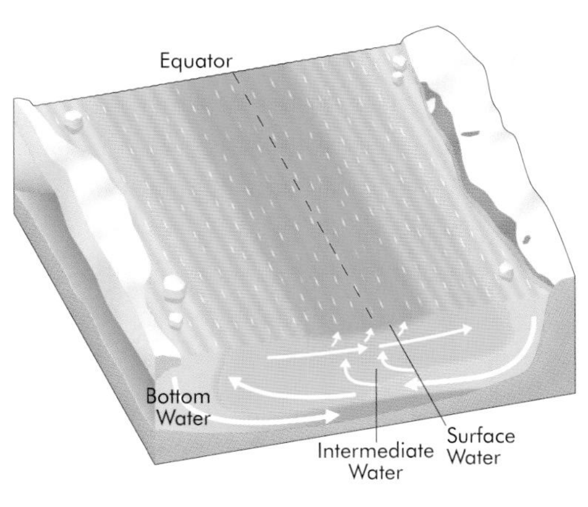
Equator
Bottom Water
Intermediate Water
Surface Water

Limits of the Oceans and Seas

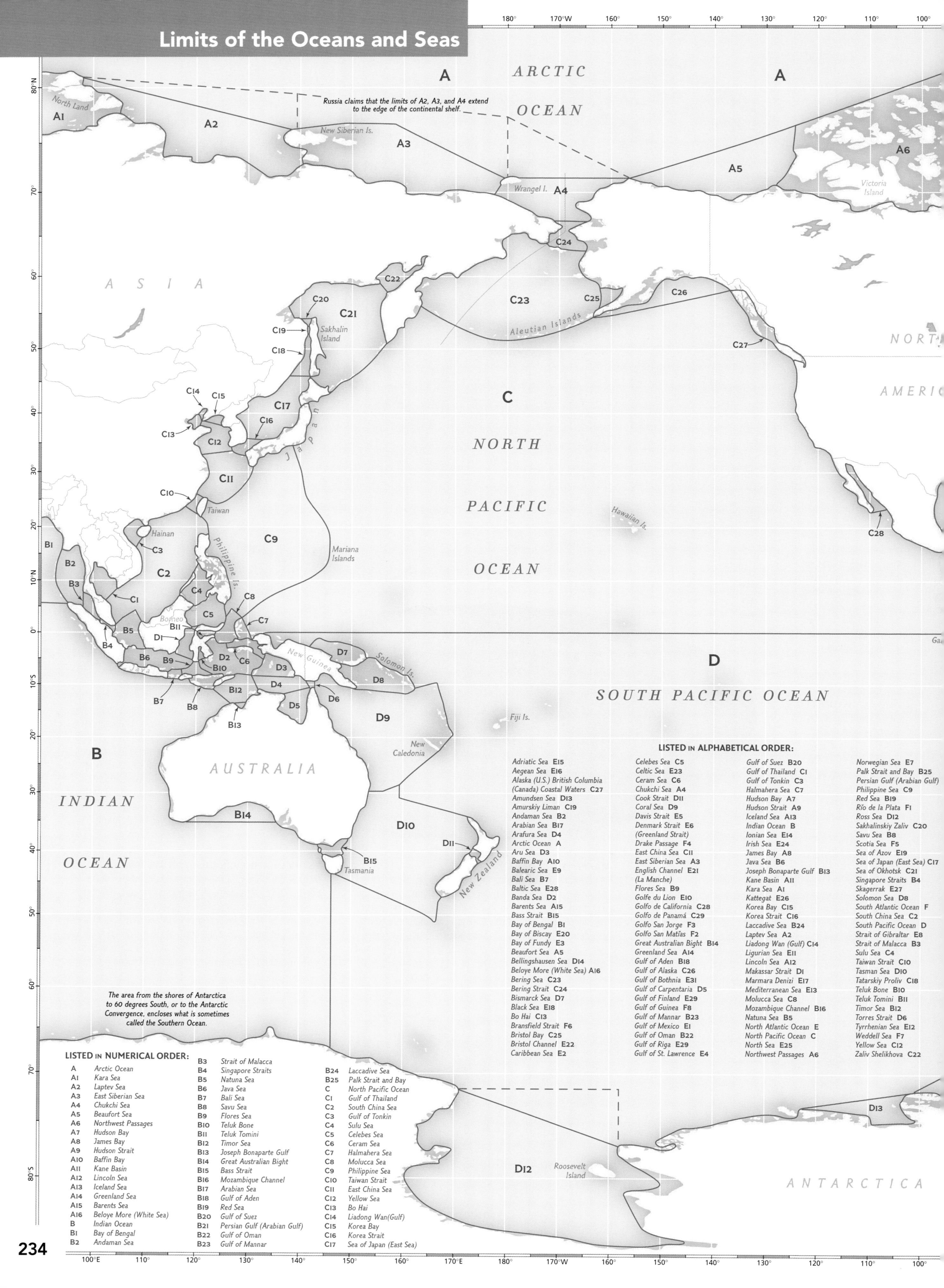

180° 170°W 160° 150° 140° 130° 120° 110° 100°
80°N 70° 60° 50° 40° 30° 20° 10°N 0° 10°S 20° 30° 40° 50° 60° 70° 80°S
100°E 110° 120° 130° 140° 150° 160° 170°E 180° 170°W 160° 150° 140° 130° 120° 110° 100°
ARCTIC OCEAN
Russia claims that the limits of A2, A3, and A4 extend to the edge of the continental shelf.
North Land
New Siberian Is.
Wrangel I.
Victoria Island
ASIA
Sakhalin Island
Japan
Taiwan
Hainan
Philippine Is.
Mariana Islands
Borneo
Java
New Guinea
Solomon Is.
Aleutian Islands
Hawaiian Is.
NORTH PACIFIC OCEAN
NORTH AMERICA
SOUTH PACIFIC OCEAN
Fiji Is.
New Caledonia
AUSTRALIA
Tasmania
New Zealand
INDIAN OCEAN
Roosevelt Island
ANTARCTICA
A A1 A2 A3 A4 A5 A6
B B1 B2 B3 B4 B5 B6 B7 B8 B9 B10 B11 B12 B13 B14 B15
C C1 C2 C3 C4 C5 C6 C7 C8 C9 C10 C11 C12 C13 C14 C15 C16 C17 C18 C19 C20 C21 C22 C23 C24 C25 C26 C27 C28
D D1 D2 D3 D4 D5 D6 D7 D8 D9 D10 D11 D12 D13
The area from the shores of Antarctica to 60 degrees South, or to the Antarctic Convergence, encloses what is sometimes called the Southern Ocean.
LISTED IN ALPHABETICAL ORDER:
Adriatic Sea E15
Aegean Sea E16
Alaska (U.S.) British Columbia (Canada) Coastal Waters C27
Amundsen Sea D13
Amurskiy Liman C19
Andaman Sea B2
Arabian Sea B17
Arafura Sea D4
Arctic Ocean A
Aru Sea D3
Baffin Bay A10
Balearic Sea E9
Bali Sea B7
Baltic Sea E28
Banda Sea D2
Barents Sea A15
Bass Strait B15
Bay of Bengal B1
Bay of Biscay E20
Bay of Fundy E3
Beaufort Sea A5
Bellingshausen Sea D14
Beloye More (White Sea) A16
Bering Sea C23
Bering Strait C24
Bismarck Sea D7
Black Sea E18
Bo Hai C13
Bransfield Strait F6
Bristol Bay C25
Bristol Channel E22
Caribbean Sea E2
Celebes Sea C5
Celtic Sea E23
Ceram Sea C6
Chukchi Sea A4
Cook Strait D11
Coral Sea D9
Davis Strait E5
Denmark Strait E6 (Greenland Strait)
Drake Passage F4
East China Sea C11
East Siberian Sea A3
English Channel E21 (La Manche)
Flores Sea B9
Golfe du Lion E10
Golfo de California C28
Golfo de Panamá C29
Golfo San Jorge F3
Golfo San Matías F2
Great Australian Bight B14
Greenland Sea A14
Gulf of Aden B18
Gulf of Alaska C26
Gulf of Bothnia E31
Gulf of Carpentaria D5
Gulf of Finland E29
Gulf of Guinea F8
Gulf of Mannar B23
Gulf of Mexico E1
Gulf of Oman B22
Gulf of Riga E29
Gulf of St. Lawrence E4
Gulf of Suez B20
Gulf of Thailand C1
Gulf of Tonkin C3
Halmahera Sea C7
Hudson Bay A7
Hudson Strait A9
Iceland Sea A13
Indian Ocean B
Ionian Sea E14
Irish Sea E24
James Bay A8
Java Sea B6
Joseph Bonaparte Gulf B13
Kane Basin A11
Kara Sea A1
Kattegat E26
Korea Bay C15
Korea Strait C16
Laccadive Sea B24
Laptev Sea A2
Liadong Wan (Gulf) C14
Ligurian Sea E11
Lincoln Sea A12
Makassar Strait D1
Marmara Denizi E17
Mediterranean Sea E13
Molucca Sea C8
Mozambique Channel B16
Natuna Sea B5
North Atlantic Ocean E
North Pacific Ocean C
North Sea E25
Northwest Passages A6
Norwegian Sea E7
Palk Strait and Bay B25
Persian Gulf (Arabian Gulf)
Philippine Sea C9
Red Sea B19
Río de la Plata F1
Ross Sea D12
Sakhalinskiy Zaliv C20
Savu Sea B8
Scotia Sea F5
Sea of Azov E19
Sea of Japan (East Sea) C17
Sea of Okhotsk C21
Singapore Straits B4
Skagerrak E27
Solomon Sea D8
South Atlantic Ocean F
South China Sea C2
South Pacific Ocean D
Strait of Gibraltar E8
Strait of Malacca B3
Sulu Sea C4
Taiwan Strait C10
Tasman Sea D10
Tatarskiy Proliv C18
Teluk Bone B10
Teluk Tomini B11
Timor Sea B12
Torres Strait D6
Tyrrhenian Sea E12
Weddell Sea F7
Yellow Sea C12
Zaliv Shelikhova C22
LISTED IN NUMERICAL ORDER:
A Arctic Ocean
A1 Kara Sea
A2 Laptev Sea
A3 East Siberian Sea
A4 Chukchi Sea
A5 Beaufort Sea
A6 Northwest Passages
A7 Hudson Bay
A8 James Bay
A9 Hudson Strait
A10 Baffin Bay
A11 Kane Basin
A12 Lincoln Sea
A13 Iceland Sea
A14 Greenland Sea
A15 Barents Sea
A16 Beloye More (White Sea)
B Indian Ocean
B1 Bay of Bengal
B2 Andaman Sea
B3 Strait of Malacca
B4 Singapore Straits
B5 Natuna Sea
B6 Java Sea
B7 Bali Sea
B8 Savu Sea
B9 Flores Sea
B10 Teluk Bone
B11 Teluk Tomini
B12 Timor Sea
B13 Joseph Bonaparte Gulf
B14 Great Australian Bight
B15 Bass Strait
B16 Mozambique Channel
B17 Arabian Sea
B18 Gulf of Aden
B19 Red Sea
B20 Gulf of Suez
B21 Persian Gulf (Arabian Gulf)
B22 Gulf of Oman
B23 Gulf of Mannar
B24 Laccadive Sea
B25 Palk Strait and Bay
C North Pacific Ocean
C1 Gulf of Thailand
C2 South China Sea
C3 Gulf of Tonkin
C4 Sulu Sea
C5 Celebes Sea
C6 Ceram Sea
C7 Halmahera Sea
C8 Molucca Sea
C9 Philippine Sea
C10 Taiwan Strait
C11 East China Sea
C12 Yellow Sea
C13 Bo Hai
C14 Liadong Wan(Gulf)
C15 Korea Bay
C16 Korea Strait
C17 Sea of Japan (East Sea)

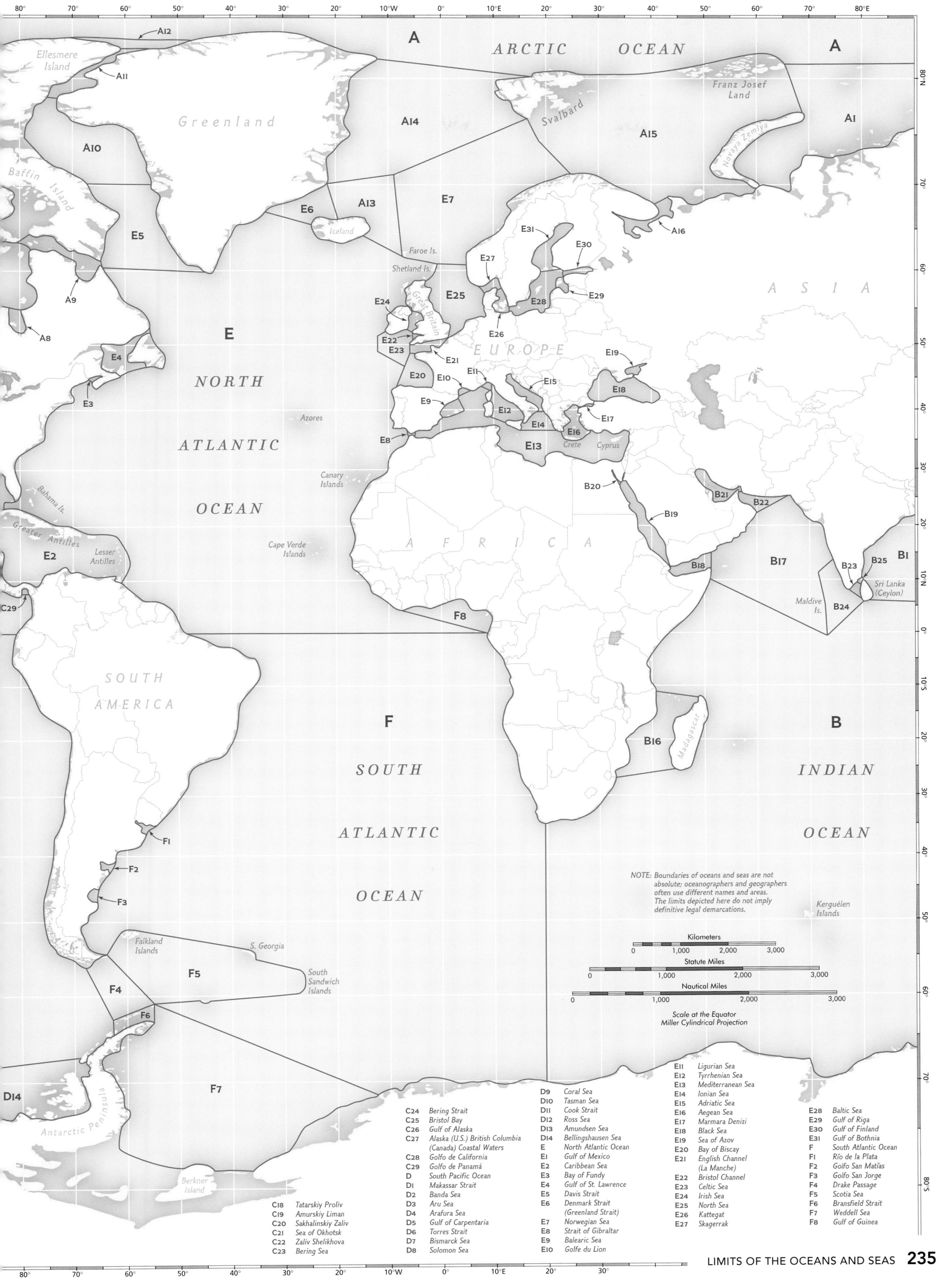
ARCTIC OCEAN
A
Ellesmere Island
Greenland
Baffin Island
Iceland
Faroe Is.
Shetland Is.
Svalbard
Franz Josef Land
Novaya Zemlya
A1
A8
A9
A10
A11
A12
A13
A14
A15
A16
E
NORTH ATLANTIC OCEAN
Azores
Canary Islands
Cape Verde Islands
Bahama Is.
Greater Antilles
Lesser Antilles
Great Britain
EUROPE
ASIA
AFRICA
Crete
Cyprus
E2
E3
E4
E5
E6
E7
E8
E9
E10
E11
E12
E13
E14
E15
E16
E17
E18
E19
E20
E21
E22
E23
E24
E25
E26
E27
E28
E29
E30
E31
B
INDIAN OCEAN
Maldive Is.
Sri Lanka (Ceylon)
Madagascar
Kerguélen Islands
B1
B16
B17
B18
B19
B20
B21
B22
B23
B24
B25
C29
F
SOUTH ATLANTIC OCEAN
SOUTH AMERICA
Falkland Islands
S. Georgia
South Sandwich Islands
Antarctic Peninsula
Berkner Island
D14
F1
F2
F3
F4
F5
F6
F7
F8
NOTE: Boundaries of oceans and seas are not absolute; oceanographers and geographers often use different names and areas. The limits depicted here do not imply definitive legal demarcations.
Kilometers
0 1,000 2,000 3,000
Statute Miles
0 1,000 2,000 3,000
Nautical Miles
0 1,000 2,000 3,000
Scale at the Equator
Miller Cylindrical Projection
80° 70° 60° 50° 40° 30° 20° 10°W 0° 10°E 20° 30° 40° 50° 60° 70° 80°E
80°N 70° 60° 50° 40° 30° 20° 10°N 0° 10°S 20° 30° 40° 50° 60° 70° 80°S
C18 Tatarskiy Proliv
C19 Amurskiy Liman
C20 Sakhalinskiy Zaliv
C21 Sea of Okhotsk
C22 Zaliv Shelikhova
C23 Bering Sea
C24 Bering Strait
C25 Bristol Bay
C26 Gulf of Alaska
C27 Alaska (U.S.) British Columbia (Canada) Coastal Waters
C28 Golfo de California
C29 Golfo de Panamá
D South Pacific Ocean
D1 Makassar Strait
D2 Banda Sea
D3 Aru Sea
D4 Arafura Sea
D5 Gulf of Carpentaria
D6 Torres Strait
D7 Bismarck Sea
D8 Solomon Sea
D9 Coral Sea
D10 Tasman Sea
D11 Cook Strait
D12 Ross Sea
D13 Amundsen Sea
D14 Bellingshausen Sea
E North Atlantic Ocean
E1 Gulf of Mexico
E2 Caribbean Sea
E3 Bay of Fundy
E4 Gulf of St. Lawrence
E5 Davis Strait
E6 Denmark Strait (Greenland Strait)
E7 Norwegian Sea
E8 Strait of Gibraltar
E9 Balearic Sea
E10 Golfe du Lion
E11 Ligurian Sea
E12 Tyrrhenian Sea
E13 Mediterranean Sea
E14 Ionian Sea
E15 Adriatic Sea
E16 Aegean Sea
E17 Marmara Denizi
E18 Black Sea
E19 Sea of Azov
E20 Bay of Biscay
E21 English Channel (La Manche)
E22 Bristol Channel
E23 Celtic Sea
E24 Irish Sea
E25 North Sea
E26 Kattegat
E27 Skagerrak
E28 Baltic Sea
E29 Gulf of Riga
E30 Gulf of Finland
E31 Gulf of Bothnia
F South Atlantic Ocean
F1 Río de la Plata
F2 Golfo San Matías
F3 Golfo San Jorge
F4 Drake Passage
F5 Scotia Sea
F6 Bransfield Strait
F7 Weddell Sea
F8 Gulf of Guinea

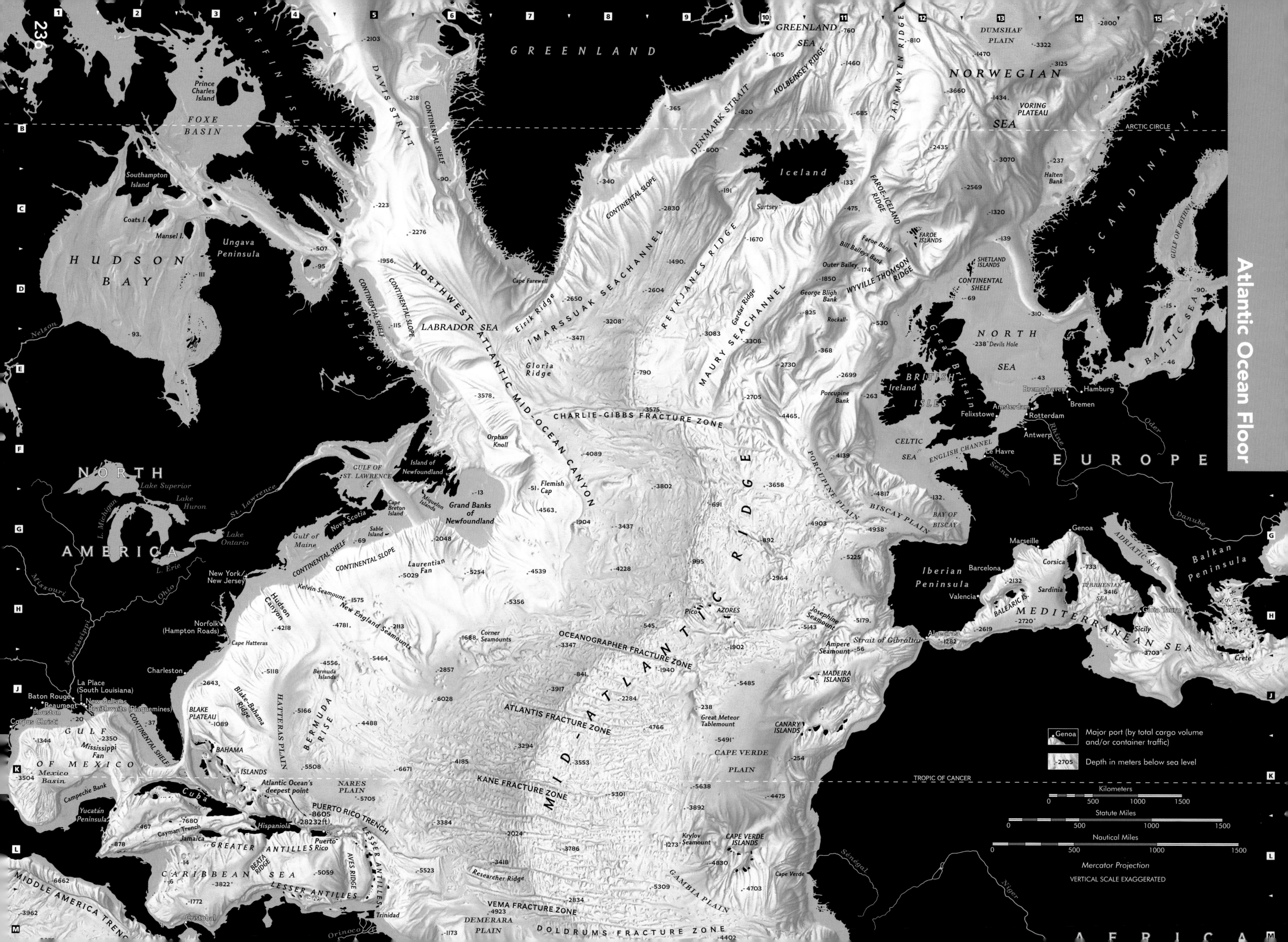

Atlantic Ocean Floor
GREENLAND
GREENLAND SEA
NORWEGIAN SEA
DUMSHAF PLAIN
VORING PLATEAU
JAN MAYEN RIDGE
KOLBEINSEY RIDGE
DENMARK STRAIT
Iceland
Surtsey
FAROE-ICELAND RIDGE
FAROE ISLANDS
Faroe Bank
Bill Baileys Bank
Outer Bailey
WYVILLE THOMSON RIDGE
George Bligh Bank
Rockall
Porcupine Bank
SHETLAND ISLANDS
CONTINENTAL SHELF
NORTH SEA
238 Devils Hole
Halten Bank
SCANDINAVIA
ARCTIC CIRCLE
GULF OF BOTHNIA
BALTIC SEA
Oder
Hamburg
Bremen
Bremerhaven
Amsterdam
Rotterdam
Antwerp
Rhine
Felixstowe
Le Havre
Seine
Great Britain
BRITISH ISLES
Ireland
CELTIC SEA
ENGLISH CHANNEL
BAY OF BISCAY
BISCAY PLAIN
PORCUPINE PLAIN
EUROPE
Danube
Balkan Peninsula
Crete
ADRIATIC SEA
Genoa
Marseille
Corsica
Sardinia
TYRRHENIAN SEA
Sicily
MEDITERRANEAN SEA
BALEARIC IS.
Barcelona
Valencia
Iberian Peninsula
Algeciras
Strait of Gibraltar
TROPIC OF CANCER
Josephine Seamount
Ampere Seamount
MADEIRA ISLANDS
CANARY ISLANDS
AZORES
Pico
Great Meteor Tablemount
CAPE VERDE PLAIN
CAPE VERDE ISLANDS
Cape Verde
Krylov Seamount
GAMBIA PLAIN
Sénégal
Niger
AFRICA
MAURY SEACHANNEL
Gardar Ridge
REYKJANES RIDGE
CONTINENTAL SLOPE
IMARSSUAK SEACHANNEL
Eirik Ridge
Cape Farewell
Gloria Ridge
CHARLIE-GIBBS FRACTURE ZONE
MID-ATLANTIC RIDGE
NORTHWEST ATLANTIC MID-OCEAN CANYON
LABRADOR SEA
Labrador
Orphan Knoll
Flemish Cap
Grand Banks of Newfoundland
OCEANOGRAPHER FRACTURE ZONE
ATLANTIS FRACTURE ZONE
KANE FRACTURE ZONE
VEMA FRACTURE ZONE
DOLDRUMS FRACTURE ZONE
Researcher Ridge
DEMERARA PLAIN
Corner Seamounts
Laurentian Fan
New England Seamounts
Kelvin Seamount
BERMUDA RISE
Bermuda Islands
NARES PLAIN
PUERTO RICO TRENCH
Atlantic Ocean's deepest point
-8605 (-28232 ft)
Puerto Rico
HATTERAS PLAIN
Hudson Canyon
Blake-Bahama Ridge
BLAKE PLATEAU
BAHAMA ISLANDS
Cape Hatteras
LESSER ANTILLES
AVES RIDGE
GREATER ANTILLES
BEATA RIDGE
CARIBBEAN SEA
Hispaniola
Cuba
Jamaica
Cayman Trench
Trinidad
Orinoco
Cristobal
Yucatán Peninsula
Campeche Bank
GULF OF MEXICO
Mississippi Fan
Mexico Basin
MIDDLE AMERICA TRENCH
Houston
Corpus Christi
Beaumont
New Orleans
Braithwaite (Plaquemines)
Baton Rouge
La Place (South Louisiana)
Charleston
Norfolk (Hampton Roads)
New York/New Jersey
Mississippi
Missouri
Ohio
L. Erie
Lake Ontario
Lake Huron
Lake Superior
L. Michigan
St. Lawrence
GULF OF ST. LAWRENCE
Island of Newfoundland
Miquelon Islands
Cape Breton Island
Sable Island
Nova Scotia
Gulf of Maine
NORTH AMERICA
DAVIS STRAIT
BAFFIN ISLAND
FOXE BASIN
Prince Charles Island
Southampton Island
Coats I.
Mansel I.
Ungava Peninsula
HUDSON BAY
Nelson
Genoa Major port (by total cargo volume and/or container traffic)
-2705 Depth in meters below sea level
Kilometers
Statute Miles
Nautical Miles
Mercator Projection
VERTICAL SCALE EXAGGERATED

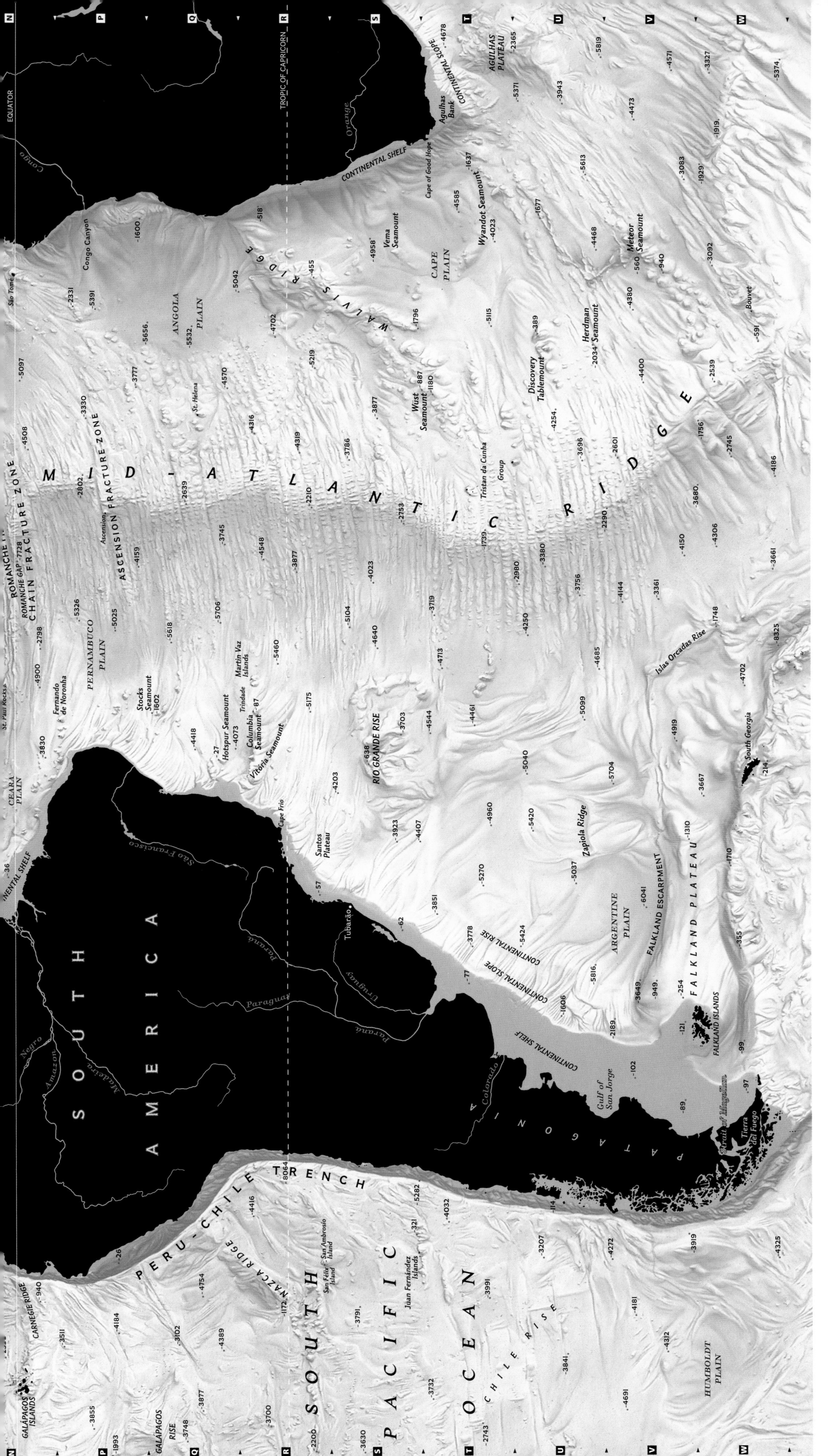

MID-ATLANTIC RIDGE
SOUTH AMERICA
SOUTH PACIFIC OCEAN
PERU-CHILE TRENCH
WALVIS RIDGE
ANGOLA PLAIN
CAPE PLAIN
PERNAMBUCO PLAIN
ARGENTINE PLAIN
FALKLAND PLATEAU
FALKLAND ESCARPMENT
FALKLAND ISLANDS
RIO GRANDE RISE
ASCENSION FRACTURE ZONE
PATAGONIA
NAZCA RIDGE
CHILE RISE
HUMBOLDT PLAIN
AGULHAS PLATEAU
TROPIC OF CAPRICORN
EQUATOR

The ragged spine of the Mid-Atlantic Ridge fills the center of the Atlantic Ocean Basin from north to south. This prominent spreading ridge was not discovered until the middle of the 20th century.

ASIA
SEA OF OKHOTSK
BERING SEA
ALEUTIAN BASIN
ALEUTIAN ISLANDS
ALEUTIAN TRENCH
KURIL TRENCH
KURIL BASIN
SEA OF JAPAN (East Sea)
YELLOW SEA
EAST CHINA SEA
JAPAN TRENCH
IZU TRENCH
BONIN TRENCH
NORTHWEST PACIFIC BASIN
EMPEROR SEAMOUNTS
EMPEROR TROUGH
HESS RISE
SHATSKIY RISE
CHINOOK TROUGH
NORTHWEST HAWAIIAN RIDGE
HAWAIIAN RIDGE
MID-PACIFIC MOUNTAINS
PHILIPPINE SEA
WEST MARIANA BASIN
MARIANA TRENCH
EAST MARIANA BASIN
SOUTH CHINA SEA
INDOCHINA PENINSULA
CAROLINE ISLANDS
CENTRAL PACIFIC BASIN
INDONESIA
GREATER SUNDA ISLANDS
BANDA SEA
JAVA TRENCH
New Guinea
SOLOMON ISLANDS
CORAL SEA
AUSTRALIA
TROPIC OF CANCER
TROPIC OF CAPRICORN
EQUATOR
TASMAN SEA
NEW ZEALAND
KERMADEC TRENCH
TONGA TRENCH
LOUISVILLE RIDGE
CHATHAM RISE
CAMPBELL PLATEAU
INDIAN OCEAN
SOUTHEAST INDIAN RIDGE
SOUTH AUSTRALIAN BASIN
Challenger Deep -10920 (-35827ft) World's greatest ocean depth
-7125 (-23376ft) Indian Ocean's deepest point

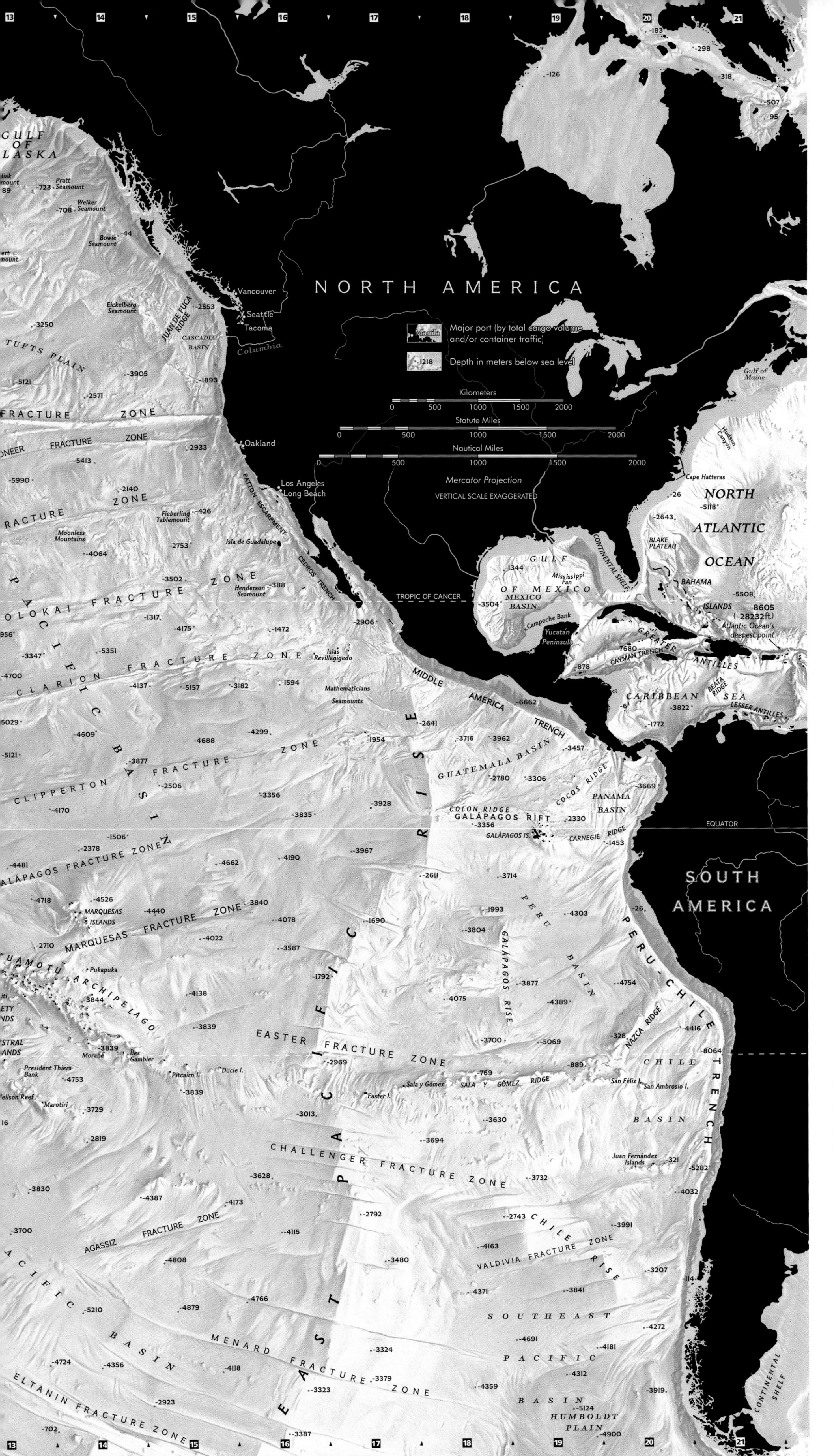
NORTH AMERICA
SOUTH AMERICA
NORTH ATLANTIC OCEAN
GULF OF MEXICO
CARIBBEAN SEA
Major port (by total cargo volume and/or container traffic)
Depth in meters below sea level
Kilometers
Statute Miles
Nautical Miles
Mercator Projection
VERTICAL SCALE EXAGGERATED
TROPIC OF CANCER
EQUATOR
EAST PACIFIC RISE
Vancouver
Seattle
Tacoma
Oakland
Los Angeles
Long Beach
CLARION FRACTURE ZONE
CLIPPERTON FRACTURE ZONE
MOLOKAI FRACTURE ZONE
MARQUESAS FRACTURE ZONE
EASTER FRACTURE ZONE
CHALLENGER FRACTURE ZONE
MENARD FRACTURE ZONE
ELTANIN FRACTURE ZONE
AGASSIZ FRACTURE ZONE
VALDIVIA FRACTURE ZONE
GALÁPAGOS FRACTURE ZONE
MIDDLE AMERICA TRENCH
PERU-CHILE TRENCH
GUATEMALA BASIN
PERU BASIN
CHILE BASIN
PANAMA BASIN
SOUTHEAST PACIFIC BASIN
GALÁPAGOS RIFT
GALÁPAGOS IS.
CARNEGIE RIDGE
COCOS RIDGE
NAZCA RIDGE
GALÁPAGOS RISE
CHILE RISE
SALA Y GÓMEZ RIDGE
Easter I.
Juan Fernández Islands
TUAMOTU ARCHIPELAGO
MARQUESAS ISLANDS
Pitcairn I.
HUMBOLDT PLAIN
Cape Hatteras
BAHAMA ISLANDS
-8605 (-28232ft) Atlantic Ocean's deepest point
GREATER ANTILLES
LESSER ANTILLES
CAYMAN TRENCH
Yucatán Peninsula
CONTINENTAL SHELF

The Pacific Ocean Basin is shrinking as it is subsumed under surrounding continents on all sides.

Dead Sea
(-1365ft)-416
World's lowest point
Mt. Everest
(29035ft)8850
World's highest point
Major port (by total cargo volume and/or container traffic)
Depth in meters below sea level
Kilometers
Statute Miles
Nautical Miles
Mercator Projection
VERTICAL SCALE EXAGGERATED
TROPIC OF CANCER
EQUATOR
TROPIC OF CAPRICORN
S A H A R A
A F R I C A
A S I A
A R A B I A N
P E N I N S U L A
I N D I A
ARABIAN SEA
ARABIAN BASIN
BAY OF BENGAL
PERSIAN GULF
GULF OF OMAN
GULF OF ADEN
RED SEA
SOMALI BASIN
MASCARENE BASIN
MASCARENE PLAIN
MADAGASCAR BASIN
NATAL BASIN
MADAGASCAR PLATEAU
MID-INDIAN BASIN
MID-INDIAN RIDGE
NINETYEAST RIDGE
CARLSBERG RIDGE
CHAGOS-LACCADIVE PLATEAU
OWEN FRACTURE ZONE
SOUTHWEST INDIAN RIDGE
SOUTHEAST
CROZET BASIN
AGULHAS BASIN
AGULHAS PLATEAU
KERGUELEN PLATEAU
ATLANTIC-INDIAN RIDGE
MOZAMBIQUE ESCARPMENT
PRINCE EDWARD FRACTURE ZONE
INDOMED FRACTURE ZONE
ATLANTIS II FRACTURE ZONE
RODRIGUES FRACTURE ZONE
VEMA FRACTURE ZONE
EGERIA FRACTURE ZONE
MAURITIUS TRENCH
AMIRANTE TRENCH
CHAGOS TRENCH
Madagascar
Sri Lanka (Ceylon)
Nile
Euphrates
Tigris
Indus
Ganges
Brahmaputra
Zambezi
Limpopo
Shire
Lake Victoria
Lake Malawi
Richards Bay
Cape Agulhas
Agulhas Bank
Dubai
Colombo
Socotra
Seychelles
Chagos Archipelago
Diego Garcia
Maldive Islands
Lakshadweep
Mauritius
Réunion
Kerguelen Islands
Crozet Islands
Prince Edward Islands
Amsterdam
St. Paul
Ob' Tablemount
Walters Shoal
Nikitin Seamount
COCO-DE-MER SEAMOUNTS
Andaman Islands
Nicobar Islands

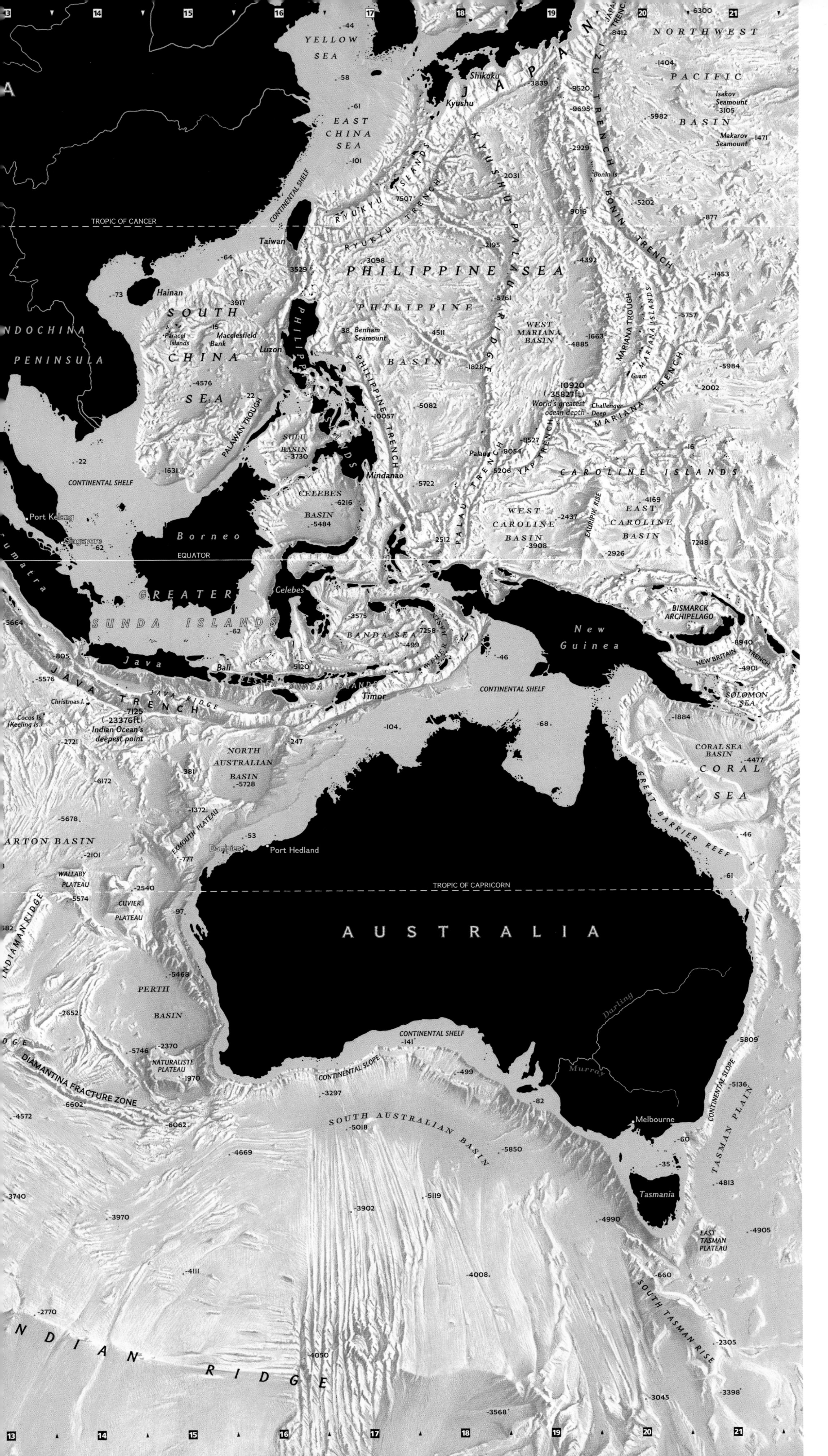
YELLOW SEA
EAST CHINA SEA
JAPAN
Shikoku
Kyushu
NORTHWEST PACIFIC BASIN
Isakov Seamount
Makarov Seamount
JAPAN TRENCH
IZU TRENCH
BONIN TRENCH
Bonin Is.
RYUKYU ISLANDS
RYUKYU TRENCH
KYUSHU-PALAU RIDGE
CONTINENTAL SHELF
TROPIC OF CANCER
Taiwan
PHILIPPINE SEA
PHILIPPINE BASIN
Benham Seamount
WEST MARIANA BASIN
MARIANA TROUGH
MARIANA ISLANDS
MARIANA TRENCH
Guam
-10920 (-35827ft) World's greatest ocean depth
Challenger Deep
Hainan
SOUTH CHINA SEA
Paracel Islands
Macclesfield Bank
INDOCHINA PENINSULA
Luzon
PHILIPPINE ISLANDS
PHILIPPINE TRENCH
PALAWAN TROUGH
SULU BASIN
Mindanao
Palau
PALAU TRENCH
YAP TRENCH
CAROLINE ISLANDS
WEST CAROLINE BASIN
EAST CAROLINE BASIN
EAURIPIK RISE
CELEBES BASIN
Port Kelang
Singapore
Borneo
EQUATOR
Sumatra
GREATER SUNDA ISLANDS
Celebes
BANDA SEA
WEBER DEEP
Java
Bali
Timor
New Guinea
BISMARCK ARCHIPELAGO
NEW BRITAIN TRENCH
SOLOMON SEA
JAVA TRENCH
JAVA RIDGE
Christmas I.
Cocos Is. (Keeling Is.)
-7125 (-23376ft) Indian Ocean's deepest point
NORTH AUSTRALIAN BASIN
CONTINENTAL SHELF
CORAL SEA BASIN
CORAL SEA
GREAT BARRIER REEF
EXMOUTH PLATEAU
Dampier
Port Hedland
WHARTON BASIN
WALLABY PLATEAU
CUVIER PLATEAU
TROPIC OF CAPRICORN
NINETYEAST RIDGE
AUSTRALIA
PERTH BASIN
Darling
Murray
NATURALISTE PLATEAU
DIAMANTINA FRACTURE ZONE
CONTINENTAL SHELF
CONTINENTAL SLOPE
SOUTH AUSTRALIAN BASIN
Melbourne
TASMAN PLAIN
Tasmania
EAST TASMAN PLATEAU
SOUTH TASMAN RISE
SOUTHEAST INDIAN RIDGE

The Ninety East Ridge, the longest linear feature in the world, formed as ocean crust moved north over a hot spot deep in the Earth.

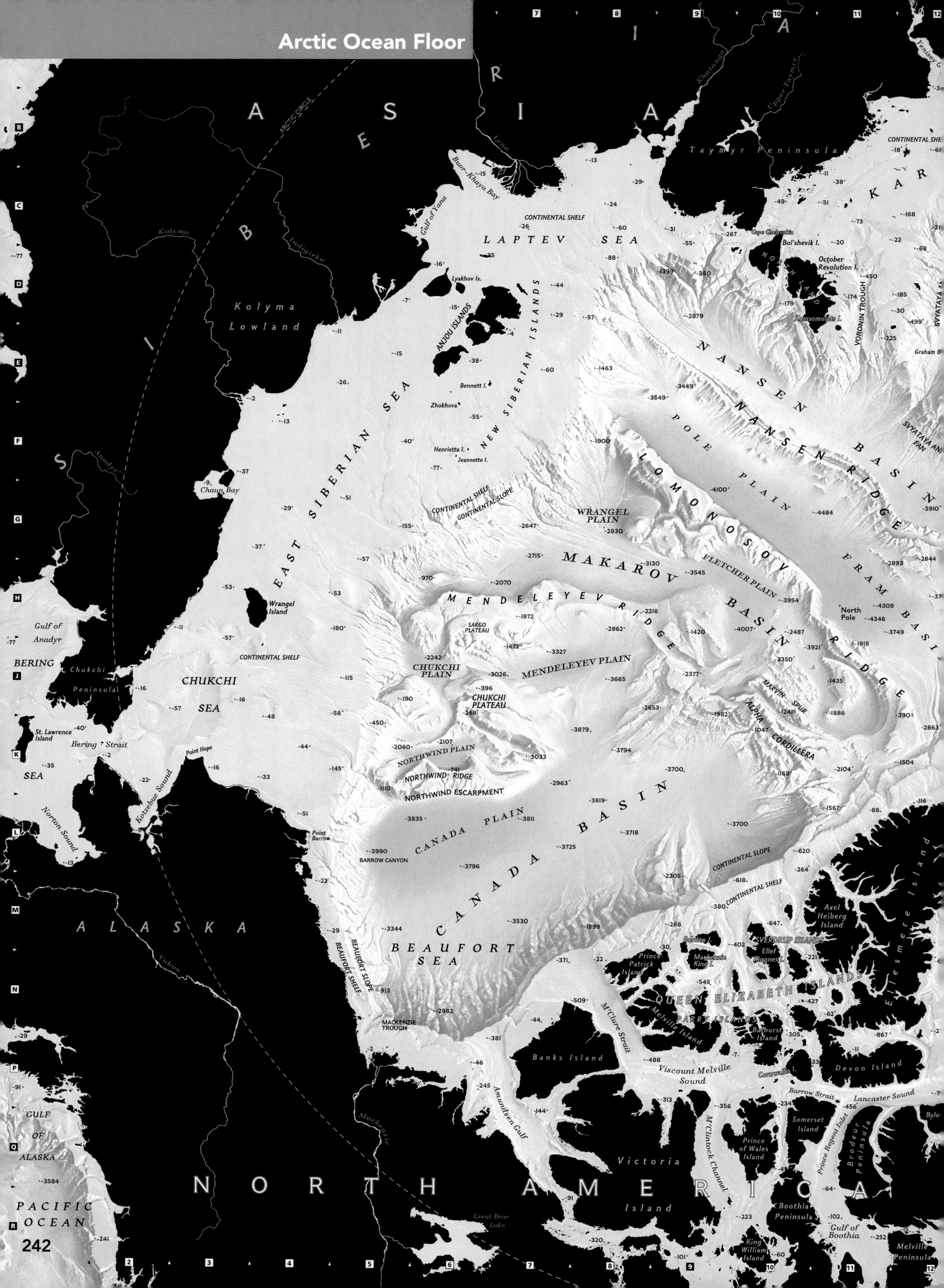
ASIA
SIBERIA
LAPTEV SEA
CONTINENTAL SHELF
EAST SIBERIAN SEA
NEW SIBERIAN ISLANDS
ANJOU ISLANDS
Lyakhov Is.
Bennett I.
Zhokhova
Henrietta I.
Jeannette I.
Kolyma Lowland
Chaun Bay
Wrangel Island
CHUKCHI SEA
Chukchi Peninsula
BERING SEA
Gulf of Anadyr
St. Lawrence Island
Bering Strait
Point Hope
Kotzebue Sound
Norton Sound
Point Barrow
ALASKA
GULF OF ALASKA
PACIFIC OCEAN
NORTH AMERICA
Taymyr Peninsula
Cape Chelyuskin
Bol'shevik I.
October Revolution I.
Komsomolets I.
VORONIN TROUGH
KARA
NANSEN BASIN
NANSEN RIDGE
POLE PLAIN
LOMONOSOV RIDGE
FRAM BASIN
North Pole
WRANGEL PLAIN
MAKAROV BASIN
FLETCHER PLAIN
MENDELEYEV RIDGE
SARGO PLATEAU
MENDELEYEV PLAIN
CHUKCHI PLAIN
CHUKCHI PLATEAU
NORTHWIND PLAIN
NORTHWIND RIDGE
NORTHWIND ESCARPMENT
MARVIN SPUR
ALPHA CORDILLERA
CANADA PLAIN
CANADA BASIN
BARROW CANYON
CONTINENTAL SLOPE
BEAUFORT SEA
BEAUFORT SHELF
BEAUFORT SLOPE
MACKENZIE TROUGH
QUEEN ELIZABETH ISLANDS
SVERDRUP ISLANDS
PARRY ISLANDS
Axel Heiberg Island
Ellesmere Island
Borden I.
Mackenzie King I.
Ellef Ringnes I.
Prince Patrick Island
Melville Island
Bathurst Island
Cornwallis I.
Devon Island
Banks Island
M'Clure Strait
Viscount Melville Sound
Barrow Strait
Lancaster Sound
Amundsen Gulf
Victoria Island
M'Clintock Channel
Prince of Wales Island
Somerset Island
Prince Regent Inlet
Brodeur Peninsula
Boothia Peninsula
Gulf of Boothia
King William Island
Melville Peninsula
Great Bear Lake

EUROPE
BARENTS SEA
NORWEGIAN SEA
GREENLAND SEA
GREENLAND
ATLANTIC OCEAN
SCANDINAVIA
WHITE SEA
GULF OF BOTHNIA
SVALBARD
Iceland
Arctic Ocean's deepest point
Molloy Hole
-5669
(-18599ft)
Depth in meters below sea level
Kilometers
Statute Miles
Nautical Miles
Azimuthal Equidistant Projection
VERTICAL SCALE EXAGGERATED

Water depths in the Arctic Ocean must often be measured from submarines under the ice. They discovered three almost parallel ridges crossing the Arctic Basin.

Ocean Floor Around Antarctica

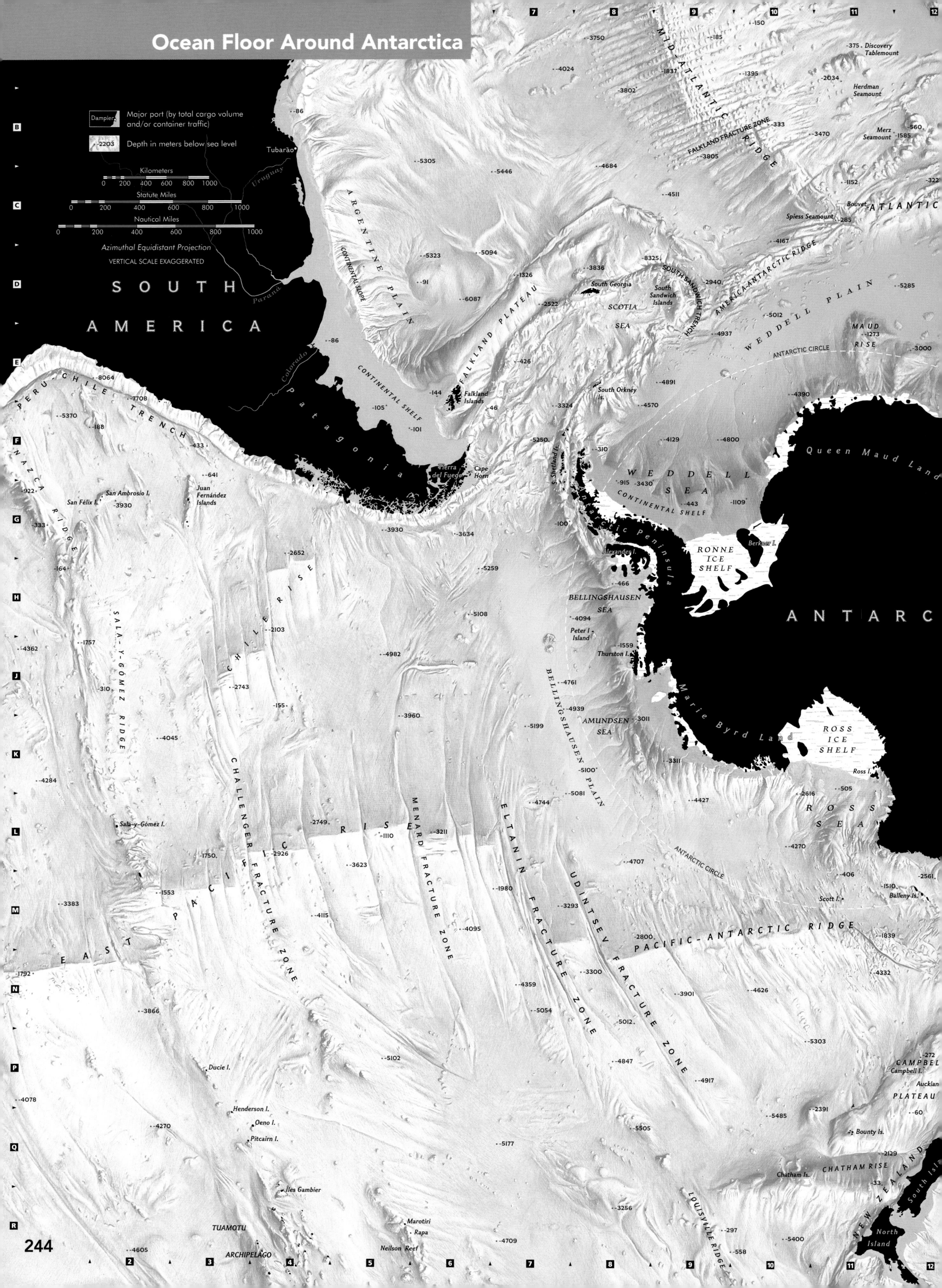
Major port (by total cargo volume and/or container traffic)
Depth in meters below sea level
Kilometers
Statute Miles
Nautical Miles
Azimuthal Equidistant Projection
VERTICAL SCALE EXAGGERATED

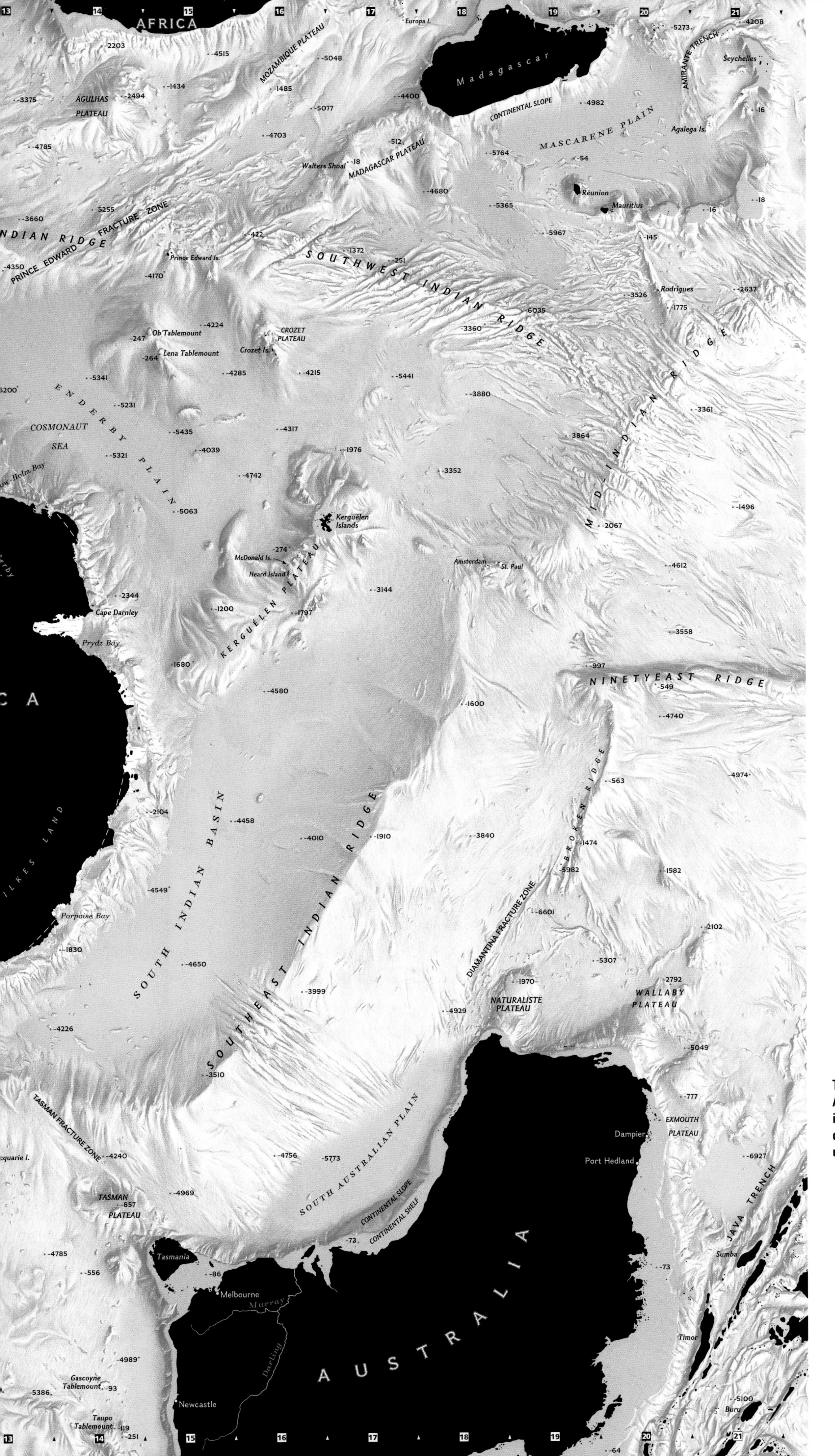
AFRICA
Europa I.
Madagascar
Seychelles
AMIRANTE TRENCH
Agalega Is.
MOZAMBIQUE PLATEAU
AGULHAS PLATEAU
CONTINENTAL SLOPE
MASCARENE PLAIN
Walters Shoal
MADAGASCAR PLATEAU
Réunion
Mauritius
INDIAN RIDGE
PRINCE EDWARD FRACTURE ZONE
Prince Edward Is.
SOUTHWEST INDIAN RIDGE
Rodrigues
Ob' Tablemount
Lena Tablemount
CROZET PLATEAU
Crozet Is.
MID-INDIAN RIDGE
ENDERBY PLAIN
COSMONAUT SEA
Kerguélen Islands
McDonald Is.
Heard Island
KERGUÉLEN PLATEAU
Amsterdam
St. Paul
Cape Darnley
Prydz Bay
NINETYEAST RIDGE
BROKEN RIDGE
SOUTH INDIAN BASIN
SOUTHEAST INDIAN RIDGE
DIAMANTINA FRACTURE ZONE
Porpoise Bay
NATURALISTE PLATEAU
WALLABY PLATEAU
TASMAN FRACTURE ZONE
SOUTH AUSTRALIAN PLAIN
EXMOUTH PLATEAU
Dampier
Port Hedland
TASMAN PLATEAU
CONTINENTAL SLOPE
CONTINENTAL SHELF
JAVA TRENCH
Tasmania
Melbourne
Murray
Darling
AUSTRALIA
Sumba
Timor
Gascoyne Tablemount
Taupo Tablemount
Newcastle
Buru

The ice-covered Antarctic continent is surrounded by deep, fairly flat underwater plains.

Space

In the first decade of the new millennium, astronomers are conducting extensive surveys of new frontiers in space, registering millions of galaxies, each composed of billions of stars. New orbiters and surface rovers explored Mars, confirming the presence of liquid water in its distant past and detecting methane in its atmosphere. A probe descended through the atmosphere of Titan, a moon of Saturn, and returned the first pictures from its surface, showing a strange, cold new world. A capsule traveling through space returned samples of the sun, and another spacecraft is now en route to Pluto. Meanwhile, a copper "cannonball" deployed from a spacecraft created the first man-made impact crater on a comet while another returned comet dust to Earth.

Wherever we look, we see evidence of cataclysmic events, indicating that we live in a 13-billion-year-old universe that is still evolving. Some suns, their atmospheres curiously enriched with telltale elements, may be "death stars" that swallowed whole planets long ago. Our own Milky Way is gradually devouring a small galaxy in the constellation Sagittarius, and elsewhere larger galaxies collide and distort each other. The universe began with a big bang and has been expanding ever since. A mysterious "dark energy" that exceeds all known forms of energy is thought to cause this expansion; space is also pervaded by unseen "dark matter," the dominant component of the universe. In laboratories on Earth and on the drawing boards of aerospace engineers, we are preparing to explore the next frontier of astronomical observation, looking for gravitational waves that may disturb the very fabric of space and time.

A composite view of two images, one taken from the WIYN Telescope in Arizona and the other from the Hubble Space Telescope, shows in amazing detail the outbursts in the Helix Nebula, a glowing gaseous shell of a dying sun-like star. Closest planetary nebula to the Earth, Helix Nebula is estimated to be approximately 650 light-years away from our planet. High-resolution images from Hubble and other telescopes are showing new details that enable us to understand the evolution of stars and other mysteries of the universe.

THE YOUNG EARTH HAD NO MOON. At some point in Earth's early history, an object larger than Mars struck Earth a great, glancing blow. Instantly, most of the rogue body and a sizable chunk of Earth were vaporized. The ensuing cloud rose to above 14,000 miles (22,500 km) altitude, where it condensed into innumerable solid particles that orbited Earth as they aggregated into ever larger moonlets, eventually combining to form the moon. This "giant impact" hypothesis of the moon's origin is based on computer simulations and on laboratory analyses of lunar rocks gathered by six teams of Apollo astronauts. It also fits with data on the lunar topography and environment recorded by the United States' Clementine and Lunar Prospector spacecraft.

The airless lunar surface bakes in the sun at up to 243°F (117°C) for two weeks at a time. All the while, it is sprayed with the solar wind of subatomic particles. Then, for an equal period, the same spot is in the dark, cooling to about minus 272°F (-169°C) when the sun sets. Day and night, the moon is bombarded by micrometeoroids and larger space rocks. The moon's rotation is synchronized with Earth's in such a way that it always shows the same face to Earth. One hemisphere, the near side, always faces us, while the other, the far side, always faces away. The far side has been photographed only from spacecraft. *(Continued on page 250)*

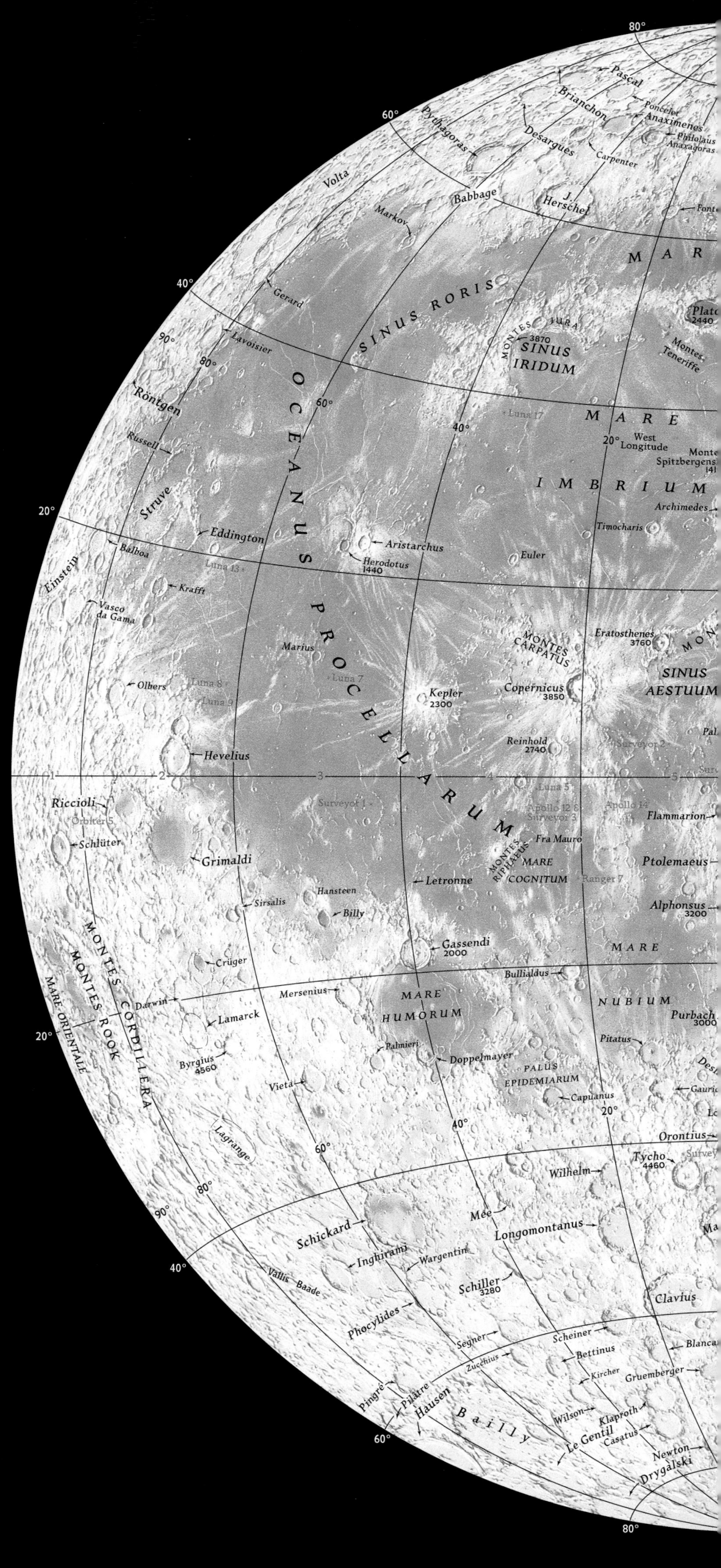

OCEANUS PROCELLARUM
SINUS RORIS
SINUS IRIDUM
MONTES JURA
3870
MARE IMBRIUM
West Longitude
MARE HUMORUM
MARE COGNITUM
MARE NUBIUM
PALUS EPIDEMIARUM
SINUS AESTUUM
MONTES CARPATUS
MONTES RIPHAEUS
MONTES CORDILLERA
MONTES ROOK
MARE ORIENTALE
Montes Teneriffe
Montes Spitzbergensis
Pascal
Brianchon
Poncelet
Anaximenes
Philolaus
Anaxagoras
Pythagoras
Desargues
Carpenter
Volta
Babbage
J. Herschel
Markov
Gerard
Lavoisier
Röntgen
Russell
Struve
Eddington
Einstein
Balboa
Luna 13
Krafft
Vasco da Gama
Aristarchus
Herodotus
1440
Luna 17
Archimedes
Timocharis
Euler
Marius
Luna 7
Eratosthenes
3760
Kepler
2300
Copernicus
3850
Olbers
Luna 8
Luna 9
Reinhold
2740
Surveyor 2
Hevelius
Riccioli
Orbiter 5
Schlüter
Surveyor 1
Luna 5
Apollo 12 & Surveyor 3
Apollo 14
Flammarion
Fra Mauro
Ptolemaeus
Grimaldi
Letronne
Ranger 7
Alphonsus
3200
Sirsalis
Hansteen
Billy
Gassendi
2000
Crüger
Bullialdus
Mersenius
Darwin
Lamarck
Purbach
3000
Pitatus
Byrgius
4560
Palmieri
Doppelmayer
Vieta
Capuanus
Lagrange
Orontius
Tycho
4460
Wilhelm
Schickard
Inghirami
Wargentin
Mee
Longomontanus
Vallis Baade
Schiller
3280
Clavius
Phocylides
Segner
Scheiner
Bettinus
Zucchius
Kircher
Gruemberger
Pingré
Pilâtre
Hausen
Bailly
Wilson
Klaproth
Casatus
Le Gentil
Newton
Drygalski

One square centimeter on this Lambert Azimuthal Equal-Area projection equals 28,700 square kilometers on the moon; elevations of prominent features are stated in meters. Impact craters, including those (labeled in blue) commemorating the seven *Challenger* astronauts, predominate on the far side. Landing site labels are in red.

Clementine Digital Elevation Map

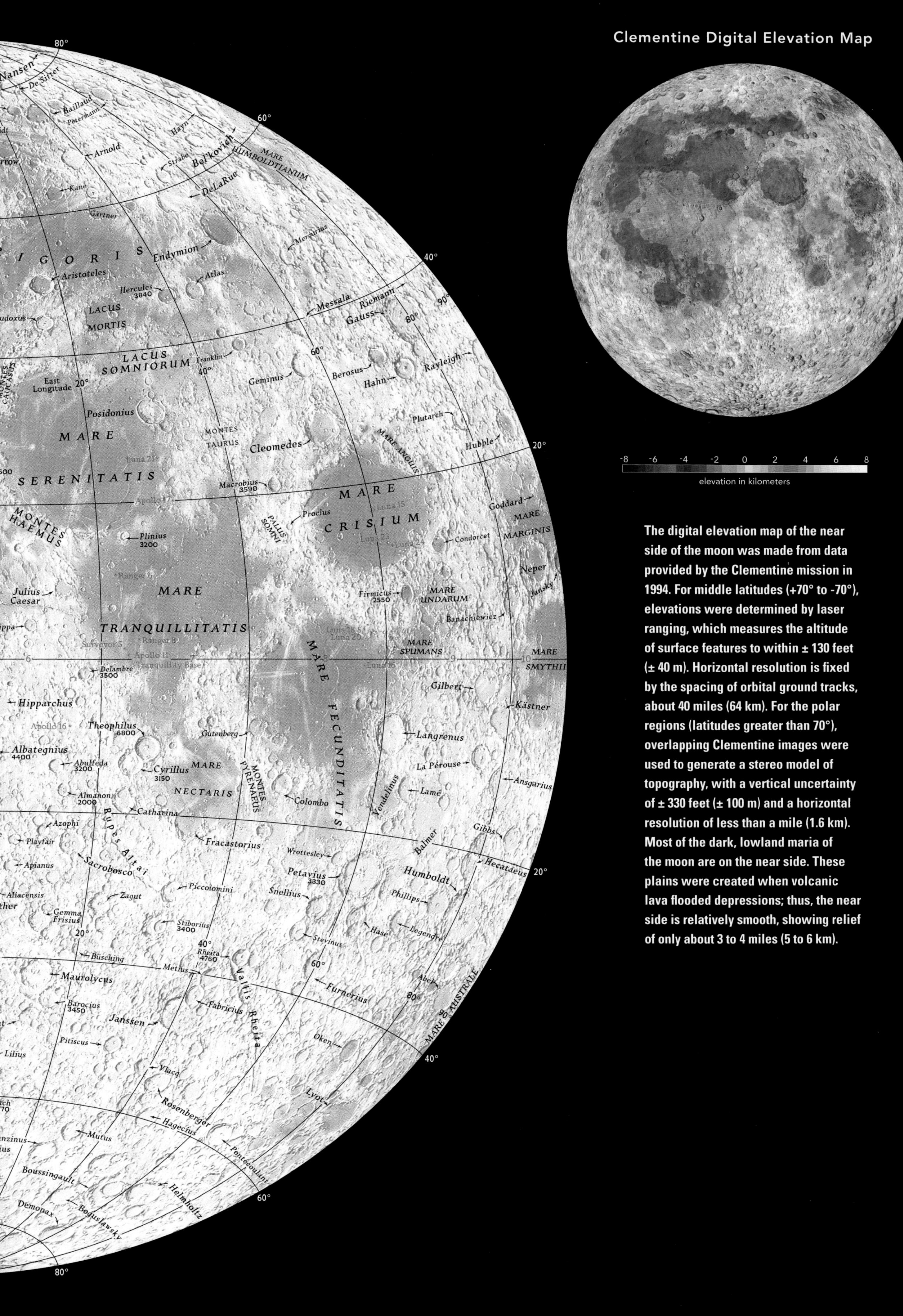

-8 -6 -4 -2 0 2 4 6 8
elevation in kilometers
Nansen
De Sitter
Baillaud
Petermann
Barrow
Arnold
Hayn
Strabo
Bel'kovich
MARE HUMBOLDTIANUM
DeLaRue
Kane
Gärtner
Mercurius
Endymion
Aristoteles
Atlas
Hercules 3840
LACUS MORTIS
Eudoxus
Messala
Riemann
Gauss
LACUS SOMNIORUM
Franklin
East Longitude
MONTES CAUCASUS
Gemimus
Berosus
Hahn
Rayleigh
Posidonius
MARE SERENITATIS
MONTES TAURUS
Luna 21
Plutarch
Cleomedes
MARE ANGUIS
Hubble
4500
Macrobius 3590
Apollo 17
MARE CRISIUM
Luna 15
Goddard
MARE MARGINIS
MONTES HAEMUS
Proclus
PALUS SOMNI
Plinius 3200
Luna 23
Luna 24
Condorcet
Neper
Ranger 6
Jansky
Julius Caesar
MARE TRANQUILLITATIS
Firmicus 2550
MARE UNDARUM
Banachiewicz
Agrippa
Luna 18
Luna 20
Ranger 8
Surveyor 5
MARE SPUMANS
Apollo 11 (Tranquillity Base)
MARE SMYTHII
Luna 16
Delambre 3500
MARE FECUNDITATIS
Gilbert
Hipparchus
Kästner
Apollo 16
Theophilus 6800
Gutenberg
Langrenus
Albategnius 4400
Abulfeda 3200
Cyrillus 3150
MARE NECTARIS
MONTES PYRENAEUS
La Pérouse
Almanon 2000
Colombo
Vendelinus
Lamé
Ansgarius
Catharina
Rupes Altai
Azophi
Playfair
Gibbs
Fracastorius
Balmer
Apianus
Sacrobosco
Wrottesley
Hecataeus
Petavius 3330
Humboldt
Aliacensis
Zagut
Piccolomini
Snellius
Phillips
Walther
Gemma Frisius
Stiborius 3400
Hase
Legendre
Stevinus
Büsching
Rheita 4760
Metius
Maurolycus
Vallis Rheita
Furnerius
Abel
MARE AUSTRALE
Barocius 3450
Fabricius
Janssen
Pitiscus
Oken
Lilius
Vlacq
Lyot
Zach 3770
Rosenberger
Hagecius
Mutus
Manzinus
Pontécoulant
Boussingault
Helmholtz
Demonax
Boguslawsky

The digital elevation map of the near side of the moon was made from data provided by the Clementine mission in 1994. For middle latitudes (+70° to -70°), elevations were determined by laser ranging, which measures the altitude of surface features to within ± 130 feet (± 40 m). Horizontal resolution is fixed by the spacing of orbital ground tracks, about 40 miles (64 km). For the polar regions (latitudes greater than 70°), overlapping Clementine images were used to generate a stereo model of topography, with a vertical uncertainty of ± 330 feet (± 100 m) and a horizontal resolution of less than a mile (1.6 km). Most of the dark, lowland maria of the moon are on the near side. These plains were created when volcanic lava flooded depressions; thus, the near side is relatively smooth, showing relief of only about 3 to 4 miles (5 to 6 km).

(Continued from page 248)

The rocks and materials brought back by the Apollo missions are extremely dry; the moon has no indigenous water. However, it is bombarded by water-rich comets and meteoroids. Most of this water is lost to space, but some is trapped in permanently shadowed areas near the moon's poles.

To the unaided eye, the bright lunar highlands and the dark maria (Latin for "seas") make up the "man in the moon." A telescope shows that they consist of a great variety of round impact features, scars left by objects that struck the moon long ago. In the highlands, craters are closely packed together. In the maria, they are fewer. The largest scars are the impact basins, ranging up to about 1,500 miles (2,400 km) across. The basin floors were flooded with lava some time after the titanic collisions that formed them. The dark lava flows are what the eye discerns as maria. Wrinkled ridges, domed hills, and fissures mark the maria, all familiar aspects of volcanic landscapes. Young craters are centers of radial patterns of bright ejecta, material thrown from the impacts that made them. Because the force of gravity is weaker on the moon, blocks of rock hurled from impacts travel farther than they would on Earth.

The moon has no mountains like the Himalaya, produced by one tectonic plate bumping into another. There is no continental drift. Everywhere, the lunar surface is sheathed in regolith, a rocky rubble created by the constant bombardment by meteoroids, asteroids, and comets. Lunar mountains consist of volcanic domes and the central peaks and rims of impact craters.

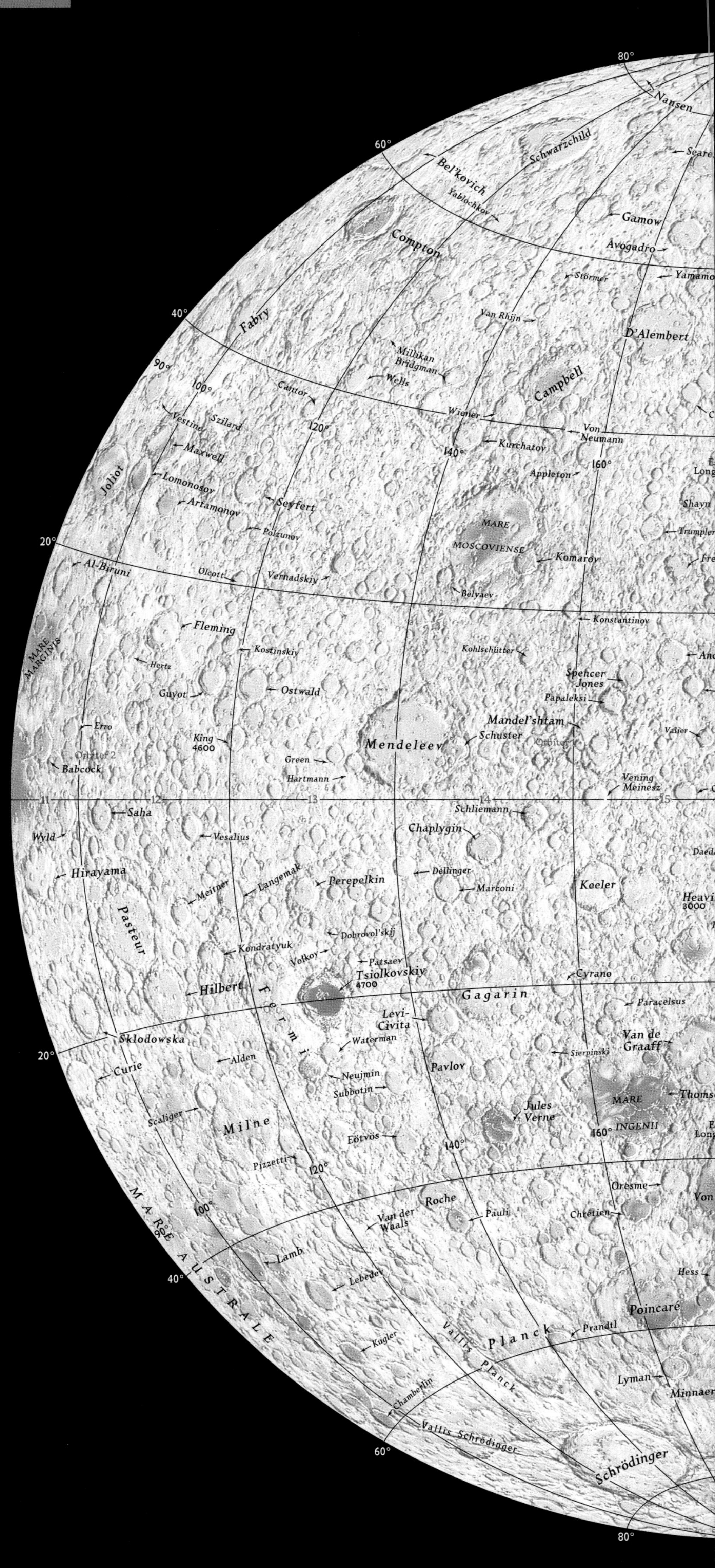
Nansen
Schwarzschild
Bel'kovich
Yablochkov
Gamow
Avogadro
Compton
Störmer
Van Rhijn
D'Alembert
Fabry
Millikan
Bridgman
Wells
Campbell
Cantor
Wiener
Von Neumann
Szilard
Vestine
Kurchatov
Maxwell
Appleton
Joliot
Lomonosov
Artamonov
Seyfert
MARE MOSCOVIENSE
Komarov
Polzunov
Al-Biruni
Olcott
Vernadskiy
Belyaev
Konstantinov
Fleming
MARE MARGINIS
Kostinskiy
Kohlschütter
Hertz
Spencer Jones
Guyot
Ostwald
Papaleksi
Mandel'shtam
Erro
King 4600
Schuster
Mendeleev
Babcock
Green
Hartmann
Vening Meinesz
Saha
Schliemann
Wyld
Vesalius
Chaplygin
Hirayama
Langemak
Perepelkin
Dellinger
Marconi
Keeler
Meitner
Pasteur
Dobrovol'skij
Kondratyuk
Volkov
Patsaev
Tsiolkovskiy 4700
Cyrano
Hilbert
Fermi
Gagarin
Paracelsus
Levi-Civita
Sklodowska
Waterman
Van de Graaff
Sierpinski
Curie
Alden
Pavlov
Neujmin
Subbotin
MARE INGENII
Jules Verne
Scaliger
Milne
Eötvös
Pizzetti
Oresme
Roche
Van der Waals
Pauli
Chrétien
MARE AUSTRALE
Lamb
Lebedev
Hess
Poincaré
Kugler
Vallis Planck
Planck
Prandtl
Lyman
Chamberlin
Vallis Schrödinger
Schrödinger

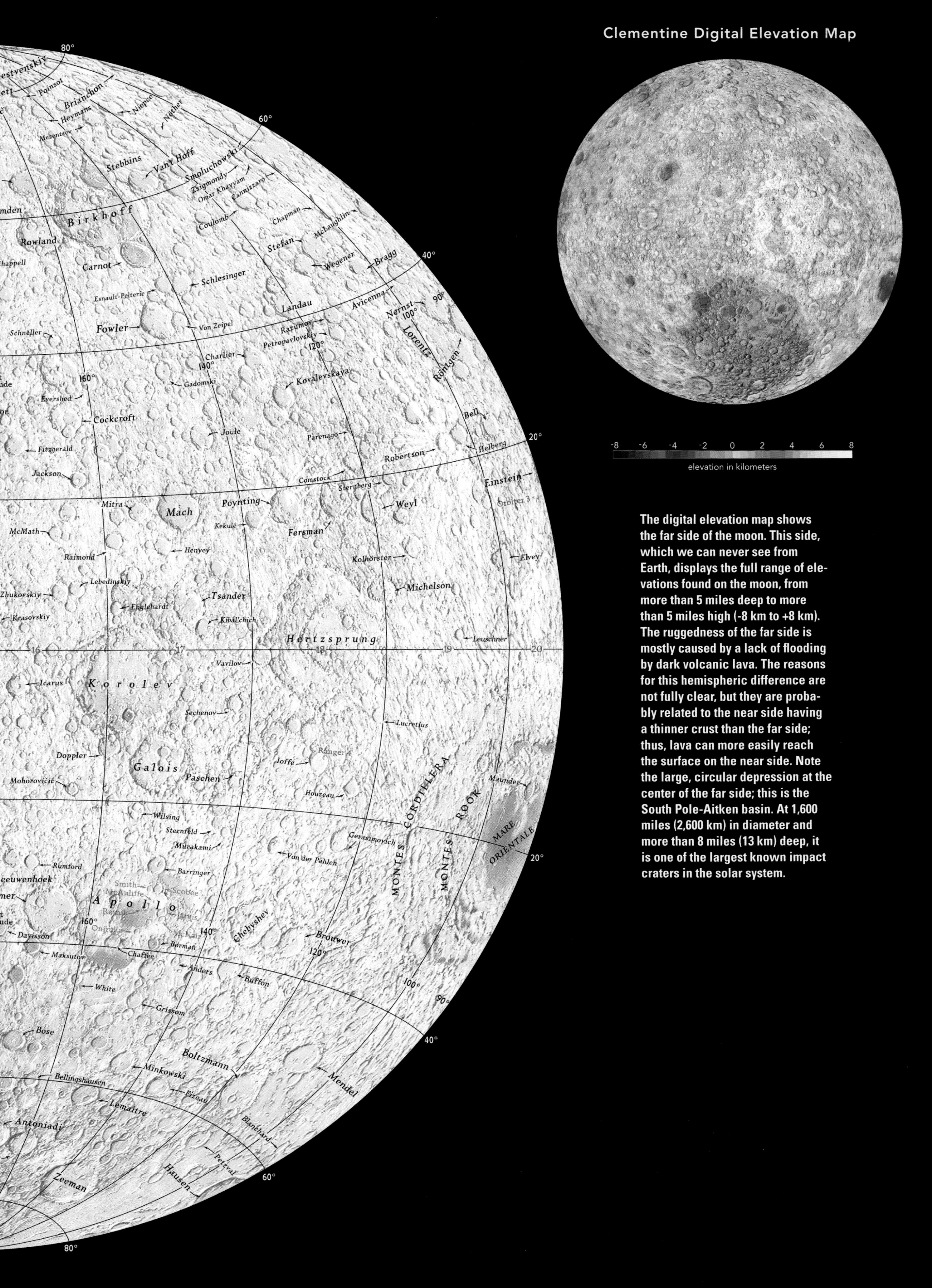
Poinsot
Brianchon
Heymans
Niepce
Mezentsev
Nöther
Stebbins
Van't Hoff
Smoluchowski
Zsigmondy
Omar Khayyam
Cannizzaro
Birkhoff
Coulomb
Chapman
McLaughlin
Rowland
Stefan
Carnot
Wegener
Bragg
Schlesinger
Esnault-Pelterie
Landau
Avicenna
Nernst
Schneller
Fowler
Von Zeipel
Razumov
Petropavlovskiy
Lorentz
Charlier
Röntgen
Gadomski
Kovalevskaya
Evershed
Cockcroft
Joule
Bell
Parenago
Helberg
Fitzgerald
Robertson
Jackson
Comstock
Sternberg
Einstein
Mitra
Mach
Poynting
Weyl
McMath
Kekulé
Fersman
Henyey
Raimond
Kolhörster
Elvey
Lebedinskiy
Michelson
Zhukovskiy
Tsander
Englehardt
Krasovskiy
Kibal'chich
Hertzsprung
Leuschner
Vavilov
Icarus
Korolev
Sechenov
Lucretius
Doppler
Ioffe
Galois
Paschen
Maunder
Mohorovičić
Houzeau
Montes Cordillera
Montes Rook
Mare Orientale
Wilsing
Sternfeld
Gerasimovich
Murakami
Von der Pahlen
Rumford
Barringer
Leeuwenhoek
Apollo
Chebyshev
Davisson
Brouwer
Borman
Maksutov
Chaffee
Anders
Buffon
White
Grissom
Bose
Boltzmann
Minkowski
Bellingshausen
Mendel
Lemaître
Antoniadi
Blanchard
Zeeman
Hausen
Clementine Digital Elevation Map
-8 -6 -4 -2 0 2 4 6 8
elevation in kilometers

Clementine Digital Elevation Map

The digital elevation map shows the far side of the moon. This side, which we can never see from Earth, displays the full range of elevations found on the moon, from more than 5 miles deep to more than 5 miles high (-8 km to +8 km). The ruggedness of the far side is mostly caused by a lack of flooding by dark volcanic lava. The reasons for this hemispheric difference are not fully clear, but they are probably related to the near side having a thinner crust than the far side; thus, lava can more easily reach the surface on the near side. Note the large, circular depression at the center of the far side; this is the South Pole-Aitken basin. At 1,600 miles (2,600 km) in diameter and more than 8 miles (13 km) deep, it is one of the largest known impact craters in the solar system.

THE MARTIAN LANDSCAPE is both familiar and alien. All of its features, from rugged riverbeds to shifting sand dunes, are also found on Earth. Yet Mars, with its lower gravity and thinner atmosphere, imprints its own character on these features: The volcanoes are taller, the canyons wider, the ice caps more ephemeral than on Earth.

Compiled from NASA spacecraft data, the map at right depicts the remarkable terrain of the red planet. Mars's polar caps have frozen water, like our Arctic and Antarctic, but during the winters frozen carbon dioxide also coats the poles. The huge crater at far left is a caldera atop Olympus Mons, a Missouri-size volcano three times the height of Mount Everest. Three more large calderas, to the right of Olympus Mons, mark the peaks of three other volcanoes along the Tharsis rise. To the right of Tharsis, the dark canyons of the Valles Marineris (Mariner Valleys) extend more than 4,000 kilometers (2,500 mi). To the right of center, the dark patch running north-south is Syrtis Major, often the easiest feature to spot with a small telescope.

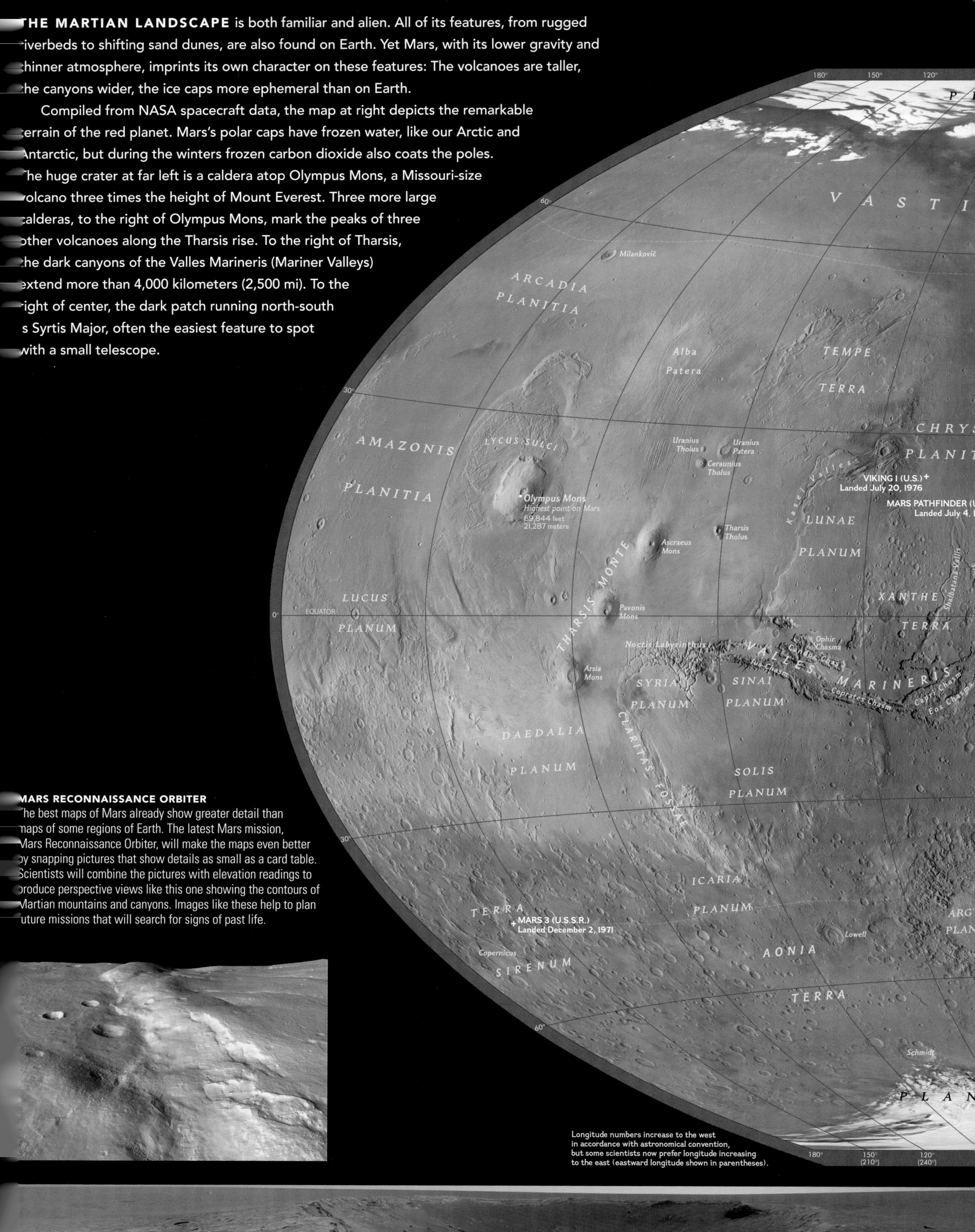
180°
150°
120°
60°
30°
0°
EQUATOR
30°
60°
VASTI
Milanković
ARCADIA PLANITIA
Alba Patera
TEMPE TERRA
CHRYS
PLANIT
AMAZONIS PLANITIA
LYCUS SULCI
Uranius Tholus
Uranius Patera
Ceraunius Tholus
VIKING I (U.S.)
Landed July 20, 1976
MARS PATHFINDER
Landed July 4,
Olympus Mons
Highest point on Mars
69,844 feet
21,287 meters
Kasei Valles
LUNAE PLANUM
Tharsis Tholus
Ascraeus Mons
THARSIS MONTES
Pavonis Mons
XANTHE TERRA
Shalbatana Vallis
LUCUS PLANUM
Noctis Labyrinthus
Ophir Chasma
Arsia Mons
VALLES MARINERIS
SYRIA PLANUM
SINAI PLANUM
Coprates Chasma
Capri Chasma
Eos Chasma
DAEDALIA PLANUM
CLARITAS FOSSAE
SOLIS PLANUM
ICARIA PLANUM
TERRA SIRENUM
MARS 3 (U.S.S.R.)
Landed December 2, 1971
Copernicus
Lowell
ARG
PLAN
AONIA TERRA
Schmidt
PLAN
Longitude numbers increase to the west in accordance with astronomical convention, but some scientists now prefer longitude increasing to the east (eastward longitude shown in parentheses).
180°
150° (210°)
120° (240°)

MARS RECONNAISSANCE ORBITER

The best maps of Mars already show greater detail than maps of some regions of Earth. The latest Mars mission, Mars Reconnaissance Orbiter, will make the maps even better by snapping pictures that show details as small as a card table. Scientists will combine the pictures with elevation readings to produce perspective views like this one showing the contours of Martian mountains and canyons. Images like these help to plan future missions that will search for signs of past life.

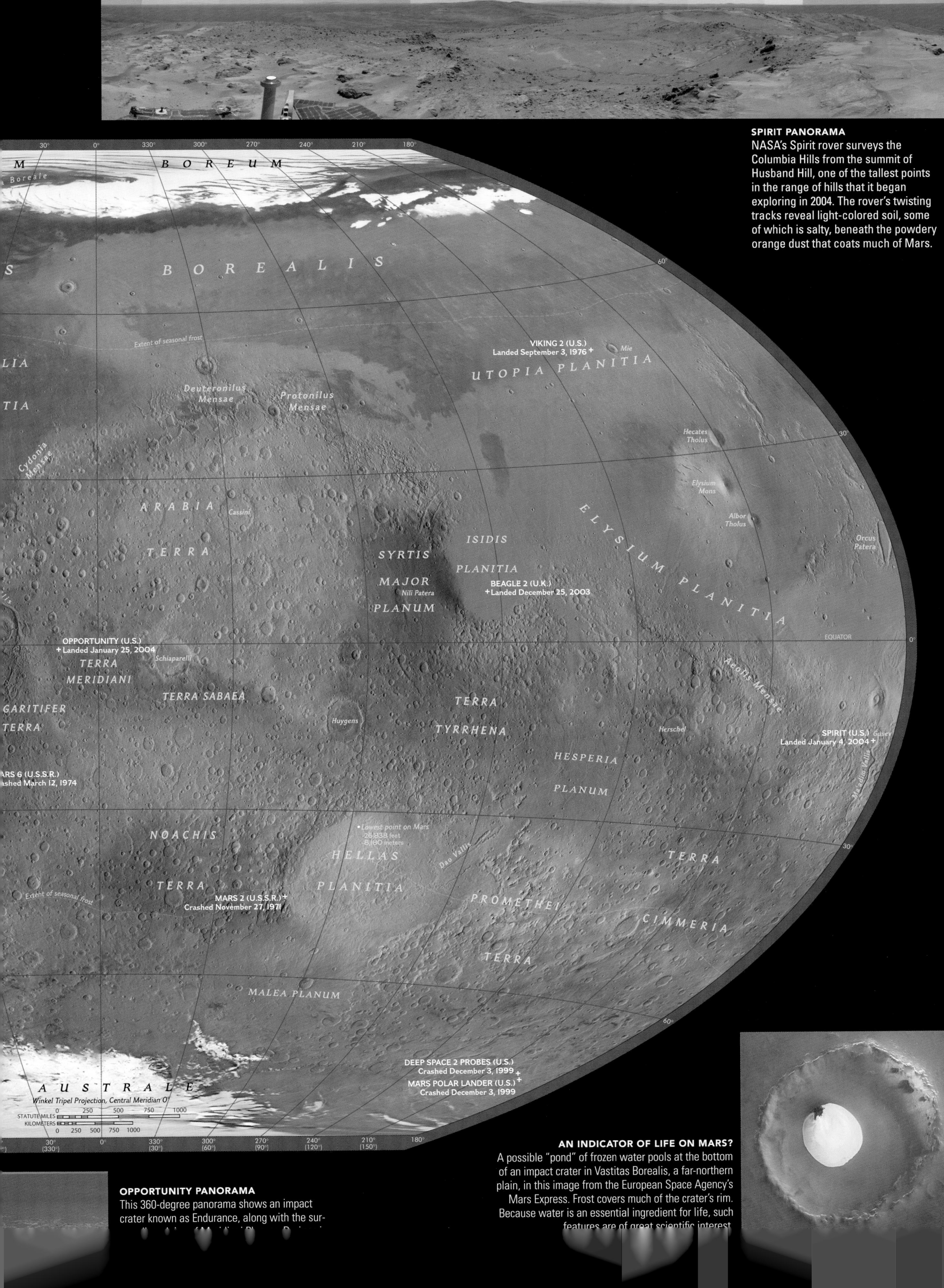
B O R E U M
B O R E A L I S
Extent of seasonal frost
VIKING 2 (U.S.)
Landed September 3, 1976
Mie
UTOPIA PLANITIA
Deuteronilus Mensae
Protonilus Mensae
Cydonia Mensae
Hecates Tholus
Elysium Mons
Albor Tholus
Orcus Patera
ARABIA TERRA
Cassini
ISIDIS PLANITIA
SYRTIS MAJOR PLANUM
Nili Patera
BEAGLE 2 (U.K.)
Landed December 25, 2003
ELYSIUM PLANITIA
EQUATOR
OPPORTUNITY (U.S.)
Landed January 25, 2004
Schiaparelli
TERRA MERIDIANI
TERRA SABAEA
Aeolis Mensae
ARITIFER TERRA
Huygens
TERRA TYRRHENA
Herschel
SPIRIT (U.S.)
Landed January 4, 2004
Gusev
Ma'adim Vallis
HESPERIA PLANUM
RS 6 (U.S.S.R.)
ashed March 12, 1974
Lowest point on Mars
26,838 feet
8,180 meters
NOACHIS TERRA
HELLAS PLANITIA
Dao Vallis
TERRA CIMMERIA
MARS 2 (U.S.S.R.)
Crashed November 27, 1971
PROMETHEI TERRA
MALEA PLANUM
DEEP SPACE 2 PROBES (U.S.)
Crashed December 3, 1999
MARS POLAR LANDER (U.S.)
Crashed December 3, 1999
A U S T R A L E
Winkel Tripel Projection, Central Meridian 0°
STATUTE MILES 0 250 500 750 1000
KILOMETERS 0 250 500 750 1000

SPIRIT PANORAMA
NASA's Spirit rover surveys the Columbia Hills from the summit of Husband Hill, one of the tallest points in the range of hills that it began exploring in 2004. The rover's twisting tracks reveal light-colored soil, some of which is salty, beneath the powdery orange dust that coats much of Mars.

AN INDICATOR OF LIFE ON MARS?
A possible "pond" of frozen water pools at the bottom of an impact crater in Vastitas Borealis, a far-northern plain, in this image from the European Space Agency's Mars Express. Frost covers much of the crater's rim. Because water is an essential ingredient for life, such features are of great scientific interest.

OPPORTUNITY PANORAMA
This 360-degree panorama shows an impact crater known as Endurance, along with the sur-

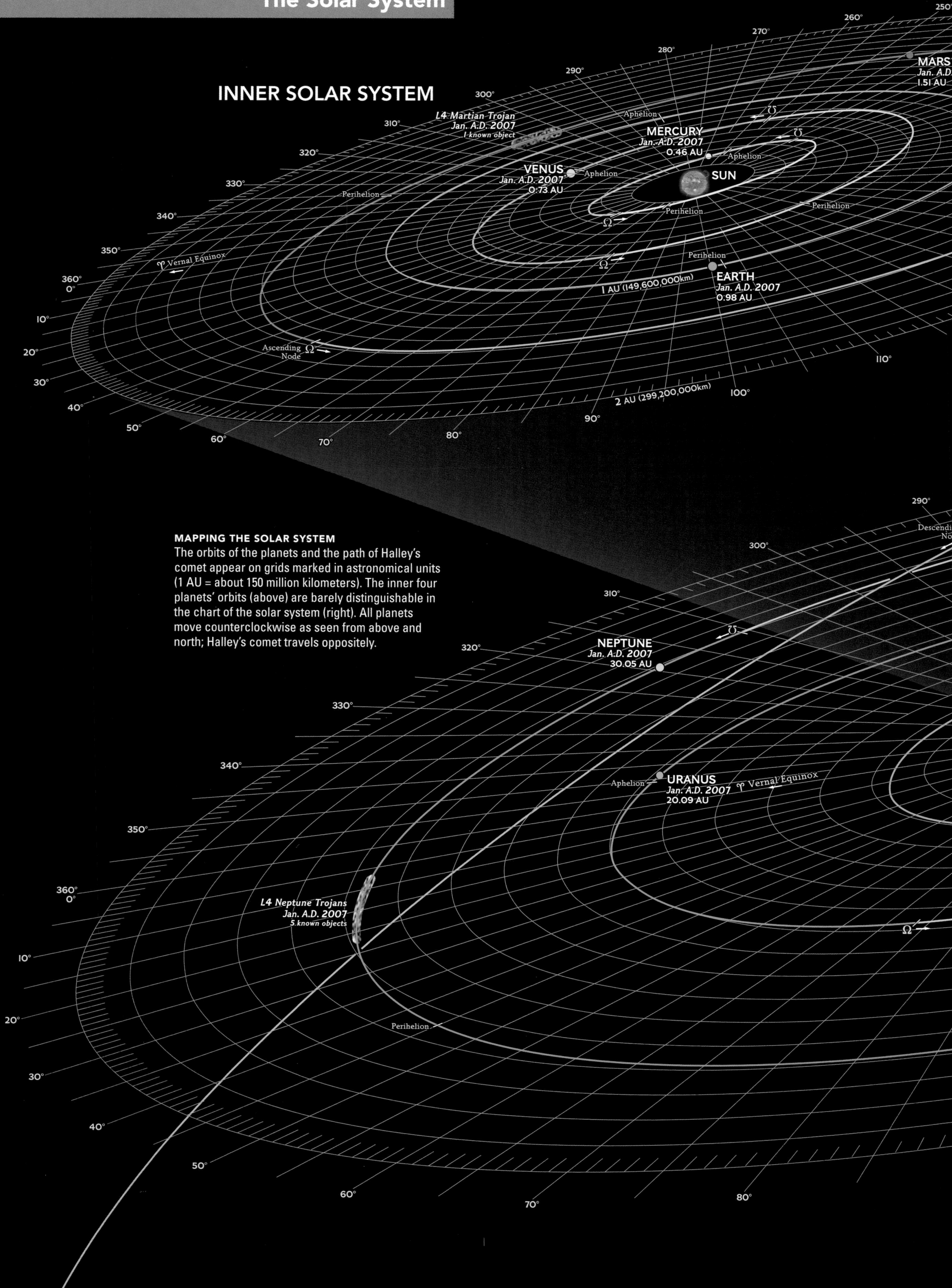
INNER SOLAR SYSTEM
L4 Martian Trojan
Jan. A.D. 2007
1 known object
MERCURY
Jan. A.D. 2007
0.46 AU
VENUS
Jan. A.D. 2007
0.73 AU
SUN
EARTH
Jan. A.D. 2007
0.98 AU
MARS
Jan. A.D.
1.51 AU
Aphelion
Perihelion
Vernal Equinox
Ascending Node
1 AU (149,600,000km)
2 AU (299,200,000km)
NEPTUNE
Jan. A.D. 2007
30.05 AU
URANUS
Jan. A.D. 2007
20.09 AU
L4 Neptune Trojans
Jan. A.D. 2007
5 known objects

MAPPING THE SOLAR SYSTEM
The orbits of the planets and the path of Halley's comet appear on grids marked in astronomical units (1 AU = about 150 million kilometers). The inner four planets' orbits (above) are barely distinguishable in the chart of the solar system (right). All planets move counterclockwise as seen from above and north; Halley's comet travels oppositely.

ASTEROIDS
Remnants from the age of planetary formation, the largest asteroids are spherical, like planets, but most others have irregular shapes, like potatoes. They sometimes collide and break up. A few are known to have tiny moons.

COMETS
Comets are composed of ice and other frozen substances, mixed in with interplanetary dust. As they approach the sun, the ices vaporize and the coma, or atmosphere, grows. Then, a long tail or tails sweep back in the antisolar direction.

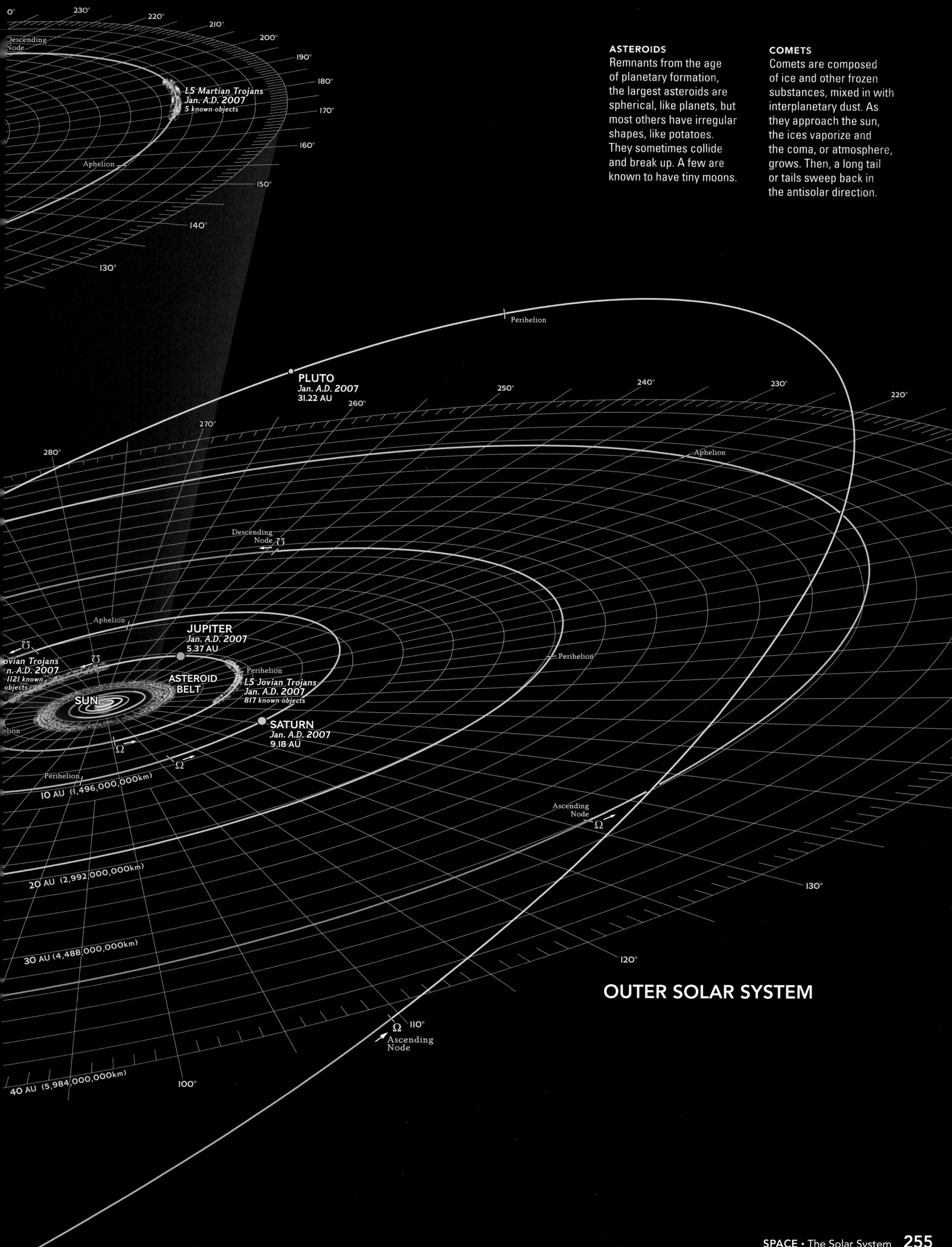

230°
220°
210°
200°
190°
180°
170°
160°
150°
140°
130°
Descending Node
L5 Martian Trojans
Jan. A.D. 2007
5 known objects
Aphelion
Perihelion
PLUTO
Jan. A.D. 2007
31.22 AU
280°
270°
260°
250°
240°
230°
220°
Aphelion
Descending Node
Aphelion
JUPITER
Jan. A.D. 2007
5.37 AU
ASTEROID BELT
SUN
Perihelion
L5 Jovian Trojans
Jan. A.D. 2007
817 known objects
SATURN
Jan. A.D. 2007
9.18 AU
Perihelion
Perihelion
10 AU (1,496,000,000km)
Ascending Node
20 AU (2,992,000,000km)
130°
30 AU (4,488,000,000km)
120°
110°
Ascending Node
40 AU (5,984,000,000km)
100°

OUTER SOLAR SYSTEM

The Planets

JUPITER

WHAT IS A PLANET?

Due to improvements in telescopic observation, we're continually learning more about our solar system, its planets and planet-like objects, and their evolution. Yet even as scientists learn and discover more, there is not yet uniform agreement among them about what actually defines a planet. In the last decade or so, observatories around the Earth have detected evidence of large bodies orbiting other stars. Are they also planets? The question is difficult to answer because beyond tradition, there is currently no universally accepted definition.

The solar system has two classes of planets whose origins can be partially explained or understood. The Inner planets (Mercury, Venus, Earth, and Mars) have solid surfaces and mean densities that suggest a rocky core. The Outer planets, called gas giants (Jupiter, Saturn, Uranus, and Neptune), are primarily hydrogen and helium gas and thus have much lower mean densities. Planets within our solar system vary widely in other ways as well: for example, in overall size, and in whether they have moons, rings, irregular shapes, and/or internal heat sources.

The discovery of yet another planet-like object, Xena, in 2005 has once again raised the question of "What is a planet?" The International Astronomical Union (IAU), an organization of professional astronomers, is at work on addressing this issue.

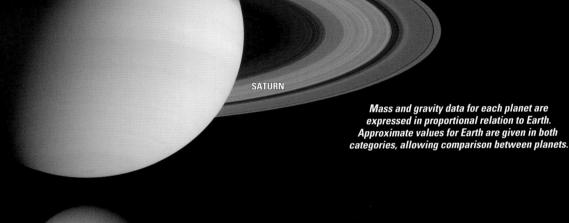

MERCURY	
Average distance from the sun:	57,900,000 km
Perihelion:	46,000,000 km
Aphelion:	69,820,000 km
Revolution period:	88 days
Average orbital speed:	47.9 km/s
Average temperature:	167°C
Rotation period:	58.9 days
Equatorial diameter:	4,879 km
Mass (Earth=1):	0.055
Density:	5.43 g/cm^3
Surface gravity (Earth=1):	0.38
Known satellites:	none

Image by: Mariner 10

SATURN

Mass and gravity data for each planet are expressed in proportional relation to Earth. Approximate values for Earth are given in both categories, allowing comparison between planets.

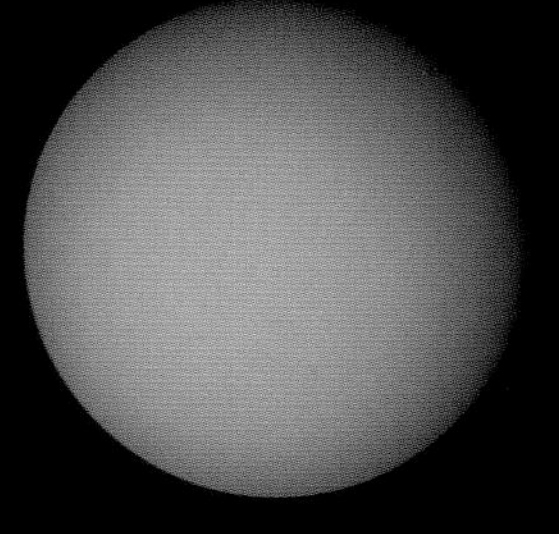

URANUS

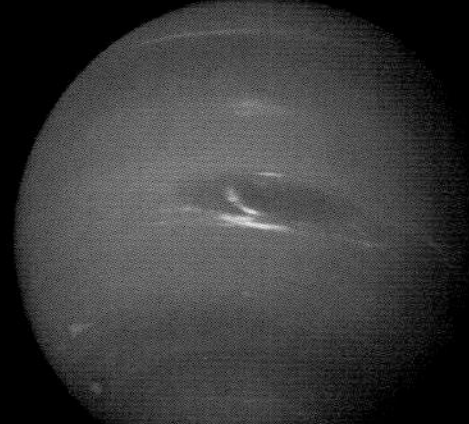

NEPTUNE

RELATIVE SCALE

The planets are shown here in proportionate size to one another. See the Planetary Orbits diagram in the upper right of this plate for their proper relationship to the Sun.

EARTH

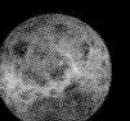

VENUS

MARS

MERCURY

PLUTO

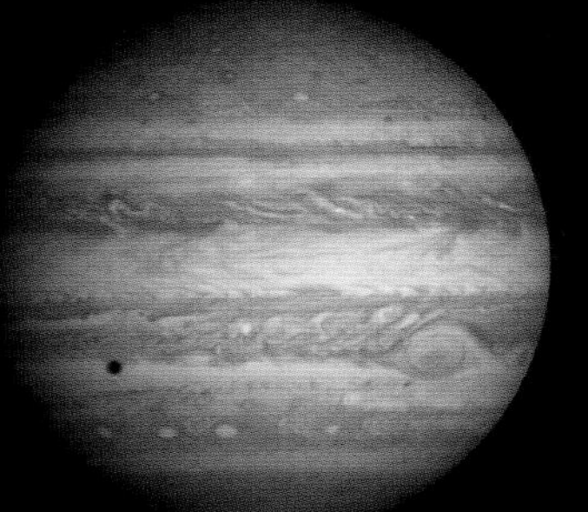

JUPITER	
Average distance from the sun:	778,600,000 km
Perihelion:	740,520,000 km
Aphelion:	816,620,000 km
Revolution period:	11.87 years
Average orbital speed:	13.1 km/s
Average temperature:	-110°C
Rotation period:	9.9 hours
Equatorial diameter:	142,984 km
Mass (Earth=1):	317.8
Density:	1.33 g/cm^3
Surface gravity (Earth=1):	2.36
Known satellites:	63
Largest satellites:	Ganymede, Callisto, Io, Europa

Image by: Cassini Orbiter

SATURN	
Average distance from the sun:	1,433,500,000 km
Perihelion:	1,352,550,000 km
Aphelion:	1,514,500,000 km
Revolution period:	29.44 years
Average orbital speed:	9.7 km/s
Average temperature:	-140°C
Rotation period:	10.7 hours
Equatorial diameter:	120,536 km
Mass (Earth=1):	95.2
Density:	0.69 g/cm^3
Surface gravity (Earth=1):	0.92
Known satellites:	47
Largest satellites:	Titan, Rhea, Iapetus, Dione, Tethys

Image by: Cassini Orbiter

SUN

Average surface temperature:	5,505°C
Average core temperature	16,000,000°C
Rotation period:	25 days
Equatorial diameter:	1,392,000 km
Mass (Earth=1):	332,950
Density:	1.41 g/cm^3
Surface gravity (Earth=1):	28.0

PLANETARY ORBITS

(see also page 259)

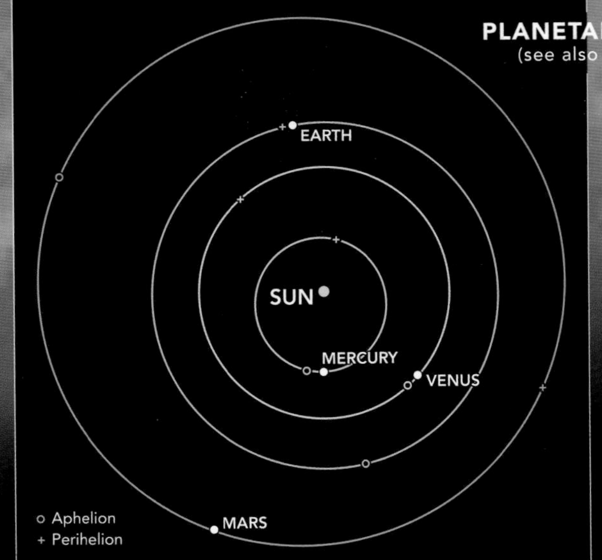

EARTH
SUN
MERCURY
VENUS
MARS
o Aphelion
+ Perihelion

INNER SOLAR SYSTEM

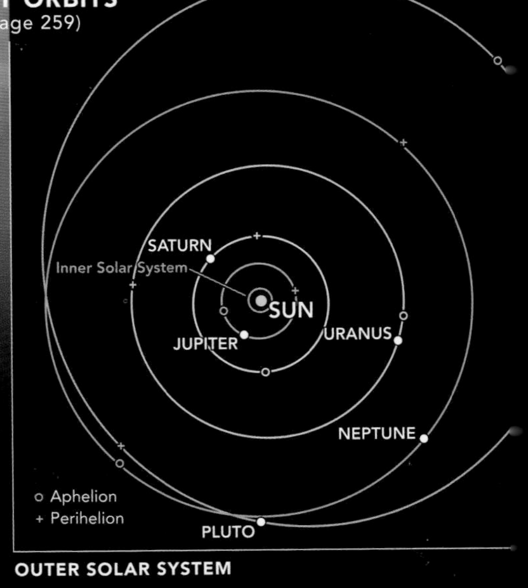

SATURN
Inner Solar System
SUN
JUPITER
URANUS
NEPTUNE
PLUTO
o Aphelion
+ Perihelion

OUTER SOLAR SYSTEM

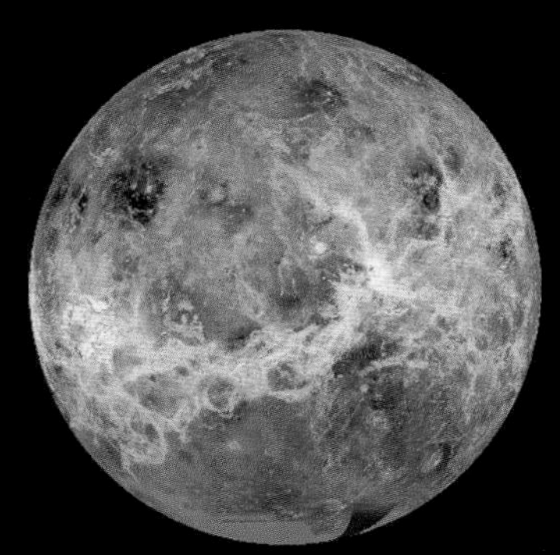

VENUS

Average distance from the sun:	108,200,000 km
Perihelion:	107,480,000 km
Aphelion:	108,940,000 km
Revolution period:	224.7 days
Average orbital speed:	35 km/s
Average temperature:	464°C
Rotation period:	244 days
Equatorial diameter:	12,104 km
Mass (Earth=1):	0.816
Density:	5.24 g/cm^3
Surface gravity (Earth=1):	0.91
Known satellites:	none

Image by: Magellan

EARTH

Average distance from the sun:	149,600,000 km
Perihelion:	147,090,000 km
Aphelion:	152,100,000 km
Revolution period:	365.2 days
Average orbital speed:	29.8 km/s
Average temperature:	15°C
Rotation period:	23.9 hours
Equatorial diameter:	12,756 km
Mass :	5,974,000,000,000,000,000,000 metric tons
Density:	5.52 g/cm^3
Surface gravity	9.81 m/s^2
Known satellites:	1
Largest satellite:	Earth's Moon

Image by: Galileo Orbiter

MARS

Average distance from the sun:	227,900,000 km
Perihelion:	206,620,000 km
Aphelion:	249,230,000 km
Revolution period:	687 days
Average orbital speed:	24.1 km/s
Average temperature:	-65°C
Rotation period:	24.6 hours
Equatorial diameter:	6,794 km
Mass (Earth=1):	0.107
Density:	3.93 g/cm^3
Surface gravity (Earth=1):	0.38
Known satellites:	2
Largest satellites:	Phobos, Deimos

Image by: Mars Global Surveyor

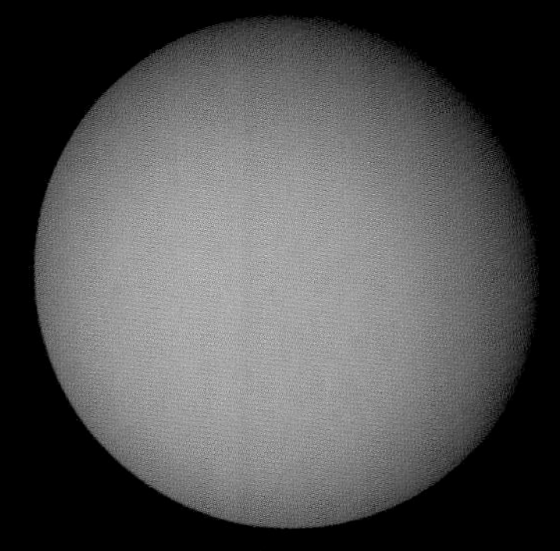

URANUS

Average distance from the sun:	2,872,500,000 km
Perihelion:	2,741,300,000 km
Aphelion:	3,003,620,000 km
Revolution period:	83.81 years
Average orbital speed:	6.8 km/s
Average temperature:	-195°C
Rotation period:	17.2 hours
Equatorial diameter:	51,118 km
Mass (Earth=1):	14.5
Density:	1.27 g/cm^3
Surface gravity (Earth=1):	0.89
Known satellites:	27
Largest satellites:	Titania, Oberon, Umbriel, Ariel

Image by: Hubble Space Telescope

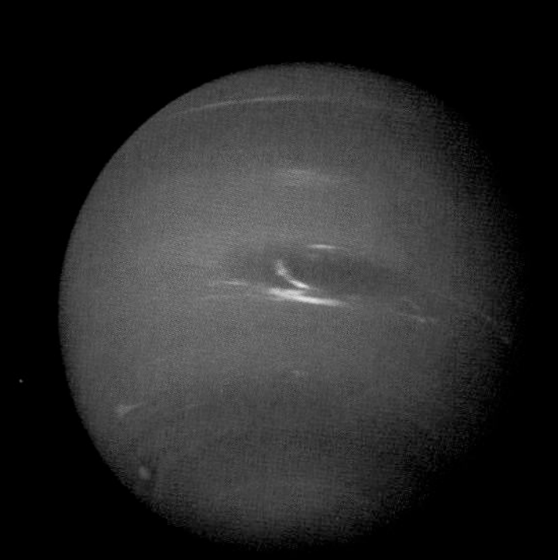

NEPTUNE

Average distance from the sun:	4,495,100,000 km
Perihelion:	4,444,450,000 km
Aphelion:	4,545,670,000 km
Revolution period:	163.84 years
Average orbital speed:	5.4 km/s
Average temperature:	-200°C
Rotation period:	16.1 hours
Equatorial diameter:	49,528 km
Mass (Earth=1):	17.1
Density:	1.64 g/cm^3
Surface gravity (Earth=1):	1.12
Known satellites:	13
Largest satellite:	Triton

Image by: Voyager II

PLUTO

Average distance from the sun:	5,870,000,000 km
Perihelion:	4,436,820,000 km
Aphelion:	7,375,930,000 km
Revolution period:	248.19 years
Average orbital speed:	4.7 km/s
Average temperature:	-225°C
Rotation period:	6.4 days
Equatorial diameter:	2,390 km
Mass (Earth=1):	0.002
Density:	1.75 g/cm^3
Surface gravity (Earth=1):	0.06
Known satellites:	1
Largest satellite:	Charon

Image by: Hubble Space Telescope

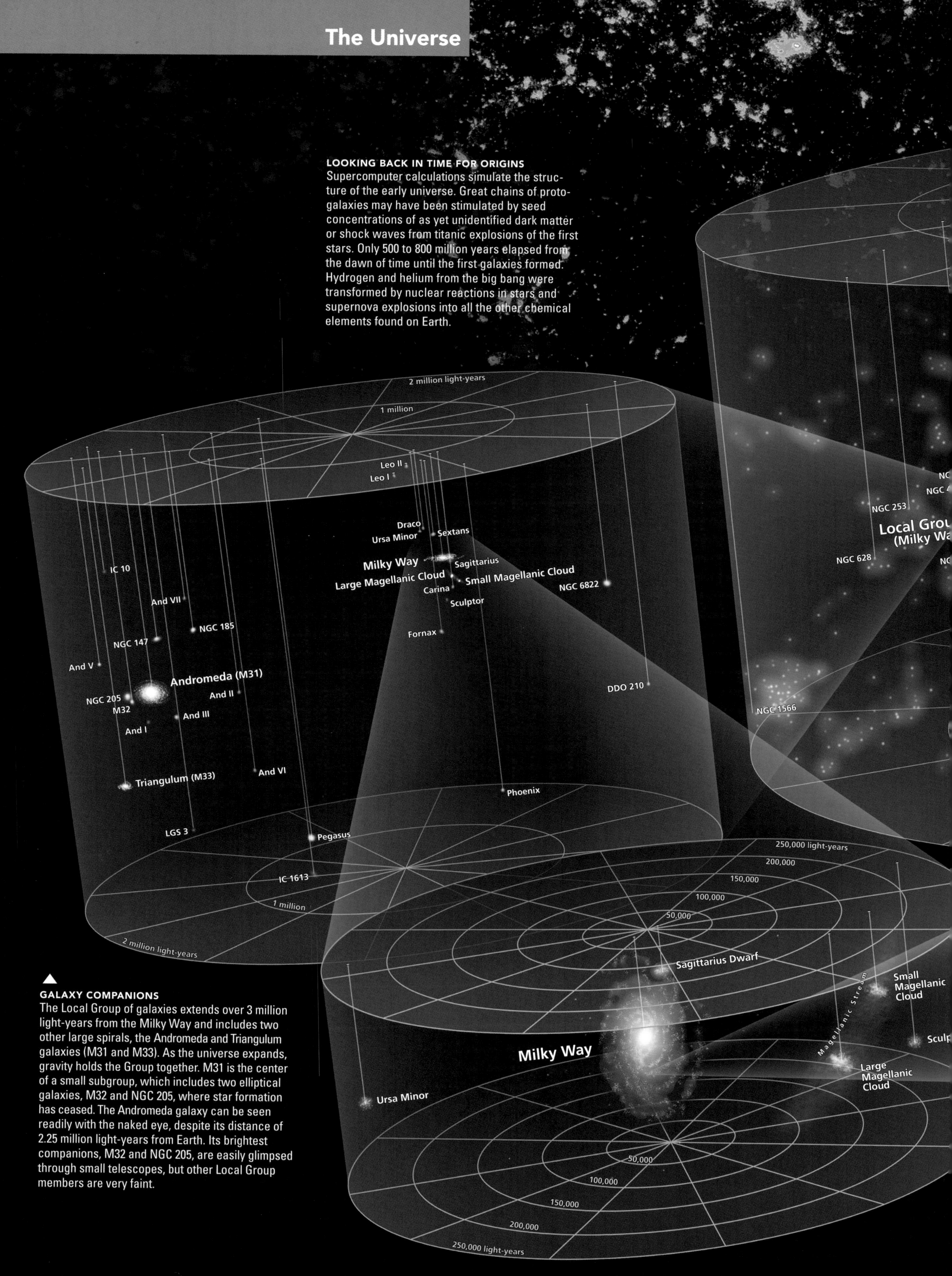
2 million light-years
1 million
Leo II
Leo I
Draco
Ursa Minor
Sextans
Milky Way
Sagittarius
Large Magellanic Cloud
Small Magellanic Cloud
Carina
Sculptor
NGC 6822
Fornax
IC 10
And VII
NGC 185
NGC 147
And V
Andromeda (M31)
And II
NGC 205
M32
And III
And I
DDO 210
Triangulum (M33)
And VI
Phoenix
LGS 3
Pegasus
IC 1613
1 million
2 million light-years
250,000 light-years
200,000
150,000
100,000
50,000
Sagittarius Dwarf
Small Magellanic Cloud
Magellanic Stream
Milky Way
Large Magellanic Cloud
Ursa Minor
50,000
100,000
150,000
200,000
250,000 light-years
NGC 253
NGC 628
NGC 1566

LOOKING BACK IN TIME FOR ORIGINS Supercomputer calculations simulate the structure of the early universe. Great chains of protogalaxies may have been stimulated by seed concentrations of as yet unidentified dark matter or shock waves from titanic explosions of the first stars. Only 500 to 800 million years elapsed from the dawn of time until the first galaxies formed. Hydrogen and helium from the big bang were transformed by nuclear reactions in stars and supernova explosions into all the other chemical elements found on Earth.

▲ **GALAXY COMPANIONS** The Local Group of galaxies extends over 3 million light-years from the Milky Way and includes two other large spirals, the Andromeda and Triangulum galaxies (M31 and M33). As the universe expands, gravity holds the Group together. M31 is the center of a small subgroup, which includes two elliptical galaxies, M32 and NGC 205, where star formation has ceased. The Andromeda galaxy can be seen readily with the naked eye, despite its distance of 2.25 million light-years from Earth. Its brightest companions, M32 and NGC 205, are easily glimpsed through small telescopes, but other Local Group members are very faint.

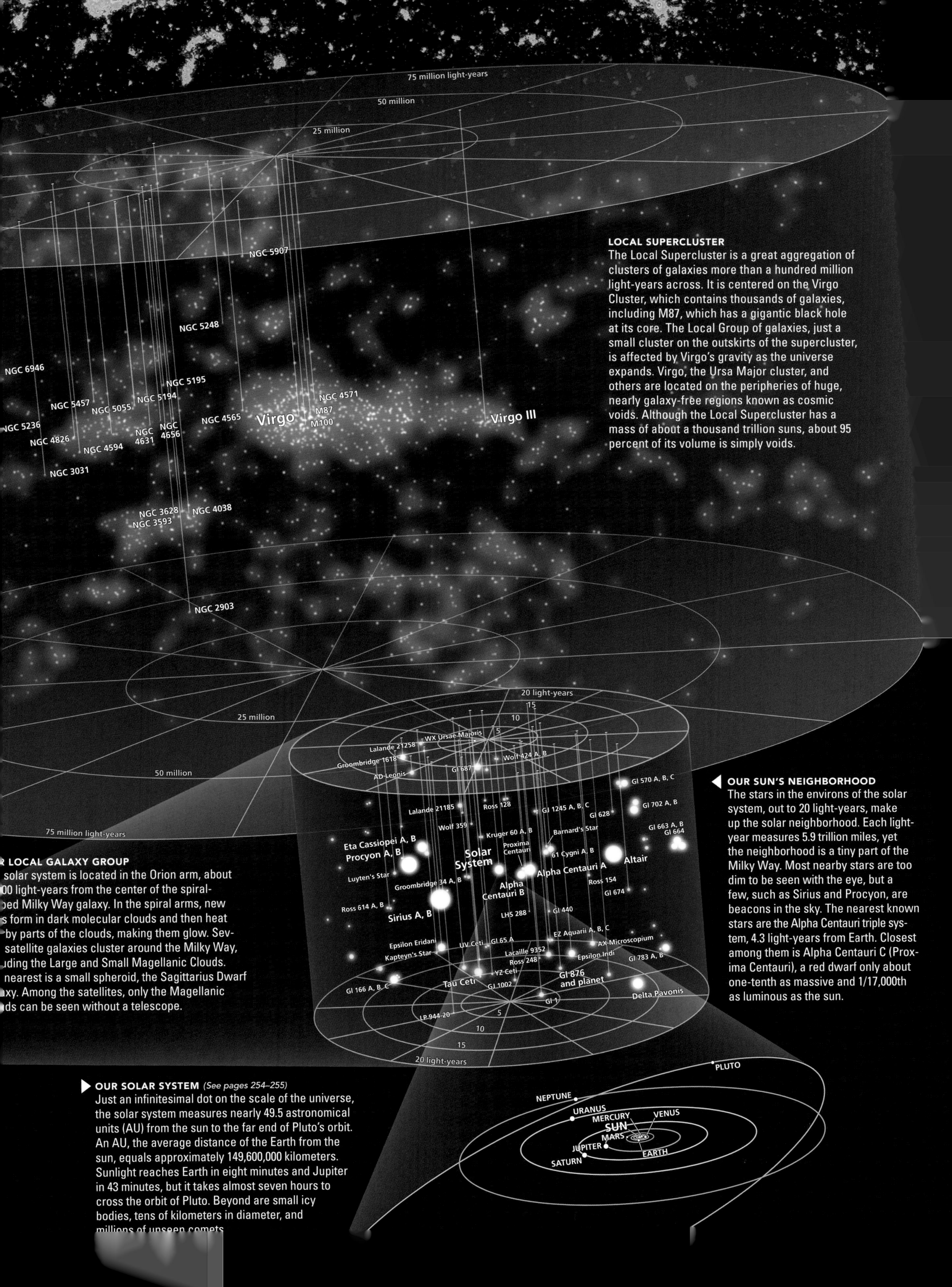
75 million light-years
50 million
25 million
NGC 5907
NGC 5248
NGC 6946
NGC 5195
NGC 5457
NGC 5055
NGC 5194
NGC 4571
M87
M100
NGC 5236
NGC 4826
NGC 4594
NGC 4631
NGC 4656
NGC 4565
Virgo
Virgo III
NGC 3031
NGC 3628
NGC 3593
NGC 4038
NGC 2903
LOCAL SUPERCLUSTER
The Local Supercluster is a great aggregation of clusters of galaxies more than a hundred million light-years across. It is centered on the Virgo Cluster, which contains thousands of galaxies, including M87, which has a gigantic black hole at its core. The Local Group of galaxies, just a small cluster on the outskirts of the supercluster, is affected by Virgo's gravity as the universe expands. Virgo, the Ursa Major cluster, and others are located on the peripheries of huge, nearly galaxy-free regions known as cosmic voids. Although the Local Supercluster has a mass of about a thousand trillion suns, about 95 percent of its volume is simply voids.
25 million
50 million
75 million light-years
r LOCAL GALAXY GROUP
solar system is located in the Orion arm, about 00 light-years from the center of the spiral-
bed Milky Way galaxy. In the spiral arms, new s form in dark molecular clouds and then heat by parts of the clouds, making them glow. Sev- satellite galaxies cluster around the Milky Way, uding the Large and Small Magellanic Clouds. nearest is a small spheroid, the Sagittarius Dwarf axy. Among the satellites, only the Magellanic ds can be seen without a telescope.
20 light-years
15
10
5
WX Ursae Majoris
Lalande 21258
Groombridge 1618
Wolf 424 A, B
AD Leonis
Gl 687
Gl 570 A, B, C
Lalande 21185
Ross 128
Gl 702 A, B
GJ 1245 A, B, C
Gl 628
Wolf 359
Gl 663 A, B
Gl 664
Kruger 60 A, B
Barnard's Star
Eta Cassiopei A, B
Procyon A, B
Solar System
Proxima Centauri
61 Cygni A, B
Altair
Alpha Centauri A
Luyten's Star
Groombridge 34 A, B
Alpha Centauri B
Ross 154
Gl 674
Ross 614 A, B
Sirius A, B
LHS 288
Gl 440
EZ Aquarii A, B, C
Epsilon Eridani
UV Ceti
Gl 65 A
AX Microscopium
Kapteyn's Star
Lacaille 9352
Epsilon Indi
Ross 248
Gl 783 A, B
YZ Ceti
Tau Ceti
Gl 876 and planet
Gl 166 A, B, C
GJ 1002
Delta Pavonis
Gl 1
LP 944-20
20 light-years
OUR SUN'S NEIGHBORHOOD
The stars in the environs of the solar system, out to 20 light-years, make up the solar neighborhood. Each light-year measures 5.9 trillion miles, yet the neighborhood is a tiny part of the Milky Way. Most nearby stars are too dim to be seen with the eye, but a few, such as Sirius and Procyon, are beacons in the sky. The nearest known stars are the Alpha Centauri triple system, 4.3 light-years from Earth. Closest among them is Alpha Centauri C (Proxima Centauri), a red dwarf only about one-tenth as massive and 1/17,000th as luminous as the sun.
OUR SOLAR SYSTEM (See pages 254–255)
Just an infinitesimal dot on the scale of the universe, the solar system measures nearly 49.5 astronomical units (AU) from the sun to the far end of Pluto's orbit. An AU, the average distance of the Earth from the sun, equals approximately 149,600,000 kilometers. Sunlight reaches Earth in eight minutes and Jupiter in 43 minutes, but it takes almost seven hours to cross the orbit of Pluto. Beyond are small icy bodies, tens of kilometers in diameter, and millions of unseen comets.
PLUTO
NEPTUNE
URANUS
MERCURY
VENUS
SUN
MARS
JUPITER
EARTH
SATURN

Space Exploration Timeline

1957

First Artificial Satellite
U.S.S.R.
Oct. 4, 1957
Sputnik I was launched; it transmitted radio signals back to Earth for a short time.

First Live Animal in Space
U.S.S.R.
Nov. 3, 1957
Dog named Laika lived eight days in space aboard Sputnik 2.

1958

First American Satellite
U.S.
Jan. 31, 1958
Explorer I discovered radiation belts around the Earth.

Creation of NASA
U.S.
Oct. 1, 1958
National Aeronautics and Space Administration (NASA) was established.

1959

First Man-made Object to Achieve Solar Orbit
U.S.S.R.
Jan. 4, 1959
Luna 1

First Spacecraft to Impact on The Moon
U.S.S.R.
Sept. 14, 1959
Luna 2

First View of Moon's Far Side
U.S.S.R.
Oct. 7, 1959
Luna 3 photographed 70 percent of the far side.

1960

First Weather Satellite
U.S.
Apr. 1, 1960
Tiros 1 established satellites as a useful tool for studying weather conditions.

1961

First Man in Space
U.S.S.R.
Apr. 12, 1961
Yuri Gagarin orbited Earth once in Vostok I, completing the trip in 108 minutes.

First American in Space
U.S.
May 5, 1961
Alan Shepard's Freedom 7 flight lasted 15 minutes and did not reach orbit.

President John F. Kennedy's Historic Speech
U.S.
May 25, 1961
Kennedy challenged nation to land man on moon by end of decade.

1967

First U.S. Space Tragedy
U.S.
Jan. 27, 1967
Three astronauts were killed in a fire during a test.

First Spaceflight Casualty
U.S.S.R.
Apr. 24, 1967
Soyuz 1 crashed, killing one.

First Venus Probe Launched
U.S.S.R.
June 12, 1967
Venera 4 compiled data on Venusian atmosphere.

1968

First Moon Orbit
U.S.S.R.
Sept. 15, 1968
Zond 5

First Manned Apollo Mission
U.S.
Oct. 11, 1968
Apollo 7 orbited Earth once.

First Manned Moon Orbit
U.S.
Dec. 24, 1968
Apollo 8 made ten orbits on six-day mission.

1969

First Manned Moon Landing
U.S.
July 20, 1969
Neil Armstrong and Edwin Aldrin Jr. were first to set foot on the moon.

1970

Apollo 13 Launch
U.S.
Apr. 11, 1970
After oxygen tanks exploded three astronauts were nearly killed; mission control coordinated their dramatic rescue.

First Automated Return of Lunar Soil
U.S.S.R.
Sept. 12, 1970
Luna 16, an automated spacecraft, returned lunar soil samples.

First Robotic Lunar Mission
U.S.S.R.
Nov. 10, 1970
Robot controlled from Earth

1971

First Landing on Venus
U.S.S.R.
Dec. 15, 1970
Venera 7 transmitted from Venus' surface for 23 minutes.

1977

Launch of Voyager Missions
U.S.
Aug.–Sept. 1977
Voyager I and II traveled to Jupiter and Saturn; they were the first spacecraft sent to explore these planets.

1978

Arrival of U.S. Probes at Venus
U.S.
Dec. 1978
U.S. probes obtained data on the atmosphere and mapped the surface.

1979

Arrival of Voyager 1 at Jupiter
U.S.
Mar. 5, 1979
Voyager 1 transmitted pictures of the planet and its moons.

Arrival of Voyager 2 at Jupiter
U.S.
July 9, 1979
Voyager 2 transmitted images of the planet and its moons.

First Images of Saturn
U.S.
Sept. 1, 1979
Space probe Pioneer 11

1980

Arrival of Voyager 1 at Saturn
U.S.
Nov. 12, 1980
Probe transmitted images of the planet and its moons.

1981

First Space Shuttle Launch
U.S.
Apr. 12, 1981
First mission of the Space Transportation System (STS-1)

Arrival of Voyager 2 at Saturn
U.S.
Aug. 25, 1981
Probe transmitted images of the planet and its moons.

1987

1988

New Space Endurance Record
U.S.S.R.
Dec. 29, 1987
Yuri Romanenko inhabited Mir for 326 days.

1989

Arrival of Voyager 2 at Neptune
U.S.
Aug. 25, 1989
First close-up images of Neptune and its moons were transmitted.

1990

Launch of Hubble Space Telescope
U.S.
Apr. 24, 1990
Telescope was successfully deployed, but a flawed mirror resulted in fuzzy images.

Arrival of Magellan at Venus
U.S.
Aug. 10, 1990
Magellan used radar to map the Venusian surface.

1991

1997

Landing of Mars Pathfinder on Mars
U.S.
July 4, 1997
Spacecraft examined terrain and returned images of the planet's surface.

1998

Return of John Glenn to Space
U.S.
Oct. 29, 1998
Glenn returned to space for first time in 36 years.

Launch of First Module of I.S.S. (International Space Station)
Russia
Nov. 20, 1998
Russian rocket carried first component of I.S.S.

1999

First American I.S.S. Module
U.S.
Dec. 4, 1998
New module was attached to Russian module.

2000

100th Space Shuttle Mission
U.S.
Oct. 11, 2000
The 28th *Discovery* mission

First Landing on an Asteroid
U.S.
Feb. 12, 2001
NEAR spacecraft landed on asteroid Eros and sent back images.

100th U.S. Space Walk
U.S.
Feb. 14, 2001
Space walk was necessary to install a new module for the I.S.S.

2001

New Space Walk Record
U.S.
Mar. 11, 2001
Susan Helms and Jim Voss spent 8 hours, 56 minutes installing new I.S.S. module.

First Tourist in Space
U.S.- Russia
Apr. 28, 2001
Dennis Tito paid 20 million dollars to fly in a Russian Soyuz space capsule and board the I.S.S.

962 | 1963 | 1964 | 1965 | 1966

First American in Orbit
U.S.
Feb. 20, 1962
John Glenn orbited the Earth three times on Friendship 7.

First Woman in Space
U.S.S.R.
June 16, 1963
Valentina Tereshkova

First Space Walk
U.S.S.R.
Mar. 18, 1965
Alexei Leonov's tethered space walk lasted 12 minutes.

First Images of Mars
U.S.
July 14, 1965
Pictures from Mariner 4 showed no evidence of life on Mars.

First Spacecraft to Land on the Moon
U.S.S.R.
Feb. 3, 1966
Luna 9 demonstrated the moon's surface strong enough to support large spacecraft.

First American Spacecraft on the Moon
U.S.
June 2, 1966
Surveyor I soft-landed on the moon and transmitted photographs.

972 | 1973 | 1974 | 1975 | 1976

First Space Station
U.S.S.R.
Apr. 19, 1971
Salyut I orbited for more than two years.

First Occupation of Space Station
U.S.S.R.
June 7, 1971
Three cosmonauts occupied Salyut 1 for several weeks.

First Lunar Rover Mission
U.S.
July 30, 1971
Astronauts explored the moon's surface with a rover.

First Spacecraft to Orbit Another Planet
U.S.
Nov. 13, 1971
Mariner 9 orbited Mars and mapped the surface.

First Black Hole Candidate
U.S.
Dec. 1972
Cignus X-1 was designated as first probable black hole.

First U.S. Space Station
U.S.
May 14, 1973
Skylab was launched for science experiments.

First Skylab Crew
U.S.
May 25, 1973
Crew repaired damage to Skylab sustained during launch.

First Inter-National Space Rendezvous
U.S. - U.S.S.R.
July 17, 1975
American Apollo 18 and Soviet Soyuz 19 docked together.

First Surface Images of Venus
U.S.S.R.
Oct. 1975
Venera 9 and 10

First Surface Images of Mars
U.S.
July 20, 1976
Viking 1 represented first U.S. attempt at landing on another planet.

Discovery of Water Frost on Mars
U.S.
Sept. 1976
Viking 2 found water frost on Utopia Planitia.

982 | 1983 | 1984 | 1985 | 1986

First Venus Soil Samples
U.S.S.R.
Mar. 1, 1982
Venera 13

First Operational Space Shuttle Mission
U.S.
Nov. 11, 1982
Space shuttle *Columbia* deployed two satellites.

New Space Endurance Record
U.S.S.R.
Dec. 11, 1982
Two Soviet cosmonauts inhabited space station Salyut 7 for 211 days.

Maiden Voyage of *Challenger*
U.S.
Apr. 4, 1983
America's second space shuttle

First American Woman in Space
U.S.
June 18, 1983
Sally Ride traveled on *Challenger* mission STS-7.

First Untethered Space Walk
U.S.
Feb. 3, 1984
Astronaut Bruce McCandless used the new Manned Maneuvering Unit.

Maiden Voyage of *Discovery*
U.S.
Aug. 30, 1984
America's third space shuttle

Maiden Voyage of *Atlantis*
U.S.
Oct. 3, 1985
America's fourth space shuttle

Arrival of Voyager 2 at Uranus
U.S.
Jan. 24, 1986
Captured the first close-up views of Uranus and its moons

***Challenger* Tragedy**
U.S.
Jan. 28, 1986
Shuttle's crew of seven were killed in an explosion when a leak ignited the fuel tank shortly after liftoff.

Launch of *Mir* Space Station
U.S.S.R.
Feb. 20, 1986
First module successfully launched into orbit.

992 | 1993 | 1994 | 1995 | 1996

Maiden Voyage of *Endeavour*
U.S.
May 7, 1992
Launch brought the number of orbiters in the shuttle fleet back to four.

50th Space Shuttle Mission
U.S.
Sept. 12, 1992
The second *Endeavour* mission

First H.S.T. Servicing Mission
U.S.
Dec. 2, 1993
Endeavour began the first servicing mission of the Hubble Space Telescope.

First Russian Cosmonaut Aboard Shuttle
U.S.- Russia
Feb. 3, 1994
Sergei Krikalev flew aboard *Discovery.*

First Female Shuttle Pilot
U.S.
Feb. 3, 1995
Eileen M. Collins piloted *Discovery* on mission STS-63.

New Space Endurance Record
Russia
Mar. 22, 1995
Valeriy Polyakov spent 438 days aboard *Mir.*

First Shuttle Docking with *Mir*
U.S.- Russia
June 29, 1995
American space shuttle *Atlantis* rendezvoused with the Russian space station.

Arrival of Galileo at Jupiter
U.S.
Dec. 7, 1995
Studies were made of the planet and its atmosphere.

75th Space Shuttle Mission
U.S.
Feb. 22, 1996
The 19th *Columbia* mission

Return of Shannon Lucid From *Mir*
U.S.- Russia
Sept. 26, 1996
Lucid set U.S. space endurance record of 188 days aboard *Mir.*

:002 | 2003 | 2004 | 2005 | 2006 | FUTURE

Launch of Shenzhou IV
China
Dec. 30, 2002
China launched its Shenzhou IV spacecraft in a test launch to prepare for manned space voyages.

Space Shuttle *Columbia* Mission
U.S.
Feb. 1, 2003
The shuttle *Columbia* broke up during its return descent, killing all seven crew members.

Successful Chinese Orbit
China
Oct. 15, 2003
China launched a human into space, who returned safely after orbiting Earth for two days.

Spirit Rover on Mars
U.S.
Jan. 15, 2004
The NASA Rover Spirit rolled onto the surface of Mars after bouncing to a landing nearly two weeks earlier.

Data From Titan
U.S.
Jan. 14, 2005
Huygens made a parachute-assisted descent through the atmosphere of Titan (a moon of Saturn), collecting data.

First Probe into a Comet
U.S.
Jul. 4, 2005
In a planned collision, Deep Impact became the first space mission to probe inside the surface of a comet.

Mission to Pluto
U.S.
Jan. 15–19, 2006
Stardust Capsule returned to Earth, bringing samples of Comet Wild. A few days later, a mission was launched to explore Pluto.

Discovery of Ice Volcanoes
U.S.
Mar. 9, 2006
NASA announced discovery of ice volcanoes on Enceladus.

E.S.A. Venus Express
Europe
Apr. 11, 2006
European Space Agency's (ESA) Venus Express went into orbit around Venus.

In 2007, India will launch its first mission to the moon. In 2008, NASA plans to launch the Lunar Reconnaissance Orbiter for making detailed maps of the moon to be used in future manned missions. A few years later, NASA's second New Frontiers Mission, Juno, is expected to be launched. Juno will become the first solar-powered spacecraft to orbit Jupiter, collect information about its interior, and reveal new information about the formation and evolution of the solar system.

Appendix

Airline Distances in Kilometers

	BEIJING	CAIRO	CAPE TOWN	CARACAS	HONG KONG	HONOLULU	LONDON	MELBOURNE	MÉXICO	MONTRÉAL	MOSCOW	NEW DELHI	NEW YORK	PARIS	RIO DE JANEIRO	ROME	SAN FRANCISCO	SINGAPORE	STOCKHOLM	TOKYO
BEIJING		7557	12947	14411	1972	8171	8160	9093	12478	10490	5809	3788	11012	8236	17325	8144	9524	4465	6725	2104
CAIRO	7557		7208	10209	8158	14239	3513	13966	12392	8733	2899	4436	9042	3215	9882	2135	12015	8270	3404	9587
CAPE TOWN	12947	7208		10232	11867	18562	9635	10338	13703	12744	10101	9284	12551	9307	6075	8417	16487	9671	10334	14737
CARACAS	14411	10209	10232		16380	9694	7500	15624	3598	3932	9940	14221	3419	7621	4508	8363	6286	18361	8724	14179
HONG KONG	1972	8158	11867	16380		8945	9646	7392	14155	12462	7158	3770	12984	9650	17710	9300	11121	2575	8243	2893
HONOLULU	8171	14239	18562	9694	8945		11653	8862	6098	7915	11342	11930	7996	11988	13343	12936	3857	10824	11059	6208
LONDON	8160	3513	9635	7500	9646	11653		16902	8947	5240	2506	6724	5586	341	9254	1434	8640	10860	1436	9585
MELBOURNE	9093	13966	10338	15624	7392	8862	16902		13557	16730	14418	10192	16671	16793	13227	15987	12644	6050	15593	8159
MÉXICO	12478	12392	13703	3598	14155	6098	8947	13557		3728	10740	14679	3362	9213	7669	10260	3038	16623	9603	11319
MONTRÉAL	10490	8733	12744	3932	12462	7915	5240	16730	3728		7077	11286	533	5522	8175	6601	4092	14816	5900	10409
MOSCOW	5809	2899	10101	9940	7158	11342	2506	14418	10740	7077		4349	7530	2492	11529	2378	9469	8426	1231	7502
NEW DELHI	3788	4436	9284	14221	3770	11930	6724	10192	14679	11286	4349		11779	6601	14080	5929	12380	4142	5579	5857
NEW YORK	11012	9042	12551	3419	12984	7996	5586	16671	3362	533	7530	11779		5851	7729	6907	4140	15349	6336	10870
PARIS	8236	3215	9307	7621	9650	11988	341	16793	9213	5522	2492	6601	5851		9146	1108	8975	10743	1546	9738
RIO DE JANEIRO	17325	9882	6075	4508	17710	13343	9254	13227	7669	8175	11529	14080	7729	9146		9181	10647	15740	10682	18557
ROME	8144	2135	8417	8363	9300	12936	1434	15987	10260	6601	2378	5929	6907	1108	9181		10071	10030	1977	9881
SAN FRANCISCO	9524	12015	16487	6286	11121	3857	8640	12644	3038	4092	9469	12380	4140	8975	10647	10071		13598	8644	8284
SINGAPORE	4465	8270	9671	18361	2575	10824	10860	6050	16623	14816	8426	4142	15349	10743	15740	10030	13598		9646	5317
STOCKHOLM	6725	3404	10334	8724	8243	11059	1436	15593	9603	5900	1231	5579	6336	1546	10682	1977	8644	9646		8193
TOKYO	2104	9587	14737	14179	2893	6208	9585	8159	11319	10409	7502	5857	10870	9738	18557	9881	8284	5317	8193	

Abbreviations

Adm. *Administrative*
Af. *Africa*
Afghan. *Afghanistan*
Agr. *Agriculture*
Ala. *Alabama*
Alas. *Alaska*
Alban. *Albania*
Alg. *Algeria*
Alta. *Alberta*
Arch. *Archipelago, Archipiélago*
Arg. *Argentina*
Ariz. *Arizona*
Ark. *Arkansas*
Arm. *Armenia*
Atl. Oc. *Atlantic Ocean*
Aust. *Austria*
Austral. *Australia*
Azerb. *Azerbaijan*
B. *Baai, Baía, Baie, Bahía, Bay, Buḩayrat*
B.C. *British Columbia*
Belg. *Belgium*
Bol. *Bolivia*
Bosn. & Herzg. *Bosnia and Herzegovina*
Braz. *Brazil*
Bulg. *Bulgaria*
C. *Cabo, Cap, Cape, Capo*
Calif. *California*
Can. *Canada*
Cen. Af. Rep. *Central African Republic*
C.H. *Court House*
Chan. *Channel*
Chap. *Chapada*
Cmte. *Comandante*
Cnel. *Coronel*
Co.-s. *Cerro-s*
Col. *Colombia*
Colo. *Colorado*
Conn. *Connecticut*
Cord. *Cordillera*
C.R. *Costa Rica*
Cr. *Creek, Crique*
C.S.I. Terr. *Coral Sea Islands Territory*
D.C. *District of Columbia*
Del. *Delaware*
Den. *Denmark*
Dom. Rep. *Dominican Republic*
D.R.C. *Democratic Republic of the Congo*
E. *East-ern*
Ecua. *Ecuador*
El Salv. *El Salvador*
Eng. *England*
Ens. *Ensenada*
Eq. *Equatorial*
Est. *Estonia*
Eth. *Ethiopia*
Exp. *Exports*
Falk. Is. *Falkland Islands*
Fd. *Fiord, Fiordo, Fjord*
Fin. *Finland*
Fk. *Fork*
Fla. *Florida*
Fn. *Fortín*
Fr. *France, French*
F.S.M. *Federated States of Micronesia*
ft *feet*
Ft. *Fort*
G. *Golfe, Golfo, Gulf*
Ga. *Georgia*
Ger. *Germany*
Gl. *Glacier*
Gr. *Greece*
Gral. *General*
Hbr. *Harbor, Harbour*
Hist. *Historic, -al*
Hond. *Honduras*
Hts. *Heights*
Hung. *Hungary*
Hwy. *Highway*
I.-s. *Île-s, Ilha-s, Isla-s, Island-s, Isle, Isol-a, -e*
Ice. *Iceland*
I.H.S. *International Historic Site*
Ill. *Illinois*
Ind. *Indiana*
Ind. *Industry*
Ind. Oc. *Indian Ocean*
Intl. *International*
Ire. *Ireland*
It. *Italy*
Jap. *Japan*
Jct. *Jonction, Junction*
Kans. *Kansas*
Kaz. *Kazakhstan*
Kep. *Kepulauan*
Ky. *Kentucky*
Kyrg. *Kyrgyzstan*
L. *Lac, Lago, Lake, Límni Loch, Lough*
La. *Louisiana*
Lab. *Labrador*
Lag. *Laguna*
Latv. *Latvia*
Leb. *Lebanon*
Lib. *Libya*
Liech. *Liechtenstein*
Lith. *Lithuania*
Lux. *Luxembourg*
m *meters*
Maced. *Macedonia*
Madag. *Madagascar*
Maurit. *Mauritius*
Mass. *Massachusetts*
Md. *Maryland*
Me. *Maine*
Medit. Sea *Mediterranean Sea*
Mex. *Mexico*
Mgne. *Montagne*
Mich. *Michigan*
Minn. *Minnesota*
Miss. *Mississippi*
Mo. *Missouri*
Mon. *Monument*
Mont. *Montana*
Mor. *Morocco*
Mt.-s. *Mont-s, Mount-ain-s*
N. *North-ern*
Nat. *National*
Nat. Mem. *National Memorial*
Nat. Mon. *National Monument*
N.B. *National Battlefield*
N.B. *New Brunswick*
N.C. *North Carolina*
N. Dak. *North Dakota*
N.E. *Northeast*
Nebr. *Nebraska*
Neth. *Netherlands*
Nev. *Nevada*
Nfld. *Newfoundland*
N.H. *New Hampshire*
Nicar. *Nicaragua*
Nig. *Nigeria*
N. Ire. *Northern Ireland*
N.J. *New Jersey*
N. Mex. *New Mexico*
N.M.P. *National Military Park*
N.M.S. *National Marine Sanctuary*
Nor. *Norway*
N.P. *National Park*
N.S. *Nova Scotia*
N.S.W. *New South Wales*
N.V.M. *National Volcanic Monument*
N.W.T. *Northwest Territories*
N.Y. *New York*
N.Z. *New Zealand*
O. *Ostrov, Oued*
Oc. *Ocean*
Okla. *Oklahoma*
Ont. *Ontario*
Oreg. *Oregon*
Oz. *Ozero*
Pa. *Pennsylvania*
Pac. Oc. *Pacific Ocean*
Pak. *Pakistan*
Pan. *Panama*
Para. *Paraguay*
Pass. *Passage*
Peg. *Pegunungan*
P.E.I. *Prince Edward Island*
Pen. *Peninsula, Péninsule*
Pk. *Peak*
P.N.G. *Papua New Guinea*
Pol. *Poland*
Pol. *Poluostrov*
Port. *Portugal, Portuguese*
P.R. *Puerto Rico*
Prov. *Province, Provincial*
Pt.-e. *Point-e*
Pta. *Ponta, Punta*
Qnsld. *Queensland*
Que. *Quebec*
R. *Río, River, Rivière*
Ra.-s. *Range-s*
Rec. *Recreation*
Rep. *Republic*
Res. *Reservoir, Reserve, Reservatório*
R.I. *Rhode Island*
Rom. *Romania*
Russ. *Russia*
S. *South-ern*
Sa.-s. *Serra, Sierra-s*
S. Af. *South Africa*
Sask. *Saskatchewan*
S.C. *South Carolina*
Scot. *Scotland*
Sd. *Sound*
S. Dak. *South Dakota*
Serb. & Mont. *Serbia and Montenegro*
Sev. *Severn-yy, -aya, -oye*
Sk. *Shankou*
Slov. *Slovenia*
Sp. *Spain, Spanish*
Spr.-s. *Spring-s*
Sta. *Santa*
St.-e. *Saint-e, Sankt, Sint*
Str.-s. *Straat, Strait-s*
Switz. *Switzerland*
Syr. *Syria*
Taj. *Tajikistan*
Tas. *Tasmania*
Tenn. *Tennessee*
Terr. *Territory*
Tex. *Texas*
Tg. *Tanjung*
Thai. *Thailand*
Trin. *Trinidad*
Tun. *Tunisia*
Turk. *Turkey*
Turkm. *Turkmenistan*
U.A.E. *United Arab Emirates*
U.K. *United Kingdom*
Ukr. *Ukraine*
U.N. *United Nations*
Uru. *Uruguay*
U.S. *United States*
Uzb. *Uzbekistan*
Va. *Virginia*
Vdkhr. *Vodokhranilishche*
Vdskh. *Vodoskhovyshche*
Venez. *Venezuela*
V.I. *Virgin Islands*
Vic. *Victoria*
Viet. *Vietnam*
Vol. *Volcán, Volcano*
Vt. *Vermont*
W. *Wadi, Wādī, Webi*
W. *West-ern*
Wash. *Washington*
Wis. *Wisconsin*
W. Va. *West Virginia*
Wyo. *Wyoming*
Yug. *Yugoslavia*
Zakh. *Zakhod-ni, -nyaya, -nye*
Zimb. *Zimbabwe*

QUICK REFERENCE CHART FOR METRIC TO ENGLISH CONVERSION

1 METER	1 METER = 100 CENTIMETERS
1 FOOT	1 FOOT = 12 INCHES
1 KILOMETER	1 KILOMETER = 1,000 METERS
1 MILE	1 MILE = 5,280 FEET

METERS	1	10	20	50	100	200	500	1,000	2,000	5,000	10,000
FEET	3.281	32.81	65.62	164.05	328.1	656.2	1,640.5	3,281.0	6,562.0	16,405.0	32,810.0

KILOMETERS	1	10	20	50	100	200	500	1,000	2,000	5,000	10,000
MILES	0.621	6.21	12.42	31.05	62.1	124.2	310.5	621.0	1,242.0	3,105.0	6,210.0

CONVERSION FROM METRIC MEASURES

SYMBOL	WHEN YOU KNOW	MULTIPLY BY	TO FIND	SYMBOL
		LENGTH		
cm	centimeters	0.39	inches	in
m	meters	3.28	feet	ft
m	meters	1.09	yards	yd
km	kilometers	0.62	miles	mi
		AREA		
cm^2	square centimeters	0.16	square inches	in^2
m^2	square meters	10.76	square feet	ft^2
m^2	square meters	1.20	square yards	yd^2
km^2	square kilometers	0.39	square miles	mi^2
ha	hectares	2.47	acres	—
		MASS		
g	grams	0.04	ounces	oz
kg	kilograms	2.20	pounds	lb
t	metric tons	1.10	short tons	—
		VOLUME		
mL	milliliters	0.06	cubic inches	in^3
mL	milliliters	0.03	liquid ounces	liq oz
L	liters	2.11	pints	pt
L	liters	1.06	quarts	qt
L	liters	0.26	gallons	gal
m^3	cubic meters	35.31	cubic feet	ft^3
m^3	cubic meters	1.31	cubic yards	yd^3
		TEMPERATURE		
°C	degrees Celsius (centigrade)	9/5 then add 32	degrees Fahrenheit	°F

CONVERSION TO METRIC MEASURES

SYMBOL	WHEN YOU KNOW	MULTIPLY BY	TO FIND	SYMBOL
		LENGTH		
in	inches	2.54	centimeters	cm
ft	feet	0.30	meters	m
yd	yards	0.91	meters	m
mi	miles	1.61	kilometers	km
		AREA		
in^2	square inches	6.45	square centimeters	cm^2
ft^2	square feet	0.09	square meters	m^2
yd^2	square yards	0.84	square meters	m^2
mi^2	square miles	2.59	square kilometers	km^2
—	acres	0.40	hectares	ha
		MASS		
oz	ounces	28.35	grams	g
lb	pounds	0.45	kilograms	kg
—	short tons	0.91	metric tons	t
		VOLUME		
in^3	cubic inches	16.39	milliliters	mL
liq oz	liquid ounces	29.57	milliliters	mL
pt	pints	0.47	liters	L
qt	quarts	0.95	liters	L
gal	gallons	3.79	liters	L
ft^3	cubic feet	0.03	cubic meters	m^3
yd^3	cubic yards	0.76	cubic meters	m^3
		TEMPERATURE		
°F	degrees Fahrenheit	5/9 after subtracting 32	degrees Celsius (centigrade)	°C

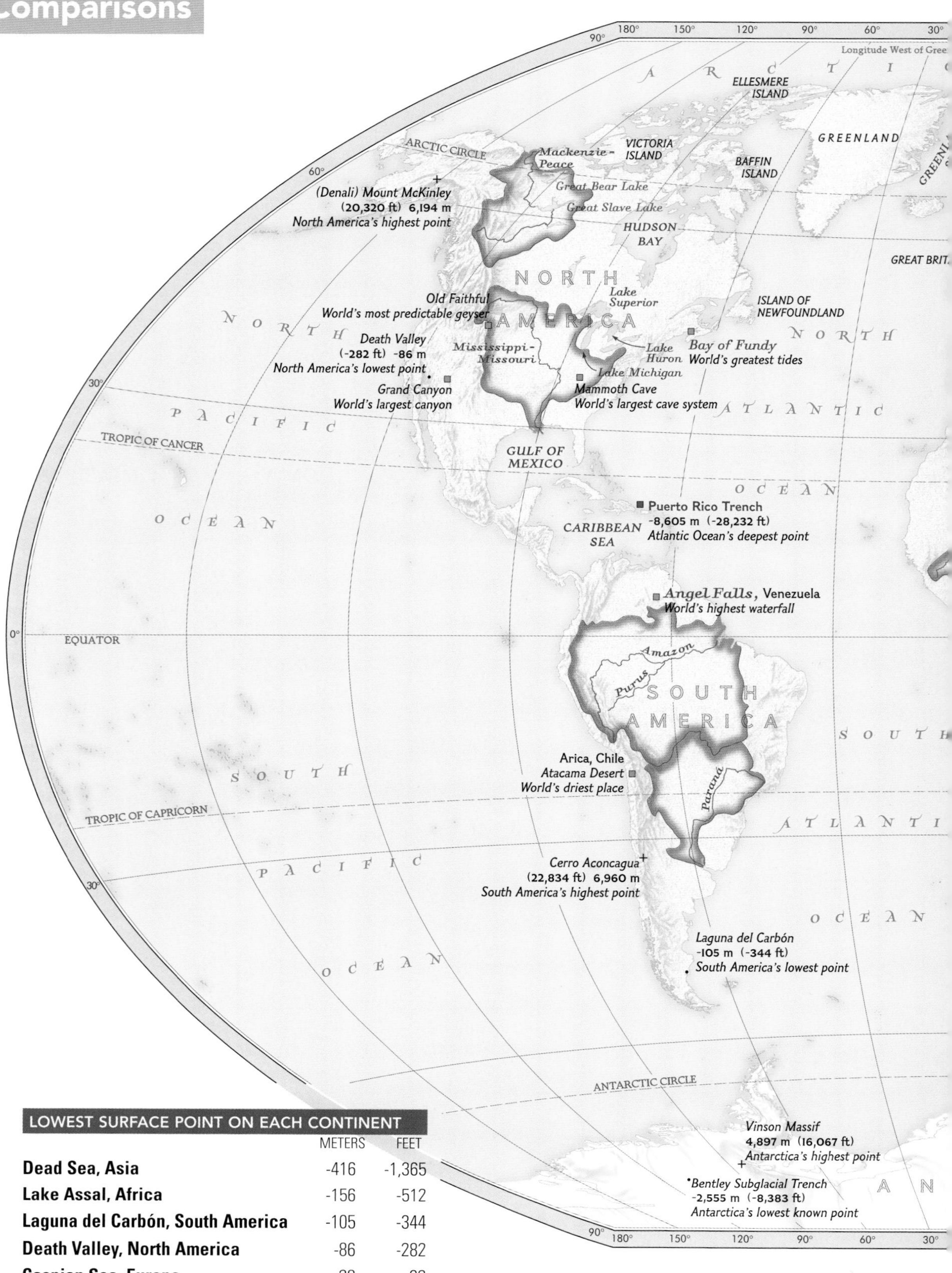

Longitude West of Greenwich
ELLESMERE ISLAND
GREENLAND
VICTORIA ISLAND
BAFFIN ISLAND
ARCTIC CIRCLE
Mackenzie-Peace
Great Bear Lake
Great Slave Lake
(Denali) Mount McKinley
(20,320 ft) 6,194 m
North America's highest point
HUDSON BAY
GREAT BRIT.
NORTH AMERICA
Lake Superior
ISLAND OF NEWFOUNDLAND
Old Faithful
World's most predictable geyser
Death Valley
(-282 ft) -86 m
North America's lowest point
Mississippi-Missouri
Lake Huron
Lake Michigan
Bay of Fundy
World's greatest tides
Grand Canyon
World's largest canyon
Mammoth Cave
World's largest cave system
NORTH PACIFIC OCEAN
NORTH ATLANTIC OCEAN
TROPIC OF CANCER
GULF OF MEXICO
Puerto Rico Trench
-8,605 m (-28,232 ft)
Atlantic Ocean's deepest point
CARIBBEAN SEA
Angel Falls, Venezuela
World's highest waterfall
EQUATOR
Amazon
Purus
SOUTH AMERICA
Arica, Chile
Atacama Desert
World's driest place
Paraná
TROPIC OF CAPRICORN
SOUTH PACIFIC OCEAN
SOUTH ATLANTIC OCEAN
Cerro Aconcagua
(22,834 ft) 6,960 m
South America's highest point
Laguna del Carbón
-105 m (-344 ft)
South America's lowest point
ANTARCTIC CIRCLE
Vinson Massif
4,897 m (16,067 ft)
Antarctica's highest point
*Bentley Subglacial Trench
-2,555 m (-8,383 ft)
Antarctica's lowest known point

THE EARTH

Mass: 5,974,000,000,000,000,000,000 (5.974 sextillion) metric tons

Total Area: 510,066,000 sq km (196,938,000 sq mi)

Land Area: 148,647,000 sq km (57,393,000 sq mi), 29.1% of total

Water Area: 361,419,000 sq km (139,545,000 sq mi), 70.9% of total

Population: 6,477,451,000

THE EARTH'S EXTREMES

Hottest Place: Dalol, Danakil Depression, Ethiopia, annual average temperature 34°C (93°F)

Coldest Place: Plateau Station, Antarctica, annual average temperature -56.7°C (-70°F)

Hottest Recorded Temperature: Al Aziziyah, Libya 58°C (136.4°F), September 3, 1922

Coldest Recorded Temperature: Vostok, Antarctica -89.2°C (-128.6°F), July 21, 1983

Wettest Place: Mawsynram, Assam, India, annual average rainfall 1,187 cm (467 in)

Driest Place: Arica, Atacama Desert, Chile, rainfall barely measurable

Highest Waterfall: Angel Falls, Venezuela 979 m (3,212 ft)

Largest Hot Desert: Sahara, Africa 9,000,000 sq km (3,475,000 sq mi)

Largest Ice Desert: Antarctica 13,209,000 sq km (5,100,000 sq mi)

Largest Canyon: Grand Canyon, Colorado River, Arizona 446 km (277 mi) long along river, 180 m (600 ft) to 29 km (18 mi) wide, about 1.8 km (1.1 mi) deep

Largest Cave Chamber: Sarawak Cave, Gunung Mulu National Park, Malaysia 16 hectares and 79 meters high (40.2 acres and 260 feet)

Largest Cave System: Mammoth Cave, Kentucky, over 530 km (330 mi) of passageways mapped

Most Predictable Geyser: Old Faithful, Wyoming, annual average interval 66 to 80 minutes

Longest Reef: Great Barrier Reef, Australia 2,300 km (1,429 mi)

Greatest Tidal Range: Bay of Fundy, Canadian Atlantic Coast 16 m (52 ft)

AREA OF EACH CONTINENT

	SQ KM	SQ MI	PERCENT OF EARTH'S LAND
Asia	44,579,000	17,212,000	30.0
Africa	30,065,000	11,608,000	20.2
North America	24,474,000	9,449,000	16.5
South America	17,819,000	6,880,000	12.0
Antarctica	13,209,000	5,100,000	8.9
Europe	9,938,000	3,837,000	6.7
Australia	7,687,000	2,968,000	5.2

HIGHEST POINT ON EACH CONTINENT

	METERS	FEET
Mount Everest, Asia	8,850	29,035
Cerro Aconcagua, South America	6,960	22,834
Mount McKinley (Denali), N. America	6,194	20,320
Kilimanjaro, Africa	5,895	19,340
El'brus, Europe	5,642	18,510
Vinson Massif, Antarctica	4,897	16,067
Mount Kosciuszko, Australia	2,228	7,310

LOWEST SURFACE POINT ON EACH CONTINENT

	METERS	FEET
Dead Sea, Asia	-416	-1,365
Lake Assal, Africa	-156	-512
Laguna del Carbón, South America	-105	-344
Death Valley, North America	-86	-282
Caspian Sea, Europe	-28	-92
Lake Eyre, Australia	-16	-52
Bentley Subglacial Trench, Antarctica	-2,555	-8,383

LARGEST ISLANDS

		AREA SQ KM	AREA SQ MI
1	**Greenland**	2,166,000	836,000
2	**New Guinea**	792,500	306,000
3	**Borneo**	725,500	280,100
4	**Madagascar**	587,000	226,600
5	**Baffin Island**	507,500	196,000
6	**Sumatra**	427,300	165,000
7	**Honshu**	227,400	87,800
8	**Great Britain**	218,100	84,200
9	**Victoria Island**	217,300	83,900
10	**Ellesmere Island**	196,200	75,800
11	**Sulawesi (Celebes)**	178,700	69,000
12	**South Island (New Zealand)**	150,400	58,100
13	**Java**	126,700	48,900
14	**North Island (New Zealand)**	113,700	43,900
15	**Island of Newfoundland**	108,900	42,000

LARGEST DRAINAGE BASINS

		AREA SQ KM	AREA SQ MI
1	**Amazon, South America**	7,050,000	2,721,000
2	**Congo, Africa**	3,700,000	1,428,000
3	**Mississippi-Missouri, North America**	3,250,000	1,255,000
4	**Paraná, South America**	3,100,000	1,197,000
5	**Yenisey-Angara, Asia**	2,700,000	1,042,000
6	**Ob-Irtysh, Asia**	2,430,000	938,000
7	**Lena, Asia**	2,420,000	934,000
8	**Nile, Africa**	1,900,000	733,400
9	**Amur, Asia**	1,840,000	710,000
10	**Mackenzie-Peace, North America**	1,765,000	681,000
11	**Ganges-Brahmaputra, Asia**	1,730,000	668,000
12	**Volga, Europe**	1,380,000	533,000
13	**Zambezi, Africa**	1,330,000	513,000
14	**Niger, Africa**	1,200,000	463,000
15	**Chang Jiang (Yangtze), Asia**	1,175,000	454,000

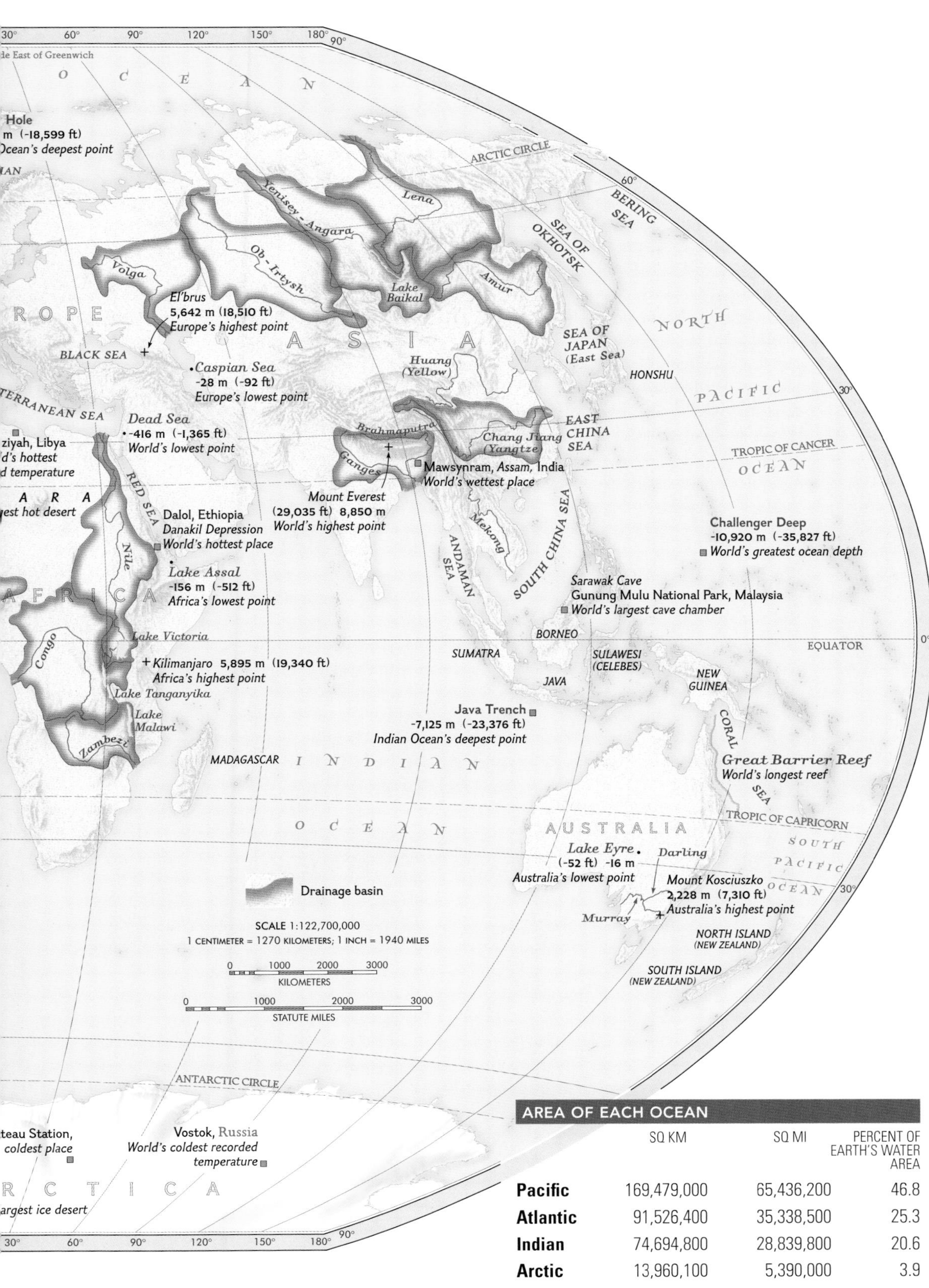

ARCTIC CIRCLE
Molloy Hole
-5,669 m (-18,599 ft)
Arctic Ocean's deepest point
EUROPE
Volga
El'brus
5,642 m (18,510 ft)
Europe's highest point
BLACK SEA
Caspian Sea
-28 m (-92 ft)
Europe's lowest point
MEDITERRANEAN SEA
Dead Sea
-416 m (-1,365 ft)
World's lowest point
ASIA
Yenisey-Angara
Lena
Ob-Irtysh
Lake Baikal
Amur
BERING SEA
SEA OF OKHOTSK
SEA OF JAPAN (East Sea)
HONSHU
NORTH PACIFIC OCEAN
Huang (Yellow)
Chang Jiang (Yangtze)
EAST CHINA SEA
Brahmaputra
Ganges
Mawsynram, Assam, India
World's wettest place
Mount Everest
(29,035 ft) 8,850 m
World's highest point
TROPIC OF CANCER
RED SEA
Dalol, Ethiopia
Danakil Depression
World's hottest place
Nile
Lake Assal
-156 m (-512 ft)
Africa's lowest point
AFRICA
Challenger Deep
-10,920 m (-35,827 ft)
World's greatest ocean depth
ANDAMAN SEA
Mekong
SOUTH CHINA SEA
Sarawak Cave
Gunung Mulu National Park, Malaysia
World's largest cave chamber
BORNEO
EQUATOR
Lake Victoria
Congo
Kilimanjaro 5,895 m (19,340 ft)
Africa's highest point
Lake Tanganyika
Lake Malawi
Zambezi
SUMATRA
SULAWESI (CELEBES)
JAVA
NEW GUINEA
Java Trench
-7,125 m (-23,376 ft)
Indian Ocean's deepest point
MADAGASCAR
INDIAN OCEAN
CORAL SEA
Great Barrier Reef
World's longest reef
TROPIC OF CAPRICORN
AUSTRALIA
Lake Eyre
(-52 ft) -16 m
Australia's lowest point
Darling
Murray
Mount Kosciuszko
2,228 m (7,310 ft)
Australia's highest point
SOUTH PACIFIC OCEAN
NORTH ISLAND (NEW ZEALAND)
SOUTH ISLAND (NEW ZEALAND)
Drainage basin
SCALE 1:122,700,000
1 CENTIMETER = 1270 KILOMETERS; 1 INCH = 1940 MILES
KILOMETERS
STATUTE MILES
ANTARCTIC CIRCLE
Plateau Station, coldest place
Vostok, Russia
World's coldest recorded temperature
ANTARCTICA
Largest ice desert

GEOPOLITICAL EXTREMES

Largest Country: Russia 17,075,400 sq km (6,592,850 sq mi)

Smallest Country: Vatican City 0.4 sq km (0.2 sq mi)

Most Populous Country: China 1,333,827,000 people

Least Populous Country: Vatican City 1,000 people

Most Crowded Country: Monaco 16,500 per sq km (41,250 per sq mi)

Least Crowded Country: Mongolia 1.7 per sq km (4.4 per sq mi)

Largest Metropolitan Area: Tokyo 34,997,000 people

Country with the Greatest Number of Bordering Countries: China 14, Russia 14

ENGINEERING WONDERS

Tallest Office Building: Taipei 101, Taipei, Taiwan 508 m (1,667 ft)

Tallest Tower (Freestanding): CN Tower, Toronto, Canada 553 m (1,815 ft)

Tallest Manmade Structure: KVLY TV tower, near Fargo, North Dakota 629 m (2,063 ft)

Longest Wall: Great Wall of China, approx. 3,460 km (2,150 mi)

Longest Road: Pan-American highway (not including gap in Panama and Colombia), more than 24,140 km (15,000 mi)

Longest Railroad: Trans-Siberian Railroad, Russia 9,288 km (5,772 mi)

Longest Road Tunnel: Laerdal Tunnel, Laerdal, Norway 24.5 km (15.2 mi)

Longest Rail Tunnel: Seikan submarine rail tunnel, Honshu to Hokkaido, Japan 53.9 km (33.5 mi)

Highest Bridge (over water): Royal Gorge Bridge, Colorado 321 m (1,053 ft) above water

Longest Highway Bridge: Lake Pontchartrain Causeway, Louisiana 38.4 km (23.9 mi)

Longest Suspension Bridge: Akashi-Kaikyo Bridge, Japan 3,911 m (12,831 ft)

Longest Boat Canal: Grand Canal, China, over 1,770 km (1,100 mi)

Longest Irrigation Canal: Garagum Canal, Turkmenistan, nearly 1,100 km (700 mi)

Largest Artificial Lake: Lake Volta, Volta River, Ghana 9,065 sq km (3,500 sq mi)

Tallest Dam: Rogun Dam, Vakhsh River, Tajikistan 335 m (1,099 ft)

Tallest Pyramid: Great Pyramid of Khufu, Egypt 137 m (450 ft)

Deepest Mine: Savuka Mine, South Africa approx. 4 km (2.5 mi) deep

Longest Submarine Cable: Sea-Me-We 3 cable, connects 33 countries on four continents, 39,000 km (24,200 mi) long

AREA OF EACH OCEAN

	SQ KM	SQ MI	PERCENT OF EARTH'S WATER AREA
Pacific	169,479,000	65,436,200	46.8
Atlantic	91,526,400	35,338,500	25.3
Indian	74,694,800	28,839,800	20.6
Arctic	13,960,100	5,390,000	3.9

LONGEST RIVERS

		KM	MI
1	**Nile, Africa**	6,825	4,241
2	**Amazon, South America**	6,437	4,000
3	**Chang Jiang (Yangtze), Asia**	6,380	3,964
4	**Mississippi-Missouri, North America**	5,971	3,710
5	**Yenisey-Angara, Asia**	5,536	3,440
6	**Huang (Yellow), Asia**	5,464	3,395
7	**Ob-Irtysh, Asia**	5,410	3,362
8	**Amur, Asia**	4,416	2,744
9	**Lena, Asia**	4,400	2,734
10	**Congo, Africa**	4,370	2,715
11	**Mackenzie-Peace, North America**	4,241	2,635
12	**Mekong, Asia**	4,184	2,600
13	**Niger, Africa**	4,170	2,591
14	**Paraná-Río de la Plata, S. America**	4,000	2,485
15	**Murray-Darling, Australia**	3,718	2,310
16	**Volga, Europe**	3,685	2,290
17	**Purus, South America**	3,380	2,100

DEEPEST POINT IN EACH OCEAN

	METERS	FEET
Challenger Deep, Pacific Ocean	-10,920	-35,827
Puerto Rico Trench, Atlantic Ocean	-8,605	-28,232
Java Trench, Indian Ocean	-7,125	-23,376
Molloy Hole, Arctic Ocean	-5,669	-18,599

LARGEST LAKES BY AREA

		AREA		MAXIMUM DEPTH	
		SQ KM	SQ MI	METERS	FEET
1	**Caspian Sea**	371,000	143,200	1,025	3,363
2	**Lake Superior**	82,100	31,700	406	1,332
3	**Lake Victoria**	69,500	26,800	82	269
4	**Lake Huron**	59,600	23,000	229	751
5	**Lake Michigan**	57,800	22,300	281	922
6	**Lake Tanganyika**	32,600	12,600	1,470	4,823
7	**Lake Baikal**	31,500	12,200	1,637	5,371
8	**Great Bear Lake**	31,300	12,100	446	1,463
9	**Lake Malawi**	28,900	11,200	695	2,280
10	**Great Slave Lake**	28,600	11,000	614	2,014

LARGEST SEAS BY AREA

		AREA		AVGERAGE DEPTH	
		SQ KM	SQ MI	METERS	FEET
1	**Coral Sea**	4,183,510	1,615,260	2,471	8,107
2	**South China Sea**	3,596,390	1,388,570	1,180	3,871
3	**Caribbean Sea**	2,834,290	1,094,330	2,596	8,517
4	**Bering Sea**	2,519,580	972,810	1,832	6,010
5	**Mediterranean Sea**	2,469,100	953,320	1,572	5,157
6	**Sea of Okhotsk**	1,625,190	627,490	814	2,671
7	**Gulf of Mexico**	1,531,810	591,430	1,544	5,066
8	**Norwegian Sea**	1,425,280	550,300	1,768	5,801
9	**Greenland Sea**	1,157,850	447,050	1,443	4,734
10	**Sea of Japan**	1,008,260	389,290	1,647	5,404
11	**Hudson Bay**	1,005,510	388,230	119	390
12	**East China Sea**	785,990	303,470	374	1,227
13	**Andaman Sea**	605,760	233,890	1,061	3,481
14	**Red Sea**	436,280	168,450	494	1,621
15	**Black Sea**	410,150	158,360	1,336	4,383

Political Entities and Status

ALL OF THE EARTH'S LANDS are grouped into four categories on pages 266 through 269: independent states, dependencies, areas of special status, and areas geographically separated from their mainland countries. At right, a world map uses different colors to show the distribution of lands within each category.

Each of the 192 countries listed in the independent states category (below) is a recognized territory whose government is the highest legal authority over the land and people within its boundaries.

A dependency, on the other hand, is a region whose territory is controlled by another, often very distant, country; it is not, however, considered an inherent part of the controlling country. Most dependencies are inhabited and have some form of local government with limited autonomy.

An area of special status is a region of ambiguous political status. Most of these areas can be described as disputed territory, territory not recognized as independent by other countries, or territory leased by one government to another. In the fourth category are populated lands considered integral parts of independent states, but they are separated from the rest of their countries by a significant distance.

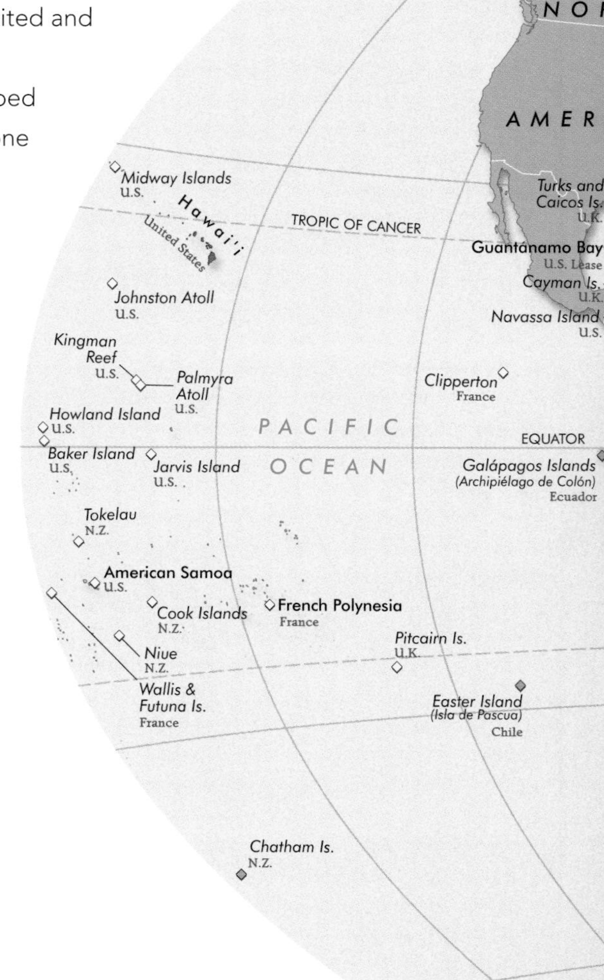

Alaska
U.S.
Midway Islands
U.S.
Hawai'i
United States
TROPIC OF CANCER
Turks and Caicos Is.
U.K.
Guantánamo Bay
U.S. Lease
Cayman Is.
U.K.
Navassa Island
U.S.
Johnston Atoll
U.S.
Kingman Reef
U.S.
Palmyra Atoll
U.S.
Howland Island
U.S.
Baker Island
U.S.
Jarvis Island
U.S.
PACIFIC
OCEAN
Clipperton
France
EQUATOR
Galápagos Islands
(Archipiélago de Colón)
Ecuador
Tokelau
N.Z.
American Samoa
U.S.
Cook Islands
N.Z.
French Polynesia
France
Pitcairn Is.
U.K.
Niue
N.Z.
Wallis & Futuna Is.
France
Easter Island
(Isla de Pascua)
Chile
Chatham Is.
N.Z.

INDEPENDENT STATES OF THE WORLD

COUNTRY	CAPITAL	2005 POPULATION	DATE OF INDEPENDENCE
AFGHANISTAN	Kabul	29,929,000	Aug. 19, 1919
ALBANIA	Tirana	3,170,000	Nov. 28, 1912
ALGERIA	Algiers	32,814,000	July 5, 1962
ANDORRA	Andorra la Vella	74,000	1278
ANGOLA	Luanda	15,375,000	Nov. 11, 1975
ANTIGUA AND BARBUDA	St. John's	80,000	Nov. 1, 1981
ARGENTINA	Buenos Aires	38,592,000	July 9, 1816
ARMENIA	Yerevan	3,033,000	Sept. 21, 1991
AUSTRALIA	Canberra	20,351,000	Jan. 1, 1901
AUSTRIA	Vienna	8,151,000	1156
AZERBAIJAN	Baku	8,388,000	Aug. 30, 1991
BAHAMAS	Nassau	319,000	July 10, 1973
BAHRAIN	Manama	731,000	Aug. 15, 1971
BANGLADESH	Dhaka	144,233,000	Dec. 16, 1971
BARBADOS	Bridgetown	258,000	Nov. 30, 1966
BELARUS	Minsk	9,776,000	Aug. 25, 1991
BELGIUM	Brussels	10,458,000	July 21, 1831
BELIZE	Belmopan	292,000	Sept. 21, 1981
BENIN	Porto-Novo, Cotonou	8,439,000	Aug. 1, 1960
BHUTAN	Thimphu	970,000	Aug. 8, 1949
BOLIVIA	La Paz, Sucre	8,922,000	Aug. 6, 1825
BOSNIA AND HERZEGOVINA	Sarajevo	3,840,000	Mar. 1, 1992
BOTSWANA	Gaborone	1,640,000	Sept. 30, 1966
BRAZIL	Brasília	184,184,000	Sept. 7, 1822
BRUNEI	Bandar Seri Begawan	363,000	Jan. 1, 1984
BULGARIA	Sofia	7,741,000	Mar. 3, 1878
BURKINA FASO	Ouagadougou	13,925,000	Aug. 5, 1960
BURUNDI	Bujumbura	7,795,000	July 1, 1962
CAMBODIA	Phnom Penh	13,329,000	Nov. 9, 1953
CAMEROON	Yaoundé	16,380,000	Jan. 1, 1960
CANADA	Ottawa	32,225,000	Dec. 11, 1931
CAPE VERDE	Praia	476,000	July 5, 1975
CENTRAL AFRICAN REPUBLIC	Bangui	4,238,000	Aug. 13, 1960
CHAD	N'Djamena	9,657,000	Aug. 11, 1960
CHILE	Santiago	16,136,000	Sept. 18, 1810
CHINA	Beijing	1,303,701,000	221 B.C.
COLOMBIA	Bogotá	46,039,000	July 20, 1810
COMOROS	Moroni	671,000	July 6, 1975
CONGO	Brazzaville	3,999,000	Aug. 15, 1960
CONGO, DEMOCRATIC REPUBLIC OF THE	Kinshasa	60,764,000	June 30, 1960
COSTA RICA	San José	4,331,000	Sept. 15, 1821
CÔTE D'IVOIRE	Yamoussoukro, Abidjan	18,154,000	Aug. 7, 1960
CROATIA	Zagreb	4,438,000	June 25, 1991
CUBA	Havana	11,275,000	May 20, 1902
CYPRUS	Nicosia	965,000	Aug. 16, 1960
CZECH REPUBLIC	Prague	10,212,000	Jan. 1, 1993
DENMARK	Copenhagen	5,418,000	10th century
DJIBOUTI	Djibouti	793,000	June 27, 1977
DOMINICA	Roseau	70,000	Nov. 3, 1978
DOMINICAN REPUBLIC	Santo Domingo	8,862,000	Feb. 27, 1844
ECUADOR	Quito	13,032,000	May 24, 1822
EGYPT	Cairo	74,033,000	Feb. 28, 1922
EL SALVADOR	San Salvador	6,881,000	Sept. 15, 1821
EQUATORIAL GUINEA	Malabo	504,000	Oct. 12, 1968
ERITREA	Asmara	4,670,000	May 24, 1993
ESTONIA	Tallinn	1,345,000	May 1919
ETHIOPIA	Addis Ababa	77,431,000	circa 1 A.D.
FIJI ISLANDS	Suva	842,000	Oct. 10, 1970
FINLAND	Helsinki	5,246,000	Dec. 6, 1917
FRANCE	Paris	60,742,000	486
GABON	Libreville	1,384,000	Aug. 17, 1960
GAMBIA	Banjul	1,595,000	Feb. 18, 1965
GEORGIA	T'bilisi	4,501,000	April 9, 1991
GERMANY	Berlin	82,490,000	Jan. 18, 1871
GHANA	Accra	22,019,000	Mar. 6, 1957
GREECE	Athens	11,100,000	1829
GRENADA	St. George's	101,000	Feb. 7, 1974
GUATEMALA	Guatemala	12,701,000	Sept. 15, 1821
GUINEA	Conakry	9,453,000	Oct. 2, 1958
GUINEA-BISSAU	Bissau	1,586,000	Sept. 24, 1973
GUYANA	Georgetown	751,000	May 26, 1966
HAITI	Port-au-Prince	8,288,000	Jan. 1, 1804
HONDURAS	Tegucigalpa	7,212,000	Sept. 15, 1821
HUNGARY	Budapest	10,086,000	1001
ICELAND	Reykjavík	295,000	June 17, 1944
INDIA	New Delhi	1,103,596,000	Aug. 15, 1947
INDONESIA	Jakarta	221,932,000	Aug. 17, 1945
IRAN	Tehran	69,515,000	Apr. 1, 1979
IRAQ	Baghdad	28,807,000	Oct. 3, 1932
IRELAND	Dublin	4,125,000	Dec. 6, 1921
ISRAEL	Jerusalem	7,105,000	May 14, 1948
ITALY	Rome	58,742,000	Mar. 17, 1861
JAMAICA	Kingston	2,666,000	Aug. 6, 1962
JAPAN	Tokyo	127,728,000	660 B.C.
JORDAN	Amman	5,795,000	May 25, 1946
KAZAKHSTAN	Astana	15,079,000	Dec. 16, 1991
KENYA	Nairobi	33,830,000	Dec. 12, 1963
KIRIBATI	Tarawa	92,000	July 12, 1979
KOREA, NORTH	Pyongyang	22,912,000	Aug. 15, 1945
KOREA, SOUTH	Seoul	48,294,000	Aug. 15, 1945
KUWAIT	Kuwait	2,589,000	June 19, 1961
KYRGYZSTAN	Bishkek	5,172,000	Aug. 31, 1991
LAOS	Vientiane	5,924,000	July 19, 1949
LATVIA	Riga	2,300,000	Dec. 1919
LEBANON	Beirut	3,779,000	Nov. 22, 1943
LESOTHO	Maseru	1,804,000	Oct. 4, 1966
LIBERIA	Monrovia	3,283,000	July 26, 1847
LIBYA	Tripoli	5,766,000	Dec. 24, 1951
LIECHTENSTEIN	Vaduz	35,000	Jan. 23, 1719
LITHUANIA	Vilnius	3,415,000	April 1919
LUXEMBOURG	Luxembourg	457,000	1839
MACEDONIA	Skopje	2,039,000	Sept. 17, 1991
MADAGASCAR	Antananarivo	17,308,000	June 26, 1960
MALAWI	Lilongwe	12,341,000	July 6, 1964
MALAYSIA	Kuala Lumpur	26,121,000	Aug. 31, 1957
MALDIVES	Male	294,000	July 26, 1965
MALI	Bamako	13,518,000	Sept. 22, 1960
MALTA	Valletta	405,000	Sept. 21, 1964
MARSHALL ISLANDS	Majuro	59,000	Oct. 21, 1986
MAURITANIA	Nouakchott	3,069,000	Nov. 28, 1960
MAURITIUS	Port Louis	1,243,000	Mar. 12, 1968
MEXICO	Mexico	107,029,000	Sept. 16, 1810
MICRONESIA, FEDERATED STATES OF	Palikir	108,000	Nov. 3, 1986
MOLDOVA	Chisinau	4,206,000	Aug. 27, 1991
MONACO	Monaco	33,000	1419
MONGOLIA	Ulaanbaatar	2,646,000	July 11, 1921
MOROCCO	Rabat	30,704,000	Mar. 2, 1956
MOZAMBIQUE	Maputo	19,420,000	June 25, 1975
MYANMAR (BURMA)	Yangon (Rangoon)	50,519,000	Jan. 4, 1948
NAMIBIA	Windhoek	2,031,000	Mar. 21, 1990
NAURU	Yaren	13,000	Jan. 31, 1968
NEPAL	Kathmandu	25,371,000	1768
NETHERLANDS	Amsterdam	16,296,000	1579
NEW ZEALAND	Wellington	4,107,000	Sept. 26, 1907
NICARAGUA	Managua	5,774,000	Sept. 15, 1821
NIGER	Niamey	13,957,000	Aug. 3, 1960

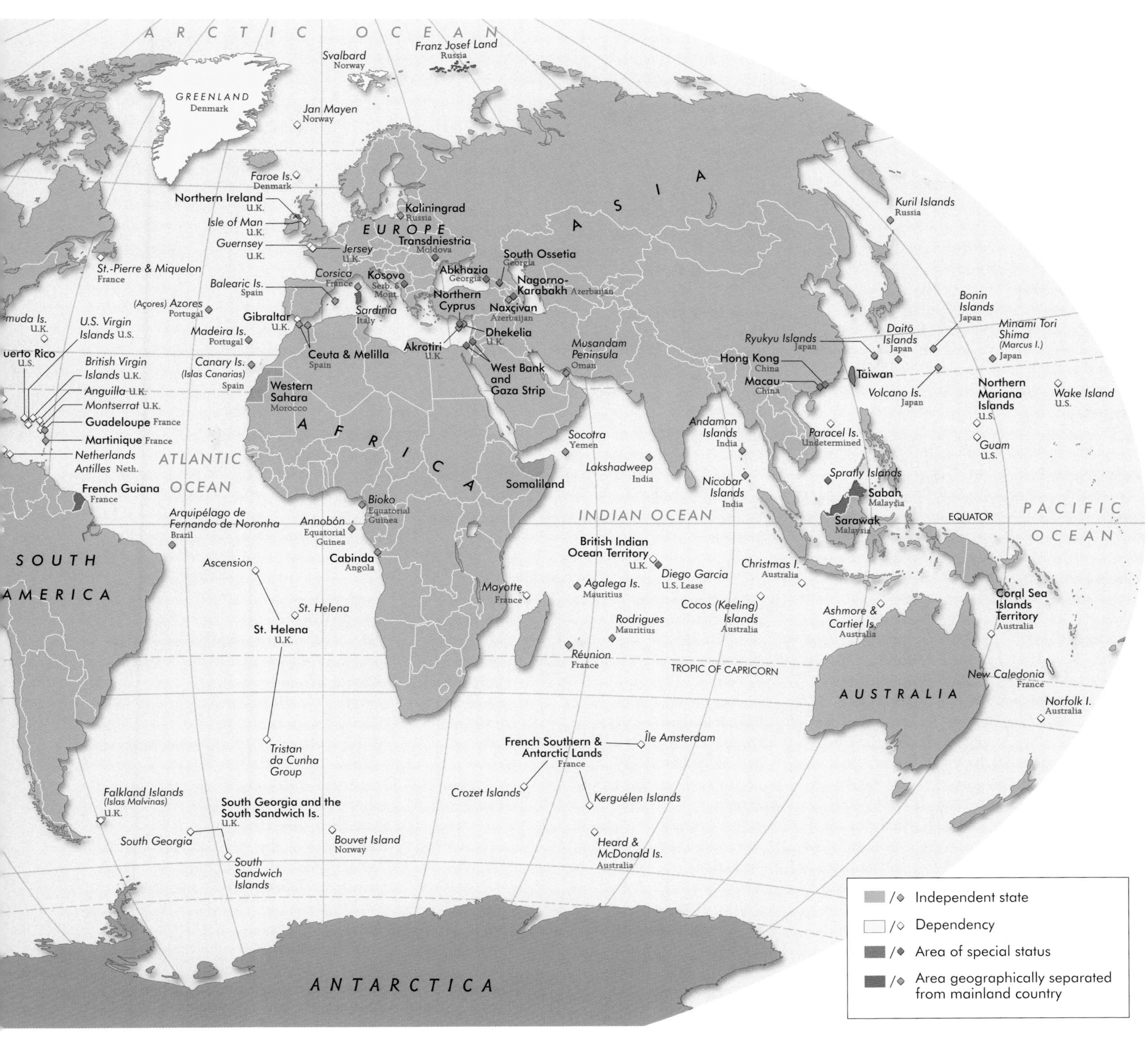

ARCTIC OCEAN
Franz Josef Land
Russia
Svalbard
Norway
GREENLAND
Denmark
Jan Mayen
Norway
Faroe Is.
Denmark
Northern Ireland
U.K.
Isle of Man
U.K.
Guernsey
U.K.
Jersey
U.K.
Kaliningrad
Russia
EUROPE
Transdniestria
Moldova
ASIA
Kuril Islands
Russia
St.-Pierre & Miquelon
France
Corsica
France
Kosovo
Serb. & Mont.
Abkhazia
Georgia
South Ossetia
Georgia
Nagorno-Karabakh
Azerbaijan
Balearic Is.
Spain
(Açores) Azores
Portugal
Sardinia
Italy
Northern Cyprus
Naxçivan
Azerbaijan
Dhekelia
U.K.
Akrotiri
U.K.
Gibraltar
U.K.
Madeira Is.
Portugal
Bermuda Is.
U.K.
U.S. Virgin Islands U.S.
Puerto Rico
U.S.
British Virgin Islands U.K.
Anguilla U.K.
Montserrat U.K.
Guadeloupe France
Martinique France
Netherlands Antilles Neth.
Canary Is.
(Islas Canarias)
Spain
Ceuta & Melilla
Spain
Western Sahara
Morocco
West Bank and Gaza Strip
Musandam Peninsula
Oman
Ryukyu Islands
Japan
Hong Kong
China
Macau
China
Taiwan
Daitō Islands
Japan
Bonin Islands
Japan
Minami Tori Shima
(Marcus I.)
Japan
Volcano Is.
Japan
Northern Mariana Islands
U.S.
Wake Island
U.S.
Guam
U.S.
ATLANTIC OCEAN
AFRICA
Socotra
Yemen
Andaman Islands
India
Paracel Is.
Undetermined
Lakshadweep
India
Nicobar Islands
India
Spratly Islands
Sabah
Malaysia
Sarawak
Malaysia
Somaliland
French Guiana
France
Bioko
Equatorial Guinea
Arquipélago de Fernando de Noronha
Brazil
Annobón
Equatorial Guinea
INDIAN OCEAN
EQUATOR
PACIFIC OCEAN
SOUTH AMERICA
Ascension
Cabinda
Angola
British Indian Ocean Territory
U.K.
Diego Garcia
U.S. Lease
Christmas I.
Australia
Mayotte
France
Agalega Is.
Mauritius
St. Helena
St. Helena
U.K.
Rodrigues
Mauritius
Cocos (Keeling) Islands
Australia
Ashmore & Cartier Is.
Australia
Coral Sea Islands Territory
Australia
Réunion
France
TROPIC OF CAPRICORN
New Caledonia
France
AUSTRALIA
Norfolk I.
Australia
Tristan da Cunha Group
French Southern & Antarctic Lands
France
Île Amsterdam
Crozet Islands
Kerguélen Islands
Falkland Islands
(Islas Malvinas)
U.K.
South Georgia and the South Sandwich Is.
U.K.
South Georgia
Bouvet Island
Norway
Heard & McDonald Is.
Australia
South Sandwich Islands
ANTARCTICA
Independent state
Dependency
Area of special status
Area geographically separated from mainland country

COUNTRY	CAPITAL	2005 POPULATION	DATE OF INDEPENDENCE
NIGERIA	Abuja	131,530,000	Oct. 1, 1960
NORWAY	Oslo	4,620,000	June 7, 1905
OMAN	Muscat	2,436,000	1650
PAKISTAN	Islamabad	162,420,000	Aug. 14, 1947
PALAU	Koror	21,000	Oct. 1, 1994
PANAMA	Panama	3,232,000	Nov. 3, 1903
PAPUA NEW GUINEA	Port Moresby	5,887,000	Sept. 16, 1975
PARAGUAY	Asunción	6,158,000	May 14, 1811
PERU	Lima	27,947,000	July 28, 1821
PHILIPPINES	Manila	84,765,000	July 4, 1946
POLAND	Warsaw	38,163,000	Nov. 11, 1918
PORTUGAL	Lisbon	10,576,000	1140
QATAR	Doha	768,000	Sept. 3, 1971
ROMANIA	Bucharest	21,612,000	Mar. 26, 1881
RUSSIA	Moscow	143,025,000	Aug. 24, 1991
RWANDA	Kigali	8,722,000	July 1, 1962
ST. KITTS AND NEVIS	Basseterre	48,000	Sept. 19, 1983
ST. LUCIA	Castries	163,000	Feb. 22, 1979
ST. VINCENT AND THE GRENADINES	Kingstown	111,000	Oct. 27, 1979
SAMOA	Apia	188,000	Jan. 1, 1962
SAN MARINO	San Marino	30,000	Sept. 3, 301
SAO TOME AND PRINCIPE	São Tomé	153,000	July 12, 1975
SAUDI ARABIA	Riyadh	24,573,000	Sept. 23, 1932
SENEGAL	Dakar	11,658,000	Aug. 20, 1960
SERBIA AND MONTENEGRO	Belgrade, Podgorica	10,722,000	Apr. 27, 1992
SEYCHELLES	Victoria	81,000	June 29, 1976
SIERRA LEONE	Freetown	5,525,000	Apr. 27, 1961
SINGAPORE	Singapore	4,296,000	Aug. 9, 1965
SLOVAKIA	Bratislava	5,382,000	Jan. 1, 1993
SLOVENIA	Ljubljana	1,998,000	June 25, 1991
SOLOMON ISLANDS	Honiara	472,000	July 7, 1978
SOMALIA	Mogadishu	8,592,000	July 1, 1960
SOUTH AFRICA	Pretoria, Cape Town, Bloemfontein	46,923,000	May 31, 1910
SPAIN	Madrid	43,484,000	1492
SRI LANKA	Colombo	19,722,000	Feb. 4, 1948
SUDAN	Khartoum	40,187,000	Jan. 1, 1956
SURINAME	Paramaribo	447,000	Nov. 25, 1975
SWAZILAND	Mbabane, Lobamba	1,138,000	Sept. 6, 1968
SWEDEN	Stockholm	9,029,000	June 6, 1523
SWITZERLAND	Bern	7,446,000	Aug. 1, 1291
SYRIA	Damascus	18,389,000	Apr. 17, 1946
TAJIKISTAN	Dushanbe	6,813,000	Sept. 9, 1991
TANZANIA	Dar es Salaam, Dodoma	36,481,000	Apr. 26, 1964
THAILAND	Bangkok	65,002,000	1238
TIMOR-LESTE (EAST TIMOR)	Dili	947,000	May 20, 2002
TOGO	Lomé	6,145,000	Apr. 27, 1960
TONGA	Nuku'alofa	102,000	June 4, 1970
TRINIDAD AND TOBAGO	Port-of-Spain	1,305,000	Aug. 31, 1962
TUNISIA	Tunis	10,043,000	Mar. 20, 1956
TURKEY	Ankara	72,907,000	Oct. 29, 1923
TURKMENISTAN	Ashgabat	5,240,000	Oct. 27, 1991
TUVALU	Funafuti	10,000	Oct. 1, 1978
UGANDA	Kampala	26,907,000	Oct. 9, 1962
UKRAINE	Kiev	47,110,000	Aug. 24, 1991
UNITED ARAB EMIRATES	Abu Dhabi	4,618,000	Dec. 2, 1971
UNITED KINGDOM	London	60,068,000	10th century
UNITED STATES	Washington, D.C.	296,483,000	July 4, 1776
URUGUAY	Montevideo	3,419,000	Aug. 25, 1825
UZBEKISTAN	Tashkent	26,444,000	Sept. 1, 1991
VANUATU	Port-Vila	218,000	July 30, 1980
VATICAN CITY	Vatican City	1,000	Feb. 11, 1929
VENEZUELA	Caracas	26,749,000	July 5, 1811
VIETNAM	Hanoi	83,305,000	Sept. 2, 1945
YEMEN	Sanaa	20,727,000	May 22, 1990
ZAMBIA	Lusaka	11,227,000	Oct. 24, 1964
ZIMBABWE	Harare	13,010,000	Apr. 18, 1980

DEPENDENCIES OF THE WORLD

DEPENDENCY	POPULATION	LOCATION	CAPITAL OR CHIEF CITY	DEPENDENCY OF	POLITICAL STATUS (SYSTEM)*
AMERICAN SAMOA	63,000	South Pacific Ocean	Pago Pago	United States	Unincorporated territory
ANGUILLA	13,000	Caribbean Sea	The Valley	United Kingdom	Overseas territory
ARUBA	97,000	Caribbean Sea	Oranjestad	Netherlands	Part of the Netherlands (parliamentary democracy)
ASHMORE AND CARTIER ISLANDS	no indigenous inhabitants	Indian Ocean	Administered from Canberra	Australia	Territory
BAKER ISLAND	uninhabited	North Pacific Ocean	Administered from Washington, D.C.	United States	Unincorporated territory
BERMUDA	62,000	North Atlantic Ocean	Hamilton	United Kingdom	Overseas territory (parliamentary government)
BOUVET ISLAND	uninhabited	South Atlantic Ocean	Administered from Oslo	Norway	Territory
BRITISH INDIAN OCEAN TERRITORY[1]	no indigenous inhabitants	Indian Ocean	Administered from London	United Kingdom	Overseas territory
BRITISH VIRGIN ISLANDS	22,000	Caribbean Sea	Road Town	United Kingdom	Overseas territory
CAYMAN ISLANDS	44,000	Caribbean Sea	George Town	United Kingdom	Overseas territory (British crown colony)
CHRISTMAS ISLAND	500	Indian Ocean	The Settlement	Australia	Territory
CLIPPERTON	uninhabited	North Pacific Ocean	Administered from French Polynesia	France	Possession of France
COCOS (KEELING) ISLANDS	600	Indian Ocean	West Island	Australia	Territory
COOK ISLANDS	13,000	South Pacific Ocean	Avarua	New Zealand	Free association with New Zealand (parliamentary democracy)
CORAL SEA ISLANDS TERRITORY	no indigenous inhabitants	South Pacific Ocean	Administered from Canberra	Australia	Territory
FALKLAND ISLANDS[2]	3,000	South Atlantic Ocean	Stanley	United Kingdom	Overseas territory
FAROE ISLANDS	50,000	North Atlantic Ocean	Tórshavn	Denmark	Part of Denmark (self-governing overseas division)
FRENCH POLYNESIA	255,000	South Pacific Ocean	Papeete	France	Overseas territory
FRENCH SOUTHERN AND ANTARCTIC LANDS[3]	no indigenous inhabitants	Indian Ocean	Administered from Paris	France	Overseas territory
GIBRALTAR	29,000	Europe	Gibraltar	United Kingdom	Overseas territory
GREENLAND (KALAALLIT NUNAAT)	57,000	North Atlantic Ocean	Nuuk (Godthåb)	Denmark	Part of Denmark (self-governing overseas division)
GUAM	169,000	North Pacific Ocean	Hagåtña (Agana)	United States	Unincorporated territory
GUERNSEY (Channel Islands)[4]	65,000	English Channel	St. Peter Port	United Kingdom	British crown dependency
HEARD AND MCDONALD ISLANDS	uninhabited	Indian Ocean	Administered from Canberra	Australia	Territory
HOWLAND ISLAND	uninhabited	North Pacific Ocean	Administered from Washington, D.C.	United States	Unincorporated territory
ISLE OF MAN	78,000	Irish Sea	Douglas	United Kingdom	British crown dependency (parliamentary democracy)
JAN MAYEN[5]	no indigenous inhabitants	Norwegian Sea	Administered from Oslo	Norway	Territory
JARVIS ISLAND	uninhabited	South Pacific Ocean	Administered from Washington, D.C.	United States	Unincorporated territory
JERSEY (Channel Islands)	91,000	English Channel	St. Helier	United Kingdom	British crown dependency
JOHNSTON ATOLL	uninhabited	North Pacific Ocean	Administered from Washington, D.C.	United States	Unincorporated territory
KINGMAN REEF	uninhabited	North Pacific Ocean	Administered from Washington, D.C.	United States	Unincorporated territory
MAYOTTE	181,000	Mozambique Channel	Mamoudzou	France	Territorial collectivity
MIDWAY ISLANDS	no indigenous inhabitants	North Pacific Ocean	Administered from Washington, D.C.	United States	Unincorporated territory
MONTSERRAT	5,000	Caribbean Sea	Plymouth (abandoned)	United Kingdom	Overseas territory
NAVASSA ISLAND	uninhabited	Caribbean Sea	Administered from Washington, D.C.	United States	Unincorporated territory
NETHERLANDS ANTILLES[6]	187,000	Caribbean Sea	Willemstad	Netherlands	Part of the Netherlands (parliamentary government)
NEW CALEDONIA	227,000	South Pacific Ocean	Nouméa	France	Overseas territory
NIUE	1,600	South Pacific Ocean	Alofi	New Zealand	Free association with New Zealand (parliamentary democracy)
NORFOLK ISLAND	2,000	South Pacific Ocean	Kingston	Australia	Territory
NORTHERN MARIANA ISLANDS	80,000	North Pacific Ocean	Saipan	United States	Commonwealth in political union with the U.S. (commonwealth government)
PALMYRA ATOLL	no indigenous inhabitants	North Pacific Ocean	Administered from Washington, D.C.	United States	Incorporated territory
PARACEL ISLANDS[7]	no indigenous inhabitants	South China Sea	Administered from China	undetermined	NA
PITCAIRN ISLANDS	45	South Pacific Ocean	Adamstown	United Kingdom	Overseas territory
PUERTO RICO	3,912,000	Caribbean Sea	San Juan	United States	Commonwealth associated with the U.S. (commonwealth government)
ST. HELENA[8]	6,000	South Atlantic Ocean	Jamestown	United Kingdom	Overseas territory
SAINT-PIERRE AND MIQUELON	7,000	North Atlantic Ocean	Saint-Pierre	France	Self-governing territorial collectivity
SOUTH GEORGIA AND THE SOUTH SANDWICH ISLANDS[2]	no indigenous inhabitants	South Atlantic Ocean	Administered from Stanley	United Kingdom	Overseas territory
SVALBARD	2,700	Arctic Ocean	Longyearbyen	Norway	Territory
TOKELAU	1,500	South Pacific Ocean	Administered from Wellington	New Zealand	Territory
TURKS AND CAICOS ISLANDS	21,000	North Atlantic Ocean	Cockburn Town (on Grand Turk Island)	United Kingdom	Overseas territory
U.S. VIRGIN ISLANDS	109,000	Caribbean Sea	Charlotte Amalie	United States	Unincorporated territory
WAKE ISLAND	no indigenous inhabitants	North Pacific Ocean	Administered from Washington	United States	Unincorporated territory
WALLIS AND FUTUNA ISLANDS	15,000	South Pacific Ocean	Matâ'utu	France	Overseas territory

NOTES TO DEPENDENCIES OF THE WORLD

* *The political status of dependencies is based on the designation provided by the administering country. The variety of political designations reflects the diverse nature of the relationship dependencies have with their controlling countries.*

[1] Chagos Archipelago

[2] Dependent territory of the United Kingdom (also claimed by Argentina).

[3] The French Southern and Antarctic Lands dependency includes Île Amsterdam, Île Saint-Paul, the Crozet Islands, and the Kerguélen Islands in the southern Indian Ocean. It also includes Terre Adélie, the French-claimed sector of Antarctica; the French claim to this region is not internationally recognized, however (see "Areas of Special Status," opposite, for information on claims to Antarctica).

[4] The Bailiwick of Guernsey includes the islands of Alderney, Guernsey, Herm, and Sark, as well as smaller islands nearby.

[5] Jan Mayen is administered from Oslo, Norway, through a governor resident in Longyearbyen, Svalbard.

[6] Netherlands Antilles comprises two groupings of islands: Curaçao and Bonaire are located off the coast of Venezuela; Saba, Sint Eustatius, and Sint Maarten (the Dutch two-fifths of the island of Saint Martin) lie 500 miles (800 km) to the northeast.

[7] South China Sea islands are occupied by China but claimed by Vietnam.

[8] The territory of Saint Helena includes the island group of Tristan da Cunha, far to the southwest Saint Helena also administers Ascension Island, lying to the northwest.

AREAS OF SPECIAL STATUS

AREA	POPULATION	LOCATION
ABKHAZIA	537,500	Part of Georgia

Following the collapse of the Soviet Union in 1991 and Georgia's subsequent independence, the Abkhazian parliament declared its sovereignty and restoration of its 1925 constitution. In 1992 Georgian troops invaded, but by 1993 the Georgian government lost control of the entire area of Abkhazia. Years of negotiations have not resulted in movement toward a settlement.

ANTARCTICA **no indigenous inhabitants** **Territory south of 60 degrees south latitude**

Seven countries claim Antarctic territory, but these claims are not legally recognized by the Antarctic Treaty of 1959. This treaty prohibits military activities and dedicates Antarctica to peaceful use and free exchange of scientific information. Individual nations maintain bases, and the research projects they support typically involve collaborators from many countries.

DIEGO GARCIA **military base** **Indian Ocean**

Diego Garcia constitutes the southernmost island of the British Indian Ocean Territory, a dependency of Great Britain. In 1966, the United States leased Diego Garcia for 50 years and established a joint military base with Great Britain on the island. The U.S. lease will expire in 2016. Diego Garcia, along with the Chagos Archipelago, is claimed by Mauritius.

GUANTÁNAMO BAY **military base** **Cuba**

After helping Cuba gain independence in 1902, the United States leased 45 square miles (116 sq km) of territory around Guantánamo Bay. This lease was reaffirmed in a 1934 treaty stipulating that the return of Guantánamo Bay to Cuba could only be arranged through the mutual consent of the U.S. and Cuba. Though Guantánamo Bay remains sovereign Cuban territory, the American lease does not have a termination date.

HONG KONG **6,921,000** **Part of China**

Hong Kong became a Special Administrative Region (SAR) of China on July 1, 1997. China has promised that under its "one country, two systems" formula, China's socialist economic system will not be practiced in Hong Kong and that Hong Kong will enjoy a high degree of autonomy in all matters, except foreign and defense affairs, for the next 50 years.

KOSOVO **2,473,000** **Part of Serbia and Montenegro**

Hostilities broke out in Kosovo in 1998. Ethnic Albanians, who make up 90 percent of the local population, sought an independent state, while Serbs fought to keep Kosovo part of Serbia and Montenegro. NATO air strikes helped bring about an agreement to end the fighting, and the UN began administering Kosovo in June 1999.

MACAU **474,000** **Part of China**

After more than 400 years as a Portuguese outpost, Macau reverted to China in December 1999 as a Special Administrative Region, a status it will maintain for 50 years. Like Hong Kong, it enjoys a high degree of autonomy in all matters except foreign and defense affairs.

NAGORNO-KARABAKH **192,400** **Part of Azerbaijan**

A predominantly ethnic Armenian enclave within Azerbaijan, Nagorno-Karabakh sought to unite with Armenia in 1988. Azerbaijani forces attempted to reestablish control in 1992, but were met with fierce resistance. More than 30,000 have died and over a million people have been displaced as a result of the fighting. A cease-fire was signed in 1994, and international efforts to resolve the conflict are ongoing.

NORTHERN CYPRUS **200,000** **Eastern Mediterranean Sea**

Following a Greek-led coup and the landing of Turkish forces on the island in 1974, Cyprus split into two hostile territories. The internationally recognized Greek Cypriot government controls the southern portion of the island whereas Turkish Cypriots, bolstered by a Turkish military force, control the northern portion. Turkish Cypriots unilaterally declared independence in 1983, but their claims have not been recognized by any nation other than Turkey.

SOMALILAND **3,500,000** **Horn of Africa**

The government of Somalia collapsed in 1991, after a bloody civil war. Somaliland claims independence and governs some three million people in the north—an area that roughly corresponds to the former British Somaliland. The United Nations does not recognize Somaliland as an independent state.

SOUTH OSSETIA **99,800** **Part of Georgia**

In 1990 South Ossetia, wishing to unite with North Ossetia in the Russian Federation, declared independence from Georgia. Armed clashes resulted between Georgian forces and separatists. A cease-fire was signed in 1992, but peace remains fragile.

SPRATLY ISLANDS **no indigenous inhabitants** **South China Sea**

The scattered islands and reefs known as the Spratly Islands are claimed in part by Brunei, Malaysia, the Philippines, and entirely by China, Taiwan, and Vietnam.

TAIWAN **22,731,000** **Southeast of China**

The People's Republic of China claims the island of Taiwan as its 23rd province. The government of Taiwan (Republic of China) maintains that there is one China—but two political entities.

TRANSDNIESTRIA **634,000** **Part of Moldova**

In 1992 separatist forces, made up largely of Ukrainian and Russian minorities, declared a "Dniester Republic" between the east bank of the Dniester River and the Ukrainian border. Armed conflict occurred between Moldovan government forces and Transdniestrian separatists. Negotiations to resolve the conflict continue, and a cease-fire is still in effect.

WEST BANK AND GAZA STRIP **3,762,000** **Adjacent to Israel**

The West Bank and Gaza Strip were captured by Israel in the 1967 Six Day War. A peace agreement was signed in 1993, which gave areas of the West Bank and Gaza Strip limited Palestinian autonomy. In August of 2005 Israel evacuated the Gaza Strip, removing settlers and military personnel. The future of the autonomous regions, and more than 3.7 million Palestinians, are subject to Israeli-Palestinian negotiations.

WESTERN SAHARA **341,000** **Southwest of Morocco**

Formerly Spanish Sahara, Western Sahara was annexed by Morocco in the late 1970s and brought under Moroccan administration. The Polisario Front, a resistance group that repudiated Moroccan sovereignty, fought a guerrilla war that ended in a 1991 cease-fire administered by the United Nations. A referendum on the final status of Western Sahara has repeatedly been postponed.

AREAS GEOGRAPHICALLY SEPARATED FROM MAINLAND COUNTRIES

REGION	POPULATION	COUNTRY	LOCATION
AGALEGA ISLANDS	300	Mauritius	Indian Ocean
AKROTIRI	military base	United Kingdom	Cyprus
ALASKA	664,000	United States	North America
ANDAMAN ISLANDS	314,000	India	Indian Ocean
ANNOBÓN	5,000	Equatorial Guinea	Gulf of Guinea
ARQUIPÉLAGO DE FERNANDO DE NORONHA	2,100	Brazil	South Atlantic Ocean
AZORES	241,000	Portugal	North Atlantic Ocean
BALEARIC ISLANDS	982,000	Spain	Mediterranean Sea
BIOKO	260,000	Equatorial Guinea	Gulf of Guinea
BONIN ISLANDS	2,800	Japan	North Pacific Ocean
CABINDA	100,000	Angola	Africa
CANARY ISLANDS	1,938,000	Spain	North Atlantic Ocean
CEUTA AND MELILLA	138,000	Spain	North Africa
CHATHAM ISLANDS	700	New Zealand	South Pacific Ocean
CORSICA	268,000	France	Mediterranean Sea
DAITO ISLANDS	2,100	Japan	North Pacific Ocean
DHEKELIA	military base	United Kingdom	Cyprus
EASTER ISLAND	4,000	Chile	South Pacific Ocean
FRANZ JOSEF LAND	not permanently inhabited	Russia	Arctic Ocean
FRENCH GUIANA	195,000	France	South America
GALÁPAGOS ISLANDS	19,000	Ecuador	Pacific Ocean
GUADELOUPE	450,000	France	Caribbean Sea
HAWAI'I	1,275,000	United States	North Pacific Ocean
KALININGRAD	955,000	Russia	Europe
KURIL ISLANDS	30,000	Russia	North Pacific Ocean
LAKSHADWEEP	61,000	India	Indian Ocean
MADEIRA ISLANDS	244,000	Portugal	North Atlantic Ocean
MARTINIQUE	397,000	France	Caribbean Sea
MUSANDAM PENINSULA	28,000	Oman	Arabian Peninsula
NAXÇIVAN	370,000	Azerbaijan	Asia
NICOBAR ISLANDS	42,000	India	Indian Ocean
NORTHERN IRELAND	1,710,000	United Kingdom	Ireland
RÉUNION	782,000	France	Indian Ocean
RODRIGUES	36,000	Mauritius	Indian Ocean
RYUKYU ISLANDS	1,492,000	Japan	North Pacific Ocean
SABAH AND SARAWAK	4,675,000	Malaysia	Borneo
SARDINIA	1,650,000	Italy	Mediterranean Sea
SOCOTRA	44,000	Yemen	Indian Ocean
VOLCANO ISLANDS	no indigenous inhabitants	Japan	North Pacific Ocean

DISCLAIMER

The list of geographically separate areas includes places that do not fit conveniently into any of the three previous categories. Politically, these areas are integral parts of independent countries; thus, they are not dependencies. Nor are they areas of special status. They warrant inclusion in this category simply because they lie a significant distance, across either land or water, from the rest of their countries' land areas. In compiling this list, we chose to include only the areas that are populated at least part of the year. This means that we have not listed myriad uninhabited islands. Determining exactly what constitutes sufficient geographical separation to justify inclusion involves a certain degree of subjectivity. For this reason, the fourth category of Earth's lands should not be considered an official grouping. Instead, it should be viewed only as one way of classifying areas that do not fall neatly into the three other categories—but which are significant enough to deserve special attention.

Special Flags

IF WE COULD BRING A SNAPSHOT back from the future, few images would tell us more about what lies ahead than a flag chart showing the banners of all countries. The independence of new nations, the breakup of empires, even changing political and religious currents—all would be reflected in the symbols and colors of the national flags. This is dramatically evident in the changing flag of the United States (below), but similar visual statements could be made for most countries.

Germany provides another example. In the Middle Ages a gold banner with a black eagle proclaimed its Holy Roman Emperor a successor to the Caesars. A united 19th-century German Empire adopted a black-white-red tricolor for Bismarck's "blood and iron" policies. The liberal Weimar and Federal Republics (1919-1933 and since 1949) hailed a black-red-gold tricolor. The dark years from 1933 to 1945 were under the swastika flag of the Nazi regime. These and similar flags in other countries are more than visual aids to history: Their development and use are a fundamental part of the political and social life of a community.

Like maps, flags are ways to communicate information in condensed form. The study of geography is paralleled by the study of flags, known as vexillology (from the Latin word vexillum, for "small sail" or flag). Books, journals, Web sites, and other sources convey information on vexillology; there are also organizations and institutions around the world linked by the International Federation of Vexillological Associations. Even very young students can gain understanding of countries, populations, political changes, religious movements, and historical events by learning about flags.

All flags embody myths and historical facts, whether they are displayed at the Olympic Games, carried by protesters, placed at a roadside shrine, or arrayed at a ceremony of national significance, such as a presidential inauguration. Flags are powerful symbols, attractive to groups of all kinds; hence their once prominent display by Nazis and Communists to manipulate the masses, their waving by the East Timorese after a successful struggle for independence, and their spontaneous use by people in the United States after September 11, 2001.

Flags of nations may be the most significant flags today, but they are far from the only ones. Sport teams, business enterprises, religious groups, ethnic groups, schools, and international organizations frequently rally, reward, and inspire people through the use of flags. An observant person will also notice advertising banners, nautical signals, warning flags, decorative pennants, the rank flags of important individuals, and many related symbols such as coats of arms and logos. Examples of flags, as presented on these two pages, only hint at the rich possibilities of design, usage, and symbolism. The vexillophile (flag hobbyist) can easily and inexpensively acquire a substantial collection of flags and flag-related items. The vexillographer (flag designer) can create flags for self or family, club or team, or even for a city or county. The vexillologist (flag scholar) will find endless connections between flags and history, political science, communications theory, social behavior, and other areas. As with geography, the knowledge gained by a study of flags can be a richly rewarding personal experience.

Development of the Stars and Stripes

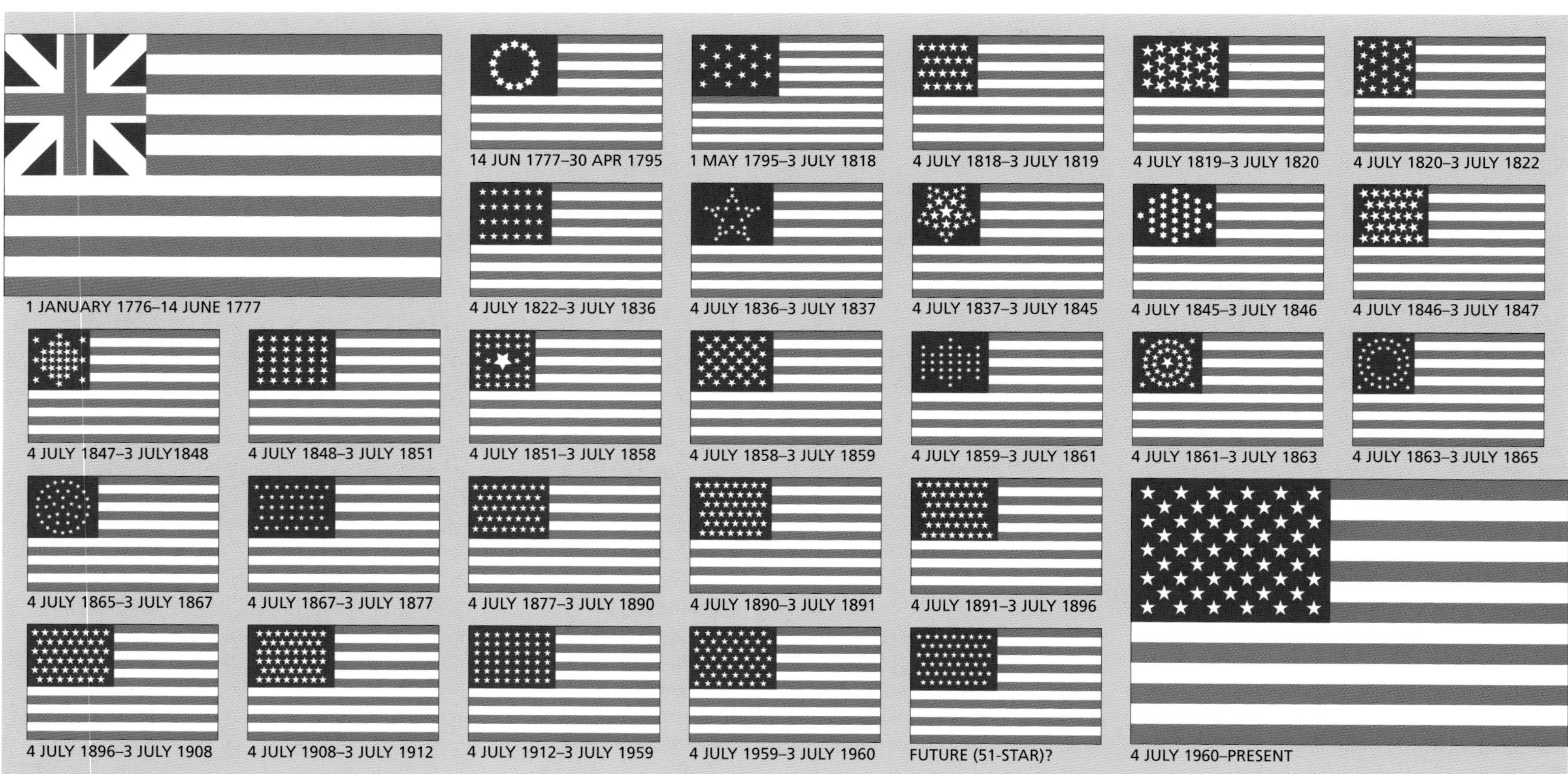

1 JANUARY 1776–14 JUNE 1777
14 JUN 1777–30 APR 1795
1 MAY 1795–3 JULY 1818
4 JULY 1818–3 JULY 1819
4 JULY 1819–3 JULY 1820
4 JULY 1820–3 JULY 1822
4 JULY 1822–3 JULY 1836
4 JULY 1836–3 JULY 1837
4 JULY 1837–3 JULY 1845
4 JULY 1845–3 JULY 1846
4 JULY 1846–3 JULY 1847
4 JULY 1847–3 JULY1848
4 JULY 1848–3 JULY 1851
4 JULY 1851–3 JULY 1858
4 JULY 1858–3 JULY 1859
4 JULY 1859–3 JULY 1861
4 JULY 1861–3 JULY 1863
4 JULY 1863–3 JULY 1865
4 JULY 1865–3 JULY 1867
4 JULY 1867–3 JULY 1877
4 JULY 1877–3 JULY 1890
4 JULY 1890–3 JULY 1891
4 JULY 1891–3 JULY 1896
4 JULY 1896–3 JULY 1908
4 JULY 1908–3 JULY 1912
4 JULY 1912–3 JULY 1959
4 JULY 1959–3 JULY 1960
FUTURE (51-STAR)?
4 JULY 1960–PRESENT

No country has changed its flag as frequently as the United States. The Continental Colors (top left) represented the Colonies during the early years of the American Revolution. Its British Union Jack, which signified loyalty to the crown, was replaced on June 14, 1777, by "13 stars...representing a new constellation." Congressman Francis Hopkinson was the designer.

The number of stars and stripes was increased to 15 in 1795. In 1817 Congressman Peter Wendover wrote the current flag law. The number of stripes was permanently limited to 13; the stars were to correspond to the number of states, with new stars added to the flag the following Fourth of July.

Star arrangement was not specified, however, and throughout the 19th century a variety of exuberant star designs—"great luminaries," rings, ovals, and diamonds—were actually used. With the increasing number of states, the modern alternating rows of stars became standard. Finally, in 1912, President Taft set forth exact regulations for all flag details.

If a new state joins the Union, a 51-star flag will be needed. There is a logical design for it: alternating rows of nine and eight stars, as shown above.

International Flags

MOURNING
The black flag signals death, piracy, protest, and danger. It is also a symbol of mourning for the dead.

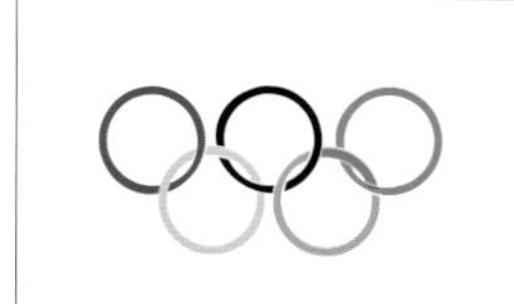

OLYMPIC GAMES
The colors refer to those in the national flags of participating countries. The Olympic flag was created in 1913.

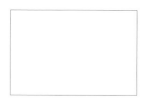

RED CRESCENT
In Muslim nations, Geneva Convention organizations rejected the red cross in favor of a red crescent, officially recognized in 1906.

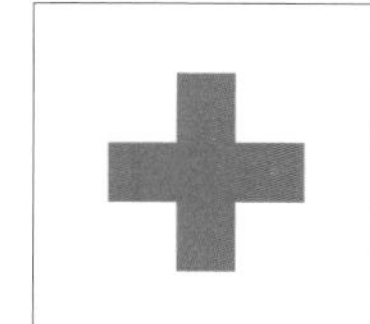

RED CROSS
The Geneva Convention chose its symbol and flag in 1864 to identify people, vehicles, and buildings protected during wartime.

TRUCE/PEACE
For a thousand years a white flag has served as a symbol of truce, surrender, noncombatant status, neutrality, and peace.

UNITED NATIONS
Olive branches of peace and a world map form the symbol adopted by the United Nations in 1946. The flag dates from 1947.

Regional Flags

ARAB LEAGUE
The color green and the crescent are often symbols in member countries of the League of Arab States, founded in 1945.

ASEAN
A stylized bundle of rice, the principal local crop, appears on the flag of the Association of South East Asian Nations (ASEAN).

COMMONWEALTH
Once the British Empire, the modern Commonwealth under this flag informally links countries with common goals.

EUROPEAN UNION
The number of stars for this flag, adopted in 1955, is permanently set at 12. The ring is a symbol for unity.

OAS
Flags of member nations appear on the flag of the Organization of American States; each new member prompts a flag change.

PACIFIC COMMISSION
The palm tree, surf, and sailboat are found in all of the member nations; each star on the flag represents a country.

Religious Flags

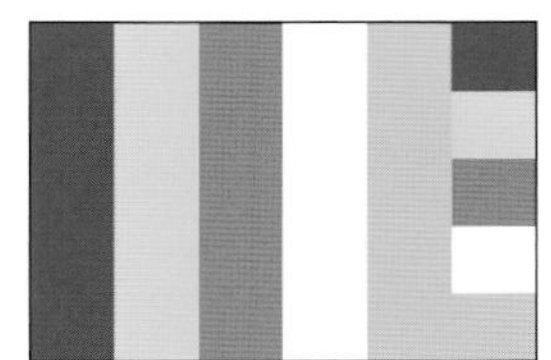

BUDDHISM
Designed in 1885 by Henry Olcott of the United States, the Buddhist flag features the auras associated with the Buddha.

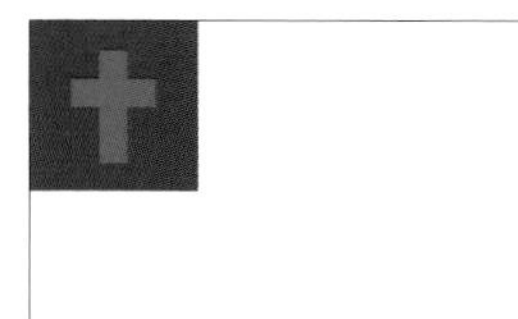

CHRISTIANITY
The sacrifice of Christ on the Cross is heralded in this 1897 flag, which features a white field for purity.

ISLAM
"There Is No God But Allah and Muhammad Is the Prophet of Allah" is written on this widely used but unofficial flag.

Ethnic Flags

LA RAZA
Crosses for the ships of Columbus and a golden Inca sun recall the Spanish and Indian heritage of Latin Americans.

PALESTINIANS
Since 1922 Palestinians have used this flag, with traditional Arab dynastic colors, as a symbol of the statehood they desire.

ROMA (GYPSIES)
Against a background of blue sky and green grass, a wheel represents the vehicles (and homes) of the nomadic Roma people.

Specialized Flags

ANARCHISTS
Opposition to all forms of authority is hinted at in the "hand-drawn" rendition of an encircled A in the anarchist flag.

BLUE FLAG
The campaign for the improvement of the environment presents this flag as an award for success.

BOY SCOUTS
Created in 1961, this flag shows the traditional Boy Scout fleur-de-lis within a rope tied with a reef knot.

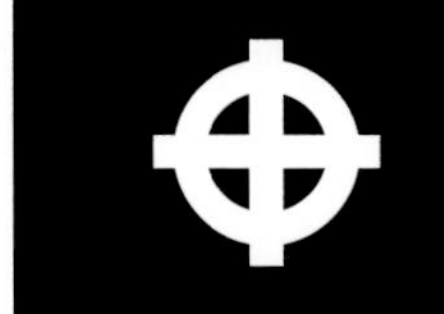

CIRCLE CROSS
This ancient religious symbol, related to the swastika, is widely used as a neo-Nazi symbol in Europe and North America.

CONFEDERATE BATTLE FLAG
In many countries this flag represents protest against established authority in culture, politics, and lifestyle.

DIVERS FLAG
As a warning signal to other boats, this flag flies wherever divers are underwater nearby—and at divers' clubhouses.

ESPERANTO
On the flag promoting Esperanto as a world language, a star signifies unity; green, traditionally, is a symbol of hope.

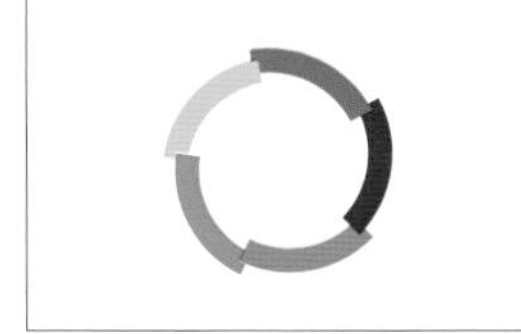

FRANCOPHONIE
French speakers share their common language and culture in periodic conferences and activities held under this flag.

GAY PRIDE
The Rainbow Flag, in various configurations, has been flown since 1978 by the gay and lesbian community and their families.

GIRL SCOUTS
The trefoil with a compass needle adorns the World Flag of Girl Guides and Girl Scouts, which was adopted in May 1991.

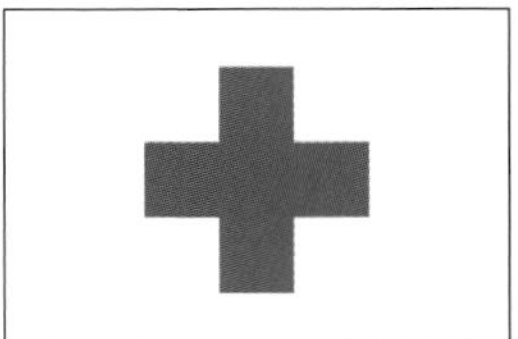

GREEN CROSS
Organizations that display this flag promote public safety in natural disasters, transportation, and the workplace.

MASONS
The unofficial flag of the Masons displays their traditional logo with symbolic square and compass.

Aaglet *well*
Aain *spring*
Aauinat *spring*
Āb *river, water*
Ache *stream*
Açude *reservoir*
Ada,-si *island*
Adrar *mountain-s, plateau*
Aguada *dry lake bed*
Aguelt *water hole, well*
'Ain, Aïn *spring, well*
Aïoun-et *spring-s, well*
Aivi *mountain*
Ákra, Akrotírion *cape, promontory*
Alb *mountain, ridge*
Alföld *plain*
Alin' *mountain range*
Alpe-n *mountain-s*
Altiplanicie *high-plain, plateau*
Alto *hill-s, mountain-s, ridge*
Älv-en *river*
Āmba *hill, mountain*
Anou *well*
Anse *bay, inlet*
Ao *bay, cove, estuary*
Ap *cape, point*
Archipel, Archipiélago *archipelago*
Arcipelago, Arkhipelag *archipelago*
Arquipélago *archipelago*
Arrecife-s *reef-s*
Arroio, Arroyo *brook, gully, rivulet, stream*
Ås *ridge*
Ava *channel*
Aylagy *gulf*
'Ayn *spring, well*

Ba *intermittent stream, river*
Baai *bay, cove, lagoon*
Bāb *gate, strait*
Badia *bay*
Bælt *strait*
Bagh *bay*
Bahar *drainage basin*
Bahía *bay*
Bahr, Baḩr *bay, lake, river, sea, wadi*
Baía, Baie *bay*
Bajo-s *shoal-s*
Ban *village*
Bañado-s *flooded area, swamp-s*
Banc, Banco-s *bank-s, sandbank-s, shoal-s*
Band *lake*
Bandao *peninsula*
Baño-s *hot spring-s, spa*
Baraj-ı *dam, reservoir*
Barra *bar, sandbank*
Barrage, Barragem *dam, lake, reservoir*
Barranca *gorge, ravine*
Bazar *marketplace*
Ben, Benin *mountain*
Belt *strait*
Bereg *bank, coast, shore*
Berg-e *mountain-s*
Bil *lake*
Biq'at *plain, valley*
Bir, Bîr, Bi'r *spring, well*
Birket *lake, pool, swamp*
Bjerg-e *mountain-s, range*
Boca, Bocca *channel, river, mouth*
Bocht *bay*
Bodden *bay*
Boğaz, -i *strait*
Bögeni *reservoir*
Boka *gulf, mouth*
Bol'sh-oy, -aya, -oye *big*
Bolsón *inland basin*
Boubairet *lagoon, lake*
Bras *arm, branch of a stream*
Braţ, -ul *arm, branch of a stream*
Bre, -en *glacier, ice cap*
Bredning *bay, broad water*
Bruch *marsh*
Bucht *bay*
Bugt-en *bay*
Buḩayrat, Buheirat *lagoon, lake, marsh*
Bukhta, Bukta, Bukt-en *bay*
Bulak, Bulaq *spring*
Bum *hill, mountain*
Burnu, Burun *cape, point*
Busen *gulf*
Buuraha *hill-s, mountain-s*
Buyuk *big, large*

Cabeza-s *head-s, summit-s*
Cabo *cape*
Cachoeira *rapids, waterfall*
Cal *hill, peak*
Caleta *cove, inlet*
Campo-s *field-s, flat country*
Canal *canal, channel, strait*
Caño *channel, stream*
Cao Nguyen *mountain, plateau*
Cap, Capo *cape*
Capitán *captain*
Càrn *mountain*
Castillo *castle, fort*
Catarata-s *cataract-s, waterfall-s*
Causse *upland*
Çay *brook, stream*
Cay-s, Cayo-s *island-s, key-s, shoal-s*
Cerro-s *hill-s, peak-s*
Chaîne, Chaînons *mountain chain, range*
Chapada-s *plateau, upland-s*
Chedo *archipelago*
Chenal *river channel*
Chersónisos *peninsula*
Chhung *bay*
Chi *lake*
Chiang *bay*
Chiao *cape, point, rock*
Ch'ih *lake*
Chink *escarpment*
Chott *intermittent salt lake, salt marsh*
Chou *island*
Ch'ü *canal*
Ch'üntao *archipelago, islands*
Chute-s *cataract-s, waterfall-s*
Chyrvony *red*
Cima *mountain, peak, summit*
Ciudad *city*
Co *lake*
Col *pass*
Collina, Colline *hill, mountains*
Con *island*
Cordillera *mountain chain*
Corno *mountain, peak*
Coronel *colonel*
Corredeira *cascade, rapids*
Costa *coast*
Côte *coast, slope*
Coxilha, Cuchilla *range of low hills*
Crique *creek, stream*
Csatorna *canal, channel*
Cul de Sac *bay, inlet*

Da *great, greater*
Daban *pass*
Dağ, -ı, Dagh *mountain*
Dağlar, -ı *mountains*
Dahr *cliff, mesa*
Dake *mountain, peak*
Dal-en *valley*
Dala *steppe*
Dan *cape, point*
Danau *lake*
Dao *island*
Dar'ya *lake, river*
Daryācheh *lake, marshy lake*
Dasht *desert, plain*
Dawan *pass*
Dawḩat *bay, cove, inlet*
Deniz, -i *sea*
Dent-s *peak-s*
Deo *pass*
Desēt *hummock, island, land-tied island*
Desierto *desert*
Détroit *channel, strait*
Dhar *hills, ridge, tableland*
Ding *mountain*
Distrito *district*
Djebel *mountain, range*
Do *island-s, rock-s*
Doi *hill, mountain*
Dome *ice dome*
Dong *village*
Dooxo *floodplain*
Dzong *castle, fortress*

Eiland-en *island-s*
Eilean *island*
Ejland *island*
Elv *river*
Embalse *lake, reservoir*
Emi *mountain, rock*
Enseada, Ensenada *bay, cove*
Ér *rivulet, stream*
Erg *sand dune region*
Est *east*
Estación *railroad station*
Estany *lagoon, lake*
Estero *estuary, inlet, lagoon, marsh*
Estrecho *strait*
Étang *lake, pond*
Eylandt *island*
Ežeras *lake*
Ezers *lake*

Falaise *cliff, escarpment*
Farvand-et *channel, sound*
Fell *mountain*
Feng *mount, peak*
Fiord-o *inlet, sound*
Fiume *river*
Fjäll-et *mountain*
Fjällen *mountains*
Fjärd-en *fjord*
Fjardar, Fjördur *fjord*
Fjeld *mountain*
Fjell-ene *mountain-s*
Fjöll *mountain-s*
Fjord-en *inlet, fjord*
Fleuve *river*
Fljót *large river*
Flói *bay, marshland*
Foci *river mouths*
Főcsatorna *principal canal*
Förde *fjord, gulf, inlet*
Forsen *rapids, waterfall*
Fortaleza *fort, fortress*
Fortín *fortified post*
Foss-en *waterfall*
Foum *pass, passage*
Foz *mouth of a river*
Fuerte *fort, fortress*
Fwafwate *waterfalls*

Gacan-ka *hill, peak*
Gal *pond, spring, waterhole, well*
Gang *harbor*
Gangri *peak, range*
Gaoyuan *plateau*
Garaet, Gara'et *lake, lake bed, salt lake*
Gardaneh *pass*
Garet *hill, mountain*
Gat *channel*
Gata *bay, inlet, lake*
Gattet *channel, strait*
Gaud *depression, saline tract*
Gave *mountain stream*
Gebel *mountain-s, range*
Gebergte *mountain range*
Gebirge *mountains, range*
Geçidi *mountain pass, passage*
Geçit *mountain pass, passage*
Gezâir *islands*
Gezîra-t, Gezîret *island, peninsula*
Ghats *mountain range*
Ghubb-at, -et *bay, gulf*
Giri *mountain*
Gletscher *glacier*
Gobernador *governor*
Gobi *desert*
Gol *river, stream*
Göl, -ü *lake*
Golets *mountain, peak*
Golf, -e, -o *gulf*
Gor-a, -y, Gór-a, -y *mountain,-s*
Got *point*
Gowd *depression*
Goz *sand ridge*
Gran, -de *great, large*
Gryada *mountains, ridge*
Guan *pass*
Guba *bay, gulf*
Guelta *well*
Guntō *archipelago*
Gunung *mountain*
Gura *mouth, passage*
Guyot *table mount*

Haḍabat *plateau*
Haehyŏp *strait*
Haff *lagoon*
Hai *lake, sea*
Haihsia *strait*
Haixia *channel, strait*
Hakau *reef, rock*
Hakuchi *anchorage*
Halvø, Halvøy-a *peninsula*
Hama *beach*
Hamada, Ḩammādah *rocky desert*
Hamn *harbor, port*
Hāmūn, Hamun *depression, lake*
Hana *cape, point*
Hantō *peninsula*
Har *hill, mound, mountain*
Ḩarrat *lava field*
Hasi, Hassi *spring, well*
Hauteur *elevation, height*
Hav-et *sea*
Havn, Havre *harbor, port*
Hawr *lake, marsh*
Hāyk' *lake, reservoir*
Hegy, -ség *mountain, -s, range*
Heiau *temple*
Ho *canal, lake, river*
Hoek *hook, point*
Hög-en *high, hill*
Höhe, -n *height, high*
Høj *height, hill*
Holm, -e, Holmene *island-s, islet -s*
Ḩolot *dunes*
Hon *island-s*
Hor-a, -y *mountain, -s*
Horn *horn, peak*
Houma *point*
Hoved *headland, peninsula, point*
Hraun *lava field*
Hsü *island*
Hu *lake, reservoir*
Huk *cape, point*
Hüyük *hill, mound*

Idehan *sand dunes*
Île-s, Ilha-s, Illa-s, Îlot-s *island-s, islet-s*
Îlet, Ilhéu-s *islet, -s*
Irhil *mountain-s*
'Irq *sand dune-s*
Isblink *glacier, ice field*
Is-en *glacier*
Isla-s, Islote *island-s, islet*
Isol-a, -e *island, -s*
Istmo *isthmus*
Iwa *island, islet, rock*

Jabal, Jebel *mountain-s, range*
Järv, -i, Jaure, Javrre *lake*
Jazā'ir, Jazīrat, Jazīreh *island-s*
Jehīl *lake*
Jezero, Jezioro *lake*
Jiang *river, stream*
Jiao *cape*
Jibāl *hill, mountain, ridge*
Jima *island-s, rock-s*
Jøkel, Jökull *glacier, ice cap*
Joki, Jokka *river*
Jökulsá *river from a glacier*
Jūn *bay*

Kaap *cape*
Kafr *village*
Kaikyō *channel, strait*
Kaise *mountain*
Kaiwan *bay, gulf, sea*
Kanal *canal, channel*
Kangri *mountain, peak*
Kap, Kapp *cape*
Kavīr *salt desert*
Kefar *village*
Kënet' *lagoon, lake*
Kep *cape, point*
Kepulauan *archipelago, islands*
Khalīg, Khalīj *bay, gulf*
Khirb-at, -et *ancient site, ruins*
Khrebet *mountain range*
Kinh *canal*
Klint *bluff, cliff*
Kō *bay, cove, harbor*
Ko *island, lake*
Koh *island, mountain, range*
Köl-i *lake*
Kólpos *gulf*
Kong *mountain*
Körfez, -i *bay, gulf*
Kosa *spit of land*
Kou *estuary, river mouth*
Kowtal-e *pass*
Krasn-yy, -aya, -oye *red*
Kryazh *mountain range, ridge*
Kuala *estuary, river mouth*
Kuan *mountain pass*
Kūh, Kūhhā *mountain-s, range*
Kul', Kuli *lake*
Kum *sandy desert*
Kundo *archipelago*
Kuppe *hill-s, mountain-s*
Kust *coast, shore*
Kyst *coast*
Kyun *island*

La *pass*
Lac, Lac-ul, -us *lake*
Lae *cape, point*
Lago, -a *lagoon, lake*
Lagoen, Lagune *lagoon*
Laguna-s *lagoon-s, lake-s*
Laht *bay, gulf, harbor*
Laje *reef, rock ledge*
Laut *sea*
Lednik *glacier*
Leida *channel*
Lhari *mountain*
Li *village*
Liedao *archipelago, islands*
Liehtao *archipelago, islands*
Liman-ı *bay, estuary*
Límni *lake*
Ling *mountain-s, range*
Linn *pool, waterfall*
Lintasan *passage*
Liqen *lake*
Llano-s *plain-s*
Loch, Lough *lake, arm of the sea*
Loma-s *hill-s, knoll-s*

Mal *mountain, range*
Mal-yy, -aya, -oye *little, small*
Mamarr *pass, path*
Man *bay*
Mar, Mare *large lake, sea*

Marsa, Marsá *bay, inlet*
Masabb *mouth of river*
Massif *massif, mountain-s*
Mauna *mountain*
Mēda *plain*
Meer *lake, sea*
Melkosopochnik *undulating plain*
Mesa, Meseta *plateau, tableland*
Mierzeja *sandspit*
Minami *south*
Mios *island*
Misaki *cape, peninsula, point*
Mochun *passage*
Mong *town, village*
Mont-e, -i, -s *mount, -ain, -s*
Montagne, -s *mount, -ain, -s*
Montaña, -s *mountain, -s*
More *sea*
Morne *hill, peak*
Morro *bluff, headland, hill*
Motu, -s *islands*
Mouïet *well*
Mouillage *anchorage*
Muang *town, village*
Mui *cape, point*
Mull *headland, promontory*
Munkhafad *depression*
Munte *mountain*
Munţi-i *mountains*
Muong *town, village*
Mynydd *mountain*
Mys *cape*

Nacional *national*
Nada *gulf, sea*
Næs, Näs *cape, point*
Nafūd *area of dunes, desert*
Nagor'ye *mountain range, plateau*
Nahar, Nahr *river, stream*
Nakhon *town*
Namakzār *salt waste*
Ne *island, reef, rock-s*
Neem *cape, point, promontory*
Nes, Ness *peninsula, point*
Nevado-s *snow-capped mountain-s*
Nez *cape, promontory*
Ni *village*
Nísi, Nísia, Nisís, Nísoi *island-s, islet-s*
Nisídhes *islets*
Nizhn-iy, -yaya, -eye *lower*
Nizmennost' *low country*
Noord *north*
Nord-re *north-ern*
Nørre *north-ern*
Nos *cape, nose, point*
Nosy *island, reef, rock*
Nov-yy, -aya, -oye *new*
Nudo *mountain*
Numa *lake*
Nunatak, -s, -ker *peak-s surrounded by ice cap*
Nur *lake, salt lake*
Nuruu *mountain range, ridge*
Nut-en *peak*
Nuur *lake*

Ö-n, Ø-er *island-s*
Oblast' *administrative division, province, region*
Oceanus *ocean*
Odde-n *cape, point*
Øer-ne *islands*
Oglat *group of wells*
Oguilet *well*
Ór-os, -i *mountain, -s*
Órmos *bay, port*
Ort *place, point*
Øst-er *east*
Ostrov, -a, Ostrv-o, -a *island, -s*
Otoci, Otok *islands, island*
Ouadi, Oued *river, watercourse*
Øy-a *island*
Øyane *islands*
Ozer-o, -a *lake, -s*

Pää *mountain, point*
Palus *marsh*
Pampa-s *grassy plain-s*
Pantà *lake, reservoir*
Pantanal *marsh, swamp*
Pao, P'ao *lake*
Parbat *mountain*
Parque *park*
Pas, -ul *pass*
Paso, Passo *pass*
Passe *channel, pass*
Pasul *pass*
Pedra *rock*
Pegunungan *mountain range*
Pellg *bay, bight*
Peña *cliff, rock*
Pendi *basin*
Penedo-s *rock-s*
Péninsule *peninsula*
Peñón *point, rock*
Pereval *mountain pass*
Pertuis *strait*
Peski *sands, sandy region*
Phnom *hill, mountain, range*
Phou *mountain range*
Phu *mountain*
Piana-o *plain*
Pic, Pik, Piz *peak*
Picacho *mountain, peak*
Pico-s *peak-s*
Pistyll *waterfall*
Piton-s *peak-s*
Pivdennyy *southern*
Plaja, Playa *beach, inlet, shore*
Planalto, Plato *plateau*
Planina *mountain, plateau*
Plassen *lake*
Ploskogor'ye *plateau, upland*
Pointe *point*
Polder *reclaimed land*
Poluostrov *peninsula*
Pongo *water gap*
Ponta, -l *cape, point*
Ponte *bridge*
Poolsaar *peninsula*
Portezuelo *pass*
Porto *port*
Poulo *island*
Praia *beach, seashore*
Presa *reservoir*
Presidente *president*
Presqu'île *peninsula*
Prokhod *pass*
Proliv *strait*
Promontorio *promontory*
Průsmyk *mountain pass*
Przylądek *cape*
Puerto *bay, pass, port*
Pulao *island-s*
Pulau, Pulo *island*
Puncak *peak, summit, top*
Punt, Punta, -n *point, -s*
Pun *peak*
Puu *hill, mountain*
Puy *peak*

Qal'eh *castle, fort*
Qā' *depression, marsh, mud flat*
Qal'at *fort*
Qanâ *canal*
Qārat *hill-s, mountain-s*
Qaşr *castle, fort, hill*
Qila *fort*
Qiryat *settlement, suburb*
Qolleh *peak*
Qooriga *anchorage, bay*
Qoz *dunes, sand ridge*
Qu *canal*
Quebrada *ravine, stream*
Qullai *peak, summit*
Qum *desert, sand*
Qundao *archipelago, islands*
Qurayyāt *hills*

Raas *cape, point*
Rabt *hill*
Rada *roadstead*
Rade *anchorage, roadstead*
Rags *point*
Ramat *hill, mountain*
Rand *ridge of hills*
Rann *swamp*
Raqaba *wadi, watercourse*
Ras, Râs, Ra's *cape*
Ravnina *plain*
Récif-s *reef-s*
Regreg *marsh*
Represa *reservoir*
Reservatório *reservoir*
Restinga *barrier, sand area*
Rettō *chain of islands*
Ri *mountain range, village*
Ría *estuary*
Ribeirão *stream*
Río, Rio *river*
Rivière *river*
Roca-s *cliff, rock-s*
Roche-r, -s *rock-s*
Rosh *mountain, point*
Rt *cape, point*
Rubha *headland*
Rupes *scarp*

Saar *island*
Saari, Sar *island*
Sabkha-t, Sabkhet *lagoon, marsh, salt lake*
Sagar *lake, sea*
Sahara, Şaḩrā' *desert*
Sahl *plain*
Saki *cape, point*
Salar *salt flat*
Salina *salt pan*
Salin-as, -es *salt flat-s, salt marsh-es*
Salto *waterfall*
Sammyaku *mountain range*
San *hill, mountain*
San, -ta, -to *saint*
Sandur *sandy area*
Sankt *saint*
Sanmaek *mountain range*
São *saint*
Sarīr *gravel desert*
Sasso *mountain, stone*
Savane *savanna*
Scoglio *reef, rock*
Se *reef, rock-s, shoal-s*
Sebjet *salt lake, salt marsh*
Sebkha *salt lake, salt marsh*
Sebkhet *lagoon, salt lake*
See *lake, sea*
Selat *strait*
Selkä *lake, ridge*
Semenanjung *peninsula*
Sen *mountain*
Seno *bay, gulf*
Serra, Serranía *range of hills or mountains*
Severn-yy, -aya, -oye *northern*
Sgùrr *peak*
Sha *island, shoal*
Sha'ib *ravine, watercourse*
Shamo *desert*
Shan *island-s, mountain-s, range*
Shankou *mountain pass*
Shanmo *mountain range*
Sharm *cove, creek, harbor*
Shaţţ *large river*
Shi *administrative division, municipality*
Shima *island-s, rock-s*
Shō *island, reef, rock*
Shotō *archipelago*
Shott *intermittent salt lake*
Shuiku *reservoir*
Shuitao *channel*
Shyghanaghy *bay, gulf*
Sierra *mountain range*
Silsilesi *mountain chain, ridge*
Sint *saint*
Sinus *bay, sea*
Sjö-n *lake*
Skarv-et *barren mountain*
Skerry *rock*
Slieve *mountain*
Sø *lake*
Sønder, Søndre *south-ern*
Sopka *conical mountain, volcano*
Sor *lake, salt lake*
Sør, Sör *south-ern*
Sory *salt lake, salt marsh*
Spitz-e *peak, point, top*
Sredn-iy, -yaya, -eye *central, middle*
Stagno *lake, pond*
Stantsiya *station*
Stausee *reservoir*
Stenón *channel, strait*
Step'-i *steppe-s*
Štít *summit, top*
Stor-e *big, great*
Straat *strait*
Straum-en *current-s*
Strelka *spit of land*
Stretet, Stretto *strait*
Su *reef, river, rock, stream*
Sud *south*
Sudo *channel, strait*
Suidō *channel, strait*
Şummān *rocky desert*
Sund *sound, strait*
Sunden *channel, inlet, sound*
Svyat-oy, -aya, -oye *holy, saint*
Sziget *island*

Tagh *mountain-s*
Tall *hill, mound*
T'an *lake*
Tanezrouft *desert*
Tang *plain, steppe*
Tangi *peninsula, point*
Tanjong, Tanjung *cape, point*
Tao *island-s*
Tarso *hill-s, mountain-s*
Tassili *plateau, upland*
Tau *mountain-s, range*
Taūy *hills, mountains*
Tchabal *mountain-s*
Te Ava *tidal flat*
Tel-l *hill, mound*
Telok, Teluk *bay*
Tepe, -si *hill, peak*
Tepuí *mesa, mountain*
Terara *hill, mountain, peak*
Testa *bluff, head*
Thale *lake*
Thang *plain, steppe*
Tien *lake*
Tierra *land, region*
Ting *hill, mountain*
Tir'at *canal*
Tó *lake, pool*
To, Tō *island-s, rock-s*
Tonle *lake*
Tope *hill, mountain, peak*
Top-pen *peak-s*
Träsk *bog, lake*
Tso *lake*
Tsui *cape, point*
Tübegi *peninsula*
Tulu *hill, mountain*
Tunturi-t *hill-s, mountain-s*

Uad *wadi, watercourse*
Udde-m *point*
Ujong, Ujung *cape, point*
Umi *bay, lagoon, lake*
Ura *bay, inlet, lake*
'Urūq *dune area*
Uul, Uula *mountain, range*
'Uyûn *springs*

Vaara *mountain*
Vaart *canal*
Vær *fishing station*
Vaïn *channel, strait*
Valle, Vallée *valley, wadi*
Vallen *waterfall*
Valli *lagoon, lake*
Vallis *valley*
Vanua *land*
Varre *mountain*
Vatn, Vatten, Vatnet *lake, water*
Veld *grassland, plain*
Verkhn-iy, -yaya, -eye *higher, upper*
Vesi *lake, water*
Vest-er *west*
Via *road*
Vidda *plateau*
Vig, Vík, Vik, -en *bay, cove*
Vinh *bay, gulf*
Vodokhranilishche *reservoir*
Vodoskhovyshche *reservoir*
Volcan, Volcán *volcano*
Vostochn-yy, -aya, -oye *eastern*
Vötn *stream*
Vozvyshennost' *plateau, upland*
Vozyera *lake-s*
Vrchovina *mountains*
Vrch-y *mountain-s*
Vrh *hill, mountain*
Vrŭkh *mountain*
Vyaliki *big, large*
Vysočina *highland*

Wabē *stream*
Wadi, Wâdi, Wādī *valley, watercourse*
Wâhât, Wāḩat *oasis*
Wald *forest, wood*
Wan *bay, gulf*
Water *harbor*
Webi *stream*
Wiek *cove, inlet*

Xia *gorge, strait*
Xiao *lesser, little*

Yanchi *salt lake*
Yang *ocean*
Yarymadasy *peninsula*
Yazovir *reservoir*
Yōlto *island group*
Yoma *mountain range*
Yü *island*
Yumco *lake*
Yunhe *canal*
Yuzhn-yy, -aya, -oye *southern*

Zaki *cape, point*
Zaliv *bay, gulf*
Zan *mountain, ridge*
Zangbo *river, stream*
Zapadn-yy, -aya, -oye *western*
Zatoka *bay, gulf*
Zee *bay, sea*
Zemlya *land*

M X W V U T S R Q P O N
GREENLAND (KALAALLIT NUNAAT) Denmark
ICELAND
Reykjavík
CANADA
ALASKA U.S.
RUSSIA
UNITED STATES
MEXICO
BRAZIL
ARGENTINA
CHILE
NORTH PACIFIC OCEAN
SOUTH PACIFIC OCEAN
NORTH ATLANTIC OCEAN
SOUTH ATLANTIC OCEAN
All of Alaska except Atka, Adak, Shemya and Attu islands in the westernmost Aleutians uses "V" zone time. The exceptions use "W" zone.
Date Line
Monday Sunday
M+120
M+60
W+30
V+30
Q+30
M+45
DATE LINE
The 180° meridian represents, theoretically, the Date Line. When crossing the 180° meridian from west longitude to east longitude the date must be advanced by one day; when crossing the 180° meridian from east longitude to west longitude the date is retarded one day. Because of frontiers and in order to ensure that all islands of a group are to the east or west of the date line, local modifications to the line are necessary. Consequently, the date line does not coincide with the theoretical line of the 180° meridian.
LEGEND
1. Time zones are identified by letters. The bold maroon lines represent time zone boundaries. Zone time in the land areas within these boundaries is indicated by pointers bridging the zone at the top of the map and a stationary time scale, calibrated in five minute increments.
2. Where a time zone extends vertically to the top of the map without being blocked off by a boundary line, its associated pointer indicates the time for that zone. (example: zone Z)
3. Where a time zone is blocked off and does not extend vertically to the top of the map, applicable time is indicated by reference to the pointer identified with the same letter as that placed within the boundaries of the zone. (example: Finland, zone B)
4. Countries and zones in which time differs by a fraction of an hour are identified by a letter plus numerals. Applicable time is indicated on the time scale by the pointer identified with the same letter, to which is added the number of minutes indicated by the numeral. (example: India, E+30)
12 AM 1 AM 2 AM 3 AM 4 AM 5 AM 6 AM 7 AM 8 AM 9 AM 10 AM 11 AM
180° 165° 150° 135° 120° 105° 90° 75° 60° 45° Longitide West 30° of Greenwich 15°
+12- -11 -10 -9 -8 -7 -6 -5 -4 -3 -2 -1

The numeral in each tab directly above shows the number of hours to be added to, or subtracted from, Coordinated Universal Time (UTC), formerly Greenwich Mean Time (GMT).

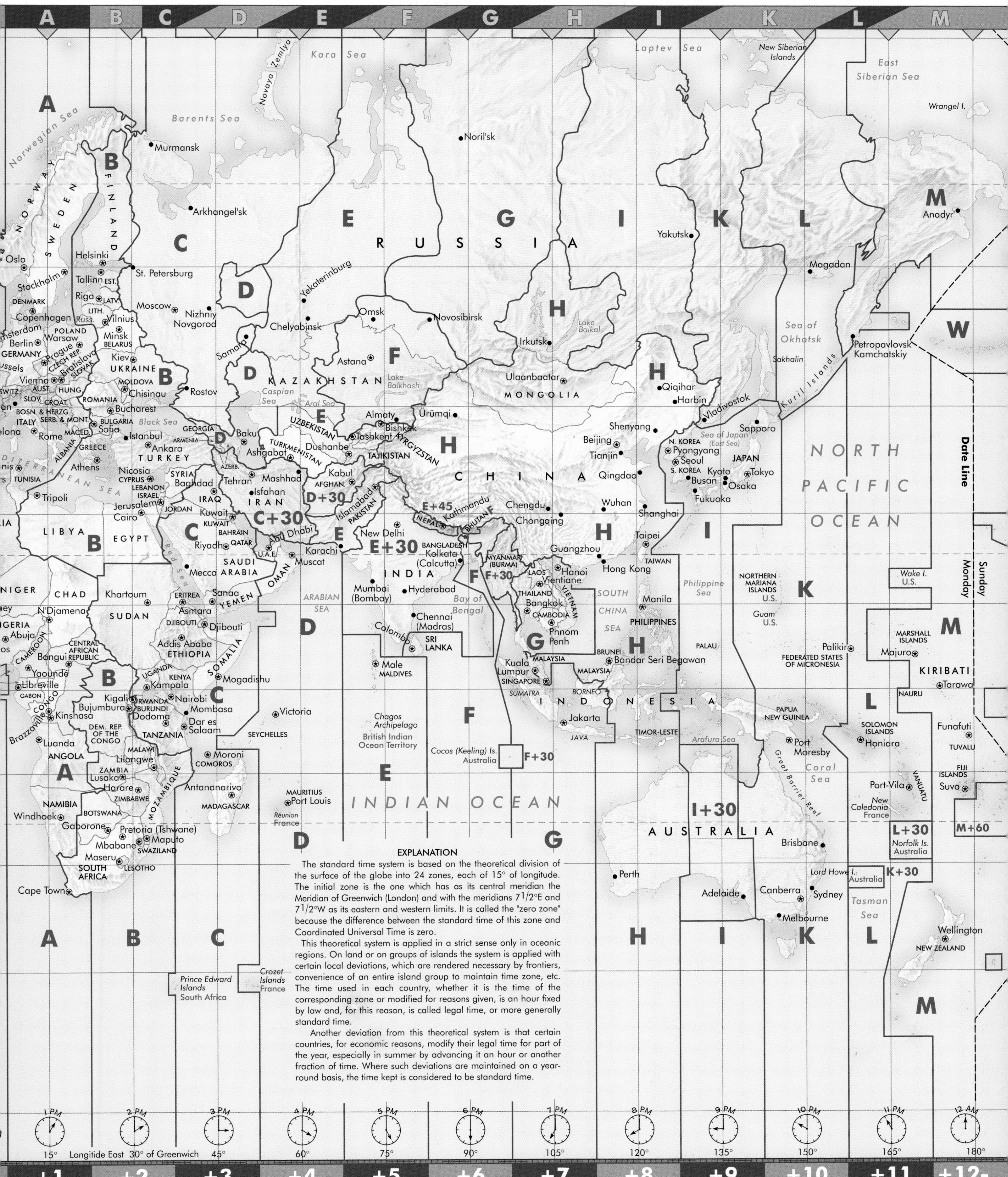
A B C D E F G H I K L M
Kara Sea
Laptev Sea
New Siberian Islands
East Siberian Sea
Wrangel I.
Barents Sea
Norwegian Sea
Novaya Zemlya
Noril'sk
Murmansk
Arkhangel'sk
NORWAY
SWEDEN
FINLAND
RUSSIA
Yakutsk
Anadyr
Magadan
Oslo
Helsinki
St. Petersburg
Stockholm
Tallinn
EST.
Riga
LATV.
DENMARK
LITH.
Copenhagen
Vilnius
Moscow
Nizhniy Novgorod
Yekaterinburg
Omsk
Novosibirsk
Chelyabinsk
Samara
Amsterdam
Berlin
POLAND
Warsaw
Minsk
BELARUS
GERMANY
Prague
CZECH REP.
Bratislava
SLOVAK
Brussels
Vienna
AUST.
HUNG.
Kiev
UKRAINE
MOLDOVA
Chisinau
Rostov
ROMANIA
Bucharest
SWITZ.
SLOV.
CROAT.
BOSN. & HERZG.
ITALY
SERB. & MONT.
BULGARIA
Sofia
Black Sea
Rome
MACED.
ALBANIA
GREECE
Athens
Istanbul
Ankara
TURKEY
GEORGIA
ARMENIA
AZERB.
Baku
Caspian Sea
KAZAKHSTAN
Astana
Lake Balkhash
Aral Sea
UZBEKISTAN
TURKMENISTAN
Ashgabat
Tashkent
Dushanbe
TAJIKISTAN
Bishkek
KYRGYZSTAN
Almaty
Ürümqi
Irkutsk
Lake Baikal
Ulaanbaatar
MONGOLIA
Qiqihar
Harbin
Vladivostok
Sea of Okhotsk
Sakhalin
Kuril Islands
Petropavlovsk Kamchatskiy
Sapporo
Sea of Japan (East Sea)
N. KOREA
Pyongyang
Seoul
S. KOREA
Busan
JAPAN
Kyoto
Tokyo
Osaka
Fukuoka
Shenyang
Beijing
Tianjin
Qingdao
CHINA
Wuhan
Shanghai
Chengdu
Chongqing
Taipei
TAIWAN
Guangzhou
Hong Kong
NORTH PACIFIC OCEAN
Date Line
Sunday
Monday
Mediterranean Sea
Tunis
TUNISIA
Tripoli
Nicosia
CYPRUS
SYRIA
LEBANON
ISRAEL
Beirut
Baghdad
IRAQ
Tehran
Mashhad
Isfahan
IRAN
Kabul
AFGHAN.
Islamabad
PAKISTAN
Jerusalem
Cairo
JORDAN
Kuwait
KUWAIT
BAHRAIN
QATAR
Riyadh
Abu Dhabi
U.A.E.
Muscat
OMAN
Karachi
New Delhi
NEPAL
Kathmandu
BHUTAN
BANGLADESH
Kolkata (Calcutta)
INDIA
Mumbai (Bombay)
Hyderabad
Chennai (Madras)
Bay of Bengal
ARABIAN SEA
Colombo
SRI LANKA
Male
MALDIVES
MYANMAR (BURMA)
LAOS
Vientiane
Hanoi
THAILAND
Bangkok
VIETNAM
CAMBODIA
Phnom Penh
SOUTH CHINA SEA
Manila
PHILIPPINES
Philippine Sea
NORTHERN MARIANA ISLANDS U.S.
Guam U.S.
Wake I. U.S.
MARSHALL ISLANDS
Majuro
PALAU
FEDERATED STATES OF MICRONESIA
Palikir
KIRIBATI
Tarawa
NAURU
LIBYA
EGYPT
SAUDI ARABIA
Mecca
Red Sea
YEMEN
Sanaa
ERITREA
Asmara
DJIBOUTI
Djibouti
SUDAN
Khartoum
CHAD
N'Djamena
NIGER
NIGERIA
Abuja
CAMEROON
CENTRAL AFRICAN REPUBLIC
Bangui
Yaoundé
Libreville
GABON
CONGO
Brazzaville
Kinshasa
DEM. REP. OF THE CONGO
Luanda
ANGOLA
ETHIOPIA
Addis Ababa
SOMALIA
Mogadishu
UGANDA
KENYA
Kampala
Nairobi
RWANDA
Kigali
BURUNDI
Bujumbura
Mombasa
Dodoma
TANZANIA
Dar es Salaam
MALAWI
Lilongwe
ZAMBIA
Lusaka
Harare
ZIMBABWE
MOZAMBIQUE
Moroni
COMOROS
SEYCHELLES
Victoria
Antananarivo
MADAGASCAR
MAURITIUS
Port Louis
Réunion France
NAMIBIA
Windhoek
BOTSWANA
Gaborone
Pretoria (Tshwane)
Maputo
Mbabane
SWAZILAND
Maseru
LESOTHO
SOUTH AFRICA
Cape Town
Chagos Archipelago
British Indian Ocean Territory
Cocos (Keeling) Is. Australia
INDIAN OCEAN
Kuala Lumpur
MALAYSIA
SINGAPORE
SUMATRA
BORNEO
BRUNEI
Bandar Seri Begawan
INDONESIA
Jakarta
JAVA
TIMOR-LESTE
Arafura Sea
PAPUA NEW GUINEA
Port Moresby
Coral Sea
Great Barrier Reef
SOLOMON ISLANDS
Honiara
Funafuti
TUVALU
VANUATU
Port-Vila
FIJI ISLANDS
Suva
New Caledonia France
AUSTRALIA
Perth
Adelaide
Canberra
Sydney
Melbourne
Brisbane
Lord Howe I. Australia
Norfolk Is. Australia
Tasman Sea
Wellington
NEW ZEALAND
Prince Edward Islands South Africa
Crozet Islands France
W
C+30 D+30 E+30 E+45 F+30 I+30 K+30 L+30 M+60
1 PM 2 PM 3 PM 4 PM 5 PM 6 PM 7 PM 8 PM 9 PM 10 PM 11 PM 12 AM
15° Longitude East 30° of Greenwich 45° 60° 75° 90° 105° 120° 135° 150° 165° 180°
+1 +2 +3 +4 +5 +6 +7 +8 +9 +10 +11 +12-
Mercator Projection

EXPLANATION

The standard time system is based on the theoretical division of the surface of the globe into 24 zones, each of 15° of longitude. The initial zone is the one which has as its central meridian the Meridian of Greenwich (London) and with the meridians 7 1/2°E and 7 1/2°W as its eastern and western limits. It is called the "zero zone" because the difference between the standard time of this zone and Coordinated Universal Time is zero.

This theoretical system is applied in a strict sense only in oceanic regions. On land or on groups of islands the system is applied with certain local deviations, which are rendered necessary by frontiers, convenience of an entire island group to maintain time zone, etc. The time used in each country, whether it is the time of the corresponding zone or modified for reasons given, is an hour fixed by law and, for this reason, is called legal time, or more generally standard time.

Another deviation from this theoretical system is that certain countries, for economic reasons, modify their legal time for part of the year, especially in summer by advancing it an hour or another fraction of time. Where such deviations are maintained on a year-round basis, the time kept is considered to be standard time.

Major Cities of the World

NOTES ON MAJOR CITY DATA

The population figures in the following list are from *World Urbanization Prospects: the 2003 Revision*, prepared by the United Nations. The list shows urban agglomerations with at least 1,000,000 inhabitants in the year 2003. An "urban agglomeration" is a contiguous territory with an urban level of population density; it includes one or more cities or towns and adjacent thickly settled areas. Thus, its geographic extent roughly coincides with the limits of a built-up urban area as seen from on high. Because an urban agglomeration is basically a metropolitan area, the population figure given for each area on the list will naturally be greater than the city-proper population figure cited in many other publications.

It is difficult to compare city populations because definitions of cities and metropolitan areas, as well as the availability of statistics, vary widely among countries. Also, the names given to metropolitan areas and the regions that comprise them may vary. As a result, some of the urban agglomeration names and population figures used in this atlas differ from names and figures given for the same general areas included on lists in other publications.

Spellings may vary, too. The UN list sometimes uses spellings that do not agree with ones used on National Geographic maps. In such cases, we have listed the place-names as they appear in the *Family Reference Atlas*. We did not change a UN spelling if we included it in the atlas as a parenthetical name or used it as a conventional name on world or physical maps.

Some of the names on the following list do not appear at all on maps in the atlas because they are regions rather than cities (Germany's Rhein-Ruhr South, for example). Others (some cities in China, for instance) were not included because of space limitations due to map scale.

CITY	COUNTRY	POPULATION
AACHEN	Germany	1,071,000
ABIDJAN	Côte d'Ivoire	3,337,000
ACCRA	Ghana	1,847,000
ADANA	Turkey	1,199,000
ADDIS ABABA	Ethiopia	2,723,000
ADELAIDE	Australia	1,124,000
AGRA	India	1,431,000
AHMADABAD	India	4,869,000
ALEXANDRIA	Egypt	3,653,000
ALGIERS	Algeria	3,060,000
ALLAHABAD	India	1,106,000
ALMATY	Kazakhstan	1,115,000
AMMAN	Jordan	1,237,000
AMRITSAR	India	1,092,000
AMSTERDAM	Netherlands	1,145,000
ANKARA	Turkey	3,428,000
ANSHAN	China	1,457,000
ANTANANARIVO	Madagascar	1,678,000
ASANSOL	India	1,187,000
ASUNCIÓN	Paraguay	1,639,000
ATHENS	Greece	3,215,000
ATLANTA	United States	3,999,000
AUCKLAND	New Zealand	1,117,000
AUSTIN	United States	1,028,000
BAGHDAD	Iraq	5,620,000
BAKU	Azerbaijan	1,816,000
BALTIMORE	United States	2,141,000
BAMAKO	Mali	1,264,000
BANDUNG	Indonesia	3,765,000
BANGALORE	India	6,141,000
BANGKOK	Thailand	6,486,000
BAOTOU	China	1,348,000
BARCELONA	Spain	4,406,000
BARRANQUILLA	Colombia	1,830,000
BASRA	Iraq	1,150,000
BEIHEI	China	1,026,000
BEIJING (PEKING)	China	10,848,000
BEIRUT	Lebanon	1,792,000
BELÉM	Brazil	1,956,000
BELGRADE	Serb. & Mont.	1,118,000
BELO HORIZONTE	Brazil	5,048,000
BERLIN	Germany	3,327,000
BHOPAL	India	1,563,000
BIELEFELD	Germany	1,309,000
BIRMINGHAM	U. K.	2,224,000
BOGOTÁ	Colombia	7,290,000
BOSTON	United States	4,212,000
BRASÍLIA	Brazil	3,099,000
BRAZZAVILLE	Congo	1,080,000
BRISBANE	Australia	1,712,000
BUCARAMANGA	Colombia	1,019,000
BUCHAREST	Romania	1,853,000
BUDAPEST	Hungary	1,708,000
BUENOS AIRES	Argentina	13,047,000
BURSA	Turkey	1,320,000
BUSAN (PUSAN)	South Korea	3,579,000
CAIRO	Egypt	10,834,000
CALGARY	Canada	1,014,000
CALI	Colombia	2,452,000
CAMPINAS	Brazil	2,488,000
CAPE TOWN	South Africa	2,967,000
CARACAS	Venezuela	3,226,000
CASABLANCA	Morocco	3,578,000
CHANGCHUN	China	3,010,000
CHANGDE	China	1,438,000
CHANGSHA	China	1,935,000
CHELYABINSK	Russia	1,077,000
CHENGDU	China	3,404,000
CHENNAI (MADRAS)	India	6,691,000
CHICAGO	United States	8,568,000
CHIFENG (ULANHAD)	China	1,119,000
CHITTAGONG	Bangladesh	3,794,000
CHONGQING	China	4,848,000
CINCINNATI	United States	1,552,000
CIUDAD JUÁREZ	Mexico	1,381,000
CLEVELAND	United States	1,814,000
COCHIN (KOCHI)	India	1,412,000
COIMBATORE	India	1,544,000
COLUMBUS	United States	1,190,000
CONAKRY	Guinea	1,366,000
COPENHAGEN	Denmark	1,066,000
CÓRDOBA	Argentina	1,533,000
CURITIBA	Brazil	2,721,000
DAEGU	South Korea	2,502,000
DAEJEON (TAEJON)	South Korea	1,426,000
DAKAR	Senegal	2,167,000
DALIAN (DAIREN)	China	2,677,000
DALLAS-FORT WORTH	United States	4,446,000
DAMASCUS	Syria	2,228,000
DAQING	China	1,101,000
DAR ES SALAM	Tanzania	2,441,000
DATONG	China	1,134,000
DAVAO	Philippines	1,254,000
DELHI	India	14,146,000
DENVER	United States	2,135,000
DETROIT	United States	3,951,000
DHAKA	Bangladesh	11,560,000
DHANBAD	India	1,135,000
DNIPROPETROVSK	Ukraine	1,052,000
DONETSK	Ukraine	1,005,000
DONGGUAN	China	1,217,000
DOUALA	Cameroon	1,858,000
DUBLIN	Ireland	1,015,000
DURBAN	South Africa	2,551,000
EAST RAND	South Africa	2,808,000
ESFAHAN	Iran	1,480,000
FAISALABAD	Pakistan	2,370,000
FARIDABAD	India	1,200,000
FORTALEZA	Brazil	3,107,000
FUSHUN	China	1,420,000
FUYU	China	1,051,000
FUZHOU	China	1,398,000
GHAZIABAD	India	1,129,000
GOIÂNIA	Brazil	1,770,000
GRANDE VITÓRIA	Brazil	1,521,000
GUADALAJARA	Mexico	3,825,000
GUANGZHOU (CANTON)	China	3,887,000
GUAYAQUIL	Ecuador	2,262,000
GUIYANG	China	2,402,000
GUJRANWALA	Pakistan	1,366,000
GWANGJU (KWANGJU)	South Korea	1,410,000
HAIPHONG	Vietnam	1,755,000
HALAB (ALEPPO)	Syria	2,379,000
HAMBURG	Germany	2,681,000
HANDAN	China	2,070,000
HANGZHOU	China	1,883,000
HANNOVER	Germany	1,293,000
HANOI	Vietnam	3,977,000
HARARE	Zimbabwe	1,469,000
HARBIN	China	2,911,000
HAVANA	Cuba	2,189,000
HEFEI	China	1,288,000
HELSINKI	Finland	1,075,000
HEZE	China	1,743,000
HO CHI MINH CITY (SAIGON)	Vietnam	4,851,000
HONG KONG	China	7,049,000
HOUSTON	United States	4,118,000
HUAINAN	China	1,394,000
HUAIYIN	China	1,271,000
HUZHOU	China	1,092,000
HYDERABAD	India	5,864,000
HYDERABAD	Pakistan	1,319,000
IBADAN	Nigeria	2,284,000
INCHEON	South Korea	2,575,000
INDIANAPOLIS	United States	1,318,000
INDORE	India	1,800,000
ISTANBUL	Turkey	9,371,000
IZMIR	Turkey	2,388,000
JABALPUR	India	1,180,000
JAIPUR	India	2,575,000
JAKARTA	Indonesia	12,296,000
JAMSHEDPUR	India	1,179,000
JEDDAH	Saudi Arabia	3,557,000
JILIN	China	1,471,000
JINAN	China	2,619,000
JINGMEN	China	1,197,000
JINING	China	1,068,000
JINXI	China	1,800,000
JOHANNESBURG	South Africa	3,084,000
KABUL	Afghanistan	2,956,000
KADUNA	Nigeria	1,273,000
KAMPALA	Uganda	1,246,000
KANO	Nigeria	2,763,000
KANPUR	India	2,879,000
KANSAS CITY	United States	1,398,000
KAOHSIUNG	China	1,489,000
KARACHI	Pakistan	11,078,000
KARAJ	Iran	1,165,000
KATOWICE	Poland	2,962,000
KAZAN	Russia	1,108,000
KHARKIV	Ukraine	1,455,000
KHARTOUM	Sudan	4,286,000
KHULNA	Bangladesh	1,401,000
KIEV	Ukraine	2,618,000
KINSHASA	D. R. C.	5,277,000
KITAKYUSHU	Japan	2,777,000
KOLKATA (CALCUTTA)	India	13,806,000
KUALA LUMPUR	Malaysia	1,352,000
KUNMING	China	1,729,000
KUWAIT CITY	Kuwait	1,222,000
KYOTO	Japan	1,806,000
LA PAZ	Bolivia	1,477,000
LAGOS	Nigeria	10,103,000
LAHORE	Pakistan	5,989,000
LANZHOU	China	1,765,000
LAS VEGAS	United States	1,568,000

CITY	COUNTRY	POPULATION
LEEDS	U.K.	1,406,000
LEÓN	Mexico	1,383,000
LESHAN	China	1,158,000
LILLE	France	1,021,000
LIMA	Peru	7,899,000
LINYI	China	1,993,000
LISBON	Portugal	1,962,000
LONDON	U.K.	7,619,000
LOS ANGELES	United States	12,018,000
LUAN	China	1,934,000
LUANDA	Angola	2,623,000
LUBUMBASHI	D. R. C.	1,012,000
LUCKNOW	India	2,439,000
LUDHIANA	India	1,496,000
LUOYANG	China	1,535,000
LUPANSHUI	China	2,080,000
LUSAKA	Zambia	1,394,000
LYON	France	1,391,000
MACEIÓ	Brazil	1,062,000
MADRID	Spain	5,103,000
MADURAI	India	1,222,000
MANAGUA	Nicaragua	1,098,000
MANAUS	Brazil	1,559,000
MANCHESTER	U.K.	2,203,000
MANILA	Philippines	10,352,000
MAPUTO	Mozambique	1,221,000
MARACAIBO	Venezuela	2,073,000
MARACAY	Venezuela	1,090,000
MARSEILLE	France	1,373,000
MASHHAD	Iran	2,080,000
MECCA	Saudi Arabia	1,446,000
MEDAN	Indonesia	2,010,000
MEDELLÍN	Colombia	3,099,000
MEERUT	India	1,260,000
MELBOURNE	Australia	3,577,000
MEMPHIS	United States	1,016,000
MENDOZA	Argentina	1,025,000
MEXICO CITY	Mexico	18,660,000
MIAMI	United States	5,216,000
MIANYANG	China	1,129,000
MILAN	Italy	4,064,000
MILWAUKEE	United States	1,330,000
MINNEAPOLIS-ST. PAUL	United States	2,476,000
MINSK	Belarus	1,705,000
MOGADISHU	Somalia	1,175,000
MONTERREY	Mexico	3,422,000
MONTEVIDEO	Uruguay	1,341,000
MONTRÉAL	Canada	3,471,000
MOSCOW	Russia	10,469,000
MOSUL	Iraq	1,163,000
MULTAN	Pakistan	1,376,000
MUMBAI (BOMBAY)	India	17,431,000
MUNICH	Germany	2,312,000
NAGOYA	Japan	3,164,000
NAGPUR	India	2,251,000
NAIROBI	Kenya	2,575,000
NAMPO	North Korea	1,124,000
NANCHANG	China	1,696,000
NANCHONG	China	1,045,000
NANJING	China	2,780,000
NANNING	China	1,361,000
NAPLES	Italy	2,934,000
NASIK	India	1,287,000
NEIJIANG	China	1,427,000
NEWCASTLE	U.K.	1,031,000
NEW ORLEANS	United States	1,005,000
NEW YORK	United States	18,252,000
NINGBO	China	1,182,000
NIZHNIY NOVGOROD	Russia	1,306,000
NORFOLK-VIRGINIA BEACH-NEWPORT NEWS	United States	1,424,000
NOVOSIBIRSK	Russia	1,430,000
NÜRNBERG	Germany	1,203,000
ODESA	Ukraine	1,021,000
OMSK	Russia	1,137,000
ORLANDO	United States	1,244,000
OSAKA	Japan	11,244,000
OTTAWA	Canada	1,093,000
PALEMBANG	Indonesia	1,569,000
PARIS	France	9,794,000
PATNA	India	1,898,000
PERTH	Australia	1,442,000
PESHAWAR	Pakistan	1,176,000
PHILADELPHIA	United States	5,261,000
PHNOM PENH	Cambodia	1,157,000
PHOENIX	United States	3,218,000
PINGXIANG	China	1,538,000
PITTSBURGH	United States	1,770,000
PORT-AU-PRINCE	Haiti	1,961,000
PORTLAND-VANCOUVER	United States	1,718,000
PORTO	Portugal	1,283,000
PORTO ALEGRE	Brazil	3,682,000
PRAGUE	Czech Republic	1,170,000
PRETORIA	South Africa	1,209,000
PROVIDENCE-PAWTUCKET	United States	1,211,000
PUEBLA	Mexico	1,876,000
PUNE	India	4,144,000
P'YONGYANG	North Korea	3,228,000
QINGDAO	China	2,385,000
QIQIHAR	China	1,445,000
QUITO	Ecuador	1,451,000
RABAT	Morocco	1,759,000
RAJKOT	India	1,110,000
RAWALPINDI	Pakistan	1,680,000
RECIFE	Brazil	3,411,000
RHEIN-MAIN	Germany	3,712,000
RHEIN-NECKAR	Germany	1,620,000
RHEIN-RUHR MIDDLE	Germany	3,301,000
RHEIN-RUHR NORTH	Germany	6,560,000
RHEIN-RUHR SOUTH	Germany	3,076,000
RIO DE JANEIRO	Brazil	11,214,000
RIVERSIDE-SAN BERNARDINO	United States	1,614,000
RIYADH	Saudi Arabia	5,126,000
ROME	Italy	2,665,000
ROSARIO	Argentina	1,280,000
ROSTOV NA DONU	Russia	1,075,000
ROTTERDAM	Netherlands	1,104,000
SACRAMENTO	United States	1,487,000
SALVADOR	Brazil	3,187,000
SAMARA	Russia	1,155,000
SAN ANTONIO	United States	1,386,000
SAN DIEGO	United States	2,766,000
SAN FRANCISCO-OAKLAND	United States	3,300,000
SAN JOSE	United States	1,584,000
SAN JOSÉ	Costa Rica	1,085,000
SAN JUAN	Puerto Rico	2,332,000
SAN SALVADOR	El Salvador	1,424,000
SANAA	Yemen	1,469,000
SANTA CRUZ	Bolivia	1,231,000
SANTIAGO	Chile	5,478,000
SANTO DOMINGO	Dominican Republic	1,865,000
SANTOS	Brazil	1,569,000
SÃO PAULO	Brazil	17,857,000
SAPPORO	Japan	1,800,000
SEATTLE	United States	2,870,000
SEOUL	South Korea	9,714,000
SHANGHAI	China	12,759,000
SHANTOU (SWATOW)	China	1,281,000
SHENYANG	China	4,882,000
SHENZHEN	China	1,221,000
SHIJIAZHUANG	China	1,680,000
SHIRAZ	Iran	1,186,000
SINGAPORE	Singapore	4,253,000
SOFIA	Bulgaria	1,076,000
SRINAGAR	India	1,037,000
ST. LOUIS	United States	2,110,000
ST. PETERSBURG	Russia	5,286,000
STOCKHOLM	Sweden	1,697,000
STUTTGART	Germany	2,697,000
SUINING	China	1,483,000
SUQIAN	China	1,230,000
SURABAYA	Indonesia	2,616,000
SURAT	India	3,261,000
SUWON	South Korea	1,073,000
SUZHOU	China	1,168,000
SYDNEY	Australia	4,274,000
TABRIZ	Iran	1,346,000
TAIAN	China	1,531,000
TAICHUNG	China	1,018,000
TAIPEI	China	2,505,000
TAIYUAN	China	2,476,000
TAMPA-ST. PETERSBURG-CLEARWATER	United States	2,168,000
TANGSHAN	China	1,732,000
TASHKENT	Uzbekistan	2,155,000
TBILISI	Georgia	1,064,000
TEGUCIGALPA	Honduras	1,007,000
TEHRAN	Iran	7,190,000
TEL AVIV-YAFO	Israel	2,917,000
TIANJIN (TIENTSIN)	China	9,271,000
TIANMEN	China	1,878,000
TIANSHUI	China	1,236,000
TIJUANA	Mexico	1,465,000
TOKYO	Japan	34,997,000
TOLUCA	Mexico	1,778,000
TORONTO	Canada	4,880,000
TORREÓN	Mexico	1,039,000
TRIPOLI	Libya	2,006,000
TUNIS	Tunisia	1,996,000
TURIN	Italy	1,203,000
UFA	Russia	1,043,000
UJUNGPANDANG	Indonesia	1,140,000
ULSAN	South Korea	1,042,000
URUMQI	China	1,501,000
VADODARA	India	1,596,000
VALENCIA	Venezuela	2,160,000
VANCOUVER	Canada	2,059,000
VARANASI (BENARES)	India	1,259,000
VIENNA	Austria	2,179,000
VIJAYAWADA	India	1,055,000
VISHAKHAPATNAM	India	1,404,000
VOLGOGRAD	Russia	1,016,000
WANXIAN	China	1,879,000
WARSAW	Poland	2,200,000
WASHINGTON, D.C.	United States	4,098,000
WEIFANG	China	1,331,000
WENZHOU	China	1,394,000
WUHAN	China	5,653,000
WUXI	China	1,166,000
XIAN	China	3,203,000
XIANTAO	China	1,699,000
XIAOSHAN	China	1,128,000
XINGHUA	China	1,575,000
XINTAI	China	1,330,000
XINYI	China	1,002,000
XUZHOU	China	1,621,000
YANCHENG	China	1,631,000
YANGON (RANGOON)	Myanmar	3,874,000
YANTAI	China	1,667,000
YAOUNDÉ	Cameroon	1,616,000
YEKATERINBURG	Russia	1,292,000
YEREVAN	Armenia	1,079,000
YIXING	China	1,121,000
YIYANG	China	1,441,000
YONGZHOU	China	1,148,000
YUEYANG	China	1,256,000
YULIN	China	1,637,000
YUZHOU	China	1,205,000
ZAOYANG	China	1,174,000
ZAOZHUANG	China	2,131,000
ZHANJIANG	China	1,481,000
ZHENGZHOU (CHENGCHOW)	China	2,176,000
ZIBO	China	2,735,000
ZIGONG	China	1,102,000

World Temperature and Rainfall

Average daily high and low temperatures and monthly rainfall for selected world locations:

	JAN.			FEB.			MARCH			APRIL			MAY			JUNE			JULY			AUG.			SEPT.			OCT.			NOV.			DEC.		
CANADA																																				
CALGARY, *Alberta*	-4	-16	14	-2	-14	15	3	-9	20	11	-3	27	17	3	54	20	7	82	24	9	65	23	8	57	18	3	40	12	-1	18	3	-9	16	-2	-13	14
CHARLOTTETOWN, *P.E.I.*	-3	-11	100	-3	-12	83	1	-7	83	7	-1	77	14	4	79	20	10	75	24	14	78	23	14	86	18	10	91	13	5	106	6	0	106	0	-7	111
CHURCHILL, *Manitoba*	-23	-31	15	-22	-30	12	-15	-25	18	-6	-15	23	2	-5	27	11	1	43	17	7	55	16	7	62	9	2	53	2	-4	44	-9	-16	31	-18	-26	18
EDMONTON, *Alberta*	-9	-18	23	-5	-15	18	0	-9	19	10	-1	24	17	5	45	21	9	79	23	12	87	22	10	64	17	5	36	11	0	20	0	-8	18	-6	-15	22
FORT NELSON, *B.C.*	-18	-27	23	-11	-23	21	-2	-15	21	8	-4	20	16	3	44	21	8	65	23	10	76	21	8	58	15	3	39	6	-4	28	-9	-17	26	-16	-24	23
GOOSE BAY, *Nfld.*	-12	-22	1	-10	-21	4	-4	-15	4	3	-7	15	10	0	46	17	5	97	21	10	119	19	9	98	14	4	87	6	-2	58	0	-8	21	-9	-18	7
HALIFAX, *Nova Scotia*	0	-8	139	0	-9	121	3	-5	123	8	0	109	14	5	110	18	9	96	22	13	93	22	14	103	19	10	93	13	5	127	8	1	142	2	-5	141
MONTRÉAL, *Quebec*	-6	-15	71	-4	-13	66	2	-7	71	11	1	74	18	8	69	24	13	84	26	16	87	25	14	91	20	10	84	13	4	76	5	-2	90	-3	-11	85
MOOSONEE, *Ontario*	-14	-27	39	-12	-25	32	-5	-19	37	3	-8	36	11	0	55	18	5	72	22	9	79	20	8	78	15	5	77	8	0	66	-1	-9	53	-11	-21	41
OTTAWA, *Ontario*	-6	-16	67	-5	-15	59	1	-8	67	11	0	60	19	7	72	24	12	82	27	15	86	25	13	80	20	9	77	13	3	69	4	-3	70	-4	-12	74
PRINCE RUPERT, *B.C.*	4	-3	237	6	-1	198	7	0	202	9	2	179	12	5	133	14	8	110	16	10	115	16	10	149	15	8	218	11	5	345	7	1	297	5	-1	275
QUÉBEC, *Quebec*	-7	-17	85	-6	-16	75	0	-9	79	8	-1	76	17	5	93	22	10	108	25	13	112	23	12	109	18	7	113	11	2	89	3	-4	100	-5	-13	104
REGINA, *Saskatchewan*	-12	-23	17	-9	-21	13	-2	-13	18	10	-3	20	18	3	45	23	9	77	26	11	59	25	10	44	19	4	35	11	-2	20	0	-11	16	-8	-19	14
SAINT JOHN, *N.B.*	-3	-14	141	-2	-14	115	3	-7	111	10	-1	111	17	4	116	22	9	103	25	12	100	24	11	100	19	7	108	14	2	118	6	-3	149	-1	-10	157
ST. JOHN'S, *Nfld.*	-1	-8	69	-1	-9	69	1	-6	74	5	-2	80	10	1	91	16	6	95	20	11	78	20	11	122	16	8	125	11	3	147	6	0	122	2	-5	91
TORONTO, *Ontario*	-1	-8	68	-1	-9	60	3	-4	66	11	2	65	17	7	71	23	13	68	26	16	77	25	15	70	21	11	73	14	5	62	7	0	70	1	-6	67
VANCOUVER, *B.C.*	5	0	146	8	1	121	10	2	102	13	5	69	17	8	56	19	11	47	22	13	31	22	13	37	19	10	60	14	6	116	9	3	155	6	1	172
WHITEHORSE, *Yukon*	-14	-23	17	-9	-18	13	-2	-13	13	5	-5	9	13	1	14	18	5	30	20	8	37	18	6	39	12	3	31	4	-3	21	-6	-13	20	-12	-20	19
WINNIPEG, *Manitoba*	-13	-23	21	-10	-21	19	-2	-13	26	9	-2	34	18	5	55	23	10	81	26	14	74	25	12	66	19	6	55	12	1	35	-1	-9	26	-9	-18	22
YELLOWKNIFE, *N.W.T.*	-24	-32	14	-20	-30	12	-12	-24	11	-1	-13	10	10	0	16	18	8	20	21	12	35	18	10	39	10	4	29	1	-4	32	-10	-18	23	-20	-28	17
UNITED STATES																																				
ALBANY, *New York*	-1	-12	61	1	-10	59	7	-4	76	14	2	77	21	7	86	26	13	83	29	15	80	27	14	87	23	10	78	17	4	77	9	-1	80	2	-8	74
AMARILLO, *Texas*	9	-6	13	12	-4	14	16	0	23	22	6	28	26	11	71	31	16	88	33	19	70	32	18	74	28	14	50	23	7	35	15	0	15	10	-5	15
ANCHORAGE, *Alaska*	-6	-13	20	-3	-11	21	1	-8	17	6	-2	15	12	4	17	16	8	26	18	11	47	17	10	62	13	5	66	5	-2	47	-3	-9	29	-5	-12	28
ASPEN, *Colorado*	0	-18	32	2	-16	26	5	-11	35	10	-6	28	16	-2	39	22	1	34	26	5	44	25	4	45	21	0	34	15	-5	36	6	-10	31	1	-15	32
ATLANTA, *Georgia*	10	0	117	13	1	117	18	6	139	23	10	103	26	15	100	30	19	92	31	21	134	31	21	93	28	18	91	23	11	77	17	6	95	12	2	105
ATLANTIC CITY, *N.J.*	5	-6	83	6	-5	78	11	0	98	16	4	86	22	10	82	27	15	63	29	18	103	29	18	103	25	13	78	19	7	72	13	2	84	7	-3	81
AUGUSTA, *Maine*	-2	-11	76	0	-10	71	4	-5	84	11	1	92	19	7	95	23	12	85	26	16	85	25	15	84	20	10	80	14	4	92	7	-1	114	0	-8	93
BIRMINGHAM, *Alabama*	11	0	128	14	1	114	19	6	150	24	10	114	27	14	112	31	18	97	32	21	132	32	20	95	29	17	105	24	10	75	18	5	103	13	2	120
BISMARCK, *N. Dak.*	-7	-19	12	-3	-15	11	4	-8	20	13	-1	37	20	6	56	25	11	74	29	14	59	28	12	44	22	6	38	15	0	21	4	-8	14	-4	-16	12
BOISE, *Idaho*	2	-6	38	7	-3	28	12	0	32	16	3	31	22	7	31	27	11	22	32	14	8	31	14	9	25	9	16	18	4	18	9	-1	35	3	-5	35
BOSTON, *Massachusetts*	2	-6	95	3	-5	91	8	0	100	13	5	93	19	10	84	25	15	79	28	18	73	27	18	92	23	14	82	17	8	87	11	4	110	5	-3	105
BROWNSVILLE, *Texas*	21	10	37	22	11	36	26	15	16	29	19	41	31	22	64	33	24	74	34	24	39	34	24	69	32	23	134	30	19	89	26	15	41	22	11	30
BURLINGTON, *Vermont*	-4	-14	46	-3	-13	44	4	-6	55	12	1	71	20	7	78	24	13	85	27	15	90	26	14	101	21	9	85	14	4	77	7	-1	76	-1	-9	59
CHARLESTON, *S.C.*	14	3	88	16	4	80	20	9	114	24	12	71	28	17	97	31	21	155	32	23	180	32	22	176	29	20	135	25	14	77	21	8	63	16	5	82
CHARLESTON, *W. Va.*	5	-5	87	7	-4	82	14	2	100	19	6	85	24	11	99	28	15	92	30	18	126	29	17	102	26	14	81	20	7	67	14	2	85	8	-2	85
CHEYENNE, *Wyoming*	3	-9	10	5	-8	11	7	-6	26	13	-1	35	18	4	64	24	9	56	28	13	51	27	12	42	22	7	31	16	1	19	8	-5	15	4	-9	10
CHICAGO, *Illinois*	-1	-10	48	1	-7	42	8	-1	72	15	5	97	22	10	83	27	16	103	29	19	103	28	18	89	24	14	79	18	7	70	9	1	73	2	-6	65
CINCINNATI, *Ohio*	3	-6	89	5	-4	67	12	1	97	18	7	94	24	12	101	28	17	99	30	19	102	30	18	86	26	14	75	19	8	62	12	3	81	5	-3	75
CLEVELAND, *Ohio*	1	-7	62	2	-6	58	8	-2	78	15	4	85	21	9	90	26	14	89	28	17	88	27	16	86	23	12	80	17	7	65	10	2	80	3	-4	70
DALLAS, *Texas*	13	1	47	15	4	58	20	8	74	25	13	105	29	18	125	33	22	86	35	24	56	35	24	60	31	20	82	26	14	100	19	8	64	14	3	60
DENVER, *Colorado*	6	-9	14	8	-7	16	11	-3	34	17	1	45	22	6	63	27	11	43	31	15	47	30	14	38	25	9	28	19	2	26	11	-4	23	7	-8	15
DES MOINES, *Iowa*	-2	-12	26	1	-9	30	8	-2	57	17	4	85	23	11	103	28	16	108	30	19	97	29	18	105	24	13	80	18	6	58	9	-1	46	0	-9	31
DETROIT, *Michigan*	-1	-7	42	1	-7	43	7	-2	62	14	4	75	21	10	69	26	15	85	29	18	86	27	18	87	23	14	78	16	7	55	9	2	67	2	-4	67
DULUTH, *Minnesota*	-9	-19	31	-6	-16	21	1	-9	44	9	-2	59	17	4	84	22	9	105	25	13	102	23	12	101	18	7	95	11	2	62	2	-6	48	-6	-15	32
EL PASO, *Texas*	13	-1	11	17	1	11	21	5	8	26	9	7	31	14	9	36	18	17	36	20	38	34	19	39	31	16	34	26	10	20	19	4	11	14	-1	14
FAIRBANKS, *Alaska*	-19	-28	14	-14	-26	11	-5	-19	9	5	-6	7	15	3	15	21	10	35	22	11	45	19	8	46	13	2	28	0	-8	21	-12	-21	18	-17	-26	19
HARTFORD, *Connecticut*	1	-9	83	2	-7	79	8	-2	97	16	3	97	22	9	95	27	14	85	29	17	86	28	16	104	24	11	101	18	5	99	11	0	105	3	-6	99
HELENA, *Montana*	-1	-12	15	3	-9	12	7	-5	18	13	-1	24	19	4	45	24	9	53	29	12	28	28	11	27	21	5	28	15	0	19	6	-6	14	0	-12	16
HONOLULU, *Hawai'i*	27	19	80	27	19	68	28	20	72	28	20	32	29	21	25	30	22	10	31	23	15	32	23	14	31	23	18	31	22	53	29	21	67	27	19	89
HOUSTON, *Texas*	16	4	98	19	6	75	22	10	88	26	15	91	29	18	142	32	21	133	34	22	85	34	22	95	31	20	106	28	14	120	22	10	97	18	6	91
INDIANAPOLIS, *Indiana*	1	-8	69	4	-6	61	11	0	92	17	5	94	23	11	98	28	16	98	30	18	111	29	17	88	25	13	74	19	6	69	11	1	89	4	-5	77
JACKSONVILLE, *Florida*	18	5	83	19	6	89	23	10	100	26	13	77	29	17	92	32	21	140	33	22	164	33	22	186	31	21	199	27	15	99	23	10	52	19	6	65
JUNEAU, *Alaska*	-1	-7	139	1	-5	116	4	-3	113	8	0	105	13	4	109	16	7	88	18	9	120	17	8	160	13	6	217	8	3	255	3	-2	186	0	-5	153
KANSAS CITY, *Missouri*	2	-9	30	5	-6	32	12	0	67	18	7	88	24	12	138	29	17	102	32	20	115	30	19	99	26	14	120	20	8	83	11	1	56	4	-6	43
LAS VEGAS, *Nevada*	14	0	14	17	4	12	20	7	13	25	10	5	31	16	5	38	21	3	41	25	9	40	23	13	35	19	7	28	12	6	20	6	11	14	1	10
LITTLE ROCK, *Arkansas*	9	-1	85	12	1	88	17	6	120	23	11	134	26	15	141	31	20	84	33	22	83	32	21	80	28	18	85	23	11	102	16	6	153	10	1	123
LOS ANGELES, *California*	19	9	70	19	10	61	19	10	51	20	12	20	21	14	3	22	15	1	24	17	1	25	18	2	25	17	5	24	15	7	21	12	38	19	9	43
LOUISVILLE, *Kentucky*	5	-5	85	7	-3	88	14	2	113	20	7	101	24	13	114	29	17	90	31	20	106	30	19	84	27	15	76	21	8	68	14	3	92	7	-2	89
MEMPHIS, *Tennessee*	9	-1	118	12	2	114	17	6	136	23	11	142	27	16	126	32	21	98	34	23	101	33	22	87	29	18	83	24	11	74	17	6	124	11	2	135
MIAMI, *Florida*	24	15	52	25	16	53	26	18	63	28	20	82	30	22	150	31	24	227	32	25	152	32	25	198	31	24	215	29	22	178	27	19	80	25	16	47
MILWAUKEE, *Wisconsin*	-3	-11	32	-1	-8	31	5	-3	54	12	2	87	18	7	73	24	13	87	27	17	85	26	16	94	22	12	95	15	6	66	7	-1	65	0	-7	53
MINNEAPOLIS, *Minnesota*	-6	-16	21	-3	-13	22	4	-5	45	14	2	58	21	9	80	26	14	103	29	17	97	27	16	95	22	10	70	15	4	49	5	-4	37	-4	-12	24
NASHVILLE, *Tennessee*	8	-3	108	10	-1	100	16	4	127	22	9	104	26	14	118	30	18	99	32	21	99	31	20	85	28	16	89	23	9	67	16	4	101	10	-1	112
NEW ORLEANS, *Louisiana*	16	5	116	18	7	148	22	11	124	26	15	119	29	18	135	32	22	147	33	23	167	32	23	157	30	21	138	26	15	76	22	11	101	18	7	132
NEW YORK, *New York*	3	-4	80	4	-3	76	9	1	99	15	7	94	21	12	93	26	17	80	29	21	101	28	20	107	24	16	85	18	10	81	12	5	96	6	-1	90
OKLAHOMA CITY, *Okla.*	8	-4	28	11	-1	36	17	4	61	22	9	76	26	14	145	31	19	107	34	21	74	34	21	65	29	17	97	23	10	80	16	4	43	10	-2	37
OMAHA, *Nebraska*	-1	-12	18	2	-9	21	9	-2	61	17	5	73	23	11	118	28	16	105	30	19	96	29	18	95	24	13	90	18	6	60	9	-1	35	1	-9	23
PENSACOLA, *Florida*	15	5	109	17	7	126	21	11	150	25	15	112	28	19	105	32	22	168	32	23	187	32	23	176	30	21	166	26	15	102	21	11	91	17	7	105
PHILADELPHIA, *Pa.*	3	-5	82	5	-4	70	11	1	95	17	6	88	23	12	94	28	17	87	30	20	108	29	19	97	25	15	86	19	8	67	13	3	85	6	-2	86
PHOENIX, *Arizona*	19	3	21	22	5	21	25	7	30	29	9	7	33	13	5	38	18	3	39	23	21	38	22	30	36	18	23	30	12	14	23	7	18	19	3	28
PITTSBURGH, *Pa.*	1	-8	66	3	-7	60	9	-1	85	16	4	80	21	9	92	26	14	91	28	16	98	27	16	83	24	12	74	17	6	61	10	1	69	4	-4	71
PORTLAND, *Oregon*	7	1	133	11	2	105	13	4	92	16	5	61	20	8	53	23	12	38	27	14	15	27	14	23	24	11	41	18	7	76	11	4	135	8	2	149
PROVIDENCE, *R.I.*	3	-7	101	4	-6	91	8	-2	111	14	3	102	20	9	89	25	14	77	28	17	77	27	17	102	24	12	88	18	6	93	12	2	117	5	-4	110
RALEIGH, *N.C.*	9	-2	89	11	0	88	17	4	94	22	8	70	26	13	96	29	18	91	31	20	111	30	20	110	27	16	79	22	9	77	17	4	76	12	0	79
RAPID CITY, *S. Dak.*	2	-12	10	4	-10	12	8	-6	26	14	0	52	20	6	84	25	12	89	30	15	63	29	13	43	23	7	32	17	1	26	8	-5	12	3	-11	10
RENO, *Nevada*	7	-6	28	11	-4	24	14	-2	20	18	1	11	23	5	17	28	8	11	33	11	7	32	10	6	26	5	9	20	1	10	12	-3	19	8	-7	27
ST. LOUIS, *Missouri*	3	-6	50	6	-4	54	13	2	84	19	8	97	25	13	100	30	19	103	32	21	92	31	20	76	27	16	73	20	9	70	13	3	78	5	-3	64
SALT LAKE CITY, *Utah*	2	-7	32	6	-4	30	11	0	45	16	3	52	22	8	46	28	13	23	33	18	18	32	17	21	26	11	27	19	5	34	10	-1	34	3	-6	34
SAN DIEGO, *California*	19	9	56	19	10	41	19	12	50	20	13	20	21	15	5	22	17	2	25	19	1	25	20	2	25	19	5	24	16	9	21	12	30	19	9	35
SAN FRANCISCO, *Calif.*	14	8	112	16	9	77	16	9	78	17	10	34	17	10	10	18	11	4	18	12	1	19	13	2	20	13	7	20	13	28	17	11	73	14	8	91

RED FIGURES: Average daily high temperature (°C) **BLUE FIGURES:** Average daily low temperature (°C) **BLACK FIGURES:** Average monthly rainfall (mm)
1 millimeter = 0.039 inches

	JAN.			FEB.			MARCH			APRIL			MAY			JUNE			JULY			AUG.			SEPT.			OCT.			NOV.			DEC.		
UNITED STATES																																				
SANTA FE, *New Mexico*	6	-10	11	9	-7	9	13	-5	12	18	-1	13	24	4	23	29	9	31	31	12	52	29	11	64	25	7	38	20	1	32	13	-5	14	7	-9	12
SEATTLE, *Washington*	7	2	141	10	3	107	12	4	94	14	5	64	18	8	42	21	11	38	24	13	20	24	13	27	21	11	47	15	8	89	10	5	149	7	2	149
SPOKANE, *Washington*	1	-6	52	5	-3	39	9	-1	37	14	2	28	19	6	35	24	10	33	28	12	15	28	12	16	22	8	20	15	2	31	5	-2	51	1	-6	57
TAMPA, *Florida*	21	10	54	22	11	73	25	14	90	28	16	44	31	20	76	32	23	143	32	24	189	32	24	196	32	23	160	29	18	60	25	14	46	22	11	54
VICKSBURG, *Mississippi*	14	2	155	16	3	131	21	8	160	25	12	147	29	16	130	32	20	88	33	22	106	33	21	80	30	18	85	26	12	106	20	8	126	16	4	168
WASHINGTON, *D.C.*	6	-3	71	8	-2	66	14	3	90	19	8	72	25	14	94	29	19	80	31	22	97	31	21	104	27	17	84	21	10	78	15	5	76	8	0	79
WICHITA, *Kansas*	4	-7	19	8	-5	23	14	1	57	20	7	57	25	12	99	30	18	105	34	21	82	33	20	78	27	15	85	21	8	62	13	1	37	6	-5	29
MIDDLE AMERICA																																				
ACAPULCO, *Mexico*	29	21	8	31	21	1	31	21	0	31	22	1	32	23	36	32	24	325	32	24	231	32	24	236	31	24	353	31	23	170	31	22	30	31	21	10
BALBOA, *Panama*	31	22	34	32	22	16	32	22	14	32	23	73	31	23	198	30	23	203	31	23	176	31	23	200	30	23	197	29	23	271	29	23	260	31	23	133
CHARLOTTE AMALIE, *V.I.*	28	23	50	27	22	41	28	23	49	28	23	63	29	24	105	30	25	67	31	26	71	31	26	112	31	26	132	31	25	139	29	24	131	28	23	69
GUATEMALA, *Guatemala*	23	12	4	25	12	5	27	14	10	28	14	32	29	16	110	27	16	257	26	16	197	26	16	193	26	16	235	24	16	98	23	14	33	22	13	13
GUAYMAS, *Mexico*	23	13	17	24	14	6	26	16	5	29	18	1	31	21	2	34	24	1	34	27	46	35	27	71	35	26	28	32	22	17	28	18	8	23	13	18
HAVANA, *Cuba*	26	18	71	26	18	46	27	19	46	29	21	58	30	22	119	31	23	165	32	24	124	32	24	135	31	24	150	29	23	173	27	21	79	26	19	58
KINGSTON, *Jamaica*	30	19	29	30	19	24	30	20	23	31	21	39	31	22	104	32	23	96	32	23	46	32	23	107	32	23	127	31	23	181	31	22	95	31	21	41
MANAGUA, *Nicaragua*	33	21	2	33	21	3	35	22	4	36	23	3	35	24	136	32	23	237	32	23	132	32	23	121	33	23	213	32	23	315	32	22	42	32	22	10
MÉRIDA, *Mexico*	28	17	30	29	17	23	32	19	18	33	21	20	34	22	81	33	23	142	33	23	132	33	23	142	32	23	173	31	22	97	29	19	33	28	18	33
MEXICO, *Mexico*	19	6	8	21	6	5	24	8	11	25	11	19	26	12	49	24	13	106	23	12	129	23	12	121	23	12	110	21	10	44	20	8	15	19	6	7
MONTERREY, *Mexico*	20	9	18	22	11	23	24	14	16	29	17	29	31	20	40	33	22	68	32	22	62	33	22	76	30	21	151	27	18	78	22	13	26	18	10	20
NASSAU, *Bahamas*	25	18	48	25	18	43	26	19	41	27	21	65	29	22	132	31	23	178	31	24	153	32	24	170	31	24	180	29	23	171	27	21	71	26	19	43
PORT-AU-PRINCE, *Haiti*	31	20	32	31	20	50	32	21	79	32	22	156	32	22	218	33	23	96	34	23	73	34	23	139	33	23	166	32	22	164	31	22	84	31	21	35
PORT-OF-SPAIN, *Trinidad*	29	19	69	30	19	41	31	19	46	31	21	53	32	21	94	31	22	193	31	21	218	31	22	246	31	22	193	31	22	170	31	21	183	30	21	124
SAN JOSÉ, *Costa Rica*	24	14	11	24	14	5	26	15	14	26	17	46	27	17	224	26	17	276	25	17	215	26	16	243	26	16	326	25	16	323	25	16	148	24	14	42
SAN JUAN, *Puerto Rico*	27	21	75	27	21	56	27	21	59	28	22	95	29	23	156	29	24	112	29	24	115	29	24	133	30	24	136	29	24	140	29	23	148	27	22	118
SAN SALVADOR, *El Salv.*	32	16	7	33	16	7	34	17	13	34	18	53	33	19	179	31	19	315	32	18	312	32	19	307	31	19	317	31	18	230	31	17	40	32	16	12
SANTO DOMINGO, *Dom. Rep.*	29	19	57	29	19	43	29	19	49	29	21	77	30	22	179	31	22	154	31	22	155	31	23	162	31	22	173	31	22	164	30	21	111	29	19	63
TEGUCIGALPA, *Honduras*	25	13	9	27	14	4	29	14	8	30	17	32	29	18	151	28	18	159	28	17	82	28	17	87	28	17	185	27	17	135	26	16	38	25	15	12
SOUTH AMERICA																																				
ANTOFAGASTA, *Chile*	24	17	0	24	17	0	23	16	0	21	14	0	19	13	0	18	11	1	17	11	1	17	11	1	18	12	0	19	13	0	21	14	0	22	16	0
ASUNCIÓN, *Paraguay*	35	22	150	34	22	133	33	21	142	29	18	145	25	14	120	22	12	73	23	12	51	26	14	48	28	16	83	30	17	136	32	18	144	34	21	142
BELÉM, *Brazil*	31	22	351	30	22	412	31	23	441	31	23	370	31	23	282	31	22	164	31	22	154	31	22	122	32	22	129	32	22	105	32	22	101	32	22	202
BOGOTÁ, *Colombia*	19	9	48	20	9	52	19	10	81	19	11	119	19	11	103	18	11	61	18	10	47	18	10	48	19	9	58	19	10	142	19	10	115	19	9	67
BRASÍLIA, *Brazil*	27	18	262	27	18	213	28	18	202	28	17	103	26	13	20	25	11	4	26	11	4	28	13	6	31	16	35	28	18	140	28	19	238	26	18	329
BUENOS AIRES, *Arg.*	29	17	93	28	17	81	26	16	117	22	12	90	18	8	77	14	5	64	14	6	59	16	6	65	18	8	78	21	10	97	24	13	89	28	16	96
CARACAS, *Venezuela*	24	13	41	25	13	27	26	14	22	27	16	20	27	17	36	26	17	52	26	16	53	26	16	53	27	16	48	26	16	47	25	16	50	26	14	58
COM. RIVADAVIA, *Arg.*	26	13	16	25	13	11	22	11	21	18	8	21	13	6	34	11	3	21	11	3	25	12	3	22	14	5	13	19	9	13	22	10	13	24	12	15
CÓRDOBA, *Argentina*	31	16	110	30	16	102	28	14	96	24	11	45	21	7	25	18	3	10	18	3	10	21	4	13	23	7	27	25	11	69	28	13	97	30	16	118
GUAYAQUIL, *Ecuador*	31	21	224	31	22	278	31	22	287	32	22	180	31	20	53	31	20	17	29	19	2	30	18	0	31	19	2	30	20	3	31	20	3	31	21	30
LA PAZ, *Bolivia*	17	6	130	17	6	105	18	6	72	18	4	47	18	3	13	17	1	6	17	1	9	17	2	14	18	3	29	19	4	40	19	6	50	18	6	93
LIMA, *Peru*	28	19	1	28	19	1	28	19	1	27	17	0	23	16	1	20	14	2	19	14	4	19	13	3	20	14	3	22	14	2	23	16	1	26	17	1
MANAUS, *Brazil*	31	24	264	31	24	262	31	24	298	31	24	283	31	24	204	31	24	103	32	24	67	33	24	46	33	24	63	33	24	111	33	24	161	32	24	220
MARACAIBO, *Venezuela*	32	23	5	32	23	5	33	23	6	33	24	39	33	25	65	34	25	55	34	24	25	34	25	53	34	25	76	33	24	119	33	24	55	33	24	22
MONTEVIDEO, *Uruguay*	28	17	95	28	16	100	26	15	111	22	12	83	18	9	76	15	6	74	14	6	86	15	6	84	17	8	90	20	9	98	23	12	78	26	15	84
PARAMARIBO, *Suriname*	29	22	209	29	22	149	29	22	168	30	23	219	30	23	307	30	23	302	31	23	227	32	23	163	33	23	80	33	23	82	32	23	117	30	22	204
PUNTA ARENAS, *Chile*	14	7	35	14	7	28	12	5	39	10	4	41	7	2	42	5	1	32	4	-1	34	6	1	33	8	2	28	11	3	24	12	4	29	14	6	32
QUITO, *Ecuador*	22	8	113	22	8	128	22	8	154	21	8	176	21	8	124	22	7	48	22	7	20	23	7	24	23	7	78	22	8	127	22	7	109	22	8	103
RECIFE, *Brazil*	30	25	62	30	25	102	30	24	197	29	24	252	28	23	301	28	23	302	27	22	254	27	22	156	28	23	78	29	24	36	29	24	29	29	25	40
RIO DE JANEIRO, *Brazil*	29	23	135	29	23	124	28	22	134	27	21	109	25	19	78	24	18	52	24	17	45	24	18	46	24	18	62	25	19	82	26	20	100	28	22	137
SANTIAGO, *Chile*	29	12	3	29	11	3	27	9	5	23	7	13	18	5	64	14	3	84	15	3	76	17	4	56	19	6	30	22	7	15	26	9	8	28	11	5
SÃO PAULO, *Brazil*	27	17	225	28	18	208	27	17	160	26	14	71	23	12	67	22	11	54	22	9	35	23	11	48	23	12	77	24	14	117	26	15	139	27	16	185
VALPARAÍSO, *Chile*	22	13	0	22	13	0	21	12	0	19	11	22	17	10	38	16	9	100	16	8	111	16	8	42	17	9	27	18	10	15	21	11	15	22	12	1
EUROPE																																				
AJACCIO, *Corsica*	13	3	76	14	4	58	16	5	66	18	7	56	21	10	41	25	14	23	27	16	71	28	16	18	26	15	43	22	11	97	18	7	112	15	4	79
AMSTERDAM, *Neth.*	4	1	79	5	1	44	8	3	89	11	6	39	16	10	50	18	13	60	21	15	73	20	15	60	18	13	80	13	9	104	8	5	76	5	2	72
ATHENS, *Greece*	13	6	48	14	7	41	16	8	41	20	11	23	25	16	18	30	20	7	33	23	5	33	23	8	29	19	10	24	15	53	19	12	55	15	8	62
BARCELONA, *Spain*	13	6	38	14	7	38	16	9	47	18	11	47	21	14	44	25	18	38	28	21	28	28	21	44	25	19	76	21	15	96	16	11	51	13	8	44
BELFAST, *N. Ireland*	6	2	83	7	2	55	9	3	59	12	4	51	15	6	56	18	9	65	18	11	79	18	11	78	16	9	82	13	7	85	9	4	75	7	3	84
BELGRADE, *Serb. & Mont.*	3	-3	42	5	-2	39	11	2	43	18	7	57	23	12	73	26	15	84	28	17	63	28	17	53	24	13	47	18	8	50	11	4	55	5	0	52
BERLIN, *Germany*	2	-3	43	3	-3	38	8	0	38	13	4	41	19	8	49	22	12	64	24	14	71	23	13	62	20	10	44	13	6	44	7	2	46	3	-1	48
BIARRITZ, *France*	11	4	106	12	4	93	15	6	92	16	8	95	18	11	97	22	14	93	23	16	64	24	16	74	22	15	102	19	11	129	15	7	135	12	5	134
BORDEAUX, *France*	9	2	76	11	2	65	15	4	66	17	6	65	20	9	71	24	12	65	25	14	52	26	14	59	23	12	70	18	8	87	13	5	88	9	3	86
BRINDISI, *Italy*	12	6	57	13	7	61	15	8	67	18	11	35	22	14	26	26	18	20	29	21	9	29	21	25	26	18	47	22	15	71	18	11	72	14	8	65
BRUSSELS, *Belgium*	4	-1	82	7	0	51	10	2	81	14	5	53	18	8	74	22	11	74	23	12	58	22	12	42	21	11	69	15	7	85	9	3	61	6	0	68
BUCHAREST, *Romania*	1	-7	44	4	-5	37	10	-1	35	18	5	46	23	10	65	27	14	86	30	16	56	30	15	56	25	11	35	18	6	28	10	2	45	4	-3	42
BUDAPEST, *Hungary*	1	-4	41	4	-2	36	10	2	41	17	7	49	22	11	69	26	15	71	28	16	53	27	16	53	23	12	45	16	7	52	8	3	58	4	-1	49
CAGLIARI, *Sardinia*	14	7	53	15	7	52	17	9	45	19	11	35	23	14	27	27	18	10	30	21	3	30	21	10	27	19	29	23	15	57	19	11	56	16	9	55
CANDIA, *Crete*	16	9	94	16	9	76	17	10	41	20	12	23	23	15	18	27	19	3	29	21	1	29	22	3	27	19	18	24	17	43	21	14	69	18	11	102
COPENHAGEN, *Denmark*	2	-2	42	2	-3	25	5	-1	35	10	3	40	16	8	42	19	11	52	22	14	67	21	14	75	18	11	51	12	7	53	7	3	52	4	1	51
DUBLIN, *Ireland*	7	2	64	8	2	51	10	3	52	12	5	49	14	7	56	18	9	55	19	11	65	19	11	77	17	10	62	14	7	73	10	4	69	8	3	69
DURAZZO, *Albania*	11	6	76	12	6	84	13	8	99	17	13	56	22	17	41	25	21	48	28	23	13	28	22	48	24	18	43	20	14	180	14	11	216	12	8	185
EDINBURGH, *Scotland*	6	1	55	6	1	41	8	2	47	11	4	39	14	6	50	17	9	50	18	11	64	18	11	69	16	9	63	12	7	62	9	4	63	7	2	61
FLORENCE, *Italy*	9	2	64	11	3	62	14	5	69	19	8	71	23	12	73	27	15	56	30	18	34	30	17	47	26	15	83	20	11	99	14	7	103	11	4	79
GENEVA, *Switzerland*	4	-2	55	6	-1	53	10	2	60	15	5	63	19	9	76	23	13	81	25	15	72	24	14	90	21	12	90	14	7	91	8	3	81	4	0	66
HAMBURG, *Germany*	2	-2	61	3	-2	40	7	-1	52	13	3	47	18	7	55	21	11	74	22	13	81	22	12	79	19	10	68	13	6	62	7	3	65	4	0	71
HELSINKI, *Finland*	-3	-9	46	-4	-9	37	0	-7	35	6	-1	37	14	4	42	19	9	46	22	13	62	20	12	75	15	8	67	8	3	69	3	-1	66	-1	-5	55
LISBON, *Portugal*	14	8	95	15	8	87	17	10	85	20	12	60	21	13	44	25	15	18	27	17	4	28	17	5	26	17	33	22	14	75	17	11	100	15	9	97
LIVERPOOL, *England*	7	2	69	7	2	48	9	3	38	11	5	41	14	8	56	17	11	51	19	13	71	18	13	79	16	11	66	13	8	76	9	5	76	7	3	64
LONDON, *England*	7	2	62	7	2	36	11	8	50	13	4	43	17	7	45	21	11	46	23	13	46	22	12	44	19	11	43	14	7	73	9	4	45	7	2	59
LUXEMBOURG, *Lux.*	3	-1	66	4	-1	54	10	1	55	14	4	53	18	8	66	21	11	65	23	13	70	22	12	69	19	10	62	13	6	70	7	3	71	4	0	74
MADRID, *Spain*	9	2	45	11	2	43	15	5	37	18	7	45	21	10	40	27	15	25	31	17	9	30	17	10	25	14	29	19	10	46	13	5	64	9	2	47
MARSEILLE, *France*	10	2	49	12	2	40	15	5	45	18	8	46	22	11	46	26	15	26	29	17	15	28	17	24	25	15	63	20	10	94	15	6	76	11	3	59

World Temperature and Rainfall

Average daily high and low temperatures and monthly rainfall for selected world locations:

EUROPE	JAN.			FEB.			MARCH			APRIL			MAY			JUNE			JULY			AUG.			SEPT.			OCT.			NOV.			DEC.		
	High	Low	Rain	High	Low	Rain	High	Low	Rain	High	Low	Rain	High	Low	Rain	High	Low	Rain	High	Low	Rain	High	Low	Rain	High	Low	Rain	High	Low	Rain	High	Low	Rain	High	Low	Rain
MILAN, *Italy*	5	0	61	8	2	58	13	6	72	18	10	85	23	14	98	27	17	81	29	20	68	28	19	81	24	16	82	17	11	116	10	6	106	6	2	75
MUNICH, *Germany*	1	-5	49	3	-5	43	9	-1	52	14	3	70	18	7	101	21	11	123	23	13	127	23	12	112	20	9	83	13	4	62	7	0	54	2	-4	51
NANTES, *France*	8	2	79	9	2	62	13	4	62	15	6	54	19	9	61	22	12	55	24	14	50	24	13	54	21	12	70	16	8	89	11	5	91	8	3	86
NAPLES, *Italy*	12	4	94	13	5	81	15	6	76	18	9	66	22	12	46	26	16	46	29	18	15	29	18	18	26	16	71	22	12	130	17	9	114	14	6	137
NICE, *France*	13	4	77	13	5	73	15	7	73	17	9	64	20	13	49	24	16	37	27	18	19	27	18	32	25	16	65	21	12	111	17	8	117	13	5	88
OSLO, *Norway*	-2	-7	41	-1	-7	31	4	-4	34	10	1	36	16	6	45	20	10	59	22	13	75	21	12	86	16	8	72	9	3	71	3	-1	57	0	-4	49
PALERMO, *Italy*	16	8	44	16	8	35	17	9	30	20	11	29	24	14	14	27	18	9	30	21	2	30	21	8	28	19	28	25	16	59	21	12	66	18	10	68
PALMA DE MALLORCA, *Spain*	14	6	39	15	6	35	17	8	37	19	10	35	22	13	34	26	17	20	29	20	8	29	20	18	27	18	52	23	14	77	18	10	54	15	8	54
PARIS, *France*	6	1	46	7	1	39	12	4	41	16	6	44	20	10	56	23	13	57	25	15	57	24	14	55	21	12	53	16	8	57	10	5	54	7	2	49
PRAGUE, *Czech. Rep.*	1	-4	21	3	-2	19	7	1	26	13	4	36	18	9	59	22	13	68	23	14	67	23	14	62	18	11	41	12	7	30	5	2	27	1	-2	23
RIGA, *Latvia*	-4	-10	32	-3	-10	24	2	-7	26	10	1	35	16	6	42	21	9	58	22	11	72	21	11	68	17	8	66	11	4	54	4	-1	52	-2	-7	39
ROME, *Italy*	11	5	80	13	5	71	15	7	69	19	10	67	23	13	52	28	17	34	30	20	16	30	19	24	26	17	69	22	13	113	16	9	111	13	6	97
SEVILLE, *Spain*	15	6	56	17	7	74	20	9	84	24	11	58	27	13	33	32	17	23	36	20	3	36	20	3	32	18	28	26	14	66	20	10	94	16	7	71
SOFIA, *Bulgaria*	2	-4	34	4	-3	34	10	1	38	16	5	54	21	10	69	24	14	78	27	16	56	26	15	43	22	11	40	17	8	35	9	3	52	4	-2	44
SPLIT, *Croatia*	10	5	80	11	5	65	14	7	65	18	11	62	23	16	62	27	19	48	30	22	28	30	22	43	26	19	66	20	14	87	15	10	111	12	7	113
STOCKHOLM, *Sweden*	-1	-5	31	-1	-5	25	3	-4	26	8	1	29	14	6	34	19	11	44	22	14	64	20	13	66	15	9	49	9	5	51	5	1	44	2	-2	39
VALENCIA, *Spain*	15	6	23	16	6	38	18	8	23	20	10	30	23	13	28	26	17	33	29	20	10	29	20	13	27	18	56	23	13	41	19	10	64	16	7	33
VALETTA, *Malta*	14	10	84	15	10	58	16	11	38	18	13	20	22	16	10	26	19	3	29	22	1	29	23	5	27	22	33	24	19	69	20	16	91	16	12	99
VENICE, *Italy*	6	1	51	8	2	53	12	5	61	17	10	71	21	14	81	25	17	84	27	19	66	27	18	66	24	16	66	19	11	94	12	7	89	8	3	66
VIENNA, *Austria*	1	-4	38	3	-3	36	8	1	46	15	6	51	19	10	71	23	14	69	25	15	76	24	15	69	20	11	51	14	7	25	7	3	48	3	-1	46
WARSAW, *Poland*	0	-6	28	0	-6	26	6	-2	31	12	3	37	20	9	50	23	12	66	24	15	77	23	14	72	19	10	47	13	5	41	6	1	38	2	-3	35
ZÜRICH, *Switzerland*	2	-3	61	5	-2	61	10	1	68	15	4	85	19	8	101	23	12	127	25	14	128	24	13	124	20	11	98	14	6	83	7	2	71	3	-2	72

ASIA	JAN.			FEB.			MARCH			APRIL			MAY			JUNE			JULY			AUG.			SEPT.			OCT.			NOV.			DEC.		
ADEN, *Yemen*	27	23	8	27	23	7	29	24	8	31	26	4	34	28	3	35	29	1	34	28	2	33	27	3	34	28	4	32	26	2	29	24	2	27	23	4
ALMATY, *Kazakhstan*	-5	-14	33	-3	13	23	4	-6	56	13	3	102	20	10	94	24	14	66	27	16	36	27	14	30	22	8	25	13	2	51	4	-5	48	-2	-9	33
ANKARA, *Turkey*	4	-4	49	6	-3	52	11	-1	45	17	4	44	23	9	56	26	12	37	30	15	13	31	15	8	26	11	28	21	7	21	14	3	28	6	-2	63
ARKHANGEL'SK, *Russia*	-12	-20	30	-10	-18	28	-4	-13	28	5	-4	18	12	2	33	17	6	48	20	10	66	19	10	69	12	5	56	4	-1	48	-2	-7	41	-8	-15	33
BAGHDAD, *Iraq*	16	4	27	18	6	28	22	9	27	29	14	19	36	19	7	41	23	0	43	24	0	43	24	0	40	21	0	33	16	3	25	11	20	18	6	26
BALIKPAPAN, *Indonesia*	29	23	243	30	23	221	30	23	249	29	23	226	29	23	258	29	23	252	28	23	259	29	23	257	29	23	201	29	23	186	29	23	176	29	23	245
BANGKOK, *Thailand*	32	20	11	33	22	28	34	24	31	35	25	72	34	25	189	33	24	152	32	24	158	32	24	187	32	24	320	31	24	231	31	22	57	31	20	9
BEIJING, *China*	2	-9	4	5	-7	5	12	-1	8	20	7	18	27	13	33	31	18	78	32	22	224	31	21	170	27	14	58	21	7	18	10	-1	9	3	-7	3
BEIRUT, *Lebanon*	17	11	187	17	11	151	19	12	96	22	14	51	26	18	19	28	21	2	31	23	0	32	23	0	30	23	6	27	21	48	23	16	119	18	13	176
BRUNEI	30	24	371	30	24	193	31	24	198	32	24	249	32	24	277	31	24	241	31	25	229	31	24	185	31	24	300	31	24	368	31	24	386	30	24	330
CHENNAI (MADRAS), *India*	29	19	29	31	20	9	33	22	9	35	26	17	38	28	44	38	27	52	36	26	99	35	26	124	34	25	125	32	24	285	29	22	345	29	21	138
CHONGQING, *China*	9	5	18	13	7	21	18	11	38	23	16	94	27	19	148	29	22	174	34	24	151	35	25	128	28	22	144	22	16	103	16	12	49	13	8	23
COLOMBO, *Sri Lanka*	30	22	84	31	22	64	31	23	114	31	24	255	31	26	335	29	25	190	29	25	129	29	25	96	29	25	158	29	24	353	29	23	308	29	22	152
DAMASCUS, *Syria*	12	2	39	14	4	32	18	6	23	24	9	13	29	13	5	33	16	1	36	18	0	37	18	0	33	16	0	27	12	9	19	8	26	13	4	42
DAVAO, *Philippines*	31	22	117	32	22	110	32	22	109	33	22	149	32	23	223	31	23	205	31	22	171	31	22	161	32	22	177	32	22	184	32	22	139	31	22	139
DHAKA, *Bangladesh*	26	13	8	28	15	21	32	20	58	33	23	116	33	24	267	32	26	358	31	26	399	31	26	317	32	26	256	31	24	164	29	19	30	26	14	6
HANOI, *Vietnam*	20	13	20	21	14	30	23	17	64	28	21	91	32	23	104	33	26	284	33	26	302	32	26	386	31	24	254	29	22	89	26	18	66	22	15	71
HO CHI MINH CITY, *Viet.*	32	21	14	33	22	4	34	23	9	35	24	51	33	24	213	32	24	309	31	24	295	31	24	271	31	23	342	31	23	261	31	23	119	31	22	47
HONG KONG, *China*	18	13	27	17	13	44	19	16	75	24	19	140	28	23	298	29	26	399	31	26	371	31	26	377	29	25	297	27	23	119	23	18	38	20	15	25
IRKUTSK, *Russia*	-16	-26	13	-12	-25	10	-4	-17	8	6	-7	15	13	1	33	20	7	56	21	10	79	20	9	71	14	2	43	5	-6	18	-7	-17	15	-16	-24	15
ISTANBUL, *Turkey*	8	3	91	9	2	69	11	3	62	16	7	42	21	12	30	25	16	28	28	18	24	28	19	31	24	16	48	20	13	66	15	9	92	11	5	114
JAKARTA, *Indonesia*	29	23	342	29	23	302	30	23	210	31	24	135	31	24	108	31	23	90	31	23	59	31	23	48	31	23	69	31	23	106	30	23	139	29	23	208
JEDDAH, *Saudi Arabia*	29	19	5	29	18	1	29	19	1	33	21	1	35	23	1	36	24	0	37	23	1	37	27	1	36	25	1	35	23	1	33	22	25	30	19	30
JERUSALEM, *Israel*	13	5	140	13	6	111	18	8	116	23	10	17	27	14	6	29	16	0	31	17	0	31	18	0	29	17	0	27	15	11	21	12	68	15	7	129
KABUL, *Afghanistan*	2	-8	33	4	-6	54	12	1	70	19	6	66	26	11	21	31	13	1	33	16	5	33	15	1	29	11	2	23	6	4	17	1	11	8	-3	21
KARACHI, *Pakistan*	25	13	7	26	14	10	29	19	10	32	23	3	34	26	0	34	28	10	33	27	90	31	26	58	31	25	27	33	22	3	31	18	3	27	14	5
KATHMANDU, *Nepal*	18	2	17	19	4	15	25	7	30	28	12	37	30	16	102	29	19	201	29	20	375	28	20	325	28	19	189	27	13	56	23	7	2	19	3	10
KOLKATA (CALCUTTA), *India*	27	13	12	29	15	25	34	21	32	36	24	53	36	25	129	33	26	291	32	26	329	32	26	338	32	26	266	32	23	131	29	18	21	26	13	7
KUNMING, *China*	16	3	11	18	4	14	21	7	17	24	11	20	26	14	90	25	17	175	25	17	205	25	17	203	24	15	126	21	12	78	18	7	40	17	3	13
LAHORE, *Pakistan*	21	4	25	22	7	24	28	12	27	35	17	15	40	22	17	41	26	39	38	27	155	36	26	135	36	23	63	35	15	10	28	8	3	23	4	14
LHASA, *China*	7	-10	0	9	-7	3	12	-2	4	16	1	6	19	5	24	24	9	72	23	9	132	22	9	128	21	7	58	17	1	9	13	-5	1	9	-9	1
MANAMA, *Bahrain*	30	14	14	21	15	16	24	17	11	29	21	8	33	26	1	36	28	0	37	29	0	38	29	0	36	27	0	32	24	0	28	21	7	22	16	17
MANDALAY, *Myanmar*	28	13	2	31	15	13	36	19	7	38	25	35	37	26	142	34	26	124	34	26	83	33	25	113	33	24	155	32	23	125	29	19	45	27	14	10
MANILA, *Philippines*	30	21	21	31	21	10	33	22	15	34	23	30	34	24	123	33	24	262	31	24	423	31	24	421	31	24	353	31	23	197	31	22	135	30	21	65
MOSCOW, *Russia*	-9	-16	38	-6	-14	36	0	-8	28	10	1	46	19	8	56	21	11	74	23	13	76	22	12	74	16	7	48	9	3	69	2	-3	43	-5	-10	41
MUMBAI (BOMBAY), *India*	28	19	3	28	19	1	30	22	1	32	24	2	33	27	14	32	26	518	29	25	647	29	24	384	29	24	276	32	24	55	32	23	15	31	21	2
MUSCAT, *Oman*	25	19	28	25	19	18	28	22	10	32	26	10	37	30	1	38	31	3	36	31	1	33	29	1	34	28	0	34	27	3	30	23	10	26	20	18
NAGASAKI, *Japan*	9	2	75	10	2	87	14	5	124	19	10	190	23	14	191	26	18	326	29	23	284	31	23	187	27	20	236	22	14	108	17	9	89	12	4	80
NEW DELHI, *India*	21	7	23	24	9	20	31	14	15	36	20	10	41	26	15	39	28	68	36	27	200	34	26	200	34	24	123	34	18	19	29	11	3	23	8	10
NICOSIA, *Cyprus*	15	5	70	16	5	50	19	7	35	24	10	21	29	14	26	34	18	9	37	21	1	37	21	2	33	18	6	28	14	23	22	10	41	17	7	74
ODESA, *Ukraine*	0	-6	25	2	-4	18	5	-1	18	12	6	28	19	12	28	23	16	48	26	18	41	26	18	36	21	14	28	16	9	36	10	4	28	4	-2	28
PHNOM PENH, *Cambodia*	31	21	7	32	22	9	34	23	32	34	24	73	33	24	149	33	24	149	32	24	151	32	24	157	31	24	231	31	24	259	30	23	129	30	22	38
PONTIANAK, *Indonesia*	31	23	275	32	23	213	32	23	242	33	23	280	33	23	279	32	23	228	32	23	178	32	23	206	32	23	245	32	23	356	31	23	385	31	23	321
RIYADH, *Saudi Arabia*	21	8	14	23	9	10	28	13	30	32	18	30	38	22	13	42	25	0	42	26	0	42	24	0	39	22	0	34	16	1	29	13	5	21	9	11
ST. PETERSBURG, *Russia*	-7	-13	25	-5	-12	23	0	-8	23	8	4	25	15	6	41	20	11	51	21	13	64	20	13	71	15	9	53	9	4	46	2	-2	36	-3	-8	30
SANDAKAN, *Malaysia*	29	23	454	29	23	271	30	23	200	31	23	118	32	23	153	32	23	196	32	23	185	32	23	205	32	23	240	31	23	263	31	23	356	30	23	470
SAPPORO, *Japan*	-2	-12	100	-1	-11	79	2	-7	70	11	0	61	16	4	59	21	10	65	24	14	86	26	16	117	22	11	136	16	4	114	8	-2	106	1	-8	102
SEOUL, *South Korea*	0	-9	21	3	-7	28	8	-2	49	17	5	105	22	11	88	27	16	151	29	21	384	31	22	263	26	15	160	19	7	49	11	0	43	3	-7	24
SHANGHAI, *China*	8	1	47	8	1	61	13	4	85	19	10	95	25	15	104	28	19	174	32	23	145	32	23	137	28	19	138	23	14	69	17	7	52	12	2	37
SINGAPORE, *Singapore*	30	23	239	31	23	165	31	24	174	31	24	166	32	24	171	31	24	163	31	24	150	31	24	171	31	24	164	31	23	191	31	23	250	31	23	269
TAIPEI, *China*	19	12	95	18	12	141	21	14	162	25	17	167	28	21	209	32	23	280	33	24	248	33	24	277	31	23	201	27	19	112	24	17	76	21	14	76
T'BILISI, *Georgia*	6	-2	16	7	-1	21	12	2	30	18	7	52	23	12	83	27	16	73	31	19	49	31	19	40	26	15	44	20	9	39	13	4	32	8	0	21
TEHRAN, *Iran*	7	-3	42	10	0	37	15	4	39	22	9	33	28	14	15	34	19	3	37	22	2	36	22	2	32	18	2	24	12	9	17	6	24	11	1	32
TEL AVIV-YAFO, *Israel*	17	9	165	18	9	64	19	10	58	23	12	13	27	16	3	29	18	0	31	21	0	31	21	0	30	20	1	29	18	14	25	15	85	19	11	144
TOKYO, *Japan*	8	-2	50	9	-1	72	12	2	106	17	8	129	22	12	144	24	17	176	28	21	136	30	22	149	26	19	216	21	13	194	16	6	96	11	1	54
ULAANBAATAR, *Mongolia*	-19	-32	1	-13	-29	1	-4	-22	3	7	-8	5	13	-2	8	21	7	25	22	11	74	21	8	48	14	2	20	6	-8	5	-6	-20	5	-16	-28	3
VIENTIANE, *Laos*	28	14	7	30	17	18	33	19	41	34	23	88	32	23	212	32	24	216	31	24	209	31	24	254	31	24	244	31	21	81	29	18	16	28	16	5
VLADIVOSTOK, *Russia*	-11	-18	8	-6	-14	10	1	-7	18	8	1	30	13	6	53	17	11	74	22	16	84	24	18	119	20	13	109	13	5	48	2	-4	30	-7	-13	15

RED FIGURES: Average daily high temperature (°C) **BLUE FIGURES:** Average daily low temperature (°C) **BLACK FIGURES:** Average monthly rainfall (mm)
1 millimeter = 0.039 inches

ASIA	JAN.			FEB.			MARCH			APRIL			MAY			JUNE			JULY			AUG.			SEPT.			OCT.			NOV.			DEC.		
WUHAN, *China*	8	1	41	9	2	57	14	6	92	21	13	136	26	18	165	31	23	212	34	26	165	34	26	114	29	21	73	23	16	74	17	9	49	11	3	30
YAKUTSK, *Russia*	-43	-47	8	-33	-40	5	-18	-29	3	-3	-14	8	9	-1	10	19	9	28	23	12	41	19	9	33	10	1	28	-5	-12	13	-26	-31	10	-39	-43	8
YANGON (RANGOON), *Myanmar*	32	18	4	33	19	4	36	22	17	36	24	47	33	25	307	30	24	478	29	24	535	29	24	511	30	24	368	31	24	183	31	23	62	31	19	11
YEKATERINBURG, *Russia*	-14	-21	8	-10	-17	10	-4	-12	5	6	-3	8	14	4	15	18	9	48	21	12	38	18	10	53	12	5	46	3	-2	23	-7	-12	10	-12	-18	8
AFRICA																																				
ABIDJAN, *Côte d'Ivoire*	31	23	22	32	24	47	32	24	110	32	24	142	31	24	309	29	23	543	28	23	238	28	22	36	28	23	74	29	23	172	31	23	168	31	23	85
ACCRA, *Ghana*	31	23	15	31	24	29	31	24	57	31	24	90	31	24	136	29	23	199	27	23	50	27	22	19	27	23	43	29	23	64	31	24	34	31	24	20
ADDIS ABABA, *Ethiopia*	24	6	17	24	8	38	25	9	68	25	10	86	25	10	86	23	9	132	21	10	268	21	10	281	22	9	186	24	7	28	23	6	11	23	5	10
ALEXANDRIA, *Egypt*	18	11	52	19	11	28	21	13	13	23	15	4	26	18	1	28	21	0	29	23	0	31	23	0	30	23	1	28	20	8	25	17	35	21	13	55
ALGIERS, *Algeria*	15	9	93	16	9	73	17	11	67	20	13	52	23	15	34	26	18	14	28	21	2	29	22	5	27	21	33	23	17	77	19	13	96	16	11	114
ANTANANARIVO, *Madag.*	26	16	287	26	16	262	26	16	194	24	14	57	23	12	18	21	10	9	20	9	8	21	9	10	23	11	16	27	12	61	27	14	153	27	16	290
ASMARA, *Eritrea*	23	7	0	24	8	0	25	9	1	26	11	7	26	12	23	26	12	48	22	12	114	22	12	123	23	13	49	22	12	4	22	10	3	22	9	0
BAMAKO, *Mali*	33	16	0	36	19	0	39	22	3	39	24	19	39	24	59	34	23	131	32	22	229	31	22	307	32	22	198	34	22	63	34	18	7	33	17	0
BANGUI, *Cen. Af. Rep.*	32	20	20	34	21	39	33	22	107	33	22	133	32	21	163	31	21	143	29	21	181	29	21	225	31	21	190	31	21	202	31	20	93	32	19	29
BEIRA, *Mozambique*	32	24	267	32	24	259	31	23	263	30	22	117	28	18	67	26	16	40	25	16	34	26	17	33	28	18	25	31	22	34	31	22	121	31	23	243
BENGHAZI, *Libya*	17	10	66	18	11	41	21	12	20	23	14	5	26	17	3	28	20	1	29	22	1	29	22	1	28	21	3	27	19	18	23	16	46	19	12	66
BUJUMBURA, *Burundi*	29	20	97	29	20	97	29	20	126	29	20	129	29	20	64	29	19	11	30	19	3	30	19	17	31	20	43	31	20	62	29	20	98	29	20	100
CAIRO, *Egypt*	18	8	5	21	9	4	24	11	4	28	14	2	33	17	1	35	20	0	36	21	0	35	22	0	32	20	0	30	18	1	26	14	3	20	10	6
CAPE TOWN, *S. Africa*	26	16	16	26	16	15	25	14	22	22	12	50	19	9	92	18	8	105	17	7	91	18	8	83	18	9	54	21	11	40	23	13	24	24	14	19
CASABLANCA, *Morocco*	17	7	57	18	8	53	19	9	51	21	11	38	22	13	21	24	16	6	26	18	0	27	19	1	26	17	6	24	14	34	21	11	65	18	8	73
CONAKRY, *Guinea*	31	22	1	31	23	1	32	23	6	32	23	21	32	24	141	30	23	503	28	22	1210	28	22	1016	29	23	664	31	23	318	31	24	106	31	23	14
DAKAR, *Senegal*	26	18	1	27	17	1	27	18	0	27	18	0	29	20	1	31	23	15	31	24	75	31	24	215	32	24	146	32	24	42	30	23	3	27	19	4
DAR ES SALAAM, *Tanzania*	31	25	66	31	25	66	31	24	130	30	23	290	29	22	188	29	20	33	28	19	31	28	19	30	28	19	30	29	21	41	30	22	74	31	24	91
DURBAN, *S. Africa*	27	21	119	27	21	126	27	20	132	26	18	84	24	14	56	23	12	34	22	11	35	22	13	49	23	15	73	24	17	110	25	18	118	26	19	120
HARARE, *Zimbabwe*	26	16	190	26	16	177	26	14	107	26	13	33	23	9	10	21	7	3	21	7	1	23	8	2	26	12	7	28	14	32	27	16	93	26	16	173
JOHANNESBURG, *S. Africa*	26	14	150	25	14	129	24	13	110	22	10	48	19	6	24	17	4	6	17	4	10	20	6	10	23	9	25	25	12	65	25	13	126	26	14	141
KAMPALA, *Uganda*	28	18	58	28	18	68	27	18	128	26	18	185	26	17	134	25	17	71	25	17	55	26	16	87	27	17	100	27	17	119	27	17	142	27	17	95
KHARTOUM, *Sudan*	32	15	0	34	16	0	38	19	0	41	22	0	42	25	4	41	26	7	38	25	49	37	24	69	39	25	21	40	24	5	36	20	0	33	17	0
KINSHASA, *D.R.C.*	31	21	138	31	22	148	32	22	184	32	22	220	31	22	145	29	19	5	27	18	3	29	18	4	31	20	40	31	21	133	31	22	235	30	21	156
KISANGANI, *D.R.C.*	31	21	97	31	21	107	31	21	172	31	21	190	31	21	162	30	21	128	29	19	114	28	20	178	29	20	164	30	20	233	29	20	207	30	20	105
LAGOS, *Nigeria*	31	23	27	32	25	44	32	26	98	32	25	146	31	24	252	29	23	414	28	23	253	28	23	69	28	23	153	29	23	197	31	24	66	31	24	25
LIBREVILLE, *Gabon*	31	23	164	31	22	137	32	23	248	32	23	232	31	22	181	29	21	24	28	20	3	29	21	6	29	22	69	30	22	332	30	22	378	31	22	197
LIVINGSTONE, *Zambia*	29	19	175	29	19	160	29	18	95	30	15	25	28	11	5	25	7	1	25	7	0	28	10	0	32	15	2	34	19	26	33	19	78	31	19	176
LUANDA, *Angola*	28	23	34	29	24	35	30	24	90	29	24	127	28	23	18	25	20	0	23	18	0	23	18	1	24	19	2	26	22	6	28	23	32	28	23	23
LUBUMBASHI, *D.R.C.*	28	16	253	28	17	256	28	16	210	28	14	51	27	10	4	26	7	1	26	6	0	28	8	0	32	11	6	33	14	31	31	16	150	28	17	272
LUSAKA, *Zambia*	26	17	213	26	17	172	26	17	104	26	15	22	25	12	3	23	10	0	23	9	0	25	12	0	29	15	1	31	18	14	29	18	86	27	17	200
LUXOR, *Egypt*	23	6	0	26	7	0	30	10	0	35	15	0	40	21	0	41	21	0	42	23	0	41	23	0	39	22	0	37	18	1	31	12	0	26	7	0
MAPUTO, *Mozambique*	30	22	153	31	22	134	29	21	99	28	19	52	27	16	29	25	13	18	24	13	15	26	14	13	27	16	32	28	18	51	28	19	78	29	21	94
MARRAKECH, *Morocco*	18	4	27	20	6	31	23	9	36	26	11	32	29	14	17	33	17	7	38	19	2	38	20	3	33	17	7	28	14	20	23	9	37	19	6	28
MOGADISHU, *Somalia*	30	23	0	30	23	0	31	24	8	32	26	58	32	25	59	29	23	78	28	23	67	28	23	42	29	23	21	30	24	30	31	24	40	30	24	9
MONROVIA, *Liberia*	30	23	5	29	23	3	31	23	112	31	23	297	30	22	340	27	23	917	27	22	615	27	23	472	27	22	759	28	22	640	29	23	208	30	23	74
NAIROBI, *Kenya*	25	12	45	26	13	43	25	14	73	24	14	160	22	13	119	21	12	30	21	11	13	21	11	13	24	11	26	24	13	42	23	13	121	23	13	77
N'DJAMENA, *Chad*	34	14	0	37	16	0	40	21	0	42	23	8	40	25	31	38	24	62	33	22	150	31	22	215	33	22	91	36	21	22	36	17	0	33	14	0
NIAMEY, *Niger*	34	14	0	37	18	0	41	22	3	42	25	6	41	27	35	38	25	75	34	23	143	32	23	187	34	23	90	38	23	16	38	18	1	34	15	0
NOUAKCHOTT, *Maurit.*	29	14	1	31	15	3	32	17	1	32	18	1	34	21	1	33	23	3	32	23	13	32	24	104	34	24	23	33	22	10	32	18	3	28	13	1
TIMBUKTU, *Mali*	31	13	0	34	14	0	38	19	0	42	22	1	43	26	4	43	27	19	39	25	62	36	24	79	39	24	33	40	23	3	37	18	0	32	13	0
TRIPOLI, *Libya*	16	8	69	17	9	40	19	11	27	22	14	13	24	16	5	27	19	1	29	22	0	30	22	1	29	22	11	27	18	38	23	14	60	18	9	81
TUNIS, *Tunisia*	14	6	62	16	7	52	18	8	46	21	11	38	24	13	22	29	17	10	32	20	3	33	21	7	31	19	32	25	15	55	20	11	54	16	7	63
WADI HALFA, *Sudan*	24	9	0	27	10	0	31	14	0	36	18	0	40	22	1	41	24	0	41	25	1	41	25	0	40	24	0	37	21	0	30	15	0	25	11	0
YAOUNDÉ, *Cameroon*	29	19	26	29	19	55	29	19	140	29	19	193	28	19	216	27	19	163	27	19	62	27	18	80	27	19	216	27	18	292	28	19	120	28	19	28
ZANZIBAR, *Tanzania*	32	24	75	33	24	61	33	25	150	30	25	350	29	24	251	28	23	54	28	22	44	28	22	39	29	22	48	30	23	86	32	24	201	32	24	145
ZOMBA, *Malawi*	27	18	299	27	18	269	26	18	230	26	17	85	24	14	23	22	12	13	22	12	8	24	13	8	27	15	8	29	18	29	29	19	124	27	18	281
ATLANTIC ISLANDS																																				
ASCENSION ISLAND	29	23	4	31	23	8	31	24	23	31	24	27	31	23	10	29	23	14	29	22	12	28	22	10	28	22	8	28	22	7	28	22	4	29	22	3
FALKLAND ISLANDS	13	6	71	13	5	58	12	4	64	9	3	66	7	1	66	5	-1	53	4	-1	51	5	-1	51	7	1	38	9	2	41	11	3	51	12	4	71
FUNCHAL, *Madeira Is.*	19	13	87	18	13	88	19	13	79	19	14	43	21	16	22	22	17	9	24	19	2	24	19	3	24	19	27	23	18	85	22	16	106	19	14	87
HAMILTON, *Bermuda Is.*	20	14	112	20	14	119	20	14	122	22	15	104	24	18	117	27	21	112	29	23	114	30	23	137	29	22	132	26	21	147	23	17	127	21	16	119
LAS PALMAS, *Canary Is.*	21	14	28	22	14	21	22	15	15	22	16	10	23	17	3	24	18	1	25	19	1	26	21	0	26	22	6	26	19	18	24	18	37	22	16	32
NUUK, *Greenland*	-7	-12	36	-7	-13	43	-4	-11	41	-1	-7	30	4	-2	43	8	1	36	11	3	56	11	3	79	6	1	84	2	-3	64	-2	-7	48	-5	-10	38
PONTA DELGADA, *Azores*	17	12	105	17	11	91	17	12	87	18	12	62	20	13	57	22	15	36	25	17	25	26	18	34	25	17	75	22	16	97	20	14	108	18	12	98
PRAIA, *Cape Verde*	25	20	1	25	19	2	26	20	0	26	21	0	27	21	0	28	22	0	28	24	7	29	24	63	29	25	88	29	24	44	28	23	15	26	22	5
REYKJAVÍK, *Iceland*	2	-2	86	3	-2	75	4	-1	76	6	1	56	10	4	42	12	7	45	14	9	51	14	8	62	11	6	71	7	3	88	4	0	83	2	-2	84
THULE, *Greenland*	-17	-27	7	-20	-29	8	-19	-28	4	-13	-23	4	-2	-9	5	5	-1	6	8	2	14	6	1	17	1	-6	13	-5	-13	11	-11	-19	11	-18	-27	5
TRISTAN DA CUNHA	19	15	103	20	16	110	19	14	133	18	14	137	16	12	153	14	11	153	14	10	54	13	9	162	13	9	157	15	11	148	16	12	124	18	14	131
PACIFIC ISLANDS																																				
APIA, *Samoa*	30	24	437	29	24	360	30	23	356	30	24	236	29	23	174	29	23	135	29	23	100	29	24	111	29	23	144	29	24	206	30	23	259	29	23	374
AUCKLAND, *New Zealand*	23	16	70	23	16	86	22	15	77	19	13	96	17	11	115	14	9	126	13	8	131	14	8	112	16	9	94	17	11	93	19	12	82	21	14	78
DARWIN, *Australia*	32	25	396	32	25	331	33	25	282	33	24	97	33	23	18	31	21	3	31	19	1	32	21	4	33	23	15	34	25	60	34	26	130	33	26	239
DUNEDIN, *New Zealand*	19	10	81	19	10	70	17	9	78	15	7	75	12	5	78	9	4	78	9	3	70	11	3	61	13	5	61	15	6	70	17	7	79	18	9	81
GALÁPAGOS IS., *Ecuador*	30	22	20	30	24	36	31	24	28	31	24	18	30	23	1	28	22	1	27	21	1	27	19	1	27	19	1	27	19	1	27	20	1	28	21	1
GUAM, *Mariana Is.*	29	24	138	29	23	116	29	24	121	31	24	108	31	25	164	31	25	150	30	24	274	30	24	368	30	24	374	30	24	334	30	25	231	29	24	160
HOBART, *Tasmania*	22	12	51	22	12	38	20	11	46	17	9	51	14	7	46	12	5	51	11	4	51	13	5	49	15	6	47	17	8	60	19	9	52	21	11	57
MELBOURNE, *Australia*	26	14	48	26	14	47	24	13	52	20	11	57	17	8	58	14	7	49	13	6	49	15	6	50	17	8	59	19	9	67	22	11	60	24	12	59
NAHA, *Okinawa*	19	13	125	19	13	126	21	15	159	24	18	165	27	20	252	29	24	280	32	25	178	31	25	270	31	24	175	27	21	165	24	18	133	21	14	111
NOUMÉA, *N. Caledonia*	30	22	111	29	23	130	29	22	155	28	21	121	26	19	106	25	18	107	24	17	91	24	16	73	26	17	56	27	18	53	28	20	55	30	21	77
PAPEETE, *Tahiti*	32	22	335	32	22	292	32	22	165	32	22	173	31	21	124	30	21	81	30	20	66	30	20	48	30	21	58	31	21	86	31	22	165	31	22	302
PERTH, *Australia*	29	17	9	29	17	13	27	16	19	24	14	45	21	12	122	18	10	182	17	9	174	18	9	136	19	10	80	21	12	53	24	14	21	27	16	13
PORT MORESBY, *P.N.G.*	32	24	179	31	24	196	31	24	190	31	24	120	30	24	65	29	23	39	28	23	27	28	23	26	29	23	33	30	24	35	31	24	56	32	24	121
SUVA, *Fiji Islands*	30	23	305	30	23	293	30	23	367	29	23	342	28	22	261	27	21	166	26	20	142	26	20	184	27	21	200	27	21	217	28	22	266	29	23	296
SYDNEY, *Australia*	26	18	103	26	18	111	24	17	131	22	14	130	19	11	123	16	9	129	16	8	103	17	9	80	19	11	69	22	13	83	23	16	81	25	17	78
WELLINGTON, *N.Z.*	21	13	79	21	13	80	19	12	85	17	11	98	14	8	121	13	7	124	12	6	139	12	6	121	14	8	99	16	9	105	17	10	88	19	12	90

A

abyssal plain a flat, relatively featureless region of the deep ocean floor extending from the mid-ocean ridge to a continental rise or deep-sea trench

acculturation the process of losing the traits of one cultural group while assimilating with another cultural group

alloy a substance that is a mixture of two metals or a metal and a nonmetal

alluvial fan a depositional, fan-shaped feature found where a stream or channel gradient levels out at the base of a mountain

antipode a point that lies diametrically opposite any given point on the surface of the Earth

Archaean (Archean) eon the second eon of Earth's geologic history, ending around 2,500 million years ago

archipelago an associated group of scattered islands in a large body of water

asthenosphere the uppermost zone of Earth's mantle; it consists of rocks in a "plastic" state, immediately below the lithosphere

atmosphere the thin envelope of gases surrounding the solid Earth and comprising mostly nitrogen, oxygen, and various trace gases

atoll a circular coral reef enclosing a lagoon

B

barrier island a low-lying, sandy island parallel to a shoreline but separated from the mainland by a lagoon

basin a low-lying depression in the Earth's surface; some basins are filled with water and sediment, while others are dry most of the time

bathymetry the measurement of depth within bodies of water or the information gathered from such measurements

bay an area of a sea or other body of water bordered on three sides by a curved stretch of coastline but usually smaller than a gulf

biodiversity a broad concept that refers to the variety and range of species (flora and fauna) present in an ecosystem

biogeography the study of the distribution patterns of plants and animals and the processes that produce those patterns

biological weapon a weapon that uses an organism or toxin, such as a bacteria or virus, to harm individuals

biome a very large ecosystem made up of specific plant and animal communities interacting with the physical environment (climate and soil)

biosphere the realm of Earth that includes all plant and animal life-forms

bluff a steep slope or wall of consolidated sediment adjacent to a river or its floodplain

bog soft, spongy, waterlogged ground consisting chiefly of partially decayed plant matter (peat)

breakwater a stone or concrete structure built near a shore to prevent damage to watercraft or construction

butte a tall, steep-sided, flat-topped tower of rock that is a remnant of extensive erosional processes

C

caldera a large, crater-like feature with steep, circular walls and a central depression resulting from the explosion and collapse of a volcano

canal an artificially made channel of water used for navigation or irrigation

canopy the ceiling-like layer of branches and leaves that forms the uppermost layer of a forest

capitalism an economic system characterized by resource allocation primarily through market mechanisms; means of production are privately owned (by either individuals or corporations), and production is organized around profit maximization

capture fishery all of the variables involved in the activities to harvest a given fish (e.g., location, target resource, technology used, social characteristic, purpose, season)

carbon cycle one of the several geochemical cycles by which matter is recirculated through the lithosphere, hydrosphere, atmosphere, and biosphere

carbon neutral process a process resulting in zero net change in the balance between emission and absorption of carbon

carrying capacity the maximum number of animals and/or people a given area can support at a given time under specified levels of consumption

cartogram a map designed to present statistical information in a diagrammatic way, usually not to scale

cartographer a person who interprets, designs, and creates maps and other modes of geographic representation

chemical weapon a weapon that uses toxic properties of chemical substances to harm individuals

chlorofluorocarbon a molecule of industrial origin containing chlorine, fluorine, and carbon atoms; causes severe ozone destruction

civilization a cultural concept suggesting substantial development in the form of agriculture, cities, food and labor surplus, labor specialization, social stratification, and state organization

climate the long-term behavior of the atmosphere; it includes measures of average weather conditions (e.g., temperature, humidity, precipitation, and pressure), as well as trends, cycles, and extremes

colonialism the political, social, or economic domination of a state over another state or people

commodity an economic good or product that can be traded, bought, or sold

composite image a product of combining two or more images

coniferous trees and shrubs with thin leaves and producing cones; also a forest or wood composed of these trees

continental drift a theory that suggests the continents were at one time all part of a prehistoric supercontinent that broke apart; according to the theory, the continents slowly "drifted" across the Earth's surface to their present positions

continental shelf the submerged, offshore extension of a continent

continental slope the steeply graded sea floor connecting the edge of the continental shelf to the deep-ocean floor

convection the transfer of heat within a gas or solid of nonuniform temperature from mass movement or circulatory motion due to gravity and uneven density within the substance

convergent boundary where tectonic plates move toward each other along their common boundary, causing subduction

core the dense, innermost layer of Earth; the outer core is liquid, while the inner core is solid

Coriolis effect the deflection of wind systems and ocean currents (as well as freely moving objects not in contact with the solid Earth) to the right in the Northern Hemisphere and to the left in the Southern Hemisphere as a consequence of the Earth's rotation

crust the rocky, relatively low density, outermost layer of Earth

cultural diffusion the spread of cultural elements from one group to another

culture the "way of life" for a group; it is transmitted from generation to generation and involves a shared system of meanings, beliefs, values, and social relations; it also includes language, religion, clothing, music, laws, and entertainment

D

dead zone oxygen-starved areas in oceans and lakes where marine life cannot be supported, often linked to runoff of excess nutrients

deciduous trees and shrubs that shed their leaves seasonally; also a forest or wood mostly composed of these trees

deformation general term for folding and faulting of rocks due to natural shearing, compression, and extension forces

delta a flat, low-lying, often fan-shaped region at the mouth of a river; it is composed of sediment deposited by a river entering a lake, an ocean, or another large body of water

demography the study of population statistics, changes, and trends based on various measures of fertility, mortality, and migration

denudation the overall effect of weathering, mass wasting, and erosion, which ultimately wears down and lowers the continental surface

desert a region that has little or no vegetation and averages less than 10 inches of precipitation a year

desertification the spread of desert conditions in arid and semiarid regions; desertification results from a combination of climatic changes and increasing human pressures in the form of overgrazing, removal of natural vegetation, and cultivation of marginal land

developed country general term for an industrialized country with a diversified and self-sustaining economy, strong infrastructure, and high standard of living

developing country general term for a non-industrialized country with a weak economy, little modern infrastructure, and low standard of living

dialect a regional variation of one language, with differences in vocabulary, accent, pronunciation, and syntax

diffuse plate boundary a zone of faulting and earthquakes extending to either side of a plate boundary

digital elevation model (DEM) a digital representation of Earth's topography in which data points representing altitude are assigned coordinates and viewed spatially; sometimes called a digital terrain model (DTM)

disconformity a discontinuity in sedimentary rocks in which the rock beds remain parallel

divide a ridge separating watersheds

dormant volcano an active volcano that is temporarily in repose, but expected to erupt in the future

E

earthquake vibrations and shock waves caused by volcanic eruptions or the sudden movement of Earth's crustal rocks along fracture zones called faults

easterlies a regular wind that blows from the east

ecosystem a group of organisms and the environment with which they interact

elevation the height of a point or place above an established datum, sometimes mean sea level

El Niño a pronounced warming of the surface waters along the coast of Peru and the equatorial region of the east Pacific Ocean; it is caused by weakening (sometimes reversal) of the trade winds, with accompanying changes in ocean circulation (including cessation of upwelling in coastal waters)

emigrant a person migrating away from a country or area; an out-migrant

endangered species a species at immediate risk of extinction

endemic typical to or native of a particular area, people, or environment

endogeneous introduced from or originating within a given organism or system

environment the sum of the conditions and stimuli that influence an organism

eon the largest time unit on the geologic time scale; consists of several shorter units called eras

Equator latitude 0°; an imaginary line running east and west around Earth and dividing it into two equal parts known as the Northern and Southern Hemispheres; the Equator always has approximately 12 hours of daylight and 12 hours of darkness

equinox the time of year (usually September 22-23 and March 21-22) when the length of night and day are about equal, and the sun is directly overhead at the Equator

era a major subdivision of time on the geologic time scale; consists of several shorter units called periods

erosion the general term for the removal of surface rocks and sediment by the action of water, air, ice, or gravity

escarpment a cliff or steep rock face that separates two comparatively level land surfaces

estuary a broadened seaward end or extension of a river (usually a drowned river mouth), characterized by tidal influences and the mixing of fresh and saline water

ethnic group minority group with a collective self-identity within a larger host population

ethnocentrism a belief in the inherent superiority of one's own ethnic group and culture; a tendency to view all other groups or cultures in terms of one's own

eutrophication the process that occurs when large amounts of nutrients from fertilizers or animal wastes enter a water body and bacteria break down the nutrients; the bacterial action causes depletion of dissolved oxygen

Exclusive Economic Zone (EEZ) an oceanic zone extending up to 200 nautical miles (370 km) from a shoreline, within which a coastal state claims jurisdiction over fishing, mineral exploration, and other economically important activities

exogenous introduced from or originating outside a given organism or system

external debt debt owed to non-residents; repayable in foreign currency, goods, or services

F

fault a fracture or break in rock where the opposite sides are displaced relative to each other

fjord a coastal inlet that is narrow and deep and reaches far inland; it is usually formed by the sea filling in a glacially scoured valley or trough

flood basalt a huge lava flow that produces thick accumulations of basalt layers over a large area

floodplain a wide, relatively flat area adjacent to a stream or river and subject to flooding and sedimentation; it is the most preferred land area for human settlement and agriculture

food chain the feeding pattern of organisms in an ecosystem, through which energy from food passes from one level to the next in a sequence

fork the place where a river separates into branches; also may refer to one of those branches

fossil fuel fuel in the form of coal, petroleum, or natural gas derived from the remains of ancient plants and animals trapped and preserved in sedimentary rocks

G

galaxy a collection of stars, gas, and dust bound together by gravity; there are billions of galaxies in the universe, and the Earth is in the Milky Way galaxy

genocide the intentional destruction, in whole or in part, of a national, ethnic, racial, or religious group

genome the complete set of genetic material of an organism

geochemistry a branch of geology focusing on the chemical composition of earth materials

geographic information system (GIS) an integrated hardware-software system used to store, organize, analyze, manipulate, model, and display geographic information or data

geography literally means "Earth description"; as a modern academic discipline, geography is concerned with the explanation of the physical and human characteristics and patterns of Earth's surface

geomorphology the study of planetary surface features, especially the processes of landform evolution on Earth

geopolitics the study of how factors such as geography, economics, and demography affect the power and foreign policy of a state

glaciation a period of glacial advancement through the growth of continental ice sheets and/or mountain glaciers

glacier a large, natural accumulation of ice that spreads outward on the land or moves slowly down a slope or valley

global positioning system (GPS) a system of artificial satellites that provides information on three-dimensional position and velocity to users at or near the Earth's surface

global warming the warming of Earth's average global temperature due to a buildup of "greenhouse gases" (e.g., carbon dioxide and methane) released by human activities; increased levels of these gases cause enhanced heat absorption by the atmosphere

globe a scale model of the Earth that correctly represents not only the area, relative size, and shape of physical features but also the distance between points and true compass directions

great circle the largest circle that can be drawn around a sphere such as a globe; a great circle route is the shortest route between two points on the surface of a sphere

greenhouse effect an enhanced near-surface warming that is due to certain atmospheric gases absorbing and re-radiating long-wave radiation that might otherwise have escaped to space had those gases not been present in the atmosphere

gross domestic product (GDP) the total market value of goods and services produced by a nation's economy in a given year using global currency exchange rates

gross national income (GNI) the income derived from the capital and income belonging to nationals employed domestically or abroad

gravitational waves ripples in the fabric of space and time, usually caused by the interaction of two or more large masses

gulf a very large area of an ocean or a sea bordered by coastline on three sides

gyre a large, semicontinuous system of major ocean currents flowing around the outer margins of every major ocean basin

H

habitat the natural environment (including controlling physical factors) in which a plant or animal is usually found or prefers to exist

hemisphere half a sphere; cartographers and geographers, by convention, divide the Earth into the Northern and Southern Hemispheres at the Equator and the Eastern and Western Hemispheres at the prime meridian (longitude 0°) and 180° meridian

herbaceous a type of plant lacking woody tissue, and usually with a life of just one growing season

hot spot a localized and intensely hot region or mantle plume beneath the lithosphere; it tends to stay relatively fixed geographically as a lithospheric plate migrates over it

human geography one of the two major divisions of systematic geography; it is concerned with the spatial analysis of human population, cultures, and social, political, and economic activities

hurricane a large, rotating storm system that forms over tropical waters, with very low atmospheric pressure in the central region and winds in excess of 74 mph (119km/h); it is called a typhoon over the western Pacific Ocean and a cyclone over the northern Indian Ocean

hydrologic cycle the continuous recirculation of water from the oceans, through the atmosphere, to the continents, through the biosphere and lithosphere, and back to the sea

hydrosphere all of the water found on, under, or over Earth's surface

hypsometry the measurement of contours and elevation of land above sea level

I

ice age a period of pronounced glaciation usually associated with worldwide cooling, a greater proportion of global precipitation falling as snow, and a shorter snowmelt period

igneous the rock type formed from solidified molten rock (magma) that originates deep within Earth; the chemical composition of the magma and its cooling rate determine the final rock type

immigrant a person migrating into a particular country or area; an in-migrant

impact crater a circular depression on the surface of a planet or moon caused by the collision of another body, such as an asteroid or comet

indigenous native to or occurring naturally in a specific area or environment

industrial metabolism a concept that describes the process of converting raw materials into a final product and waste through energy and labor

infrastructure transportation and communications networks that allow goods, people, and information to flow across space

inorganic not relating to or being derived from living things

interdependence mutual reliance among beings or processes

internally displaced person a person who flees his/her home, to escape danger or persecution, but does not leave the country

International Date Line an imaginary line that roughly follows the 180° meridian in the Pacific Ocean; immediately west of the date line the calendar date is one day ahead of the calendar date east of the line; people crossing the date line in a westward direction lose one calendar day, while those crossing eastward gain one calendar day

intertropical convergence zone (ITCZ) a zone of low atmospheric pressure created by intense solar heating, thereby leading to rising air and horizontal convergence of northeast and southeast trade winds; over the oceans, the ITCZ is usually found between 10° N and 10° S, and over continents the seasonal excursion of the ITCZ is much greater

isthmus a relatively narrow strip of land with water on both sides and connecting two larger land areas

J

jet stream a high-speed west-to-east wind current; jet streams flow in narrow corridors within upper-air westerlies, usually at the interface of polar and tropical air

K

karst a region underlain by limestone and characterized by extensive solution features such as sinkholes, underground streams, and caves

L

lagoon a shallow, narrow water body located between a barrier island and the mainland, with freshwater contributions from streams and saltwater exchange through tidal inlets or breaches throughout the barrier system

La Niña the pronounced cooling of equatorial waters in the eastern Pacific Ocean

latitude the distance north or south of the Equator; lines of latitude, called parallels, are evenly spaced from the Equator to the North and South Poles (from 0° to 90° N and S latitude); latitude and longitude (see below) are measured in terms of the 360 degrees of a circle and are expressed in degrees, minutes, and seconds

leeward the side away from or sheltered by the wind

lingua franca a language used beyond its native speaker population as a common or commercial language

lithosphere the rigid outer layer of the Earth, located above the asthenosphere and comprising the outer crust and the upper, rigid portion of the mantle

longitude the distance measured in degrees east or west of the prime meridian (0° longitude) up to 180°; lines of longitude are called meridians (compare with latitude, above)

M

macroscopic concerned with or considered in large units

magma molten, pressurized rock in the mantle that is occasionally intruded into the lithosphere or extruded to the surface of the Earth by volcanic activity

magnetic pole the points at Earth's surface at which the geomagnetic field is vertical; the location of these points constantly changes

mantle the dense layer of Earth below the crust; the upper mantle is solid and with the crust, forms the lithosphere, the zone containing tectonic plates; the lower mantle is partially molten, making it the pliable base upon which the lithosphere "floats"

map projection the geometric system of transferring information about a round object, such as a globe, to a flat piece of paper or other surface for the purpose of producing a map with known properties and quantifiable distortion

maria volcanic plains on the moon's surface that appear to the naked eye as smooth, dark areas

meridian a north-south line of longitude used to reference distance east or west of the prime meridian (longitude 0°)

mesa a broad, flat-topped hill or mountain with marginal cliffs and/or steep slopes formed by progressive erosion of horizontally bedded sedimentary rocks

metamorphic the rock type formed from preexisting rocks that have been substantially changed from their original igneous, sedimentary, or earlier metamorphic form; catalysts of this change include high heat, high pressure, hot and mineral-rich fluids, or, more commonly, some combination of these

metric ton (tonne) unit of weight equal to 1,000 kilograms or 2,205 pounds

micrometeoroids a tiny particle of rock or dust in space, usually weighing less than a gram

microscopic considered in or concerned with small units

migration the movement of people across a specified boundary for the purpose of establishing a new place of residence

mineral an inorganic solid with a distinctive chemical composition and a specific crystal structure that affect its physical characteristics

moment magnitude scale a measure of the total energy released by an earthquake; preferred to the Richter scale because it more accurately measures strong earthquakes and can be used with data for distant earthquakes

monsoon a seasonal reversal of prevailing wind patterns, often associated with pronounced changes in moisture

N

nation a cultural concept for a group of people bound together by a strong sense of shared values and cultural characteristics, including language, religion, and common history

nebula a cloud of interstellar gas and dust

node a point where distinct lines or objects intersect

Normalized Difference Vegetation Index (NDVI) a measurement of plant growth density over the Earth's surface, measured on a scale of 0.1 to 0.8 (low to high vegetation)

North Pole the most northerly geographic point on the Earth; the northern end of the Earth's axis of rotation; 90° N

nuclear weapon a weapon which uses nuclear reactions to derive destructive force

O

oasis a fertile area with water and vegetation in a desert

ocean current the regular and persistent flow of water in the oceans, usually driven by atmospheric wind and pressure systems or by regional differences in water density (temperature, salinity)

offshoring relocating business processes to another country, where they are performed by either another branch of the parent company or an external contractor (international outsourcing)

organic relating to or derived from living things

oxbow lake a crescent-shaped lake or swamp occupying a channel abandoned by a meandering river

outsourcing delegating non-core processes from within a business to an external entity such as a subcontractor

ozone a bluish gas composed of three oxygen atoms and harmful to breathe

ozone layer region of Earth's atmosphere where ozone concentration is relatively high; the ozone layer absorbs harmful ultraviolet rays from the sun

P

paleo-geographic map a map depicting the past positions of the continents, developed from historic magnetic, biological, climatological, and geologic evidence

Pangaea the supercontinent from which today's continents are thought to have originated

peninsula a long piece of land jutting out from a larger piece of land into a body of water

period a basic unit of time on the geologic time scale, generally 35 to 70 million years in duration; a subdivision of an era

Phanerozoic eon an eon of Earth's geologic history that comprises the Paleozoic, Mesozoic, and Cenozoic eras

photosynthesis process by which plants convert carbon dioxide and water to oxygen and carbohydrates

physical geography one of the two major divisions of systematic geography; the spatial analysis of the structure, process, and location of Earth's natural phenomena, such as climate, soil, plants, animals, water, and topography

pilgrimage a typically long and difficult journey to a special place, often of religious importance

plain an extensive, flat-lying area characterized generally by the absence of local relief features

planetary nebula an interstellar cloud of gas and dust formed when a star runs out of central nuclear fuel, finally ejecting its outer layers in a gaseous shell

plate tectonics the theory that Earth's lithospheric plates slide or shift slowly over the asthenosphere and that their interactions cause earthquakes, volcanic eruptions, movement of landmasses, and other geologic events

plateau a landform feature characterized by high elevation and gentle upland slopes

politicide the intentional destruction, in whole or in part, of a group of people based on their political or ideological beliefs

point a sharp prominence or headland on the coast that juts out into a body of water

pollution a direct or indirect process resulting from human activity; part of the environment is made potentially or actually unsafe or hazardous to the welfare of the organisms that live in it

porphyry an igneous rock characterized by large crystals within a matrix of much finer crystals

primary energy energy sources as they are found naturally—i.e., before they have been processed or transformed into secondary sources

prime meridian the line of 0° longitude that runs through Greenwich, England, and separates the Eastern and Western Hemispheres

Priscoan eon the earliest eon of Earth's geologic history; also known as the Hadean eon

proliferation the process of growing rapidly and suddenly

Proterozoic eon the eon of geologic time that includes the interval between the Archean and Phanerozoic eons and is marked by rocks that contain fossils indicating the first appearance of eukaryotic organisms (as algae)

protogalaxy a cloud of gas, possibly consisting of dark matter, hydrogen, and helium, that is forming into a galaxy

purchasing power parity (PPP) a method of measuring gross domestic product that compares the relative value of currencies based on what each currency will buy in its country of origin; PPP provides a good comparison between national economies and is a decent indicator of living standards

R

rain shadow the dry region on the downwind (leeward) side of a mountain range

raster data spatial data represented as a unified grid of equal-area cells, each with a single numerical value; best-suited for contiguous data such as elevation

red dwarf a relatively small, cool, and faint star with a very long estimated lifespan; the most common type of star

reef a strip of rocks or sand either at or just below the surface of water

refugee a person who flees his/her country of origin to escape danger or persecution for reasons of, for example, race, religion, or political opinion

regolith a layer of disintegrated or partly decomposed rock overlying unweathered parent materials; regolith is usually found in areas of low relief where the physical transport of debris is weak

remote sensing the measurement of some property of an object by means other than direct contact, usually from aircraft or satellites

renewable resource a resource that can be regenerated or maintained if used at rates that do not exceed natural replenishment

Richter scale a logarithmic scale devised to represent the relative amount of energy released by an earthquake; moment magnitude has superceded the Richter scale as the preferred measurement of earthquake magnitude

rift a long, narrow trough created by plate movement at a divergent boundary

rift valley a long, structural valley formed by the lowering of a block between two parallel faults

Ring of Fire (also Rim of Fire) an arc of volcanoes and tectonic activity along the perimeter of the Pacific Ocean

S

salinization the accumulation of salts in soil

satellite data information collected by a vehicle orbiting a celestial body

savanna a tropical grassland with widely spaced trees; it experiences distinct wet and dry seasons

seamount a submerged volcano rising from the ocean floor

sedimentary the rock type formed from preexisting rocks or pieces of once-living organisms; deposits accumulate on Earth's surface, generally with distinctive layering or bedding

solar radiation energy emitted by the sun

solar wind the stream of atoms and ions moving outward from the solar corona at 300 to 500 kilometers per second

solstice a celestial event that occurs twice a year (usually June 20-21 and December 21-22), when the sun appears directly overhead to observers at the Tropic of Cancer or the Tropic of Capricorn

sound a broad channel or passage of water connecting two larger bodies of water or separating an island from the mainland

South Pole the most southerly geographic point on the Earth; the southern end of the Earth's axis of rotation; 90° S

spatial resolution a measure of the smallest distinguishable separation between two objects

spectral resolution a measure of the ability of a sensing system to distinguish electromagnetic radiation of different frequencies

spit beach extension that forms along a shoreline with bays and other indentations

spreading boundary where plates move apart along their common boundary, creating a crack in the Earth's crust (typically at the mid-ocean ridge), which is then filled with upwelling molten rock; also called a divergent boundary

steppe semiarid, relatively flat, treeless region that receives between 10 and 20 inches of precipitation yearly

state an area with defined and internationally acknowledged boundaries; a political unit

strait a narrow passage of water that connects two larger bodies of water

subduction the tectonic process by which the down-bent edge of one lithospheric plate is forced underneath another plate

subatomic particle a part of an atom, such as a proton, neutron, or electron

T

tariff a surcharge on imports levied by a state; a form of protectionism designed to increase imports' market price and thus inhibit their consumption

tectonic plate (also lithospheric or crustal plate) a section of the Earth's rigid outer layer that moves as a distinct unit upon the plastic-like mantle materials in the asthenosphere

temperate mild or moderate

temporal resolution a measure of the frequency with which a sensing system gathers data

terrestrial radiation natural sources of radiation found in earth materials

threatened species species at some, but not immediate, risk of extinction

tide the regular rise and fall of the ocean, caused by the mutual gravitational attraction between the Earth, moon, and sun, as well as the rotation of the Earth-moon system around its center of gravity

ton a unit of weight equal to 2,000 pounds in the U.S. or 2,240 pounds in the U.K.

tonne (see metric ton)

topography the relief features that are evident on a planetary surface

tornado a violently rotating, funnel-shaped column of air characterized by extremely low atmospheric pressures and exceptional wind speeds generated within intense thunderstorms

tradewind a wind blowing persistently from the same direction; particularly from the subtropical high-pressure centers toward the equatorial low-pressure zone

transgenic an organism artificially or naturally containing one or more genes from a different type of organism

tributary a river or stream flowing into a larger river or stream

tropical warm and moist; occuring in or characteristic of the Tropics

Tropic of Cancer latitude 23.5° N; the farthest northerly excursion of the sun when it is directly overhead

Tropic of Capricorn latitude 23.5° S; the farthest southerly excursion of the sun when it is directly overhead

tsunami a series of ocean waves, often very destructive along coasts, caused by the vertical displacement of the seafloor during an earthquake, submarine landslide, or volcanic eruption

tundra a zone in cold, polar regions (mostly in the Northern Hemisphere) that is transitional between the zone of polar ice and the limit of tree growth; it is usually characterized by low-lying vegetation, with extensive permafrost and waterlogged soils

U

unconformity a discontinuity in sedimentary rocks caused by erosion or nondeposition

uplift the slow, upward movement of Earth's crust

upwelling the process by which water rich in nutrients rises from depth toward the ocean surface; it is usually the result of diverging surface waters

urban agglomeration a group of several cities and/or towns and their suburbs

urbanization a process in which there is an increase in the percentage of people living and working in urban places as compared to rural places; a process of change from a rural to urban lifestyle

V

vector data spatial data represented as as nodes and connectors identified by geographic coordinates, and related to one another to symbolize geographic features; best-suited for geographic features that can be represented as points, lines, or polygons

volcanism the upward movement and expulsion of molten (melted) material and gases from within the Earth's mantle onto the surface where it cools and hardens, producing characteristic terrain

W

watershed the drainage area of a river and its tributaries

weathering the processes or actions that cause the physical disintegration and chemical decomposition of rock and minerals

westerlies a regular wind that blows from the west

wetland an area of land covered by water or saturated by water sufficiently enough to support vegetation adapted to wet conditions

wilderness a natural environment that has remained essentially undisturbed by human activities and, increasingly, is protected by government or nongovernment organizations

windward the side toward or unsheltered from the wind

xerophyte a plant that thrives in a dry environment

yazoo a tributary stream that runs parallel to the main river for some distance

Z

zenith the point in the sky that is immediately overhead; also the highest point above the observer's horizon obtained by a celestial body

zoning the process of subdividing urban areas as a basis for land-use planning and policy

Place-Name Index

THE FOLLOWING SYSTEM is used to locate a place on a map in the National Geographic Family Reference Atlas of the World. The boldface type after an entry refers to the plate on which the map is found. The letter-number combination refers to the grid on which the particular place-name is located. The edge of each map is marked horizontally with numbers and vertically with letters. In between, at equally spaced intervals, are index ticks (▲). If these ticks were connected with lines, each page would be divided into a 12- by 16-square grid. Take Abilene, Kansas, for example. The index entry reads "**Abilene, *Kans., U.S.* 105 S8**." On page 105, Abilene is located within the grid square where row S and column 8 intersect.

A place-name may appear on several maps, but the index lists only the best presentation. Usually, this means that a feature is indexed to the largest-scale map on which it appears in its entirety. (Note: Rivers are often labeled multiple times even on a single map. In such cases, the rivers are indexed to labels that are closest to their mouths.) The name of the country or continent in which a feature lies is shown in italic type and is usually abbreviated. (A full list of abbreviations appears on page 262.)

The index lists more than proper names. Some entries include a description, as in "**Elba, island, *It.* 150 J5**" and "**Urubamba, river, *Peru* 130 H5.**" In languages other than English, the description of a physical feature may be part of the name; e.g., the "Berg" in "**Kleine Berg, *Neth. Antilles, Neth.* 121 P14**" means "mountain." The Glossary of Foreign Terms on page 272 translates such terms into English.

When a feature or place can be referred to by more than one name, both may appear in the index with cross-references. These are especially useful for finding major cities in China, where the phonetic Pinyin system has replaced the Wade-Giles system for the romanization of the Chinese language. For example, the entry for Canton reads "**Canton *see* Guangzhou, *China* 183 R4**." That entry is "**Guangzhou (Canton), *China* 183 R4**."

A

Aachen, Ger. 148 F4
Aalen, Ger. 148 J7
Aalsmeer, Neth. 146 J12
Aalst, Belg. 146 L11
Aansluit, S. Af. 202 J9
Aare, river, Switz. 150 A3
Aarschot, Belg. 146 L12
Aasu, Amer. Samoa, U.S. 218 M7
Aba, China 180 K11
Aba, Dem. Rep. of the Congo 198 H12
Aba, Nigeria 201 H14
Abā as Saʻūd, Saudi Arabia 172 N9
Abaco Island, Bahamas 120 C6
Ābādān, Iran 172 F11
Ābādeh, Iran 173 F13
Abadla, Alg. 196 C9
Abaetetuba, Braz. 131 D13
Abaiang, island, Kiribati 214 G8
Abaji, Nigeria 201 G14
Abajo Peak, Utah, U.S. 107 P9
Abakan, Russ. 159 L13
Abancay, Peru 130 H5
Abaokoro, island, Kiribati 217 F17
Abashiri, Japan 184 E15
Abashiri Wan, Japan 184 E15
Abay, Kaz. 175 E14
Ābaya Hāyk', Eth. 199 H14
Abbaye, Point, Mich., U.S. 98 E7
Abbeville, Ala., U.S. 101 M17
Abbeville, Fr. 146 M9
Abbeville, La., U.S. 100 Q8
Abbeville, S.C., U.S. 96 K7
Abbeyfeale, Ire. 143 T3
Abbeyleix, Ire. 143 T5
Abbiategrasso, It. 150 E4
Abbot Ice Shelf, Antarctica 226 J6
Abbotsford, B.C., Can. 82 M8
Abbotsford, Wis., U.S. 98 H4
Abbottabad, Pak. 176 M11
ʻAbda (Eboda), ruin, Israel 171 P5
ʻAbd al ʻAzīz, Jabal, Syr. 170 D13
ʻAbd al Kūrī, island, Yemen 173 R13
Abéché, Chad 197 H16
Ab-e Istadeh-ye Moqor, lake, Afghan. 177 P7
Abemama, island, Kiribati 214 G8
Abengourou, Côte d'Ivoire 200 H9
Åbenrå, Den. 140 P11
Abeokuta, Nigeria 200 G12
Aberaeron, Wales, U.K. 143 U9
Aberdare, Wales, U.K. 143 V10
Aberdaron, Wales, U.K. 143 T8
Aberdaugleddau see Milford Haven, Wales, U.K. 143 V8
Aberdeen, Idaho, U.S. 106 H6
Aberdeen, Md., U.S. 96 C14
Aberdeen, Miss., U.S. 101 J13
Aberdeen, N.C., U.S. 96 J11
Aberdeen, S. Dak., U.S. 104 J6
Aberdeen, Scot., U.K. 142 K11
Aberdeen, Wash., U.S. 108 D2
Aberdeen Lake, Nunavut, Can. 83 H14
Aberffraw, Wales, U.K. 143 S9
Abergele, Wales, U.K. 143 S10
Abergwaun see Fishguard, Wales, U.K. 143 U8
Abernathy, Tex., U.S. 102 J5
Abert, Lake, Oreg., U.S. 108 K6
Abertawe see Swansea, Wales, U.K. 143 V9
Aberteifi see Cardigan, Wales, U.K. 143 U9
Abertillery, Wales, U.K. 143 V10
Aberystwyth, Wales, U.K. 143 U9
Abhā, Saudi Arabia 172 N8
Abidjan, Côte d'Ivoire 200 H9
Abilene, Kans., U.S. 105 S8
Abilene, Tex., U.S. 102 L8
Abingden Downs, Qnsld., Austral. 211 R12
Abingdon see Pinta, Isla, island, Ecua. 128 N9
Abingdon, Eng., U.K. 143 V12
Abingdon, Ill., U.S. 99 Q4
Abingdon, Va., U.S. 96 G8
Abiquiu, N. Mex., U.S. 107 R12
Abisko, Sw. 141 D13
Abitibi, river, N. Amer. 80 H8
Abitibi, Lake, N. Amer. 80 H8
Abkhazia, Rep. of Georgia 169 A15
Åbo see Turku, Fin. 141 K15
Abohar, India 178 E4
Abomey, Benin 200 G11
Abraham Lincoln Birthplace National Historic Site, Ky., U.S. 101 C16
Abraham's Bay, Bahamas 117 H16
Abra Pampa, Arg. 132 D9
Abreú, Dom. Rep. 117 L19
Abrolhos, Arquipélago dos, Braz. 131 K16
Absalom, Mount, Antarctica 226 E11
Absaroka Range, Wyo., U.S. 106 F9
Absarokee, Mont., U.S. 106 E9
Absheron Yarymadasy, peninsula, Azerb. 169 D23
Abū al Abyaḑ, island, U.A.E. 173 J14
Abu al Ḩuşayn, Qāʻ, Jordan 170 M10
Abū ʻAlī, island, Saudi Arabia 172 H12
Abū Baḩr, plain, Saudi Arabia 172 L11
Abu Ballâș, peak, Egypt 194 E8
Abū Daghmah, Syr. 170 D10
Abu Dhabi see Abū Z̧aby, U.A.E. 173 J14
Abu Durba, Egypt 171 T2
Abu Hamed, Sudan 199 C13
Abuja, Nigeria 201 F14
Abū Kamāl, Syr. 170 H14
Abū Madd, Ra's, Saudi Arabia 172 J6
Abu Matariq, Sudan 198 F11
Abunã, river, Bol., Braz. 130 G7
Abunã, Braz. 130 G7
Abū Qumayyiş, Ra's, Saudi Arabia 173 J13
Abu Rudeis, Egypt 171 S2
Abu Rūjmayn, Jabal, Syr. 170 G10
Abu Shagara, Ras, Sudan 199 C14
Abu Simbel, site, Egypt 197 F19
Abuta, Japan 184 G13
Ābuyē Mēda, peak, Eth. 199 F15
Abu Zabad, Sudan 198 F12
Abū Z̧aby (Abu Dhabi), U.A.E. 173 J14
Abu Zenîma, Egypt 171 S2
Abwong, Sudan 199 G13
Abyad, El Bahr el (White Nile), Sudan 199 F13
Abyek, Iran 172 C12
Academy Glacier, Antarctica 226 H10
Acadia National Park, Me., U.S. 95 F18
A Cañiza, Sp. 144 C6
Acaponeta, Mex. 114 G9
Acapulco, Mex. 114 K11
Acaraú, Braz. 131 D16
Acarigua, Venez. 128 C8
Acatenango, Volcán de, Guatemala 115 L15
Acatlán, Mex. 114 J12
Accomac, Va., U.S. 96 E15
Accra, Ghana 200 H11
Accumoli, It. 150 J9
Achach, island, F.S.M. 217 C14
Acharacle, Scot., U.K. 142 L7
Achavanich, Scot., U.K. 142 H10
Achayvayam, Russ. 159 D21
Achill Island, Ire. 143 R3
Achim, Ger. 148 C7
Achinsk, Russ. 159 K13
Achna, Cyprus 160 P9
Achnasheen, Scot., U.K. 142 J8
Acıgöl, lake, Turk. 168 G5
Acıpayam, Turk. 168 H5
Ackerman, Miss., U.S. 100 K12
Ackley, Iowa, U.S. 105 N12
Acklins, The Bight of, Bahamas 117 H15
Acklins Island, Bahamas 117 H15
Acoma Pueblo, N. Mex., U.S. 107 S11
Aconcagua, Cerro, Arg. 132 K7
Aconcagua, Río, Chile 132 K6
Açores see Azores, islands, Atl. Oc. 204 C3
A Coruña, Sp. 144 A6
Acquaviva, San Marino 161 J14
Acqui Terme, It. 150 F3
Acraman, Lake, Austral. 210 J9
Acre, river, Braz., Peru 130 G6
Acre see ʻAkko, Israel 170 K5
Acteon, Groupe, Fr. Polynesia, Fr. 219 G22
Actium, battle, Gr. 154 G7
Açu, Braz. 131 F17
Ada, Ghana 200 H11
Ada, Minn., U.S. 104 G8
Ada, Ohio, U.S. 99 Q12
Ada, Okla., U.S. 102 H12
Ada, Serb. & Mont. 152 D10
Adair, Cape, Nunavut, Can. 83 E17
Adak Island, Alas., U.S. 110 N5
Adalia see Antalya, Turk. 168 H6
Adam, Oman 173 K16
Adámandás, Gr. 155 M13
Adamello, peak, It. 150 C6
Adams, Minn., U.S. 104 L12
Adams, Wis., U.S. 98 K5
Adams, Mount, Wash., U.S. 108 E5
Adam's Peak, Sri Lanka 179 T7
Adam's Rock, Pitcairn I., U.K. 219 Q23
Adamstown, Pitcairn I., U.K. 219 Q23
Adamsville, Tenn., U.S. 101 G13
ʻAdan (Aden), Yemen 172 R9
Adana, Turk. 168 J10
ʻAdan aş Şughrá, cape, Yemen 172 R9
Adang, Teluk, Indonesia 188 K12
Adare, Cape, Antarctica 227 R13
Adavale, Qnsld., Austral. 211 U12
Adda, river, It. 150 E5
Ad Dahnā', desert, Saudi Arabia 172 H10
Ad Dakhla, W. Sahara, Mor. 196 E5
Ad Dammām, Saudi Arabia 172 H12
Ad Dār al Ḩamrā', Saudi Arabia 172 H6
Ad Darb, Saudi Arabia 172 N8
Ad Dawādimī, Saudi Arabia 172 J9
Ad Dawḩah (Doha), Qatar 173 J13
Ad Dibdibah, region, Iraq, Kuwait, Saudi Arabia 172 G10
Ad Dilam, Saudi Arabia 172 K11
Addis Ababa see Ādīs Ābeba, Eth. 199 G15
Ad Dīwānīyah, Iraq 172 E10
Addu Atoll, Maldives 179 X3
Ad Duwayd, Saudi Arabia 172 F8
Addy, Wash., U.S. 108 B8
Adel, Ga., U.S. 97 P6
Adel, Iowa, U.S. 105 P11
Adel, Oreg., U.S. 108 L6
Adelaide, Bahamas 120 B10
Adelaide, S. Aust., Austral. 211 Y10
Adelaide Island, Antarctica 226 E4
Adelaide Peninsula, Nunavut, Can. 83 F14
Adelaide River, N. Terr., Austral. 211 P7
Adelfi, island, Gr. 155 G13
Adélie Coast, Antarctica 227 Q18
Aden see ʻAdan, Yemen 172 R9
Aden, Gulf of, Ind. Oc. 240 E5
Aderbissinat, Niger 196 H12
Adieu, Cape, Austral. 210 J8
Adige, river, It. 150 E7
Ādīgrat, Eth. 199 E15
Adilabad, India 178 L6
Adímilos, island, Gr. 155 M13
Adin, Calif., U.S. 108 M5
Adinkerke, Belg. 146 L10
Adíparos, island, Gr. 155 L14
Adirondack Mountains, N.Y., U.S. 94 G11
Ādīs Ābeba (Addis Ababa), Eth. 199 G15
Adi Ugri, Eritrea 199 E15
Adıyaman, Turk. 169 H13
Adjud, Rom. 153 D16
Adjuntas, P.R., U.S. 120 N3
Adlavik Islands, Nfld. & Lab., Can. 83 K22
Adler, Russ. 157 U11
Admiralty Inlet, Nunavut, Can. 83 E16
Admiralty Inlet, Wash., U.S. 108 B4
Admiralty Island, Alas., U.S. 84 Q7
Admiralty Island National Monument, Alas., U.S. 111 L22
Admiralty Islands, P.N.G. 213 B19
Admiralty Mountains, Antarctica 227 Q14
Abou Deïa, Chad 197 J15
Adour, river, Fr. 147 X7
Adra, Sp. 144 M11
Adrano, It. 151 S11
Adrar, Alg. 196 D10
Adrar, region, Mauritania 196 F6
Adrar des Iforas, range, Mali 196 F10
Adraskan, Afghan. 177 N2
Adria, It. 150 E8
Adrian, Mich., U.S. 99 N11
Adrian, Minn., U.S. 104 L9
Adrian, Tex., U.S. 102 G4
Adrianople see Edirne, Turk. 168 B3
Adriatic Sea, Eur. 138 J7
Adun Gol, China 182 B2
Ādwa, Eth. 199 E15
Adyakit, Gora, Russ. 159 F14
Aegean Sea, Eur. 138 K9
Aegina see Égina, island, Gr. 154 K12
Aegir Ridge, Arctic Oc. 243 J20
Aej, island, Marshall Is. 216 G8
Aeon Point, Kiribati 217 C24
Afaahiti, Fr. Polynesia, Fr. 219 P17
Afándou, Gr. 155 N20
Afar, region, Eth. 199 E16
Afareaitu, Fr. Polynesia, Fr. 219 N14
Affric, Glen, Scot., U.K. 142 K8
Afghanistan, Asia 167 U6
ʻAfīf, Saudi Arabia 172 K8
Afiq, Israel 170 K6
Afitos, Gr. 154 D12
Afmadow, Somalia 199 J16
Afobaka, Suriname 129 E16
Afognak Island, Alas., U.S. 111 L15
Afono Bay, Amer. Samoa, U.S. 218 L8
ʻAfrīn, Syr. 170 D8
Afşin, Turk. 168 G12

B

Batukelau, *Indonesia* **188** J11
Bat'umi, *Rep. of Georgia* **169** C16
Batu Pahat, *Malaysia* **187** V10
Batuputih, *Indonesia* **188** H12
Baturaja, *Indonesia* **188** L7
Baturité, *Braz.* **131** E17
Bat Yam, *Israel* **170** M5
Batz, Île de, *Fr.* **147** P3
Bau, island, *Fiji Is.* **218** J7
Baubau, *Indonesia* **189** L14
Baucau, *Timor-Leste* **189** M15
Bauchi, *Nigeria* **201** F15
Baudette, *Minn., U.S.* **104** E10
Baudó, Serranía de, *S. Amer.* **126** B2
Baugé, *Fr.* **147** R7
Bauges, range, *Fr.* **147** U14
Baun, *Indonesia* **189** N14
Baunatal, *Ger.* **148** F7
Baures, river, *Bol.* **130** H8
Bauru, *Braz.* **131** L13
Baús, *Braz.* **130** K11
Bautino, *Kaz.* **174** G5
Bautzen, *Ger.* **148** F11
Bavaria, region, *Ger.* **148** J8
Bawal, island, *Indonesia* **188** K9
Bawean, island, *Indonesia* **188** L10
Bawku, *Ghana* **200** F11
Baxkorgan, *China* **180** G8
Baxley, *Ga., U.S.* **97** N7
Baxoi, *China* **180** L9
Baxter, *Minn., U.S.* **104** H10
Baxter Springs, *Kans., U.S.* **105** V10
Bay'ah, *Oman* **173** J15
Bayamo, *Cuba* **116** K12
Bayamón, *P.R., U.S.* **120** M4
Bayan, *Mongolia* **180** E9
Bayanaūyl, *Kaz.* **175** D15
Bayandalay, *Mongolia* **180** F11
Bayanga, *Cen. Af. Rep.* **198** J8
Bayan Gol *see* Dengkou, *China* **182** C1
Bayan Har Shan, *China* **180** J9
Bayan Har Shankou, *China* **180** J10
Bayanhongor, *Mongolia* **180** E11
Bayanmönh, *Mongolia* **181** D13
Bayano, Lago, *Pan.* **115** N22
Bayan Obo, *China* **182** B3
Bayan Range, *Afghan.* **176** M5
Bayard, *N. Mex., U.S.* **107** V10
Bayard, *Nebr., U.S.* **105** P1
Bayat, *Turk.* **168** F6
Bayāz, *Iran* **173** F15
Bayboro, *N.C., U.S.* **96** J14
Bayburt, *Turk.* **169** E15
Bay City, *Mich., U.S.* **98** K12
Bay City, *Tex., U.S.* **103** S13
Baydarata Bay, *Arctic Oc.* **243** A14
Baydaratskaya Guba, *Russ.* **158** F11
Baydhabo (Baidoa), *Somalia* **199** J16
Bayès, Cap, *New Caledonia, Fr.* **218** C7
Bayeux, *Fr.* **147** N7
Bayfield, *Wis., U.S.* **98** E4
Bayghanīn, *Kaz.* **174** E8
Bayḩān al Qişāb, *Yemen* **172** Q10
Bayındır, *Turk.* **168** G3
Bay Islands, *N. Amer.* **80** P7
Bayjī, *Iraq* **172** C9
Baykal, Ozero, *Russ.* **159** L16
Baykan, *Turk.* **169** G16
Baykonur *see* Bayqongyr, *Kaz.* **174** G10
Baykonur Cosmodrome, *Kaz.* **174** G11
Baykurt, *China* **180** F4
Bay Minette, *Ala., U.S.* **101** N14
Bay of Whales, station, *Antarctica* **226** N11
Bayonne, *Fr.* **147** X5
Bayqongyr (Baykonur, Leninsk), *Kaz.* **174** G10
Bayramaly, *Turkm.* **174** M10
Bayramiç, *Turk.* **168** E2
Bayreuth, *Ger.* **148** H9
Bay St. Louis, *Miss., U.S.* **100** P12
Bay Springs, *Miss., U.S.* **100** M12
Bayt al Faqīh, *Yemen* **172** Q8
Bayt Laḩm (Bethlehem), *W. Bank* **170** M5
Baytown, *Tex., U.S.* **103** Q14
Baza, *Sp.* **144** L12
Baza'i Gonbad, *Afghan.* **176** K11
Bazar Dyuzi, peak, *Azerb.* **169** C21
Bazar-e Panjva'i, *Afghan.* **177** Q5
Bazar-e Taleh, *Afghan.* **176** L7
Bazar-Kurgan, *Kyrg.* **176** F10
Bazartöbe, *Kaz.* **174** D6
Bazas, *Fr.* **147** W7
Bazkovskaya, *Russ.* **157** P11
Bazmān, Kūh-e, *Iran* **173** G17
Be, Nosy, *Madagascar* **203** D18
Beach, *N. Dak., U.S.* **104** G1
Beach Haven, *N.J., U.S.* **94** Q11
Beachy Head, *Eng., U.K.* **143** W14
Beagle Bay, *W. Aust., Austral.* **211** R4
Béar, Cap, *Fr.* **147** Z11
Bearden, *Ark., U.S.* **100** J8
Beardmore Glacier, *Antarctica* **227** L13
Beardstown, *Ill., U.S.* **99** R4
Bear Island, *Ire.* **143** V2
Bear Islands *see* Medvezh'i Ostrova, *Russ.* **159** C19
Bear Lake, *Idaho, Utah, U.S.* **106** J8
Bear Paw Mountains, *Mont., U.S.* **84** C8
Bear River Range, *Idaho, Utah, U.S.* **106** J7
Bears Paw Mountains, *Mont., U.S.* **106** B9
Beasain, *Sp.* **144** B12
Beata, Cabo, *Dom. Rep.* **117** N17
Beata, Isla, *Dom. Rep.* **117** N17
Beata Ridge, *Atl. Oc.* **236** L4
Beatrice, *Nebr., U.S.* **105** R8
Beatrice, Cape, *Austral.* **210** B10
Beattock, *Scot., U.K.* **143** N10
Beatton River, *B.C., Can.* **82** J9
Beatty, *Nev., U.S.* **109** T10
Beau Bassin, *Mauritius* **205** G19
Beaucaire, *Fr.* **147** X12
Beauchêne Island, *Falkland Is., U.K.* **133** W12
Beaufort, *Lux.* **160** J10
Beaufort, *Malaysia* **188** G11
Beaufort, *N.C., U.S.* **96** J14
Beaufort, *S.C., U.S.* **96** M9
Beaufort Sea, *Arctic Oc.* **242** M5
Beaufort Shelf, *Arctic Oc.* **242** N5
Beaufort Slope, *Arctic Oc.* **242** N5
Beaufort West, *S. Af.* **202** L9
Beaugency, *Fr.* **147** R9
Beaumanoir, Port du, *Fr. Polynesia, Fr.* **219** Q17
Beaumont, *Tex., U.S.* **103** Q15
Beaune, *Fr.* **147** S13
Beausoleil, *Fr.* **147** X16
Beausoleil, Town Hall of, *Fr.* **161** C21
Beautemps Beaupré, Île, *New Caledonia, Fr.* **218** C8
Beauvais, *Fr.* **147** N9
Beauvoir, *Fr.* **147** S5
Beaver, *Alas., U.S.* **111** E17
Beaver, river, *Okla., U.S.* **102** E6
Beaver, *Okla., U.S.* **102** E7
Beaver, *Oreg., U.S.* **108** F2
Beaver, *Utah, U.S.* **107** N6
Beaver Bay, *Minn., U.S.* **104** F13
Beaver City, *Nebr., U.S.* **105** R5
Beaver Creek, *Kans., U.S.* **105** R4
Beaver Creek, *Mont., U.S.* **106** B10
Beaver Dam, *Ky., U.S.* **101** C15
Beaver Dam, *Wis., U.S.* **98** L6
Beaver Falls, *Pa., U.S.* **94** N3
Beaver Glacier, *Antarctica* **227** C19
Beaverhead, river, *Mont., U.S.* **106** F6
Beaverhead Mountains, *Mont., U.S.* **106** F6
Beaver Island, *Mich., U.S.* **98** G9
Beaver Lake, *Ark., U.S.* **100** E6
Beaverton, *Oreg., U.S.* **108** F3
Beawar, *India* **178** G4
Bebar, *India* **178** H1
Bebiram, *Indonesia* **213** B14
Beccles, *Eng., U.K.* **143** T16
Bečej, *Serb. & Mont.* **152** E10
Becerreá, *Sp.* **144** B7
Béchar, *Alg.* **196** C9
Becharof Lake, *Alas., U.S.* **111** L14
Beckerich, *Lux.* **160** J9
Beckley, *W. Va., U.S.* **96** E8
Beddouza, Cap, *Mor.* **196** B7
Bedford, *Eng., U.K.* **143** U13
Bedford, *Ind., U.S.* **99** T9
Bedford, *Iowa, U.S.* **105** Q10
Bedford, *Pa., U.S.* **94** P5
Bedford, *Va., U.S.* **96** F10
Bedford, Cape, *Austral.* **210** C13
Bedfort Point, *Grenada* **121** J23
Bedonia, *It.* **150** F5
Bedourie, *Qnsld., Austral.* **211** U10
Bedous, *Fr.* **147** Y6
Beebe, *Ark., U.S.* **100** G9
Beech Grove, *Ind., U.S.* **99** R9
Beef Island, *Virgin Islands, U.K.* **120** Q7
Beenleigh, *Qnsld., Austral.* **211** V15
Be'ér Menuḩa, *Israel* **171** Q5
Be'er Ora, *Israel* **171** R5
Beersheba *see* Be'ér Sheva', *Israel* **171** N5
Be'ér Sheva' (Beersheba), *Israel* **171** N5
Beetaloo, *N. Terr., Austral.* **211** R8
Beethoven Peninsula, *Antarctica* **226** F6
Beeville, *Tex., U.S.* **103** T10
Bega, *N.S.W., Austral.* **211** Z14
Bega, river, *Rom.* **152** D12
Bega, Canalul, *Rom.* **152** E10
Begejski Kanal, *Serb. & Mont.* **152** E10
Beggars Point, *Antigua & Barbuda* **121** A21
Bègles, *Fr.* **147** V6
Begusarai, *India* **178** H10
Behagle *see* Laï, *Chad* **197** K14
Behbehān, *Iran* **172** F12
Behring Point, *Bahamas* **116** E11
Behshahr, *Iran* **173** B14
Bei, river, *China* **181** N14
Bei'an, *China* **181** C17
Beida *see* Al Bayḑā', *Lib.* **197** B16
Beihai, *China* **183** S1
Beijing (Peking), *China* **182** D7
Beilen, *Neth.* **146** H14
Beiliu, *China* **183** R2
Beilul, *Eritrea* **199** E16
Beipiao, *China* **182** B9
Beira, *Mozambique* **203** G13
Beirut *see* Beyrouth, *Leb.* **170** H6
Bei Shan, *China* **180** F9
Beitbridge, *Zimb.* **202** H11
Beït ed Dîne, *Leb.* **170** J6
Beiuş, *Rom.* **152** C12
Beizhen, *China* **182** B10
Beja, *Port.* **144** K6
Beja, *Tun.* **196** A12
Bejaïa, *Alg.* **196** A11
Béjar, *Sp.* **144** F8
Bejestān, *Iran* **173** D16
Bekaa Valley, *Leb.* **170** J7
Bekdash *see* Karabogaz, *Turkm.* **174** J6
Békés, *Hung.* **149** M17
Békéscsaba, *Hung.* **149** M17
Bekily, *Madagascar* **203** J16
Bekja, island, *Marshall Is.* **216** K8
Bekkai, *Japan* **184** F16
Bekobod, *Taj.* **176** G8
Bekobod, *Uzb.* **175** L13
Bekoropoka-Antongo, *Madagascar* **203** H16
Bekwai, *Ghana* **200** H10
Bela, *Pak.* **177** V5
Belaga, *Malaysia* **188** H11
Bel Air, *Mauritius* **205** G20
Belalcázar, *Sp.* **144** J9
Belarus, *Eur.* **139** T9
Bela Vista, *Braz.* **130** L10
Belaya, river, *Russ.* **138** D14
Belaya, Gora, *Russ.* **159** C20
Belaya Glina, *Russ.* **157** S11
Belaya Gora, *Russ.* **159** E18
Belaya Kalitva, *Russ.* **157** Q11
Belaya Zemlya, Ostrova, *Russ.* **159** C13
Bełchatów, *Pol.* **149** F15
Belcheragh, *Afghan.* **176** L5
Belcher Islands, *Nunavut, Can.* **83** L17
Belcik, *Turk.* **168** E11
Belcoo, *N. Ire., U.K.* **143** Q5
Belderg, *Ire.* **143** Q3
Belding, *Mich., U.S.* **98** L10
Beledweyne, *Somalia* **199** H17
Belele, *W. Aust., Austral.* **211** V3
Belém, *Braz.* **131** D13
Belén, *Arg.* **132** G8
Belen, *N. Mex., U.S.* **107** S12
Bélep, Îles, *New Caledonia, Fr.* **218** B6
Bélep, Îles, *New Caledonia, Fr.* **214** K7
Belev, *Russ.* **156** L9
Belfast, *Me., U.S.* **95** F17
Belfast, *N. Ire., U.K.* **143** Q7
Belfast Lough, *N. Ire., U.K.* **143** P7
Belfield, *N. Dak., U.S.* **104** G2
Belfort, *Fr.* **147** R15
Belgaum, *India* **179** N4
Belgica Bank, *Arctic Oc.* **243** J15
Belgica Mountains, *Antarctica* **227** C16
Belgium, *Eur.* **139** T5
Belgodère, *Fr.* **150** J4
Belgorod, *Russ.* **157** N9
Belgrade, *Mont., U.S.* **106** E8
Belgrade *see* Beograd, *Serb. & Mont.* **152** F10
Belgrano II, station, *Antarctica* **226** E10
Belhaven, *N.C., U.S.* **96** H14
Belidzhi, *Russ.* **157** U16
Belilou *see* Peleliu, island, *Palau* **216** Q10
Belinyu, *Indonesia* **188** K8
Belitung (Billiton), island, *Indonesia* **188** K9
Belize, *N. Amer.* **81** P19
Belize City, *Belize* **115** K16
Bel'kachi, *Russ.* **159** H19
Bel'kovskiy, Ostrov, *Russ.* **159** D16
Bella Bella, *B.C., Can.* **82** K7
Bellac, *Fr.* **147** T8
Bella Coola, *B.C., Can.* **82** K8
Bellaire, *Mich., U.S.* **98** H10
Bellaire, *Ohio, U.S.* **99** R15
Bellaire, *Tex., U.S.* **103** R14
Bellary, *India* **179** N5
Bella Unión, *Uru.* **132** J13
Bella Vista, *Arg.* **132** G9
Bella Vista, *Arg.* **132** H13
Bellavista, *Peru* **130** F2
Belle-Anse, *Haiti* **117** M17
Belledonne, Chaîne de, *Fr.* **147** U14
Bellefontaine, *Martinique, Fr.* **121** F22
Bellefontaine, *Ohio, U.S.* **99** Q12
Bellefonte, *Pa., U.S.* **94** N6
Belle Fourche, *S. Dak., U.S.* **104** K1
Belle Fourche, river, *Wyo., U.S.* **106** G13
Belle Fourche Reservoir, *S. Dak., U.S.* **104** K1
Bellegarde, *Fr.* **147** Q10
Bellegarde, *Fr.* **147** T14
Belle Glade, *Fla., U.S.* **97** V10
Belle-Île, *Fr.* **147** R4
Belle Isle, *Nfld. & Lab., Can.* **83** L23
Belle Isle, Strait of, *Nfld. & Lab., Can.* **83** L22
Bellême, *Fr.* **147** Q8
Belle Plaine, *Iowa, U.S.* **105** N13
Belle Plaine, *Minn., U.S.* **104** K11
Belleville, *Fr.* **147** T12
Belleville, *Ill., U.S.* **99** T4
Belleville, *Kans., U.S.* **105** R7
Bellevue, *Iowa, U.S.* **105** N14
Bellevue, *Nebr., U.S.* **105** Q9
Bellevue, *Ohio, U.S.* **99** P13
Bellevue, *Tex., U.S.* **102** K10
Bellevue, *Wash., U.S.* **108** C4
Bellingham, *Wash., U.S.* **108** A4
Bellingshausen, station, *Antarctica* **226** C3
Bellingshausen Plain, *Antarctic Oc.* **244** J7
Bellingshausen Sea, *Antarctica* **226** H4
Bellinzona, *Switz.* **150** C4
Bello, *Col.* **128** E4
Bellona Island, *Solomon Is.* **217** Q18
Bellows Falls, *Vt., U.S.* **95** J13
Bellpat, *Pak.* **177** S7
Bell Peninsula, *Nunavut, Can.* **83** H17
Bell Point, *St. Martin, Fr.* **121** A14
Bell Rock (Inchcape), *Scot., U.K.* **142** L11
Bells, *Tenn., U.S.* **100** F12
Belluno, *It.* **150** C8
Bell Ville, *Arg.* **132** K11
Bellville, *Tex., U.S.* **103** Q12
Belmond, *Iowa, U.S.* **104** M11
Belmont, *Grenada* **121** L22
Belmont, *Miss., U.S.* **101** H13
Belmont, *N.C., U.S.* **96** J9
Belmonte, *Port.* **144** F7
Belmonte, *Sp.* **144** H12
Belmonte, *Braz.* **131** J16
Belmopan, *Belize* **115** K16
Belmullet, *Ire.* **143** Q3
Belogorsk, *Russ.* **159** K19
Belo Horizonte, *Braz.* **131** L14
Beloit, *Kans., U.S.* **105** S7
Beloit, *Wis., U.S.* **98** M6
Belomorsk, *Russ.* **158** D8
Belorado, *Sp.* **144** C11
Belorechensk, *Russ.* **157** T11
Belo-Tsiribihina, *Madagascar* **203** G16
Beloūsovka, *Kaz.* **175** D18
Beloye, Lake *see* Beloye, Ozero, *Russ.* **138** C10
Beloye More, *Russ.* **158** D8
Beloye Ozero, *Russ.* **156** F9
Belozersk, *Russ.* **156** F9
Belpre, *Ohio, U.S.* **99** S15
Belt, *Mont., U.S.* **106** C8
Belterra, *Braz.* **130** D11
Belton, *S.C., U.S.* **96** K7
Belton, *Tex., U.S.* **103** P11
Belton Lake, *Tex., U.S.* **103** N11
Belukha, peak, *Russ.* **166** F8
Belukha, Gora, *Russ.* **158** M12
Belush'ya Guba, *Russ.* **158** D10
Belvedere Courtyard, *Vatican City* **161** P16
Belvedere Marittimo, *It.* **151** P13
Belvès, *Fr.* **147** V8
Belvidere, *Ill., U.S.* **98** M6
Belvidere, *S. Dak., U.S.* **104** L4
Belvís de la Jara, *Sp.* **144** G9
Belyando, river, *Austral.* **210** F13
Belyy, *Russ.* **156** J7
Belyy, Ostrov, *Russ.* **158** E12
Belzoni, *Miss., U.S.* **100** K10
Bemaraha, plateau, *Madagascar* **203** G16
Bembe, *Angola* **202** B6
Bembibre, *Sp.* **144** C8
Bemidji, *Minn., U.S.* **104** F10
Benāb, *Iran* **172** B10
Benabarre, *Sp.* **145** D15
Benadir, region, *Somalia* **194** K11
Benasque, *Sp.* **145** C15
Benavente, *Sp.* **144** D9
Benavides, *Tex., U.S.* **103** U10
Benbecula, island, *Scot., U.K.* **142** J6
Bend, *Oreg., U.S.* **108** H5
Bendals, *Antigua & Barbuda* **121** B20
Bendena, *Qnsld., Austral.* **211** V13
Bender, *Mold.* **157** R5
Bender Cassim *see* Boosaaso, *Somalia* **199** F18
Bendern, *Liech.* **160** M2
Bendigo, *Vic., Austral.* **211** Z12
Bené Beraq, *Israel* **170** M5
Benetutti, *It.* **151** N4
Benevento, *It.* **150** M11
Bengal, Bay of, *Ind. Oc.* **166** K8
Bengara, *Indonesia* **188** H12
Bengbu, *China* **182** J7
Benghazi *see* Banghāzī, *Lib.* **197** C15
Benghisa Point, *Malta* **161** L23
Bengkalis, island, *Indonesia* **188** H6
Bengkalis, *Indonesia* **188** H6
Bengkayang, *Indonesia* **188** J9
Bengkulu, *Indonesia* **188** K6
Bengo, Baía do, *Angola* **202** C5
Benguela, *Angola* **202** D5
Benguerir, *Mor.* **196** B8
Beni, river, *Bol.* **130** H7
Beni Abbes, *Alg.* **196** C9
Benicarló, *Sp.* **145** F15
Benidorm, *Sp.* **145** J15
Benifaió, *Sp.* **145** H14
Beni Mazâr, *Egypt* **197** D18
Benin, *Af.* **195** H16
Benin, Bight of, *Af.* **194** J4
Benin City, *Nigeria* **201** H13
Beni Ounif, *Alg.* **196** B10
Beni Suef, *Egypt* **197** D18
Benitses, *Gr.* **154** F6
Benjamin, *Tex., U.S.* **102** K8
Benjamin Constant, *Braz.* **130** E5
Benjamín Hill, *Mex.* **114** C7
Benkelman, *Nebr., U.S.* **105** R3
Benlidi, *Qnsld., Austral.* **211** U13
Bennett, Ostrov, *Russ.* **159** C17
Bennett Peak, *N. Mex., U.S.* **107** Q10
Bennettsville, *S.C., U.S.* **96** J10
Ben Nevis, peak, *Scot., U.K.* **142** L8
Benneydale, *N.Z.* **213** K19
Bennington, *Vt., U.S.* **94** J12
Benoud, *Alg.* **196** B10
Bensbach, *P.N.G.* **213** E17
Bensheim, *Ger.* **148** H6
Benson, *Ariz., U.S.* **107** V8
Benson, *Minn., U.S.* **104** J9
Benson, *N.C., U.S.* **96** H12
Benson Point, *Kiribati* **217** B22
Bent, *Iran* **173** H17
Benta, *Malaysia* **188** G6
Bentham's, *Barbados* **121** J18
Bentinck Island, *Myanmar* **187** P7
Bentiu, *Sudan* **198** G12
Bentley Subglacial Trench, *Antarctica* **226** K10
Benton, *Ark., U.S.* **100** H8
Benton, *Ill., U.S.* **99** U6
Benton, *Ky., U.S.* **101** D13
Benton, *La., U.S.* **100** K6
Bentong, *Indonesia* **189** L13
Bentong, *Malaysia* **187** U9
Benton Harbor, *Mich., U.S.* **99** N9
Benton Lake, *Mont., U.S.* **106** C8
Bentonville, *Ark., U.S.* **100** E6
Bent's Old Fort National Historic Site, *Colo., U.S.* **107** N15

C

D

E

F

Faial, island, Azores 144 P3
Faibus Point, N. Mariana Is., U.S. 216 B7
Faichuk, island, F.S.M. 217 C14
Faie, Fr. Polynesia, Fr. 219 G14
Faie, Baie de, Fr. Polynesia, Fr. 219 G14
Faihava Passage, Tonga 218 L11
Faioa, island, Tonga 218 L12
Faïoa, island, Wallis & Futuna, Fr. 218 C11
Fairbanks, Alas., U.S. 111 G17
Fairborn, Ohio, U.S. 99 R12
Fairburn, Ga., U.S. 96 L5
Fairbury, Ill., U.S. 99 Q6
Fairbury, Nebr., U.S. 105 R8
Fairfax, Okla., U.S. 102 E11
Fairfax, S.C., U.S. 96 M9
Fairfield, Ala., U.S. 101 J15
Fairfield, Calif., U.S. 109 R4
Fairfield, Idaho, U.S. 106 H5
Fairfield, Ill., U.S. 99 T6
Fairfield, Iowa, U.S. 105 Q13
Fairfield, Mont., U.S. 106 C7
Fairfield, Ohio, U.S. 99 S11
Fairfield, Tex., U.S. 103 N12
Fair Haven, Vt., U.S. 94 H12
Fairhope, Ala., U.S. 101 P14
Fair Isle, Scot., U.K. 142 F11
Fairmont, Minn., U.S. 104 L10
Fairmont, W. Va., U.S. 96 C9
Fairport, Mich., U.S. 98 G8
Fairport, N.Y., U.S. 94 J7
Fairview, Mont., U.S. 106 C13
Fairview, Okla., U.S. 102 F9
Fairview, Qnsld., Austral. 211 Q12
Fairview, Tenn., U.S. 101 E15
Fairview, Utah, U.S. 106 M7
Fairweather, Mount, Alas., U.S. 111 K21
Fais, island, F.S.M. 214 F3
Faisalabad, Pak. 177 Q11
Faith, S. Dak., U.S. 104 J3
Faizabad, India 178 G8
Fajardo, P.R., U.S. 120 M6
Fajardo, P.R., U.S. 117 M23
Fakahiku, island, Tonga 218 Q6
Fakahina, island, Fr. Polynesia, Fr. 219 E20
Fakakakai, Tonga 218 P7
Fakaofu, island, Tokelau, N.Z. 214 H10
Fakarava, island, Fr. Polynesia, Fr. 219 E18
Fakel, Russ. 156 G16
Fakenham, Eng., U.K. 143 T15
Fakfak, Indonesia 189 K18
Faku, China 182 B11
Fala Ane Point, Amer. Samoa, U.S. 218 Q3
Falaise, Pointe, St. Martin, Fr. 121 B14
Falakró, Óros, Gr. 155 B13
Falamae, Solomon Is. 217 L14
Falciano, San Marino 161 G17
Falcon, Cape, Oreg., U.S. 108 E2
Falcon, Presa, Mex. 114 E12
Falconara Marittima, It. 150 H9
Falcone, Capo del, It. 150 M3
Falconer, N.Y., U.S. 94 K4
Falcon Reservoir, Tex., U.S. 103 V8
Falealupo, Samoa 218 K1
Faleasao, Amer. Samoa, U.S. 218 P3
Falefatu, island, Tuvalu 217 L23
Falelatie, Samoa 218 L3
Falelima, Samoa 218 K1
Falémé, river, Mali, Senegal 196 H6
Faleniu, Amer. Samoa, U.S. 218 M7
Falfurrias, Tex., U.S. 103 V10
Falkenberg, Sw. 140 N12
Falkensee, Ger. 148 D10
Falkirk, Scot., U.K. 142 M9
Falkland Escarpment, Atl. Oc. 237 V6
Falkland Fracture Zone, Antarctic Oc. 244 B9
Falkland Islands (Islas Malvinas), Falkland Is., U.K. 133 W12
Falkland Plateau, Atl. Oc. 237 V6
Falkland Sound, Falkland Is., U.K. 133 W12
Falknis, peak, Liech., Switz. 160 R3
Falkonéra, island, Gr. 154 M12
Falköping, Sw. 140 M12
Fallbrook, Calif., U.S. 109 Y9
Fallen Jerusalem, island, Virgin Islands, U.K. 120 R8
Fallières Coast, Antarctica 226 E5
Fallon, Nev., U.S. 109 P7
Fall River, Mass., U.S. 95 L15
Fall River Lake, Kans., U.S. 105 U9
Fall River Mills, Calif., U.S. 108 M4
Falls City, Nebr., U.S. 105 R9
Falmouth, Antigua & Barbuda 121 B21
Falmouth, Eng., U.K. 143 Y8
Falmouth, Jam. 120 H7
Falmouth, Ky., U.S. 101 A18
Falmouth, Me., U.S. 95 H16
Falmouth Harbour, Antigua & Barbuda 121 B21
False Bay, S. Af. 194 R7
False Cape, N. Amer. 80 N3
False Divi Point, India 179 N8
False Pass, Alas., U.S. 110 N11
False Point, India 178 K11
Falset, Sp. 145 E16
Falso, Cabo, Dom. Rep. 117 N17
Falso, Cabo, Mex. 114 G7
Falster, island, Den. 140 P12
Fălticeni, Rom. 153 B15
Falun, Sw. 141 K13
Famagusta see Ammochostos, Cyprus 160 P10
Fanaik, island, F.S.M. 217 D16
Fanan, island, F.S.M. 217 C16
Fanananei, Mochun, F.S.M. 217 B14
Fanangat, island, F.S.M. 217 B15
Fanannon, island, F.S.M. 217 C15
Fanapanges, island, F.S.M. 217 C14
Fanasich, island, F.S.M. 217 C14
Fanchang, China 182 K8
Fancy, St. Vincent & the Grenadines 121 J16
Fanemoch, island, F.S.M. 217 B15
Faneno, island, F.S.M. 217 B15
Fanew, island, F.S.M. 217 C15
Fanew, Mochun, F.S.M. 217 C15
Fangak, Sudan 198 G12
Fangale'ounga, Tonga 218 P7
Fangasito, island, Tonga 218 M11
Fangatau, island, Fr. Polynesia, Fr. 219 E20
Fangataufa, island, Fr. Polynesia, Fr. 219 H21
Fangcheng, China 182 J4
Fangshan, China 182 E4
Fangxian, China 182 J3
Fanning Island see Tabuaeran, Kiribati 214 F12
Fano, It. 150 G9
Fanos, island, F.S.M. 217 B15
Fanshan, China 183 N9
Fanshi, China 182 D5
Fanūdah, Saudi Arabia 172 J7
Fañunchuluyan, Bahia, N. Mariana Is., U.S. 216 B6
Fanurmot, island, F.S.M. 217 C14
Fanxian, China 182 G6
Farafangana, Madagascar 203 H17
Farâfra Oasis, Egypt 197 D18
Farah, river, Afghan. 177 P2
Farah, Afghan. 177 P2
Farallon de Medinilla, island, N. Mariana Is., U.S. 216 C2
Farallon de Pajaros, island, N. Mariana Is., U.S. 214 D4
Farallon Islands, Calif., U.S. 84 G2
Faranah, Guinea 200 F6
Farasān, Jazā'ir, Saudi Arabia 172 P8
Faraulep Atoll, F.S.M. 216 Q4
Fare, Fr. Polynesia, Fr. 219 G14
Fareara, Pointe, Fr. Polynesia, Fr. 219 Q17
Fareera, Passe, Fr. Polynesia, Fr. 219 G14
Fareham, Eng., U.K. 143 W13
Farewell, Cape see Nunap Isua, Greenland, Den. 81 D22
Farewell, Cape, N.Z. 213 M17
Farga de Moles, Sp. 160 K2
Fargo, N. Dak., U.S. 104 G8
Farg'ona, Uzb. 175 K14
Faribault, Minn., U.S. 104 K11
Faridkot, India 178 D4
Farim, Guinea-Bissau 200 E4
Farīmān, Iran 173 C16
Fariones, Punta, Canary Is. 204 P8
Farkhor, Taj. 176 K8
Farmakonísion, Gr. 155 L18
Farmersville, Tex., U.S. 102 K12
Farmerville, La., U.S. 100 K8
Farmington, Ill., U.S. 99 Q4
Farmington, Me., U.S. 95 F16
Farmington, Mo., U.S. 105 U15
Farmington, N. Mex., U.S. 107 Q10
Farmington, Utah, U.S. 106 K7
Farmville, Va., U.S. 96 F12
Farnham, N.Y., U.S. 94 K4
Fårö, island, Sw. 141 L14
Faro, Port. 144 L6
Faro, Punta del, It. 151 R12
Faroe Bank, Atl. Oc. 236 C12
Faroe-Iceland Ridge, Atl. Oc. 236 C11
Faroe Islands (Føroyar), Den. 140 J5
Farquhar, Atoll de, Seychelles 203 C19
Farrell, Pa., U.S. 94 M3
Fārs, region, Iran 173 G14
Fársala, Gr. 154 F10
Farsund, Nor. 140 M10
Fartak, Ra's, Yemen 173 P13
Far'ûn (Coral Island), Egypt 171 R5
Farwell, Tex., U.S. 102 H3
Fasā, Iran 173 G14
Fasano, It. 150 M14
Fastiv, Ukr. 157 N5
Fastnet Rock, Ire. 143 V3
Fataka (Mitre Island), Solomon Is. 214 J8
Fatato, island, Tuvalu 217 K23
Fatehabad, India 178 E5
Fatehgarh, India 178 F7
Fatehpur, India 178 G7
Fátima, Port. 144 G5
Fatsa, Turk. 168 D12
Fatu Hiva, island, Fr. Polynesia, Fr. 215 H15
Fatumanini, Passe, Wallis & Futuna, Fr. 218 B11
Fatumanongi, island, Tonga 218 P6
Fatumu, Tonga 218 J12
Faucilles, Monts, Fr. 147 Q14
Faulkton, S. Dak., U.S. 104 J6
Fauna Nui, Lac, Fr. Polynesia, Fr. 219 G14
Fauro, island, Solomon Is. 217 K15
Fauske, Nor. 140 E12
Faversham, Eng., U.K. 143 V15
Favignana, Isola, It. 151 S8
Faxaflói, bay, Ice. 140 F2
Faya-Largeau, Chad 197 G15
Fayaoué, New Caledonia, Fr. 218 C8
Fayaoué, Baie de, New Caledonia, Fr. 218 C8
Fayd, Saudi Arabia 172 H8
Fayette, Ala., U.S. 101 J14
Fayette, Miss., U.S. 100 M10
Fayette, Mo., U.S. 105 S12
Fayetteville, Ark., U.S. 100 E6
Fayetteville, N.C., U.S. 96 J11
Fayetteville, Tenn., U.S. 101 G15
Fayetteville, W. Va., U.S. 96 E8
Fazilka, India 178 E4
Fdérik, Mauritania 196 E6
Fear, Cape, N.C., U.S. 96 K12
Fécamp, Fr. 147 N8
Federal, Arg. 132 J13
Federated States of Micronesia, Pac. Oc. 214 F4
Fedorovka, Kaz. 174 B10
Fefen, island, F.S.M. 217 C15
Fehmarn, island, Ger. 148 B9
Feijó, Braz. 130 F5
Feilding, N.Z. 213 L19
Feira de Santana, Braz. 131 H16
Feixi, China 182 K7
Feke, Turk. 168 G11
Felanitx, Sp. 145 H18
Feldbach, Aust. 148 M12
Feldberg, peak, Ger. 148 K6
Feldkirch, Aust. 148 L7
Feldkirch, Aust. 160 M3
Félicité Island, Seychelles 205 M21
Felidu Atoll, Maldives 179 V3
Felipe Carrillo Puerto, Mex. 115 H17
Felixstowe, Eng., U.K. 143 U15
Fellowship, Jam. 120 J11
Fellowship, Jam. 120 J7
Feltre, It. 150 D7
Femund, lake, Nor. 140 J11
Fen, river, China 182 F4
Fena Valley Reservoir, Guam, U.S. 216 D10
Fen Country, Eng., U.K. 143 T14
Fene, Sp. 144 A6
Feneppi, island, F.S.M. 217 D15
Fengari, peak, Gr. 155 D15
Fengcheng, China 182 C11
Fengcheng, China 183 N6
Fenghuang, China 183 N2
Fengjie, China 182 K2
Fengkai, China 183 R3
Fenglin, Taiwan, China 183 R10
Fengning, China 182 C7
Fengshan, Taiwan, China 183 S9
Fengtai, China 182 J7
Fengxian, China 180 K12
Fengyüan, Taiwan, China 183 R9
Fengzhen, China 182 C5
Feni Islands, P.N.G. 213 C22
Feno, Cap de, Fr. 150 L4
Feno, Capo di, Fr. 150 K3
Fenua Fu, island, Wallis & Futuna, Fr. 218 C11
Fenualoa, island, Solomon Is. 217 P23
Fenua Roa, island, Fr. Polynesia, Fr. 219 K16
Fenxi, China 182 F4
Fenyang, China 182 F4
Feodosiya, Ukr. 157 S8
Feolin Ferry, Scot., U.K. 142 M7
Fer, Point au, La., U.S. 100 R9
Fera, island, Solomon Is. 217 M18
Ferdows, Iran 173 D16
Féres, Gr. 155 C16
Fērfēr, Eth. 199 H17
Fergana Valley, Uzb. 175 K14
Fergus Falls, Minn., U.S. 104 H9
Ferguson Seamount, Pac. Oc. 238 F9
Fergusson Island, P.N.G. 213 E21
Feridu, island, Maldives 179 U3
Ferit, island, F.S.M. 217 B16
Ferkéssédougou, Côte d'Ivoire 200 F8
Fermo, It. 150 H10
Fermont, Que., Can. 83 L20
Fermoselle, Sp. 144 E8
Fermoy, Ire. 143 U4
Fernandez Bay, Bahamas 120 E11
Fernandina, Isla (Narborough), Ecua. 128 Q7
Fernandina Beach, Fla., U.S. 97 Q8
Fernando de Noronha, S. Amer. 126 E12
Fernando de Noronha, Arquipélago de, Braz. 131 E19
Fernan Vaz see Omboué, Gabon 201 L15
Ferndale, Calif., U.S. 109 N1
Ferndale, Wash., U.S. 108 A4
Fern Grotto, Hawai'i, U.S. 112 B6
Fern Gully, Jam. 120 H9
Fernlee, Qnsld., Austral. 211 V13
Fernley, Nev., U.S. 109 P7
Ferrara, It. 150 F7
Ferrato, Capo, It. 151 P4
Ferré, Cap, Martinique, Fr. 121 G23
Ferreira do Alentejo, Port. 144 K5
Ferreira Gomes, Braz. 130 C12
Ferreñafe, Peru 130 F2
Ferret, Cap, Fr. 147 W6
Ferrette, Fr. 147 R15
Ferriday, La., U.S. 100 M9
Ferro see Hierro, island, Canary Is. 204 R3
Ferro, Ilhéu de, Madeira 204 L5
Ferrol, Sp. 144 A6
Ferrolana, Eq. Guinea 204 M6
Ferrysburg, Mich., U.S. 98 L9
Fertile, Minn., U.S. 104 F8
Fès (Fez), Mor. 196 B9
Feshi, Dem. Rep. of the Congo 198 M8
Fessenden, N. Dak., U.S. 104 F5
Festus, Mo., U.S. 105 T15
Feteşti, Rom. 153 F17
Fethiye, Turk. 168 J4
Fethiye Körfezi, Turk. 168 J4
Fetlar, island, Scot., U.K. 142 D12
Fetoa, island, Tonga 218 Q6
Fetokopunga, island, Tonga 218 Q7
Fetuna, Fr. Polynesia, Fr. 219 C23
Feuet, Lib. 196 E12
Feuilles, Rivière aux, Que., Can. 83 K19
Feurs, Fr. 147 U12
Fevzipaşa, Turk. 168 H11
Feyzabad, Afghan. 176 K9
Fez see Fès, Mor. 196 B9
Fezzan, region, Lib. 197 E13
Fianarantsoa, Madagascar 203 H17
Fichtelberg, peak, Ger. 148 G10
Fidenza, It. 150 E5
Fieberling Tablemount, Pac. Oc. 239 F15
Fields Find, W. Aust., Austral. 211 W3
Fier, Albania 152 L9
Fier-Shegan, Albania 152 L9
Fife Lake, Mich., U.S. 98 J10
Fife Ness, Scot., U.K. 142 M11
Fifth Cataract, Sudan 199 D13
Figari, Capo, It. 150 M5
Figeac, Fr. 147 W9
Fig Tree, St. Kitts & Nevis 121 C18
Figueira da Foz, Port. 144 F5
Figueres, Sp. 145 C18
Figuig, Mor. 196 B9
Fiji Islands, Pac. Oc. 214 J9
Fiji Islands Plateau, Pac. Oc. 238 L10
Filabres, Sierra de los, Sp. 144 L12
Filadelfia, Parag. 130 L9
Filchner Ice Sheet, Antarctica 226 F10
Filey, Eng., U.K. 143 Q13
Filfla, island, Malta 161 M22
Filiaşi, Rom. 153 F13
Filiátes, Gr. 154 E7
Filiatrá, Gr. 154 L9
Filicudi, Isola, It. 151 R11
Filiourí, river, Gr. 155 B15
Filipiáda, Gr. 154 F7
Filipstad, Sw. 140 K12
Fillmore, Calif., U.S. 109 W7
Fillmore, Utah, U.S. 107 N7
Filyos, river, Turk. 168 C8
Fimbul Ice Shelf, Antarctica 226 A12
Fimi, river, Dem. Rep. of the Congo 198 K8
Fiñana, Sp. 144 L12
Fındıklı, Turk. 169 C15
Findlay, Ohio, U.S. 99 P12
Findochty, Scot., U.K. 142 J10
Fineveke, Wallis & Futuna, Fr. 218 B11
Finger Lakes, N.Y., U.S. 94 K7
Fíngoè, Mozambique 202 E12
Fínikas, Gr. 155 K14
Finike, Turk. 168 J5
Finisterre, Cape, Sp. 138 H2
Finke, river, N. Terr., Austral. 211 U9
Finke, N. Terr., Austral. 211 U9
Finland, Eur. 139 Q9
Finland, Minn., U.S. 104 F13
Finland, Gulf of, Est., Fin. 141 K16
Finlay, river, B.C., Can. 82 J9
Finley, N. Dak., U.S. 104 F7
Finley Cay, Bahamas 120 E5
Finnmark Plateau, Nor. 138 A8
Finnsmark-vidda, region, Nor. 141 C14
Finschhafen, P.N.G. 213 D20
Finsteraarhorn, peak, Switz. 150 C3
Fionn Loch, Scot., U.K. 142 J8
Fionnphort, Scot., U.K. 142 L7
Fiorentino, San Marino 161 K15
Fiorina, river, San Marino 161 H16
Fiorina, San Marino 161 H16
Frías, Arg. 132 H9
Firat (Euphrates), river, Turk. 169 E15
Fire Island National Seashore, N.Y., U.S. 94 N12
Firenze (Florence), It. 150 G7
Firenzuola, It. 150 G7
Firmat, Arg. 132 K11
Firminy, Fr. 147 U12
Firozabad, India 178 G6
Firoz Koh, region, Afghan. 176 M4
First Cataract, Egypt 197 E19
First Sugar Mill, Hawai'i, U.S. 112 C5
Fīrūzābād, Iran 173 G13
Fish, river, Namibia 202 J7
Fisher, river, Mont., U.S. 106 B5
Fisher, S. Aust., Austral. 211 W7
Fisher Glacier, Antarctica 227 F18
Fisher Strait, Nunavut, Can. 83 H16
Fishguard (Abergwaun), Wales, U.K. 143 U8
Fishing Cays, Bahamas 120 C10
Fish Lake, Utah, U.S. 107 N7
Fiskárdo, Gr. 154 H7
Fismes, Fr. 147 N11
Fisterra, Sp. 144 B5
Fisterra, Cabo, Sp. 144 B5
Fitchburg, Mass., U.S. 95 K14
Fitii, Fr. Polynesia, Fr. 219 G14
Fitii, Baie de, Fr. Polynesia, Fr. 219 G14
Fitiuta, Amer. Samoa, U.S. 218 N4
Fito, Mount, Samoa 218 L3
Fitri, Lac, Chad 197 J15
Fitzgerald, Alta., Can. 82 J11
Fitzgerald, Ga., U.S. 97 P6
Fitzroy, river, Qnsld., Austral. 210 F15
Fitzroy, river, W. Aust., Austral. 211 R5
Fitzroy Crossing, W. Aust., Austral. 211 R5
Fiume see Rijeka, Croatia 152 E4
Fiumicello, river, San Marino 161 J16
Fivaku, island, Maldives 179 T3
Five Island Harbour, Antigua & Barbuda 121 B20
Five Islands Village, Antigua & Barbuda 121 B20

G

Guayaguayare Bay, *Trinidad & Tobago* **121** Q23
Guayama, *P.R., U.S.* **120** N4
Guayaquil, *Ecua.* **128** K2
Guayaquil, Gulf of, *S. Amer.* **126** D1
Guaymas, *Mex.* **114** D7
Guaynabo, *P.R., U.S.* **120** M4
Gûbâl, Strait of, *Egypt* **171** U3
Gubbio, *It.* **150** H8
Gubin, *Pol.* **148** E11
Gubkin, *Russ.* **157** N9
Gucheng, *China* **182** J3
Gudalur, *India* **179** Q5
Gudaut'a, *Abkhazia* **169** A15
Gudermes, *Russ.* **157** T14
Gudgeon Bay, *Pitcairn I., U.K.* **219** Q23
Gudur, *India* **179** P7
Guebwiller, *Fr.* **147** Q15
Guelb er Rîchât, peak, *Mauritania* **196** F6
Guelmim, *Mor.* **196** C7
Güeppí, *Peru* **130** C3
Guéra Massif, *Chad* **194** G7
Guerara, *Alg.* **196** B11
Guéret, *Fr.* **147** T9
Guernsey, island, *Ch. Is.* **143** Z11
Guernsey, *Wyo., U.S.* **106** J13
Guernsey Reservoir, *Wyo., U.S.* **106** J13
Gueydan, *La., U.S.* **100** P8
Gugegwe, island, *Marshall Is.* **216** M6
Guguan, island, *N. Mariana Is., U.S.* **216** B2
Gui, river, *China* **183** R2
Guía de Isora, *Canary Is.* **204** Q4
Guiana Highlands, *S. Amer.* **126** B6
Guiana Island, *Antigua & Barbuda* **121** B21
Guichi, *China* **182** L7
Guide, *China* **180** J11
Guienne, region, *Fr.* **147** W7
Guiglo, *Côte d'Ivoire* **200** G7
Guijá, *Mozambique* **202** J12
Guijuelo, *Sp.* **144** F8
Guildford, *Eng., U.K.* **143** W13
Guilford, *Me., U.S.* **95** E16
Guilin, *China* **183** Q2
Guillaume-Delisle, Lac, *Que., Can.* **83** L18
Guillestre, *Fr.* **147** V15
Guimarães, *Port.* **144** D6
Guimarães, *Braz.* **131** D15
Guin, *Ala., U.S.* **101** J14
Guinchos Cay, *Cuba* **116** G11
Guinea, *Af.* **195** H14
Guinea, Gulf of, *Af.* **194** J4
Guinea-Bissau, *Af.* **195** G13
Güines, *Cuba* **116** G6
Guingamp, *Fr.* **147** P4
Guiping, *China* **183** R2
Güira de Melena, *Cuba* **116** G6
Güiria, *Venez.* **128** B12
Guisborough, *Eng., U.K.* **143** Q12
Guitiriz, *Sp.* **144** B6
Guixi, *China* **183** N7
Guixian, *China* **183** R1
Guiyang, *China* **183** P4
Guiyang, *China* **180** N12
Gujar Khan, *Pak.* **177** N11
Gujranwala, *Pak.* **177** P12
Gujrat, *Pak.* **177** P11
Gulang, *China* **180** H11
Gulbarga, *India* **178** M5
Gulbene, *Latv.* **141** L17
Gul'cha, *Kyrg.* **176** G11
Gulf Islands National Seashore, *Fla., U.S.* **97** Q2
Gulf Islands National Seashore, *Miss., U.S.* **101** P13
Gulfport, *Miss., U.S.* **100** P12
Gulf Shores, *Ala., U.S.* **101** P14
Gulgong, *N.S.W., Austral.* **211** X14
Guling, *China* **182** M6
Guliston, *Uzb.* **175** K13
Gulitel, Mount, *Palau* **216** M12
Gulja *see* Yining, *China* **180** E6
Gulkana, *Alas., U.S.* **111** H18
Güllük, *Turk.* **168** H3
Gülnar, *Turk.* **168** J8
Gülşehir, *Turk.* **168** F10
Gulu, *Uganda* **199** J13
Gülübovo, *Bulg.* **153** J15
Gulya, *Russ.* **159** K18
Gulyantsi, *Bulg.* **153** G14
Guma *see* Pishan, *China* **180** G4
Gumdag, *Turkm.* **174** L6
Gumla, *India* **178** J9
Gummi, *Nigeria* **201** E13
Gümüşhacıköy, *Turk.* **168** D10
Gümüşhane, *Turk.* **169** D14
Gümüşören, *Turk.* **168** G10
Gumzai, *Indonesia* **189** L19
Guna, *India* **178** H6
Gun Bay, *Cayman Is., U.K.* **120** J4
Gun Cay, *Bahamas* **116** D9
Gun Creek, *Virgin Islands, U.K.* **120** Q9
Gundagai, *N.S.W., Austral.* **211** Y13
Gundlupet, *India* **179** Q5
Gündoğmuş, *Turk.* **168** J7
Güney, *Turk.* **168** G4
Gungu, *Dem. Rep. of the Congo* **198** L9
Gun Hill, *Barbados* **121** K19
Gunib, *Russ.* **157** U15
Gunnbjørn, peak, *N. Amer.* **80** B10
Gunnedah, *N.S.W., Austral.* **211** W14
Gunners Quoin, island, *Mauritius* **205** F20
Gunnewin, *Qnsld., Austral.* **211** U14
Gunnison, *Colo., U.S.* **107** N11
Gunnison, *Utah, U.S.* **106** M7
Gunsan, *S. Korea* **182** G13
Gunt, river, *Taj.* **176** J10
Guntersville, *Ala., U.S.* **101** H16
Guntersville Lake, *Ala., U.S.* **101** H16
Guntur, *India* **179** N7
Gunungsugih, *Indonesia* **188** L7
Guoyang, *China* **182** J6
Gupis, *Pak.* **176** L11
Gurabo, *P.R., U.S.* **120** N5
Gurage, peak, *Eth.* **194** H10
Gura Humorului, *Rom.* **153** B15
Gura Portiıei, strait, *Rom.* **153** F18
Gurban Obo, *China* **181** F14
Gurdaspur, *India* **177** P13
Gurdon, *Ark., U.S.* **100** J7
Güre, *Turk.* **168** F5
Gurer, island, *Marshall Is.* **216** L3
Gurguan Point, *N. Mariana Is., U.S.* **216** B7
Guri Dam, *Venez.* **128** D12
Guri i Topit, peak, *Albania* **152** L10
Gurimatu, *P.N.G.* **213** D19
Gurkovo, *Bulg.* **153** J15
Gurney, *P.N.G.* **213** E21
Gürün, *Turk.* **168** F12
Gurupá, *Braz.* **130** D12
Gurupá Island, *S. Amer.* **126** D8
Gurupi, river, *Braz.* **131** D14
Gurupi, *Braz.* **131** G13
Gurupi, Cape, *S. Amer.* **126** D9
Gurupi, Serra do, *Braz.* **131** E13
Gurvan Bogd Uul, range, *Mongolia* **180** E11
Gusau, *Nigeria* **201** E14
Gusev, *Russ.* **156** J2
Guşgy, river, *Turkm.* **174** N10
Guşgy, *Turkm.* **174** P10
Gushan, *China* **182** D11
Gushi, *China* **182** K6
Gushikawa, *Japan* **185** Y1
Gusikha, *Russ.* **159** E15
Gusinaya Bank, *Arctic Oc.* **243** C16
Gusinoozersk, *Russ.* **159** L16
Gus' Khrustal'nyy, *Russ.* **156** J11
Guspini, *It.* **151** P3
Güssing, *Aust.* **148** M12
Gustavia, *St.-Barthélemy* **119** F15
Gustine, *Calif., U.S.* **109** S5
Güstrow, *Ger.* **148** C9
Gutâiu, peak, *Rom.* **153** B13
Gutcher, *Scot., U.K.* **142** C12
Gutenberg Castle, *Liech.* **160** Q2
Gütersloh, *Ger.* **148** E6
Guthrie, *Ky., U.S.* **101** D15
Guthrie, *Okla., U.S.* **102** F11
Guthrie, *Tex., U.S.* **102** K7
Guthrie Center, *Iowa, U.S.* **105** P10
Gutian, *China* **183** P8
Guttenberg, *Iowa, U.S.* **104** M14
Güvem, *Turk.* **168** D8
Guwahati, *India* **178** G13
Guyana, *S. Amer.* **127** B18
Guyandotte, river, *W. Va., U.S.* **96** E7
Guyang, *China* **182** C3
Guymon, *Okla., U.S.* **102** E5
Guyonneau, Anse, *Guadeloupe, Fr.* **121** F14
Guyra, *N.S.W., Austral.* **211** W15
Guyuan, *China* **182** B6
Güzeloluk, *Turk.* **168** J9
Güzelyurt, *Turk.* **168** G9
Guzhang, *China* **182** M2
G'uzor, *Uzb.* **174** M12
Gwa, *Myanmar* **186** K5
Gwadar, *Pak.* **177** W2
Gwai, *Zimb.* **202** G10
Gwalior, *India* **178** G6
Gwanda, *Zimb.* **202** G11
Gwangju (Kwangju), *S. Korea* **182** G13
Gwardafuy, Cape, *Somalia* **194** G12
Gwatar Bay, *Pak.* **177** W1
Gweebarra Bay, *Ire.* **143** P4
Gweru, *Zimb.* **202** G11
Gwinn, *Mich., U.S.* **98** F7
Gwinner, *N. Dak., U.S.* **104** H7
Gwoza, *Nigeria* **201** F16
Gwydir, river, *Austral.* **210** J14
Gyamysh, peak, *Azerb.* **169** D20
Gyangzê, *China* **180** L7
Gyaring Co, *China* **180** K7
Gyaring Hu, *China* **180** J9
Gydan *see* Kolymskoye Nagor'ye, range, *Russ.* **159** D20
Gydanskiy Poluostrov, *Russ.* **158** F12
Gyda Peninsula, *Russ.* **166** C8
Gyêgu, *China* **180** K9
Gyeongju (Kyŏngju), *S. Korea* **182** G15
Gympie, *Qnsld., Austral.* **211** V15
Gyöngyös, *Hung.* **149** L15
Győr, *Hung.* **149** L14
Gypsum, *Kans., U.S.* **105** T7
Gyula, *Hung.* **149** M17
Gyumri, *Arm.* **169** D18
Gyzylarbat, *Turkm.* **174** L7
Gyzyletrek, *Turkm.* **174** M6
Gyzylgaya, *Turkm.* **174** K7
Gyzylsuw, *Turkm.* **174** K6
Gżira, *Malta* **161** K23

H

Ha'afeva, island, *Tonga* **218** Q6
Haag, *Switz.* **160** N2
Ha'akame, *Tonga* **218** J11
Ha'alaufuli, *Tonga* **218** L12
Haamaire, Baie, *Fr. Polynesia, Fr.* **219** K14
Haamene, Baie de, *Fr. Polynesia, Fr.* **219** A23
Ha'ano, island, *Tonga* **218** P7
Ha'apai Group, *Tonga* **214** K10
Haapamäki, *Fin.* **141** H15
Haapiti, *Fr. Polynesia, Fr.* **219** N14
Haapsalu, *Est.* **141** K16
Haapu, *Fr. Polynesia, Fr.* **219** H14
Haarlem, *Neth.* **146** J12
Ha'asini, *Tonga* **218** J12
Haast, *N.Z.* **213** P15
Haast Bluff, *N. Terr., Austral.* **211** T8
Haava, Canal, *Fr. Polynesia, Fr.* **219** N20
Hab, river, *Pak.* **177** V6
Habahe, *China* **180** C7
Ḩabarūt, *Oman* **173** N14
Habomai, *Japan* **184** F16
Habomai Islands, *Russ.* **184** G6
Haboro, *Japan* **184** E13
Hachijō Jima, *Japan* **185** S12
Hachiman, *Japan* **185** P10
Hachinohe, *Japan* **184** J13
Hachiōji, *Japan* **185** P12
Hachirō Gata, *Japan* **184** K12
Hachita, *N. Mex., U.S.* **107** V10
Hacıbektaş, *Turk.* **168** F9
Hadarba, Ras, *Sudan* **199** B14
Ḩadd, Ra's al, *Oman* **173** K17
Haddummati Atoll, *Maldives* **179** W3
Hadejia, river, *Nigeria* **194** G5
Ḩadera, *Israel* **170** L5
Hadhramaut *see* Ḩaḑramawt, region, *Yemen* **166** J3
Hadīboh (Tamrida), *Yemen* **173** R14
Ḩadīdah, *Syr.* **170** D10
Hadım, *Turk.* **168** H7
Ḩadīthah, *Iraq* **172** D8
Hadja, *Solomon Is.* **217** P20
Hadley Bay, *Nunavut, Can.* **83** E13
Ha Dong, *Vietnam* **186** H12
Ḩaḑramawt, region, *Yemen* **172** Q11
Hadrian's Wall, *Eng., U.K.* **143** P11
Hadyach, *Ukr.* **157** N7
Haeju, *N. Korea* **182** E12
Hā'ena, *Hawai'i, U.S.* **113** M22
Haenam, *S. Korea* **182** H13
Ḩafar al Bāţin, *Saudi Arabia* **172** G10
Hafik, *Turk.* **168** E12
Ḩafīt, Jabal, *U.A.E.* **173** K15
Hafizabad, *Pak.* **177** P11
Hagåtña (Agana), *Guam, U.S.* **216** C10
Hagemeister Island, *Alas., U.S.* **110** L12
Hagen, *Ger.* **148** F6
Hagerman, *N. Mex., U.S.* **107** U14
Hagerman Fossil Beds National Monument, *Idaho, U.S.* **106** H4
Hagerstown, *Md., U.S.* **96** B12
Häggenås, *Sw.* **140** H12
Hagi, *Japan* **185** Q5
Ha Giang, *Vietnam* **186** G11
Hagia Triada, ruin, *Gr.* **155** R14
Hagman, Puntan, *N. Mariana Is., U.S.* **216** C5
Hagoi Susupe, lake, *N. Mariana Is., U.S.* **216** C4
Hags Head, *Ire.* **143** S3
Hague, Cap de la, *Fr.* **147** N5
Haguenau, *Fr.* **147** P15
Haha Jima Rettō, *Japan* **184** K5
Hai, Hon, *Vietnam* **187** Q14
Hai'an, *China* **182** J9
Hai'an, *China* **181** Q13
Haicheng, *China* **182** C10
Hai Duong, *Vietnam* **186** H12
Haifa *see* Ḩefa, *Israel* **170** K5
Haifeng, *China* **183** S5
Haig, *W. Aust., Austral.* **211** W6
Haiger, *Ger.* **148** G6
Haikang, *China* **183** T1
Haikou, *China* **183** T2
Ha'iku, *Hawai'i, U.S.* **113** G17
Ḩā'il, *Saudi Arabia* **172** H8
Hailar, *China* **181** C15
Hailey, *Idaho, U.S.* **106** G5
Hails, *China* **182** B1
Hailuoto, island, *Fin.* **141** F15
Haimen *see* Jiaojiang, *China* **182** M10
Haimen Wan, *China* **183** R6
Hainan, island, *China* **183** U2
Haines, *Alas., U.S.* **111** K21
Haines, *Oreg., U.S.* **108** G8
Haines City, *Fla., U.S.* **97** U8
Haines Junction, *Yukon, Can.* **82** G7
Hainiya Point, *N. Mariana Is., U.S.* **216** E8
Haiphong, *Vietnam* **186** H12
Haiti, *N. Amer.* **81** N22
Haiya, *Sudan* **199** D14
Haiyan, *China* **182** L9
Haiyan, *China* **180** H11
Haizhou Wan, *China* **182** H8
Hajdúböszörmény, *Hung.* **149** L17
Hajdúszoboszló, *Hung.* **149** L17
Hajiki Saki, *Japan* **184** L11
Haji Pir Pass, *India, Pak.* **177** N11
Ḩajjah, *Yemen* **172** P9
Ḩājjīābād, *Iran* **173** G15
Hajnáčka, *Slovakia* **149** K15
Hajnówka, *Pol.* **149** D18
Hakalau, *Hawai'i, U.S.* **113** L21
Hakamaru, island, *Cook Is., N.Z.* **219** B15
Hakataramea, *N.Z.* **213** Q16
Hakauata, island, *Tonga* **218** P7
Hakha, *Myanmar* **186** G4
Hakkari, *Turk.* **169** H18
Hakken San, *Japan* **185** Q9
Hakodate, *Japan* **184** H13
Hakui, *Japan* **185** N10
Hakupa Pass, *Solomon Is.* **217** J18
Hakupu, *Niue, N.Z.* **219** B20
Hala, *Pak.* **177** V7
Halaaniyaat, Juzor al (Kuria Muria Islands), *Oman* **173** N15
Ḩalab (Aleppo), *Syr.* **170** D9
Ḩalabān, *Saudi Arabia* **172** K9
Halachó, *Mex.* **115** H16
Halāli'i Lake, *Hawai'i, U.S.* **112** C3
Halalo, Pointe, *Wallis & Futuna, Fr.* **218** C11
Hala'ula, *Hawai'i, U.S.* **113** K19
Halawa, *Hawai'i, U.S.* **113** K19
Hālawa, Cape, *Hawai'i, U.S.* **113** F15
Hālawa Bay, *Hawai'i, U.S.* **113** F15
Halayeb, *Egypt* **197** F20
Halba, *Leb.* **170** G7
Halban, *Mongolia* **180** C10
Halberstadt, *Ger.* **148** E8
Halcon, Mount, *Philippines* **189** D13
Haldwani, *India* **178** E7
Hale, *Mich., U.S.* **98** J12
Haleakalā Crater, *Hawai'i, U.S.* **113** H17
Haleakalā National Park, *Hawai'i, U.S.* **113** H18
Haleakalā Observatories, *Hawai'i, U.S.* **113** H17
Hale Center, *Tex., U.S.* **102** J5
Hale'iwa, *Hawai'i, U.S.* **112** D10
Haleki'i-Pihana Heiaus, *Hawai'i, U.S.* **113** G16
Haleyville, *Ala., U.S.* **101** H14
Halfeti, *Turk.* **168** H12
Half Moon Bay, *Antigua & Barbuda* **121** B21
Halfway, *Oreg., U.S.* **108** G9
Halgan, Cape, *F.S.M.* **217** A19
Halifax, *N.S., Can.* **83** P22
Halifax, *Qnsld., Austral.* **211** R13
Halifax, *Va., U.S.* **96** F11
Halkett, Cape, *Alas., U.S.* **111** B16
Hálki, island, *Gr.* **155** N19
Hálki, island, *Gr.* **155** N19
Hálkí, *Gr.* **154** F10
Halkída (Chalkis), *Gr.* **154** H12
Halkidikí, peninsula, *Gr.* **154** D12
Hall, *Aust.* **148** L8
Hallandale, *Fla., U.S.* **97** W10
Hall Basin, *Nunavut, Can.* **83** A17
Hall Beach, *Nunavut, Can.* **83** F16
Halle, *Belg.* **146** L12
Halle, *Ger.* **148** F9
Hallein, *Aust.* **148** L10
Hallettsville, *Tex., U.S.* **103** R12
Halley, station, *Antarctica* **226** D10
Halliday, *N. Dak., U.S.* **104** F3
Hallim, *S. Korea* **182** J13
Hall Islands, *F.S.M.* **216** Q6
Hällnäs, *Sw.* **141** G14
Hallock, *Minn., U.S.* **104** E8
Hall Peninsula, *Nunavut, Can.* **83** H19
Halls, *Tenn., U.S.* **100** F12
Halls Creek, *W. Aust., Austral.* **211** R6
Hallstatt, *Aust.* **148** L10
Halmahera, island, *Indonesia* **189** H16
Halmahera Sea, *Indonesia* **189** J17
Halmeu, *Rom.* **152** A12
Halmstad, *Sw.* **140** N12
Halola, *Solomon Is.* **217** L14
Halsa, *Nor.* **140** H10
Halstead, *Eng., U.K.* **143** U15
Halstead, *Kans., U.S.* **105** U7
Haltdalen, *Nor.* **140** H11
Halten Bank, *Atl. Oc.* **236** C14
Halulu Heiau, *Hawai'i, U.S.* **113** G14
Halys *see* Kızılırmak, river, *Turk.* **168** D9
Ham, *Fr.* **147** N10
Hamada, *Japan* **185** Q6
Hamadān, *Iran* **172** D11
Hamaguir, *Alg.* **196** C9
Ḩamāh (Hamath), *Syr.* **170** F8
Hāmākua, region, *Hawai'i, U.S.* **113** L20
Hamamatsu, *Japan* **185** Q10
Hamamet, Gulf of, *Tun.* **194** C6
Hamar, *Nor.* **140** K11
Hamasaka, *Japan* **185** P8
Hamâta, Gebel, *Egypt* **197** E20
Hamath *see* Ḩamāh, *Syr.* **170** F8
Hamatombetsu, *Japan* **184** D14
Hamburg, *Ark., U.S.* **100** K9
Hamburg, *Ger.* **148** C8
Hamburg, *Iowa, U.S.* **105** Q9
Hamburg, *Mo., U.S.* **105** Q9
Hamburg, *N.Y., U.S.* **94** J5
Ḩamḑah, *Saudi Arabia* **172** M9
Ḩamdānah, *Saudi Arabia* **172** M7
Hamden, *Conn., U.S.* **94** M12
Hämeenlinna, *Fin.* **141** J16
Hamelin, *W. Aust., Austral.* **211** V1
Hameln, *Ger.* **148** E7
Hamersley Range, *Austral.* **210** F3
Hamhŭng, *N. Korea* **182** D13
Hami (Kumul), *China* **180** F9
Hamilton, *Ala., U.S.* **101** H14
Hamilton, *Bermuda, U.K.* **120** B2
Hamilton, *Ill., U.S.* **99** Q3
Hamilton, *Mo., U.S.* **105** R11
Hamilton, *Mont., U.S.* **106** D5
Hamilton, *N.Y., U.S.* **94** J9
Hamilton, *N.Z.* **213** K19
Hamilton, *Ohio, U.S.* **99** S11
Hamilton, *Ont., Can.* **83** R18
Hamilton, *Scot., U.K.* **142** M9
Hamilton, *Tas., Austral.* **211** Z16
Hamilton, *Tex., U.S.* **103** N10
Hamilton, *Vic., Austral.* **211** Z11
Hamilton, Lake, *Ark., U.S.* **100** H7
Hamilton Harbour, *Bermuda, U.K.* **120** B2
Hamilton Inlet, *Nfld. & Lab., Can.* **83** K22
Hamina, *Fin.* **141** J17

I

Island Pond, Vt., U.S. 95 F13
Islands, Bay of, N.Z. 213 H18
Islas Orcadas Rise, Atl. Oc. 237 V9
Islay, island, Scot., U.K. 142 M7
Isle of Man, Isle of Man, U.K. 143 Q9
Isle Royale National Park, Mich., U.S. 98 D6
Islote Bay, Trinidad & Tobago 121 Q21
Ismâ‘ilîya, Egypt 171 P1
Isna, Egypt 197 E19
Isoka, Zambia 202 C12
Isola di Capo Rizzuto, It. 151 Q14
Isonzo, river, It., Slov. 150 D9
Isparta, Turk. 168 G6
Ispas, Turkm. 174 L10
Ispikan, Pak. 177 V2
İspir, Turk. 169 D15
Israel, Asia 167 T3
Isrīyah, ruin, Syr. 170 F9
Issano, Guyana 129 E14
Issime, It. 150 D3
Issoudun, Fr. 147 S9
Ist, island, Croatia 152 F4
İstanbul (Constantinople), Turk. 168 C5
İstanbul Boğazi (Bosporus), Turk. 168 C5
Istaravshan (Ŭroteppa), Taj. 176 G7
Istiéa, Gr. 154 G11
Isto, Mount, Alas., U.S. 111 C18
Istokpoga, Lake, Fla., U.S. 97 V9
Istres, Fr. 147 X13
Istria, peninsula, Croatia 152 E4
Itabaianinha, Braz. 131 H17
Itabuna, Braz. 131 J16
Itacoatiara, Braz. 130 D10
Itaetê, Braz. 131 H16
Itaipú Dam, Braz., Parag. 130 M11
Itaituba, Braz. 130 E10
Itajaí, Braz. 131 N13
Italia, Monte, Chile 133 Y8
Italy, Eur. 139 W7
Itambé, Pico de, Braz. 131 K15
Itanagar, India 178 F14
Itapetinga, Braz. 131 J16
Itapipoca, Braz. 131 E16
Itasca, Tex., U.S. 102 M11
Itasca, Lake see Mississippi, Source of the, Minn., U.S. 104 G9
Itatupã, Braz. 130 C12
Itbayat, island, Philippines 189 A14
Itéa, Gr. 154 H10
Iténez, river, Bol., Braz. 130 H9
Itezhi-Tezhi, Lake, Zambia 202 E10
Ithaca see Itháki, island, Gr. 154 H7
Ithaca, Mich., U.S. 98 L11
Ithaca, N.Y., U.S. 94 K8
Itháki (Ithaca), island, Gr. 154 H7
Itháki (Vathý), Gr. 154 H7
Ítilo, Gr. 154 M10
Itimbiri, river, Dem. Rep. of the Congo 194 J7
Itiquira, river, Braz. 130 J10
Itō, Japan 185 Q12
Itoman, Japan 185 Y1
Itta Bena, Miss., U.S. 100 J11
Ittiri, It. 150 M3
Ittoqqortoormiit, Greenland, Den. 81 B22
Itu Aba Island, Spratly Is. 188 E11
Ituí, river, Braz. 130 E5
Ituiutaba, Braz. 131 K13
Ituni, Guyana 129 E14
Iturama, Braz. 130 K12
Iturup (Etorofu), island, Russ. 159 J23
Ituxi, river, Braz. 130 F7
Ituzaingó, Arg. 132 G14
Itzehoe, Ger. 148 B7
Iuka, Miss., U.S. 101 G13
Iul'tin, Russ. 159 B20
Ivaí, river, Braz. 130 M11
Ivalo, Fin. 141 D15
Ivangrad, Serb. & Mont. 152 H9
Ivanhoe, N.S.W., Austral. 211 X12
Ivanhoe, W. Aust., Austral. 211 Q6
Ivanić Grad, Croatia 152 D6
Ivanjica, Serb. & Mont. 152 G10
Ivano-Frankivs'k, Ukr. 157 P2
Ivanovo, Russ. 156 H11
Ivanteyevka, Russ. 156 L15
Ivatsevichy, Belarus 156 L3
Ivaylovgrad, Bulg. 153 K15
Ivdel', Russ. 158 G9
Ivirairai, Mont, Fr. Polynesia, Fr. 219 P16
Ivisa see Ibiza, island, Sp. 145 H17
Ivory Coast, Cote dIvoire 194 J2
Ivrea, It. 150 D3
Ivujivik, Que., Can. 83 H17
Iwadate, Japan 184 J12
Iwaki, Japan 185 N13
Iwakuni, Japan 185 Q6
Iwamizawa, Japan 184 F13
Iwanuma, Japan 184 L13
Iwate, Japan 184 K13
Iwembere Steppe, Tanzania 194 K9
Iwo, Nigeria 200 G12
Iwo Jima, Japan 184 L5
Ixtapa, Mex. 114 K10
Iyo, Japan 185 R6
Iž, island, Croatia 152 G5
Īzad Khvāst, Iran 173 E13
Izamal, Mex. 115 H16
Izberbash, Russ. 157 U16
Izbica, Pol. 149 D14
Izena Shima, Japan 185 X1
Izhevsk, Russ. 156 G16
Izhevsk, Russ. 158 H8
Izhma, river, Russ. 138 B12
Izmayil, Ukr. 157 S4
İzmir (Smyrna), Turk. 168 F3
İznik (Nicaea), Turk. 168 D5
İznik Gölü, Turk. 168 D5
Izozog, Bañados del, S. Amer. 126 H5
Izra‘, Syr. 170 K7
Izu Hantō, Japan 185 Q11
Izuhara, Japan 185 Q3
Izu Islands, Japan 166 F14
Izumo, Japan 185 P6
Izu Shichitō, Japan 185 Q12
Izu Shotō, Japan 184 J5
Izu Trench, Pac. Oc. 238 F6
Izyaslav, Ukr. 157 N4
Izyum, Ukr. 157 P9

J

Jaba, P.N.G. 217 K14
Jabalpur, India 178 J7
Jabal Zuqar, Jazīrat, Yemen 172 Q8
Jabbūl, Syr. 170 E9
Jabbūl, Sabkhat al, Syr. 170 E9
Jabel Abyad Plateau, Sudan 194 F8
Jabiru, N. Terr., Austral. 211 P8
Jablah, Syr. 170 F7
Jablaničko Jezero, Bosn. & Herzg. 152 G7
Jablonec, Czech Rep. 148 G11
Jabnoren, island, Marshall Is. 216 K7
Jaboatão, Braz. 131 G18
Jabor, Marshall Is. 216 M8
Jäbrayyl, Azerb. 169 E21
Jabuka, island, Croatia 152 H5
Jabwot Island, Marshall Is. 216 H4
Jaca, Sp. 145 C14
Jacareacanga, Braz. 130 E10
Jaciparaná, Braz. 130 G7
Jackman, Me., U.S. 95 D15
Jackpot, Nev., U.S. 108 L12
Jacksboro, Tex., U.S. 102 K10
Jackson, Ala., U.S. 101 M14
Jackson, Barbados 121 K19
Jackson, Calif., U.S. 109 R5
Jackson, Ga., U.S. 96 L5
Jackson, La., U.S. 100 N9
Jackson, Mich., U.S. 98 M11
Jackson, Minn., U.S. 104 L10
Jackson, Miss., U.S. 100 L11
Jackson, Mo., U.S. 105 U16
Jackson, Ohio, U.S. 99 S13
Jackson, S.C., U.S. 96 L8
Jackson, Tenn., U.S. 101 F13
Jackson, Wyo., U.S. 106 H8
Jackson, Ostrov, Russ. 158 C12
Jackson Bay, N.Z. 213 P15
Jackson Lake, Ga., U.S. 96 L5
Jackson Lake, Wyo., U.S. 106 G8
Jacksonport, Wis., U.S. 98 H8
Jacksonville, Ala., U.S. 101 J16
Jacksonville, Ark., U.S. 100 G9
Jacksonville, Fla., U.S. 97 Q8
Jacksonville, Ill., U.S. 99 R4
Jacksonville, N.C., U.S. 96 J13
Jacksonville, Tex., U.S. 102 M14
Jacksonville Beach, Fla., U.S. 97 R9
Jacmel, Haiti 117 M16
Jacobabad, Pak. 177 T7
Jacob Lake, Ariz., U.S. 107 Q7
Jacquinot Bay, P.N.G. 213 C21
Jacumba, Calif., U.S. 109 Z11
J.A.D. Jensen Nunatakker, peak, N. Amer. 80 D10
Jadraque, Sp. 144 E12
Jaén, Peru 130 F2
Jaén, Sp. 144 K11
Jaffa, Cape, Austral. 210 L10
Jaffna, Sri Lanka 179 R7
Jafr, Qā‘ al, Jordan 171 Q7
Jagdalpur, India 178 L8
Jāghir Bāzār, Syr. 170 C14
Jaghjagh, river, Syr. 170 C14
Jagodina, Serb. & Mont. 152 G11
Jagraon, India 178 D5
Jagtial, India 178 L6
Jaguarão, Braz. 130 Q11
Jahanabad, India 178 H10
Jahorina, peak, Bosn. & Herzg. 152 G8
Jahrom, Iran 173 G14
Jaicoa, Cordillera, P.R., U.S. 120 M2
Jaicós, Braz. 131 F16
Jaigarh, India 178 M3
Jaintiapur, Bangladesh 178 H13
Jaipur, India 178 G5
Jaisalmer, India 178 F2
Jājarm, Iran 173 B15
Jajpur, India 178 K10
Jakar, Bhutan 178 F13
Jakarta, Indonesia 188 L8
Jakeru, island, Marshall Is. 216 L3
Jakhau, India 178 H1
Jakobstad (Pietarsaari), Fin. 141 G15
Jal, N. Mex., U.S. 107 V15
Jalaihai Point, Guam, U.S. 216 D11
Jalalabad, Afghan. 176 M9
Jalal-Abad, Kyrg. 176 F10
Jalasjärvi, Fin. 141 H15
Jalaun, India 178 G7
Jaldak, Afghan. 177 P6
Jaleswar, India 178 K11
Jalgaon, India 178 K5
Jalgaon, India 178 K5
Jalingo, Nigeria 201 G16
Jalkot, Pak. 176 L11
Jaloklab, island, Marshall Is. 216 G10
Jalón, river, Sp. 145 E13
Jalor, India 178 G3
Jalpaiguri, India 178 G12
Jālq, Iran 173 G18
Jáltipan, Mex. 115 K14
Jaluit, island, Marshall Is. 216 M8
Jaluit Atoll, Marshall Is. 216 H4
Jaluit Lagoon, Marshall Is. 216 M8
Jamaame, Somalia 199 K16
Jamaica, N. Amer. 81 P21
Jamaica, island, N. Amer. 80 N9
Jamaica Cay, Bahamas 117 G13
Jamalpur, Bangladesh 178 H12
Jamanota, peak, Aruba, Neth. 121 Q17
Jaman Pass, Afghan., Taj. 176 J12
Jambi, Indonesia 188 K7
Jambusar, India 178 J3
James see San Salvador, Isla, island, Ecua. 128 P9
James, river, N. Dak., U.S. 104 G6
James, river, S. Dak., U.S. 104 M7
James, river, Va., U.S. 96 E11
James Bay, N. Amer. 80 G8
James Cistern, Bahamas 120 E6
James Point, Bahamas 120 D6
James Range, Austral. 210 F8
James Ross Island, Antarctica 226 C4
Jamestown, N. Dak., U.S. 104 G6
Jamestown, N.Y., U.S. 94 K4
Jamestown National Historic Site, Va., U.S. 96 F13
Jamestown Reservoir, N. Dak., U.S. 104 G6
Jammu, India 177 P12
Jamnagar, India 178 J2
Jampur, Pak. 177 S9
Jämsä, Fin. 141 J15
Jamshedpur, India 178 J10
Jamuna, river, Bangladesh 178 H12
Janaúba, Braz. 131 J15
Jan Bulaq, Afghan. 176 K6
Jand, Pak. 177 N10
Jandaq, Iran 173 D14
Jandia, peak, Canary Is. 204 Q7
Jandia, Punta de, Canary Is. 204 Q7
Jandiatuba, river, Braz. 130 E6
Jandola, Pak. 177 P8
Jan Doran, Neth. Antilles, Neth. 121 Q18
Janesville, Wis., U.S. 98 M6
Jangain, island, P.N.G. 217 H14
Jangaon, India 178 M7
Jangeru, Indonesia 188 K12
Jangheung, S. Korea 182 H13
Jangipur, India 178 H11
Jani Kheyl, Afghan. 177 P7
Janīn, W. Bank 170 L6
Jan Mayen, island, Nor. 81 A22
Jan Mayen Fracture Zone, Arctic Oc. 243 J18
Jan Mayen Ridge, Arctic Oc. 243 J19
Janów Lubelski, Pol. 149 F17
Jansenville, S. Af. 202 M9
Jan Thiel, Lagún, Neth. Antilles, Neth. 121 Q15
Januária, Braz. 131 J14
Jaora, India 178 H4
Japan, Asia 167 T14
Japan, Sea of (East Sea), Asia 166 F13
Japan Trench, Pac. Oc. 238 E6
Japtan, island, Marshall Is. 216 H9
Japurá, Braz. 130 D7
Jaquot, Pointe, Dominica 121 D18
Jarābulus, Syr. 170 C10
Jaramillo, Arg. 133 T9
Jaranwala, Pak. 177 Q11
Jarash (Gerasa), Jordan 170 L6
Jarbidge, river, Idaho, U.S. 106 J4
Jarbidge, Nev., U.S. 108 L11
Jardim, Braz. 130 L10
Jardines de la Reina, islands, Cuba 116 J10
Jargalant, Mongolia 181 D14
Jargalant, Mongolia 180 E10
Jarghan, Afghan. 176 L5
Jari, river, Braz. 130 C12
Jarocin, Pol. 149 E13
Jarosław, Pol. 149 G17
Jarud Qi, China 181 E16
Järvenpää, Fin. 141 J16
Jarvis Island, Pac. Oc. 214 G12
Järvsö, Sw. 141 J13
Jashpurnagar, India 178 J9
Jāsk, Iran 173 J16
Jasło, Pol. 149 H17
Jason Islands, Falkland Is., U.K. 133 V11
Jason Peninsula, Antarctica 226 D5
Jasonville, Ind., U.S. 99 S8
Jasper, Ala., U.S. 101 J14
Jasper, Alta., Can. 82 L9
Jasper, Ark., U.S. 100 E7
Jasper, Fla., U.S. 97 Q7
Jasper, Ga., U.S. 96 K5
Jasper, Ind., U.S. 99 T8
Jasper, Tex., U.S. 103 P15
Jastrowie, Pol. 149 C13
Jastrzębie-Zdrój, Pol. 149 H14
Jászberény, Hung. 149 L15
Jataí, Braz. 130 K12
Jati, Pak. 177 W7
Jatibonico, Cuba 116 H9
Jatobal, Braz. 131 E13
Jaú, river, Braz. 130 D8
Jauaperi, river, Braz. 130 C9
Jaunpur, India 178 G8
Java (Jawa), island, Indonesia 188 M9
Javari, river, Braz., Peru 130 E4
Java Ridge, Ind. Oc. 241 H15
Java Sea, Indonesia 188 L10
Java Trench, Ind. Oc. 241 H14
Jávea (Xàbia), Sp. 145 J15
Javhlant see Uliastay, Mongolia 180 D10
Jawa see Java, island, Indonesia 188 M9
Jawhar (Giohar), Somalia 199 J17
Jawi, Indonesia 188 J9
Jaworzno, Pol. 149 G15
Jay, Okla., U.S. 102 E14
Jaya, Puncak, Indonesia 213 C16
Jaya Peak, Indonesia 166 L16
Jayapura, Indonesia 189 K21
Jayawijaya, Pegunungan, Indonesia 189 L20
Jay Em, Wyo., U.S. 106 J13
Jayton, Tex., U.S. 102 K7
Jayuya, P.R., U.S. 120 N3
Jaz Mūrīan, Hāmūn-e, Iran 173 H16
Jbail (Byblos), Leb. 170 H6
Jeanerette, La., U.S. 100 Q9
Jeanette, Ostrov, Russ. 159 C17
Jean Marie River, N.W.T., Can. 82 H10
Jean-Rabel, Haiti 117 L16
Jebba, Nigeria 201 F13
Jebel, Bahr el (Mountain Nile), Sudan 199 H13
Jebri, Pak. 177 U5
Jebus, Indonesia 188 K7
Jeddah, Saudi Arabia 172 L7
Jedrol, island, Marshall Is. 216 H8
Jędrzejów, Pol. 149 G16
Jefferson, Ga., U.S. 96 K6
Jefferson, Iowa, U.S. 105 N10
Jefferson, river, Mont., U.S. 106 E7
Jefferson, Tex., U.S. 102 L15
Jefferson, Wis., U.S. 98 L6
Jefferson, Mount, Nev., U.S. 109 Q10
Jefferson, Mount, Oreg., U.S. 108 G4
Jefferson City, Mo., U.S. 105 T13
Jefferson City, Tenn., U.S. 101 E19
Jeffersonville, Ind., U.S. 99 T10
Jeffrey City, Wyo., U.S. 106 J11
Jef Jef el Kebir, desert, Chad 197 F15
Jega, Nigeria 201 E13
Jégun, Fr. 147 X8
Jeju (Cheju), S. Korea 182 J13
Jeju-Do, S. Korea 182 J13
Jeju Strait, S. Korea 182 H13
Jekyll Island, Ga., U.S. 97 P8
Jelbart Ice Shelf, Antarctica 226 A12
Jelenia Góra, Pol. 148 F12
Jelgava (Mitau), Latv. 141 M16
Jellico, Tenn., U.S. 101 D18
Jemaja, island, Indonesia 188 H8
Jember, Indonesia 188 M11
Jembongan, island, Malaysia 188 F12
Jemez Pueblo, N. Mex., U.S. 107 R12
Jeminay, China 180 D7
Jemo Island, Marshall Is. 216 F4
Jena, Fla., U.S. 97 R6
Jena, Ger. 148 F9
Jena, La., U.S. 100 M8
Jengish Chokusu (Pik Pobedy, Victory Peak), China, Kyrg. 176 E15
Jenkins, Ky., U.S. 101 C20
Jennings, La., U.S. 100 P8
Jenny Point, Dominica 121 F20
Jensen, Utah, U.S. 106 L9
Jensen Beach, Fla., U.S. 97 V10
Jens Munk Island, Nunavut, Can. 83 F16
Jenu, Indonesia 188 J9
Jeongeup, S. Korea 182 G13
Jeonju, S. Korea 182 G13
Jequié, Braz. 131 H16
Jequitinhonha, river, Braz. 131 J16
Jerantut, Malaysia 187 T10
Jerba Island, Tun. 197 B13
Jérémie, Haiti 117 M15
Jeremoabo, Braz. 131 G17
Jerez de la Frontera, Sp. 144 M8
Jeréz de los Caballeros, Sp. 144 J7
Jericho see Arīḩā, W. Bank 170 M6
Jericoacoara, Point, S. Amer. 126 D10
Jerid, Chott el, Tun. 196 B12
Jerilderie, N.S.W., Austral. 211 Y12
Jerimoth Hill, R.I., U.S. 95 L14
Jerome, Idaho, U.S. 106 H5
Jerramungup, W. Aust., Austral. 211 Y3
Jersey, island, Ch. Is. 143 Z11
Jersey Bay, Virgin Islands, U.S. 120 N10
Jersey City, N.J., U.S. 94 N11
Jersey Shore, Pa., U.S. 94 M7
Jerseyside, Nfld. & Lab., Can. 83 M24
Jerseyville, Ill., U.S. 99 S4
Jerusalem, Israel 170 M5
Jervis see Rábida, Isla, island, Ecua. 128 Q9
Jervis Bay, Austral. 210 L14
Jervis Bay Territory, Austral. 211 Y14
Jerzu, It. 151 P4
Jesenice, Slov. 152 C4
Jeseník, Czech Rep. 149 G13
Jesi, It. 150 H9
Jessore, Bangladesh 178 J12
Jesup, Ga., U.S. 97 P8
Jesús María, Arg. 132 J10
Jetmore, Kans., U.S. 105 T5
Jetpur, India 178 J2
Jewel Cave National Monument, S. Dak., U.S. 104 L1
Jewell, Iowa, U.S. 105 N11
Jewett, Tex., U.S. 103 N12
Jeypore, India 178 L8
Jezercë, Maja, Albania 152 J9
Jezioro Shiardwy, Pol. 149 B16
Jezzîne, Leb. 170 J6
Jhalawar, India 178 H5
Jhal Jhao, Pak. 177 V5
Jhang, Pak. 177 Q10
Jhansi, India 178 H6
Jharsuguda, India 178 K9
Jhatpat, Pak. 177 T7
Jhelum, river, Pak. 177 Q10
Jhelum, Pak. 177 P11
Jhimpir, Pak. 177 W7
Jhudo, Pak. 177 W8

K

Kajiki, *Japan* **185** T4
Kaka, *Sudan* **199** F13
Kaka, *Turkm.* **174** M9
Kākā, Lae 'O, *Hawai'i, U.S.* **113** H16
Kakamas, *S. Af.* **202** K8
Kakana, *India* **179** S14
Kakaramea, *N.Z.* **213** L18
Kakdwip, *India* **178** J11
Kake, *Alas., U.S.* **111** L22
Kake, *Japan* **185** Q6
Kakeroma Jima, *Japan* **185** W3
Kākhk, *Iran* **173** D16
Kakhovka, *Ukr.* **157** R7
Kakhovka Reservoir, *Ukr.* **138** G11
Kakinada (Cocanada), *India* **178** M8
Kakogawa, *Japan* **185** Q8
Kakshaal Range, *China, Kyrg.* **176** F14
Kaktovik, *Alas., U.S.* **111** C18
Kakuda, *Japan* **184** M13
Kala, *Azerb.* **169** D23
Kalaallit Nunaat *see* Greenland, *N. Amer.* **81** C21
Kalabagh, *Pak.* **177** P9
Kalabakan, *Malaysia* **188** G12
Kalabo, *Zambia* **202** E9
Kalach, *Russ.* **157** N11
Kalach na Donu, *Russ.* **157** P12
Kalae (South Point), *Hawai'i, U.S.* **113** Q19
Kalafrana, *Malta* **161** L23
Kalahari Desert, *Botswana, Namibia* **202** H8
Kalāheo, *Hawai'i, U.S.* **112** C5
Kal'ai Khumb, *Taj.* **176** J9
Kalalea, Heiau o, *Hawai'i, U.S.* **113** Q19
Kalalua, peak, *Hawai'i, U.S.* **113** N21
Kalam, *Pak.* **176** L10
Kalama, *Wash., U.S.* **108** E3
Kalamáta, *Gr.* **154** L9
Kalamazoo, river, *Mich., U.S.* **98** M9
Kalamazoo, *Mich., U.S.* **98** M10
Kalambáka, *Gr.* **154** E9
Kálamos, island, *Gr.* **154** H7
Kalamotí, *Gr.* **155** J16
Kalannie, *W. Aust., Austral.* **211** W3
Kalao, island, *Indonesia* **189** M13
Kalaoa, *Hawai'i, U.S.* **113** M18
Kalaotoa, island, *Indonesia* **189** M14
Kalasin, *Thai.* **186** L10
Kalat *see* Qalat, *Afghan.* **177** P6
Kalat, *Pak.* **177** S5
Kalaupapa, *Hawai'i, U.S.* **113** F14
Kalaupapa National Historic Park, *Hawai'i, U.S.* **113** F14
Kalávrita, *Gr.* **154** J9
Kalawao, site, *Hawai'i, U.S.* **113** F15
Kalaýmor, *Turkm.* **174** N10
Kalay-wa, *Myanmar* **186** F5
Kalb, Ra's al, *Yemen* **172** Q11
Kälbäjär, *Azerb.* **169** E20
Kalbān, *Oman* **173** M17
Kalbarri, *W. Aust., Austral.* **211** V1
Kaldar, *Afghan.* **176** K6
Kale, *Turk.* **168** J5
Kalealoa, cape, *Hawai'i, U.S.* **112** E10
Kale Burnu, *Turk.* **169** D14
Kalecik, *Turk.* **168** E9
Kaledupa, island, *Indonesia* **189** L14
Kalemie, *Dem. Rep. of the Congo* **198** M12
Kalemyo, *Myanmar* **186** F5
Kalenyy, *Kaz.* **174** D6
Kaleybar, *Iran* **172** A11
Kalgoorlie, *W. Aust., Austral.* **211** W4
Kaliakoúda, peak, *Gr.* **154** G9
Kaliakra, Nos, *Bulg.* **153** H18
Kalianda, *Indonesia* **188** L8
Kalihi Wai, *Hawai'i, U.S.* **112** B5
Kalihi Wai Bay, *Hawai'i, U.S.* **112** A6
Kalí Límni, *Gr.* **155** P18
Kalima, *Dem. Rep. of the Congo* **198** K11
Kalimantan *see* Borneo, region, *Indonesia* **188** J10
Kálimnos, island, *Gr.* **155** L18
Kálimnos, *Gr.* **155** L18
Kalimpang, *India* **178** G11
Kaliningrad, *Russ.* **156** J1
Kaliningrad Oblast, *Russ.* **156** J2
Kalinino, *Arm.* **169** C18
Kalinino, *Russ.* **157** S10
Kalininsk, *Russ.* **156** M13
Kalinkavichy, *Belarus* **156** M5
Kalispell, *Mont., U.S.* **106** B5
Kalisz, *Pol.* **149** E14
Kalix, *Sw.* **141** F14
Kalkan, *Turk.* **168** J5
Kalkaska, *Mich., U.S.* **98** J10
Kallithéa, *Gr.* **154** J12
Kallsjön, lake, *Sw.* **140** H12
Kalmar, *Sw.* **141** N13
Kalnai, *India* **178** J9
Kalnik, peak, *Croatia* **152** D6
Kalo Chorio, *Cyprus* **160** Q7
Kalohi Channel, *Hawai'i, U.S.* **113** G14
Kaloko-Honokōhau National Historic Park, *Hawai'i, U.S.* **113** M18
Kaloli Point, *Hawai'i, U.S.* **113** M22
Kaloní, *Gr.* **155** F16
Kalonís, Kólpos, *Gr.* **155** G16
Kalpa, *India* **178** D6
Kalpeni Island, *India* **179** R3
Kalpitiya, *Sri Lanka* **179** S7
Kalskag, *Alas., U.S.* **111** J13
Kalsubai, peak, *India* **178** L4
Kaltag, *Alas., U.S.* **111** G14
Kaluga, *Russ.* **156** K9
Kalumburu, *W. Aust., Austral.* **211** Q6
Kalush, *Ukr.* **157** P2
Kal'ya, *Russ.* **158** G9
Kalyan, *India* **178** L3
Kalyazin, *Russ.* **156** H9
Kama, river, *Russ.* **158** H8
Kamaing, *Myanmar* **186** E6
Kamaishi, *Japan* **184** K14
Kamakal, island, *Fr. Polynesia, Fr.* **219** R20
Kamakou, peak, *Hawai'i, U.S.* **113** F15
Kamalino, *Hawai'i, U.S.* **112** C3
Kaman, *Turk.* **168** F9
Kamárai, *Gr.* **155** L14
Kamarān, island, *Yemen* **172** P8
Kama Reservoir, *Russ.* **138** C13
Kamariotissa, *Gr.* **155** D15
Kamarod, *Pak.* **177** T3
Kamar Zard, *Afghan.* **177** N2
Kambang, *Indonesia* **188** K6
Kambanós, Akrotírio, *Gr.* **155** J14
Kambove, *Dem. Rep. of the Congo* **198** N11
Kamchatka, Poluostrov, *Russ.* **159** F22
Kamchatka Peninsula *see* Kamchatskiy Poluostrov, *Russ.* **166** C13
Kamchatskiy Poluostrov, *Russ.* **159** E22
Kamchiya, river, *Bulg.* **153** H17
Kamdesh, *Afghan.* **176** L9
Kamehameha I Birthplace, *Hawai'i, U.S.* **113** J18
Kamen, Gora, *Russ.* **159** G14
Kaména Voúrla, *Gr.* **154** G11
Kamenka, *Kaz.* **174** C6
Kamenka, *Russ.* **156** L12
Kamenka, *Russ.* **158** E9
Kamenskiy, *Russ.* **157** N13
Kamensk Shakhtinskiy, *Russ.* **157** Q11
Kamensk Ural'skiy, *Russ.* **158** J9
Kamiah, *Idaho, U.S.* **106** D4
Kamieskroon, *S. Af.* **202** L7
Kamileroi, *Qnsld., Austral.* **211** S11
Kamiloloa, *Hawai'i, U.S.* **113** F14
Kamina, *Dem. Rep. of the Congo* **198** M10
Kamin'-Kashyrs'kyy, *Ukr.* **156** M3
Kaminone Shima, *Japan* **185** W3
Kamino Shima, *Japan* **185** Q3
Kamitsuki, *Japan* **185** R12
Kamitsushima, *Japan* **185** Q3
Kamiyaku, *Japan* **185** U4
Kamkhat Muḩaywir, ruin, *Jordan* **171** N7
Kamloops, *B.C., Can.* **82** M9
Kammuri, peak, *Japan* **185** Q6
Kamo, *Arm.* **169** D19
Kamoa Mountains, *Guyana* **129** G14
Kamoenai, *Japan* **184** F12
Kamōhio Bay, *Hawai'i, U.S.* **113** H16
Kamoke, *Pak.* **177** P12
Kamo'oloa, *Hawai'i, U.S.* **112** D10
Kampala, *Uganda* **199** K13
Kampar, *Malaysia* **187** T9
Kampen, *Neth.* **146** H13
Kamphaeng Phet, *Thai.* **186** L8
Kâmpóng Cham, *Cambodia* **187** N12
Kampong Kuala Besut, *Malaysia* **187** S10
Kampos, *Cyprus* **160** P6
Kampot, *Cambodia* **187** P11
Kamrau, Teluk, *Indonesia* **213** C15
Kamsack, *Sask., Can.* **83** M13
Kamsar, *Guinea* **200** F4
Kamuela *see* Waimea, *Hawai'i, U.S.* **113** K19
Kamui Misaki, *Japan* **184** F12
Kam'yanets'-Podil's'kyy, *Ukr.* **157** P3
Kam'yanka-Dniprovs'ka, *Ukr.* **157** R8
Kamyshin, *Russ.* **157** N13
Kamyzyak, *Russ.* **157** R15
Kanab, *Utah, U.S.* **107** Q6
Kanab Creek, *Ariz., Utah, U.S.* **107** Q6
Kanacea, island, *Fiji Is.* **218** H9
Kanaga Island, *Alas., U.S.* **110** N5
Kanak, river, *Turk.* **168** E10
Kanaláki, *Gr.* **154** F7
Kananga, *Dem. Rep. of the Congo* **198** L10
Kanapou Bay, *Hawai'i, U.S.* **113** H16
Kanarraville, *Utah, U.S.* **107** P6
Kanash, *Russ.* **156** J14
Kanatea, island, *Tonga* **218** J11
Kanawha, river, *W. Va., U.S.* **96** D7
Kanazawa, *Japan* **185** N9
Kanbalu, *Myanmar* **186** F6
Kanchenjunga, peak, *India, Nepal* **178** F11
Kanchipuram, *India* **179** Q7
Kandahar, *Afghan.* **177** Q5
Kandalaksha, *Russ.* **158** D8
Kandalakshskiy Zaliv, *Russ.* **158** D8
Kandangan, *Indonesia* **188** K11
Kándanos, *Gr.* **154** Q12
Kandersteg, *Switz.* **150** C3
Kandhkot, *Pak.* **177** T8
Kandi, *Benin* **200** F12
Kandi, *India* **178** H11
Kandiaro, *Pak.* **177** U7
Kandíla, *Gr.* **154** K10
Kandıra, *Turk.* **168** C6
Kandrach, *Pak.* **177** V5
Kandrian, *P.N.G.* **213** D20
Kandudu, island, *Maldives* **179** W3
Kandudu, island, *Maldives* **179** X3
Kandu-ye Bala, *Afghan.* **177** N5
Kandy, *Sri Lanka* **179** T7
Kane, *Pa., U.S.* **94** L5
Kane Basin, *Nunavut, Can.* **83** B16
Kane Fracture Zone, *Atl. Oc.* **236** K7
Kanengo, Note, *Solomon Is.* **217** P22
Kāne'ohe, *Hawai'i, U.S.* **112** E11
Kanevskaya, *Russ.* **157** S10
Kang, *Afghan.* **177** Q2
Kangaamiut, *Greenland, Den.* **81** D21
Kangal, *Turk.* **168** F12
Kangan, *Iran* **173** G13
Kangān, *Iran* **173** H16
Kanganpur, *Pak.* **177** Q12
Kangar, *Malaysia* **187** S8
Kangaroo Island, *S. Aust., Austral.* **211** Y10
Kangbao, *China* **182** B6
Kangding, *China* **180** L11
Kangean, Kepulauan, *Indonesia* **188** M11
Kangeeak Point, *Nunavut, Can.* **83** F19
Kangerlussuaq, *Greenland, Den.* **81** D21
Kangertittivaq, bay, *N. Amer.* **80** B10
Kanggava Bay, *Solomon Is.* **217** Q19
Kanggye, *N. Korea* **182** C13
Kangiqsualujjuaq, *Que., Can.* **83** J20
Kangiqsujuaq, *Que., Can.* **83** J18
Kangirsuk, *Que., Can.* **83** J19
Kangmar, *China* **180** M7
Kango, *Gabon* **201** K15
Kangping, *China* **182** B11
Kangpokpi, *India* **178** G14
Kangrinboqê Feng, peak, *China* **180** K5
Kangto, peak, *China, India* **178** F14
Kaniama, *Dem. Rep. of the Congo* **198** M10
Kaniere, *N.Z.* **213** N17
Kanif, *F.S.M.* **217** D18
Kanigiri, *India* **179** N7
Kanin, Poluostrov, *Russ.* **158** E9
Kanin Nos, Mys, *Russ.* **158** D9
Kanin Peninsula *see* Kanin, Poluostrov, *Russ.* **138** A11
Kanish, ruin, *Turk.* **168** F10
Kanita, *Japan* **184** J13
Kaniv, *Ukr.* **157** P6
Kanjarkot, site, *Pak.* **177** W8
Kanjiža, *Serb. & Mont.* **152** D10
Kankakee, *Ill., U.S.* **99** P7
Kankakee, river, *Ill., Ind., U.S.* **99** P8
Kankan, *Guinea* **200** F7
Kanker, *India* **178** K8
Kanmaw Kyun, *Myanmar* **187** P7
Kanmen, *China* **183** N10
Kannapolis, *N.C., U.S.* **96** H9
Kannari, *Japan* **184** L13
Kannauj, *India* **178** G7
Kano, *Nigeria* **201** E14
Kanokupolu, *Tonga* **218** H11
Kanopolis, *Kans., U.S.* **105** T7
Kanorado, *Kans., U.S.* **105** S3
Kanosh, *Utah, U.S.* **107** N6
Kanoya, *Japan* **185** T4
Kanpur, *India* **178** G7
Kansas, river, *Kans., U.S.* **105** S8
Kansas, *U.S.* **105** T4
Kansas City, *Kans., U.S.* **105** S10
Kansas City, *Mo., U.S.* **105** S10
Kansk, *Russ.* **159** K14
Kant, *Kyrg.* **176** D11
Kantankufri, *Ghana* **200** G11
Kantara Castle, *Cyprus* **160** N10
Kanton, island, *Kiribati* **214** G10
Kanuku Mountains, *Guyana* **129** F14
Kanye, *Botswana* **202** J9
Kao, island, *Tonga* **218** P6
Kaohsiung, *Taiwan, China* **183** S9
Kaoka Bay, *Solomon Is.* **217** N19
Kaokoland, region, *Namibia* **202** G5
Kaolack, *Senegal* **196** H4
Kaoma, *Zambia* **202** E9
Kapa, island, *Tonga* **218** M11
Kapa'a, *Hawai'i, U.S.* **112** B6
Kapa'au, *Hawai'i, U.S.* **113** K19
Kapadvanj, *India* **178** J3
Kapan, *Arm.* **169** F20
Kapanga, *Dem. Rep. of the Congo* **198** M10
Kapela, range, *Croatia* **152** E5
Kapfenberg, *Aust.* **148** L12
Kapıdağı, peak, *Turk.* **168** D4
Kapingamarangi Atoll, *F.S.M.* **214** G5
Kapiri Mposhi, *Zambia* **202** E11
Kapisillit, *Greenland, Den.* **81** D22
Kapiskau, river, *Ont., Can.* **83** M17
Kapit, *Malaysia* **188** H10
Kaplan, *La., U.S.* **100** Q8
Kapoeta, *Sudan* **199** H13
Kapoho Crater, *Hawai'i, U.S.* **113** M22
Kaposvár, *Hung.* **149** N14
Kappar, *Pak.* **177** V2
Kapuāiwa Coconut Grove, *Hawai'i, U.S.* **113** F14
Kapulena, *Hawai'i, U.S.* **113** K20
Kapunda, *S. Aust., Austral.* **211** X10
Kapurthala, *India* **178** D5
Kapuskasing, *Ont., Can.* **83** N17
Kapydzhik, peak, *Arm.* **169** F20
Kara-Balta, *Kyrg.* **176** E11
Karabiga, *Turk.* **168** D3
Karabogaz (Bekdash), *Turkm.* **174** J6
Karabük, *Turk.* **168** C8
Kara Burun, *Turk.* **168** J7
Karaburun, peninsula, *Albania* **152** M9
Karaburun, *Turk.* **168** F2
Karacabey, *Turk.* **168** D4
Karaca Dağ, *Turk.* **169** H14
Karacadağ, *Turk.* **169** H14
Karacaköy, *Turk.* **168** C4
Karachala, *Azerb.* **169** E22
Karachev, *Russ.* **156** L8
Karachi, *Pak.* **177** W6
Karad, *India* **178** M4
Kara Dağ, *Turk.* **169** H18
Kara Dağ, *Turk.* **168** H8
Karadag, *Azerb.* **169** D23
Karaginskiy, Ostrov, *Russ.* **159** E22
Karahallı, *Turk.* **168** G5
Karahüyük, *Turk.* **168** G7
Karaisalı, *Turk.* **168** H10
Karaj, *Iran* **172** C12
Karakeçi, *Turk.* **169** H14
Karakelong, island, *Indonesia* **189** G16
Karakoçan, *Turk.* **169** F14
Kara-Köl, *Kyrg.* **176** F10
Karakol (Przheval'sk), *Kyrg.* **176** E14
Karakoram Pass, *China, India* **176** L14
Karakoram Range, *India, Pak.* **176** K12
Karakul', *Taj.* **176** H11
Karakulino, *Russ.* **156** H16
Karakuwisa, *Namibia* **202** G8
Karam, *Russ.* **159** K15
Karaman, *Turk.* **168** H8
Karamay, *China* **180** D7
Karamea, *N.Z.* **213** M17
Karamea Bight, *N.Z.* **213** M17
Karamürsel, *Turk.* **168** D5
Karanja, *India* **178** K6
Karapınar, *Turk.* **168** H9
Kara-Say, *Kyrg.* **176** E14
Karasburg, *Namibia* **202** K7
Kara Sea, *Arctic Oc.* **242** C11
Karasjok, *Nor.* **141** C14
Karas Mountains, *Namibia* **194** Q7
Karasu, river, *Turk.* **169** E15
Karasu, river, *Turk.* **169** F18
Karasu, *Turk.* **168** C6
Karasuk, *Russ.* **158** K11
Karataş, *Turk.* **168** J10
Karatepe, *Turk.* **168** H11
Karathuri, *Myanmar* **187** P7
Karatsu, *Japan* **185** R4
Karatung, island, *Indonesia* **189** G16
Karaul, *Russ.* **159** F13
Karavas, *Cyprus* **160** N8
Karávia, island, *Gr.* **154** M12
Karavostasi, *Cyprus* **160** P7
Karavostassás, *Gr.* **155** M14
Karawanken, range, *Slov.* **152** C4
Karayazı, *Turk.* **169** E16
Karayün, *Turk.* **168** E12
Karbalā', *Iraq* **172** E9
Karcag, *Hung.* **149** L16
Kardámila, *Gr.* **155** H16
Kardamíli, *Gr.* **154** L10
Karditsa, *Gr.* **154** F9
Kardiva (Karidu), island, *Maldives* **179** U3
Kardiva Channel, *Maldives* **179** U3
Kärdla, *Est.* **141** K15
Karesuando, *Sw.* **141** D14
Kargı, *Turk.* **168** D10
Kargil, *India* **176** M13
Kargilik *see* Yecheng, *China* **180** G4
Kari, *Nigeria* **201** F15
Kariba, *Zimb.* **202** F11
Kariba, Lake, *Zambia, Zimb.* **202** F10
Karidu *see* Kardiva, island, *Maldives* **179** U3
Kariés, *Gr.* **154** L10
Karikari, Cape, *N.Z.* **213** H18
Karimata, island, *Indonesia* **188** K9
Karimata, Kepulauan, *Indonesia* **188** K9
Karimganj, *India* **178** H14
Karimnagar, *India* **178** L7
Karimunjawa, Kepulauan, *Indonesia* **188** L9
Káristos, *Gr.* **155** J13
Karitane, *N.Z.* **213** Q16
Karitena, *Gr.* **154** K9
Karizak, *Afghan.* **177** P1
Karkar, island, *P.N.G.* **213** C19
Karkinits'ka Zatoka, *Ukr.* **157** S7
Karkūk (Kirkuk), *Iraq* **172** C9
Karlıova, *Turk.* **169** F15
Karlovac, *Croatia* **152** E5
Karlovássi, *Gr.* **155** J17
Karlovy Vary, *Czech Rep.* **148** G10
Karlshamn, *Sw.* **141** N13
Karlskrona, *Sw.* **141** N13
Karlsruhe, *Ger.* **148** J6
Karlstad, *Minn., U.S.* **104** E8
Karlstad, *Sw.* **140** L12
Karmala, *India* **178** L4
Karmir Blur, ruin, *Arm.* **169** E18
Karnali, river, *Nepal* **178** E8
Karnaphuli Reservoir, *Bangladesh* **178** J14
Karnes City, *Tex., U.S.* **103** S10
Karnobat (Polyanovgrad), *Bulg.* **153** J16
Karoi, *Zimb.* **202** F11
Karokh, *Afghan.* **176** M2
Karoko, *Fiji Is.* **218** G8
Karompa, island, *Indonesia* **189** M14
Karonga, *Malawi* **203** C13
Karonie, *W. Aust., Austral.* **211** W5
Karosa, *Indonesia* **189** K13
Karpasia Peninsula, *Cyprus* **160** M11
Kárpathos, *Gr.* **155** P18
Kárpathos (Carpathos), island, *Gr.* **155** P18
Kárpathos Stenón, *Gr.* **155** P19
Karpeníssi, *Gr.* **154** G9
Karperó, *Gr.* **154** E9
Karratha, *W. Aust., Austral.* **211** S2
Karre Mountains, *Cen. Af. Rep.* **194** H6
Karridale, *W. Aust., Austral.* **211** Y2
Kars, *Turk.* **169** D17
Kartal, *Turk.* **168** C5
Karumba, *Qnsld., Austral.* **211** R11
Kārūn, river, *Iran* **172** F11
Karunjie, *W. Aust., Austral.* **211** Q6
Karviná, *Czech Rep.* **149** H14
Karwar, *India* **179** N4
Karwi, *India* **178** H8
Karyaí, *Gr.* **155** D13
Kar'yepol'ye, *Russ.* **158** E9
Karynzharyk, desert, *Kaz.* **174** J6
Kaş, *Turk.* **168** J5
Kas, *Sudan* **198** E10

L

M

Medvezh'i Ostrova (Bear Islands), Russ. 159 C19
Medvezh'yegorsk, Russ. 158 D7
Medyado, island, Marshall Is. 216 L8
Medyai, island, Marshall Is. 216 L8
Meekatharra, W. Aust., Austral. 211 V3
Meeker, Colo., U.S. 106 L10
Meerut, India 178 F6
Meeteetse, Wyo., U.S. 106 G10
Mega, Indonesia 189 J18
Mēga, Eth. 199 H15
Megálo Horió, Gr. 155 M18
Megalópoli, Gr. 154 K9
Mégara, Gr. 154 J12
M̃égham, Vanuatu 218 D3
Meghri, Arm. 169 F20
Megiddo, Israel 170 L5
Megion, Russ. 158 H11
Megísti (Kastellórizon), Gr. 155 N22
Mehadia, Rom. 152 F12
Mehamn, Nor. 141 B14
Mehar, Pak. 177 U6
Meharry, Mount, Austral. 210 F3
Meherrin, river, Va., U.S. 96 F12
Mehetia, island, Fr. Polynesia, Fr. 219 F17
Mehola, W. Bank 170 L6
Mehrīz, Iran 173 E14
Mehtar Lam, Afghan. 176 M8
Meichang, China 181 L16
Meiganga, Cameroon 201 G17
Meighan Island, Nunavut, Can. 83 B14
Meigs, Ga., U.S. 97 Q5
Meihekou, China 182 B12
Meiktila, Myanmar 186 H6
Meiningen, Ger. 148 G8
Meissen, Ger. 148 F10
Meizhou, China 183 R6
Mejatto, island, Marshall Is. 216 K1
Mejillones, Chile 132 E6
Mejillones del Sur, Bahía de, Chile 132 E7
Mejit Island, Marshall Is. 216 F5
Mékambo, Gabon 201 K17
Mek'elē, Eth. 199 E15
Mekerrhane, Sebkha, Alg. 196 D10
Mekhtar, Pak. 177 R8
Mekiro, island, Fr. Polynesia, Fr. 219 Q20
Meknès, Mor. 196 B8
Mekong, river, Asia 166 K11
Mekong River Delta, Vietnam 187 Q13
Mekoryuk, Alas., U.S. 110 J11
Melanesia, islands, Pac. Oc. 214 G4
Melbourne, Fla., U.S. 97 T10
Melbourne, Vic., Austral. 211 Z12
Melbourne, Mount, Antarctica 227 P14
Mele, Capo, It. 150 G3
Mélé Bay, Vanuatu 218 F3
Melegnano, It. 150 E4
Melekeiok, Palau 216 N12
Melekeiok Point, Palau 216 N12
Melenki, Russ. 156 J11
Melfi, Chad 197 J15
Melfi, It. 150 M12
Melfort, Sask., Can. 82 M12
Melgar de Fernamental, Sp. 144 C10
Melide, Sp. 144 B6
Meligalás, Gr. 154 L9
Melilla, Sp. 144 P11
Melinka, Chile 133 R6
Melipilla, Chile 132 L6
Melita see Mljet, island, Croatia 152 J7
Melitopol', Ukr. 157 R8
Mellansel, Sw. 141 H13
Melle, Fr. 147 T7
Melle, Ger. 148 E6
Mellen, Wis., U.S. 98 F4
Mellieħa, Malta 161 J21
Mellieħa Bay, Malta 161 J21
Mělník, Czech Rep. 148 G11
Melo, Uru. 132 K15
Melolo, Indonesia 189 N13
Melos see Mílos, island, Gr. 155 M13
Melrhir, Chott, Alg. 196 B12
Melrose, Minn., U.S. 104 J10
Melrose, W. Aust., Austral. 211 V4
Mels, Switz. 150 B5
Meltaus, Fin. 141 E15
Melton, Vic., Austral. 211 Z12
Meluan, Malaysia 188 H10
Melun, Fr. 147 Q10
Melvich, Scot., U.K. 142 G9
Melville, Sask., Can. 82 N12
Melville, Lake, Nfld. & Lab., Can. 83 K22
Melville Bay, N. Amer. 80 C8
Melville Hills, N.W.T., Nunavut, Can. 82 E11
Melville Island, N. Terr., Austral. 211 N7
Melville Island, N.W.T., Nunavut, Can. 83 D13
Melville Peninsula, Nunavut, Can. 83 F16
Melvin, Tex., U.S. 103 N8
Melvin, Lough, Ire., U.K. 143 Q5
Mé Maoya, peak, New Caledonia, Fr. 218 D7
Memba, Mozambique 203 E15
Memboro, Indonesia 189 N13
Memmingen, Ger. 148 K7
Memphis, Mo., U.S. 105 Q13
Memphis, Tenn., U.S. 100 G11
Memphis, Tex., U.S. 102 H7
Mena, Ark., U.S. 100 G6
Mena, Ukr. 156 M7
Menahga, Minn., U.S. 104 G10
Menai Strait, Wales, U.K. 143 S9
Ménaka, Mali 196 H10
Menard, Tex., U.S. 103 P8
Menard Fracture Zone, Pac. Oc. 239 Q15
Menasha, Wis., U.S. 98 J6
Mende, Fr. 147 W11
Mendebo Mountains, Eth. 194 H10
Mendeleyev Plain, Arctic Oc. 242 J7
Mendeleyev Ridge, Arctic Oc. 242 H6
Mendeleyevsk, Russ. 156 H16
Mendelssohn Seamount, Pac. Oc. 238 G12
Mendenhall, Miss., U.S. 100 M11
Mendi, P.N.G. 213 D18
Mendī, Eth. 199 F14
Mendip Hills, Eng., U.K. 143 W11
Mendocino, Calif., U.S. 109 P2
Mendocino, Cape, Calif., U.S. 84 E2
Mendocino Fracture Zone, Pac. Oc. 238 E12
Mendota, Calif., U.S. 109 T6
Mendota, Ill., U.S. 99 P5
Mendoza, Arg. 132 K8
Menehune Ditch, Hawai'i, U.S. 112 B5
Meneng, region, Nauru 217 F23
Meneng Point, Nauru 217 F23
Menetés, Gr. 155 P18
Meng, river, Aust. 160 P4
Menge, island, Marshall Is. 216 M8
Mengen, Turk. 168 D7
Mengene Dağı, Turk. 169 G18
Menghai, China 180 Q10
Mengzi, China 180 P11
Meningie, S. Aust., Austral. 211 Y10
Menkere, Russ. 159 F17
Menno, S. Dak., U.S. 104 M7
Menominee, Mich., U.S. 98 H7
Menominee, river, Mich., Wis., U.S. 98 G7
Menomonee Falls, Wis., U.S. 98 L7
Menomonie, Wis., U.S. 98 H2
Menongue, Angola 202 E7
Menor, Mar, Sp. 145 K14
Menorca (Minorca), Sp. 145 G20
Men'shikova, Mys, Russ. 158 E11
Mentasta Lake, Alas., U.S. 111 H18
Mentawai, Kepulauan, Indonesia 188 K5
Mentawai Islands, Indonesia 166 M10
Menton, Fr. 147 X16
Mentor, Ohio, U.S. 99 N15
Menyamya, P.N.G. 213 D19
Menzies, W. Aust., Austral. 211 W4
Menzies, Mount, Antarctica 227 F18
Me'ona, Israel 170 K6
Meppel, Neth. 146 H13
Meppen, Ger. 148 D6
Mequinenza, Embalse de, Sp. 145 E15
Meramangye, Lake, Austral. 210 H8
Meramec, river, Mo., U.S. 105 T14
Merampit, island, Indonesia 189 G16
Merano, It. 150 C7
Meratus, Pegunungan, Indonesia 188 K11
Merauke, Indonesia 189 N21
Merca see Marka, Somalia 199 J17
Mercan Dağları, Turk. 169 F14
Mercara, India 179 Q5
Merced, Calif., U.S. 109 S5
Mercedario, Cerro, S. Amer. 126 L4
Mercedes, Arg. 132 H13
Mercedes, Arg. 132 L12
Mercedes, Arg. 132 L9
Mercedes, Tex., U.S. 103 W10
Mercedes, Uru. 132 K13
Merceditas, Chile 132 H7
Mercherchar (Eil Malk), island, Palau 216 P11
Mercy, Cape, Nunavut, Can. 83 G19
Mercy Bay, N.W.T., Can. 82 D12
Meredith, Cape, Falkland Is., U.K. 133 W11
Meredith, Lake, Tex., U.S. 102 G5
Mereeg, Somalia 199 H17
Merefa, Ukr. 157 P9
M̃éré Lava, island, Vanuatu 218 B2
Mergenevo, Kaz. 174 D6
Mergui Archipelago, Myanmar 187 N7
Meriç, river, Turk. 168 C2
Meriç, Turk. 168 C2
Mérida, Mex. 115 H16
Mérida, Sp. 144 H8
Mérida, Venez. 128 C7
Mérida, Cordillera de, Venez. 128 C7
Meriden, Conn., U.S. 94 M12
Meridian, Idaho, U.S. 106 G3
Meridian, Miss., U.S. 101 L13
Meridian, Tex., U.S. 102 M10
Mérig, island, Vanuatu 218 B2
Merimbula, N.S.W., Austral. 211 Z14
Merir, island, Palau 214 F2
Meritxell, Andorra 160 H4
Merizo, Guam, U.S. 216 E10
Merkel, Tex., U.S. 102 L7
Merkine, Lith. 141 P17
Meroe, ruin, Sudan 199 D13
Merowe, Sudan 199 D13
Merredin, W. Aust., Austral. 211 X3
Merrick Mountains, Antarctica 226 G7
Merrill, Oreg., U.S. 108 L4
Merrill, Wis., U.S. 98 H5
Merrillville, Ind., U.S. 99 P8
Merrimack, river, N.H., U.S. 95 J14
Merriman, Nebr., U.S. 104 M3
Merritt Island, Fla., U.S. 97 T10
Mer Rouge, La., U.S. 100 K9
Merryville, La., U.S. 100 N6
Mersch, Lux. 160 J10
Merseburg, Ger. 148 F9
Mersey River, Eng., U.K. 143 S10
Mersin see İçel, Turk. 168 J9
Mersing, Malaysia 187 U11
Merta Road, India 178 G4
Mertert, Lux. 160 J11
Merthyr Tydfil, Wales, U.K. 143 V10
Mértola, Port. 144 K6
Mertz Glacier, Antarctica 227 Q17
Mertz Glacier Tongue, Antarctica 227 R17
Mertzon, Tex., U.S. 103 N6
Méru, Fr. 147 N10
Meru, Kenya 199 K14
Merzifon, Turk. 168 D10
Merzig, Ger. 148 H5
Merz Seamount, Antarctic Oc. 244 B11
Mesa, Ariz., U.S. 107 U7
Mesabi Range, Minn., U.S. 85 C14
Mesach Mellet, region, Lib. 197 E13
Mesa Verde National Park, Colo., U.S. 107 Q10
Mescit Tepe, Turk. 169 D15
Meseong, island, F.S.M. 217 D15
Meseta, plateau, Sp. 138 J2
Me Shima, Japan 185 S2
Meskéné see Maskanah, Syr. 170 E10
Mesocco, Switz. 150 C4
Mesopotamia, region, Iraq 172 C8
Mesopotamia, St. Vincent & the Grenadines 121 K16
Mesquite, Nev., U.S. 109 T13
Mesquite, Tex., U.S. 102 L12
Messarás, Kólpos, Gr. 155 R14
Messene, ruin, Gr. 154 L9
Messina, It. 151 R12
Messina, S. Af. 202 H11
Messina, Stretto di, It. 151 R12
Messíni, Gr. 154 L9
Messiniakós Kólpos, Gr. 154 M9
Messolóngi, Gr. 154 H8
Mestá, Gr. 155 H16
Mestia, Rep. of Georgia 169 A17
Mestre, It. 150 D8
Mesudiye, Turk. 168 D12
Meta, river, Venez. 128 E8
Meta Incognita Peninsula, Nunavut, Can. 83 H19
Metairie, La., U.S. 100 Q11
Metalanim, F.S.M. 217 F14
Metalanim Harbor, F.S.M. 217 F14
Metaline Falls, Wash., U.S. 108 A9
Metallifere, Colline, It. 150 H6
Metán, Arg. 132 F9
Metaponto, It. 151 N14
Metaxádes, Gr. 155 B16
Meteora, ruin, Gr. 154 E9
Meteor Crater, Ariz., U.S. 107 S8
Meteor Seamount, Atl. Oc. 237 V14
Méthana, Gr. 154 K12
Methánon, island, Gr. 154 K12
Methóni, Gr. 154 M9
Metković, Croatia 152 H7
Metlakatla, Alas., U.S. 111 N24
Metlili Chaamba, Alg. 196 B11
Metolius, Oreg., U.S. 108 G5
Métoma, island, Vanuatu 218 A1
Metropolis, Ill., U.S. 99 V6
Métsovo, Gr. 154 E8
Metter, Ga., U.S. 97 N8
Mettlach, Ger. 160 K11
Mettur Dam, India 179 Q6
Metz, Fr. 147 P14
Meulan, Fr. 147 P9
Meuse, river, Belg., Fr. 146 M12
Mexia, Tex., U.S. 103 N12
Mexiana, Ilha, Braz. 131 C13
Mexicali, Mex. 114 A5
Mexican Hat, Utah, U.S. 107 Q9
México, Mex. 114 J11
Mexico, Me., U.S. 95 F15
Mexico, Mo., U.S. 105 S13
Mexico, N. Amer. 81 N17
Mexico, Gulf of, N. Amer. 80 M7
Mexico Basin, Atl. Oc. 236 K1
Meyanodas, Indonesia 213 D14
Meydan Shahr, Afghan. 176 M7
Meymaneh, Afghan. 176 L4
Meyrargues, Fr. 147 X13
Mezdra, Bulg. 153 H13
Mezen', river, Russ. 158 F9
Mezen', Russ. 158 E9
Mezen' Bay, Russ. 138 A11
Mezhdusharskiy, Ostrov, Russ. 158 E10
Mézidon-Canon, Fr. 147 P7
Mézin, Fr. 147 W7
Mezőtúr, Hung. 149 M16
Mezzolombardo, It. 150 C7
Mġarr, Malta 161 H20
Mġarr, Malta 161 K21
Miahuatlán, Mex. 115 K13
Miajadas, Sp. 144 H8
Miami, Fla., U.S. 97 X10
Miami, river, N. Amer. 80 K7
Miami, Okla., U.S. 102 E14
Miami, Tex., U.S. 102 G7
Miami Beach, Fla., U.S. 97 X10
Miamisburg, Ohio, U.S. 99 R11
Mianchi, China 182 H4
Mīāndowāb, Iran 172 B10
Miandrivazo, Madagascar 203 G16
Mīāneh, Iran 172 B11
Miani Hor, bay, Pak. 177 V5
Mianrud, Pak. 177 T3
Mianwali, Pak. 177 P9
Mianyang, China 180 L12
Miaodao, island, China 182 E9
Miaoli, Taiwan, China 183 Q9
Miarinarivo, Madagascar 203 G17
Miass, Russ. 158 J8
Michalovce, Slovakia 149 J17
Miches, Dom. Rep. 117 M20
Michigan, U.S. 98 F7
Michigan, Lake, U.S. 85 F16
Michigan City, Ind., U.S. 99 N8
Michurinsk, Russ. 156 L11
Micoud, St. Lucia 121 L14
Micronesia, islands, Pac. Oc. 214 E4
Midai, island, Indonesia 188 H8
Mid-Atlantic Ridge, Atl. Oc. 236 K7
Middelburg, Neth. 146 K11
Middelburg, S. Af. 202 L9
Middle Alkali Lake, Calif., U.S. 108 M6
Middle America Trench, Pac. Oc. 239 H18
Middle Andaman, island, India 179 Q14
Middle Bight, Bahamas 116 F11
Middlebury, Vt., U.S. 94 G12
Middlegate, Norfolk I., Austral. 217 F20
Middle Island, St. Kitts & Nevis 121 B17
Middle Loup, river, Nebr., U.S. 105 P5
Middlemarch, N.Z. 213 Q16
Middle Park, Qnsld., Austral. 211 S12
Middleport, Ohio, U.S. 99 S14
Middle Quarters, Jam. 120 J7
Middle River, Minn., U.S. 104 E9
Middlesboro, Ky., U.S. 101 D19
Middlesbrough, Eng., U.K. 143 Q12
Middleton, Wis., U.S. 98 L5
Middletown, Conn., U.S. 95 M13
Middletown, N.Y., U.S. 94 M10
Middletown, Ohio, U.S. 99 S11
Midelt, Mor. 196 B9
Midi, Canal du, Fr. 147 X9
Mid-Indian Basin, Ind. Oc. 240 H10
Mid-Indian Ridge, Ind. Oc. 240 G8
Midland, Mich., U.S. 98 K11
Midland, S. Dak., U.S. 104 L4
Midland, Tex., U.S. 102 M5
Midlothian, Tex., U.S. 102 L11
Mid-Pacific Mountains, Pac. Oc. 238 G7
Midu, island, Maldives 179 X3
Midway Islands, U.S. 112 K2
Midwest, Wyo., U.S. 106 H12
Midwest City, Okla., U.S. 102 G11
Midyat, Turk. 169 H16
Midžor, peak, Bulg., Serb. & Mont. 152 H12
Międzyrzecz, Pol. 148 D12
Miélan, Fr. 147 X7
Mielec, Pol. 149 G16
Miercurea Ciuc, Rom. 153 D15
Mieres, Sp. 144 B9
Miguel Calmon, Braz. 131 H16
Migyaunglaung, Myanmar 186 M7
Mihalıççık, Turk. 168 E7
Mijas, Sp. 144 M9
Mijdaḩah, Yemen 172 Q11
Mijek, W. Sahara, Mor. 196 E6
Mijikadrek, island, Marshall Is. 216 G8
Mikhaylovka, Russ. 157 N12
Mikkeli, Fin. 141 H16
Míkonos, island, Gr. 155 K15
Míkonos, Gr. 155 K15
Mikrí Préspa, Límni, Gr. 154 C8
Mikun', Russ. 158 F8
Mikura Jima, Japan 185 R12
Milaca, Minn., U.S. 104 H11
Miladummadulu Atoll, Maldives 179 T3
Milagro, Ecua. 128 K2
Milan see Milano, It. 150 D4
Milan, Mo., U.S. 105 R12
Milan, Tenn., U.S. 101 F13
Milano (Milan), It. 150 D4
Milas, Turk. 168 H3
Milazzo, Capo di, It. 151 R12
Milbank, S. Dak., U.S. 104 J8
Milbridge, Me., U.S. 95 F18
Mildenhall, Eng., U.K. 143 T14
Mildura, Vic., Austral. 211 X11
Mile, China 180 P11
Mile and a Quarter, Barbados 121 J18
Mile Gully, Jam. 120 J8
Mil Entrance, F.S.M. 217 C18
Miles, Qnsld., Austral. 211 V14
Miles, Tex., U.S. 103 N7
Miles City, Mont., U.S. 106 D12
Mileto, It. 151 R13
Miletto, Monte, It. 150 L11
Miletus, ruin, Turk. 168 G3
Mileura, W. Aust., Austral. 211 V3
Milford, Del., U.S. 96 C15
Milford, Iowa, U.S. 104 M10
Milford, Mass., U.S. 95 K14
Milford, Nebr., U.S. 105 Q8
Milford, Utah, U.S. 107 N6
Milford Bay, Trinidad & Tobago 121 N17
Milford Haven (Aberdaugleddau), Wales, U.K. 143 V8
Milford Lake, Kans., U.S. 105 S8
Milford Sound, N.Z. 213 Q15
Milgarra, Qnsld., Austral. 211 R11
Milgun, W. Aust., Austral. 211 U3
Mili Atoll, Marshall Is. 216 H5
Miliés, Gr. 154 F11
Milikapiti, N. Terr., Austral. 211 N7
Mililani Town, Hawai'i, U.S. 112 E11
Milingimbi, N. Terr., Austral. 211 P9
Milk, river, Mont., U.S. 106 B11
Milk, Wadi el, Sudan 198 D12
Mil'kovo, Russ. 159 F22
Milk River Bath, Jam. 120 K8
Millars Sound, Bahamas 120 B11
Millau, Fr. 147 W11
Mill City, Oreg., U.S. 108 G4
Milledgeville, Ga., U.S. 96 M6
Mille Lacs Lake, Minn., U.S. 104 H11
Millen, Ga., U.S. 96 M8
Miller, S. Dak., U.S. 104 K6
Millerovo, Russ. 157 P11
Miller Peak, Ariz., U.S. 107 W8
Miller Point, Solomon Is. 217 R24
Millersburg, Ohio, U.S. 99 Q14

Niafounké, Mali 196 H8
Niagara, river, N.Y., U.S. 94 H5
Niagara, Wis., U.S. 98 G7
Niagara Falls, Can., U.S. 85 E19
Niah, Malaysia 188 G11
Niamey, Niger 196 J10
Niangara, Dem. Rep. of the Congo 198 H11
Niangua, river, Mo., U.S. 105 U12
Nianiau, Pu'u, Hawai'i, U.S. 113 G17
Nianzishan, China 181 C16
Nias, island, Indonesia 188 H4
Niau, island, Fr. Polynesia, Fr. 219 E17
Nibok, region, Nauru 217 E23
Nicaea see İznik, Turk. 168 D5
Nicaragua, N. Amer. 81 Q20
Nicaragua, Lago de, Nicar. 115 M18
Nicaragua, Lake see Nicar., Lago de, N. Amer. 80 Q8
Nicastro, It. 151 Q13
Nice, Fr. 147 X16
Nicephorium see Ar Raqqah, Syr. 170 E11
Niceville, Fla., U.S. 97 Q2
Nichinan, Japan 185 T5
Nicholas Channel, Bahamas, Cuba 116 F8
Nicholasville, Ky., U.S. 101 B18
Nicholls' Town, Bahamas 116 E11
Nicholson, W. Aust., Austral. 211 R7
Nicholson Range, Austral. 210 H2
Nickavilla, Qnsld., Austral. 211 U12
Nickerson, Kans., U.S. 105 T7
Nicobar Islands, India 179 S14
Nicopolis, ruin, Gr. 154 G7
Nicosia see Lefkosia, Cyprus 160 N8
Nicosia, It. 151 S11
Nicoya, Península de, Costa Rica 115 N18
Nicoya Peninsula see Nicoya, Península de, N. Amer. 80 Q8
Nida, Lith. 141 N15
Nidzh, Azerb. 169 C21
Nidzica, Pol. 149 C15
Niederanven, Lux. 160 J10
Niedere Tauern, Aust. 148 L11
Nienburg, Ger. 148 D7
Nieuw Amsterdam, Suriname 129 E16
Nieuw Nickerie, Suriname 129 E15
Nieuwpoort, Neth. Antilles, Neth. 121 Q15
Nieves, Pico da las, Canary Is. 204 R5
Nif, F.S.M. 217 D18
Nifiloli, island, Solomon Is. 217 P23
Niğde, Turk. 168 G10
Niger, Af. 195 G17
Niger, river, Af. 194 H5
Niger, Source of the, Guinea 194 H2
Niger Delta, Nigeria 201 J13
Nigeria, Af. 195 H17
Nightingale Island, Tristan da Cunha Is., U.K. 194 R2
Nigríta, Gr. 154 C12
Nihing, river, Pak. 177 V2
Nihiru, island, Fr. Polynesia, Fr. 219 E19
Nihoa, island, Hawai'i, U.S. 112 M8
Nihonmatsu, Japan 184 M13
Niigata, Japan 184 M11
Niihama, Japan 185 R7
Ni'ihau, island, Hawai'i, U.S. 112 C3
Niimi, Japan 185 Q7
Nii Shima, Japan 185 Q12
Nijmegen, Neth. 146 J13
Nikalap Aru, island, F.S.M. 217 G13
Nikao, Cook Is., N.Z. 218 Q9
Nikaupara, Cook Is., N.Z. 218 Q11
Níkea, Gr. 154 F10
Nikel', Russ. 158 C9
Nikiboko, Neth. Antilles, Neth. 121 Q19
Nikítas, Gr. 154 D12
Nikitin Seamount, Ind. Oc. 240 G10
Nikolai, Alas., U.S. 111 H15
Nikolayevsk, Russ. 157 N13
Nikolayevskiy, Russ. 159 J19
Nikolayevsk na Amure, Russ. 159 J21
Nikol'sk, Russ. 156 K13
Nikolski, Alas., U.S. 110 P8
Nikol'skoye, Russ. 157 Q14
Nikol'skoye, Russ. 159 E23
Nikopol', Ukr. 157 Q8
Nīk Pey, Iran 172 B11
Niksar, Turk. 168 D12
Nīkshahr, Iran 173 H17
Nikšić, Serb. & Mont. 152 J8
Nikumaroro, island, Kiribati 214 H10
Nil, Russ. 159 K18
Nilandu, island, Maldives 179 V3
Nilandu, island, Maldives 179 W3
Nilandu Atoll, Maldives 179 V3
Nile, river, Af. 194 E9
Nile, Sources of the, Burundi, Rwanda 194 K9
Nile River Delta, Egypt 194 D9
Niles, Mich., U.S. 99 N9
Niles, Ohio, U.S. 99 P15
Nilgiri Hills, India 179 Q5
Nimach, India 178 H4
Nimbahera, India 178 H4
Nimba Mountains, Côte d'Ivoire 200 G7
Nimbin, N.S.W., Austral. 211 W15
Nîmes, Fr. 147 X12
Nímos, island, Gr. 155 M19
Nimrod Glacier, Antarctica 227 L13
Ninati, Indonesia 189 L21
Nine Degree Channel, India 179 S3
Ninetyeast Ridge, Ind. Oc. 240 K11
Ninety Mile Beach, Austral. 210 M13
Ninety Mile Beach, N.Z. 213 H18
Nineveh, ruin, Iraq 172 C9
Ninfas, Punta, Arg. 133 R10
Ningbo, China 182 L10
Ningcheng, China 182 C8
Ningde, China 183 P8
Ningdu, China 183 P6
Ningguo, China 182 L8
Ningshan, China 182 H1
Ningwu, China 182 D4
Ningyuan, China 183 P3
Ninh Binh, Vietnam 186 H12
Ninh Hoa, Vietnam 187 N14
Ninigo Group, P.N.G. 213 B18
Ninilchik, Alas., U.S. 111 K16
Niniva, island, Tonga 218 P6
Ninnescah, river, Kans., U.S. 105 U7
Ninni, island, Marshall Is. 216 N5
Ninnis Glacier, Antarctica 227 Q16
Nīnole, Hawai'i, U.S. 113 L21
Nīnole, Hawai'i, U.S. 113 P20
Ninove, Belg. 146 L11
Nioaque, Braz. 130 L10
Niobrara, river, Nebr., U.S. 104 M5
Nioro du Sahel, Mali 196 H6
Niort, Fr. 147 T7
Nioumachoua, Comoros 205 N15
Nipawin, Sask., Can. 82 M12
Nipe, Bahía de, Cuba 117 K13
Nipigon, Ont., Can. 83 P16
Nipigon, Lake, Ont., Can. 83 N16
Nipton, Calif., U.S. 109 V12
Niquelândia, Braz. 131 J13
Niquero, Cuba 116 K11
Nīr, Iran 172 B11
Nirmal, India 178 L6
Niš, Serb. & Mont. 152 H11
Nişāb, Saudi Arabia 172 G10
Nişāb, Yemen 172 Q10
Nišava, river, Serb. & Mont. 152 H12
Nishikō, Japan 185 S4
Nishine, Japan 184 K13
Nishinoomote, Japan 185 U4
Nishino Shima, Japan 185 P6
Nishtūn, Yemen 173 P13
Nissi, Est. 141 K16
Níssiros, island, Gr. 155 M18
Nisswa, Minn., U.S. 104 H10
Niţā', Saudi Arabia 172 H11
Niterói, Braz. 131 M15
Nitra, Slovakia 149 K14
Nitro, W. Va., U.S. 96 D8
Niuafo'ou, island, Tonga 214 J9
Niuatoputapu, island, Tonga 214 J10
Niu Aunfo Point, Tonga 218 H11
Niue, island, N.Z., Pac. Oc. 214 K10
Niulakita, island, Tuvalu 214 J9
Niutao, island, Tuvalu 214 H9
Niutoua, Tonga 218 H12
Niutou Shan, China 182 M10
Nixon, Tex., U.S. 103 R10
Nixon's Harbor, Bahamas 120 C8
Niya see Minfeng, China 180 H6
Nizamabad, India 178 L6
Nizamghat, India 178 F15
Nizam Sagar, lake, India 178 M6
Nizao, Dom. Rep. 117 M19
Nizhnekamsk, Russ. 156 H16
Nizhneshadrino, Russ. 159 J13
Nizhneudinsk, Russ. 159 L14
Nizhnevartovsk, Russ. 158 H11
Nizhneyansk, Russ. 159 E17
Nizhniy Baskunchak, Russ. 157 Q14
Nizhniy Bestyakh, Russ. 159 G18
Nizhniy Lomov, Russ. 156 L12
Nizhniy Novgorod, Russ. 156 J12
Nizhniy Tagil, Russ. 158 H9
Nizhnyaya Tunguska, river, Russ. 159 H13
Nizhnyaya Tura, Russ. 158 H9
Nizhyn, Ukr. 157 N6
Nizip, river, Turk. 168 H12
Nizip, Turk. 168 H12
Nizwá, Oman 173 K16
Nizza Monferrato, It. 150 F3
Nizzana (El 'Auja), Israel 171 P4
Njegoš, peak, Serb. & Mont. 152 H8
Njombe, Tanzania 199 N13
Nkhata Bay, Malawi 203 D13
Nkhotakota, Malawi 203 D13
Nkongsamba, Cameroon 201 H15
Nmai, river, Myanmar 186 D7
Noatak, river, Alas., U.S. 84 M3
Noatak, Alas., U.S. 111 D13
Noatak National Preserve, Alas., U.S. 111 D14
Nouans-les-Fontaines, Fr. 147 S9
Nobeoka, Japan 185 S5
Noblesville, Ind., U.S. 99 R9
Nobo, Indonesia 189 M14
Noboribetsu, Japan 184 G13
Nocera Terinese, It. 151 Q13
Nocona, Tex., U.S. 102 J10
Nodales, Bahía de los, Arg. 133 U9
Nodaway, river, Mo., U.S. 105 Q10
Nofre, Peña, Sp. 144 D7
Nogáles, Mex. 114 B7
Nogales, Ariz., U.S. 107 W8
Nogara, It. 150 E6
Nōgata, Japan 185 R4
Nogent-le-Rotrou, Fr. 147 Q8
Nogent-sur-Seine, Fr. 147 Q11
Noginsk, Russ. 156 J10
Nogoyá, Arg. 132 K12
Nogu Dabu, island, P.N.G. 217 H18
Nogueira, peak, Port. 144 D7
Nohar, India 178 E4
Noheji, Japan 184 J13
Nohili Point, Hawai'i, U.S. 112 B4
Nohona o Hae, peak, Hawai'i, U.S. 113 L19
Nohta, India 178 J7
Noia, Sp. 144 B5
Noire, Montagne, Fr. 147 X10
Noires, Montagnes, Fr. 147 Q3
Noirmoutier, Île de, Fr. 147 S5
Nojima Zaki, Japan 185 Q12
Noka, Solomon Is. 217 P22
Nokaneng, Botswana 202 G8
Nokia, Fin. 141 J15
Nok Kundi, Pak. 177 S2
Nokomis, Ill., U.S. 99 S5
Nokuku, Vanuatu 218 C1
Nola, Cen. Af. Rep. 198 H8
Noli, It. 150 F3
Nolinsk, Russ. 156 G15
Noma Misaki, Japan 185 T4
Nomans Land, island, Mass., U.S. 95 M15
Nome, Alas., U.S. 110 F12
Nomgon, Mongolia 180 F12
Nomoneas, island, F.S.M. 217 B15
Nomo Saki, Japan 185 S3
Nomuka, island, Tonga 218 Q6
Nomuka Group, Tonga 218 Q6
Nomuka Iki, island, Tonga 218 Q6
Nomwin Atoll, F.S.M. 216 Q6
Nonancourt, Fr. 147 P9
Nondalton, Alas., U.S. 111 K15
Nongjrong, India 178 G14
Nong Khai, Thai. 186 K10
Nonouti, island, Kiribati 214 G8
Nonpareil, Grenada 121 J22
Nonsuch Bay, Antigua & Barbuda 121 B21
Nonsuch Island, Bermuda, U.K. 120 B4
Nonthaburi, Thai. 186 M9
Nonume, Solomon Is. 217 Q22
Nonza, Fr. 150 J4
Noole, Solomon Is. 217 Q22
Noonan, N. Dak., U.S. 104 D2
Noord, Aruba, Neth. 121 Q16
Noordkaap, cape, Aruba, Neth. 121 Q17
Noordpunt, cape, Neth. Antilles, Neth. 121 N13
Noormarkku, Fin. 141 J15
Noorvik, Alas., U.S. 111 E13
Nóqui, Angola 202 B5
Nora, ruin, It. 151 Q4
Nora Hazel Point, Virgin Islands, U.K. 120 Q7
Norak, Taj. 176 J8
Norborne, Mo., U.S. 105 S11
Norcia, It. 150 J9
Nord, Greenland, Den. 81 A20
Nord, Baie du, Mauritius 205 J20
Nord, Pointe, Comoros 205 L14
Nord, Pointe, Wallis & Futuna, Fr. 218 E11
Nord, Pointe, St. Martin, Fr. 121 A15
Nordaustlandet, island, Norway 167 N7
Norden, Ger. 148 C6
Norderstedt, Ger. 148 C8
Nord Est, Grande Récif du, Mayotte, Fr. 205 N17
Nordeste, Azores 144 Q5
Nordfjordeid, Nor. 140 J10
Nordhausen, Ger. 148 F8
Nordhorn, Ger. 148 D5
Nordkapp, cape, Nor. 141 B14
Nordkjosbotn, Nor. 141 D13
Nordli, Nor. 140 G12
Nordoyar, island, Faroe Is., Den. 140 J6
Nore, river, Ire. 143 T5
Norfolk, Nebr., U.S. 105 N7
Norfolk, Va., U.S. 96 F14
Norfolk Island, Austral. 214 L7
Norfolk Ridge, Pac. Oc. 238 M8
Norfork Lake, Ark., U.S. 100 E9
Noril'sk, Russ. 159 F13
Normal, Ill., U.S. 99 Q6
Norman, Ark., U.S. 100 H7
Norman, river, Austral. 210 D11
Norman, Okla., U.S. 102 G11
Norman, Lake, N.C., U.S. 96 H9
Normanby Island, P.N.G. 213 E21
Normandy, region, Fr. 147 P6
Norman's Cay, Bahamas 120 G5
Norman's Pond Cay, Bahamas 120 E8
Normanton, Qnsld., Austral. 211 R11
Norman Wells, N.W.T., Can. 82 F10
Norna, Mount, Austral. 210 E11
Nornalup, W. Aust., Austral. 211 Y3
Ñorquincó, Arg. 133 Q7
Norris Lake, Tenn., U.S. 101 E18
Norristown, Pa., U.S. 94 P9
Norrköping, Sw. 141 L13
Norrsundet, Sw. 141 J13
Norseman, W. Aust., Austral. 211 X4
Norsk, Russ. 159 K19
Norsup, Vanuatu 218 D2
Nort, Fr. 147 R6
Norte, Cabo, Braz. 131 C13
Norte, Punta, Arg. 132 M13
Norte, Serra do, Braz. 130 G9
North, Cape, N.S., Can. 83 N22
North Adams, Mass., U.S. 94 J12
North Albanian Alps, Albania 152 J9
Northampton, Eng., U.K. 143 U13
Northampton, Mass., U.S. 95 K13
Northampton, W. Aust., Austral. 211 W2
Northampton Seamounts, Hawai'i, U.S. 112 L4
North Andaman, island, India 179 P14
North Aral Sea, Kaz. 174 G10
North Arm, N.W.T., Can. 82 H11
North Augusta, S.C., U.S. 96 L8
North Aulatsivik Island, Nfld. & Lab., Can. 83 J20
North Australian Basin, Ind. Oc. 241 J16
North Battleford, Sask., Can. 82 M11
North Bay, Ont., Can. 83 P18
North Belcher Islands, Nunavut, Can. 83 L17
North Bend, Oreg., U.S. 108 J2
North Bimini, island, Bahamas 120 B8
North Branch, Minn., U.S. 104 J12
North Branch Potomac, river, Md., W. Va., U.S. 96 C10
North Caicos, island, Turks & Caicos Is., U.K. 117 H17
North Canadian, river, Okla., U.S. 102 F9
North Cape, N.Z. 213 G18
North Cape see Nordkapp, Nor. 138 A8
North Cape, Kiribati 217 B20
North Carolina, U.S. 96 H7
North Cascades National Park, Wash., U.S. 108 A5
North Channel, Mich., U.S. 98 F12
North Channel, N. Ire., Scot., U.K. 143 N7
North Charleston, S.C., U.S. 96 M10
North Chicago, Ill., U.S. 98 M7
North China Plain, China 166 G11
Northcliffe, W. Aust., Austral. 211 Y3
North Comino Channel, Malta 161 H21
North Dakota, U.S. 104 F2
North Downs, Eng., U.K. 143 V14
North East, Pa., U.S. 94 K3
Northeast Cay, Jam. 116 P11
Northeast Pacific Basin, Pac. Oc. 238 D11
Northeast Pass, Marshall Is. 216 L8
Northeast Passage, Solomon Is. 217 R24
North East Point, Cayman Is., U.K. 116 L9
North East Point, Kiribati 217 B23
Northeast Point, Bahamas 117 G15
Northeast Point, Jam. 120 J11
Northeast Providence Channel, Bahamas 116 D12
Northeim, Ger. 148 E7
North Entrance, Palau 216 K12
Northern Cyprus, Cyprus 160 M8
Northern Dvina, river, Russ. 138 B11
Northern European Plain, Eur. 138 F5
Northern Ireland, U.K. 143 P6
Northern Karroo, region, Lesotho, S. Af. 194 Q7
Northern Light Lake, Minn., U.S. 104 E14
Northern Mariana Islands, U.S., Pac. Oc. 214 D4
Northern Perimeter Highway, Braz. 130 C10
Northern Range, Trinidad & Tobago 121 N22
Northern Sporades see Vóries Sporádes, islands, Gr. 155 F13
Northern Territory, Austral. 211 R8
Northern Uvals, Russ. 138 C12
Northfield, Minn., U.S. 104 K11
Northfield, Vt., U.S. 95 G13
North Fiji Islands Basin, Pac. Oc. 238 L9
North Fond du Lac, Wis., U.S. 98 K6
North Fork, Calif., U.S. 109 S7
North Fork Clearwater, river, Idaho, U.S. 106 D4
North Fork Flathead, river, Mont., U.S. 106 A5
North Fork Payette, river, Idaho, U.S. 106 F4
North Fork Red, river, Okla., Tex., U.S. 102 H8
North Fork Salt, river, Mo., U.S. 105 R13
North Friar's Bay, St. Kitts & Nevis 121 B18
North Frisian Islands, Ger. 148 A7
North Geomagnetic Pole 2005, Nunavut, Can. 83 B16
North Head, N.Z. 213 J18
North Island, N.Z. 213 K18
North Island, Seychelles 205 N19
North Korea, Asia 167 T12
North Lakhimpur, India 178 F14
North Land, islands, Russ. 166 B9
North Land see Severnaya Zemlya, Russ. 159 C14
North Las Vegas, Nev., U.S. 109 U12
North Little Rock, Ark., U.S. 100 G8
North Loup, river, Nebr., U.S. 105 N5
North Magnetic Pole 2006, N.W.T., Can. 83 A13
North Malosmadulu Atoll, Maldives 179 U3
North Manchester, Ind., U.S. 99 P9
North Mole, Gibraltar, U.K. 161 N22
North Myrtle Beach, S.C., U.S. 96 K12
North Naples, Fla., U.S. 97 W8
North Negril Point, Jam. 120 H5
North Olmsted, Ohio, U.S. 99 P14
North Palmetto Point, Bahamas 120 E6
North Pass, Marshall Is. 216 K4
North Perry, Ohio, U.S. 99 N15
North Pioa, peak, Amer. Samoa, U.S. 218 M8
North Platte, river, Nebr., U.S. 105 P2
North Platte, Nebr., U.S. 105 Q4
North Point, Barbados 121 J18
North Point, Cook Is., N.Z. 219 A14
North Point, Mich., U.S. 98 H12
North Point, Seychelles 205 N20
Northport, Ala., U.S. 101 K14
Northport, Wash., U.S. 108 A8
North Powder, Oreg., U.S. 108 F8
North Raccoon, river, Iowa, U.S. 105 P11
North Rock, Bahamas 120 A8
North Roe, Scot., U.K. 142 D12
North Ronaldsay, island, Scot., U.K. 142 F11
North Saskatchewan, river, Alta., Can. 82 L11
North Sea, Eur. 138 E5
North Sentinel Island, India 179 Q14

P

Puluwat Atoll, F.S.M. 216 Q5
Pumpkin Creek, Mont., U.S. 106 E12
Puná, Isla, Ecua. 128 K2
Puna, region, Hawai'i, U.S. 113 N21
Punaauia, Fr. Polynesia, Fr. 219 P15
Punaauia, Pointe, Fr. Polynesia, Fr. 219 P15
Puna de Atacama, region, S. Amer. 126 J4
Punaeroa, Passe, Fr. Polynesia, Fr. 219 C23
Punakha, Bhutan 178 F12
Punalu'u, Hawai'i, U.S. 113 P20
Punan, Indonesia 188 H11
Puncak Jaya, peak, Indonesia 189 L20
Punch, India 177 N11
Pune, India 178 L4
Punitaqui, Chile 132 J6
Puno, Peru 130 J6
Punta, Cerro de, P.R., U.S. 120 N3
Punta Aguja, range, Peru 130 F1
Punta Alta, Arg. 133 N11
Punta Arenas, Chile 133 X8
Punta Coles, range, Peru 130 K5
Punta del Este, Uru. 132 L14
Punta Delgada, Arg. 133 R10
Punta Gorda, Belize 115 K16
Punta Gorda, Fla., U.S. 97 V8
Punta Negra, range, Peru 130 F1
Punta Pariñas, range, Peru 130 E1
Punta Prieta, Mex. 114 C5
Puntarenas, Costa Rica 115 N18
Punta Umbría, Sp. 144 L7
Puntland, region, Somalia 199 G18
Punto Fijo, Venez. 128 A8
Puntudo, Cerro, Arg. 133 U8
Punxsutawney, Pa., U.S. 94 M5
Puohine, Fr. Polynesia, Fr. 219 C23
Puqi, China 182 L5
Puquio, Peru 130 J4
Puranpur, India 178 F7
Purari, river, P.N.G. 213 D19
Purcell, Okla., U.S. 102 H11
Purcell Mountains, Can., U.S. 106 A4
Purdy Islands, P.N.G. 213 B19
Purgatoire, river, Colo., U.S. 107 P14
Puri, India 178 L10
Purmerend, Neth. 146 H12
Purna, river, India 178 K5
Purnia, India 178 G11
Pursat, Cambodia 187 N11
Purus, river, Braz. 130 E8
Purvis, Miss., U.S. 100 N12
Pusad, India 178 L6
Pusan see Busan, S. Korea 182 G14
Pushkin, Russ. 156 F6
Pushkino, Russ. 156 M14
Pusht-i-Rud, region, Afghan. 177 P3
Puta, Azerb. 169 D23
Putangaroa, island, Cook Is., N.Z. 219 C15
Putao, Myanmar 186 D7
Putian, China 183 Q8
Putilovo, Russ. 156 F12
Putina, Peru 130 J6
Puting, Tanjung, Indonesia 188 K10
Puto, P.N.G. 217 J13
Putorana, Plato, Russ. 159 G14
Putrachoique, Cerro, Arg. 133 R7
Puttalam, Sri Lanka 179 S7
Puttelange, Fr. 147 P15
Puttur, India 179 P7
Putumayo, river, Col. 128 K7
Putumayo, river, Ecua., Peru 128 H4
Pütürge, Turk. 169 G13
Pu'uanahulu, Hawai'i, U.S. 113 L19
Pu'uhonua o Hōnaunau National Historic Park (City of Refuge National Historic Park), Hawai'i, U.S. 113 N18
Pu'ukohola Heiau National Historic Site, Hawai'i, U.S. 113 K19
Pu'uwai, Hawai'i, U.S. 112 C3
Puwe, island, F.S.M. 217 B15
Puxian, China 182 F3
Puyallup, Wash., U.S. 108 C4
Puyang, China 182 G6
Puy de Sancy, peak, Fr. 147 U10
Puy-Guillaume, Fr. 147 U11
Puysegur Point, N.Z. 213 R14
Puzak, Hamun-e, Afghan. 177 Q2
Pweto, Dem. Rep. of the Congo 198 M12
Pya, Lake, Russ. 138 B9
P'yagina, Poluostrov, Russ. 159 F21
Pyasinskiy Zaliv, Russ. 159 E13
Pyatigorsk, Russ. 157 T13
P'yatykhatky, Ukr. 157 Q7
Pyay, Myanmar 186 J5
Pydna, battle, Gr. 154 D10
Pyeonghae, S. Korea 182 F14
Pyhäjoki, Fin. 141 G15
Pyhäselkä, lake, Fin. 141 H17
Pyinkayaing, Myanmar 186 L5
Pyinmana, Myanmar 186 J6
Pyin-U-Lwin, Myanmar 186 G6
Pymatuning Reservoir, Ohio, Pa., U.S. 99 N16
P'yŏng-sŏng, N. Korea 182 D12
P'yŏngyang, N. Korea 182 D12
Pyote, Tex., U.S. 103 N3
Pyramides, Pointe, Wallis & Futuna, Fr. 218 E11
Pyramid Lake, Nev., U.S. 109 P6
Pyramid Rock, China 188 B10
Pyramids and Sphinx, ruin, Egypt 197 C18
Pyrenees, range, Eur. 138 H4
Pýrgos, Gr. 155 R15
Pyryatyn, Ukr. 157 N7
Pytalovo, Russ. 156 H5
Pyu, Myanmar 186 J6

Qabanbay, Kaz. 175 G18
Qabqa, China 180 J10
Qāḏub, Yemen 173 R14
Qaeanā, Syr. 170 J7
Qā'emābād, Iran 173 E17
Qā'emshahr, Iran 173 C13
Qagan Nur, China 182 A6
Qagan Nur, China 182 A5
Qagan Us see Dulan, China 180 J10
Qahar Youyi Houqi, China 182 B5
Qahar Youyi Zhongqi, China 182 C5
Qaidam Basin, China 166 G9
Qaidam Pendi, China 180 H9
Qairouan, Tun. 197 A13
Qala, Malta 161 H21
Qalamcheshmeh, Afghan. 177 N4
Qalansīyah, Yemen 173 R14
Qalat (Kalat), Afghan. 177 P6
Qal'at al Azlam, ruin, Saudi Arabia 172 H5
Qal'at Bīshah, Saudi Arabia 172 M8
Qal'eh Shahr, Afghan. 176 L5
Qal'eh-ye Fath, Afghan. 177 R2
Qal'eh-ye Gaz, Afghan. 177 P4
Qal'eh-ye Now, Afghan. 176 M3
Qal'eh-ye Sarkari, Afghan. 176 L6
Qalhāt, Oman 173 K17
Qallabat, Eth. 199 E14
Qamar, Ghubbat al, Yemen 173 P13
Qamdo, China 180 L9
Qamea, island, Fiji Is. 218 G8
Qamīnis, Lib. 197 C15
Qammieh Point, Malta 161 J21
Qamystybas, Kaz. 174 G10
Qandala, Somalia 199 F18
Qapshaghay, Kaz. 175 H16
Qapshaghay Reservoir, Kaz. 175 H17
Qarabutaq, Kaz. 174 D9
Qaraghandy, Kaz. 175 E14
Qaraghayly, Kaz. 175 E15
Qarah Bagh, Afghan. 177 N7
Qaraqoynn Köli, Kaz. 175 G13
Qaratal, river, Kaz. 175 G16
Qarataū, Kaz. 175 J14
Qarataū Zhotasy, range, Kaz. 174 H13
Qaratöbe, Kaz. 174 D7
Qaraton, Kaz. 174 F7
Qaraūyl, Kaz. 175 E17
Qarazhal, Kaz. 175 F14
Qarchi Gak, Afghan. 176 K6
Qardho, Somalia 199 F18
Qarokŭl, lake, Taj. 176 H11
Qarqan, river, China 180 G7
Qarqaraly, Kaz. 175 E15
Qarqin, Afghan. 176 K5
Qarsaqbay, Kaz. 174 F12
Qarshi, Uzb. 174 L12
Qaryat al 'Ulyā, Saudi Arabia 172 H11
Qaryat az Zuwaytīnah, Lib. 197 C15
Qaşr-e Qand, Iran 173 H17
Qaşr Farāfra, Egypt 197 D17
Qaşr Ḩamām, Saudi Arabia 172 L10
Qa'ţabah, Yemen 172 Q9
Qatar, Asia 167 V4
Qaţīnah, Buḩayrat, Syr. 170 G8
Qattara Depression, Egypt 197 C17
Qax, Azerb. 169 C20
Qāyen, Iran 173 D16
Qayghy, Kaz. 174 D11
Qaynar, Kaz. 175 E16
Qazakh, Azerb. 169 C19
Qazaly, Kaz. 174 G10
Qazaq Shyghanaghy, Kaz. 174 J6
Qazi Deh, Afghan. 176 K10
Qazimämmäd, Azerb. 169 D22
Qazvīn, Iran 172 C12
Qeissan, Sudan 199 F13
Qele Levu, island, Fiji Is. 218 G9
Qena, Egypt 197 D19
Qeqertarsuaq (Godhavn), Greenland, Den. 81 C21
Qeqertarsuatsiaat, Greenland, Den. 81 D22
Qerqertarsuaq, island, N. Amer. 80 C8
Qeshm, island, Iran 173 H15
Qeshm, Iran 173 H15
Qeysar, Afghan. 176 L4
Qianjiang, China 181 L13
Qianxian, China 182 G1
Qianyang, China 182 G1
Qianyang, China 183 N2
Qidong, China 182 K10
Qidong, China 183 P3
Qiemo, China 180 G6
Qijiaojing, China 180 E8
Qikiqtarjuaq, island, Nunavut, Can. 83 H20
Qikiqtarjuaq, Nunavut, Can. 83 F19
Qila Ladgasht, Pak. 177 T2
Qila Safed, Pak. 177 S1
Qila Saifullah, Pak. 177 R7
Qilian Shan, China 166 G9
Qimantag, range, China 180 H8
Qimen, China 182 L7
Qing, river, China 182 L3
Qingdao, China 182 G9
Qinghai Hu, China 180 H10
Qingjian, China 182 F3
Qingjiang, China 183 N6
Qingshuihe, China 182 D4
Qingtian, China 183 N9
Qingxu, China 182 E4
Qingyang, China 182 F1
Qingyuan, China 182 B12
Qingyuan, China 183 R4
Qingzhou, China 182 F8
Qinhuangdao, China 182 D9
Qin Lin, range, China 166 G11
Qin Ling, China 182 H1
Qinxian, China 182 F4
Qionghai (Jiaji), China 183 U2
Qiongshan, China 183 U2
Qiongzhou Haixia, strait, China 183 T1
Qiqian, China 181 B15
Qiqihar, China 181 C16
Qiryat Shemona, Israel 170 K6
Qishn, Yemen 173 P13
Qitai, China 180 E8
Qitaihe, China 181 D18
Qixia, China 182 F9
Qiyang, China 183 P3
Qiyl, river, Kaz. 174 D7
Qızılağac Körfäzi, Azerb. 169 F22
Qizilqum, desert, Uzb. 174 J10
Qom, river, Iran 172 D12
Qom, Iran 172 D12
Qomsheh, Iran 173 E13
Qonaqkänd, Azerb. 169 C22
Qongyrat, Kaz. 175 F15
Qo'qon, Uzb. 175 K14
Qorakŭl, Uzb. 174 L11
Qoraqalpog'iston, region, Uzb. 174 H8
Qormi, Malta 161 K22
Qosköl, Kaz. 174 E12
Qosshaghyl, Kaz. 174 F7
Qostanay, Kaz. 174 B11
Qowryah, Afghan. 177 Q4
Qrendi, Malta 161 L22
Quairading, W. Aust., Austral. 211 X3
Quakertown, Pa., U.S. 94 N9
Quamby, Qnsld., Austral. 211 S11
Quanah, Tex., U.S. 102 J8
Quan Dao Nam Du, island, Vietnam 187 Q11
Quanery, Anse, Dominica 121 F20
Quang Ngai, Vietnam 186 L14
Quang Tri, Vietnam 186 K13
Quannan, China 183 Q5
Quanshuigou, China 176 L15
Quanzhou, China 183 P3
Quanzhou, China 183 Q8
Quaraí, Braz. 130 P10
Quartier d'Orléans, St. Martin, Fr. 121 B15
Quartier du Colombier, St. Martin, Fr. 121 B14
Quartu Sant'Elena, It. 151 Q4
Quartzsite, Ariz., U.S. 107 T5
Quatre Bornes, Mauritius 205 G19
Quba, Azerb. 169 C22
Qūchān, Iran 173 B16
Qudaym, Syr. 170 G10
Queanbeyan, N.S.W., Austral. 211 Y14
Quebec, Can. 83 M20
Québec, Que., Can. 83 P20
Quebracho Coto, Arg. 132 F10
Quebradillas, P.R., U.S. 120 M2
Queen Adelaida Archipelago, S. Amer. 126 R4
Queen Alexandra Range, Antarctica 227 L13
Queen Charlotte Islands, B.C., Can. 82 J6
Queen Charlotte Sound, B.C., Can. 82 K7
Queen Elizabeth Islands, Nunavut, Can. 83 B15
Queen Elizabeth Range, Antarctica 227 L13
Queen Fabiola Mountains (Yamato Mountains), Antarctica 227 C17
Queen Ka'ahumanu Highway, Hawai'i, U.S. 113 L18
Queen Mary Coast, Antarctica 227 J21
Queen Maud Gulf, Nunavut, Can. 83 F14
Queen Maud Land, Antarctica 226 C11
Queen Maud Mountains, Antarctica 226 K12
Queensland, Austral. 211 T12
Queenstown, N.Z. 213 Q15
Queenstown, S. Af. 202 L10
Queenstown, Tas., Austral. 211 Z15
Queen Victoria's Profile, Hawai'i, U.S. 112 C6
Queets, Wash., U.S. 108 C2
Queiros, Cape, Vanuatu 218 C1
Quelimane, Mozambique 203 F14
Quellón, Chile 133 R6
Quemado, N. Mex., U.S. 107 T10
Quemado, Tex., U.S. 103 S6
Quemoy see Kinmen, island, Taiwan, China 183 R8
Quemú Quemú, Arg. 132 M10
Quequén, Arg. 133 N12
Quercy, region, Fr. 147 W9
Querétaro, Mex. 114 H11
Quesada, Costa Rica 115 N19
Queshan, China 182 J5
Quesnel, B.C., Can. 82 L8
Que Son, Vietnam 186 L13
Questa, N. Mex., U.S. 107 Q13
Quetta, Pak. 177 R6
Quetzaltenango, Guatemala 115 L15
Quezon City, Philippines 189 C13
Qufu, China 182 G7
Quibala, Angola 202 D6
Quibdó, Col. 128 E4
Quiberon, Presqu'île de, Fr. 147 R4
Quijotoa, Ariz., U.S. 107 V6
Quilá, Mex. 114 F8
Quilcene, Wash., U.S. 108 B3
Quillan, Fr. 147 Y10
Quillota, Chile 132 K6
Quilon (Kollam), India 179 S5
Quilpie, Qnsld., Austral. 211 V12
Quimilí, Arg. 132 G11
Quimper, Fr. 147 Q3
Quimperlé, Fr. 147 Q3
Quinault, river, Wash., U.S. 108 C2
Quinault, Wash., U.S. 108 C2
Quince Mil, Peru 130 H5
Quincy, Calif., U.S. 109 P5
Quincy, Fla., U.S. 97 Q5
Quincy, Ill., U.S. 99 R3
Quincy, Mass., U.S. 95 K15
Quines, Arg. 132 K9
Quinhagak, Alas., U.S. 110 K12
Qui Nhon, Vietnam 186 M14
Quinn, river, Nev., U.S. 108 L8
Quintanar de la Orden, Sp. 144 G11
Quinter, Kans., U.S. 105 S4
Quintin, Fr. 147 Q4
Quinto, Sp. 145 E14
Quintus Rocks, Bahamas 120 E5
Quipungo, Angola 202 E6
Quirindi, N.S.W., Austral. 211 X14
Quissanga, Mozambique 203 D15
Quissico, Mozambique 203 J13
Quitaque, Tex., U.S. 102 J6
Quitilipi, Arg. 132 G12
Quitman, Ga., U.S. 97 Q6
Quitman, Miss., U.S. 101 M13
Quito, Ecua. 128 J3
Quixadá, Braz. 131 E17
Qujiang, China 183 Q4
Qujing, China 180 N11
Qulan, Kaz. 175 J15
Qulandy, Kaz. 174 G9
Qulbān Banī Murrah, ruin, Jordan 171 Q8
Qullai Ismoili Somoni (Communism Peak), Taj. 176 H10
Qulsary, Kaz. 174 F7
Qundao, island, China 182 E9
Qŭnghirot, Uzb. 174 J8
Quobba, W. Aust., Austral. 211 U1
Quogue, N.Y., U.S. 95 N13
Qurayyāt, Oman 173 K16
Qŭrghonteppa, Taj. 176 J7
Quryq, Kaz. 174 H5
Qusar, Azerb. 169 C22
Quşeir, Egypt 197 D19
Qusmuryn, Kaz. 174 C11
Qusmuryn Köli, Kaz. 174 C11
Quwo, China 182 G4
Quxian, China 180 L12
Qüxü, China 180 L7
Quy Chau, Vietnam 186 J11
Quyghan, Kaz. 175 G15
Quy Hop, Vietnam 186 J11
Quzhou, China 182 F6
Quzhou, China 182 M8
Qvareli, Rep. of Georgia 169 B19
Qyzan, Kaz. 174 G6
Qyzylorda, Kaz. 174 H11

Raahe, Fin. 141 G15
Raas, island, Indonesia 188 M11
Raasay, island, Scot., U.K. 142 J7
Raasay, Sound of, Scot., U.K. 142 J7
Rab, island, Croatia 152 E4
Raba, Indonesia 189 M13
Rabacca, St. Vincent & the Grenadines 121 K17
Rabastens, Fr. 147 X7
Rabat see Victoria, Malta 161 H20
Rabat, Malta 161 K22
Rabat, Mor. 196 B8
Rabaul, P.N.G. 213 C21
Rabga Pass, China, Nepal 178 F11
Rabi (Rambi), island, Fiji Is. 218 G8
Rábida, Isla (Jervis), Ecua. 128 Q9
Rābigh, Saudi Arabia 172 K7
Racale, It. 151 N15
Răcari, Rom. 153 F15
Racconigi, It. 150 E2
Raccoon Cay, Bahamas 117 H13
Raccoon Point, La., U.S. 100 R10
Race, Cape, Nfld. & Lab., Can. 83 M24
Raceland, La., U.S. 100 Q10
Rachaïya, Leb. 170 J6
Rach Gia, Vietnam 187 Q11
Racine, Wis., U.S. 98 M7
Raco, Mich., U.S. 98 F10
Rădăuţi, Rom. 153 A15
Radcliff, Ky., U.S. 101 C16
Radford, Va., U.S. 96 F9
Radhanpur, India 178 H3
Radisson, Que., Can. 83 M18
Radix, Point, Trinidad & Tobago 121 Q23
Radnevo, Bulg. 153 J15
Radom, Pol. 149 F16
Radomsko, Pol. 149 F15
Radomyshl', Ukr. 157 N5
Radviliškis, Lith. 141 N16
Raḑwá, Jabal, Saudi Arabia 172 J6
Radzyń Podlaski, Pol. 149 E17
Rae Bareli, India 178 G8
Rae-Edzo, N.W.T., Can. 82 H11
Raeford, N.C., U.S. 96 J11
Rae Isthmus, Nunavut, Can. 83 G16
Rae Lakes, N.W.T., Can. 82 G11
Raeside, Lake, Austral. 210 H4
Raetihi, N.Z. 213 L19
Rāf, Jabal, Saudi Arabia 172 G7
Rafa', Gaza Strip 171 N4

S

T

Taplejung, *Nepal* **178** F11
Tapora, Passe, *Fr. Polynesia, Fr.* **219** P17
Tappahannock, *Va., U.S.* **96** E13
Tapu, Motu, *Fr. Polynesia, Fr.* **219** K13
Tapuaenuku, peak, *N.Z.* **213** N18
Tapuaetai, island, *Cook Is., N.Z.* **218** Q12
Tapuamu, *Fr. Polynesia, Fr.* **219** A23
Tapueraha, Passe de, *Fr. Polynesia, Fr.* **219** Q17
Tapul Group, *Philippines* **189** G13
Tapunui, island, *Cook Is., N.Z.* **219** A17
Tapurucuará, *Braz.* **130** C7
Taputapu, Cape, *Amer. Samoa, U.S.* **218** M6
Taputimu, *Amer. Samoa, U.S.* **218** N7
Ţaqah, *Oman* **173** P14
Taquari, river, *Braz.* **130** K10
Tar, river, *N.C., U.S.* **96** H12
Tara, *Qnsld., Austral.* **211** V14
Tara, *Russ.* **158** J10
Tara, river, *Serb. & Mont.* **152** H9
Tara, Hill of, *Ire.* **143** R6
Ţarābulus (Tripoli), *Lib.* **197** B13
Tarakan, island, *Indonesia* **188** H12
Tarakan, *Indonesia* **188** H12
Tarakite-iti, island, *Cook Is., N.Z.* **219** C14
Taranaki, Mount (Mt. Egmont), *N.Z.* **213** L18
Tarancón, *Sp.* **144** G11
Taransay, island, *Scot., U.K.* **142** H6
Taranto, *It.* **151** N14
Taranto, Golfo di, *It.* **151** N14
Tarapacá, *Col.* **128** K8
Tarapaina, *Solomon Is.* **217** N20
Tarapoto, *Peru* **130** F3
Taraqu, ruin, *Afghan.* **177** R1
Tarara, *P.N.G.* **217** K14
Tarare, *Fr.* **147** U12
Tarasa Dwip, island, *India* **179** S15
Tarascon, *Fr.* **147** Y9
Tarata, *Peru* **130** K6
Taratai, island, *Kiribati* **217** F17
Taratai, *Kiribati* **217** F17
Tarauacá, river, *Braz.* **130** F5
Tarauacá, *Braz.* **130** F5
Taravai, island, *Fr. Polynesia, Fr.* **219** Q20
Taravai, *Fr. Polynesia, Fr.* **219** Q20
Taravao, *Fr. Polynesia, Fr.* **219** P17
Taravao, Baie de, *Fr. Polynesia, Fr.* **219** P17
Taravo, river, *Fr.* **150** K4
Tarawa (Bairiki), *Kiribati* **217** G17
Tarawera, Mount, *N.Z.* **213** K19
Taraz, *Kaz.* **175** J14
Tarazit Massif, *Niger* **194** F5
Tarazona, *Sp.* **145** D13
Tarazona de la Mancha, *Sp.* **145** H13
Tarbagannakh, Gora, *Russ.* **159** G19
Tarbaghatay Zhotasy, *Kaz.* **175** F18
Tarbat Ness, *Scot., U.K.* **142** J9
Tarbert, *Scot., U.K.* **142** J6
Tarbert, *Scot., U.K.* **142** M8
Tarbes, *Fr.* **147** Y7
Tarboro, *N.C., U.S.* **96** H13
Tarbrax, *Qnsld., Austral.* **211** S12
Tarcoola, *S. Aust., Austral.* **211** W9
Tardun, *W. Aust., Austral.* **211** W2
Taree, *N.S.W., Austral.* **211** X15
Ţarfā, Ra's aţ, *Saudi Arabia* **172** N8
Tarfaya, *Mor.* **196** C6
Tarfside, *Scot., U.K.* **142** K10
Targhee Pass, *Idaho, Mont., U.S.* **106** F8
Târgu Mureş, *Rom.* **153** C14
Tari, *P.N.G.* **213** D18
Ţarīf, *U.A.E.* **173** K14
Tarifa, *Sp.* **144** N8
Tarifa, Punta de, *Sp.* **144** N8
Tarija, *Bol.* **130** L7
Tarikere, *India* **179** P5
Tariku-Taritatu Plain, *Indonesia* **189** K20
Tarim, river, *China* **180** F6
Tarim Basin, *China* **166** G8
Tarim Pendi, *China* **180** F5
Tarin Kowt, *Afghan.* **177** P5
Taritatu, river, *Indonesia* **213** C17
Tarkastad, *S. Af.* **202** L10
Tarkhankut, Mys, *Ukr.* **157** S7
Tarkio, *Mo., U.S.* **105** Q9
Tarko Sale, *Russ.* **158** G12
Tarkwa, *Ghana* **200** H10
Tarlac, *Philippines* **189** C13
Tarma, *Peru* **130** H4
Tarn, river, *Fr.* **147** X9
Tärnaby, *Sw.* **140** F12
Tarnak, river, *Afghan.* **177** Q5
Tarnobrzeg, *Pol.* **149** G17
Tarnogskiy Gorodok, *Russ.* **156** E12
Tarnów, *Pol.* **149** G16
Ţārom, *Iran* **173** G15
Taroom, *Qnsld., Austral.* **211** U14
Tarpon Springs, *Fla., U.S.* **97** U7
Tarpum Bay, *Bahamas* **120** E6
Tarpum Bay, *Bahamas* **120** F6
Tarquinia, *It.* **150** K7
Tarrabool Lake, *Austral.* **210** D9
Tarrafal, *Cape Verde* **205** B14
Tarrafal, *Cape Verde* **205** B15
Tarrafal, *Cape Verde* **205** D16
Tarragona, *Sp.* **145** E16
Tarraleah, *Tas., Austral.* **211** Z16
Tarras, *N.Z.* **213** Q16
Tarsia, *It.* **151** P13
Tarsus, *Turk.* **168** J10
Tarta, *Turkm.* **174** K6
Tartagal, *Arg.* **132** D10
Tartas, *Fr.* **147** X6
Tartu, *Est.* **141** K17
Ţarţūs (Tortosa), *Syr.* **170** G7
Taruia Passage, *Cook Is., N.Z.* **219** B17
Tarutao, Ko, *Thai.* **187** S8
Tarutung, *Indonesia* **188** H5
Tarvisio, *It.* **150** C9
Tarxien, *Malta* **161** K23
Tasāwah, *Lib.* **197** E13
Tasböget, *Kaz.* **174** H11
Tascosa, *Tex., U.S.* **102** G4
Tasek Dampar, lake, *Malaysia* **187** U10
Taseyevo, *Russ.* **159** K14
Tashanta, *Russ.* **158** M12
Tash Gozar, *Afghan.* **176** K6
Tashk, Daryācheh-ye, *Iran* **173** F14
Tashkent *see* Toshkent, *Uzb.* **175** K13
Tash-Kömür, *Kyrg.* **176** F10
Tasiilaq, *Greenland, Den.* **81** C22
Tasikmalaya, *Indonesia* **188** M9
Tasiusaq, *Greenland, Den.* **81** C20
Taskan, *Russ.* **159** F20
Taskesken, *Kaz.* **175** F18
Taşköprü, *Turk.* **168** C9
Tasman, *N.Z.* **213** M18
Tasman Bay, *N.Z.* **213** M18
Tasman Fracture Zone, *Antarctic Oc.* **245** N14
Tasmania, island, *Austral.* **210** M16
Tasmania, *Austral.* **211** Z15
Tasman Peninsula, *Austral.* **210** M16
Tasman Plain, *Pac. Oc.* **238** P7
Tasman Sea, *Pac. Oc.* **238** P7
Tăşnad, *Rom.* **152** B12
Taşova, *Turk.* **168** D11
Tassialouc, Lac, *Que., Can.* **83** K18
Tas Tumus, *Russ.* **159** G17
Tasure, *Solomon Is.* **217** L15
Tataacho Point, *N. Mariana Is., U.S.* **216** D7
Tatabánya, *Hung.* **149** L14
Tatafa, island, *Tonga* **218** P7
Tatakoto, island, *Fr. Polynesia, Fr.* **219** E21
Tatamba, *Solomon Is.* **217** M18
Tatarbunary, *Ukr.* **157** S5
Tatarsk, *Russ.* **158** K11
Tatarskiy Proliv, *Russ.* **159** J21
Tatar Strait, *Russ.* **166** D13
Tate, *Ga., U.S.* **96** K5
Tateyama, *Japan* **185** Q12
Tathlina Lake, *N.W.T., Can.* **82** H10
Tathlīth, *Saudi Arabia* **172** M9
Tatkon, *Myanmar* **186** H6
Tatnam, Cape, *Man., Can.* **83** L15
Tatry, range, *Pol., Slovakia* **149** J15
Tattershall, *Eng., U.K.* **143** S14
Tatuí, *Braz.* **131** M13
Tatum, *N. Mex., U.S.* **107** U15
Tatvan, *Turk.* **169** G16
Tau, island, *Amer. Samoa, U.S.* **218** P3
Tau, *Amer. Samoa, U.S.* **218** P3
Tau, island, *Tonga* **218** H12
Tauá, *Braz.* **131** F16
Tauak Passage, *F.S.M.* **217** F13
Tauanap, Mochun, *F.S.M.* **217** B14
Taubaté, *Braz.* **131** M14
Tauenai Channel, *F.S.M.* **217** G13
Tauere, island, *Fr. Polynesia, Fr.* **219** E20
Taugarau, island, *Fr. Polynesia, Fr.* **219** K18
Tauhunu, island, *Cook Is., N.Z.* **219** B13
Tauhunu, *Cook Is., N.Z.* **219** B13
Taula, island, *Tonga* **218** M11
Taulaga, *Amer. Samoa, U.S.* **218** R3
Taumako, island, *Solomon Is.* **217** N24
Taumarunui, *N.Z.* **213** L19
Taumatawhakatangihangakoauauotamateapokaiwhenuakitanatahu, peak, *N.Z.* **213** M19
Taum Sauk Mountain, *Mo., U.S.* **105** U15
Taunga, island, *Tonga* **218** M11
Taunggok, *Myanmar* **186** J5
Taunggyi, *Myanmar* **186** H6
Taungoo, *Myanmar* **186** J6
Taungup Pass, *Myanmar* **186** J5
Taunsa, *Pak.* **177** R9
Taunton, *Eng., U.K.* **143** W10
Taunton, *Mass., U.S.* **95** L15
Taupo, *N.Z.* **213** K19
Taupo, Lake, *N.Z.* **213** L19
Taupo Tablemount, *Pac. Oc.* **238** N7
Tauragė, *Lith.* **141** N16
Tauranga, *N.Z.* **213** K19
Taurere, Pointe, *Fr. Polynesia, Fr.* **219** L14
Taurus *see* Toros Dağları, range, *Turk.* **168** J8
Taūshyq, *Kaz.* **174** G5
Tauste, *Sp.* **145** D13
Tautama, island, *Pitcairn I., U.K.* **219** Q23
Tautau, island, *Fr. Polynesia, Fr.* **219** A23
Tautira, *Fr. Polynesia, Fr.* **219** P17
Tautu, *Cook Is., N.Z.* **218** Q11
Tautua, island, *Cook Is., N.Z.* **219** B18
Tauu Islands, *P.N.G.* **217** H16
Tavaerua, island, *Cook Is., N.Z.* **218** Q12
Tavai, *Wallis & Futuna, Fr.* **218** E11
Tavan Bogd Uul *see* Youyi Feng, peak, *China, Mongolia* **180** C8
Tavannes, *Switz.* **150** A2
Tavas, *Turk.* **168** G4
Tavda, *Russ.* **158** H9
Taverna, *It.* **151** Q14
Taverner Bay, *Nunavut, Can.* **83** G18
Tavernes, *Fr.* **147** X14
Tavernes de la Valldigna, *Sp.* **145** H15
Tavernier, *Fla., U.S.* **97** Y10
Taveuni, island, *Fiji Is.* **218** H8
Tavropoú, Límni, *Gr.* **154** F9
Tavşanlı, *Turk.* **168** E5
Tavua, *Fiji Is.* **218** H6
Tavu-Na-Sici, island, *Fiji Is.* **218** J9
Tawai, *India* **178** F16
Tawake, *Fiji Is.* **218** G8
Tawakoni, Lake, *Tex., U.S.* **102** L13
Tawang, *India* **178** F13
Tawas City, *Mich., U.S.* **98** J12
Tawau, *Malaysia* **188** G12
Tawi Tawi, island, *Philippines* **189** G13
Tawu, *Taiwan, China* **183** S9
Taxco, *Mex.* **114** J11
Taxkorgan, *China* **180** G4
Tay, Firth of, *Scot., U.K.* **142** L11
Tay, Loch, *Scot., U.K.* **142** L9
Tayan, *Indonesia* **188** J9
Tayandu, Kepulauan, *Indonesia* **189** L18
Taygonos, Poluostrov, *Russ.* **159** E21
Taylakova, *Russ.* **158** J11
Taylor, *Mich., U.S.* **98** M12
Taylor, *Tex., U.S.* **103** P11
Taylor, Mount, *N. Mex., U.S.* **107** S11
Taylor Glacier, *Antarctica* **227** N14
Taylor Highway, *Alas., U.S.* **111** G19
Taylors, *S.C., U.S.* **96** J7
Taylorsville, *Miss., U.S.* **100** M12
Taylorville, *Ill., U.S.* **99** S5
Taymā', *Saudi Arabia* **172** G6
Taymyr, Lake, *Russ.* **166** C9
Taymyr, Ozero, *Russ.* **159** E14
Taymyr, Poluostrov, *Russ.* **159** E14
Taymyr Peninsula, *Russ.* **166** C9
Tay Ninh, *Vietnam* **187** P12
Taypaq, *Kaz.* **174** E6
Tayshet, *Russ.* **159** K14
Taytay, *Philippines* **189** E13
Ţayyebāt, *Iran* **173** C17
Tayynsha (Krasnoarmeysk), *Kaz.* **175** B13
Taz, river, *Russ.* **158** G12
Taza, *Mor.* **196** B9
Tazawa Ko, *Japan* **184** K13
Tazawako, *Japan* **184** K13
Tazewell, *Va., U.S.* **96** F8
Tāzirbū, *Lib.* **197** E16
Tazovskiy, *Russ.* **158** G12
Tazovskiy Poluostrov, *Russ.* **158** F12
Tba P'arvani, lake, *Rep. of Georgia* **169** C18
T'bilisi (Tiflis), *Rep. of Georgia* **169** C18
Tchabal Gangdaba, range, *Cameroon* **201** G16
Tchad, Lac *see* Chad, Lake, *Af.* **197** J13
Tchibanga, *Gabon* **201** M16
Tchin-Tabaradène, *Niger* **196** H11
Tczew, *Pol.* **149** B14
Teaehoa, Pointe, *Fr. Polynesia, Fr.* **219** N20
Te Afualiku, island, *Tuvalu* **217** J23
Teague, *Tex., U.S.* **103** N12
Teahupoo, *Fr. Polynesia, Fr.* **219** Q17
Teaiti Point, *Cook Is., N.Z.* **218** Q9
Teakava, island, *Fr. Polynesia, Fr.* **219** Q21
Te Anau, *N.Z.* **213** Q15
Te Anau, Lake, *N.Z.* **213** Q15
Teaoraereke, *Kiribati* **217** G17
Tearinibai, *Kiribati* **217** F17
Tea Tree, *N. Terr., Austral.* **211** T8
Teava Moa, Passe, *Fr. Polynesia, Fr.* **219** B24
Teavanui, Passe, *Fr. Polynesia, Fr.* **219** K13
Teavapiti, Passe, *Fr. Polynesia, Fr.* **219** B23
Teavaraa, Passe de, *Fr. Polynesia, Fr.* **219** P16
Teavaro, *Fr. Polynesia, Fr.* **219** N14
Teberda, *Russ.* **157** U12
Tébessa, *Alg.* **196** B12
Tebingtinggi, *Indonesia* **188** H5
Techirghiol, *Rom.* **153** G18
Techla, *W. Sahara, Mor.* **196** E5
Technití Límni Kremastón, *Gr.* **154** G8
Tecka, *Arg.* **133** R7
Tecomán, *Mex.* **114** J9
Tecpan, *Mex.* **114** K11
Tecuala, *Mex.* **114** G9
Tecuci, *Rom.* **153** D16
Tecumseh, *Mich., U.S.* **98** N11
Tecumseh, *Nebr., U.S.* **105** R9
Tecumseh, *Okla., U.S.* **102** G11
Teec Nos Pos, *Ariz., U.S.* **107** Q9
Teel, *Mongolia* **180** D11
Tefala, island, *Tuvalu* **217** L22
Tefarerii, *Fr. Polynesia, Fr.* **219** H14
Tefé, river, *Braz.* **130** E7
Tefé, *Braz.* **130** D7
Tefenni, *Turk.* **168** H5
Tegal, *Indonesia* **188** M9
Teglio, *San Marino* **161** L14
Tégua, island, *Vanuatu* **218** A1
Tegucigalpa, *Hond.* **115** L17
Teguise, *Canary Is.* **204** P7
Tehachapi, *Calif., U.S.* **109** V8
Tehachapi Mountains, *Calif., U.S.* **109** W8
Tehachapi Pass, *Calif., U.S.* **109** V8
Te Hapua, *N.Z.* **213** G17
Tehek Lake, *Nunavut, Can.* **83** H14
Tehoohaivei, Cap, *Fr. Polynesia, Fr.* **219** M21
Tehrān, *Iran* **173** C13
Tehuacán, *Mex.* **114** J12
Tehuantepec, *Mex.* **115** K13
Tehuantepec, Golfo de, *Mex.* **115** L14
Tehuantepec, Gulf of *see* Tehuantepec, Golfo de, *N. Amer.* **80** P6
Tehuantepec, Isthmus of *see* Tehuantepec, Istmo de, *N. Amer.* **80** P6
Tehuantepec, Istmo de, *Mex.* **115** K14
Tehuata (Rekareka), island, *Fr. Polynesia, Fr.* **219** E19
Teide, Pico de, *Canary Is.* **204** Q4
Teignmouth, *Eng., U.K.* **143** X10
Teiko, Motu, *Fr. Polynesia, Fr.* **219** R20
Tejen, *Turkm.* **174** M9
Tejenstroy, *Turkm.* **174** N9
Tejo (Tagus), river, *Port.* **144** H5
Tekamah, *Nebr., U.S.* **105** P9
Te Karaka, *N.Z.* **213** K20
Tekax, *Mex.* **115** H16
Tekeli, *Kaz.* **175** G17
Tekirdağ, *Turk.* **168** C3
Tekirova, *Turk.* **168** J6
Tekkali, *India* **178** L9
Tekman, *Turk.* **169** E16
Teknaf, *Bangladesh* **178** K14
Tekoa, *Wash., U.S.* **108** C9
Tekokota, island, *Fr. Polynesia, Fr.* **219** E19
Tekopua, island, *Cook Is., N.Z.* **218** Q12
Te Koutu Point, *Cook Is., N.Z.* **218** Q11
T'elavi, *Rep. of Georgia* **169** B19
Tel Aviv-Yafo, *Israel* **170** M5
Telde, *Canary Is.* **204** R6
Telebekelel Ngerael, *Palau* **216** K11
Telefomin, *P.N.G.* **213** C17
Telegraph Creek, *B.C., Can.* **82** H8
Telekitonga, island, *Tonga* **218** R7
Telekivavau, island, *Tonga* **218** Q7
Telele, island, *Tuvalu* **217** L23
Telén, *Arg.* **132** M9
Telescope Peak, *Calif., U.S.* **109** U9
Telescope Point, *Grenada* **121** K23
Teles Pires (São Manuel), river, *Braz.* **130** F10
Teljo, Jebel, *Sudan* **194** G8
Tell Atlas, *Alg., Tun.* **194** C4
Tell City, *Ind., U.S.* **99** U8
Teller, *Alas., U.S.* **110** F11
Tellicherry, *India* **179** Q4
Telloh *see* Lagash, ruin, *Iraq* **172** E10
Tell Tayinat, ruin, *Turk.* **168** J11
Telluride, *Colo., U.S.* **107** P11
Telsen, *Arg.* **133** R9
Telšiai, *Lith.* **141** N16
Telukbutun, *Indonesia* **188** G9
Telukdalem, *Indonesia* **188** J4
Teluk Intan, *Malaysia* **187** T9
Tema, *Ghana* **200** H11
Te Manga, peak, *Cook Is., N.Z.* **218** Q9
Tematagi, island, *Fr. Polynesia, Fr.* **219** H20
Tembagapura, *Indonesia* **189** L20
Tembenchi, *Russ.* **159** H14
Témbi, range, *Gr.* **154** E10
Temerin, *Serb. & Mont.* **152** E9
Temerloh, *Malaysia* **187** U10
Teminabuan, *Indonesia* **189** J18
Teminikov, *Russ.* **156** K12
Temirtaū, *Kaz.* **175** D14
Temoe (Timoe), island, *Fr. Polynesia, Fr.* **219** H23
Temora, *N.S.W., Austral.* **211** Y13
Tempe, *Ariz., U.S.* **107** U7
Tempio, *It.* **150** M4
Temple, *Okla., U.S.* **102** J10
Temple, *Tex., U.S.* **103** P11
Temple Bay, *Austral.* **210** B12
Temryuk, *Russ.* **157** S9
Temryukskiy Zaliv, *Russ.* **157** S9
Temse, *Belg.* **146** K12
Temuco, *Chile* **133** P6
Temuka, *N.Z.* **213** P17
Tena, *Ecua.* **128** J3
Tenali, *India* **179** N7
Tenao, *Monaco* **161** B22
Tenararo, island, *Fr. Polynesia, Fr.* **219** G22
Ténaro, Akrotírio (Taenarum), *Gr.* **154** N10
Tenarunga, island, *Fr. Polynesia, Fr.* **219** G22
Tenasserim, region, *Myanmar* **186** M7
Tenasserim, *Myanmar* **187** N8
Tende, *Fr.* **147** W16
Ten Degree Channel, *India* **179** R14
Tendō, *Japan* **184** L13
Tendürek Dağı, *Turk.* **169** F18
Ténéré, region, *Niger* **196** F12
Tenerife, island, *Canary Is.* **204** Q5
Tengako, island, *Tuvalu* **217** J24
Tengasu, island, *Tuvalu* **217** L22
Tengchong, *China* **180** N10
Te Nggano, *Solomon Is.* **217** R19
Tengiz, oil field, *Kaz.* **174** G7
Tengiz, Lake, *Kaz.* **166** E7
Tengiz Köli, *Kaz.* **175** D13
Tengxian, *China* **182** G7
Tengxian, *China* **183** R2
Tenino, *Wash., U.S.* **108** D3
Tenjo, Mount, *Guam, U.S.* **216** C10
Tenkasi, *India* **179** S5
Tenke, *Dem. Rep. of the Congo* **198** N11
Tenkiller Ferry Lake, *Okla., U.S.* **102** F14
Tenkodogo, *Burkina Faso* **200** E11

U

Uníon, Bahía, Arg. 133 P11
Union City, Ohio, U.S. 99 Q11
Union City, Pa., U.S. 94 L3
Union City, Tenn., U.S. 100 E12
Union Point, Ga., U.S. 96 L6
Union Springs, Ala., U.S. 101 L16
Uniontown, Ala., U.S. 101 L14
Uniontown, Pa., U.S. 94 P3
Unionville, Mo., U.S. 105 Q12
Unionville, Nev., U.S. 109 N8
United Arab Emirates, Asia 167 V4
United Estates, Bahamas 120 E12
United Kingdom, Eur. 139 S4
United States, N. Amer. 81 K18
Unity, Oreg., U.S. 108 G8
University Park, N. Mex., U.S. 107 V12
Unnao, India 178 G7
Unst, island, Scot., U.K. 142 C12
Ünye, Turk. 168 D12
Unzha, Russ. 156 G12
Uoleva, island, Tonga 218 P7
Upata, Venez. 128 C12
Upemba, Lake, Dem. Rep. of the Congo 194 L8
Upernavik Kujalleq, Greenland, Den. 81 C20
Upham, N. Dak., U.S. 104 E4
Upington, S. Af. 202 K8
Upolu, island, Samoa 218 L3
'Upolu Point, Hawai'i, U.S. 113 J19
Upper Arlington, Ohio, U.S. 99 R13
Upper Bogue, Bahamas 120 D5
Upper Darby, Pa., U.S. 94 P9
Upper Guinea, region, Af. 194 H3
Upper Hutt, N.Z. 213 M19
Upper Kama Upland, Russ. 138 C13
Upper Klamath Lake, Oreg., U.S. 108 K4
Upper Lake, Calif., U.S. 108 L6
Upper Lough Erne, N. Ire., U.K. 143 Q5
Upper Manzanilla, Trinidad & Tobago 121 P23
Upper Missouri River Breaks National Monument, Mont., U.S. 106 C10
Upper Peninsula, Mich., U.S. 98 F6
Upper Red Lake, Minn., U.S. 104 E10
Upper St. Clair, Pa., U.S. 94 N3
Upper Sandusky, Ohio, U.S. 99 Q12
Uppsala, Sw. 141 K14
Upshi, India 178 C6
Upton, Wyo., U.S. 106 G13
'Uqayribāt, Syr. 170 F9
Ur, ruin, Iraq 172 F10
Urabá, Golfo de, Col. 128 D4
Urad Houqi, China 182 B1
Urad Qianqi, China 182 C2
Urad Zhongqi, China 182 B2
Urakawa, Japan 184 G14
Ural, river, Kaz., Russ. 166 E5
Ural, river, Russ. 158 J8
Uralla, N.S.W., Austral. 211 W15
Ural Mountains, Russ. 166 D7
Urana, N.S.W., Austral. 211 Y13
Urandangi, Qnsld., Austral. 211 S10
Urania, La., U.S. 100 M8
Uranium City, Sask., Can. 82 J12
Uranu, island, F.S.M. 217 B14
Uraricoera, river, Braz. 130 B8
Uraricoera, Braz. 130 B9
Uravan, Colo., U.S. 107 N10
Urawa, Japan 185 P12
Urbana, Ill., U.S. 99 R7
Urbana, Ohio, U.S. 99 R12
Urbandale, Iowa, U.S. 105 P11
Urbano Noris, Cuba 116 K12
Urbett, island, Marshall Is. 216 K7
Urbino, It. 150 G8
Urbión, Picos de, Sp. 144 D12
Urdos, Fr. 147 Y6
Uren', Russ. 156 G13
Uréparapara, island, Vanuatu 218 A2
Urganch, Uzb. 174 K9
Urgut, Uzb. 174 L12
Uriah, Mount, N.Z. 213 N17
Uribia, Col. 128 A6
Uriondo, Bol. 130 L7
Uritskoye, Russ. 159 H17
Urla, Turk. 168 F2
Urlaţi, Rom. 153 E15
Urlins, Antigua & Barbuda 121 B20
Urmia, Lake see Orūmīyeh, Daryācheh-ye, Iran 172 B10
Uroševac, Serb. & Mont. 152 J11
Ŭroteppa see Istaravshan, Taj. 176 G7
Urt Moron, China 180 H8
Uruana, Braz. 131 J13
Uruapan, Mex. 114 J10
Urubamba, river, Peru 130 H5
Urucará, Braz. 130 D10
Uruçuí, Braz. 131 F15
Uruçuí, Serra do, S. Amer. 126 F9
Urugi, Japan 185 P10
Uruguai, river, Braz. 130 N11
Uruguaiana, Braz. 130 P10
Uruguay, S. Amer. 127 L19
Uruguay, river, S. Amer. 126 K7
Urukthapel (Ngeruktabel), island, Palau 216 P11
Ürümqi, China 180 E7
Uruno Point, Guam, U.S. 216 B11
Urup, island, Russ. 159 J23
Uryupinsk, Russ. 157 N12
Ürzhar, Kaz. 175 F18
Urzhum, Russ. 156 G15
Urziceni, Rom. 153 F16
Usa, Japan 185 R7
Usa, river, Russ. 138 A12
Uşak, Turk. 168 F5
Usakos, Namibia 202 H6
Usarp Mountains, Antarctica 227 Q15
Usedom, island, Ger. 148 B11
Useldange, Lux. 160 J9
Ushakova, Ostrov, Russ. 159 C13
Ushakovskoye, Russ. 159 B19
Üsharal, Kaz. 175 F18
Ushibuka, Japan 185 S4
Ushi Point, N. Mariana Is., U.S. 216 A8
Üshtöbe, Kaz. 175 G17
Ushuaia, Arg. 133 X9
Ushumun, Russ. 159 K19
Usinsk, Russ. 158 F10
Usman', Russ. 156 M10
Usol'ye Sibirskoye, Russ. 159 L15
Usove, Ukr. 156 M4
U.S. Range, Nunavut, Can. 83 A16
U.S.S. Arizona Memorial, Hawai'i, U.S. 112 E11
Ussel, Fr. 147 U10
Ussuri, river, China, Russ. 166 E12
Ussuriysk, Russ. 159 M21
Uster, Switz. 150 A4
Ustica, It. 151 R9
Ustica, Isola di, It. 151 R9
Ust' Ilimpeya, Russ. 159 H15
Ust' Ilimsk, Russ. 159 K15
Ustí nad Labem, Czech Rep. 148 G11
Ustka, Pol. 149 B13
Ust' Kamchatsk, Russ. 159 E22
Ust' Kamenogorsk see Öskemen, Kaz. 175 D18
Ust' Kamo, Russ. 159 J14
Ust' Kut, Russ. 159 K15
Ust' Labinsk, Russ. 157 S11
Ust' Maya, Russ. 159 G19
Ust' Mil', Russ. 159 H19
Ust' Nera, Russ. 159 F19
Ust' Olenek, Russ. 159 E16
Ust' Omchug, Russ. 159 F20
Ust' Ordynskiy, Russ. 159 L15
Ust' Usa, Russ. 158 F10
Ust' Yansk, Russ. 159 E17
Ust' Yudoma, Russ. 159 H19
Ustyurt Plateau, Kaz., Uzb. 174 H7
Ustyuzhna, Russ. 156 G9
Usu, China 180 E7
Usuki, Japan 185 R5
Usumacinta, river, N. Amer. 80 P6
Usvyaty, Russ. 156 J6
Uta, Indonesia 189 L19
Utah, U.S. 106 M6
Utah Beach, Fr. 147 N6
Utah Lake, Utah, U.S. 106 L7
Utara, Bunguran see Natuna Besar, Kepulauan, Indonesia 188 G8
Ute Creek, N. Mex., U.S. 107 Q14
Utete, Tanzania 199 M15
Uthai Thani, Thai. 186 L8
Uthal, Pak. 177 V5
Utiariti, Braz. 130 H10
Utica, N.Y., U.S. 94 J9
Utiel, Sp. 145 H14
Utirik Atoll, Marshall Is. 216 F4
Utkela, India 178 L9
Utnur, India 178 L6
Utopia, N. Terr., Austral. 211 T9
Utraula, India 178 G8
Utrecht, Neth. 146 J12
Utsunomiya, Japan 185 N12
Utta, Russ. 157 R14
Uttaradit, Thai. 186 K8
Utuado, P.R., U.S. 120 N3
Utuloa, Wallis & Futuna, Fr. 218 B11
Utupua, island, Solomon Is. 217 Q23
Uturoa, Fr. Polynesia, Fr. 219 B23
Utva, river, Kaz. 174 D7
Utwa, F.S.M. 217 B18
Uummannaq, Greenland, Den. 81 C21
Uusikaupunki, Fin. 141 J15
Uva, Russ. 156 G16
Uvalde, Tex., U.S. 103 R8
Uvarovo, Russ. 156 M12
Uvéa see Ouvéa, Île, island, New Caledonia, Fr. 218 C8
Uvea, island, Wallis & Futuna, Fr. 218 B11
Uvinza, Tanzania 198 L12
Uvol, P.N.G. 213 D21
Uvs Nuur, Mongolia 180 C9
Uwajima, Japan 185 R6
'Uwayrid, Ḩarrat al, Saudi Arabia 172 H6
'Uweinat, Jebel, Sudan 198 C11
Uxin Qi (Dabqig), China 182 E2
Uxmal, ruin, Mex. 115 H16
Uyar, Russ. 159 K13
Uyuni, Bol. 130 L7
Uyuni, Salar de, Bol. 130 L7
Uzbekistan, Asia 167 T6
Uzbel Shankou, China, Taj. 176 H11
Uzerche, Fr. 147 U9
Uzès, Fr. 147 W12
Uzhhorod, Ukr. 157 P1
Užice, Serb. & Mont. 152 G9
Uzlovaya, Russ. 156 K9
Üzümlü, Turk. 168 H4
Uzunköprü, Turk. 168 C3
Uzynköl, Kaz. 174 B11

V

Vaal, river, S. Af. 202 K10
Vaals, Neth. 146 L13
Vaasa, Fin. 141 H14
Vác, Hung. 149 L15
Vacaville, Calif., U.S. 109 R4
Vache, Île à, Haiti 117 N15
Vacía Talega, Punta, P.R., U.S. 120 M5
Vacoas, Mauritius 205 G20
Vadodara, India 178 J3
Vadsø, Nor. 141 C15
Vaduz, Liech. 160 P2
Vaduz Castle, Liech. 160 P2
Værøy, island, Nor. 140 E11
Vaga, river, Russ. 138 C11
Vágar, island, Faroe Is., Den. 140 J5
Vaghena, island, Solomon Is. 217 L16
Vagthus Point, Virgin Islands, U.S. 120 R3
Váh, river, Slovakia 149 J14
Vahanga, island, Fr. Polynesia, Fr. 219 G22
Vahitahi, island, Fr. Polynesia, Fr. 219 F21
Vahituri, island, Fr. Polynesia, Fr. 219 L17
Vaiaau, Fr. Polynesia, Fr. 219 B23
Vaiau, Passe, Fr. Polynesia, Fr. 219 Q17
Vaiden, Miss., U.S. 100 K11
Vaiea, Niue, N.Z. 219 B20
Vaiere, island, Cook Is., N.Z. 219 C17
Vaigalu, Samoa 218 L4
Vaihiria, Lac, Fr. Polynesia, Fr. 219 P16
Vail, Colo., U.S. 106 M12
Vaila, island, Scot., U.K. 142 D11
Vailala, Wallis & Futuna, Fr. 218 B11
Vailoa, Samoa 218 K2
Vailoatai, Amer. Samoa, U.S. 218 N7
Vaimalau, Wallis & Futuna, Fr. 218 B11
Vaini, Tonga 218 J11
Vaionifa, Passe, Fr. Polynesia, Fr. 219 P18
Vaipae, Cook Is., N.Z. 218 Q11
Vaipaee, Fr. Polynesia, Fr. 219 N23
Vaipeka, Cook Is., N.Z. 218 P11
Vairaatea, island, Fr. Polynesia, Fr. 219 F21
Vairo, Fr. Polynesia, Fr. 219 Q17
Vaitahu, Fr. Polynesia, Fr. 219 N20
Vaïtape, Fr. Polynesia, Fr. 219 K14
Vaitoare, Fr. Polynesia, Fr. 219 B23
Vaitogi, Amer. Samoa, U.S. 218 N7
Vaitupu, island, Tuvalu 214 H9
Vaitupu, Wallis & Futuna, Fr. 218 B11
Vai'utukakau Bay, Tonga 218 L11
Vaka'eitu, island, Tonga 218 M11
Vakfıkebir, Turk. 169 D14
Vakhan, region, Afghan. 176 K10
Vakhrushev, Russ. 159 J22
Vakhsh, river, Taj. 176 H9
Vakhtan, Russ. 156 G13
Valamaz, Russ. 156 G15
Valcheta, Arg. 133 Q9
Valdagno, It. 150 D7
Valdahon, Fr. 147 S14
Valdai Hills, Russ. 138 D10
Valdayskaya Vozvyshennost', Russ. 156 J7
Valdepeñas, Sp. 144 J11
Valderrobres, Sp. 145 F15
Valdes, Península, Arg. 133 R10
Valdez, Alas., U.S. 111 J18
Valdez, Ecua. 128 H2
Valdivia, Chile 133 P6
Valdivia, Col. 128 D4
Valdivia Fracture Zone, Pac. Oc. 239 P19
Val-d'Or, Que., Can. 83 P18
Valdosta, Ga., U.S. 97 Q6
Valdragone, San Marino 161 J15
Vale, Oreg., U.S. 108 H9
Valea lui Mihai, Rom. 152 B11
Valença, Port. 144 D5
Valença, Braz. 131 H16
Valence, Fr. 147 V13
Valence, Fr. 147 W8
Valencia, Sp. 145 H14
Valencia, Venez. 128 B9
Valencia, Golfo de, Sp. 145 H15
Valencia, Lake, S. Amer. 126 A4
Valenciennes, Fr. 146 M11
Valentia Island, Ire. 143 U2
Valentine, Nebr., U.S. 104 M4
Valentine, Tex., U.S. 103 P1
Valenza, It. 150 E4
Valera, Venez. 128 C7
Valga, Est. 141 L17
Valguarnera Caropepe, It. 151 S11
Valier, Mont., U.S. 106 B7
Valinco, Golfe de, Fr. 150 L4
Valira, river, Andorra 160 J3
Valira del Nort, river, Andorra 160 J3
Valira d'Orient, river, Andorra 160 H4
Valjevo, Serb. & Mont. 152 F9
Valka, Latv. 141 L17
Valkeakoski, Fin. 141 J15
Valkenswaard, Neth. 146 K13
Valkyrie Dome, Antarctica 227 D15
Valladolid, Mex. 115 H16
Valladolid, Sp. 144 D10
Valle de la Pascua, Venez. 128 C10
Valledupar, Col. 128 B6
Valle Fértil, Sierra del, Arg. 132 J8
Valle Formozo, Sao Tome and Principe 205 D20
Vallegrande, Bol. 130 K8
Vallehermoso, Canary Is. 204 Q4
Vallejo, Calif., U.S. 109 R3
Vallenar, Chile 132 H6
Valletta, Malta 161 K23
Valley Center, Kans., U.S. 105 U7
Valley City, N. Dak., U.S. 104 G7
Valley Falls, Kans., U.S. 105 S9
Valley Falls, Oreg., U.S. 108 K6
Valley Mills, Tex., U.S. 103 N11
Valley Station, Ky., U.S. 101 B16
Vallo della Lucania, It. 151 N12
Vallorbe, Switz. 150 B1
Valls, Sp. 145 E16
Valmeyer, Ill., U.S. 99 T4
Valmiera, Latv. 141 L17
Valmy, Fr. 147 P12
Valona see Vlorë, Albania 152 M9
Valozhyn, Belarus 156 K4
Valparaiso, Fla., U.S. 97 Q2
Valparaiso, Ind., U.S. 99 P8
Valparaíso, Chile 132 K6
Valparaíso, Mex. 114 G10
Vals, Tanjung, Indonesia 213 D16
Valsad, India 178 K3
Valüna, valley, Liech. 160 Q3
Valuyevka, Russ. 157 R13
Valuyki, Russ. 157 N10
Valverde, Canary Is. 204 R3
Valverde del Camino, Sp. 144 K7
Van, Turk. 169 G17
Van, Lake, Turk. 166 F4
Vana, Solomon Is. 217 R23
Vanadzor, Arm. 169 D18
Van Alstyne, Tex., U.S. 102 K12
Vanavana, island, Fr. Polynesia, Fr. 219 G21
Vanavara, Russ. 159 J15
Van Blommestein Meer, Suriname 129 E16
Van Buren, Ark., U.S. 100 F6
Van Buren, Me., U.S. 95 A18
Vanceboro, Me., U.S. 95 D19
Vanceboro, N.C., U.S. 96 H13
Vanceburg, Ky., U.S. 101 A19
Vancouver, B.C., Can. 82 M8
Vancouver, Wash., U.S. 108 F3
Vancouver Island, B.C., Can. 82 L7
Vandalia, Ill., U.S. 99 S5
Vandalia, Mo., U.S. 105 S14
Vandalia, Ohio, U.S. 99 R11
Vanderbilt, Mich., U.S. 98 H11
Vanderford Glacier, Antarctica 227 M20
Van Diemen, Cape, Austral. 210 A7
Van Diemen Gulf, Austral. 210 A8
Vänern, lake, Sw. 140 L12
Vangaindrano, Madagascar 203 H17
Van Gölü, Turk. 169 G17
Vangunu, island, Solomon Is. 217 M17
Vangunu, Mount, Solomon Is. 217 M16
Vangviang, Laos 186 J10
Van Horn, Tex., U.S. 103 N1
Vanikolo, island, Solomon Is. 217 R23
Vanikolo Islands, Solomon Is. 217 R23
Vanimo, P.N.G. 213 B17
Vanino, Russ. 159 K21
Vanj, Taj. 176 J9
Vankarem, Russ. 159 A20
Vännäs, Sw. 141 G14
Vannes, Fr. 147 R4
Van Ninh, Vietnam 187 N14
Vannøy, island, Nor. 141 C13
Vanoise, Massif de la, Fr. 147 U15
Vanrhynsdorp, S. Af. 202 L7
Vanrook, Qnsld., Austral. 211 R12
Vansbro, Sw. 140 K12
Vansittart Island, Nunavut, Can. 83 G16
Van Tassell, Wyo., U.S. 106 H14
Vanua, island, Fiji Is. 218 H9
Vanua Lava, island, Vanuatu 218 B2
Vanua Levu, island, Fiji Is. 218 G7
Vanua Masi, island, Fiji Is. 218 J9
Vanuatu, Pac. Oc. 214 K8
Vanua Vatu, island, Fiji Is. 218 J9
Vanuca, island, Fiji Is. 218 J6
Van Wert, Ohio, U.S. 99 Q11
Vao, New Caledonia, Fr. 218 E9
Vao, Nosy, Madagascar 203 F16
Varadero, Cuba 116 G7
Varanasi (Banaras), India 178 H9
Varangerfjorden, bay, Nor. 141 C15
Varangerhalvøya, peninsula, Nor. 141 B15
Varano, Lago di, It. 150 K12
Varas, Afghan. 177 N4
Varaždin, Croatia 152 D6
Varazze, It. 150 F3
Varberg, Sw. 140 M12
Vardar, river, Maced. 152 K12
Vardø, Nor. 141 B15
Varėna, Lith. 141 N17
Varennes, Fr. 147 N13
Varese, It. 150 D4
Varilhes, Fr. 147 Y9
Varkaus, Fin. 141 H16
Varna, Bulg. 153 H17
Varnavino, Russ. 156 H12
Varnenski Zaliv, Bulg. 153 H17
Varnensko Ezero, Bulg. 153 H17
Varnville, S.C., U.S. 96 M9
Varosha, Cyprus 160 P10
Varto, Turk. 169 F16
Vārts Järv, Est. 141 L17
Varungga Point, Solomon Is. 217 L16
Varzob, Taj. 176 H7
Varzy, Fr. 147 R11
Vasafua, island, Tuvalu 217 K22
Vasiliko, Cyprus 160 Q8
Vasil'yevo, Russ. 156 J14
Vaskess Bay, Kiribati 217 B22

Z

Moon Index

Pavlov, **250** L10
Perepelkin, **250** J8
Petavius, **249** L17
Petermann, **249** B14
Petropavlovskiy, **251** E17
Petzval, **251** P15
Phillips, **249** L18
Philolaus, **248** B12
Phocylides, **248** P9
Piccolomini, **249** L15
Pilâtre, **248** Q9
Pingré, **248** P9
Pitatus, **248** L11
Pitiscus, **249** N14
Pizzetti, **250** M8
Planck, **250** P10
Planck, Vallis, **250** P10
Plaskett, **251** B13
Plato, **248** D12
Playfair, **249** L13
Plinius, **249** G14
Plutarch, **249** F18
Poincaré, **250** N11
Poinsot, **251** B13
Polzunov, **250** F8
Poncelet, **248** B11
Pontécoulant, **249** P16
Posidonius, **249** F15
Poynting, **251** G16
Prandtl, **250** P11
Procellarum, Oceanus, **248** E8
Proclus, **249** G16
Ptolemaeus, **248** J12
Purbach, **248** L12
Putredinis, Palus, **249** F13
Pyrenaeus, Montes, **249** K16
Pythagoras, **248** B10

R

Racah, **250** K12
Raimond, **251** G14
Rayleigh, **249** E18
Razumov, **251** E17
Reinhold, **248** H11
Resnik, **251** M15
Rheita, **249** M16
Rheita, Vallis, **249** M16
Riccioli, **248** J6
Riemann, **249** D18
Riphaeus, Montes, **248** J10
Robertson, **251** F18
Roche, **250** M10
Röntgen, **251** E18
Rook, Montes, **248** L6
Roris, Sinus, **248** D9
Rosenberger, **249** P15
Rowland, **251** D13
Rozhdestvenskiy, **251** B13
Rumford, **251** L14
Russell, **248** E7

S

Sacrobosco, **249** L14
Saha, **250** J6
Scaliger, **250** L7
Scheiner, **248** P11
Schickard, **248** N9
Schiller, **248** N10
Schlesinger, **251** D15
Schliemann, **250** J10
Schlüter, **248** J6
Schneller, **251** E14
Schomberger, **249** Q13
Schrödinger, **250** Q11
Schrödinger, Vallis, **250** Q10
Schuster, **250** H10
Schwarzchild, **250** B11
Scobee, **251** L15
Scott, **249** Q13
Seares, **250** B12
Sechenov, **251** J16
Segner, **248** P10
Serenitatis, Mare, **249** F14
Seyfert, **250** F8
Sharonov, **250** G12
Shayn, **250** F12
Short, **248** Q12
Sierpinski, **250** L11
Sirsalis, **248** K8
Sklodowska, **250** L6
Smith, **251** L15
Smoluchowski, **251** B16
Smythii, Mare, **249** H19
Snellius, **249** L17
Sommerfeld, **251** C13
Somni, Palus, **249** G16
Somniorum, Lacus, **249** E15
Spencer Jones, **250** G11
Spitzbergensis, Montes, **248** E12
Spumans, Mare, **249** H18
Stebbins, **251** C14
Stefan, **251** D16
Sternberg, **251** G17
Sternfeld, **251** L15
Stevinus, **249** M16
Stiborius, **249** M15
Stöfler, **249** M13
Störmer, **250** C11
Strabo, **249** C15
Struve, **248** F7
Subbotin, **250** L9
Szilard, **250** E7

T

Taurus, Montes, **249** F16
Teneriffe, Montes, **248** D12
Theaetetus, **249** E13
Theophilus, **249** J15
Thomson, **250** L12
Tikhov, **250** C12
Timocharis, **248** F11
Tranquillitatis, Mare, **249** H15
Trumpler, **250** F12
Tsander, **251** H15
Tsiolkovskiy, **250** K9
Tycho, **248** M12

U

Undarum, Mare, **249** H18

V

Valier, **250** H12
Van de Graaff, **250** L12
Van der Waals, **250** N9
Van Rhijn, **250** D10
Van't Hoff, **251** C15
Vaporum, Mare, **249** G13
Vasco da Gama, **248** G6
Vavilov, **251** J16
Vendelinus, **249** K17
Vening Meinesz, **250** H11
Vernadskiy, **250** F9
Vesalius, **250** J7
Vestine, **250** E7
Vieta, **248** L8
Vlacq, **249** N15
Volkov, **250** K8
Volta, **248** C9
Von der Pahlen, **251** L16
Von Kármán, **250** M12
Von Neumann, **250** E11
Von Zeipel, **251** E15

W

Walther, **249** L13
Wargentin, **248** N9
Waterman, **250** L9
Wegener, **251** D17
Wells, **250** D9
Werner, **249** L13
Weyl, **251** G17
White, **251** N14
Wiechert, **250** Q12
Wiener, **250** E10
Wilhelm, **248** M11
Wilsing, **251** K15
Wilson, **248** Q11
Wrottesley, **249** L17
Wyld, **250** J6

Y

Yablochkov, **250** C10
Yamamoto, **250** C12

Z

Zach, **249** P13
Zagut, **249** L14
Zeeman, **251** Q14
Zhukovskiy, **251** H14
Zsigmondy, **251** C16
Zucchius, **248** P10

SPACECRAFT LANDING OR IMPACT SITES

Apollo 11 (Tranquillity Base) **249** H15
Apollo 12 **248** J11
Apollo 14 **248** J11
Apollo 15 **249** F13
Apollo 16 **249** J14
Apollo 17 **249** G15
Luna 2 **249** F13
Luna 5 **248** J10
Luna 7 **248** H9
Luna 8 **248** H7
Luna 9 **248** H7
Luna 13 **248** F8
Luna 15 **249** G17
Luna 16 **249** J17
Luna 17 **248** E10
Luna 18 **249** H17
Luna 20 **249** H17
Luna 21 **249** F15
Luna 23 **249** G17
Luna 24 **249** G18
Orbiter 1 **250** H11
Orbiter 2 **250** H6
Orbiter 3 **251** G19
Orbiter 5 **248** J6
Ranger 4 **251** K17
Ranger 6 **249** G14
Ranger 7 **248** J11
Ranger 8 **249** H15
Ranger 9 **248** K12
Surveyor 1 **248** J9
Surveyor 2 **248** H12
Surveyor 3 **248** J11
Surveyor 4 **248** H12
Surveyor 5 **249** H14
Surveyor 6 **248** H12
Surveyor 7 **248** M12

Printed in Verona, Italy

Acknowledgments

WORLD THEMATIC SECTION

Introduction pp. 14–15

CONSULTANTS
John Morrison
World Wildlife Fund (WWF)

GRAPHICS
ECOREGIONS: Terrestrial Ecoregions of the World were developed by D.M. Olson, E. Dinerstein, E.D. Wikramanayake, N.D. Burgess, G.V.N. Powell, E.C. Underwood, J.A. D'Amico, I. Itoua, H.E. Strand, J.C. Morrison, C.J. Loucks, T.F. Allnutt, T.H. Ricketts, Y. Kura, J.F. Lamoreux, W.W. Wettengel, P. Hedao, K.R. Kassem, World Wildlife Fund. Marine Ecoregions of the World (MEOW) were developed by the MEOW Working Group, co-chaired by The Nature Conservancy and the World Wildlife Fund (Mark Spalding, Helen Fox, Gerald Allen, Nick Davidson, Zach Ferdana, Max Finlayson, Ben Halpern, Miguel Jorge, Al Lombana, Sara Lourie, Kirsten Martin, Edmund McManus, Jennifer Molnar, Kate Newman, Cheri Recchia, James Robertson).

Structure of the Earth pp. 22–23

CONSULTANTS
Laurel M. Bybell
U.S. Geological Survey (USGS)
Robert I. Tilling
U.S. Geological Survey (USGS)

GRAPHICS
CONTINENTS ADRIFT IN TIME: Christopher R. Scotese/PALEOMAP Project
CUTAWAY OF THE EARTH: Tibor G. Tóth
TECTONIC BLOCK DIAGRAMS: Susan Sanford
PLATE TECTONICS: *National Geographic Atlas of the World,* 8th ed., Washington, D.C.: The National Geographic Society, 2005
GEOLOGIC TIME: National Geographic Books

Earth's Rocky Exterior pp. 24–25

CONSULTANTS
Jon Spencer
Arizona Geological Survey
Robert I. Tilling
U.S. Geological Survey (USGS)

GRAPHICS
ROCK CYCLE AND READING EARTH HISTORY: ChrisOrr.com and XNR Productions
GLOBAL DISTRIBUTION OF ROCK TYPES: Global distribution of surface rock from *The National Geographic Desk Reference.* Washington, D.C.: The National Geographic Society, 1999. Age of oceanic crust from Simkin et al., *This Dynamic Planet: World Map of Volcanoes, Earthquakes, Impact Craters, and Plate Tectonics,* 3rd ed. USGS, 2006

PHOTOGRAPHS
PAGE 24, (UP) R.D. Griggs, USGS; **(CT)** Sharon Johnson; **(LO)** David Muench
PAGE 25, Raymond Gehman/NGS Image Collection

Landforms pp. 26–29

CONSULTANTS
Sharon Johnson
University of California, Berkeley
Mike Slattery
Texas Christian University

GRAPHICS
FICTIONAL LANDFORMS: *National Geographic World Atlas for Young Explorers.* Washington, D.C.: The National Geographic Society, 2003
DUNES: ChrisOrr.com
RIVERS: Steven Fick/Canadian Geographic
GLACIAL LANDFORMS: Steven Fick

SATELLITE IMAGES
MISSISSIPPI RIVER DELTA: Centre National d'Etudes Spatiales (CNES)

PHOTOGRAPHS
PAGE 26, (LE) Joel Sartore/www.joelsartore.com; **(CT)** Science Photo Library/CORBIS; **(UP RT)** George F. Mobley; **(LO RT)** James D. Balog
PAGE 27, (UP LE) Wolfgang Kaehler/CORBIS; **(UP CT)** Lyle Rosbotham; **(UP RT)** Adriel Heisey; **(LO LE)** Marc Moritsch/NGS Image Collection; **(LO CT)** Peter Essick; **(LO RT)** Sam Abell, NGS
PAGE 28, (LE) Peter Essick; **(CT)** Douglas R. Grant; **(RT)** Tom and Pat Leeson
PAGE 29, (UP CT) Rob Brander; **(UP RT)** George Veni and James Jasek; **(LO LE)** Sharon Johnson; **(LO RT)** Douglas R. Grant/Parks Canada

Surface of the Earth pp. 30–31

CONSULTANTS
Peter W. Sloss
NOAA National Geophysical Data Center (NGDC)

SATELLITE IMAGES
EARTH SURFACE ELEVATIONS AND DEPTHS, A SLICE OF EARTH, AND HYPSOMETRY: Peter Sloss, NOAA National Geophysical Data Center
SNOW DEPTH AND SEA ICE: Data provided by NASA/GSFC, Don Cavalieri, Dorothy Hall, and Gene Carl Feldman
CLOUD COVER: Data provided by NASA/GISS, William B. Rossow, and Gene Carl Feldman
DAY AND NIGHT TEMPERATURE DIFFERENCE: Data provided by NASA/GSFC, Joel Susskind and Gene Carl Feldman
VEGETATION COVER : Data provided by NASA/GSFC, Compton J. Tucker, and Gene Carl Feldman

Land Cover pp. 32–33

CONSULTANTS
Paul Davis
The Global Land Cover Facility, University of Maryland

SATELLITE IMAGES
GLOBAL LAND COVER COMPOSITION: M. Hansen, R. DeFries, J.R.G. Townshend, and R. Sohlberg. 1998. "Global land cover classification at 1km spatial resolution using a classification tree approach." 1 Km Land Cover Classification Derived from AVHRR; College Park, Maryland: The Global Land Cover Facility. (Note: Data were derived from NOAA AVHRR and NASA Landsat imagery.)

PHOTOGRAPHS
PAGE 32, (UP LE) Tom and Pat Leeson/Photo Researchers; **(UP RT)** Michael Nichols/NGS Image Collection; **(LO LE)** Stephen J. Krasemann/Photo Researchers; **(LO CT LE)** Rod Planck/Photo Researchers; **(CT LE)** Jim Steinberg/Photo Researchers; **(CT RT)** Matthew C. Hansen, University of Maryland; **(LO CT RT)** Gregory G. Dimijian/Photo Researchers; **(LO RT)** Sharon Johnson
PAGE 33, (LE) Georg Gerster/Photo Researchers; **(LO CT LE)** Rod Planck/Photo Researchers; **(LE CT)** Jim Richardson; **(RT CT)** George Steinmetz; **(LO CT RT)** Steve McCurry; **(RT)** B. and C. Alexander/Photo Researchers

Climate pp. 34–37

CONSULTANTS
William Burroughs
H. Michael Mogil
Certified Consulting Meteorologist (CCM)
Vladimir Ryabinin
World Climate Research Programme

GRAPHICS
TOPOGRAPHY: ChrisOrr.com and XNR Productions
GLOBAL AIR TEMPERATURE CHANGES, 1850–2000: Reproduced by kind permission of the Climatic Research Unit.

SATELLITE IMAGES
Images originally created for the GLOBE program by NOAA's National Geophysical Data Center, Boulder, Colorado, U.S.A.
CLOUD COVER: International Satellite Cloud Climatology Project (ISCCP); National Aeronautics and Space Administration (NASA); Goddard Institute for Space Studies (GISS)
PRECIPITATION: Global Precipitation Climatology Project (GPCP); International Satellite Land Surface Climatology Project (ISLSCP)
SOLAR ENERGY: Earth Radiation Budget Experiment (ERBE); Greenhouse Effect Detection Experiment (GEDEX)
TEMPERATURE: National Center for Environmental Prediction (NCEP); National Center for Atmospheric Research (NCAR); National Weather Service (NWS)

PHOTOGRAPHS
PAGE 35, Sharon G. Johnson.

Weather pp. 38–39

CONSULTANTS
Gerry Bell
National Oceanic and Atmospheric Administration (NOAA)
H. Michael Mogil
Certified Consulting Meteorologist (CCM)

GRAPHICS
WATER CYCLE, AIR MASSES, JET STREAM, WEATHER FRONTS, CLOUD TYPES: ChrisOrr.com

SATELLITE IMAGES
HURRICANE IMAGE: NASA Goddard Space Flight Center (GSFC), data from NOAA
EL NIÑO IMAGE SEQUENCE: Courtesy Robert M. Carey, NOAA
LIGHTNING IMAGE: NASA Marshall Space Flight Center Lightning Imaging Sensor (LIS) Instrument Team, Huntsville, Alabama

Biosphere pp. 40–41

CONSULTANTS
Manuel Colunga-Garcia (Entomology), Patrick J. Webber (Plant Biology), David T. Long (Geological Sciences), Stuart H. Gage (Entomology), Craig K. Harris (Sociology)
Earth System Science Education Program, Michigan State University
Jane Robertson Vernhes
World Network of Biosphere Reserves, UNESCO

GRAPHICS
BIOSPHERE DYNAMICS: Earth Science System Education Program, Michigan State University, and ChrisOrr.com
EARTH SYSTEM DYNAMICS: Edward Gazsi
SIZE OF THE BIOSPHERE: The COMET Program and ChrisOrr.com
BIOSPHERE OVER TIME: Earth Science System Education Program, Michigan State University

SATELLITE IMAGES
BIOSPHERE FROM SPACE: SeaWiFS, NASA/Goddard Space Flight Center, Gene Carl Feldman and ORBIMAGE

Biodiversity pp. 42–43

CONSULTANTS
Craig Hilton-Taylor
International Union for Conservation of Nature and Natural Resources (IUCN)
Mike Hoffmann
Conservation International
John Morrison
World Wildlife Fund (WWF)

GENERAL REFERENCES
Conservation International: www.biodiversityhotspots.org

International Union for Conservation of Nature and Natural Resources (IUCN): www.iucnredlist.org

GRAPHICS
THE NATURAL WORLD, SPECIES DIVERSITY, AND PROJECTED BIODIVERSITY: Biodiversity. NG Maps for National Geographic Magazine, February 1999

Population pp. 44–47

CONSULTANTS
Carl Haub
Population Reference Bureau
Gregory Yetman
Center for International Earth Science Information Network (CIESIN), Columbia University

GENERAL REFERENCES
Center for International Earth Science Information Network (CIESIN), Columbia University: www.ciesin.org

International Migration, 2002. Population Division of the Department of Economic and Social Affairs of the United Nations Secretariat. New York: United Nations, 2002

Population Reference Bureau: www.prb.org

United Nations World Population Prospects: The 2004 Revision Population Database: esa.un.org/unpp

World Urbanization Prospects: The 2003 Revision. Population Division of the Department of Economic and Social Affairs of the United Nations Secretariat. New York: United Nations, 2004

GRAPHICS
POPULATION DENSITY: Center for International Earth Science Information Network (CIESIN), Columbia University, and Centro Internacional de Agricultura Tropical (CIAT), 2005. Gridded Population of the World Version 3 (GPWv3): Population Density Grids—World Population Density, 2005 [map]. Palisades, New York: Socioeconomic Data and Applications Center (SEDAC), Columbia University. Available at http://sedac.ciesin.columbia.edu/gpw. Accessed April 2006

SATELLITE IMAGES
LIGHTS OF THE WORLD: Composite image: MODIS imagery; ETOPO-2 relief; NOAA/NGDC and DMSP lights at night data

Languages pp. 48–49

CONSULTANTS
Bernard Comrie
Max Planck Institute for Evolutionary Anthropology

GRAPHICS
VOICES OF THE WORLD, HOW MANY SPEAK WHAT?, VANISHING LANGUAGES, MAJOR LANGUAGE FAMILIES TODAY: *National Geographic Atlas of the World,* 8th ed., Washington, D.C.: The National Geographic Society, 2005
EVOLUTION OF LANGUAGES: *National Geographic Almanac of Geography,* Washington, D.C.: The National Geographic Society, 2005

Religions pp. 50–51

CONSULTANTS
William M. Bodiford
University of California—Los Angeles
Todd Johnson
Center for the Study of Global Christianity, Gordon-Conwell Theological Seminary

GENERAL REFERENCES
World Christian Database: Center for the Study of Global Christianity, Gordon-Conwell Theological Seminary
www.worldchristiandatabase.org

GRAPHICS
MAJOR RELIGIONS *National Geographic Atlas of the World,* 8th ed., Washington, D.C.: The National Geographic Society, 2005

PHOTOGRAPHS
PAGE 50, (LE) Jodi Cobb, National Geographic Photographer; **(RT)** James L. Stanfield
PAGES 50–51, Tony Heiderer
PAGE 51, (LE) Thomas J. Abercrombie; **(RT)** Annie Griffiths Belt

Health and Education pp. 52–53

CONSULTANTS
Carlos Castillo-Salgado
Pan American Health Organization (PAHO)/
World Health Organization (WHO)
George Ingram and Annababette Wils
Education Policy and Data Center
Margaret Kruk
United Nations Millennium Project and
University of Michigan School of Public Health
Ruth Levine
Center for Global Development

GENERAL REFERENCES
2004 Report on the Global AIDS Epidemic. World Health Organization and the Joint United Nations Programme on HIV/AIDS, 2004

Education Policy and Data Center: www.epdc.org

Global Burden of Disease Estimates. Geneva: World Health Organization, 2004

Human Development Report, 2005. New York: United Nations Development Programme (UNDP), 2005

UN Millennium Development Goals: www.un.org/millenniumgoals

The State of the World's Children 2006. Table 5: Education. New York: UNICEF, 2006

The World Health Report 2005. Annex table 5. Selected national health accounts indicators. Geneva: World Health Organization, 2005

World Bank list of economies, 2005. Washington, D.C.: World Bank

World Health Organization: www.who.int

Youth (15–24) and Adult (15+) Literacy Rates by Country and by Gender for 2000–2004. New York: UNESCO Institute for Statistics, 2005

GRAPHICS
ACCESS TO IMPROVED SANITATION: Adapted from *WHO Water Supply and Sanitation Monitoring Mid-Term Report, 2004.*
DEVELOPING HUMAN CAPITAL: Adapted from Human Capital Projections developed by Education Policy and Data Center.

Conflict and Terror pp. 54–55

CONSULTANTS
Barbara Harff
U.S. Naval Academy
Monty G. Marshall
Center for Systemic Peace and Center for Global Policy, George Mason University
Christian Oxenboll
United Nations High Commissioner for Refugees (UNHCR)

GENERAL REFERENCES
Global Statistics. Internal Displacement Monitoring Centre (iDMC). 2006: www.internal-displacement.org

Marshall, Monty G., and Ted Robert Gurr. *Peace and Conflict.* Center for International Development & Conflict Management. University of Maryland, College Park, MD: 2005

Proliferation News and Resources. Carnegie Endowment for International Peace. 2005: www.carnegieendowment.org/npp

United Nations High Commissioner for Refugees (UNHCR): www.unhcr.org

United Nations Peacekeeping: www.un.org/Depts/dpko

Economy pp. 56–57

CONSULTANTS
William Beyers
University of Washington
Michael Finger
World Trade Organization (WTO)
Richard R. Fix
World Bank
Susan Martin
Institute for the Study of International Migration

GENERAL REFERENCES
CIA World Factbook: www.cia.gov

International Monetary Fund: www.imf.org

International Telecommunication Union: www.itu.int

International Trade Statistics, 2005. Geneva, Switzerland: World Trade Organization

UNESCO Institute for Statistics: www.uis.unesco.org

World Development Indicators, 2005, Washington, D.C.: World Bank

Note: GDP and GDP (PPP) data on this spread are from the IMF.

GRAPHICS
LABOR MIGRATION: *National Geographic Atlas of the World,* 8th ed., Washington, D.C.: The National Geographic Society, 2005

Trade pp. 58–59

CONSULTANTS
Peter Werner and Michael Finger
World Trade Organization (WTO)

United Nations Conference on Trade and Development (UNCTAD)

GENERAL REFERENCES
International Trade Statistics, 2005, Geneva, Switzerland: World Trade Organization

United Nations Conference on Trade and Development: www.unctad.org

World Trade Organization: www.wto.org

GRAPHICS
GROWTH OF WORLD TRADE: World Trade Organization

Food pp. 60–61

CONSULTANTS
Freddy Nachtergaele, Sachiko Tsuji, Vincent Ngendakumana, Edward Gillin, Guy Nantel, Giulia Cimino
Food and Agriculture Organization of the United Nations (FAO)
Birgit Meade
Economic Research Service,
U.S. Department of Agriculture (USDA)
Shahla Shapouri
Economic Research Service, U.S. Department of Agriculture (USDA) and Food and Agriculture Organization of the United Nations (FAO)

GENERAL REFERENCES
Food and Agriculture Organization of the United Nations (FAO) Statistics Division (agricultural data): faostat.fao.org/faostat

GRAPHICS
WORLD GRAIN PRODUCTION: *National Geographic Almanac of Geography,* Washington, D.C.: The National Geographic Society, 2005

PHOTOGRAPHS
PAGE 61, (LE) Steven L. Raymer/NGS Image Collection; (CT) Richard Olsenius/NGS Image Collection; (RT) Jim Richardson

Energy pp. 62–63

CONSULTANTS
Connie Brooks
Sandia National Laboratories
George Douglas, Dennis Elliott, Donna Heimiller, Gary Schmitz, Thomas Stoffel
National Renewable Energy Laboratory (NREL)
Michael Grillot
U.S. Energy Information Administration
Elena Nekhaev
World Energy Council
Simon Walker
Independent Editorial and Technical Services

GENERAL REFERENCES
American Wind Energy Association. *Global Wind Energy Market Report,* 2003

Bertani, Ruggero. World Geothermal Power Generation in the Period 2001–2005. *Geothermics,* Volume 34, Number 6, December 2005, p. 651–690

BP Statistical Review of World Energy 2005

Energy Information Administration, U.S. Department of Energy: www.eia.doe.gov

National Renewable Energy Laboratory: www.nrel.gov

Power Reactor Information System. International Atomic Energy Agency: www.iaea.org/programmes/a2/index.html

Survey of Energy Resources: Biomass. World Energy Council: www.worldenergy.org

The LNG industry. Groupe International des Importateurs de Gaz Naturel Liquefie, 2004

GRAPHICS
FOSSIL FUEL EXTRACTION: ChrisOrr.com and XNR Productions

PHOTOGRAPHS
PAGE 63, (UP) Jim Richardson; (UP CT) Mark C. Burnett/Photo Researchers; (CT) Courtesy National Renewable Energy Laboratory; (LO CT) John Mead/Science Photo Library/Photo Researchers; (LO) John Mead/Science Photo Library/Photo Researchers

Minerals pp. 64–65

CONSULTANTS
Philip Brown
University of Wisconsin—Madison
Nelson Fugate
Mineral Information Institute
W. David Menzie and J. Michael Eros
USGS Minerals Information Team

GENERAL REFERENCES
USGS Minerals Information: minerals.usgs.gov/minerals

PHOTOGRAPHS
PAGE 64, (UP LE) Philip Brown; (CT LE) Philip Brown; (LO LE) Philip Brown; (UP CT) Phillip Hayson/Photo Researchers; (CT) Mark A. Schneider/Photo Researchers; (LO CT) Steven Holt/Stockpix.com; (UP RT) Mineral Information Institute/www.mii.org; (CT RT) Russ Lappa/Photo Researchers; (LO RT) Russ Lappa/Photo Researchers;
PAGE 65, (UP LE) U.S. Geological Survey; (CT LE) E.R. Degginger/Photo Researchers; (LO LE) U.S. Geological Survey; (UP CT) U.S. Geological Survey; (CT) Mineral Information Institute/www.mii.org; (LO CT) U.S. Geological Survey; (UP RT) Kenneth W. Larsen, Courtesy Smithsonian Institution, NMNH; (CT RT) Kenneth W. Larsen, Courtesy Smithsonian Institution, NMNH; (LO RT) Philip Brown

Environmental Stresses pp. 66–67

CONSULTANTS
Christian Lambrechts
Division of Early Warning and Assessment (DEWA), United Nations Environment Programme (UNEP)

GENERAL REFERENCES
Acidification and eutrophication of developing country ecosystems. Swedish University of Agricultural Sciences (SLU), 2002

Centre of Documentation, Research and Experimentation on Accidental Water Pollution (Cedre): www.le-cedre.fr

EM-DAT: The OFDA/CRED International Disaster Database. Université Catholique de Louvain, Brussels, Belgium: www.em-dat.net

Energy Information Administration. U.S. Department of Energy: www.eia.doe.gov

Global Forest Resources Assessment. Forestry Department of the Food and Agriculture Organization of the United Nations, 2005

United Nations Environment Programme-World Conservation and Monitoring Program (UNEP-WCMC): www.unep-wcmc.org

GRAPHICS
HUMAN FOOTPRINT: *National Geographic Atlas of the World,* 8th ed., Washington, D.C.: The National Geographic Society, 2005

SATELLITE IMAGES
DEPLETION OF THE OZONE LAYER: Ozone Processing Team at NASA/Goddard Space Flight Center

Protected Areas pp. 68–69

CONSULTANTS
Simon Blyth
UNEP World Conservation Monitoring Centre (UNEP-WCMC)

UNESCO World Heritage Centre

GENERAL REFERENCES
Antarctic Protected Areas Information Archive: www.cep.aq/apa

Protected areas map and statistics produced from the World Database on Protected Areas (WDPA) in March 2006 by UNEP World Conservation Monitoring Centre (WDPA custodian) (www.unep-wcmc.org), Cambridge, UK

UNEP-WCMC: www.unep-wcmc.org

UNESCO World Heritage Centre: whc.unesco.org

PHOTOGRAPHS
PAGE 69, (UP) James P. Blair; (LO LE) Art Wolfe/Getty Images; (LO CT) Richard Nowitz/NGS Image Collection; (LO RT) Sarah Leen

Acknowledgments

Globalization
pp. 70–71

CONSULTANTS

Mary Amiti
International Monetary Fund (IMF)

Janet Pau
Global Business Policy Council, A.T. Kearney, Inc.

Shang-Jin Wei
International Monetary Fund (IMF) and
National Bureau of Economic Research (NBER)

GENERAL REFERENCES

Airports Council International: www.airports.org

Amiti, Mary, and Shang-Jin Wei, 2004, "Demystifying Outsourcing." *Finance & Development*, December 2004, pp. 36–39.

Balance of Payments Statistics, 2003. Washington, D.C.: International Monetary Fund.

International Telecommunication Union: www.itu.int

"Measuring Globalization." *Foreign Policy*, May/June 2005: 52–60. Globalization Index is developed by A.T. Kearney, Inc. and Foreign Policy (Carnegie Endowment for International Peace).

World Investment Report, 2005. Geneva, Switzerland: United Nations Conference on Trade and Development.

GRAPHICS

TRANSNATIONAL CORPORATIONS: Adapted from *The Times Complete History of the World*, 6th ed. New York: Barnes & Noble Books, 2004.
EXTREMES OF GLOBALIZATION: Adapted from "Measuring Globalization." *Foreign Policy*, May/June 2005.
IMPORTS IN BUSINESS SERVICES AS A SHARE OF GDP: Adapted from Amiti, Mary, and Shang-Jin Wei, 2004, "Demystifying Outsourcing." *Finance & Development*, December 2004, pp. 36–39.

Technology and Communication
pp. 72–73

CONSULTANTS

Tim Kelly
Strategic Planning Unit,
International Telecommunication Union

Sarah Parkes
Media Works Creative

GENERAL REFERENCES

International Telecommunication Union: www.itu.int

GRAPHICS

CENTERS OF TECHNOLOGICAL INNOVATION: *Human Development Report 2001*, United Nations Development Programme (source data updated by Human Development Report Office in 2006) and World Intellectual Property Organization.
MILESTONES IN TECHNOLOGY: Adapted from *Human Development Report 2001*, United Nations Development Programme.
THE DIGITAL DIVIDE: NG Maps. Source data provided by TeleGeography Research, a division of PriMetrica, Inc. (www.telegeography.com) and the International Telecommunication Union. The Fuller Projection map design is a trademark of the Buckminster Fuller Institute © 1938, 1967, and 1992. All rights reserved.

Internet
pp. 74–75

CONSULTANTS

Josh Polterock and Brad Huffaker
Cooperative Association for Internet Data Analysis (CAIDA)

GENERAL REFERENCES

Cooperative Association for Internet Data Analysis (CAIDA): www.caida.org

International Telecommunication Union: www.itu.int

GRAPHICS

All images provided by the Cooperative Association for Internet Data Analysis (CAIDA), located at the San Diego Supercomputer Center (SDSC). CAIDA is a research unit of the University of California at San Diego (UCSD). URL: www.caida.org. Sponsors of this work include CAIDA Members, Cisco Systems, Department of Homeland Security (DHS, award NBCHC-040159), National Science Foundation (NSF, awards OCI-0137121, CNS-0433668, and CCR-0311690), and WIDE. Images copyright © 2006 The Regents of the University of California.

MAPPING THE SPREAD OF A COMPUTER VIRUS: Cooperative Association for Internet Data Analysis (CAIDA) "Nyxem Virus Analysis." Copyright © 2006 The Regents of the University of California. All rights reserved. Used by permission.
GLOBAL INTERNET CONNECTIVITY: Cooperative Association for Internet Data Analysis (CAIDA) "Skitter" Internet Map, 2005. Copyright © 2005 The Regents of the University of California. All rights reserved. Used by permission.
WORLDWIDE DISTRIBUTION OF INTERNET RESOURCES: Cooperative Association for Internet Data Analysis (CAIDA) "BGP Geopolitical Analysis Visualization." Copyright © 2006 The Regents of the University of California. All rights reserved. Used by permission.

ADDITIONAL CONSULTANTS

Regional Thematic Maps

Carl Haub
Population Reference Bureau

W. David Menzie and J. Michael Eros
USGS Minerals Information Team

Freddy Nachtergaele
Food and Agriculture Organization of the United Nations (FAO)

Gregory Yetman
Center for International Earth Science Information Network (CIESIN), Columbia University

Flags and Facts

Carl Haub
Population Reference Bureau

Whitney Smith
Flag Research Center

Antarctica
pp. 222–229

Graham Bartram
The Flag Institute

Scott Borg
National Science Foundation (NSF)—Antarctic Division

Mark R. Drinkwater
European Space Agency

Kenneth Jezek
Byrd Polar Research Center, Ohio State University

Tony K. Meunier
USGS Polar Program

Whitney Smith
Flag Research Center

David G. Vaughan
Bedmap Consortium, British Antarctic Survey

Roland Warner
Antarctic Cooperative Research Centre and Australian Antarctic Division

Oceanography
pp. 232–233

Eric J. Lindstrom
National Aeronautics and Space Administration (NASA)

Keelin Kuipers
National Atmospheric and Oceanic Administration (NOAA)

Bob Molinari
NOAA

Bruce Parker
NOAA/National Ocean Service (NOS)

Richard A. Schmalz, Jr.
NOAA

Limits of the Oceans & Seas

Adam J. Kerr pp. 234–235
International Hydrographic Management Consulting

Space
pp. 246–261

Sanjay S. Limaye and Rosalyn A. Pertzborn
Space Science and Engineering Center, University of Wisconsin—Madison

Stephen P. Maran

Robert E. Pratt
National Geographic Maps

The Moon
pp. 248–251

Paul D. Spudis
Lunar and Planetary Institute, Houston, Texas

Mars
pp. 252–253

Damond Benningfield
StarDate radio series

The Solar System
pp. 254–255

Lucy McFadden
University of Maryland, College Park

The Planets
pp. 256–257

Henry Kline
NASA Jet Propulsion Laboratory (JPL)

The Universe
pp. 258–259

Todd J. Henry
Harvard-Smithsonian Center for Astrophysics

Edmund Bertschinger
Massachusetts Institute of Technology

Donald P. Schneider
Pennsylvania State University

Marc Postman
Space Telescope Science Institute (STScI)

Christopher D. Impey
University of Arizona

R. Brent Tully
University of Hawai'i

August E. Evrard
University of Michigan

Geographic Comparisons

John Kammerer pp. 264–265
National Geospatial-Intelligence Agency (NGA)

George Sharman
NOAA/NESDIS/NGDC

Peter H. Gleick
Pacific Institute for Studies in Development, Environment, and Security

R.L. Fisher
Scripps Institution of Oceanography

Philip Micklin
Western Michigan University

Political Entities and Status

Leo Dillon pp. 266–269
Department of State, Office of the Geographer

Harm J. de Blij
Michigan State University

Carl Haub
Population Reference Bureau

Whitney Smith
Flag Research Center

Special Flags
pp. 270–271

Whitney Smith
Flag Research Center

Glossary
pp. 282–284

Rex Honey
University of Iowa

Bernard O. Bauer
University of Southern California

PHYSICAL AND POLITICAL MAPS

Bureau of the Census,
U.S. Department of Commerce

Bureau of Land Management,
U.S. Department of the Interior

Central Intelligence Agency (CIA)

National Geographic Maps

National Geospatial-Intelligence Agency (NGA)

National Park Service,
U.S. Department of the Interior

Office of the Geographer,
U.S. Department of State

U.S. Board on Geographic Names (BGN)

U.S. Geological Survey,
U.S. Department of the Interior

PRINCIPAL REFERENCE SOURCES

Columbia Gazetteer of the World. Cohen, Saul B., ed. New York: Columbia University Press, 1998

Encarta World English Dictionary. New York: St. Martin's Press and Microsoft Encarta, 1999

Human Development Report, 2005. New York: United Nations Development Programme (UNDP), Oxford University Press, 2005

International Trade Statistics, 2005. Geneva, Switzerland: World Trade Organization

McKnight, Tom L. *Physical Geography: A Landscape Appreciation.* 5th ed. Upper Saddle River, New Jersey: Prentice Hall, 1996

National Geographic Atlas of the World, 8th ed., Washington, D.C.: The National Geographic Society, 2005

Strahler, Alan and Arthur Strahler. *Physical Geography: Science and Systems of the Human Environment.* 2nd ed., John Wiley & Sons, Inc, 2002

Tarbuck, Edward J. and Frederick K. Lutgens. *Earth: An Introduction to Physical Geology.* 7th ed. Upper Saddle River, New Jersey: Prentice Hall, 2002

World Development Indicators, 2005. Washington, D.C.: World Bank

The World Factbook 2006. Washington, D.C.: Central Intelligence Agency, 2006

The World Health Report 2005. Geneva: World Health Organization, 2001

World Investment Report, 2005. New York and Geneva: United Nations Conference on Trade and Development, 2005

Cambridge Dictionaries Online
dictionary.cambridge.org

Central Intelligence Agency
www.cia.gov

CIESIN
www.ciesin.org

Conservation International
www.conservation.org

Energy Information Agency
www.eia.doe.gov

Food and Agriculture Organization of the UN
www.fao.org

International Monetary Fund
www.imf.org

Merriam-Webster OnLine
www.m-w.com

National Aeronautics and Space Administration
www.nasa.gov

National Atmospheric and Oceanic Administration
www.noaa.gov

National Climatic Data Center
www.ncdc.noaa.gov

National Geophysical Data Center
www.ngdc.noaa.gov

National Park Service
www.nps.gov

National Renewable Energy Laboratory
www.nrel.gov

Population Reference Bureau
www.prb.org

United Nations
www.un.org

UN Conference on Trade and Development
www.unctad.org

UN Development Programme
www.undp.org

UN Educational, Cultural, and Scientific Organization
www.unesco.org

UNESCO Institute for Statistics
www.uis.unesco.org

UNEP-WCMC
www.unep-wcmc.org

UN Millennium Development Goals
www.un.org/millenniumgoals

UN Population Division
www.unpopulation.org

UN Refugee Agency
www.unhcr.org

UN Statistics Division
unstats.un.org

U.S. Board on Geographic Names
geonames.usgs.gov

U.S. Bureau of Economic Analysis
www.bea.gov

U.S. Census Bureau
www.census.gov

U.S. Geological Survey
www.usgs.gov

World Bank
www.worldbank.org

World Health Organization
www.who.int

World Trade Organization
www.wto.org

WWF
www.worldwildlife.org

SATELLITE IMAGES

CONTINENTAL SATELLITE IMAGES: NASA/Jet Propulsion Laboratory (JPL)/California Institute of Technology/Advanced Very High Resolution Radiometer (AVHRR) Project/Cartographic Applications Group (CAG)

The Cartographic Applications Group manipulated more than 500 NOAA weather satellite images acquired by the AVHRR instrument to create satellite coverages at one-kilometer resolution (one pixel of data equals one kilometer on the Earth). Using hundreds of multidate NOAA AVHRR satellite scenes and imaging in the visible and near-infrared wavelengths, the mosaics were created in a rapid fashion using semiautomated software procedures based on JPL's VICAR/IBIS image processing and GIS software.

FRONT JACKET, ANTARCTICA FROM SPACE: WorldSat International Inc., www.skyviewcafe.com, and NG Books

TITLE PAGE (PAGE 2), Peter Sloss, NOAA (National Geophysical Data Center)

PAGE 29, MISSISSIPPI RIVER DELTA: Centre National d'Etudes Spatiales (CNES)

PAGES 32–33, GLOBAL LAND COVER CLASSIFICATION AT 1KM SPATIAL RESOLUTION USING A CLASSIFICATION TREE APPROACH: M. Hansen, R. DeFries, J.R.G. Townshend, and R. Sohlberg. 1998. 1 Km Land Cover Classification Derived from AVHRR. College Park, Maryland: The Global Land Cover Facility (Note: Data was derived from NOAA AVHRR and NASA Landsat imagery.)

PAGE 34, *Images created originally for the GLOBE program by NOAA's National Geophysical Data Center, Boulder, Colorado, U.S.A.*
CLOUD COVER: International Satellite Cloud Climatology Project (ISCCP); National Aeronautics and Space Administration (NASA); Goddard Institute for Space Studies (GISS). **PRECIPITATION:** Global Precipitation Climatology Project (GPCP); International Satellite Land Surface Climatology Project (ISLSCP). **SOLAR ENERGY:** Earth Radiation Budget Experiment (ERBE); Greenhouse Effect Detection Experiment (GEDEX). **TEMPERATURE:** National Center for Environmental Prediction (NCEP); National Center for Atmospheric Research (NCAR); National Weather Service (NWS).

PAGE 38, HURRICANE IMAGE: NASA Goddard Space Flight Center (GSFC), data from NOAA

PAGE 39, EL NIÑO IMAGE SEQUENCE: Courtesy Robert M. Carey, NOAA; **LIGHTNING IMAGE:** NASA Marshall Space Flight Center Lightning Imaging Sensor (LIS) Instrument Team, Huntsville, Alabama

PAGE 40, BIOSPHERE FROM SPACE: SeaWiFS, NASA/Goddard Space Flight Center, Gene Carl Feldman and ORBIMAGE

PAGE 44, LIGHTS OF THE WORLD: Composite image: MODIS imagery; ETOPO-2 relief; NOAA/NGDC and DMSP lights at night data

PAGE 66, DEPLETION OF THE OZONE LAYER: Ozone Processing Team at NASA/Goddard Space Flight Center

PAGE 228, SURFACE ELEVATION: Byrd Polar Research Center, Ohio State University. **ICE SHEET THICKNESS:** Bedmap Project. **ICE FLOW VELOCITY:** Roland Warner, Antarctic Cooperative Research Centre and Australian Antarctic Division. **SEA ICE MOVEMENT AND WIND FLOW: SEA ICE VELOCITY DATA:** Mark R. Drinkwater and Xiang Liu, Jet Propulsion Laboratory/California Institute of Technology. **SURFACE WINDS:** Based on data from David H. Bromwich, Ohio State University, and Thomas R. Parish, University of Wyoming.

PAGES 246–247, UGC10214 ("TADPOLE GALAXY") IMAGE: NASA/Holland Ford, Johns Hopkins University; Mark Clampin and George Hartig, Space Telescope Science Institute; Garth Illingworth, University of California Observatories/Lick Observatory

PAGES 249 AND 251, CLEMENTINE TOPOGRAPHIC MAP OF THE MOON: Courtesy of the Lunar and Planetary Institute, Houston, Texas

PAGES 256 AND 257, THE PLANETS: Courtesy of NASA/JPL/Caltech

PAGE 384, ETOPO-2 relief; Digital Chart of the World

PHOTOGRAPHS

Front Jacket
(LE) Jodi Cobb/NGS Image Collection
(CT LE) Robert B. Haas/NGS Image Collection
(RT) Paul Chesley/NGS Image Collection

Interior
PAGE 24, (UP) R.D. Griggs, USGS
PAGE 24, (CT) Sharon Johnson
PAGE 24, (LO) David Muench
PAGE 25, Raymond Gehman/NGS Image Collection
PAGE 26, (LE) Joel Sartore/www.joelsartore.com
PAGE 26, (CT) Science Photo Library/CORBIS
PAGE 26, (UP RT) George F. Mobley
PAGE 26, (LO RT) James D. Balog
PAGE 27, (UP LE) Wolfgang Kaehler/CORBIS
PAGE 27, (UP CT) Lyle Rosbotham
PAGE 27, (UP RT) Adriel Heisey
PAGE 27, (LO LE) Marc Moritsch/NGS Image Collection
PAGE 27, (LO CT) Peter Essick
PAGE 27, (LO RT) Sam Abell, NGS
PAGE 28, (LE) Peter Essick
PAGE 28, (CT) Douglas R. Grant
PAGE 28, (RT) Tom and Pat Leeson
PAGE 29, (UP CT) Rob Brander
PAGE 29, (UP RT) George Veni and James Jasek
PAGE 29, (LO LE) Sharon Johnson
PAGE 29, (LO RT) Douglas R. Grant/Parks Canada
PAGE 32, (UP LE) Tom and Pat Leeson/Photo Researchers
PAGE 32, (UP RT) Michael Nichols/NGS Image Collection
PAGE 32, (LO LE) Stephen J. Krasemann/Photo Researchers
PAGE 32, (LO CT LE) Rod Planck/Photo Researchers
PAGE 32, (CT LE) Jim Steinberg/Photo Researchers
PAGE 32, (CT RT) Matthew C. Hansen, University of Maryland
PAGE 32, (LO CT RT) Gregory G. Dimijian/Photo Researchers
PAGE 32, (LO RT) Sharon Johnson
PAGE 33, (LE) Georg Gerster/Photo Researchers
PAGE 33, (LO CT LE) Rod Planck/Photo Researchers
PAGE 33, (LE CT) Jim Richardson
PAGE 33, (RT CT) George Steinmetz
PAGE 33, (LO CT RT) Steve McCurry
PAGE 33, (RT) B. and C. Alexander/PhotoResearchers
PAGE 35, Sharon Johnson
PAGE 50, (LE) Jodi Cobb/National Geographic Photographer
PAGE 50, (RT) James L. Stanfield
PAGES 50–51 Tony Heiderer
PAGE 51, (LE) Thomas J. Abercrombie
PAGE 51, (RT) Annie Griffiths Belt;
PAGE 61, (LE) Steven L. Raymer/NGS Image Collection
PAGE 61, (CT) Richard Olsenius/NGS Image Collection
PAGE 61, (RT) Jim Richardson
PAGE 63, (UP) Jim Richardson
PAGE 63, (UP CT) Courtesy National Renewable Energy Laboratory
PAGE 63, (LO CT) John Mead/Science Photo Library/Photo Researchers
PAGE 63, (LO) John Mead/Science Photo Library/Photo Researchers
PAGE 64, (UP LE) Philip Brown
PAGE 64, (CT LE) Philip Brown
PAGE 64, (LO LE) Philip Brown
PAGE 64, (UP CT) Phillip Hayson/Photo Researchers
PAGE 64, (CT) Mark A. Schneider/Photo Researchers
PAGE 64, (LO CT) Steven Holt/Stockpix.com
PAGE 64, (UP RT) Mineral Information Institute/www.mii.org
PAGE 64, (CT RT) Russ Lappa/Photo Researchers
PAGE 64, (LO RT) Russ Lappa/Photo Researchers
PAGE 65, (UP LE) U.S. Geological Survey
PAGE 65, (CT LE) E.R. Degginger/Photo Researchers
PAGE 65, (LO LE) U.S. Geological Survey
PAGE 65, (UP CT) U.S. Geological Survey
PAGE 65, (CT) Mineral Information Institute/www.mii.org
PAGE 65, (LO CT) U.S. Geological Survey
PAGE 65, (UP RT) Kenneth W. Larsen, Courtesy Smithsonian Institution, NMNH
PAGE 65, (CT RT) Kenneth W. Larsen, Courtesy Smithsonian Institution, NMNH
PAGE 65, (LO RT) Philip Brown
PAGE 69, (UP) James P. Blair
PAGE 69, (LO LE) Art Wolfe/Getty Images
PAGE 69, (LO CT) Richard Nowitz/NGS Image Collection
PAGE 69, (LO RT) Sarah Leen
PAGES 76–77, Ron Watts/CORBIS
PAGE 79, W.E. Garrett/NGS Image Collection
PAGES 122–123, Skip Brown/NGS Image Collection
PAGE 125, L. Scott Shelton
PAGES 134–135, George F. Mobley/NGS Image Collection
PAGE 137, Winfield I. Parks, Jr.
PAGES 162–163, J. Yip/Imagestate/Panoramic Images
PAGE 165, Steve McCurry/NGS Image Collection
PAGES 190–191, Beverly Joubert/NGS Image Collection
PAGE 193, David Boyer/NGS Image Collection
PAGES 206–207, Theo Allofs/CORBIS
PAGE 209, Pam Gardner/Frank Lane Picture Agency/CORBIS
PAGES 222–223, Paul A. Souders/CORBIS
PAGE 225, Maria Stenzel

KEY TO FLAGS AND FACTS

The National Geographic Society, whose cartographic policy is to recognize de facto countries, counted 192 independent nations in the spring of 2006. Within this atlas, fact boxes for independent nations, most dependencies, and U.S. states are placed on or next to regional maps that show the areas they represent. Each box includes the flag of the political entity, as well as important statistical data. Boxes for some dependencies show two flags—a local flag and the flag of the administering country. Because Paraguay and the state of Oregon have different designs on the obverse and reverse sides of their flags, their fact boxes show both sides of their flags.

The statistical data provide highlights of geography, demography, and economy. These details offer a brief overview of each entity; they present general characteristics and are not intended to be comprehensive studies. The structured nature of the text results in some generic collective or umbrella terms. The industry category, for instance, includes services in addition to traditional manufacturing sectors. Space limitations dictate the amount of information included. For example, the only languages listed for the U.S. are English and Spanish, although many others are spoken.

Fact boxes are arranged alphabetically by the conventional short forms of the country or dependency names (except for the Oceania, Islands of Africa, and Europe's Smallest Countries fact boxes, where country and dependency boxes are grouped separately). The short-form names for dependencies are followed by the name of the administering country in parentheses. The short-form names for Côte d'Ivoire, Myanmar, and Timor-Leste are followed by alternate, commonly refered to names in parentheses. The conventional long-form names of the country or dependency appear within colored stripes below the short-form names; if there are no long forms, the short forms are repeated. This policy has two exceptions: For U.S. states, nicknames are shown inside the colored stripes, and for French overseas departments, the words "Overseas Department of France" appear inside the colored stripes. These departments of France are the equivalent of states in the United States, and thus not considered dependencies.

AREA accounts for the total area of a country, U.S. state, or dependency, including all land and inland water delimited by international boundaries, intranational boundaries, or coastlines.

In the POPULATION category, the figures for U.S. state populations are from the U.S. Census Bureau's 2005 midyear estimates. Two population figures are listed for the CAPITAL and LARGEST CITY of each state. The city-proper figure, from data provided by the U.S. Census Bureau, shows the estimated number of people who lived within the incorporated city limits on July 1st of 2004. The larger metro-area figure represents the number of people who live within a U.S. Office of Management and Budget-defined metropolitan statistical area—a broader designation that includes both a city proper and the surrounding urbanized region. These July 1st, 2004 estimates are from the U.S. Census Bureau's table of Annual Estimates of the Population of Metropolitan and Micropolitan Statistical Areas. Metropolitan statistical areas and their geographic boundaries can cross state borders and are defined on the basis of population as well as other factors. Some state capitals with small populations are not defined as part of a metropolitan statistical area; in those cases, only city-proper population figures are shown.

POPULATION figures for independent nations and dependencies are mid-2005 figures from the Population Reference Bureau in Washington, D.C. Next to CAPITAL is the name of the seat of government, followed by the city's population. Capital city populations for both independent nations and dependencies are from 2003 United Nations estimates and represent the population of the city's urban agglomeration, which usually includes both city proper and adjacent suburbs. Both POPULATION and CAPITAL population figures for countries, dependencies, and U.S. states are rounded to the nearest thousand.

Under RELIGION, the most widely practiced faith appears first. "Traditional" or "indigenous" connotes beliefs of important local sects, such as Maya in Middle America. Under LANGUAGE, the most widely spoken language is listed first. Official languages are denoted using the parenthetical (official) following the language. Both RELIGION and LANGUAGE are in rank ordering, taken from the CIA World Factbook.

LITERACY generally indicates the percentage of the population above the age of 15 who can read and write. There are no universal standards of literacy, so these estimates (from the CIA World Factbook) are based on the most common definition available for a nation. LIFE EXPECTANCY (from 2005 Population Reference Bureau data) represents the average number of years a group of infants born in the same year can be expected to live if the mortality rate at each age remains constant in the future.

GDP PER CAPITA is Gross Domestic Product divided by midyear population estimates. GDP estimates for independent nations are from the UN Statistics Division and follow their methodology for data estimation (for details, see http://unstats.un.org). Estimates for dependencies are from the CIA World Factbook. All are measured in purchasers' prices (i.e., they take into account the purchasing powers of different currencies). For U.S. states, equivalent measurements to GDP on the intranational level have been used. PCPI, or Per Capita Personal INCOME, figures from the U.S. Bureau of Economic Analysis are presented; PCPI divides the total personal income of all residents of a state by the midyear population.

Individual income estimates such as GDP PER CAPITA and PCI are among the many indicators used to assess a nation's well-being. As statistical averages, they hide extremes of poverty and wealth. Furthermore, they take no account of factors that affect quality of life, such as environmental degradation, educational opportunities, and health care.

ECONOMY information for the independent nations and dependencies is divided into three general categories: Industry, Agriculture, and Exports. Because of structural limitations, only the primary industries (Ind), agricultural commodities (Agr), and exports (Exp) as listed in the CIA World Factbook are reported. Agriculture serves as an umbrella term for not only crops but also livestock, products, and fish. In the interest of conciseness, agriculture for the independent nations presents, when applicable but not limited to, three major crops, followed respectively by leading entries for livestock, products, and fish. For the other two categories, the four leading industries and export products are listed where data and space limitations allow. The information provided for each category is listed in rank order, starting with the largest by value or importance.

NA indicates that data are not available.

NATIONAL
GEOGRAPHIC
Family
REFERENCE
SECOND EDITION
Atlas
OF THE
WORLD

Published by the National Geographic Society

John M. Fahey, Jr. — *President and Chief Executive Officer*

Gilbert M. Grosvenor — *Chairman of the Board*

Nina D. Hoffman — *Executive Vice President, President, Books Publishing Group*

Prepared by the Book Division

Kevin Mulroy — *Senior Vice President and Publisher*

Marianne R. Koszorus — *Design Director*

Staff for this Atlas

Carl Mehler — *Project Editor and Director of Maps*

Nicholas P. Rosenbach — *Supervisor of Map Edit*

Timothy J. Carter, Laura Exner, Steven D. Gardner, Thomas L. Gray, Joseph F. Ochlak — *Map Editors*

Matt Chwastyk, Sam Chernawsky, Gregory Ugiansky, and XNR Productions — *Map Research and Compilation*

Matt Chwastyk, Gregory Ugiansky — *Map Production Managers*

Steven D. Gardner, James Huckenpahler, Kyle T. Rector, Martin S. Walz, and XNR Productions — *Map Production*

David B. Miller — *Contributing Geographer*

Rebecca Lescaze; Principal, Carolinda E. Averitt, Laura Exner, K. M. Kostyal, Jane Sunderland — *Text Editors*

Elisabeth B. Booz, Patrick Booz, Philip Brown, William Burroughs, Carlos Castillo-Salgado, Manuel Colunga-Garcia, Byron Crape, Ellen Ficklen, Michael Finger, Richard Fix, Stuart H. Gage, Matthew C. Hansen, Craig K. Harris, Mike Hoffmann, Tim Kelly, K. M. Kostyal, Ruth Levine, Eric Lindstrom, David T. Long, Enrique Loyola-Elizondo, Stephen P. Maran, Carl Mehler, W. David Menzie, H. Michael Mogil, John Morrison, Rhea Muchow, Ted Munn, Margaret Murray, Sarah Parks, Janet Pau, Josh Polterock, Antony Shugaar, Brad Singer, Peter W. Sloss, Whitney Smith, Paul D. Spudis, Robert Tilling, Simon Walker, Patrick J. Webber, Joe Yogerst — *Contributing Writers*

Sam Chernawsky, Elizabeth B. Booz, Victoria Garrett Jones, Rhea Muchow, Joseph F. Ochlak, Anne E. Withers — *Text Researchers*

Marty Ittner, Principal; Jennifer Christiansen, Megan McCarthy, Susan K. White — *Book Design*

ChrisOrr.com, Tibor G. Tóth — *Art and Illustrations*

Dana Chivvis, Sadie Quarrier — *Photo Editors*

Abby Lepold, Meredith C. Wilcox — *Photo Assistants*

Rebecca Hinds — *Managing Editor*

R. Gary Colbert — *Production Director*

Manufacturing and Quality Control

Christopher A. Liedel — *Chief Financial Officer*

Phillip L. Schlosser — *Vice President*

John T. Dunn — *Technical Director*

Vincent P. Ryan — *Director*

Maryclare Tracy — *Manager*

Reproduction by Quad/Graphics, Alexandria, Virginia

Printed and Bound by Mondadori S.p.A., Verona, Italy

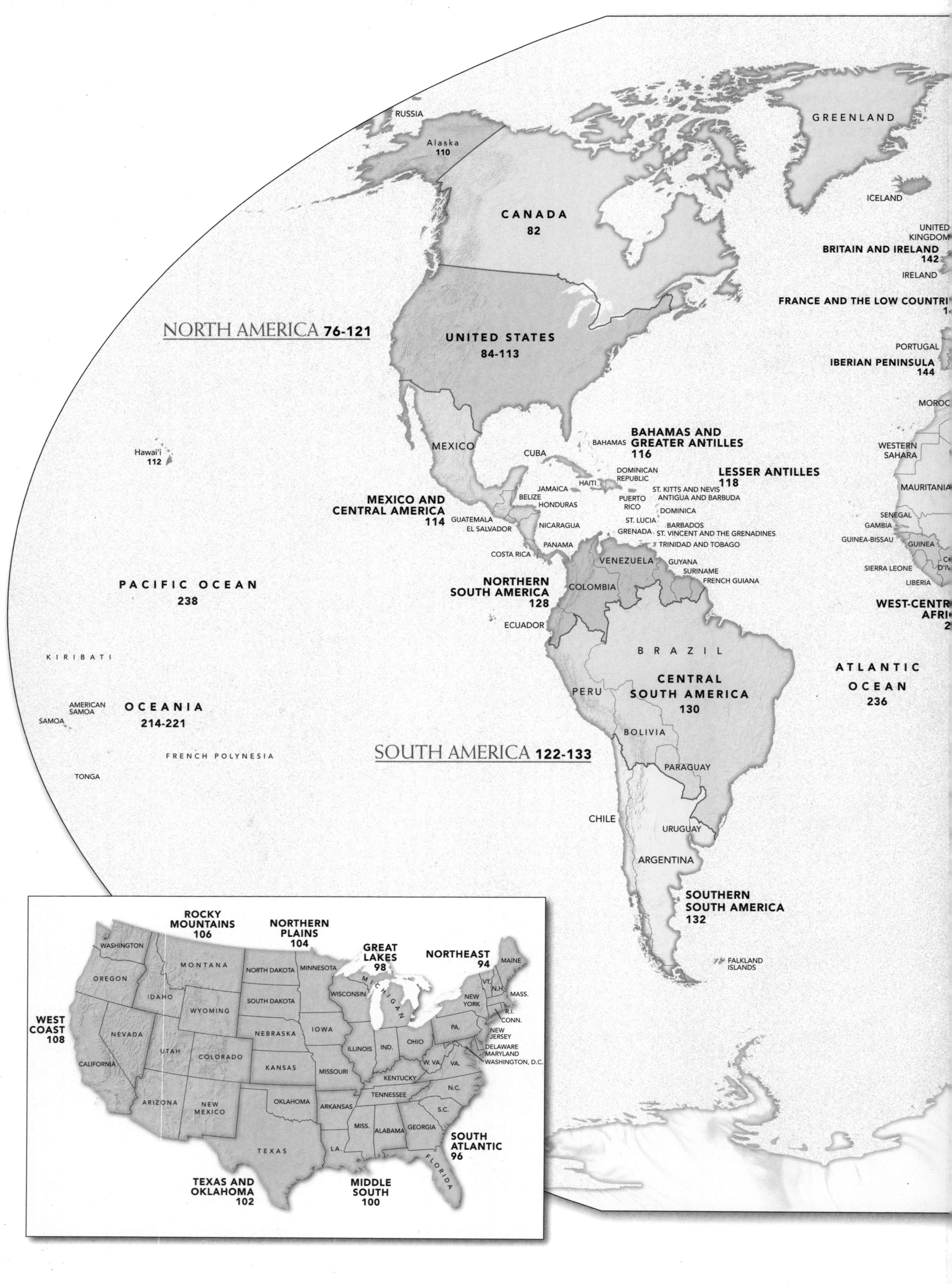

RUSSIA
Alaska
110
GREENLAND
ICELAND
CANADA
82
UNITED KINGDOM
BRITAIN AND IRELAND
142
IRELAND
FRANCE AND THE LOW COUNTRI
NORTH AMERICA 76-121
UNITED STATES
84-113
PORTUGAL
IBERIAN PENINSULA
144
MOROC
BAHAMAS
BAHAMAS AND GREATER ANTILLES
116
WESTERN SAHARA
Hawai'i
112
MEXICO
CUBA
DOMINICAN REPUBLIC
LESSER ANTILLES
118
HAITI
JAMAICA
ST. KITTS AND NEVIS
ANTIGUA AND BARBUDA
MAURITANIA
MEXICO AND CENTRAL AMERICA
114
BELIZE
HONDURAS
PUERTO RICO
DOMINICA
GUATEMALA
EL SALVADOR
NICARAGUA
ST. LUCIA
BARBADOS
GRENADA
ST. VINCENT AND THE GRENADINES
TRINIDAD AND TOBAGO
PANAMA
COSTA RICA
SENEGAL
GAMBIA
GUINEA-BISSAU
GUINEA
SIERRA LEONE
LIBERIA
VENEZUELA
GUYANA
SURINAME
FRENCH GUIANA
COLOMBIA
PACIFIC OCEAN
238
NORTHERN SOUTH AMERICA
128
ECUADOR
WEST-CENTR AFRI
BRAZIL
KIRIBATI
ATLANTIC OCEAN
236
CENTRAL SOUTH AMERICA
130
PERU
AMERICAN SAMOA
SAMOA
OCEANIA
214-221
BOLIVIA
FRENCH POLYNESIA
SOUTH AMERICA 122-133
TONGA
PARAGUAY
CHILE
URUGUAY
ARGENTINA
SOUTHERN SOUTH AMERICA
132
FALKLAND ISLANDS
ROCKY MOUNTAINS
106
NORTHERN PLAINS
104
GREAT LAKES
98
NORTHEAST
94
WASHINGTON
MONTANA
NORTH DAKOTA
MINNESOTA
MAINE
OREGON
VT.
N.H.
MASS.
IDAHO
SOUTH DAKOTA
WISCONSIN
MICHIGAN
NEW YORK
WYOMING
R.I.
CONN.
WEST COAST
108
NEBRASKA
IOWA
PA.
NEW JERSEY
NEVADA
UTAH
ILLINOIS
IND.
OHIO
DELAWARE
MARYLAND
COLORADO
WASHINGTON, D.C.
W. VA.
VA.
CALIFORNIA
KANSAS
MISSOURI
KENTUCKY
N.C.
TENNESSEE
ARIZONA
NEW MEXICO
OKLAHOMA
ARKANSAS
S.C.
MISS.
ALABAMA
GEORGIA
SOUTH ATLANTIC
96
TEXAS
LA.
FLORIDA
TEXAS AND OKLAHOMA
102
MIDDLE SOUTH
100